RITUAL AND BELIEF

Readings in the Anthropology of Religion

EDITED BY

David Hicks

State University of New York at Stony Brook

Boston   Burr Ridge, IL   Dubuque, IA   Madison, WI   New York   San Francisco   St. Louis
Bangkok   Bogotá   Caracas   Kuala Lumpur   Lisbon   London   Madrid   Mexico City
Milan   Montreal   New Delhi   Santiago   Seoul   Singapore   Sydney   Taipei   Toronto

McGraw-Hill Higher Education ⚛

A Division of The **McGraw-Hill** Companies

RITUAL AND BELIEF:
Readings in the Anthropology of Religion
Published by McGraw-Hill, an imprint of The McGraw-Hill Companies, Inc. 1221 Avenue of the Americas, New York, NY, 10020. Copyright © 2002, 1999 by The McGraw-Hill Companies, Inc. All rights reserved. No part of this publication may be reproduced or distributed in any form or by any means, or stored in a data base or retrieval system, without the prior written consent of The McGraw-Hill Companies, Inc., including, but not limited to, in any network or other electronic storage or transmission, or broadcast for distance learning.

Some ancillaries, including electronic and print components, may not be available to customers outside the United States.

This book is printed on acid-free paper.

4 5 6 7 8 9 BKM BKM 0 9 8 7 6

ISBN-13: 978-0-07-241489-9

ISBN-10: 0-07-241489-8

Publisher: *Phillip A. Butcher*
Executive sponsoring editor: *Carolyn Henderson*
Editorial assistant: *Julie Abodeely*
Marketing manager: *Daniel M. Loch*
Project manager: *Jill Howell*
Production supervisor: *Carol A. Bielski*
Media producer: *Shannon Rider*
Designer: *Jennifer McQueen*
Supplement producer: *Cathy L. Tepper*
Photo research: *Jeremy Cheshareck*
Cover design: *Crispin Prebys*
Cover image: *Stephanie Maze/NGS Image Collection*
Typeface: *10/12 Times Roman*
Compositor: *Carlisle Publishers Services*

Library of Congress Cataloging-in-Publication Data
Ritual and belief : readings in the anthropology of religion / edited by David Hicks.— [2nd ed.].
    p. cm.
  Includes bibliographical references and index.
  ISBN 0-07-241489-8 (alk. paper)
  1. Ethnology—Religious aspects. 2. Religion. 3. Religions. I. Hicks, David, 1939–
BL256 .R58 2002
291—dc21

2001030796

www.mhhe.com

To the Memory of My Brother,
Alfred "Bill" Hicks
1940-1997

ABOUT THE AUTHOR

DAVID HICKS studied anthropology at the University of Oxford, where he earned his doctorate after carrying out 19 months of field research in the country that is now East Timor, in Southeast Asia. He subsequently carried out field research on the neighboring island of Flores in eastern Indonesia. Dr. Hicks is chairman and professor of anthropology at the State University of New York at Stony Brook. He has received research awards from the National Science Foundation, the Wenner-Gren Foundation for Anthropological Research, and the United States Institute of Peace, and in 1997 he received the honor of a residency at the Rockefeller Study/Conference Center in Bellagio, Italy. He has also served as a consultant for the World Bank. In 1999, he returned to East Timor with funding from the Harry Frank Guggenheim Foundation and the American Philosophical Society. In August 1999, Dr. Hicks served as a delegate of the Carter Center monitoring the United Nations plebiscite in East Timor. He is the author of *Tetum Ghosts & Kin* (1976); *Structural Analysis in Anthropology: Case Studies from Indonesia and Brazil* (1978); *A Maternal Religion: The Role of Women in Tetum Myth and Ritual* (1984); and *Kinship and Religion in Eastern Indonesia* (1990). He is coauthor, with Margaret A. Gwynne, of *Cultural Anthropology* (1994, 1996).

PREFACE

Ritual and Belief: Readings in the Anthropology of Religion is designed for undergraduate courses in the Anthropology of Religion or Comparative Religions. It may be used as either a stand-alone text or as a supplement. In compiling this reader, my purpose has been to offer a text that is more instructor- and student-friendly than any other anthology currently available.

Any anthology, of course, reflects its compiler's own preferences and sense of what other teachers may want, and the present reader is no exception. My choice of readings is eclectic: No single anthropological approach or theoretical perspective dominates the text. Theoretical significance, scholarly eminence of the author, and inherent interest provide the principal criteria, but each reading is also selected to complement the chapter, in which it appears. It is important to note that these chapters are pedagogically coherent rather than ad hoc assemblages, a critical difference between this anthology and certain other anthologies. Included among the theoretical perspectives are structural-functionalism, structuralism, Malinowskian functionalism, cultural materialism, and cultural evolutionism; also included are the synchronic and diachronic approaches. The book offers a mix of classic readings and more recent contributions, and the "world religions" are included along with examples from the religions of traditionally nonliterate cultures. In short, I have sought to embrace as diverse a range of religious traditions as possible, from an assortment of times and places.

THE SECOND EDITION

The Second Edition of *Ritual and Belief* has, as a result of many suggestions made by a number of industrious reviewers:

- More readings overall.
- 13 new selections:
  Robin Horton: *Neo-Tylorianism;* Edmund Leach: *Genesis as Myth;* Lyle B. Steadman, Craig T. Palmer, and Christopher F. Tilley: *The Universality of Ancestor Worship;* Arnold van Gennep: *Conclusions;* Victor W. Turner: *Religious Specialists;* Beth A. Conklin: *"Thus are Our Bodies, Thus Was Our Custom: Mortuary Cannibalism in An Amazonian Society;"* Jeanne Favret-Saada: *The Way Things Are Said;* Serena Nanda: *The Hijras of India: Cultural and Individual Dimensions of an Institutionalized Third Gender Role;* Stansilav Andreski: *The Syphilitic Shock;* Evon Z. Vogt: *Water Witching: An Interpretation of a Ritual Pattern in a Rural American Community;* Eileen Barker: *The Unification Church;* Loretta Orion: *The Transforming Influence of American Gatherings;* Barry Chavannes: *The Rastafari Abroad,* and 4 new "Religion in the News" boxes: "A Legendary Hero Guides a Reborn Kyrgyzstan"; "Mozambique Enlists Healers in AIDS Prevention"; "Pastor and His Wife Are Acquitted on All Charges in Sex-Abuse Case"; "An Apocalyptic Mystery."
- A new chapter, "New Religious Movements" (Chapter 12), on alternative religions.
- More cross-references between "Readings," chapter "Introductions," and "Commentaries," so that students have access to previous contexts in which the author, topic, or idea was earlier encountered.
- The expansion of the "Introductions" to the chapters and the "Commentaries" on the readings to facilitate greater student comprehension of each chapter's set of readings.
- An expanded glossary at the end of the book, which includes terms that might be unfamiliar to students who have not studied anthropology in depth.
- A listing of important web sources for ritual and belief so that students have the opportunity to learn something of what scholars of religion are currently doing as well as increase their bibliographic knowledge.

ORGANIZATION

Each chapter discusses a specific topic: Chapter 1—perspectives; Chapter 2—myth, cosmology, and symbolic classification; Chapter 3—gods, spirits, and souls; Chapter 4—ritual; Chapter 5—practitioners of ritual; Chapter 6—body and mind; Chapter 7—magic and witchcraft; Chapter 8—death; Chapter 9—

sexuality and gender; Chapter 10—the natural environment; Chapter 11—agents of change; Chapter 12—new religious movements.

Each chapter follows a standard format:

- A brief "Introduction" to the general topic designed to establish the context for the chapter's readings.
- A "Commentary" to introduce each reading. (Since the selections vary in difficulty and character, I have been flexible in regard to both the length and the content of these "Commentaries"; some situate the reading in its theoretical context, others offer more of an evaluative interpretation.)

Because comparative religion involves concepts that often defy neat categorization, most of the selections in this anthology might have been assigned to one or more different chapters. But editorial judgment had to be exercised and, while the chapter assignments must not be regarded as definitive, they should be regarded as working compromises between the claims of scholarly convention and the conveniences of pedagogy. Since this reader includes classic studies as well as modern works, students must anticipate a wide variety of stylistic conventions both in vocabulary and in assumptions about the nature of other cultures. For instance, the sharp distinction scholars once made between "us" and "them" is no longer part of mainstream thinking; the use of such terms as "primitive" or "savage" to describe the customs of other people are outdated modes of reference which may, as such, give us more insight into the assumptions of our own not-too-distant scholarly ancestors than into the thinking of members of other cultures.

PEDAGOGICAL AIDS

- A map included at the beginning of the text identifies the location of the major world religions and the approximate number of those religions' adherents.
- An annotated set of further readings enables students to deepen their understanding of material included in the readings or to broaden their knowledge of related topics.
- An annotated set of suggested videos illustrating the topics discussed in the chapter. This list contains, where verifiable, information on each video's running time, date of distribution, purchase cost, rental cost, and distributor. Costs, of course, are liable to change.
- An "Ask Yourself" sidebar designed to stimulate students' reflections on the readings and help them prepare for more fruitful classroom discussions.
- A "Religion in the News" box, in relevant chapters, consisting of articles selected from the news media that demonstrate the part beliefs and rituals currently play in the real world.

INSTRUCTOR SUPPLEMENTS PACKAGE

As a full-service publisher of quality educational products, McGraw-Hill does much more than just sell textbooks. The company creates and publishes an extensive array of print, video, and digital supplements for students and instructors. This edition of *Ritual and Belief* is accompanied by the following:

- Instructor's Manual/Testbank—chapter outlines, suggested videos, chapter summaries, lecture notes, essay questions, and an objective question testbank.

This Instructor's Manual is provided free of charge to students and instructors. Orders of new (versus used) textbooks help us defray the cost of developing such supplements, which is substantial. Please contact your local McGraw-Hill representative for more information on any of the above supplements.

ACKNOWLEDGMENTS

I gratefully acknowledge the following for their assistance in preparing this reader for publication and for their helpful suggestions: my editor, Ms. Carolyn Henderson; and Mr. Robert Gilpin. My thanks also to the staff of the Emma Clark Library, in East Setauket, Long Island, for their invariably gracious assistance, as well as to Robin Davis Miller and the Author's Guild for the continual support they give authors, including, I am happy to say, myself. I thank the following reviewers for their suggestions, which helped to shape this reader: Daniel Varisco, Hofstra University; William Stuart, University of Maryland; Joseph Bastien, University of Texas; Morris Foster, University of Oklahoma; Marjorie Snipes, State University of West Georgia; David Knowlton, University of Utah; William Abruzzi, Muhlenberg College; and Pam Frese, College of Wooster.

CONTENTS

INTRODUCTION

Religion offers inexhaustible scope for anyone interested in humanity, whether in the behavior or the thought of *Homo sapiens*. In its beliefs and rituals, something of the riches that constitute the genetic endowments of our imaginative capacities are revealed at the same time that they demonstrate the pragmatic adjustments these products of the imagination must make to the demands of experience if those who profess them are to prosper in the "real" world. Not surprisingly, then, we encounter religion in many of the diverse media of our times—in newspapers and magazines, on television, in political discussions (for Americans the constitutional divide between religion and the state is a perennial source of controversy and the issue of whether public funds, in the form of vouchers, be used to pay for parochial education is a current contention), in novels, and in the classroom. In the academic world, the study of religion is a well-established field of scholarly endeavor, and departments of Theology, Judaic Studies, Christian Studies, Islamic Studies, and Comparative Religion make it their focus of inquiry. In anthropology and sociology, the study of religion is a major topic, and a few specialists in religion have emerged over the years as great scholars in those two fields.

This collection of readings is concerned with how religion manifests itself in the beliefs and rituals of many different societies, at the same time as taking into account two related phenomena, magic and witchcraft. Therefore, to situate the readings in a proper scholarly framework, in this Introduction I shall consider some of the more important ideas anthropologists and sociologists rely upon in attempting to understand what human beings are doing when they perform rituals and justify their performance in beliefs. The meaning of rituals and beliefs, as we shall see from the present collection of readings, comes about from the use of symbols, and since symbols are fundamental to ritual and beliefs, I shall start our discussion with them.

SYMBOLS

The *American Heritage Dictionary* defines a symbol as "something that represents something else by association, resemblance, or convention," a usage I favor in this book. A rectangular piece of cloth imprinted with a design consisting of a conventional arrangement of stars and stripes in specific colors symbolizes the United States of America, and for U.S. citizens displaying this object, reciting the Pledge of Allegiance to it, or saluting, it symbolizes their loyalty to their country and their agreement with the ideals on which the U.S. government is based.

This everyday example of a symbol suggests four important properties of symbols. First, a symbol can be an object (such as a flag), a series of words (such as a pledge), or an action (such as a salute). Second, to use a symbol is to communicate something—an attitude, a feeling, or an abstract idea (such as freedom or democracy). Third, symbols may be arbitrary; there is no intuitively obvious connection between a piece of printed cloth and the concept of democracy. And fourth, the meaning of a symbol is not necessarily immediate; it may convey meaning back into the past or forward into the future.

In every society, symbols are the most important vehicles by which culture is transmitted. Whether in the form of language, actions, or objects, people constantly employ symbols in doing, thinking, saying, and making things. Moreover, the symbols used by members of a society often coalesce into integrated symbolic systems. A language, for instance, is made up of many sounds, many gestures, and many tones of voice, every one of which not only has meaning in its own right but also takes on added meaning when employed in conjunction with the others.

While some symbols are unique to the cultures that employ them, others are found in several or many different cultures. Certain symbols are so widely used cross-culturally that they seem to be virtually universal. For example, in all cultures about which we have the relevant information, the right hand or right side is considered superior to left. Further, right usually symbolizes goodness and strength, whereas left is associated with evil and weakness. Nevertheless, the meaning of most symbols does vary cross-culturally. Take colors, for example: these may have different symbolic meanings depending upon the society that uses them. In Western cultures, brides traditionally wear white, and black is associated with death. But in India and certain other Asian countries, white symbolizes death, and brides dress in red.

By employing symbols—words, gestures, colors, and every type of medium that can be used for symbolization—societies give life to their beliefs and meaning to their rituals.

BELIEFS

Beliefs may be contained in formal canons or systematic dogmas, as in Islam, Judaism, or Christianity. Or they may consist of ideas, perhaps quite flexibly linked together in myths, that allow plenty of room for alternative interpretations. Anthropologists carrying out fieldwork in other societies commonly report that their informants seem to have no consistent views regarding such issues as the persistence of life after death or on the origins of humanity, and that they frequently contradict themselves in different situations as they attempt to answer questions put to them by the anthropologist. The traditional beliefs the Crow Indians of the Great Plains are a good example of this lack of ideological organization. Crow beliefs were not organized into inflexible doctrines to which every member of the society had to adhere, and no one would be denounced as a heretic for expressing unconventional beliefs (Lowie 1970, 30). The absence of a dogma permitted a variety of interpretations.

People believe in the existence of gods, witches, immortality, and the efficacy of magic for many reasons. One factor undoubtedly is the innate human tendency to bring order to our lives, a desire to classify, for either practical or symbolic purposes. Practical classification identifies ideas and objects for scientific purposes or to satisfy the requirements of everyday life, whereas symbolic classification systematically organizes ideas or groups for symbolic purposes (Needham 1979, 3) (see Chapter 2).

A second factor is the human desire to understand. Unexplained phenomena can create some measure of intellectual frustration, and beliefs that provide an explanation may be welcomed for the intellectual comfort they can provide. This is especially so when they also impose a degree of order on experience. Clifford Geertz, an American anthropologist, describes how, during his fieldwork in a Javanese village, a large deformed toadstool sprouted from the ground in a remarkably short time (1965, 16). So peculiar was this event people came from miles around to marvel. Their fascination did not lie in the importance of toadstools in Javanese culture, for toadstools have no special significance. The phenomenon's odd shape and rapid growth brought about this interest because the toadstool fit neither into the local system of symbolic classification nor into its practical classification. It thereby assaulted the local community's sense of what was orderly and proper (see Chapter 2), and it rather abruptly forced villagers to confront the notion that perhaps their traditional way of classifying reality might be somehow inadequate. They therefore felt compelled to contrive some explanation. Geertz cites several possible alternatives the villagers invented. They came up with two practical reasons and one religious reason. The practical reasons were either that the toadstool was a fake someone had planted or that the toadstool resulted from the unusually heavy rains the region had recently experienced. Their religious reason was that the toadstool had been fashioned by spirits, and this explanation satisfied their intellects sufficiently for them to select it as their preferred explanation.

A third factor may be found in the human desire to control (empirically or symbolically) events or to exercise some influence over nature. These ends may be accomplished through the mediating agency of spirits or not, as the case may be. Over 10,000 years ago, Cro-Magnon cave dwellers may have been expressing this need in their wall paintings when they drew pictures of game animals with spears in their sides. Perhaps by drawing a successful hunt they hoped to bring it about.

Alternatively, whether organized or not, beliefs may constitute defining components of a moral code. This occurs in Islam, Judaism, and Christianity, and the beliefs lend support to the maintenance of social discipline. Religious beliefs may also provide philosophical comfort to human beings in circumstances of misfortune and on the inevitable occasion of death. Certainly, adherence to a common complex of beliefs offers pragmatic benefits to a community. Beliefs held in common by individuals in the same society (what the French sociologist, Emile Durkheim, called *réprésentations collectives ["collective representations"]*) have been identified as contributors to social cohesion, while rituals that are performed collectively encourage feelings of common identity.

We shall never know what stimulated our earliest ancestors to conceive of the existence of spirits, but we do have ample case material showing how beliefs undergo change through time. Over the last several centuries many small-scale societies have undergone social, economic, and political upheavals, often as a result of contact with Western societies, and these new conditions have generated new religious beliefs and rituals—or variations on old ones—which, in turn, have emerged as popular movements for radical social change (see Chapter 11). Western societies, too, have undergone major religious changes. The Reformation in the 16th century is an outstanding example of how religion can be transformed by events. Today, religious movements in North America and Europe, such as the Unification Church and wiccan, are not only responding to new social and psychological needs of individuals, they are themselves as transforming influences on society (see Chapter 12). Typically, as with the wiccan movement, the new beliefs and rituals that are created or reinvented find justification in myth.

MYTHS

Myths are stories set in a vaguely remote period of time that describe the origins of significant phenomena in human experience, including death, fire, agriculture, humanity, customs, beliefs, and landscape features. They often describe the exploits of culture heroes—spirits, animals, quasi-human beings, or inanimate objects—who play important roles in shaping the human world. Myths, accordingly, "confront us with at least one event or situation which is physically or humanly impossible" (van Baal 1977, 165). They also satisfy the human desire for explanation. In nonliterate societies, where religious traditions are transmitted down the generations by the spoken word instead of by means of the written word, beliefs are rarely codified into an immutable canon; instead myths often provide repositories for beliefs as well as providing vehicles for transmitting them.

RITUALS

The term "ritual" is open to a number of definitions. Most, however, incorporate some reference to repetitive forms of behavior that are carried out on socially prescribed occasions and that convey messages whose meaning may—or may not—be explicitly known to the participants. As with the repetitive actions involved in celebrating the American flag, rituals provide a medium by which human beings use symbols to communicate ideas, values, and sentiments. Some scholars prefer to apply the term "ritual" only to repetitive acts that involve spirits or magic. Other scholars use a broader definition. For them, nonreligious and nonmagical forms of repetitive behavior also constitute ritual. Shaking hands, for example, would not be considered a ritual according to the more limited definition, whereas in the broader definition it would. In this book, I use the term "ritual" in the more inclusive sense.

The form of behavior we usually refer to as "ritual" varies widely in the form it takes, and it serves a multitude of purposes. One common mode is sacrificial, in which an offering is made to some spiritual agency. A common intention of sacrifice is to establish or reinforce a bond between the human gift giver and the spirit who receives the gift. Another purpose is to propitiate a spirit who has been offended by human conduct. Another reason for offering a sacrifice may be to ensure fertility, good crops, success in hunting, or an improvement in health. The person offering the sacrifice may act on his or her own behalf, on behalf of selected others, or on behalf of the community. The term sacrificer, or *sacrificateur* (in the French original), was coined in 1899 by Henri Hubert and Marcel Mauss in an article in which they suggest how rituals in which sacrifices are offered to gods are structured. Insightful as this essay was, one flaw Hubert and Mauss were guilty of was in regarding "sacrifice" as constituting a distinctive category of ritual. This tendency remains a habit of thought in cultural anthropology. Anthropologists are still fond of classifying rituals according to what they consider their main function or purpose is, or in light of some other criteria. Thus we have "rites of passage," "divinatory rituals," "rites of affliction," "propitiatory rituals," "expiatory rituals," "ancestral rituals," "fertility rituals," and so on. Typically, in fact, ritual will usually have more than one function or purpose, and in a given society sacrifices may be offered during the celebration of practically all of the above categories of ritual. Only in an artificial sense, therefore, can one isolate "sacrifice" as a distinct ritual category, isolated from all other rituals. This is not to say that these labels do not sometimes have a use. They serve as rough indicators of what to expect when a particular ritual is to be discussed in an anthropological work, but they should not be expected to hold more weight than they can carry. The problem of categorizing rituals is well demonstrated in the article on revitalization rituals by

Anthony C. F. Wallace (Chapter 11). It also raises the issue of definition in more general terms.

RELIGION, MAGIC, AND WITCHCRAFT

In discussing rituals and beliefs one key problem that may arise concerns the difficulty of defining what we mean by the terms "religion" and "magic." Take religion first. When scholars study religion cross-culturally, they typically commence by attempting to define what they mean by the term "religion." The problem, of course, is that we are relying on definitions and terms that have developed in cultures in Western societies and in then taking for granted that they are just as applicable in the local contexts of other, often quite different, societies. A brief examination of the etymology of the English-language term "religion" might help as a starting point, since it will give us some idea how varied—even in European usage—are the meanings associated with the term and its derivations. The first thing we need to note is that there is no consensus among scholars regarding the word's origins. There is no word common to the Indo-European languages that can be translated as "religion." Nor is there exact correspondent in either Greek or Latin. Even the Latin etymology is uncertain. The word religion may derive from *ligare,* to tie. On the other hand, it may come from *legere,* to collect, which may refer to the notion of recollect, that is, "to go back on a previous step and to make a new choice; for example, as in being religious, checked by scruple in the performance of rites." In discussing this etymology, Rodney Needham (1981, 72) points out that "what is indicated [here] is an inner state, not an objective property of certain things or a set of beliefs and practices."

Wilfred Cantwell Smith (1991, 19), while offering a somewhat different etymological interpretation, also makes clear that the term's antecedents bear little relation to the famous definitions proposed by anthropologists and sociologists over the course of the last 100 years. Smith traces the word religion to *religio,* although it was "a term that eventually was used in a great variety of senses . . . without precision" (p. 20). Western civilization's early church fathers, medieval scholars and philosophers, and modern philosophers and social scientists contributed to the development of various Western culture-specific meanings that we associate with the concepts of religion and sacred. As a result, we use these terms to refer to Western customs, and we typically associate the concepts of religion and the sacred with morality to suggest that they connote such qualities as holiness or godliness, and to distinguish religion from magic. The traditions of many cultures, however, do not make a connection between religion and morality, nor make a distinction between religion and magic.

Chapter 1 reflects upon the alternative definitions favored by influential scholars in the field of religion, but to get us started I shall suggest as a working definition the one proposed in 1873 by the English anthropologist, Edward Tylor, who defined religion as "the belief inspiritual beings." This, of course, would exclude Buddhism, one of the great world religions, but as we shall see, no useful definition is without its exceptions, and if we keep Buddhism in mind as a notable exception to this working definition, a definition framed in terms of spirit will serve us well enough as we read about the diverse beliefs of many different peoples. Although religion is definable in a lot of different ways, if we include in our definition some reference to spirits or to some form of life after death we are probably justified in assuming that religion is a cultural universal. Even the official atheism of the Soviet Union was itself partly a response to the religious traditions of its populations. Of course, not every person, even in a strongly religious community, may subscribe to that community's ideological conventions, but in such instances the beliefs of the individual are overshadowed by the collectivity of which he or she is part.

"Magic," as the term is generally used in anthropology, differs from religion in that it refers to rituals that are performed without the benefit of spiritual agencies in order to secure immediately practical results. These were two features of magic James George Frazer (see Chapter 7) used as defining differences between the two phenomena. Nevertheless, magic rituals, like those of religion, are also made up of symbols and may also make symbolic statements.

Another concept we frequently associate with religion and magic is witchcraft. Anthropologists find it useful applying the term "witchcraft" to the belief that certain individuals, called "witches," have the innate capacity to injure others, not by using ritual as in magic, but by mental techniques or by uttering "deadly words" (see Chapter 7). Personifying misfortune in the image of a witch is a common way people in many societies explain misfortunes, and for believers, misfortune is thought to occur not randomly or because its victims merit it, but because of other people (witches). When some misfortune seems to lack any empirical explanation, the presence of witchcraft may serve to provide the answer. For example, a Zande person (Zande is the adjectival form of Azande, an ethnic group living in Central Africa) who stumbles over the stump of a tree knows perfectly well the cut on his toe was caused by violent contact with a sharp object (Evans-Pritchard, 1937). But he wonders what caused him to fail to spot such an obvious obstacle. In this situation, the Azande consider several possible reasons under such circumstances: carelessness, stupidity, a failure to observe appropriate taboos, or a lapse in respect toward the ancestral ghosts. If, however, given the facts of a particular instance, these reasons have to be discarded—as they so often apparently are!—the default explanation is that a witchcraft is the culprit.

Whether spirits, magic, or witchcraft are held to be the agents responsible, misfortunes—whether trivial mishaps or traumatic disasters—are inevitable ingredients of the human condition. How people the world over—contemporary folk as well as those in earlier periods—have sought to account for these negative aspects of living, as well as explain or construct life's pleasanter components, affords us alternative perspectives to our own. In this reader, we shall learn something of how scholars, mainly anthropologists, but from other disciplines, too, have attempted to offer insights into how human beings have devised ways—in ritual and belief—of grappling with the quandaries of existence.

THE SOCIOLOGY OF RELIGION

The two scholars who are generally considered to have made the most influential contributions to the sociology of religion are the Frenchman, Emile Durkheim (1858–1916) and the German, Max Weber (1864–1920). The influence of Durkheim is attested to in the many citations made to his work by anthropologists (this tendency is made clear in the readings contained in this book). An important component in his attaining the importance he did lay his leadership of the *Année sociologique* school, a group of great French sociologists, who around the turn of the 20th century worked together to produce dozens of important studies. These scholars included Henri Hubert and Marcel Mauss, whose classic contribution to the field of sacrifice has already been cited. Weber's influence has been somewhat less. Durkheim's conviction that beliefs and institutions intermesh in a synchronic manner (see below) was a feature of his work that anthropological fieldworkers came to appreciate. His idea matched the conditions typically found in the societies in which they carried out their field research. Because these societies lacked the tradition of writing, there was no documentation of their past by the people themselves. Furthermore, the researcher normally resided among them only for a short time. The absence of access to a documented past, coupled with this relatively brief period of residence in the field combined to reduce the anthropologist's awareness of social changes taking place in the society being studied.

Nevertheless, Max Weber managed to engage some anthropological attention. His notion of charisma (see Chapter 5), for example, has proved useful to understanding power, and he examined to a greater depth than Durkheim religion as a dynamic force in social change. In his *The Protestant Ethic and the Spirit of Capitalism,* he argued the case that religious ideas could influence economic forces, a view that contracted the arguments of Karl Marx (1818–1883), the German economist, philosopher, and revolutionary, who emphasized the importance of economic factors on religion—a perspective taken up in the 20th century by the cultural-material school of anthropological analysis (see below). Reading 11–4 exemplifies this aspect of Weber's thought.

THE ANTHROPOLOGY OF RELIGION

The most profound contribution anthropologists have made to the study of religion is in providing huge quantities of information about rituals and beliefs in other societies. Since the great majority of readings offered here are the work of cultural anthropologists whose writings assume readers are familiar with concepts used in anthropology, it may be useful to summarize several of those that occur most frequently.

A *synchronic approach* investigates rituals and beliefs during a particular period of time, minimizing the factor of social change. This is the Durkheimian approach. A *diachronic approach,* by contrast, examines institutions and collective representations as they change through time. Reading 4–5 is an example of a synchronic approach, and 7–3 is an example of a diachronic approach. These two approaches are often expressed by anthropologists as an opposition respectively between *structure* and *process.* The work of Durkheim and the British school of structural-functionalists, who were influenced by him, analyzed societies synchronically, and so we find that in such works as E. E. Evans-Pritchard's *Nuer Religion* the impression we receive is of a set of rituals and beliefs balancing one another out in a motionless condition of stasis. To some extent the limited time ethnographers spent in the field made it hard for them to notice any but the most dramatic changes that were taking place about them, of course, and this handicap was exacerbated by the absence of written records made by the people themselves, who were usually nonliterate. The *structural-functional approach* (see Reading 3–3) is a fairly inclusive perspective that includes the more sociological slant of A. R. Radcliffe-Brown (1881–1951) who viewed institutions in terms of the part they play in maintaining the "social structure" and the more purely structuralist perspective of E. E. Evans-Pritchard (1902–1973), whose work was more akin to the later structural approach of the contemporary French scholar, Claude Lévi-Strauss. A *structuralist approach,* or structural analysis, examines the manner in which collective representations are ordered in a given society, and the anthropologist making this kind of analysis relies upon certain principles of thought that order the thinking of all human beings regardless of their culture. Among the most common of these principles are opposition, complementarity, and analogy. Certain scholars, most famously Lévi-Strauss and the English writer, Edmund Leach (Reading 2–2), include in their structural interpretations attempts to discern "messages" they believe are "encoded" in the rituals or myths they are seeking to interpret. A very different approach is that of the cultural-materialist, and it is an approach famously associated with the American anthropologist, Marvin Harris, who was strongly influenced by the ideas of Karl Marx. In Harris's reworking of the Marxian thesis, empirical factors such as the natural environment or technology are emphasized as the controlling determinants that shape religion. An example of this approach, by another anthropologist, Roy A. Rappaport, appears in Reading 10–2.

Another anthropological term is "participant observation," which can be described as the signature research technique of anthropology. Participant observation is the involvement (as well as the observation) by the anthropologist in the lives of members of the community in which he or she is collecting information. This process of collecting data is known as "ethnography," and the information thus gathered as "ethnographic information." While engaged in this process, the anthropologist is often referred to as an "ethnographer"—as distinct from a Victorian scholar or a modern-day anthropologist working in his or her office away from the field. Finally, this ethnographic information will then be written up in the form of a book, which is also called "an ethnography."

An equally important concept in anthropology is "cultural relativism." This is the notion that the beliefs and behaviors of a particular people should be assessed, not according to the values of the observer's own society, but within the context of these peoples' own values. For example, sacrificing an animal as part of a ritual performance is a form of behavior some Westerners would find objectionable, yet it is a feature of many religions in the Third World. The cultural relativist would argue that—in the absence of any universal yardstick against which cultures can be measured and compared—no ethnic group, society, or culture can be said to be superior to another. Who, then, is to say that the Western attitude is preferable? Or, for that matter, the superior attitude? The contrary attitude, ethnocentrism, is of a piece with the belief that one's own ethnic group, society, or culture is superior to others.

WORLD RELIGIONS AND LOCAL RELIGIONS

Edward Tylor (1832–1917), James George Frazer (1854–1941), Emile Durkheim (1858–1916), Sigmund Freud (1856–1939), and the other early scholars of religion never had the opportunity to participate in rituals or witness with their own eyes the complex situations in which beliefs are put into effect. They were knowledgeable enough about Judaism and Christianity, and some had an acquaintance with Islam or Hinduism or Buddhism. But their interest in these religions lay in the teachings contained in the *Bible,* the *Koran,* the *Upanishads,* and the other great religious texts of the world religions. The moral prescriptions and other beliefs elaborated by generations of sophisticated religious scholars embedded in these texts constituted for them the very essence for the study of these religions. This is not to say that the beliefs of the great world religions are entirely systematic and coherent, of course, but in part because they have been set down in literate form they are, to a far greater degree than the religions of nonliterate folk, standarized. However, as I said earlier, most religions do not have specialists whose job it is to reflect upon their religion and bring their society's beliefs into something resembling a systematic and coherent theology or set of prescriptions—such as those contained in the famous *Catechism of the Catholic Church.* Nor did literacy become widespread until the 20th century. Hence, ethnographers typically report that the people they discuss local religion with often give conflicting interpretations of their beliefs and that the rituals they carry out can vary unpredictably from performance to performance. So when we read such ethnographic studies as *Nuer Religion, Manus Religion,* and *Lugbara Religion,* what we find is that their authors, respectively, Evans-Pritchard, John Middleton, and Reo Fortune have, in effect, themselves become the theologians of the local religion. They have put into a coherent framework what are often only fragments of belief thereby making local religions seem rather more systematic than they really are and conveying the idea that it is normal for religious beliefs to coalesce into a systematic theology.

Modern anthropological scholarship, in contrast, pays more attention to how beliefs are conceptualized and rituals performed "in practice" by local populations rather than specialists' texts. The wider social context in which beliefs and rituals have their existence plays a crucial part in any anthropological discussion of religion. To give an example: anthropologists' interest what has been called "practical religion" (Leach 1968:1) make them curious about why many Mexicans regard the Virgin Mary as a goddess rather than as merely the greatest of the saints, as the *Catechism of the Catholic Church* insists. They would, like Eric Wolf (Reading 9–2), regard it as entirely legitimate that people would find this heresy (as defined by the official Catholic dogma) worth ascribing to, and they would look to local attitudes and social behavior for an explanation. The result, as you will find in reading Wolf's article, is convincing. Textual scholarship has yielded important insights into religion, and anthropologists have used the findings of their textual colleagues to advance their own understanding of the nature of religion. At the same time they offer their own distinctive contribution, and this is, above all, to portray how religion, magic, and witchcraft enable individuals to come to terms with the fact that they are human.

FURTHER READINGS

Child, Alice B., and Irvin L. Child. *Religion and Magic in the Life of Traditional Peoples.* Englewood Cliffs, N.J.: Prentice-Hall, 1992. This text is particularly helpful for cross-cultural study.

Evans-Pritchard, E. E. *Theories of Primitive Religion.* Oxford: Clarendon Press, 1965. In this book, one of the most influential scholars of religion and magic offers his distinctively personal view of the contributions certain of his predecessors—including Edward Tylor, James George Frazer, Emile Durkheim, and Bronislaw Malinowski—made to our knowledge of these concepts.

Pals, Daniel L. *Seven Theories of Religion.* New York and Oxford: Oxford University Press, 1996. This book is a clearly written introduction to ritual and belief, brimming with information and packed with critical insights. It deals with the work of some of the scholars discussed by Evans-Pritchard—Tylor, Frazer, and Durkheim—but brings the anthropological study of religion up-to-date by including the work of Edward Evans-Pritchard himself and Clifford Geertz.

SUGGESTED RESOURCE FOR VIDEOS

Heider, Karl G., and Carol Hermer. *Films for Anthropological Teaching,* 8th ed. Special Publication 29. Washington, D.C.: American Anthropological Association, 1995. Although the films and videos included in this authoritative compilation cover the entire discipline of anthropology, many concern ritual and religious ideas (see pp. 20–22), making this an essential handbook for the teaching of these topics.

WEB-SITE RESOURCES

http://www.rai.anthropology.org.uk
http://www.ameranthassn.org
http://www.films.com

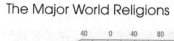

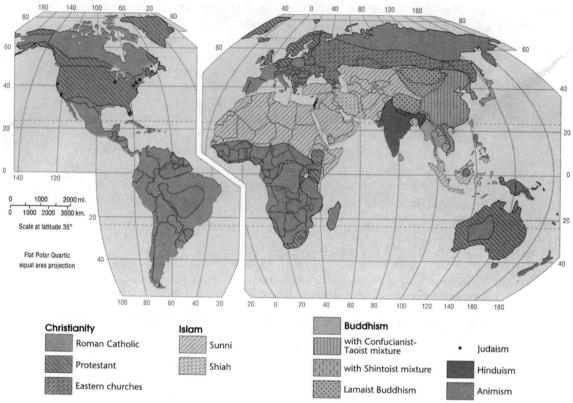

Approximate Statistics for the Five Principal World Religions, 1995

Religion	*Approximate number of adherents*
Buddhism	323,894,000
Christianity	1,927,953,000
Hinduism	780,547,000
Judaism	14,117,000
Islam	1,099,634,000

Note: These figures are to be regarded as approximate, but they do illustrate a rough idea of the relative demographic strengths of the major world religions (Brunner 1998).

Source: From *The Human Mosaic: A Thematic Introduction to Cultural Geography,* 8th ed. by Terry G. Jordan-Bychkov and Mona Domosh. Copyright © 1999 by Addison-Wesley Educational Publisher, Inc. Reprinted by permission of W. H. Freeman and Company.

Rituals and beliefs are expressed and transmitted from generation to generation by means of symbols. A symbol is something that stands for something else. A flag bearing a particular arrangement of stars and stripes symbolizes the United States of America, and saluting this flag symbolizes loyalty to the nation.

Photo courtesy of Maxine Hicks

CHAPTER 1

PERSPECTIVES

The readings in this chapter demonstrate that beliefs and rituals can be legitimately studied from a variety of different perspectives. The readings by Edward Tylor, Sigmund Freud, and Emile Durkheim illustrate the English anthropologist, Edward Evans-Pritchard's (1965) three perspectives, or what he referred to as "theories," of religion and magic. Robin Horton's article takes another look at Tylor's approach as that of a modern-day professional anthropologist. The readings offer distinctive insights into the nature of ritual and belief, since, as noted in the Introduction, intellectual, emotional, and sociological factors influence religion. Indeed, given the biological makeup of human beings how could it be otherwise? But, despite the confident assertions of those who proposed them, none of these theories can be regarded as offering an exclusive or definitive "theory of religion."

Emile Durkheim considered religion so effective a mechanism for social coherence that he chose to define religion in terms that were sociological—"a unified system of beliefs and practices relative to sacred things . . . which unite into one single moral community, called a Church, all those who [follow] them" (1965, p. 62). This characterization underscored Durkheim's conviction that—whatever else it might be, the result of intellectual speculation or perhaps a product of psychology—the essence of religion lay in its character as a sociological phenomenon. People acquire their religious beliefs, learn to carry out rituals, and assimilate the appropriate religious sentiments, he pointed out, as part of their process of socialization; adding that since beliefs are generated within the context of society they are therefore valid for that society. "There are no religions which are false," Durkheim wrote. "All are true in their own fashion; all answer, though in different ways, to the given conditions of human existence" (p. 15). Durkheim went on to claim that society can be regarded as possessing godlike properties. It exerts immense power over its members, instills a sense of dependence on them, and is the object of inordinate respect. Beliefs, he concluded, are the collective representations by which believers explain to themselves the nature of their society.

In contrast, the English scholar Edward Tylor (1873) argued for the intellectual perspective on religion. Beliefs evolved from the intellect's desire to explain the natural world. Taking beliefs in unseen beings as a common element of religion everywhere, Tylor (as we saw in the Introduction) defined religion as "the belief in spiritual beings" (1873, p. 424). Having first made clear what he meant by the term "religion," Tylor then speculated about its origins among our earliest ancestors. He conjectured that beliefs in spiritual beings arose from dreams. While dreaming, the sleeper would inevitably find himself or herself among not only the living but also the dead. Tylor tried to imagine what construction early human beings might have put on this experience, and he concluded they probably reasoned some part of the human self existed as an insubstantial entity that complemented the material body and survived death. Thus did the idea of the soul come into being. Then, over the course of time, ideas about these phantoms evolved into beliefs in the existence of spirits, which (unlike souls) were supernatural agencies entirely distinct from human beings. To win their favors, sacrifices would have been made and so the first rituals were invented. As time went on, increasingly powerful spirits were imagined, and polytheism came into being. Eventually, monotheism evolved (See Fig. 1).

Monotheism, of course, was a feature of the predominant religion of Tylor's own society, Christianity. His view was typical of anthropological thinking at that time, an ethnocentric conjecture implying that monotheism was the logical end product of a long evolutionary process of religious thought, in which an antecedent set of simpler beliefs evolved into increasingly complex ideologies. Science, however, he believed, would eventually climax this evolution, and religion would fade away. Comparative research later revealed that monotheism, even in the rather restricted sense of a single almighty spirit, is in fact rare among the religions of the world. Indeed, on the pages of the Bible the Christian God himself concedes the existence of other gods. The Bible tells how God

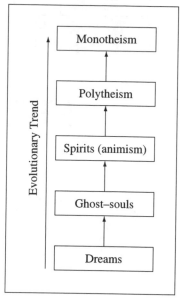

FIGURE 1

demands that his devotees worship no other god but himself—"Thou shalt not have strange gods before me!" Paul Radin (1954, 3–4), an anthropological authority on religion well-known for his ethnographic studies of the Plains Indians, remarks that "Pure monotheism in the late Hebraic, Christian and Mohammedan sense of the term is rare. It is clearly encountered in certain parts of Africa, especially West Africa, and in Polynesia. Its occurrence in aboriginal America and Australia, it seems to me, is more than doubtful. As an essentially philosophic belief entertained by a few deeply religious individuals and connected with origin myths it may, however, appear everywhere."

Beliefs and rituals are frequently charged with sentiments, a link that has persuaded some students of religion to put a psychological cast on religion, most notably, Sigmund Freud, who suggested that guilt is the main driving force inspiring it. Couching his argument in Oedipal terms, he wrote a scenario that he appeared to have imagined could have taken place in primeval times, one in which early human hunting groups were led by an elder male—their father—who commandeered the females in the group for his own pleasure. Frustrated, his sons revolted against his tyranny, killing him and then eating his corpse. Subsequently overcome by feelings of guilt, the murderers reconstructed their victim as a culture hero who in time became apotheosized into a god.

Reading 1–4, by Robin Horton, a specialist in the religions of West Africa, defends Tylor's intellectualist position from the point of view of an anthropologist who (unlike Tylor) actually carried out modern field research and who has the advantage of drawing upon a huge wealth of ethnographic data collected by trained ethnographers over a period of eighty years. In advocating certain key ideas offered by his intellectualist predecessor, Horton emphasizes that although these ideas are justified by the information we now possess (and which Tylor lacked), other approaches to our understanding of religious beliefs are also valid, most notably the sociological approach, which gained currency only after Tylor had published his *Primitive Culture.*

READING 1–1

ANIMISM

Edward B. Tylor

Edward Tylor sought to explain why human beings came to believe in spirits, and in doing so came up with the notion of what he called the "ghost-soul." This led him to develop his theory in such a manner as to extend the world of souls outside the domain of human beings. It might have seemed reasonable to early human beings, he said, to credit natural objects, such as animals, trees, and stars, as well has human beings, with souls. Tylor claimed this type of belief constituted the first religion, and he called it animism. *Tylor's thesis reflected Charles Darwin's biological model and was in tune with the evolutionary thought of the time, but it eventually succumbed to the sociological approach of Emile Durkeim. Although*

bolstered by a huge number of ethnographic examples from all over the world, the beliefs Tylor used as his data were, for the most part, useless as evidence because he had failed to see what Durkheim later stressed, viz., that beliefs require an ethnographic context to be properly understood. Then, too, he failed to take into account the problem of verifiability. How could his thesis be proved? Nevertheless, Edward Tylor properly drew attention to the intellectual nature of many so-called "primitive" beliefs, and his term "animism," by proving to have some descriptive value in comparative studies, has become part of the vocabulary of comparative religion.

The first requisite in a systematic study of the religions of the lower races, is to lay down a rudimentary definition of religion. By requiring in this definition the belief in a supreme deity or of judgment after death, the adoration of idols or the practice of sacrifice, or other partially-diffused doctrines or rites, no doubt many tribes may be excluded from the category of religious. But such narrow definition has the fault of identifying religion rather with particular developments than with the deeper motive which underlies them. It seems best to fall back at once on this essential source, and simply to claim, as a minimum definition of Religion, the belief in Spiritual Beings. If this standard be applied to the descriptions of low races as to religion, the following results will appear. It cannot be positively asserted that every existing tribe recognizes the belief in spiritual beings, for the native condition of a considerable number is obscure in this respect, and from the rapid change or extinction they are undergoing, may ever remain so. It would be yet more unwarranted to set down every tribe mentioned in history, or known to us by the discovery of antiquarian relics, as necessarily having possessed the defined minimum of religion. Greater still would be the unwisdom of declaring such a rudimentary belief natural or instinctive in all human tribes of all times; for no evidence justifies the opinion that man, known to be capable of so vast an intellectual development, cannot have emerged from a non-religious condition, previous to that religious condition in which he happens at present to come with sufficient clearness within our range of knowledge. It is desirable, however, to take our basis of enquiry in observation rather than from speculation. Here, so far as I can judge from the immense mass of accessible evidence, we have to admit that the belief in spiritual beings appears among all low races with whom we have attained to thoroughly intimate acquaintance; whereas the assertion of absence of such belief must apply either to ancient tribes, or to more or less imperfectly described modern ones. The exact bearing of this state of things on the problem of the origin of religion may be thus briefly stated. Were it distinctly proved that non-religious savages exist or have existed, these might be at least plausibly claimed as representatives of the condition of Man before he arrived at the religious stage of culture. It is not desirable, however, that this argument should be put forward, for the asserted existence of the non-religious tribes in question rests, as we have seen, on evidence often mistaken and never conclusive. The argument for the natural evolution of religious ideas among mankind is not invalidated by the rejection of an ally too weak at present to give effectual help. Non-religious tribes may not exist in our day, but the fact bears no more decisively on the development of religion, than the impossibility of finding a modern English village without scissors or books or Lucifer-matches bears on the fact that there was a time when no such things existed in the land.

I purpose here, under the name of Animism, to investigate the deep-lying doctrine of Spiritual Beings, which embodies the very essence of Spiritualistic as opposed to Materialistic philosophy. Animism is not a new technical term, though now seldom used . . .

Animism characterizes tribes very low in the scale of humanity, and thence ascends, deeply modified in its transmission, but from first to last preserving an unbroken continuity, into the midst of high modern culture. Doctrines adverse to it, so largely held by individuals or schools, are usually due not to early lowness of civilization, but to later changes in the intellectual course, to divergence

from, or rejection of, ancestral faiths; and such newer developments do not affect the present enquiry as to the fundamental religious condition of mankind. Animism is, in fact, the groundwork of the Philosophy of Religion, from that of savages up to that of civilized men. And although it may at first sight seem to afford but a bare and meagre definition of a minimum of religion, it will be found practically sufficient; for where the root is, the branches will generally be produced. It is habitually found that the theory of Animism divides into two great dogmas, forming parts of one consistent doctrine; first, concerning souls of individual creatures, capable of continued existence after the death or destruction of the body; second, concerning other spirits, upward to the rank of powerful deities. Spiritual beings are held to affect or control the events of the material world, and man's life here and hereafter; and it being considered that they hold intercourse with men, and receive pleasure or displeasure from human actions, the belief in their existence leads naturally, and it might almost be said inevitably, sooner or later to active reverence and propitiation. Thus Animism, in its full development, includes the belief in souls and in a future state, in controlling deities and subordinate spirits, these doctrines practically resulting in some kind of active worship. One great element of religion, that moral element which among the higher nations forms its most vital part, is indeed little represented in the religion of the lower races. It is not that these races have no moral sense or no moral standard, for both are strongly marked among them, if not in formal precept, at least in that traditional consensus of society which we call public opinion, according to which certain actions are held to be good or bad, right or wrong. It is that the conjunction of ethics and Animistic philosophy, so intimate and powerful in the higher culture, seems scarcely yet to have begun in the lower. I propose here hardly to touch upon the purely moral aspects of religion, but rather to study the animism of the world so far as it constitutes, as unquestionably it does constitute, an ancient and world-wide philosophy, of which belief is the theory and worship is the practice. Endeavouring to shape the materials for an enquiry hitherto strangely undervalued and neglected, it will now be my task to bring as clearly as may be into view the fundamental animism of the lower races, and in some slight and broken outline to trace its course into higher regions of civilization. Here let me state once for all two principal conditions under which the present research is carried on. First, as to the religious doctrines and practices examined, these are treated as belonging to theological systems devised by human reason, without supernatural aid or revelation; in other words, as being developments of Natural Religion. Second, as to the connexion between similar ideas and rites in the religions of the savage and the civilized world. While dwelling at some length on doctrines and ceremonies of the lower races, and sometimes particularizing for special reasons the related doctrines and ceremonies of the higher nations, it has not seemed my proper task to work out in detail the problems thus suggested among the philosophies and creeds of Christendom. Such applications, extending farthest from the direct scope of a work on primitive culture, are briefly stated in general terms, or touched in slight allusion, or taken for granted without remark . . .

The first branch of the subject to be considered is the doctrine of human and other Souls, an examination of which will occupy the rest of the present chapter. What the doctrine of the soul is among the lower races, may be explained in stating the present theory of its development. It seems as though thinking men, as yet at a low level of culture, were deeply impressed by two groups of biological problems. In the first place, what is it that makes the difference between a living body and a dead one; what causes waking, sleep, trance, disease, death? In the second place, what are those human shapes which appear in dreams and visions? Looking at these two groups of phenomena, the ancient savage philosophers probably made their first step by the obvious inference that every man has two things belonging to him, namely, a life and a phantom. These two are evidently in close connexion with the body, the life as enabling it to feel and think and act, the phantom as

being its image or second self; both, also, are perceived to be things separable from the body, the life as able to go away and leave it insensible or dead, the phantom as appearing to people at a distance from it. The second step would seem also easy for savages to make, seeing how extremely difficult civilized men have found it to unmake. It is merely to combine the life and the phantom. As both belong to the body, why should they not also belong to one another, and be manifestations of one and the same soul? Let them then be considered as united, and the result is that well-known conception which may be described as an apparitional-soul, a ghost-soul. This, at any rate, corresponds with the actual conception of the personal soul or spirit among the lower races, which may be defined as follows: It is a thin unsubstantial human image, in its nature a sort of vapour, film, or shadow; the cause of life and thought in the individual it animates; independently possessing the personal consciousness and volition of its corporeal owner, past or present; capable of leaving the body far behind, to flash swiftly from place to place; mostly impalpable and invisible, yet also manifesting physical power, and especially appearing to men waking or asleep as a phantasm separate from the body of which it bears the likeness; continuing to exist and appear to men after the death of that body; able to enter into, possess, and act in the bodies of other men, of animals, and even of things. Though this definition is by no means of universal application, it has sufficient generality to be taken as a standard, modified by more or less divergence among any particular people . . .

The early animistic theory of vitality, regarding the functions of life as caused by the soul, offers to the savage mind an explanation of several bodily and mental conditions, as being effects of a departure of the soul or some of its constituent spirits. This theory holds a wide and strong position in savage biology. . . . Among the Algonquin Indians of North America, we hear of sickness being accounted for by the patient's "shadow" being unsettled or detached from his body, and of the convalescent being reproached for exposing himself before his shadow was safely settled down in him; where we should say that a man was ill and recovered, they would consider that he died, but came again . . .

Such temporary exit of the soul has a world-wide application to the proceedings of the sorcerer, priest, or seer himself. He professes to send forth his spirit on distant journeys, and probably often believes his soul released for a time from its bodily prison . . .

Death is the event which, in all stages of culture, brings thought to bear most intensely, though not always most healthily, on the problems of psychology. The apparition of the disembodied soul has in all ages been thought to bear especial relation to its departure from its body at death . . .

That the apparitional human soul bears the likeness of its fleshly body, is the principle implicitly accepted by all who believe it really and objectively present in dreams and visions. My own view is that nothing but dreams and visions could have ever put into men's minds such an idea as that of souls being ethereal images of bodies. It is thus habitually taken for granted in animistic philosophy, savage or civilized, that souls set free from the earthly body are recognized by a likeness to it which they still retain, whether as ghostly wanderers on earth or inhabitants of the world beyond the grave . . .

Departing from the body at the time of death, the soul or spirit is considered set free to linger near the tomb, to wander on earth or flit in the air, or to travel to the proper region of spirits—the world beyond the grave. The principal conceptions of the lower psychology as to a Future Life will be considered in the following chapters, but for the present purpose of investigating the theory of souls in general, it will be well to enter here upon one department of the subject. Men do not stop short at the persuasion that death releases the soul to a free and active existence, but they quite logically proceed to assist nature, by slaying men in order to liberate their souls for ghostly uses. Thus there arises one of the most wide-spread, distinct, and intelligible rites of animistic religion—that of funeral human sacrifice for the service of the dead. When a man of rank dies and his soul departs to its own place, wherever and

whatever that place may be, it is a rational inference of early philosophy that the souls of attendants, slaves, and wives, put to death at his funeral, will make the same journey and continue their service in the next life, and the argument is frequently stretched further, to include the souls of new victims sacrificed in order that they may enter upon the same ghostly servitude. It will appear from the ethnography of this rite that it is not strongly marked in the very lowest levels of culture, but that, arising in the higher savagery, it develops itself in the barbaric stage, and thenceforth continues or dwindles in survival.

READING 1–2

THE RETURN OF TOTEMISM IN CHILDHOOD

Sigmund Freud

The most famous proponent of the emotional approach to the study of ritual and belief was the psychoanalyst Sigmund Freud, and here he sets forth his ideas concerning the origins of religion. The belief in a god, he says, originated in feelings of guilt. As Evans-Pritchard has remarked (1965, p. 63), for the French sociologist Emile Durkheim, god was society; for Freud, god was the father. In a figurative sense, at least, Durkheim had the facts on his side. Freud's hypothesis, in contrast, was mere fancy, supported by neither data nor illuminating metaphor. Nevertheless, Freud's insistence on the importance of the emotions involved in religious behavior served as a corrective to Tylor's one-sided emphasis on the intellectual character of religion and his resulting focus upon belief as the generator of ritual. Freud's thesis set the stage for the functional link Malinowski would later try to establish between ritual and the psychological health of the individual. As a corrective for the sociological approach it also reminds us that religion is as much an individual matter as a sociological phenomenon. The emotional side of religion was continued in the work of the American anthropologist, Robert H. Lowie (1970), for whom religion was a "sense of the Extraordinary, Mysterious, or Supernatural" (p. xvi). An anthro-

pologist of a later generation, Victor Turner (Reading 4–2), in the 1960s, following an extraordinary productive period of ethnographic research in central Africa, was to make use of, and merge into his own distinctive style of analysis, all three approaches—intellectual, sociological, and emotional—thus providing us with an especially convincing portrait of a religious system, that of the Ndembu, of Zambia, Central Africa.

Let us call up the spectacle of a totem meal of the kind we have been discussing, amplified by a few probable features which we have not yet been able to consider. The clan is celebrating the ceremonial occasion by the cruel slaughter of its totem animal and is devouring it raw—blood, flesh and bones. The clansmen are there, dressed in the likeness of the totem and imitating it in sound and movement, as though they are seeking to stress their identity with it. Each man is conscious that he is performing an act forbidden to the individual and justifiable only through the participation of the whole clan; nor may anyone absent himself from the killing and the meal. When the deed is done, the slaughtered animal is lamented and bewailed. The mourning is obligatory, imposed by dread of a threatened retribution. As Robertson Smith (1894, 412) remarks of an analogous occasion, its chief purpose is to disclaim responsibility for the killing.

But the mourning is followed by demonstrations of festive rejoicing: every instinct is unfettered and there is license for every kind of gratification. Here we have easy access to an understanding of the nature of festivals in general. A festival is a permitted, or rather an obligatory, excess, a solemn breach of a prohibition. It is not that men commit the excesses because they are feeling happy as a result of some injunction they have received. It is rather that excess is of the essence of a festival; the festive feeling is produced by the liberty to do what is as a rule prohibited.

What are we to make, though, of the prelude to this festive joy—the mourning over the death of the animal? If the clansmen rejoice over the killing of the totem—a normally forbidden act—why do they mourn over it as well?

As we have seen, the clansmen acquire sanctity by consuming the totem: they reinforce their iden-

tification with it and with one another. Their festive feelings and all that follows from them might well be explained by the fact that they have taken into themselves the sacred life of which the substance of the totem is the vehicle.

Psycho-analysis has revealed that the totem animal is in reality a substitute for the father; and this tallies with the contradictory fact that, though the killing of the animal is as a rule forbidden, yet its killing becomes a festive occasion—the fact that it is killed and yet mourned. The ambivalent emotional attitude, which to this day characterizes the father-complex in our children and which often persists into adult life, seems to extend to the totem animal in its capacity as substitute for the father.

If, now, we bring together the psycho-analytic translation of the totem with the fact of the totem meal and with Darwin's theories of the earliest state of human society, the possibility of a deeper understanding emerges—a glimpse of a hypothesis which may seem fantastic but which offers the advantage of establishing an unsuspected correlation between groups of phenomena that have hitherto been disconnected.

There is, of course, no place for the beginnings of totemism in Darwin's primal horde. All that we find there is a violent and jealous father who keeps all the females for himself and drives away his sons as they grow up. This earliest state of society has never been an object of observation. The most primitive kind of organization that we actually come across—and one that is in force to this day in certain tribes—consists of bands of males; these bands are composed of members with equal rights and are subject to the restrictions of the totemic system, including inheritance through the mother. Can this form of organization have developed out of the other one? and if so along what lines?

If we call the celebration of the totem meal to our help, we shall be able to find an answer. One day[1] the brothers who had been driven out came together, killed and devoured their father and so made an end of the patriarchal horde. United, they had the courage to do and succeeded in doing what would have been impossible for them individually.

(Some cultural advance, perhaps, command over some new weapon, had given them a sense of superior strength.) Cannibal savages as they were, it goes without saying that they devoured their victim as well as killing him. The violent primal father had doubtless been the feared and envied model of each one of the company of brothers: and in the act of devouring him they accomplished their identification with him, and each one of them acquired a portion of his strength. The totem meal, which is perhaps mankind's earliest festival, would thus be a repetition and a commemoration of this memorable and criminal deed, which was the beginning of so many things—of social organization, of moral restrictions and of religion.[2]

In order that these latter consequences may seem plausible leaving their premises on one side, we need only suppose that the tumultuous mob of brothers were filled with the same contradictory feelings which we can see at work in the ambivalent father-complexes of our children and of our neurotic patients. They hated their father, who presented such a formidable obstacle to their craving for power and their sexual desires; but they loved and admired him too. After they had got rid of him, had satisfied their hatred and had put into effect their wish to identify themselves with him, the affection which had all this time been pushed under was bound to make itself felt.[3] It did so in the form of remorse. A sense of guilt made its appearance, which in this instance coincided with the remorse felt by the whole group. The dead father became stronger than the living one had been—for events took the course we so often see them follow in human affairs to this day. What had up to then been prevented by his actual existence was thenceforward prohibited by the sons themselves, in accordance with the psychological procedure so familiar to us in psycho-analyses under the name of "deferred obedience." They revoked their deed by forbidding the killing of the totem, the substitute for their father; and they renounced its fruits by resigning their claim to the women who had now been set free. They thus created out of their filial sense of guilt the two fundamental taboos of totemism,

which for that very reason inevitably corresponded to the two repressed wishes of the Œdipus complex. Whoever contravened those taboos became guilty of the only two crimes with which primitive society concerned itself.[4]

The two taboos of totemism with which human morality has its beginning, are not on a par psychologically. The first of them, the law protecting the totem animal, is founded wholly on emotional motives: the father had actually been eliminated, and in no real sense could the deed be undone. But the second rule, the prohibition of incest, has a powerful practical basis as well. Sexual desires do not unite men but divide them. Though the brothers had banded together in order to overcome their father, they were all one another's rivals in regard to the women. Each of them would have wished, like his father, to have all the women to himself. The new organization would have collapsed in a struggle of all against all, for none of them was of such over-mastering strength as to be able to take on his father's part with success. Thus the brothers had no alternative, if they were to live together, but—not, perhaps, until they had passed through many dangerous crises—to institute the law against incest, by which they all alike renounced the women whom they desired and who had been their chief motive for dispatching their father. In this way they rescued the organization which had made them strong—and which may have been based on homosexual feelings and acts, originating perhaps during the period of their expulsion from the horde. Here, too, may perhaps have been the germ of the institution of matriarchy, described by Bachofen (1861), which was in turn replaced by the patriarchal organization of the family.

On the other hand, the claim of totemism to be regarded as a first attempt at a religion is based on the first of these two taboos—that upon taking the life of the totem animal. The animal struck the sons as a natural and obvious substitute for their father; but the treatment of it which they found imposed on themselves expressed more than the need to exhibit their remorse. They could attempt, in their relation to this surrogate father, to allay their burning sense of guilt, to bring about a kind of reconciliation with their father. The totemic system was, as it were, a covenant with their father, in which he promised them everything that a childish imagination may expect from a father— protection, care and indulgence—while on their side they undertook to respect his life, that is to say, not to repeat the deed which had brought destruction on their real father. Totemism, moreover, contained an attempt at self-justification: "If our father had treated us in the way the totem does, we should never have felt tempted to kill him." In this fashion totemism helped to smooth things over and to make it possible to forget the event to which it owed its origin.

Features were thus brought into existence which continued thenceforward to have a determining influence on the nature of religion. Totemic religion arose from the filial sense of guilt, in an attempt to allay that feeling and to appease the father by deferred obedience to him. All later religions are seen to be attempts at solving the same problem. They vary according to the stage of civilization at which they arise and according to the methods which they adopt; but all have the same end in view and are reactions to the same great event with which civilization began and which, since it occurred, has not allowed mankind a moment's rest.

ENDNOTES

1. To avoid possible misunderstanding, I must ask the reader to take into account the final sentences of the following footnote as a corrective to this description.

2. This hypothesis, which has such a monstrous air, of the tyrannical father being overwhelmed and killed by a combination of his exiled sons was also arrived at by Atkinson (1903, 220 f.) as a direct implication of the state of affairs in Darwin's primal horde: "The patriarch had only one enemy whom he should dread . . . a youthful band of brothers living together in forced celibacy, or at most in polyandrous relation with some single female captive. A horde as yet weak in their impubescence they are, but they would, when strength was gained with time, inevitably wrench by combined attacks, renewed again and again, both wife and life from the paternal tyrant." Atkinson, who incidentally passed his whole life in New Caledonia and had unusual opportunities for studying the natives, also pointed out that the conditions which Darwin assumed to prevail in the primal horde may easily be observed in herds of wild oxen

and horses and regularly lead to the killing of the father of the herd (Ibid., 222 f.). He further supposed that, after the father had been disposed of, the horde would be disintegrated by a bitter struggle between the victorious sons. Thus any new organization of society would be precluded: there would be "an ever-recurring violent succession to the solitary paternal tyrant, by sons whose parricidal hands were so soon again clenched in fratricidal strife" (Ibid., 228). Atkinson, who had no psycho-analytic hints to help him and who was ignorant of Robertson Smith's studies, found a less violent transition from the primal horde to the next social stage, at which numbers of males live together in a peaceable community. He believed that through the intervention of maternal love the sons—to begin with only the youngest, but later others as well—were allowed to remain with the horde, and that in return for this toleration the sons acknowledged their father's sexual privilege by renouncing all claim to their mother and sisters (Ibid., 231 ff.).

Such is the highly remarkable theory put forward by Atkinson. In its essential feature it is in agreement with my own; but its divergence results in its failing to effect a correlation with many other issues.

The lack of precision in what I have written in the text above, its abbreviation of the time factor and its compression of the whole subject-matter, may be attributed to the reserve necessitated by the nature of the topic. It would be as foolish to aim at exactitude in such questions as it would be unfair to insist upon certainty.

3. This fresh emotional attitude must also have been assisted by the fact that the deed cannot have given complete satisfaction to those who did it. From one point of view it had been done in vain. Not one of the sons had in fact been able to put his original wish—of taking his father's place—into effect. And, as we know, failure is far more propitious for a moral reaction than satisfaction.

4. "Murder and incest, or offences of a like kind against the sacred laws of blood, are in primitive society the only crimes of which the community as such takes cognizance." (Smith, 1894, 419.)

READING 1–3

THE ELEMENTARY FORMS OF THE RELIGIOUS LIFE

Emile Durkheim

In this reading Durkheim draws a distinction between sacred and profane (or secular), which he sees as a key feature of both religion and magic. Sacred things are things set apart as special. Profane things are the commonplace matters of everyday life. Durkheim also sought to distinguish religion from magic, contrasting the communal character of religion with what he considered the individual character of magic (see Chapter 7). Both these famous statements are true to some extent, but modern ethnographic research has to some extent contradicted Durkheim. It has demonstrated the relativity of the concepts of sacred and secular (see Reading 6–4). Sacred objects, for example, can be merely profane in certain contexts. Among the Oglala, an Indian group of the North American Plains, the sweat lodge is a sacred building when used for religious rituals. When it is not being so used it is not sacred at all. Magic rituals, too, can, at times, be communal affairs (see Reading 4–5), and just simply, as Durkheim claimed, social events.

Despite the attraction a sociological approach held for him, Durkheim was not averse to appealing to psychological facts, as when he offered his own version of how religion originated. Religious ideas, he argued, were generated in ritual situations in which participants reacted with intense emotion to their activities. In these highly charged, emotional performances, participants came to feel the presence of immaterial beings living unseen among them, and who evidently came from some world other than the profane world (see Reading 8–4). This was the sacred world, and its inhabitants, the gods, were thus only creations in the collective representations of society. They were only projects of society itself: god = society. Again, as with Freud's thesis of religious origins and that of Tylor's, Durkheim, in this particular argument, could not offer any reliable ethnographic evidence in support of his assertions.

Religious phenomena are naturally arranged in two fundamental categories: beliefs and rites. The first are states of opinion, and consist in representations; the second are determined modes of action. Between these two classes of facts there is all the difference which separates thought from action.

The rites can be defined and distinguished from other human practices, moral practices, for example, only by the special nature of their object. A moral rule prescribes certain manners of acting to us, just as a rite does, but which are addressed to a different class of objects. So it is the object of the rite which must be characterized, if we are to characterize the rite itself. Now it is in the beliefs that the special nature of this object is expressed. It is possible to define the rite only after we have defined the belief.

All known religious beliefs, whether simple or complex, present one common characteristic: they presuppose a classification of all the things, real and ideal, of which men think, into two classes or opposed groups, generally designated by two distinct terms which are translated well enough by the words *profane* and *sacred* (*profane, sacré*). This division of the world into two domains, the one containing all that is sacred, the other all that is profane, is the distinctive trait of religious thought; the beliefs, myths, dogmas and legends are either representations or systems of representations which express the nature of sacred things, the virtues and powers which are attributed to them, or their relations with each other and with profane things. But by sacred things one must not understand simply those personal beings which are called gods or spirits; a rock, a tree, a spring, a pebble, a piece of wood, a house, in a word, anything can be sacred. A rite can have this character; in fact, the rite does not exist which does not have it to a certain degree. There are words, expressions and formulæ which can be pronounced only by the mouths of consecrated persons; there are gestures and movements which everybody cannot perform. If the Vedic sacrifice has had such an efficacy that, according to mythology, it was the creator of the gods, and not merely a means of winning their favour, it is because it possessed a virtue comparable to that of the most sacred beings. The circle of sacred objects cannot be determined, then, once for all. Its extent varies infinitely, according to the different religions. That is how Buddhism is a religion: in default of gods, it admits the existence of sacred things, namely, the four noble truths and the practices derived from them.

Up to the present we have confined ourselves to enumerating a certain number of sacred things as examples: we must now show by what general characteristics they are to be distinguished from profane things.

One might be tempted, first of all, to define them by the place they are generally assigned in the hierarchy of things. They are naturally considered superior in dignity and power to profane things, and particularly to man, when he is only a man and has nothing sacred about him. One thinks of himself as occupying an inferior and dependent position in relation to them; and surely this conception is not without some truth. Only there is nothing in it which is really characteristic of the sacred. It is not enough that one thing be subordinated to another for the second to be sacred in regard to the first. Slaves are inferior to their masters, subjects to their king, soldiers to their leaders, the miser to his gold, the man ambitious for power to the hands which keep it from him; but if it is sometimes said of a man that he makes a religion of those beings or things whose eminent value and superiority to himself he thus recognizes, it is clear that in any case the word is taken in a metaphorical sense, and that there is nothing in these relations which is really religious.

On the other hand, it must not be lost to view that there are sacred things of every degree, and that there are some in relation to which a man feels himself relatively at his ease. An amulet has a sacred character, yet the respect which it inspires is nothing exceptional. Even before his gods, a man is not always in such a marked state of inferiority; for it very frequently happens that he exercises a veritable physical constraint upon them to obtain what he desires. . . . Moreover, if it is true that man depends upon his gods, this dependence is reciprocal. The gods also have need of man; without offerings and sacrifices they would die. We shall even have occasion to show that this dependence of the gods upon their worshippers is maintained even in the most idealistic religions.

But if a purely hierarchic distinction is a criterium at once too general and too imprecise, there is nothing left with which to characterize the sacred in its relation to the profane except their heterogeneity. However, this heterogeneity is sufficient to characterize this classification of things and to distinguish it from all others, because it is very particular: *it is absolute*. In all the history of human thought there exists no other example of two categories of things so profoundly differentiated or so radically opposed to one another. The traditional

opposition of good and bad is nothing beside this; for the good and the bad are only two opposed species of the same class, namely morals, just as sickness and health are two different aspects of the same order of facts, life, while the sacred and the profane have always and everywhere been conceived by the human mind as two distinct classes, as two worlds between which there is nothing in common. The forces which play in one are not simply those which are met with in the other, but a little stronger; they are of a different sort. In different religions, this opposition has been conceived in different ways. Here, to separate these two sorts of things, it has seemed sufficient to localize them in different parts of the physical universe; there, the first have been put into an ideal and transcendental world, while the material world is left in full possession of the others. But howsoever much the forms of the contrast may vary, the fact of the contrast is universal . . .

The opposition of these two classes manifests itself outwardly with a visible sign by which we can easily recognize this very special classification, wherever it exists. Since the idea of the sacred is always and everywhere separated from the idea of the profane in the thought of men, and since we picture a sort of logical chasm between the two, the mind irresistibly refuses to allow the two corresponding things to be confounded, or even to be merely put in contact with each other; for such a promiscuity, or even too direct a contiguity, would contradict too violently the dissociation of these ideas in the mind. The sacred thing is *par excellence* that which the profane should not touch, and cannot touch with impunity. To be sure, this interdiction cannot go so far as to make all communication between the two worlds impossible; for if the profane could in no way enter into relations with the sacred, this latter could be good for nothing. But, in addition to the fact that this establishment of relations is always a delicate operation in itself, demanding great precautions and a more or less complicated initiation, it is quite impossible, unless the profane is to lose its specific characteristics and become sacred after a fashion and to a certain degree itself. The two classes cannot even approach each other and keep their own nature at the same time . . .

The real characteristic of religious phenomena is that they always suppose a bipartite division of the whole universe, known and knowable, into two classes which embrace all that exists, but which radically exclude each other. Sacred things are those which the interdictions protect and isolate: profane things, those to which these interdictions are applied and which must remain at a distance from the first. Religious beliefs are the representations which express the nature of sacred things and the relations which they sustain, either with each other or with profane things. Finally, rites are the rules of conduct which prescribe how a man should comport himself in the presence of these sacred objects . . .

However, this definition is not yet complete, for it is equally applicable to two sorts of facts which, while being related to each other, must be distinguished nevertheless: these are magic and religion.

Magic, too, is made up of beliefs and rites. Like religion, it has its myths and its dogmas; only they are more elementary, undoubtedly because, seeking technical and utilitarian ends, it does not waste its time in pure speculation. It has its ceremonies, sacrifices, lustrations, prayers, chants and dances as well. The beings which the magician invokes and the forces which he throws in play are not merely of the same nature as the forces and beings to which religion addresses itself; very frequently, they are identically the same. Thus, even with the most inferior societies, the souls of the dead are essentially sacred things, and the object of religious rites. But at the same time, they play a considerable rôle in magic . . .

The really religious beliefs are always common to a determined group, which makes profession of adhering to them and of practising the rites connected with them. They are not merely received individually by all the members of this group; they are something belonging to the group, and they make its unity. The individuals which compose it feel themselves united to each other by the simple fact that they have a common faith. A society whose members are united by the fact that they think in the same way in regard to the sacred world and its rela-

tions with the profane world, and by the fact that they translate these common ideas into common practices, is what is called a Church. In all history, we do not find a single religion without a Church. Sometimes the Church is strictly national, sometimes it passes the frontiers; sometimes it embraces an entire people (Rome, Athens, the Hebrews), sometimes it embraces only a part of them (the Christian societies since the advent of Protestantism); sometimes it is directed by a corps of priests, sometimes it is almost completely devoid of any official directing body. But wherever we observe the religious life, we find that it has a definite group as its foundation. Even the so-called private cults, such as the domestic cult or the cult of a corporation, satisfy this condition; for they are always celebrated by a group, the family or the corporation. Moreover, even these particular religions are ordinarily only special forms of a more general religion which embraces all: these restricted Churches are in reality only chapels of a vaster Church which, by reason of this very extent, merits this name still more.

It is quite another matter with magic. To be sure, the belief in magic is always more or less general; it is very frequently diffused in large masses of the population, and there are even peoples where it has as many adherents as the real religion. But it does not result in binding together those who adhere to it, nor in uniting them into a group leading a common life. *There is no Church of magic.* Between the magician and the individuals who consult him, as between these individuals themselves, there are no lasting bonds which make them members of the same moral community, comparable to that formed by the believers in the same god or the observers of the same cult. The magician has a clientele and not a Church, and it is very possible that his clients have no other relations between each other, or even do not know each other; even the relations which they have with him are generally accidental and transient; they are just like those of a sick man with his physician. The official and public character with which he is sometimes invested changes nothing in this situation; the fact that he works openly does not unite him more regularly or more durably to those who have recourse to his services . . .

Thus we arrive at the following definition: *A religion is a unified system of beliefs and practices relative to sacred things, that is to say, things set apart and forbidden—beliefs and practices which unite into one single moral community called a Church, all those who adhere to them.* The second element which thus finds a place in our definition is no less essential than the first; for by showing that the idea of religion is inseparable from that of the Church, it makes it clear that religion should be an eminently collective thing.

NEO-TYLORIANISM: SOUND SENSE OR SINISTER PREJUDICE?

Robin Horton
University of Ibadan, Nigeria

Robin Horton revisits the intellectual approach to the study of belief and ritual, and he offers a defense against scholars who have attempted to undermine it. His central point is that Tylor was perfectly correct in remarking that the religious beliefs of nonliterate people frequently explain, to their advocates' own satisfaction apparently, features of the natural world and of their own societies that they feel need explaining. Now, this may seem reasonable enough to non-anthropologists, but you will recall that for Durkheim religious beliefs were merely symbols. The same was true for Freud. The beliefs of the followers of religion, in other words, should not be taken literally. They are not what religious people really believe. At a deeper level—but one, of course, capable of being accessed by the scholar—beliefs stood for other things—society, god as a father, and so on. We should not take them seriously in their own right as local explanations of how the world worked, but only as symbols that believers could not adequately understand. In Chapter 2 we shall see how, for scholars who favor the structuralist

approach—Edmund Leach, whom Horton singles out for strong criticism, was one of its leading advocates—it is the way in which beliefs are arranged in a system of order that is the most meaningful characteristic of such beliefs, and therefore what anthropologists should study. Horton, however, urges us to take seriously the contents *of religious beliefs. If people, for instance, say that sickness is punishment from their ancestral ghosts, why should the ethnographer prefer to seek some deeper, more obscure explanation? Beliefs such as this may indeed have some emotional basis or sociological consequences, but these alternative forms of explanation, though useful as additional perspectives, Horton would argue, should not prevent us from accepting it as a fact of ethnography that people in this society really do explain illness in this way, and that this fact is one that the anthropologist must take into account in devising his or her own interpretation of that religion.*

Over the last year or two a new pejorative, 'neo-Tylorian', has entered the vocabulary of British social anthropologists. What error is it supposed to castigate?

The short answer seems to be that when someone in a pre-literate society answers questions about the cause of an event by making a statement concerning the activities of invisible personal beings, the neo-Tylorian (following his ancestor Sir E. B. Tylor) takes the statement at its face value. He accepts it as an attempt at explanation, and goes on to ask why members of the culture in question should try to explain things in this unfamiliar way.

To the layman, this intellectualist approach is likely to seem self-evidently sensible. To the orthodox social anthropologist, however, it is misguided in the extreme. For the anthropologist, it is the height of error to take pre-literate religious belief-statements at their face value. Such statements may be many things; but they are not really attempts at explanation, and should not be analysed as such.[1]

This is a very odd position. And its oddity stands out all the more clearly when one reflects that nothing of the kind has ever occurred to members of any other discipline concerned with the study of human beliefs. Thus historians of ideas have long been engaged in trying to answer questions as to why

Europeans of earlier ages should have sought to explain worldly events in theoretical terms very different from those to which we are now accustomed. But however strange these theoretical terms have seemed, the historians have never stopped to doubt whether they should take the statements containing them at their face value. For the historians, such statements give every appearance of being attempts at explanation, and should therefore be analysed and interpreted as such.[2]

Why should the intellectualist approach, which is perfectly satisfactory to the historian of earlier European ideas, appear so unsatisfactory to the social anthropologist dealing with the ideas of pre-literate, non-European cultures? Certainly results can have very little to do with the matter. For the historian of ideas, operating on the premiss that 'things are what they seem,' has been forging ahead most successfully with his interpretation of the European thought-tradition; but the social anthropologist, operating on the premiss that 'things are *not* what they seem,' has had little success in explaining why pre-literate peoples have the kind of ideas they do. If the anthropologist is so adamant in refusing to return to the more straightforward and apparently more productive methods favoured by the historian of ideas, he must have some very powerful negative arguments to support him. In this article, I shall try to identify these arguments and examine their worth. There seem, in fact, to be five principal arguments involved; and in what follows, I shall review them one by one. For illustration, I shall draw principally on the African material with which I am most familiar.

1. *In the sort of pre-literate cultures that social anthropologists study, there has been little development of that ideal of objective understanding of the world which is so central to the modern Western ethos. Hence intellectualist interpretations of the ideas of such cultures are out of order.[3]*

Now I think it is fair to say that the emergence of the ideal of objectivity is something peculiar to modern Western culture. But anthropologists using this fact to rule out intellectualist interpretation in non-Western cultures seem to have misunderstood

what is involved. Thus the emergence of an ideal of objectivity does not mean the growth of an interest in explanation where there was none before. Rather, it means the growth of a conviction that this interest, if it is to be pursued effectively, must be segregated from the influence of political manipulation, aesthetic values, wish-fulfillment, and so on. Pre-objective cultures, then, are not cultures where the desire to make sense of the world is absent. They are cultures where this desire is still intricately interwoven with many others. Hence what is required in studying them is not an abstention from intellectualist analysis, but a delicate balancing of intellectualist with political, aesthetic and other analysis.

Even with such a balanced, many-angled approach, there is good reason for thinking that, so far as beliefs and ideas are concerned, the intellectualist analysis must take precedence over others. The force of this contention is greatest in relation to the question of political manipulation. Modern social anthropologists have been fascinated by the political manipulation of ideas—perhaps because it is one of the most obvious bridges between the Senior Common Room and the Assembly Place Under the Iroko Tree. However, their analysis of such manipulation has a curious unreality; and I think it can be shown that this unreality is a direct outcome of the policy of rushing in with a political analysis before having made an intellectualist analysis.

An extreme illustration of this point is provided by Edmund Leach's *Political systems of highland Burma* (1954). Leach maintains that Kachin ideas about *nats* (spirits) are nothing but counters in the language of political argument; and it is precisely this contention which convinces one that his analysis is unreal. One cannot help protesting that if the *nats* are nothing more than counters in the power game, why do Kachins waste so much time talking about them? Why do they not couch their political arguments more directly? Less extreme but more instructive is John Middleton's *Lugbara religion* (1960). Here is a book which starts with a vivid but rather conventional analysis of the way in which influential members of Lugbara communities manipulate ideas of ancestral power for political purposes, and ends with what is perhaps the most brilliant intellectualist analysis of an African system of religious ideas yet made. Reading this book in the order in which it was written, one gets the same feeling of unreality as one had from Leach. Why do these people not get on with the politics? Rereading it with the intellectualist analysis put in before the political, one immediately regains a sense of reality. Now it becomes obvious why the old men spend such a lot of time talking about ancestral power and witchcraft when they are struggling for political position. It is because these ideas mean so much to Lugbara as intellectual tools for making sense of the world, that they are such powerful instruments in the hands of the politicians. If they meant nothing in intellectual terms, they would be nothing in the hands of the politicians.

It is because he *has* got things in the right order that a novelist of traditional African life like Chinua Achebe gives us a sense of reality missing from the work of the anthropologists. His *Arrow of God* (1964) in particular, deals with the intricate relations between religious beliefs and power struggles. Indeed, its two principal protagonists are priestly politicians. As backcloth to the struggle between the Eze Ulu and the Eze Idemili, Achebe gives us a compelling picture of the key place that their deities, Ulu and Idemili, occupy in the village world view. It is this backcloth that makes us see not only what powerful tools these deities are in the hands of would-be manipulators, but also what strict limits there must be to manipulation when those involved believe in and live by the ideas they are manipulating. Achebe's book, of course, is a novel and not a work of analysis; but a careful reading of it would do much to help anthropologists regain a sense of proportion in these matters.

To conclude, it is clear that social anthropologists have been seriously misled by the glib phrase 'manipulation of ideas'. What politicians manipulate is not ideas, but people's dependence on ideas as means of ordering, explaining, predicting and controlling their world. Only a prior analysis of the nature of this dependence can pave the way for an adequate grasp of the scope and limitations of manipulation.

2. *Members of pre-literate cultures tend to be of a practical rather than of a theoretical bent. Hence analyses that treat the religious ideas of such cultures as explanatory theories are beside the point.*[4]

My first comment on this argument is that the truth of the premiss is dubious. West African experience certainly makes one very chary of asserting that preliterate cultures lack people whose interest in theory outruns their practical concern. Nearly all of us who have worked in this area know the occasional old men who, having retired from the hurly-burly of everyday life, spend much of their time thinking it through and trying to make sense of it. And although there may be few such people in any particular community, they often play a disproportionate part in transmitting ideas to the next generation.

My second comment is that the argument appears to be based on the misleading colloquial opposition of 'theory' and 'practice.' As I have pointed out in a recent article, one of the principal intellectual functions of traditional African religious theory is that of placing everyday events in a wider causal context than common sense provides (Horton 1967a: 53–8). Traditional religious theory, indeed, complements common sense in its concern for the diagnosis, prediction and control of events. It is thus as intimately linked as is common sense with the practical concerns of its users. Conversely, it is reasonable to suppose that these practical concerns have played as great a part in stimulating the development of theory as they have in stimulating the development of common sense. So even if there were such a thing as a culture carried entirely by hard-headed pragmatists, one would still expect to find plenty of theory in it. Even in such a culture, then, there would be room for an intellectualist analysis.

3. *The ideas of pre-literate cultures seldom form logically consistent systems. Hence in such cultures an intellectualist analysis, which assumes a search for logical consistency, is inappropriate.*[5]

A short answer to this argument is that the modern Western world-view is far from forming a logically consistent whole —especially where ideas about the nature of man are concerned! But this in no way stops us from interpreting the history of Western thought in terms of a striving for consistency. The achievement of consistency is one thing; the striving for it quite another.

Some social anthropologists go so far as to admit the reality of this striving in pre-literate cultures, but suggest that those involved are few in number and highly atypical.[6] Here, in fact, we are back with our old men whose interest in theory outruns their practical concern; and the answer is much the same as that given to argument 2. These people may be few and atypical, but they characteristically play a crucial part in the transmission of ideas to the next generation. Hence the ideas of the general population bear the stamp of their interests.

In traditional Africa, the most significant index of the striving for consistency is the well-nigh ubiquitous presence of the idea of a supreme being who is the sustainer of all the lesser spiritual agencies, and who is indeed the ultimate prime mover of everything. If it is nothing else, this concept is surely an assertion that beneath the diversity and apparent haphazardness of the world of appearance, there is an ultimate unity and an ultimate consistency. The ways of the supreme being are often said to be somewhat inscrutable as compared with the ways of the lesser spirits—an admission that the details of this ultimate unity and consistency are perhaps beyond the power of men to work out. But the very existence of the concept is a profession of faith that it is there.

4. *The ideas which neo-Tylorians treat as explanatory are religious ideas, and we know from our experience in modern Western culture that religious ideas do not 'really' attempt to explain the events in the space-time world. They are concerned with other things.*[7]

Here we have the fallacy of regarding belief in spiritual beings as something which serves the same basic human aspiration wherever it occurs. A little thought should remind us that over the last fifteen hundred years of European history, religion has slowly abdicated a very considerable interest in the explanation, prediction and control of worldly

events to the emerging sciences (Firth 1950). Hence modern western Christianity's lack of interest in these things is a very poor index by which to judge early Christianity. It is an even poorer index by which to judge traditional religions in pre-literate cultures.

All this was brought home to me very vividly by an aspect of my own fieldwork experience among the Kalabari people of the Niger delta. In Kalabari communities, traditional religious practitioners, orthodox Christian churches and breakaway spiritualist sects form a most interesting triangle. In this triangle, traditional practitioners and spiritualist sects are sworn enemies, whilst both compete for the friendship of the orthodox churches. Why should this be so? In the first place, the traditional practitioners and the spiritualists are direct competitors. Both diagnose and attempt to cure a variety of misfortunes and diseases, and their claims to significance are based on these activities. The diagnostic and curative techniques of the spiritualists are in fact so similar to those of the traditionalists that the latter often accuse them of stealing traditional stock-in-trade only to bring out again under a Christian label. With the aid of some very convincing biblic exegesis, however, the spiritualists claim they are reverting, not to tradition. Kalabari beliefs and practices, but to early Christian beliefs and practices. As spectator on the sidelines, I am inclined to think that both claims are correct, and that in their overriding concern for the explanation, prediction and control of worldly events, the spiritualists draw inspiration both from Kalabari traditionalists and from elements in the Bible that reflect early Christian ideas. Both traditionalists and spiritualists are able to adopt an amiable attitude toward the orthodox churches precisely because the latter abstain from this-worldly predictive and explanatory claims, and centre their work on the business of salvation. As several attenders at spiritualist prayer houses have put it to me: 'The prayer houses cure our sicknesses and the churches pilot [*sic*] our souls'.

Although this is only one example, it could be paralleled in many parts of Africa. It does, I think, serve to bring home to us the fact that modern western Christianity, as a religion, is somewhat peculiar in its lack of concern with the explanation of this-worldly events. This characteristic, therefore, cannot be used to justify opposition to intellectualist analysis of other religious systems.

5. *If we are wrong-headed enough to treat them as explanations, we have to admit that traditional religious beliefs are mistaken. And the only possible interpretation of such mistakes is that they are the product of childish ignorance. Neo-Tylorians who take traditional beliefs at their face value therefore subscribe to the stereotype of the 'ignorant savage' and are illiberal racists. If on the other hand we treat them as having intention, which, despite appearances, are quite other than explanatory, we no longer have to evaluate traditional beliefs in the light of the canons of adequacy current in the sciences Anthropologists who take this line are therefore not committed to the 'ignorant savage' stereotype. They are good liberals.*

The germs of this argument, if argument it can be called, are to be found in Lévy-Bruhl's early criticism of Tylor and Frazer.[8] Hints of it recur in many expositions of the orthodox anti-intellectualist position over the last two decades; and it has recently been given a highly explicit formulation by Leach.[9] My own feeling is that it is this sort of attitude that underpins and lends force to all the other arguments we have considered. In assessing its appeal, we shall do well to note its affinities with that other powerful offspring of Lévy-Bruhl's work, the militant ideology of Negritude.

There is a short and sharp answer to this whole line of thought. It is that, by all normal criteria of assessment, many of the religious beliefs of pre-literate cultures *are* primarily explanatory in intent; that by the criteria of the sciences, many of them *are* mistaken; and that to wriggle out of admitting this by the pretence that such beliefs are somehow not really what they obviously are is simply to distort facts under the influence of extraneous values. In this respect liberal anthropology is no better than Fascist anthropology, racist anthropology, or what-have-you.

So much for the straight case against the liberals. It seems unlikely, however, that a frontal attack of this kind will ever carry a position defended by irrational obstacles of the strength we are facing here. What we have to do is weaken the liberal position by persuading its adherents that the facts do not really come into conflict with their most cherished values.

Let us start by asking: what is so very dreadful about holding theories which later turn out to be mistaken? The liberals, of course, are very put off by Tylor's contention that the mistaken theories of pre-literate peoples are the outcome of a childish mentality. But surely we do not have to follow Tylor in thinking that childishness is the only possible explanation for mistaken theories. On the contrary, it seems the least plausible of all conceivable explanations. In recent articles, I myself have explored what seems a fairly convincing interpretation of such mistakes, and one that casts no slur at all on the mental capacity or maturity of the peoples concerned (Horton 1967*a*).

For those who will not easily see the point when it is made about pre-literate peoples, let us move over to the history of European ideas, and more specifically to the history of the sciences. Contrary to the view of many social anthropologists, science, though progressive, is not in any simple sense cumulative. It progresses through the overthrow of a goodish theory by one that gives wider coverage of the data; through the overthrow of this better theory by one that gives still wider coverage, and so on.[10] Under this system, today's intellectual hero is inevitably tomorrow's mistaken man. But the quality of his achievement will still stand tomorrow. Indeed, it is his achievement which has made possible the further advance that proclaims him mistaken. Newton is no less a hero for the overthrow of classical physics. Heisenberg will be no less a hero for the overthrow of quantum theory.

The trouble with the liberals, as I see it, is the belief that although their own theoretical framework may be elaborated by future generations, it will not be found radically mistaken. It is this belief which makes them feel there is something illiberal about imputing mistakes to pre-literate theorists. But if what I have said about the nature of scientific progress is correct, their view of their own conceptual framework is unduly optimistic. And if their own framework is inevitably going to be tomorrow's mistake, what is illiberal about imputing mistakes to pre-literates?

From here it is but a small step to my final piece of persuasion. I should like to suggest to the liberals that in certain fields the dichotomies 'wrong/right,' 'mistaken/correct' are in fact far too strong to do justice to the relation between the beliefs of pre-literates and those of modern Westerners.

One of the things that makes the liberals see pre-literate explanatory theories as totally wrong-headed is the fact that they characteristically feature invisible personal beings. Here the positivist background of so many of them obtrudes itself. As positivists, they view themselves as revolutionaries in action against the old, pre-scientific order. And like most revolutionaries, their besetting error is that, in trying to liquidate the old order, they throw out the baby with the bathwater. Thus because many of the explanatory beliefs of pre-scientific Europe happen to have been couched in personal terms, they have declared any theory couched in such terms as *ipso facto* beyond the pale of the rational. In so doing, however, they have thrown out the basic canon of scientific method which lays it down that no type of theory can be judged right or wrong solely on the grounds of its content.

A very vivid exposition of this canon is to be found in the astronomer Fred Hoyle's science-fiction novel *The black cloud*. Here we find an international committee of scientists trying to explain the nature and behaviour of a terrible opaque cloud which, coming between the earth and the sun, threatens to freeze up the planet. In what is clearly intended as a sermon on scientific method, Hoyle takes as his hero a gruff, monosyllabic Russian. All the others laugh at this man because, whenever they ask for his views, he simply repeats 'Bastard in cloud!'—thus showing himself to be either a joker in poor taste or a deluded animist. Later, however, it is the animist who has the laugh; for his theory and his alone covers the various puzzling aspects of the phenomenon, and provides a basis for the prediction of its behaviour.

Animistic explanations, then, have nothing *prima facie* unreasonable about them; and the liberal has no cause to blush when he meets them in pre-literate cultures.

The liberal can, of course, concede all that has been said so far, and still object that when it comes to accounting for the facts, the animistic beliefs of pre-literate cultures, considered as theories, make a very poor showing alongside the impersonal theories of the West. This is certainly true enough where we are dealing with inanimate matter, with plants, and with lower animals; but the nearer we come to the 'higher' activities of man, the more dubious it becomes. Traditional beliefs have very little of interest to say to the physicist, the chemist, and the biologist; but they have a surprising amount to say to the psychologist and the sociologist.

The truth of this contention is well illustrated by Evans-Pritchard's classic *Witchcraft, oracles and magic among the Azande* (1937). This monograph was the first to document in detail the way in which members of a traditional African culture used a corpus of explanatory 'mystical' theory to make sense of and cope with the vicissitudes of their everyday lives. In particular, it highlighted the connexion made by Zande theory between human misfortune and disturbance in the social fabric—a connection which later research showed was typical of traditional thought. When this book came out thirty years ago, both the author and his readers talked on the assumption that, judged by the criteria of the sciences, Zande ideas on this subject were mistakes. Today, I think many commentators would be hesitant about making such an assumption. In an age where social disturbance, operating via psychological disturbance, is recognised as a probable contributor to a whole spectrum of human misfortunes ranging from high blood pressure to falling under a bus, it is no longer so easy to say that the Zande thinker is just mistaken. Now what brought about this change in Western beliefs? One factor at least seems to have been inspiration by just those pre-literate beliefs that once were considered so erroneous. It is not for nothing that Walter B. Cannon, commonly acknowledged as 'the father of psycho-somatic medicine', called one of his early articles on the subject 'Voodoo death' (1965).

Another book which is likely to be seminal in this respect is Fortes's *Oedipus and Job in west African religion* (1959). This book deals with what may be called Tallensi social psychology. It reveals a system of concepts in many ways uncannily similar to those of Western psychoanalysts, but with certain significant differences. Notably, Tallensi concepts postulate a somewhat different distribution of motives as between conscious and unconscious sectors of the mind (Horton 1961). In a decade in which psychiatrists are becoming increasingly aware of the culture-bound nature of Western psychodynamic concepts, this and other west African social psychologies clearly merit a respectful hearing.

If the reader feels tempted to smile patronisingly at the last two paragraphs, he should ask himself the following question. After all the sound and the fury and the self-congratulation have been discounted, just how far have psychoanalysis, behaviourism, structural-functionalism, and other basic Western theories of higher human behaviour really advanced our understanding of ourselves? If he answers honestly, I think he will stop smiling.

Let me sum up on all of this. Behind the liberal's concern to play down the explanatory aspect of pre-literate religious beliefs lies a strong streak of patronage. Basically, he believes that, so far as explanatory value is concerned, his theories are in some absolute and final sense right, whilst pre-literate theories are in some equally absolute sense wrong. What I have tried to point out here is that the rightness of the current western belief-system is in the nature of things transitory; and that in the sphere of 'higher' human behaviour, at least, pre-literate belief-systems may from time to time be the source of insights that seriously shake some Western foundations. In reminding the liberal of these things, I hope I have done something towards removing the sentimental obstacles which have hitherto prevented him from considering the intellectualist approach on its merits.

I should like to end this rather polemical article on a note of reconciliation. Social anthropologists often talk as though one had to chose between an intellectualist and a sociological analysis of pre-literate beliefs. In fact, however, such a choice is neither necessary nor desirable.

Tylor's intellectualism, it is true, was innocent of any sociological overtones. To the question of why some cultures had 'animistic' and others 'scientific' world-views, his ultimate answer was that members of the first lot of cultures had a childish mentality, whilst members of the second lot had an adult mentality. Whatever else this was, it was certainly not a sociological explanation. But, as I said earlier, we can be intellectualists without following Tylor in other respects.

As I see it, the only thing the intellectualist is entitled to ask is that we begin by analysing pre-literate belief statements in terms of the overt explanatory ends they serve. After this, he should welcome all comers—sociologists, psychoanalysts, the lot. In point of fact, it is almost impossible to make an intellectualist analysis of belief statements without doing some sociology in the process. This was borne in upon me most forcibly when I embarked on a generalised comparison of African and Western thought-traditions. I was driven to an intellectualist approach to this task by the singular failure of the anti-intellectualist establishment to make any headway with it. In trying to make intellectualist analyses of various traditional African religious theories, however, I came up against the fact that they were above all theories of society and of the individual's place in it. Hence it was impossible to gain understanding of them without taking detailed account of the social organisations whose workings they were concerned to make sense of. Much the same thing happened when I tried to understand why African traditional cultures favoured personalised models for their explanatory tasks, whilst Western culture favoured impersonal models. In tackling the question, I started out with the intellectualist assumption that both the gods and spirits of traditional Africa and the ultimate particles and forces of the Western world-view were alternative means to what was basically the same explanatory end. This assumption led to the further question of why the theoretical models of the two sets of cultures were founded on such very different analogies. And in trying to answer this second question, I found I had to take into account such unambiguously sociological variables as stability and complexity of social organisation, and the relation between society and its non-human environment (Horton 1967*a*: 64–5).

On the basis of my own work, then, I regard the intellectualist approach as a healthy corrective to certain current fashions in social anthropology. I do not regard it as an alternative to sociological analysis.

ENDNOTES

1. Complaints about a 'Neo-Tylorian' or 'Back to Frazer' movement seem to have been touched off by a number of recent challenges to the anti-intellectualist establishment in British social anthropology. One of the first of these was made by Jarvie (1964), in a colourful plea for a return to intellectualism roughly as practised by Frazer. Later came provocative articles by Geertz and Spiro (1966) in a volume resulting from a confrontation of British and American social anthropologists. At a more particular level, the return to intellectualism was advocated in Young's (1966) paper on the Jukun kingship. Three of my own recent papers have taken much the same intellectualist line (Horton 1964; 1967*a*; 1967*b*).

   The response to these intellectualist views has been a grumbling one. Jarvie's book got a generally ill-tempered reception, typical of which was Ardener's (1965) review. Among more concerted statements of opposition, one may single out Beattie's (1966) programmatic paper, which puts very strongly the thesis that pre-literate magico-religious beliefs are 'not what they seem'. One may also note the anti-intellectualist injunctions in Ch. 5 of Douglas's brilliant *Purity and danger* (1966)—injunctions which come a little surprisingly from the author of a revolutionary intellectualist interpretation of pollution behaviour. Finally, there is Leach's strongly worded condemnation (1967), which contends that the intellectualist approach to preliterate beliefs is not only wrong, but symptomatic of vicious prejudice.
2. For a good account of the intellectualist assumption of modern historians of science, see the Introduction to Kuhn (1962).
3. Douglas (1966: ch. 5) warns against intellectualist approaches to those cultures which, as she puts it, have not developed a 'conscious reaching for objectivity'.
4. This again is implied in Douglas (1966: ch. 5). See for instance p. 89: 'It is a practical interest in living and not an

academic interest in metaphysics which has produced these beliefs . . .' For an earlier formulation, see Gluckman (1963), especially p. 141: 'They had elaborate theologies, but these were developed in social relations, rather than in intellectual speculations'.
5. Richards (1967: 291) remarks on the general reluctance of British social anthropologists to make the striving for consistency the starting-point of their analyses. This reluctance is exemplified by Douglas (1966: ch. 5).
6. Richards (1967: 291) comments: 'Sceptical British anthropologists have also suggested from time to time that such consistent and logical systems as those described in the case of the Dogon must be the product of a single mind and a philosophical one at that—an Ogotemmeli in fact.'
7. This is one of the arguments in Leach (1967). For instance: 'An alternative way of explaining a belief which is factually untrue is to say that it is a species of religious dogma; the truth which it expresses does not relate to the ordinary matter-of-fact world of everyday things but to metaphysics.'
8. See the critique of 'L'Ecole Anglaise' in the introduction to Lévy-Bruhl (1910).
9. The whole tone of Leach (1967) is one of strong moral disapproval of the intellectualist approach. Thus he accuses Spiro of being 'positively eager to believe that the aborigines were ignorant' and says that intellectualists 'seem to gain assurance from supposing that the people they study have the simple-minded ignorance of small children'.

   Since submitting this article, I have read Spiro's rejoinder to Leach (Spiro 1968). Although his argument is very similar to my own, I have left the text of the article unamended as I think it carries the argument somewhat further than he himself has taken it.
10. For a very clear picture of this process see Kuhn (1962), especially the closing chapter on 'Progress through revolutions'.

REFERENCES

Achebe, C. 1964. *Arrow of God.* London: Heinemann.

Ardener, E. 1965. Review of *The revolution in anthropology, Man* **65**, 57–8.

Beattie, J. 1966. Ritual and social change. *Man* (N.S.) **I**, 60–74.

Cannon, W. B. 1965. Voodoo death. In *A reader in comparative religion* (eds) W. A. Lessa & E. Z. Vogt. New York: Harper & Row.

Douglas, M. 1966. *Purity and danger.* London: Routledge & Kegan Paul.

Evans-Pritchard, E. E. 1937. *Witchcraft, oracles and magic among the Azande.* Oxford: Clarendon Press.

Firth, R. 1950. Religious belief and personal adjustment. *J. R. anthrop. Inst.* **78**, 25–43.

Fortes, M. 1959. *Oedipus and Job in west African religion.* Cambridge: Univ. Press.

Geertz, C. 1966. Religion as a cultural system. In *Anthropological approaches to the study of religion* (ed.) M. Banton (Monogr. Ass. social Anthrop. 3). London: Tavistock Publications.

Gluckman, M. 1963. *Order and rebellion in tribal Africa.* London: Cohen & West.

Horton, R. 1961. Destiny and the unconscious in west Africa. *Africa* **31,** 110–16.

———. 1964. Ritual man in Africa. *Africa* **34,** 85–104.

———. 1967a. African traditional thought and western science. I. *Africa* **37,** 50–71.

———. 1967b. African traditional thought and western science. 2. *Africa* **37,** 155–87.

Hoyle, F. 1960. *The black cloud.* Harmondsworth: Penguin.

Jarvie, I. C. 1964. *The revolution in anthropology.* London: Routledge & Kegan Paul.

Kuhn, T. 1962. *The structure of scientific revolutions.* Chicago: Univ. Press.

Leach, E. R. 1954. *Political systems of highland Burma.* London: Bell.

———. 1967. Virgin birth. *Proc. R. anthrop. Inst.* **1966,** 39–49.

Levy-Bruhl, L. 1910. *Les fonctions mentales dans les societes inferieures.* Paris: Presses Universitaires de France.

Middleton, J. 1960. *Lugbara religion.* London: Oxford Univ. Press.

Richards, A. I. 1967. African systems of thought: an Anglo-French dialogue. *Man* (N.S.) **2,** 286–98.

Spiro, M. E. 1966. Religion: problems of definition and explanation. In *Anthropological approaches to the study of religion* (ed.) M. Banton (Monogr. Ass. social Anthrop. 3). London: Tavistock Publications.

———. 1968. Virgin birth, parthenogenesis and physiological paternity: an essay in cultural interpretation. *Man* (N.S.) **3,** 242–61.

Young, M. 1966. The divine kingship of the Jukun. *Africa* **36,** 135–53.

FURTHER READINGS

Cunningham, Graham. *Religion and Magic: Approaches and Theories.* New York: New York University Press. 1999. A brief overview of the most important anthropologists who have contributed to the study of ritual and belief. The author discusses, among others, Tylor, Frazer, Durkheim, Malinowski, Evans-Pritchard, and van Gennep.

Geertz, Clifford. "Religion as a Cultural System." In *Anthropological Approaches to the Study of Religion,* ed. Michael Banton. London: Tavistock, Association of Social Anthropologists Monographs, no. 3, 1966, pp. 1–46. This article is considered a classic by anthropologists. By elaborating on the definitions of Tylor and Durkheim, Clifford Geertz attempts in this essay to define religion in the most widely embracing manner possible. More elaborate than Tylor's definition, or even Durkheim's, Geertz's definition acknowledges the emotional aspects of human experience, the intellectual framework for beliefs, the means whereby believers are convinced to believe, and religion as an integrated component of society. After defining what he means by the term religion, Geertz goes on to examine the five "pillars" of his definition, in the course of which he gives us a series of profound, thought-provoking insights. The five key phrases in his definition are a system of symbols, moods and motivations, general order of existence, aura of factuality, and uniquely realistic.

Hardacre, Helen. *Marketing the Menacing Fetus in Japan.* Berkeley: University of California Press, 1997. This study complements the video on abortion recommended below, by describing the Japanese institution of *mizuko kuyo.* The *mizuko kuyo* consists of ritual activities that memorialize the spirits of aborted fetuses, which are comforted and honored.

Morris, Brian. *Anthropological Studies of Religion.* Cambridge: Cambridge University Press. 1987. A comprehensive guide to all anthropological aspects of religion. Another introduction to religion, but rather more demanding than that of Cunningham's. It deals with the main theorists and offers a well-thought-out original perspective on the topic.

ASK YOURSELF

Consider carefully the various definitions of religion you have read in this chapter. If none should seem to fit your own understanding of what religion is, try to compose a more satisfactory alternative. Would you include Buddhism as a religion (it lacks a belief in spirits)? Would Communism be a religion in your definition (it fits Durkheim's definition)?

Klass, Morton. *Ordered Universes: Approaches to the Anthropology of Religion.* Boulder: Westview Press. 1995. A fine survey of religion, well-written and, for its size, comprehensive.

SUGGESTED VIDEOS

"Abortion: The Moral Dilemma." Religious beliefs often find expression in moral codes. Catholic morality prohibits abortion, yet millions of Catholics either ignore the prohibition or find their personal lives riven by the tensions that result from obeying it. In this video, Caroline and Roger are a couple who have watched two of their babies die from an inherited disease. They have one healthy child, but want a second. The questions they face are these: Should they risk another pregnancy, and, if so, what should they do if the baby proves to be unhealthy or suffers unduly? Would they have an abortion, despite supporting, in principle, their Church's prohibition against it? 28 minutes; 1995; $149 (sale); $75 (rental); #KB4628. Films for the Humanities & Sciences, P.O. Box 2053, Princeton, NJ.

"The Five Pillars of Islam." The religion of Islam rests upon five principles, or "pillars." This documentary describes and places them in their historical contexts. Included also is a discussion of the conflict between the traditional teachings of the Prophet and the influences of 20th-century industrialization. 30 minutes; 1995; $89.95 (sale); #KB708. Films for the Humanities & Sciences, P.O. Box 2053, Princeton, NJ.

"The Principles and Practice of Zen." The process leading to satori—the state of spiritual enlightenment—is examined in this documentary. It shows the rigors and aesthetic sensibility, the abnegation of the self, and the devotion to principles that defy expression in words.

The documentary depicts the path of a student priest journeying around Japan and engaging in verbal duels with priests of different philosophical persuasions. The tea ceremony and flower arrangement are included, as are exquisite specimens of Japanese temple architecture. 100 minutes; $159 (sale); #KB1669. Films for the Humanities & Sciences, P.O. Box 2053, Princeton, NJ.

"Women Serving Religion." One of the most contentious issues facing Christianity, Judaism, and Islam is the issue of women's role in religion. In the past, women's roles in these three great institutions has been limited, but today there is much debate about their participation. This film examines women's roles in these religions and considers the influence of feminism on such matters as the ordination of woman. Color. 29 minutes. #KB5741. $89.95 (sale). Films for the Humanities & Sciences. P.O. Box 2053, Princeton, NJ 08543-2053.

Source: Edward B. Tylor, "Animism," in *Primitive Culture: Researches into the Development of Mythology, Philosophy, Religion, Language, Art, and Custom,* vol. 1, 2nd ed. (London: John Murray, 1873), pp. 424–58.

Source: Sigmund Freud, "The Return of Totemism in Childhood," in *Totem and Taboo,* trans. James Strachey (New York: W. W. Norton and Company, 1950), pp. 140–45. Reprinted with permission by Routledge and Kegan Paul.

Source: Abridgement reprinted with the permission of The Free Press, a Division of Simon & Schuster from *The Elementary Forms of the Religious Life* by Emile Durkheim, trans. by Joseph Ward Swain. Copyright © 1965 by The Free Press.

Source: Man. Volume 3 (Number 4), pages 625–634.

Although the meaning of Stonehenge is lost in the mists of the past, one theory proposed is that the standing stones are arranged in a circle for ritual purposes associated with astrological observations involving the cosmological notions of people living 5,000 years ago in southern England. *Photo courtesy of Maxine Hicks*

CHAPTER 2

MYTH, COSMOLOGY, AND SYMBOLIC CLASSIFICATION

The British anthropologist Bronislaw Malinowski argued that some myths, he called them "sociological charters," justified social inequities. They might, for example, justify the political privileges nobles claimed or account for the fact that only members of a certain group had the right to perform certain rituals. Ritual, as it happens, is sometimes rather closely associated with myth, and Malinowski was right in supposing that myths can explain how certain rituals first came to be performed and even specify the precise way in which future generations must carry it out. In this way, some rituals can be said to reproduce the incidents originally described in myth.

Malinowski influenced Mircea Eliade, a scholar of comparative religion, who, unlike Malinowski, had not carried out fieldwork and therefore had not had the opportunity to see how myths functioned in nonliterate societies. Nevertheless, Eliade accepted Malinowski's thesis that myth served social ends. However, after examining a huge body of myths from all over the world and seeking their general features he eventually reached the conclusion that

myths could have a multiplicity of meanings rather than single functions. His favorite mythic theme was that of the "eternal return" (Eliade, 1954), by which he meant that an essential feature of myths was to recount the first occurrence of some phenomenon crucial to humankind, e.g., the origin of agriculture, and that those who recite the myth believe they are making conditions favorable for the maintenance of that phenomenon. Eliade correctly asserted that the origins of phenomena essential for the existence of humanity typically provide the focus for myths, but he went astray in claiming those who told and heard these myths invariably came to think that by the mere recital of these tales they could ensure that these essential things continued. Another scholar of myth was Joseph Campbell, who earned considerable public fame by demonstrating how certain motifs, such as death, birth, fertility, and the after-life, kept reappearing in a huge number of myths in many cultures around the world.

A much less obvious route to interpreting myths is structural analysis. The French anthropologist, Claude Lévi-Strauss, like Eliade and Campbell, approached the study of myth by library research rather than by fieldwork, and he based his ideas upon his reading of thousands of myths from all over the world. Lévi-Strauss suggested that myths contained concealed "messages" that contained ideas of fundamental significance to those who heard the stories. Instead of these messages being delivered in Malinowskian style as straightforward and explicit statements, however, Lévi-Strauss said they had to be "decoded" from oblique hints given in the narratives. Lévi-Strauss's attempt to "decode" the meaning of these myths extends far beyond the analysis of a single myth, however, for he includes within his structural analysis all the variants of the same myth, and then extends the analysis to include clusters of myths that he regards as similar in theme. Lévi-Strauss's major work on myth was published in four volumes, of which the first, *The Raw and the Cooked,* attempts to demonstrate that certain formal relations essential for human thinking, such as opposition, analogy, complementarity, and reciprocity, appear in these narratives as a means of ordering material categories such as raw/cooked, fresh/decayed, and dry/burnt, and conceptual categories like time and space, in such ways as to pose and "resolve" certain logical dilemmas or philosophical quandaries which human beings encounter and which otherwise defy logical resolution. Incest, death, marriage, and birth are the most prominent experiences of life that provide opportunities for human beings to worry about the meaning of life, and Lévi-Strauss argues that one way we resolve the puzzles these worries involve is through myths. Myths do this by subtly converting insoluble conundrums into puzzles that *can* be solved—if the structural analyst can decode the story correctly. The formal relations that organize the incidents, figures, and episodes contained in the myths are, in his view, common to the thinking of all peoples, whatever their culture, for they are the genetically endowed properties of the human brain. Myths are especially useful for revealing these properties of the mind since myths are the direct products of the human imagination and thus are less constrained by the "hard" facts of

experience than, say, ritual or religious beliefs, which must take some account, at the very least, of the "real" world. Myths accordingly offer us a direct window into the working of the human mind and its capacity to order ideas.

The reading given here is a structural analysis of the Book of Genesis by an English follower of Lévi-Strauss, the social anthropologist, Edmund Leach. Leach tended to be more faithful to the original details of the narratives he was studying than Lévi-Strauss, and I include Leach's analysis as an example of the structural approach here partly for this reason and partly because Leach pilots us more explicitly through every step of his reasoning than is usually the case with Lévi-Strauss.

Another scholar of myth identified with the structural school of anthropology is Georges Dumézil, whose method of analysis overlapped with that of Lévi-Strauss. He differs in some important ways, however, most notably in the fact that whereas Lévi-Strauss is concerned with attempting to discover how the mind works and has simply chosen myths as his vehicle, Dumézil's entire scholarly life has centered about the myths of the ancient Indo-Europeans, the ancestors of, among others, most of the population of Europe. Dumézil's field of study is often referred to as "comparative mythology," and though he was not an anthropologist his work was very much influenced by anthropology and sociology—more especially by the writings of the *Année sociologique* School (see Introduction).

Some myths do much more than just describe the origins of the material world and its creatures, though; they also provide believers with an all-embracing system of classification, called a *cosmology* that explains how the cosmos—a single, orderly model of the universe—came into existence. The spiritual world is also accorded a place in this all-embracing harmonious whole, as is humanity. In the traditional cosmology of the Zuni of New Mexico, for example, all beings and things in nature—such as the sun, moon, and Earth, as well as human beings, animals, and plants—were arranged into fixed places in the cosmos (Cushing,

1896). The cosmos itself was divided into seven regions: north, south, east, west, zenith, nadir, and center. Everything in the cosmos was allocated to one or other of these regions.

Although modes of symbolic classification based on the number seven and those based upon nine are not universal, all societies impose some measure of classification upon their world. Yet in so doing societies invariably find that in some important ways their classification, which is a cultural construction or reconfiguration of empirical reality, clashes with their experience of reality. One strategy by which society evades this conflict is, according to Lévi-Strauss, myth. An alternative strategy to cope with such apparent contradictions has been proposed by Mary Douglas (Reading 2–4). This is the concept of pollution.

A given myth does not necessarily correspond to a given ritual (see Reading 4–1), but there *are* societies where myths are dramatized in rituals. A good example is to be found among the Australian Aboriginal societies, whose rituals are an essential feature of their cosmology, whose dominant concept is that of the "Dreaming," a notion that refers to a time when the world was created and before human beings appeared. In myths of the Dreaming, the Earth is often imagined as starting with a flat plain, unmarked by any topographic features, after which ancestral beings commence to emerge from within the Earth and begin shaping its topography. Myths describe how every action of the ancestral beings has an impact on the landscape. The opening from which an ancestral being emerged from the ground might become a waterhole or perhaps the entrance to a cave; at sites where ancestral beings stuck their digging sticks into the ground, trees might sprout. These ancestral beings were complex forms of energy capable of transforming their own bodies into the shapes of such creatures as the kangaroo and caterpillar or into the shapes of inanimate objects like rocks and trees, and ritual provides the means whereby the Aborigines can tap into the resources of the Dreaming and exploit them for their present-day lives. In performing these rituals, Aborigines are able to assume the identities of their Dreamtime ancestors and once having done so command the awesome power these supernaturals possess (Morphy 1998, p. 185).

READING 2–1

THE ROLE OF MYTH IN LIFE

Bronislaw Malinowski

Malinowski argues here that myth is "a hard-working, extremely important cultural force," rejecting the claim that myths can be considered as texts loaded with meaning accessible only through symbols or tools for exercises in cognitive problem solving. His position is thus the opposite of that of Lévi-Strauss, and he further differs from Lévi-Strauss in downplaying the "mere examination of texts." Malinowski properly insists on extending the meaning of narratives to include their manner of recitation and the social contexts in which they are recited since performance, he correctly observes, is an essential aspect of myth. The way the narrator presents himself or herself, the response the audience makes to the narrator's presentation, and the narrator's own reaction to the audience members' responses are, in Malinowski's view, as essential in the study of myth as the narrative.

Field research has demonstrated that myth-as-charter, myth-as-performance, and myth-as-text are viable alternatives as media for interpretation. Indeed, there are other interesting perspectives, including myth-as-history, myth-as-ethnography, and myth-as-psychoanalysis.

Bronislaw Malinowski's considerable reputation was built upon his skill as an indomitable fieldworker and this reading reveals his ethnographic expertise at work. Thus, in classifying the different genres of narrative, Malinowski quite correctly insists on using the indigenous categories of the local society itself rather than rely on the alien Western categories of narrative. Most anthropologists would probably take issue with his characterizing folktales as something "seasonal," however, and would wish him to define "legend" more precisely, but we should

Source: Bronislaw Malinowski, "The Role of Myth in Life," in magic, science and religion and other essays (Westport, Conn.: Greenwood Press, 1984 [1948]), pp. 96–11)

note that it is only after he has told us how the Trobrian-
ders themselves classify oral literature that he imposes
his western labels. A generation of ethnographers—
including Edward Evans-Pritchard, Raymond Firth, and
Edmund Leach—was inspired by the abundance and
exactitude of the information Malinowski collected
during his fieldwork, but mythology, however, figured low
on their list of research priorities. Only as late as 1955,
with the publication of a paper by Lévi-Strauss entitled
"The Structural Study of Myth," did myth return as a
major anthropological concern.

By the examination of a typical Melanesian culture and by a survey of the opinions, traditions, and
behavior of these natives, I propose to show how
deeply the sacred tradition, the myth, enters into
their pursuits, and how strongly it controls their
moral and social behavior. In other words, the thesis
of the present work is that an intimate connection
exists between the word, the mythos, the sacred
tales of a tribe, on the one hand, and their ritual acts,
their moral deeds, their social organization, and
even their practical activities, on the other.

In order to gain a background for our description
of the Melanesian facts, I shall briefly summarize
the present state of the science of mythology. Even
a superficial survey of the literature would reveal
that there is no monotony to complain of as regards
the variety of opinions or the acrimony of polemics.
To take only the recent up-to-date theories advanced
in explanation of the nature of myth, legend, and
fairy tale, we should have to head the list, at least as
regards output and self-assertion, by the so-called
school of Nature-mythology which flourishes
mainly in Germany. The writers of this school maintain that primitive man is highly interested in natural
phenomena, and that his interest is predominantly of
a theoretical, contemplative, and poetical character.
In trying to express and interpret the phases of the
moon, or the regular and yet changing path of the
sun across the skies, primitive man constructs symbolic personified rhapsodies. To writers of this
school every myth possesses as its kernel or ultimate
reality some natural phenomenon or other, elabo-
rately woven into a tale to an extent which sometimes almost masks and obliterates it. There is not

much agreement among these students as to what
type of natural phenomenon lies at the bottom of
most mythological productions. There are extreme
lunar mythologists so completely moonstruck with
their idea that they will not admit that any other phenomenon could lend itself to a savage rhapsodic
interpretation except that of earth's nocturnal satel-
lite. The Society for the Comparative Study of
Myth, founded in Berlin in 1906, and counting
among its supporters such famous scholars as
Ehrenreich, Siecke, Winckler, and many others, carried on their business under the sign of the moon.
Others, like Frobenius for instance, regard the sun as
the only subject around which primitive man has
spun his symbolic tales. Then there is the school of
meteorological interpreters who regard wind,
weather, and colors of the skies as the essence of
myth. To this belonged such well-known writers of
the older generation as Max Müller and Kuhn. Some
of these departmental mythologists fight fiercely for
their heavenly body or principle; others have a more
catholic taste, and prepare to agree that primeval
man has made his mythological brew from all the
heavenly bodies taken together.

I have tried to state fairly and plausibly this naturalistic interpretation of myths, but as a matter of
fact this theory seems to me to be one of the most
extravagant views ever advanced by an anthropologist or humanist—and that means a great deal. It has
received an absolutely destructive criticism from
the great psychologist Wundt, and appears
absolutely untenable in the light of any of Sir James
Frazer's writings. From my own study of living
myths among savages, I should say that primitive
man has to a very limited extent the purely artistic
or scientific interest in nature; there is but little
room for symbolism in his ideas and tales; and
myth, in fact, is not an idle rhapsody, not an aimless
outpouring of vain imaginings, but a hard-working,
extremely important cultural force. Besides ignor-
ing the cultural function of myth, this theory
imputes to primitive man a number of imaginary
interests, and it confuses several clearly distinguishable types of story, the fairy tale, the legend,
the saga, and the sacred tale or myth.

In strong contrast to this theory which makes myth naturalistic, symbolic, and imaginary, stands the theory which regards a sacred tale as a true historical record of the past. This view, recently supported by the so-called Historical School in Germany and America, and represented in England by Dr. Rivers, covers but part of the truth. There is no denying that history, as well as natural environment, must have left a profound imprint on all cultural achievements, hence also on myths. But to take all mythology as mere chronicle is as incorrect as to regard it as the primitive naturalist's musings. It also endows primitive man with a sort of scientific impulse and desire for knowledge. Although the savage has something of the antiquarian as well as of the naturalist in his composition, he is, above all, actively engaged in a number of practical pursuits, and has to struggle with various difficulties; all his interests are tuned up to this general pragmatic outlook. Mythology, the sacred lore of the tribe, is, as we shall see, a powerful means of assisting primitive man, of allowing him to make the two ends of his cultural patrimony meet. We shall see, moreover, that the immense services to primitive culture performed by myth are done in connection with religious ritual, moral influence, and sociological principle. Now religion and morals draw only to a very limited extent upon an interest in science or in past history, and myth is thus based upon an entirely different mental attitude.

The close connection between religion and myth which has been overlooked by many students has been recognized by others. Psychologists like Wundt, sociologists like Durkheim, Hubert, and Mauss, anthropologists like Crawley, classical scholars like Miss Jane Harrison have all understood the intimate association between myth and ritual, between sacred tradition and the norms of social structure. All of these writers have been to a greater or lesser extent influenced by the work of Sir James Frazer. In spite of the fact that the great British anthropologist, as well as most of his followers, have a clear vision of the sociological and ritual importance of myth, the facts which I shall present will allow us to clarify and formulate more

precisely the main principles of a sociological theory of myth.

I might present an even more extensive survey of the opinions, divisions, and controversies of learned mythologists. The science of mythology has been the meeting point of various scholarships: the classical humanist must decide for himself whether Zeus is the moon, or the sun, or a strictly historical personality; and whether his ox-eyed spouse is the morning star, or a cow, or a personification of the wind—the loquacity of wives being proverbial. Then all these questions have to be rediscussed upon the stage of mythology by the various tribes of archaeologists, Chaldean and Egyptian, Indian and Chinese, Peruvian and Mayan. The historian and the sociologist, the student of literature, the grammarian, the Germanist and the Romanist, the Celtic scholar and the Slavist discuss, each little crowd among themselves. Nor is mythology quite safe from logicians and psychologists, from the metaphysician and the epistemologist—to say nothing of such visitors as the theosophist, the modern astrologist, and the Christian Scientist. Finally, we have the psychoanalyst who has come at last to teach us that the myth is a daydream of the race, and that we can only explain it by turning our back upon nature, history, and culture, and diving deep into the dark pools of the subconscious, where at the bottom there lie the usual paraphernalia and symbols of psychoanalytic exegesis. So that when at last the poor anthropologist and student of folklore come to the feast, there are hardly any crumbs left for them!

If I have conveyed an impression of chaos and confusion, if I have inspired a sinking feeling towards the incredible mythological controversy with all the dust and din which it raises, I have achieved exactly what I wanted. For I shall invite my readers to step outside the closed study of the theorist into the open air of the anthropological field, and to follow me in my mental flight back to the years which I spent among a Melanesian tribe of New Guinea. There, paddling on the lagoon, watching the natives under the blazing sun at their garden work, following them through the patches of jungle, and on the winding beaches and reefs, we shall learn about their life. And again, observing their ceremonies in the cool of the afternoon or in the shadows of the evening, sharing their meals round their fires, we shall be able to listen to their stories.

For the anthropologist—one and only among the many participants in the mythological contest—has the unique advantage of being able to step back behind the savage whenever he feels that his theories become involved and the flow of his argumentative eloquence runs dry. The anthropologist is not bound to the scanty remnants of culture, broken tablets, tarnished texts, or fragmentary inscriptions. He need not fill out immense gaps with voluminous, but conjectural, comments. The anthropologist has the myth-maker at his elbow. Not only can he take down as full a text as exists, with all its variations, and control it over and over; he has also a host of authentic commentators to draw upon; still more he has the fullness of life itself from which the myth has been born. And as we shall see, in this live context there is as much to be learned about the myth as in the narrative itself.

Myth as it exists in a savage community, that is, in its living primitive form, is not merely a story told but a reality lived. It is not of the nature of fiction, such as we read today in a novel, but it is a living reality, believed to have once happened in primeval times, and continuing ever since to influence the world and human destinies. This myth is to the savage what, to a fully believing Christian, is the Biblical story of Creation, of the Fall, of the Redemption by Christ's Sacrifice on the Cross. As our sacred story lives in our ritual, in our morality, as it governs our faith and controls our conduct, even so does his myth for the savage.

The limitation of the study of myth to the mere examination of texts has been fatal to a proper understanding of its nature. The forms of myth which come to us from classical antiquity and from the ancient sacred books of the East and other similar sources have come down to us without the context of living faith, without the possibility of obtaining comments from true believers, without the concomitant knowledge of their social organization, their practiced morals, and their popular cus-

toms—at least without the full information which the modern fieldworker can easily obtain. Moreover, there is no doubt that in their present literary form these tales have suffered a very considerable transformation at the hands of scribes, commentators, learned priests, and theologians. It is necessary to go back to primitive mythology in order to learn the secret of its life in the study of a myth which is still alive—before, mummified in priestly wisdom, it has been enshrined in the indestructible but lifeless repository of dead religions.

Studied alive, myth, as we shall see, is not symbolic, but a direct expression of its subject matter; it is not an explanation in satisfaction of a scientific interest, but a narrative resurrection of a primeval reality, told in satisfaction of deep religious wants, moral cravings, social submissions, assertions, even practical requirements. Myth fulfills in primitive culture an indispensable function: it expresses, enhances, and codifies belief; it safeguards and enforces morality; it vouches for the efficiency of ritual and contains practical rules for the guidance of man. Myth is thus a vital ingredient of human civilization; it is not an idle tale, but a hard-worked active force; it is not an intellectual explanation or an artistic imagery, but a pragmatic charter of primitive faith and moral wisdom.

I shall try to prove all these contentions by the study of various myths; but to make our analysis conclusive it will first be necessary to give an account not merely of myth, but also of fairy tale, legend, and historical record.

Let us then float over in spirit to the shores of a Trobriand lagoon, and penetrate into the life of the natives—see them at work, see them at play, and listen to their stories. Late in November the wet weather is setting in. There is little to do in the gardens, the fishing season is not in full swing as yet, overseas sailing looms ahead in the future, while the festive mood still lingers after the harvest dancing and feasting. Sociability is in the air, time lies on their hands, while bad weather keeps them often at home. Let us step through the twilight of the approaching evening into one of their villages and sit at the fireside, where the flickering light draws more and more people as the evening falls and the conversation brightens. Sooner or later a man will be asked to tell a story, for this is the season of fairy tales. If he is a good reciter, he will soon provoke laughter, rejoinders, and interruptions, and his tale will develop into a regular performance.

At this time of the year folk tales of a special type called kukwanebu are habitually recited in the villages. There is a vague belief, not very seriously taken, that their recital has a beneficial influence on the new crops recently planted in the gardens. In order to produce this effect, a short ditty in which an allusion is made to some very fertile wild plants, the kasiyena, must always be recited at the end.

Every story is "owned" by a member of the community. Each story, though known by many, may be recited only by the "owner"; he may, however, present it to someone else by teaching that person and authorizing him to retell it. But not all the "owners" know how to thrill and to raise a hearty laugh, which is one of the main ends of such stories. A good raconteur has to change his voice in the dialogue, chant the ditties with due temperament, gesticulate, and in general play to the gallery. Some of these tales are certainly "smoking-room" stories, of others I will give one or two examples.

Thus there is the maiden in distress and the heroic rescue. Two women go out in search of birds' eggs. One discovers a nest under a tree, the other warns her: "These are eggs of a snake, don't touch them." "Oh, no! They are eggs of a bird," she replies and carries them away. The mother snake comes back, and finding the nest empty starts in search of the eggs. She enters the nearest village and sings a ditty:

I wend my way as I wriggle along,

The eggs of a bird it is licit to eat;

The eggs of a friend are forbidden to touch.

This journey lasts long, for the snake is traced from one village to the other and everywhere has to sing her ditty. Finally, entering the village of the two women, she sees the culprit roasting the eggs, coils around her, and enters her body. The victim is laid down helpless and ailing. But the hero is nigh; a

man from a neighboring village dreams of the dramatic situation, arrives on the spot, pulls out the snake, cuts it to pieces, and marries both women, thus carrying off a double prize for his prowess.

In another story we learn of a happy family, a father and two daughters, who sail from their home in the northern coral archipelagoes, and run to the southwest till they come to the wild steep slopes of the rock island Gumasila. The father lies down on a platform and falls asleep. An ogre comes out of the jungle, eats the father, captures and ravishes one of the daughters, while the other succeeds in escaping. The sister from the woods supplies the captive one with a piece of lawyer cane, and when the ogre lies down and falls asleep they cut him in half and escape.

A woman lives in the village of Okopukopu at the head of a creek with her five children. A monstrously big stingaree paddles up the creek, flops across the village, enters the hut, and to the tune of a ditty cuts off the woman's finger. One son tries to kill the monster and fails. Every day the same performance is repeated till on the fifth day the youngest son succeeds in killing the giant fish.

A louse and a butterfly embark on a bit of aviation, the louse as a passenger, the butterfly as aeroplane and pilot. In the middle of the performance, while flying overseas just between the beach of Wawela and the island of Kitava, the louse emits a loud shriek, the butterfly is shaken, and the louse falls off and is drowned.

A man whose mother-in-law is a cannibal is sufficiently careless to go away and leave her in charge of his three children. Naturally she tries to eat them; they escape in time, however, climb a palm, and keep her (through a somewhat lengthy story) at bay, until the father arrives and kills her. There is another story about a visit to the Sun, another about an ogre devastating gardens, another about a woman who was so greedy that she stole all food at funeral distributions, and many similar ones.

In this place, however, we are not so much concentrating our attention on the text of the narratives, as on their sociological reference. The text, of course, is extremely important, but without the context it remains lifeless. As we have seen, the interest of the story is vastly enhanced and it is given its proper character by the manner in which it is told. The whole nature of the performance, the voice and the mimicry, the stimulus and the response of the audience mean as much to the natives as the text; and the sociologist should take his cue from the natives. The performance, again, has to be placed in its proper time setting—the hour of the day, and the season, with the background of the sprouting gardens awaiting future work, and slightly influenced by the magic of the fairy tales. We must also bear in mind the sociological context of private ownership, the sociable function and the cultural role of amusing fiction. All these elements are equally relevant; all must be studied as well as the text. The stories live in native life and not on paper, and when a scholar jots them down without being able to evoke the atmosphere in which they flourish he has given us but a mutilated bit of reality.

I pass now to another class of stories. These have no special season, there is no stereotyped way of telling them, and the recital has not the character of a performance, nor has it any magical effect. And yet these tales are more important than the foregoing class; for they are believed to be true, and the information which they contain is both more valuable and more relevant than that of the kukwanebu. When a party goes on a distant visit or sails on an expedition, the younger members, keenly interested in the landscape, in new communities, in new people, and perhaps even new customs, will express their wonder and make inquiries. The older and more experienced will supply them with information and comment, and this always takes the form of a concrete narrative. An old man will perhaps tell his own experiences about fights and expeditions, about famous magic and extraordinary economic achievements. With this he may mix the reminiscences of his father, hearsay tales and legends, which have passed through many generations. Thus memories of great droughts and devastating famines are conserved for many years, together with the descriptions of the hardships, struggles, and crimes of the exasperated population.

A number of stories about sailors driven out of their course and landing among cannibals and hos-

tile tribes are remembered, some of them set to song, others formed into historic legends. A famous subject for song and story is the charm, skill, and performance of famous dancers. There are tales about distant volcanic islands; about hot springs in which once a party of unwary bathers were boiled to death; about mysterious countries inhabited by entirely different men or women; about strange adventures which have happened to sailors in distant seas; monstrous fish and octopi, jumping rocks and disguised sorcerers. Stories again are told, some recent, some ancient, about seers and visitors to the land of the dead, enumerating their most famous and significant exploits. There are also stories associated with natural phenomena; a petrified canoe, a man changed into a rock, and a red patch on the coral rock left by a party who ate too much betel nut.

We have here a variety of tales which might be subdivided into historical accounts directly witnessed by the narrator, or at least vouched for by someone within living memory; legends, in which the continuity of testimony is broken, but which fall within the range of things ordinarily experienced by the tribesmen; and hearsay tales about distant countries and ancient happenings of a time which falls outside the range of present-day culture. To the natives, however, all these classes imperceptibly shade into each other; they are designated by the same name, libwogwo; they are all regarded as true; they are not recited as a performance, nor told for amusement at a special season. Their subject matter also shows a substantial unity. They all refer to subjects intensely stimulating to the natives; they all are connected with activities such as economic pursuits, warfare, adventure, success in dancing and in ceremonial exchange. Moreover, since they record singularly great achievements in all such pursuits, they redound to the credit of some individual and his descendants or of a whole community; and hence they are kept alive by the ambition of those whose ancestry they glorify. The stories told in explanation of peculiarities of features of the landscape frequently have a sociological context, that is, they enumerate whose clan or family performed the deed. When this is not the case, they are isolated fragmentary comments upon some natural feature, clinging to it as an obvious survival.

In all this it is once more clear that we can neither fully grasp the meaning of the text, nor the sociological nature of the story, nor the natives' attitude towards it and interest in it, if we study the narrative on paper. These tales live in the memory of man, in the way in which they are told, and even more in the complex interest which keeps them alive, which makes the narrator recite with pride or regret, which makes the listener follow eagerly, wistfully, with hopes and ambitions roused. Thus the essence of a legend, even more than that of a fairy tale, is not to be found in a mere perusal of the story, but in the combined study of the narrative and its context in the social and cultural life of the natives.

But it is only when we pass to the third and most important class of tales, the sacred tales or myths, and contrast them with the legends, that the nature of all three classes comes into relief. This third class is called by the natives liliu, and I want to emphasize that I am reproducing prima facie the natives' own classification and nomenclature, and limiting myself to a few comments on its accuracy. The third class of stories stands very much apart from the other two. If the first are told for amusement, the second to make a serious statement and satisfy social ambition, the third are regarded, not merely as true, but as venerable and sacred, and they play a highly important cultural part. The folk tale, as we know, is a seasonal performance and an act of sociability. The legend, provoked by contact with unusual reality, opens up past historical vistas. The myth comes into play when rite, ceremony, or a social or moral rule demands justification, warrant of antiquity, reality, and sanctity.

In the subsequent chapters of this book we will examine a number of myths in detail, but for the moment let us glance at the subjects of some typical myths. Take, for instance, the annual feast of the return of the dead. Elaborate arrangements are made for it, especially an enormous display of food. When this feast approaches, tales are told of how death began to chastise man, and how the power of eternal rejuvenation was lost. It is told why the spir-

its have to leave the village and do not remain at the fireside, finally why they return once in a year. Again, at certain seasons in preparation for an overseas expedition, canoes are overhauled and new ones built to the accompaniment of a special magic. In this there are mythological allusions in the spells, and even the sacred acts contain elements which are only comprehensible when the story of the flying canoe, its ritual, and its magic are told. In connection with ceremonial trading, the rules, the magic, even the geographical routes are associated with corresponding mythology. There is no important magic, no ceremony, no ritual without belief; and the belief is spun out into accounts of concrete precedent. The union is very intimate, for myth is not only looked upon as a commentary of additional information, but it is a warrant, a charter, and often even a practical guide to the activities with which it is connected. On the other hand the rituals, ceremonies, customs, and social organization contain at times direct references to myth, and they are regarded as the results of mythical event. The cultural fact is a monument in which the myth is embodied; while the myth is believed to be the real cause which has brought about the moral rule, the social grouping, the rite, or the custom. Thus these stories form an integral part of culture. Their existence and influence not merely transcend the act of telling the narrative, not only do they draw their substance from life and its interests—they govern and control many cultural features, they form the dogmatic backbone of primitive civilization.

This is perhaps the most important point of the thesis which I am urging: I maintain that there exists a special class of stories, regarded as sacred, embodied in ritual, morals, and social organization, and which form an integral and active part of primitive culture. These stories live not by idle interest, not as fictitious or even as true narratives; but are to the natives a statement of a primeval, greater, and more relevant reality, by which the present life, fates, and activities of mankind are determined, the knowledge of which supplies man with the motive for ritual and moral actions, as well as with indications as to how to perform them.

In order to make the point at issue quite clear, let us once more compare our conclusions with the current views of modern anthropology, not in order idly to criticize other opinions, but so that we may link our results to the present state of knowledge, give due acknowledgment for what we have received, and state where we have to differ clearly and precisely.

It will be best to quote a condensed and authoritative statement, and I shall choose for this purpose of definition an analysis given in *Notes and Queries on Anthropology,* by the late Miss C. S. Burne and Professor J. L. Myres. Under the heading "Stories, Sayings, and Songs," we are informed that "this section includes many intellectual efforts of peoples" which "represent the earliest attempt to exercise reason, imagination, and memory." With some apprehension we ask where is left the emotion, the interest, and ambition, the social role of all the stories, and the deep connection with cultural values of the more serious ones? After a brief classification of stories in the usual manner we read about the sacred tales: "Myths are stories which, however marvelous and improbable to us, are nevertheless related in all good faith, because they are intended, or believed by the teller, to explain by means of something concrete and intelligible an abstract idea or such vague and difficult conceptions as Creation, Death, distinctions of race or animal species, the different occupations of men and women; the origins of rites and customs, or striking natural objects or prehistoric monuments; the meaning of the names of persons or places. Such stories are sometimes described as etiological, because their purpose is to explain why something exists or happens.[1]

Here we have in a nutshell all that modern science at its best has to say upon the subject. Would our Melanesians agree, however, with this opinion? Certainly not. They do not want to "explain," to make "intelligible" anything which happens in their myths—above all not an abstract idea. Of that there can be found to my knowledge no instance either in Melanesia or in any other savage community. The few abstract ideas which the natives possess carry their concrete commentary in the very word which expresses them. When being is described by verbs to lie, to sit, to stand, when cause and effect are expressed by words signifying foundation and the past standing upon it, when various concrete nouns tend towards the meaning of space, the word and the relation to concrete reality make the abstract idea sufficiently "intelligible." Nor would a Trobriander or any other native agree with the view that "Creation, Death, distinctions of race or animal species, the different occupations of men and women" are "vague and difficult conceptions." Nothing is more familiar to the native than the different occupations of the male and female sex; there is nothing to be explained about it. But though familiar, such differences are at times irksome, unpleasant, or at least limiting, and there is the need to justify them, to vouch for their antiquity and reality, in short to buttress their validity. Death, alas, is not vague, or abstract, or difficult to grasp for any human being. It is only too hauntingly real, too concrete, too easy to comprehend for anyone who has had an experience affecting his near relatives or a personal foreboding. If it were vague or unreal, man would have no desire so much as to mention it; but the idea of death is fraught with horror, with a desire to remove its threat, with the vague hope that it may be, not explained, but rather explained away, made unreal, and actually denied. Myth, warranting the belief in immortality, in eternal youth, in a life beyond the grave, is not an intellectual reaction upon a puzzle, but an explicit act of faith born from the innermost instinctive and emotional reaction to the most formidable and haunting idea. Nor are the stories about "the origins of rites and customs" told in mere explanation of them. They never explain in any sense of the word; they always state a precedent which constitutes an ideal and a warrant for its continuance, and sometimes practical directions for the procedure.

We have, therefore, to disagree on every point with this excellent though concise statement of present-day mythological opinion. This definition would create an imaginary, non-existent class of narrative, the etiological myth, corresponding to a non-existent desire to explain, leading a futile existence as an "intellectual effort," and remaining outside native culture and social organization with their pragmatic interests. The whole treatment appears to us faulty, because myths are treated as mere stories, because they are regarded as a primitive intellectual armchair occupation, because they are torn out of their life context, and studied from what they look like on paper, and not from what they do in life. Such a definition would make it impossible either to see clearly the nature of myth or to reach a satisfactory classification of folk tales. In fact we would also have to disagree with the definition of legend and of fairy tale given subsequently by the writers in *Notes and Queries on Anthropology.*

But above all, this point of view would be fatal to efficient field work, for it would make the observer satisfied with the mere writing down of narratives. The intellectual nature of a story is exhausted with its text, but the functional, cultural, and pragmatic aspect of any native tale is manifested as much in its enactment, embodiment, and contextual relations as in the text. It is easier to write down the story than to observe the diffuse, complex ways in which it enters into life, or to study its function by the observation of the vast social and cultural realities into which it enters. And this is the reason why we have so many texts and why we know so little about the very nature of myth.

ENDNOTE

1. Quoted from *Notes and Queries on Anthropology,* pp. 210 and 211.

READING 2-2

*GENESIS AS MYTH**

Edmund Leach

Edmund Leach (1910–1989), was an outstanding British social anthropologist of the period after World War II, who adopted various approaches to the study of human

---

*References such as (iv. 3) refer to the third verse of the fourth chapter of the book Genesis (English Authorized Version) unless otherwise stated.
Source: In Genesis is as Myth and Other Essays, by Edmund Leach. London, United Kingdom: Jonathan Cape, 1969. Pages 7-23.

behavior in society, among them the structural-functional, and in the 1950s became attracted to the structural approach that Lévi-Strauss was just pioneering. During the 1960s and 1970s, he produced a series of structural analyses on myths drawn from the Bible, in part because he wanted to show how Lévi-Strauss's approach could be useful not just for obscure myths told by nonliterate people, but to give us fresh perspectives on literary narratives familiar to Westerners. "Genesis as Myth" is chosen as a case study in the structural analysis of myth because since it is one of his earliest structural studies, Leach takes particular pains to make explicit the basic assumptions underlying the structural approach. Note that he insists (following Lévi-Strauss) that all variants of a narrative be included in the analysis—not just a single one, however famous it may be, or the most complete, or the earliest version. Nor is he at all concerned with trying to determine which version of Genesis is the "best" or most "original." He explains the importance complementary (or binary) oppositions, and the significance of mediation. In true structuralist manner, we are presented with repetitions and inversions galore, and Leach ends up claiming to detect three "messages" in the stories. The term, endogamy, it might be worth noting here, means marrying within one's own group.

Although this kind of analysis has been challenged by some scholars as being too dependent upon the analyst's own interpretation, even critics concede that structural analysis has returned myth to a central place in anthropology, and this reading demonstrates why.

A distinguished German theologian has defined myth as 'the expression of unobservable realities in terms of observable phenomena.[1] All stories which occur in the Bible are myths for the devout Christian, whether they correspond to historical fact or not. All human societies have myths in this sense, and normally the myths to which the greatest importance is attached are those which are the least probable. The non-rationality of myth is its very essence, for religion requires a demonstration of faith by the suspension of critical doubt.

But if myths do not mean what they appear to mean, how do they come to mean anything at all? What is the nature of the esoteric mode of communication by which myth is felt to give 'expression to unobservable realities'?

This is an old problem which has lately taken on a new shape because, if myth be a mode of communication, then a part of the theory which is embodied in digital computer systems ought to be relevant. The merit of this approach is that it draws special attention to precisely those features of myth which have formerly been regarded as accidental defects. It is common to all mythological systems that all important stories recur in several different versions. Man is created in Genesis (i. 27) and then he is created all over again (ii. 7). And, as if two first men were not enough, we also have Noah in chapter viii. Likewise in the New Testament, why must there be four gospels each telling the 'same' story yet sometimes flatly contradictory on details of fact? Another noticeable characteristic of mythical stories is their markedly binary aspect; myth is constantly setting up opposing categories: 'In the beginning God created the heaven and the earth'; 'They crucified Him and two others with him, on either side one, and Jesus in the midst'; 'I am the Alpha and the Omega, the beginning and the end, saith the Lord.' So always it is in myth—God against the world and the world itself for ever dividing into opposites on either side: male and female, living and dead, good and evil, first and last . . .

Now, in the language of communication engineers, the first of these common characteristics of myth is called *redundancy*, while the second is strongly reminiscent of the unit of information—the *bit*. 'Information' in this technical sense is a measure of the freedom of choice in selecting a message. If there are only two messages and it is arbitrary which you choose then 'information is unity', that is $= 1$ bit.*[2]

Communication engineers employ these concepts for the analysis of problems which arise when a particular individual (the sender) wishes to transmit a coded message correctly to another individual (the receiver) against a background of interference (noise). 'Information' refers on the one hand to the degrees of choice open to the sender in encoding his transmission, and on the other to the degrees of

choice open to the receiver in interpreting what he receives (which will include noise in addition to the original transmitted signal). In this situation a high level of redundancy makes it easy to correct errors introduced by noise.

Now in the mind of the believer, myth does indeed convey messages which are the Word of God. To such a man the redundancy of myth is a very reassuring fact. Any particular myth in isolation is like a coded message badly snarled up with noisy interference. Even the most confident devotee might feel a little uncertain as to what precisely is being said. But, as a result of redundancy, the believer can feel that, even when the details vary, each alternative version of a myth confirms his understanding and reinforces the essential meaning of all the others.

The anthropologist's viewpoint is different. He rejects the idea of a supernatural sender. He observes only a variety of possible receivers. Here redundancy increases information—that is the uncertainty of the possible means of decoding the message. This explains what is surely the most striking of all religious phenomena—the passionate adherence to sectarian belief. The whole of Christendom shares a single corpus of mythology so it is surely very remarkable that the members of each particular Christian sect are able to convince themselves that they alone possess the secret of revealed truth. The abstract propositions of communication theory help us to understand this paradox.

But if the true believer can interpret his own mythology in almost any way he chooses, what principle governs the formation of the original myth? Is it random chance that a myth assumes one pattern rather than another? The binary structure of myth suggests otherwise.

Binary oppositions are intrinsic to the process of human thought. Any description of the world must discriminate categories in the form 'p is what not-p is not'. An object is alive or not alive and one could not formulate the concept 'alive' except as the converse of its partner 'dead'. So also human beings are male or not male, and persons of the opposite sex are either available as sexual partners or not avail-

---

*Bit stands for 'binary digit'.

able. Universally these are the most fundamentally important oppositions in all human experience.

Religion everywhere is preoccupied with the first, the antinomy of life and death. Religion seeks to deny the binary link between the two words; it does this by creating the mystical idea of 'another world', a land of the dead where life is perpetual. The attributes of this other world are necessarily those which are not of this world; imperfection here is balanced by perfection there. But this logical ordering of ideas has a disconcerting consequence— God comes to belong to the other world. The central 'problem' of religion is then to re-establish some kind of bridge between Man and God.

This pattern is built into the structure of every mythical system; the myth first discriminates between gods and men and then becomes preoccupied with the relations and intermediaries which link men and gods together. This much is already implicit in our initial definition.

So too with sex relations. Every human society has rules of incest and exogamy. Though the rules vary they always have the implication that for any particular male individual all women are divided by at least one binary distinction, there are women of *our kind* with whom sex relations would be incestuous and there are women of the *other kind* with whom sex relations are allowed. But here again we are immediately led into paradox. How was it in the beginning? If our first parents were persons of two kinds, what was that other kind? But if they were both of our kind, then their relations must have been incestuous and we are all born in sin. The myths of the world offer many different solutions to this childish intellectual puzzle, but the prominence which it receives shows that it entails the most profound moral issues. The crux is as before. If the logic of our thought leads us to distinguish *we* from *they,* how can we bridge the gap and establish social and sexual relations with 'the others' without throwing our categories into confusion?

So, despite all variations of theology, this aspect of myth is a constant. In every myth system we will find a persistent sequence of binary discriminations as between human/superhuman, mortal/immortal,

male/female, legitimate/illegitimate, good/bad . . . followed by a 'mediation' of the paired categories thus distinguished.

'Mediation' (in this sense) is always achieved by introducing a third category which is 'abnormal' or 'anomalous' in terms of ordinary 'rational' categories. Thus myths are full of fabulous monsters, incarnate gods, virgin mothers. This middle ground is abnormal, non-natural, holy. It is typically the focus of all taboo and ritual observance.

This approach to myth analysis derives originally from the techniques of structural linguistics associated with the name of Roman Jakobson[3] but is more immediately due to Claude Lévi-Strauss, one of whose examples may serve to illustrate the general principle.

Certain Pueblo Indian myths focus on the opposition between life and death. In these myths we find a threefold category distinction: agriculture (means to life), war (means to death), and hunting (a mediating category since it is means to life for men but means to death for animals). Other myths of the same cluster deploy a different triad: grass-eating animals (which live without killing), predators (which live by killing), and carrion-eating creatures (mediators, since they eat meat but do not kill in order to eat). In accumulation this total set of associated symbols serves to imply that life and death are *not* just the back and the front of the same penny, that death is *not* the necessary consequence of life.[4]

My Fig. 1 has been designed to display an analogous structure for the case of the first four chapters of Genesis. The three horizontal bands of the diagram correspond to (i) the story of the seven-day creation, (ii) the story of the Garden of Eden, and (iii) the story of Cain and Abel. The diagram can also be read vertically: column 1 in band (ii) corresponds to column 1 in band (i) and so on. The detailed analysis is as follows:—

UPPER BAND

First Day. (i. 1–5; not on diagram). Heaven distinguished from Earth; Light from Darkness; Day from Night; Evening from Morning.

Second Day. (i. 6–8; col. 1 of diagram). (Fertile) water (rain) above; (infertile) water (sea) below. Mediated by firmament (sky).

Third Day. (i. 9–10; col. 2 and i. 11–12; col. 3). Sea opposed to dry land. Mediated by 'grass, herb-yielding seed (cereals), fruit trees'. These grow on dry land but need water. They are classed as things 'whose seed is in itself' and thereby contrasted with bisexual animals, birds, etc.

The creation of the world as a static (that is, dead) entity is now complete and this whole phase of the creation is opposed to the creation of moving (that is, living) things.

Fourth Day. (i. 13–18; col. 4). Mobile sun and moon are placed in the fixed firmament of col. 1. Light and darkness become alternations (life and death become alternates).

Fifth Day. (i. 20–3; col. 5). Fish and birds are living things corresponding to the sea/land opposition of col. 2 but they also mediate the col. 1 oppositions between sky and earth and between salt water and fresh water.

Sixth Day. (i. 24–5; col. 6). Cattle (domestic animals), beasts (wild animals), creeping things. These correspond to the static triad of col. 3. But only the grass is allocated to the animals. Everything else, including the meat of the animals, is for Man's use (i. 29–30). Later at Leviticus xi creatures which do not fit this exact ordering of the world—for instance water creatures with no fins, animals and birds which eat meat or fish, etc.—are classed as 'abominations' Creeping Things are anomalous with respect to the major categories, Fowl, Fish, Cattle, Beast, and are thus abominations *ab initio* (Leviticus xi. 41–2). This classification in turn leads to an anomalous contradiction. In order to allow the Israelites to eat locusts the author of Leviticus xi had to introduce a special qualification to the prohibition against eating creeping things: 'Yet these *ye may* eat: of every flying creeping thing that goeth on all four which have legs above their feet, to leap withal upon the earth' (v. 21). The procedures of binary discrimination could scarcely be carried further!

(i. 26–7; col. 7). Man and Woman are created simultaneously.

The whole system of living creatures is instructed to 'be fruitful and multiply', but the problems of Life versus Death, and Incest versus Procreation are not faced at all.

CENTRE BAND

The Garden of Eden story which now follows tackles from the start these very problems which have been evaded in the first version. We start again with the opposition Heaven versus Earth, but this is mediated by a fertilizing mist drawn from the dry infertile earth (ii. 4–6). This theme, which blurs the distinction life/death, is repeated. Living Adam is formed from the dead dust of the ground (ii. 7); so are the animals (ii. 19); the garden is fertilized by a river which 'went out of Eden' (ii. 10); finally fertile Eve is formed from a rib of infertile Adam (ii. 22–3).

The opposition Heaven/Earth is followed by further oppositions—Man/Garden (ii. 15); Tree of Life/Tree of Death (ii. 9, 17); the latter is called the tree of the 'knowledge of good and evil' which means the knowledge of sexual difference.

Recurrent also is the theme that unity in the other world (Eden, Paradise) becomes duality in this world. Outside Eden the river splits into four and divides the world into separate lands (ii. 10–14). In Eden, Adam can exist by himself, Life can exist by itself; in this world, there are men and women, life and death. This repeats the contrast between monosexual plants and bisexual animals which is stressed in the first story.

The other living creatures are now created specifically because of the loneliness of Man in Eden (ii. 18). The categories are Cattle, Birds, Beasts. None of these are adequate as a helpmeet for Man. So finally Eve is drawn from Adam's rib . . . 'they are of one flesh' (ii. 18–24).

Comparison of Band 1 and Band 2 at this stage shows that Eve in the second story replaces the 'Creeping Things' of the first story. Just as Creeping Things were anomalous with respect to Fish, Fowl,

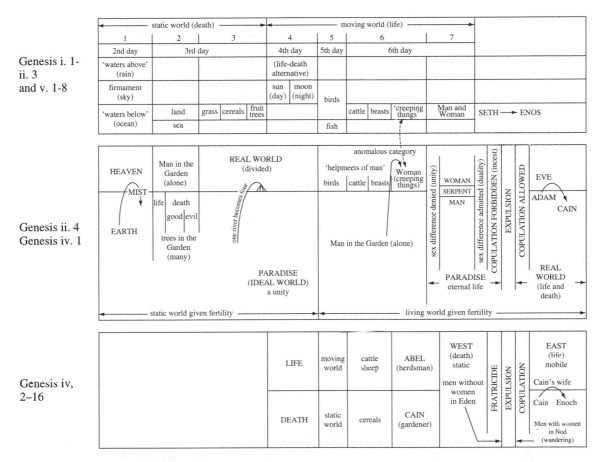

FIGURE 1 The four chapters of Genesis contain three separate creation stories. Horizontal bands correspond to (a) seven-day creation; (b) Garden of Eden; and (c) Cain and Abel. Each story sets up the opposition Death versus Life, God versus Man. World is 'made alive' by using categories of 'woman' and 'creeping thing' to mediate this opposition.

Cattle and Beast so Eve is anomalous to the opposition Man versus Animal. And, as a final mediation (chapter iii), the Serpent, a creeping thing, is anomalous to the opposition Man versus Woman.

Christian artists have always been sensitive to this fact; they manage to give the monster a somewhat hermaphrodite appearance while still indicating some kind of identification between the Serpent and Eve herself. Hugo Van der Goes, in 'The Fall' at the Kunsthistorisches Museum, Vienna, puts Eve and the Serpent in the same posture. Michaelangelo makes Adam and Eve both gaze with loving adoration on the Serpent, but the Serpent has Eve's face.[5]

Adam and Eve eat the forbidden fruit and become aware of sexual difference; death becomes inevitable (iii. 3–8). But now for the first time pregnancy and reproduction become possible. Eve does not become pregnant until after she has been expelled from Paradise (iv. 1).

LOWER BAND

Cain the Gardener and Abel the Herdsman repeat the antithesis between the first three days of the Creation and the last three days in the first story. Abel's living world is more pleasing to God (iv.

4–5). Cain's fratricide compares with Adam's incest and so God's questioning and cursing of Cain (iv. 9–12) has the same form and sequence as God's questioning and cursing of Adam, Eve and the Serpent (ii. 9–19). The latter part of iii. 16 is later repeated exactly (iv. 7), so Cain's sin was not only fratricide but also incestuous homosexuality. In order that immortal monosexual existence in Paradise may be exchanged for fertile heterosexual existence in reality, Cain, like Adam, must acquire a wife (iv. 17). To this end Adam must eliminate a sister: Cain a brother. The symmetry is complete.

The issue here is the logical basis of incest categories and closely analogous patterns must occur in all mythologies regardless of their superficial content. Cross-cultural comparison becomes easier if we represent the analysis as a systematic pattern of binary discriminations as in Fig. 2.

Adam/Eve and Cain/Abel are then seen to be variants of a theme which can also occur in other forms, as in the well-known myth of Oedipus. The actual symbolism in these two cases is nearly identical. Oedipus, like Adam and Cain, is initially earthbound and immobile. The conclusion of the Athenian version of the Oedipus story is that he is an exiled wanderer, protected by the gods. So also is Cain (iv. 14–15). The Bible also includes the converse of this pattern. In Genesis xxviii Jacob is a lonely exile and wanderer under God's protection, but (xxxii. 24–32) he is renamed Israel and thus given the status of a first ancestor with a territorial autochthonous base, and he is tamed by God. Although Jacob dies abroad in Egypt he is buried on his own ancestral soil in Israel (xl. 29–32; l. 5–7).

In the Oedipus story, in place of Eve's Serpent we have Jocasta's Sphinx. Like Jocasta the Sphinx is female, like Jocasta the Sphinx commits suicide, like the Serpent the Sphinx leads men to their doom by verbal cunning, like the Serpent the Sphinx is an anomalous monster. Eve listens to the Serpent's words and betrays Adam into incest; Oedipus solves the Sphinx riddle and is led into incest. Again, Oedipus's patricide replaces Cain's fratricide—Oedipus, incidentally, meets Laius 'at a cross roads'.

Perfect Ideal categories	Confused anomalous categories (sacred)	Imperfect real categories
HEAVEN The other world Paradise, Eden	FIRMAMENT Sky	EARTH This world
Things by themselves LIGHT DARKNESS DAY NIGHT DUST		Things in pairs DAY+ SUN NIGHT+ MOON
Life by itself Immortality Good by itself Unity ONE RIVER	Death Evil	Air Sea Freshwater Land BIRDS FISH PLANTS Life+Death Mortality Good +Evil Division FOUR RIVERS
Things whose seed is in themselves CEREALS FRUIT GRASS	CREEPING THINGS	Things with two sexes CATTLE BEASTS
Dust–MAN (by himself)		Meat
	ADAM EVE brother sister SERPENT incest	
Cereals	CAIN ABEL fratricide homosexual incest	Castle
WEST	EXPULSION FROM PARADISE	EAST Beginning of real life in real world Adam+Eve (as wife) Cain+Wife Procreation

FIGURE 2   Incest categories have a logical basis in all myths. Similarity between myths is seen most clearly if they are analyzed in a binary form as shown in this table.

Parallels of this kind seem too close to be accidental, but this kind of algebra is unfamiliar and more evidence will be needed to convince the skeptical. Genesis contains several further examples of first ancestors.

Firstly, Noah survived the destruction of the world by flood together with three sons and their wives. Prior to this the population of the world had included three kinds of being—'sons of God', 'daughters of men' and 'giants' who were the offspring of the union of the other two (vi. 1–4). Since the forbears of Noah's daughters-in-law have all been destroyed by the Flood, Noah becomes a unique ancestor of all mankind without the implication of incest. Chapter ix. 1–7 addressed to Noah is almost the duplicate of i. 27–30 addressed to Adam.

Though heterosexual incest is evaded, the theme of homosexual incest in the Cain and Abel story recurs in the Noah saga when drunken Noah is seduced by his own son Ham (ix. 21–5). The Canaanites, descendants of Ham, are for this reason accursed. (That a homosexual act is intended is evident from the language 'Ham saw the nakedness of his father'. Compare Leviticus xviii. 6–19, where 'to uncover the nakedness of' consistently means to have sexual relations with.)

In the second place Lot survives the destruction of the world by fire together with two nubile daughters. Drunken Lot is seduced by his own daughters (xix. 30–8). The Moabites and the Ammonites, descendants of these daughters, are for this reason accursed. In chapter xix the men of Sodom endeavour to have homosexual relations with two angels who are visiting Lot. Lot offers his nubile daughters instead but they escape unscathed. The implication is that Lot's incest is less grave than heterosexual relations with a foreigner, and still less grave than homosexual relations.

Thirdly, the affair of the Sodomites and the Angels contains echoes of 'the sons of God' and 'the daughters of men' but links superficially with chapter xviii where Abraham receives a visit from God and two angels who promise that his ageing and barren wife Sarah shall bear a son. Sarah is Abraham's half-sister by the same father (xx. 12) and his relations with her are unambiguously incestuous (Leviticus xviii. 9). Abraham *loans* Sarah to Pharaoh saying that she is his sister (xii. 19). He does the same with King Abimelech (xx. 2). Isaac repeats the game with Abimelech (xxvi. 9–11) but with a difference. Isaac's wife Rebekah is his father's brother's son's daughter (second cousin) and the relation is *not* in fact incestuous. The barrenness of Sarah is an aspect of her incest. The supernatural intervention which ultimately ensures that she shall bear a child is evidence that the incest is condoned. Pharaoh and Abimelech both suffer supernatural penalties for the lesser

offence of adultery, but Abraham, the incestuous husband, survives unscathed.

There are other stories in the same set. Hagar, Sarah's Egyptian slave, bears a son Ishmael to Abraham whose descendants are wanderers of low status. Sarah's son Isaac is marked out as of higher status than the sons of Abraham's concubines, who are sent away to 'the east country' (c.f. wandering Cain who made his home in Nod 'eastward of Eden'). Isaac marries a kinswoman in preference to a Canaanite woman. Esau's marriage to a Hittite woman is marked as a sin. In contrast his younger and favoured twin brother Jacob marries two daughters of his mother's brother who is in turn Jacob's father's father's brother's son's son.

All in all, this long series of repetitive and inverted tales asserts:

(a) the overriding virtue of close kin endogamy;
(b) that the sacred hero-ancestor Abraham can carry this so far that he marries his paternal half-sister (an incestuous relationship). Abraham is thus likened to Pharaoh, for the Pharaohs of Egypt regularly married their paternal half-sisters; and
(c) that a rank order is established which places the tribal neighbours of the Israelites in varying degrees of inferior status depending upon the nature of the defect in their original ancestry as compared with the pure descent of Jacob (Israel).

The myth requires that the Israelites be descended unambiguously from Terah the father of Abraham. This is achieved only at the cost of a breach of the incest rule; but by reciting a large number of similar stories which entail even greater breaches of sexual morality the relations of Abraham and Sarah finally stand out as uniquely virtuous. Just as Adam and Eve are virtuous as compared to Cain and Abel, so Abraham's incest can pass unnoticed in the context of such outrageous characters as Ham, Lot's daughters, and the men of Sodom.

I have concentrated here upon the issue of sexual rules and transgressions so as to show how

a multiplicity of repetitions, inversions and variations can add up to a consistent 'message'. I do not
wish to imply that this is the only structural pattern
which these myths contain.

The novelty of the analysis which I have presented does not lie in the facts but in the procedure. Instead of taking each myth as a thing in
itself with a 'meaning' peculiar to itself it is
assumed, from the start, that every myth is one of
a complex and that any pattern which occurs in
one myth will recur, in the same or other variations, in other parts of the complex. The structure
that is common to all variations becomes apparent
when different versions are 'superimposed' one
upon the other.

Whenever a corpus of mythology is recited in
its religious setting such structural patterns are
'felt' to be present, and convey meaning much as
poetry conveys meaning. Even though the ordinary listener is not fully conscious of what has
been communicated, the 'message' is there in a
quite objective sense. If the labour of program-
ming could be performed the actual analysis could
be done by a computer far better than by any
human. Furthermore it seems evident that much
the same patterns exist in the most diverse kinds of
mythology. This seems to me to be a fact of great
psychological, sociological and scientific significance. Here truly are observable phenomena
which are the expression of unobservable realities.

NOTES

1. J. Schniewind in H. W. Bartsch, 'Kerygma and Myth: a Theological Debate' (London, S.P.C.K., 1953), p. 47.
2. C. Shannon and W. Weaver, 'The Mathematical Theory of
   Communication' (Urbana, University of Illinois Press, 1949).
3. R. Jakobson and M. Halle, 'Fundamentals of Language' (The
   Hague, Mouton, 1956).
4. C. Lévi-Strauss, 'The Structural Study of Myth,' *Myth: a
   Symposium,* ed. T. A. Sebeok (Bloomington, University of
   Indiana Press, 1955).
5. G. Groddeck, 'The World of Man' (London, C. W. Daniel,
   1934).
See also E. R. Leach, 'Lévi-Strauss in the Garden of Eden,'
Transactions of the New York Academy of Sciences, 23, 4 (New
York, 1961), pp. 386–96.

READING 2–3

THE DOGON

Marcel Griaule and Germaine Dieterlen

*The cosmological ingenuity myths can reveal is seen to
advantage in the traditions of the Dogon, a population
living in Mali. Dogon myths seek to account for the origin
of the cosmos and the place of humanity within it. As a
blueprint for the creation of the cosmos and its development, as well as the order inherent in human organization, the Dogon cycle of myths is intriguingly subtle.
Although abbreviated, Griaule and Dieterlen's summary
of Dogon myths conveys a sense of the harmony that
blends the individual, society, and cosmos into a single,
all-embracing unity.*

*The Dogon are well-known among religious scholars
for the intricacy of their beliefs and rituals. Marcel Griaule and Germaine Dieterlen, together with other French
ethnographers, spent decades of fieldwork researching
them. This reading, though lacking any explicit theoretical slant or analytical focus gives us an excellent corrective to the presumptions of scholars such as Tylor, Frazer,
Freud, and Durkheim that "primitive" religion lacked the
sophistication of the world religions.*

INTRODUCTION

At the present stage of studies of the Dogon, and
precisely because these studies seek to penetrate
deeply into the mentality of the people, it is not possible to present a brief and clear-cut account of the
relationship between their cosmogony and their
social organization. The reader is warned from the
outset, therefore, that he will not find here an
exhaustive presentation of Dogon thought from the
point of view with which this book is concerned;
only certain institutions and concepts among those

Source: Marcel Griaule and Germaine Dieterlen, "The Dogon,"
in *African Worlds: Studies in the Cosmological Ideas and Social
Values of African Peoples*, ed. Daryll Forde (London: Oxford
University Press, 1954), pp. 83–89. Reprinted with permission.

for which adequate documentation exists will be selected for discussion.

The ideas of the Dogon may perhaps best be understood by considering the forms in which they express them. The basis of their thought concerning the universe and man's place in it is the "sign," most fully elaborated in the form of a "table of signs."[1] The Dogon hold that a "sign" or symbol and that which it symbolizes are reversible; that signs, substitutes, and images constitute a vast system of correspondences, in which every term is interlocked within what seem to be specific categories. These categories in their turn, whether linked or opposed, are themselves correlated.

Social institutions and, in general, all organized human activities constitute a scheme of representations. By analogy, a parallel scheme of myths reproduces the former, but with persons, places, times, and functions transposed. This second scheme, whether esoteric or not, provides for the natives a system of references and explanations of their social institutions.

Among the Dogon, exoteric myths correspond to a "superficial knowledge"[2] common to the greater part of the population; on the other hand, esoteric myths, parallel to these, present other identifications and much wider connections. Finally, within and beyond this totality of beliefs appears a logical scheme of symbols expressing a system of thought which cannot be described simply as myth. For this conceptual structure, when studied, reveals an internal coherence, a secret wisdom, and an apprehension of ultimate realities equal to that which we Europeans conceive ourselves to have attained. The Dogon, in this system of myths and symbols, are able to express a correspondence between their social organization and the world order as they conceive it. For them social life reflects the working of the universe and, conversely, the world order depends on the proper ordering of society.

Furthermore, the social order is projected in the individual, the indivisible cell which, on the one hand, is a microcosm of the whole, and, on the other, has a circumscribed function, like a cog in a machine; not only is a person the product of his institutions, he is also their motive power. Lacking any special power in himself, but because he is the representative of the whole, the individual affects the cosmic order which he also displays.

THE MYTHS OF THE DOGON

In order to understand the Dogon view of their own social organization it is necessary to know their myths of creation, and a brief analytical summary of these will be given below. Their conception of the universe is based, on the one hand, on a principle of vibrations of matter, and on the other, on a general movement of the universe as a whole. The original germ of life is symbolized by the smallest cultivated seed—*digitaria exilis*—commonly known as fonio and also called by the Dogon *kize uzi,* "the little thing." this seed, quickened by an internal vibration, bursts the enveloping sheath, and emerges to reach the uttermost confines of the universe. At the same time this unfolding matter moves along a path which forms a spiral or helix[3] (see Fig. 1). Two fundamental notions are thus expressed: on the one hand the perpetual helical movement signifies the conservation of matter; further, this movement, which is presented diagrammatically as a zigzag line (*ozu tonnolo*) on the facades of shrines, is held to represent

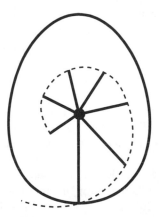

FIGURE 1   The First Seven Vibrations of the Egg of the World.

FIGURE 2   The Prefiguring of Man in the Egg of the World.

the perpetual alternation of opposites—right and left, high and low, odd and even, male and female—reflecting a principle of twin-ness, which ideally should direct the proliferation of life. These pairs of opposites support each other in an equilibrium which the individual being conserves within itself. On the other hand, the infinite extension of the universe is expressed by the continual progression of matter along this spiral path.

These primordial movements are conceived in terms of an ovoid form—"the egg of the world" (*aduno tal*)—within which lie, already differentiated, the germs of things; in consequence of the spiral movement of extension the germs develop first in seven segments of increasing length, representing the seven fundamental seeds of cultivation, which are to be found again in the human body, and which, with the *Digitaria,* indicate the predominance of the Ogdoad or Divine Octet in this system of thought: the organization of the cosmos, of man, and of society (Fig. 2). At the seventh vibration the segment breaks its envelope. This segment is the symbol of the seed which plays a primary role in the life and thought of the Dogon—the *emme ya,* female sorghum, which represents life, the ideal food, immune from impurity.

Having broken its wrapping the creative process emerges to follow the predestined and predetermined movement of being. For inside the first seed, and forming its central core, was an oblong plate

divided into four sectors in which lay the signs corresponding to the twenty-two categories into which the universe is classified, each placed under the direction of one of the four elements: air, fire, earth, and water. In the rotatory movement of creation this plate, turning on itself, flings off the signs into space, where they come to rest, each one on the things which it symbolizes and which till then existed only potentially. At their touch every being comes into existence and is automatically placed in the predetermined category.

All these images seem to relate to an effort of discovery, an attempt to apprehend the infinitely small at its point of departure towards the immeasurably vast. In fact, the order of the heavens, as it is observed and conceived by the Dogon, is no more than a projection, infinitely expanded, of events and phenomena which occur in the infinitely small.

The starting-point of creation is the star which revolves round Sirius and is actually named the "*Digitaria* star"; it is regarded by the Dogon as the smallest and the heaviest of all the stars; it contains the germs of all things. Its movement on its own axis and around Sirius upholds all creation in space. We shall see that its orbit determines the calendar.

Just as on the vegetal plane seven seeds came out of the first, so in the same way on the astral plane, from the first star came seven others bearing the names of the seven corresponding seeds. But from the moment when beings became conscious of themselves and capable of purposive action, the course of creation developed, in Dogon thought, in a less simple fashion. Personalities appeared who, after the chief person, the Creator God *Amma,* moved in a world of feeling, resembling man's ideas of himself and his own activities.

The preceding events, as already mentioned, took place inside an enormous egg (*aduno tal*), a world situated in infinite space and containing the appointed model of the creation, *Nommo,* the son of God. This egg was divided into two twin placenta,[4] each of which should have contained a pair of twin

Nommo, direct emanations and sons of God, according to the Dogon, and prefigurations of man. Like all other creatures these twin beings, living images of the fundamental principle of twin-ness in creation, were each equipped with two spiritual principles of opposite sex; each of them, therefore, was in himself a pair. We shall see how these images dominate the organization of society and of the family.

In one placenta, however, the male person, for reasons which are obscure, did not await the usual period of gestation appointed by *Amma* but emerged prematurely from the egg. Moreover, he tore a fragment from his placenta and with it came down through space outside the egg; this fragment became the earth. This being, *Yurugu,* brought the fonio with him intending to make a world of his own, modelled on the first but surpassing it.

This irregular procedure at the outset disorganized *Amma's* order of creation; the earth thus constituted was provided with a male soul only, since the being who made it was thus imperfect. From this imperfection arose the notion of impurity: earth and *Yurugu* were, from the beginning, solitary and impure. *Yurugu,* realizing that this situation would effectually prevent him from carrying out his task on earth, returned to heaven to try and find the rest of his placenta with his twin soul. But at his revolt, *Amma* had handed over this twin soul to the remaining pair in the other part of the egg, and had put her in their charge. *Yurugu* could not retrieve her; and from that time he has been engaged in a perpetual and fruitless search for her. He returned to the dry earth where now there began in the darkness to come into existence single, incomplete beings, offspring of incest; in fact he procreated in his own placenta, in the earth, that is, with his mother. Here we have the prefiguration of certain kinship ties and sentiments.

Seeing this, *Amma* decided to send to earth the *Nommo* of the other half of the egg, creators of the sky and the stars. They came down to earth on a gigantic arch, at the centre of which stood the two *Nommo* of the sky, who had assumed the guise of blacksmiths. At the four cardinal points were four other pairs of *Nommo,* avatars of the first and the

ancestors of man. The four male ancestors were named Amma Seru, Lébé Seru, Binu Seru, and Dyongu Seru. The arch constituted a new, undefiled earth; its descent coincided with the appearance of light in the universe, which till then had been in darkness. Water, in the form of rain, purified and fertilized the soil in which were sown the eight seeds which the mythical ancestors brought with them—each bearing a seed; human beings, animals, and plants forthwith came into existence. The 8 ancestors first gave birth to 12 offspring consisting of 4 pairs of twins—3 of mixed sexes and 1 male pair—as well as 2 males and 2 females. Thus the first 3 mythical generations comprised 22 persons, 10 of whom were female and 12 male.[5] With the aid of the skills taught by *Nommo,* social life was organized. In this way everything which had been created in the egg was then made manifest.

The advent of the arch of *Nommo* denotes not only the delimitation of space but also the measurement of times and seasons: the year was linked to the apparent movement of the sun, avatar of the other portion of the placenta of *Yurugu;* days alternated with nights and the seasons followed each other.

This period of the ordering of creation extended over twenty-two years, during which all social institutions were established. The first four years correspond to the first four seed-times, which today are symbolized by the actions of the totem priests who, at the rituals of sowing, cast the millet seeds to the four cardinal points. These four sowings, which denote the planting of the whole world, were necessary to ensure the perennial resurgence of plant life, that is, symbolically, the procreation of human beings. From the fifth sowing onwards a rite was celebrated of which the name, *bulu,* indicates its purpose, for its meaning is "to make alive again."

Death made its appearance in consequence of events connected with the position of *Yurugu* in the new organization. In the myth the dry, uncultivated, uninhabited earth belongs to *Yurugu,* a being of night, whereas *Nommo,* a being of the day, associated with the sky, water, and fertility, rules the cultivated, habitable land.

MAN

Man is the "seed" of the universe: that is to say, he was prefigured in the seed *Digitaria,* the vibrations and extensions of which produced the world.

This notion is expressed in the interpretation of the first seven segmentary vibrations which occurred in the first envelope. The first and the sixth produced the legs, the second and fifth the arms, the third and fourth the head, the seventh the scx organs of man (see Fig. 2). The first movements of creation were thus the first prefiguration of the being around whom everything was to be organized. But the link between man and the first creative act does not end here. The original seed first produced the image of man; conversely, man in his own person presents the image of the seed; the seven segment-vibrations also represent seven seeds, to which should be added the original *Digitaria* itself. These eight seeds are to be found in man's clavicles and symbolize his substance as well as his sustenance. We shall see that this notion of a vegetal series, in its various modifications, plays a dominant part in human society.

Man is the image not only of creation's first beginning but also of the existing universe. The egg of the world is represented by a diagram in which it is shown filled with germinating cells, one of which extrudes downwards, while a second lies horizontally across the first at its point of exit; these two constitute the setting of the world and establish the four cardinal points. A third cell, pressing on the first, takes its place and forces it to curve on itself, forming an open egg-shape symmetrical in position with the first (Fig. 3).[6] The *Dogon* thus produce a diagram which they call "the life of the world" and which is interpreted not only as the microcosmic man but also as the heavenly placenta (the upper egg-form) and the earthly placenta (the lower egg-form) which are separated by the space represented by the cross. In this diagram there may also be seen a reference to the principle of twin-ness: the two egg-shapes and the two segments form two pairs of twins recalling the four primordial beings each possessing two souls. From

FIGURE 3 "The Life of the World." The Heavenly and Earthly Placentas.

this it follows that the supreme expression of the individual's identity with creation, the perfect creation, is a pair of twins.

Like these primordial beings, man possesses two souls of opposite sexes, one of which inhabits his body while the other dwells in the sky or in water and links it to him. The vital force (*nyama*), which flows in his veins with his blood, is associated with the eight seeds which are distributed equally between his two clavicles. These seeds, united in pairs, are the basis of various notions concerning human personality and the changes it undergoes and they also recall the original groups of four pairs of twins (cf. p. 63). The series so constituted, the terms of which may vary from one social group to another, does not occur in the same order for every individual in the same group. Thus, within the same family the order applicable to a man will be inverted in the case of a woman; some seeds are excluded for certain social ranks or functions; they are held to be the chief factors of social differentiation. Since the condition of a person mirrors the condition of the universe, everything which affects the one has repercussions on the other; that is to say, in some way all a man's actions and all his circumstances must be conceived as closely connected with the functioning of things in general.

The seeds symbolize the food of mankind; they are the pivot on which turns the life of the cultivator, which depends as much on the seasonal renewal of vegetation as on the daily intake of food. They recall also the renewal of human life itself, which vanishes momentarily from its possessor only to be reborn in his descendants. Finally, the regular and appointed series attributed to the seeds is the sign of the universal order established on earth since the descent of *Nommo.*

Disorder among the seeds, which for an individual results especially from the breaking of the rules of life, prefigures the universal disorder which spreads by stages from the individual to his close kinsmen, his family, his clan, his people. But the disorder may be arrested and removed at any stage by appropriate rituals. Exact and complicated, they make it possible both for the individual to be restored and the general order to be preserved. Thus the individual, through his family and the society in which he lives, is linked in his structure and in his evolution with the universe; and this connection operates in both directions.

A human being in his development manifests the development of *Nommo,* symbol of the ordered world. Thus the new-born infant at birth is the head of *Nommo;* when later he becomes a herdboy, he is the chest, at betrothal the feet, at marriage the arms, and when fully adult he is the complete *Nommo*; as an elder and still more as a supreme chief he is both *Nommo* and the totality of the world and mankind.

ENDNOTES

1. See M. Griaule and G. Dieterlen, *Signes graphiques soudanais,* Paris, 1951.
2. For the knowledge possessed by the peoples of the French Sudan see G. Dieterlen, *Essai sur la religion bambara,* Paris, 1951.
3. The circular outward and/or upward motion is represented by a helical or spiral form in Dogon signs (Ed.).
4. In ordinary conversation the Dogon constantly use the term *me* for both the placenta and the amnion. We use "placenta" here because their symbolic representations are mainly associated with that organ.
5. Totemism among the Dogon is closely linked with this descent system.
6. See also "Signes graphiques Dogon" in *Signes graphiques soudanais.*

READING 2–4

POLLUTION

Mary Douglas

Mary Douglas's main point here is that the concepts of pollution, taboo, and dirt apply to things that do not fit neatly into the classificatory pigeonholes, or categories, created by society. Drawing on psychology and the work of Lévi-Strauss, Douglas claims that social categories are artificial because society imposes them on the continuum of sensory perception. They are therefore vulnerable to reality and must be hedged about by taboos to protect them. The concept of pollution serves to mark off areas where categories diverge too much from reality. Taboo is an important concept in this reading, and here Douglas— following Edmund Leach, another exponent of the structuralist school of anthropology—demonstrates its application to the classification of categories.

One of the great puzzles in comparative studies of religion has been the reconciliation of the concept of pollution, or defilement, with that of holiness. In the last half of the nineteenth century, Robertson Smith asserted that the religion of primitive peoples developed out of the relation between a community and its gods, who were seen as just and benevolent. Dependent on a sociological approach to religion, Robertson Smith continued always to draw a line between religious behavior, concerned with ethics and gods, and nonreligious, magical behavior. He used the term taboo to describe nonreligious rules of conduct, especially those concerned with pollution, in order to distinguish them from the rules of holiness protecting sanctuaries, priests, and everything pertaining to gods. The latter behavior he held to be intelligible and praiseworthy and the former to be

---

Source: "Pollution" by Mary Douglas. Reprinted, with slight deletions, by permission of Macmillan Library Reference USA, a Simon & Schuster Macmillan Company, from International Encyclopedia of the Social Sciences, David L. Sills, editor. Vol. 12, pp. 336–341. Copyright © 1968 by Crowell Collier and Macmillan, Inc.

primitive, savage, and irrational—"magical superstition based on mere terror."

He clearly felt that magic and superstition were not worth a scholar's attention. But Sir James Frazer, who dedicated *The Golden Bough* to Robertson Smith, tried to classify and understand the nature of magical thinking. He formulated the two principles of sympathetic magic: action by contagion and action by likeness. Frazer followed Robertson Smith in assuming that magic was more primitive than religion, and he worked out an evolutionary scheme in which primitive man's earliest thinking was oriented to mechanical ideas of contagion. Magic gradually gave way to another cosmology, the idea of a universe dominated by supernatural beings similar to man but greatly superior to him. Magic thus came to be accepted as a word for ritual which is not enacted within a cult of divine beings. But obviously there is an overlap between nonreligious ideas of contagion and rules of holiness. Robertson Smith accounted for this by making the distinction between holiness and uncleanness a criterion of the advanced religions:

> The person under taboo is not regarded as holy, for he is separated from approach to the sanctuary as well as from contact with men, but his act or condition is somehow associated with supernatural dangers, arising, according to the common savage explanation, from the presence of formidable spirits which are shunned like an infectious disease. In most savage societies no sharp line seems to be drawn between the two kinds of taboo . . . And even in more advanced nations the notions of holiness and uncleanness often touch . . . [to] distinguish between the holy and the unclean, marks a real advance above savagery. ([1889] 1927, p. 153)

Frazer echoes the notion that confusion between uncleanness and holiness marks primitive thinking. In a long passage in which he considers the Syrian attitude to pigs, he concludes: "Some said this was because the pigs were unclean; others said it was because the pigs were sacred. This . . . points to a hazy state of religious thought in which the ideas of sanctity and uncleanness are not yet sharply distinguished, both being blent in a sort of vaporous solu-

tion to which we give the name of taboo" ([1890] 1955, vol. 2, part 5, p. 23).

The work of several modern-day students of comparative religion derives not directly from Frazer but from the earlier work of Durkheim, whose debt to Robertson Smith is obvious in many ways. On the one hand, Durkheim was content to ignore aspects of defilement which are not part of a religious cult. He developed the notion that magical injunctions are the consequence of primitive man's attempt to explain the nature of the universe. Durkheim suggested that experimentation with magical injunctions, having thus arisen, has given way to medical science. But on the other hand, Durkheim tried to show that the contagiousness of the sacred is an inherent, necessary, and peculiar part of its character.

His idea of the sacred as the expression of society's awareness of itself draws heavily on Robertson Smith's thesis that man's relation to the gods, his religious behavior, is an aspect of prescribed social behavior. It followed, for Durkheim, that religious ideas are different from other ideas. They are not referable to any ultimate material reality, since religious shrines and emblems are only themselves representations of abstract ideas. Religious experience is an experience of a coercive moral force. Consequently, religious ideas are volatile and fluid; they float in the mind, unattached, and are always likely to shift, or to merge into other contexts at the risk of losing their essential character: there is always the danger that the sacred will invade the profane and the profane invade the sacred. The sacred must be continually protected from the profane by interdictions. Thus, relations with the sacred are always expressed through rituals of separation and demarcation and are reinforced with beliefs in the danger of crossing forbidden boundaries.

If contemporary thinkers were not already well prepared to accept the idea that "religious" restrictions were utterly different from primitive superstitions about contagion, this circular distinction between two kinds of contagion could hardly have gone unchallenged. How can it be argued that contagiousness is the peculiar characteristic of ideas about the sacred when another kind of contagiousness has been bracketed away by definition as irrelevant?

This criticism of Durkheim's treatment of sacred contagion is implicit in Lévy-Bruhl's massive work on primitive mentality (1922). Lévy-Bruhl documented a special kind of outlook on the universe, one in which the power to act and to be acted upon regardless of restrictions of space and time is widely attributed to symbolical representations of persons and animals. He himself explained the belief in such remote contagion by the dominance of the idea of the supernatural in the primitive view of the world. And since he would expect "supernatural" to be equated with Durkheim's "sacred," he seems to have seen no conflict between his and the master's views.

We cannot accept Durkheim's argument that there are two kinds of contagion, one the origin of primitive hygiene and the other intrinsic to ideas about the sacred, because it is circular. If we approach the problem of contagion in Lévy-Bruhl's terms, then the scope of the answer is broadened: there is not simply a residual area of magical behavior that remains to be explained after primitive religious behavior has been understood but rather a whole mentality, a view of how the universe is constituted. This view of the universe differs essentially from that of civilized man in that sympathetic magic provides the key to its control. Lévy-Bruhl is open to criticism: his statement of the problem is oversimple. He bluntly contrasts primitive mentality with scientific thought, not fully appreciating what a rare and specialized activity scientific thinking is and in what well-defined and isolated conditions it takes place. His use of the word "pre-logical" in his first formulation of primitive thinking was unfortunate, and he later discarded it. But although his work seems to be discredited at present, the general problem still stands. There is a whole class of cultures, call them what you will, in which great attention is paid to symbolic demarcation and separation of the sacred and the profane and in which dangerous consequences are expected to follow from neglect of the rituals of separation. In these cultures lustrations, fumigations, and purifications of various kinds are applied to avert the dangerous effect of breach of the rules, and symbolic actions based on likeness to real causes are used as instruments for creating positive effects.

THE CULTURAL DEFINITION

If we are not to follow Robertson Smith in treating the rules of uncleanness as irrational and beyond analysis, we need to clear away some of the barriers which divide up this whole field of inquiry. While the initial problem is posed by the difference between "our" kind of thinking and "theirs," it is a mistake to treat "us" the moderns and "them" the ancients as utterly different. We can only approach primitive mentality through introspection and understanding of our own mentality. The distinction between religious behavior and secular behavior also tends to be misleadingly rigid. To solve the puzzle of sacred contagion we can start with more familiar ideas about secular contagion and defilement. In English-speaking cultures, the key word is the ancient, primitive, and still current "dirt." Lord Chesterfield defined dirt as matter out of place. This implies only two conditions, a set of ordered relations and a contravention of that order. Thus the idea of dirt implies a structure of ideas. For us dirt is a kind of compendium category for all events which blur, smudge, contradict, or otherwise confuse accepted classifications. The underlying feeling is that a system of values which is habitually expressed in a given arrangement of things has been violated.

This definition of defilement avoids some historical peculiarities of Western civilization. For example, it says nothing about the relation between dirt and hygiene. We know that the discovery of pathogenic organisms is recent, but the idea of dirt antedates the idea of pathogenicity. It is therefore more likely to have universal application. If we treat all pollution behavior as the reaction to any event likely to confuse or contradict cherished classifications, we can bring two new approaches to bear on the problem: the work of psychologists on perception and of anthropologists on the structural analysis of culture.

Perception is a process in which the perceiver actively interprets and, in the course of his interpreting, adapts and even supplements his sensory experiences. Hebb has shown that in the process of perception, the perceiver imposes patterns of organization on the masses of sensory stimuli in the environment (1949; 1958). The imposed pattern organizes sequences into units—fills in missing events which would be necessary to justify the recognition of familiar units. The perceiver learns to adjust his response to allow for modification of stimuli according to changes in lighting, angle of regard, distance, and so forth. In this way the learner develops a scheme or structure of assumptions in the light of which new experiences are interpreted. Learning takes place when new experience lends itself to assimilation in the existing structure of assumption or when the scheme of past assumptions is modified in order to accommodate what is unfamiliar. In the normal process of interpretation, the existing scheme of assumptions tends to be protected from challenge, for the learner recognizes and absorbs cues which harmonize with past experience and usually ignores cues which are discordant. Thus, those assumptions which have worked well before are reinforced. Because the selection and treatment of new experiences validates the principles which have been learned, the structure of established assumptions can be applied quickly and automatically to current problems of interpretation. In animals this stabilizing, selective tendency serves the biological function of survival. In men the same tendency appears to govern learning. If every new experience laid all past interpretations open to doubt, no scheme of established assumptions could be developed and no learning could take place.

This approach may be extended to the learning of cultural phenomena. Language, for example, learned and spoken by individuals, is a social phenomenon produced by continuous interaction between individuals. The regular discriminations which constitute linguistic structure are the spontaneous outcome of continual control, exercised on an individual attempting to communicate with others. Expressions which are ambiguous or which deviate from the norm are less effective in communication, and speakers experience a direct feedback encouraging conformity. Language has more loosely and more strictly patterned domains in which ambiguity has either more or less serious repercussions on effective communication. Thus there are certain domains in which ambiguity can be better tolerated than in others (Osgood & Sebeok 1954, p. 129).

Similar pressures affect the discrimination of cultural themes. During the process of enculturation the individual is engaged in ordering newly received experiences and bringing them into conformity with those already absorbed. He is also interacting with other members of his community and striving to reduce dissonance between his structure of assumptions and theirs (Festinger 1957). Frenkel-Brunswik's research among schoolchildren who had been variously exposed to racial prejudice illustrates the effects of ambiguity on learning at this level. The children listened to stories which they were afterwards asked to recall. In the stories the good and bad roles were not consistently allocated to white and Negro characters. When there was dissonance between their established pattern of assumptions about racial values and the actual stories they heard, an ambiguous effect was received. They were unable to recall the stories accurately. There are implications here for the extent to which a culture (in the sense of a consistent structure of themes, postulates, and evaluations) can tolerate ambiguity. It is now common to approach cultural behavior as if it were susceptible to structural analysis on lines similar to those used in linguistics (Lévi-Strauss 1958; Leach 1961). For a culture to have any recognizable character, a process of discrimination and evaluation must have taken place very similar to the process of language development—with an important difference. For language the conditions requiring clear verbal communication provide the main control on the pattern which emerges, but for the wider culture in which any language is set, communication with others is not the only or principal function. The culture affords a hierarchy of goals and values which the community can apply as a general guide to action in a wide variety of contexts. Cultural interaction, like linguistic interaction, involves the individual in communication with others. But it also helps the individual to reflect upon and order his own experience.

The general processes by which language structure changes and resists change have their analogues at the higher level of cultural structure. The response to ambiguity is generally to encourage clearer discrimination of differences. As in language, there are different degrees of tolerance of ambiguity. Linguistic intolerance is expressed by avoidance of ambiguous utterances and by pressure to use well-discriminated forms where differences are important to interpretation and appropriate responses. Cultural intolerance of ambiguity is expressed by avoidance, by discrimination, and by pressure to conform.

THE FUNCTIONS OF POLLUTION BELIEFS

To return to pollution behavior, we have already seen that the idea of dirt implies system. Dirt avoidance is a process of tidying up, ensuring that the order in external physical events conforms to the structure of ideas. Pollution rules can thus be seen as an extension of the perceptual process: insofar as they impose order on experience, they support clarification of forms and thus reduce dissonance.

Much attention has been paid to the sanctions by which pollution rules are enforced (see Steiner 1956, p. 22). Sometimes the breach is punished by political decree, sometimes by attack on the transgressor, and sometimes by grave or trivial sanctions; the sanction used reflects several aspects of the matter. We can assume that the community, insofar as it shares a common culture, is collectively interested in pressing for conformity to its norms. In some areas of organization the community is capable of punishing deviants directly, but in others this is not practicable. This may happen, for example, if political organization is not sufficiently developed or if it is developed in such a way as to make certain offenses inaccessible to police action. Homicide is a type of offense which is variously treated according to the relationship between killer and victim. If the

offender is himself a member of the victim's group and if this is the group which is normally entrusted with protection of its members' interests, it may be held contradictory and impossible for the group to inflict punishment. Then the sanction is likely to be couched in terms of a misfortune that falls upon the offender without human intervention. This kind of homicide is treated as a pollution.

We would expect to find that the pollution beliefs of a culture are related to its moral values, since these form part of the structure of ideas for which pollution behavior is a protective device. But we would not expect to find any close correspondence between the gravity with which offenses are judged and the danger of pollution connected with them. Some moral failings are likely to be met with prompt and unpleasant social consequences. These self-punishing offenses are less likely to be sanctioned by pollution beliefs than by other moral rules. Pollution beliefs not only reinforce the cultural and social structure, but they can actively reduce ambiguity in the moral sphere. For example, if two moral standards are applied to adultery, so that it is condemned in women and tolerated in men, there will inevitably be some ambiguity in the moral judgment since adultery involves a man and a woman. A pollution belief can reduce the ambiguity. If the man is treated as dangerously contagious, his adulterous condition, while not in itself condemned, endangers the outraged husband or the children; moral support can be mustered against him. Alternatively, if attention is focused on the pollution aspect of the case, a rite of purification can mitigate the force of the moral condemnation.

This approach to pollution allows further applications of Durkheimian analysis. If we follow him in assuming that symbolism and ritual, whether strictly religious or not, express society's awareness of its own configuration and necessities, and if we assume that pollution rules indicate the areas of greater systematization of ideas, then we have an additional instrument of sociological analysis. Durkheim held that the dangerous powers imputed to the gods are, in actual fact, powers vested in the social structure for defending itself, as a structure, against the deviant behavior of its members. His approach is strengthened by including all pollution rules and not merely those which form part of the religious cult. Indeed, deriving pollution behavior from processes similar to perception comes close to Durkheim's intention of understanding society by developing a social theory of knowledge.

Pollution rules in essence prohibit physical contact. They tend to be applied to products or functions of human physiology; thus they regulate contact with blood, excreta, vomit, hair clippings, nail clippings, cooked food, and so on. But the anthropologist notes that the incidence of beliefs in physiological pollution varies from place to place. In some communities menstrual pollution is gravely feared and in others not at all; in some, pollution by contact with the dead is feared, in others pollution of food or blood. Since our common human condition does not give rise to a common pattern of pollution observances, the differences become interesting as an index of different cultural patterning. It seems that physiological pollutions become important as symbolic expressions of other undesirable contacts which would have repercussions on the structure of social or cosmological ideas. In some societies the social definition of the sexes is more important than in others. In some societies social units are more rigorously defined than in others. Then we find that physical contact between sexes or between social units is restricted even at second or third remove. Not only may social intercourse be restricted, but sitting on the same chair, sharing the same latrine, or using the same cooking utensils, spoons, or combs may be prohibited and negatively sanctioned by pollution beliefs. By such avoidances social definitions are clarified and maintained. Color bars and caste barriers are enforced by these means. As to the ordered relation of social units and the total structure of social life, this must depend on the clear definition of roles and allegiances. We would therefore expect to find pollution concepts guarding threatened disturbances of the social order. On this, nearly everything has been said by van Gennep. His metaphor of society as a kind of house divided into rooms and corridors, the compartments carefully

isolated and the passages between them protected by ceremonial, shows insight into the social aspects of pollution. So also does his insistence on the relative character of the sacred:

> Sacredness as an attribute is not absolute; it is brought into play by the nature of particular situations. . . . Thus the "magic circles" pivot, shifting as a person moves from one place in society to another. The categories and concepts which embody them operate in such a way that whoever passes through the various positions of a lifetime one day sees the sacred where before he has seen the profane, or vice versa. Such changes of condition do not occur without disturbing the life of society and the individual, and it is the function of rites of passage to reduce their harmful effects. (Gennep [1909] 1960, pp. 12–13)

Van Gennep saw that rites of transition treat all marginal or ill-defined social states as dangerous. His treatment of margins is fully compatible with the sociological approach to pollution. But van Gennep's ideas must be vastly expanded. Not only marginal social states, but all margins, the edges of all boundaries which are used in ordering the social experience, are treated as dangerous and polluting.

Rites of passage are not purificatory but are prophylactic. They do not redefine and restore a lost former status or purify from the effect of contamination, but they define entrance to a new status. In this way the permanence and value of the classifications embracing all sections of society are emphasized.

When we come to consider cosmological pollution, we are again faced with the problem unresolved by Lévy-Bruhl. Cosmological pollution is to the Westerner the most elusive, yet the most interesting case. Our own culture has largely given up the attempt to unify, to interpenetrate, and to cross-interpret the various fields of knowledge it encompasses. Or rather, the task has been taken over by natural science. A major part of pollution behavior therefore lies outside the realm of our own experience: this is the violent reaction of condemnation provoked by anything which seems to defy the apparently implicit categories of the universe. Our culture trains us to believe that anomalies are only due to a temporarily inadequate formulation of general natural laws. We have to approach this kind of pollution behavior at second hand.

The obvious source of information on the place of cosmic abnormality in the mind of the primitive is again Lévy-Bruhl. Earthquakes, typhoons, eclipses, and monstrous births defy the order of the universe. If something is thought to be frightening because it is abnormal or anomalous, this implies a conception of normality or at least of categories into which the monstrous portent does not fit. The more surprising that anomaly is taken to be, the clearer the evidence that the categories which it contradicts are deeply valued.

At this point we can take up again the question of how the culture of civilization differs from that which Lévy-Bruhl called primitive. Recalling that dirt implies system and that pollution beliefs indicate the areas of greatest systematization, we can assume that the answer must be along the same lines. The different elements in the primitive world view are closely integrated; the categories of social structure embrace the universe in a single, symbolic whole. In any primitive culture the urge to unify experience to create order and wholeness has been effectively at work. In "scientific culture" the apparent movement is the other way. We are led by our scientists to specialization and compartmentalism of spheres of knowledge. We suffer the continual breakup of established ideas. Lévy-Bruhl, looking to define the distinction between the scientific and the primitive outlook, would have been well served if he had followed Kant's famous passage on his own Copernican revolution. Here Kant describes each great advance in thought as a stage in the process of freeing "mind" from the shackles of its own subjective tendencies. In scientific work the thinker tries to be aware of the provisional and artificial character of the categories of thought which he uses. He is ready to reform or reject his concepts in the interests of making a more accurate statement.

Any culture which allows its guiding concepts to be continually under review is immune from cosmological pollutions. To the extent that we have no established world view, our ways of thinking are different from those of people living in primitive cul-

tures. For the latter, by long and spontaneous evolution, have adapted their patterns of assumption from one context to another until the whole of experience is embraced. But such a comprehensive structure of ideas is precarious to the extent that it is an arbitrary selection from the range of possible structures in the same environment. Other ways of dividing up and evaluating reality are conceivable. Hence, pollution beliefs protect the most vulnerable domains, where ambiguity would most weaken the fragile structure.

EMOTIONAL ASPECTS OF POLLUTION BEHAVIOR

Pollution beliefs are often discussed in terms of the emotions which they are thought to express. But there is no justification for assuming that terror, or even mild anxiety, inspires them any more than it inspires the housewife's daily tidying up. For pollution beliefs are cultural phenomena. They are institutions that can keep their forms only by bringing pressure to bear on deviant individuals. There is no reason to suppose that the individual in a primitive culture experiences fear, still less unreasoning terror, if his actions threaten to modify the form of the culture he shares. His position is exactly comparable to a speaker whose own linguistic deviations cause him to produce responses which vary with his success in communicating. The dangers and punishments attached to pollution act simply as means of enforcing conformity.

As to the question of the rational or irrational character of rules of uncleanness, Robertson Smith is shown to have been partly right. Pollution beliefs certainly derive from rational activity, from the process of classifying and ordering experience. They are, however, not produced by strictly rational or even conscious processes but rather as a spontaneous by-product of these processes.

BIBLIOGRAPHY

Douglas, Mary. 1966. *Purity and Danger: A Comparative Study of Concepts of Pollution and Taboo.* London: Routledge.

Durkheim, Émile. (1912) 1954. *The Elementary Forms of the Religious Life.* London: Allen & Unwin; New York: Macmillan.

First published as *Les formes élémentaires de la vie religieuse, le système totémique en Australie*. A paperback edition was published in 1961 by Collier.

Eliade, Mircea. (1957) 1959. *The Sacred and the Profane: The Nature of Religion*. New York: Harcourt. First published in German. A paperback edition was published in 1961 by Harper.

Festinger, Leon. 1957. *A Theory of Cognitive Dissonance*. Evanston, Ill.: Row.

Frazer, James. (1890) 1955. *The Golden Bough: A Study in Magic and Religion*. 3rd ed., Rev. & Enl. 13 vols. New York: St. Martins; London: Macmillan. An abridged edition was published in 1922 and reprinted in 1955.

Frenkel-Brunswik, Else. 1949. *Intolerance of Ambiguity as an Emotional and Perceptual Personality Variable*. Journal of Personality 18:108–143.

Gennep, Arnold van. (1909) 1960. *The Rites of Passage*. London: Routledge; Univ. of Chicago Press. First published in French.

Hebb, Donald O. 1949. *The Organization of Behavior: A Neuropsychological Theory*. New York: Wiley.

———. 1958. *A Textbook of Psychology*. Philadelphia: Saunders.

Leach, Edmund R. 1961. *Rethinking Anthropology*. London School of Economics and Political Science Monographs on Social Anthropology, no. 22. London: Athlone.

Lévi-Strauss, Claude. (1958) 1963. *Structural Anthropology*. New York: Basic Books. First published in French.

Lévy-Bruhl, Lucien. (1910) 1926. *How Natives Think*. London: Allen & Unwin. First published as *Les fonctions mentales dans les sociétés primitives*.

———. (1922) 1923. *Primitive Mentality*. Macmillan. First published in French.

Osgood, Charles E.; and Sebeok, Thomas A. (editors). (1954) 1965. *Psycholinguistics: A Survey of Theory and Research Problems*. Bloomington: Indiana Univ. Press.

Smith, William Robertson. (1889) 1927. *Lectures on the Religion of the Semites*. 3d ed. New York: Macmillan.

Steiner, Franz. 1956. *Taboo*. New York: Philosophical Library.

RELIGION IN THE NEWS

A LEGENDARY HERO GUIDES A REBORN KYRGYZSTAN

The social value of myth is attested to among modern-day citizens of Kyrgyzstan, a republic in central Asia, whose citizens—the Kyrgyz—lack a strong religious ideology and tradition of political unity to help make their society more cohesive. Their collective self-realization in what the article calls "the legend of Manas" provides them with a measure of cohesion, inculcating as it does moral values and generating a sense of collective pride. The improbable feats of the hero, Manas, which includes uprooting trees and hurling boulders

from the top of mountains, suggests that we are justified in regarding this oral narrative as much myth as legend. Malinowski would appreciate evidence here of his concept of "charter" heavily at work: the mythic past is being manipulated to serve the contemporary political vision President Askar Akayev has for his young nation.

Source: Stephen Kinzer, "A Legendary Hero Guides a Reborn Kyrgyzstan." The New York Times, January 2, 2000, page 3.

ASK YOURSELF

Critics of the structural approach maintain the binary oppositions, reversals, and mediators that structural anthropologists claim to have discovered do not really exist in the stories themselves, but are superimposed on them by the author. Think about Reading 2–2 again, and ask yourself if you are convinced that Edmund Leach is really onto something or whether the author

was suffering from an unduly overheated imagination when he sought to discover "messages" in these biblical myths. And what of the three "messages?" Are you convinced Leach has demonstrated that they exist? If you are—or even if you are not—has Leach made you think about Genesis with any greater insight than before you read him?

FURTHER READINGS

Endicott, Kirk. *Batek Negrito Religion.* Oxford: Clarendon Press, 1979. The cosmos of a nomadic hunting and gathering people living in the rain forest of the Malay Peninsula is examined in relation to the indigenous attitudes toward the natural environment, conceptions of humanity, divinities, and ritual practices. This is a brilliant analysis of the cosmological notions of a technologically simple society.

Kirk, G. S. *Myth: Its Meaning and Functions in Ancient and Other Cultures.* London: Cambridge University Press, and Berkeley and Los Angeles: University of California Press, 1970. The author, a classical scholar, evaluates the merits of the different approaches to myth by examining their power to help us make sense of the narratives of ancient times and—more restrictedly—those of nonliterate societies. This is an admirable introduction to myth—authoritative yet engagingly readable.

Lévi-Strauss, Claude. "The Structural Study of Myth" in *Structural Anthropology,* Volume 1. 1963 New York: HarperCollins Publishers, Inc. Some myths seem to hide attempts to resolve certain philosophical puzzles. In analyzing the story of Oedipus in this article, Lévi-Strauss argues that the myth attempts to resolve a dilemma brought about by two apparently contradictory beliefs held in classic Greek society. On the one hand, he says, the Greeks believed that human beings were born from the earth. On the other, they denied this belief. The myth, he tries to show, enabled them to evade the puzzle in a manner that (presumably) satisfied their sense of logic.

Lévi-Strauss, Claude. *The raw & cooked: introduction to a science of mythology,* Vol. 1, Trans. John and Doreen Weightman. New York and Evanston: Harper & Row, 1969. In this book, the most famous of all students of mythology begins by analyzing a single myth from a Brazilian tribe. He gradually adds more and more as he extends his geographical range. By the end of the book he has analyzed 183 myths. And there are another three volumes before he gets to North American myths! Very tough going, but an indispensable work for anyone seriously interested in myth.

Needham, Rodney. *Symbolic Classification.* Santa Monica, Calif. 1979. A brief overview of this topic. Among the matters discussed are the various forms symbolic classification may take, opposition, and transformations.

Radin, Paul. The Trickster: *A Study in American Indian Mythology.* New York: Schocken. 1972 (1956). The trickster is a world-wide motif, occurring in the folklore of many societies. In this book we see how he reveals his distinctive attributes among the Winnebago, Assiniboine, and Tlingit peoples, of North America.

SUGGESTED VIDEOS

"Popol Vuh: The Creation Myth of the Maya." This video uses imagery from ancient Maya ceramics to create a captivating depiction of the Popol Vuh, the Maya creation narrative, which is the foundation myth for many Native American beliefs. After the Maya are introduced, the narrative unfolds. It starts with the creation of the world and ends with the victory of the hero twins over the evil lords of the underworld. A teacher's guide is available. 60 minutes; 1992; $295 (sale), $70 (rental). Catalog #38183. "World Cultures on Film and Video," University of California Extension, Center for Media and Independent Learning, 2000 Center Street, Fourth Floor, Berkeley, CA 94704.

"Tracking the Pale Fox: Studies on the Dogon." This film describes the history of research into Dogon culture. It begins with the original fieldwork of Marcel Griaule in 1931, which it locates within the framework of the French Anthropology of the time, and includes interviews with Dogon Elders and researcher Germaine Dieterlen. 48 minutes; RA/VHS 212; $72; Film Officer, RAI, 50 Fitzroy Street, London W1P 5HS, United Kingdom.

"Watunna." This animation video has five tales from the creation myths of the Yekuana Indians, who live in the rain forests of Venezuela. They describe the origin of evil, sex, night, fire, and food. The animation consists of handpainted watercolors using designs that are drawn in part from ancient Yekuana art. 24 minutes; 1990; $195 (sale), $50 (rental). Catalog #37907. "World Cultures on Film and Video," University of California Extension, Center for Media and Independent Learning, 2000 Center Street, Fourth Floor, Berkeley, Ca 94704.

"My Country Djarrakpi." For the Australian Aborigines, paintings and ritual form part of a unitary complex that includes social organization since every painting or design is owned by a particular clan and celebrates occurrences in the clan's "Ancestral Past." This film portrays a member of the Yolngu tribe talking about his land at Djarrakpi, a site of great sacredness for his clan. We see an exhibition of his paintings at the

Australian National University in Canberra, where he interprets his bark painting of Djarrakpi and then we are taken to the sand dunes of Djarrakpi itself where he describes the meaning of some of the physical features of the local landscape. £15. By Ian Dunlop. Producer: Film Australia. 1981. Length: 16 minutes. VC.RA98. Film Officer, Royal Anthropological Institute (RAI), 50 Fitzroy Street, London W1P 5HS, United Kingdom.

On the island of Flores, in eastern Indonesia, men from different villages slash at each other with buffalo-hide whips in a ritual performed so that local spirits will make crops fertile. If blood is drawn, villages believe a good rice harvest will follow.

Photo courtesy of David Hicks

CHAPTER 3

GODS, SPIRITS, AND SOULS

Unfettered by physical limitations, the human imagination might be thought capable of creating a virtually infinite diversity of gods, spirits, and souls, yet cross-culturally we find a surprising similarity between the distinct features of spiritual agencies. Beliefs in beings that created the cosmos and humanity are certainly widespread, but cross-cultural research suggests they are not as universal as beliefs that ancestral ghosts exist and that these agencies have the power to influence human affairs (Reading 3–4). Very frequently, indeed, we find that ghosts of this kind are believed to control the behavior of their living relatives by punishing misbehavior or the neglect of duty with sickness or even death. The same is true of other categories of spiritual agency. Ethnographers often comment on the degree to which human beings live their lives in continual awareness of the influence gods and spirits exercise upon them, an influence that may be integrated into a philosophy of misfortune, so that political setbacks, crop failure, a lack of success in love, and other vicissitudes that make up human experience are explained in terms of their punitive sanctions. In this respect, spiritual agencies share a common denominator with sorcerers (bad magicians) and witches.

Like ghosts, souls are spiritual entities primarily associated with the human body—although Edward Tylor's animism, of course, included the notion that other natural objects can possess souls as well as human beings. The soul's presence in—or temporary or permanent absence from—the body often indicates health or brings about sickness, life or death. A spirit is usually defined as a spiritual agency that is not associated with a physical place of residence, and there are nature spirits, agricultural spirits, spirit-guardians of animals, and demons. These may "exist" in their own right, independently of deities, but in some systems of belief spirits represent specific aspects of a single god, so that, for example, helpful spirits represent the god's compassionate side and malignant spirits represent the god's punitive side. Like ancestral ghosts and spirits, therefore, gods also serve as sanctioning agents.

The influence of spiritual agencies on human life is striking on the island of Bali, in Indonesia, where a local form of Hinduism exists. Balinese-Hinduism has a cosmos consisting of three worlds. Gods and spirits, like ancestral ghosts, reside in the upper world; demons live in the lower world; and human beings dwell in the middle world. Human beings exist at the pleasure of these spirits to whose whims their fate is hostage since prosperity in the middle world ultimately comes from the spirits without whose fertility-conferring powers life would be impossible. Another essence of existence is decay, a force that lies under the control of the demons, so that, like the gods, demons help to keep the never-ending cycle of life going. But the spirits also need nourishment given by human beings, and so sacrifices are offered to them—ugly things to the demons and beautiful things to the gods. Were the Balinese to disregard their duty to satisfy the needs of the gods and demons, the latter would disregard the human need for human, agricultural, and animal fertility. The cycle of life would stall.

Spirits, therefore, are fundamentally important in religion, and we can readily see why Tylor decided to define religion with reference to them. James George Frazer, his contemporary, used the presence or absence of spiritual agencies to distinguish religion from magic, and in doing so established a distinction between the two phenomena that has stood the test of time. Frazer's distinction is a famous one, and we commence this chapter's readings with it.

READING 3–1

MAGIC AND RELIGION

James G. Frazer

This excerpt from The Golden Bough *contains Frazer's definition of religion. It is consistent with that of Tylor, and brings into relief Frazer's view of magic. Religion, according to Frazer, was "a propitiation or conciliation of powers superior to man which are believed to direct*

Source: Reprinted with the permission of Simon & Schuster from "Magic and Religion," in *The Golden Bough: A Study in Magic and Religion*, Vol. 1 by Sir James George Frazer. Copyright © 1922 by Macmillan Publishing Company, renewed 1950 by Barclays Bank Ltd.

and control the course of nature and of human life." The reading also includes Frazer's equally celebrated arguments about the nature of magic, religion, and science. These, however, betray his lack of field research. Had he studied a community that practiced magic, he would have discovered that these three concepts may coexist in the same society. Furthermore, his theory that there is an evolutionary progression from a stage of magic, to a stage of religion, to a stage of science is not affirmed by ethnography. If science is understood to include the application of technology (however simple) to nature, virtually all societies combine magic, religion, and science.

Wherever sympathetic magic occurs in its pure unadulterated form it assumes that in nature one event follows another necessarily and invariably without the intervention of any spiritual or personal agency. Thus its fundamental conception is identical with that of modern science; underlying the whole system is a faith, implicit but real and firm, in the order and uniformity of nature. The magician does not doubt that the same causes will always produce the same effects, that the performance of the proper ceremony, accompanied by the appropriate spell, will inevitably be attended by the desired result, unless, indeed, his incantations should chance to be thwarted and foiled by the more potent charms of another sorcerer. He supplicates no higher power: he sues the favour of no fickle and wayward being: he abases himself before no awful deity. Yet his power, great as he believes it to be, is by no means arbitrary and unlimited. He can wield it only so long as he strictly conforms to the rules of his art, or to what may be called the laws of nature as conceived by him. To neglect these rules, to break these laws in the smallest particular, is to incur failure, and may even expose the unskilful practitioner himself to the utmost peril. If he claims a sovereignty over nature, it is a constitutional sovereignty rigorously limited in its scope and exercised in exact conformity with ancient usage. Thus the analogy between the magical and the scientific conceptions of the world is close. In both of them the succession of events is assumed to be perfectly regular and certain, being determined by immutable laws, the operation of which can be foreseen and calculated precisely; the elements of caprice, of chance, and of accident are banished from the course of nature. Both of them open up a seemingly boundless vista of possibilities to him who knows the causes of things and can touch the secret springs that set in motion the vast and intricate mechanism of the world. Hence the strong attraction which magic and science alike have exercised on the human mind; hence the powerful stimulus that both have given to the pursuit of knowledge. . . .

The fatal flaw of magic lies not in its general assumption of a sequence of events determined by law, but in its total misconception of the nature of the particular laws which govern that sequence. If we analyse the various cases of sympathetic magic which have been passed in review in the preceding pages, and which may be taken as fair samples of the bulk, we shall find, as I have already indicated, that they are all mistaken applications of one or other of two great fundamental laws of thought, namely, the association of ideas by similarity and the association of ideas by contiguity in space or time. A mistaken association of similar ideas produces homoeopathic or imitative magic: a mistaken association of contiguous ideas produces contagious magic. The principles of association are excellent in themselves, and indeed absolutely essential to the working of the human mind. Legitimately applied they yield science; illegitimately applied they yield magic, the bastard sister of science. It is therefore a truism, almost a tautology, to say that all magic is necessarily false and barren; for were it ever to become true and fruitful, it would not longer be magic but science. From the earliest times man has been engaged in a search for general rules whereby to turn the order of natural phenomena to his own advantage, and in the long search he has scraped together a great hoard of such maxims, some of them golden and some of them mere dross. The true or golden rules constitute the body of applied science which we call the arts; the false are magic.

If magic is thus next of kin to science, we have still to enquire how it stands related to religion. But the view we take of that relation will necessarily be coloured by the idea which we have formed of the nature of religion itself; hence a writer may reasonably be expected to define his conception of religion before he proceeds to investigate its relation to magic. There is probably no subject in the world about which opinions differ so much as the nature of religion, and to frame a definition of it which would satisfy every one must obviously be impossible. All that a writer can do is, first, to say clearly what he means by religion, and afterwards to employ the word consistently in that sense throughout his work. By religion, then, I understand a propitiation or conciliation of powers superior to man which are believed to direct and control the course of nature and of human life. Thus defined, religion consists of two elements, a theoretical and a practical, namely, a belief in powers higher than man and an attempt to propitiate or please them. Of the two, belief clearly comes first, since we must believe in the existence of a divine being before we can attempt to please him. But unless the belief leads to a corresponding practice, it is not a religion but merely a theology; in the language of St. James, "faith, if it hath not works, is dead, being alone." In other words, no man is religious who does not govern his conduct in some measure by the fear or love of God. On the other hand, mere practice, divested of all religious belief, is also not religion. Two men may behave in exactly the same way, and yet one of them may be religious and the other not. If the one acts from the love or fear of God, he is religious; if the other acts from the love or fear of man, he is moral or immoral according as his behaviour comports or conflicts with the general good. Hence belief and practice or, in theological language, faith and works are equally essential to religion, which cannot exist without both of them. But it is not necessary that religious practice should always take the form of a ritual; that is, it need not consist in the offering of sacrifice, the recitation of prayers, and other outward ceremonies. Its aim is to please the deity, and if the deity is one who delights in charity and mercy and purity more than in oblations of blood, the chanting of hymns, and the fumes of incense, his worshippers will best please him, not by prostrating themselves before him, by intoning his praises, and by filling his temples with costly gifts, but by being pure and merciful and charitable towards men, for in so doing they will imitate, so far as human infirmity allows, the perfections of the divine nature. It was this ethical side of religion which the Hebrew prophets, inspired with a noble ideal of God's goodness and holiness, were never weary of inculcating. . . .

But if religion involves, first, a belief in superhuman beings who rule the world, and, second, an attempt to win their favour, it clearly assumes that the course of nature is to some extent elastic or variable, and that we can persuade or induce the mighty beings who control it to deflect, for our benefit, the current of events from the channel in which they would otherwise flow. Now this implied elasticity or variability of nature is directly opposed to the principles of magic as well as of science, both of which assume that the processes of nature are rigid and invariable in their operation, and that they can as little be turned from their course by persuasion and entreaty as by threats and intimidation. The distinction between the two conflicting views of the universe turns on their answer to the crucial question, Are the forces which govern the world conscious and personal, or unconscious and impersonal? Religion, as a conciliation of the superhuman powers, assumes the former member of the alternative. For all conciliation implies that the being conciliated is a conscious or personal agent, that his conduct is in some measure uncertain, and that he can be prevailed upon to vary it in the desired direction by a judicious appeal to his interests, his appetites, or his emotions. Conciliation is never employed towards things which are regarded as inanimate, nor towards persons whose behaviour in the particular circumstances is known to be determined with absolute certainty. Thus in so far as religion assumes the world to be directed by conscious agents who may be turned from their purpose by persuasion, it stands in fundamental antagonism to magic as well as to science, both of which take for granted that the course of nature is determined, not by the passions or caprice of personal beings, but by the operation of immutable laws acting mechanically. In magic, indeed, the assumption is only implicit, but in science it is explicit. It is true that

magic often deals with spirits, which are personal agents of the kind assumed by religion; but whenever it does so in its proper form, it treats them exactly in the same fashion as it treats inanimate agents, that is, it constrains or coerces instead of conciliating or propitiating them as religion would do. Thus it assumes that all personal beings, whether human or divine, are in the last resort subject to those impersonal forces which control all things, but which nevertheless can be turned to account by any one who knows how to manipulate them by the appropriate ceremonies and spells . . .

Yet though magic is . . . found to fuse and amalgamate with religion in many ages and in many lands, there are some grounds for thinking that this fusion is not primitive, and that there was a time when man trusted to magic alone for the satisfaction of such wants as transcended his immediate animal cravings. In the first place a consideration of the fundamental notions of magic and religion may incline us to surmise that magic is older than religion in the history of humanity. We have seen that on the one hand magic is nothing but a mistaken application of the very simplest and most elementary processes of the mind, namely the association of ideas by virtue of resemblance or contiguity; and that on the other hand religion assumes the operation of conscious or personal agents, superior to man, behind the visible screen of nature. Obviously the conception of personal agents is more complex than a simple recognition of the similarity or contiguity of ideas; and a theory which assumes that the course of nature is determined by conscious agents is more abstruse and recondite, and requires for its apprehension a far higher degree of intelligence and reflection, than the view that things succeed each other simply by reason of their contiguity or resemblance. The very beasts associate the ideas of things that are like each other or that have been found together in their experience; and they could hardly survive for a day if they ceased to do so. But who attributes to the animals a belief that the phenomena of nature are worked by a multitude of invisible animals or by one enormous and prodigiously strong animal behind the scenes? It is probably no injustice to the brutes to assume that the honour of devising a theory of this latter sort must be reserved for human reason. Thus, if magic be deduced immediately from elementary processes of reasoning, and be, in fact, an error into which the mind falls almost spontaneously, while religion rests on conceptions which the merely animal intelligence can hardly be supposed to have yet attained to, it becomes probable that magic arose before religion in the evolution of our race, and that man essayed to bend nature to his wishes by the sheer force of spells and enchantments before he strove to coax and mollify a coy, capricious, or irascible deity by the soft insinuation of prayer and sacrifice . . .

If an Age of Religion has thus everywhere, as I venture to surmise, been preceded by an Age of Magic, it is natural that we should enquire what causes have led mankind, or rather a portion of them, to abandon magic as a principle of faith and practice and to betake themselves to religion instead. When we reflect upon the multitude, the variety, and the complexity of the facts to be explained, and the scantiness of our information regarding them, we shall be ready to acknowledge that a full and satisfactory solution of so profound a problem is hardly to be hoped for, and that the most we can do in the present state of our knowledge is to hazard a more or less plausible conjecture. With all due diffidence, then, I would suggest that a tardy recognition of the inherent falsehood and barrenness of magic set the more thoughtful part of mankind to cast about for a truer theory of nature and a more fruitful method of turning her resources to account. The shrewder intelligences must in time have come to perceive that magical ceremonies and incantations did not really effect the results which they were designed to produce, and which the majority of their simpler fellows still believed that they did actually produce. This great discovery of the inefficacy of magic must have wrought a radical though probably slow revolution in the minds of those who had the sagacity to make it. The discovery amounted to this, that men for the first time recognised their inability to manipulate at pleasure certain natural forces which hitherto they had believed to be completely within their control. It was a confession of human ignorance and weak-

ness. Man saw that he had taken for causes what were no causes, and that all his efforts to work by means of these imaginary causes had been vain. His painful toil had been wasted, his curious ingenuity had been squandered to no purpose. He had been pulling at strings to which nothing was attached; he had been marching, as he thought, straight to the goal, while in reality he had only been treading in a narrow circle. Not that the effects which he had striven so hard to produce did not continue to manifest themselves. They were still produced, but not by him. The rain still fell on the thirsty ground: the sun still pursued his daily, and the moon her nightly journey across the sky: the silent procession of the seasons still moved in light and shadow, in cloud and sunshine across the earth: men were still born to labour and sorrow, and still, after a brief sojourn here, were gathered to their fathers in the long home hereafter. All things indeed went on as before, yet all seemed different to him from whose eyes the old scales had fallen. For he could no longer cherish the pleasing illusion that it was he who guided the earth and the heaven in their courses, and that they would cease to perform their great revolutions were he to take his feeble hand from the wheel. In the death of his enemies and his friends he no longer saw a proof of the resistless potency of his own or of hostile enchantments; he now knew that friends and foes alike had succumbed to a force stronger than any that he could wield, and in obedience to a destiny which he was powerless to control.

Thus cut adrift from his ancient moorings and left to toss on a troubled sea of doubt and uncertainty, his old happy confidence in himself and his powers rudely shaken, our primitive philosopher must have been sadly perplexed and agitated till he came to rest, as in a quiet haven after a tempestuous voyage, in a new system of faith and practice, which seemed to offer a solution of his harassing doubts and a substitute, however precarious, for that sovereignty over nature which he had reluctantly abdicated. If the great world went on its way without the help of him or his fellows, it must surely be because there were other beings, like himself, but far stronger, who, unseen themselves, directed its course and brought about all the varied series of events which he had hitherto believed to be dependent on his own magic. It was they, as he now believed, and not he himself, who made the stormy wind to blow, the lightning to flash, and the thunder to roll; who had laid the foundations of the solid earth and set bounds to the restless sea that it might not pass; who caused all the glorious lights of heaven to shine; who gave the fowls of the air their meat and the wild beasts of the desert their prey; who bade the fruitful land to bring forth in abundance, the high hills to be clothed with forests, the bubbling springs to rise under the rocks in the valleys, and green pastures to grow by still waters; who breathed into man's nostrils and made him live, or turned him to destruction by famine and pestilence and war. To these mighty beings, whose handiwork he traced in all the gorgeous and varied pageantry of nature, man now addressed himself, humbly confessing his dependence on their invisible power, and beseeching them of their mercy to furnish him with all good things, to defend him from the perils and dangers by which our mortal life is compassed about on every hand, and finally to bring his immortal spirit, freed from the burden of the body, to some happier world, beyond the reach of pain and sorrow, where he might rest with them and with the spirits of good men in joy and felicity for ever.

READING 3–2

THE PROBLEM OF SYMBOLS

E. E. Evans-Pritchard

Another prominent instance of how beliefs in spiritual beings can dominate the ritual life of a population was described by E. E. Evans-Pritchard for the Nuer, a cattle-raising people of the Sudan, in Northeast Africa.

Source: E. E. Evans-Pritchard, "The Problem of Symbols," in *Nuer Religion* (Oxford: Clarendon Press, 1956), pp. 123–35. Reprinted by permission of Oxford University Press.

The Nuer are divided into clans, which are in turn divided into lineages. These lineages are divided into smaller units, which themselves are divided into even smaller subunits. At the bottom of this social hierarchy is the individual. Under the influence of Durkheim, but developing a structural-functional approach of his own, Evans-Pritchard argued that Nuer ideas about spirits correspond to this social structure (1956:117–119). The tribe, the largest social unit, is identified with the supreme Nuer god (kwoth). Descending through the structural hierarchy, each Nuer clan has its own major spirit, which ranks below this supreme god; each lineage has its own spirit, which ranks below the clan spirit; and so on right down the ranking to the individual. At this point in the structure, each Nuer individual has a soul, which occupies the lowest ranking in the hierarchy of spirits. The term kwoth, *Evans-Pritchard explains, in its widest sense means "spirit," a transcendent category of being. In describing the correspondence between the social groups and their different categories of spiritual counterpart, he argues that each group-spirit is a "refraction" of this transcendent category of* kwoth, *whose precise meaning thus shifts depending upon the perspective of the observer.*

A critic might reiterate the concern cited in the Commentary to Reading 3–2 and raise the question: Where do these complementary oppositions and analogies come from? Are they really in the Nuer's own ethnography? Or does Evans-Pritchard's interpretation of Nuer beliefs really come from his own commitment to the structural-functional approach and his admiration of Durkheim? This criticism has not been leveled at the work of Evans-Pritchard with anything like the consistency it has been made of Lévi-Strauss—possibly because the former's dedication to ethnographic research excites admiration.

In this reading, Evans-Pritchard also uses data from fieldwork to dismiss the claim made by such scholars as Lucien Lévy-Bruhl and Edward Tylor that nonliterate peoples confuse the ideal (or symbolic) with the real. He does so by analyzing two Nuer religious statements. One of these is "Twins are birds." Although at face value this assertion would seem to be a case of misconceived identity, Evans-Pritchard shows it to be a metaphoric way of saying that, in respect to kwoth, twins and birds have a similar character: Nuer thought represents both as "persons of the above." The other Nuer phrase, which like its companion has attained classic status in the anthropological literature, is "A cucumber is an ox." Again, this statement might appear to suggest confusion of thought, but Evans-Pritchard points out that only in ritual are cucumbers equated with oxen, and only then in the sense that they are sacrificial substitutes.

In the last chapter I discussed how the Nuer conception of Spirit is figured in different ways to different persons and categories and groups. In this chapter I consider the material forms in which Spirit manifests itself or is represented. God is, properly speaking, not figured in any material representations, nor are almost all the spirits of the above, though both God and his supra-terrestrial refractions may reveal themselves in signs. But the spirits of the below are represented in creatures and things. Our problem chiefly concerns these spirits of the below. It can be simply stated by the question: What meaning are we to attach to Nuer statements that such-and-such a thing is *kwoth,* spirit? The answer is not so simple.

There are several ways in which what we would render as "is" is indicated in the Nuer language. The one which concerns us here is the particle *e.* It is used to tell the listener that something belongs to a certain class or category and hence about some character or quality it has, as "*e dit,*" "it is a bird," "*gat nath e car,*" "the Nuer is black," and "*Duob e ram me goagh,*" "Duob is a good man." The question we are asking is what meaning or meanings it has for Nuer when they say of something, "*e kwoth,*" "it is Spirit" (in the sense either of God or of a divine refraction).

Nuer do not claim to see God, nor do they think that anyone can know what he is like in himself. When they speak about his nature they do so by adjectives which refer to attributes, such as "great" and "good," or in metaphors taken from the world around them, likening his invisibility and ubiquity to wind and air, his greatness to the universe he has created, and his grandeur to an ox with widespread horns. They are no more than metaphors for Nuer, who do not say that any of these things is God, but only that he is like (*cere*) them. They express in these poetic images as best they can what they think must be some of his attributes.

Nevertheless, certain things are said, or may be said, "to be" God—rain, lightning, and various other natural—in the Nuer way of speech, created—things which are of common interest. There is here an ambiguity, or an obscurity, to be elucidated, for Nuer are not now saying that God or Spirit is like this or that, but that this or that "is" God or Spirit. Elucidation here does not, however, present great difficulties.

God being conceived of as in the sky, those celestial phenomena which are of particular significance for Nuer, rain and lightning, are said, in a sense we have to determine, to be him. There is no noun denoting either phenomenon and they can only be spoken of by verbs indicating a function of the sky, as "*ce nhial deam,*" "the sky rained," and "*ce nhial mar,*" "the sky thundered." Also pestilences, murrains, death, and indeed almost any natural phenomenon significant for men are commonly regarded by Nuer as manifestations from above, activities of divine being. Even the earthly totems are conceived of as a relationship deriving from some singular intervention of Spirit from above in human affairs. It is chiefly by these signs that Nuer have knowledge of God. It might be held, therefore, that the Nuer conception of God is a conceptualization of events which, on account of their strangeness or variability as well as on account of their potentiality for fortune or misfortune, are said to be his activities or his activities in one or other of his hypostases or refractions. Support for such a view might be found in the way Nuer sometimes speak of one or other of these effects. They may say of rain or lightning or pestilence "*e kwoth,*" "it is God," and in storms they pray to God to come to earth gently and not in fury—to come gently, it will be noted, not to make the rain come gently.

I do not discuss this ontological question here beyond saying that were we to suppose that such phenomena are in themselves regarded as God we would misunderstand and misrepresent Nuer religious thought, which is pre-eminently dualistic. It is true that for them there is no abstract duality of natural and supernatural, but there is such a duality between *kwoth,* Spirit, which is immaterial rather than supernatural, and *cak,* creation, the material world known to the senses. Rain and lightning and pestilences and murrains belong to this created world and are referred to by Nuer as *nyin kwoth,* instruments of God.

Nevertheless, they and other effects of significance for men are διοσημʹια, signs or manifestations of divine activity; and since Nuer apprehend divine activity in these signs, in God's revelation of himself to them in material forms, the signs are, in a lower medium, what they signify, so that Nuer may say of them "*e kwoth,*" "it is God." Rain and pestilence come from God and are therefore manifestations of him, and in this sense rain and pestilence are God, in the sense that he reveals himself in their falling. But though one can say of rain or pestilence that it is God one cannot say of God that he is rain or pestilence. This would make no sense for a number of reasons. In the first place, the situation could scarcely arise, God not being an observable object, in which Nuer would require or desire to say about him that he is anything. In the second place, the word *kwoth* does not here refer to a particular refraction of Spirit, a spirit, but to Spirit in its oneness, God, and he could not be in any way identified with any one of his manifestations to the exclusion of all the others. A third, and the most cogent, reason is that rain is water which falls from the sky and pestilence is a bodily condition and they are therefore in their nature material things and not Spirit. Indeed, as a rule, rain is only thought of in connexion with Spirit, and is therefore only said to be Spirit, when it does not fall in due season or falls too much or too violently with storm and lightning—when, that is, the rain has some special significance for human affairs. This gives us a clue to what is meant when Nuer say of something that it is God or that it is a spirit of the air, as thunder may be said to be the spirit *wiu* or a prophet of the spirit *deng* may be said to be *deng*—especially as Nuer readily expand such statements by adding that thunder, rain, and pestilence are all instruments (*nyin*) of God or that they are sent by (*jak*) God, and that the

spirit *deng* has filled (*gwang*) the prophet through whom it speaks. In the statement here that something is Spirit or a spirit the particle *e,* which we translate "is," cannot therefore have the meaning of identity in a substantial sense. Indeed, it is because Spirit is conceived of in itself, as the creator and the one, and quite apart from any of its material manifestations, that phenomena can be said to be sent by it or to be its instruments. When Nuer say of rain or lightning that it is God they are making an elliptical statement. What is understood is not that the thing in itself is Spirit but that it is what we would call a medium or manifestation or sign of divine activity in relation to men and of significance for them. What precisely is posited by the hearer of any such elliptical statement depends on the nature of the situation by reference to which it is made. A vulture is not thought of as being in itself Spirit; it is a bird. But if it perches on the crown of a byre or hut Nuer may say "*e kwoth,*" "it is Spirit," meaning that its doing so is a spiritual signal presaging disaster. A lion is not thought of as being in itself Spirit; it is a beast. But it may, on account of some event which brings it into a peculiar relation to man, such as being born, as Nuer think sometimes happens, as twin to a human child, be regarded as a revelation of Spirit for a particular family and lineage. Likewise, diseases, or rather their symptoms, are not thought of as being in themselves Spirit, but their appearance in individuals may be regarded as manifestations of Spirit for those individuals. Spirit acts, and thereby reveals itself, through these creatures. This distinction between the nature of a thing and what it may signify in certain situations or for certain persons is very evident in totemic relationships. A crocodile is Spirit for certain persons, but it is not thought to be in its nature Spirit, for others kill and eat it. It is because Nuer separate, and quite explicitly when questioned about the matter, spiritual conceptions from such material things as may nevertheless be said "to be" the conceptions, that they are able to maintain the unity and autonomy of Spirit in spite of a great diversity of accidents and are able to speak of Spirit without reference to any of its material manifestations.

So far I have been mostly speaking of the conception of God and of those of his refractions which belong to the category of the sky or of the above. With two possible exceptions,[1] we cannot say that the things said "to be" these spirits are material symbols or representations of them; at any rate not in the same sense as we can speak of things being symbols of those lesser refractions of Spirit Nuer call spirits of the earth or of the below, in which God stands in a special relationship to lineages and individuals—such diverse things as beasts, birds, reptiles, trees, phosphorescent objects, and pieces of wood. These lesser refractions of Spirit, regarded as distinct spirits in relation to each other, cannot, unlike the spirits of the air, easily be thought of except in relation to the things by reference to which they derive their individuality, and which are said "to be" them.

When, therefore, Nuer say that the pied crow is the spirit *buk* or that a snake is Spirit, the word "is" has a different sense from what it has in the statement that rain is Spirit. The difference does not merely lie in the fact that kwoth has here a more restricted connotation, being spoken of in reference to a particular and exclusive refraction—a spirit— rather than comprehensively as God or Spirit in its oneness. It lies also in the relation understood in the statement between its subject (snake or crow) and its predicate (Spirit or a spirit). The snake in itself is not divine activity whereas rain and lightning are. The story accounting for a totemic relationship may present it as arising from a revelation of divine activity, but once it has become an established relationship between a lineage and a natural species, the species is a representation or symbol of Spirit to the lineage. What then is here meant when it is said that the pied crow "is" *buk* or that a snake "is" Spirit: that the symbol "is" what it symbolizes? Clearly Nuer do not mean that the crow is the same as buk, for buk is also conceived of as being in the sky and also in rivers, which the pied crow certainly is not; nor that a snake is the same as some spiritual refraction, for they say that the snake just crawls on the earth while the spirit it is said to be is in the sky. What then is being predicated about the crow or snake in the statement that either is Spirit or a spirit?

It will be simpler to discuss this question in the first place in relation to a totemic relationship. When a Nuer says of a creature "*e nyang,*" "it is a crocodile," he is saying that it is a crocodile and not some other creature, but when he says, to explain why a person behaves in an unusual manner towards crocodiles "*e kwothdien,*" "it (the crocodile) is their spirit," he is obviously making a different sort of statement. He is not saying what kind of creature it is (for it is understood that he is referring to the crocodile) but that what he refers to is Spirit for certain people. But he is also not saying that the crocodile is Spirit—it is not so for him—but that certain people so regard it. Therefore a Nuer would not make a general statement that "*nyang e kwoth,*" "crocodile is Spirit," but would only say, in referring to the crocodile, "*e kwoth,*" "it is Spirit," the distinction between the two statements being that the first would mean that the crocodile is Spirit for everyone whereas the second, being made in a special context of situation, means that it is Spirit for certain persons who are being discussed, or are understood, in that context. Likewise, whilst it can be said of the crocodile that it is Spirit, it cannot be said of Spirit that it is the crocodile, or rather, if a statement is framed in this form it can only be made when the word *kwoth* has a pronominal suffix which gives it the meaning of "his spirit," "their spirit," and so forth; in other words, where the statement makes it clear that what is being spoken of is Spirit conceived of in relation to particular persons only. We still have to ask, however, in what sense the crocodile is Spirit for these persons.

Since it is difficult to discuss a statement that something which can be observed, crocodile, is something more than what it appears to be when this something more, Spirit, cannot be observed, it is helpful first to consider two examples of Nuer statements that things are something more than they appear to be when both the subject term and the predicate term refer to observable phenomena.

When a cucumber is used as a sacrificial victim Nuer speak of it as an ox. In doing so they are asserting something rather more than that it takes the place of an ox. They do not, of course, say that cucumbers are oxen, and in speaking of a particular cucumber as an ox in a sacrificial situation they are only indicating that it may be thought of as an ox in that particular situation; and they act accordingly by performing the sacrificial rites as closely as possible to what happens when the victim is an ox. The resemblance is conceptual, not perceptual. The "is" rests on qualitative analogy. And the expression is asymmetrical, a cucumber is an ox, but an ox is not a cucumber.

A rather different example of this way of speaking is the Nuer assertion that twins are one person and that they are birds.[2] When they say "twins are not two persons, they are one person" they are not saying that they are one individual but that they have a single personality. It is significant that in speaking of the unity of twins they only use the word *ran,* which, like our word "person," leaves sex, age, and other distinguishing qualities of individuals undefined. They would not say that twins of the same sex were one *dhol,* boy, or one *nyal,* girl, but they do say, whether they are of the same sex or not, that they are one *ran,* person. Their single social personality is something over and above their physical duality, a duality which is evident to the senses and is indicated by the plural form used when speaking of twins and by their treatment in all respects in ordinary social life as two quite distinct individuals. It is only in certain ritual situations, and symbolically, that the unity of twins is expressed, particularly in ceremonies connected with marriage and death, in which the personality undergoes a change. Thus, when the senior of male twins marries, the junior acts with him in the ritual acts he has to perform; female twins ought to be married on the same day; and no mortuary ceremonies are held for twins because, for one reason, one of them cannot be cut off from the living without the other. A woman whose twin brother had died some time before said to Miss Soule, to whom I am indebted for the information, "Is not his soul still living? I am alive, and we are really children of God."

There is no mortuary ceremony even when the second twin dies, and I was told that twins do not attend the mortuary ceremonies held for their dead

kinsfolk, nor mourn them, because a twin is a *ran nhial,* a person of the sky or of the above. He is also spoken of as *gat kwoth,* a child of God. These dioscuric descriptions of twins are common to many peoples, but the Nuer are peculiar in holding also that they are birds. They say "a twin is not a person *(ran),* he is a bird *(dit),*" although, as we have just seen, they assert, in another sense, that twins are one person *(ran).* Here they are using the word *ran* in the sense of a human being as distinct from any other creature. The dogma is expressed in various ways. Very often a twin is given the proper name *Dit,* bird, *Gwong,* guineafowl, or *Ngec,* francolin.[3] All Nuer consider it shameful, at any rate for adults, to eat any sort of bird or its eggs, but were a twin to do this it would be much more than shameful. It would be *nueer,* a grave sin, for twins respect *(thek)* birds, because, Nuer say, birds are also twins, and they avoid any sort of contact with them. The equivalence of twins and birds is expressed particularly in connexion with death. When an infant twin dies people say "*ce par,*" "he has flown away," using the word denoting the flight of birds. Infant twins who die, as so often happens, are not buried, as other infants are, but are covered in a reed basket or winnowing-tray and placed in the fork of a tree, because birds rest in trees. I was told that birds which feed on carrion would not molest the bodies but would look at their dead kinsmen—twins and birds are also said to be kin, though the usage may be regarded as metaphorical—and fly away again. When I asked a Nuer whether adult twins would be buried like other people he replied "no, of course not, they are birds and their souls go up into the air." A platform, not used in the normal mode of burial, is erected in the grave and a hide placed over it. The body is laid on this hide and covered with a second hide. Earth is then carefully patted over the upper hide instead of being shovelled in quickly, as in the burial of an ordinary person. I was told that the corpse is covered with earth lest a hyena eat it and afterwards drink at a pool, for men might drink at the same pool and die from contamination *(nueer).*

It is understandable that Nuer draw an analogy between the multiple hatching of eggs and the dual birth of twins. The analogy is explicit, and, through an extension of it, the flesh of crocodiles and turtles is also forbidden to twins on the ground that these creatures too, like birds, lay eggs. Miss Soule once had a girl twin in her household who refused fish for the same reason—the only case of its kind known to either of us. But the analogy between multiple births in birds and men does not adequately explain why it is with birds that human twins are equated when there are many other creatures which habitually bear several young at the same time and in a manner more closely resembling human parturition. It cannot be just multiple birth which leads Nuer to say that twins are birds, for these other creatures are not respected by twins on that account. The prohibition on eating eggs is clearly secondary, and it is extended to include crocodiles and turtles—and by Miss Soule's girl fish also—not because they lay eggs but because their laying eggs makes them like birds. Moreover, it is difficult to understand why a resemblance of the kind should in any case be made so much of. The multiple hatching of chicks is doubtless a resemblance which greatly strengthens the idea of twins being birds, but it is only part of a more complex analogical representation which requires to be explained in more general terms of Nuer religious thought. A twin, on account of his peculiar manner of conception is, though not Spirit himself, a special creation, and, therefore, manifestation of Spirit; and when he dies his soul goes into the air, to which things associated with Spirit belong. He is a *ran nhial,* a person of the above, whereas an ordinary person is a *ran piny,* a person of the below. A bird, though also not in itself Spirit, belongs by nature to the above and is also what Nuer call, using "person" metaphorically, a *ran nhial,* a person of the above, and being such is therefore also associated with Spirit. It cannot, of course, be determined for certain whether a twin is said to be a person of the above because he is a bird or whether he is said to be a bird because he is a person of the above, but the connexion in thought between twins and birds is certainly not simply derived from the multiple birth similitude but also, and in my view primarily, from both birds and twins

being classed by Nuer as *gaat kwoth,* children of God. Birds are children of God on account of their being in the air, and twins belong to the air on account of their being children of God by the manner of their conception and birth.

It seems odd, if not absurd, to a European when he is told that a twin is a bird as though it were an obvious fact, for Nuer are not saying that a twin is like a bird but that he is a bird. There seems to be a complete contradiction in the statement; and it was precisely on statements of this kind recorded by observers of primitive peoples that Lévy-Bruhl based his theory of the prelogical mentality of these peoples, its chief characteristic being, in his view, that it permits such evident contradictions—that a thing can be what it is and at the same time something altogether different. But, in fact, no contradiction is involved in the statement, which, on the contrary, appears quite sensible, and even true, to one who presents the idea to himself in the Nuer language and within their system of religious thought. He does not then take their statements about twins any more literally than they make and understand them themselves. They are not saying that a twin has a beak, feathers, and so forth. Nor in their everyday relations with twins do Nuer speak of them as birds or act towards them as though they were birds. They treat them as what they are, men and women. But in addition to being men and women they are of a twin-birth, and a twin-birth is a special revelation of Spirit; and Nuer express this special character of twins in the "twins are birds" formula because twins and birds, though for different reasons, are both associated with Spirit and this makes twins, like birds, "people of the above" and "children of God," and hence a bird a suitable symbol in which to express the special relationship in which a twin stands to God. When, therefore, Nuer say that a twin is a bird they are not speaking of either as it appears in the flesh. They are speaking of the *anima* of the twin, what they call his *tie,* a concept which includes both what we call the personality and the soul; and they are speaking of the association birds have with Spirit through their ability to enter the realm to which Spirit is likened in metaphor and where Nuer think it chiefly is, or may be. The formula does not express a dyadic relationship between twins and birds but a triadic relationship between twins, birds, and God. In respect to God twins and birds have a similar character.

It is because Nuer do not make, or take, the statement that twins are birds in any ordinary sense that they are fully aware that in ritual relating to twins the actions are a kind of miming. This is shown in their treatment of the corpse of a twin, for, according to what they themselves say, what is a bird, the *tie* or *anima,* has gone up into the air and what is left and treated—in the case of adults platform burial being a convenient alternative to disposal in trees— as though it might be a bird is only the ring, the flesh. It is shown also in the convention that should one of a pair of twins die, the child who comes after them takes his place, counting as one of them in the various ceremonies twins have to perform and respecting birds as rigorously as if he were himself a twin, which he is not. The ceremonies have to be performed for the benefit of the living twin and their structure and purpose are such that there have to be two persons to perform them, so a brother or sister acts in the place of the dead.

This discussion of what is meant by the statement that a twin is a bird is not so far away from the subject of totemism as it might seem to be, for the stock explanation among the Nuer of a totemic relationship is that the ancestor of a lineage and a member of a natural species were born twins. The relationship of lineage to species is thereby made to derive not only from the closest of all possible relationships but also from a special act of divine revelation; and since the link between a lineage and its totem is the tutelary spirit of the lineage associated with the totem it is appropriate that the relationship should be thought of as having come about by an event which is a direct manifestation of Spirit.

However, an examination of the Nuer dogma that twins are birds was made not on account of totemic relationships commonly being explained in terms of twinship but because it was hoped that it would be easier to understand, in the light of any conclusions reached about what is meant by the statement that a twin is a bird, what Nuer mean when they say that some totemic creature, such as the crocodile, is Spirit. Certainly there is here neither the sort of metaphor nor the sort of ellipsis we found in earlier statements. Nor can Nuer be understood to mean that the creature is identical with Spirit, or even with a spirit, Spirit conceived of in a particular totemic refraction. They say quite definitely themselves that it is not; and it is also evident, for Nuer as well as for us, that a material symbol of Spirit cannot, by its very nature, be that which it symbolizes.

Nevertheless, though crocodile and Spirit are quite different and unconnected ideas, when the crocodile is for a certain lineage a symbol of their special relationship to God, then in the context of that relationship symbol and what it symbolizes are fused. As in the case of the "twins are birds" formula, the relation is a triadic one, between a lineage and a natural species and God. There are obvious and significant differences between the creature–Spirit expression and the cucumber–ox and bird–twin expressions. Cucumber, ox, man, and bird are all things which can be known by the senses; but where Spirit is experienced other than in thought it is only in its effects or through material representations of it. We can, therefore, easily see how Nuer regard it as being in, or behind, the crocodile. The subject and predicate terms of the statement that something is Spirit are here no longer held apart by two sets of visible properties. Consequently, while Nuer say that totemic spirits and totems are not the same they sometimes not only speak of, but act towards, a totem as if the spirit were in it. Thus they give some meat of a sacrifice to the lion-spirit to lions, and when they sacrifice to the durra-bird-spirit they address also the birds themselves and tell them that the victim is for them. Nevertheless, they make it clear in talking about their totems that what respect they show for them is on account of their representing the spirits associated with them and not for their own sake.

Another difference is that whereas in the cases of the cucumber–ox and twin–bird expressions the equivalence rests on analogies which are quite obvious even to us once they are pointed out—the cucumber being treated in the ritual of sacrifice as an ox is, and twins and birds both being "children of God" and also multiple births—analogy is lacking in the creature–Spirit expression. There is no resemblance between the idea of Spirit and that of crocodile. There is nothing in the nature of crocodiles which evokes the idea of Spirit for Nuer, and even for those who respect crocodiles the idea of Spirit is evoked by these creatures because the crocodile is a representation of Spirit in relation to their lineage and not because there is anything crocodile-like about Spirit or Spirit-like about crocodiles. We have passed from observation of resemblances to thought by means of symbols in the sort of way that the crocodile is used as a symbol for Spirit.

We are here faced with the same problem we have been considering earlier, but in what, in the absence of analogical guidance to help us, is a more difficult form. The difficulty is increased by Nuer symbols being taken from an environment unfamiliar to us and one which, even when we familiarize ourselves with it, we experience and evaluate differently. We find it hard to think in terms of crocodiles, snakes, and fig-trees. But reflection shows us that this problem is common to all religious thought, including our own; that a religious symbol has always an intimate association with what it represents, that which brings to the mind with what it brings to the mind. Nuer know that what they see is a crocodile, but since it represents Spirit to some of them it is for those people, when thought of in that way, also what it stands for. The relationship of members of a Nuer lineage to Spirit is represented by a material symbol by which it can be thought of concretely, and therefore as a relationship distinct from the relationships of other lineages to Spirit. What the symbols stand for is the same thing. It is they, and not what they stand for, which differentiate the relationships. There results, when what acts as a symbol is regarded in this way, a fusion between Spirit, as so represented, and its material representation. I would say that then Nuer regard Spirit as being in some way in, or behind, the creature in which in a sense it is beholden.

The problem is even more difficult and complex than I have stated it, because we might say that what are fused are not so much the idea of Spirit and its material representation as the idea of Spirit and the idea of its material representation. It is rather the idea of crocodile than the saurian creatures themselves which stands for Spirit to a lineage. If a Nuer cannot see Spirit he likewise in some cases seldom, if ever, sees his totem; so that it is no longer a question of a material object symbolizing an idea but of one idea symbolizing another. I doubt whether those who respect monorchid bulls or waterbuck often see a member of the class or species, and children in these and other cases must often be told about their totemic attachments before they have seen their totems. There must also be Nuer who respect dom palms who live in parts of Nuerland to the east of the Nile where this tree does not grow.[4] Indeed, I feel confident that one totem, the *lou* serpent, a kind of Loch Ness monster, does not exist, and if this is so, a totem can be purely imaginary. As this point has some theoretical importance for a study of totemism I draw attention to a further significant fact. Nuer do not speak of the spirit of crocodiles, lions, tamarind-trees, and so on, but always of the spirit of crocodile, lion, and tamarind-tree, and they would never say that crocodiles, lions, and tamarind-trees were somebody's spirit but always that crocodile, lion, and tamarind-tree was his spirit. The difference in meaning between the plural and singular usage is not, perhaps, very obvious in English but it is both clear and vital in Nuer. It is the difference between crocodiles thought of as they are seen in rivers and crocodiles thought of as crocodile or as the crocodile, as a type of creature, crocodile as a conception. The point I am making is exemplified by the story . . . of a man who gave up respecting lions because they killed his cattle. He still regarded lion-spirit, Spirit in the representation of lion, as a spirit connected with his family. But if a totemic relationship may be an ideal one, and has always something of the ideal in it, I would still say that Nuer regard Spirit as being in some way in, or behind, totemic creatures when they think of them as representations of Spirit.

This must be all the more so with the other spirits of the below, the *bieli,* nature sprites, and the *kulangni,* fetishes. In general much of what has been said in this chapter about the totemic spirits applies to these other spirits also, but there is one important difference. In the statement "crocodile is their spirit" both terms of the proposition can be thought of quite separately and are indeed so presented in the statement. This is partly because the crocodile is Spirit only for some persons and not for others, and also because, even for those for whom it is Spirit, it also exists in its own right as a reptile and may be so regarded by them without the idea of Spirit being involved. The reptile can be said to be Spirit only because it is something which may represent it and is, therefore, different from it. But in the case of a luminescence, such as will-o'-the-wisp from rotting swamp vegetation, the appearance can scarcely be represented in thought apart from what appears in it. It does not seem to be regarded, as rain may be, as a manifestation of Spirit through a medium which can be said to be sent by, or to be an instrument of, Spirit, but as an emanation of Spirit or as Spirit itself revealed in the light, a theophany like the burning bush in Midian. Nuer speak of it sometimes as the spirit's fire, and of its fire burning. Nor is it, as a crocodile may be, regarded as a representation of Spirit which, being apart from what it represents, can be said to be what it represents. On the contrary, whilst the lights are easily kept apart in the mind from the things on which they are accustomed to appear—swamp vegetation, hippopotamuses, meteorites, and other objects—they are not themselves conceived of as other than Spirit in the form of *bieli* and under that name. They are not something that is thought to exist in its own right but can be said to be Spirit. They are in themselves Spirit, in however lowly a form. Consequently, though they have a special significance for those persons who have acquired a relationship to the *bieli* spirits, they are Spirit also for those not directly concerned with them. Rain and crocodiles are created things with which Spirit may, or may not, be associated, according to circumstances and persons, but a will-o'-the-wisp is a property of Spirit, fractionally conceived of as a spirit of a special kind, and it cannot be thought of in terms other than of Spirit.

So when a Nuer says of a light in the bush that it is Spirit the problem we have been considering has changed its form and, at least on first consideration, seems to elude, if not altogether to escape, us. For us the light is a gas arising from swamp vegetation, so that the statement that it is Spirit is of the same kind as the statement that a crocodile is Spirit; and whatever meaning might be attached to the one would be the same for the other. But we cannot say that they are statements of the same kind for Nuer. For them, whereas the crocodile is a thing conceived of separately from Spirit, even though in a certain sense and for certain people it may be said to be Spirit, the phosphorescence is a descent of Spirit in the form of light on to something which is not in any way said to be Spirit, such as a hippopotamus, and on which it may appear at certain times and places and not at other times and places. So we are no longer asking what sense it has for Nuer when one of them says of a thing, which is not for them in itself Spirit, that it is Spirit. We are asking what sense it has for them when one of them says of a thing which has no meaning for them other than an emanation of Spirit that it is Spirit. In the case of the crocodile what is perceived is the reptile, and in certain circumstances it may be conceived of as Spirit for certain persons. In the case of the *bieli* what is perceived may indeed be said to be just light but it can only be conceived of as Spirit, for it has no other name which differentiates it from any other sort of light or fire than *bieli.* When, regarding such a light, Nuer say "it is Spirit" they are no longer saying that something is something else but are merely giving a name to what is observed; so that here "it is Spirit" belongs to the same class of statements as "it is a crocodile," and it might be held that the question we have been examining does not properly arise. Nevertheless, this is not entirely the case, as I will explain later.

What has been said of the lights of the nature sprites can be said also of the little bundles of wood in which the *kulangni,* the fetish spirits, have their abode, but for a different reason. A bundle of wood in which a fetish spirit has its abode is not a symbol of spirit, as a crocodile may be. Nor is it, like the *bieli,* a visible appearance of Spirit. It is a thing where a particular spirit abides. Nevertheless, it must be difficult for a fetish-owner to regard the bundle as being just anything which serves as a lodging for the spirit. It is before the bundle that he makes his offerings and it is the bundle he points at an enemy he wishes the spirit to harm. Moreover, the bundles are fashioned solely as habitations for spirits and have no significance other than is derived from this purpose and use. Hence when Nuer say of a fetish-bundle that it is Spirit they are not saying that something which also has for them a separate meaning as something in itself, which is other than Spirit, is something else, namely Spirit, but that something which has no meaning of any kind outside its being an abode and a material sign of Spirit is Spirit. So the fetish-bundles cannot easily be thought of, as can rain or crocodile, either in terms of Spirit or in terms of their purely material natures, but only in terms of Spirit.

But though in the case of both the lights and the bundles there seems to be a more complete and fixed fusion between things and Spirit than in the case of the totems, the problem of something being something else is still present, though in a more complex, and also a more obscure and roundabout, form. Here again, although it can be said of a light in the bush or of a fetish-bundle that it is Spirit, the statement cannot be reversed. It cannot be said of Spirit that it is the light or the bundle, for that would mean to Nuer that Spirit in its oneness, conceived of as God, is entirely in the light or the bundle, which would make no sense to them. In the statement that the light or bundle is Spirit what, therefore, has to be understood by Spirit is a refraction of Spirit, or a spirit. But, even so, the "is" is not one of identity, for though a phosphorescent light is a nature sprite exhibiting itself and is not conceived of as anything else, the nature sprite may be thought of independently of the light; and though the fetish-bundle may be a meaningless object except in relation to the fetish-spirit which occupies it, the spirit which

occupies it can be thought of independently of it. When the light is no longer visible the *biel* sprite is none the less present for certain people as their sprite, which is Spirit in relation to them as an idea quite apart from its sporadic appearances as a light. A fetish-spirit takes its abode in a fetish-bundle of wood and it may leave it; and it is also present for certain people as Spirit in relation to them as an idea quite apart from its material home. In either case the spirits are thought to come, or at some time to have come, from above to earth and to be independent, as Spirit, of any material forms. Consequently the same nature sprite or fetish-spirit can be in different lights or in different bundles at the same time, just as an air-spirit can be in different prophets at the same time or a totemic spirit can be in any number of members of a species at the same time.

There is a further fact to be taken into consideration. When Nuer speak of lights in the bush or of fetish-bundles as Spirit they normally would not use the generic word for Spirit, *kwoth,* or even its plural and fractionary form *kuth,* spirits. They would say of them that they were *bieli* or *kulangni.* So whilst it is true that *bieli* and *kulangni* are *kuth piny,* spirits of the below, the fact that they are given distinctive class names and that consequently it is possible for Nuer to explain them by saying that they are Spirit or that they are spirits attached to certain persons shows that though they are regarded as Spirit or spirits they are also somehow regarded differently from the way in which Spirit is usually regarded. So the problem here is further complicated by a third term being understood in the statement about something that it is something else: the light *is bieli,* and the *bieli* are Spirit; the bundle is *kulangni,* and the *kulangni* are Spirit. This added complication may be supposed to be due to the fact that though these spirits cannot be said to be identical with things they are more closely bound to them than is the case with other, and higher, spiritual conceptions; and the more Spirit is thought to be bound to visible forms the less it is thought of as Spirit and the more it is thought of in terms of what it is bound to. In other words, there are gradations of the conception of Spirit from pure unattached Spirit to

Spirit associated with human, animal, and lifeless objects and more and more closely bound to what it is associated with the farther down the scale one goes. This scale of Spirit, as I have explained earlier, is related to segmentation of the social order and is represented by Nuer by levels of space as well as by levels and degrees of immanence. So when Nuer say of something that it is Spirit we have to consider not only what "is" means but also what "Spirit" means. Nevertheless, though the sense of "*kwoth*" varies with the context, the word refers always to something of the same essence; and what is being said, directly or indirectly, in the statements is always the same, that something is that essence.

We can make some contribution towards a solution of the problem in the light of this discussion. When Nuer say of something "*e kwoth*," "it is Spirit," or give it a name of which it can be further said "that is Spirit," the "is" does not in all instances have the same connotation. It may be an elliptical statement, signifying that the thing referred to is a manifestation of Spirit in the sense of God revealing himself in instruments or effects. Or it may be a symbolical statement, signifying that what in itself is not Spirit but represents Spirit to certain persons is for these persons Spirit in such contexts as direct attention to the symbolic character of an object to the exclusion of whatever other qualities it may possess. Or it may be a statement signifying something closer to identity of the thing spoken of with what it is said to be, Spirit. The statements never, however, signify complete identity of anything with Spirit, because Nuer think of Spirit as something more than any of its modes, signs, effects, representations, and so forth, and also as something of a different nature from the created things which they are. They are not able to define what it is, but when it acts within the phenomenal world they say it has come from above, where it is conceived to be and whence it is thought to descend. Consequently Spirit in any form can be detached in the mind from the things said to be it, even if they cannot always be so easily detached from the idea of Spirit.

I can take the analysis no farther; but if it is inconclusive it at least shows, if it is correct, how

wide of the mark have been anthropological attempts to explain the kind of statements we have been considering. Anthropological explanations display two main errors. The first, best exemplified in the writings of Lévy-Bruhl, is that when a people say that something is something else which is different they are contravening the Law of Contradiction and substituting for it a law of their own prelogical way of thinking, that of mystical participation.[5] I hope at least to have shown that Nuer do not assert identity between the two things. They may say that one is the other and in certain situations act towards it as though it were that other, or something like it, but they are aware, no doubt with varying degrees of awareness, and readily say, though with varying degrees of clarity and emphasis, that the two things are different. Moreover, it will have been noted that in the seemingly equivocal statements we have considered, with perhaps one exception, the terms cannot be reversed. The exception is the statement that twins are birds, because it can also be said that birds are twins. That a hatch of birds are twins is a statement, to which we also can give assent, which does not derive logically from the statement that twins are birds but from a perception independent of that proposition; so it does not concern our problem. Rain may be said to be God but God cannot be said to be rain; a cucumber may be called an ox but an ox cannot be called a cucumber; and the crocodile may be said to be Spirit but Spirit cannot be said to be the crocodile. Consequently these are not statements of identity. They are statements not that something is other than it is but that in a certain sense and in particular contexts something has some extra quality which does not belong to it in its own nature; and this quality is not contrary to, or incompatible with, its nature but something added to it which does not alter what it was but makes it something more, in respect to this quality, than it was. Consequently, no contradiction, it seems to me, is involved in the statements.

Whether the predicate refers to a conception or to a visible object the addition makes the subject equivalent to it in respect to the quality which both now have in common in such contexts as focus the attention on that quality alone. The things referred to are not the same as each other but they are the same in that one respect, and the equivalence, denoted by the copula, is not one of substance but of quality. Consequently we cannot speak here, as Lévy-Bruhl does, of mystical participation, or at any rate not in his sense of the words, because the two things are not thought to be linked by a mystical bond but simply by a symbolic nexus. Therefore, what is done to birds is not thought to affect twins, and if a totem is harmed the spirit of that totem may be offended but it is not harmed by the harm done to the totemic creature.

That the relation between the thing said to be something else and that something else it is said to be is an ideal one is indeed obvious, but anthropological explanations of modes of primitive thought as wide apart as those of Tylor, Max Müller, and Lévy-Bruhl, are based on the assumption that though for us the relation is an ideal one primitive peoples mistake it for a real one; and those anthropologists who sponsor psychological explanations often make the same assumption. This is the second error. If my interpretation is correct, Nuer know very well when they say that a crocodile is Spirit that it is only Spirit in the sense that Spirit is represented to some people by that symbol just as they know very well that a cucumber is only an ox in the sense that they treat it as one in sacrifice. That they do not mistake ideal relations for real ones is shown by many examples . . . : the identification of a sacrificial spear with that of the ancestor . . . , the identification of man with ox in sacrifice . . . , the identification of a man's herd with that of the ancestor of his clan . . . , the identification of sickness and sin in a sacrificial context . . . , and the identification of the left hand with death and evil. . . . It is shown also in the symbolism of many of their rites, where their purpose is expressed in mimicry . . .

I think that one reason why it was not readily perceived that statements that something is something else should not be taken as matter-of-fact statements is that it was not recognized that they are made in relation to a third term not mentioned in them but understood. They are statements, as far as the Nuer are concerned, not that *A* is *B*, but that *A* and *B* have something in common in relation to *C*. This is evident when we give some thought to the matter. A cucumber is equivalent to an ox in respect to God who accepts it in the place of an ox. A crocodile is equivalent to Spirit only when conceived of as a representation of God to a lineage. Consequently, though Nuer do not mistake ideal relations for real ones, an ideal equivalence is none the less true for them, because within their system of religious thought things are not just what they appear to be but as they are conceived of in relation to God.

This implies experience on an imaginative level of thought where the mind moves in figures, symbols, metaphors, analogies, and many an elaboration of poetic fancy and language; and another reason why there has been misunderstanding is that the poetic sense of primitive peoples has not been sufficiently allowed for, so that it has not been appreciated that what they say is often to be understood in that sense and not in any ordinary sense. This is certainly the case with the Nuer, as we see in this chapter and in many places elsewhere in this book, for example, in their hymns. In all their poems and songs also they play on words and images to such an extent that no European can translate them without commentary from Nuer, and even Nuer themselves cannot always say what meaning they had for their authors. It is the same with their cattle- and dance-names, which are chosen both for euphony and to express analogies. How Nuer delight in playing with words is also seen in the fun they have in making up tongue-twisters, sentences which are difficult to pronounce without a mistake, and slips of the tongue, usually slips in the presence of mothers-in-law, which turn quite ordinary remarks into obscenities. Lacking plastic and visual arts, the imagination of this sensitive people finds its sole expression in ideas, images, and words.

In this and the last chapter I have attempted to lay bare some features of the Nuer conception of Spirit. We are not asking what Spirit is but what is the Nuer conception of *kwoth*, which we translate

"Spirit." Since it is a conception that we are inquiring into, our inquiry is an exploration of ideas. In the course of it we have found that whilst Nuer conceive of Spirit as creator and father in the heavens they also think of it in many different representations (what I have called refractions of Spirit) in relation to social groups, categories, and persons. The conception of Spirit has, we found, a social dimension (we can also say, since the statement can be reversed, that the social structure has a spiritual dimension). We found also that Spirit, in the Nuer conception of it, is experienced in signs, media, and symbols through which it is manifested to the senses. Fundamentally, however, this is not a relation of Spirit to things but a relation of Spirit to persons through things, so that, here again, we are ultimately concerned with the relation of God and man, and we have to consider not only what is the God-to-man side of the relationship, to which attention has so far mostly been given, but also the man-to-God side of it, to which I now turn.

ENDNOTES

1. The spear *wiu* may be said to stand for the spirit *wiu* . . ., and the pied crow may be said to stand for the spirit *buk* which is the most terrestrially conceived of among the greater spirits . . .
2. I have given a more detailed account in "Customs and Beliefs Relating to Twins among the Nilotic Nuer," *Uganda Journal*, 1936.
3. That the names, at least all those I have heard, are taken from birds lowest in the scale of Nuer reckoning requires comment, especially in view of the argument I later develop. It may be due to the Nuer habit of speaking of their relation to God—the birth of twins constitutes such a context—by comparing themselves with lowly things. On the other hand, it may be simply in keeping with the logic of the analogy. Twins belong to the class of the above but are below; just as guineafowl and francolin belong to the class of birds, which as a class is in the category of the above, but are almost earthbound.
4. Dr. Lienhardt tells me that a number of lineages in western Dinkaland respect creatures which no longer exist there. A Dinka who travelled with him to other parts of the Southern Sudan was astonished when he first saw his totem, an elephant. Nana Kobina Nketsia IV of Sekondi permits me to say that the first time he saw his totem, the buffalo, was last year in a film at Oxford. Professor I. Schapera tells me that the ruling family of the senior tribe in the Bechuanaland Protectorate, the Kwena, have been living for a hundred years in a region where their totem, the crocodile, is unknown (see also what he says in *The Tswana* (International African Institute),

1953, p. 35, and Hugh Ashton, *The Basuto,* 1952, p. 14). Other examples could be cited. It may help us to appreciate the point better if we consider the nearest parallels in our own country. When we think of the lion as our national symbol we do not think of the mangy creatures of the African bush or in zoos. Nor does it incommode us that there are no unicorns and never have been any.
5. I refer to his earlier writings, in particular *Les Fonctions mentales dans les sociétés inférieures* (1910) and *La Mentalité primitive* (1922). The second part of his last book, *L'Expérience mystique et les symboles chez les primitifs* (1938), which took account of modern research, is a brilliant discourse on the problems we have been discussing.

READING 3–3

THE GHOST CULT IN BUNYORO[1]

J. H. M. Beattie

The Nyoro, a people living in East Africa, make very clear the influence of ancestral ghosts on human life. The ghost ritual provides one way of reducing stress and embodies an effective sanction against certain forms of socially disapproved behavior. This ritual, John Beattie suggests, offers a means by which the anxieties produced by sickness (very common among the Nyoro) can be lessened. Beattie explains how the ghost cult functions as an inducement to good behavior: when persons who have been ill-treated die and become ghosts, they are believed to take revenge on those who hurt them. The social ideal of behaving kindly toward living members of society is thus reinforced by religious beliefs.

We have here a variation of the structural-functional approach in that Beattie, who was a student of Evans-Pritchard's in Oxford, attempts to demonstrate how one institution (the ghost cult) influences another aspect of society, i.e., conduct that is deemed socially acceptable. In this respect his analysis resembles that of his teacher's comparison of Zande and Trobriand magic (Reading 4–5) and Boyer's and Nissenbaum's study of Salem witchcraft (Reading 7–3).

When a Nyoro[2] suffers illness, childlessness, or other misfortune, his traditional culture provides three

Source: John Beattie, "The Ghost Cult in Bunyoro," *Ethnology,* Vol. 3, no. 2, April 1964, pp. 127–51. Reprinted with permission.

broad types of explanation of why this should be, each with its associated pattern of cultural response. It may be due to sorcery (*burogo*) by some living person; it may be due to one or more of the wide range of nonhuman *mbandwa* spirits; or it may be due to the activity of a ghost. I have given some account elsewhere of Nyoro beliefs about sorcery (Beattie 1963) and of the Nyoro spirit mediumship cult (Beattie 1957, 1961). In this essay I consider Nyoro ideas about ghosts, the kinds of social situations in which their activity is diagnosed, and what is done about them (for a brief outline of the pattern of Nyoro attitudes to ghosts see Beattie 1960: 75–77).

A ghost (*muzimu,* plural *mizimu*) is the disembodied spirit of someone who has died. When a man is alive this vital principle is called *mwoyo* (plural *myoyo*), which may be rather loosely translated as "soul," and it is believed to dwell in the breast or diaphragm. But a ghost is not just a person who has died; it is a being of quite a different order from the living. Though it possesses human attributes it is not human. A Nyoro who wishes to threaten another with posthumous vengeance for some injury does not say, "I shall haunt you when I die"; he says, "I shall leave you a ghost" (*ndikulekera muzimu*). Ghosts are left by people, but they are not people. This is implied also by the fact that the noun class to which the word muzimu belongs is not that of "people" (*muntu,* plural *bantu*) but that of a certain class of things, a class which includes in particular most kinds of trees and other plants.

Ghosts are thought of as somehow diffused through space, "like wind" (*nk'omuyaga*). An informant said:

> When a man dies, his soul (*mwoyo*), which dwells inside him [he pointed to his diaphragm], is spread all around, like water. Afterwards it goes and lives underground, in the country of Nyamiyonga, the king of the dead. There it meets all other people who have died, and lives for ever. A man's soul can go away from his body and visit other places while he is asleep. It is no good killing a man or an animal while he is fast asleep; he will not die, or at least not so soon, if his soul is not there. You must wake

him up a little first; as soon as he begins to stir, then you can kill him.

Thus ghosts are particularly associated with the underworld, Okuzimu, and it is significant that the phrase most commonly used for spirit possession refers to the ghost's "mounting into the head" (*kutemba ha mutwe*) of its medium. Okuzimu is sometimes thought of as a real place, and Nyoro myth tells of an early king, Isaza, who was enticed away into the world of ghosts by its ruler Nyamiyonga, who sent him some beautiful cattle which vanished into a pit in the ground, whither the infatuated ruler followed them (Beattie 1960: 13–14). As in European belief, ghosts are also sometimes associated with particular places which they frequented when alive, and with their graves. The color black is appropriate to them; we shall see that a goat which is sacrificed or dedicated to a ghost should be black.

Unlike its European counterpart, a Nyoro ghost is never seen, although it may appear in dreams in the form of the dead person whose ghost it is. Rather it makes itself known to the living by causing them illness or other misfortune, and its agency can only be diagnosed by a diviner (*muraguzi,* plural *baraguzi;* a doctor-diviner who can treat as well as diagnose ghostly activity is called *mufumu,* plural *bafumu*), whom the victim consults. For the most part ghosts are inimical, but they are not always so, and the ghost of a man's dead father, especially, is thought to retain some concern for the well-being of his sons and his other descendants. We shall see that the Nyoro do not have a highly developed ancestral cult, but a person may look to the ghost of his father (and to other patrilineal ghosts) for support, as he does to his father while he is alive. Nyoro say that a man can call on the help of his dead father by sprinkling an offering of *nsigosigo* (a dry mixture of millet and sesame) on his grave and asking him for assistance. I was told that a girl whose brother was forcing her into a marriage against her will, to obtain the bridewealth for her, might call on her dead father's ghost in this way and ask him to thwart her brother's plans and prevent her marriage.

Here is a Christian informant's account of help given to him by his father's ghost:

> I dreamed that my father appeared up above, accompanied by an angel. They were surrounded by a very bright light, which got brighter and brighter. The angel said, "Don't be afraid." Then suddenly they disappeared, and there was intense darkness, out of which a savage lion approached to kill me. But my father again appeared and said, "Don't fear; I shall not let it hurt you." Then I woke up. Another night I dreamed that a neighbor of mine, who I knew hated me, was approaching me with a horn (*ihembe,* used in sorcery) held in his outstretched hand and pointed at me. I knew that he was making sorcery against me, and I was very frightened. But at that moment my father appeared and stopped him, saying, "Leave off bewitching my son." I then woke up feeling very scared. The next morning when I went out into my compound I saw something sticking in the ground, and when I went to see what it was I found that it was a horn. So I knew that my enemy had really come to make sorcery against me in the night. That day I burned that horn; while it was being burnt it cried out "eeeeh! eeeeh!" That same day a goat and two of my fowls died. Two weeks later that man died; my father's ghost had killed him for having tried to make sorcery against me.

On the whole, however, ghosts are thought to be maleficent, which is what we should expect, for like other spirit agents they usually become socially relevant only when illness or other misfortune strikes. Nyoro say that when a relative dies he ceases to think of his kin as "his" people; the ghost no longer takes a warm and friendly human interest in the welfare of his living kin, as his own flesh and blood. "*Amara kufu taba wawe,*" Nyoro sometimes say, i.e., "A person who is dead is no longer 'your' person." But they are not absolutely consistent about this, for there is another saying, "A ghost follows its own" (*omuzimu gukuratira akagwo*)—though of course the pursuit may not be inspired wholly by benevolence. We shall see that just as people are dependent on the good will of ghosts, or at least on the suspension of their ill will, so ghosts

are also thought to be dependent on people who, through rites of sacrifice and possession, provide them with what they need. Like most social relationships, Nyoro relations with ghosts are ambivalent. But for the most part ghosts are feared, not loved, and much of the ritual concerned with them is aimed at keeping them at a distance, rather than achieving closer relations with them.

Ordinarily the Nyoro do not like speaking of the dead. "A person who speaks the name of a dead parent or close relative feels unhappy at once," one of my assistants told me. He added that his mother refused to have a photograph of her dead husband on the wall of her house for this reason. If a man mentions the name of his dead father he should say, "I haven't spoken your name, father; when I die I'll see you" (*tinkugambire tata, ndifa ndikusanga*). He means that he has meant no injury to the dead man.

Though a victim of illness or other misfortune may suspect ghostly activity, this is always confirmed by divination (*buraguzi*). The sufferer visits a local diviner (*muraguzi*), of whom there are still several in every Nyoro locality. Using one of the accepted techniques of divination—the most popular is the one which involves throwing nine prepared cowry shells on a mat (see Beattie 1960: 71–73)—the diviner determines whether his client's trouble is due to sorcery, to the agency of nonhuman spirits, or to a ghost. If ghostly agency is diagnosed, then further divination, combined with skillful questioning of the patient, may establish the ghost's identity.

This is not always very difficult, though sometimes it is. Like sorcerers, ghosts generally attack people against whom they have a grudge. So when ghostly activity is diagnosed, the ghost is usually that of someone who was injured or offended before he died—or in certain cases of someone whose ghost was neglected after he died. But the ghost may not confine its vengeance to the person who actually offended it; often, indeed, the offender may not be directly attacked at all. In eight out of fifteen cases on which I have details (see Table 1) where ghostly activity was diagnosed, the original offender was not attacked directly but through his children, and in two others he was long since dead and vengeance was wreaked on his descendants. The biblical reference to "visiting the iniquity of the fathers upon the children unto the third and fourth generation" makes good sense to traditionally minded Nyoro.

There follows an informant's account of a case in which a woman's miscarriage was attributed to the ghost of a household slave or servant (*mwiru rubale*) who had been a member of the household long ago. The ghosts of such persons, who in pre-European times were usually people who had been captured in war, probably as children, and were thus often members of other tribes, are thought to be particularly dangerous. I return later to the "social sanction" aspect of the Nyoro ghost cult, but it may be remarked here that this belief must have conduced to the reasonable treatment of such captives, who usually lived as for all practical purposes members of the family of their captors. Certainly the Nyoro say that it was always advisable for families which owned such domestic slaves to treat them well.

> Case 1. When this ghost came into my house I consulted a doctor-diviner (*mufumu*), who said that it was that of a former household slave in my father's family. It was making my wife ill and had caused her to have a miscarriage. We did not know the name of that slave, and you know that it is very difficult to catch a ghost whose name is not known. First you have to sing songs to call that ghost. When it comes into the head of its medium you ask it what its name is. It generally refuses to say, and this is what happened in our case. So the diviner had to make special preparations. He made two pots and fired them on that very same day. I had to provide a black billy-goat and two red fowls. And the *mufumu* brought a number of special charms (*bihambo*), which were small pieces of various kinds of wood and other plants.
>
> I remember the names of some of these. One was called *kiboha,* which means "that which ties up." It was a small, creeping plant for "tying up" the ghost so that it should not return to our house. Another was called *kinamiro,* which means "that which stoops," and another was called *kyombera busa.* This last means something that makes a lot of noise for nothing, and it suggests that the ghost should go shamefully away and not come back. Other charms were: a

> piece of wood from a tree called *mutatembwa,* which means that it cannot be climbed (its bark is very smooth); a piece of tree stump called *bahumaho* (so that the ghost should stumble on it); a plant called ihozo, "that which makes cool;" another called *ruhunahune,* "that which is silent" (so that the ghost may remain still and peaceful); and a kind of grass named *ntahinduka,* "I shall not turn round." The *mufumu* put all these charms into the pots he had made.
>
> Then, when the ghost had mounted into my wife's head after the usual seance with singing, the shaking of gourd rattles, and so on, the goat and the chickens were shown to it and slaughtered. Then the ghost [through its medium] spat on the goat's head; the head of an animal sacrificed is always given to the ghost. After this head was put into one of the pots, and the ghost was persuaded by the *mufumu* to leave my wife and go into the pot. Then we hastily took both the pots and buried them at the foot of a tree near the front of the house. This meant that if the ghost tried to return it would not get any further than the place where the pots were buried. After that we planted some of the grass called *ntahinduka* over the place, so that the ghost should not turn round and come back to trouble my wife. The *mufumu* then said that my wife would soon bear children. She has not borne any yet, but I hope that she will do so soon.

Although this text does not describe in detail the process of possession and ghost transference, it indicates one of the ways in which ghosts may be dealt with, i.e., by "catching" them and either destroying them or (as in the present case) insuring that they are kept away for good. Also it provides some interesting examples of the symbolism involved in ghost ritual. If it be accepted that ritual is a kind of language, it is plain enough what is being said in this case through the kinds of charms used and the Nyoro names given to them. Especially interesting is the symbolic "tying up" of the ghost. A brief text from another informant further develops the same notion:

> When a ghost has caused a woman to have miscarriages, the *mufumu* may make a horn called *ruboha* as medicine for her. He takes a goat's horn and cleans it and puts special medicines consisting of pieces of wood and other plants in it. Then he smears it with the

TABLE 1
Cases of Attack by Ghosts

Case No.	How Manifested?	Relationship of Ghost to Victim	Who Had Offended Ghost?	How?	Did Ghost Attack Offender?		Action Taken?	Successful?
					Directly?	Through Relative of Offender?		
1	Miscarriage	Household slave of patrilineal ancestor	Household head long ago	Cruelty	No	Yes, through descendant	Ghost caught and buried	Not yet
2	Epilepsy	Co-wife of mother's mother	Its co-wife	Practiced sorcery against her	No	Yes, through daughter's child	Victim's mother became ghost's medium	Not recorded
3	Ulcer on leg	Mother's father	Its daughter	Neglect	No	Yes, through son	Victim's mother became ghost's medium	Yes
4	Sudden seizure	Younger brother	Its elder brother	Retained property bequeathed to sisters	Yes	No	Younger sister became ghost's medium	Yes
5	Illness	Father's father	Its son	Prevented wife from taking food to father	No	Yes, through child and brother's child	Mediumship; sacrifice; brothers to live together	Yes
6	Miscarriages	Mother	Its husband	Deprived her of goat by refusing bridewealth for daughter	No	Yes, through daughter	Ghost-hut built, goat dedicated	Not yet
7	Leprosy, beaten by children	Wife	Its husband	Cruelty	Yes	No	Various means	No
8	Death and illness	Mother's sister's son	Its mother's mother	Refused goat for sacrifice to help sick grandchild (ghost)	No	Yes, through daughter's children	Victim's father became ghost's medium; sacrifice	Not recorded

T A B L E 1 (*Concluded*)
Cases of Attack by Ghosts

Case No.	How Manifested?	Relationship of Ghost to Victim	Who Had Offended Ghost?	How?	Did Ghost Attack Offender?			Action Taken?	Successful?
					Directly?	Through Relative of Offender?			
9	Miscarriages	Household slave of father's father's father	Household head long ago	Cruelty	No	Yes, through son's child		Ghost caught and burnt	Yes
10	Property burnt	Husband	Its wife	Not recorded	Yes recorded	No		Victim became ghost's medium; sacrifice	Yes
11	Miscarriages	Pat. half brother	Its parents	Not keeping child at their home after it died	No	Yes, through daughter		Various means	No
12	Painful swellings	Father	Its daughter	Marrying against wishes	Yes	No		Sacrifice; probably possession	No
13	Epilepsy	Mother	Its husband	Accepting brideweath for daughter against her last wishes	No	Yes, through daughter		Mother's wishes complied with (bridewealth returned)	Yes
14	Allergy to goat meat	Wife	Its husband	Keeping goat given to her	Yes	No		None	—
15	Epilepsy	Mother's mother	Its son and his wife	Neglect when ill	No	Yes, through children		Not recorded	No

slimy juice of a plant called *rucuhya* [*Sida rhombifolia*, a plant with tiny white flowers].[3] When the goat provided for the ghost is being slaughtered, blood from its neck is allowed to flow over the horn. The horn is then given to the woman to keep. The *mufumu* names that horn *ruboha* because the ghost has been "tied up" (*kuboha*) by the medicine in it, and it will protect that woman from further attack by that ghost.

Of interest, also, in Case 1 is the notion that nameless ghosts are especially difficult to deal with. An old man told me:

Nameless ghosts generally come from outside the household, perhaps from very far away. They come especially from men who were killed with women [i.e., in war]; perhaps speared and thrown into pits. These increased very much in the time of King Kabarega, because at that time there was much raiding and killing. These nameless ghosts may make impossible demands. I once heard of one which asked for buffalo milk, a dog's horn, and the tendon of a nkuba, a fabulous fowl associated with thunder and lightening. It said that it wanted to drink buffalo milk in the dog's horn. If it doesn't get what it wants, it may kill off a whole settlement. One such group of agnates (*kika*) lived at Kiswaza, and now not a single person of that group remains.

However the ghost is dealt with (and, as we shall see below, not all ghosts can be destroyed or sent away), it must first be induced, through possession ritual, to "mount into the head" of the affected person, or sometimes—as, for example, when the person affected is a small child—into the head of someone who represents the victim. In this way it is enabled to enter into communication with the living, and they with it. This possession can only be brought about by a doctor-diviner (*mufumu*) who is an initiated member of one or more of the Nyoro spirit mediumship cults, as most *bafumu* are. There follows a text dictated to me by some women who were formerly pagan but had recently been converted to the revivalist branch of the Native Anglican Church known as the *balokole* ("saved"). It gives some account of the ritual of possession.

When the *mufumu* comes to the house, food is cooked, and they eat. Then they cut some *ngando* wood [a wood which burns with a white flame], and special medicines are put on the head and body of the sick person. When the time for the possession has come, usually at night, the people sit around the hearth, where a fire is glowing. The *mufumu* begins to shake his gourd rattle (*nyege*) rhythmically, and everyone present begins to sing special songs. The words of one song are *Rwitakwanga araire omu rubale nagaranga omunaku wabu* [meaning roughly "Rwakitanga died, and his body was left among the rocks; on account of his poverty there was no one to bury him"].

Another song is *Karota Karota ija turole*, which means "Karota, Karota, come so that we may see you!" Karota is the name of a magic horn which the mufumu may put in the initiate's hands; it is then called upon to bring the ghost (*Karota leta muzimu!*). The singing may go on for a long time.

If the ghost does not come, they may take the sick man "to search for the ghost" (*kusera muzimu*). First the *mufumu* takes a torch of burning grass and thrusts it in all four directions. Then he takes the sick man outside, and he and the other *bafumu* present ask him if he has ever been initiated as a spirit medium. If he says "No," they explain to him what he has to do, and he agrees. Then they bring him into the house again and put the horn Karota in his hands, and they go on singing the appropriate songs. Soon the sick man begins to weep bitterly, without words but noisily. The mufumu says, "The ghost is coming!" Then they sing another song, the words of which are *Lira muno, tiguli muzimu, idomora* ("Weep much; this is not [just] a ghost, it is a terribly powerful thing"). Soon the patient falls forward on his face; he has been in a sitting position. Then the mufumu addresses the ghost, which is now in the patient's head: "What would you like to eat?" (*Nogonza okulyaki?*). The ghost answers through the sick person "meat." But he uses the special vocabulary used by ghosts and calls it *kanunka* instead of the usual Nyoro word *nyama*. The *mufumu* also asks the ghost who it is (*Niwe oha?*). The ghost may give the name of someone who has died long ago.

Then the *mufumu* goes on to ask, "And what was it that annoyed you?" (*Okabihizibwaki?*). The ghost replies: "They refused to give me meat," or "They killed me," or "They didn't take proper care of me so I died," or gives some other reason.

If the ghost asks for a goat, they bring a black one (*kibogo*) and present it to the ghost. And the *mufumu* says, "The matter is finished; here is your goat. Now leave off killing people." Then they cut the goat's throat, and they cause the blood to flow into a new winnowing basket (*rugali*), which is sound and without holes. They order the patient to drink some of the blood. He drinks as well as he is able. Then the goat is skinned and divided up, and a small part of it is cooked; most of the meat is taken home by the *mufumu*.

Different *bafumu* have different techniques for inducing ghosts to mount into the heads of their clients, but always the use of medicines, singing special ghost songs,[4] and the rhythmical shaking of gourd rattles form part of the ceremony. Usually the sick person who is to be the ghost's medium is completely covered in a barkcloth, and often special medicines are burnt or infused and the patient required to inhale the fumes. Medicines, one of which is an infusion of chalk, may be rubbed on his body. An informant's account of one way of inducing possession follows.

Case 2. When I was a small boy about seven years old, one of my half brothers, who was about four, started having fits. So one day my father brought a *mufumu* to the house to catch that ghost. The diviners had told him that was the ghost of a co-wife of the child's maternal grandmother, who was said to have practiced sorcery against that co-wife long ago. The ghost was now avenging this injury by attacking her co-wife's daughter's child.

The ghost was made to come into the head of that child's mother, Nyezi, as the boy was too young to be a medium. When the *mufumu* came, we had our evening meal, and then, after it was dark, we gathered round the fire inside the house. The *mufumu* took a rope, of the kind used for tethering goats, and he tied one end of this to the center pole of the house. Nyezi was made to hold the other end with both hands by means of a stick to which the rope was tied. The *mufumu* sat beside the rope; he draped certain kinds of leaves over it and held others in his hand. He also had various medicines spread out on a mat in front of him. Then he started rhythmically shaking his gourd rattle and singing; other people who were present and knew the songs joined in. Nyezi did not sing, but she gradually started swaying backwards and forwards with the rope in her hands. Suddenly she cried out in a loud voice: *Mawe! Mawe!* ("Mother! mother!"—a cry of

distress). Then we knew that the ghost had come into her head.

Soon after that I fell asleep, and I do not know how the ghost was eventually caught. But I was told afterwards that it was caught in a pot and thrown away. *Rafumu* often do this; they put dry banana leaves in the pot and sometimes a small lizard, which makes little rustling sounds in the pot and also itself makes a funny little noise, almost like a person.

Another technique is to make a hole in the roof of the house and to pass a rope through the hole. To the end of the rope is attached the flower sheath, called *nkonombo* in Nyoro, which grows at the end of a bunch of bananas. The rope, with the *nkonombo* at the end, hangs down inside the room where people have assembled for the seance, and as it proceeds a close watch is kept on the rope. As soon as the *nkonombo* is seen to shake, the *mufumu* leaps up and says that the ghost has come and is shaking the rope. He may then persuade it to pass, via the medium, into a pot prepared for it, and so encompass its own destruction.

Alternatively, the *nkonombo* may be suspended outside the house, as in the case recorded in the following text, written by one of my assistants:

The ghost of a person outside the family or lineage (*kika*) can be burnt, but not that of a close relative. Ghosts of slaves or other unrelated persons may be burnt. For example, if a thirsty traveler were refused a drink of water at a certain house, and then died of thirst on his way, his ghost might attack the members of that household and could be burnt.

Such unrelated ghosts are caught at night. They may be caught with the help of certain *mbandwa* spirits [for an account of these see Beattie 1961]. The *mbandwa* spirits that I know of which can do this are Irungu, the spirit of the bush, and Kapumpuli, the spirit of smallpox; both of these spirits can divine when they are in their mediums' heads. After rattles have been played and the songs of *kubandwa* sung, the *mbandwa* spirit comes into the medium's head, and it begins to talk to the ghost. In this way the ghost may be persuaded to leave the sick person and to come into the head of the doctor-diviner, who is already being possessed by the *mbandwa* spirit. Then the spirit and the ghost talk while both are in the medium's head.

Here is a new way of catching a ghost that I observed. The *mufumu* came with his assistant, called *ow'ensaho* (bag carrier). In the bag were many kinds of medicines, plants, cowries, and other things; also a knife for cutting meat. The patient's family were told to find six strong people, who had to stay outside the house to catch the ghost. Inside, where the seance was being held, a rope had been attached to the patient's wrist and passed through the roof, so that it hung down over the edge of the thatch. To the end of the rope the *mufumu* had tied an *nkonombo* [banana flower sheath]. An opening had been made in this, and the *mufumu* had spat in it. He then told the people outside that if, after the rattles and singing had gone on inside the house for some time, they should see the rope shaking, then they must seize the rope firmly and not let it go; if they released it, the ghost would escape and might throw some of them down and kill them. The people were very frightened of the *mufumu*, and they did as they were told.

Indoors, the *mufumu* began to talk to the ghost, which was now in the patient's head: "What is it? What is it? You shall not kill this person. What is the trouble between you?" (*Kiki? Kiki? Omuntu ota-muita. Baitu muturaineki?*). The ghost replied: "Now I shall really destroy this man. Why did they leave me alone in the house to die?" (*Omuntu onu hati nimu-gonola lelo; bakandekelaki omunyegamo ninfwa?*). It was using the ghost vocabulary, not everyday Nyoro. The *mufumu* pleaded with it: "Leave off, my friend [literally my blood-partner']; please leave off!" *Deka, munywani wange; pai deka!*).

Then the *mufumu* took some dried wood of a kind called *kitimazi*, literally "dung-wood," which has a smell like human ordure, and he fumigated the patient with this, in order to drive the ghost out of him. [He probably burnt some of it and caused the smoke to penetrate the barkcloth wherein the patient was swathed.] He also rubbed other medicines on him. And the rattles were shaken hard and fast. Then the ghost left the patient and passed along the rope to the banana flower sheath which was hanging outside.

When the people who were outside saw the rope shaking violently, they seized it very firmly, as they had been told, and the people came rushing out of the house. The *mufumu* quickly sealed the hole which he had made in the *nkonombo* and untied it from the rope. Then he ordered the people to cut firewood early in the morning and to make a big fire. The next morning

this was done, and the *mufumu* threw that thing on the fire. He did not allow anyone else to approach the fire while he did so, and after he had thrown it in the fire he ran away very quickly. As he did so we heard a shriek; I think that this noise was made by a friend of the *mufumu* who was hiding near the fire, but I did not see anybody.

A further brief account tells in more detail how a ghost may be induced to enter a pot, and how it may be disposed of:

When the ghost is in the medium's head, they may burn a little meat for it. They take the ears of the goat that has been slaughtered and char them so that there is a smell of burning. Then the *mufumu* throws these into a pot which has been smeared with clay; the pot is shaped rather like a water jar (*nfumbi*). With them he puts into the pot a certain kind of reeds (*busagazi*); while he is doing these things the people are singing, and gourd rattles are being shaken. Then he takes hold of the head of the person who is being possessed and looks closely into his nose and mouth. [Then the ghost passes] into the pot, which the patient has been given to hold. The pot is taken from him quickly. If they hear the reeds rustling inside the pot, they close it with mud as quickly as they can, for now the ghost has been captured. Then they put the pot on one side, and everybody is pleased, because the ghost has been caught. Next someone who is very strong takes up the pot, holding it very carefully so that it won't burst. He has to hold it very firmly, for the whole pot may be shaking and its contents churning about (*kucundacunda*). In this way they know that they really have caught the ghost. Sometimes some of the people there may say that the man is just pretending, and they take hold of the pot too. In this way everyone may confirm for himself that the ghost is truly there.

Then there is a discussion as to how they should destroy it. Some say that it should be burned; others that it should be buried. If they agree to bury it, they dig a hole about five feet deep. And if they decide to burn it, they cut firewood and burn it in the bush some distance away from the house, perhaps two hundred yards away. If the fire is not strong enough, so that it just burns the plantain-fiber ropes with which the pot is bound, the ghost may suddenly escape. If it does, it may there and then kill the people who have caught it and go on to kill others. But if the fire is a really strong one, it doesn't matter when the rope is burnt; the ghost will not be able to escape from the flames and will be consumed. Then the patient will recover, and that ghost will never return to do more harm.

As well as being destroyed, a ghost may also be, as it were, kept permanently at bay. After the sacrifice of a goat and the performance of the possession ritual the *mufumu* may "keep" that ghost in front of the homestead. He does this by burying the goat's head in front of the courtyard; on the goat's head he has placed a small quantity of saliva procured from the ghost when it was possessing its victim. This will satisfy the ghost that it has eaten its goat, and so it will not want to come into the house and injure people. A speckled cock (*rusanja*) may also be buried with the goat. On top of these things the grass called *ejubwa* is planted.

But not all ghosts can be finally disposed of in these ways. Ghosts which can be burned are those of domestic slaves (*bairu rubale*), of blood partners (*banywani*), and of parents-in-law. The ghost of a close relative, or of a spouse, cannot be destroyed, but must be enabled to enter into an enduring relationship with the living by means of the possession cult. Here is an informant's account of what happens:

The *mufumu* and others present play their rattles and sing the songs which are sung to raise ghosts. The fire is dim and glowing, not blazing. When the ghost comes into the medium's head it makes a small fawning noise, like a dog welcoming someone it knows, before it starts to talk. Then it begins to speak in a small, far-away voice, like a dying person. It may say: "We have died; we live in the country of Nyamiyonga [the king of the ghosts] far underground where the termites live" (*Itwe tukagolomoka; tuikala owanyamiyonga owa nkubebe*). The *mufumu* asks it, "Who are you?" (*niwe oha?*), and the ghost replies, "I am so-and-so" (*ninyowe nanka*). The mufumu continues, "What do you want?" (*noyendaki?*), and the ghost answers, "I want to eat" (*ninyenda kwehila*). The ghost is now using ghost words instead of ordinary Nyoro; thus *kwehila* (to eat) is *kulya* in everyday speech. The *mufumu* then asks it, "What do you want to eat?" (*noyenda kwehilaki?*), and the ghost replies, "I want to eat meat and millet porridge" (*ninyenda*

kwehila akanunka na kazuzu). *Kanunka* is the ghost term for meat (*nyama*), and *kazuzu* is the ghost term for millet (*oburo*).

Then the *mufumu* explains to the patient's relatives what the ghost has said. A black goat is produced; this is the meat which ghosts eat. If the ghost is a man's, the goat should be male; if it is a woman's, it should be female. But if a man who has been caught by a man's ghost cannot obtain a male goat, then they take a female goat and kill it. But first they tie 25 cents, or perhaps 5 cents, on to its head, and so turn it into a male goat. When they have done this they cut the meat up, and they give the ghost the goat's head with these cents tied to it. The cents are buried with the goat's head; the *mufumu* says that he cannot take them himself, for if he were to try to cheat the ghost he would die.

Thus in the course of the initial possession the ghost states what it wants. Almost always this involves the immediate provision of a goat. But it may also involve the making of periodic sacrifices to it (entailing further mediumistic ritual), perhaps the dedication of an animal to it, often the erection and maintenance of a special ghost hut for it, sometimes the carrying out of specific obligations or commitments which have been neglected. In the fifteen cases of ghostly activity which I recorded in some detail, six ghosts were quite close maternal kin of their victims, four were quite close paternal kin, three were spouses. In none of these cases could the ghost be destroyed or sent away. There follows a long account, by a young man who had had some secondary education, of how a ghost, avenging neglect by a daughter when it was alive, attacked that daughter's child. The account is of some interest also as showing that the conflict between modern Western ideas and traditional ones arises in the context of the ghost cult, as in many other contexts.

Case 3. When I was at school in Hoima [the capital of Bunyoro] I used to stay in the home of a woman called Kabasika. I called her my *nyinento* [mother's sister, literally "little mother"] because she was born in the same clan as my mother. She lived about two miles from the town, and I used to walk in to school every day.

In May, 1954, her son Turumanya, a boy of about seven, became affected (*yakwatwa,* literally "was caught") by a big ulcer on his leg. It hurt him very much, and when medicine was put on it it would not stay there but fell off at once. After about two weeks the ulcer was enormous; I used to treat it myself with powder which I got from the hospital, but it got no better. One afternoon my *nyinento* said to me: "This child of mine is being made sick by a ghost, perhaps by a ghost of this very household (*eka*)." Early the next morning when I went to greet her I found that she had left the house. After a while my cousin Turumanya and I saw her returning. As soon as she came in, and before I had time to ask her where she had been, she called me aside. "Come behind the house with me, Apuli" (a pet name), she said, "I want to tell you something." We went out behind the house and sat down. She was holding a small bunch of a special kind of grass (*etete,* lemon grass) and *rweza* (literally "that which whitens or purifies," a small herb with a pretty white blossom, perhaps a celosia). Then she said to me: "Atenyi—this is my *mpako* name[5]—do you know what has made that mother's child of yours sick?" I said "No," and she went on: "He's been made sick by the ghost of his grandfather Kahanda, my father; it wants to eat. And if it is given meat to eat and can then be persuaded to spit on Turumanya, so conveying its blessing to him, then that ulcer will get better. This is what took me out so early in the morning; I have been to the diviner Karoli to find out what the matter was."

Then she said: "Now, Atenyi, let me start with a prayer (*kambanze ndame*). Then I must prepare millet porridge and meat for the ghost, so that my child may get well." Then she went into the house. I stayed outside, but I could hear what she said when she prayed at the *ihangirro* (shrine or sacred place) in the corner of her room. This is what I heard her saying, after she had knelt down: "Ai, father, I know that it is you who has made this child of mine sick, because a long time has passed without my cooking anything for you to eat. Ai, all you good people who have died, release this child of yours so that he may be all right again. I am just going to prepare a meal for you so that you may eat." (*Ai, tata, manyire niwe orwaize omwana wange onu, habwokutwara omwanya mwingi ntaku-cumbira okalya; ai, inywena abarungi abayegoro-moire mutaise omwana wanyu onu abeho kurungi; nyowe kantekanize mbacumbire mwehire.*)

After this my *nyinento* prepared millet, and she sent me to buy some beef at Hoima market; I bought just two pounds. When I got home I wanted the meat to be cooked at once so that I could have some of it. But she refused, saying, "That meat is not for you, or for your brother either; no, this is my private affair!" So I left it. That evening she prepared our evening meal for us as usual and we ate; but we did not have any of that meat, no! And after we had eaten, she started cooking food for that ghost. She cooked it like any other food, but when she had finished dishing the millet porridge she called me to carry that food into the house. I did so.

Soon after this a neighbor, a married woman who was a friend of my *nyinento* and a kind of interpreter (*muhinduzi*) for the world of ghosts i.e., she was an initiate in the Nyoro spirit mediumship cult: came to the house, to tell the ghost that its food had been prepared for it. She sat down on the ground by the hearth. My *nyinento* went to her room and took a barkcloth. When she returned she called me and my young brother (who was also staying there at that time) into the house, but we refused and went to sit on the verandah. But the boy Turumanya was with his mother; he sat beside her while she was being possessed by her father's ghost. However, we did come into the house a little later, and these are the things which I heard and saw.

My *nyinento* was sitting in the room near the *ihangirro;* she was stooped over and completely covered by the barkcloth. She was quite silent for some minutes. Then she started to make little grunting noises (*kuhuna*): "Nnn, nnn." Then she began to speak, but her voice was quite changed; it was small and high-pitched. She said, "I have come back!" (*ntarukire*); this is the ghost's way of saying *ngarukire,* "I have returned." And the neighbor who was there to speak to the ghost said "Return!" (*taruka!*). Then the ghost greeted the people present: "Are you all right there? And I'm here, all right. [This is a usual form of greeting in Bunyoro.] I died, alas! alas! So it's you people, well! well!" (*Muloho kulungi; nanyowe ndoho; nkagoromoka, ai, ai; niinywe, bambi*).

The woman replied and told the ghost that its food was ready for it: "I have called you; come and eat. I have cooked a little millet for you and some meat; help yourself and eat with your children. Because I know that it was you who made this child of mine sick." (*Nkwesere oije olye, ncumbire akaro kenaku hamu nakanunka; oyehire nabana bawe habwokuba nkamanya niwe warwaize omwana wange onu.*) And the ghost answered, "You, is the child there? Bring him so that I can have a look at him" (*Wewe, araha mulete murole*). Then the boy was brought forward to be spat upon by his grandfather's ghost. And the ghost spat lightly on him and said: "Apuli, recover from your ulcer; grow strong; do a man's work!" (*Apuli, okire ekihoya, oyomere, opakase masaija!*). While the ghost spat on him, it moved him about by his head, shoulders, and arms. And it gave him a small morsel of millet porridge, which it had spat on, and a piece of meat, which the boy ate. Then the ghost wanted to spit on me as well, but I refused and ran out into the kitchen with my young brother, and stayed there.

Then I heard the woman explaining to the ghost: "These children are schoolboys (*basomi,* literally 'readers'); they are people of the Europeans, outsiders (*balimwoyo,* a term used to denote people who have not been initiated into the possession cult). That is why they are not able to come near." Then she shouted to us: "You there! Take care of yourselves in matters like these. You could easily die or be caught by a terrible disease!" And she called to us again to go in. But we refused because we were attending school, and they had forbidden us there to have anything to do with things of this sort or to eat such food. They are absolutely forbidden by the Catholic religion.

After my *nyinento* had finished being possessed by her father Kahande's ghost, she put the barkcloth back in its place. Then she came back and said to the other woman: "My dear friend, hunger is killing me; give me some of that millet which is there to eat." I said to her: "But you've just been eating millet porridge and meat!" She answered, "My child, do you think it was I who was just eating?" I said, "Yes," and she went on: "It was the ghost that was eating, not I. Well, perhaps I was eating, but I do not know where the food has gone. These are things of the devil (*Sitani*)."

From that time the boy Turumanya began to recover, and after one month his ulcer was quite gone.

There are gaps in this account. Possession is usually induced by singing and the shaking of gourd rattles, but there is no mention of this here; also it is not stated whether the ghost required a ghost-hut to be erected for it. Nevertheless, the account illustrates some points already made. We noted, for example, that a ghost may attack the person who has offended it not directly but indirectly, and in the account it was not Kabasika but her child Turumanya, who had never done anything to annoy his late grandfather, who was inflicted with a painful ulcer. Although individualism has increased in Bunyoro, as elsewhere, with the coming of Western influence, the bonds of family and lineage are still sufficiently strong for an attack on one member of the lineage or domestic group to be thought of as an attack on all.

It is significant, moreover, that Kabasika was not thinking of her relationship with the ghost world solely in interindividual terms. It is true that her direct concern was with her father's ghost, which was supposed to be offended because she had neglected it, but she also expressed her concern with "all you good people who have died," that is, with the ancestral ghosts as in some sense a collectivity. Furthermore, in this case the possession was by proxy. The usual pattern is for the victim himself to be formally possessed by the ghost which is afflicting him, but where the victim is a small child, and hence presumably incapable of understanding and memorizing the quite complex pattern of behavior required, the ghost may be induced to possess his mother or another close relative as a substitute.

Finally, the case reveals the conflict which prevails between traditional Nyoro ritual practices and the new Christian-inspired ideas being disseminated by both church and state. My informant and his young brother had attended a mission school [almost all education in Bunyoro is in mission hands, and the Protestant Church Missionary Society has had much influence on the native rulers]. The missionary attitude to traditional religious and magical practices in Bunyoro has, I believe, been exceptionally repressive. This has created, at least during the present period of transition, a painful dilemma for many schoolchildren from traditional homes. Strong pressures may be put on them by their parents and relatives to participate in traditional rites, and refusal may be regarded not merely as a regrettable indifference to the old customs but as an act of deliberate injury to family and kin.

Another detailed text, related by a Christian informant with a secondary education, also involves possession by proxy, though it is likewise of interest on other grounds. Mission influence, though not directly mentioned, may well have been reflected, directly or indirectly, in the chosen medium's reluctance to participate.

Case 4. A neighbor of ours called Yowana died. He had several brothers and sisters, and when he was dying he said that his goats should be given to his eldest sister, except for a few which should go to a younger sister. But his older brother Isoke was a greedy man, and as soon as Yowana was dead he took those goats into his own house. He did not trouble to obey his brother's wishes; he said to himself, "He's dead and will never know." But Yowana's ghost said to itself:

"Ma! Shall I not say God forbid that you should steal my property! You have shown your hatred for me, and now that I am dead you flatter yourself that you can help yourself to what is mine! You cheat!" (*Ma! tinikyo nafukize ekyo iwe kutunga ebyange; okanoba nindora hati wabona nafa wanyebugira notwara ebyange; odupa!*). And the ghost caught that man Isoke and threw him on the ground in a fit. People cried, "What is it? What is it? What is killing him?" (*Kiki? kiki? yaitwaki?*), and those who were near rushed to help him. And they called to his relatives, "Go quickly to the diviners and find out what is killing him!" So his mother went to a diviner, and the diviner threw his shells and said, "It's his brother's ghost; this man has taken (*akalya*, literally 'he has eaten') what was refused to him and given to his sisters."

His mother asked the diviner, "What shall we do?" He said that first the property should be divided up as the dead man had ordered. Next they should find a doctor-diviner (*mufumu*) to come and arrange for the ghost to possess someone (*kutendeka*); otherwise her son would die. The mother replied, "But my son is as good as dead already; it is finished; shall I go and help him when he is already dead?" (*Omwana wange afuire; kihoire ndaija kumujuna afuire*). The diviner threw his shells again and saw that they had fallen in a straight line (*muhingo*). So he said to her, "He's not dead yet; but if you don't do as I have told you he will not eat again until he has seen the gateway of the pit" (*Hati tafe baitu obumutakole ebinkusoboroire taija kulya arozire irembo ly'ekina*).

The woman wept, and after she had wept she gave her son medicines to calm him, rubbing them in his armpits and groin. Then he began to come to his senses, and she explained to him that it would be well to give the goats to their proper owners; if this were not done he would die. So Isoke softened and agreed to divide up the property. She went on to tell him that the diviner had said the ghost should be enabled to possess a member of the family, after which it would cease to trouble him (*guraculera*, literally "it would calm down").

So the young man called a *mufumu* to arrange for the possession. He came, summoned everybody in the household, and spread out his medicines. He had told them to collect the wood called *ngando* and to make a fire in the house, so that he could call the ghost into the sick man's head and talk to it. He threw some medicine on the fire, and other medicine was put in a potsherd which was placed on the embers and the patient made to inhale it. After this the *mufumu* took the potsherd in his hands and circled the sick man's head with it. While he did this he called upon the ghost to cease making him ill. Then he asked it what it wanted and whom it wished as its medium. But that day the ghost refused to explain what it wanted done. So that night after dark he continued to talk to it, and at last it said that it wanted to have its youngest sister as its medium. When that sister heard about this the following morning she was afraid, for she knew that possession by a ghost sometimes entails rough handling, and she ran away and hid herself in a neighbor's house. But the mother set out to track her until she found her. When she caught her she beat her very much, bound her legs so that she should not run away again, and tied her arms behind her back. That night the *mufumu* continued to talk with the ghost, and the ghost said that it wanted a black goat killed for it and that it would eat the meat while it was "in the head" of its medium. The next evening, after the evening meal, the *mufumu* ordered that the girl who was to be the medium should be prepared. Her legs and arms were untied, and she was made to sit near the fire. The goat was brought and slaughtered, and one leg was cooked at once. The *mufumu* rubbed medicine on the girl, and he put other medicine in the potsherd which was by the fire; this he then moved in a circle round her head.

Then the ghost descended (*kusirimuka*)[6] into its medium. When it had entered her [*kumugwera*, literally "fell upon her"], it began to hurl her about and choke her. She knew nothing of this; others explained it to her later. But the next day her throat was so sore that she could not even swallow her own saliva.

As soon as the *mufumu* saw that the ghost had seized her and was choking her so fiercely, he began to talk and plead with it and to put more medicine on it [i.e., on the medium], until it calmed down. Then he fed it with the meat which had been cooked for it, and the others present ate as well. There was also millet porridge. The *mufumu* gave the ghost pellets of food by putting them into its [i.e., the medium's] mouth, and the ghost also began to give the people who were there morsels of food in the same way, and told them to eat.[7] When the meal was finished, the *mufumu* released the ghost to go back to its own place, and it was all finished. Then the ghost's strength left the girl. From that time the ghost has been quiet and has brought no more trouble. My informant told me that he afterwards asked the girl what it felt like to be possessed by a ghost. She replied that it had made her feel strange and unwell; she had felt impelled to weep, that she was being moved by some power outside herself, that she was being strangled and knocked down; she did not remember anything more.

This case well illustrates the sanctioning aspect of the ghost cult. When Isoke fell ill, the diviner's diagnosis and advice were powerful incentives for him to carry out his dead brother's wishes and give the goats bequeathed to his sisters to their rightful owners. It may be presumed that Isoke's meanness and dishonesty in this matter were common knowledge in the neighborhood; it is very unlikely that the cheated sisters had kept silent. It is possible, too, that Isoke felt a certain uneasiness at having defied the wishes of his dead brother. So the diviner's findings can hardly have been unexpected.

Belief in the power of ghosts also served as a powerful sanction for conformity with accepted social norms in the following case.

Case 5. An old man called Yozefu was ill, and Mariya, the wife of his second son Yonasani, cooked some food for him and took it to him to eat. She was intercepted by her husband Yonasani, who angrily threw the food away, saying abusively to Mariya: "Why do you want to cook for him? Hasn't he got a wife of his own?" A day or two later the old man Yozefu died.

Shortly afterwards Yozefu's ghost appeared in a dream to Rumondo, his eldest son, and said that his [Yozefu's] daughter Eseri should become its medium. Also, at about the same time, Rumondo's small daughter became ill, and the diviners said that this was due to Yozefu's ghost. So Rumondo called a doctor-diviner to deal with the matter. The *mufumu* spoke with the ghost through the sick child, and the ghost said that the child would get better, but that unless the possession were arranged quickly it would find another victim in the family. A day or two later Yonasani's son, a lad of about twenty, fell ill; he seemed to be going out of his mind and kept falling down. The girl Eseri was duly initiated, and various *bafumu* were consulted, but the young man remained ill for several months.

Then Yozefu's ghost again appeared to Rumondo in a dream and told him to call an old friend of his [Yozefu's], who was also a medium. This man came, there was another seance, and at last the ghost spoke through its medium Eseri. It said that a sheep should be bought and slaughtered for it, a feast held, and a small ghost-hut erected for it in the courtyard. It also said that Rumondo's two brothers should come back and live together with Rumondo at the family home (at that time they were living far apart, and only Rumondo was living at his father's place). All these things were done as directed. At once the sick boy got better, and that was the end of the matter.

Here again the actual offender was not attacked directly but indirectly, first through his brother's child and then through his own. A man is especially vulnerable through his children, and particularly through his sons. The Nyoro, like other peoples with a classificatory kinship terminology, think of a brother's sons as being, in a real sense, one's own sons too. In predominantly patrilineal Bunyoro a man looks to his sons to continue his line and perhaps, after his death, to provide his ghost with the attentions it needs. This case is interesting also in its sanctioning aspect, as vividly expressing the traditional value of agnatic solidarity, which is nowadays giving way before the new individualistic values of contemporary Bunyoro. In traditional times adult brothers often lived together in large compound families, which formed real corporate agnatic units in relation to other similar units.

Though this is no longer the norm, many brothers still do live near one another and look to one another for co-operation and support. Even though many do not, the story of Yozefu's ghost shows that the belief that they ought to do so is still an important value for some Nyoro.

In the cases just quoted, the action taken at the ghost's behest is reported to have been successful. But this is not always so. Kiboko had a ghost-hut (*kibali*) under the eaves of his thatched, mud-and-wattle hut to the right of the doorway; in it was a small piece of a kind of ant-mound called *mpike*. I asked him for what ghost it had been erected, and he replied:

Case 6. My wife had many miscarriages and failed to give birth to a live child, so I went to the diviners, and they said that the trouble was due to the ghost of my wife's dead mother. She had been annoyed before she died because she had not received "the goat of the bride's mother" when her daughter was married. This was my wife's father's fault; he had refused to accept bridewealth for her. Had he done so, then one of the goats which I would have paid would have gone to her mother. When I consulted a *mufumu* and made contact with the ghost, it told me to make a ghost-hut for it and dedicate a black goat to it. I did all these things, but that wife has not yet had a child.

When I asked Kiboko whether he thought that it was still possible that the action he had taken might be effective, he replied skeptically, "Will a woman of forty begin to bear children?"

Ghost-huts are of standardized pattern, usually untidy-looking conical huts of sticks and grass about eighteen inches high. Here is an informant's description of a *kibali*.

The frame is made of sticks of a tree called *bijegejege* or *ebosa* [I have not been able to identify these]. The sticks are tied together in the shape of a small cone about a foot or eighteen inches high; they are tied with the bark of *ebosa* or with *esojo* grass. On the floor of the hut they spread *esojo* grass, not *etete* [lemon grass], which is used in huts for embandwa spirits only. If the hut is for a male ghost a stick of a tree called *rusinga* is placed upright in the hut as a spear is in a real house; this stick is the ghost's spear. [Real

spears are made of *rusinga* wood, which grows strong and straight.] All the bones of the goat which was eaten at the possession feast are buried in a hole dug beside the entrance to the ghost-hut, except the lower jawbone, which is placed on top of the hole after it has been filled in. Sometimes a black goat is kept in the household permanently for the ghost, and when the ghost says it wants to eat they may kill it and replace it with another goat. In this case only the bones of the first goat that is killed are buried in this hole. A piece of a special kind of anthill called *mpike* [these are small, hard, dome-shaped mounds, sometimes used as cooking stones] is brought and may be put on top of the jawbone. This is the ghost's stool, for it to sit on when it comes there. The *mufumu* also puts a small piece of barkcloth in the ghost-hut; this is to provide clothing for the ghost. The tail of a chameleon may also be put there; this is because a chameleon can look in all directions at once, so that the ghost may not approach unseen.

Some ghosts are believed to be so inimical that none of the measures described above are effective against them. Here is an informant's statement about the powers of different kinds of ghosts:

The ghost of a sister's child (*mwihwa*) does not have a hut built for it, nor can it be "caught." If a *mwihwa's* ghost attacks a family it finishes off the whole household; this is something about *baihwa* which causes them to be very much feared.[8] The ghost of a person's mother's brother (*nyinarumi*) or mother's sister (*nyinento*) is also very strong; such ghosts are stronger than those of parents (*bazaire*, literally "those who have begotten or borne one"), which may have huts built for them.

The ghost of an infant (*nkerembe*) is stronger than that of an adult, but it is not as strong as that of a sister's child. An infant's ghost cannot be burnt; they simply do what it wants. It can cry like a real infant. An *nkerembe* can leave a ghost for three reasons—perhaps because they have thrown it away (*kunagwa*), perhaps because they have left it in a burning house and run away, perhaps because it has been killed by its mother. Those ghosts which have huts built for them are usually those of the father's side.

Particularly dangerous is the ghost of a person who has committed suicide because of some injury or slight. The following text illustrates the fate of a man attacked by the ghost of his late wife, who had killed herself because of his unkindness to her.

Case 7. Tito left his wife at home in Bunyoro looking after his home and farm while he went to Kampala to work. He stayed away for six years, and during this time his half brother by the same father, Asafu, came to his house and helped his wife with the farm, giving her presents of clothes and other things and eventually, a child. When Tito returned, he was very angry about this. He had no right to be so; it was not as though his wife had taken up with a stranger. The child was of his clan and house, and the blood was the same. In Nyoro custom, if a man sleeps with the wife of his brother by the same father, there is no adultery. Also it was unreasonable to expect a woman to remain faithful through six years of separation. In fact, the Native Government had recently made a law that if a man left his wife for two years or more he would have no claim if she went elsewhere or had a child by another man, and he would have no right to compel her to return to him.

However Tito did not see things in this light. He never left off reproaching his wife, and he constantly abused and beat her. After some time she went off into the bush and hanged herself on a tree. She left a very powerful ghost. The first thing that happened was that the child who had been born during Tito's absence died, a week after her own death. Then the children of Tito and his dead wife began to fight with their father and beat him. A year later he contracted leprosy, and he has suffered from this ever since. He does not die, but he is weak, cannot walk, and is wasted away. Sometimes he seems to get a bit better, and then he relapses and seems about to die, and then he recovers a little again. This is because the ghost wishes him to suffer as much as possible. Even now, in his present state, his eldest son beats him from time to time when he is drunk. Tito has tried every means to get rid of that ghost and has bought many medicines, but they could never succeed in catching it.

Where it is suspected that a dying person is likely to leave a ghost to afflict the living, the Nyoro say that the danger may be averted by premortem treatment (though I have never heard of an actual case).

If a man who is always cursing people and threatening to leave a ghost to injure them falls sick, sometimes when they see that he is just about to die they find some clay, and they suffocate him by putting this in his mouth. They also put some in his anus, and after that they bury him. Thus that man cannot leave a ghost, because they have "caught" it before he died.

In three of the seven cases cited, the ghost was a relative on the victim's mother's side, in two a patrilateral relative, in one a spouse, and in one a domestic slave (*mwiru rubale*). In all these cases the ghost was an individual believed to have been offended before death by the victim or by a near relative of the victim. And in all of them, except that of the old man Yozefu whose ghost first announced itself in a dream, illness or other misfortune was the first intimation that a ghost might be active. Even in Yozefu's case, illness in the family followed hard on the heels of this announcement. Is there, then, any sense in which we can say that the Nyoro have, or traditionally had, an ancestral cult, in which the ancestors are "worshiped" and sacrificed to as a collectivity? Or is the ghost cult simply an individual and *ad hoc* reaction to illness or other misfortune, like sorcery and certain other kinds of spirit possession?

It is plain, I think, from the cases already given that it is mostly the latter, but there is a little more to it than this. It would be misleading to say that the traditional religion of the Nyoro was ancestor worship. In fact, their traditional religion centers on the Cwezi spirits, which are associated with a wonderful race of people supposed to have come to Bunyoro many centuries ago, to have ruled the country for a couple of generations and performed many wonderful things, and then to have vanished as mysteriously as they came. These spirits, of which there were traditionally nineteen, are linked with the Nyoro clan system, one or more of them being specially associated with each of the local agnatic descent groups in which the Nyoro are said to have been traditionally organized. The cult of these spirits was also a mediumistic one (Beattie 1961).

Nonetheless, there are traces of an ancestral cult in some parts of Bunyoro. Although in most of the country it is either not practiced at all or is of negligible importance, everybody knows what it is and that it is, or was, practiced by some Nyoro. We noted, in Case 3, that Kabasika was concerned with her father's ghost not solely as an individual but also as associated with a collectivity of ancestors. It is significant that the region where the ancestral cult is still much spoken of and practiced is the Lake Albert littoral—an area which is largely isolated from the rest of Bunyoro by a steep escarpment and where the inhabitants, unlike those of upland Bunyoro, live in compact settlements of villages which are territorially organized on a lineage basis. The large settlement of Tonya, for example, consisting of about 130 households, comprises four distinct subdivisions or wards, each named after one clan of which practically all the adult men in the ward are members. In this lakeshore region membership in a group defined by agnatic descent is very much more important than it is for the members of the more dispersed communities of upland Bunyoro, where residence is comparatively little determined by descent.

To perform a special rite of prayer and sacrifice for the father's ghost is called *kubembeka*. It can be carried out only by a son, and, if there are several sons, by the father's heir. In Bunyoro there is only one heir (*mugwetwa*); the patrimonial authority is always transmitted undivided. In the *kubembeka* rite, remoter patrilineal forebears are always implicitly or explicitly associated with the father's ghost; the Nyoro say that other ghosts of the father's line are always present. A special shrine is constructed and maintained by the man who has authority to perform the rite. This is quite different from the ordinary ghost-hut, which, as we have noted, is a flimsy conical construction of sticks and grass. The *ibembo* shrine consists of four short stakes stuck in the ground in a straight line so that they stand about four inches above the surface and about two or three inches apart. Each stake is neatly bound with grass. Usually they are placed under a flimsy rectangular stand made of sticks. I could obtain no explanation of the form of the *ibembo* shrine, but it is relevant to note that in a number of ritual contexts in Bunyoro the number four is associated with men, three with women. The stakes are

said to be made of the wood of a tree fern (called *mulere*) and are called *bikondo* or *bibibi*.

Though one informant told me that in Tonya and other lakeshore communities prayers are addressed to the patrilineal ghosts at every new moon, my impression is that *ibembo* is likely to be performed about once a year. Even then, my informants agreed that it would very often be neglected until the man responsible for arranging it was reminded of it by seeing his father in a dream, or by an illness in his family which the diviners attributed to his neglect of the *ibembo* shrine. The ceremony would be attended by all the brothers of the dead man and their families. It could also be attended by wives and sisters' children (the latter being "children" of their mothers' clan), but not by more distant affines or by mothers' brothers (*nyinarumi*). The rite might or might not include possession; if it did not, it probably amounted to little more than a prayer and the placing at the shrine of a little millet or beer. I was told in Tonya that an offering of fish could also appropriately be made; when this was done the fish offered should be the species called *ngasa* (tiger fish). Unlike most Lake Albert fish, this species is equipped with extremely sharp teeth. It may be that, like Tallensi totems (Fortes 1945: 145), this implied aggressiveness makes them particularly appropriate to represent the ancestors, but the Nyoro to whom I suggested this, though amused, were unwilling to confirm it! The following is a Tonya informant's account of what takes place at *ibembo*:

Yowasi is the head of all the Basaigi clan in Tonya, and he performs the *ibembo* ceremony for his dead father on behalf of them all. The *ibembo* is for other ancestors of the Basaigi besides Yowasi's father; the names of some of these ancestors are Karasi, Rwemera, Karongo, Miigo, and Kiiza. The members of the Basaigi clan gather at Yowasi's shrine (*bikondo*). They do not do so at regular intervals, only when there has been some kind of misfortune (*bujune*), like someone being sick, a woman failing to bear children, or a man becoming impotent. In such a case the victim would have consulted the diviners first, and they would have advised that *ibembo* should be held. It might occur once a year or more often.

At this ceremony a goat is killed, and fish and millet porridge are also prepared. When the goat is being brought to be sacrificed, it is a good thing if it urinates on the way. This shows that there is no evil ahead, that the ghosts will do no harm to anyone in that house, that they wish them to give birth and to have good health, and that the ghosts are pleased with the goat that is being brought for them. But if the goat defecates, that is a bad sign and shows that the ghosts are not pleased. Beer may or may not be provided.

In the ceremony different ancestral ghosts enter into Yowasi and speak through him. Yowasi speaks in his ordinary voice, but it is the ghosts who are speaking and not he. He is dressed in a barkcloth. While Yowasi is in a state of possession members of his group may ask him for what they want. Thus women may say, "We want to give birth" (*tukwenda kuzara*), and the ghost which is possessing Yowasi says, "You will give birth" (*murazara*); it spits in the outstretched hands of the suppliant women, who then wipe the saliva [which conveys the ghost's blessing] on their faces and heads. Or a person may say, "I'm sick, cure me," and the ghost may reply, "You will recover" (*orakira*), and convey its blessing in the same way. After this the food is brought and the ghosts eat, being still in the head of Yowasi. Sometimes a goat is not slaughtered there and then but is kept for the ancestors; it may be eaten at a later *ibembo*.

This ceremony is usually carried out in the early afternoon. Yowasi had to be initiated into the possession cult in order to receive these ghosts. Initiation takes place in the bush at night and is carried out by old men of the Basaigi clan who are members of the possession cult.

To the question whether Nyoro have an ancestral cult, then, the answer must be that they know what is meant by such a cult and that some of them practice it. But the presence or absence of such a cult is very much a matter of degree. Most Nyoro, although they know that their fathers and their fathers' fathers left ghosts behind them when they died and that these ghosts can injure them, are little concerned with their ancestral ghosts as such. Ghosts, whether ancestral or otherwise, are for the most part thought of as individuals who can injure the living when they are offended. At least outside the sparsely populated lakeshore region, where residence is still largely based on unilineal descent, there is in Bunyoro little idea (though there is some) of "the ancestors" as a kind of unindividuated power, a collectivity—an idea which is still strongly held by some neighboring peoples such as the Lugbara (see Middleton 1960).

In the foregoing pages I have set out, with some ethnographic illustration, how the Nyoro think about ghosts and what they do about them. Let me recapitulate the principal stages in the ghost ritual. To begin with, a person (or someone close to him) falls ill or suffers some other misfortune, e.g., repeated abortion in the case of a woman. He or she consults a diviner, who is likely to diagnose one of three possible causes of the trouble: sorcery by some living person, the activity of nonhuman *mbandwa* spirits, or the action of a ghost. If ghostly activity is diagnosed, two broad types of action may follow, depending on the nature of the ghost and its relationship to the victim. First, it may be destroyed or otherwise permanently got rid of; second, an enduring relationship with it may be entered into, expressed through periodic sacrifice and prayer, the dedication to it of an animal, and the erection of a ghost-hut for it. But in either case the ghost must first of all be induced, through the spirit mediumship cult, to mount into the head of either the sick person or his accredited representative. When there, it may be either removed or disposed of, or propitiated, depending on the kind of ghost it is.

In some parts of Bunyoro an enduring relationship of this kind may be entered into especially with patrilineal ghosts, and to this extent the Nyoro may be said to have an ancestral cult. But in by far the greater part of the country, and in most respects in all of it, the ghost-victim relationship is an individual and interpersonal one, supposed to derive from some real or imagined slight, injury, or neglect either by the victim or by one of his close relatives. When all the culturally prescribed action has been properly carried out, the sufferer should recover. Some do; in six of the fifteen cases which I have recorded the victims are said to have recovered, in five not to have done so, and in two (both cases of repeated miscarriage) the victims had still not given up hope that the treatment would be effective.

I conclude by considering a little further the social and psychological implications of the Nyoro ghost cult. Functionally, like the other institutionalized forms of Nyoro spirit mediumship which I have discussed elsewhere, the ghost ritual is effective on two levels. First, it provides one way of thinking about and dealing with situations of stress and anxiety, and, second, it embodies an effective social sanction against certain kinds of socially disapproved behavior.

In Bunyoro, as in other relatively underdeveloped countries (though here as elsewhere the situation is rapidly changing), there is still much ill health, especially in infancy and childhood, and miscarriage is common. In rural areas access to modern means of dealing with these misfortunes is not yet easily or readily available. But the traditional culture provides a means of coming to terms with them, and even though these means are not (or at least not wholly) satisfying clinically, they do nonetheless provide emotional relief for the sufferer and his relatives. It may be, indeed, as I have remarked elsewhere, that the length and complexity of the ritual involved is psychologically beneficial rather than the reverse. In situations of stress what is important is to have something to do; to be compelled to remain inactive and impotent in the face of illness or other misfortune is psychologically unendurable.

But like the other Nyoro mediumistic cults, the ghost cult does more than offer its practitioners something useless to do merely for the sake of doing something. To begin with, it is by no means to be assumed that it is wholly useless. Subjection to treatment through ghost mediumship, whether the supposed medium's attitude to it is credulous, wholly skeptical, or a mixture of the two—I return to this point below—is a vivid and traumatic experience. Even for a man in the pink of condition, the darkness, the close group of people in the small warm hut, the monotonous but exciting rhythm of gourd rattles shaken close to his ears, the singing, and perhaps the fumes from burning or boiling herbs and other medicines can hardly fail to have a powerful physical and emotive effect. On a person who is sick and impressionable the effect must be

very much greater. High excitement, profuse perspiration, and perhaps final collapse may afford a kind of shock therapy which, at least in some cases, may well relieve certain kinds of symptoms.

Even where dissociation is not achieved or is incomplete, the dramatic, cathartic effect of the performance is important. As in other Nyoro possession ritual, the medium takes on the voice and gestures of the ghost which is supposed to be possessing him, and it is plain from some of the cases recorded in this paper that professional mediums may possess considerable histrionic talent. Whatever else it is, a mediumistic seance is evidently a thrilling dramatic performance. It is "expressive" rather than, or at least as much as, it is "instrumental." Or perhaps it would be more accurate to say that it is thought to be instrumental precisely because it is expressive. It is not a practical technique like pottery or basket-making, to be varied and improved in the light of experiment and experience. It is a symbolic procedure, to be understood rather by reference to what is being said than just by reference to what it is being sought to achieve. And it is the whole rite, not the instruments or techniques used, taken by themselves, which is believed to be effective.

When I was investigating the *mbandwa* possession cult in Bunyoro, an informant told me that she knew even before she was initiated into the cult that possession was not genuine, but simulated. But even so, she told me, she thought that it was a good thing to go through with the prescribed ritual. For her, although it involved pretence, it was not just pretence. If it is thought that ghosts, like other spirits, exist and can harm the living (and this is still widely believed in Bunyoro today, as it is in many other countries), then it may be supposed that these ghosts are gratified, and may be appeased, by the rituals which are performed on their behalf. This is so even though these rituals be regarded not as scientific procedures (and therefore "true"), but rather as symbolic ones. As among the ancient Greeks, it is held appropriate to approach the spirit world through drama, through vivid symbolic statements of what is feared and desired, not through empirically tested, practical techniques. To suppose other-

wise is to fall into the Frazerian fallacy of interpreting religious behavior as though it were a kind of
inferior and misguided science.

The Nyoro ghost cult, then, like the other Nyoro
spirit cults, is a drama. At the same time, in some of
its forms (as in *kubembeka*) it is an expression of
worship and piety toward beings whose existence is
still widely acknowledged.

I turn now to a few comments about the cult's
aspect as a sanction for good behavior. Obviously
the belief that ghosts can injure and even kill living
people, and that they are likely to do this if they are
ill-treated or neglected while they are alive, is a
powerful incentive to treat one's fellow men properly. Every one of the cases quoted in this paper
exhibits this aspect. Cruelty, neglect, cheating, and
failure to maintain good brotherly relations are
socially disapproved modes of behavior. And in
every case some such delict was diagnosed as
having given cause for ghostly punishment. Thus,
in its traditional form, the cult was essentially a
moral one. For the Nyoro, as for members of many
Western European societies not so long ago, illness
and other misfortune are thought of as often being
somehow "deserved." And just as orthodox Christianity threatened wrongdoers with hell fire in the
afterlife, so the Nyoro ghost cult threatens them
with illness or other misfortune in this life.

It is of interest that it is the kind of relationship
between ghost and victim, even more than the
degree of enormity of the precipitating offense, that
is held to determine the severity of the ghost's
attack. A man's closest ties are with his father and
his kin, but although the father's ghost can and
sometimes does punish his children, its attack is
rarely fatal, and often it is thought (unlike other
ghosts) to be benevolent. This is not surprising, for
a man in a sense lives through his children, who will
remember him and honor his name, and a Nyoro
thinks of himself as "of one blood" with his father
and with the surviving members of the agnatic
descent group to which he belongs. Here also other
and more pragmatic sanctions come into play. Even
after his father's death, a man probably has—and
certainly would have had in traditional times—
other agnatic kinsmen with whom in his own inter-

est he is bound to maintain friendly and co-operative
relations.

This is less so in regard to one's mother's people,
who belong to a lineage and clan other than one's
own (though here, at least as regards the mother, the
relationship is usually tempered by close affection).
Thus a mother's brother's ghost, and even her
sister's, are said to be more dangerous than paternal
ghosts. But the most dangerous of all related ghosts
is that of a sister's son, who is an "outsider" as no
other relative is; "a sister's son is outside" (*omwihwa
aheru*), say the Nyoro. Though a man's mother's
brothers are all members of the same clan or descent
group, his classificatory sisters' children are likely to
be scattered in many groups and so to be widely dispersed. His relationship with them is consequently
ambivalent; though he is their "male mother," and
they are his "children," they are also in some sense
strangers, "outsiders," for they are not members of
his own or his mother's clan but of "outside" clans
whose members have married women of his own
clan (see Beattie 1958 on the ambivalence of the relationship between mother's brother and sister's son).

The more "outside" a ghost is, the more dangerous it can be. Thus unrelated ghosts, as we saw earlier, may be among the most dangerous of all. The
ghosts of former domestic slaves, of blood partners
(who are by definition of separate clans), and of
wandering unnamed ghosts are among the most difficult to deal with. Outsiders are feared, and they
must therefore be treated with special care and consideration. This fear is expressed in the ghost cult.

There is yet another aspect to this way of distinguishing between ghosts in terms of their potency.
In Bunyoro most social relationships are hierarchi-
cally conceived, so that in any relationship one partner is thought to be superordinate, the other subordinate. In several contexts, it seems that occupation
of a role of social or political subordination may be,
as it were, compensated for by the ascription to the
inferior of a kind of ritual superiority. Thus the
Nyoro say that a sister's son has ritual (though not
of course secular) power over his mother's brother,
whom he is said to "rule" (*kulema*), even though he
stands to him in the subordinate and inferior relationship of "child." And it may be supposed, as was

noted earlier, that the ascription of a special ritual potency to captives used as household slaves (who of course had no secular means of enforcing any claims against their owners) must have operated as a strong sanction against maltreating them.

An effect of culture contact, and especially of the advent of a cash economy, on Nyoro possession cults and on the techniques of divination with which they are associated has been to increase the profits available to ritual specialists, and so to further the proliferation of many such cults. All Nyoro believe that some diviners and mediums are charlatans, but few believe that all of them are. But although Western influence has led to a great proliferation of cult activity in the context of the spirit (*mbandwa*) cult, it seems to have had no comparable effect on the ghost cult.

This is simply explained. It follows from the nature of the ghost cult that it should exhibit less structural modification under the influence of Western contact than either the mbandwa spirit cult (which has readily assimilated many new and inimical forces deriving from the contact situation by turning them into *mbandwa* spirits) or the complex of sorcery beliefs, in which some *mbandwa* spirits play a significant role. For ghosts are personal powers, they are left by people with whom one has had dealings when they were alive, and for all practical purposes these are now, as they have always been, other Nyoro. Unlike other kinds of spirits, therefore, ghosts cannot proliferate into a variety of new kinds any more than people themselves can. Ghosts are, as they always were, spirits of the dead; they cannot be anything else.

Consistently with this, it is my impression (though one that in the nature of the case it is difficult to confirm) that, although recourse to spirit mediumship has certainly not declined in recent years, and may even be increasing, explanation by diviners of illness and miscarriage as due to ghosts is decreasing and is giving way to explanation in terms of the now very extensive Nyoro pantheon of nonhuman spirits. Certainly I have recorded many more cases of possession by *mbandwa* spirits than of possession by ghosts. Further, as we have noted, except in one small and distinctive region of Bunyoro the cult of the patrilineal ancestral ghosts, regarded as in some

sense a collectivity, is no longer practiced. I have, indeed, no firm evidence that it was more widely practiced in the past than it is now, but the Nyoro say that it was, and the term for the ancestral cult, *ibembo,* is known throughout Bunyoro. Such a decline would be consistent with the breakdown of an older type of residential grouping in which, even if residence was never wholly in lineage terms as it is among some neighboring peoples, local groups were firmly centered on patrilineal descent groups, and solidarity among a group of close agnates was a primary social value at the community level.

ENDNOTES

1. I carried out field work in Bunyoro, western Uganda, for about 22 months, during 1951–53 and 1955, mostly under the auspices of the Treasury Committee for Studentships in Foreign Languages and Cultures, whose support I gratefully acknowledge. The Nyoro are, for good reasons, very unwilling to discuss their traditional cults, and much of the information given in this paper could not have been obtained without the help of my two Nyoro assistants, the late Perezi Mpuru and the late Lameki Kikubebe. The deaths of these two young men, one while I was in the field and the other last year, are a grievous loss to Nyoro ethnography.

2. In the Nyoro language (*Lunyoro* or *Runyoro*) one Nyoro is a *Munyoro,* two or more are *Banyoro.* In the interest of simplicity I omit these prefixes except in the name of the country itself, Bunyoro. I also omit initial vowels throughout, except in reproduced texts, for the same reason; thus I write *muzimu* (ghost) instead of *omuzimu,* and so on.

3. I owe this and other plant identifications to Davis 1938.

4. I give below the words of four such songs. Like *mbandwa* songs (Beattie 1961: 33–35), they contain a good deal of repetition as well as unverbalized humming and ululation. They are sung to the accompaniment of the gourd rattles of the *bafumu* who are present. I was unable to get a clear account of the meaning of all of them (if indeed they all have clear meanings), but they may be worth putting on record nonetheless.

   (1) *Tiguli muzimu idobora ahaha idobora:*
       It is not a ghost, ahaha, it is a very very big thing.

   (2) *Tete alemere balete nyamukanura ahaha ehehe Tete alemere:*
       Tete has been overcome; let them bring the sudden destroyer; ahaha, ehehe, Tete has been overcome.

   (3) *Eihembe karondoza, ihembe karondoza; alire enaku, ihembe:*
       The Horn which Searchs Things Out, the Horn which Searches Things Out; he may cry poverty, the Horn.

   (4) *Kahembe ruiragura tema enkorra nonaga; bwoya bw'atorogo terebukire:*
       The Small Black Horn, cut bean leaves and throw them away; the hair of atorogo [?] has slipped away [i.e., has escaped].

5. Every Nyoro child is given one of the eleven or so special *mpako* names, which are supposedly of Nilotic origin. Their use in everyday discourse implies friendly intimacy.

6. The use of this word seems to contradict the idea that ghosts "rise" into the head of the medium, but the implication here is of violent attack.

7. This rite of putting food into another's mouth is called *kubegera*. It symbolizes amity and close attachment, as between a mother and her child.

8. This may reflect the fact that the relationship between mother's brother and sister's son in Bunyoro is an ambivalent and highly institutionalized one, with specific ritual obligations on both sides (cf. Beattie 1958: 17–22).

BIBLIOGRAPHY

Beattie, J. H. M. 1957. Initiation into the Cwezi Spirit Possession Cult in Bunyoro. African Studies 16:150–161.

____. 1958. Nyoro Marriage and Affinity. Africa 28: 1–22.

____. 1960. Bunyoro: An African Kingdom. New York.

____. 1961. Group Aspects of the Nyoro Spirit Mediumship Cult. Rhodes-Livingstone Journal 30: 11–38.

____. 1963. Sorcery in Bunyoro. Witchcraft and Sorcery in East Africa, ed. J. Middleton, pp. 27–55. London.

Davis, M. B. 1938. A Lunyoro-Lunyankole-English and English-Lunyoro-Lunyankole Dictionary. London.

Fortes, M. 1945. The Dynamics of Clanship among the Tallensi. London.

Middleton, J. 1960. Lugbara Religion. London.

READING 3–4

THE UNIVERSALITY OF ANCESTOR WORSHIP

Lyle B. Steadman, Craig T. Palmer, and Christopher F. Tilley

The three authors of this article have searched the published works on spiritual agencies and conclude that ancestor worship is universal. They further find that ancestor rituals appear to be more widely performed than rituals directed toward a creator-god. The evidence they provide is quite convincing, though some anthropologists would probably argue that in order to bring some of their ethnographic examples within the framework of their def-

Source: Ethnology 35, no. 1 (1996), pp. 63–76.

initions they have stretched the term "ancestor worship" too generously. Even if this objection is sustainable the extensive occurrence of rituals by which human beings signal their respect for spirits related to them by kinship is striking, and is consistent with the importance they assume in Tylor's theory about the evolution of religious beliefs, though of course this generality does not "prove" the theory correct.

A "professional malpractice of anthropologists to exaggerate the exotic character of other cultures" (Bloch 1977:285) has been detrimental to the study of cultural universals. This is highly regrettable because "universals not only exist but are important to any broad conception of the task of anthropology" (Brown 1991:5). Further, in the anthropological study of indigenous religions, a focus on differences has caused an apparently universal aspect of religion to be overlooked: the claim that ancestors influence the living and/or are influenced by the living. We argue here that such claims of communication between the dead and their descendants are universal and may be the key to understanding the universality of religious belief.

Claims of ancestor interaction with the living have not been recognized as universal because the anthropologists' stress on differences has caused them to be overly narrow in their definitions of both "ancestor" and "worship." Hence, they have tended to overlook the fundamental similarities between religions that have ancestor worship and those that are said to lack it. This division is theoretically significant because even when ancestor worship is found in a majority of the cultures used in a study (e.g., Swanson 1964), its nonuniversality requires it to be explained in terms of unique aspects of certain cultures (see Swanson 1964:97–108). If ancestor worship were recognized as a universal aspect of religion, its explanation would offer a deeper understanding of religious behavior.

One reason for the inability to recognize the universality of ancestor worship is that the term is often reserved for those societies where the dead are explicitly called by a term that is translated as ancestor, thus excluding societies whose religious practices concern ghosts, shades, spirits, souls, totemic plants and animals, or merely the dead. For example, Lehmann and Myers (1993:284) state that

> [a] major problem with Spencer's argument [that ancestor worship was the first religion] is that many societies at the hunting-and-gathering level do not practice ancestor worship. The Arunta of Australia, for example, worshiped their totemic plants and animals, but not their human ancestors.

Distinguishing between ancestors and totemic plants and animals is questionable since totems are clearly ancestral in that they identify a person with a line of ancestors (e.g., one's father, father's father, etc.). Indeed, Harris (1989:405) points out that the Australian form of totemism "is a form of diffuse ancestor worship . . . [because by] taking the name of an animal such as kangaroo . . . people express a communal obligation to the founders of their kinship group."

The role of ancestors is also obscured in many descriptions of societies whose religions are based on more general, and hence, supposedly nonancestral, spirits or gods. An example of this is the hunters and gatherers living in the Kalahari who are often referred to as the !Kung. Although Lee (1984:103) does state that the !Kung's "religious universe is inhabited by a high god, a lesser god, and a host of minor animal spirits," he also states that "the main actors in [the !Kung's religious] world are the *//gangwasi,* the ghosts of recently deceased !Kung" (Lee 1984:103).

The failure to see the connection between ancestors and spirits or gods often causes societies to be excluded from the ancestor worship category. For example, Lehmann and Myers (1993:284) state that

> [w]hen the living dead are forgotten in the memory of their group and dropped from the genealogy as a result of the passing of time (four or five generations), they are believed to be transformed into "nameless spirits," non-ancestors. . . .

Similarly, Tonkinson (1978:52) claims that the Mardu lack ancestor worship because they cannot remember the names of specific distant ancestors, despite the fact that their religious rituals focus on "Ancestral Beings." The Yanomamo provide a similar example because their religion is said to be shamanic and concerned with spirits instead of ancestors. Although it is true that Yanomamo religion centers on shamans ingesting hallucinogenic drugs and controlling spirits, Chagnon (1983:92) reports that "when the original people [the *no badabo*] died, they turned into spirits: *hekura.*" Since the no badabo were clearly the original Yanomamo, ancestors are actually central to Yanomamo religion (see Steadman and Palmer 1994). Indeed, it is crucial to realize that whenever there is reference to ghosts, spirits, or the dead in a society's religion, ancestors will be present, if not predominant, in this category.

An overly narrow definition of the term, worship, is also often used to claim that certain societies lack ancestor worship. Many societies indeed do if the meaning of worship is restricted to elaborate ceremonies involving ritualized sacrifices. If, however, the term worship is used in its broader sense of reverence or respect, the claim that ancestor worship is not universal is open to question. Further, several anthropologists have pointed out that worship may not be the most accurate term to describe even those societies unquestionably assumed to have ancestor worship. For example, in a discussion of some of the classic ancestral cults of Africa, Abraham (1966:63) states that the rituals associated with ancestors "are not rites of worship but methods of communication."

If the essence of ancestor worship is the claim that there is communication between ancestors and the living, then this behavior should be tested as a possible universal aspect of religion. Hence, we reexamined the ethnographic material used in what is perhaps the most famous cross-cultural study of religion (Swanson 1964) to determine if there is evidence of claims that ancestors can influence or be influenced by the living, even in those societies coded in the study as lacking ancestor worship.

METHODOLOGY

The societies coded in Swanson's (1964) sample were selected for two reasons. First, the study is well respected, often cited, and adequately deals with many of the problems involved in cross-cultural research (see Naroll 1970; Palmer 1989a). Second, the question relevant to the issue of communication between ancestors and the living (column 29 in Swanson 1964) is worded in a way nearly perfect for the purposes of the present study:

Active Ancestral Spirits:
0. Absent—dead ancestors do not influence the living
1. Present—nature of activity unspecified
2. Present—aid or punish living humans
3. Present—are invoked by the living to assist in earthly affairs (Swanson 1964:210–11)

Category 2 clearly indicates the presence of the claim that ancestors influence the living, and category 3 implies the claim that the dead can be influenced by the living. Hence, this study will examine the sixteen societies (32 percent of the sample) coded as "0" (Absent—ancestors do not influence the living) and the eight societies (16 percent of the sample) coded as "1" (Present—nature of activity unspecified). The purpose of this re-examination is not to discredit Swanson's valuable work, but to determine if a universal aspect of religious behavior lies undiscovered within the ethnographic data he surveyed.

RESULTS

The Sixteen Cultures Coded: "Ancestors Absent"

Azande   The Azande represented the geographical region of Africa-Equitoria. Zande life is filled with references to witches, ghosts, and other supernatural phenomena, and descriptions by Evans-Pritchard make it clear that these include ancestors who are claimed to both influence and be influenced by the living. For example, Evans-Pritchard (1937:39) states:

We may ask whether the distinction between witches, *aboro mangu,* and those who are not witches, *amokundu,* is maintained beyond the grave? I have never been given a spontaneous statement to this effect, but in answer to direct and leading questions I

have on one or two occasions been told that when witches die they become evil ghosts (*agirisa*). [These evil ghosts contrast with] *Atoro,* the ordinary ghosts, [who] are benevolent beings, at least as benevolent as a Zande father of the family, and their occasional participation in the world they have left behind them is on the whole orderly and conducive to the welfare of their children.

The passage indicates that the Azande did sometimes claim that ancestors influence the living. Evans-Pritchard (1974:101) also describes a plea from the living to the dead that demonstrates that the Azande also claimed that ancestors can be influenced by the living:

O Deleakowe are not the ghosts with God? If you favour me as you favoured me in your lifetime! Since you died leaving your son, your son has been very unhappy, for his kinsmen dislike him. O our father, our husband, give us fortune together with your son so we may praise the ghosts and say that the ghosts judge well. Since you died things have gone ill with your offspring, he has not begotten children. It would seem that the ghosts refuse him a child. May he beget a child after this blessing with which we have come today to bless him.

Aztec   The Aztecs represented the geographical region of Mexico. Although Vaillant (1944) claims that the Aztecs lacked ancestor worship, he makes several statements demonstrating that the living were claimed to be able to influence ancestors; e.g., "The rest of the dead passed to Mictlan, the underworld. They had to overcome several hazards before they could take up their life there, so they were equipped [by the living] with charms and gifts for the journey" (Vaillant 1944:179). Another example of the living being claimed to influence the dead is the statement that "[t]hen he [the deceased person] reached a broad river which he crossed on the back of a little red dog, sometimes included in the grave furniture for the purpose" (Vaillant 1944:179). Further, Conrad and Demarest (1984:152) state that the Aztec had "a dividing line between life and death so blurred that living people conversed and partied with the dead."

Blackfoot The Blackfoot represented the North America-Plains region. McClintock's (1910) description of their ghost stories clearly indicates that the Blackfoot claimed that the dead could influence the living: "She [a woman named Mistina], like many others, had been deeply impressed by the fact that many well-known Indians had died during the summer and their spirits had been appearing to the living, bringing fear and sometimes even death" (McClintock 1910:139–40). That these dead include ancestors is demonstrated in the ghost story of Two Strikes and Running Rabbit: "[S]he beheld the spirit of her father, Running Rabbit, who had touched her. Not long afterwards Two Strikes died very suddenly and her family believe that Running Rabbit took her with him to the spirit world" (McClintock 1910:141). The fact that the Blackfoot took elaborate care of their dead, sometimes carrying a skeleton "in a raw hide bag for many years" (McClintock 1910:150), also suggests that the dead could be influenced by kindly treatment.

Cuna The Cuna represented the South America-Circum-Caribbean region. Stout (1947:40–42) makes numerous references to living Cuna making offerings to dead relatives, whose "souls" or "spirits" sometimes appear to them and cause "illness, misfortune, and death."

Iban The Iban represented the Oceania-Indonesia region. Their conception of the *ngarong* (secret helper) indicates that they sometimes claimed that ancestors could influence the living. Although the *ngarong* is not always claimed to be an ancestor, Hose and McDougall (1912:92) state that it "seems to be usually the spirit of some ancestor or dead relative . . . [who] becomes the special protector of some individual Iban." Iban discourse about *ngarong* also suggests that the living can influence the dead. For example, an informant stated that "[h]e himself has none *[ngarong],* but he will not kill the gibbon because the *ngarong* of his grandfather, who died twenty years ago, was a gibbon" (Hose and McDougall 1912:91). Although the man may have avoided killing gibbons solely out of respect for his grandfather, this statement suggests

that killing the gibbon would have negatively affected his dead grandfather.

Lengua The Lengua represented the South American-Gran Chaco region. Their description is full of examples of claims both that the living could influence the dead and that ancestors could influence the living.

> There is a general belief that ghosts linger around a camp and are dangerous, or at least unpleasant to meet. . . . The near relatives of the deceased or, if he were a chief, the members of the extended family, took a new name hoping to deceive the ghost, who might have been tempted to return and drag his fellow tribesmen with him to the afterworld. (Metraux 1963:333)

Metraux (1963:334) also states that "Lengua mourners, fearful of ghosts, often sought the hospitality of some other band. These Indians believed that the chilly spirit of the departed man would return to his deserted camp looking for a fire." Finally, the Lengua "did not like to leave this world without atoning for wrongs done to a fellow member of the band, lest the quarrel be continued in the hereafter" (Metraux 1963:334).

Lepcha The Lepcha represented the Eurasia-Central Asia region. They appear to represent a case similar to that of the Yanomamo in that the ancestral nature of their deities and spirits has been overlooked by anthropologists. For example, von Furer-Haimendorf (1987:327) describes their religion as "based on the worship of local deities and a variety of nature spirits, whose cult is in the hands of shamans." The ancestral nature of these deities and spirits, however, becomes clear in the subsequent description:

> In the old Lepcha religion the ability to act as priest depends on possession by a spirit attached to a lineage of priestly character. The chief function of a priest is to ward off the misfortunes and afflictions caused by malevolent spirits; this can be achieved by animal sacrifices as well as by direct communication with supernatural powers. On certain occasions, priests become possessed by their tutelary spirit, to whom they owe the gift of prophecy. At funerary ceremonies the priest summons the soul of the deceased to speak his last

words through the priest's mouth and then conducts it into the sphere of the gods. (von Furer-Haimendorf 1987:327)

This statement indicates that Lepcha priests were claimed to assist the dead and be influenced by the dead, and evidence suggests that the spirits in Lepcha religion were not just vague spirits, but the spirits of deceased Lepcha:

> On some occasions of great importance a Lepcha shaman, who may be male or female, becomes possessed by the spirit of a semilegendary Lepcha chieftain believed to have ruled the Lepcha country when the first Tibetan settlers arrived in Sikkim. (von Furer-Haimendorf 1987:327).

Gorer (1938:231) also states that the "Mun worship two supernaturals, *Hit rum* and *De num,* who are considered to be ancestral gods who look after all dead Lephchas."

Nez Perces   The Nez Perces represented the North America-Plateau region. Beal (1966) makes it clear that the "Guardian Spirit," *Wyakin,* who forms the center of Nez Perces religion, was closely associated with the spirits of the dead, which presumably included ancestors:

> [T]he Nez Perces believed in immortality of all life. The individual's relationship to the spirits (powers and principalities) might be intimate indeed. He could invoke them to serve in the role of guide and protector. The key to this relationship was known as *Wyakin.* (Beal 1966:12)

Pomo   The Pomo Indians represent the North America-California region.[1] Bean and Theodoratus (1978:297) describe a "ghost impersonating ceremony [that] was traditionally performed as an act of atonement for offenses against the dead." The Pomo also made offerings to dead relatives: "A second burning took place one year later, at which time friends and relatives brought additional gifts for offering to the deceased" (Bean and Theodoratus 1978:297).

Romans   The Romans represent the Eurasia-Europe region. Fustel de Coulanges (1956) indicates that ancestor worship was a vital part of

Roman life, and there are clear examples of claims that ancestors influence the living and are influenced by the living even in the descriptions of Roman religion given by authors who say that the Romans did not practice ancestor worship. For example, Bailey (1932:39–40) argues that the Romans lacked ancestor worship because the "evil spirits" involved in religious rituals "are thought of vaguely and collectively: in no case are they in any sense individualized." But he states that the Lemuria festival "represents a very primitive attitude towards the family dead, in which they are regarded as tiresome ghosts" (Bailey 1932:98–99), and describes the festival:

> The father of the house rises at midnight and after purification by washing of hands, takes black beans and casts them over his shoulder without looking back, saying at the time "with these beans I redeem myself and my family." Nine times he repeats the spell and the charm, and the ghosts come behind him and gather up the beans. He washes once more and clangs brass vessels. Nine times he repeats the formula "Ghosts of my fathers, depart," and then the purification is complete. (Bailey 1932:39)

Samoyed   The Samoyed, specifically the Ostyak Samoyed, represented the Eurasia-Arctic Eurasia region. Czaplicka (1951:176) states that, "[w]ith the exception of the Ostyak Samoyed, the Samoyedic tribes are much more given to ancestor- and hero-worship than to animal worship." But even with the animal worship of the Ostyak Samoyed, ancestors are claimed to influence, and be influenced by, the living. "Kai Donner found that along the river Tym the Ostyak Samoyed consider their highest god the 'grandfather of the clan,' who is worshipped under various names, while the Ostyak Samoyed along the river Ket symbolize him by a living bear" (Czaplicka 1951:175). The claim that the Ostyak Samoyed practice animal worship instead of ancestor worship is another instance of failing to realize that the totem animal is simply a symbol for the ancestor. Indeed, not only does Czaplicka (1951:175) report that these people "believe in the transformation of man into an animal, and vice versa," he states that

Itte, the hero of the epic of the Ostyak Samoyed recorded by Kai Donner, had by one of his wives, the daughter of Massullozi, "Forest-Spirit," a son, "Bear-spirit" (*Pargaikuorgai lozi* or *Pargai* meaning "bear-spirit"); from this son the Samoyed of the Ket river derive their descent. For this reason they call themselves *Kuorgai-Tamder,* "race of bears." (Czaplicka 1951:177)

Finally, Czaplicka contradicts his original exclusion of the Ostyak Samoyed from the category of societies possessing ancestor worship when he states that "[t]he worshipping of a tribal ancestor is common to all the Samoyed, and endowing him with the form of a bear may merely indicate his unusual origin" (Czaplicka 1951:177).

Donner (1954) reports that "[t]he most important deity in the religious life of the Samoyed and the one who has the most decisive significance is undoubtedly *Kuodargup* or the tribal father of each individual tribe" (Donner 1954:71). He also describes offerings to the dead and says that "[t]he spirits of powerful shamans, who have been dead for a long time, can bewitch people for years to come" (Donner 1954:75).

Shoshoni   The Shoshoni represented the North America-Great Basin region. Hints of ancestors are found in Trenholm's and Carley's (1964:8) statement that the Shoshoni's "vague imaginings for religion' amounted to a simple faith dependent upon the spirit, the *mugua,* and the ghost, the *tsoap.*" More explicit references are found in Shoshoni origin mythology concerning Coyote: "The Northern Shoshonis accept the fact that Coyote and his unnamed sorceress were their ancestors" (Trenholm and Carley 1964:35). Coyote was often referred to as "father," and sometimes took human form: "I had seen the Father. He was a handsome Indian" (Trenholm and Carley 1964:35). That the Shosoni were careful not to "displease Coyote" (Trenholm and Carley 1964:36) suggests that Shosoni claimed ancestors could be influenced by the living.

Todas   The Todas represented the Eurasia-Greater India region. Rivers (1906) asserts that the Todas do not practice ancestor worship, evidently on the basis that the Todas worship certain hills that are the residences of gods. These gods, however, were

linked to known persons: "In the case of Kwoten, the account of his life is so circumstantial as to leave little doubt that he was a real man who was deified after a mysterious disappearance" (Rivers 1906:446). It is also clear that these deified Todas, who were regularly claimed to be influenced by the living, were often explicitly associated with ancestors: "Thus, when Teitnir gave a buffalo after the death of his wife, some said it was given to the gods, while others said it was given to Teitnir's grandfather, and when I tried to inquire more definitely into this point the two things were said to be the same" (Rivers 1906:446–47).

Trumai   The Trumai represented the Mato-Grosso region of South America. It is clear that ancestors played a major role in Trumai religion because Murphy and Quain (1955:72) refer to the Trumai's anthropomorphic creator deities who existed "in the dim past of the 'grandfathers of all the Trumai.'" Although they state that "the day-to-day world of the Trumai was little influenced by extra-corporeal forces or personages" (Murphy and Quain 1955:72), they make several statements indicating that the ancestral personages could be influenced by, and influence, the living (e.g., "offerings" were made during the *ole* ceremony to supernatural entities such as *Nukekerehe,* who was said to eat people who stayed up too late); and that "numerous cooking utensils . . . were buried with both male and female deceased" (Murphy and Quain 1955:90) suggests that the Trumai thought that such gifts could be used by their deceased kin.

Winnebago   The Winnebago represented the North America-Prairie region. Radin (1963) reports numerous instances of ancestors influencing the living similar to the following statement concerning ritual fasting: "Then another spirit would come and say, 'Well, grandson, I have taken pity upon you and I bless you with all the good things that the earth holds'" (Radin 1963:7).

Yurok   The Yurok represented the North America-Northwest Coast region. That the Yurok claimed to be able to influence the dead is clearly indicated by the fact that the Yurok man makes "a fire on the grave to keep his dead kinsman warm" (Hartland 1951:417). Meyer (1971:268) also states that Yurok religion teaches a man to "love his relatives even after death."

The Eight Cultures Coded: "Ancestors Present—Nature of Activity Unspecified"

Arunta The Arunta represented the Australia region. Spencer and Gillen's (1968) description of the ancestral spirit, *Ulthana,* reveals claims of the dead influencing, and being influenced by, the living:

> During the period of mourning . . . no person must mention the name of the deceased . . . for fear of disturbing and annoying the man's spirit, which in ghost form, or as they call it, *Ulthana,* walks about. If the *Ulthana* hears his name he comes to the conclusion that his relatives are not properly mourning for him . . . and so he will come and trouble them in their sleep, to show them that he's not pleased. (Spencer and Gillen 1968:498; see also 494–97)

Carib The Carib represented the Guiana geographic region. Rouse (1963) provides clear indications of interaction between ancestors and the living among the Carib when he reports that the people, probably family members, built fires around "the grave to purify it and to prevent the deceased from catching cold. . . . [I]n prehistoric times a slave or dog was killed and put in the grave to care for the dead person" (Rouse 1963:559). Each Carib took one of these spirits as his or her personal deity (*ichieri*), who was given offerings because such spirits could "insure good crops and safeguard crops" or, in the case of evil spirits (*maboya*) be blamed for "disagreeable and frightening occurrences" (Rouse 1963:562). The ancestral nature of these spirits is confirmed by Rouse's statement (1963:562) that "[s]ome shamans kept in their houses the hair or bones of their ancestors, which were supposed to contain *maboya.*"

Carrier The Carrier represented the Subarctic America region. Morice (1951) reports claims of the dead (presumably including ancestors) interacting with the living. Indeed, this may be the basis for their name:

> When the ashes of the pyer had cooled down, she [the widow] would go, shedding many a dutiful tear, and pick up the few remnants of bones which had escaped the flames. These she placed in a small satchel, which thenceforth she had to carry on her person till the day—three or four years later—of her liberation from the unspeakably hard bondage into which she had entered. This custom, which seems to have no parallel among the American aborigines, is responsible for the distinctive name of the Carrier tribe. . . .

> A further proof of the Carriers' belief in the immortality of the soul may be gathered from their dread of ghosts, which they declare to be very sensitive to the mention of the names they bore in their earthly existence; hence, mention of these names is carefully avoided. (Morice 1951:230)

Dobuans The Dobuans represented Melanesia. Fortune (1932) provides clear evidence that talk about the spirits of ancestors interacting with the living played a large part in both their totemism and the elaborate magic for which the Dobuans are famous:

> In Melanesia generally if misfortune is not attributed to the black art [magic] it is attributed to the spirits of the dead. . . . We have seen that a few spirits of the first ancestors of man are conceived as the familiars who do the magician's bidding. (Fortune 1932: 178)

Further, "the first ancestors still exist, and exert the same influence that legend vouches for their having exerted some five generations ago" (Fortune 1932:99).

Iroquois The Iroquois represented the eastern woodlands of North America. Burland (1985:64) states that the Iroquois have "a great number of ancestral spirits. Not only did the ancestors watch over men in their daily activities, but they could also be visited in dreams." According to St. John (1989:136), "Iroquois both respect and fear the dead and therefore conduct a number of feasts for them."

Yagua The Yagua represented Amazonia. Steward and Metraux's (1963) summary of Fejos (1943) makes it clear that the Yagua claim that ancestors interact with the living:

> The souls of the dead are thought to dwell on a hill and to have no interest in living people except when they

return for a chicha feast, at which men wearing Ficus bast masks impersonate them and drink the chicha. Yagua belief assigns souls a place in the sky, where they do not eat or work but from which they occasionally return unseen to drink chicha and to play tricks on the living. (Steward and Metraux 1963:735–36)

Yahgan The Yahgan represented Patagonia, and although Cooper (1963:102) claims that "no organized cult existed and the dead were not prayed to," he also provides evidence that ancestors are claimed to interact with the living:

> There was a distinct fear of the dead; . . . the souls of the dead shamans entered into the beliefs and practices of the medicine men. . . . There was a very definite belief in a Supreme Being called *Watauinewa* or *Watanuineiwa,* who was also called by other names meaning "The Powerful One," "The Highest One," and especially by the name of "My Father." (Cooper 1963:102–03)

Yukots The Yukots represented California. Wallace (1978) provides evidence for ancestors interacting with the living. First he states that "[a] totem symbol peculiar to his paternal line was transmitted by a father to all his children; it was an animal or bird that no member would kill or eat and that was dreamed of and prayed to" (Wallace 1978:453). He also states that "[v]arious personal effects of the deceased were interred with the body and a dog was sometimes sacrificed" (Wallace 1978:455). Kroeber (1925:509) also notes that "[t]o ward off danger of the dead person's return, a short prayer was addressed to him. . . ."

DISCUSSION

Evidence of claims that ancestors influence the living and/or are influenced by the living have been found in all 24 of the societies coded by Swanson as lacking ancestor worship. This means that such claims about communication between ancestors and their living descendants are found in all of the societies in Swanson's cross-cultural sample. This

suggests that such behavior may be a universal aspect of religion.

This suggestion lies midway between the generally accepted views exemplified by the following statement: "Although the worship of ancestors is not universal, a belief in the immortality of the dead occurs in all cultures" (Lehmann and Myers 1993:283). That is, even if ancestor worship is not universal (which may be true if ancestor worship is defined in its most restrictive sense) all religions may have more in common than the mere assertion of the immortality of the dead.

This is important because the explanation of belief in an afterlife is that it fulfills the human need to reduce the anxiety felt when confronted with death. Although widely cited, this explanation, usually credited to Malinowski (1922, 1948) but owing more of its origin to Marrett (1914), has been subject to several criticisms (see Kroeber 1948; Radcliffe-Brown 1939; Evans-Pritchard 1965; Palmer 1989b). The anxiety reduction explanation also fails to account for the findings presented here. If anxiety reduction were the function of religious behavior, the claim of the continued existence of souls in an afterlife would be sufficient. Hence, the anxiety reduction hypothesis cannot account for the apparently universal additional claim of communication between the living and the dead.

To explain why claims of communication between the living and the dead appear to occur universally, we suggest that it is necessary to understand that the spirits of the dead are those of ancestors. This suggests that religions are closely linked to kinship relations in indigenous society because "[i]n such societies, it might not be an exaggeration to say that kinship relations are tantamount to social relations" (Ferraro 1992:175). Ancestors are particularly important to indigenous societies because they are the source of a society's traditions: "a system of information, support and guidance" (Hefner 1991:123) on how to relate to one's physical and social environment (Steadman and Palmer In press). The Lugbara of sub-Saharan Africa say that "the rules of social behavior are 'the words of our ancestors' " (Middleton 1960: 27), and Rivers

(1906:445) states that "[t]he Todas are the slaves of their traditions and the laws and regulations which have been handed down to them by their ancestors."

Religious rituals that focused on ancestors could strengthen kinship ties and the traditions on which they depend:

> Evidently the family-cult in primitive times, must have greatly tended to maintain the family bond: alike by causing periodic assemblings for sacrifice, by repressing dissensions, and by producing conformity to the same injunctions. (Spencer 1972:218)

The claim that ancestors can influence the living and be influenced by them may have been a part of such rituals because it strengthened kin ties and the transmission of traditions in two ways. First, the reference to long-dead ancestors provided a means of involving many more co-descendants than the few who could trace their common ancestry through only a few generations. Second, as Rappaport (1979:262) points out, supernatural claims, such as that ancestors influence the living or are influenced by them, establish "the quality of unquestionable truthfulness." Such claims about ancestors promote the acceptance of traditions because, "although one can argue to a point with an elder, no one questions the wisdom and authority of an ancestor" (Lehmann and Myers 1993:285; see also Fortes 1976:2; Steadman and Palmer 1994, 1995).

In kinship-based societies the connection between religion and ancestors is fairly direct. Not only do their religious leaders communicate with ancestors (Steadman and Palmer 1994), they often memorize the genealogies of the people in their society. Under such conditions the "ancestor" in "ancestor worship" can often be taken quite literally.

Finally, a comment about world religions. If ancestor worship really lies at the heart of religion, there should be evidence of this even in world religions. Although a discussion of world religions is beyond the scope of this article, we suggest that what distinguishes world religions is that they are not confined to groups of people who consider

themselves kin. Hence, references to actual ancestors would not serve the function of creating close social bonds among the members of the religion. Such bonds would have to be only kinship-like. Perhaps this is why world religions often lack references to actual ancestors, but sometimes place great emphasis on metaphorical common ancestors, such as "God the Father," that can serve as a basis for co-operative relations among the members of a world religion (Steadman and Palmer 1995).

ENDNOTE

1. Swanson (1964) specifies "northern groups" without further precision. For this re-examination, using Pomo may unintentionally misrepresent the practices of "northern groups" of Pomo. Also of note, the Pomo had participated in the Peyote Cult of 1889, and it is unclear what effect this movement may have had with respect to their talk about ghosts, spirits, etc.

BIBLIOGRAPHY

Abraham, W. E. 1966. The Mind of Africa. Chicago.

Bailey, C. 1932. Phases in the Religion of Ancient Rome. Berkeley.

Beal, M. D. 1966. I Will Fight No More Forever. Seattle.

Bean, L. J., and D. Theodoratus. 1978. Western Pomo and Northeastern Pomo. Handbook of North American Indians, Vol. 8, ed. R. F. Heizer, pp. 289–305. Washington DC.

Bloch, M. 1977. The Past and the Present in the Present. Man 12:278–92.

Brown, D. T. 1991. Human Universals. New York.

Burland, C. 1985. North American Indian Mythology. New York.

Chagnon, N. 1983. Yanomamo: The Fierce People. New York.

Conrad, G. W., and A. A. Demarest. 1984. Religion and Empire. Cambridge.

Cooper, J. M. 1963. The Yahgan. Handbook of South American Indians, ed. J. Steward, pp. 81–105. New York.

Czaplicka, M. A. 1951. Samoyed. Encyclopedia of Religion and Ethics, Vol. 11, eds. J. Hastings, J. A. Selbie, and L. H. Gray, pp. 172–77. New York.

Donner, K. 1954. Among the Samoyed in Siberia, transl. R. Kyler. New Haven.

Evans-Pritchard, E. E. 1937. Witchcraft, Oracles and Magic Among the Azande. New York.

———. 1965. Theories of Primitive Religion. New York.

———. 1974. Man and Woman Among the Azande. New York.

Fejos, P. 1943. Ethnography of the Yagua. New York.

Ferraro, G. 1992. Cultural Anthropology: An Applied Perspective. St. Louis.

Fortes, M. 1976. An Introductory Commentary. Ancestors, ed. W. H. Newell, pp. 1–16. The Hague.

Fortune, R. F. 1932. Sorcerers of Dobu. New York.

Fustel de Coulanges, N. D. 1956. The Ancient City. Garden City NJ.

Gorer, G. 1938. Himalayan Village, An Account of the Lepchas of Sikkim. London.

Harris, M. 1989. Our Kind. New York.

Hartland, E. S. 1951. Death and Disposal of the Dead. Encyclopedia of Religion and Ethics, Vol. 4, eds. J. Hastings, J. A. Selbie, and L. H. Gray, pp. 411–44. New York.

Hefner, P. 1991. Myth and Morality: The Love Command. Zygon 26:115–36.

Hose, C., and W. McDougall. 1912. The Pagan Tribes of Borneo. London.

Kroeber, A. L. 1925. Elements of Culture in Native California. The California Indians: A Source Book, eds. R. F. Heizer and M. A. Whipple, pp. 3–65. Berkeley.

———. 1948. Anthropology. New York.

Lee, R. 1984. The Dobe !Kung. New York.

Lehmann, A. C., and J. E. Myers. 1993. Ghosts, Souls, and Ancestors: Power of the Dead. Magic, Witchcraft, and Religion, eds. A. C. Lehmann and J. E. Myers, pp. 283–86. Mountain View CA.

Malinowski, B. 1922. Argonauts of the Western Pacific. New York.

———. 1948. Magic, Science and Religion. Garden City NY.

Marrett, R. R. 1914 (1909). The Threshold of Religion. London.

McClintock, W. 1910. The Old North Trail, or Life, Legends, and Religion of the Blackfeet Indians. Lincoln NB.

Metraux, A. 1963. Ethnography of the Chaco. Handbook of South American Indians, ed. J. H. Steward, pp. 197–370. New York.

Meyer, C. 1971. The Yurok of Trinidad Bay, 1851. The California Indians: A Source Book, eds. R. F. Heizer and M. A. Whipple, pp. 391–430. Berkeley.

Middleton, J. 1960. Lugbara Religion. Oxford.

Morice, A. G. 1951. Carrier Indians. Encyclopedia of Religion and Ethics, Vol. 3, eds. J. Hastings, J. A. Selbie, and L. H. Gray, pp. 229–30. New York.

Murphy, R. F., and B. Quain. 1955. The Trumai Indians of Central Brazil. Monographs of the American Ethnological Society #24, ed. E. S. Goldrank, pp. 1–108. Seattle.

Naroll, R. 1970. What Have We Learned from Cross-Cultural Surveys? American Anthropologist 72:1227–88.

Palmer, C. T. 1989a. Is Rape a Cultural Universal? A Reexamination of the Ethnographic Evidence. Ethnology 28(1):1–16.

———. 1989b. The Ritual-Taboos of Fishermen: An Alternative Explanation. Maritime Anthropological Studies 2 (1):59–68.

Radcliffe-Brown, R. R. 1939. Taboo. Cambridge.

Radin, P. 1963. The Autobiography of a Winnebago Indian. New York.

Rappaport, R. A. 1979. Ritual, Sanctity, and Cybernetics. Reader in Comparative Religion, ed. W. A. Lessa and E. Z. Vogt, pp. 327–31. New York.

Rivers, W. H. R. 1906. The Todas. London.

Rouse, I. 1963. The Carib. Handbook of South American Indians, ed. J. Steward, pp. 547–66. New York.

Spencer, B., and F. J. Gillen. 1968 (1899). The Native Tribes of Central Australia. New York.

Spencer, H. 1972. On Social Evolution. Chicago.

St. John, D. P. 1989. Iroquois. Native American Religions: North America, ed. L. E. Sullivan, pp. 133–38. New York.

Steadman, L. B., and C. T. Palmer. 1994. Visiting Dead Ancestors: Shamans as Interpreters of Religious Traditions. Zygon 29(2):173–89.

———. 1995. Religion as an Identifiable Traditional Behavior Subject to Natural Selection. Journal of Social and Evolutionary Systems 18(2):149–64.

———. In Press. Myths as Instructions From Ancestors: The Example of Oedipus. Zygon.

Steward, J. H., and A. Metraux. 1963. The Peban Tribes. Handbook of South American Indians, ed. J. Steward, pp. 727–36. New York.

Stout, D. B. 1947. San Blas Cuna Acculturation: An Introduction. New York.

Swanson, G. 1964 (1960). The Birth of the Gods. Ann Arbor.

Tonkinson, R. 1978. The Mardudjara Aborigines. New York.

Trenholm, V. C., and M. Carley. 1964. The Shoshoni: Sentinels of the Rockies. Norman OK.

Vaillant, G. C. 1944. Aztecs of Mexico. Garden City NY.

von Furer-Haimendorf, C. 1987. Himalayan Religions. The Encyclopedia of Religion, ed. M. Eliade, pp. 325–29. New York.

Wallace, W. 1978. Southern Valley Yokuts. Handbook of North American Indians, Vol. 8, ed. R. F. Heizer, pp. 448–61. Washington DC.

ASK YOURSELF

When we compare beliefs about gods and spirits we almost always discover that in their various moral and even visual attributes they bear a striking similarity to human beings. The Scriptures declare that "Man was born in God's image and likeness," but the unbeliever might well invert that assertion and say that "God was born in Man's image and likeness." Do you think all gods and spirits *have* to be anthropomorphic, i.e., attributing human motivation, features, or behavior to non-human beings or things? Are there other possibilities? Think of a supernatural agent and describe it. Then classify the characteristics you have identified as being either (a) human attributes or (b) supernatural attributes. Are there, in fact, any purely "supernatural" attributes or are they all human, but on a magnified scale?

FURTHER READINGS

Evans-Pritchard, E. E. *Nuer Religion.* Oxford: Clarendon Press, 1956. In applying certain Durkheimian ideas to the religion of this Sudanese people, the author refines them in this classic example of structural-functional analysis.

Gordon, Bruce and Marshall, Peter. *The Place of the Dead: Death and Remembrance in Late Medieval and Early Modern Europe.* Cambridge: University Press. 2000. Historical scholarship and anthropology are joined in this anthology of 15 studies of how human beings have "interacted" with the ghosts their imaginations have devised.

Harman, William P. *The Sacred Marriage of a Hindu Goddess.* Bloomington and Indianapolis: Indiana University Press, 1989. The author here interprets a Hindu religious festival, performed each year in the presence of around half a million pilgrims in the city of Madurai in southern India. The ritual involves a goddess and her sacred marriage, and Harman discusses the concept of marriage in its human dimension and in relation to the nature of female divinities. This engrossing book should be read in conjunction with a documentary film about the Madurai ritual, "Wedding of the Goddess," first distributed in 1976 by the South Asian Center of the University of Wisconsin in Madison. It comes in two parts. The first part (36 minutes) sets forth the historical background. The second part (40 minutes) encompasses the ritual itself.

SUGGESTED VIDEOS

"A Month for the Entertainment of Spirits." This documentary describes the rituals of African-Guyanese who maintain their African traditions of making contact with local spirits. Its centerpiece is a libation ritual and four *comfa* rituals, which are examined in relation to other rituals by which human beings communicate with spirits. 30 minutes; 1992; $195 (sale), $50 (rental); Catalog #38143. "World Cultures on Film and Video," University of California Extension, Center for Media and Independent Learning, 2000 Center Street, Fourth Floor, Berkeley, CA 94704.

"Mammy Water: In Search of the Water Spirits in Nigeria." The term "Mammy Water" is the pidgin designation for a local water goddess worshiped by the Ibibio-, Ijaw-, and Igbo-speaking peoples of Nigeria. The water goddess endows wealth and children upon believers, compensates them formisfortunes, helps with sickness, and alleviates need. The deity is especially helpful to women, and her various cults are directed, for the most part, by priestesses. 59 minutes; 1991; $295 (sale), $70 (rent); Catalog #38097. "World Cultures on Film and Video," University of California

Extension, Center for Media and Independent Learning, 2000 Center Street, Fourth Floor, Berkeley, CA 94704.

"The Guardian of the Forces." Control over ancestral spirits and voodoo divinities by Sikavi, a "fetish priest," operating in Togo, west Africa, is here examined in the context of possession and sacrifice. We see the meaning of human-spirit interaction for healing practices, life, and death in a culture in which the traditional and modern blend. 52 minutes; 1991; Film Officer, Royal Anthropological Institute (RAI), 50 Fitzroy Street, London W1P 5HS, United Kingdom.

"Tayuban: Dancing the Spirit in Java." With sexually-charged undercurrents, every year a village on Java performs a ritual in which men dance with professional female dancers, performances intended as a gift to local spirits in exchange for benefits to the community.

Ritual reaffirms common values. Every year, on the Feast of the Epiphany (January 6), no matter how chilling the water, young men of the Greek Orthodox religion dive in Mount Sinai Harbor, in New York State, to retrieve the paramount Christian symbol, a cross, which the local bishop has thrown in to commemorate the visit of the three kings (or magi) to the Christ child in the manger at Bethlehem.

Photo courtesy of Maxine Hicks

CHAPTER 4

RITUAL

As I remarked in the Introduction, those repetitive and symbolic actions that we term "rituals" are forms of behavior by which human beings communicate ideas, values, and sentiments they share in common. Various theories have been advanced to account for their universality. Perhaps the most radical is that of Rodney Needham's (1985: 177). Human beings, he suggests, perform rituals because it is in human nature to do so. "Considered in its most characteristic features, [ritual] is a kind of activity—like speech or dancing—that man as a ceremonial animal happens naturally to perform." This is an appeal to the genetic makeup of *Homo sapiens,* of course, and were it true would remove the study of ritual's essential character from the psychological and sociological contexts in which anthropologists have hitherto sought to explain it.

These contexts have, however, provided generations of scholars with the opportunity to display their intellectual ingenuity, and their discussions have generated some provocative insights into the meaning of ritual. Among the most prominent were those of the English functionalist, Bronislaw Malinowski (1954), who proposed a psychological explanation. Malinowski suggested that in situations of peril and threat, human beings resort to rituals as a means of coping with anxiety. We never possess every scrap of knowledge required to overcome all of life's potential challenges, Malinowski argued, and since nonliterate people lack the more sophisticated technology possessed by Westerners they are therefore especially in need of, and likely to resort to, rituals as a substitute for more practical actions. The Trobriand Islanders are famous for embarking on long trading expeditions on the high seas in wooden canoes that are far more dangerous than western vessels. To compensate for their lack of a technology that would reduce the dangers and nudge away their fears, Malinowski said, the sailors would perform rituals before setting out. Even though they might not realize the "real" reason why they were doing so, the very act of carrying the rituals out acted to reduce the tension generated by the Trobrianders' sense of helplessness. The rituals generated much the same feeling of security the islanders would have attained had they possessed a technology to handle the dangers more adequately. As he put it, when they fish in the calm waters of lagoons Trobriand sailors do not bother performing rituals!

Another influential line of thought was contained in Emile Durkheim's sociological explanation. He and the structural-functionalists whom he influenced, such as A. R. Radcliffe-Brown, saw in ritual a means by which society could maintain its cohesion. By collectively performing rituals, he claimed, individuals transcended their selfish individuality and experienced the feeling they were part of some transcendental entity (which was society). This feeling fostered a communal spirit that strengthened the bonds that united individuals to such a degree that when the ritual was over individuals retained the feeling that they were part of an entity that was larger than their individual selves. Carrying out rituals from time to time recharged this feeling. Seen from this perspective, therefore, ritual is a function of social interaction.

The work of Edmund Leach acknowledges both the structural-function school and the symbolic approach favored by Victor Turner, his English colleague, though they approached symbolism from different direction. Thus, whereas in Reading 4–1 Leach discusses ritual as a general phenomenon and describes how scholars have sought to explain it, Turner's article (Reading 4–2) is concerned to demonstrate how symbols are used in the rituals of a single society, the Ndembu. In doing so, he vividly depicts symbols as a medium of communication. The other two readings in this chapter combine the sociological and the communicative aspects of ritual at the same time as they show how symbols enable these aspects to have an influence on society and its members.

Note that Leach and Turner define ritual in different ways. Leach's definition of ritual conforms to the usage I follow in this volume, that is, the term "ritual" includes both sacred and secular (Durkheim's "profane") spheres of action. For

Turner, however, ritual is an activity that, by definition, involves *spirits.* "By 'ritual,' " he writes (1967:19), "I mean prescribed formal behavior for occasions not given over to technological routine, having reference to beliefs in mystical beings or powers."

READING 4–1

RITUAL

Edmund R. Leach

In this article, Edmund Leach evaluates the contributions of Emile Durkheim, Edward Tylor, James Frazer, Bronislaw Malinowski, A. R. Radcliffe-Brown, Max Gluckman, and others to the problems of ritual, belief, myth, and magic. He points out that these scholars fall into the trap of seeking to define ritual in absolute terms. Leach, in contrast, points out that ritual is not something given in nature. A ritual is a concept, an abstraction whose meaning is defined by social context. Leach further argues that ritual is primarily a medium of communication. He also resurrects a question Tylor and his contemporary, William Robertson Smith, both raised. Which has priority: ritual or belief? Leach sides with Robertson Smith. "The rite," he states, "is prior to the explanatory belief." Despite the earlier views of Tylor, Frazer, and Durkheim, Leach's contention that ritual should be granted primacy over explanatory beliefs is supported by research that has shown that beliefs associated with particular rituals change more easily over time than the rituals themselves.

Leach is on weaker ground in seeing an invariable connection between ritual and myth. Here he follows Malinowski, who thought that the only narratives that could properly be termed "myths" were those that accompanied rituals and served as "sacred charters."

Source: "Ritual," by Edmund R. Leach. Reprinted with permission of Macmillan Library Reference USA, a Simon & Schuster Macmillan Company, from *International Encyclopedia of the Social Sciences,* ed. David L. Sills. Vol. 13, pp. 520–526 (references deleted). Copyright © 1968 by Crowell Collier and Macmillan, Inc.

Leach, in his book Political Systems of Highland Burma (1954:13) contended that "Myth, in my terminology, is the counterpart of ritual; myth implies ritual, ritual implies myth, they are one and the same," adding, by way of emphasis, "myth regarded as a statement in words 'says' the same thing as ritual regarded as a statement in action." Comparative ethnography, on the contrary, finds no invariable link; nor is evidence from Western history especially supportive of their claim either. Does the myth of Genesis have a ritual counterpart?

Citations in the *Oxford English Dictionary* from the fourteenth century on reveal two distinct trends of common usage for the words *rite (ritual), ceremony (ceremonial),* and *custom (customary).* On the one hand, these terms have been used interchangeably to denote any noninstinctive predictable action or series of actions that cannot be justified by a "rational" means-to-ends type of explanation. In this sense the English custom of shaking hands is a ritual, but the act of planting potatoes with a view to a harvest is not. But rationality is not easily defined. A psychiatrist may refer to the repeated hand washing of a compulsive neurotic as a "private ritual" even when, in the actor's judgment, the washing is a rational means to cleanliness. Likewise, a high-caste Hindu is required by his religion to engage in elaborate washing procedures to ensure his personal purity and cleanliness; the rationality or otherwise of such actions is a matter of cultural viewpoint. In this case, anthropologists who distinguish between ritual cleanliness and actual cleanliness are separating two aspects of a single state rather than two separate states. The distinction between cleanliness and dirt is itself a cultural derivation that presupposes an elaborate hierarchy of ritual values. If "nonrationality" is made a criterion of *ritual,* it must be remembered that the judge of what is rational is the observer, not the actor. The other trend of usage has been to distinguish the three categories: ritual, ceremony, and custom. Ritual is then usually set apart as a body of custom specifically associated with religious performance, while ceremony and custom become residual categories for the description of secular activity. Where religion is the specific concern of fully institutionalized churches, as in Europe, a religious delimitation of ritual is unambiguous and easy to apply; in the exotic societies studied by anthropologists this is not the case. Recognizing this problem, some contemporary authors have argued that ambiguity in the data may be overcome by the multiplication of analytic concepts (e.g., Firth 1956, p. 46; Wilson 1954, p. 240; Gluckman 1962, pp. 20–24). Gluckman, in particular, favors an elaborate vocabulary giving clearly distinguishable meanings to *ceremony, ceremonious, ritual, ritualism,* and *ritualization,* but the circumstances in which precision might be useful are hard to imagine. Ritual is clearly not a fact of nature but a concept, and definitions of concepts should be operational; the merits of any particular formula will depend upon how the concept is being used.

In short, to understand the word *ritual* we must take note of the user's background and prejudices. A clergyman would probably assume that all ritual necessarily takes place inside a church in accordance with formally established rules and rubrics; a psychiatrist may be referring to the private compulsions of individual patients; an anthropologist will probably mean "a category of standardized behavior (custom) in which the relationship between the means and the end is not 'intrinsic' " (Goody 1961, p. 159), but he will interpret this definition loosely or very precisely according to individual temperament. The associated terms *ceremonial* and *customary* are also used in very varied ways, even by professionals from the same discipline.

HISTORICAL USAGE OF THE CONCEPT

The views of Robertson Smith (1889) are of particular relevance in arriving at a definition of terms. As a former professor of divinity, he advocated the study of comparative religion. He assumed that the boundaries between what is religion and what is not religion are self-evident. Modern religion (Christianity) consists of beliefs (dogma) and practices (ritual); "in the antique religions mythology takes the place of dogma." Myth is merely "an explanation of a religious usage." Hence, "the study of ancient religion must begin, not with myth, but with ritual and traditional usage." The thesis that religion consists essentially of beliefs *and* rituals and that, of the two, ritual is in some sense prior has influenced many later writers in many different fields.

Durkheim ([1912] 1954, p. 47) defined religion as "a unified system of beliefs and practices (rites) relative to sacred things, that is to say, things set apart and forbidden—beliefs and practices which unite into a single moral community called a Church, all those who adhere to them." Rites, for Durkheim, are "the rules of conduct which prescribe how a man should comport himself in the presence of these sacred objects" (*ibid.*, p. 41). Negative (ascetic) rites are the customs that we commonly label *taboo*. Positive rites include "imitative rites," which are in fact the same practices that Frazer called "homeopathic magic"; "representative or commemorative rites," which are the cults of ancestor worship; sacrifice; and piacular rites, or memorials to misfortune, such as mourning. The overprecision of Durkheim's classification leads to some difficulties. He asserts dogmatically that "the division of the world into two domains, the one containing all that is sacred, the other all that is profane, is the distinctive trait of religious thought" (*ibid.*, p. 37). In his system, magic belongs to the sphere of the profane, even though "magic, too, is made up of beliefs and rites" (*ibid.*, p. 42).

The same set of rituals may readily be classified in other ways. Thus van Gennep (1908) proposed a category to cover all individual life-crisis ceremonials (e.g., those associated with birth, puberty, marriage, death) and also recurrent calendric ceremonials such as birthdays and New Year's Day. He called these "rites of passage." In practice, van Gennep's schema has proved more useful than Durkheim's (see Gluckman 1962).

If Durkheim seems to be excessively rigid, Frazer, who was Robertson Smith's pupil, errs in the opposite direction. In the pages of *The Golden Bough* (1890) the words *custom, ceremonial, rite,* and *ritual* seem to be interchangeable. Belief and

rite are assumed to be so closely interdependent that if evidence concerning either is available the author may confidently "conjecture" as to the other, which he does very freely. Employing similar assumptions, later writers have felt entitled to make the most sweeping reconstructions of ancient religious systems on the basis of slender archeological residues of ritual practice (Hooke 1958).

A more profitable development of Robertson Smith's theme was the inquiry by Jane Harrison (1912; 1913) into the relationship between ritual and art. Harrison noted that the Greek word *drama* is derived from *dromenon* (religious ritual, literally: "things done"). She attached special importance to Durkheim's category of "imitative rites": "Primitive man . . . tends to re-enact whatever makes him feel strongly; any one of his manifold occupations, hunting, fighting, later ploughing and sowing, provided it be of sufficient interest and importance, is material for a *dromenon* or rite" ([1913] 1951, p. 49). Thus ritual is seen as a magical dramatization of ordinary activities, while in turn the drama is a secular recapitulation of ritual. Although ritual is distinguished from nonritual by the presence or absence of a religious context, the details of this distinction remain imprecise.

Harrison was a classical scholar who profited from the writings of anthropologists; the succeeding generation of anthropologists in turn profited from hers. Malinowski and Radcliffe-Brown introduced the concept of functionalism into British social anthropology; they were both indebted to Harrison, though both were also, and quite independently, the propagators of Durkheim's ideas. The concept of "ritual value," which Radcliffe-Brown developed in *The Andaman Islanders* (1922) and later writings, is essentially that espoused by Harrison. Objects to which ritual value attaches are objects that are socially important for secular reasons. Radcliffe-Brown, however, added the proposition that the performance of ritual generates in the actors certain "sentiments" that are advantageous to the society as a whole. In their discussions of this theme both Radcliffe-Brown and Malinowski tend to assume that economic value depends upon utility rather than scarcity, and they attempt to distinguish ritual value as something other than economic value. Radcliffe-Brown shows that the Andamanese attached "ritual value" to objects (including foods) that were scarce luxuries, but he makes an unnecessary mystery of this fact. Karl Marx had a much clearer understanding of what is, after all, our common experience. Marx observed that the value of commodities in the market is quite different from the value of the same goods considered as objects of utility. He distinguishes the extra value that goods acquire by becoming market commodities as "fetichistic value" (1867–1879). This concept is closely akin to Radcliffe-Brown's "ritual value," though in Marx's argument the magical element is only an aspect of the commodity value, rather than the value as a whole. Furthermore, where Radcliffe-Brown urged that ritual is to the advantage of society, Marx claimed that it is to the disadvantage of the individual producer. The Marxist thesis is that in the activities of the secular market—where all values are supposed to be measured by the strictest canons of rationality—judgments are in fact influenced by mystical nonrational criteria. A full generation later Mauss (1925), developing his general theory of gift exchange from an entirely different viewpoint, reached an identical conclusion. Exchanges that *appear* to be grounded in secular, rational, utilitarian needs turn out to be compulsory acts of a ritual kind in which the objects exchanged are the vehicles of mystical power.

Of the authors I have mentioned, Durkheim, Harrison, Radcliffe-Brown, and Mauss all started out with the assumption that every social action belongs unambiguously to one or the other of two readily distinguishable categories: the nonrational, mystical, nonutilitarian, and sacred or the rational, common-sense, utilitarian, and profane. Each author would clearly like to distinguish a specific category, *ritual,* which could refer unambiguously and exhaustively to behavior relevant to things sacred. Each author ends up by demonstrating that no such discrimination is possible—that all "sacred things" are also, under certain conditions, "profane things," and vice versa. Malinowski sought to avoid this dilemma. For him, the essential issue was that of rationality rather than religion. Those who followed Frazer in thinking of magic as "a false scientific technique" necessarily classed magic as a profane activity, but according to Malinowski, primitive man has a clear understanding of the difference between a technical act and a magical rite. Magic and religion both belong to a single sphere, the magico–religious; ". . . every ritual performance, from a piece of primitive Australian magic to a Corpus Christi procession, from an initiation ceremony to the Holy Mass, is a traditionally enacted miracle. . . . Man needs miracles not because he is benighted through primitive stupidity, [or] through the trickery of a priesthood . . . but because he realizes at every stage of his development that the powers of his body and of his mind are limited" ([1923–1939] 1963, pp. 300–301).

But if ethnography offers little support to Durkheim, it offers still less to Malinowski. Most people in most societies have only the haziest ideas about the distinction either between sacred and profane or between rational and nonrational; it is a scholastic illusion to suppose that human actions are everywhere ordered to accord with such discriminations. Some authors still hold that a specific category is delimited by the phrase "behavior accounted for by mystical action": in my view they are mistaken.

RITUAL AND COMMUNICATION

In this whole discussion two elements are involved which have so far been scarcely mentioned. Human actions can serve to *do* things, that is, alter the physical state of the world (as in lighting a bonfire), or they can serve to *say* things. Thus, the Englishman's handshake makes a complicated statement such as, "I am pleased to meet you and willing to converse." All speech is a form of customary behavior, but, likewise, all customary behavior is a form of speech, a mode of communicating information. In our dress, in our manners, even in our most trivial gestures we are constantly "making statements" that others can understand. For the most part these statements refer to human relationships and to status.

The actions that "say things" in this way are not as a rule intrinsically different from those that "do things." If I am cold, I am likely to put on more clothes, and this is a rational action to alter the state of the world; but the kinds of clothes I put on and the way I wear them will serve to "say things" about myself. Almost every human action that takes place in culturally defined surroundings is divisible in this way; it has a technical aspect which does something and an aesthetic, communicative aspect which says something.

In those types of behavior that are labeled ritual by any of the definitions so far discussed, the aesthetic, communicative aspect is particularly prominent, but a technical aspect is never entirely absent. The devout Christian eats and drinks as part of a sacrament, but he also says grace as a preface to an ordinary meal. These are plainly "ritual" matters. But it is equally a matter of "ritual" that whereas an Englishman would ordinarily eat with a knife and fork, a Chinese would use chopsticks, and an Indian his right hand (but not his left, which for complex reasons is deemed polluted).

The Meaning of Ritual   Whether we use a narrow or a broad definition of ritual, one major problem is that of interpretation. What does ritual mean? If a ritual act be deemed to say something, how do we discover what it says? Clearly the actor's own view is inadequate. With minor variations the ritual of the Christian Mass is the same throughout Christendom, but each individual Christian will explain the performance by reference to his own sectarian doctrine. Such doctrines vary quite widely; the social scientist who seeks to understand why a particular ritual sequence possesses the content and form that he observes can expect little help from the rationalizations of the devout. But intuition is equally unreliable. Sacrifice, in the sense of the ritual killing of an animal victim, is an institution with a worldwide distribution. How can we explain this? Why

should this particular kind of rite be considered an appropriate kind of action in the situations in which it is observed? There is no lack of theory. Some argue that the victim is identified with God and then sacramentally eaten; others that the victim is a gift or a bribe to the gods; others that the victim stands in substitution for the giver of the sacrifice; others that the victim is a symbolic representation of sin; and so on. All these explanations may be true or partly true for particular situations, but they cannot all be true at once, and none of them reach into the heart of the problem, which is, Why should the killing of an animal be endowed with sacramental quality at all?

Some interpretative approaches are more clearly formulated than others and deserve special attention. Radcliffe-Brown (1922) postulated that human beings always manipulate their thought categories consistently. We can discover what a ritual symbol means by observing the diverse uses of that symbol in both ritual and secular contexts. This is a powerful but by no means foolproof interpretative device. For example, the English speak of "high" status versus "low" status. We might then suppose that in ritual drama the person who is "higher" will always be superior. Up to a point this applies. Persons of authority are raised on a dais; a suppliant kneels; an orator stands when his audience sits. But there are also situations where persons of extreme eminence sit (e.g., a king on his throne) when all others stand. The regularities are not simple.

This should not surprise us. In seeking to understand ritual we are, in effect, trying to discover the rules of grammar and syntax of an unknown language, and this is bound to be a very complicated business.

Lévi-Strauss (1962) is inclined to see ritual procedures as integral with processes of thought. The drama of ritual breaks up the continuum of visual experience into sets of categories with distinguishable names and thereby provides us with a conceptual apparatus for intellectual operations at an abstract and metaphysical level. Such an approach implies that we should think of ritual as a language in a quite literal sense. Various theorems of communication engineering and of structural linguistics should thus be applicable. We can, for example, start to investigate the role played by "redundancy" in ritual. Do binary contrasts in ritual correspond to phonemic contrasts in verbal speech forms? Can we discover, in any particular culture, rules concerning the development of a ritual sequence that would be comparable to the rules of generative grammar which Chomsky (1957) suggests must govern the modes by which each individual composes a verbal utterance? This is a field in which exploration has hardly begun.

Ritual as Social Communication   Most modern anthropologists would agree that culturally defined sets of behaviors can function as a language, but not all will accept my view that the term *ritual* is best used to denote this communicative aspect of behavior. Although we are still very much in the dark as to how ritual behaviors manage to convey messages, we understand roughly what the messages are about and at least part of what they say. Social anthropologists and sociologists alike claim that their special field is the study of systems of social relationship. This notion of social relationship is a verbal derivation based on inference. We do not observe relationships; we observe individuals behaving toward one another in customary, ritually standardized ways, and whatever we have to say about social relationships is, in the last analysis, an interpretation of these "ritual" acts. All of us in our private daily lives manipulate the symbols of an intricate behavioral code, and we readily decode the behavioral messages of our associates; this we take for granted. Comparable activities on a collective scale in the context of a religious institution are rated mysterious and irrational. Yet their functional utility seems plain enough. Our day-to-day relationships depend upon a mutual knowledge and mutual acceptance of the fact that at any particular time any two individuals occupy different positions in a highly complex network of status relationships; ritual serves to reaffirm what these status differences are. It is characteristic of all

kinds of ritual occasion that all participants adopt special forms of dress, which emphasize in an exaggerated way the formal social distinctions that separate one individual from another. Thus, ritual serves to remind the congregation just where each member stands in relation to every other and in relation to a larger system. It is necessary for our day-to-day affairs that we should have these occasional reminders, but it is also reassuring. It is this reassurance perhaps that explains why, in the absence of scientific medicine, ritual forms of therapy are often strikingly successful.

Here the argument seems to have come full circle. For if ritual be that aspect of customary behavior that "says things" rather than "does things" (cf. Parsons' instrumental–expressive dichotomy), how is it that, in the view of the actors (and even of some analysts), ritual may "do things" as well as "say things?" The most obvious examples are healing rituals which form a vast class and have a world-wide distribution, but here we may also consider role-inversion rituals, which Gluckman (1962) has classed as "rituals of rebellion" and which he perceives as fulfilling a positive cathartic function.

Ritual as Power   From the viewpoint of the actor, rites can alter the state of the world because they invoke power. If the power is treated as inherent in the rite itself, the analyst calls the action magic; if the power is believed to be external to the situation—a supernatural agency—the analyst says it is religious. Current argument on this theme is highly contentious, and I must declare my own position: I hold that the rite is prior to the explanatory belief. This will be recognized as essentially the view of Robertson Smith.

The concept of power itself is a derivation. We observe as an empirical fact that an individual *A* asserts dominance over another individual *B;* we observe that *B* submits to *A,* and we say that "*A* has power over *B*." And then in a ritual context we observe another individual *A1* going through a performance that he believes will coerce a fourth individual *B1;* or alternatively, we observe *B1* making a ritual act of submission to an unseen presence *C1*. The normal classification declares that the acts of *A* and *B* are rational but that the acts of *A1* and *B1* are irrational. To me it seems that they are all actions of the same kind. The "authority" by which *A* is able to coerce and control the behavior of *B* in a secular situation is just as abstract and metaphysical as the magical power by which *A1* seeks to coerce *B1* or the religious power that *B1* seeks to draw from *C1*. Ideas about the relations between supernatural agencies and human beings or about the potency of particular ritual behaviors are modeled on first-hand experience of real-life relationships between real human beings. But conversely, every act by which one individual asserts his authority to curb or alter the behavior of another individual is an invocation of metaphysical force. The submissive response is an ideological reaction, and it is no more surprising that individuals should be influenced by magical performances or religious imprecations than that they should be influenced by the commands of authority. The power of ritual is just as actual as the power of command.

Ritual as Belief   Unlike Robertson Smith, Tylor (1871) assumed the priority of belief over ritual. In England a Neo-Tylorian view has a number of contemporary advocates. According to their argument, it is the belief accompanying the behavior, rather than any quality of the behavior itself, that distinguishes ritual. Since the participants in a religious ritual claim that their actions are designed to alter the state of the world by bringing coercive influence upon supernatural agencies, why should we not accept this statement at its face value? Why invoke the proposition that the actions in question are, as Durkheim would have it, "symbolic representations of social relationships?" Goody counterposes the intellectualized interpretation of social behavior made by the observer to the statement of the actor himself. "What happens, then," writes Goody (1961, p. 157), "is that symbolic acts are defined in opposition to rational acts and constitute a residual category to which 'meaning' is assigned by the observer in order to make sense of [the] oth-

erwise irrational. . . ." Ritual acts are to be interpreted in the context of belief: they mean what the actors say they mean. This common-sense approach clearly has its attractions. Yet it may be argued that if culturally defined behavior can only be interpreted by the actors, all cross-cultural generalization is impossible, and all attempts to make a rational analysis of the irrational must necessarily be fallacious (see Goody 1961, p. 155). In contrast, I, along with other Durkheimians, continue to insist that religious behavior cannot be based upon an illusion.

Jane Harrison's thesis that "ritual is a dramatisation of myth" was reformulated by Malinowski in the assertion that "myth is a charter for social action." According to this argument, myth and ritual are not merely interdependent; they jointly provide a model for "correct" moral attitudes in secular life. But although it is easy to cite examples in which rituals enshrine in a quite straightforward way the most strongly felt values of society, there are many striking exceptions. The characters of myth frequently break all the moral conventions of mundane society in the most glaring way, and in many rituals the actors are required to behave in a manner precisely contrary to that which they would be expected to adopt in ordinary life. Two very different types of explanation have been offered for facts of this kind. One sees this role inversion as symbolic; the events of myth and ritual refer to the space-time of "the other world"; they belong to Durkheim's category of the *sacred,* and to express this fact their content systematically inverts whatever is appropriate to "this world," the *profane*. In contrast, Gluckman, in an argument that has wide application (see Norbeck 1961, pp. 205–211), stresses the aggressive elements present in role-reversal ceremonies, which he aptly names "rituals of rebellion" (Gluckman 1962). The performers, he suggests, act out in dramatic form hostilities that are deeply felt but may not be expressed in normal secular relationships. This acted aggression serves as a cathartic release mechanism, and by relieving tension these inverted behaviors actually serve to strengthen the moral code they appear to deny. It is an ingenious argument but hard to validate. Once again we are faced with the difficulty that sharply contrasted interpretations seem to afford partial explanations of the same ethnographic facts, so that choice of theory becomes a matter of personal predilection.

Nineteenth-century positivist thinkers made a triadic distinction between reason, magic, and religion. Various authors have attempted to fit ritual to this triad and also to the two dichotomies: sacred-profane, rational-nonrational. Some of the resulting difficulties have been considered. It is argued that no useful distinction may be made between ritual acts and customary acts but that in discussing ritual we are concerned with aspects of behavior that are expressive (aesthetic) rather than instrumental (technical). Ritual action, thus conceived, serves to express the status of the actor vis-à-vis his environment, both physical and social; it may also serve to alter the status of the actor. When ritual functions in this latter sense, it is a manifestation of power; thus, the universal belief in the potency of ritual action is by no means an illusion. No attempt has been made to discuss the forms of ritual. Any form of secular activity, whether practical or recreational, can be stylized into dramatic performance and made the focus of a ritual sequence. Such stylization tends to distort the secular norm in either of two directions: the emphasis may be ascetic, representing the intensification of formal restraint, or ecstatic, signifying the elimination of restraint. Ascetic and ecstatic elements are present in most ceremonial sequences, and the contrast may form part of the communication code (Leach 1961, chapter 6). Finally, it has been stressed that even among those who have specialized in this field there is the widest possible disagreement as to how the word ritual should be used and how the performance of ritual should be understood.

BIBLIOGRAPHY

Chomsky, Noam. (1957) 1964. *Syntactic Structures*. The Hague: Mouton.

Durkheim, Émile. (1912) 1954. *The Elementary Forms of the Religious Life*. London: Allen & Unwin; New York: Macmil-lan. First published as *Les formes élémentaires de la vie religieuse, le systégme totémique en Australie*. A paperback edition was published in 1961 by Collier.

Firth, Raymond. 1956. Ceremonies for Children and Social Frequency in Tikopia. Oceania 27:12–55.

Frazer, James. (1890) 1955. *The Golden Bough*. 13 vols., 3d ed., rev. & enl. New York: St. Martins; London: Macmillan.

Gennep, Arnold van. (1909) 1960. *The Rites of Passage*. London: Routledge: Univ. of Chicago Press. First published in French.

Gluckman, Max. 1962. Les rites de passage. Pages 1–52 in Max Gluckman (editor), *Essays on the Ritual of Social Relations*. Manchester (England) Univ. Press.

Goody, J. R. 1961. Religion and Ritual: The Definitional Problem. *British Journal of Sociology* 12:142–164.

Harrison, Jane E. (1912) 1937. *Themis: A Study of the Social Origins of Greek Religion*. 2d ed., rev. Cambridge Univ. Press.

——. (1913) 1951. *Ancient Art and Ritual*. Rev. ed. New York: Oxford Univ. Press.

Hooke, Samuel H. (editor). 1958. *Myth, Ritual, and Kingship*. Oxford: Clarendon.

Leach, Edmund R. 1961. *Rethinking Anthropology*. London School of Economics and Political Science, Monographs on Social Anthropology, No. 22. London: Athlone.

Lévi-Strauss, Claude. (1962) 1966. *The Savage Mind*. Univ. of Chicago Press. First published in French.

Malinowski, Bronislaw. (1913–1941) 1962. *Sex, Culture and Myth*. New York: Harcourt. See especially pages 295–336, "The Foundations of Faith and Morals."

Marx, Karl. (1867–1879) 1925–1926. *Capital: A Critique of Political Economy*. 3 vols. Chicago: Kerr. Volume 1: *The Process of Capitalist Production*. Volume 2: *The Process of Circulation of Capital*. Volume 3: *The Process of Capitalist Production as a Whole*. The manuscripts of Volumes 2 and 3 were written between 1867 and 1879. They were first published posthumously in German in 1885 and 1894.

Mauss, Marcel. (1925) 1954. *The Gift: Forms and Functions of Exchange in Archaic Societies*. Glencoe, Ill.: Free Press. First published as *Essai sur le don: Forme et raison de l'échange dans les sociétés archaïques*.

Norbeck, Edward. 1961. *Religion in Primitive Society*. New York: Harper.

Radcliffe-Brown, A. R. (1922) 1948. *The Andaman Islanders*. Glencoe, Ill.: Free Press.

Smith, William Robertson. (1889) 1956. *The Religion of the Semites*. New York: Meridian.

Srinivas, Mysore N. 1952. *Religion and Society Among the Coorgs of South India*. Oxford: Clarendon.

Tylor, Edward B. (1871) 1958. *Primitive Culture: Researches into the Development of Mythology, Philosophy, Religion, Art and Custom*. 2 vols. Gloucester, Mass.: Smith. Volume 1: *Origins of Culture*. Volume 2: *Religion in Primitive Culture*.

Wilson, Monica. 1954. Nyakyusa Ritual and Symbolism. *American Anthropologist* New Series 56:228–241.

READING 4–2

RITUAL SYMBOLISM, MORALITY, AND SOCIAL STRUCTURE AMONG THE NDEMBU

V. W. Turner

Victor Turner was one of the two leading exponents of the Manchester School of social anthropology in England. Max Gluckman, who founded the school, was the other (see Reading 4–1). Unlike structural-functionalism, this school follows an approach to the study of society that emphasizes the dynamics *of social life rather than studying social structure as a static abstraction. Integral to this approach is a concern with how real persons interact with one another in adjusting to circumstances of daily life, a focus that expresses itself in the careful attention members of the Manchester School pay to real situations that actually crop up in the course of social life. The ethnographies proponents of this school write abound in case studies that portray individuals competing and cooperating with one another as they seek to accomplish their aims. In ritual, this social interaction is made possible, of course, by symbols, and in this reading Victor Turner demonstrates, in great detail, the ways in which symbols used in Ndembu ritual maintain bonds between individuals.*

The Ndembu, of Zambia in Central Africa, notice that when the thin bark of a local tree they call mudyi *is scratched, a milky white sap oozes out. For the Ndembu, this sap is the tree's most important physical property, and on it they base an ever-widening network of symbols. The white sap itself is the starting point for this network and by means of it the white liquid comes to symbolize many things. The sap's immediate referent is human milk, which in turn symbolizes the female breast from which the*

Source: Victor Turner, "Ritual Symbolism, Morality, and Social Structure among the Ndembu," in *African Systems of Thought,* ed. Meyer Fortes and G. Dieterlen (London: Oxford University Press, for the International African Institute, 1965), pp. 75–95. Reprinted with permission by the International African Institute.

milk flows. The breast itself symbolizes the suckling of infants, an activity that symbolizes the mother–child bond. This bond of mother–child symbolizes the family, a social group basic to Ndembu society, and the family, finally, symbolizes the whole of Ndembu society.

The Ndembu have thus incorporated into their culture a progression of symbols in which each object, action, or institution serves to symbolize another symbol that is of even greater abstraction. The network starts with tangible symbols—beads of latex, milk, the female breast—and progresses to abstract ones. First an action (breast feeding), then social institutions (the mother–child relationship, the family, Ndembu society). No single referent, therefore, can convey the full symbolic meaning of the milk tree to the Ndembu: the tree's total meaning resides in the combination of all its referents, any one of which can only be fully understood as part of the whole system.

This article is typical of Turner's earlier anthropology—ethnographically precise, original in its theoretical suggestions, and intellectually provocative. It also shows how Turner understood that psychological, sociological, and symbolic factors could work together in a ritual context. One problem with his type of analysis, however, is that because it results from an unusually close empathy between ethnographer and informant we are sometimes left unclear about which idea comes from Turner and which is genuinely Nedmbu.

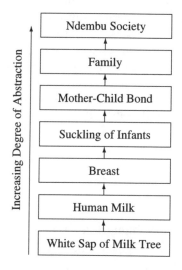

FIGURE 2   The Ndembu Tree Milk.

THE NDEMBU OF
MWINILUNGA DISTRICT

The Ndembu, numbering about 17,000, today inhabit the western portion of Mwinilunga District in the North-Western Province of Northern Rhodesia, approximately between 11° and 12° South latitude. They claim to have come as invaders some three centuries ago from the Northern Lunda empire (Luunda) of Mwantiyanvwa and to have conquered or received the submission of small scattered groups of indigenous Mbwela or Lukolwe.

On their well-wooded plateau the Ndembu practise a form of subsistence cultivation in which cassava growing is associated with hunting. In addition to cassava, finger millet is grown by small circle ash-planting methods mainly for beer-making, and maize is cultivated in streamside gardens for food and beer.

They are a matrilineal, virilocal people with high personal spatial mobility, and inhabit small villages with cores of male matrikin, of whom the oldest member of the senior genealogical generation is usually the headman.

The Ndembu did not have the high degree of political centralization enjoyed by their northern Lunda ancestors. Villages in pre-European times possessed considerable political autonomy. Under British rule, however, a hierarchy has been established consisting of a Chief (the "Native Authority") and four Sub-Chiefs. Formerly, these Sub-Chiefs belonged to a class of senior village headmen who held renowned historical titles but had little real power.

ASPECTS OF NDEMBU RITUAL
SYMBOLISM

In this paper I wish to discuss the semantic structure and properties of some of the principal symbols found in Ndembu ritual. Each kind of ritual may be regarded as a configuration of symbols, a sort of "score" of which the symbols are the notes. The symbol is the smallest unit of specific structure in Ndembu ritual. The vernacular term for it is *chinjikikilu,* from *ku-jikijila,* "to blaze a trail"—by cutting marks on a tree with one's axe or by breaking and bending branches to serve as guides back from the unknown bush to known paths. A symbol, then, is a blaze or landmark, something that connects the unknown with the known. The Ndembu term comes from the vocabulary of hunting and exemplifies the high ritual value attached to this pursuit. Furthermore, in discussing their symbols with Ndembu one finds them constantly using the term *ku-solola,* "to make visible" or "to reveal," and they associate this term with aspects of the chase. Indeed, in their ritual vocabulary derivatives of this verb are frequent. For example, the temporary shrine erected for ritual to propitiate the spirits of deceased hunter relatives very often consists of a forked branch taken from the *musoli* tree. Ndembu tell me that this tree is used as a symbol in hunters' ritual because its fruit and young shoots are much appreciated by duiker and other woodland animals who emerge from concealment to eat them, and may be easily shot by a hidden hunter or caught in his snares. The tree, they say, makes the game "visible." Hence portions of it are used as medicines (*yitumbu*) in rituals performed to rid hunters of misfortune. It is said that these medicines will "make animals appear quickly to the hunter" when next he goes into the bush. *Musoli* medicines are also used in rituals performed to make barren women fruitful; they will "make children visible," say Ndembu.

Another use of *musoli* is worth mentioning. Ndembu have a ritual called *Ihamba,* the main aim of which is to remove by cupping horns from a patient's body the upper central incisor (also called *ihamba*) of a dead hunter relative which has imbedded itself under the skin. The spirit, materialized as a tooth, is said to "bite" its victim because the latter has forgotten to pour out a libation of blood at its grave after making a kill, or else because there has been quarreling in the victim's village. The victim may not necessarily have been guilty himself of quarrelsome behaviour, but may have been selected as a representative of the disordered kin-group. The specialist who supervises the ritual procedure usually insists on those village members who have grudges (*yitela*) against one another or against the patient (*muyeji*) coming forward and making a public confession of their hidden animosities. Only after this, he says, will the *ihamba* consent to being caught in a cupping horn. Now the principal medicine of this ritual, the one at which an invocation to the spirit is made, the one which is collected before all others, consists of the tap-root of a *musoli* tree. My informants told me that the root stood for the *ihamba* tooth and that the *musoli* species was used: (a) "to make the *ihamba* tooth come out quickly," and (b) "so that people would speak truly (*ku-hosha chalala*) and openly." Here the idea is clearly that relief is brought both to the patient and to the disturbed social group if hidden ill-feeling is brought to light.

Another derivative of *ku-solola,* "to reveal," is *isoli* or *chisoli,* terms which designate "a place of revelation." They refer to specially consecrated sites, used only in the final phases of important rituals, where esoteric rites are performed and secret matters are revealed to the initiated.

Finally, the term *Musolu* stands for a type of ritual performed only by chiefs and senior headmen to bring on or "make visible" delayed rains.

One aspect of the process of ritual symbolization among the Ndembu is, therefore, to make visible, audible, and tangible beliefs, ideas, values, sentiments, and psychological dispositions which cannot directly be perceived. Associated with this process of revealing the unknown, invisible, or the hidden is the process of making public what is private, or making social what is personal. Anything that cannot be shown to be in conformity with the norms or in terms of the values of Ndembu society is potentially dangerous to its cohesion and continuity. Hence the importance of the public confession in the *Ihamba* ritual. By exposing their ill-feeling in a ritual context to beneficial ritual forces, individuals are purged of rebellious wishes and emotions and willingly conform once more to the public mores.

In an Ndembu ritual each symbol makes visible and accessible to purposive public action certain elements of Ndembu culture and society. It also tends to relate these elements to certain natural and physiological regularities. Thus in various contexts *musoli* relates the value of public confession to the restoration of health and of female fertility. This brings me to another important property of many ritual symbols, their polysemy or multivocality. By these terms I mean that a single symbol may stand for many things. This property of individual symbols is true of ritual as a whole. For a few symbols have to represent a whole culture and its material environment. Ritual may be described, in one aspect, as quintessential custom in that it represents a distillate or condensation of many secular customs and natural regularities. Certain dominant or focal symbols conspicuously possess this property of multivocality which allows for the economic representation of key aspects of culture and belief. Each dominant symbol has a "fan" or "spectrum" of referents, which are interlinked by what is usually a simple mode of association, its very simplicity enabling it to interconnect a wide variety of *significata*. For example, the associational link provided by "whiteness" enables white clay (*mpemba*) to stand for a multiplicity of ideas and phenomena, ranging from biological referents as "semen," to abstract ideas such as "ritual purity," "innocence" from witchcraft, and "solidarity with the ancestor spirits."

When we talk about the "meaning" of a symbol, we must be careful to distinguish between at least three "levels" or "fields" of meaning. These I propose to call:

1. the level of indigenous interpretation (or, briefly, the exegetical meaning);
2. the operational meaning; and
3. the positional meaning.

The exegetical meaning is obtained from questioning indigenous informants about observed ritual behaviour. Here again one must distinguish between information given by ritual specialists and information given by laymen, i.e. between esoteric and exoteric interpretations. One must also be careful to ascertain whether a given explanation is truly representative of either of these categories or whether it is a uniquely personal view.

On the other hand, much light may be shed on the role of the ritual symbol by equating its meaning with its use, by observing what the Ndembu do with it, and not only what they say about it. This is what I call the operational meaning, and this level has the most bearing on problems of social dynamics. For the observer must consider not only the symbol but the structure and composition of the group which handles it or performs mimetic acts with direct reference to it. He must further note the affective qualities of these acts, whether they are aggressive, sad, penitent, joyful, derisive, and so on. He must also inquire why certain persons and groups are absent on given occasions, and if absent, whether and why they have been ritually excluded from the presence of the symbol.

The positional meaning of a symbol derives from its relationship to other symbols in a totality, a *Gestalt,* whose elements acquire their significance from the system as a whole. This level of meaning is directly related to the important property of ritual symbols mentioned earlier—their polysemy. Such symbols possess many senses, but contextually it may be necessary to stress one or a few of them only. Thus the *mukula* tree viewed in abstraction from any given ritual context may stand for "matriliny," "huntsmanship," "menstrual blood," "the meat of wild animals," and many other concepts and things. The associational link between its various senses is provided by the red gum it secretes, which Ndembu liken to blood. Now in the boys' circumcision ritual (*Mukanda*) the meaning of *mukula* is determined by its symbolic context. A log of this wood is placed near the site where the boys are circumcised. They are circumcised under a mudyi tree, which, as we shall see, stands *inter alia* for motherhood and the mother–child relationship. Then they are lifted over a cutting of the *muyombu* tree, which is customarily planted quick-set as a shrine to the village ancestor spirits, and placed still bleeding on the *mukula* log. Here the *mukula* log stands mainly for two things. It represents the wish of the elders that the circumcision wounds will heal quickly—from the fact that *mukula* quickly coagulates like a scab. But it also represents, I was told,

masculinity (*wuyala*), and the life of an adult male, who as hunter and warrior has to shed blood. The rite represents (a) the removal of the boy from dependence on his mother (the passage from the *mudyi* tree); (b) his ritual death and subsequent association with the ancestors (the passage over the *muyombu* tree); and (c) his incorporation into the male moral community of tribesmen (the collective setting on the *mukula* tree where the boys are ceremonially fed as though they were infants by the circumcisers and by their fathers. Each boy was given a ball of cassava mush to be eaten directly from the circumciser's knife). In this rite the position of the *mukula* symbol with reference to other symbolic objects and acts is the crucial semantic factor.

The same symbol may be reckoned to have different senses at different phases in a ritual performance, or rather different senses become paramount at different times. Which sense shall become paramount is determined by the ostensible purpose of the phase of the ritual in which it appears. For a ritual, like a space-rocket, is phased, and each phase is directed towards a limited end which itself becomes a means to the ultimate end of the total performance. Thus the act of circumcision is the aim and culmination of a symbol-loaded phase of the *Mukanda* ritual, but itself becomes a means to the final end of turning a boy into a tribesman. There is a consistent relationship between the end or aim of each phase in a ritual, the kind of symbolic configuration employed in that phase, and the senses which become paramount in multivocal symbols in that configuration.

I should now like to consider the exegetical meaning of one of the principal Ndembu ritual symbols, the *mudyi* tree. This symbol is found in more than half a dozen different kinds of ritual. But its *locus classicus* is in the girl's puberty ritual (*Nkang'a*). The novice is laid, wrapped in a blanket, at the foot of a slender young *mudyi* sapling. Ndembu say that its pliancy stands for the youth of the girl. The sapling has been previously consecrated by the novice's ritual instructress (*nkong'u*) and her mother. They trampled down the grass in a circle around the tree, thus making it sacred—"set

apart" (*chakumbodyi*) or "forbidden" (*chakujila*).
The site, like that of circumcision for the boys, is
called *ifwilu* or "the place of dying." Both sites are
also known as *ihung'u* "the place of suffering" or
"ordeal." *Ihung'u* is also applied to a hut where a
woman is in labour. It is a "place of suffering"
because the novice must not move her limbs until
nearly nightfall on penalty of being pinched all over
by the older women. Nor may she eat or speak all
day. The association of the *mudyi* tree with suffering and dying should be borne in mind as an aspect
of its positional meaning.

Ndembu begin the exposition of *mudyi's* meaning by pointing out that if its bark is scratched beads
of milky latex are promptly secreted. For this
reason, they say that *mudyi* or "milk-tree" is a
symbol (*chinjikijilu*) for "breasts" and "breast
milk"—both called in Chindembu *mayeli*. They go
on from there to say that *mudyi* means "a mother
and her child," i.e. a social relationship. They further extend this sense to signify a matrilineage
(*ivumu*—literally "a womb or stomach"). A text
which I collected well expresses this view:

*Mudyi diku kwakaminiyi nkakulula hakumutembwisha
    aninkakulula*
    The milk-tree is the place where slept the (founding)
    ancestress, where they initiated her and another
    ancestress

*mukwawu nimukwawu ni kudi nkaka ni kudi mama
    ninetu anyana;*
    and (then) another down to the grandmother and the
    mother and ourselves the children;

*diku kumuchidi wetu kutwatachikili ni amayala nawa
    chochu hamu.*
    It is the place where our tribe (or tribal custom—
    literally "kind") began, and also the men in just the
    same way.

My informant then added the following comments: The milk-tree is the place of all mothers; it
is the ancestress of men and women. *Ku-tembwisha,*
"to initiate a girl," means to dance round and round
the milk-tree where the novice lies. The milk-tree is
the place where our ancestors slept, to be initiated
there means to become ritually pure or white. An
uninitiated girl, a menstruating woman, or an uncircumcised boy is called "one who lacks whiteness"
(*wunabulakutooka*).

Contextually, a particular novice's milk-tree
may be termed "her matrilineage." At one phase of
the ritual, the leaves of this tree are said to represent
"the novice's children"—a sense which is concerned with a future wished-for state of affairs
rather than with the past or present.

In other phases of the *Nkang'a* ritual the milk-
tree is said to stand for "the women" and for "womanhood." It also has the situational sense of "married womanhood."

Finally, the milk-tree stands for the process
of learning (*ku-diza*), especially for learning
"women's sense" or "wisdom" (*mana yawambanda*).
An informant said that "mudyi" is like going to
school; "the girl drinks sense as a baby drinks
milk."

The semantic structure of *mudyi* may itself be
likened to a tree. At the root is the primary sense of
"breast milk" and from this proceeds by logical
steps series of further senses. The general direction
is from the concrete to the increasingly abstract, but
there are several different branches along which
abstraction proceeds. One line develops as follows:
breast, mother–child relationship, matriliny, the
Ndembu tribe or tribal custom of which matriliny is
the most representative principle. Another line runs:
development of the breasts, womanhood, married
womanhood, childbearing. Yet another goes from
suckling to learning the tasks, rights, and duties of
womanhood. As with many other Ndembu symbols, derivative senses themselves become symbols
pointing to ideas and phenomena beyond themselves. Thus "matriliny," a derivative sense from
"the mother–child relationship," and "breast-milk,"
by the principle of *pars pro toto,* itself becomes a
symbol for Ndembu culture in its totality.

But despite this multiplicity of senses Ndembu
speak and think about the milk-tree as a unity,
almost as a unitary *power.* They can break down the
concept "milk-tree" cognitively into many attributes, but in ritual practice they view it as a single
entity. For them it is something like Goethe's "eter-

nal womanly," a female or maternal principle pervading society and nature. For it must not be forgotten that ritual symbols are not merely signs representing known things; they are felt to possess ritual efficacy, to be charged with power from unknown sources, and to be capable of acting on persons and groups coming in contact with them in such a way as to change them for the better or in a desired direction. Symbols, in short, have an orectic as well as a cognitive function. They elicit emotion and express and mobilize desire.

Indeed it is possible further to conceptualize the exegetic meaning of dominant symbols in polar terms. At one pole cluster a set of referents of a grossly physiological character, relating to general human experience of an emotional kind. At the other pole cluster a set of referents to moral norms and principles governing the social structure. If we call these semantic poles respectively the "orectic" and the "normative" pole, and consider Ndembu ritual symbols in terms of this model, we find that the milk-tree stands at one and the same time for the physiological aspect of breast-feeding with its associated affectual patterns, and for the normative order governed by matriliny. In brief, a single symbol represents both the obligatory and the desirable. Here we have an intimate union of the moral and the material. An exchange of qualities may take place in the psyches of the participants under the stimulating circumstances of the ritual performance, between orectic and normative poles; the former, through its association with the latter, becomes purged of its infantile and regressive character, while the normative pole becomes charged with the pleasurable effect associated with the breast-feeding situation. In one aspect, the tie of milk, under matriliny, develops into the primary structural tie. But in another aspect, and here the polar model is apposite, the former stands opposed to and resists the formation of the latter.

Other important Ndembu symbols have a similar polar structure. *Mukula,* for example, in the context of *Nkula,* a ritual performed to cure menstrual disorders, represents at its orectic pole the "blood of birth," while at the normative pole, it represents

matriliny and also the historical connexion between the Ndembu and the empire of Mwantiyanvwa in the Congo, whose first incumbent, a female chief called Luweji Ankonde, suffered from menorxhagia. The tough *chikoli* thorn-tree, which plays an important role in the boys' circumcision ritual, is said to stand for "masculinity" in the moral and social sense. It is said to stand for courage (*wulobu*), skill at hunting, and for "speaking well in legal cases." But *chikoli* also has its physiological pole. To quote one informant: "*Chikoli* is a very strong tree, its wood is very hard. One name for it is *chikang' anjamba,* from *ku-kang' anya,* "to fail," and *njamba,* "the elephant." The elephant fails to break it. Neither wind or rain can break it, and white ants cannot eat it. It stands upright like the male organ, or a man's strong body. That is why we say it represents strength (*wukolu*)." *Chikoli,* like *wukolu,* is derived from *ku-kola,* "to be strong or potent." I could cite many other Ndembu examples, if time permitted, of this polarity, which I consider to be a universal feature of ritual symbols of any semantic complexity.

But let us return to the *mudyi* tree, this time to observe what takes place near and around it on the day of the novice's ordeal, the phase of *Kwing'ija,* or "Putting in," with which the girl's puberty ritual (*Nkang'a*) begins. For now we are going to consider the operational meaning of the milk-tree. Immediately we are confronted with a problem. For whereas it can be argued that on the exegetic level of meaning, the structural referents of the milk-tree are concerned with the harmonious and solidary aspects of groups and relationships organized by matriliny or femininity, it is immediately obvious that much of the behaviour observable in connexion with it represents a mimesis of conflict within those very groups and relationships.

For example, in the early hours of the morning only the senior women of the novice's own village may dance around the *mudyi* tree. Later on, only women and not men, may dance there, and the women attack the men in jeering and lampooning songs. Moreover, for a long time the girl's mother may not approach the *mudyi* tree, and when she eventually does so, she is mocked by the senior women. I might also mention an episode in which all the senior women compete to be first to snatch a spoon of cassava mush and beans, called "the porridge of *chipwampwilu,*" from the ritual instructress. This porridge represents fertility, and in particular the novice's fertility. If a woman from a distant village grabs the spoon first, this is thought to mean that the novice will bear her children far away from her mother's place of residence. This episode represents competition between the principles of matriliny and virilocality. Other episodes in Nkang'a also signify this conflict, though most of them do not have direct reference to the milk-tree.

Thus, during different episodes, the value attached to the solidarity of women is contradicted in practice by the conflict between the novice's mother and the adult women who are ritually incorporating her daughter into their married ranks and removing her from her mother's knee. It is further contradicted by the separation of the novice's village members from the other women, and by the rivalry, on a village basis, between the women for the novice's fertility, and between individual women for fertility. The unity of the tribe is contradicted by the mobilization of the women around the milk-tree in jeering opposition to the men. And the novice's ordeal, with the threat of punishment if she moves, represents one aspect of the conflict between senior women and girls.

What is interesting is that indigenous informants do not relate these conflicts, stereotyped though they be, to their orthodox interpretations of the symbolism of the milk-tree. Yet these mimed conflicts have to take place at the *ifwilu,* the novice's "dying-place," which is located next to the milk-tree. A psychoanalyst of the Kleinian school might be tempted perhaps to relate the contrast between the exegetic and operational levels of meaning, between the emphasis on harmony and the emphasis on discord, to the infant's ambivalent attitude to the mother's breast, which both soothes him and arouses hostility by its apparently capricious absences. He might regard the lack of interpretation

of the conflict behaviour as due to the psychological "splitting" mechanism which separates the hostile from the loving attitude to the breast and thrusts this hostility into the unconscious psyche. But it is theoretically inadmissible to explain social facts, such as ritual symbols, by the concepts of depth psychology. A sociological hypothesis to account for the contradiction between these levels of meaning might be advanced to the effect that on the exegetic level, the principle of matriliny is abstracted from its social context and appears in its ideal purity. The conflicts within groups and relationships articulated by matriliny which are exhibited at the operational level are not due to the structural inadequacies of matriliny or to human frailty with regard to keeping rules, but rather result from other principles of social organization which constantly and consistently interfere with the harmonious working of matriliny. Age and sex differences cut across matrilineal affiliation. Virilocal marriage strikes into the cohesion of a local matrilineage. The matricentric family makes rival demands on the loyalty of members of a matrilineage. Type-conflicts of these kinds are acted out before the milk-tree, the arch-symbol of matrilineal continuity, and of the ultimate dependence of Ndembu society on the mother's breast. The puberty ritual asserts that though matriliny may regularly be challenged by other principles and trends, yet it persists and triumphs.

In conclusion, I would like to draw attention to the relationship between the milk-tree symbolism and the symbolic principle of "whiteness" (*wutooka*) on the exegetic level of interpretation. At the apex of the total symbolic system of the Ndembu is the colour triad, white—red—black. At certain esoteric episodes in the boys' circumcision ritual and in the initial ritual of the men's and women's funerary associations of *Mung'ong'i* and *Chiwila* the meanings of these three colours are taught to young Ndembu. Whiteness is most commonly represented by powdered white clay (*mpemba* or *mpeza*), redness by powdered red clay (*mukundu, ng'ula,* or *mukung'u*), and blackness by charcoal (*makala*). These substances are not so much symbols as tokens of three vital principles, akin to the Hindu "strands of life" mentioned in the Bhagavadgita. I have collected many texts and made many observations of the use of these colours in ritual, and may therefore state briefly that whiteness stands, inter alia, for "goodness (*ku-waha*), health (*ku-koleka*), ritual purity (*ku-tooka*), freedom from misfortune (*ku-bula ku-halwa*), for political authority (*wanta*), and for assembling with the spirits (*kudibomba niakishi*)." To sum up drastically: it represents the entire moral order plus the fruits of virtue; health, strength, fertility, the respect of one's fellows, and the blessing of one's ancestors. Whiteness differs from redness in that it stresses harmony, cohesion, and continuity, while redness, associated with blood-spilling as well as with blood-kinship, tends to denote discontinuity, strength acquired through breach of certain rules, and male aggressiveness (as in hunting, which is represented in many rituals by red clay and red symbols).

Now there are many symbols which Ndembu themselves class as "white things" and which they believe to be pervaded by the moral attributes of whiteness. The milk-tree, representing matriliny, is one of these. For Ndembu, matriliny is what Professor Fortes has called, though in a rather different connexion, an "irreducible principle"[1] of social organization, through which the moral order, with all its prescription and prohibitions, is mediated to the individual. Matriliny is the framework of those aspects of Ndembu morality which the people regard as changeless and as harmoniously interrelated nodal points. It would be possible to show that the norms and values controlling those relationships derived from the tie of milk form the "matrix" of the moral order, and have ideally what Ndembu would regard as a "white" quality. Matriliny gives a specific form and stamp to a morality which would otherwise be imprecise and general.

ENDNOTE

1. Cf. *The Web of Kinship among the Tallensi*, Oxford University Press, 1949, p. 344.

READING 4–3

CONCLUSIONS

Arnold van Gennep

This reading is the conclusion to a book that describes the most famous of all categories of ritual, "rites of passage," which was first identified by the Belgian folklorist Arnold van Gennep in 1908. Van Gennep, although a contemporary of Emile Durkheim, and not at all adverse to studying human behavior from a sociological perspective, worked independently of Durkheim's Anné sociologique school. Comparative library research led van Gennep to notice that when significant transitions in life are undergone, as at birth, puberty, marriage, and death, society often marks these transitions with what he called "rites of passage." He proposed that rites of passage in their exemplary form consist of three stages, each of which corresponds to a step in the progress of an individual or group through the complete ritual. These three stages are separation, liminality (or transition, or limen), and incorporation. In this triadic system the individual or group first undergoes separation from an original status, then is temporarily isolated from society, and finally is incorporated into a new status.

The stage of separation connotes the idea of severance from the existing status. In the traditional Western wedding, for example, the bride is symbolically separated from the rest of society by a veil. Liminality is the stage that places individuals in no man's land where they find themselves "betwixt or between" statuses. They are marginally positioned—physically, psychologically, perhaps both—somewhere between their former status and their forthcoming one. At the altar the bride is located between her father, who represents the status she is departing, and her husband-to-be, who represents the new status she is about to enter. The final stage typically entails a meal shared by all involved members of the community or maybe a dance in which the initiate rejoins society in his or her new role. At a wedding, the exit of the bride and groom, arm in arm, through a throng of well-wishers symbolizes their reintegration into society in a new status.

Source: The Rites of Passage, Translated by Monika B. Vizedom and Gabrielle L. Caffee. Chicago: The University of Chicago Press 1960 [1908].

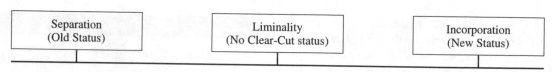

FIGURE 3 The Three Stages In a Rite of Passage.

Ethnographers have applied van Gennep's fruitful insight to their own work (see Turner 1967: 93–111), and some have shown that local populations may emphasize one or other stage at the expense of the others. Other anthropologists have developed the notion of liminality to include spheres of social life not considered by van Gennep, as Victor Turner has done with his influential notion of communitas.

Turner defines communitas as a set of "relationships between those jointly undergoing ritual transition" (Turner 1974:274), as, for instance, among initiates undergoing a rite of passage. Within this situation, and since they are outside of the social structure and the institutions of society, their relationships with each other in the state of communitas are not subject to the norms of society. Instead of being governed by the conventions upon which social structure depends, their mutual relationships are spontaneous, and their interaction uninhibited by the conventional rules imposed by status or role-playing. This is not to say that individuals in communitas merge their individual identities, Turner says, but they are liberated from social conformity. Turner sees communitas as offering some benefits to society, most notably creativity and dynamism. Having escaped—however fleetingly—from normal social restrictions individuals in a condition of communitas may, he suggests, experience feelings of unbounded exhilaration at being freed—even if temporarily—from irksome regulations. This feeling stimulates their sense of novelty, and provides those in communitas with the opportunity to take a fresh look at the social conventions they have abandoned. From this novel perspective they may even come to devise ways of improving or perhaps even replacing the traditional rituals and beliefs of society.

CONCLUSIONS

Our brief examination of the ceremonies through which an individual passes on all the most important occasions of his life has now been completed.

It is but a rough sketch of an immense picture, whose every detail merits careful study.

We have seen that an individual is placed in various sections of society, synchronically and in succession; in order to pass from one category to another and to join individuals in other sections, he must submit, from the day of his birth to that of his death, to ceremonies whose forms often vary but whose function is similar. Sometimes the individual stands alone and apart from all groups; sometimes, as a member of one particular group, he is separated from the members of others. Two primary divisions are characteristic of all societies irrespective of time and place: the sexual separation between men and women, and the magico-religious separation between the profane and the sacred. However, some special groups—such as religious associations, totem clans, phratries, castes, and professional classes—appear in only a few societies. Within each society there is also the age group, the family, and the restricted politico-administrative and territorial unit (band, village, town). In addition to this complex world of the living, there is the world preceding life and the one which follows death.

These are the constants of social life, to which have been added particular and temporary events such as pregnancy, illnesses, dangers, journeys, etc. And always the same purpose has resulted in the same form of activity. For groups, as well as for individuals, life itself means to separate and to be reunited, to change form and condition, to die and to be reborn. It is to act and to cease, to wait and rest, and then to begin acting again, but in a different way. And there are always new thresholds to cross: the thresholds of summer and winter, of a season or a year, of a month or a night; the thresholds of birth, adolescence, maturity, and old age; the threshold of death and that of the afterlife—for those who believe in it.

I am certainly not the first to have been struck by the resemblances among various components of the ceremonies discussed here. Similarities have been noted between entire rites, as well as among minor details. Thus, for example, Hartland[1] observed the resemblances between certain initiation rites and some rites of marriage; Frazer[2] perceived those between certain puberty rites and funerals; Ciszewski,[3] those among certain rites of baptism, friendship, adoption, and marriage. Diels[4] followed by Dieterich[5] and Hertz,[6] pointed out similarities among certain ceremonies of birth, marriage, and funerals, and Hertz added to the list rites for the opening of a new house (but did not present evidence) and rites of sacrifice. Goblet d'Alviella[7] pointed out the resemblance between baptism and initiation; Webster,[8] that between initiation into secret societies and the ordination of a shaman.

Hertz[9] was interested in the order of funeral rites and alluded to what he called the "transitory stage"—the period that lasts from marriage to the birth of the first child and that corresponds to the "transitory stage" of the dead in Indonesia (especially in Borneo). But except for him, all these scholars, including Crawley,[10] saw only resemblances in particulars. For instance, the communal meal (Smith's "communion sacrifice"), union through blood, and a number of other ties of incorporation furnished the subject matter for several interesting chapters by Hartland. Certain rites of separation, like temporary seclusion and dietary and sexual taboos, Frazer and Crawley found recurring in a great many sets of ceremonies. Diels, Dieterich, and, in general, all those who have been concerned with classical religions have demonstrated the importance in these religions of the so-called rites of purification (anointing, lustration, etc.). It was inevitable that marked resemblances would appear when a specific rite, such as the exchange of blood, was isolated for analysis in a monograph and when contexts were superimposed.

A host of ethnographers and folklorists have demonstrated that among the majority of peoples, and in all sorts of ceremonies, identical rites are performed for identical purposes. In this way, and

thanks first to Bastian, then to Tylor, and later to Andree, a great many unilateral theories were destroyed. Today their orientation is of interest because, in the long run, it will make possible the delineation of cultural sequences and the stages of civilization.

The purpose of this book is altogether different. Our interest lies not in the particular rites but in their essential significance and their relative positions within ceremonial wholes—that is, their order. For this reason, some rather lengthy descriptions have been included in order to demonstrate how rites of preliminary or permanent separation, transition, and incorporation are placed in relation to one another for a specific purpose. Their positions may vary, depending on whether the occasion is birth or death, initiation or marriage, but the differences lie only in matters of detail. The underlying arrangement is always the same. Beneath a multiplicity of forms, either consciously expressed or merely implied, a typical pattern always recurs: *the pattern of the rites of passage.*

The second fact to be pointed out—whose generality no one seems to have noticed previously—is the existence of transitional periods which sometimes acquire a certain autonomy. Examples of these are seen in the novitiate and the betrothal. It is this concept of transition that provides an orientation for understanding the intricacies and the order of rites preliminary to marriage.

Third, it seems important to me that the passage from one social position to another is identified with a *territorial passage,* such as the entrance into a village or a house, the movement from one room to another, or the crossing of streets and squares. This identification explains why the passage from one group to another is so often ritually expressed by passage under a portal,[1] or by an "opening of the doors." These phrases and events are seldom meant as "symbols"; for the semicivilized the passage is actually a territorial passage. In fact, the spatial separation of distinct groups is an aspect of social organization. The children live with the women up to a certain age; boys and girls live separated from married people, sometimes in a special house or section or in a special kraal; at marriage one of the two spouses, if not both, changes residence; warriors do not keep company with blacksmiths, and sometimes each professional class has its assigned place of residence.[2] In the Middle Ages the Jews were isolated in their ghettos, just as the Christians of the first centuries lived in remote sections. The territorial separation between clans may also be very definite,[3] and each Australian band camps in a specific place when on the march.[4] In short, a change of social categories involves a change of residence, and this fact is expressed by the rites of passage in their various forms.

As I have said several times, I do not maintain that all rites of birth, initiation, etc., are rites of passage only, or that all peoples have developed characteristic rites of passage for birth, initiation, and so forth. Funeral ceremonies in particular, since they depend on local beliefs concerning man's fate after death, may consist primarily of defensive procedures against the soul of the deceased and rules of prophylaxis against the contagion of death; in that case they present only a few aspects of the typical pattern. Nevertheless, it is always wise to be careful about such conclusions; the pattern may not appear in a summary description of the funeral ceremonies of a particular people, although it is clearly evident in a more detailed account. Similarly, among some peoples who do not consider the woman impure during her pregnancy and who allow anyone to be present at delivery, childbirth is only an ordinary act, painful but normal. But in that case the pattern will be transposed to the rites of childhood, or it may be included in the rites of betrothal and marriage.

The units of ceremonial life among certain peoples sometimes differ from those which are prevalent in our own and most other societies and those around which the chapters of this book have been organized. It has been pointed out, for example, that among the Todas there is a single set of ceremonies extending from the parents' adolescence to the birth of the first child and that it would be arbitrary to divide this set into ceremonies preliminary to puberty, pertaining to puberty, to marriage, to preg-

nancy, to delivery, to birth, and to childhood. This amalgamation recurs among many other groups, but in the last analysis this effort at synthesis is not affected by it. Although the pattern of the rites of passage occurs in a different form in these instances, it is present nonetheless, and it is clearly elaborated.

Another general observation seems pertinent. The preceding analysis has shown variations in the internal division of societies, the relation of the diverse sections to one another, and the breadth of the barriers between them, which range from a simple imaginary line to a vast neutral region. Thus it would be possible to draw a diagram for each people in which the peaks of a zigzag line would represent recognized stages and the valleys the intervening periods. The apexes would sometimes be sharp peaks and sometimes flattened lines of varying length. For example, among certain peoples there are practically no betrothal rites except a meal shared at the moment of the preliminary agreement; the marriage ceremonies begin immediately afterward. Among others, on the contrary, there is a whole series of stages from the time of the betrothal (at an early age) until the newly married couple's return to ordinary life, and each of these stages possesses a certain degree of autonomy.

Whatever the intricacies of the pattern, the order from birth until death must often consists of successive stages best represented in rectilinear form. Among certain peoples like the Lushae, however, it is circular, so that all individuals go through the same endless series of rites of passage from life to death and from death to life. This extreme cyclical form of the pattern has acquired in Buddhism an ethical and philosophical significance, and for Nietzsche, in his theory of the eternal return, a psychological significance.

Finally, the series of human transitions has, among some peoples, been linked to the celestial passages, the revolutions of the planets, and the phases of the moon. It is indeed a cosmic conception that relates the stages of human existence to those of plant and animal life and, by a sort of prescientific divination, joins them to the great rhythms of the universe.

ENDNOTES

1. Hartland, *The Legend of Perseus,* II, 335–99.
2. Frazer, *The Golden Bough,* pp. 204–7, 209, 210 ff., 418, etc.
3. Ciszewski, *Künstliche Verwandschaft bei den Südslaven,* pp. 1–4, 31, 36, 53, 54, 107–11, 114, etc.
4. Hermann Diels, *Sibyllinische Blätter,* p. 48.
5. Dieterich, *Mutter Erde,* pp. 56–57.
6. Hertz, "La représentation collective de la mort," pp. 104, 117, 126–27.
7. Goblet d'Alviella, "De quelques problèmes relatifs aux mystères d'Élcusis," p. 340.
8. Webster, *Primitive Secret Societies,* p. 176.
9. Hertz, "La représentation collective de la mort," p. 130, n. 5.
10. Crawley (*The Mystic Rose.*) points out the precise similarities in the rites of marriage and funerals (p. 369) and rites of marriage and initiation (p. 326); on the last point, see also Reinach, *Cultes, mythes, et religions,* I, 309.
1. Trumbull has even noted (*The Threshold Covenant,* pp. 252–57)—among the Chinese, the Greeks, the Hebrews, and others—an identification of the woman and the door.
2. [The reader will note that all these instances are not equally applicable to all societies.]
3. See the separation of the clans in the Pueblo villages as described, among others, by Cosmos Mindeleff, *Localization of Tusayan Clans.* (Nineteenth Annual Report of The Bureau of American Ethnology [1897–98], Part II [Washington, D.C.: Government Printing Office, 1900]), pp. 635–53.
4. See, among others, Howitt, *The Native Tribes of South East Australia,* pp. 773–77 (on camping rules).

READING 4–4

RETURN TO THE WOMB

David Hicks

This reading is an example of a structural approach to the analysis of ritual. But besides deriving its inspiration from the work of Claude Lévi-Strauss, the analysis owes a debt to Arnold van Gennep (Reading 4–3) whose three stages are clearly seen in the Tetum death ritual. Here death produces three residual categories: the corpse, the deceased's soul, and the deceased's kinsfolk. We find that each of these three entities undergoes its own distinct

Source: David Hicks, "Return to the Womb," in *A Maternal Religion: The Role of Women in Tetum Myth and Ritual.* (De Kalb: Northern Illinois University, Center for Southeast Asian Studies, 1984), pp. 107–24. Reprinted by permission of the author.

rites of passage, which are signposted by symbols representing severance, liminality, and incorporation.

Another influence apparent in this reading is Robert Herz's study of death as a collective representation (see Introduction to Chapter 8). In particular, the ritual specifies that during the time when the ethnographer was collecting the information, i.e., in the late 1960s, the transitional period lasted three days. However, in former times, after the rites of separation had been observed, the corpse would be placed in a tree, remaining there for as much as seven years before being permanently interred in the ground. This is an instance of Herz's "double burial." Herz accounted for this custom in terms of the psychological need to permit the sense of loss suffered by the survivors to gradually atrophy over an extended period of time and to allow the gap made in the deceased's network of social relations to be gradually effaced. This is an outside analyst's interpretation and may or may not accord with local perspectives. For the record, Tetum villagers gave as their reason for this traditional practice the need to ensure everyone entitled to view the corpse had the opportunity to do so. An ordinary villager, with no political ties, would need to be seen only by his or her relatives, and so the period between the two burials would be short. On the other hand, the remains of a king would need to be viewed by non-related persons as well as by relatives, and it might take years for his entire political constituency to be accommodated.

RESTORING ORDER

On Timor, an island lying just north of Australia, live a population known as the Tetum. Their cosmos consists of the human world and an underworld inhabited by spirits. The inhabitants of each world normally keep their distance from one another. But when human beings break taboos, the spirits enter the human upperworld, thereby breaching the boundary separating the two domains. Sickness and other misfortunes are thought to be expressions of the disorder represented by the conflation of the two worlds.

The paradigm par excellence of disorder in the cosmos, however, is death. Cosmic order is destroyed for the dead person, and for his affines and agnates. In effect, this means everyone in Mamulak and Mane Hat; and for normal life to continue, cosmic order must be restored. The ritual of death accomplishes this separation-leading-to-restoration, and it is because the emphasis is on separation rather than union that women do not play such a prominent part in the death ritual as in most unifying rituals.

The disjunctive motif of the death ritual restructures three anomalies. Although associated with the underworld, the corpse (*lolon maté*), the dead soul, and the deceased's agnates (*ema maté,* "people of death"), are still predominantly upperworld figures. The corpse is tangible, yet inclines toward the unknown world below, since it no longer functions as a normal human being. The dead soul is invisible and intangible, yet for a year can move freely in the world above. The agnates are visible, yet descent links them with the corpse.

The ritual consists of three series of rites of passage, and it works to make each of these three anomalies clear-cut members of either the sacred world, or the secular world. One series transforms the corpse into a full-fledged member of the world below. The second does likewise for the dead soul. The third restores kin to full community existence in the upperworld.

In van Gennep fashion, the Tetum ritual consists of three stages, with each anomaly going through each stage. The corpse's separation from the upperworld is marked by the destruction of his possessions. Three days' isolation, in a building especially erected to receive it, the house of death (*uma maté*), signals the corpse's transition. Interment, the third stage, integrates the corpse into the underworld. For the corpse and kin these disjunctive rites occupy three days.

A full year must follow upon the burial for the dead soul to be considered safely integrated into the sacred world. So the entire duration of this ritual is actually twelve months and three days. During this period the deceased's kin continue to fear the dead soul, and the deceased's spouse is prohibited from remarrying.

The agnates of the dead person, the "people of death" (*ema maté*), are contrasted with his affines (*ema moris,* "people who give life"). The "people of death" is a category that, strictly speaking, should include all members of the deceased's clan. At most funerals, however, only the members of the same

hamlet as the dead person and those lineage agnates who expressly join with the hamlet for the event actually perform the activities incumbent upon the people of death. The people who give life thus include some agnates as well as affines, but in deference to local classification, I shall refer to them as "affines." The agnates, then, are the people of death; the affines, the people who give life.

That the people of death is an anomalous category is suggested by the evidence that, though physically alive, persons in this category are, in fact, termed people of death. They are separated in the first stage from the community, when their hair is cut. Next, together with the corpse, they are isolated in the house of death. Then, within an hour or so of the interment they re-enter the community and upperworld participation in a rite of commensality with their affines, after which meal they cease to be called people of death. Other than as keeners, the people of death remain passive throughout most of the ritual. Only when the coffin is about to be taken from their hamlet are they roused into any kind of involvement with the people who give life, an action that actually emphasizes their intimate association with the corpse. By way of contrast, the people of life busy themselves in constructing kitchens, eating houses, and the house of death, making the coffin, fetching water, cooking, washing up, clipping their agnates' hair, destroying the deceased's property, preparing the corpse for burial, carrying the coffin to the cemetery, and burying it.

Tama maté ("to enter or be buried in the underworld") is the term for death ritual, and applies to both the entire ritual and, more specifically, to that action which gives its name to the total set of rites, that is, the burial itself. In Caraubalo, Christians are interred in the cemetery of Santa Cruz, a place located near the dato wain's hamlet in Barique. Pagans are interred near Baria Laran hamlet.

The form of the ritual I shall describe is the most common type practiced in Caraubalo. When, in ancient days, a king died, the ritual was somewhat different; otherwise, neither sex, class, nor religious affiliations make for much variation from the pattern of activities I describe now.

THE RITES OF SEPARATION

A normal death, like birth, takes place in the house womb. Even while an ailing person is dying, his hamlet fellows select two persons of the deceased's lineage (if male) or of the deceased husband's lineage (if female), so that when the expected death occurs, they can set out immediately to visit every hamlet whose lineage is related either by descent or affinity to that of the dead person's lineage. This means that the emissaries must travel to every aristocratic hamlet in the princedom, in other words, all the hamlets of Mamulak and Mane Hat.

In each hamlet a woman comes forward to offer the messengers lime, seven pieces of areca, and seven betel leaves, after which the head messenger addresses her:

1. You lived here
2. You, our mother-in-law, Cassa Bo
3. The deceased used to come here many times
4. Seven of your daughters may perhaps follow us to become pregnant
5. Seven may carry the root
6. But as yet your hand has not followed
7. But as yet your foot has not followed
8. Some water has been slopped
9. A little water has been spilt
10. It flows down to you, our affines
11. Whom we grasp, whom we hold tightly
12. Indeed, you, mother-in-law, and we, are one person
13. In two persons
14. You, siblings-in-law, and we, are one person
15. In two persons
16. To whom we always give water
17. Who always address us in ritual words
18. Who rebuke us
19. The tree of the rat
20. The rat in the tree
21. We don't like it, we don't like it; we cut it down
22. Run from the carrying basket
23. Until you arrive at the place of many houses
24. Until you arrive at the place of many midwives
25. Come to your sister
26. You, our mother, our hand
27. Our foot; come to listen
28. Come and join us
29. To find your eldest sister, you must leave your hamlet
30. But go no further
31. And all your relatives, too
32. And your senior males
33. They and their rebukes must come
34. You are our trouble removers
35. A corpse, a corpse
36. Force yourselves to see
37. Look at the tree
38. High! Its branches are high
39. Climb to place the coffin at its summit
40. Climb the stalk [kain]
41. Change the dog, mother-in-law
42. Change the chicken, mother-in-law

The messengers take their leave.

The term *kain* (line 40) is part of an injunction to the people who give life to climb the tree mentioned in the three previous lines, the tree at whose summit the coffin used to be placed in former days. The term *kain* is used here with the sense of "link," a connection which, since the tree in the birth ritual is the clan tree, enables us to discern an important notion hitherto unsuspected, namely, that the tree symbolizes the tie between the individual and his ancestral ghosts. As formerly practiced, therefore, the ritual returns the deceased person to the place whence he emerged at birth, and because his origins lie in the underworld this world receives him at death. And so, human existence in the upperworld is a transitory episode in a cycle which begins and ends in the underworld.

Lines 34–35 establish the intention of the ritual: to remove the "trouble" plaguing the people of death. Though only the corpse is mentioned, I was told the lines also referred to the dead soul and to the contagious state of the people of death. In the final couplet, the affines (represented by the mother-in-law) are urged to act out their role as transformers. Between lines 10–15, and on line 2, the "link" between the two groups is intensely expressed. Indeed, lines 12–15 admirably present an image of unity-in-the-dyad. The "root" mentioned on line 5 is a metaphor for the affinal bond.

The woman of the affinal hamlet, though addressed as if her group had actually given women to that of the deceased's, need not actually be a member of a wife-giving descent-group. Yet the hamlets in Mamulak and Mane Hat intermarry so much the likelihood is that she almost certainly is. The contrast being made is between the people of death and the people who give life, and such is the force of dualism in Tetum thinking that it defines all hamlets (apart from the hamlet of death) as affinal, that is, as of the people who give life.

The death ritual is, as I have said, a ritual whose purpose is to restore the disjunction between the upperworld and the underworld, but—as certain metaphors in the above speech show, and as revealed by metaphors in the following speech—images of union abound. These involve the bonds uniting the people of death with their affines and the reason they appear is that the people of death are reminding their affines of the responsibilities the affines owe them, one of which is carrying out the death ritual.

Let us examine them. Water, in lines 8–10, is said to have slopped onto the ground and flows downhill. The image presented here is of a stream flowing from the people of death to their affines, and uniting them. It is reinforced by line 16: "To whom we always give water." Lines 4–5 contain the usual reference to the number seven. The allusion to daughters who "may carry the root" (lines 4–5), reminds the affines they supply brides who will one day become "pregnant." The "sister" (line 25) is any female they have ever provided, and line 29 specifies, more exactly, "elder sister." Elder sisters generally marry before younger sisters, they become the "mothers" of the people of death (line 26). The people who give life are urged to "run from" their hamlet (line 22) to where there are "many houses" (line 23) and "many midwives" (line 24), that is, to the deceased's hamlet. The large number of its midwives implies there will be many offspring. The messengers' speech (line 1) at the birth ritual introduced the terms "hand" and "leg."

They return here (lines 6, 7, 26, 27). The people who give life are asked to come to the people of death. Cassa Bo ("Cassa-the-Great") is a pseudonym given to the female representative of the affinal hamlet, "out of respect for" Cassa Sonek, whose name is thus evoked at both birth and death rituals. The "tree of the rat" (lines 19–21), i.e. the sago palm, is cut down for the coffin.

While the messengers are traveling from hamlet to hamlet, those members of the people of life category who arrive first at the hamlet of death commence their prescribed tasks. After their machetes have struck down a suitable sago palm, younger members of the party hollow out its inside, while others cut down another tree, and split off a flat piece of wood for the coffin lid.

Female people who give life weave a white cloth that is to be wrapped around the coffin after it has been placed in the death house. When this has been done, men tack nails into the cloth at either end of the casket. Each set of nails is so patterned that when red and yellow threads are wound around it they form a starlike shape the villagers liken to the sun. Only royalty was allowed to display this emblem three or four generations ago, but today the coffin of even the lowliest commoner can be thus embellished.

Other people who give life meanwhile cut the hair of the female people of death, a rite of separation carried out on the verandas of the houses owned by the people of death. In another separation rite, people who give life wash the corpse, remove its clothes, destroy the deceased's weapons, utensils, and personal effects, and dress the corpse in its ceremonial finery.

Still other people who give life erect the eating house and the death house. Spinsters and young bachelors prepare food. Until the death house has been constructed and the coffin filled, the hamlet of death is a hive of activity, but by the time the death house has been erected, only cooks remain at work.

People of death keen in the house where the death occurred and continue later inside the death house. There they keep up their wails for hours at a stretch until the coffin is finally carried away.

The Death House

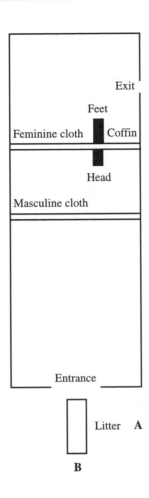

A- Place of the ritual dressing and ritual ablution

B- Site of the *hakáss*

house is internally segmented like a regular house. This second line consists of feminine cloths, which hang down over the coffin, as it straddles both rear sections of the house, an arrangement consistent with the corpse's transitional character. The corpse is to be dispatched to the underworld where it now belongs, and so is deposited nearer the feminine part of the building, just as (in the house where the death befell) it lay in the house womb, near the sacred pillar. It is from the house womb that a person emerges as an infant, and into it he returns. Here occurs conception, and here—within the womb—occurs death.

When the death house is ready, and the coffin inside awaits its occupant, males of the people who give life carry the corpse to it. Once it is inside they nail the lid down. Those people of death most closely related to the deceased person follow the people who give life to the death house, where they begin wailing. The others remain within, silent.

Those people who give life who have performed these ritual activities wash their hands in warm water from a jar. If the cool jar symbolizes a healthy person, we might expect the hot jar to symbolize a sick person, and in the death ritual perhaps even to stand for the dead person. Its destruction and removal from the hamlet is consistent with this inference. Thus:

hot jar	—	cool jar
deceased	—	living person
corpse	—	living body

THE LIMINAL STAGE

For both corpse and people of death the transition period extends over three days. Inside the death house the corpse lies undisturbed while at its head the widowed person, parents, siblings, and children kneel side by side, heads covered with black cloths, and arms around one another's shoulders, keening "words of death." From time to time an impassioned mourner will sway forward until her (his) head touches the coffin before righting herself (himself), and from time to time recently arrived

The death house [see figure] is also termed the "black house" (*uma metan*), another association between dark colors and death. Roughly ten feet from the ground to its ridge and fourteen feet long, the house is raised three or four feet on piles. Its entrance is at the front, and to one side is its exit. If the deceased were Christian, somewhere in the house religious pictures, and perhaps a rosary, dangle from one or the other beam. From a pillar near the exit a piece of rope extends to an opposite pillar. Hanging down from it in such a way as to separate the rear of the house from the front are a few pieces of cloth. They are said to be "masculine." Another cloth partition divides the remainder of the building into two sections, so that the death people who give life will quietly enter the building and start wailing at the other end of the coffin. When their obligation is concluded they leave.

Another of their obligations consists of tendering gifts to the hamlet of death. They do this through the lord of death (*maté na'in*), a senior male of the dead person's hamlet. A close relative of the dead person is not normally chosen, for it is thought that such a person should be crying over the corpse rather than enacting the role of lord of death, and it would be too incompatible with his position as a liminal figure for a male so closely associated with the deceased.

The representative of every group among the people who give life that arrives in the hamlet goes at once to the lord of death, and gives him corn, rice, and a pig. A second gift is given, "the four patacas," which is intended to provide part of the bridewealth of the next male from the hamlet of death who marries, so the deceased's descent group can obtain a replacement. This interaction is suggested in the speech made by gift-giver to lord of death:

1. We are talking about [name of hamlet where death occurred]
2. We come about your female affines
3. Your mother
4. Noko Rubik
5. Nai Lequik
6. These words do not concern corn
7. They are not about rice
8. Instead, they concern Nai Lequik
9. Noko Rubik
10. [We] your affines
11. Those two who come to give you a new child
12. A fresh, green, child
13. But we have not forgotten your male kin
14. Your father
15. Funo Lequik
16. Lequi Rubik
17. Your baby is below
18. There below
19. Go and seize it
20. Walk and seize it
21. Come, the banana's male agnates
22. His father

23. Funo Lequik
24. Lequi Rubik
25. Seize it again
26. Come, too, his female affines
27. His mother
28. Noko Rubik
29. The four of you
30. Your banana
31. Your boat
32. The white life is arriving
33. The red life is arriving
34. In its body
35. In its body
36. Seize and hold tightly
37. The *pataca lima nulu*
38. Your banana is coming
39. The earth is shaking
40. His male agnates
41. His father
42. Funo Lequik
43. Lequi Rubik
44. Seize it
45. Seize and hold tightly
46. The four *patacas*
47. Come and shake the ground more
48. The earth is shaking
49. Noko Rubik
50. Funo Lequik
51. The four of you
52. Now, look at your gifts
53. For you have listened to our words.

These words do not concern corn

They are not about rice

With these phrases the gift-giver reminds the lord of death that his statements are metaphoric. "White life" is the infant's soul; "red life" (line 33), its blood.

In common with such Indonesian peoples as the Ngaju (Schärer, 1963:91–5, et passim), the Tetum make an association between boats and coffins. In past times, people would place the corpse of a king in a coffin that was termed "foreign boat," a designation that also applied to the king's death house. Combined with an earlier inference concerning the

Tetum view of human life, this association provides *us* with one possible interpretation of the reference to "boat" (line 31). By creating a parallel between "banana" and "coffin," this line and line 30 may be intended as an elliptical statement as to the cyclical pattern of the individual's existence, i.e. emergence (as a "banana") from the earth, and a return to the place in the coffin at death. You will recall that in Text 11 the younger brother's corpse is first put into a tree; then a boat; is taken on a sea voyage to the "other side," that is to say, to the sacred world; then restored to life.

The female figures, Noko Rubik and Nai Lequik (lines 4, 5, 8, 9, 28, 49) are names that stand for the people who give life. Their male complements, Funo Lequik and Lequi Rubik (lines 15, 16, 23, 24, 42, 43, 50), are names that stand for the people of death. The relationship terms, *ina* (lines 3, 27) and *feton* (lines 2, 26), like Noko Rubik and Nai Lequik, symbolize the people who give life (affines); the terms *aman* (lines 14, 22, 41) and *alin* (line 13), and Funo Lequik and Lequi Rubik symbolize the people of death (agnates).

Line 11 underscores one intention of the visit. The people who give life, as affines, come "to give . . . a new child" to the people of death. In the Tetum cycle of life the people who give life are thus commissioned to place the dead in the underworld and encourage a baby to emerge from the underworld into the upperworld. The people of death (lines 19, 20, 25, 36, 44, 45) are urged to seize the "banana," *pataca lima nulu, pataca ha'at,* and baby, which have been given by the people who give life. The infant, nevertheless, is a product of the two groups uniting, so on line 13 comes the reminder that the creative role of the people of death has not been "forgotten." The references to "earth" and "ground" (lines 39, 47, 48) accord with the grand theme of the cycle of life. As is literally the case with the banana, but only figuratively with the *pataca lima nulu,* the infant emerges from the "ground," or mother goddess "earth," who is said to shake like a human woman giving birth. The infant must be "seized," "held tightly" (lines 19, 20, 25, 36, 44, 45) as it comes up from "below" (lines 17, 18).

While the gift-givers leave to keen, the lord of death walks into the dead person's house. There, he places the money in a basket standing on the sacred shelf. After the commensal meal, the total offering becomes the property of the widowed person, or, if the deceased himself were widowed, of the eldest son (or daughter), who may use it as he (or she) desires.

At noon on the third day when everyone who has come to the hamlet has had a chance to wail, and the grave has been dug, senior male people who give life command a group of about eighteen young men to carry a bamboo litter to the death house. In mustering before its entrance, the lads bring the liminal stage to a close, and start the final stage, that of integration.

THE RITES OF INTEGRATION

The young men hold the litter at right angles to the house; half of them holding one side, half holding the other. When they have taken a firm grasp of the litter, they begin swaying rhythmically and in unison, from side to side. As the litter rocks gently they chant these words:

1. You poor, poor orphan
2. You poor one, your mother is not here
3. Your father is not here
4. Your mother no longer exists
5. Your father no longer exists
6. We are very near burying you
7. In Santa Cruz cemetery
8. Ancestors
9. Ancestors, come
10. Walk near us
11. Approach us
12. Enter our door.

Lines 1–5 inform the dead soul it is no longer part of the upperworld, and that it has been deprived of its kin (*aman*) and affines (*inan*). Lines 6–7 are self-explanatory, but the remaining five lines are rather less so. The ghostly ancestors of the deceased are asked to enter the death house (where the soul is thought to lurk) and conduct it to the underworld, at the same time that the people of death carry the corpse to the grave. Thus, though one journey is visible, and the other is invisible, they parallel each other in dispatching an undesirable to the other world.

While the recitation proceeds, two spinster people who give life each put on a sarong, more colorful than usual, an embroidered blouse, a bracelet, earrings, hairpins, and a head cloth. Two girls help them, and all four stand on a mat of the same type that the groom and bride sit on during the marriage ritual. While preparing themselves, the spinsters step off the mat only to have their feet washed in a bowl of water. When the two girls have dressed, they are joined by two young men dressed as old-time warriors. In his left hand, each warrior grasps a spear, and in his right, a war sword, weapons signifying the power of the people of life to defend the upperworld folk from the dead soul. The eighteen litter bearers clamber into the death house. Inside, they lift the coffin and bring it out. On the ground, in front of the house, they tie it firmly to the litter with stout cords.

Every person of death hastens to the front of the death house, where the widowed person (for convenience I shall assume it is a woman) is kneeling at the feet of one of the warriors. She puts her arms around his feet, and rests her forehead on the ground, careful not to touch his legs with her head or hands, pleading that the corpse be allowed to remain with her in the hamlet of death. She rises, and repeats her precatory rite at the second warrior's feet. Both ignore her, and move to the spot marked *B* (in the figure on page 137) to perform an action called *hakass,* in which, shoulder to shoulder, they shuffle forward and backwards, right feet leading, twisting their weapons about with short movements of their forearms. After a minute or so they shuffle up to the coffin, and gently touch it at a point over the corpse's head with the tips of their swords and spears, as though to tap the dead soul from the corpse's head, should it have taken up lodgings there. They shuffle back, and return six more times, after which they advance in a normal manner towards the

coffin, as though to carry it off to the cemetery. They reach it, and, as if on a cue, a tremendous cry erupts from somewhere in the depths of the death house, and, brandishing his own sword high in the air, the lord of death, galvanized into action, leaps onto the frontal veranda, in a ritualized attempt to keep the corpse among its kin.

Far from being intimidated by this electrifying apparition, the two warriors advance towards it, threatening to use their swords and spears, saying:

1. We have beaten it strongly
2. We have beaten it strongly
3. It has departed
4. The hamlet group was broken
5. The corpse constantly demands the words
6. Even you must speak them
7. These words must come
8. You must speak them loudly
9. They must be uttered forcefully
10. "We have beaten it strongly"
11. "We have beaten it strongly"

Lines 1–3 imply the soul has been dislodged from the body. Line 4 remarks death has fractured the integrity of the hamlet, and Line 5 refers to the presence of the corpse, which provokes the words, "We have beaten it strongly." These words must be allowed to "come" (line 7), and, it is said, despite his reluctance to permit the corpse to be taken away, the lord of death, too, must force from his lips the same words (lines 6, 7, 8, 9), and help expel the dead soul.

The warriors return to their starting position, and the lord of death joins his fellow people of death. To the accompaniment of raucous shouting by all, the coffin bearers lift the stretcher. With the corpse's feet pointing towards the cemetery, they and the rest of the people who give life begin to enter the forest. Just before they clear the confines of the hamlet, the widower and a few people of death make one final attempt to prevent it leaving, pushing past the bachelors to place their hands on the coffin. For a couple of moments the bachelors allow this, before pressing on to the grave by a route that does not pass near any other hamlet. For these are "hamlets of life" (*knua moris*).

Holding a small tray of flowers covered with a white cloth, the two spinsters lead the procession. From the left wrist of each girl dangles a "pouch of death" (*kohé maté*), and from the right wrist a "pouch of life" (*kohé moris*). Inside both are betel ingredients.

Later, after they have added a little earth to the contents of the two pouches of death ("because the soul and corpse live in the earth") as the coffin is being lowered into the grave, the girls drop the pouches of death on the coffin. The people who give life distribute the betel-chewing ingredients in the pouches of life among themselves as they cluster around the graveside, and when the burial is over take them to the hamlet of death where one of them is hung from a beam in the death house. The other is refilled with lime, areca, and betel, and is taken to the house womb of the deceased, to be tied to the sacred shelf for a year. During this time it is known as "the dead soul's pouch," for when the dead soul takes to wandering around the hamlet, the villagers say, it will be so eager to devour the ingredients placed inside, it will be too preoccupied to trouble them.

Following immediately upon the spinsters come the two warriors. Next comes the corpse, and, bringing up the rear, the rest of Mamulak and Mane Hat. The journey to the cemetery is punctuated by the opposing sets of coffin bearers tussling with one another seven times. The bearers on one side of the litter represent the forces of the upperworld and the ones on the opposite side represent the underworld. Each time the upperworld triumphs as its rivals sprawl on the ground. These scuffles are called the *dun malu* (dun = "to banish," "to separate," "to intimidate"; *malu* = "each other"): "to separate one from the other." Were the forces of the underworld to succeed in overpowering those of the upperworld the soul would be able to pry open the coffin lid and unite with the corpse. After each tussle the coffin bearers continue on their way until the next struggle. The seventh tussle ends just outside the entrance to the cemetery, and marks the soul's acquiescence in the loss of its former body.

At the graveside, the bachelors place the coffin on some wide teak leaves that adorn flat stones near the pit, the "vagina" of the grave, whose depths are known as the womb of the earth. The actual burial itself is called either the *tama rai* ("to enter the earth") or the *tama maté*. To prevent the earth from touching the coffin, a feminine cloth known as *hena laka* lines the bottom of the pit. The bachelors, and any male who can get a grip on the supporting ropes, lower the casket to the bottom, and when it touches the cloth a man jumps down to wrap the ends of the cloth over the coffin top. He next fastens them together with large pins, and finally places a black and red masculine cloth over it.

The wrapping provided by the feminine cloth intensifies the womb-like circumstance of the corpse, already enveloped in the womb of the earth. The masculine cloth conjoining with the feminine cloth is an analogy of the sexual congress which has to precede the birth of a child, so the cyclical character of Tetum religion is again present: birth-to-death-to-birth.

Each person throws a clod of earth onto the coffin, which is so oriented that the head faces the east, with the right side of the corpse towards the north. After every member of the congregation has contributed some earth, the two warriors, who are standing at the head of the coffin, say:

1. His head has become white
2. His leg has become white
3. His head is buried
4. But his leg remains out
5. His leg is buried
6. But his head remains out
7. Tomorrow
8. His head will be laid to rest
9. His leg will be laid to rest.

The first six lines betray the uncertain feelings of the villagers towards the dead person's body, which has now been integrated into the earth womb. Yet his invisible soul may be anywhere. Lines 3–6 contrast the corpse's clear-cut position in the underworld with the uncertainty the villagers feel about the soul's ambiguous status, for they must await the *keta maté* ritual, enacted "tomorrow" (line 7), that is, twelve months hence, to be definitely integrated in the underworld. The warriors keep watch, as a few men toss earth into the pit, and when the grave has been filled in, the two girls deposit the flowers they have been holding at the head of the grave. Afterwards, everyone leaves the cemetery. In days to come, the flowers eventually wither, the girls replace them, and with the decay of the second bunch, a third and final posy is placed on the grave. When these flowers, too, have withered, some men who were formerly people who give life raze the death house to the ground, and destroy its contents. From the time the corpse is interred to the time this building is destroyed, only the two flower-carrying spinsters may enter it, to hang the pouch of life inside.

After the burial, the terms "people of death," "people who give life" and "death house" are dropped. Distinctions between the two groups are now unnecessary, and the kin are ritually reintegrated into the upperworld when they share the funeral feast in the house built for just this purpose.

The integration stage for the soul (the *keta maté*), whose liminal stage has thus lasted a year, occupies part of one afternoon and continues as a festival into the night. By this simple rite the soul is conclusively severed from the upperworld by the affines, who smash the deceased's sacred jar and cut up the second pouch of life. The pieces they throw about the wilderness immediately adjacent to the hamlet where the death occurred. There, away from any path, the debris is left for rain and sun to remove. It is dangerous, and none can touch it.

CONCLUDING REMARKS

I have tried to register something of the confusion the socially unauthorized union of underworld and upperworld causes if human beings do not speedily restore cosmic order. Disorder is at its most extreme in death, when the three anomalies—the corpse, its soul, and the dead person's kin—are created. The death ritual transforms the corpse and soul from anomalies into clear-cut beings of the underworld,

and restores the kin to the upperworld. Separation restores order.

READING 4–5

THE MORPHOLOGY AND FUNCTION OF MAGIC: A COMPARATIVE STUDY OF TROBRIAND AND ZANDE RITUAL AND SPELLS

E. E. Evans-Pritchard

This comparative study of Zande and Trobriand magic is a typical example in structural-functional analysis. Its premise, that magic "takes on the mould of the society in which it has its place and function," might be considered unremarkable today, but writing in the 1920s, Evans-Pritchard still felt obliged to counter the influence of evolutionary-minded anthropologists whose idea of comparative analysis was to analyze institutions independently of their social contexts. By employing a structural-functional approach Evans-Pritchard is able to isolate a range of problems involving magic. Why, for example, do the words uttered in Trobriand magic take the form of formulae whereas Zande spells are more in the manner of impromptu utterances? Evans-Pritchard finds that his answer lies in the different institutions of each society.

THE USE OF THE COMPARATIVE METHOD

A working hypothesis should never be allowed to become a settled conviction until it has been tested and re-tested, but every first-hand investigation requires some theoretical view to start with. In the

---

Source: E. E. Evans-Pritchard, "The Morphology and Function of Magic: A Comparative Study of Trobriand and Zande Ritual and Spells." Reproduced by permission of the American Anthropological Association from *American Anthropologist* 31:4, 1929. Not for further reproduction.

present attempt I shall have especially in view the entire range of magic in two societies.

Very little work has yet been accomplished by specialists in the field towards presenting a full descriptive and analytical account of magic. One cannot therefore make wide comparisons which would yield general principles based on an intensive study of many primitive communities. Moreover, the work which has been accomplished has been done mainly in Melanesia and the social incidence of magic in Melanesia appears to differ considerably from the social incidence of magic in Africa. This is due in general to the difference in form between the two types of society and in particular to the bias given by a strict association of magic with a definite social grouping which profoundly affects the structure and the functional occasions of the magic. I shall attempt to demonstrate in this paper that the principles of magic deduced from Melanesian data and formulated as general laws for all societies have, in view of a study of African peoples, to be reformulated and possibly modified.

I shall show how this is so by a comparison between the magic of a Melanesian society described by Professor Malinowski and the magic of an African society investigated by myself. The Melanesian community is that of the Trobriand islands, a coral archipelago lying to the northeast of New Guinea. The African tribe is a section of the Azande nation which lives in the Bahr-el-Ghazal province of the Anglo-Egyptian Sudan. I shall build up my argument mainly on the data furnished by the Trobrianders and the Azande but shall draw upon any other societies of whose magic there is a good account to check my results.

In order to understand the argument it is necessary to know the sociological distribution and balance of these two societies and their main food-procuring activities. The Trobrianders live in villages which act together in communal undertakings such as agricultural labor, trading expeditions, warfare, and public ceremonial. The villages are also largely political units, though the chief may rule over the wider area of a district. Many of these chiefs are little more than village headmen, others have great prestige in virtue of belonging to certain "families" of the four totemic clans. None wield great executive power. The four totemic clans are scattered but the "families" or sub-clans are localized. The Trobrianders are patrilocal and matrilineal, the girl going to live in her husband's village, but membership of the clan group and inheritance of wealth and rank are passed to a man's sister's son instead of to his own natural offspring. Girls are married from their father's home whilst boys as a rule return to their mother's village before marriage. The main economic activity of the Trobriander is the cultivation of his gardens. Fishing plays a great part in maintaining his food supply and is of far greater importance than hunting owing to the absence of mammalian fauna in these coral islands.[1]

The social organization of the Azande is as different from that of the Trobrianders as are the islands of the South Seas from the vast inland tracts of Central Africa. The Azande have no village life but live in homesteads widely separated from each other. In consequence they have fewer communal undertakings. Politically they are organized into tribes which stretch over an enormous area and are governed by one chief. The tribes are divided into a number of ill-defined sections each under the leadership of a chief's deputy. The chiefs all belong to one ruling class and exercise great power. There are a large number of totemic clans which are scattered all over the country and possess little social solidarity. The Azande are patrilocal and patrilineal. Girls live in the homesteads of their husbands and inheritance of wealth and rank pass from a man to his sons and brothers. Gardening forms the main work of a Zande. Hunting and the collection of edible termites are important activities, fishing contributing little to the food supply.

If we study any such institution as magic, religion, law, or economic life, we shall find that it takes on the mould of the society in which it has its place and function. Where the morphology of society differs as between the Trobrianders and the Azande we shall expect to find that the sociological role of magic amongst these two peoples differs accordingly.

FUNCTION OF MAGIC

Professor Malinowski was the first writer to demonstrate clearly from a detailed study of one society wherein lies the function of magic.[2] He showed how magic filled a gap left by lack of knowledge in man's pragmatic pursuits, e.g., wind magic, and how it provided an alternative means of expression for thwarted human desires, e.g., black magic. His general conclusions as to the function of magic in society are fully borne out by a study of Zande data.

For example, the Zande uses magic to protect himself, his children, his agricultural and hunting activities from the malign power of witchcraft. He uses productive magic to multiply his crops, to ensure success in netting game, in encouraging the termites to embark on their nuptial swarmings, in smelting and forging iron, in increasing the number of his subjects. He uses magic to give him confidence in love-making or in singing, to protect his property from theft and his wife from illicit intercourse. He consults the magic of the oracles to give him confidence before circumcision, before marriage, before building a new homestead. Magic plays its part in all the main biological and social occasions of a Zande's life. I could multiply examples, and an analysis of the social context of each would endorse Professor Malinowski's conclusions as to the psychological and sociological role of magic.

But suppose that a Trobriand Argonaut were to make an unusually long and perilous voyage, were to paddle his dug-out canoe two thousand miles up the placid and dreary waters of the Nile, were to make his way to Zandeland, were to learn the tongue of the Azande and enter into their customs, how would he find that their magic conforms to or differs from the principles of his own society?

He would find that Zande "white" magic, whether protective or productive in character, like his own is never looked upon as one of the forces of nature which can be utilized by man, but is regarded as a cherished cultural possession which derives its powers from man's abstinence and from his knowledge of tradition. He would find that the Azande, like his own people, believe magic to have come into the world with man and not to have been acquired by subsequent discovery in the world of nature. The Zande would reject as strongly as himself the idea of magic as a universal impersonal power as expressed in the concepts *mana* in Polynesia and *wakan* and orenda in North America.[3] Also neither the Trobriander nor the Zande consider magic to be a gift from the spirits of the dead.

The sex and food taboos which precede all acts of magic would conform to the tradition of the Trobriand visitor. Nor would he find anything in the rites of magic which would appear to him to be inconceivable or unreal. But where the Trobriander would be confused would be in noticing that whilst in structure Zande magic is similar to his own, it stresses some of its component parts which he regards as of less importance than others, whereas some of the parts upon which he lays the greatest stress in his island home are performed by the Zande with a shocking freedom and carelessness. In both societies all important acts of magic consist of the rite, the spell, the condition of the performer, and the tradition of the magic, but the emphasis placed on each by the two peoples is different.

THE SPELL

To peoples such as the Trobrianders and the Maori the spell is a rigid unalterable formula which is transmitted intact from generation to generation, and the slightest deviation from its traditional form would invalidate the magic.[4] The spell is "occult, handed over in magical filiation, known only to the practitioner." Knowledge of the magic is knowledge of the spell, the ritual centers round it, it is always the core of the magical performance (Malinowski 1922:68). Now to the Zande the spell is nearly always essential to the act of magic in all forms of "white" magic, but it is not stressed in the same way as in the Trobriand islands or in New Zealand. Indeed, the qualities of the spell in Zande magic are the direct opposite of those which we have been told characterize Trobriand magic. It is a saying rather than a formula, it is familiar, it is handed over without strict reference to genealogical ties, the knowledge of it is not confined to the practitioner.

I will give an example of owned Zande magic from my collection of texts. It is a typical hunting spell, which is pronounced over a pot in which the magical ingredients are being cooked in oil. The practitioner stirs the pot and says:

bingia (name of magic)	nga are	mu you	mi I	ye come	ka to
ra cook	ru you	ware thus	mu you	ti fall	na with
ana animals	fo for	ri me	mi I	imi kill	mbaga bushbuck
ana animals	dunduko all	mi I	ara cook	ru you	ti for
ana animals	mi I	imi kill	ana animals	gbe much	

"You are *bingia* magic, I come to cook you thus. You bring me animals. I kill bushbuck-all animals. I cook you on my behalf. I kill animals much."

This spell is not a set formula learnt by heart and repeated without variation by all who use the same magic, nor one which is handed down intact from generation to generation. It is a saying adapted to the purpose of the magic and uttered in the common form and phraseology of all Zande spells but it will vary in its word formation. The practitioner will change words on different occasions and different men will insert different details.

To make this variation in the spells quite clear I will give one more example, which embodies two texts given to me by the same informant on different occasions. There is an oil-bearing plant, a species of sesame, called *kpagu,* which yields a regular yearly crop to the Azande. The material used in this magic is a tall grass with a feather-like form of its branching stems, called *bingba,* and is known to everyone. It is a common grass which springs up on arable land and is used for thatching the roofs of the huts. Now a man who wishes to increase the yield of his *kpagu* will pluck some of these grass stems and hurling them like a dart will transfix the broad leaves of the oil-plant. The spell accompanying this action was given me in the first instance as follows:

kpagu (name of plant)	nga are	mu you	du is	le here	mu you
zunga be	a zu very fruitful	wa as	kina truly	bingba (name of grass)	
ni with	dunga many	he it			

"You are *kpagu* here, you be exceeding fruitful, indeed as *bingba,* with much fruit."

On a second occasion my informant gave me the spell for the same magic as follows:

bingba (name of grass)	nga are	mu you	sele oil		
ida consent	ida very much	wa as	kina truly	bingba (name of grass)	
gi my	kpagu (name of plant)	mu you be	zungu fruitful	gbe much	ka not
mo you	kanga refuse	ya not			

"*Bingba* are you, oil plant take very well, just like *bingba.* My *kpagu be* exceeding fruitful, do not refuse."

It will at once be seen by a comparison between these two spells that there is more difference than similarity in the wording. The sense is the same but we find that the words are so little part of a formula that in the first spell the plant is addressed, whereas in the second spell both the plant and its magic are called upon by name.

It is true that the example I have given is of an unowned type of magic and a type of magic which has no part in communal undertakings. As will be seen later, it is consequent upon my argument that the more strictly owned is magic and the more the occasion on which it is practised is of common interest, the more it will tend to become formulated, the less it will vary from traditional form. But I will return to a consideration of this point later.

Here it is possible to make a useful distinction between the "saying" spell and the "formula" spell. The psychological background of all magic demands that utterance shall accompany the rite if its function is to be performed but it does not determine the form of the utterance. The form of the spell is dependent upon social causes not to be found in a study of the magic itself save in relation to the whole society and culture in which it is practised.

THE MATERIAL ELEMENT IN MAGIC

But if the spell in Trobriand culture is the essential part of magic, what takes its place in Zande culture? In the morphology of Zande magic it is the material element in the magic which is occult and which is known only to the practitioner. Usually this consists of strange woods and rare roots. Indeed the Zande word for magic is ngwa, which generally means wood and only in special contexts refers to magic. There is an interesting linguistic comparison in the Trobriand islands, for there, on the contrary, the native uses the same word for spell and magic, generally *megwa,* the material element in the ritual being of minor importance.

That it is to the material component in the ritual and not to the spell that the Azande attach main importance can be shown from many of my fieldwork experiences, but it is more satisfactory to illustrate their opinion from their own stories. Many of these stories, about the Zande culture-hero Ture, centre around magical powers once possessed but now lost. In one of these stories a man, called Yangayma, possessed magical feathers which enabled him to fly after performing a ritual dance and chanting a song-spell:

yu	yangayma	gi	swe	ku	ba
(untranslatable)	(name of man)	these	feathers	of	father

ba	fu	yangayma
father	gave	(name of man)

"Yu Yangayma, these feathers of father, father gave Yangayma."

The culture-hero Ture stole these feathers and chanted the song-spell, substituting his name for that of their rightful owner: "Yu yu Ture, these feathers of father, father gave Ture." In stealing the feathers, however, Ture dropped one of them and when Yangayma found this he put it in his hat and singing the spell as above he gave pursuit into the air and deprived Ture of all the stolen feathers so that the culture-hero fell to the ground and was killed.[5]

In another story Ture was walking with a man called Depago who possessed magic which enabled him to enter into the ground. When it began to rain he took some medicine from his horn where he kept it and wiped it on an ant-hill. On the ant-hill opening they both entered and Ture was amazed to see the fine village and the wealth of Depago under the ground. In order to leave the ant-hill Depago wiped some more of his magic on to the earth and said:

Depago Depago Depago	nzinginzingi	sende
(name of man)	muddy	earth

Depago	na	yera	ngalimo
(name of man)	is	cutting	deep

sende	nzinginzingi	sende
earth	muddy	earth

"Depago, Depago, Depago, quagmire, Depago is cutting a big pit, a quagmire."

As Ture was departing he stole some of the magical soot. He went home and persuaded all his wives, with the exception of his first wife Nanzagbe who knew his ways, to burn their huts and come and live with him under the ground. He went with his wives to an ant-hill and wiped some of the magic on the ground and said "Deture, Deture, Deture, a quagmire, Deture is cutting a big pit, a quagmire." The ant-hill opened and they entered only to find grass and they became very hungry. Meanwhile Nanzagbe went and told Depago what had happened and he came and rescued Ture and his wives.[6]

This story is in need of native commentary as it is not clear why Ture could not have got out of the ant-hill. Those natives whom I have questioned on this point have replied that he could not get out because he had not enough magical soot since he had foolishly wiped it all on the outside of the ant-hill.

In yet another story Ture tries to copy someone whom he has seen putting out a bush fire by placing a magical fat on his head. But in this story we are distinctly told that Ture used a different fat so that his efforts ended in failure.

I could give other instances from the folk-lore of the Zande to illustrate the manner in which the importance of the magical substance itself is stressed more than other aspects of the performance, but these three will suffice. We have seen that in the first story it was the theft of the feathers which enabled Ture to fly and that it was the loss of these feathers which caused his subsequent fall, just as it was the finding of the one dropped feather which gave Yangayma power to pursue him from the earth. In the second story it was the theft of the magical soot by which Ture entered the ant-hill and its absence which prevented him from getting out again. In the third story it was the use of a secret fat which gave power over fire and it was Ture's attempt to control fire by a different fat which led to failure.

On these occasions Ture copied the spell correctly—I do not wish to underestimate its importance in the magical performance—but it was the loss of the material of the rite which made the act of magic invalid. This is the whole point of the stories.

Now just as we found that the emphasis placed on different elements of the magic in the Trobriand islands and in Zandeland has a parallel in different linguistic symbols, *ngwa* and *megwa,* we shall find a similar parallel between the significance of the stories given above and the significance of some Trobriand myths.

Once upon a time in these South Sea islands there lived a man Mokatuboda of the Lukuba clan with his three sisters and his younger brother Toweyre'i. Mokatuboda possessed the magic of the flying canoes and the myth describes his success in a trading expedition and the envy of the other natives whose canoes had to sail on the water whilst his flew through the air. Next year they cultivated their gardens. There was a terrible drought and the rain fell only on the garden of Mokatuboda because he made an evil magic of the rain. Angry and jealous, his brothers and maternal nephews killed him, believing that they had been taught the magic (i.e., the spells) and could use it on his decease. But Mokatuboda had not taught them the real spells, neither the magic of the adze nor of the rain nor of the lashing creeper nor of the coconut oil nor of the staff. His younger brother Toweyre'i thought that he had already received all the magic but he had only part, and next year when they prepared to

make a big trading expedition he discovered that by his fratricide he had deprived mankind of one of its most powerful cultural possessions, the magic of the flying canoe. The whole point of this story is that the magic was invalid because Mokatuboda had not taught all the spells to his brother.[7]

I shall leave the spell, to return to it later, and will draw attention to another profound difference between Trobriand and Zande magic.

TRADITION

In the Trobriand islands "in the case of any important magic we invariably find the story accounting for its existence." "All important magic has its tradition and is buttressed by its myth." Do we find the same background of belief amongst the Azande?

Since all magic tends to create its own myth it would be indeed surprising if there were no tradition of a simple kind associated with Zande magic. I found that there is always a current tradition, a cycle of everyday myth encircling and generated by the magic.[8] When I asked a Zande how he knew that his magic was of any use he told me a story from his own experience or from that of his friends or neighbors. He told me how when gathering termites by night his friend had blown his magic elephant whistle and how soon afterwards they heard the tramping and trumpeting of the elephants and next morning saw their deep spoor in the moist earth. Another told me how he had always wished to be a fine singer but had never shown any ability in the art until a famous song leader gave him medicine to eat. Another told me how his brother, and a neighboring chief also, had a swollen penis and had become impotent because of the use of a certain type of "black" magic. Always there is this halo of rumor and wonder around magic of the Azande.

We know well, for Goldenweiser[9] has shown us, how in our own society magic is always associated with wonder-working, with strange coincidences too numerous to be accounted for by chance, with the rumor of uncanny personal experience, with the borrowed plumes of eastern mysticism. "There is no faith without miracles."

But this current tradition, this everyday myth is loose and short-lived whether in Melanesia, Africa, or Europe, and can be easily distinguished from the set legend and socially inherited myth by its loose form, its restricted range, and its absence of longevity.

I did not find, save in rare instances, myth of this kind associated with Zande magic. Often magic has been taken over by the Azande from some stranger people, and they will tell you how they learnt it by making blood-brotherhood with the foreigner. If you press the native to tell you how man first became acquainted with any magic he will say that Mböli, the Supreme Being, gave it to him. Thus though the myth of Mböli forms the final background of belief for all ritual, there is no specific myth for each specific type of magic.

Occasionally, however, I have found amongst the Azande a specific myth accounting for the origin of a magic, or a legend, proving its potency. Thus the clan of the Amazungu have a myth telling how they obtained their magic for healing fractures. Into the clan was born a baby quite round like a pot. The bewildered father was instructed in a dream by Mböli to incinerate the child and to use the cinders to heal broken bones. I will give another example. The corporation of medicine-men possess powerful magic known only to the members of the corporation. That their magic is genuine is proved by legends which show how in the past great medicine-men performed remarkable feats through its medium. In the Golden Age of their magic the magician Rëpa, a primitive Moses, went with his chief to wage war beyond the great Uelle river of the Congo. On their return northwards the army found themselves with the enemy in their rear and the wide river to their front. In this crisis Rëpa threw some of his magic into the water so that the waters parted, leaving a dry channel of sand, on which they passed over to the other side. When the enemy pursued them into the centre of the river Rëpa, like his Hebrew prototype, closed the waters upon their fighting men.

Like Moses in the last story, his end was like the end of Elijah.

Rëpa dances exceedingly the dance of the medicine-men. He rose on high. Then the bells say wia wia wia wia. He rose and rose and rose for ever on high. He went quite out of sight so that the eyes of men did not see him again. He dropped the bells from his hands. The bells kept on falling and falling and falling: they fell here to earth. They plunged and plunged to the earth right into the centre of an ant-hill so that no one saw them.

Many were the mighty deeds performed by Rëpa and his son Bokoparanga in virtue of their magic.

The myth of the Amazunga clan and the legends of the medicine-men are, however, quite exceptional. Generally I have failed to find any story accounting for the existence of magic. Just as it was possible to make a useful distinction between the saying and the formula in the rite of magic, so it is possible to make a similar analysis of the tradition of magic. The psychological function of magic demands a background of belief in its tradition, but it does not determine the form of these traditions. Whether they exist only as loose current tradition and short-lived everyday myths or whether they become set into the mould of a compact myth or legend, depends upon the place they occupy in each society, and upon their relation to other parts of the culture in which they exist.

I shall shortly return to a consideration of tradition and the place which this conclusion occupies in my argument. Absence of formulae and absence of specific myths are the two main characteristics which in Zandeland present a contrast with the magic of the Trobriand isles. There are smaller differences which will be noted in the following section.

THE RITE, THE CONDITIONS OF THE RITE, THE CONDITIONS OF THE PERFORMER

Were I to describe fully the ritual of several types of Zande magic, the reader would notice a laxity in the performance which would horrify a Melanesian. He would find confusing variations in the sequence and in the procedure of the ritual. The slightest slip in the ceremonial, a minute omission in the performance of the rite, an insignificant change in its sequence, does not, as amongst many primitive peoples, the Trobrianders and the Maori for instance, invalidate the whole act of magic.

Nothing acts more strongly in conserving tradition and compelling conformity in ritual than the publicity of the performance. Amongst the Trobrianders some rites of magic

> are ceremonial and have to be attended by the whole community, all are public in that it is known when they are going to happen and anyone can attend them (p. 31).

Amongst the Azande there is very little ceremonial in magic. There are certainly no big public ceremonies which must or may be attended by others than the family of the man concerned or his friends or by a few old men. Privacy is characteristic of Zande magic.

Lack of conservative discipline in the performance of the rites has its counterpart in the lack of uniformity in the time during which a man must observe the sex and food taboos which accompany all magic. Though agreeing in the main, different practitioners will give one different time estimates and some will observe a wider range of food restrictions than others. There is also considerable laxity in the observation of the taboos. These are often neglected, though a practitioner would always say that they had been observed as they are supposed to be.

In Zande magic the taboos and the rites are subject to variation, the spell is diffuse and unformulated, the tradition is not standardized, the performance is neither public nor ceremonial; the whole act of magic is less rigidly defined and less amenable to set form than the magic acts of Melanesia.

GROUP OWNERSHIP OF MAGIC

What then are the social causes which determine these differences between the ritual of the Trobriand islands and the ritual of the Azande of the Nile-Uelle divide? I think that they are to be found in a comparative study of the ownership of magic in the two areas. In the Trobriands

> Magic tends in all its manifestations to become specialized, exclusive and departmental, and hereditary within a family or clan (p. 45).

Amongst the Azande magic is seldom specialized within or exclusive to a family or clan, but is spread widely amongst the community without reference to kindred ties.

If you ask a Zande whence he obtained his magic he will tell you that he received it from his father for it is handed from father to son like any other wealth; or he will tell you that he or his father bought the magic, for magic, being the property of an individual, can be bought and sold; or he will tell you that one of his friends told him about the magic out of comradeship, or that knowledge of that type of magic is possessed by everybody.

Trobriand magic presents a contrast in that in its most important systems, such as garden magic, fishing magic, the ritual of weather, rain, and sun, it must be transmitted through the binding custom of kinship which compels a man to hand over his knowledge of spells with his other property to the son of his sister. It is true that some magic can be bought, but its transference is always accompanied and restricted by social qualifications. Very little magic is unowned.

In this difference between Trobriand magic owned by the family or clan, not open to sale and purchase outside these groups, and Zande magic, owned by the individual and able to be transmitted beyond the restricted domain of genealogical or clan relationship, it is possible to see a solution to the problem of formulae and standardized tradition.

The formula is surety of undisputed ownership of magic and compels filiation of the magic in the family or clan, for the long set formula is a value which can only be handed over laboriously and slowly. But amongst the Azande magic is not generally associated with any social group, being diffused widely without reference to ties of relationship. Consequently there is no need for the formula which tends to restrict the use of the magic to the group already possessing it. Moreover, the core of the magic being not the spell but the material element, it is easily transferred from one person to another. To the Trobriander the spell is the most important part of the magic, in a sense is the magic, because the formula keeps the magic in the group with which it is traditionally associated, whereas the Azande have no magical formulae, but only sayings, because magic is not generally associated with any social grouping. The formula is correlated with group ownership. I attribute the emphasis placed upon tradition to the same social cause. The function of the myth is to project the facts of group ownership into the realms of belief, to provide a convincing sanction to the ownership. This is the rôle which it plays in the Trobriand islands, but as Zande magic is not associated exclusively with any section of the community there is no need for the myth as it would have no social function to fulfil.

If this explanation is correct, then in those exceptional cases in which Zande magic is associated with a social grouping it should also be associated with myth. This is what we do find, and I have already given examples from the clan of the Amazungu and the corporation of the medicine-men. Inversely the Trobriand "white" magic, which is not owned by any segment of society, should be found without a background of myth and is so found.

The conclusion drawn is that an utterance is an essential psychological accompaniment of all magical rites and that tradition is an essential sanction for their performance, but that these only crystallize into the set formula and standardized myth when the social mobility of the magic is restricted by its ownership being invested in the family or clan or some departmental grouping. Ownership is always a conservative and standardizing agent in society.

This thesis can be illustrated more widely than by the two areas from which my data have mainly been drawn, but I do not wish to make a compilation, for not only magical but all exceptional privileges invested in one class in society require the halo of myth. Thus amongst the Azande only those clans which are differentiated from the rest of the Zande totemic clans by a special social function have specific clan mythology. In some societies all the clans have differentiated social functions with associated myths, as, for example, the Winnebago Indians.[10]

It will be found also that all important magic in any society is restricted in use to a few members of the community whether these few persons derive their credentials from membership of a family, kinship, or departmental grouping or not. By important magic I refer to all magic associated with those pursuits on which the life of the community depends; magic used in communal undertakings such as agriculture, fishing, hunting, trading expeditions; magic practised on behalf of the whole community such as the magic of rain and of the sun, magic to increase the totem animal or plant; magic used to reinforce some essential function of society such as government and leadership in war.

In the Trobriand islands all really important magic performances are carried out by men who have received their knowledge of the spells from their mother's brother according to the law of this matrilineal society. If a man passes on the spells to his own son, this latter may use them but may not teach them to another. Important magic is consequently restricted to a very few men who practise in virtue of membership of family or clan. To take another example, amongst the Kiwai Papuans,[11] a society in which group ownership of magic appears to be unknown and where knowledge of the rites and spells is common property, important communal activities such as house-building agricultural and fishing pursuits, and other collective acts of labor have their magic performed by one old man and one old woman who know the secret parts of the rites and whose death is a certain result of the performance.

Amongst the Azande there are only occasional communal activities in contrast to the Trobriand islanders or the Kiwai Papuans, but the stronger and more important medicines are known only to a few men.

POSSIBLE RESULTS OF SPREAD OF MAGIC

If all the more important magic is in the hands of a few individuals in any society, the logical inference to be drawn is that the wider spread the magic the less important the social function it fulfils; the more the performance of magic becomes public property, the less social utility it possesses. This inference can be checked from observation.

Amongst the Trobrianders such magic as is known to all members of the community has very little social significance. The same is true of the Azande, amongst whom much magic is common property and much can be bought so cheaply that it is not even sought after by most men.

In a society such as this, where magic is not restricted in use to members of a group, but is characterized by its social mobility, it is possible to suggest tentatively that certain features in the domain of magic are due to the absence of exclusive ownership. I think that it is possible that the great extension of the magic of oracles, divination, and ordeal amongst the Azande and in many other parts of Africa in contrast to the little importance attached to them throughout Polynesia and Melanesia, may be attributed to the absence of hereditary ownership, set formulae, and standardized tradition. For it must be remembered that, although the object of oracles is to know about future events and not to produce or influence them, nevertheless it fulfils the same psychological function as other types of magic by giving man confidence in his social and economic undertakings. We have, therefore, various types of magic fulfilling the same function. However, in the present state of my researches into Zande customs I do not wish to stress this point too much.

This same phenomenon, this reduplication of rôle in many types of Zande magic, is seen in the special associations for the practice of magic (secret societies). Insofar as I have investigated these associations I have found that the purpose of their magic is already covered by other types of magic. The spread and popularity of these societies may, I believe, be accounted for by the need to systematize and stabilize magic by affiliating its use to an association and by this means enhancing its social utility. In these societies the knowledge of the magic is restricted to the leader of the society. However, the secret societies at present found in Zandeland are of recent introduction. Generally they are of easy access, short-lived, and replaced by other associations of a like nature.

CREATION OF NEW MAGIC

Not only have all the secret societies of the Azande of the Bahr-el-Ghazal entered from across the Congo border, but many hunting and other medicines are learnt from the Baka, Mundu, Avokaiya, and Moro peoples to the East, the Pambia to the West, the Bongo and Bellanda to the North, the Mangbettu, Amade, Abarambo to the South. Medicines have also been incorporated into Zande culture from the many peoples who now call themselves Azande, but who a generation ago spoke their own language and had their own distinctive customs. The territorial spread of magic is quick and far-reaching. In at least one instance the Azande have borrowed magic from even the distant and hostile Dinka tribes. The Azande find in the magic of their neighbors a constant source of new and powerful medicine.

Nor do I think that all Zande magic is of great age. We have already noted that all Zande magic has its current tradition, its halo of rumor, mystery, and wonder, the birthplace in all societies from which springs transmitted tradition, set legend, and standardized myth, stabilized by group ownership and handed over by the customary procedure of kinship, or other social machinery. However, in saying that magic creates its own mythology the problem has been simplified. Does not belief create magic? Often a native will tell you, for example, that a certain man has powerful magic to kill leopards. If you ask your informant what magic is possessed by the hunter, he will say that he does not know, but that he must own some magic or he would not be so successful in killing leopards.

Actual achievement is demanded of the man who wishes to sell his magic. The fate of unsuccessful magicians, especially rainmakers in many parts of the world, is evidence of this demand. But the production of rain is a supposed and not an actual achievement. Amongst the Moro of the Yei river in the Southern Sudan it is only when a man becomes renowned as a hunter that he plants medicine roots at the side of his hut and becomes a practitioner.[12]

It would be a barren discussion whether the myth follows the practice of the magic in all cases or whether sometimes the practice of the magic springs out of current tradition. The rite of magic and the myth always interlace and shape each other. I only wish to suggest that new magic is constantly being created, and that it is created by successful men influenced by the rumors of magic which attend their success, and that whilst magic gives men confidence in their undertakings, it also represents a record of man's actual achievement. Primitive man is not a romantic but a practical hardheaded being, even in his magic, and there is no magic to attempt the impossible.

FUNCTIONAL OCCASIONS OF MAGIC

So far I have endeavored to show by correlations how the morphology of magic amongst the Trobrianders and the Azande is determined by the social structure of the two societies. The same is true of the functional occasions of magic. This cannot be demonstrated at length, as it would then be necessary to describe fully the occasions of use and the specific function of all magic in both communities. Moreover the statement is so obvious in simpler instances that it hardly requires demonstration. The Zande has no canoe magic because he has no canoes. The Trobriander has no magic of ironforging because he lives in a stone age.

The problem becomes more complicated when we consider the sociological aspects of magic. It is clear that the communal garden magic of the Trobrianders is absent from Zande life because the Azande do not cultivate their gardens by joint labor.

It is more difficult to see why the Trobriand chief uses magic as part of his machinery of government, whereas the Zande chief does not use this weapon of chastisement, but this difference can readily be understood when the position of the chief is known in both societies. The Trobriand chief was unable to exercise great executive power as may readily be judged from the almost entire absence of corporal punishment, whereas the mutilations and executions inflicted on their subjects by the Zande chiefs are one of the many signs of their real power. The Zande chief, therefore, had little need of magic to enforce his rule.

On the other hand, the Azande move their homesteads freely over the countryside and a chief who has angered his people may lose his subjects. Also a young chief anxious to conquer or acquire new territory by peaceful means has to rely entirely upon his popularity to attract followers. Hence we find a system of magic for attracting dependents.

Magic used in communal undertakings such as we find in the Trobriands, in garden work, in trading expeditions, in building canoes, and in other forms of economic enterprise has no counterpart in Zande life. This is because there is a lack of cohesion in Zande social life, solidarity either due to close aggregation of dwellings or good means of communication, being absent. Thus while magic amongst the Kiwai Papuans or the Trobrianders is often associated with village activities, this cannot be so amongst the Azande because there are no villages.

Also amongst the Azande we do not find the institution of magic associated, save in one instance, with the clan. This is because the clans have little solidarity. Political functions are in the hands of a class and the clans also lack the cohesion which localization would give them. For magic is an important social institution, and for it to be orientated after a group, that group must have solidarity without which it cannot exercise important social functions.

SUMMARY AND CONCLUSIONS

I set out at the commencement of this paper to show that the social incidence of magic in Melanesia differs from the social incidence of magic in Africa and that this difference affects the structure and functional occasions of the magic. I have attempted to do this by a comparison between the data of the Trobriand islands and the data of the Azande of the Nile-Uelle divide. I explained how the Trobriander and the Zande regarded magic not as a force of nature, but as a cultural heritage, not as something discovered but as something co-existent in time with man, not as a vague impersonal power but as a tangible weapon of culture, not activated by the spirits of the dead but deriving its power from the knowledge of tradition and the abstinence of living men.

I then analyzed the structure of magic in these two societies and showed how the spell amongst the Trobrianders is a standardized formula whilst amongst the Azande it is only a saying adapted to the purpose of the magic and accompanying the rite. I concluded that the psychological purpose of magic is not served unless an utterance is made in conjunction with the rite, but that the crystallization of the utterance into a standardized formula is determined by the affiliation of the magic with a group through the institution of ownership.

The analysis of magic in the two societies showed also that amongst the Trobrianders myth, like the spell, is a standardized formula, a set story transmitted intact to the succeeding generation by the social mechanism of kinship, whilst among the Azande magic generates only a loose current myth and everyday tradition, save in exceptional instances in which the magic is owned by a restricted social grouping and a stereotyped and permanent element of culture takes the place of the ephemeral mythology. For here again I concluded that the psychological purpose of magic is not served unless the ritual has a background of belief in mythology, a halo of stories about its wonder-working powers, but that the crystallization of these stories into standardized myth is determined by the affiliation of the magic with a group through the institution of ownership.

I suggested that any section of society enjoying special privileges, whether magical or otherwise, produces its own mythology, the function of the myth being to give sanction to the possession of the exclusive privileges.

I suggested that important magic, that is, magic which plays its role in large communal undertakings or is practised on behalf of the whole community or reinforces an essential function of society such as war or government, is always to be found in the hands of a few men. I gave some examples to support this view. Since all important magic is in the hands of a few individuals the more it becomes spread among the members of the community at large, the more it loses its importance and social utility. This gives rise to the creation of new magic,

magical redundancy, and an attempt to stabilize the magic through new groups or associations.

I have described how today magic is taken over by one people from another. This is one way in which new magic comes into being, but it is also created by individuals and I have discussed the manner of its birth.

In the earlier part of my paper I attempted to show that the form of magic depends upon the structure of society as a whole, and at the end I indicated that the functional occasions of magic are also determined by the social structure. Examples were given to show how the occasion on which magic is used, the social activities with which it is correlated, and the groups after which it is orientated differ with differences of social structure.

It is one of the aims of social anthropology to interpret all differences in the form of a typical social institution by reference to difference in social structure. In this paper I have attempted to show that differences in the form of the institution of magic, in particular between two societies, can be explained by showing the variation in social structure between these societies.

By the method of correlation we attempted to show that the formalization of the components of magic rites depends on the factor of ownership. It may be asked why magic is owned by the kin or clan groups in the Trobriand isles and not amongst the Azande. The answer is that in the Trobriands these groups have important social and economic functions to carry out which we do not find associated with the same groups amongst the Azande. Now since the role of magic is to enable these social and economic processes to be carried out, it is naturally associated with the groups fulfilling these functions. The purpose of this paper was to show how such an association affects the form of the magic.

ENDNOTES

1. Seligman, The Melanesians of New Guinea, chap. 49, 1910. Malinowski Argonauts of the Western Pacific, passim, 1922.
2. Magic, Science and Religion, published in Science, Religion and Reality (ed. J. Needham), 1925. References will be to this paper when not stated otherwise. For the detailed

facts on which Prof. Malinowski bases his views see Arg-
onauts of the Western Pacific, chapters on Magic, Myth
(Psyche Miniatures), 1926; Crime and Custom, 1926; and
Sexual Life of Savages, 1929.

3. I do not wish to state that these forces are conceived of as
impersonal by the natives themselves, but that they have
been described as such by ethnographers and theoretical
writers, such as Marett, Preuss, Hubert and Mauss,
Durkheim, and others.

4. For Maori magic, see R. W. Firth's Primitive Economics of
the New Zealand Maori (London: Routledge), 1929.

5. See Plas and Lagac, Zande Grammar, 1921.
6. See Rev. C. Gore's forthcoming Zande Grammar.
7. Argonauts of the Western Pacific, 311 ff.
8. See also Malinowski, ibid., 76–77.
9. Goldenweiser, Early Civilization, 193 ff., 1921.
10. Radin, The Winnebago Tribe. 37th Annual Report of the
Bureau of American Ethnology, 1915–16.
11. G. Landtman, Kiwai Papuans, passim, 1927.
12. From my unpublished notes.

ASK YOURSELF

Consider what ritual actions you might have performed
recently. Did you shake hands with some new acquaintance? What would have happened had you disre-
garded this little ritual? Next time you walk into your
professor's office start your conversation without the
customary greeting, such as "Hi!" and note what
response you get. What would you anticipate that
would be?

FURTHER READINGS

Bell, Catherine. *Ritual: Perspectives and Dimensions.*
Oxford: Oxford University Press. 1967. Heavy on
ethnography and thoroughly grounded in history, this
study of ritual delves in considerable detail into the different ways in which some of the most influential
thinkers have understood ritual.

Hubert, Henri, and Marcel Mauss. *Sacrifice: Its Nature
and Function,* trans. W. D. Halls. Chicago: University
of Chicago Press, 1964. This is the authoritative analysis of sacrifice mentioned in the introduction to this
book. Although now outdated, Hubert and Mauss's
work exerted an influence on several generations of
scholars, and is a characteristic product of Durkheim's
famous *Année sociologique* School.

Muir, Edward. *Ritual in Early Modern Europe.* Cambridge: Cambridge University Press, 1997. Between
about 1400 and 1700, argues Muir, a revolution in
ritual theory occurred in Europe, completely transforming concepts of time, the body, and the presence of
spiritual agencies in the human world.

Turner, Victor, and Edith Turner. *Image and Pilgrimage
in Christian Culture: Anthropological Perspectives.*
New York: Columbia University Press, 1978. The
institution of the pilgrimage is certainly not
unknown among nonliterate societies; but it is only
within the context of the major historical religions,
of Hinduism, Buddhism, Judaism, Christianity, and
Islam, that it becomes a prominent ritual activity.
Among the topics described in this study are pilgrimages as a liminal category (as in a rite of passage), the devotion to the Virgin Mary (including her
manifestation in Guadalupe [Reading 9–2]), apparitions, and miracles.

SUGGESTED VIDEOS

"Altar of Fire." This documentary focuses on a detailed
record of what has been claimed to be the world's
oldest surviving ritual, dating as far back as 3,000
years ago. This is the Agnicayana, a Vedic sacrifice to
Agni, the god of fire. The 12-day ritual is shown as it
was performed in 1975 in a village in southwestern
India. 45 minutes; 1976; $297 (sale), $60 (rental); Catalog #37360. "World Cultures on Film and Video,"
University of California Extension, Center for Media
and Independent Learning, 2000 Center Street, Fourth
Floor, Berkeley, CA 94704.

"Religion and Magic." This documentary examines religion from an anthropological perspective, portraying
rituals from a variety of cultures, including the carving
of a medicine mask by Native Americans, the Eka Dasa

Rudra ritual performed once a century by the people of Bali, and the rituals of the Maya, of Central America. It explores the purposes of ritual in general and of these rituals in particular, and then portrays revitalization movements and the functions of religion in industrialized societies. 30 minutes; 1983; $119 (sale); Catalog #SJ19. Insight Media, 121 West 85th Street, New York, NY 10024.

"Sweating Indian Style: Conflicts over Native American Ritual." A group of New Age women in Ojai, California, construct a new sweat lodge and perform their own ritual. This documentary shows the women preparing themselves and discussing their reasons for carrying out a performance. Also included are selected opinions of Native Americans. Some dislike their sacred rituals being shared with outsiders; other Native Americans are more tolerant of sincere, albeit non-indigenous, seekers of the truth. 57 minutes; 1994; $145 (sale), $40 (rental); Documentary Education Resources, 101 Morse Street, Watertown, MA 02172.

"The King Does not Lie: The Initiation of a Shango Priest." This video follows the initiation of a priest of the Santeria religion, through a series of ritual stages which constitute his rite of passage. Produced by Judith Gleason and Elisa Mereghetti. 50 Min. Sale $395. Rental $75. Filmakers Library, 124 East 40th Street, New York, NY 10016.

Priests, in contrast to shamans and prophets, undergo a period of education for their vocation and must pass through a rite of passage to attain their position. Here we see novices undergoing ordination by a senior practitioner, a bishop, who himself had been ordained years earlier.

Photo courtesy of Maxine Hicks

CHAPTER 5

PRACTITIONERS OF RITUAL

Anthropologists find it useful classifying practitioners of ritual into three categories: (a) shamans, (b) priests, and (c) prophets. The characteristics of the practitioners anthropologists rely on to classify them in this way overlap, but cross-cultural studies of ritual leaders lend substantial ethnographic support for this three-fold classification.

The term *shaman* is borrowed from the vocabulary of a Siberian group, the Evenks, and can be translated as "one who is excited or moved." The practice of shamanism was once common among the North American Indians, and today remains common in South America and in many parts of Asia. Korea, in particular, is famous for its shamans.

Shamans may also be termed *healers, curers, medicine men,* or *witch doctors,* designations that alert us to the varied functions shamans carry out. Like priests, shamans mediate between spirits and human beings. Unlike priests, though, shamans usually require to a pronounced degree that personal quality known as "charisma" in his or her personality. Shamans, again like priests, can be of either sex, or they may be bisexual in some respects. Among certain North American Indian groups in the last century shamans could be men dressed up as women. Their transsexual identity neatly captured the most essential feature of shamanism—the shaman's dual nature—for the shaman works in two worlds: the world of human beings and the world of the spirits.

Shamans offer practical benefits to society. Human beings are vulnerable to misfortunes of many kinds—we cannot always expect to succeed in our undertakings, we suffer the loss of loved ones, we become ill, we suffer the pains of aging, and we die. As we saw in Chapter 3 people in many societies believe that spirits can bring about such misfortunes, which come about because spirits punish persons who misbehave. Therefore, when persons fall ill one response they may make is to think what misconduct they might have indulged in. Have they neglected to offer sacrifices to the spirits? Have they stolen anything? Is there some offense they have committed, but which they cannot recall without prompting? In this circumstance, a shaman may be called upon to diagnose the cause, identify the offended spirit, and suggest what ritual sacrifice would appease it.

How does a person become a shaman? An aspiring shaman may undergo a period of training and/or observe established shamans at work, but having the right personality is essential. Charisma is very desirable and an ability to enter into trances usually essential. Necessary also, is an ability to identify psychologically with patients so as to understand where their real problems may lie. Being a clever actor is a useful advantage, and having a talent for mimicry or ventriloquism, is another big help.

In the majority of cases, a person wishing to become a shaman must have undergone some psychologically difficult experience or endured some physical hardship that has transformed his or her personality in some radical way. The community, too, must be ready to accept the transformed personality that has emerged. On occasion, an individual becomes a shaman almost without intention. There are numerous cases on record where a sick person is at death's door, yet somehow survives, though with a personality radically transformed. The person may then have a strange story indeed to tell his or her kin and neighbors. Survivors typically describe how their soul departed the ailing body and was escorted to the supernatural world with the aid of spirits. There the soul talked with its spirit hosts and was instructed in many matters useful to the human community, including instruction in how to cure sick persons.

Upon the person's return to the human community, the traveler to this unknown land might feel so altered by his or her unique encounter with the spirits as to believe they have granted him or her the power to cure other afflicted individuals. So the person begins attempting cures. Should these effects succeed he or she will attract a steadily increasing list of clients, and from then on the person's career depends upon his or her skills. An evocative example of this process is reported in Reading 5–4.

Shamans typically experience hallucinations and trances, states often induced by drugs. Followers may believe that while in these states shamans are possessed by spirits or that their souls have left their bodies for a temporary visit to the other world. In some cases, before a shaman can practice "controlled" spirit possession, he or she must suffer the "uncontrolled" invasions of such beings, an experience at times so traumatic that a shaman who has undergone it successfully is sometimes said to have died and been reborn.

Visions among the Jíavaro (Reading 5–3) are brought about by drugs, whereas in some societies, like the Chukchee of Siberia, shamans enter trances by allowing their minds to be overcome by the constant beating of drums. In Chukchee trances, the shaman's mind and body become possessed by spirits, and spectators, packed tightly into the small room where the ritual is taking place, know instantly when this moment occurs. The shaman begins to beat his drum faster, shake his head furiously; a strange, chattering noise erupts from his lips, and he shouts hysterically. He is the mouthpiece for the spirits his drumming has conjured up. Waldemar Bogoras, who attended various Chukchee rituals, relates in his book *The Chukchee* (1904–1905) how spectacular possessions can get when a shaman happens to be a talented ventriloquist. Some especially talented individuals who are subject to possession by several spirits will have a different voice for each spirit. In this way a certain spirit-voice might seem to come from one corner of the room where the ritual is being held, another from the roof, another from the ground, another from between someone's legs, and others from various other locations. Sometimes a voice will be heard first as a faint distant noise. Then, as it gradually approaches, the voice grows louder, then louder, until it climaxes by rushing into the room, passing by the spectators and exiting. They then hear it getting fainter and fainter again, until the voice is finally extinguished. Some of the shaman's voices are those of the various animal spirits who can possess him, and so the shaman will at different times roar like a bear spirit, snort like a reindeer spirit, or howl like a wolf spirit. Or even have these voices conduct a conversation on the same occasion!

A shaman will incorporate magic into his or her ritual, and this may include leechcraft, a practice in which the alleged cause of a complaint is sucked out of a patient's body. This "cause" may actually be a sliver of wood or bone that the shaman tucked into his or her cheek before commencing the "cure."

Successful shamanism is more about psychology than medicine, and practitioners usually avoid attempting cures they know are unattainable since too many failures will cost them their reputations and clients, and ultimately means their livelihoods. In communities where there is access to Western medicines, shamans may actually counsel patients suffering from illnesses such as cancer to go to a physician. A shaman most often succeeds when clients suffer from mental problems or physical problems caused by psychological difficulties.

It goes almost without saying that shamans need to possess a thorough knowledge of the personal circumstances of their clients and of their patients' relationships with other members of the community. Armed with this knowledge, a shaman who has a solid reputation for successful healing has a fighting chance of convincing a patient whose real problem is mental that his or her illness can be cured. Typically, a shaman enters a trance, visits the supernatural world, and asks its inhabitants the cause of and cure for his client's illness. Upon his "return" he informs the patient what he has learnt—a ritual offering of food to the spirits often suffices to restore health. A great shaman cures a patient partly because her reputation is so great so that the invalid consults her in full confidence he will be cured. After all has she not "cured" many fellow sufferers in the past?

One question anthropologists have concerned themselves with from time to time is the issue of whether or not shamans are psychologically disturbed individuals. Descriptions of performances such as those described above may suggest at least some Chukchee shamans—and shamans elsewhere—may be to some degree psychologically

unusual. Some anthropologists have even gone so far as to argue that "spirit possession" is little more than a socially acceptable way for mentally disturbed individuals to dramatize their plight. But most fieldworkers show that in order to understand their client's problems and the personality and social relationships that have helped to bring them about, shamans needs to have a strong grasp of reality—and keep control over their behavior. A mentally impaired shaman is unlikely to be of use to anyone.

What is unarguable, however, is that community acceptance is essential for a shaman to function as a shaman. Societies like the Chukchee typically have criteria for determining whether a particular individual who claims to be possessed by a spirit and therefore eligible for being considered a shaman is the "genuine" article or someone who is either mentally unbalanced or fraudulent. In light of these criteria kin and neighbors will compare a candidate's behavior to that of established shamans, assess his or her claims in light of his or her previous personal history, and make a judgment call. The hopeful candidate may then be given a chance to try and cure someone. Or else the person's claims may be promptly ignored. The relative stringency of this requirement would seem to militate against the argument that shamans are mentally ill. In the article by Margery Wolf (Reading 5–2) the possibility that the local aspirant to the status of shaman may not be mentally stable is quite obviously of relevance to those of her neighbors who must pass judgment on her claims.

It is hardly a wonder, then, that shamanism is so widespread. Besides providing psychological reassurance to sick individuals and combating psychosomatic complaints, by seeking out social problems as possible causes of illness shamans help repair troubled social relationships. They also provide explanations for all manner of misfortunes and they encourage harmonious dialogue between human beings and spirits.

The terms *shaman, sorcerer,* and *magician* are often used interchangeably, a point that Claude Lévi-Strauss illustrates with clarity in Reading 4–4.

More discerning usage might require that the designations *sorcerer* and *magician* be regarded as synonyms for practitioners who engage in magical rituals without going into trances, whereas the term *shaman* be applied to a ritual functionary for whom trances are a customary procedure.

Priests are more familiar to Western societies than shamans, of course. Unlike shamans, however, priests (and priestesses) occupy formal positions or offices, and although they also mediate between human beings and spirits, they normally become practitioners by undertaking a period of training ending with initiation into the priesthood. The complex rite of passage—the ordination—an initiate into the Catholic priesthood must undergo is the climax of years of strenuous education instruction and moral self-conditioning. Charisma is rarely a job requirement for the office of priest, whose authority derives from the rights and obligations that define the position, not from the incumbent's personality. Because the office of priest and the position of shaman are embedded in the structure of society it is generally the case that his or her office is a force for the conservation of tradition rather than force for social change. Priests, like shamans, have a major stake in society as it is constituted, and as such their functions merge into those of other leaders in society, such as politicians and bureaucrats. In light of Durkheim's proposition that god = society we can easily understand how securely the office priest fits into the social structure. Indeed, in certain societies in the past the offices of priest and king were united in one and the same person. In these instances the priest-king symbolized the society and the cosmos he or she headed, and the physical condition of the body of the incumbent of such an office could be of immense significance. A vigorous body implied that society was healthy whereas a decrepit body suggested society was dissolute. Reading 8–4 gives an example of how body and society could be viewed in this manner.

An entirely different category of religious practitioner is the *prophet*. Over the last several centuries, many small-scale societies have been wrenched into social, economic, and political turmoil, often as a result of contact with Western culture. During these upheavals, when people come to feel disaffected and develop the sense that society no longer fulfills their needs, prophets (or *messiahs*) may emerge as leaders of what are sometimes called *revitalization movements*. Prophets are agents of change. They are usually men who have experienced intense spiritual experiences. Thus inspired, a charismatic prophet feels impelled to undertake a spiritual mission to transform society and in so doing sometimes either founds a new religion, like the Buddha, Jesus Christ, and Mohammed, or drives his adherents to destruction, like the Reverend Jim Jones (Reading 12–1).

As with shamans, one quality possessed by prophets is charisma, which can be observed, too, in certain political leaders worldwide. This concept was introduced into modern sociology by Max Weber (1947), who defined charisma as "a certain quality of an individual personality by virtue of which he is set apart from ordinary men and treated as endowed with supernatural, superhuman, or at least specifically exceptional powers or qualities. These are not accessible to the ordinary person, but are regarded as of divine origin or as exemplary, and on the basis of them the individual concerned is treated as a leader" (pp. 358–359).

The Handsome Lake religion of the Iroquois of upper New York State was founded by one such figure (Kehoe 1989, 113–127). After the American victory in the Revolutionary War, the Iroquois, who had supported the British, were dispersed in reservations as white settlers took over their lands. By 1800, the Iroquois were suffering wretched social and economic conditions, during which an Iroquois chief called Handsome Lake announced that he had experienced visions in which spirits warned him that the Iroquois would be destroyed unless they mended their ways. Forcefully preaching this message to his people, the charismatic Handsome Lake succeeded not only in initiating radical economic changes—traditional Iroquois farming methods were replaced by more effective European methods, for example—but also in founding a new religion based on traditional Iroquois beliefs and rituals.

During the last decades of the 19th century, the native groups of the Great Plains also had their prophets. These had arisen in response to socioeconomic upheavals similar to those that had led to the advent of Handsome Lake among the Iroquois. The Plains Indians had suffered from considerable cultural deprivation. Their vast bison herds had been all but wiped out, and their crops had repeatedly failed. White people had seized their lands and herded them onto reservations. Alcohol, measles, and whooping cough, all introduced by the whites, had killed thousands. The relentless Western expansion of pioneers had resulted in massacres and left a trail of broken peace treaties in its wake. Native Americans' feelings of frustration had grown increasingly desperate.

In this context, a series of charismatic characters emerged. These prophets guaranteed that if only people would follow them, the whites would be overcome, the great bison herds would return, and lands forfeited under duress to the Europeans would be recovered. Furthermore, sickness and death would disappear, dead kinsmen would be restored to life, and everlasting prosperity and happiness would reign (Kehoe, 1989). What was needed to bring about the millennium was for people to have faith, pray, and partake in a ritual called the Ghost Dance, a ceremony attended by the ancestral ghosts. Since such promises seemed to offer the only hope of survival, ghost dancing was widely practiced. But to no avail.

An example of a prophet in the Christian religion is Jesus, a man who broke with religious orthodoxy during a time of social upheaval and persuaded people to give up their customary way of life to become his disciples. In the process, he adapted traditional Judaic beliefs to the changing times and to his personality. After his death, the church he founded continued under Peter, a less charismatic man, and in the course of time eventually became an institution run by office-holders.

READING 5–1

RELIGIOUS SPECIALISTS

Victor W. Turner

Victor Turner (see also Reading 4–2) was one of the most influential anthropological experts on ritual and belief. His reputation was established in the 1960s with a series of articles and books analyzing in great ethnographic detail the ritual symbolism of the Ndembu. The fieldwork which generated the massive quantity of meticulously recorded information had been amassed at the beginning of the 1950s, and after he had completed publishing his Ndembu material he extended his research, and consolidated his reputation, into more comparative work. He thus commenced to reflect upon the work of other scholars and matured his own mode of interpretation in such concepts as "communitas" (See Introduction to Chapter 4). Turner's work, as noted in Chapter 4, is representative of the Manchester School of anthropology, and combines psychological insights with an appreciation for the dynamism of social processes.

This reading gives us a very informative anthropological summary of the kind of work religious practitioners perform. Many of the differences that Turner uses to distinguish them have already been discussed in the Introduction to this chapter, but he organizes them in his own distinctive manner. His approach here is typological, i.e., Turner is concerned to place each of the three categories, together with that of diviner, into a system of classification. Given the summary nature of his account, inevitably there are exceptions to his generalizations. For example, shamanism not only occurs in hunting and gathering societies. It can be an important feature of religion in modern industrialized societies, too, as we find in Korea. Again, we should note that Turner's definition of religion in terms of gods excludes Buddhism, which many scholars would regard as religion.

Source: "Religious Specialists," from International Encyclopedia of the Social Sciences, Volume 13 by David L. Sills, ed. (New York: Macmillan Company & The Free Press.

ANTHROPOLOGICAL STUDY

A religious specialist is one who devotes himself to a particular branch of religion or, viewed organizationally, of a religious system. "Religion" is a multivocal term whose range of meanings varies in different social and historical contexts. Nevertheless, most definitions of religion refer to the recognition of a transhuman controlling power that may be either personal or impersonal. A religious specialist has a culturally defined status relevant to this recognition. In societies or contexts where such power is regarded as impersonal, anthropologists customarily describe it as *magic,* and those who manipulate the power are magicians. Wherever power is personalized, as deity, gods, spirits, daemons, genii, ancestral shades, ghosts, or the like, anthropologists speak of *religion.* In reality, religious systems contain both magical and religious beliefs and procedures: in many of them the impersonal transhuman (or mystical, or nonempirical, or supernatural) power is considered to be a devolution of personal power, as in the case of the mystical efficacy or rites established *in illo tempore* by a deity or divinized ancestor.

Priest and prophet   Scholars have tended to distinguish between two polarities of religious specialization. Max Weber, for example, although well aware of numerous historical instances of their overlap and interpenetration, contrasts the roles of priest and prophet. He begins by making a preliminary distinction between priest and magician. A priest, he writes, is always associated with "the functioning of a regularly organized and permanent enterprise concerned with influencing the gods—in contrast with the individual and occasional efforts of magicians." Accordingly, the crucial feature of priesthood is that it represents the "specialization of a particular group of persons in the continuous operation of a cultic enterprise, permanently associated with particular norms, places and times, and related to specific social groups." In Weber's view, the prophet is distinguished from the priest by "personal call." The priest's claim to religious authority derives from his service in a sacred tradition; the

authority of the prophet is founded on revelation and personal "charisma." This latter term has been variously defined by Weber (in some contexts it seems almost to represent the *Führerprinzip*), but it may broadly be held to designate extraordinary powers. These include, according to Weber, "the capacity to achieve the ecstatic states which are viewed, in accordance with primitive experience, as the preconditions for producing certain effects in meteorology, healing, divination and telepathy." But charisma may be either ascribed or achieved. It may be an inherent faculty ("primary charisma") or it may be "produced artificially in an object or person through some extraordinary means." Charisma may thus be "merited" by fastings, austerities, or other ordeals. Even in such cases, Weber asserts, there must be some dormant capacity in the persons or objects, some "germ" of extraordinary power, already vested in them. The prophet, then, is a "purely individual bearer of charisma," rather than the representative of a sacred tradition. He produces discontinuity in that cultic enterprise which it is the priest's major role to keep "in continuous operation." Weber's prophet feels that he has a "mission" by virtue of which he "proclaims a religious doctrine or divine commandment." Weber refuses to distinguish sharply between a "renewer of religion" who preaches "an older revelation, actual or suppositious" and a "founder of religion" who claims to bring completely new "deliverances," for, he says, "the two types merge into one another." In Weber's view, the charisma of a prophet appears to contain, in addition to ecstatic and visionary components, a rational component, for he proclaims "a systematic and distinctively religious ethic based upon a consistent and stable doctrine which purports to be a revelation" [(1922); *see also* CHARISMA *and* WEBER, MAX].

Weber's distinction between priest and prophet has its main relevance in an analytical frame of reference constructed to consider the relationship between religion as "a force for dynamic social change" and religion as "a reinforcement of the stability of societies" (Parsons 1963). It has been found effective by such anthropologists as Evans-

Pritchard (1949; 1956) and Worsley (1957*a;* 1957*b*) who are dealing directly with social transitions and "the prophetic break," or what Parsons calls "the primary decision point [between] a direction which makes for a source of evolutionary change in the . . . established or traditional order, and a direction which tends either to reinforce the established order or at least not to change it drastically" (1963, p. xxix in 1964 edition).

Priest and shaman   Anthropologists who are less concerned than Weber with the genesis of religions and with internal developments in complex societies or their impact on the "primitive" world are inclined to contrast priest not with prophet but with shaman or spirit medium and to examine the relationship between these statuses as part of the normal working of the religious system in the simpler societies. In their excellently representative *Reader in Comparative Religion* (1958), the editors W. A. Lessa and E. Z. Vogt devote a whole section to this distinction.

Often, where there is a priest the shaman is absent, and vice versa, although both these roles may be found in the same religion, as among the Plains Indians. According to Lowie (1954), a Plains Indian shaman is a ritual practitioner whose status is acquired through a personal communication from a supernatural being, whereas a priest does not necessarily have a face-to-face relationship with the spirit world but must have competence in conducting ritual. Lessa and Vogt ([1958] 1965, p. 410) expand these differences: a shaman's powers come by "divine stroke," a priest's power is inherited or is derived from the body of codified and standardized ritual knowledge that he learns from older priests and later transmits to successors. They find that shamanism tends to predominate in food-gathering cultures, where the shaman most frequently performs a curing rite for the benefit of one or more patients and within the context of an extended family group. Shamanistic rites are "noncalendrical," or contingent upon occasions of mishap and illness. The priest and priestly cult organization are characteristically found in the more structurally

elaborated food-producing—usually agricultural—societies, where the more common ceremonial is a public rite performed for the benefit of a whole village or community. Such rites are often calendrical, or performed at critical points in the ecological cycle.

Shaman and medium   Raymond Firth (1964*a*, p. 638) regards shamanism as itself "that particular form of spirit mediumship in which a specialist (the *shaman*) normally himself a medium, is deemed to exercise developed techniques of control over spirits, sometimes including mastery of spirits believed to be possessing another medium." This definition, like that of Howells (1948), stresses the *control* exercised over spirits. Howells describes the shaman as "bullyragging" gods or spirits and emphasizes his intellectual qualities as a leader. This element of mastery makes the shaman a distinctive type of spirit medium, one who is believed to be "possessed by a spirit (or closely controlled by a spirit) [and who] can serve as a means of communication between other human beings and the spirit world" (Firth 1964*b,* p. 689). The spirit medium per se need not exert mastery; he is rather the vessel or vehicle of the transhuman entity.

Thus, although we sometimes find the two functions of priest and shaman combined in the same individual (Piddington 1950), mediums, shamans, and prophets clearly constitute subtypes of a single type of religious functionary. The priest communicates with transhuman entities through ritual that involves cultural objects and activities. The medium, shaman, and prophet communicate in a person-to-person manner: they are in what Buber (1936) would describe as an I–thou relationship with the deities or spirits. The priest, on the other hand, is in what may be called an I–it relationship with the transhuman. Between the priest and the deity intervenes the institution: Priests may therefore be classified as institutional functionaries in the religious domain, while medium, shaman, and prophet may be regarded as subtypes of inspirational functionaries. This distinction is reflected in characteristically different modes of operation. The priest presides over a rite; the shaman or medium conducts a seance. Symbolic forms associated with these occasions differ correlatively: the symbols of a rite are sensorily perceptible to a congregation and have permanence in that they are culturally transmissible, while those of a seance are mostly in the mind of the entranced functionary as elements of his visions or fantasies and are often generated by and limited to the unique occasion. The inspirational functionary may describe what he has clairvoyantly perceived (or "been shown" as he might put it), but the institutional functionary manipulates symbolic objects with prescribed gestures in full view of this congregation.

Sociocultural correlates   Since the priest is an actor in a culturally "scripted" drama, it is but rarely that priests become innovators, or "dramatists." If they do assume this role it is mainly as legislative reformers—by altering the details of liturgical procedure—that they do so. If a priest becomes a radical innovator in religion, he is likely to become a prophet to his followers and a heretic to his former superiors. From the priestly viewpoint it is the office, role, and script that are sacred and "charismatic" and not the incumbent of priestly office. The priest is concerned with the conservation and maintenance of a deposit of beliefs and practices handed down as a sacred trust from the founders of the social or religious system. Since its symbols at the semantic level tend to condense the critical values, norms, and principles of the total cultural system into a few sensorily perceptible representations, the sanctification of these symbols is tantamount to a preservative of the entire culture. What the priest is and does keeps cultural change and individual deviation within narrow limits. But the energy and time of the inspirational functionary is less bound up with the maintenance of the total cultural system. His practice has more of an *ad hoc* flavor; he is more sensitive and responsive than the priest to the private and personal, to the mutable and idiosyncratic. This type of functionary thrives in loosely structured food-gathering cultures, where he deals individually with specific occasions of trouble, or

during periods of social turbulence and change, when societal consensus about values is sharply declining and numerically significant classes of persons and social groups are becoming alienated from the orthodox social order. The shaman subtype is completely a part of the cultural system of the food-gatherers; the prophet may well stand outside the cultural system during such a period of decomposition and propose new doctrines, ethics, and even economic values.

The shaman is not a radical or a reformer, since the society he services is traditionally flexible and mobile; the prophet is an innovator and reformer, for he confronts a tightly structured order that is moribund and points the way to religious forms that will either provide an intensified cognitive dynamic for sociocultural change or codify the new moral, ideational, and social structures that have been inarticulately developing.

There are of course significant differences in the scale of the societies in which shaman and prophet operate. The shaman enacts his roles in small-scale, multifunctional communities whose religious life incorporates beliefs in a multitude of deities, daemons, nature spirits, or ancestral shades—societies that Durkheim might have described as possessing mechanical solidarity, low moral density, and segmental organization. The prophet tends to come into his own when the division of labor is critically replacing "mechanical" by "organic" solidarity, when class antagonisms are sharpened, or when small-scale societies are decisively invaded by the powerful personnel, ideas, techniques, and cultural apparatus (including military skills and armaments) of large-scale societies. The shaman deals in a personal and specific way with spirits and lesser deities; the prophet enters into dialogue, on behalf of his whole community, with the Supreme Being or with the major deities of a traditional pantheon, whose tutelary scope embraces large numbers of persons and groups, transcending and transecting their traditional divisions and animosities. Alternatively he communicates with the generalized ancestors or *genii loci,* conceived to be a single anonymous and homogeneous collectivity rather than a structure of known and named shades, each representing a specific segment of society. Whereas the shaman's function is associated with looseness of structure in small-scale societies, the prophet's is linked with loosening of structure in large-scale societies or with incompatibilities of scale in culture-contact situations.

Divination and religious specialists   In its strict etymological sense the term "divination" denotes inquiry about future events or matters, hidden or obscure, directed to a deity who, it is believed, will reply through significant tokens. It usually refers to the process of obtaining knowledge of secret or future things by mechanical means or manipulative techniques—a process which may or may not include invoking the aid of nonempirical (transhuman) persons or powers but does not include the empirical methods of science.

In the analysis of preliterate societies divination often is concerned with the immediate problems and interests of individuals and subgroups and but seldom with the destinies of tribes and nations. It is this specificity and narrowness of reference that primarily distinguishes divination from prophecy. Nadel (1954, p. 64) has called the kind of guidance it offers "mechanical and of a case-to-case kind." The diviner "can discover and disentangle some of the hidden influences which are at work always and everywhere . . . he cannot uncover any more embracing design. . . . Yet within the limits set to it divination has a part to play, providing some of the certainty and guidance required for provident action." Thus, although its range and scope are more circumscribed than those of prophecy, divination is believed to reveal what is hidden and in many cases to forecast events, auspicious and inauspicious.

Divination further refers to the analysis of past events, especially untoward events; this analysis often includes the detection and ascription of guilt with regard to their perpetrators, real or alleged. Where such untoward events are attributed to sorcerers and witches the diviner has great freedom of judgment in detecting and determining guilt. Divin-

ers are frequently consulted by victims' relatives and show intuitive and deductive virtuosity in discovering quarrels and grudges in their clients' kin groups and local communities. Social anthropologists find important clues to areas and sources of social strain and to the character and strength of supportive social norms and values in the diviners' diagnoses.

There is evidence that mediums, shamans, and priests in various cultures have practiced divination. The medium and shaman often divine without mechanical means but with the assistance of a tutelary spirit. In the work of Lessa and Vogt there is a translation of a vivid first-person account by a Zulu informant of a diviner's seance. This mediumistic female diviner

> dramatically utilizes some standard procedures of her art—ventriloquism, prior knowledge of the clients, the overhearing of the client's unguarded conversation, and shrewd common sense—to enable her spirits to provide the clients with advice. In this example, . . . a boy is suffering from a convulsive ailment. The spirits discover that an ancestral spirit is spitefully causing the boy's illness: the spirits decree that the location of the family's village must be moved; a goat must be sacrificed to the ancestor and the goat's bile poured over the boy; the boy must drink *Itongo* medicine. The treatment thus ranges from physical to social actions—from propitiation of wrathful ancestors to prescription of a medicinal potion. (Lessa & Vogt [1958] 1965, p. 340)

Similar accounts of shamanistic divinatory seances have been recorded by anthropologists working among North and South American Indians, Eskimos, and Siberian tribes, in many parts of Africa, and among Afro–Americans.

Divination was a function of members of the priesthood in many of the complex religious systems of Polynesia, west Africa, and ancient Mexico; in the religions of Israel, Greece, Etruria, and Rome; in Babylonia, India, China, Japan, and among the Celts. According to Wach,

> The Etruscans made these practices so much a part of their culture that the discipline has been named after

them (disciplina Etrusca or auquralis). Different phenomena and objects were used as media to ascertain the desires of the gods (regular and irregular celestial events, lightning, fire, and earthquakes, the shape or utterances of animals, flights of birds, movements of serpents, barking of dogs, forms of liver or entrails). Both in Etruria and Rome a numerous and well-organized hierarchy of functionaries existed for the practice of the sacred arts. (1958, p. 111 in 1961 edition)

Indeed, diffused through the Roman world, many of these techniques passed into medieval and modern culture.

Diviner and doctor Callaway's account (1868–1870) of the combined divinatory and curative seance in Zululand emphasizes the close relationship believed to hold in many preliterate societies between the functions of divination and therapy. Sometimes, as in the case cited, the diviner and "doctor" are the same person, but more often the roles are specialized and performed by different individuals. Modern therapy is taking increasingly into account the psychosomatic character of many maladies and the importance of sociological factors in their etiology. In most preliterate societies bodily symptoms are regarded as signs that the soul or life principle of the patient is under attack or has been abstracted by spiritual forces or beings. Furthermore, it is widely held that these attacks are motivated by animosities provoked by breaches of cultural, mainly religious, prescriptions and/or by breaches of social norms regarded as binding on members of kin groups or local communities. Thus, to acquire a comprehensive understanding of why and how a patient was afflicted with certain symptoms by a spirit or witch, primitives seek out a diviner who will disclose the secret antagonisms in social relations or the perhaps unconscious neglect of ritual rules (always a threat to the cultural order) that incited mystical retribution or malice. The diviner is a "diagnostician" who refers his clients to his colleague, the doctor or "therapist." The doctor in question has both shamanistic and priestly attributes. The division of labor which in more complex societies segregates and institutionalizes the functions of priest and medical man has hardly begun to

make its influence felt. The diviner–doctor dichotomy does not depend, as does the priest–shaman dichotomy, upon contrasting roles in regard to the transhuman realm but upon different phases in a social process which involves *total* human phenomena—integral personalities, many psychosomatic complexes, multiple social relationships, and multiform communities.

Modes of religious specialization As the scale and complexity of society increase and the division of labor develops, so too does the degree of religious specialization. This process accompanies a contraction in the domain of religion in social life. As Durkheim stated with typical creative exaggeration in his *Division of Labor in Society* ([1893] 1960, p. 169): "Originally [religion] pervades everything; everything social is religious; the two words are synonymous. Then, little by little, political, economic, scientific functions free themselves from the religious function, constitute themselves apart and take on a more and more acknowledged temporal character."

Simple societies In the simplest societies every adult has some religious functions and the elders have most; as their capacity to hunt or garden wanes, their priestlike role comes into ever greater prominence. Women tend to receive more recognition and scope as religious functionaries than in more developed societies. There is some tendency toward religious specialization in such societies, based on a variety of attributes, such as knowledge of herbalistic lore, skill in leechcraft, the capacity to enter a state of trance or dissociation, and sometimes physical handicap that compels a man or woman to find an alternative means of support to subsistence activities. (I have met several diviners in central Africa with maimed hands or amputated limbs.) But such specialization can hardly be defined, in the majority of cases, as more than part-time or even spare-time specialization. Michael Gelfand's description of the Shona *nganga,* variously translated in the ethnographic literature as "medicine man," "doctor," or "witch doctor," exemplifies the sociocultural situation of similar practitioners in very many preliterate societies (1964). The Shona *nganga* is at once a herbalist, a medium, and also a diviner who, possessed by a spirit of a dead relative, diagnoses both the cause of illness and of death. Yet, reports Gelfand,

> when he is not engaged in his medical practice he leads exactly the same life as the other men of his village. He cultivates his land, looks after his cattle, repairs his huts, makes blankets or other equipment needed by his family. And the same applies to a woman *nganga,* who busies herself with the tasks expected of every Shona woman. . . . The amount the *nganga* does in his village depends, of course, on the demands of his patients, but on the average he has a fair amount of spare time . . . a fair guess would be [that there is a *nganga*] to every 800 to 1,000 persons. . . . The *nganga* is given no special status in his village, his chances of being appointed headman are the same as anyone else's. (1964, pp. 22–23)

Complex societies   To bring out best the effects of increase in scale and the division of labor it is necessary to examine religious systems at the opposite end of the gradient of complexity. Religion no longer pervades all social domains; it is limited to its own domain. Furthermore, it has acquired a contractual and associational character; people may choose both the form and extent of their religious participation or may opt out of any affiliation. On the other hand, within each religious group a considerable amount of specialization has taken place. Much of this has been on the organizational level. Processes of bureaucratization, involving rationality in decision making, relative impersonality in social relations, routinization of tasks, and a hierarchy of authority and function, have produced a large number of types, grades, and ranks of religious specialists in all the major religious systems.

For example, the Catholic clerical hierarchy may be considered as (1) the hierarchy of order, whose powers are exercised in worship and in the administration of the sacraments, and (2) as the hierarchy of jurisdiction, whose power is over the members of the church. Within the hierarchy of jurisdiction alone we find such manifold statuses as pope and bishop (which are held to be of divine institution);

cardinal, patriarch, exarch, and primate (whose powers are derived by delegation expressed or implied from the holy see); metropolitan and archbishop (who derive their powers from their patriarch, exarch, or primate); archdeacon, vicar general, vicar forane, rural dean, pastor, and rector (who derive their powers from their diocesan bishop).

In addition to the clerical hierarchy there are in the Catholic church numerous institutes of the religious, that is, societies of men and women approved by ecclesiastical superiors, in which the members in conformity with the special laws of their association take vows, perpetual or temporary, and by this means aspire to religious perfection. This is defined as "the heroic exercise of the virtue of supernatural charity" and is pursued by voluntary maintenance of the vows of poverty, chastity, and obedience, by ascetical practices, through charitable works, such as care of the poor, sick, aged, and mentally handicapped, and by contemplative techniques, such as prayer. Within each religious institution or congregation there is a marked division of function and gradation of office.

Thus there are many differences of religious status, rank, and function in a developed religious system such as the Catholic church. Differences in charismata are also recognized in such terms as "contemplative," "ascetic," "mystic," "preacher," "teacher," "administrator." These gifts may appear in any of the major divisions of the church: among clergy or laity, among hermits, monks, or friars, among female as well as male religious. Certain of these charismata are institutionalized and constitute the devotional pattern particular to certain religious institutions: thus there are "contemplative orders," "friars preachers," and the like.

Medium-scale societies   Other developed religions, churches, sects, cults, and religious movements exhibit degrees of bureaucratic organization and specialization of role and function. Between the situational specialization of religious activities found in small-scale societies and the full-time and manifold specialization in large-scale societies falls a wide variety of intermediate types. A characteristic religious dichotomy is found in many of the larger, politically centralized societies of west and east Africa, Asia, Polynesia, and pre-Columbian Central and South America. National and tribal gods are worshiped in the larger towns, and minor deities, daemons, and ancestral shades are venerated in the villages. At the village level we find once more the multifunctional religious practitioner. But where there are national gods there are usually national priests, their official servants, and worship tends to take place in temples or at fixed and elaborate shrines. Parrinder writes:

> In the cults of the West African gods [for example, in Dahomey, Yoruba, and Ashanti] there are priests who are highly trained to do their work. These priests are often set aside from birth, or they may be called to the service of the god by being possessed by his spirit. They will then retire from their families and public life, and submit to the training of an older priest. The training normally lasts several years, during which time the novice has to apply himself to learn all the secrets of consulting and serving the god. The training of a priest is an arduous matter. . . . [He] has to observe chastity and strict taboos of food and actions. He frequently has to sleep on a hard floor, have insufficient food, and learn to bear hardship. He is regarded as married to the god, though later he may take a wife. Like an Indian devotee, he seeks by self-discipline to train himself to hear the voice of his god. He learns the ritual and dances appropriate to the cult, receives instruction in the laws and taboos of the god, and gains some knowledge of magical medicines. (1954, pp. 100–101)

In these west African cults of deities there is a formal division of function between priests and mediums. In general, priests control mediums and carefully regulate their experience of possession. This situation is one solution to the perennial problem posed for priesthoods by what Ronald Knox (1950) has termed "enthusiasm," that is, the notion that one can become possessed by or identified with a god or God and that one's consequent acts and words are divinely inspired, even if they transgress religious or secular laws. In Dahomey, for example (Herskovits 1938), there are communal training centers, called cult houses or "convents," for medi-

ums and assistants to priests. Here the novices are secluded for considerable periods of time. Part of their training involves the attempt to induce the return of the initial spirit possession that marked their calling. They learn later to produce coherent messages in a state of trance. During this period they are under the surveillance of priests. The Catholic church has similarly brought under its control as members of contemplative orders mystics and visionaries who claim "experiential knowledge of God's presence."

Religious and political specialization   In many primitive societies an intimate connection exists between religion and politics. If by politics we denote those behavioral processes of resolution of conflict between the common good and the interests of groups by the use of or struggle for power, then religion in such societies is pragmatically connected with the maintenance of those values and norms expressing the common good and preventing the undue exercise of power. In centralized political systems that have kings and chiefs, these dignitaries themselves have priestly functions; in many parts of Africa, for example, they take charge of observances which safeguard many of the basic needs of existence, such as rain making, sowing, and harvest rites, ritual to promote the fertility of men, domestic and wild animals, and so on. On the other hand, even where this is the case, there are frequently other specialized religious functionaries whose duties are bound up with the office of kingship. An illustration of this occurs among the Bemba of Zambia, where the *Bakabilo*

> are in charge of ceremonies at the sacred relic shrines and take possession of the *babenye* when the chief dies. They alone can purify the chief from the defilement of sex intercourse so that he is able to enter his relic shrine and perform the necessary rites there. They are in complete charge of the accession ceremonies of the paramount and the bigger territorial chiefs, and some of their number are described as *bafingo* or hereditary buriers of the chief. Besides this, each individual *mukabilo* has his own small ritual duty or privilege, such as lighting the sacred fire, or forging the

blade of the hoe that is to dig the foundations of the new capital. (Richards 1940, p. 109 in 1955 edition)

The *Bakabilo* constitute a council that exerts a check on the paramount's power, since the members are hereditary officials and cannot be removed at will. They are immune to the paramount's anger and can block the implementation of decisions that they consider to be detrimental to the interests of the Bemba people by refusing to perform the ritual functions that are necessary to the exercise of his office. A priesthood of this type thus forms a constituent part of the interior structure of the government of a primitive state.

In stateless societies in Africa and elsewhere, incumbents of certain ritual positions have similar functions in the maintenance of order and the resolution of conflict. The "leopard-skin chief" or "priest of the earth" (as this specialist has been variously called) among the Nuer of the Nilotic Sudan is a person whose ritual relationship with the earth gives him power to bless or curse, to cleanse a killer from the pollution of bloodshed, and, most important, to perform the rites of reconciliation between persons who are ready to terminate a blood feud. A similar role is performed by the "masters of the fishing spear" among the Dinka and the *tendaanas,* or earth priests, among the Tallensi and their congeners in the northern territories of Ghana. Similar religious functionaries are found in many other regions of Africa. They serve to reduce, if not to resolve, conflict within the society. As against sectional and factional interests they posit the commonweal. In these contexts, moreover, the commonweal is regarded as part of the cosmic order; breach, therefore, is mystically punished. The religious specialists are accorded the function of restoring the right relation that should obtain between society, the cosmos, and the deities or ancestral shades.

VICTOR W. TURNER

BIBLIOGRAPHY

BUBER, MARTIN (1936) 1958 *I and Thou*. 2d ed. New York: Scribner. First published in German.

CALLAWAY, HENRY (1868–1870) 1885 *The Religious System of the Amazulu*. Folk-lore Society Publication No. 15. London: Trübner.

DURKHEIM, ÉMILE (1893) 1960 *The Division of Labor in Society*. Glencoe, Ill.: Free Press. First published as *De la division du travail social*.

ELWIN, VERRIER 1955 *The Religion of an Indian Tribe*. Bombay: Oxford Univ. Press.

EVANS-PRITCHARD, E. E. (1949) 1954 *The Sanusi of Cyrenaica*. Oxford: Clarendon.

EVANS-PRITCHARD, E. E. (1956) 1962 *Nuer Religion*. Oxford: Clarendon.

FIRTH, R. W. 1964*a* Shaman. Pages 638–639 in Julius Gould and William L. Kolb (editors), *A Dictionary of the Social Sciences*. New York: Free Press.

FIRTH, R. W. 1964*b* Spirit Mediumship. Page 689 in Julius Gould and William L. Kolb (editors), *A Dictionary of the Social Sciences*. New York: Free Press.

GELFAND, MICHAEL 1964 *Witch Doctor: Traditional Medicine Man of Rhodesia*. London: Harvill.

HERSKOVITS, MELVILLE J. 1938 *Dahomey: An Ancient West African Kingdom*. 2 vols. New York: Augustin.

HOWELLS, WILLIAM W. 1948 *The Heathens: Primitive Man and His Religions*. Garden City, N.Y.: Doubleday. A paperback edition was published in 1962.

KNOX, RONALD A. 1950 *Enthusiasm: A Chapter in the History of Religion; With Special Reference to the XVII and XVIII Centuries*. New York: Oxford Univ. Press.

LESSA, WILLIAM A.; and VOGT, EVON Z. (editors) (1958) 1965 *Reader in Comparative Religion: An Anthropological Approach*. 2d ed. New York: Harper. See especially the unsigned introduction to Henry Callaway's article on p. 340.

LOWIE, ROBERT H. 1954 *Indians of the Plains*. American Museum of Natural History, Anthropological Handbook No. 1. New York: McGraw-Hill.

NADEL, SIEGFRIED F. 1954 *Nupe Religion*. London: Routledge.

PARRINDER, EDWARD G. 1954 *African Traditional Religion*. London: Hutchinson's University Library.

PARSONS, TALCOTT 1963 Introduction. In Max Weber, *The Sociology of Religion*. Boston: Beacon. A paperback edition was published in 1964.

PIDDINGTON, RALPH 1950 *Introduction to Social Anthropology*. 2 vols. New York: Praeger. See especially Volume 1.

RICHARDS, AUDREY I. (1940) 1961 The Political System of the Bemba Tribe: Northeastern Rhodesia. Pages 83–120 in Meyer Fortes and E. E. Evans-Pritchard (editors), *African Political Systems*. Oxford Univ. Press.

WACH, JOACHIM 1958 *The Comparative Study of Religions*. New York: Columbia Univ. Press. A paperback edition was published in 1961.

WEBER, MAX (1922) 1963 *The Sociology of Religion*. Boston: Beacon. First published in German. A paperback edition was published in 1964.

Worsley, P. M. 1957a Millenarian Movements in Melanesia. *Rhodes-Livingstone Journal* 21: 18–31.

Worsley, P. M. 1957b *The Trumpet Shall Sound: A Study of "Cargo" Cults in Melanesia.* London: MacGibbon & Kee.

READING 5–2

THE WOMAN WHO DIDN'T BECOME A SHAMAN

Margery Wolf

A shaman cannot function as a shaman without the continual appreciation of clients. This study of a woman, who lived in a village in Taiwan, and who tried hard to persuade her fellow villagers to recognize her claims to be a shaman demonstrates how social and personal dynamics contribute to a person's acceptance as a shaman. From a theoretical point of view, it also offers a very good example of how the position of shaman can be understood from a structural-functional perspective. The claimant presented her qualifications—in effect, her personality and record of involvement in the lives of her neighbors—and asked them to evaluate them. The neighbors had a range of options from which to choose. Was the woman being called on by a deity to speak on its behalf? Was she possessed by a ghost? Was she being exploited by her husband? Was she just crazy? Did she show some command of qualities necessary for a shaman to possess? In any event, her neighbors rejected her credentials, and Margery Wolf, a leading scholar of Chinese society, attempts to explain why. In pursuing this structural-functional analysis Wolf traces the connections between the dominant values in this society and social status, and identifies social marginality, gender, and an ideology of masculinity as being instrumental in the woman's ultimate rejection. We shall return to the question of social marginality and female status again, in discussing witchcraft, in Reading 7–3.

In the spring of 1960 in a then-remote village on the edge of the Taipei basin in northern Taiwan, a

Source: Margery Wolf, "The Woman Who Didn't Become a Shaman." Reproduced by permission of the American Anthropological Association from American Ethnologist 17:2, 1990, pp. 419–30. Not for further reproduction.

young mother of three lurched out of her home, crossed a village path, and stumbled wildly across a muddy rice paddy. The cries of her children and her own agonized shouts quickly drew an excited crowd out of what had seemed an empty village. Thus began nearly a month of uproar and agitation as this small community resolved the issue of whether one of their residents was being possessed by a god or was suffering from a mental illness. For Mrs. Chen, it was a month of misery and exultation; for the residents of Peihotien, it was a month of gossip, uncertainty, and heightened religious interest; for the anthropologists in the village, it was a month of confusion and fascination.

Mrs. Chen herself had less influence over the outcome of her month of trial than a foreign observer might expect. Even Wang Ming-fu, a religious specialist who lived nearby and who was given credit for making the final decision, was only one factor in a complex equation of cultural, social, ritual, and historical forces. In the pages that follow, I will attempt to reconstruct the events of that spring from field notes, journal entries, and personal recollections and evaluate what happened from the perspective of the anthropologist. I am not concerned here with shamanism per se, but with the social and cultural factors that were brought to bear by various members of the community in deciding whether Mrs. Chen was being approached by a god who wished to use her to communicate with his devotees, whether an emotional pathology included fantasies of spirit possession, or whether, as a few maintained, her feckless husband hoped to use her as a source of income.

In the hours following Mrs. Chen's precipitous trip into the mud of the rice paddies, an enormous amount of information traveled through the village about her recent behavior, her past, and the attitude of her family and neighbors. The day before, she had taken her six-month-old baby to her sister's house and left her. She had been complaining to her husband that there was a fever in her heart. She had beaten herself on the chest, pleading to be left in peace, and had jumped up and down on the bed so violently that it had broken. Her husband, commonly referred to in the village as Dumb T'ien-lai, had told one of their neighbors that she was probably going crazy "again." Nonetheless, he had done nothing about it until her very public display. Informants who were in the crowd that gathered as neighbors pulled her out of the paddy and took her back to her house reported that she begged to be allowed to go to the river to "meet someone" who was calling her. The nearby river is considered a dangerous place, full of ghosts who have either accidentally drowned or committed suicide. Water ghosts are infamous for trying to pull in the living to take their place in the dark world of unhappy ghosts.

As the long afternoon wore on, I heard other reports. People said that she pleaded with her husband, Chen T'ien-lai, to give her incense so that she could apologize to "the god who crossed the water." When he lit the incense for her, she began to tremble all over, her eyes glazed, and she began to talk in a loud male voice. One of the oldest women in the village, a woman known for her religious knowledge, came to see her and told T'ien-lai that he should call in a *tang-ki* (shaman)[1] to see if she had met a ghost. By then, however, Mrs. Chen's husband had finally taken some action on his own, and the ranting woman was hauled off under some kind of restraint in a pedicab to what was described to me as a "mental hospital" in the nearby market town.

During the three days that Mrs. Chen was out of the village, the Chen family was part of every conversation. Arthur Wolf, our assistant Wu Chieh, and I collected information about the Chens whether we wanted it or not. We discovered that even though the family was extremely poor, Mrs. Chen went regularly to the temple in Tapu and visited other temples within walking distance. Whenever her children were ill she consulted *tang-ki* in Tapu and neighboring areas. At home, she burned incense and made offerings daily to both her husband's ancestors and a variety of spirits and gods. We learned that although she was painfully shy (we had had much less contact with her than with most other villagers), Mrs. Chen was a fiercely protective mother who had quarreled in recent months with a woman from the Lin household when Mrs. Chen's young son had been slugged by a Lin boy. The Chens had lived in the village for nearly ten years, but by village tradition they were still considered newcom-

ers—it took at least a generation for a new family to be accepted among those whose grandparents and great-grandparents had been born in Peihotien. Until then, newcomers were expected to behave like guests, and guests were expected to watch their hosts' faces. It was a Lin village.

When Mrs. Chen returned to the village, pale and drugged, her mother, Mrs. Pai, was called in by Chen T'ien-lai to "help out." Mrs. Pai had none of her daughter's shyness, and the villagers soon learned from her that her daughter had had one previous "episode" of this kind of behavior. When she was a young adolescent the family had come upon hard times and had been forced to give her away "in adoption" to a family in need of a servant. The girl had done fairly well until "something happened" about which the mother was vague in detail but implied that a member of the family had either raped or attempted to rape her. The girl had run away to her mother, been returned to her adoptive family, and within a few weeks been sent back to her parents by the adoptive family because "she was crazy." She stayed with her natal family until her marriage. There had been, according to her mother, no recurrence of erratic behavior.

Mrs. Pai also cast new light on what might have precipitated her daughter's current distress. It seems that a couple of weeks earlier a sizable sum of money had been lost from the pocket of her jacket. Mrs. Chen's son said he had seen his father take it before he went out to gamble one night, but Chen T'ien-lai denied it. Mrs. Chen blamed herself for the loss, but at times seemed convinced that it had been stolen by someone from the Lin household. At some point in the days that followed, the money was miraculously found (probably supplied by sympathetic villagers), but the expectation that this would end the problem was disappointed.

Within 48 hours of her return to Peihotien, Mrs. Chen was again drawing crowds. First, she told her mother that she must *bai-bai* (worship) to "the god who crossed the ocean," a god unknown to Mrs. Pai. The old woman I mentioned earlier informed Mrs. Pai that this was probably Shang Ti Kung (a local god) and that it cost only one New Taiwan dollar (a few cents) per day to rent an image. She also urged her to bring in Shang Ti Kung's *tang-ki* to ask what was wanted. All of this was done the next day and, according to a neighbor, the *tang-ki* said that Mrs. Chen had met a ghost. Later that afternoon the image of another god, Wang Yeh, was brought in, but Mrs. Chen still was not at peace. The next day, Mrs. Chen, according to her husband, leapt out of bed shouting that the god was in her body and that T'ien-lai must go at once to get the god's image so that she could *bai-bai* to him. They tried to humor her and finally because she was getting more and more frantic, agreed to purchase the image. However, neither Chen T'ien-lai nor his mother-in-law recognized the god she described. As Chen T'ien-lai was discussing this problem with some neighbors, his mother-in-law came out of her daughter's bedroom and announced that the daughter, using a strange voice, had told her the exact place to purchase the god's image. She sent her son-in-law on his way and, according to my informants, Mrs. Chen calmed down and went to sleep as soon as she heard that he had gone to purchase "the right god."[2]

Once the new god was put on the Chen household altar, however, the activities in the Chen courtyard changed dramatically. Mrs. Chen began to "dance" like a *tang-ki,* speak in a strange language, and make oracle-like statements. For nearly a week, whenever she came out of the house, crowds would gather and she would "perform." We did not attend all of her sessions, but we were told that she revealed knowledge about people's personal lives that "only a god" would have. She behaved and spoke in ways that were most uncharacteristic of the withdrawn, depressed woman to whom the village was accustomed.

One session in which our research assistant was involved is a good example. I quote from our field notes:

Mrs. Chen suddenly jumped up and pointed at Lin Mei-ling and told her to approach. Lin Mei-ling had been chatting with some other women about some medicine she had put on her eyes, which appeared to be infected. She looked quite scared, and the others had to push her forward toward Mrs. Chen, saying, "Go on, see what she has to say." As soon as Lin Mei-

ling reached her, Mrs. Chen touched her eyes and said, "All right. This one will be well." She sounded as if she were reading a formal notice. Mrs. Chen then returned to making *bai-bai* motions with her hands, saying: "Your husband is a good man. He has a kind heart. He took me home one night on his bicycle. Your family will have peace and won't have any troubles." Lin Mei-ling was holding her baby, who began to cry very loudly. Her mother-in-law came up and tried to take Mrs. Chen's hands off Mei-ling, telling her that the baby was crying because she had to urinate. Mrs. Chen pushed her aside and said in a loud commanding voice, "Never mind." She then began to handle the baby, saying, "You will have peace and you won't have any trouble. It doesn't matter. It doesn't matter." To Mei-ling she said, "In these days everything will be all right for you. Everything will be all right." She made more *bai-bai* motions and then told Mei-ling to go home and not speak with anyone on the way. "Do you understand?" she asked. Mei-ling was still smiling, but she was probably quite frightened, for her face had turned white. She left and Mrs. Chen knelt on the threshold, making more *bai-bai* motions. She called our assistant, Wu Chieh, to come to her.

Wu Chieh was frightened and didn't want to go forward. She asked another woman what to do and was urged to comply. She was told, "Nothing is wrong. The god is in her body, that's all." Several people pushed Wu Chieh, including Mrs. Pai, Mrs. Chen's mother. Mrs. Chen moved her hands over Wu Chieh's body and face and then took her hands and began to "jump" like a *tang-ki.* Some of the people in the crowd laughed and said, "She wants to dance with you, Wu Chieh." Mrs. Chen said, "Older Sister, you come and you are very kind to all of the children. From the top of the village to the bottom, all of the children call you Older Sister. Do you like that? Do you like that?" Wu Chieh was speechless with fear. Mrs. Chen's mother told her to say something, and Wu Chieh blurted out, "Yes." Mrs. Chen hugged her close and put her face against Wu Chieh's. Mrs. Pai said, "She wants to kiss you." Mrs. Chen shouted, "No, no, no!" Her mother quickly said, "No, I am wrong. I am just an old lady who doesn't understand."

Mrs. Chen told the crowd through gestures (reaching in her pocket, smacking her lips, and so forth) that Wu Chieh gives the children candy. "Children, adults, and old people are all the same. You know that, right?" Wu Chieh nodded. Mrs. Chen then began to make wide, sweeping *bai-bai* gestures and pronounced, "People should not be judgmental, saying this person is good and that person is bad." Then she began to jump around the yard, and an older woman hissed at Wu Chieh, "Stupid child, aren't you going to run away now?" Some little boys were giggling and saying, "This crazy lady is dancing and poor Wu Chieh is going to have to wash all of her clothes." (Mrs. Chen was dirty from kneeling and falling in the dusty courtyard.) Mrs. Chen immediately turned on the boys and shouted, "Go away if you don't believe. Go away." She waved them off as if they were curious chickens, and they scattered like chickens. She turned again to Wu Chieh and rubbed her hands, telling her that everything would be peaceful with her.

As she talked, she continued to make *bai-bai* motions and to jump about, and finally she fell over backward on the ground. She lay there for some time, and Wu Chieh said that when Mrs. Chen opened her eyes, only the whites were visible. After a bit, Mrs. Chen got up and told everyone to go away, saying, "If you don't and you meet something bad [by implication, a ghost], don't blame me." People moved off to the edge of the yard, some of them whispering, some of them laughing, but after a bit the crowd slowly began to edge back toward the house. Mrs. Chen told Wu Chieh, "Because they bully me, I am not willing to continue. Do you understand? You must take me out. Do you understand that?" Wu Chieh kept agreeing at the urging of Mrs. Chen's mother, but she wasn't at all sure what was expected of her.

Mrs. Chen told Wu Chieh to go home again and not to talk with anyone she met on the way. "Listen to what I say or it won't go well for me. After you go home, then come back and take me into the house."

People urged Wu Chieh to leave then, so she started to walk away, but Mrs. Chen called her back one more time. "I haven't finished talking to you yet," she said. "If you don't listen to me things will go badly for you. Do you understand? Now, hurry up and go home and then come back and take me to my room. Will you do that? If you don't, I will come to your house and find you." She repeated these instructions several times and added, "When you come back, if I am still talking to these women, you stand here and don't say anything, do you hear?" This was all said in a loud commanding voice, totally unlike her normal voice, according to Wu Chieh. Mrs. Chen grabbed both of Wu Chieh's hands in one of hers and gestured

with the other in the "counting" motions of a *tang-ki* who is "calculating" what goes on in the world. (This is considered an indication of the god's omniscience.)

Wu Chieh finally extricated herself from this session, but returned in a few minutes and led Mrs. Chen, still gesturing and talking oddly, into her bedroom, where she got her to lie down. Wu Chieh then fled, but Mrs. Chen did not forget her. She called for her attendance several times over the next few days. Unlike Mrs. Chen, who had spent ten years in the village and was still an outsider, Wu Chieh in the year she had lived in the village had become everyone's confidante, everyone's friend, even Mrs. Chen's.

I have included this long quote from our field notes to give the reader a sense of Mrs. Chen's performances to compare with the description of the session of an experienced *tang-ki* that will be quoted below, and also to provide a glimpse of the way in which some of the villagers responded to this event. Village opinion was divided at best. Before Mrs. Chen was finally taken away "for a rest" by her mother, several village women reported smelling "puffs of fragrant air" in her room, a sure sign that a god was present; several others reported that she had told them things that only a god could know about their family affairs; she had tormented the Lin family, who had treated her so harshly over the quarrel between their children; she had been visited by a doctor who had given her heavy doses of tranquilizers; and she had held many sessions not unlike the one described above. Finally, old Wang Ming-fu, who was considered the expert in the region on matters of religion and ritual, came to talk with her. Their conversation, of which we never got a complete report, was not a happy one. He left in a huff.

We began to detect a change in village attitudes shortly after Wang Ming-fu's visit. Dumb T'ien-lai was enjoying the spectacle far too much and talking too openly about how expensive it was for him to have his wife providing free advice to anyone who asked for it. Mrs. Chen spoke too often and too much about herself as Mrs. Chen rather than behaving as a vehicle who was unaware of her pronouncements while "in trance"; her speeches rambled on too long and lost the enigmatic quality that brings authority to the *tang-ki*. And the fact that Wang Ming-fu was unlikely to recommend that she go to a temple where other *tang-ki* got training and experience seemed to end the matter. Within a week, people had begun to refer to her as "poor Mrs. Chen," to regard her displays as a nuisance, and to pressure members of her family "to do something."

Before I explore in more detail how and why this decision was reached, some background on shamanism, or spirit possession, in China and Taiwan and its role in folk religion is necessary. I will not try to sort out the peculiar amalgam of Buddhism, Taoism, and Confucianism that is involved in folk religion in Taiwan in particular and China in general. Suffice it to say that there are Buddhist temples and monasteries and that their adherents and practitioners are distinguished by dress and diet. There are no Taoist temples, but folk temples devoted to local gods are usually the locus of the activities of Taoist priests and of the lowly spirit mediums (Jordan 1972:29). The average Taiwanese citizen will make use of Buddhist and Taoist practitioners as the need arises, sometimes entertaining both during funeral rituals. Temples nearly always have at least one Buddhist worthy on their altars, and Buddhist temples sometimes have shrines for local gods in side alcoves. To add to the confusion, spirit mediums in rural areas often provide services from their own home in front of their ancestral altar—which is also a shrine to their particular god—or in the home of the family requesting the help of their god. In urban areas some *tang-ki* have shopfront shrines to their gods, and the most successful have cults of followers who may themselves perform in trance (Kleinman 1980:232).

In his study of folk religion in a Taiwanese village, David K. Jordan describes the function of the *tang-ki* at the village level:

> The *tang-ki* are the prime rural religious arbiters. It is they who diagnose a given case of familial or village disharmony as caused by ghosts; it is they who

explore the family tree or the village forts for possible ghosts and their motivations; it is they who prescribe the cure. Spirit mediums drive harmful ghosts from the village; spirit mediums perform exorcisms; and spirit mediums represent the august presence of the divine at rites performed in their name. It is likely that in the past it was the spirit mediums who had the final voice in alliances between villages [in local wars]. [1972:85]

But, as Jordan goes on to warn:

> The *tang-ki* is not a free man [sic], and his imitation of the gods is not a matter of his own caprice. Not only must he perform in trance (and therefore presumably not be guided by capricious desires but only by unconscious directives), but he is subject to charges of being possessed by ghosts rather than by gods should he become incredible. [1972:85]

And if the *tang-ki* is deemed possessed by a ghost, like any other villager, he or she will have his or her soul called back by another practitioner, essentially ending his or her legitimacy as a shaman.

My own experience with shamans in Taiwan was much more limited than that of Jordan, in part because religion was not the primary focus of my research or that of my coresearcher, Arthur Wolf, and in part because the villages we worked in did not have a resident *tang-ki*. In Peihotien, villagers used the services of an itinerant spirit medium who visited the area every few weeks or, late in our stay, of a young man who was attached to a temple in a nearby market town. Neither of these men seemed to have the kind of influence as "religious arbiter" that Jordan describes. Our field notes and the cases the staff recorded of visits to *tang-ki* certainly show that most villagers were "true believers," but we also heard a good deal of the cynicism that Jack Potter (1974) described when villagers assigned self-serving motives to some of the in-trance pronouncements of local shamans. I do not mean to suggest in any sense that I doubt Jordan's analysis for Bao-an, but only that our informants judged shamans on the basis of their success in solving individual problems—on how *ling* (strong) their gods were. Had I had the foresight to interview more widely, I might have found that spirit mediums had more influence on community matters than I assumed at the time. Considering the case I am discussing here, this would have been an extremely valuable piece of information.

In northern Taiwan, the source of my data and much of the secondary material to which I refer, the village shaman is considered simply a conduit between a god and his or her petitioners. During festivals celebrating the god, the shaman is expected to put on a display of bodily abuse, such as lying on a bed of nails or lacerating the body with swords, or a prickball. Although this is often called "mortification" in the literature (Jordan 1972:78), the purpose is not to subjugate the flesh as in early Christian ritual, but to prove that the god does not allow his vehicle to feel pain from these injuries and will protect him or her from permanent damage. The injuries do seem to heal rather quickly, and most observers comment on the absence of any expression of pain. Some shamans draw blood during each session, others only at major public events. In private sessions they rarely stage such ordeals, but they always trance.

In the literature there are a number of excellent descriptions of the performances of Chinese shamans. Some focus on the more spectacular (and bloody) feats of *tang-ki* on festival days, when they are showing off the power of their gods (see, for example, Elliott 1955), but a few give us a village perspective. Potter (1974) provides a particularly full picture of what amounts to a villagewide seance in the New Territories in Hong Kong, a seance in which the spirit medium travels through the underworld of spirits, chatting with the departed relatives of fellow villagers and allowing them to convey messages, warnings, threats, and reassurances to the living. A description by Katherine Gould-Martin (1978:46–47) of a *tang-ki*'s session in a market town not far from Mrs. Chen's home captures the relaxed familiarity of Taiwan shamanism. The god who speaks in Gould-Martin's account is Ong-ta-kong, and a cult has formed around the image of him in the living room of a very devout but otherwise not unusual family. The *tang-ki,* a laborer in his forties who lives two doors away from this family, trances every night after dinner. While petitioners, believers, or just neighbors gather to observe, comment, or seek help, the *tang-ki* wanders about the room, lights a cigarette for the god, exchanges a few words with him, and chats with friends in the crowd. In time an assistant begins to burn spirit money and to chant. As the tempo of the chant increases, the *tang-ki* begins to shake, tremble, and then to jump about, finally banging his head on a table. As Gould-Martin describes it:

> Once the *tang-ki*'s head comes down, the assistant stops chanting and begins to read off the first case: "believing man or woman," name, birthdate, address, problem. During the reading the tang-ki starts to make sounds in a strange falsetto. He continues for some time. This is considered to be the god speaking in his native dialect, i.e., that which was spoken in his area of the Chinese mainland in the T'ang Dynasty. No one can understand these sounds. The actual advice is given in Taiwanese in a voice similar to the *tang-ki*'s normal speaking voice, but deeper, more forceful, more inflected. The sentences of advice are often followed by, "Do you understand that?" They are interspersed with the falsetto noises. Often there is some discussion. The patient asks the god or the *tang-ki*'s helper a question. The god speaking through the *tang-ki* may reply or, if it is simple or the god seems annoyed, then the helper or even another patient or listener may answer the question. The god does not like to repeat himself and will be annoyed at that, but he will answer further questions. At the end the god, speaking through the *tang-ki,* says, "next case" and lapses into soft falsetto while the data of the next case are read to him. [1978:46]

Once the *tang-ki* has completed the evening's requests to Ong-ia-kong, he is brought out of his trance by the assistant's burning of more spirit money, washes his hands and face, and chats with whomever is left in the crowd; his evening's work is then over. The money contributed is divided up among the assistant, the *tang-ki,* the host family, and a money-box designated for the god's birthday celebration and a temple the group hopes to build in his honor.

The problems brought to *tang-ki* are varied, ranging from illnesses in humans and animals to economic setbacks to marital disputes to fears of infertility. In 1958–59, Arthur Wolf and his field staff collected more than 500 observations of villagers' visits to a local *tang-ki*. Over half of the problems brought to the *tang-ki* concerned illness: 53 percent of the women asked about their own or a family member's ill health, and 56 percent of the male visitors sought help for illness. Another 16 percent of the women inquired about domestic discord, and 15 percent of the women inquired about their fortune and/or asked to have it changed. Male clients did not ask as much about family disputes (4 percent) and were more interested in having their fortune tended to (14 percent), seeking help with sick animals (12 percent), or getting advice on financial decisions (8 percent). The following examples indicate the kind of information and acuity required of a practicing *tang-ki:*

> An old lady asked for advice about her husband, who was seriously ill. The shaman said: "He should have been dead by now. Your husband should have been dead yesterday. However, due to 'strengthened fortune and added longevity' [perhaps from earlier treatment?], he has been able to reach the age of 73. His original life was for only 69 years. Even so, it looks to me as if he were supposed to have died yesterday. If he survives the first day of the coming month, he will have great fortune. You can then come to me to further strengthen his fortune, but not before." He gave her a *hu-a* [charm paper].

> A 17-year-old boy asked about a large protuberance under one of his knees. The shaman said: "You have disturbed some ghosts at night." People in the boy's family admitted that he often ran around outside in the evening and said that the swelling had become larger and more painful in recent days. The shaman gave him a *hu-a* and told him to see a doctor.

> An old lady inquired about her lost gold chain. She said she had come several days earlier, but after four days of searching, she had still not found the chain. The shaman said: "Members of your family do not get along with one another and are quarreling. It doesn't matter that you have lost this chain. The quarreling is

more important. Take this *hu-a* home and burn it to ashes, mix the ashes in water, and sprinkle it on the roof. You will be in harmony and only then will the chain reappear."

> A middle-aged man asked about his chickens. "I have raised some chickens and they seem to have a lot of sickness lately. I don't know whether they have offended some dirty thing or there is some epidemic." The shaman said: "You did not choose a good date when you built the chicken house. Besides, you have offended the fox ghost. Cleanse the chicken house three times with *hu-a* ashes in water. Offer sacrifices to make the fox ghost go away. Then, everything will be all right."

As Kleinman (1980:218ff.) also notes, a client's interview with a shaman often takes only a few minutes (although as much as two hours may be spent talking with the assistants and bystanders). In order to address the problems brought before her or him, a *tang-ki* must have a quick mind as well as a keen understanding of human motivation. Most *tang-ki* recommend medical help for obvious illness and, where appropriate, are also likely to recommend the assistance of other ritual specialists, such as geomancers and herbalists. They also practice a certain amount of psychotherapy (Kleinman 1980). In the examples above, the old woman with the seriously ill husband needed resignation coupled with a bit of hope; the boy clearly needed to see a doctor; a dirty chicken house might have been causing the man's chickens to get sick; and the old lady who came back because the *tang-ki*'s last bit of advice hadn't helped her recover her gold chain needed distraction—and all families have quarrels.

A successful *tang-ki* must be quick-witted and alert to the needs of his or her clients ("guests" is the literal translation of the term used). Other researchers (Elliott 1955:92; Gould-Martin 1978:59; Kleinman 1980:217; Potter 1974:210, 214) have suggested that *tang-ki*'s successes often rest on their knowledge of the social and economic background of their clients. Kleinman (1980), who interviewed and observed urban *tang-ki* in Taipei, comments extensively on their sensitivity to potential tensions in the Chinese family, even if the particular client/patient does not happen to be known to them.

These "job qualifications" are, obviously, derived from the observation of professional, experienced shamans. My concern in this article is why Mrs. Chen was eventually considered not to be *tang-ki* material, why she was never allowed to reach this stage. A number of scholars have discussed the means by which spirit mediums are identified in China, and they report pretty much the same set of expectations (Elliott 1955; Jordan 1972; Kleinman 1980; Potter 1974). *Tang-ki* come from modest socioeconomic backgrounds; they are preferably illiterate; they must be sincere and honest; they must display clear indications that a god has chosen them to be his vehicle. People fated to become shamans are originally fated to have short, harmless, unimportant lives, but their lives are extended by the gods who possess them in order that their bodies may be put to good use. Many spirit mediums tell of illnesses in which they were brought back from the dead, after which they are troubled by a god who sends them into trances. Nearly all *tang-ki* in Taiwan report that they struggled against possession as long as they could but finally had to give in to the god's will. In Singapore, according to Elliott, some young men choose the life and train for it, but only after "something happens" to convince them that a god wants to enter them (1955:163). *Tang-ki,* incidentally, must not charge money for their services, but it is assumed that reasonable gifts will be made by grateful clients. I suspect that in rural Taiwan, few *tang-ki* receive enough in contributions to support themselves without another source of income (Gould-Martin 1978:62–63; Jordan 1972:75). As Jordan reports, in rural Taiwan there are few "divine rascals" because the living is too poor (1972:75).

Anthropologists frequently entertain the theory that spirit possession serves to provide a role for the emotionally disabled, the psychotic, or the epileptic. Kleinman, who studied the *tang-ki* in Taiwan primarily as healers, dismisses this explanation as impossible because of the complex behavior required of shamans:

Shamanistic healing clearly demands personal strengths and sensitivities incompatible with major psychopathology, especially chronic psychosis. Thus my findings argue against the view that shamanism provides a socially legitimated role for individuals suffering from schizophrenia or other severe psychiatric or neurological disorders. [1980:214]

Kleinman has extensive case material that includes detailed observations of tang-ki sessions as well as interviews with both shamans and their clients. His conclusions and those of others who have studied the Taiwan *tang-ki* are in accord with my own observations.

Nonetheless, the behavior of the beginning *tang-ki* and even of experienced *tang-ki* when they are going into trance might well be confused with that of a person who is deranged. (See, for example, the description by Elliott [1955:63].) And Kleinman himself provides us with a long case study (followed over three years) of a Hakka businessman suffering from acute anxiety and a variety of debilitating physical symptoms, who solved (to his and the shaman's satisfaction) his problems by "accepting the god" of the shrine, trancing, and essentially playing the role of lay shaman in the cult (1980:333–374). What Western observers might classify as mental illness is not necessarily so classified in Taiwan or China. The Hakka businessman in Taipei was treated for his problems for some time before he was defined as "troubled by the god" who wished to use him as a vehicle. Another of Kleinman's cases, one he classified as "acute, recurrent psychosis associated with normal inter-ictal behavior and provoked by acute stress producing extreme fear," was that of a 34-year-old mother of three who frequently attended *tang-ki* sessions (1980: 166–169). When she began to trance regularly at one of the shrines and "asked that shrine's *tang-ki* if she could become a shaman . . . he told her no (an unusual response), because it was 'too early' and she was 'not yet ready.' " According to Kleinman, the *tang-ki* did so because "the patient was unable to control her trance behavior and acted inappropriately during her trances" (1980:167). The Hakka businessman seemed to have similar difficulties at the outset, but nonetheless was accepted readily as a lay shaman.

Mrs. Chen, our heroine from Peihotien, was eventually deemed "crazy" by her community, or, as Kleinman might more delicately phrase it, to be showing signs of psychopathology. Why? She had as many shamanistic characteristics as others who went on to full *tang-ki* status. Her origins were humble; she was functionally illiterate; she was sincere, devout, and kind-hearted; she had led a harmless and unimportant life; she had a history of psychological breakdown that could be attributed to the god's attempt to make her his vehicle; she had resisted as long as she could; she went into trances and spoke in a voice other than her own. For a fortnight she convinced a fair number of respectable villagers that a god was making his wishes known to them through her. Her lack of finesse in her public performance seemed no more inappropriate than that of other novices described in the literature.[3] Why, then, did she not qualify as a likely apprentice for training?

Unfortunately, we must depend on anthropological hindsight and the randomly recorded voices of villagers for the answers to these questions. Had Mrs. Chen become a *tang-ki* in Peihotien, we would have pages of field notes on her subsequent career, for having a *tang-ki* in one's village is a source of considerable prestige (Jordan 1972:81) and certainly something that an anthropologist would want to document, no matter how peripheral ritual behavior might be to his or her project. But having a near miss became close to a nonevent. We recorded some conversations and asked a few questions, and then quickly turned to other issues. However, even without focused and detailed interviews with Mrs. Chen's neighbors, we can explore some of the reasons why her misery was not validated as divine visitation. From the perspective of her village neighbors, the question was not merely whether she was hallucinating the voice of a god or the god was in fact speaking to her. The question included another (for many villagers) more likely alternative: that a malicious ghost rather than a god

was tormenting her. When another practitioner diagnosed her illness as a ghost problem this might have ended the matter, but his treatment appeared to have no effect on Mrs. Chen whatsoever, indicating to her would-be followers that his diagnosis was wrong and the god-possession theory was still the best explanation for her behavior.

To understand why Mrs. Chen was not accepted as a vehicle for her god, we must look more closely at her position in her community. A diagnosis of "mental illness" is even less likely to produce a response of care and concern among Chinese villagers than it is among Americans. As long as a family member's oddities can be hidden or explained away, they will be; and whatever they may think privately, the neighbors will go along, for, after all, they, their parents, and their grandparents have lived and worked side by side with this family, sometimes for centuries. Condemning someone with whom your family has that kind of relationship to a status that removes him or her from participation in society as a fully adult human is not done lightly. One might say that the person's genealogical legitimacy in the community is too high.

In the hierarchy of attributes of legitimacy, Mrs. Chen simply did not rank highly enough to protect her from dismissal as a "crazy"; for the same reason, various members of the community who might have recognized her as a potential *tang-ki* decided it was not worth the risk. To begin with, her gender was against her. There are respected female *tang-ki,* but not very many of them. *Tang-ki* are expected to be and do things inappropriate for women, and even though the extraordinary circumstances of a god's demand should make it all right, the sheer incongruity of the expectations of a god's behavior and those of a woman's behavior are enough to create misgivings. *Tang-ki,* even when not in trance and speaking with a god's voice, must be assured and competent individuals. Mrs. Chen's everyday behavior did not inspire this kind of confidence, nor did that of the only known male relative associated with her, Dumb T'ien-lai.

Even had Mrs. Chen been male, I suspect that her legitimacy would still have received closer scrutiny than that of most men in the village. As noted above, the Chens were "outsiders" in a Lin village. They had no relatives in the area whose genealogy would vouch for their respectability. They were better off than the one or two mainlanders who lived nearby and who were considered totally untrustworthy because they had no family anywhere in Taiwan who could be called to account for whatever transgressions their sons might commit. Nonetheless, the Chens by virtue of their newcomer status remained objects of suspicion, people who were considered slightly dangerous because they had no family whose face their misbehavior could ruin. The arrival of Mrs. Chen's mother helped, but the presence of her father and his brothers would have helped even more. And here again, her gender was against her, for women are considered only adjunct members of their husbands' families and temporary members of their natal families. There is no solidity, no confidence in ties through females to families about whom one knows nothing.

At another level of abstraction, Mrs. Chen's failure to be judged a *tang-ki* in the making comes down to her ambiguous status in terms of the Chinese concept of the family. Any *tang-ki* treads dangerously near the edge of respectability in relation to Chinese notions of filiality, and Mrs. Chen's situation tipped her into the area of violation. From the point of view of the Chinese villager, an individual is only part of a more important unit, the family, and the individual's personal inclinations must be subordinated to the needs of that family. Choice of education, occupation, marriage partner, even of medical attention, should be determined by family elders in terms of what is best for the group—and often that group is conceived of as a long line of ancestors stretching into a hazy past and an equally long line of descendants stretching into an unknowable future. The individual is expected to be selfless—even his or her own body is the property of the ancestors. I have seen innumerable village children harshly punished by their parents for playing so carelessly as to fall and injure themselves, thus damaging the body that belongs to the family. Jordan (1972:84) also mentions this idea in relation to *tang-ki* who regularly

slash, cut, and otherwise mutilate their bodies in service to their god. Although divine intervention is supposed to prevent any permanent damage to the ancestors' property, the *tang-ki* nonetheless violates one tenet of filial piety.

More important, *tang-ki* as *tang-ki* are serving another master. They are expected to be totally selfless in that role as well, submitting themselves fully to the god's will in order to enable the god to solve his followers' problems. In fact, the needs of the ancestors and of the possessing god rarely come into conflict, for when out of trance, the *tang-ki* can fulfill all of his or her obligations to parents, grandparents, and so forth.[4] However, in theory, the *tang-ki* has given his or her person to a god to do with as he will. Thus, the *tang-ki* submits to the god that which belongs to the ancestors. This may make the *tang-ki*'s filial piety suspect, but it also highlights the sacrifice the god requires of his vessel. Mrs. Chen's assumed (although demonstrably inaccurate) rootlessness may very well have served to devalue the selflessness of her generosity in submitting to the will of the god.

Had Mrs. Chen been a wife or daughter of a Lin, there might actually have been strong pressures on her to accept the nomination of the god whether she wished to or not. In an intriguing study of shamanism in contemporary China, Ann Anagnost describes the social pressure put on a woman to assume the role of shaman (1987:52–54). During a period of failing health, Zhu Guiying exhibited symptoms that were interpreted as spirit possession. Sought out by fellow villagers as a healer, she at first resisted, but finally submitted to the social expectations of her neighbors. As Anagnost puts it, "To refuse this role would have been tantamount to a denial of social ties and the forms of reciprocity and obligation that bound the community together" (1987:53).

I wish I had been able to pursue Mrs. Chen's case in the years that followed this incident in Peihotien. It is conceivable that in another setting, one where she was known in the context of a family, she might in fact have been encouraged to continue her interactions with the god who approached her in Peihotien. If, for instance, she had moved to Taipei and become involved in some of the cults surrounding well-known urban *tang-ki,* she might have continued to go into trance and might have become a valued member of one of the groups that Kleinman (1980) describes, thereby finding peace and status. In Peihotien she was too low in all of the hierarchies to achieve legitimacy as a full member of her community. As a result, she was not able to overcome her anomaly in either world—that of the village or that of the possessed.

Mrs. Chen failed to become a shaman, by one set of measures, because of the structural context in which she lived; she was an outsider—socially and genealogically. But her failure might be accounted for by another set of reasons, reasons even more intimately associated with her gender. Feminist theorists, exploring the construction of the gendered self in white middle-class North Americans, suggest that the male self is based on a set of oppositional categories (good/bad, right/wrong, nature/culture, and so forth) and that male selves are more rigidly bounded, more conscious of a distinction between the self and the other than female selves are (Chodorow 1974; Gilligan 1982, 1988; Hartsock 1983; Martin 1988). A female—perhaps because, as Chodorow (1974) suggests, the female infant does not need to transfer her identity from her original female caretaker—has a less bounded self. It is not tied into oppositions between self and other, but is constructed instead from connectedness and continuities.[5] A good *tang-ki* must be able to separate his or her behavior as a *tang-ki* from his or her everyday behavior. With a self constructed out of dualisms, a male may find it easier to keep his relations with his deity separate from his conscious mental life. Mrs. Chen clearly could not.

In time, Mrs. Chen might have been able to achieve this separation—other female *tang-ki* have. But Mrs. Chen had a special problem. Elsewhere I have explored the construction of the Chinese female self and have suggested that it is highly dependent on the meaning given to the individual by others (Wolf 1989). Whereas the Chinese male is born into a social and spiritual community that has continuity not only in life but after death, the Chi-

nese female is born into a social community of which she is only a temporary resident, and her spiritual community after death depends upon whom she marries or, more important, whose ancestors she gives birth to. A Chinese boy's self is defined by this certainty, this continuity. A girl's sense of self develops in an environment of uncertainty—if she isn't sufficiently modest, she won't find a good family; if she isn't obedient, no mother-in-law will want her; if she is willful, she will have trouble with some unknown husband. She reads who she is in the approving or disapproving faces of those around her. The trauma of Chinese marriage, in which a very young woman is transferred to a distant village where she knows no one, not even her husband, creates for a woman a crisis of identity that is only resolved by the gradual acquisition of a new set of mirrors in which she can identify herself. Mrs. Chen came to Peihotien a stranger, and a stranger she remained. There was no family to smile or frown, no mother-in-law to approve or disapprove of her behavior, and only a husband who was himself a stranger. Without ties to a family that had an accepted place in the village social system, when Mrs. Chen was no longer a novelty, she ceased to have an identity. She was an outsider who was neither dangerous nor useful, and she was more or less ignored. She was in fact nameless, having lost her personal name at marriage (Watson 1986). Unlike other brides, her self was never reconstructed, and her mirrors remained cloudy, except for the self she saw reflected in her children and in the conversations she had with the various gods she visited.

I continue to wonder whether or not Mrs. Chen, on that fateful day when she threw herself into the rice paddy, was not, as some claimed, trying to get to the river. Suicide (often by drowning) is a solution for many (younger) Chinese women who have trouble creating a new self in a strange place. Perhaps when she was pulled out of the muck of the paddy, she made one final attempt to join the social world of the village by way of a god who had more reality for her than the people among whom she lived. Unfortunately, her self was so poorly established that she could not carry it off. The self that spoke with the gods could not be used to construct a self that could survive in a social world constructed by strangers.

ENDNOTES

Acknowledgments. I am grateful to my field assistant, Wu Chieh (fictitious name), who played a central role in the events discussed here, for her patience and persistence. I also want to thank Arthur Wolf, who made me a part of that first field experience. Mac Marshall and three anonymous reviewers have made suggestions that improved this manuscript significantly. I appreciate their help.

1. I use shamanism and spirit possession interchangeably and refer to the practitioners as shamans, spirit mediums, or *tang-ki,* the last being the local term in Taiwan.
2. We never did get a name for this god, who needed a special paint job (with half his face black and half white) but still looked and acted very much like Shang Ti Kung to some of the people in the village who knew about such things.
3. Jordan describes the initiation of another village woman: "Throngs of village people looked on as she flailed her back, shouting, sputtering, drooling, and muttering. When it was over, she was, willy-nilly, a *tang-ki*" (1972:167).
4. Gary Seaman (1980:67) reports that early in their careers shamans are ritually adopted by the gods who possess them—these gods literally buy the young shamans from their parents. I had not heard of this in northern Taiwan.
5. I am keenly aware of the dangers of applying theoretical concepts developed from Western data to the analysis of personalities constructed in a very different culture. This hypothesis in particular seems fraught with cultural pitfalls: among them the fact that Chinese children, unlike white middle-class American children, usually have a *variety of* female caretakers during their early childhood. Whether or not the explanations hypothesized by Chodorow (1974), Gilligan (1982, 1988), and others have cross-cultural viability remains to be seen, but some aspects of the resulting gender differences they describe in adults do appear to translate. See, for example, Martin's (1988:173ff.) description of a female ideology in funeral ritual that emphasizes "the unity of opposites" in contrast to a male ideology that shows "constant efforts to separate opposites"; see also Watson (1986), who uses personal naming practices in China as evidence of differences in personhood. Gender differences in personhood and the construction of the self in Chinese society are a much neglected topic. Much of the research either asserts that there are no differences (for example, Tu 1985) or ignores gender completely (for example, Yang 1989), by default taking the male self to be the Chinese self. I have begun to explore some of these ideas elsewhere (Wolf 1989 and in a manuscript in progress), and it is a rich area for investigation.

REFERENCES

Anagnost, Ann S. 1987. Politics and Magic in Contemporary China. Modern China 13(1):40–61.

Chodorow, Nancy. 1974. Family Structure and Feminine Personality. *In* Woman, Culture, and Society. Michelle Z. Rosaldo and Louise Lamphere, eds. pp. 43–66. Stanford, CA: Stanford University Press.

Elliott, Alan J. A. 1955. Chinese Spirit Medium Cults in Singapore. London School of Economics and Political Science Monographs on Social Anthropology, No. 14. London: University of London.

Gilligan, Carol. 1982. In a Different Voice: Psychological Theory and Women's Development. Cambridge, MA: Harvard University Press.

1988 Adolescent Development Reconsidered. *In* Mapping the Moral Domain. C. Gilligan, J. V. Ward, and J. M. Taylor, eds. pp. vii–xxxviii. Cambridge, MA: Harvard University Press.

Gould-Martin, Katherine. 1978. *Ong-la-Kong:* The Plague God as Modern Physician. In Culture and Healing in Asian Societies: Anthropological, Psychiatric and Public Health Studies. Arthur Kleinman, Peter Kunstadter, E. Russell Alexander, and James L. Gate, eds. pp. 41–67. Boston: G. K. Hall & Co.

Hartsock, Nancy. 1983. Money, Sex, and Power: Toward a Feminist Historical Materialism. Boston: Northeastern University Press.

Jordan, David K. 1972. Gods, Ghosts, and Ancestors: The Folk Religion of a Taiwanese Village. Berkeley: University of California Press.

Kleinman, Arthur. 1980. Patients and Healers in the Context of Culture: An Exploration of the Borderland between Anthropology, Medicine, and Psychiatry. Berkeley: University of California Press.

Martin, Emily. 1988. Gender and Ideological Differences in Representations of Life and Death. *In* Death Ritual in Late Imperial and Modern China. James L. Watson and Evelyn S. Rawski, eds. pp. 164–179. Berkeley: University of California Press.

Potter, Jack M. 1974. Cantonese Shamanism. In Religion and Ritual in Chinese Society. A. P. Wolf, ed. pp. 207–231. Stanford, CA: Stanford University Press.

Seaman, Gary. 1980. In the Presence of Authority: Hierarchical Roles in Chinese Spirit Medium Cults. *In* Normal and Abnormal Behavior in Chinese Culture. Arthur Kleinman and T. Y. Lin, eds. pp. 61–74. Boston: D. Reidel.

Tu, Wei-ming. 1985. Confucian Thought: Selfhood as Creative Transformation. Albany: State University of New York Press.

Watson, Rubie S. 1986. The Named and the Nameless: Gender and Person in Chinese Society. American Ethnologist 13:619–631.

Wolf, Margery. 1989. The Self of Others, the Others of Self: Gender in Chinese Society. Paper presented at the conference "Perceptions of the Self: China, Japan, India," August, East-West Center, University of Hawaii, Honolulu.

Yang, Mayfair Mei-hui. 1989. The Gift Economy and State Power in China. Comparative Studies in Society and History 31(1):25–54.

READING 5–3

THE SOUND OF RUSHING WATER

Michael J. Harner

This article is about shamanism in action. Once an individual has won acceptance from his or her community as a shaman, he or she typically undertakes the responsibility for entering into trances, a condition in which, as we have already seen, communication with spirits becomes possible. In this article Michael Harner, one of the first ethnographers to study the ritual use of ritual drugs, describes how trances can be induced, by using the Jívaro, a South American forest peoples, as a case study. We find that percussion instruments and dancing accompany drug-taking as a means of stimulating trances, and learn how drug-induced visions can convey a sense of the "other world." At the same time, other-worldly experiences serve to shape indigenous perceptions of the "real" world. They help the Jívaro to formulate concepts about the nature of shamanhood (there are two categories of practitioner, curer and bewitcher), spirit helpers, and ritual taboos and prescriptions. Although their source is hallucinogenic, the image of the spirit world created by the Jívaro has a logic that assembles these various elements into something resembling a coherent whole.

He had drunk, and now he softly sang. Gradually, faint lines and forms began to appear in the darkness, and the shrill music of the *tsentsak,* the spirit helpers, arose around him. The power of the drink fed them. He called, and they came. First, *pangi,* the anaconda, coiled about his head, transmuted into a crown of gold. Then *wampang,* the giant butterfly, hovered above his shoulder and sang to him with its wings. Snakes, spiders, birds, and bats danced in the air above him. On his arms appeared a thousand eyes as his demon helpers emerged to search the night for enemies.

Source: Michael J. Harner, "The Sound of Rushing Water." With permission from Natural History (June–July 1968), pp. 28–33. Copyright the American Museum of Natural History (1968).

The sound of rushing water filled his ears, and listening to its roar, he knew he possessed the power of *tsungi,* the first shaman. Now he could see. Now he could find the truth. He stared at the stomach of the sick man. Slowly, it became transparent like a shallow mountain stream, and he saw within it, coiling and uncoiling, *makanchi,* the poisonous serpent, who had been sent by the enemy shaman. The real cause of the illness had been found.

The Jívaro Indians of the Ecuadorian Amazon believe that witchcraft is the cause of the vast majority of illnesses and non-violent deaths. The normal waking life, for the Jívaro, is simply "a lie," or illusion, while the true forces that determine daily events are supernatural and can only be seen and manipulated with the aid of hallucinogenic drugs. A reality view of this kind creates a particularly strong demand for specialists who can cross over into the supernatural world at will to deal with the forces that influence and even determine the events of the waking life.

These specialists, called "shamans" by anthropologists, are recognized by the Jívaro as being of two types: bewitching shamans or curing shamans. Both kinds take a hallucinogenic drink, whose Jívaro name is *natema,* in order to enter the supernatural world. This brew, commonly called *yagé,* or *yajé,* in Colombia, ayahuasca (Inca "vine of the dead") in Ecuador and Peru, and *caapi* in Brazil, is prepared from segments of a species of the vine *Banisteriopsis,* a genus belonging to the Malpighiaceae. The Jívaro boil it with the leaves of a similar vine, which probably is also a species of *Banisteriopsis,* to produce a tea that contains the powerful hallucinogenic alkaloids harmaline, harmine, d-tetrahydroharmine, and quite possibly dimethyltryptamine (DMT). These compounds have chemical structures and effects similar, but not identical, to LSD, mescaline of the peyote cactus, and psilocybin of the psychotropic Mexican mushroom.

When I first undertook research among the Jívaro in 1956–57, I did not fully appreciate the psychological impact of the *Banisteriopsis* drink upon the native view of reality, but in 1961 I had occasion to drink the hallucinogen in the course of field work with another Upper Amazon Basin tribe. For several hours after drinking the brew, I found myself, although awake, in a world literally beyond my wildest dreams. I met bird-headed people, as well as dragon-like creatures who explained that they were the true gods of this world. I enlisted the services of other spirit helpers in attempting to fly through the far reaches of the Galaxy. Transported into a trance where the supernatural seemed natural, I realized that anthropologists, including myself, had profoundly underestimated the importance of the drug in affecting native ideology. Therefore, in 1964 I returned to the Jívaro to give particular attention to the drug's use by the Jívaro shaman.

The use of the hallucinogenic *natema* drink among the Jívaro makes it possible for almost anyone to achieve the trance state essential for the practice of shamanism. Given the presence of the drug and the felt need to contact the "real," or supernatural, world, it is not surprising that approximately one out of every four Jívaro men is a shaman. Any adult, male or female, who desires to become such a practitioner, simply presents a gift to an already practicing shaman, who administers the *Banisteriopsis* drink and gives some of his own supernatural power—in the form of spirit helpers, or *tsentsak*—to the apprentice. These spirit helpers, or "darts," are the main supernatural forces believed to cause illness and death in daily life. To the non-shaman they are normally invisible, and even shamans can perceive them only under the influence of *natema.*

Shamans send these spirit helpers into the victims' bodies to make them ill or to kill them. At other times, they may suck spirits sent by enemy shamans from the bodies of tribesmen suffering from witchcraft-induced illness. The spirit helpers also form shields that protect their shaman masters from attacks. The following account presents the ideology of Jívaro witchcraft from the point of view of the Indians themselves.

To give the novice some *tsentsak,* the practicing shaman regurgitates what appears to be—to those

who have taken *natema*—a brilliant substance in which the spirit helpers are contained. He cuts part of it off with a machete and gives it to the novice to swallow. The recipient experiences pain upon taking it into his stomach and stays on his bed for ten days, repeatedly drinking *natema.* The J;iavaro believe they can keep magical darts in their stomachs indefinitely and regurgitate them at will. The shaman donating the *tsentsak* periodically blows and rubs all over the body of the novice, apparently to increase the power of the transfer.

The novice must remain inactive and not engage in sexual intercourse for at least three months. If he fails in self-discipline, as some do, he will not become a successful shaman. At the end of the first month, a *tsentsak* emerges from his mouth. With this magical dart at his disposal, the new shaman experiences a tremendous desire to bewitch. If he casts his *tsentsak* to fulfill this desire, he will become a bewitching shaman. If, on the other hand, the novice can control his impulse and reswallow this first *tsentsak,* he will become a curing shaman.

If the shaman who gave the *tsentsak* to the new man was primarily a bewitcher, rather than a curer, the novice likewise will tend to become a bewitcher. This is because a bewitcher's magical darts have such a desire to kill that their new owner will be strongly inclined to adopt their attitude. One informant said that the urge to kill felt by bewitching shamans came to them with a strength and frequency similar to that of hunger.

Only if the novice shaman is able to abstain from sexual intercourse for five months, will he have the power to kill a man (if he is a bewitcher) or cure a victim (if he is a curer). A full year's abstinence is considered necessary to become a really effective bewitcher or curer.

During the period of sexual abstinence, the new shaman collects all kinds of insects, plants, and other objects, which he now has the power to convert into *tsentsak.* Almost any object, including living insects and worms, can become a *tsentsak* if it is small enough to be swallowed by a shaman. Different types of *tsentsak* are used to cause different kinds and degrees of illness. The greater the variety of these objects that a shaman has in his body, the greater is his ability.

According to Jívaro concepts, each *tsentsak* has a natural and supernatural aspect. The magical dart's natural aspect is that of an ordinary material object as seen without drinking the drug *natema*. But the supernatural and "true" aspect of the *tsentsak* is revealed to the shaman by taking *natema*. When he does this, the magical darts appear in new forms as demons and with new names. In their supernatural aspects, the *tsentsak* are not simply objects but spirit helpers in various forms, such as giant butterflies, jaguars, or monkeys, who actively assist the shaman in his tasks.

Bewitching is carried out against a specific, known individual and thus is almost always done to neighbors or, at the most, fellow tribesmen. Normally, as is the case with intratribal assassination, bewitching is done to avenge a particular offense committed against one's family or friends. Both bewitching and individual assassination contrast with the large-scale headhunting raids for which the Jívaro have become famous, and which were conducted against entire neighborhoods of enemy tribes.

To bewitch, the shaman takes *natema* and secretly approaches the house of his victim. Just out of sight in the forest, he drinks green tobacco juice, enabling him to regurgitate a *tsentsak*, which he throws at his victim as he comes out of his house. If the *tsentsak* is strong enough and is thrown with sufficient force, it will pass all the way through the victim's body causing death within a period of a few days to several weeks. More often, however, the magical dart simply lodges in the victim's body. If the shaman, in his hiding place, fails to see the intended victim, he may instead bewitch any member of the intended victim's family who appears, usually a wife or child. When the shaman's mission is accomplished, he returns secretly to his own home.

One of the distinguishing characteristics of the bewitching process among the Jívaro is that, as far as I could learn, the victim is given no specific indication that someone is bewitching him. The bewitcher does not want his victim to be aware that he is being supernaturally attacked, lest he take protective measures by immediately procuring the services of a curing shaman. Nonetheless, shamans and laymen alike with whom I talked noted that illness invariably follows the bewitchment, although the degree of the illness can vary considerably.

A special kind of spirit helper, called a *pasuk,* can aid the bewitching shaman by remaining near the victim in the guise of an insect or animal of the forest after the bewitcher has left. This spirit helper has his own objects to shoot into the victim should a curing shaman succeed in sucking out the *tsentsak* sent earlier by the bewitcher who is the owner of the pasuk.

In addition, the bewitcher can enlist the aid of a *wakani* ("soul," or "spirit") bird. Shamans have the power to call these birds and use them as spirit helpers in bewitching victims. The shaman blows on the *wakani* birds and then sends them to the house of the victim to fly around and around the man, frightening him. This is believed to cause fever and insanity, with death resulting shortly thereafter.

After he returns home from bewitching, the shaman may send a *wakani* bird to perch near the house of the victim. Then if a curing shaman sucks out the intruding object, the bewitching shaman sends the *wakani* bird more *tsentsak* to throw from its beak into the victim. By continually resupplying the *wakani* bird with new *tsentsak,* the sorcerer makes it impossible for the curer to rid his patient permanently of the magical darts.

While the *wakani* birds are supernatural servants available to anyone who wishes to use them, the *pasuk,* chief among the spirit helpers, serves only a single shaman. Likewise a shaman possesses only one *pasuk.* The *pasuk,* being specialized for the service of bewitching, has a protective shield to guard it from counterattack by the curing shaman. The curing shaman, under the influence of *natema,* sees the *pasuk* of the bewitcher in human form and size, but "covered with iron except for its eyes." The curing shaman can kill this *pasuk* only by shooting a *tsentsak* into its eyes, the sole vulnerable area in the *pasuk's* armor. To the person who has not taken the hallucinogenic drink, the *pasuk* usually appears to be simply a tarantula. Shamans also may kill or injure a person by using magical darts, *anamuk,* to create supernatural animals that attack a victim. If a shaman has a small, pointed armadillo bone *tsentsak,* he can shoot this into a river while the victim is crossing it on a balsa raft or in a canoe. Under the water, this bone manifests itself in its supernatural aspect as an anaconda, which rises up and overturns the craft, causing the victim to drown. The shaman can similarly use a tooth from a killed snake as a *tsentsak,* creating a poisonous serpent to bite his victim. In more or less the same manner, shamans can create jaguars and pumas to kill their victims.

About five years after receiving his *tsentsak,* a bewitching shaman undergoes a test to see if he still retains enough *tsentsak* power to continue to kill successfully. This test involves bewitching a tree. The shaman, under the influence of *natema,* attempts to throw a *tsentsak* through the tree at the point where its two main branches join. If his strength and aim are adequate, the tree appears to split the moment the *tsentsak* is sent into it. The splitting, however, is invisible to an observer who is not under the influence of the hallucinogen. If the shaman fails, he knows that he is incapable of killing a human victim. This means that, as soon as possible, he must go to a strong shaman and purchase a new supply of *tsentsak.* Until he has the goods with which to pay for this new supply, he is in constant danger, in his proved weakened condition, of being seriously bewitched by other shamans. Therefore, each day, he drinks large quantities of *natema,* tobacco juice, and the extract of yet another drug, *pirípirí.* He also rests on his bed at home to conserve his strength, but tries to conceal his weakened condition from his enemies. When he purchases a new supply of *tsentsak,* he can safely cut down on his consumption of these other substances.

The degree of illness produced in a witchcraft victim is a function of both the force with which the *tsentsak* is shot into the body, and also of the character of the magical dart itself. If a *tsentsak* is shot all the way through the body of a victim, then "there is nothing for a curing shaman to suck out," and the patient dies. If the magical dart lodges within the body, however, it is theoretically possible to cure the victim by sucking. But in actual practice, the sucking is not always considered successful.

The work of the curing shaman is complementary to that of a bewitcher. When a curing shaman is called in to treat a patient, his first task is to see if the illness is due to witchcraft. The usual diagnosis and treatment begin with the curing shaman drinking natema, tobacco juice, and *pirípirí* in the late afternoon and early evening. These drugs permit him to see into the body of the patient as though it were glass. If the illness is due to sorcery, the curing shaman will see the intruding object within the patient's body clearly enough to determine whether or not he can cure the sickness.

A shaman sucks magical darts from a patient's body only at night, and in a dark area of the house, for it is only in the dark that he can perceive the drug-induced visions that are the supernatural reality. With the setting of the sun, he alerts his *tsentsak* by whistling the tune of the curing song; after about a quarter of an hour, he starts singing. When he is ready to suck, the shaman regurgitates two *tsentsak* into the sides of his throat and mouth. These must be identical to the one he has seen in the patient's body. He holds one of these in the front of the mouth and the other in the rear. They are expected to catch the supernatural aspect of the magical dart that the shaman sucks out of the patient's body. The *tsentsak* nearest the shaman's lips is supposed to incorporate the sucked-out *tsentsak* essence within itself. If, however, this supernatural essence should get past it, the second magical dart in the mouth blocks the throat so that the intruder cannot enter the interior of the shaman's body. If the curer's two *tsentsak* were to fail to catch the supernatural essence of the tsentsak, it would pass down into the shaman's stomach and kill him. Trapped thus within the mouth, this essence is shortly caught by, and incorporated into, the material substance of one of the curing shaman's *tsentsak.* He then "vomits" out this object and displays it to the patient and his family saying, "Now I have sucked it out. Here it is."

The non-shamans think that the material object itself is what has been sucked out, and the shaman does not disillusion them. At the same time, he is not lying, because he knows that the only important thing about a *tsentsak* is its supernatural aspect, or essence, which he sincerely believes he has removed from the patient's body. To explain to the layman that he already had these objects in his mouth would serve no fruitful purpose and would prevent him from displaying such an object as proof that he had effected the cure. Without incontrovertible evidence, he would not be able to convince the patient and his family that he had effected the cure and must be paid.

The ability of the shaman to suck depends largely upon the quantity and strength of his own tsentsak, of which he may have hundreds. His magical darts assume their supernatural aspect as spirit helpers when he is under the influence of natema, and he sees them as a variety of zoomorphic forms hovering over him, perching on his shoulders, and sticking out of his skin. He sees them helping to suck the patient's body. He must drink tobacco juice every few hours to "keep them fed" so that they will not leave him.

The curing shaman must also deal with any *pasuk* that may be in the patient's vicinity for the purpose of casting more darts. He drinks additional amounts of *natema* in order to see them and engages in *tsentsak* duels with them if they are present. While the *pasuk* is enclosed in iron armor, the shaman himself has his own armor composed of his many *tsentsak.* As long as he is under the influence of *natema,* these magical darts cover his body as a protective shield, and are on the lookout for any enemy *tsentsak* headed toward their master. When these *tsentsak* see such a missile coming, they immediately close up together at the point where the enemy dart is attempting to penetrate, and thereby repel it.

If the curer finds *tsentsak* entering the body of his patient after he has killed *pasuk,* he suspects the presence of a *wakani* bird. The shaman drinks *maikau* (Datura sp.), an hallucinogen even more powerful than *natema,* as well as tobacco juice, and silently sneaks into the forest to hunt and kill the bird with *tsentsak.* When he succeeds, the curer returns to the patient's home, blows all over the house to get rid of the "atmosphere" created by the numerous *tsentsak* sent by the bird, and completes his sucking of the patient. Even after all the *tsentsak* are extracted, the shaman may remain another night at the house to suck out any "dirtiness" (*pahuri*) still inside. In the cures which I have witnessed, this sucking is a most noisy process, accompanied by deep, but dry, vomiting.

After sucking out a *tsentsak,* the shaman puts it into a little container. He does not swallow it because it is not his own magical dart and would therefore kill him. Later, he throws the *tsentsak* into the air, and it flies back to the shaman who sent it originally into the patient. *Tsentsak* also fly back to a shaman at the death of a former apprentice who had originally received them from him. Besides receiving "old" magical darts unexpectedly in this manner, the shaman may have *tsentsak* thrown at him by a bewitcher. Accordingly, shamans constantly drink tobacco juice at all hours of the day and night. Although the tobacco juice is not truly hallucinogenic, it produces a narcotized state, which is believed necessary to keep one's *tsentsak* ready to repel any other magical darts. A shaman does not even dare go for a walk without taking along the green tobacco leaves with which he prepares the juice that keeps his spirit helpers alert. Less frequently, but regularly, he must drink *natema* for the same purpose and to keep in touch with the supernatural reality.

While curing under the influence of *natema,* the curing shaman "sees" the shaman who bewitched his patient. Generally, he can recognize the person, unless it is a shaman who lives far away or in another tribe. The patient's family knows this, and demands to be told the identity of the bewitcher, particularly if the sick person dies. At one curing session I attended, the shaman could not identify the person he had seen in his vision. The brother of the dead man then accused the shaman himself of being responsible. Under such pressure, there is a strong tendency for the curing shaman to attribute each case to a particular bewitcher.

Shamans gradually become weak and must purchase *tsentsak* again and again. Curers tend to become weak in power, especially after curing a patient bewitched by a shaman who has recently received a new supply of magical darts. Thus, the most powerful shamans are those who can repeatedly purchase new supplies of *tsentsak* from other shamans.

Shamans can take back tsentsak from others to whom they have previously given them. To accomplish this, the shaman drinks *natema,* and, using his *tsentsak,* creates a "bridge" in the form of a rainbow between himself and the other shaman. Then he shoots a *tsentsak* along this rainbow. This strikes the ground beside the other shaman with an explosion and flash likened to a lightning bolt. The purpose of this is to surprise the other shaman so that he temporarily forgets to maintain his guard over his magical darts, thus permitting the other shaman to suck them back along the rainbow. A shaman who has had his *tsentsak* taken away in this manner will discover that "nothing happens" when he drinks *natema.* The sudden loss of his *tsentsak* will tend to make him ill, but ordinarily the illness is not fatal unless a bewitcher shoots a magical dart into him while he is in this weakened condition. If he has not become disillusioned by his experience, he can again purchase *tsentsak* from some other shaman and resume his calling. Fortunately for anthropology some of these men have chosen to give up shamanism and therefore can be persuaded to reveal their knowledge, no longer having a vested interest in the profession. This divulgence, however, does not serve as a significant threat to practitioners, for words alone can never adequately convey the realities of shamanism. These can only be approached with the aid of natema, the chemical door to the invisible world of the Jívaro shaman.

Claude Lévi-Strauss

The conditions society imposes on the shaman (the "shamanistic complex") and the emotional and intellectual accompaniments of successful shamanistic work are vividly expounded by Claude Lévi-Strauss, who, in this reading, applies the terms "shaman," "sorcerer," and "magician" with unusual flexibility. The key element in the practitioner Quesalid's success—as for shamans in Taiwan and among the Jívaro—is approval by his community. People believe in him. As the author insightfully puts it, "Quesalid did not become a great shaman because he cured his patients; he cured his patients because he had become a great shaman."

Since the pioneering work of Cannon, we understand more clearly the psychophysiological mechanisms underlying the instances reported from many parts of the world of death by exorcism and the casting of spells.[1] An individual who is aware that he is the object of sorcery is thoroughly convinced that he is doomed according to the most solemn traditions of his group. His friends and relatives share this certainty. From then on the community withdraws. Standing aloof from the accursed, it treats him not only as though he were already dead but as though he were a source of danger to the entire group. On every occasion and by every action, the social body suggests death to the unfortunate victim, who no longer hopes to escape what he considers to be his ineluctable fate. Shortly thereafter, sacred rites are held to dispatch him to the realm of shadows. First brutally torn from all of his family and social ties and excluded from all functions and

Source: "The Sorcerer and His Magic," from *Structural Anthropology,* Volume 1 by Claude Lévi-Strauss. (New York: Basic-Books, 1963), Vol. 1, pp. 167–85. English translation copyright © 1963 by BasicBooks, Inc. Reprinted by permission of Basic-Books, a division of HarperCollins Publishers, Inc.

activities through which he experienced self-awareness, then banished by the same forces from the world of the living, the victim yields to the combined effect of intense terror, the sudden total withdrawal of the multiple reference systems provided by the support of the group, and, finally, to the group's decisive reversal in proclaiming him—once a living man, with rights and obligations—dead and an object of fear, ritual, and taboo. Physical integrity cannot withstand the dissolution of the social personality.[2]

How are these complex phenomena expressed on the physiological level? Cannon showed that fear, like rage, is associated with a particularly intense activity of the sympathetic nervous system. This activity is ordinarily useful, involving organic modifications which enable the individual to adapt himself to a new situation. But if the individual cannot avail himself of any instinctive or acquired response to an extraordinary situation (or to one which he conceives of as such), the activity of the sympathetic nervous system becomes intensified and disorganized; it may, sometimes within a few hours, lead to a decrease in the volume of blood and a concomitant drop in blood pressure, which result in irreparable damage to the circulatory organs. The rejection of food and drink, frequent among patients in the throes of intense anxiety, precipitates this process; dehydration acts as a stimulus to the sympathetic nervous system, and the decrease in blood volume is accentuated by the growing permeability of the capillary vessels. These hypotheses were confirmed by the study of several cases of trauma resulting from bombings, battle shock, and even surgical operations; death results, yet the autopsy reveals no lesions.

There is, therefore, no reason to doubt the efficacy of certain magical practices. But at the same time we see that the efficacy of magic implies a belief in magic. The latter has three complementary aspects: first, the sorcerer's belief in the effectiveness of his techniques; second, the patient's or victim's belief in the sorcerer's power; and, finally, the faith and expectations of the group, which con-

stantly act as a sort of gravitational field within which the relationship between sorcerer and bewitched is located and defined.[3] Obviously, none of the three parties is capable of forming a clear picture of the sympathetic nervous system's activity or of the disturbances which Cannon called homeostatic. When the sorcerer claims to suck out of the patient's body a foreign object whose presence would explain the illness and produces a stone which he had previously hidden in his mouth, how does he justify this procedure in his own eyes? How can an innocent person accused of sorcery prove his innocence if the accusation is unanimous—since the magical situation is a consensual phenomenon? And, finally, how much credulity and how much skepticism are involved in the attitude of the group toward those in whom it recognizes extraordinary powers, to whom it accords corresponding privileges, but from whom it also requires adequate satisfaction? Let us begin by examining this last point.

It was in September, 1938. For several weeks we had been camping with a small band of Nambicuara Indians near the headwaters of the Tapajoz, in those desolate savannas of central Brazil where the natives wander during the greater part of the year, collecting seeds and wild fruits, hunting small mammals, insects, and reptiles, and whatever else might prevent them from dying of starvation. Thirty of them were camped together there, quite by chance. They were grouped in families under frail lean-tos of branches, which give scant protection from the scorching sun, nocturnal chill, rain, and wind. Like most bands, this one had both a secular chief and a sorcerer; the latter's daily activities—hunting, fishing, and handicrafts—were in no way different from those of the other men of the group. He was a robust man, about forty-five years old, and a bon vivant.

One evening, however, he did not return to camp at the usual time. Night fell and fires were lit; the natives were visibly worried. Countless perils lurk in the bush: torrential rivers, the somewhat improbable danger of encountering a large wild beast—jaguar or anteater—or, more readily pictured by the Nambicuara, an apparently harmless animal which is the incarnation of an evil spirit of the waters or forest. And above all, each night for the past week we had seen mysterious campfires, which sometimes approached and sometimes receded from our own. Any unknown band is always potentially hostile. After a two-hour wait, the natives were convinced that their companion had been killed in ambush and, while his two young wives and his son wept noisily in mourning for their dead husband and father, the other natives discussed the tragic consequences foreshadowed by the disappearance of their sorcerer.

Toward ten that evening, the anguished anticipation of imminent disaster, the lamentations in which the other women began to join, and the agitation of the men had created an intolerable atmosphere, and we decided to reconnoiter with several natives who had remained relatively calm. We had not gone two hundred yards when we stumbled upon a motionless figure. It was our man, crouching silently, shivering in the chilly night air, disheveled and without his belt, necklaces, and arm-bands (the Nambicuara wear nothing else). He allowed us to lead him back to the camp site without resistance, but only after long exhortations by his group and pleading by his family was he persuaded to talk. Finally, bit by bit, we extracted the details of his story. A thunderstorm, the first of the season, had burst during the afternoon, and the thunder had carried him off to a site several miles distant, which he named, and then, after stripping him completely, had brought him back to the spot where we found him. Everyone went off to sleep commenting on the event. The next day the thunder victim had recovered his joviality and, what is more, all his ornaments. This last detail did not appear to surprise anyone, and life resumed its normal course.

A few days later, however, another version of these prodigious events began to be circulated by certain natives. We must note that this band was actually composed of individuals of different origins and had been fused into a new social entity as a result of unknown circumstances. One of the groups had been decimated by an epidemic several years before and was no longer sufficiently large to lead an independent life; the other had seceded from its original tribe and found itself in the same straits. When and under what circumstances the two groups met and decided to unite their efforts, we could not discover. The secular leader of the new band came from one group and the sorcerer, or religious leader, from the other. The fusion was obviously recent, for no marriage had yet taken place between the two groups when we met them, although the children of one were usually betrothed to the children of the other; each group had retained its own dialect, and their members could communicate only through two or three bilingual natives.

This is the rumor that was spread. There was good reason to suppose that the unknown bands crossing the savanna belonged to the tribe of the seceded group of which the sorcerer was a member. The sorcerer, impinging on the functions of his colleague the political chief, had doubtless wanted to contact his former tribesmen, perhaps to ask to return to the fold, or to provoke an attack upon his new companions, or perhaps even to reassure them of the friendly intentions of the latter. In any case, the sorcerer had needed a pretext for his absence, and his kidnapping by thunder and its subsequent staging were invented toward this end. It was, of course, the natives of the other group who spread this interpretation, which they secretly believed and which filled them with apprehension. But the official version was never publicly disputed, and until we left, shortly after the incident, it remained ostensibly accepted by all.[4]

Although the skeptics had analyzed the sorcerer's motives with great psychological finesse and political acumen, they would have been greatly astonished had someone suggested (quite plausibly) that the incident was a hoax which cast doubt upon the sorcerer's good faith and competence. He had probably not flown on the wings of thunder to the Rio Ananaz and had only staged an act. But these things might have happened, they had certainly happened in other circumstances, and they belonged to the realm of real experience. Certainly the sorcerer maintains an intimate relationship with the forces of the supernatural. The idea that in a particular case he had used his power to conceal a secular activity belongs to the realm of conjecture and provides an opportunity for critical judgment. The important point is that these two possibilities were not mutually exclusive; no more than are, for us, the alternate interpretations of war as the dying gasp of national independence or as the result of the schemes of munitions manufacturers. The two explanations are logically incompatible, but we admit that one or the other may be true; since they are equally plausible, we easily make the transition from one to the other, depending on the occasion and the moment. Many people have both explanations in the back of their minds.

Whatever their true origin, these divergent interpretations come from individual consciousness not as the result of objective analysis but rather as complementary ideas resulting from hazy and unelaborated attitudes which have an experiential character for each of us. These experiences, however, remain intellectually diffuse and emotionally intolerable unless they incorporate one or another of the patterns present in the group's culture. The assimilation of such patterns is the only means of objectivizing subjective states, of formulating inexpressible feelings, and of integrating inarticulated experiences into a system.

These mechanisms become clearer in the light of some observations made many years ago among the Zuni of New Mexico by an admirable field-worker, M. C. Stevenson.[5] A twelve-year-old girl was stricken with a nervous seizure directly after an adolescent boy had seized her hands. The youth was accused of sorcery and dragged before the court of the Bow priesthood. For an hour he denied having any knowledge of occult power, but this defense proved futile. Because the crime of sorcery was at that time still punished by death among the Zuni, the accused changed his tactics. He improvised a tale explaining the circumstances by which he had been initiated into sorcery. He said he had received two substances from his teachers, one which drove

girls insane and another which cured them. This point constituted an ingenious precaution against later developments. Having been ordered to produce his medicines, he went home under guard and came back with two roots, which he proceeded to use in a complicated ritual. He simulated a trance after taking one of the drugs, and after taking the other he pretended to return to his normal state. Then he administered the remedy to the sick girl and declared her cured. The session was adjourned until the following day, but during the night the alleged sorcerer escaped. He was soon captured, and the girl's family set itself up as a court and continued the trial. Faced with the reluctance of his new judges to accept his first story, the boy then invented a new one. He told them that all his relatives and ancestors had been witches and that he had received marvellous powers from them. He claimed that he could assume the form of a cat, fill his mouth with cactus needles, and kill his victims—two infants, three girls, and two boys—by shooting the needles into them. These feats, he claimed, were due to the magical powers of certain plumes which were used to change him and his family into shapes other than human. This last detail was a tactical error, for the judges called upon him to produce the plumes as proof of his new story. He gave various excuses which were rejected one after another, and he was forced to take his judges to his house. He began by declaring that the plumes were secreted in a wall that he could not destroy. He was commanded to go to work. After breaking down a section of the wall and carefully examining the plaster, he tried to excuse himself by declaring that the plumes had been hidden two years before and that he could not remember their exact location. Forced to search again, he tried another wall, and after another hour's work, an old plume appeared in the plaster. He grabbed it eagerly and presented it to his persecutors as the magic device of which he had spoken. He was then made to explain the details of its use. Finally, dragged into the public plaza, he had to repeat his entire story (to which he added a wealth of new detail). He finished it with a pathetic speech in which he lamented the loss of his super-natural power. Thus reassured, his listeners agreed to free him.

This narrative, which we unfortunately had to abridge and strip of all its psychological nuances, is still instructive in many respects. First of all, we see that the boy tried for witchcraft, for which he risks the death penalty, wins his acquittal not by denying but by admitting his alleged crime. Moreover, he furthers his cause by presenting successive versions, each richer in detail (and thus, in theory, more persuasive of guilt) than the preceding one. The debate does not proceed, as do debates among us, by accusations and denials, but rather by allegations and specifications. The judges do not expect the accused to challenge their theory, much less to refute the facts. Rather, they require him to validate a system of which they possess only a fragment; he must reconstruct it as a whole in an appropriate way. As the field-worker noted in relation to a phase of the trial, "The warriors had become so absorbed by their interest in the narrative of the boy that they seemed entirely to have forgotten the cause of his appearance before them."[6] And when the magic plume was finally uncovered, the author remarks with great insight, "There was consternation among the warriors, who exclaimed in one voice: 'What does this mean?' Now they felt assured that the youth had spoken the truth."[7] Consternation, and not triumph at finding a tangible proof of the crime—for the judges had sought to bear witness to the reality of the system which had made the crime possible (by validating its objective basis through an appropriate emotional expression), rather than simply to punish a crime. By his confession, the defendant is transformed into a witness for the prosecution, with the participation (and even the complicity) of his judges. Through the defendant, witchcraft and the ideas associated with it cease to exist as a diffuse complex of poorly formulated sentiments and representations and become embodied in real experience. The defendant, who serves as a witness, gives the group the satisfaction of truth, which is infinitely greater and richer than the satis-faction of justice that would have been achieved by his execution. And finally, by his ingenious defense which makes his hearers progressively aware of the vitality offered by his corroboration of their system (especially since the choice is not between this system and another, but between the magical system and no system at all—that is, chaos), the youth, who at first was a threat to the physical security of his group, became the guardian of its spiritual coherence.

But is his defense merely ingenious? Everything leads us to believe that after groping for a subterfuge, the defendant participates with sincerity and—the word is not too strong—fervor in the drama enacted between him and his judges. He is proclaimed a sorcerer; since sorcerers do exist, he might well be one. And how would he know beforehand the signs which might reveal his calling to him? Perhaps the signs are there, present in this ordeal and in the convulsions of the little girl brought before the court. For the boy, too, the coherence of the system and the role assigned to him in preserving it are values no less essential than the personal security which he risks in the venture. Thus we see him, with a mixture of cunning and good faith, progressively construct the impersonation which is thrust upon him—chiefly by drawing on his knowledge and his memories, improvising somewhat, but above all living his role and seeking, through his manipulations and the ritual he builds from bits and pieces, the experience of a calling which is, at least theoretically, open to all. At the end of the adventure, what remains of his earlier hoaxes? To what extent has the hero become the dupe of his own impersonation? What is more, has he not truly become a sorcerer? We are told that in his final confession, "The longer the boy talked the more absorbed he became in his subject. . . . At times his face became radiant with satisfaction at his power over his listeners."[8] The girl recovers after he performs his curing ritual. The boy's experiences during the extraordinary ordeal become elaborated and structured. Little more is needed than for the innocent boy finally to confess to the possession of supernatural powers that are already recognized by the group.

We must consider at greater length another especially valuable document, which until now seems to have been valued solely for its linguistic interest. I refer to a fragment of the autobiography of a Kwakiutl Indian from the Vancouver region of Canada, obtained by Franz Boas.[9]

Quesalid (for this was the name he received when he became a sorcerer) did not believe in the power of the sorcerers—or, more accurately, shamans, since this is a better term for their specific type of activity in certain regions of the world. Driven by curiosity about their tricks and by the desire to expose them, he began to associate with the shamans until one of them offered to make him a member of their group. Quesalid did not wait to be asked twice, and his narrative recounts the details of his first lessons, a curious mixture of pantomime, prestidigitation, and empirical knowledge, including the art of simulating fainting and nervous fits, the learning of sacred songs, the technique for inducing vomiting, rather precise notions of auscultation and obstetrics, and the use of "dreamers," that is, spies who listen to private conversations and secretly convey to the shaman bits of information concerning the origins and symptoms of the ills suffered by different people. Above all, he learned the ars magna of one of the shamanistic schools of the Northwest Coast: The shaman hides a little tuft of down in a corner of his mouth, and he throws it up, covered with blood, at the proper moment—after having bitten his tongue or made his gums bleed—and solemnly presents it to his patient and the onlookers as the pathological foreign body extracted as a result of his sucking and manipulations.

His worst suspicions confirmed, Quesalid wanted to continue his inquiry. But he was no longer free. His apprenticeship among the shamans began to be noised about, and one day he was summoned by the family of a sick person who had dreamed of Quesalid as his healer. This first treatment (for which he received no payment, any more than he did for those which followed, since he had not completed the required four years of apprenticeship) was an outstanding success. Although Quesalid came to be known from that moment on as a "great shaman," he did not lose his critical faculties. He interpreted his success in psychological terms—it was successful "because he [the sick person] believed strongly in his dream about me."[10] A more complex adventure made him, in his own words, "hesitant and thinking about many things."[11] Here he encountered several varieties of a "false supernatural," and was led to conclude that some forms were less false than others—those, of course, in which he had a personal stake and whose system he was, at the same time, surreptitiously building up in his mind. A summary of the adventure follows.

While visiting the neighboring Koskimo Indians, Quesalid attends a curing ceremony of his illustrious colleagues of the other tribe. To his great astonishment he observes a difference in their technique. Instead of spitting out the illness in the form of a "bloody worm" (the concealed down), the Koskimo shamans merely spit a little saliva into their hands, and they dare to claim that this is "the sickness." What is the value of this method? What is the theory behind it? In order to find out "the strength of the shamans, whether it was real or whether they only pretended to be shamans" like his fellow tribesmen,[12] Quesalid requests and obtains permission to try his method in an instance where the Koskimo method has failed. The sick woman then declares herself cured.

And here our hero vacillates for the first time. Though he had few illusions about his own technique, he has now found one which is more false, more mystifying, and more dishonest than his own. For he at least gives his clients something. He presents them with their sickness in a visible and tangible form, while his foreign colleagues show nothing at all and only claim to have captured the sickness. Moreover, Quesalid's method gets results, while the other is futile. Thus our hero grapples with a problem which perhaps has its parallel in the development of modern science. Two systems which we know to be inadequate present (with respect to each other) a differential validity, from both a logical and an empirical perspective. From which frame of reference shall we judge them? On the level of fact, where they merge, or on their own level, where they take on different values, both theoretically and empirically?

Meanwhile, the Koskimo shamans, "ashamed" and discredited before their tribesmen, are also plunged into doubt. Their colleague has produced, in the form of a material object, the illness which they had always considered as spiritual in nature and had thus never dreamed of rendering visible. They send Quesalid an emissary to invite him to a secret meeting in a cave. Quesalid goes and his foreign colleagues expound their system to him: "Every sickness is a man: boils and swellings, and itch and scabs, and pimples and coughs and consumption and scrofula; and also this, stricture of the bladder and stomach aches. . . . As soon as we get the soul of the sickness which is a man, then dies the sickness which is a man. Its body just disappears in our insides."[13] If this theory is correct, what is there to show? And why, when Quesalid operates, does "the sickness stick to his hand"? But Quesalid takes refuge behind professional rules which forbid him to teach before completing four years of apprenticeship, and refuses to speak. He maintains his silence even when the Koskimo shamans send him their allegedly virgin daughters to try to seduce him and discover his secret.

Thereupon Quesalid returns to his village at Fort Rupert. He learns that the most reputed shaman of a neighboring clan, worried about Quesalid's growing renown, has challenged all his colleagues, inviting them to compete with him in curing several patients. Quesalid comes to the contest and observes the cures of his elder. Like the Koskimo, this shaman does not show the illness. He simply incorporates an invisible object, "what he called the sickness" into his head-ring, made of bark, or into his bird-shaped ritual rattle.[14] These objects can hang suspended in mid-air, owing to the power of the illness which "bites" the house-posts or the shaman's hand. The usual drama unfolds. Quesalid is asked to intervene in cases judged hopeless by his predecessor, and he triumphs with his technique of the bloody worm.

Here we come to the truly pathetic part of the story. The old shaman, ashamed and despairing because of the ill-repute into which he has fallen and by the collapse of his therapeutic technique, sends his daughter to Quesalid to beg him for an interview. The latter finds his colleague sitting under a tree and the old shaman begins thus: "It won't be bad what we say to each other, friend, but only I wish you to try and save my life for me, so that I may not die of shame, for I am a plaything of our people on account of what you did last night. I pray you to have mercy and tell me what stuck on the palm of your hand last night. Was it the true sickness or was it only made up? For I beg you have mercy and tell me about the way you did it so that I can imitate you. Pity me, friend."[15]

Silent at first, Quesalid begins by calling for explanations about the feats of the head-ring and the rattle. His colleague shows him the nail hidden in the head-ring which he can press at right angles into the post, and the way in which he tucks the head of his rattle between his finger joints to make it look as if the bird were hanging by its beak from his hand. He himself probably does nothing but lie and fake, simulating shamanism for material gain, for he admits to being "covetous for the property of the sick men." He knows that shamans cannot catch souls, "for . . . we all own a soul"; so he resorts to using tallow and pretends that "it is a soul . . . that white thing . . . sitting on my hand." The daughter then adds her entreaties to those of her father: "Do have mercy that he may live." But Quesalid remains silent. That very night, following this tragic conversation, the shaman disappears with his entire family, heartsick and feared by the community, who think that he may be tempted to take revenge. Needless fears: He returned a year later, but both he and his daughter had gone mad. Three years later, he died.

And Quesalid, rich in secrets, pursued his career, exposing the impostors and full of contempt for the profession. "Only one shaman was seen by me, who sucked at a sick man and I never found out whether he was a real shaman or only made up. Only for this reason I believe that he is a shaman; he does not allow those who are made well to pay him. I truly never once saw him laugh."[16] Thus his original attitude has changed considerably. The radical negativism of the free thinker has given way to more moderate feelings. Real shamans do exist. And what about him? At the end of the narrative we cannot tell, but it is evident that he carries on his craft conscientiously, takes pride in his achievements, and warmly defends the technique of the bloody down against all rival schools. He seems to have completely lost sight of the fallaciousness of the technique which he had so disparaged at the beginning.

We see that the psychology of the sorcerer is not simple. In order to analyze it, we shall first examine the case of the old shaman who begs his young rival to tell him the truth—whether the illness glued in the palm of his hand like a sticky red worm is real or made up—and who goes mad when he receives no answer. Before the tragedy, he was fully convinced of two things—first, that pathological conditions have a cause which may be discovered and second, that a system of interpretation in which personal inventiveness is important structures the phases of the illness, from the diagnosis to the cure. This fabulation of a reality unknown in itself—a fabulation consisting of procedures and representations—is founded on a threefold experience: first, that of the shaman himself, who, if his calling is a true one (and even if it is not, simply by virtue of his practicing it), undergoes specific states of a psychosomatic nature; second, that of the sick person, who may or may not experience an improvement of his condition; and, finally, that of the public, who also participate in the cure, experiencing an enthusiasm and an intellectual and emotional satisfaction which produce collective support, which in turn inaugurates a new cycle.

These three elements of what we might call the "shamanistic complex" cannot be separated. But they are clustered around two poles, one formed by the intimate experience of the shaman and the other by group consensus. There is no reason to doubt that sorcerers, or at least the more sincere among them, believe in their calling and that this belief is founded on the experiencing of specific states. The hardships and privations which they undergo would often be sufficient in themselves to provoke these states, even if we refuse to admit them as proof of a serious and fervent calling. But there is also linguistic evidence which, because it is indirect, is more convincing. In the Wintu dialect of California, there are five verbal classes which correspond to knowledge by sight, by bodily experience, by inference, by reasoning, and by hearsay. All five make up the category of knowledge as opposed to conjecture, which is differently expressed. Curiously enough, relationships with the supernatural world are expressed by means of the modes of knowledge—by bodily impression (that is, the most intuitive kind of experience), by inference, and by reasoning. Thus the native who becomes a shaman after a spiritual crisis conceives of his state grammatically, as a consequence to be inferred from the fact—formulated as real experience—that he has received divine guidance. From the latter he concludes deductively that he must have been on a journey to the beyond, at the end of which he found himself—again, an immediate experience—once more among his people.[17]

The experiences of the sick person represent the least important aspect of the system, except for the fact that a patient successfully treated by a shaman is in an especially good position to become a shaman in his own right, as we see today in the case of psychoanalysis. In any event, we must remember that the shaman does not completely lack empirical knowledge and experimental techniques, which may in part explain his success. Furthermore, disorders of the type currently termed psychosomatic, which constitute a large part of the illnesses prevalent in societies with a low degree of security, probably often yield to psychotherapy. At any rate, it seems probable that medicine men, like their civilized colleagues, cure at least some of the cases they treat and that without this relative success magical practices could not have been so widely diffused in time and space. But this point is not fundamental; it is subordinate to the other two. Quesalid did not become a great shaman because he cured his patients; he cured his patients because he had become a great shaman. Thus we have reached the other—that is, the collective—pole of our system.

The true reason for the defeat of Quesalid's rivals must then be sought in the attitude of the group rather than in the pattern of the rivals' successes and failures. The rivals themselves emphasize this when they confess their shame at having become the laughingstock of the group; this is a social sentiment par excellence. Failure is secondary, and we see in all their statements that they consider it a function of another phenomenon, which is the disappearance of the social consensus, re-created at their expense around another practitioner and another system of curing. Consequently, the fundamental problem revolves around the relationship between the individual and the group, or, more accurately, the relationship between a specific category of individuals and specific expectations of the group.

In treating his patient the shaman also offers his audience a performance. What is this performance? Risking a rash generalization on the basis of a few observations, we shall say that it always involves the shaman's enactment of the "call," or the initial crisis which brought him the revelation of his condition. But we must not be deceived by the word performance. The shaman does not limit himself to reproducing or miming certain events. He actually relives them in all their vividness, originality, and violence. And since he returns to his normal state at the end of the séance, we may say, borrowing a key term from psychoanalysis, that he abreacts. In psychoanalysis, abreaction refers to the decisive moment in the treatment when the patient intensively relives the initial situation from which his disturbance stems, before he ultimately overcomes it. In this sense, the shaman is a professional abreactor.

We have set forth elsewhere the theoretical hypotheses that might be formulated in order for us to accept the idea that the type of abreaction specific to each shaman—or, at any rate, to each shamanistic school—might symbolically induce an abreaction of his own disturbance in each patient.[18]

In any case, if the essential relationship is that between the shaman and the group, we must also state the question from another point of view—that of the relationship between normal and pathological thinking. From any non-scientific perspective (and here we can exclude no society), pathological and normal thought processes are complementary rather than opposed. In a universe which it strives to understand but whose dynamics it cannot fully control, normal thought continually seeks the meaning of things which refuse to reveal their significance. So-called pathological thought, on the other hand, overflows with emotional interpretations and overtones, in order to supplement an otherwise deficient reality. For normal thinking there exists something which cannot be empirically verified and is, therefore, "claimable." For pathological thinking there exist experiences without object, or something "available." We might borrow from linguistics and say that so-called normal thought always suffers from a deficit of meaning, whereas so-called pathological thought (in at least some of its manifestations) disposes of a plethora of meaning. Through collective participation in shamanistic curing, a balance is established between these two complementary situations. Normal thought cannot fathom the problem of illness, and so the group calls upon the neurotic to furnish a wealth of emotion heretofore lacking a focus.

An equilibrium is reached between what might be called supply and demand on the psychic level—but only on two conditions. First, a structure must be elaborated and continually modified through the interaction of group tradition and individual invention. This structure is a system of oppositions and correlations, integrating all the elements of a total situation, in which sorcerer, patient, and audience, as well as representations and procedures, all play their parts. Furthermore, the public must participate in the abreaction, to a certain extent at least, along with the patient and the sorcerer. It is this vital experience of a universe of symbolic effusions which the patient, because he is ill, and the sorcerer, because he is neurotic—in other words, both having types of experience which cannot otherwise be integrated—allow the public to glimpse as "fireworks" from a safe distance. In the absence of any experimental control, which is indeed unnecessary, it is this experience alone, and its relative richness in each case, which makes possible a choice between several systems and elicits adherence to a particular school or practitioner.[19]

In contrast with scientific explanation, the problem here is not to attribute confused and disorganized states, emotions, or representations to an objective cause, but rather to articulate them into a whole or system. The system is valid precisely to the extent that it allows the coalescence or precipitation of these diffuse states, whose discontinuity also makes them painful. To the conscious mind, this last phenomenon constitutes an original experience which cannot be grasped from without. Because of their complementary disorders, the sorcerer-patient dyad incarnates for the group, in vivid and concrete fashion, an antagonism that is inherent in all thought but that normally remains vague and imprecise. The patient is all passivity and self-alienation, just as inexpressibility is the disease of the mind. The sorcerer is activity and self-projection, just as affectivity is the source of symbolism. The cure interrelates these opposite poles, facilitating the transition from one to the other, and demonstrates, within a total experience, the coherence of the psychic universe, itself a projection of the social universe.

Thus it is necessary to extend the notion of abreaction by examining the meanings it acquires in psychotherapies other than psychoanalysis, although the latter deserves the credit for rediscovering and insisting upon its fundamental validity. It may be objected that in psychoanalysis there is only one abreaction, the patient's, rather than three. We are not so sure of this. It is true that in the shamanistic cure the sorcerer speaks and abreacts for the silent patient, while in psychoanalysis it is the patient who talks and abreacts against the listening therapist. But the therapist's abreaction, while not concomitant with the patient's, is nonetheless required, since he must be analyzed before he himself can become an analyst. It is more difficult to

define the role ascribed to the group by each technique. Magic readapts the group to predefined problems through the patient, while psychoanalysis readapts the patient to the group by means of the solutions reached. But the distressing trend which, for several years, has tended to transform the psychoanalytic system from a body of scientific hypotheses that are experimentally verifiable in certain specific and limited cases into a kind of diffuse mythology interpenetrating the consciousness of the group, could rapidly bring about a parallelism. (This group consciousness is an objective phenomenon, which the psychologist expresses through a subjective tendency to extend to normal thought a system of interpretations conceived for pathological thought and to apply to facts of collective psychology a method adapted solely to the study of individual psychology.) When this happens—and perhaps it already has in certain countries—the value of the system will no longer be based upon real cures from which certain individuals can benefit, but on the sense of security that the group receives from the myth underlying the cure and from the popular system upon which the group's universe is reconstructed.

Even at the present time, the comparison between psychoanalysis and older and more widespread psychological therapies can encourage the former to re-examine its principles and methods. By continuously expanding the recruitment of its patients, who begin as clearly characterized abnormal individuals and gradually become representative of the group, psychoanalysis transforms its treatments into conversions. For only a patient can emerge cured; an unstable or maladjusted individual can only be persuaded. A considerable danger thus arises: The treatment (unbeknown to the therapist, naturally), far from leading to the resolution of a specific disturbance within its own context, is reduced to the reorganization of the patient's universe in terms of psychoanalytic interpretations. This means that we would finally arrive at precisely that situation which furnishes the point of departure as well as the theoretical validity of the magico-social system that we have analyzed.

If this analysis is correct, we must see magical behavior as the response to a situation which is revealed to the mind through emotional manifestations, but whose essence is intellectual. For only the history of the symbolic function can allow us to understand the intellectual condition of man, in which the universe is never charged with sufficient meaning and in which the mind always has more meanings available than there are objects to which to relate them. Torn between these two systems of reference—the signifying and the signified—man asks magical thinking to provide him with a new system of reference, within which the thus-far contradictory elements can be integrated. But we know that this system is built at the expense of the progress of knowledge, which would have required us to retain only one of the two previous systems and to refine it to the point where it absorbed the other. This point is still far off. We must not permit the individual, whether normal or neurotic, to repeat this collective misadventure. The study of the mentally sick individual has shown us that all persons are more or less oriented toward contradictory systems and suffer from the resulting conflict; but the fact that a certain form of integration is possible and effective practically is not enough to make it true, or to make us certain that the adaptation thus achieved does not constitute an absolute regression in relation to the previous conflict situation.

The reabsorption of a deviant specific synthesis, through its integration with the normal syntheses, into a general but arbitrary synthesis (aside from critical cases where action is required) would represent a loss on all fronts. A body of elementary hypotheses can have a certain instrumental value for the practitioner without necessarily being recognized, in theoretical analysis, as the final image of reality and without necessarily linking the patient and the therapist in a kind of mystical communion which does not have the same meaning for both parties and which only ends by reducing the treatment to a fabulation.

In the final analysis we could only expect this fabulation to be a language, whose function is to provide a socially authorized translation of phenomena whose deeper nature would become once again equally impenetrable to the group, the patient, and the healer.

ENDNOTES

1. W. B. Cannon, " 'Voodoo' Death," *American Anthropologist,* n.s., XLIV (1942).
2. An Australian aborigine was brought to the Darwin hospital in April 1956, apparently dying of this type of sorcery. He was placed in an oxygen tent and fed intravenously. He gradually recovered, convinced that the white man's magic was the stronger. See Arthur Morley in the *London Sunday Times,* April 22, 1956, p. 11.
3. In this study, whose aim is more psychological than sociological, we feel justified in neglecting the finer distinctions between the several modes of magical operations and different types of sorcerers when these are not absolutely necessary.
4. C. Lévi-Strauss, *Tristes Tropiques* (Paris: 1955), Chapter XXIX.
5. M. C. Stevenson, *The Zuni Indians,* 23rd Annual Report of the Bureau of American Ethnology (Washington, D.C.: Smithsonian Institution, 1905).
6. *Ibid.,* p. 401.
7. *Ibid.,* p. 404.
8. *Ibid.,* p. 406.
9. Franz Boas, *The Religion of the Kwakiutl,* Columbia University Contributions to Anthropology, Vol. X (New York: 1930), Part II, pp. 1–41.
10. *Ibid.,* p. 13.
11. *Ibid.,* p. 19.
12. *Ibid.,* p. 17.
13. *Ibid.,* pp. 20–21.
14. *Ibid.,* p. 27.
15. *Ibid.,* p. 31.
16. *Ibid.,* pp. 40–41.
17. D. D. Lee, "Some Indian Texts Dealing with the Supernatural," *The Review of Religion* (May, 1941).
18. See "The Effectiveness of Symbols," Chapter X of the present volume.
19. This oversimplified equation of sorcerer and neurotic was justly criticized by Michel Leiris. I subsequently refined this concept in my "Introduction à l'oeuvre de Marcel Mauss," in M. Mauss, Sociologie et Anthropologie (Paris: 1950), pp. xviii–xxiii.

RELIGION IN THE NEWS

MOZAMBIQUE ENLISTS HEALERS IN AIDS PREVENTION

As we have seen, the pragmatic and the symbolic merge in rituals carried out by religious practitioners. In Korea and Java they not only blend but are officially sanctioned at the highest levels of government. Indeed, a successful politician's shaman is much sought after by politicians who strive to become his or her client in hope the shaman will help them achieve their ambitions, too. Still, only rarely do healers act as the agents of bureaucratic organizations, and in countries where shamanistic activities are regarded as "primitive" the regard with which such practitioners is socially held is usually low. In Mozambique, however, that view is being challenged...

By Rachel L. Swarns

BEIRA, Mozambique   The traditional healer stretches her hands to the heavens and her body trembles, her rattles hiss and her shack rumbles as she cries out to the spirits of her ancestors.

Then she opens her eyes and gets down to business.

"Have you ever heard of condoms?" she asks her astonished patients, who have come to whisper about two-timing husbands and sexually transmitted diseases. "You should wear the to protect yourself from these diseases."

Meet Eufrásia Fernandes, one of the newest and most unlikely foot soldiers on Mozambique's national crusades against AIDS.

For nearly two decades, government officials derided traditional healers like Ms. Fernandes as quacks and enemies of the state. They burned the healers' tools and barred them from practicing.

In the early 1990's, Ms. Fernandes had to hide her drums and sneak onto the countryside to chant and cure. During the civil war that ravaged this nation until 1992, other healers allied themselves with the rebel army, promising soldiers spiritual protection against the government's bullets.

But, today traditional healers—known as curandeiros—are being embraced by the government as vital bearers of the safe-sex message in an impoverished country where millions of people still lack adequate access to doctors and modern medicine. Next year the government plans to expand on this national strategy by linking teams of trained healers directly to hospitals, which have been overwhelmed by an influx of patients infected with H.I.V., the virus that causes AIDS.

The traditional healers will treat the patients at home—freeing up hospital beds for other sick people—and using herbs and plants that health officials here say effectively treat opportunistic ailments, like diarrhea and pneumonia, that afflict people whose immune systems are impaired by AIDS.

The program is still a small one. Fewer than 100 of the thousands of practicing healers in this country have attended the seminars on AIDS and sexually transmitted diseases, and the government is still sorting out how the linkages between hospitals and healers will work.

But health officials say they plan to expand the program, leaving the healers to marvel at their newfound freedom and to push their businesses out into the open.

In the dusty market here, where hawkers sell mangoes, bananas and colorful squares of cloth, a healer named Ousmane Ba posted a sign promising treatment of headaches, sterility and asthma. "Children under 2 don't pay," his sign said.

The regional office of the Association of Traditional Doctors of Mozambique rents an office here, and every Tuesday and Thursday, people lodge their complaints before its grievance board. The board fines healers who abuse their powers and bars amateurs from dabbling in the field.

Last year, Ms. Fernandes opened a tiny consultancy on a bustling residential block with the blessing of the local authorities. She still counsels the bewitched and exorcises spirits, but she also sells condoms and tells her patients how to avoid AIDS and other diseases.

"Before, I couldn't work openly like this, right here in the city," said Ms. Fernandes, 39. "Now, I play my drums and there's no problem."

In a country where nearly 15 percent of the population is believed to be infected with H.I.V., the government's change of heart was critically important, health officials say.

RELIGION IN THE NEWS

MOZAMBIQUE ENLISTS HEALERS IN AIDS PREVENTION
continued

Ricardo Trindade, a deputy director in the Health Ministry, said only about 50 percent of the population had access to the fledgling national health system, whose predecessor was virtually destroyed during the 16-year civil war. The rest rely almost exclusively on traditional healers.

"The majority of people in Mozambique seek treatment from curanderios, even those who go to hospitals," Mr. Trindade said. " The government's changing attitude is definitely a good thing."

The chilly relationship began warming decisively two years ago, the healers say, when the government officially recognized their professional association and began warning them about AIDS.

Health officials feared that the healers themselves were unwittingly spreading the fatal disease. The healers typically use razor blades in their treatments, making small incisions in the flesh and pressing medicines directly into the blood. And they were often using the same blade on dozens of people.

A private group, Population Services International, began offering seminars on AIDS and other sexually transmitted diseases. The healers were urged to boil razors, to encourage patients to buy their own razors and to sell condoms along with homemade remedies for malaria, cholera and other ailments.

Titosse Ofisso, the regional president of the healers' association in Nharichonga, said he welcomed the new thinking.

"People don't know you need to use clean razors or that if you don't put condoms on, you can spread your disease to someone else," said Mr. Ofisso, 22, whose rural village lacks electricity and indoor plumbing. "People don't even know what condoms are. They still ask me, 'What is this?' "

Ms. Fernandes was reluctant at first to take part in the program. But after attending the seminar, she said she no longer worried much about mixing the modern with the traditional. After all, she has always been pragmatic when it comes to patients suffering from diseases she cannot treat on her own.

"If someone comes here with diabetes and a bad spirit, I take out the bad spirit and send them to the hospital," she said. "Now, when people have sexual diseases, I tell them to wear this condom so it doesn't spread."

It is the healers' broad popularity that makes them as valuable to health officials. More than 70 percent of Mozambiques's population are rural people, who hold tight to their traditions.

Francisco Zonjo, 66, a retiree, turned to the healers when medical doctors could not explain why several relatives had fallen sick and died.

Carlitos Pereira, 19, turned to the healers when he lost his job as a bus conductor and his wife suffered several miscarriages.

Santos Aleixo, 42, a musician with a virulent skin disease, turned to the healers after a local hospital turned him away because he could not afford the doctor's fee of $12.50.

Members of the healers' association acknowledge that they cannot cure all ailments and social problems, even though some claim such powers. They say they want to work more closely with health professionals, to get some training and to share their knowledge of the herbs and plants and, maybe, to help find a cure for AIDS.

In the meantime, they are proud to have finally won the respect of government officials and to have a clear role to play in preserving the nation's health.

"The problem of AIDS is out there," said Chapal Maconha, the president of the regional healers' association here. "But the people don't have televisions and they don't know about condoms. They don't know people are dying.

"In the outskirts there are no hospitals, no clinics to help them, to tell them what is happening. But there are curandeiros. We are the secret weapon. We can spread the message. We can help save the people."

Source: The New York Times, December 6, 1999, p. A14. Copyright©1999 by The New York Times Company. Reprinted by permission.

ASK YOURSELF

You will have seen on television persons preaching the virtues of their particular religion hoping to attract more followers to their faith. Based on what you have read in this chapter can you classify them as priests, shamans, or prophets?

FURTHER READINGS

Humphrey, Caroline and Urgunge Onon. *Shamans and Elders: Experience, Knowledge, and Power among the Daur Mongols* Oxford. Clarendon Press. 1996. Approaching the phenomenon of shamanism in one society in central Asia, this captivating work treats Daur Mongol shamanism from both synchronic and diachronic perspectives, and sheds light on shamanism as a general feature of religious experience.

Johnson, Douglas, H. *Nuer Prophets: A History of Prophecy from the Upper Nile in the Nineteenth and Twentieth Centuries.* Oxford: Clarendon Press. 1994. Evans-Pritchard's study of Nuer religion provided the inspiration for this important contribution to the study of prophets in Northeast Africa. It combines the fruits of anthropological ethnography with a careful application of historical scholarship.

Lewis, I. M. *Religion in Context: Cults and Charisma.* Cambridge: Cambridge University Press. 1996. 2nd. Edition. Possession cults, shamans, and witchcraft are particularly well described in this collection of six articles and lectures, which gives us a good overview of their significance in society.

Turner, Victor. *The Drums of Affliction.* Oxford: Clarendon Press, 1968. In contrast to the static model of religion exemplified in the structural-function approach of A. R. Radcliffe-Brown and E. E. Evans-Pritchard, Turner demonstrates ritual's dynamic role in the processes of curing sick individuals among the Ndembu.

SUGGESTED VIDEOS

"Eduardo the Healer." The biography presented in this documentary illustrates several topics dealt with in this reader. It shows how one person became a shaman and illustrates the differences between imitative and contagious magic (see Chapter 7). It reveals how religious ideas (e.g., the notion of spirits) can combine with magical symbols (e.g., "force field") in ritual. And it demonstrates the power of a charismatic practitioner to ameliorate his client's depression. 55 minutes; 1979; Pennsylvania State University: Films in the Behavioral Sciences.

"New Tribes Mission." Dedicated members of the New Tribes Mission, an evangelical group of Protestant missionaries, argue their justification for converting the Yanomamo and attempting to stop them from worshiping "false demons." 1974; price unknown; 12 minutes; Documentary Educational Resources, 5 Bridge Street, Watertown, MA 02172.

"Daba / Na Shaman." After living for over 25 years without performing any type of religious ceremony, the Na, an ethnic group living on the Himalayan plateau, began in the early 1990s to publicly perform their rituals once again. Few old shamans were still alive then, but one of them was Dafa Luzo, and in this film we see him performing rituals to expel unclean spirits and demons, and honor the ancestors. Filmmaker and anthropologist: Hua Cai. Color, 40 minutes, 1999. VC.RA 256. Film Officer, Royal Anthropological Institute (RAI), 50 Fitzroy Street, London W1P 5HS, United Kingdom.

Some rituals may be a response to the human desire for control in a world where events often seem to happen randomly. On the dashboard of his car, a devout Hindu places marigold petals and incense before pictures of two Hindu gods in the belief that the gods, thus honored, will protect both car and driver.
Photo courtesy of Margaret A. Gwynne

CHAPTER 6

BODY AND MIND

Religious ideology in many societies regulates self-presentation, and rituals and beliefs help shape body and mind. Distinctive clothing often signals ritual standing: Islam, for example, mandates that women wear the *chador,* a loose robe, usually black, that covers the body from head to toe and most of the face. The body itself may be physically altered: circumcision is imposed on Jewish boys. Ritual prescriptions may even regulate behavior, thoughts, and sometimes feelings. In some religions, the pleasures of the flesh are renounced, with sexual intercourse being a common target for taboos, along with certain types of food and drink.

Yet the human body also has an impact on collective representations. Societies exploit the body as the basis for symbolization, as in symbolic classification, where many societies use the left hand and the right hand to symbolize oppositions such as in cosmological status (sacred/profane), moral notions (bad/good), or gender (female/male). Substances produced by, or emitted from, the body are among natural objects religions everywhere turn to for symbols. Blood, for instance, finds recurrent use in sac-

rificial rituals (see Chapter 8) or to represent pollution, death, or fertility (as with menstrual blood).

Blood may be a "primary factor of experience" an image naturally impressing itself upon the human brain (see Reading 7–4), and its use as a symbol in a great many societies supports this possibility. Blood is a *multivocal* symbol, a symbol that includes more than one referent. Hence its popularity for ritual, where it symbolizes qualities that tend to coalesce around two poles. At one pole coalesce positive qualities: life, fertility, and abundance. At the other pole coalesce negative qualities: death, infertility, and want. Blood spilt in battle is masculine blood, and it brings death. Blood shed menstrually is feminine blood, and it is a harbinger of life. Balinese symbolic classification, discussed in the Introduction to Chapter 3, makes thorough use of the symbolic potential of this substance.

In some cosmologies (that of the Dogon [Reading 2–3] comes readily to mind), the human body forms a microcosm of the cosmos itself, and in the exercises of Yoga, Hindu devotees apply ritual precepts for corporeal benefits. In its fullest physical sense, the body is also the focus of attention in rituals of human sacrifice or in myths in which a deity surrenders his or her body for the sake of believers. The sacrifice of a human being is an offering directed to the gods; the self-immolation of a god is a sacrifice directed to humanity. By both kinds of ritual sacrifices, however, human beings and their gods are brought into a relationship beneficial to both parties.

In 1909 a younger colleague of Emile Durkheim's, who was also a member of his *Année sociologique* group, Robert Hertz, wrote a famous paper in French demonstrating the apparently universal human imperative to exploit the lateral possibilities offered by the human body to symbolize and classify ideas, moral notions, and gender differences (Hertz 1960:89–113). He began his essay by pointing out that in all societies positive qualities are universally associated with the right hand and negative qualities with the left. He also noted that the right symbolized masculine qualities while left symbolized feminine qualities. These analogies have been confirmed by many subsequent ethnographic studies, and his ideas on lateral symbolism inspired Evans-Pritchard's study of Nuer ritual. Hertz's original study also helped to generate, 64 years after the publication of his work, a collection of 17 independent case studies each demonstrating the widespread occurrence of these associations in cultures as diverse as the Osage of North America, ancient China, the Meru of East Africa, ancient Greece, south India, and eastern Indonesia (Needham 1973).

Any given culture's cosmology imposes its symbolic classification on the body and mind, then; but the reverse is also true. Writing in Germany in the 19th century, Adolf Bastian argued the case for the "psychic unity" of humanity. He was referring to what he took to be "mental universals," or fixed patterns of thought common to all human beings irrespective of culture. Later, the Swiss psychoanalyst Carl Jung argued a similar case for his universal "archetypes," or mental patterns supposedly inherent in the collective unconscious of every person and manifested in rituals, myths, and dreams.

A different version of the "mental patterns" thesis has been put forward by Rodney Needham (1978:23–50), one based upon his examination of

the problem of how best to make sense of witchcraft. Scholars of witchcraft generally see it as a *sociological* phenomenon, and study the social dynamics linking accuser with accused. Needham, however, prefers to analyze witchcraft as a mental phenomenon. He identifies a number of qualities he believes people the world over identify with witches and uses his finding to argue that everywhere people have a consistent mental image of the witch, a fact, he concludes, that suggests that the qualities that make up this mental image are the spontaneous product of the human brain.

As we saw in Chapter 5, shamanistic powers may often be physiologically induced by artificially manipulating the processes of the human brain by the use of drugs. The ritual taking of hallucinogens, however, can also extend to ordinary members of a religious community. Peyote (or mescal, *Lophophora williamsii*) is a spineless cactus growing from northern Mexico to southern Texas. Certain Mexican Indian populations, such as the Huichol, use the drug in their rituals. By 1890 peyote had been introduced into the rituals of the Plains Indians, and the drug is now an essential element of their religion, the "peyote religion" or the "peyote way," which is regarded by its adherents as an indigenous version of Christianity. Sociologists and anthropologists consider this "religion of the body" to be a form of revitalization movement (see Chapter 11).

READING 6–1

MY ADVENTURE WITH *EBENE*: A "RELIGIOUS EXPERIENCE"

Napoleon A. Chagnon

This excerpt from Chagnon's book informs us about the activities of Christian missionaries as they pursue their

Source: Excerpts from "My Adventure with *Ebene*: A 'Religious Experience,'" in Yąnomamö: The Fierce People, by Napoleon A. Chagnon, copyright © 1983 by Holt, Rinehart, and Winston, reprinted by permission of the publisher.

mandate to convert indigenous people to Christianity. It also graphically depicts the play of hallucinogens on the mind, and as in Reading 4–2, on the Jívaro hallucinogens, provides us with a glimpse into one possible way by which people create religious concepts.

Napoleon Chagnon has carried out many months of fieldwork among the Yanomamo Indians, who live in South America's Amazon region. For his first visit to the Yanomamo in the mid-1960s, Chagnon was part of a multi-disciplinary team assembled by a university department of human genetics to do medical research. At that time the Yanomamo had had little contact with Westerners, and they lived in small villages scattered widely throughout the remote tropical forest, and spoke only their own language. He returned many times, and by doing so was able to study Yanomamo culture diachronically as well as synchronically. After collecting "baseline" ethnographic data during fifteen months of fieldwork between 1964 and 1966, he went back to visit them ten more times during a long-term research project that by 1983 added up to a total of forty-two months in the field. Between 1964 and 1983, as more and more missionaries, settlers, and miners ventured into Yanomamo territory (an area rich in gold, diamonds, and zinc), the Yanomamos' original way of life began to dissipate, a process Chagnon records in the over 80,000 feet of ethnographic film he assisted a film-maker produce. By 1983 had completed some twenty documentaries on the Yanomamo. Together with numerous articles and several books, Chagnon's films have transformed one of the least known of nonliterate peoples into one of the best known. As the following extract from his first, and most, popular book indicates, Napoleon Chagnon could be said to be an exemplary participant observer!

On one of my annual return trips I became deeply involved with Kąobawä's relationship to the Protestant missionaries. A new missionary family had moved into his village to maintain the "field station" for a period of about a year while the resident local missionary returned to the United States on a "furlough." Missionaries, I might add, utilize a good many paramilitary phrases in their work— they regard themselves as "Commandos for Christ," "wage war on the Devil," and take "furloughs" from "active duty." I did not know this particular missionary very well, for he was usually living in Yąnomamö villages in a region that fell outside the area of my field study. However, I knew

that "Pete," as I will call him here, was more prone to conduct his evangelical objectives through recourse to fire and brimstone techniques than most of the more patient, younger Protestant missionaries I had met, often flying into tirades whenever Yąnomamö would "revert" to chewing tobacco (". . . the work of the Devil . . ."), taking extra wives, or, most annoyingly, insufflating their hallucinogens and chanting to their *hekura* spirits. Pete particularly disliked the village shamans, and made extraordinary attempts to discredit them, for they constituted a serious threat to his attempts at convincing the others that there was only one true spirit and that a belief in many spirits was evil.

At first the Yąnomamö very diplomatically, but with considerable inconvenience to themselves, accommodated his peculiarities by moving off into the jungle a few miles to conduct their daily religious activities. This kept the trade goods flowing into the village. On the surface and verbally they behaved as though they had ". . . accepted Dios" and ". . . thrown their *hekura* away," for they were ". . . filthy spirits." The inconvenience, however, became too much, and eventually the shamanism and hallucinogens moved back into the village. The noisy chanting and curing ceremonies would bring an overheated Pete running into the village, screaming and yelling recriminations at the bewildered participants, embarrassing them and intimidating them. Most important, it frightened them, for Pete was not beyond showing them paintings of Yąnomamö-like people being driven off a cliff into a fiery chasm below as punishment by "Dios" for evil doings, such as shamanism. The Yąnomamö do not understand the difference between a painting and a photograph, and Pete knew this.

I tried to ignore this as much as possible, for it angered me; I knew that it would lead to bitter arguments with the missionaries and perhaps, ultimately, to trouble with the Venezuelan officials. In general, with most of the missionaries, the problem was not too serious, for most of them were relatively patient with the Yąnomamö and employed more inconspicuous and subtle methods, and a few of them were downright humane—given their ultimate goal of destroying Yąnomamö religion.

Kąobawä himself had recently taken up the use of hallucinogenic drugs and participated in the daily rituals—something he had not done during my first stay in his village. It puzzled me at first, but it ultimately made sense when I began to understand the extent to which the Protestant missionaries were intimidating and threatening his village's religious activities. It seems clear to me now that his use of hallucinogens was a calculated act to put his prestige as a leader behind the efforts of the village curers, giving them confidence and informing the missionaries that he, as the headman, approved of what they were doing.

It was a hot afternoon, threatening to rain, and the mugginess was almost unbearable. I was working on Shamatari genealogical notes in my hut when Kąobawä and Rerebawä appeared at the door, urgently demanding to speak to me about "God-teri." (The Protestant missionaries are all called "Diosi-urihi-teri"—those from the Village of God.) I let them in and could immediately see that they were very upset and were sincerely turning to me for help. For the first time I realized that I had ignored a moral question and I felt ashamed for having done so. They were beginning to question the relative potency of their spirits versus the one from God-teri. They were also very angry with the missionary, for he had just burst into the village and broke up their chanting, denouncing them violently, and "threatening" them. I asked Kąobawä what he meant when he said "threaten." He held up two fingers and explained: "He told us that if we didn't stop chanting to the *hekura,* Dios would destroy us all with fire in this many *rasha* seasons!" I was almost sick with anger and resentment. He and Rerebawä went on to explain that Pete did this regularly, and it was beginning to anger them. They asked me, quite sincerely, if I believed that Dios would destroy them with fire if they chanted to the hekura and I told them "No." I interfered in the "work" of the missionary thereby, but I felt, somehow, morally better for having done so. I did not stop there. I stripped down to my bathing trunks and said, "Let's all go chant to the *hekura!*"

We walked into the village and word soon spread that Shąki was going to chant to his *hekura,* and his *shoabe* and *oshe* were going to instruct him. I had lived among the Yąnomamö long enough by then to know quite a bit about the *hekura,* their particular songs and how to attract them into the great cosmos that resides in the breast of all shamans, where the hekura are given their intoxicating magical beverage, *braki aiamo uku.* Then they become as one with their human receptacle, flying through the air, visiting distant places, going to the edge of the universe where the layer becomes "rotten" and other *hekura* are suspended from trees, attacking enemies and devouring the *möamo* portion of their souls, inflicting sickness and death on them, or curing their loved ones.

We walked silently over to *Kąobawä's* house, for that is where the daily religious activities were to begin. "Let me decorate you, my dear brother!" said Rerebawä softly, and I knelt on the ground while all my friends generously made their special feathers and decorations available to me so that I might become more beautiful and therefore more worthy to the *hekura.* Rerebawä took his *nara* pigment out and began painting my face and, after that, my chest. Kąobawä gave me a *wisha* tail for my head; Koaseedema loaned me his turkey scalp armbands; Makuwä gave me his special *werehi* feathers; Wakewä gave me ara tail feathers. Other men began decorating me also. The village was quiet, but a happy excitement seemed to pervade the muggy air; everyone knew that some sort of confrontation between me and the missionary was inevitable, and they were looking forward to it.

Rerebawä took out his *ebene* tube and ran a stick through it to clean it out. His father-in-law, the most prominent shaman in the village, took out a package of *hisiomö* powder and made it available to us. We cleaned off an area in front of Kąobawä's hammock, for that is where we planned to parade and dance as we called to the *hekura.* "Bei!" said Rerebawä, and I knelt forward to receive the end of his filled *ebene* tube into my nostrils. I closed my eyes, knowing that it would be painful, and he filled his chest with air and blew the magical green powder deep into my head in a long, powerful breath. I coughed and retched almost immediately, rubbing the back of my head violently to relieve the pain. "Bei!" he said again, and pushed the tube toward me. I took another blast, and felt the green mucus gush out of my other nostril as he blew. More pain, more retching, and still another blast, and another. The pain seemed to diminish each time, and I squatted on my haunches, waiting for the *hisiomö* to take effect. Others began to take the drug around me, and I gradually lost interest in them as my knees grew rubbery and my peripheral vision faded. "Ai!" I said, and Rerebawä gave me more. "Ai," I said again, and he smiled: "You've had enough for now," and pointed his tube toward someone else. I was beginning to feel light and felt as though I was filled with a strange power. Songs that I had heard the shamans from a dozen villages sing began to whirr through my mind and almost involuntarily my lips began to move, and I stood up and looked to Mavaca Mountain and began singing. Blips of light and spots flashed before me, and I began the methodical prancing that I had witnessed a thousand times. My arms seemed light and began moving almost of their own accord, rhythmically up and down at my sides, and I called to Fere-fereriwä and Periboriwä, hot and meat hungry *hekura,* and asked them to come into my chest and dwell within me. I felt great power and confidence, and sang louder and louder, and pranced and danced in ever more complex patterns. I took up Makuwä's arrows, manipulating them as I had seen Dedeheiwä and other shamans manipulate them, striking out magical blows, searching the horizon for *hekura,* singing and singing and singing. Others joined me and still others hid the machetes and bows, for I announced that Rahakanariwä dwelled within my chest and directed my actions, and all know that he caused men to be violent. We pranced together and communed with the spirits and shared something between us that was as undefinable as it was fundamentally human, a freedom to create with our minds the mystical universe that began with the beginning of time, something that seemed to be lodged in the back of imagination, something hidden and remote from consciousness, and I knew intimately why the shamans went daily through the pain of taking their drugs, for the experience was exhilarating and stimulating. But the freedom to give complete reign to the imagination was the most startling and pleasurable part, to shed my cultural shackles and fetters, to cease being a North American animal up to a point and be Yąnomamö or the part of me that I and all others have in common with Yąnomamö. Wild things passed through my mind. I thought of Lévi-Strauss' argument about the wisdom of looking for the nature of human logic and thought in primitive culture because it was not contaminated with layers of accumulated precepts and intellectual entanglements—and felt it was a marvelous idea. I could hear the initial strains of Richard Strauss' *Also Sprach Zarathustra.* I didn't care what the missionary, or the startled German visitor thought about me as he clicked off photos of the mad anthropologist going native. As my high reached ecstatic proportions, I remember Kąobawä and the others groaning as I broke the arrows over my head and pranced wildly with the shambles and splinters clutched tightly in my fists, striking the ground and enjoying the soft rain that had now begun to fall.

The village became suddenly silent, and through the haze I could see a stubby figure running into the village, screaming and shouting that the *hekura* were "filthy" and that Dios would "punish" us. And through the haze the stubby figure suddenly recognized the noisiest and most active sinner: it was the anthropologist. He gawked in astonishment at me and I grinned. My arm tropismatically described a smooth, effortless arc upward in his direction, and I noticed that it had the bird finger conspicuously and rigidly raised at him, and I felt the fire in my own eyes as I lined him up on it. Pious men do not curse—at least in their own language. He returned my signal with a Yąnomamö equivalent—a bared eyeball, exposed by pulling the eyelid down—and left in disgust. The others resumed their chanting, confident that if I didn't think Dios would destroy me in fire for chanting to the *hekura,* they shouldn't be too concerned either, for was I not myself a refugee from Dios-urihi-teri, and therefore knowledgeable about the machinations of Dios and the limitations on his power to destroy men with fire?

As the effect of the drug gradually wore off and the fatigue of my wild prancing began to be noticeable, I staggered over to Kąobawä's house and collapsed into one of the empty hammocks. Rerebawä's younger children happily surrounded me and looked at me with large, admiring eyes, gently stroking my arms and legs, inquiring whether I had seen the *hekura,* but not waiting for or expecting an answer. I wondered, in a shadowy daze, why Christian missionaries differed so strongly on simple issues, such as the putative "evil" or "innocence" of hallucinogenic snuff. Padre Cocco made no attempt to discourage it and felt that it was not only relatively harmless, but had some positive features—it gave the Yąnomamö hope when they concluded that they had been "bewitched" by enemies, a sickness that the nuns could not cure with penicillin or mercurochrome. Most of the Protestants, on the other hand, were passionately opposed to it and tried to abolish its use. I thought also about the expansion of our own culture and how politics and religion reinforced each other, as they had since the inception of the state; how the expansion of political authority often followed the proselytizing attempts of religious functionaries; how the destruction of cultures by dominant groups was expressed as moral or theological necessity; and how the sword accompanied or rapidly followed the Bible.

The Protestants, mostly American Evangelists, and the Catholics, mostly Italian or Spanish Salesians, differed radically. Indeed, the Protestants did not even regard the Catholics as Christians, for they "worshipped" idols and appeared not to oppose basic evils, such as drink, drugs, and polygamy. I recalled, with some amusement, an incident that Padre Cocco related to me. He had purchased a large quantity of manioc flour from a Ye'kwana Indian, within whose tribe both Catholic and Protestant missionaries had worked. He asked the

man if he were a Protestant. The man answered: "No, Padre, I'm a Catholic. I smoke, I drink, and I have three wives."

Where the Protestants impatiently attack the whole culture and try to bring salvation to all, including adults, the Catholics are more patient and focus on the children, partially accounting for Pete's reaction to hallucinogens and shamanism and Padre Cocco's rather humane attitude about drug use. (See Asch and Chagnon, 1974; and Chagnon and Asch, 1974b for a comparison, through documentary films, of the different strategies and philosophies of Catholic and Protestant missionaries among the Yąnomamö Indians.) As early as 1967 I was aware that the Salesians had taken a few Yąnomamö youths downstream to their elementary school near Puerto Ayacucho, and that a few boys had been sent to Caracas to their trade school. I was disturbed when I learned about this, mainly because of the health hazards this raised, but in 1972/1973 I was alarmed to learn that the Salesians established a boarding school for Yąnomamö children as young as 6 or 7 years at La Esmerelda, and began taking children from many different villages away from their families and sending them to this school for months at a time. While the school was near the Yąnomamö tribal territory, it nevertheless was almost inaccessible to the parents in many villages whose children were taken away. The parents were "compensated" for their temporary losses by well-calculated gifts, but in time they wanted desperately to have their children returned to them—but were denied. This, I feel, is a terrible price to ask a Yąnomamö family to pay to insure incorporation into the nation, but an effective and ancient practice used by other dominant cultures to subdue, modify, and incorporate obdurate ethnic minorities who differ in custom and who remain independent of the nation at large:

> The Inca kings also disposed that the heirs of lords and vassals should be brought up at court and reside there until they inherited their estates so that they should be well indoctrinated and accustomed to the mentality and ways of the Incas, holding friendly converse with

them so that later, on account of this familiar inter-course, they would love them and serve them with real affection. . . . The Inca kings sought thus to oblige their vassals to be loyal to them out of gratitude, or if they should prove so ungrateful that they did not appreciate what was done for them, at least their evil desires might be checked by the knowledge that their sons and heirs were at the capital as hostages and gages of their own fidelity (Garcilaso, 1966:404–405).

The Yąnomamö children will, of course, pass a significant and critical portion of their childhood in a foreign cultural environment and acquire a knowl-edge of its ways and expectations, and unknow-ingly forfeit a significant fraction of their own cul-tural heritage. I suspect that the emotional shock of living away from parents in such an exotic and insensitive environment will lead to serious devel-opmental and emotional problems, crises of iden-tity, and personality disturbances that could be avoided. As a parent and a human being, I would question the morality of a state organization that would remove or permit the removal of my children from me in order to indoctrinate them into beliefs that, by state definition, are superior to and more desirable than my own. I was sympathetic when Kąobawä told me, in 1975, that he would never again let the missionaries take his son, Ariwari, away from him and make him live at Esmerelda.

The adult Yąnomamö in villages where the Sale-sian missions are active, either because they have a mission post there or because they now visit regu-larly, are generally ignored insofar as intensive acculturation attempts are concerned. As one of the priests once mentioned, the effective incorporation and acculturation of the Yąnomamö is still a gener-ation off—the children are the key. Thus, the adults are relatively free to do what they please, but encouraged to adopt some of the mechanical habits of Westerners, such as the use of clothing to cover up thought-provoking sex organs and standards of personal hygiene—where, when, and how to blow one's nose and what to do with the mucus when strangers from Caracas are around—and a system of etiquette that is congenial to visitors.

Yąnomamö etiquette, I should add, is rather sophisticated in many respects and quite down to earth—and somewhat difficult to modify. A visitor to one mission awoke early one morning, stepped out of the house and ran into a Yąnomamö gentle-man who was headed off to the jungle with his bow and arrows. The Western visitor was favorably impressed with the Yąnomamö man's decorum and politeness, for as the man passed by, he smiled at the visitor, and said cheerfully: "Ya shii!" The visi-tor, reciprocally, returned the greeting, whereupon the Yąnomamö again smiled and said, "Habo. Ya baröwo." When he reported his exchange of social amenities to the missionary, he was a bit distraught at the translation: "I'm on my way to defecate." Response: "I have to defecate (also)." Reply: "Come along, then; I'll lead the way."

Mission posts are, for both Catholic and Protes-tant missionaries alike, something of showpieces of what their efforts have yielded in civilizing the Indi-ans. Clothing becomes an important concern, for missionaries are unhappy about obvious proclama-tions that nakedness reveals regarding the extent to which the Indians have not assumed a changed atti-tude about Western cultural amenities. Among the Yąnomamö, clothing serves two different functions. First, it serves a very important protective func-tion—it effectively prevents the Yąnomamö from being pestered constantly by the biting gnats and mosquitoes, both of which are very noisome at cer-tain times of the year along the major rivers. One must remember that the Yąnomamö traditionally avoid larger rivers and have only moved to them in the very recent past because of the allure of exotic trade goods, such as steel tools, fishhooks, fishline, matches, aluminum cooking pots, and other desir-able items. No Yąnomamö would tolerate the dis-comfort of living near the bug-infested rivers unless there were powerful incentives, such as trade goods, to attract them there. The second function of cloth-ing at the mission posts is essentially ideological from the missionaries' viewpoint: nakedness is assumed to be objectionable to Westerners. A sign of progress in the missions is the degree to which the "naked savages" visibly show their enlightenment by covering their private, and essentially sinful, parts. The Yąnomamö probably didn't realize that the naked body gives people sexy thoughts and evil ideas until Christianity covered it up on the argument that the nude body was sexy and thought-provoking. It conveniently crippled the patient and then provided the crutch. But nakedness to the Yąnomamö is a natural condition and many of the older people gladly accept the clothing given by the missionaries for the protective function it serves, but fail to see the "moral" dimension of the institution. I was amused one day as I passed through a mission village and stopped off to greet the priest and the nuns who lived there. As we were chatting, a Yąnomamö man and his wife strolled from the garden after their afternoon's work, he in a floppy hat and oversized khaki shirt and pants, she in her gingham smock. They came over to say hello, but their presence embarrassed the priest and nuns—he had cut the crotch out of his trousers because he apparently found the zipper cumbersome, and she had cut the bosom out of her smock so she could nurse her baby more conveniently. They stood there, grinning innocently and chatting happily—only their faces, their feet, and most of their sex organs visible. The baggy clothing seemed like a large frame around that which was not covered and to which the eye should be naturally attracted.

The younger people, especially young men, eagerly seek loincloths and rapidly acquire an attitude that a piece of cloth over the genitals is prestigious. More valuable than loincloths are bathing trunks or old underwear. These items are used as decorations at first, but later become almost "necessities," and any young man without either considers himself unfortunate and, the more accustomed he has become to them, embarrassed. I recall with some astonishment making first contact with the village of Mishimishimaböwei-teri and finding a young man in the village wearing a tattered pair of jockey undershorts! The villagers had never seen a non-Yąnomamö before my visit, but a pair of undies had managed to make it into the village via the trading network that also brought the broken and battered steel tools they acquired.

READING 6–2

"THUS ARE OUR BODIES, THUS WAS OUR CUSTOM": MORTUARY CANNIBALISM IN AN AMAZONIAN SOCIETY

Beth A. Conklin

Cannibalism is a stock topic among anthropologists—as it is a popular diversion among the general public. In Beth Conklin's article on body symbolism, cannibalism comes across as a major motif in Wari' beliefs, and we learn that in the past eating kinsfolk was not only a ritual activity enabling persons to say something about the nature of Wari' society it also provided the means by which grief could be lessened and memories of the dead gradually be made to lose their poignancy. Conklin's analysis, which is of a structural-function character, integrates these psychological attributes of cannibalism into the Wari' cosmology, in which ideas of human and animal regeneration are central features. The strength of this study lies in this very fact. We see exactly the meaning the ritual consumption of human flesh plays in Wari' religious thought, feature not always obvious in studies of cannibalism.

Indeed, so vaguely have anthropologists typically discussed cannibalism that one writer, W. Arens (1979) has ventured so far as to argue that there is no satisfactory evidence proving that cannibalism as a social activity—including ritual cannibalism—has ever been practiced by any society—ever. One point substantiating his argument is that nowhere in the history of anthropological fieldwork do you find an ethnographer stating that he or she has actually witnessed the act. The evidence consists merely of informants' assurances that at some time in the past—sometimes distant, occasionally recent—they or their ancestors consumed human flesh. A common variation on this evasion is to allege that neighboring societies practice cannibalism, but of course not the informant's!

Source: Beth A. Conklin "Thus are our Bodies, Thus was our Custom": Mortuary Cannibalism in an Amazonian Society, 1995. American Ethnologist. Volume 22. Pages 75–101. Reproduced by permission of the American Anthropological Association from American Ethnologist 22–1. Not for sale or further reproduction.

The Wari'[1] (Pakaa Nova) are an indigenous population of about 1,500 people who live in the western Brazilian rain forest, in the state of Rondônia near the Bolivian border. Until the 1960s, they disposed of nearly all their dead by consuming substantial amounts of corpses' body substances. All Wari' elders living today took part in or witnessed mortuary cannibalism, and their recollections offer an opportunity to view cannibalism from the perspectives of those who participated in it. This article explores the question of why cannibalism was the preferred means for disposing of the dead, emphasizing indigenous interpretations of the logic and meanings of cannibalism.

From a cross-cultural perspective, Wari' customs appear unusual in several respects. In most other societies, mortuary cannibalism involved the consumption of only small amounts of a corpse's body substances, which typically were ingested by a dead person's consanguineal kin.[2] Among the Wari', however, the dead person's affines ideally consumed all of the roasted flesh, brains, heart, liver, and—sometimes—the ground bones. Cannibalism was the preferred treatment for all Wari' corpses, except in a few circumstances in which bodies were cremated.

The Wari' practices both exocannibalism (the eating of enemies and social outsiders) and endocannibalism (the eating of members of one's own group) but considered the two forms of anthropophagy to have little in common. The eating of enemies, which will not be examined in detail here,[3] involved overt expressions of hostility: enemy body parts were abused and treated disrespectfully, and the freshly roasted flesh was eaten off the bone *ak karawa,* "like animal meat" (see Vilaça 1992:47–130). In contrast, the very different customs of mortuary cannibalism expressed honor and respect for the dead.

This article focuses on how mortuary cannibalism fit into Wari' experiences of grief and mourning. My approach traces themes emphasized by contemporary Wari' in reflecting on their past participation in cannibalistic funerals. The question "Why did you eat the dead?" tended to draw a limited range of responses. The most common reply was *"Je' kwerexi',"* "Thus was our custom."[4] This statement should be taken seriously; for many Wari', cannibalism was simply the norm; for reasons I discuss in this article, it was considered to be the most respectful way to treat a human body. Beyond this, when older people reflected on deeper, personal motives, they tended to link cannibalism to a process of achieving emotional detachment from memories of the dead: "When we ate the body, we did not think longingly [*koromikat*] about the dead much." Numerous middle-aged and elderly people—of both sexes and in various villages—independently offered the explanation that cannibalism altered memories and the emotions of grief in ways that helped them deal with the los of a loved one. Elders were bemused and at times rather irritated by anthropologists' singular obsession with the eating of bodies, for they insisted that cannibalism cannot be understood apart from the entire complex of mortuary rites and mourning behaviors aimed at reshaping emotional and spiritual relations between the living and the dead.

To understand cannibalism's role in mourning, I propose to show that Wari' practices reflected two concepts of widespread salience in lowland South America: the idea of the human body as a locus of physically constituted social relationships and social identity, and ideas about human-nonhuman reciprocity. These concepts merged in a yearlong series of traditional mourning rites that focused on actual and symbolic transformations of a dead person's body, from human to animal form. Cannibalism was a powerful element in a social process of mourning structured around images of ancestors' regeneration as animals with ongoing, life-supporting relations to their living relatives.

Wari' testimonies concerning the affective dimensions of cannibalism are unusual in the ethnographic literature, for we have few detailed accounts of cannibalism from the viewpoint of its practitioners. Most peoples who formerly practiced it no longer do so, leaving few individuals able or willing to speak to personal experiences of people-eating. Perhaps because of this, anthropological analyses of cannibalism have tended to focus mostly on the level of societal systems of meaning and symbolism. Cannibalism as praxis is poorly understood. This is particularly striking in the case of mortuary cannibalism: although it is, by definition, a cultural response to a fellow group member's death, we know little about how the socially constituted symbols of mortuary cannibalism relate to emotions and fit into individuals' lived experiences of coming to terms with a relative's death. Wari' recollections offer insights into one people's experiences.

In the anthropology of anthropophagy, mortuary cannibalism has received rather short shrift. The ethnographic and ethnohistorical literatures are dominated by accounts of the exocannibalism of enemies, which has been reported more frequently, and described in more depth, than endo- or mortuary cannibalism. Concomitant with this predominant focus on enemy-eating, universalist theories of cannibalism have tended to interpret anthropophagy as a fundamentally antisocial act. Psychogenic theorists from Freud (1981 [1913])) to Sagan (1974) have viewed all forms of people-eating as an expression of individuals' egocentric, oral-aggressive impulses. Recent social anthropological theories also have emphasized themes of antisociality. Lewis (1986:63–77) subsumed endo- and exocannibalism alike under a model in which consumption and ingestion reflect oral and genital aggression, and agonistic desires for dominance. Arens (1979) interpreted cannibalism as a universal symbol of barbarism, otherness, and inhumanity.

Mortuary cannibalism data have a special place in cannibalism studies, for the meanings associated with consuming one's fellows tend to be quite different from the motives for eating enemies. Mortuary cannibalism systems present the greatest potential challenge to interpretations of cannibalism as an antisocial act of aggression and domination, and the few ethnographic studies of mortuary cannibalism have tended to highlight its socially integrative dimensions. Analyses of several Melanesian systems have examined the role of mortuary cannibalism as part of the assemblage of cultural symbols and rituals whereby social groups defined and

reconstituted themselves after a death (Gillison 1983; Lindenbaum 1979; Meigs 1984; Poole 1983). Sanday's (1986) cross-cultural analysis emphasized the semantic complexity of anthropophagy and showed that cannibalism may symbolize not only evil and chaos but also social order and the regeneration of life-giving cosmic forces.

Recent general theories of mortuary cannibalism have considered only a limited set of cultural motivations, however, and have focused exclusively on ethnographic data from a single region, Melanesia. The diverse Melanesian endocannibalism systems expressed a variety of cultural meanings, but they tended to share in two main ideas: the assumption that cannibalism primarily benefits those who consume human substance; and the notion of an economy of biosocial substance in which cannibalism serves as a means of acquiring body substances, vital energies, or personal attributes contained in the dead person's corpse and of transferring them to those who eat it. These concepts have been widely assumed to characterize all endocannibalism systems. In the two most recent anthropological syntheses of cannibalism theory, Sanday stated that "[e]ndocannibalism recycles and regenerates social forces that are believed to be physically constituted in bodily substances or bones" (1986:7) and Lewis asserted that "the ritual consumption of parts of the human body enables the consumer to acquire something of the body's vital energy" (1986:73). Neither interpretation applies to the Wari' case.

Although both endo- and exocannibalism were widely practiced in lowland South America well into the 20th century (Dole 1974; Métraux 1947:22–25), the Amazonian literature has received little attention in recent North American and British discourse on cannibalism, although it has been of longstanding interest among Brazilian and French anthropologists. Some Amazonian endocannibalism reflected concepts similar to the Melanesian theme of recycling dead people's energies or attributes (see, for example, Acosta Saignes 1961: 161–162; Dole 1974:307; Erikson 1986:198; Reichel-Dolmatoff 1971:138–139), but many South American systems expressed quite different ideas, often involving notions of altering relations between body and spirit or between the living and the dead. Wari' informants universally denied that their consumption of either kin or enemies had anything to do with recycling substance, attributes, or energies from the dead to those who ate them.[5] They consistently represented cannibalism not as a boon for the eaters of human flesh but as a service for those who did not eat: the deceased and their close kin.

Wari' mortuary customs reflect complex social and symbolic systems about which a great deal more can be said than is possible in this article. I refer interested readers to the works of other anthropologists who have studied Wari' society (Mason 1977; Von Graeve 1972, 1989) and the puzzle of Wari' anthropophagy (Meireles 1986; Vilaça 1989, 1992). Meireles has examined the role of cannibalism in defining self-other relations in the construction of Wari' personhood an emphasized the symbolism of fire as mediator of human-nonhuman relations. Vilaça presented symbolic-structuralism interpretations of both exo- and endocannibalism, with special attention to affinal relations, festivals, and origin myths related to anthropophagy. Her analysis has focused on Wari' conceptions of the social universe as structured around oppositions and reciprocal exchanges between predators and prey. Symbolic oppositions between the categories of *wari'* ("we, people") and *karawa* ("animals") recur in Wari' ideology and rituals at multiple levels: humans vs. animals, Wari' vs. non-Wari', consanguines vs. affines, the living vs. the dead. Vilaça (1992:291) has emphasized that mortuary cannibalism symbolically associated the dead person with the category of prey and identified the living Wari' with the category of predators.

My analysis complements Vilaça's and Meireles's interpretations by situating cannibalism in relation to three other dimensions of Wari' experience: social processes of mourning, body concepts, and the regenerative imagery of ancestors' transformations into animals. To examine relationships among the social, symbolic, and ritual systems, I first describe the ethnographic context and mortuary rites and discuss why the Wari' case does not fit the major materialist and psychogenic models proposed to explain cannibalism elsewhere. I then examine social and psychological dimensions of Wari' body concepts to show why the corpse's destruction by cannibalism or cremation was considered essential. Finally, I explore Wari' ideas about human-animal relations that suggest an answer to the question of why the Wari' preferred cannibalism rather than cremation.

ETHNOGRAPHIC CONTEXT

The Wari' speak a language in the Chapakuran language family isolate. They entered permanent relations with Brazilian national society between 1956 and 1969, when the former national Indian agency, the S.P.I. (Serviço de Proteção aos Índios), sponsored a series of pacification expeditions that terminated Wari' autonomy. The Wari' now reside in eight major villages in indigenous reserves along tributaries of the Mamoré and Madeira Rivers in the municipality of Guajará-Mirim, Rondônia. Prior to the contact they had no canoes and inhabited interfluvial (*terra firme*) areas of the rain forest, away from the larger rivers. Today, as in the past, subsistence depends on slash-and-burn farming, hunting, fishing, and foraging. Maize is the principal staple crop, and hunting is the most socially valued food-getting activity.

Precontact villages typically were comprised of about thirty people living in several nuclear family households. Contemporary Wari' communities are administered by FUNAI (Fundação Nacional do Índio), the Brazilian government Indian agency, whose policies of population concentration and sedentarization have disrupted traditional settlement patterns and social organization. Today's villages, of 80–400 people, are located at nontraditional sites near major rivers or roads accessible to transportation to town.

Wari' society is staunchly egalitarian, and social relations are characterized by a high degree of flexibility. Leadership is ephemeral; there are no "chiefs," and no formal positions of political authority above the household level. Mason (1977) categorized Wari' kinship terminology as a Crow/Omaha–type system. Wari' kin groups are ego-centered bilateral kindreds; there are no lineages, and no internal segregation based on age grades or ceremonial activities. Precontact postmarital residence was flexible, with couples free to live near either spouse's bilateral kin after initial matrilocal bride service. Of central importance for understanding mortuary customs is the role of affinity as the strongest organizing principle in Wari' society. Alliances among families related by marriage[6] are important in food sharing, mutual aid, funeral duties and, in the past, were one basis for war alliances. Wari' society is by no means conflict-free, but most decision making is consensual, and the general tenor of social relations emphasizes mutuality and reciprocity among kin, affines, and allies.

The precontact Wari' were divided into named, territorially based subgroups (Oro Nao', Oro Eo', Oro At, Oro Mon, Oro Waram, and Oro Waram-Xijein) that were the largest social units with which individuals identified. A subgroup's members were committed to peaceful coexistence and cooperation in warfare and emergencies. Amicable relations among the villages in a subgroup were affirmed and maintained by festival exchanges, including celebrations called *hüroroin* and *tamara* that are models for the human-nonhuman alliance exchanges represented in mortuary cannibalism.

After the first peaceful contacts with outsiders were established in the Rio Dois Irmãos area in 1956, government (S.P.I.) agents and New Tribes missionaries witnessed several anthropophagous funerals. Most of the Wari' population entered contact in 1961–62. News of Wari' funerary cannibalism became public knowledge in early 1962, when an S.P.I. agent sold his eyewitness account to a São Paulo newspaper (*Folha de São Paulo* 1962). In response, a competing paper sent journalists to the Rio Negro-Ocaia contact site, where they photographed dismemberment and roasting at a child's funeral (de Carvalho 1962). Brazilian anthropologists and S.P.I. officials convinced the paper not to

publish these photographs and attempted to use the ensuing publicity to call public attention to the tragic situation of the recently contacted Wari' (Cruzeiro 1962:123–125).

Contact with the pacification teams introduced devastating epidemics of measles, influenza, tuberculosis, and other cosmopolitan diseases. Within two or three years of contact, approximately 60 percent of the precontact population was dead. Chronically ill, psychologically traumatized, and unable to hunt or plant crops, the survivors became extremely dependent on outsiders for food and medical care. Missionaries and government agents manipulated this dependency to put an end to cannibalism by threatening to withhold food and medicines from those who continued to eat the dead. They insisted that corpses be buried instead. At each of the three major contact sites, Wari' initially resisted this forced change to burial.

The deadly epidemics, however, created another reason to abandon cannibalism: traditional illness concepts could not explain the unfamiliar maladies, and so people listened when missionaries told them that the new diseases were spread by eating infected corpses. Wari' began burying people who died of illness (the great majority of early postcontact deaths), but, for a while, they continued to cannibalize those whose deaths were attributed to accidents, sorcery, and other nondisease causes. Families carried corpses into the forest, to be roasted away from outsiders' eyes. However, these efforts at deception ultimately failed, and by the end of 1962 or early 1962, nearly everyone had abandoned cannibalism altogether. (The exception was a group of about thirty Oro Mon who lived autonomously until 1969.) Today, all Wari' follow Western customs of buying corpses in cemeteries in the forest.[7]

No anthropologist has witnessed Wari' anthropophagy, and many data presented here are based on retrospective reconstructions. My primary sources are the testimonies of numerous older Wari' who say that they participated in or observed mortuary cannibalism. During two years of medical anthropological field work in 1985–87, I interviewed all 198 families in the communities of Santo

André, Ribeirao, Lage, Tanajura, and Rio Negro-Ocaia (85 percent of the total Wari' population). Interviews with adults of both sexes, aimed at collecting genealogies and mortality and morbidity histories, often led to discussions of personal experiences with relatives' deaths and funerals. I observed aspects of contemporary mourning behavior, including ritual wailing and the handling of a corpse, but no one died in a village where I was present, and I attended no burials or complete funerals. Santo André, a community of 190 people was my principal residence, and I discussed issues treated in this article with all the elders and many middle-aged people there. The most detailed information and insights came from several key informants: three men and two women between ages 60 and 75, two men in their 50s, and a man a woman in their early 40s. Most Santo André residents are decendants of the precontact Rio Dois Irmãos area population, and this article describes this group's practices, which differed only in minor details from other Wari' communities.

The Wari' do not conform to Arens' (1979) assertions that alleged cannibals seldom acknowledge eating anyone and that cannibalism is primarily a symbol of inhumanity and barbarism projected upon enemies, neighbors, and uncivilized "others." Wari' anthropophagy is not merely alleged by outsiders; Wari' themselves freely affirm practicing it in the past, even though they are aware that outsiders consider it barbaric. I found no one who denied that corpses customarily were cannibalized; numerous elders spoke openly of eating human flesh. Independent descriptions of particular funerals were internally consistent and corresponded to reports by New Tribes missionaries and S.P.I. agents who observed cannibalism in the early postcontact period. By any reasonable standards for the documentation of past events not witnessed by an ethnographer, there is no question that the Wari' ate their dead.

TRADITIONAL FUNERALS

Today, as in the past, funerals generally take place in the house of a senior kinsman of the deceased.[8]

The household's sleeping platform (or raised floor) is removed to permit mourners to crowd together under the palm-thatch roof. Two loosely defined groups have prescribed roles at funerals. The first is the *iri' nari*[9] ("true kin," or close sanguines and the spouse). Wari' define consanguinity in terms of shared blood and classify spouses as consanguines by virtue of sexual transfers of body fluids that create shared blood. Between spouses, it is said, "there is only one body" (*xika pe' na kwere*). Linked to the decreased by shared body substance, the iri' nari are the principal mourners. From the time of biological death until the body is disposed of, they remain nearest the corpse, holding it in their arms and crying.

The second group of mourners, *nari paxi* ("those who are like kin but are not truly related"), most properly consists of the dead person's own affines and affines of the deceased's close kin, but the term is extended to include all non-consanguines attending the funeral. Close affines are responsible for the work of funerals: female affines prepare maize *chicha* (a sweet, unfermented drink) and maize *pamonha* (dense, unleavened bread) to feed visitors, and male affines (ideally, the dead person's brothers-in-law or sons-in-law) serve as messengers summoning people to the funeral. They prepare and dispose of the corpse and funeral apparatus and look out for the welfare of emotionally distraught mourners.

In traditional funerals, the iri' nari sat together, apart from other mourners. In contemporary funerals, the spatial division is less marked, but close kin remain nearest the corpse. All mourners press close together around the body, leaning on each other's shoulders and wailing. Death wails are of several types, including wordless crying, the singing of kinship terms for the deceased, and a more structured keening called *aka pijim* ("to cry to speak"), in which mourners recount memories of the deceased, singing of shared experiences and the person's life history, deeds, and kindnesses. (On Amazonian ritual lament, see Briggs 1992; Graham 1986; Seeger 1987; Urban 1988, 1991.) From the moment of death until the funeral's end, everyone joins in a

ceaseless, high-pitched keening that sends a haunting mantra of collective grief reverberating off the
surrounding forest.

The dead person's humanity and social connections are repeatedly affirmed in funeral actions
directed at the corpse itself, which is the constant
focus of attention. Corpses are never left to lie
alone. From the moment of death until the body is
disposed of, grieving kin constantly cradle the
corpse in their arms, hugging it, pressing their own
bodies against it. Desire for physical contact can be
so intense that, according to several Santo André
residents, there was a funeral a few years ago where
the corpse was in danger of being pulled apart by
distraught kin struggling to embrace it. Finally, a
senior kinsman enforced order by mandating that
only one person at a time could hold the body.

Numerous funeral actions express mourners' self-
identification with the dead person's physical state
and desires to join the deceased in death. Any loss of
consciousness, such as fainting, is considered a form
of death. In one common funeral practice, close relatives "die" (*mi'pin*) by lying one on top of the other,
in stacks of three or four people with the corpse on
top. When someone faints from the suffocating press
of bodies, he or she is pulled out of the pile and someone else joins the pile, in a process repeated again
and again. In a 1986 funeral, people piled into the
homemade coffin, embracing the corpse on top.

In traditional funerals, the male affine helpers constructed the ritual firewood bundle and roasting rack.
Ideally, these were made of roofbeams, decorated
with feathers and painted with red annatto (*urucú,
Bixa orellana*). A beam was taken from each house in
the dead person's village, leaving the thatched roofs
sagging in visible expression of death's violation of
the community's integrity. Funerals for infants were
less elaborate; regular, undecorated firewood was
used. When preparations were completed, the helpers
lit the fire, spread clean mats on the ground, and dismembered the body, using a new bamboo arrow tip.
Internal organs were removed first, and the heart and
liver were wrapped in leaves to be roasted. Body parts
considered inedible, including the hair, nails, genitals,
intestines, and other entrails, were burned. The
helpers then severed the head, removed the brains, cut

the limbs at the joints, and placed the body parts on
the roasting rack. Young children's body parts were
wrapped in leaves in the manner used to roast small
fish and soft foods.

Several elders recalled that the most emotionally
difficult event in a funeral was the moment when
the corpse was taken from its relatives' arms to be
dismembered. As the body was cut, wailing and
hysterical expressions of grief reached a fevered
pitch. Up to this moment, funeral activities had
been dominated by mourners' expressions of physical and affective attachments to the dead person's
body. Dismemberment represented a radical alteration of the corpse and mourners' relations to it, a
graphic severing of the attachments represented in
the body. According to these elders, it was dismemberment, not cannibalism, that provoked the most
intense emotional dissonance. Once the corpse had
been cut, eating it was considered the most respectful possible treatment, for reasons discussed below.

The dead person's close consanguine (iri' nari)
did not eat the corpse. Consumption of a close consanguine or spouse's flesh is strongly prohibited,
because eating a close relative (with whom one
shared body substance) would be tantamount to
eating one's own flesh, or autocannibalism. It is
believed to be fatal.[10]

The nari paxi, affines and other non-kin, were
responsible for consuming the corpse; they are
sometimes referred to as *ko kao'* ("those who ate").
In a married person's funeral, those who consumed
the body typically included the dead person's
spouse's siblings, spouse's parents, spouse's parents' siblings, and the deceased's children's spouses,
as well as these individuals' own close consanguines. Unmarried people typically were eaten by
their siblings' spouses, siblings' spouses' siblings'
their parents' siblings' spouses, and these individuals' close kin. Thus, Wari' cannibalized members of
the families from which their bilateral consanguines
had taken marriage partners. Meireles (1986) noted
that cannibalism restrictions generally coincided
with incest prohibitions.

Cannibalism was a primary obligation of affinity. Adult men were obliged to eat their close
affines; refusal to do so would have insulted the

dead person's family. Women were not required to participate in cannibalism but did so at their own discretion.[11] Distinctions of generation, age, or gender were largely irrelevant: male and female adults and adolescents consumed corpses of all ages and both sexes. Men's and women's corpses were treated almost identically.

Roasting usually commenced in the late afternoon and eating usually began at dusk. The dead person's closest kin divided the well-roasted brains, heart, and liver into small pieces, placed the pieces on clean mats, and called the others to begin eating. The affines (nari paxi) did not descend greedily upon the flesh but hung back, crying and expressing reluctance to eat; only after repeated insistence by the dead person's close kin (iri' nari) did they accept the flesh. The iri' nari then prepared the other body parts by removing the flesh from the bones and dividing it into small pieces. They usually arranged these on a mat along with pieces of roasted maize bread (pamonha); in some funerals, they placed the flesh in a conical clay pot and handed pieces to the eaters, cradling the pot in their laps in the affectionate position used to hold someone's head in repose or during illness. In marked contrast to the aggressive, disrespectful treatment of enemies' flesh in exocannibalism, funeral eaters did not touch the flesh with their hands but held it delicately on thin splinters like cocktail toothpicks. They ate very slowly, alternately crying and eating. There appears to have been no special significance attached to ingesting particular body parts, and no pattern determining who ate which portions.

The ideal was to consume all of the flesh, heart, liver, and brains; in practice, the amount actually eaten depended on the degree of the corpse's decay. It is considered imperative that corpses not be disposed of (by cannibalism, cremation, or burial) until all important relatives have arrived at the funeral, seen the body, and participated in the wailing eulogies. The length of time before a body was roasted traditionally varied according to the dead person's age, status, and social ties: the older and more socially prominent the deceased, the longer the delay in roasting. Before the contact, when villages were scattered over a wide territory, most adults were not roasted until two or three days after death, when decay was well-advanced.

It was considered important to consume as much flesh as possible. When, however, flesh was too putrid to stomach—as it usually was in the case of adult corpses—the eaters forced themselves to swallow small pieces from various body parts, then cremated the rest. The ideal of total consumption was realized mainly in funerals for infants and young children who, having few social ties of their own, were roasted within a day or so of their deaths and eaten entirely. Complete consumption also appears to have occurred for some terminally ill elders whose relatives gathered and commenced wailing long before biological death. In most adult and adolescent funerals, however, most of the flesh probably was burned rather than eaten.

Consumption of the corpse continued until dawn, at which time any remaining flesh was cremated. Treatment of bones varied. Sometimes they were ground into meal, mixed with honey, and consumed. In other cases, especially in the Rio Dois Irmãos area, the bones were burned, pulverized, and buried. In all cases, the clay pots, mats, roasting rack, and funeral fire remains were burned, pounded to dust, and buried in situ by the male affine helpers. The helpers then swept the earth to eradicate all traces of the funeral and replaced the household sleeping platform over the spot where the ashes were buried.

THE QUESTION OF HUMAN FLESH AS FOOD

Before examining what motivated Wari' mortuary cannibalism, it is useful to clarify what did not. The idea that institutionalized cannibalism may be motivated by needs for dietary protein was proposed by Hamer (1977) to explain Aztec human sacrifice and has been elaborated by Harris (1977, 1985: 199–234). Wari' practices involved the ingestion of significant quantities of flesh and ground bones, and the adults who consumed them would have gained some nutrients, notably protein and calcium. Two factors nevertheless militate against a materialist interpretation of the Wari' system.

First, there is no reason to assume that the pre-contact population suffered significant food shortages. Wari' controlled a large territory with low population density and abundant game, fish, and Brazil nut resources. Elders assert that hunger was infrequent, although then, as now, there were days without meat or fish. Missionaries present at the first contacts observed no signs of malnutrition, and the assumption that the precontact Wari' did not suffer protein shortages is consistent with biomedical studies of similar groups. Although protein-scarcity hypotheses were hotly debated in Amazonian cultural ecology from the late 1960s through the early 1980s, researchers have never documented protein deficiency in relatively undisturbed native Amazonian populations living in circumstances similar to the precontact Wari'. On the contrary, studies have found adequate or more than adequate protein intake (Berlin and Markell 1977; Chagnon and Hames 1979; Dufour 1983; Milton 1984). My own data on household diets in two communities, and anthropometric assessments from four communities, indicate that contemporary Wari' diets are generally adequate, even with the depletion of game and fish near today's larger, more sedentary villages.

A second argument against nutritional motivations for Wari' cannibalism is that much potentially edible flesh was burned rather than eaten, with no attempt to preserve it for later consumption. Even in cannibalizing enemies, Wari' did not maximize protein acquisition: warriors usually took only the head and limbs, discarding the fleshy trunk. Clearly, social considerations took precedence over biological functionalism in shaping Wari' practices.

THE QUESTION OF HOSTILITY

Interpretations of cannibalism as an act of hostility are a staple of Western psychoanalytic theory (see Freud 1981 [1913]; Sagan 1974), and the fact that Wari' ate their affines raises the question of whether cannibalism expressed or mediated affinal tensions. Like Freudians, Wari' recognize that eating can express hostility, as it did in the aggressive consumption of enemy flesh. My informants, however, universally rejected the notion that mortuary customs expressed any form of overt, covert, or displaced hostility. They insisted that hostility has no place at funerals; individuals on bad terms with the deceased are barred from attending, as reportedly happened a few years ago when a man was ordered away on the grounds that "you did not love him, it is not good that you come here." In addition, Wari' emphasized that funeral "table manners" sharply differentiated affinal cannibalism from acts of eating that did express aggression. As discussed below, eating has multiple cultural connotations and can express respect for that which is eaten.

Sagan (1974:28) has dismissed the possibility of cannibalism as an act of respect or compassion for the deceased, asserting that such ideas are a mere facade for covert ambivalence, hostility, and sadistic urges rooted in resentments against the dead for having abandoned the living.[12] It is difficult to assess retrospectively, the question of whether Wari' mortuary cannibalism expressed aggression or hostility, but Wari' practices and discourse on cannibalism offer little support for this interpretation. Affinal tensions appear no greater among the precontact Wari' than in many noncannibalistic societies. Wari' express few expectations of inherent affinal conflict; ideally, and to a large extent in practice, they treat affinity as a matter of amity and mutually beneficial reciprocity. Today, as in the past, most marriages are arranged or approved by the families involved, who are careful to establish and perpetuate ties only to families with whom they enjoy positive relations. Affines call each other by consanguineal kin terms (Vilaça 1989:41–45), exchange meat and fish frequently, and offer aid in emergencies. When conflicts among affines arise, there are cultural mechanisms for dealing with them, including ritual fights (*mixita*) and discussions between family heads.

AFFINITY AND EXCHANGE

Vilaça has emphasized the importance of mortuary cannibalism as a marker of Wari' affines' relations to one another: "The funeral rite . . . reveals, through the opposition between those who eat together [*comensais*] and those who do not [*não-comensais*], the opposition cognates/affines. In the interior of Wari' society, cannibalism constructs and identifies affinity" (1992:293).

Vilaça (1992:293) also observed that Wari' affinal cannibalism reflected a recurrent theme in South American mythology, identified by Lévi-Strauss in *The Raw and the Cooked* (1969): the characterization of affines (the "takers" of women) as real or potential cannibal prey. Besides the Wari', the Yanomami also practice affinal cannibalism, consuming their affines' ground bones (Albert 1985). Sixteenth-century Tupinambá exocannibalism involved another kind of affinal cannibalism: a war captive was married to a Tupinambá woman (making him an affine to her kin) before being killed and eaten (Staden 1928[1557]). In the cosmology of the Araweté of central Brazil (who bury their dead), cannibalism is seen as a transformative mechanism for creating affinal ties between humans and divinities: when Araweté die, the gods consume the human spirits (making them into beings like themselves), then rejuvenate and marry them (Viveiros de Castro 1992). Viveiros de Castro has observed that among the Araweté, Tupinambá, Yanomami, and Pakaa Nova (Wari'), cannibalism "links affines or transforms into affines those whom it links" (1992:259).[13]

Wari' affinal cannibalism might suggest a Lévi-Straussian model of exchanges of cooked meat (human flesh) for "raw" (virgin, fecund) women given in marriage (Lévi-Strauss 1969). As in many societies, eating is a Wari' metaphor for sexual intercourse, and there are obvious parallels between affinal exchanges of human flesh in funerals and the frequent exchanges of meat (which men give to female affines) and fish (which women give to male affines) that mark affinity in everyday life. From a structuralist perspective, Wari' mortuary cannibalism resonates with exchanges of meat and marriage partners, but Wari' do not see it that way. Everyone with whom I raised this issue rejected an equation of cannibalism with exchanges of sexual partners or

food; some found the suggestion insulting. Sexual and reproductive imagery has little place in Wari' mortuary practices, in marked contrast to its prominence in many other societies' mortuary rites (Bloch and Parry (1982), and in Melanesian endo-cannibalism practices linked to elaborate ideas about male and female body substances (see Gillison 1983; Poole 1983).

From an emic point of view, what was important in cannibalistic Wari' funerals was not the exchange of substance (human flesh) but the exchange of services. Disposal of the body is a primary obligation of affinity, a service performed out of respect for the dead person and his or her family. When asked why it was the affines who ate the corpse, Wari' elders invariably replied that the affines ate it because somebody had to eat it, and the dead person's consanguines (iri' nari) could not do so (because of the prohibition against eating the flesh of someone related to oneself by shared biological substance). In addition, a number of people asserted that one simply does not feel like eating anything when grieving intensely. Eating, particularly meat-eating, expresses happiness and social integration. Symbolic oppositions between sadness and oral activity (eating, drinking, singing, shouting) are numerous: adults eat little during close kin's illnesses, consume nothing at their funerals, and eat little while mourning. People considered it irrational to suggest eating flesh at a close relative's funeral.

By Wari' logic, these cultural assumptions definitively precluded cannibalism by consanguines. The task thus fell to affines, who were the only clearly defined social group that had close social ties to the dead person's family but did not share their intimate biological and affective ties to the deceased.[14] Affinal cannibalism was a matter of pragmatism.

It was also a matter of politics. Mortuary services are central in marking, strengthening, and reconstituting affinal ties after a death. Funerals draw extended families together as does no other event, and they are the most prominent occasion (aside from mixita fights) when affines act as discrete groups in complementary opposition to one another. In fulfilling mortuary obligations, including disposal of the corpse, Wari' families linked by marriage affirm continuing commitments that transcend the lifetime of any individual member.

If one accepts this indigenous view of the disposal of corpses (whether by burial, cannibalism, or cremation) as a service rendered to the family of the deceased, assigning this task to affines does not appear particularly unusual cross-culturally. In native Amazonian societies, affines perform burial and other funeral duties among the Cashinahua (Kensinger, in press), Canela (W. Crocker, in press), and Shavante (Maybury-Lewis 1974:281). Among the Mundurucú (Murphy 1960:72) and Kagwahiv (Kracke 1978:13), these tasks fall to members of the opposite moiety, the group from which the dead person's moiety takes marriage partners. Wari' mortuary cannibalism fit this pattern of delegating mortuary tasks to affines and reflected the associations between affinity and cannibalism found in other lowland South American societies' myths and cosmologies. But this does not explain why Wari' actually *ate* their affines, whereas other peoples with similar conceptual systems did not. In this article, the question to be addressed is not why the Wari' ate their affines, but why cannibalism was the preferred treatment for human corpses.

EATING AS AN ACT OF RESPECT

Pleasing the dead by consuming their bodies is a recurrent theme in Wari' discussions of mortuary cannibalism: the dead wanted to be eaten, or at least cremated, and not to have done either would have given offense. For dying individuals, the idea of being incorporated into fellow tribesmembers' bodies apparently had considerably more appeal than the alternative of being left to rot in the ground alone.[15] One man told of his great-aunt (FFZ) who, on her deathbed, summoned him and his father (normally expected to cry rather than eat at her funeral) and asked them, as a favor, to join in consuming her body. In contrast to Western views of eating as an act of objectification and domination of the thing consumed, eating can express respect and

sympathy in Wari' culture, especially in contrast to the alternative of burial. The ground is considered "dirty" and polluting. Adults who take pride in their bodies do not sit in the dirt, ritual objects must not touch the earth, and people avoid spilling food on the ground. These values influence attitudes towards burial in the earth, which informants often described as not only dirty, but also "wet" and "cold." Respectful treatment for human remains is dry and warm; the only traditional space for respectful burial was beneath household sleeping platforms, where small fires burned almost constantly, keeping the earth warm as well as dry. This is where funeral ashes were interred in the past and where placentae and miscarried fetuses continue to be buried. Before the contact, burial in the forest expressed dishonor and normally occurred in only one context: if a woman suffered multiple stillbirths or neonatal deaths, her family might request a male affine to bury her dead infant in an anthill or in wet earth beside a stream to discourage her future babies from dying and risking similarly unpleasant treatment.

In contrast to the disrespect manifest in burial, eating can be a sympathetic act, as shown in this story about the Maize Spirit (*Jaminain Mapak*) told by a Santo André man. The story explains why one should not leave maize lying on the ground:

> Long ago, a man was walking to his field carrying a basket of maize seeds to plant. A maize kernel fell to the ground on the path. The man did not see it and went on. The maize seed began to cry like a child. Another man came along and found it crying on the ground. He picked it up and *ate* it. In doing so, he *saved* it, showing that he felt sympathy [*xiram pa'*] for it. The man who ate the seed planted his field and it yielded great quantities of maize. The man who had left the seed on the ground planted his field, but nothing grew.

This parable demonstrates Wari' ideas that abandoning a spirit-being to lie on the forest floor connotes disrespect, whereas eating it expresses respect. Eating can be an act of compassion that pleases the thing consumed so that it bestows abundance on the eater.

Similar ideas about eating as an expression of respect for the eaten are evident in food taboos associated with *jami karawa,* animals whose spirits have human form (see Conklin 1989:336–350). Spirits never die, and when a hunter kills a jami karawa animal, its spirit assumes a new animal body. However, animal spirits cannot complete their transitions to new physical bodies as long as portions of their former bodies remain. To avoid provoking spirits' wrath, one must quickly roast and eat jami karawa. Animal spirits are offended by the killing and disrespectful treatment of their bodies, not by the eating of their flesh. On the contrary, eating demonstrates respect, especially in contrast to the alternative of abandoning uneaten body parts on or in the ground.

Several funeral customs expressed these values of honoring the dead by preventing their body substances from being lost to the earth. When corpses were cut, a close kinsman of the deceased sometimes lay face down, supporting the corpse on his back during the butchering, so that its fluids would spill onto his own body rather than onto the ground. Similarly, elders recalled that young children's corpses had much fat that dripped as they roasted; to prevent it from falling into the fire, a child's grieving parents and grandparents would catch the fat in a clay pot and smear it over their own heads and bodies as they cried. Mortuary cannibalism expressed similar compassion for the dead by saving their body substances from abandonment to the earth and, instead, incorporating them into a living person's body.

In the early postcontact period, many Wari' found the forced change to burial repulsive. One Santo André man told of his father's death, which occurred soon after outsiders had put an end to cannibalism. Unhappy with the prospect of being buried, the dying man requested that, as an approximation of traditional practices, his corpse be dismembered and the pieces placed in a large ceramic cooking pot to be buried by his affines. Even today, burial continues to be a source of covert dissatisfaction among some elders, who still view burial as a less loving way to treat a human body than cannibalism or cremation. They consider the body's persistence prob-lematic for close kin, whose attachments to the dead require attenuation and transformation.

ATTACHMENTS TO THE SOCIALLY CONSTRUCTED BODY

Wari' view the human body as a primary nexus of kinship, personhood, and social relations. Kinship is defined as physically constituted in shared body substance (especially blood) that is created by parental contributions to conception and gestation and augmented by interpersonal exchanges of body fluids. As individuals mature, each major change in social status (at female puberty, male initiation, marriage, childbirth, enemy killings, and shamanic initiation) is believed to involve corresponding changes in blood and flesh induced by incorporating another individual's body substances (Conklin 1989:177–239). As in numerous other lowland South American societies, ideas about the physical bases of social relatedness reflect heightened recognition of individuals' interdependence as social actors (see J. Crocker 1977; da Matta 1979:105; Melatti 1979:65–68; Seeger et al. 1979; Turner 1980). Interpersonal attachments are conceived as shared physical substance that links individual body-selves in an organic unity transcending the boundaries of discrete physical forms.

Not only are kinship and social status physically constituted, but many cognitive and emotional processes are conceptualized as organic changes in the heart and blood, and behavior is considered to be rooted in the body (see Kensinger 1991 on similar concepts among the Cashinahua). This is reflected in the term *Kwerexi*, which means "body" or "flesh" but also means "custom," "habit," and "personality." A stock Wari' response to the ethnographer's plea to know "Why do you do that?" is a shrug and the phrase "*Je' kwerexi*," "Thus is our custom," or, translated literally, "Thus are our bodies (or flesh)." Wari' consider spirits to have few personality qualities, and they account for individual behavioral differences mostly with reference to differences in body substance, not differences in mind or spirit. Peoples' habits, eccentricities, and personality quirks are explained with "His flesh is like that" (*Je' kwerekun*) or "That's the way her body is" (*Jé kwerekem*). The phrase is not merely metaphorical but reflects ideas of the physical body as a major locus of personal identity.

Westerners tend to assume that, with death, the loss of spirit or consciousness takes away most of a person's important qualities and leaves behind an empty, almost meaningless, body shell. In contrast, Wari' corses are potent embodiments of identity, social relations, and interperson bonds. Body transformations were a primary symbolic focus in traditional mortuary rites that aimed to restructure relations between the dead and the living.

DETACHMENT AND DESTRUCTION

Gradual detachment from thinking about and remembering the dead is considered a desirable social goal, for prolonged sadness (*tomi xaxa*) is believed to endanger individual health and productivity. The negative psycho-emotional process of grieving is described with the verb *koromikat,* which refers to the negative experience of nostalgia: missing, remembering, and thinking longingly about a lost or distant object (usually a kinsperson, lover, or friend). Wari' emphasize vision and hearing as primary sources of knowledge and stimuli to memory. Because the sight of material objects evokes memories, they consider it essential to destroy or transform all tangible reminders of the dead. They burn a dead person's house and personal possessions and burn, discard, or give away crops planted by the deceased. Less-easily destroyed modern possessions, such as kettles, machetes, and shotguns, usually are given to nonrelatives. Neighbors often change their houses' appearance by altering doorways and paths, and close kin cut their hair. People traditionally have avoided using dead people's names or kin referents, although in speaking to outsiders they have recently relaxed name avoidances.

The cultural rationale for these practices reflects two concerns: banishing ghosts, and removing stimuli that evoke memories of the dead.[16] Vilaça has noted:

According to the Wari', the destruction by fire of all reminders of the deceased is, in the first place, a protection against the sadness that is felt upon seeing something that belonged to the deceased or that was touched, used or made by him; but it is also a way to avoid the coming of the ghost. [1992:228]

These dual concerns are consistent with the two primary objectives identified in cross-cultural analyses of death rites: to remove the deceased from the world of the living to the symbolic world of the dead, and to facilitate survivors' acceptance of the death and the consequent alteration of social life without the dead person (Bloch and Parry 1982:4). With regard to separating the dead from the living, the destruction of material traces is believed to lessen the tendency of ghosts (*jima*) to return to earth. Jima generally do not cause illness, but they do frighten people, and, in the days following a death, the jima of the recently deceased may try to carry kin away for companionship in death. Destroying possessions and altering appearances confuse jima so that, unable to find their former homes and companions, they return to the otherworld of the dead. Some people also suggested that the smoke surrounding roasting corpses obscured and confused the vision of jima who returned during their own funerals.

Banishing spirits, or liberating spirts from their physical bodies, has been cited as a motive for cannibalism in some other lowland South American societies (Albert 1985; Clastres 1974:316; Dole 1974:306; Ramos 1990:196; Zerries 1960). Meireles asserted that the explanation for Wari' cannibalism was "based in the idea that the dead person's soul must be banished, at the risk of afflicting the living" (Meireles 1986:427). Vilaça (1992:233, 243, 262) has interpreted roasting as a dissociative mechanism required for spirits' liberation from their bodies and full transition to the afterlife.[17] this idea is clear in Wari' food taboos that require quick consumption of certain game animals to liberate the animal spirts from their bodies (Conklin 1989:345–346; Vilaça 1992:70), but it appears to be of limited relevance in explaining cannibalism. None of my informants spontaneously suggested that eating the dead liberated spirits or prevented their return. Rather, when asked if it had that effect, some agreed that it might. Others insisted that cannibalism had nothing to do with banishing spirits. As evidence, they cited the fact, which no one disputed, that the ghosts (jima) of people who are buried today do not return to wander the earth any more frequently than those who were cannibalized or cremated.

As Vilaça (1989:378) noted, the desire to dissociate body from spirit fails to explain the preference for cannibalism over cremation, except insofar as Wari' view the acts of cooking and eating as implicit in the act of making fire.[18] Because Wari' view cremation and cannibalism as equally effective in separating spirits from their bodies and from the world of the living, the preference for cannibalism must be explained in other terms.

REMEMBERING AND THE BODY

Wari' discussions of reasons for destroying corpses and possessions emphasized the need to remove reminders in order to help mourners stop dwelling on thoughts of the dead. In a cross-cultural study of grief and mourning, Rosenblatt et al. suggested that tie-breaking and "finalizing" acts (such as ghost fears, taboos on names of the dead, and destruction of personal property) facilitate survivors' transitions to new social roles:

> [I]n a long-term relationship such as marriage, innumerable behaviors appropriate to the relationship become associated with stimuli (sights, sounds, odors, textures) in the environment of the relationship. When death . . . makes it necessary to treat the relationship as ended and to develop new patterns of behavior, these stimuli inhibit the change, because they elicit old dispositions. To facilitate change, tie-breaking practices that eliminate or alter these stimuli seem to be of great value.[1976:67–68]

Battaglia has highlighted the cultural value ascribed to acts of "forgetting as a willed transformation of memory" (1991:3) in Melanesian mortuary rites that transform materially constituted aspects of the dead person's former social identity and replace them with new images. The importance that Wari' ascribe to the destruction of reminders and processual alteration of memories and images of the dead was evident in the ritual called *ton ho'* ("the sweeping"), practiced today in an attenuated form (see Vilaça 1992:227–229; for parallels among the Canela, see Crocker and Crocker 1994:121). For several months after a death, senior Wari' consanguines, especially kin of the same sex as the deceased, make repeated trips to the forest to seek out all places associated with the dead person's memory: the place where a hunter made a blind to wait for deer, sites where a woman fished or felled a fruit tree, a favorite log where the dead person liked to sit. At each spot, the kinsperson cuts the vegetation in a wide circle, burns the brush, and sweeps over the burned circle. Elders said that, while doing this, they thought intensely about the dead person, recalling and honoring events of his or her life. Afterward, the burning and sweeping have definitively altered sentiments associated with each place so that "there is not much sadness there."

The imperative to destroy tangible elements traditionally extended to the corpse itself. Given the strength of Wari' ideas about the body's social construction and the physical bases of social relatedness, it is understandable that corpses are powerful reminders.[19] A number of individuals commented that today, when people are buried rather than eaten, their thoughts return again and again to images of the body lying under its mound of earth. A Santo André father who had recently buried a young son tried to explain this to me, saying:

> I don't know if you can understand this, because you have never had a child die. But for a parent, when your child dies, it is a very sad thing to put his body in the earth. It is cold in the earth. We keep remembering our child, lying there, cold. We remember and we are sad. In the old days when the others ate the body, we did not think about [koromikat] his body much. We did not think about our child so much, and we were not so sad.

The emotional potency of mourners' subjective attachments to the dead and their physical bodies is one of the keys to understanding Wari' cannibalism.[20]

In traditional funerals, mourners' dramatic manifestations of physical identification with the dead person's body were followed by a dramatic sundering of these bonds, beginning with the corpse's dismemberment. Cutting and roasting or cremating the body initiated a processual disassembling of physical objectification of social identity and social relations. Although Wari' considered cannibalism and cremation equally effective ways of severing ties between human bodies and spirits, they considered cannibalism more effective in attenuating affective attachments. Cannibalism initiated and facilitated the construction of a new relationship between the living and the dead by evoking images of the dead person's regeneration in animal form, and human-animal reciprocity, in which endocannibalism was the mythic balance to human hunting.

PREDATION AND RECIPROCITY

Wari' myth traces the origin of endocannibalism to the establishment of mutual predator-prey relations between hunters and animals. A story called *Pinom* is a variation of a widespread Amazonian mythic theme of the origins of cooking fire (see, for example, Lévi-Strauss 1969; Overing 1986; Wilbert and Simoneau 1990:111–133). (For analysis of the Wari' *Pinom* myth, see Meireles 1986; Vilaça 1989, 1992.) The Wari' version tells how mortuary cannibalism originated as the consequence of the theft of fire, which originally was possessed by an avaricious old woman who ate children raw. Violating Wari' principles of egalitarian sharing, this cannibal-crone let people temporarily use her fire only in exchange for large payments of firewood and fish. Without fire, Wari' could not farm, could not roast and eat maize or fish (most game animals did not yet exist), and had to subsist on raw forest fruits and hearts of palm.

Finally, two boys managed to outwit the old woman and steal her fire. They and the other Wari' escaped by climbing a liana into the sky, but the old woman pursued them. At the last moment, a piranha came to their rescue and cut the vine. The cannibal-crone fell into her own fire below, and from her

burning body emerged the carnivores: jaguars, ocelots, and *orotapan* (an unidentified carnivore, probably wolf or fox). In Wari' cosmology, jaguars not only kill and eat humans but also transform themselves into other animal spirits that cause illness by capturing and eating human spirits. Other animals, including birds, monkeys, deer, and tapir, originated when the Wari' turned into animals in order to jump from the sky back to earth, and some decided to remain animals. People and animals thus share a common origin. The myth highlights Wari' ideas about the balance of human-animal opposition: game animals came into existence, but people became prey for jaguars and animal spirit predators.

The origin of endocannibalism is attributed to parallel events in this myth's second part. The two boys turned into birds to carry the fire to earth, but a man named Pinom killed them and selfishly kept the fire to himself. Others could only watch hungrily while Pinom's family alone was able to cook food. Finally, a shaman tricked Pinom, captured the cooking fire, and shared it with everyone, thereby allowing the Wari' to become a hunting and farming society. Outwitted and enraged, Pinom told the Wari': "Now you will have to roast your children!"

This is interpreted as the mythic origin of endocannibalism, even though Pinom did not specify eating the dead, or affines' roles in it. Although most Wari' are now familiar with Christian concepts of sin and retribution, no one interpreted Pinom's dictum as a terrible punishment for human misdeeds. Instead, informants saw endocannibalism as a natural balance to humanity's acquisition of fire: the price for gaining fire to roast (and eat) animals was to be roasted (and eaten) oneself.

Reciprocity in relations between humans and animals is a common cross-cultural concept, especially among native American people whose survival depends on hunting and fishing. Sanday identified this idea as a recurrent theme in native North American myths about the origins of cannibalism and suggested that it reflected the following logic: "There is a reciprocal relationship between the eater and the eaten. Just as animals are hunted, so are humans; whoever wants to get food must become food" (1986:38–39). Notions of balanced, reciprocal, human-animal predation are central in Wari' cosmology and eschatology. Mortuary cannibalism reflected ideas of a human-nonhuman alliance predicated on reciprocal predation between living people and the spirits of animals and ancestors.

AFTERLIFE AND ALLIANCE

In Wari' visions of the afterlife, the spirits of the dead reside under the waters of deep rivers and lakes. The ancestors appear as they did in life, but everyone is strong, beautiful, and free of deformity, disease, and infirmity. The ancestors' social world resembles precontact Wari' society, with villages, houses, fields, and intervillage festival exchanges. Life is easy and crops grow abundantly, but all food is vegetarian; there is no hunting or fishing because all animals have human forms underwater.

In this underworld, the Wari' ancestors are allied and intermarried with a neighboring indigenous group called "Water Spirits" (*jami kom*). The Water Spirits appear human, but they are not Wari' ancestors and have never lived on earth as ordinary people. Rather, they are primal forces that control human death, animal fertility, and destructive storms. Their leader is a giant with huge genitalia named Towira Towira (*towira* means "testicle"), who resembles the masters of animals and other mythic figures common in lowland South American cosmologies (see, for example, Reichel-Dolmatoff 1971:80–86; Zerries 1954). Towira Towira is master of the entire underworld; all its inhabitants, including Wari' ancestors, are called jami kom.

Wari' believe that when ancestral spirits emerge from the water, they assume the bodies of white-lipped peccaries (*Tayassu pecari*), a wild, pig-like animal that roams in large herds.[21] In everyday speech, *jami mijak,* "white-lipped peccary spirit," is one of the most common ways of referring to the dead. The nonancestral Water Spirits (Towira Towira's tribe) also can become white-lipped peccaries but more commonly appear as fish, especially as masses of small, easily killed fish that appear unpredictably in the flooded forest's shallow waters.

The Wari' cosmological system reflects a typically Amazonian view of cycles of reciprocal transformation and exchange between humans and animals (see, for example, Pollock 1992, in press; Reichel-Dolmatoff 1971). What is unusual about the Wari' case is that it links these ideas to an elaborate system of real cannibalism, framed in terms of symbolic and psychological rationales not previously examined in the mortuary cannibalism literature.

At the core of Wari' spiritual concerns is the idea of an alliance between Wari' society and the Water Spirits (comprised of both Wari' ancestors and Towira Towira's tribe). This is envisioned as a cyclic festival exchange identical to the earthly hüroroin and tamara festivals that affirm and reproduce amicable relations among Wari' villages. These alliance-marking rituals are structured around dramatizations of antagonistic oppositions between a host village and visitors from another community. Hüroroin culminate in the hosts' symbolic killing of male visitors by inducing an unconscious state called *itam* that is explicitly equated with death by predation (hunting or warfare).[22] The hosts revive the visitors from this "death" with a warm water bath, symbol of birth and rebirth. Revival of the slain "prey" distinguishes this "killing" by itam from mere hunting or warfare. In a process parallel to shamanic initiation (in which an animal spirit kills and revives the initiate), the hüroroin festival's symbolic killing and revival create a bond between the killer and the killed, such that the two transcend their opposition and become allies. Role reversals are inherent in festival exchanges; the first party's visitor/prey usually later sponsor a festival at which the first party's host/killer become the visitor/prey who are "killed."

Wari' relations with the Water Spirits are conceived in identical terms, as festival exchanges in which the terrestrial and underwater societies alternate in the roles of predators (hosts) and prey (visitors), enacting a reciprocity reducible to an eminently egalitarian proposition: "We'll let you kill us if you let us kill you." The Water Spirits fulfill their side of this arrangement by visiting earth as white-lipped peccaries and fish that sing tamara songs, dance, and allow Wari' to kill and eat them.[23] Wari' reciprocate at the moment of biological death, when human spirits allow themselves to be killed by the Water Spirits. This occurs when dying person's spirit (jami-) journeys to the underworld and becomes a guest at the hüroroin party that is always in progress there. The hosts, Towira Towira and his wife, offer maize beer. If the spirit accepts, it enters itam and "dies" underwater; on earth, the person's physical body dies. As in terrestrial alliance festivals, Towira Towira later bathes the spirit and resuscitates it. He then paints it with black *genipapo* dye (*Genipa americana*), marking the dead person's new identity as a Water Spirit.[24]

Each society benefits from this arrangement. Humans provide the Water Spirit society with new members who marry and bear children, enhancing the reproduction of Water Spirit society. The Water Spirits provide the living Wari' with life-sustaining animal food. For Wari', this exchange not only reproduces the primary human-nonhuman relations of their cosmology but also promises an enhancement of ecological resources important to their subsistence. White-lipped peccaries and fish are the only food animals encountered in dense concentrations in this environment; aside from the scarce and easily over-hunted tapir, they can yield the greatest quantities of animal food in return for the least expenditure of time and effort. Although they are relatively easy to kill when encountered, their appearance is highly unpredictable.[25] Given this combination of certainty and high potential productivity, it is not surprising that Wari' rituals focus on enhancing relations with peccaries and fish.

The mythic origin of the Wari' alliance with the Water Spirits is recounted in a story called *Orotapan*,[26] which tells of how Wari', who used to be the Water Spirits' prey, became their allies instead. As allies, they gained the right to kill Water Spirits (as peccaries and fish) in return for submitting to being killed by them (at the time of biological death) and subsequently hunted, as peccaries, by the living. Three elements central to Wari' socio-ecological

security originated in this myth: the festivals of intervillage alliance that ensure peace among neighbors, humans' postmortem transformations to peccaries (which ally the human and the nonhuman), and the songs that summon peccaries and fish to earth.

In the story of *Orotapan* (see note 26), the power to hunt and eat the ancestors/Water Spirits (as peccaries and fish) is balanced by humans' destiny to become peccaries to be hunted and eaten. This is a reprise of themes from the myth of *Pinom,* in which the power to hunt and eat animals was balanced by the imperative for humans to become meat to be eaten, as corpses consumed in endocannibalism. Whereas the *Pinom* story emphasizes the primal balance between human and animal predation, the myth of *Orotapan* concerns the creation of cultural institutions that transform potentially antagonistic, antisocial, predator-prey relations into cooperative, security-enhancing alliances. The alliance festivals' symbolic predation substituted for the real killing and eating of humans by animals in a precultural era. By accepting this human place in the universe, alternating between the position of eaters and the eaten, Wari' gained the animal spirits' powers of predation.

The power to summon their ancestral/Water Spirit allies to come to earth as animals is at the core of the sacred in Wari' life. In a precontact ritual that continues today in at lest one community, villagers gather at night, before communal hunting or fishing expeditions, to sing the songs from the *Orotapan* myth that invite the Water Spirits to earth. People avoid speaking of this music's power; I learned of it only because, after the one occasion when I heard the spirit-summoning songs sung collectively, the peccaries appeared early the next morning for the first time in several months. The herd passed just outside the village, and nine white-lipped were killed—three times as many as on any day in the previous two years at Santo André. The entire community ceased work to feast on this bounty of meat, a tangible embodiment of the human-nonhuman alliance.

HUNTING THE ANCESTORS

In contrast to Durkheimian views of death as a rupture in the social fabric to be mended, native Amazonian systems often treat death, not as discontinuity, but as essential for the continuation of social life (Viveiros de Castro 1992:255; see Graham 1995). The Wari' case offers a prime example of death treated as a creative moment, a productive context for extending and renegotiating social ties that regenerate the cycle of human-animal exchanges.

Human death is necessary to the reproduction of the peccaries and fish upon which Wari' subsistence and survival depend, and the perpetuation of Wari'; and Water Spirit cooperation depends on the bonds of affection that link the recently deceased to their living kin. Only the recently dead, who still remember their terrestrial kin and are remembered by them, maintain active exchange relations with the living. The spirits of the recently dead send or lead the peccary herd to their living relatives' hunting territories, or send their allies, the fish. When ancestors appear as peccaries, they approach hunters who are their own kin and offer their bodies to be shot to feed their living relatives. Before butchering, a shaman is supposed to look at each peccary carcass to identify the human spirit inside. Today, people are lax about this; sometimes shamans are summoned to view peccaries, sometimes they are not. A peccary spirit usually is identified as being a close consanguine, or occasionally an affine, of the hunter who shot it.

Wari' see nothing odd about hunting their own relatives, as I learned from a conversation that took place the day after two white-lipped peccaries were slain. An elderly shaman was chatting with a young widower still saddened by his wife's death two days earlier. The shaman mentioned that he had talked to the roasting peccaries (who were killed by the deceased wife's patrilateral parallel cousin) and that one turned out to be the dead wife. "Is that so?" responded the young man. "Is it all right in the water?" "She's fine," the shaman replied. "With the peccaries, she took a peccary husband and has a peccary baby." "That's nice," was the widower's only comment.

Eavesdropping while eating fruit nearby, I nearly choked. "Hey!" I exclaimed. "Doesn't that make you sad? Aren't you sad that your wife's cousin killed her yesterday and that you ate her today?" The young man looked perplexed at my outburst, then replied, "No; why should I be sad? He just killed her body; she isn't angry. Her children are eating meat. It doesn't hurt her; she just will have another body. Why should I be sad? The ancestors are happy that we have meat to eat."

To Wari', the idea that some of the animals they eat are beloved kin is neither morbid nor repulsive, but a natural extension of familial food giving, a concrete manifestation of the ancestors' continuing concern for their families on earth. There are numerous stories of encounters with peccaries that were interpreted as gifts of food sent by specific ancestors. One man told me that in the 1970s, when his mother was dying, she told her family that she would send the peccaries three days after her death. True to promise, on the third night, the herd thundered into the village, stampeding under elevated houses, sending women and children screaming while men scrambled for their shotguns. Most deaths are not followed by such immediate drama, but all peccary killings are potentially interpretable as visits from the ancestors. Each new death strengthens and reproduces the Water Spirits' ties to the world of the living.

FINAL RITES

The positive image of the ancestors' regeneration as animals was the central theme of the traditional sequence of mounting rites. The dead person's integration into Water Spirit society is seen as a gradual process: while the spirit is adjusting to life in the underworld, earthly survivors are adjusting to life without the deceased. The full realization of these processes traditionally was marked by a ritual hunt called *hwet mao,* meaning "the coming out" or "the reappearance." In the Rio Dois Irmãos area, it was last observed two decades ago.

Mourning is a period of attenuated sociality. Mourners withdraw from most productive activities and social interactions, do not sing, dance, or attend parties, and spend a great deal of time inside their houses. They farm, hunt, and fish less than usual, and, consequently, eat little meat. Hwet mao marked the transition back to full engagement in social life. When senior kin decided that it was time for mourning to end (typically about a month or two before the anniversary of the death), the family departed for an extended hunt deep in the forest. They killed as much game as possible and preserved it on a huge roasting rack over a smoky, slow-burning fire. It was considered especially important that certain animals present themselves to be killed as evidence of positive relations between the Wari' and their nonhuman allies. An encounter with the white-lipped peccaries could indicate that the deceased was fully integrated into life in the afterworld and, remembering loved ones on earth, had sent the herd to feed them.

At the full moon, the hunting party returned home carrying large baskets laden with game. The mourners painted their bodies for the first time since the death and made a ritual entrance into the village, ideally at the time of day when the deceased had died. Then, leaning over the baskets heaped with meat, they cried and sang kinship terms for the dead person one last time. After this final, public expression of sorrow and remembrance, an elder announced, "Sadness has ended; now happiness begins." Feasting and singing followed, initiating the return to normal social life. In feasting on game, the ex-mourners marked their acceptance of this death as part of the cycle of human-animal exchanges. Thus, the process that began with the funeral where the dead person's affines cannibalized the corpse concluded with consanguines and affines together eating the animal meat provided by the dead and their spirit allies.

EATING THE DEAD

Viewed in the context of the yearlong series of traditional mourning rites structured around the dead person's transition to white-lipped peccary, the roasting and eating of the corpse appears as a first, symbolic marker of this change. Consistent with Hertz's (1960[1907]:34, 58) insight that transformations of the corpse often parallel changes happening to the dead person's spirit, Wari' envisioned that at the moment when the cutting of the corpse commenced at the earthly funeral, Towira Towira began to bathe and resuscitate the spirit underwater.[27] This resuscitation made the deceased into a Water Spirit who eventually would return to earth as a peccary. For terrestrial mourners, the corpse's dismemberment and roasting evoked this human-to-animal transformation.

"When we made the big fire and placed the body there, it was as if the dead person became a white-lipped peccary [*ak ka mijak pin na*]," explained a male elder of Santo André. Switching to Portuguese, he emphasized, "It appeared to be peccary [*parece queixada*]." As mourners watched a beloved relative's corpse being dismembered, roasted, and eaten, the sight must have graphically impressed upon them both the death's finality and the dead person's future identity as a peccary that would feed the living. Dismembering the body that is the focus of so many notions of personhood and relatedness made a dramatic symbolic statement about the dead person's divorce from human society, and imminent change from living meat eater to animal meat to be eaten. Cannibalism appears to have been the preferred method for disposing of the dead because eating (as opposed to cremation) not only destroyed the corpse but also affirmed the dead individual's eventual regeneration as an immortal animal.

Cannibalism made a symbolic statement about the eaters as well as the eaten. At the same time that it evoked images of the dead as peccaries, numerous prior aspects of funeral rites and mourning behavior emphasized the humanity and social identity of the eaten, explicitly rejecting any equation of human flesh with animal flesh. Thus, when mourners roasted and ate human flesh, they themselves were cast as carnivores, identified with the animal powers of predation traced to the *Pinom* and *Orotapan* myths. Funeral decorations recalled these associations: firewood and roasting racks were adorned with feathers of vultures and scarlet macaws (Orotapan's sacred bird), and firewood was tied with "fire vine" (*makuri xe'*), a liana associated with warfare and predatory powers linked to the Water Spirits and the jaguar-cannibal in the myth of *Pinom*.

Eating the dead identified Wari' society as a whole with the transcendent powers of their allies, the immortal Water Spirits. Cannibalism evoked and enacted the human position in this relationship, the alternation between the positions of meat-eater and meat to be eaten. Block (1992) has argued that a wide variety of religious and political rituals is structured around a quasi-universal dynamic: the transformation of individuals from prey/victims into hunter/killers. The theme, which is explicit in the origin myths of *Pinom* and *Orotapan,* was the central image underlying the traditional Wari' mortuary ritual sequence. The death rites moved living mourners from the position of being victims of the Water Spirit forces of death to becoming hunters of Water Spirits embodied as animals. At the same time, as was consistent with the egalitarian reciprocity that permeates Wari' social arrangements, the rites also enacted the reverse dynamic, marking humans' postmortem destiny to become animals, transformed from eaters into the eaten.

MOURNING AND TRANSFORMATION

The image of the dead as peccaries dominates Wari' visions of death and the afterlife. The ancestors' return as peccaries is a powerful negation of death's finality. It promises not only reunion after death but also contacts during life through encounters with the herd that are the only interactions that ordinary people (nonshamans) have with their deceased kin. This is not just an abstract religious notion but a moving experience for the many individuals who have interpreted encounters with peccaries as visits from dead relatives.

Cannibalism represented a dramatic affirmation of this human-to-animal transformation, an affirmation of the interdependency of human mortality and animal fertility. Thematic links between death and regeneration are prominent in many societies' mortuary rites (Bloch and Parry 1982; Metcalf and Huntington 1991), and the psychological importance of ideas about the continuity of life after death is widely recognized (see Lifton 1979). The Wari' preference for cannibalism as a way to dispose of human corpses reflected the intersection between these psychological-spiritual concerns, cast in images of human spirits' regeneration as peccaries, and cultural concepts of the human body's social meanings. As a focus of social identity and psycho-emotional ties between the living and the dead, the dead person's body served as the primary locus for the playing out of transformations of mourners' memories, images, and emotions related to the deceased. Beginning with the corpse's dismemberment, roasting, and eating, and proceeding through the memory-altering "sweeping" ritual (ton ho') to the final hunt (hwet mao) and feast, the mourning rites posited a processual transmutation of socially projected images of the dead person's body. The rites aimed to move mourners from experiences of loss, embodied in images of the deceased as corpse, to acceptance of the death as part of a regenerative cycle, embodied in images of the deceased rejuvenated as an animal.

It is difficult to assess, retrospectively, the extent to which the ritual transformations that operated on the level of the culturally constructed person also operated on the level of the individual. However, contemporary Wari' emphases on cannibalism's psychological significance, as an act that facilitated mourners' detachment from all-consuming memories of the dead, and elders' expressions of emotional dissonance concerning burial, suggest that many people found the body's destruction by cannibalism meaningful in personal experiences of grief and mourning. The eating of the dead was one powerful element in a social process of mourning understood to have eased the experience of coming to terms with a loved one's death. By casting the dead in the image of the animals they would become, cannibalism overlaid images of the deceased as corpse with new images of the deceased as an animal with ongoing relations to its living kin. It affirmed the transmutation of specific kinship ties between the living and the dead into a general enhancement of life-supporting relations between humans and animals. In essence, cannibalism was the dead person's first offering of self as food.

CONCLUSION

The explanation to Wari' mortuary cannibalism cannot be reduced to a single, simple function, for it reflected a complex amalgam of myth, eschatology, ideas about the human body, and social, psychological, and ecological concerns. Extending Lévi-Strauss's (1977:65) observation about myth, these are best understood as "an *interrelation* of several explanatory levels." As a central symbol in the rites of mourning, cannibalism presented a powerful, symbolic condensation of beliefs about life's continuity after death, affirmed in the ancestors' regeneration as animals. Mortuary cannibalism's symbolic potency derived from its evocation of multiple dimensions of the social and ecological relations in which Wari' perceive their security to be grounded. In the rites of mourning, human-nonhuman oppositions merged in what Sanday (1986:226) has called a "ritual of reconciliation" that transformed unpredictable ecological and social constraints into a meaningful conceptual order. Much anthropological discourse on cannibalism has tended to treat cultural-symbolic and ecological interpretations as mutually exclusive paradigms, but, explored in indigenous terms, the Wari' system is a symbiosis of social and ecological concerns that must be considered holistically. The material motivations associated with endocannibalism were not biological needs for protein from human flesh, but concerns with structuring cultural meanings in regard to human-animal relations that were essential, not just to subsistence but to the entire social order.

In contrast to vies of anthropophagy as the ultimately antisocial act, the act of eating the dead affirmed and reproduced the bases of Wari' society. Endocannibalism was mythically linked to the origins of culture and the festival exchanges that transform potentially antagonistic relations into cooperative alliances between neighboring villages, and between humans and the nonhuman forces of death and animal fertility. As mortuary rites renewed the primary spiritual relations of the Wari' universe, so they also revitalized relations on the social plane with the gathering of affines in support of the dead person's family. Wari' cannibalism involved not the recycling of vital energies or body substances, but the renewal of vital institutions of socio-ecological security.

A Wari' elder recalled that shortly after the contact, a missionary lectured him, saying, "Eating is for animals. People are not animals, people are not meat to be eaten." In Western thought, the revulsion that cannibalism provokes is related to its apparent blurring of distinctions between humans and animals, in treating human substance like animal meat. For Wari', however, the magic of existence lies in the commonality of human and animal identities, in the movements between the human and nonhuman worlds embodied in the recognition through cannibalism of human participation in both poles of the dynamic of eating and being eaten.

ENDNOTES

Acknowledgments. My primary debt is to the people of Santo André and other Wari' communities who shared with me their understandings and experiences of death and mourning. Field research in Brazil in 1985–87 was carried out with the authorization from the CNPq and FUNAI and supported by fellowships from the Fulbright Commission and the Inter-American Foundation and a grant-in-aid from the Wenner-Gren Foundation for Anthropological Research. A Charlotte Newcombe Fellowship supported dissertation writing, and funding from the Wenner-Gren Foundation allowed me to return to Brazil in the summer of 1991 to check my interpretations and obtain additional data. A Vanderbilt University Research Council small grant facilitated bibliographic research. Among the many Brazilian colleagues who aided this project, special thanks are owed to Julio Cezar Melatti and Martin Ibañez-Novion, who sponsored my research under the auspices of the Department of Anthropology at the Universidade de Brasília; Dídimo Graciliano de Oliveira of FUNAI/Guajará-Mirim, who offered logistical support; and Aparecida Vilaça, whose insights and friendship have enriched my studies. For helpful comments on earlier versions of this paper, I am grateful to Debbora Battaglia, Brent Berlin, Michael Brown, Gertrude Dole, Frederick Dunn, Laura Graham, Thomas Gregor, Patricia Lyon, Lynn Morgan, Donald Pollock, Edward Schieffelin, and James Trostle.

1. The final syllable is stressed in all Wari' words. *Wari'* is pronounced "wa-REE," ending in a glottal stop. On the Wari'

language, see Everett and Kern (in press) and Everett (in press).

2. Most reports of endocannibalism involve eating only small bits of flesh from specific body parts (the typical Melanesian pattern) or consuming only the ashes of cremated bones, which appears to have been the most widespread Amazonian pattern (see Dole 1974; Meireles 1986; Zerries 1960). In lowland South America, consumption of substantial amounts of fellow tribesmembers' boiled or roasted flesh has been reported among the Guayakí of Paraguay (Clastres 1974) and Panoan peoples along the Peru-Brazil border (Dole 1974; Kensinger, in press).

3. In excluding exocannibalism from this discussion, I do not mean to imply that it had no relation to mortuary cannibalism. Vilaça (1992:289–294) has emphasized that Wari' cannibalism of both enemies and affines expressed a broad "cannibal logic" of reversibility in the positions of predator and prey in Wari' relations to social others. Erikson (1986), Overing (1986), and Viveiros de Castro (1992) have noted that the traditional anthropological distinction between exo- and endocannibalism blurs in the face of the complex forms of cannibalism envisioned in lowland South American myths, cosmologies, and rituals.

4. All translations of Wari' oral texts are my own, as are all translations of written texts (with foreign titles).

5. The assertion that eating corpses involved no transfer of biosocial substances or energies is consistent with the logic of Wari' ethnomedicine, conception theory, and shared substance concepts, in which attributes are transferred among individuals only by blood and its analogs (breast milk, semen, vaginal secretions, and perspiration), not by ingesting roasted flesh (see Conklin 1989:274–304). Roasting is believed to dry up or neutralize the potency of blood and other body fluids; contact with corpses is polluting, but eating well-roasted flesh was not believed to transfer any qualities from the corpse to those who ate it. Clastres reported a similar idea in Guayaki thought about endocannibalism: "On eating human flesh one does not acquire anything more, there is no positive influence" (1974:316).

6. Extensive incest prohibitions promote dispersed affinal alliances (Meireles 1986:273), and families generally intermarry with two or more different groups of affines. At the same time, there is an emphasis on repeating as well as proliferating affinal ties by taking spouses from families already linked by previous marriages.

7. The Wari' traditionally practiced cremation as an alternative way to dispose of corpses whose flesh was considered dangerous to eat because it was contaminated by specific disease conditions. Corpses were cremated, not eaten, when they had pus in their lungs, or symptoms resembling liver disorders (ascites and cirrhosis). The outsiders who suppressed Wari' cannibalism, however, did not present cremation as an option, perhaps because cremation is discouraged in Latin American Catholicism.

8. For more detailed discussions of funeral practices and variations, see Conklin (1989:407–417) and Vilaça (1992: 208–221). Funerals for people who died in massacres and epidemics often deviated from normal patterns. When a village had been attacked, or a person killed close to home, Wari' sometimes feared that the assassin(s) would return. In such cases, they dispensed with much of the usual ceremony

and quickly roasted and consumed the corpse(s). The mass death and social chaos of the contact-era epidemics brought similar disruptions of funeral practices, including painful episodes in which corpses were abandoned, and subsequently ravaged by vultures, because the survivors were too sick to cut the large amounts of firewood needed for roasting or cremation.

9. *Nari* is a verb meaning "to be related." The proper nominative designations for consanguines and affines, respectively, are *iri' ka-nari* and *oro-ka-nari paxi*. In this text, I follow Vilaça (1992) in using simplified verbal forms,. Iri' nari and nari paxi. Similarly, mixita, ton ho' and hwet mao are verbs; the normative designations are *ka-mixita-wa, ka-ton ho'-wa,* and *ka-hwet mao-wa.*

10. This antihomeopathic idea recurs in Wari' shamanism and ethnomedicine. A shaman shares body substance with his animal spirit companion and falls violently ill if he eats that animal's flesh. Similarly, certain illnesses are attributed to ingesting substances that are similar to one's own body substance, but in a more potent, incompatible state (Conklin 1989:302–312). Corpses' flesh and body fluids, transformed by putrefaction, are considered dangerous only when ingested by their close consanguines. When eaten by affines and non-kin, roasted flesh is not believed to cause illness, although it is regarded as polluting.

11. Most women in the Rio Dois Irmãos region said that they participated in mortuary cannibalism. In the Rio Negro-Ocaia region, many women said that they did not eat human flesh because they disliked its stench. Vilaça (1992: 216–217) cited one senior man who also claimed never to have eaten the dead. In addition, some women who usually participated in cannibalism told of decisions not to eat a specific affine's corpse because they felt too close, emotionally, to the dead person. Men were expected to perform impassively the duty of consuming the corpse, regardless of their feelings of intimacy with the deceased or the revulsion provoked by the smell and taste of decayed flesh.

12. Rosaldo (1989) has called attention to the power of emotions in shaping cultural responses to death. Wari' anger over relatives' deaths generally appears to have been directed outwards, into sorcery accusations against Wari' in other communities or retaliatory attacks on Brazilians or other indigenous populations. Wari' testimonies about mortuary cannibalism give little reason to think that it expressed or vented anger or resentment, although the possibility cannot be ruled out entirely.

13. In a provocative discussion that is beyond the scope of this article, Albert (1985) and Overing (1986) have discussed associations between affinity and images of cannibalism among the Yanomami and Piaroa, respectively, in relation to issues of social harmony, violence, warfare, and the internal dynamics of endogamous, egalitarian societies. Carneiro da Cunha and Viveiros de Castro (1985) have addressed related dynamics of vengeance and reciprocity in Tupinambá exocannibalism.

14. A similar rational shaped affines' roles in euthanasia: when an elderly person suffering from a terminal illness wished to die, he or she summoned a male affine to perform the killing. Funerals were only one of several contexts in which Wari' traditionally called upon affines to perform such services.

15. A horror of burial, and preference for being cannibalized or cremated, has been reported among Panoans (Erikson 1986:198), Yanomami (Lima Figueiredo 1939:44), Guayakí (Clastres 1974:319), and Tupinambá war captives (Viveiros de Castro 1992:289–290).

16. Efforts to extinguish material traces of the dead are widespread in lowland South America. Especially common are name avoidances and the destruction of dead people's houses and personal property (see, for example, Albert 1985; Gregor 1977:264; Jackson 1983:200; Kracke 1981: 262; Métraux 1947). The dual rationales of discouraging ghosts from returning to their homes, and removing reminders that cause sadness to the bereaved, are recurrent themes. Kracke commented that among the Kagwahiv, these two different rationales are given "so interchangeably that it almost seems as if they are different ways of phrasing the same thing" (1988:213–214).

17. According to Vilaça, "Only after the body is roasted and devoured, is the *jam* [spirit] of the deceased bathed under the water, and [it] passes to full living in the world of the dead" (1992:247).

18. Vilaça has emphasized that "for the Wari' culinary preparation (which is initiated with the cutting of the prey) and devouring are interrelated and indissociable processes. The cadaver is roasted in the fire that, in its origin, is cooking fire (see the myth of *Pinom*). In this sense the cadaver is prepared as prey and should be ingested as such" (1992:263).

19. Viverios de Castro (1992:213) has noted Tupi ideas of a connection between the persistence of a corpse's flesh and the persistence of memories linking the dead and the living.

20. Vilaça's Wari' informants echoed these sentiments. She cited one man's explanation: " 'If we bury, we think about where he [the deceased] walked, where he worked; we think about his skin being there in the earth still. With the fire it is good, it finishes all the body, we don't think more' " (Vilaça 1992:265).

21. White-lipped peccaries are prominent in native American myths and rituals, from Mexico south to the Argentinian Chaco (see Donkin 1985:83–94; Sowls 1984:185–187). They often are considered closely related to people. In *The Raw and the Cooked,* Lévi-Strauss (1969:84) identified peccaries as an intermediary between jaguars (the quintessential animal predators) and human beings.

22. Hüroroin parties are structured around oppositions between a host community and visitors from elsewhere who sing and dance for their hosts. Male visitors stage dramatic raids on the hosts' village, destroy property, and perform parodies of sexual intercourse with host women. Hosts punish these transgressions by forcing the visitors to drink and vomit vast quantities of maize beer. With repeated vomiting, some lose consciousness and enter itam, in which they bleed from the mouth and experience involuntary muscular contractions that force the body into a rigid fetal position. When this occurs, the party's sponsor cries, "I've killed my prey!" (*"Pa' pin' inain watamata!"*). Submission to the physically painful "death" of itam affirms both a man's physical stamina and his trust in the allies who care for and revive him (see Conklin 1989:148–154; Vilaça 1992:186–191).

23. Metaphors of reciprocity pervade relations to the peccaries. Just as precontact party hosts sent their guests home bearing gifts, Wari' hunters traditionally gave presents to the spirits of slain white-lipped peccaries, and occasionally do so today. Before butchering, a peccary carcass is surrounded with items such as bows and arrows, baskets, chichi, shotguns, clothing, and cigarettes. The peccary is told to carry the "images"(jami-) of these items home and tell fellow Water Spirits that they, too, will be given gifts when they visit the Wari'.

24. Pollock (in press) has described strikingly similar eschatological beliefs among the Kulina of Acre, Brazil. At death, Kulina spirits journey to the underworld and receive a ritual welcome from their ancestors who, as white-lipped peccaries, fall upon the spirit and consume it. Like Wari', Kulina believe that the ancestors return to earth as white-lipped peccaries that are hunted by living people. Unlike Wari', the Kulina system carries this cycle one step further: white-lipped peccary meat becomes the souls of Kulina babies.

25. Kiltie observed that "[w]hite-lippeds are distinctive among all the terrestrial herbivorous mammals in neotropical rain forests in being the only species that forms large herds, which may include over 100 individuals" (1980:542). Hunting white-lipped peccaries is an unpredictable business, for the herds range over huge territories, never lingering long in one place and disappearing for weeks or months at a time. However, when the herd does appear, it offers relatively easy targets and multiple kills are common, making white-lipped peccaries the single most important terrestrial game in the diets of the Wari' and many other native Amazonians. Fishing involves similar patterns of high potential yield with a high quotient of procurement uncertainty; in the flooded forest, dense concentrations of huge numbers of small, easily-caught fish occasionally appear, quite unpredictably, in the fluctuating waters of temporary streams and ponds.

26. In the myth called *Orotapan* or *Hujin,* Towira Towira appears as an *orotapan* carnivore and as a white-lipped peccary named Wem Parom, who established the original alliance. Here is a summary of key events in this myth:

    A man named Hujin fell into a river and was eaten by Orotapan, the Water Spirits' leader. After eating Hujin, Orotapan threw his bones in the air and made his flesh whole again so that he could devour him again. Orotapan did this over and over, until a shaman reached into the water, caught Hujin's bones and pulled him out. However, Hujin's spirit remained captive to the Water Spirits, compelled to return every day to their underwater realm. Orotapan changed into a white-lipped peccary named Wem Parom and challenged Hujin to a musical duel. Hujin won this contest by becoming the first human to master the art of songmaking, which the Wari' consider the highest of artistic accomplishments. By this supremely cultural act, he ceased to be the spirits' prey and gained the status of an equal capable of entering an alliance with the spirits. Wem Parom sent his son, in the form of a fish, to Hujin's village to receive gifts of food marking the establishment of amicable relations. Hujin then invited the Water Spirits to a party at his earthly village and instructed his own people to make large quantities of beer and new bows and arrows. The Water Spirit guests came as white-lipped peccaries who sang, danced, drank all of their hosts' beer, and ran around breaking clay pots and destroying houses. Hujin and his kinsmen shot and killed the peccaries. From their bodies emerged the scarlet macaw, which is sacred to Orotapan. Hujin, who had shamanic powers, then looked at each peccary carcass, identified its spirit, and told his people whether it was a Wari' ancestor or a nonancestral Water Spirit. It was then that the Wari' learned of their own postmortem fate to be killed by Towira Towira and become peccaries hunted by the living.

For other versions and analysis of this myth, See Vilaça 1992:255–262.

27. Although the spirit was believed to be revived when its corpse was dismembered and roasted, this revival does not appear to have been contingent on the corpse's being eaten. Several individuals described scenarios in which a spirit, revived when its corpse was cut, returned to earth and saw its own, still uneaten body roasting. Without exception, informants asserted that Towira Towira revived all spirits alike, regardless of whether their corpses were cannibalized, cremated, or buried. Vilaça (1992:265) has suggested that, since the change to burial, Wari' have come to see the rotting of the corpse as a kind of natural "cooking" that substitutes for the roasting at traditional funerals.

REFERENCES CITED

Acosta Saignes, Miguel
1961 Estudios de Etnologia Antiqua de Venezuela. (Studies of Early Ethnology of Venezuela.) Caracas, Venezuela: Universidad Central de Venezuela.

Albert, Bruce
1985 Temps du sang, temps de cendres. Représentation de la maladies, système rituel et espace politique chez les Yanomami du Sud-est (Amazonie Brésilienne). (Time of Blood, Time of Ashes. Representation of Illness, Ritual System and Political Space among the Southeastern Yanomami [Brazilian Amazon].) Ph.D. dissertation, Université de Paris X.

Arens, William
1979 The Man-Eating Myth: Anthropology and Anthropophagy. New York: Oxford University Press.

Battaglia, Debbora
1991 The Body in the Gift: Memory and Forgetting in Sabarl Mortuary Exchange. American Ethnologist 19:3–18.

Berlin, Elois Ann, and E. K. Markell
1977 An Assessment of the Nutritional and Health Status of an Aguaruna Jívaro Community, Amazonas, Peru. Ecology of Food and Nutrition 6:69–81.

Bloch, Maurice
1992 Prey into Hunter: The Politics of Religious Experience. New York: Cambridge University Press. Bloch, Maurice, and Jonathan Parry, eds.
1982 Death and the Regeneration of Life. New York: Cambridge University Press.

Briggs, Charles
1992 "Since I Am a Woman, I Will Chastise My Relatives": Gender, Reported Speech, and the (Re)production of Social Relations in Warao Ritual Wailing. American Ethnologist 19:337–361.

Carneiro da Cunha, Manuela, and Eduardo B. Viveiros de Castro
1985 Vingança e temporalidade: Os Tupinambás. (Vengeance and Temporality: The Tupinambá.) Journal de la Société des Américanistes (Paris) 71:191–208.

de Carvalho, Bernardino
1962 Pakaanovas: Antropófagos da Amazônia. (Pakaa Nova: Cannibals of Amazônia.) O Cruzeiro (São Paulo) February 10:118–124.

Chagnon, Napoleon A., and Raymond B. Hames
1979 Protein Deficiency as a Cause of Tribal Warfare in Amazonia: New Data. Science 203:910–913.

Clastres, Pierre
1974 Guayaki Cannibalism. P. Lyon, trans. In Native South Americans: Ethnology of the Least Known Continent. Patricia J. Lyon, ed. Pp. 309–321. Boston: Little, Brown.

Conklin, Beth A.
1989 Images of Health, Illness and Death Among the Wari' (Pakaas Novos) of Rondônia, Brazil. Ph.D. dissertation, University of California at San Francisco and Berkeley.

Crocker, J. Christopher
1977 The Mirrored Self: Identity and Ritual Inversion among the Eastern Bororo. Ethnology 16(2):129–145.

Crocker, William H.
In press Canela Relationships with Ghosts: This-Worldly or Other-Worldly Empowerment. Latin American Anthropology Review.

Crocker, William, and Jean Crocker
1994 The Canela: Bonding through Kinship, Ritual, and Sex. New York: Harcourt Brace.

Cruzeiro, O
1962 Pakaanovas, (Pakaa Nova.) O Cruzeiro (São Paulo), March 23:152–160.

Dole, Gertrude E.
1974 Endocannibalism among the Amahuaca Indians. In Native South Americans: Ethnology of the Least Known continent. Patricia J. Lyon, ed. Pp. 302–308. Boston: Little, Brown.

Donkin, R. A.
1985 The Peccary. Transactions of the American Philosophical Society, 75. Philadelphia: The American Philosophical Society.

Dufour, Darna L.
1983 Nutrition in the Northwest Amazon. In Adaptive Responses of Native Amazonians. Raymond B. Hames and William T. Vickers, ed. Pp. 329–355. San Francisco: Academic Press.

Erickson, Philippe
1986 Altérité, tatouage, et anthropophagite chez les Pano. (Alterity, Tatooing, and Cannibalism among Panoans.) Journal de la Société des Américanistes Paris 72:185–210.

Everett, Daniel L.
In press Wari' Morphology. In the Handbook of morphology. Andrew Spencer and Arnold Zwicky, eds. London: Basil-Blackwell.

Everett, Daniel L., and Barbara Kern
In press The Wari' Language of Western Brazil (Pacaas Novos). London: Routledge.

Folha de São Paulo
1962 Sertanista não conseguiu impedir que os Índios devorassem a menina morta. (Government Indian Agent Did Not Manage to Prevent the Indians from Devouring the Dead Gril.) Folha de São Paulo, January 13.

Freud, Sigmund
1981 [1913] Totem and Taboo. *In* The Standard Edition of the Complete Psychological Works of Sigmund Freud, 14. James Strachey, ed. Pp. 100–155. London: The Hogarth Press and The Institute of Psychoanalysis.

Gillison, Gillian
1983 Cannibalism among Women in the Eastern Highlands of Papua New Guinea. *In* The Ethnography of Cannibalism. Paula Brown and Donald Tuzin, eds. Pp. 33–50. Washington, DC: Society for Psychological Anthropology.

Graham, Laura
1986 Three Modes of Shavante Vocal Expression: Wailing, Collective Singing, and Political Oratory. *In* Native South American Discourse. Joel Sherzer and Greg Urban, eds. Pp. 83–118. New York: Mouton de Gruyter.
1995 Performing Dreams: Discourses of Immortality among the Xavante of Brazil. Austin: University of Texas Press, in press.

Gregor, Thomas
1977 Mehinaku: The Drama of Daily Life in a Brazilian Village. Chicago: University of Chicago Press.

Harner, Michael
1977 The Ecological Basis for Aztec Sacrifice. American Ethnologist 4:117–135.

Harris, Marvin
1977 Cannibalism and Kings: The Origins of Cultures. New York: Random House.
1985 The Sacred Cow and the Abominable Pig. New York: Random House.

Hertz, Robert
1960[1907] Death and the Right Hand. Glencoe, IL: Free Press.

\Jackson, Jean E.
1983 The Fish People: Linguistic Exogamy and Tukanoan Identity in Northwest Amazonia. New York: Cambridge University Press.

Kensinger, Kenneth M.
1991 A Body of Knowledge, or, the Body Knows. Expedition (University of Pennsylvania Museum) 33(3):37–45.
In press Disposing of the Dead in Cashinahua Society. Latin American Anthropology Review.

Kiltie, Richard A.
1980 More on Amazon Cultural Ecology. Current Anthropology 21:541–544.

Kracke, Waud
1978 Force and Persuasion: Leadership in an Amazonian Society. Chicago: University of Chicago Press.
1981 Kagwahiv Mourning: Dreams of a Bereaved Father. Ethos 9:258–275.
1988 Kagwahiv Mourning II. Ghosts, Grief, and Reminiscences. Ethos 16:209–222.

Lévi-Strauss, Claude
1969 The Raw and the Cooked. New York: Harper & Row.
1977 Structural Anthropology, 2. New York: Basic Books.

Lewis, I. M.
1986 Religion in Context: Cults and Charisma. New York: Cambridge University Press.

Lifton, Robert J.
1979 The Broken Connection: On Death and the Continuity of Life. New York: Simon & Schuster.

Lima Figueiredo, José
1939 Indios do Brasil. (Indians of Brazil.) Brasiliana (São Paulo), 5th ser., 163.

Lindenbaum, Shirley
1979 Kuru Sorcery. Palo Alto, CA: Mayfield.

Mason, Alan
1977 Oranao Social Structure. Ph.D. dissertation, University of California at Davis.

da Matta, Roberto
1979 The Apinayé Relationship System: Terminology and Ideology. *In* Dialectical Societies: The Gê and Bororo of Central Brazil. David Maybury-Lewis, ed. Pp. 83–127. Cambridge, MA: Harvard University Press.

Maybury-Lewis, David
1974 Akwe-Shavante Society. New York: Oxford University Press.

Meigs, Anna
1984 Food, Sex and Pollution: A New Guinea Religion. New Brunswick, NJ: Rutgers University Press.

Meireles, Denise Maldi
1986 Os Pakaas-Novos. (The Pakaa Nova.) Master's thesis, Universidade de Brasília, Brazil.

Melatti, Julio Cezar
1979 The Relationship System of the Krahó. *In* Dialectical Societies: The Gẽe and Bororo of Central Brazil. David Maybury-Lewis, ed. Pp. 46–79. Cambridge, MA: Harvard University Press.

Métraux, Alfred
1947 Mourning Rites and Burial Forms of the South American Indians. América Indígena 7(1):7–44.

Metcalf, Peter, and Richard Huntington
1991 Celebrations of Death: The Anthropology of Mortuary Ritual. 2nd 3d. New York: Cambridge University Press.

Milton, Katharine
1984 Protein and Carbohydrate Resources of the Makú Indians of Northwestern Amazonia. American Anthropologist 86:7–27.

Murphy, Robert
1960 Headhunter's Heritage. Berkeley: University of California Press.

Overing, Joanna
1986 Images of Cannibalism, Death and Domination in a "Non Violent" Society. Journal de la Société des Américanistes (Paris) 72:133–156.

Pollock, Donald
1992 Culina Shamanism: Gender, Power and Knowledge. *In* Portals of Power: Shamanism among South American Indians.

E. Jean Langdon and Gerhard Baer, eds. Pp. 25–40. Albuquerque: University of New Mexico Press.

In press Death and the Afterdeath among the Kulina. Latin American Anthropology Review.

Poole, Fitz John Porter

1983 Cannibals, Tricksters, and Witches: Anthropophagic Images Among Bimin-Kuskusmin. *In* The Ethnography of Cannibalism. Paul Brown and Donald Tuzin, eds. Pp. 6–32. Washington, DC: Society for Psychological Anthropology.

Ramos, Alcida Rita

1990 Memórias Sanumá: Espaco e tempo em uma sociedade Yanomami. (Sanumá Memories: Space and Time in a Yanomami Society.) São Paulo: Editora Marco Zero.

Reichel-Dolmatoff, Gerardo

1971 Amazonian Cosmos. Chicago: University of Chicago Press.

Rosaldo, Renato

1989 Culture and Truth: The Remaking of Social Analysis. Boston: Beacon Press.

Rosenblatt, Paul C., R. Patricia Walsh, and Douglas A. Jackson

1976 Grief and Mourning in Cross-Cultural Perspective. New Haven, CT: HRAF Press.

Sagan, Eli

1974 Cannibalism: Human Aggression and Cultural Form. San Francisco: Harper & Row.

Sanday, Peggy Reeves

1986 Divine Hunger: Cannibalism as a Cultural System. New York: Cambridge University Press.

Seeger, Anthony

1987 Why Suyá Sing: A Musical Anthropology of an Amazonian People. New York: Cambridge University Press.

Seeger, Anthony, Roberto da Matta, and E. B. Viveiros de Castro

1979 A construção da pessoa nas sociedades indígenas brasileiras. (The Construction of the Person in Brazilian Indigenous Societies.) Boletim do Museu Nacional (Rio de Janeiro), Antropologia (n.s.) 32:2–19.

Sowls, Lyle K.

1984 The Peccaries. Tucson: The University of Arizona Press.

Staden, Hans

1928[1557] Hans Staden: The True History of His Captivity, 1557. Malcolm Letts, ed. London: George Routledge & Sons.

Turner, Terence S.

1980 The Social Skin. *In* Not by Work Alone. Jeremy Cherfas and Roger Lewin, eds. Pp. 112–140. Beverly Hills, CA: Sage Publications.

Urban, Greg

1988 Ritual Wailing in Amerindian Brazil. American Anthropologist 90:385–400.

1991 A Discourse-Centered Approach to Culture. Austin: University of Texas Press.

Vilaça, Aparecida

1989 Comendo como gente: Formas do canibalismo Wari' (Pakaa Nova). (Eating Like People: Forms of Wari' Cannibal-

ism.) Master's thesis. Museu Nacional, Universidade Federal do Rio de Janeiro.

1992 Comendo como gente: Formas do canibalismo Wari'. (Eating like People: Forms of Wari' Cannibalism.) Io de Janeiro: Editora UFRJ (Universidade Federal do Rio de Janeiro).

Viveiros de Castro, Eduardo B.

1992 From the Enemy's Point of View. Chicago: University of Chicago Press.

Von Graeve, Bernard

1972 Protective Intervention and Interethnic Relations: A Study of Domination on the Brazilian Frontier. Ph.D. dissertation, University of Toronto.

1989 The Pacaa Nova: Clash of Cultures on the Brazilian Frontier. Peterborough, Canada: Broadview Press.

Wilbert, Johannes, and Karin Simoneau

1990 Folk Literature of the Yanomami Indians. Los Angeles: UCLA Latin American Center Publications.

Zerries, Otto

1954 Wild-und Buschgeister in Südamerika. (Wild- and Bush-Spirits in South America.) Studien zur Kulturkunde, 11. Wiesbaden, Germany: F. Steiner.

1960 Endocanibalismo en la América del Sur. (Endocannibalism in South America.) Revista do Museu Paulista (São Paulo), n.s., 12:125–175.

READING 6–3

"IN THY BLOOD LIVE": GENDER AND RITUAL IN THE JUDAEO-CHRISTIAN TRADITION

Leonie J. Archer

With its concern about gender hierarchy and the religious imagery in the Bible, this reading nicely complements Reading 9–1, as well as providing illustration of Mary Douglas's discussion of taboo (see Reading 2–4). Although Leonie Archer's study is not as obviously structural as that of Edmund Leach's analysis of the Book of

Source: Leonie J. Archer, "'In thy blood live': Gender and Ritual in the Judaeo-Christian Tradition," in Through the Devil's Gateway: Women, Religion, and Taboo, ed. Alison Joseph (London: SPCK, 1990), pp. 22–49. Reprinted by permission of SPCK/Channel 4 Television.

Genesis (see Reading 2–2), it nevertheless takes full advantage of the analytical possibilities offered by the oppositions and analogies discernible in Judaic beliefs— as we can show by constructing a pair of columns that display the complementary oppositions discussed in Archer's article as a set of analogies, thus:

male	*female*
superior	*inferior*
male blood	*female blood*
superior blood	*inferior blood*
active	*passive*
circumcision	*menstruation*
culture	*nature*

In this article we return to the use of blood as a symbol, a property of this substance that I referred to the Introduction. In addition to its gender function, the distinction between male blood and female blood made in the Judaic tradition is interesting because it is a local instance of a symbolic contrast made in many religions. Despite blood's use as a symbolic of separation, blood also finds a use as a symbol of union. Male blood may be superior to female blood, but blood, when all is said and done, is blood, and as such common to both sexes. In some rituals outside the bounds of Judaism blood is used as a symbolic means of communication with the gods— the preferred substance that brings human beings and spirits together (see Introduction to Chapter 4).

As part of his argument Archer exploits a complementary opposition frequently cited in anthropological texts, that between culture and nature, and he correctly notes that this contrast is a cultural construct. In other words, it is not given in nature. This being so he might perhaps have reminded us that societies do not always have this complementary opposition. The association between nature and female and the association between culture and male should therefore in no sense be regarded as universal.

Thus saith the Lord God unto Jerusalem . . . In the day that thou wast born thy navel wast not cut, neither wast thou washed in water for cleansing; thou wast not salted at all, nor swaddled at all. No eye pitied thee, to do any of these things unto thee; but thou wast cast out in the open field in the loathesomeness of thy person . . . And when I passed by thee and saw thee wallowing in thy blood, I said unto thee: in thy blood live . . . I swore unto thee, and entered into a covenant with thee, and thou becamest mine. Then washed I

thee with water; yea, I cleansed away thy blood from thee and I anointed thee with oil. (Ezek. 16.3–6, 8–9)

It is evident from even the most cursory reading of the Hebrew Bible, in particular the Five Books of Moses (the Pentateuch), that blood, mentioned in this passage several times and with various significances, played an all-important role in the ancient Jewish belief system. In the narratives, descriptions of killing are specifically and explicitly couched in terms of the shedding of another person's blood, whilst acts of lawful vengeance for clan murder are similarly spoken of in terms of effecting an expiation by blood (Lev. 20.9, 11, 12, 13, etc.; Num. 35.19ff); one of the earliest attested acts of faith centred upon the near sacrifice of a human being (Isaac, son of Abraham), replaced at the last moment by a substitute ram which was given as a burnt-offering (Gen. 22); and the first redemption of the embryonic nation Israel involved the smearing of the blood of the Passover lamb on the doorposts and lintels of the Hebrews' homes in Egypt as a sign to the Angel of Death to leave them in safety (Exod. 12.7, 13, 23).

In the law, particularly that concerned with cultic activity, blood is all-pervasive. The consecration of the High Priest to his office, the highest and most sacred in the nation, was effected by sprinkling his garments and daubing his right ear, thumb and foot with the blood of a sacrificed animal (Exod. 29.20–21; Lev. 8.22–24, 30); in sacrificial ritual generally, the main activity of the Temple at Jerusalem, the principal feature was the dashing of the blood of animals on the horns of the altar and on the floor of the sanctuary (Exod. 29; Lev. passim; Num. 18–19, 28–9). Such cultic shedding of blood was regarded as the means of connecting with the Godhead, and animals were brought to the priests for sacrifice as sin- and thank-offerings, for purging ritual impurity, covenanting and redemption of both the individual and the nation as a whole (Lev. passim; Num. 6,7,8,15,28–29). The consumption of blood by humans was absolutely forbidden for, as Leviticus 17.11 declared, ". . . the life of the flesh is in the blood." Whilst humans could eat meat, they could only do so after careful selection and preparation of the animal (Lev. 11, 17.10ff). The blood always belonged to God, for "I have given it to you upon the altar to make atonement for your souls . . . whosoever eateth any manner of blood, I will set my face against that soul . . . and will cut him off from among his people" (Lev. 17.10–11). The ceremonial accoutrements which were an essential accompaniment to the sacrificial procedure were also all of significant colour (scarlet wool, hyssop, cedar wood—Exod. 25.4,14; 26.1,31,36; 28.5ff; 35.23–6; 39.1–5,22–9; Lev. 14.6, etc.), and the most important sacrifice of the year was that of the red heifer (Num. 19).

That a deep-seated and all-embracing blood taboo unquestionably lay at the heart of so much of Jewish belief and ritual practice is clearly evidenced by the later (Christian) book of Hebrews which saw fit to characterize Judaism specifically as a covenant of blood, sanctified, purified and redeemed by the blood of cultic sacrifice:

> Even the first covenant was not ratified without blood. For when every commandment of the law had been declared by Moses to all the people, he took the blood of calves and goats, with water and scarlet wool and hyssop, and sprinkled both the book itself and all the people, saying, "This is the blood of the covenant which God commanded you." And in the same way he sprinkled with the blood both the tent and all the vessels used in worship. Indeed, under the law almost everything is purified with blood, and without the shedding of blood there is no forgiveness of sins. (Heb. 9.18–22)

The point of interest from all of these examples is not only the obvious centrality of blood to Jewish ritual thought and practice, but also the fact that virtually all of the significant references to blood derive from the book of Leviticus and other chronologically allied strands of the Old Testament. The Bible has long been recognized as a composite work spanning many centuries, not some kind of monolithic whole, and whilst opinions differ widely as to the precise dating (and methods of dating) of its constituent parts, it remains the case that a book, or indeed a chapter, may lie in the received text next to a verse or chapter some several centuries

removed in compositional/redactional terms from its neighbour. All of the references given above come from what is called the Priestly strand ("P") and as such they are to be dated to around the time of the Jews' exile to Babylon in the sixth century bc—that is, according to the still widely accepted dating of this biblical strand within the source-critical school of thought (though it must also be said that my own arguments as developed in this essay and elsewhere independently point to the exile as the time when these blood concerns and rituals would first have emerged).[1]

Additionally, and of equal significance, is the fact that within the overall blood taboo context there seems to have been a clear and hierarchical distinction made between male blood and female blood. This may be seen not only from a detailed breakdown of the sacrificial prescriptions in terms of the sex of the victim chosen for particular occasions, but more especially from an analysis of two other rituals which appeared on the scene at the same time: covenantal (male) circumcision and the regulations surrounding menstruation and childbirth.[2] Both of these involved a flow of blood, the one positively valued, the other negatively, and both had profound resonances for men's and women's involvement (or non-involvement) in public religion. It is these two rituals which will be the main focus of this essay, but before turning to their specific analysis a few more words need to be said about the general blood context and the male–female hierarchy at work within it.

Within the sacrificial procedure, the prescription was always to select male victims for the more important occasions. Thus, the cult offerings for all the major feasts, including the sabbath, new moon and Passover, were all male animals (Num. 28); the sin-offering of a priest had to be an unblemished bullock (Lev. 4.2ff, 9.3, 16.6ff); similarly sacrifice to atone for the guilt of the nation was also a bullock (idem; cf. Num. 15.22ff); the sin-offering of a ruler was a male goat without blemish (Lev. 4.22ff), whilst any guilt-offering for sin "through error in the holy things of the Lord" was an unblemished ram (Lev. 5.14ff). In all of these instances the animal's blood was daubed on the altar, the fat burned, and the meat of the carcass divided between the sacrificing priest and the offerer for consumption. In cases of individual atonement a whole burnt-offering of a male victim was made (Lev. 1.3ff). Female animals were used only for the less significant peace-offerings when animals of either sex could be sacrificed (Lev. 3.1ff) and for the sin or guilt-offering of a commoner as opposed to that of a priest or ruler (Lev. 4.27ff; cf. Num. 15.27f). The only exception to this clear male–female hierarchy was the occasion of the ceremony of the red heifer when a female was slaughtered for atonement and purification (Num. 19). Significantly, however, this ritual was not allowed to take place within the sacred precincts: the animal was burned whole "outside the camp," its blood was not offered at the altar but burned along with the carcass, and the officiating priest was required to cleanse himself after the sacrifice.

The fact that there was a clear male–female hierarchy at work within the sacrificial procedure was not unknown to or unappreciated by the ancients. That is, the material presented is not some kind of post hoc analysis imposed upon the texts in the light of present-day concerns, removed from the ancients' own understanding of the laws in their original context. Far from it. The first century ad Jewish philosopher Philo, commenting upon the sin-offering prescriptions of Leviticus 4, wrote:

> . . . we have several divisions [of sacrifice], both according to the persons concerned and the kinds of victim. As to the persons, the High Priest is distinguished from the whole nation, and the rulers . . . from the mass of the common people . . . The sins of the High Priest and those of the whole nation are purged with an animal of the same value: in both cases it is directed that a male calf should be brought. For the sins of the ruler one of less value is ordered, though this too is a male, namely a he-goat; for the sins of the commoner, one still more inferior in kind, a female offering instead of a male, that is, a she-goat. For it was proper that in matters of sacrifice the ruler should fare better than the commoner and the nation than the ruler, since the whole should always be superior to the part . . .[3]

And with regard to the most sacred sacrifice, the whole burnt-offering, Philo analyses the choice of victim in the following way:

> . . . the victim of the whole burnt-offering is a male because the male is more complete, more dominant than the female, closer akin to causal activity, for the female is incomplete and in subjection and belongs to the category of the passive rather than the active. So too with the two ingredients which constitute our life principle, the rational and the irrational; the rational which belongs to mind and reason is of the masculine gender, the irrational, the province of sense, is of the feminine. Mind belongs to a genus wholly superior to sense as man is to woman; unblemished and purged . . . it is itself the most religious of sacrifices and its whole being is highly pleasing to God.[4]

Bearing Philo's words in mind—in particular his characterization of the male as active/causal and the female as passive—we shall now turn to the main focus of this essay, that is, an examination of the rituals of circumcision and menstrual taboo.

As was noted above and as I shall explore in further detail below, both of these involved a flow of blood—the one positively valued, the other negatively, and both had profound resonances for the involvement or non-involvement of men and women in public religion. Whilst the two rituals are not normally linked together, it does seem from close examination that they are connected and that they are, in analytical terms, in fact opposite sides of the same coin. They deserve our attention not only because of their clear male–female: superior–inferior blood differentiation, but also because, of all the other blood rituals of covenanting, purifying and cleansing discussed above, only they survived the destruction of the Jerusalem Temple in ad 70 to remain rites central to the Judaism of today, with the same religious consequences for men and women as in the ancient world.

The way in which I wish to approach the subject and discuss the notion of gendered blood, as it were, in these two rituals is by means of a socially constructed opposition between culture and nature—circumcision being deemed the work of (superior) culture and menstruation the functioning of (inferior) nature. The nature-versus-culture model of analysis was first developed within anthropology to help account for the universal subordination or secondary status of women in all societies at all times.[5] Basically, the projected dichotomy of the model rests on the assumption that every society recognizes a distinction between culture and nature, with ritual being the outer manifestation or expression of this recognition and representing culture's need to regulate and control the passive functioning of its opposite, nature—"nature" itself, of course, being a construct of "culture." Regarding the social differentiation between the sexes, this conceptual schematization can result (and I stress that this is just one possibility, and one which admirably serves the needs of patriarchy) in women being perceived as closer to nature in consequence of the biological facts of childbirth and menstruation (or rather, a particular cultural interpretation thereof), whilst men, who are deemed to lack such a cycle of visible creativity (and who have other aspects of their own equally natural physiology denied), are placed within the realm of culture, manipulating their own social and political existence, and transcending the passive forces of nature. Culture, and therefore male activity within this scheme of thought, are consequently seen as superior to nature and female passivity. It must be emphasized, however, that this particular elaboration of the nature–culture split is, of course, also itself a complex social construct and one which as I said serves patriarchal needs in various ways. The split could have gone in a different direction with different characterizations and emphases within the overall framework. To use the nature–culture dichotomy for a greater understanding of a particular situation is not therefore to promote principles of immutable (socio-) biological determinism.[6] Such then, in extremely broad terms, is the essence of the nature–culture opposition, an opposition which, as I hope to show, provides one clue as to the perceived gender differentials in blood within Judaism and which may be of help in establishing an (oppositional) link between circumcision and menstrual taboo.

Before turning to the specifics of our analysis of the blood taboo in terms of a nature–culture opposition, however, it will be necessary first to sketch in a general historical picture of the changes which occurred in the religious and social ordering of the Jewish community in the centuries surrounding the exile, the time when these rituals, at least in their final form (see below), first emerged. The need for such a sketch is obvious when one recalls that ritual and ritualistic ideas can make sense only when taken in reference to a total structure of thought and system of social and historical reality (most of which I shall, of course, be able only to touch on here). They do not spring from a vacuum or according to some arbitrary whim of the people and legislators, but have their origins in the human need to control and order existence. The way in which ritual develops—or rather is developed—and the characteristics which it assumes, reflect the ordering and preoccupations peculiar to a society. Thus it is essential that we keep in mind that notions which may now seem "normal" and "natural" are in fact, as with most things, social and cultural constructs determined by a complex of reasons and situations.

Given that the rituals of circumcision and menstrual taboo, like the other blood rituals, would appear to have derived at least in their final form from the trauma of the exile to Babylon and the consequent restructuring of the Jewish community, we shall need to start our historical survey some centuries further back in time in order to locate and appreciate the profound changes which occurred in and around the sixth century bc. The survey will focus on religious and social development and will be taken largely from the woman's perspective.

From the early chronological strands of the Old Testament, it is apparent that women in the pre-exilic period of Hebrew history enjoyed a certain active involvement in the nation's religious affairs.[7] In the biblical narratives they appear as singers and dancers (see for example, Exod. 15.20–21; Judg. 21.21; Jer. 31.4; Ps. 68.12, 24–5), prophetesses (e.g. Judg. 4.4f; 2 Sam. 20.16f; 2 Kings 22.14f), sacred prostitutes and in other cultic capacities (e.g. Gen. 38; Exod. 38.8; 1 Sam. 2.22; Hos. 4.13–14).

Significantly, however, the period to which these texts refer was one in which that rigid monotheism so characteristic of later Judaism had not as yet developed. Then polytheistic belief and worship flourished and shrines to the various deities, which included a number of goddesses, dotted the countryside of Palestine (e.g. Judg. 3.7; 1 Kings 11.5f, 15.13; 2 Kings 23.7; Jer. 7.18, 44.15f). In the course of time, however, the monotheistic principle began to assert itself, and for a complex of reasons not within the scope of this essay, the god Yahweh was elevated to a position of supremacy over all other deities. With this rise to power of a single male deity and the concomitant lessening in status of the other members of the Israelite pantheon (especially its female members), the role played by women in public religion began to diminish. The first step in that direction was taken when the early Hebrew legislators forbade the practice of sacred prostitution, this ritual being fundamental to the non-Yahwistic cults and also one in which women played a central role (Deut. 23.17–18; cf. 1 Kings 15.12; 2 Kings 23.7). Women were further removed from cultic activity when the Yahwists forced the abolition of all ritual shrines in Palestine and centralized worship at the Temple in Jerusalem, a move which was again designed to rid the land of undesirable cults (cf. 1 Kings 6ff). At this central sanctuary there was no place for female officiants as the Temple's affairs were regarded as the sole responsibility of an organized, hereditary male priesthood dedicated to the service of Yahweh. But despite all efforts, worship of the old gods and goddesses continued throughout the land of Israel and even on occasion at the Temple of Jerusalem itself—as evidenced by the books of Kings and Chronicles, which refer to events of the seventh and sixth centuries. Ironically, Yahweh's final victory came with the destruction of the Temple at the hands of the Babylonians in 587 bc. For generations prior to this calamity the custodians and promoters of Yahweh—that is, the now canonized Prophets of Israel—had been warning the people that if they did not abandon their syncretistic ways, the wrath of the one true God would descend upon them. For the people as a whole, therefore, the destruction of the Temple and the exile to Babylon came to be viewed as a dramatic realization of these doom prophecies, and proof of the absolute power of the jealous God Yahweh, and—harnessing these concepts to their own pragmatic ends—the exiles set about ridding themselves of all impurity in an effort to regain his favour. To this end all records of the past were zealously preserved and older, more primitive legal traditions extensively reworked and edited in the light of developing concepts and attitudes—most of which would seem to have been the direct result of the community's change in circumstances and new needs for order and social cohesion.[8] Of particular significance and far-reaching consequence to the lives of women was the exilic legislators' obsession with ritual cleanness[9]—and in order to understand the full import of this statement, I shall momentarily have to digress from our historical outline and spend a little time analysing the reasons for the legislators' obsession and its impact.

Remembering that we are here dealing with a community first in exile and then returned to an impoverished and divided land (i.e. Palestine towards the end of the sixth and in the course of the fifth centuries bc),[10] it is significant that the principal concern of the Priestly Code (the code with which we are primarily concerned . . .) was with the laws of kashrut, pollutions from secretions of various bodily orifices, and, as we have seen above, legislation about the cult and priesthood.[11] This concern for purity and order—for that is what the legislation is about—both reflected society's concern for its own racial integrity and social cohesion, and in turn served to promote them. As Mary Douglas writes, "The idea of society is a powerful image . . . This image has form; it has external boundaries, margins, structure . . . For symbols of society any human experience of structure, margins, or boundaries is ready to hand."[12] And again, ". . . ideas about separating, purifying, demarcating and punishing transgressions have as their main function to impose system on an inherently untidy experience. It is only by exaggerating the difference between within and without, above and below, male and female, with and against, that a semblance of order is created."[13] So, for example, the laws of kashrut, whilst serving an obvious pragmatic purpose of separating and distinguishing the Jews from their neighbours, and guarding against assimilation, also served to affirm the selected symbolic system, the abomination and avoidance of crawling things being the negative side of the pattern of things approved and a function of the ordering of society.[14] Similarly, the concern for the pollution of and from bodily secretions on a practical level worked to promote the integrity and productivity (in human terms) of the family unit—a matter of prime importance for a group concerned for its very existence and reproduction—whilst on a symbolic level, the exiles' concentration upon the unity, purity and integrity of the physical body well reflected their larger concern for the threatened boundaries of the body politic. The overt rationale behind the new prescriptions was the desire to create a people which was truly holy to God.[15]

Whilst the laws of ritual purity were directed at both men and women,[16] women—in order to promote practical, patriarchal socio-economic concerns—were particularly affected.[17] Central to the legislators' notions of purity was an all-pervasive blood taboo which, as has been demonstrated above, embraced foodstuffs, sacrificial victims, humans, etc., and very definitely separated out the male from the female. The fact that, unlike men, women's periods of bodily emission followed a regular and extended (i.e. several days at a time) cycle meant that they were declared unclean for a large part of their lives (for details see below). Great attention was paid to the pollution which resulted from contact with them during these periods, with vital purification rituals being prescribed to avert the danger to both individuals and community (in particular, the male religious community, see below) and restrictions imposed on their movement, particularly with regard to access to the cult, during their times of uncleanness. For, to take just one aspect of this notion of danger, just as crawling things could be seen as the negative side of things approved, so the flow of female blood, again in symbolic terms, could be seen as the negative side of the ideal concept of society as whole and self-contained.[18] In other words, whilst necessary to the

system on both practical and symbolic levels, and a strengthening factor to the positive definition, it remained also an offence to the ideal, marginal to the correct order, and therefore dangerous.

It was also of course a source of female power by virtue of the fact that anything that threatens also wields power—a theme which has often been picked by other contributors to this volume. Female danger/power also rested on the fact that women occupied structurally marginal positions (i.e. neither fully inside nor outside the system, not wholly nature nor culture) and on the fact that society placed them in interstructural roles (as wives and daughters) with respect to alliance-making and linking disparate power groups. Although officially accorded little or no power, it could be argued that women's culturally ambiguous position within Hebrew patriarchy resulted in a type of informal sub-structural power dynamic which in turn regenerated the culturally constructed fear of women necessary to patriarchal interests and explicit power concerns.[19] One aspect of this fear was the way in which the new notion of female impurity rapidly made inroads into the popular imagination, with the result that women came to be seen as a constant stumbling block to man's improvement, a blight on the possibility of his attaining the now required (i.e. post-exilic) standard of personal purity. Thus, in the fourth century, Job:

> Man that is born of woman is of few days and full of trouble . . . Who can bring a clean thing out of an unclean? . . . What is man that he should be clean? And he that is born of woman that he should be righteous? (Job 14.1;4 15.14)

It was an easy step from this type of attitude to regard women as the source of all evil in the world, and that indeed is what happened in the exile and beyond when there emerged the concept of the Evil Woman, of wickedness personified in female form. Such developments and analysis of the inter/sub structural power dynamic are however the concern of another paper . . .[20]

Returning to our historical outline and intimately connected with this new notion of female impurity, was the development of an increased rigidity in attitude toward and definition of function within the family group—something which had gradually been happening before the sixth century but which was accelerated and refined by the experience of the exile.[21] Together with moves towards greater urbanization; more complex economic systems; shifts in societal and familial structure (in particular the movement away from the earlier extended family unit to the nucleated one),[22] there developed the situation whereby the woman's role was placed firmly and almost exclusively in the private sphere of activity as wife, mother and homemaker (a removal encouraged by the purity laws), whilst that of the man was located in the public sphere as worker and family supporter, and active participant in social, political and religious affairs (see, for example, Prov. 31.10ff). This sharp differentiation, and the various impulses and societal shifts which encouraged it (which unfortunately we do not have time to go into here) was quite different from the situation which pertained in earlier Hebrew history. In religious terms, these two exilic and post-exilic developments—i.e. the concentration upon ritual purity and the sharp differentiation in male–female social function—were to have far-reaching consequences for women. Henceforth they were denied access to active participation in the public cult and (by implication of the biblical text which concentrated upon male activity) deemed exempt from the obligation to fulfil many of the commandments—a loaded exemption given the fact that Judaism by this time was already very much a religion of performance, moving towards being a religion dominated by a plethora of commandments governing virtually every aspect of daily existence.[23] This implication was later firmed up by the Sages of the Second Commonwealth to become a fully-fledged rabbinic declaration of exemption embracing nearly all of the positive commandments whose fulfilment depended upon a specific time of the day or year—an exemption which rapidly came to be viewed in terms of actual exclusion (Kidd. 1.7; cf. Sot. 21a). So, for example, women were under no obligation to circumcise their sons (Kidd. 1.7, a point of some significance

in the context of this essay, and one to which I shall return later), or take them to the Temple for the ritual redemption of the first-born (idem); they were exempt from making the thrice-yearly pilgrimage to Jerusalem at the feasts of Passover, Pentecost and Tabernacles (Hag. 1.1); from living in the ceremonial booths at Sukkoth (Sukk. 2.8); shaking the lulab (tos. Kidd. 1.10); sounding the shofar (tos. RH 4.1); and even, at a later stage, of pronouncing the daily affirmation of faith, the Shema (Ber. 3.3).[24] Women's exemption from these time-geared precepts was the result both of their extensive periods of ritual impurity and of their designated role as closeted homemakers—though of course in making such a statement, we immediately involve ourselves in a greater degree of circularity. Anyway, unclean and in a state of domestic seclusion, they thus became increasingly less involved in matters of public religion, and the situation quickly developed wherein their non-participation was viewed in terms of actual exclusion rather than mere exemption.[25] Now, therefore, and unlike the earlier period, only men were the full participants in and officiants of the nation's religious life. In other words, they comprised the religious community; they were the sons of the new covenant as developed in the exile and beyond.

The mark of this new covenant was (and still is) circumcision. Circumcision as a rite had been performed in Israel for many centuries, but it was only with the exile that it assumed the character of a covenantal sign between God and his chosen people. Prior to that it had been viewed in terms of an individual's placatory act of redemption to the deity (or deities) and later as a rite of initiation into the tribe, so marking the male's passage firstly to ordinary, profane existence and secondly to full, public and potentially active membership of society.[26] Already at this stage of the rite's evolution, the absence of a similar rite or substitute ceremony for the girl was a loaded omission.[27] But it was the final stage in the history of circumcision which was to have the most far-reaching implications for the woman and her role in the society and religion of her people. In the exile it was decreed that circumcision was to be the official rite of initiation into Judaism and all that that now meant. It is in Genesis 17.10ff—the verses which are usually taken as belonging to the Priestly strand of the Bible—that we first find mention of the covenantal aspects of circumcision:

> And God said unto Abraham . . . This is My Covenant, which ye shall keep between Me and you and thy seed after thee: every male among you shall be circumcised. And ye shall be circumcised in the flesh of your foreskin; and it shall be a token of a covenant betwixt Me and you. And he that is eight days old[28] shall be circumcised among you, every male throughout your generations, he that is born in thy house, or bought with the money of any foreigner, that is not of thy seed . . . And the uncircumcised male who is not circumcised in the flesh of his foreskin, that soul shall be cut off from his people; he hath broken my covenant.

Henceforth, and unlike the earlier period, this was to be the dominant aspect of the rite. Now it was not simply the male, but the circumcised male who was to be the full participant in his nation's covenantal law and cultic activities. So, for example, with regard to observance of the Passover, the pre-exilic ruling was for "thee and thy son," with no further qualification, to keep the feast, whereas in the exilic and post-exilic legislation the ordinance was modified to count only those who had been circumcised.[29] Similarly, only circumcised men were under an obligation to fulfil the whole law[30] (and here I would remind you that the essence of Judaism was now legalism and observance of the commandments). In other words, they formed the public religious community, and so the words "covenant" and "circumcision" are often used interchangeably in the post-exilic writings.[31]

Another aspect of this later circumcision of particular pertinence to the present discussion is that removal of the foreskin did not on its own render the rite effective. In line with the general emphasis on blood in the exilic Priestly tradition, tremendous importance was attached to the actual blood of the circumcision, and unless several drops of blood were seen to issue from the wound, the operation was deemed invalid and valueless. Later it was even

specified that should there be for any reason no foreskin to sever, blood must still be made to flow for a rite to be effected and for the individual to enter the covenant.[32] Whilst blood would appear to have been associated with circumcision from the earliest times (witness the account of Zipporah in Exodus 4.24–6),[33] this character of the rite, as I hope shortly to show, assumed new dimensions and significances with the experience of the exile and the developments which I have just outlined.

As a clue to that significance we might first recall the way in which the laws regarding menstruation and childbirth and this new circumcision appeared at the same time in the history of the Jewish people, and remember what was earlier said about the nature–culture dichotomy and the need of culture to control or impose itself upon what it deems to be nature. Both of these points need to be placed in context of the general significance which blood, of certain types, had within Hebrew thought and society. As has been shown above, blood was perceived to be the life-giving force of the universe—an obvious conclusion on empirical grounds, but one which was elevated from the pragmatic to the sacred in Hebrew thought by the belief that in humans it was also the seat of the soul, hence the choice of terminology noted at the outset of this essay for murder and death in the Old Testament. The blood of animals was also sacred, or seen as belonging particularly to the deity, and so its shedding played a central role in Jewish cult. As we have seen, differences were made regarding the value of male sacrifices as opposed to female ones, the latter only being offered on less important or non-community based occasions. This cultic shedding of blood was controlled by men, and consecration to the priesthood was effected by daubing men with the blood of slaughtered animals.

Taking these several points in combination we come to the particular significance of the shedding of blood in the ritual of circumcision. The belief was that to ritually and voluntarily—and I stress the word "voluntarily"—shed one's own blood was to recommend oneself to and establish a link with the Creator of the Universe, and this is precisely what happened with circumcision.[34] In other words, by the culture-controlled shedding of blood at circumcision, the individual entered the covenant and joined with his fellow "circumcisees," who together formed a community or brotherhood of blood, bound to each other and God by special duties and mutual obligations. Most importantly, this brotherhood was seen as extending laterally across a generation, vertically to fathers, grandfathers, sons and grandsons, and ultimately to God—a point to which I shall return.[35] The new significance of the covenantal blood of circumcision was clearly demonstrated by the later midrashic (rabbinic) paraphrase of the biblical "life is in the blood" to "life is in the blood of circumcision."[36]

At precisely the same time as circumcision and the blood of circumcision was receiving this new casting and additional dimension, legislation about female blood—i.e. the blood of menstruation and childbirth—appeared for the first time on the scene. But the attention paid to it was of a completely different nature to that accorded to male blood. As we have seen, it was declared unclean and ritually polluting, and equated metaphorically with the defilement imparted by carrying an idol.[37] Unlike the cultic inclusion of men through the blood of circumcision, the blood of the female cycle resulted in cultic exclusion for women. So, according to the laws of Leviticus, women were forbidden to enter the Temple or touch any hallowed thing during their times of menstrual uncleanness,[38] whilst with regard to childbirth they were similarly removed from cultic activity, this time for forty days following delivery of a boy and significantly eighty days after that of a girl.[39] And here I would like to quote the Levitical ruling on childbirth for it highlights what I hope is now becoming clear, i.e. the perceived gender differentials in blood and the connection between male circumcision and the female blood cycle:

> If a woman be delivered and bear a man-child, then she shall be unclean for seven days; as in the days of the impurity of her sickness shall she be unclean. And in the eighth day the flesh of his foreskin shall be circumcised. And she shall continue in the blood of purification three and thirty days; she shall touch no

> hallowed thing, nor come into the sanctuary, until the days of her purification be fulfilled. But if she bear a maid-child, then she shall be unclean two weeks, as in her impurity; and she shall continue in the blood of purification threescore and six days. And when the days of her purification are fulfilled, for a son or for a daughter, she shall bring a lamb of the first year for a burnt offering, and a young pigeon or a turtledove, for a sin offering, unto the door of the tent of meeting, unto the priest. And he shall offer it before the Lord, and make atonement for her; and she shall be cleansed from the fountain of her blood . . . the priest shall make atonement for her, and she shall become clean. (Lev. 12.2ff)

The significant points to note from this passage are firstly the way in which the blood of delivery is unclean; secondly the way in which in the case of a boy's birth circumcision intrudes in the text and interrupts both the period of the mother's pollution and the account of that pollution; and thirdly, the way in which the woman is finally cleansed of her impurity through the blood of sacrifice as administered by a circumcised male.

It is apparent, therefore, that differentiation was made between male and female blood, and that circumcision, in its new casting, had some role to play in that context. To deal with the blood differential first: according to the later thinking of the tannaim (rabbis of the first centuries ad), the reason for the Levitical laws of menstruation and childbirth was as punishment for the sin of Eve who brought about the death of Adam. In other words, and I quote, ". . . because she shed his blood, she was punished through her blood" (Gen. Rabbah 17.13). As the quotation shows, the two types of blood were perceived as two sides of the same coin: on the one side positive male blood and on the other negative female blood.[40] However, whilst the image of the "head and tail" coin is pertinent to our understanding of the rituals, the rabbis' words provide us with little more than an appreciation of how Jewish society (or a part thereof) at the time perceived and explained the religious state of affairs. In other words, they merely represent a constructed rationale of an existing custom. To reach a fuller understanding of the blood differential—its origin, purpose and effect—it is necessary to dig a little deeper and attempt to trace the underlying reasons by means of a sociological/anthropological analysis—and this is what I have been attempting to do in the course of this essay. I would now like to reiterate and elaborate the several points which I have raised so far, and then finally bring my argument round to demonstrating the link which exists between circumcision and menstrual/childbirth taboos.

The first point is that it is generally recognized that ritual tends to increase, intensify and shift in focus at times of social crisis. In particular—and on this see the work of Mary Douglas—when the body politic is threatened, it is common to see increased attention paid to the purity, integrity and unity of the physical body.[41] This, as we have seen, is precisely what happened with the exile and in the Levitical legislation regarding ritual pollution.

Secondly, ritual, in addition to mirroring the anxieties of society, also expresses the ordering of society in all its aspects and complexity, and to use the words of Ortner, may be viewed as marking the universal human endeavour to transcend and control the world of nature (amongst other things). Indeed, to continue with Ortner's words, "the distinctiveness of culture rests precisely on the fact that it can under most circumstances transcend natural conditions and turn them to its purpose. Thus culture at some level of awareness asserts itself to be not only distinct from but superior to nature, and that sense of distinctiveness and superiority rests precisely on the ability to transform—to 'socialize' and 'culturalize'—nature,"[42] i.e. to be active and in control.

Within this scheme of thought, anything which cannot be controlled is labelled dangerous and marginal, particularly when society is working to preserve its unity and to develop more sophisticated systems of self-definition, as was the case for the Jewish community in Palestine following the exile. The blood of childbirth and menstruation, which follows a passive and unstoppable cycle, can be construed (by the powers that be) to fall within this category, and so it is required that cultural regulation step in with restrictive legislation. That cultural regulation, as we have seen, is controlled by men, for (and this brings me to the third point), within this scheme of thought, woman herself is placed more fully within the realm of nature than man in consequence of the fact that more of her time and her body are seen to be taken up with the natural processes surrounding reproduction of the species.[43] Man, on the other hand, who within this particular characterization of the nature–culture dichotomy is deemed to lack such natural and visible creative functions, is obliged, or at least has the opportunity (to use the words of Ortner), to assert his creativity externally through the medium of technology, ritual and symbol.[44] As active manipulator of his existence, he falls within the realm of culture, and so, just as culture is deemed superior to nature, so man and his activities are considered superior to woman and her world.[45]

And this brings me to my fourth point, and that is the notion of domestic–public opposition. Following the exile, it should be recalled that women, for a complex of pragmatic reasons, were confined almost exclusively to the domestic realm. This relegation—for as such it was undoubtedly construed[46]—to the domestic realm, whilst on the one hand promoting a higher status than before for women in terms of motherhood (a status generated for society's structural purposes and needs[47]), also resulted in an overall decrease in women's status generally, for, to use the well known Lévi-Straussian model, the domestic unit—i.e. the "biological" family concerned with reproducing and socializing new members of society[48]—was seen as separate from the public entity—i.e. the superimposed network of alliances and relationships which comprised society proper, as it were. And this separation—or indeed opposition—according to Lévi-Strauss, had the significance of the opposition between nature and culture.[49] Women's world could therefore be seen as inferior to the higher cultural activities of men in the public domain[50]—a fact recognized by the first century ad Jewish philosopher Philo who in his writings made much play of this gender-differentiated opposition between the public and private domains.[51] The same writer, as we have seen (. . . above), also elaborated at length on the idea of superior male rationality and causality versus inferior female irrationality and passivity. And this brings me finally to the link between circumcision and menstrual taboo.

Whilst women's role as mothers was of paramount importance to society—particularly after the exile when maternity, for various pragmatic reasons, became the means of transmitting and establishing in biological terms, as it were, religious and ethnic identity[52]—it would seem logical, given our culture–nature opposition and the fact that culture seeks to control and impose upon whatever has been construed as natural, that something had to be done in cultural terms about the natural function of childbirth. And this, I think, is where circumcision comes in. It served as a rite of cultural rebirth by which the male individual was accorded entry into the society and religion of his people. In other words, whilst women, as it were, merely conducted the animal-like repetitive tasks of carrying on the reproduction of the human race, men, by one supreme symbolic act, imposed themselves upon nature and enacted a cultural rebirth. The blood of circumcision served as a symbolic surrogate for the blood of childbirth, and because it was shed voluntarily and in a controlled manner, it transcended the bounds of nature and the passive blood flow of the mother at delivery and during the preparatory cycle for pregnancy, menstruation.[53] The blood of circumcision, just like the blood of animal sacrifice, could also be viewed as cleansing the boy of his mother's blood and acting as a rite of separation, differentiating him from the female, and allying him with the male community.[54] In a sense, therefore, circumcision actually creates a more powerful gender distinction rather than just deriving from such a distinction—but here again one gets wrapped in inevitable strands of circularity. For all of these reasons, and unlike the earlier biblical period, only men were allowed to perform the operation (see Kidd. 1.7, 29ab; Pes. 3.7). At a later time it was even decreed that should there be no male (in particular a father) available to sever the foreskin and make the blood flow, then the child should wait until he had grown up and then perform the operation himself. Under no circumstances was the mother to enact this cultural role.[55] All of this was so very different from the earlier period of Hebrew history when the first recorded occasion of a circumcision had as its central active character the woman Zipporah, and it puts in context the biblical passage, written at the time of the exile, with which this essay opened: Jerusalem, allegorized as a female in needy relation to her Lord and depicted as cleansed of her blood by the intervention of a male deity.

In the context of post-exilic Judaism, therefore, natural birth gave rise to an intergenerational line of blood; cultural rebirth created a network of brotherhood of blood which transcended generations and was superior to biological and socio-biological kinship ties. These were the two sides of the same coin which I referred to at the beginning of this essay, the nature–culture opposition and the particular characterizations and choice of emphases here explored being one explanation for the apparent gender differentials in blood within Jewish ritual practice, and one link at least between the rite of circumcision and menstrual taboo. The fact that both rituals continued to be practised even after the 70 ad fall of the Temple in Jerusalem when other cult-associated rituals fell into disuse and when the overt reason, at least, for the laws of female purity no longer pertained, demonstrates their central significance to the Jewish system of gender creation and differentiation—and the real hidden agenda behind their initial promulgation in the sixth century bc.

The menstrual taboo, originally presented and applied with explicit reference to maintaining the purity of the Temple and its cultic participants, was in the first century ad recast in terms of family law and the purity of marriage within the domestic unit. Its rationale shifted but its purpose in one respect at least remained, and orthodox women to this day follow through the ritual of purification at the mikva every month and abstain from physical contact with their husbands during their times of bleeding and for seven days thereafter (5 two weeks every month).[56] In non-orthodox circles also the blood taboo, in culturally received if not strictly religious terms, is strong and is observed to varying degrees in context of inter-personal relations.

With regard to circumcision, this too remains a central ritual. Unlike the laws of menstruation and childbirth, it had never been as intimately linked to cultic activity/purity and so no recasting was required following the events of 70 ad. It remained the sign of the covenant and as such was observed in fulfillment of divine commandment, and this remains the case today among the religious. In non-religious circles, however, it is also widely practised and families who often observe little else of the religion frequently have their male children circumcised, again as part of a cultural inheritance and as a means (usually undefined and inarticulated) of self- and collective identification. Similarly, in the various schools of reform Judaism circumcision still occupies a central place, despite the objections raised by the nineteenth-century originators of the movement to the rite's continuation on the grounds (amongst others) that there was no rite of initiation for daughters into the religion so the male ritual ought to be abandoned.[57] The continued practice underlies Spinoza's belief that observance of this rite was alone sufficient to ensure the survival of the Jewish people (Tractatus Theologico-Politicus 3:53),[58] and demonstrates the strength of the ritual's cultural entrenchment. Whilst some shifts in meaning have occurred, therefore, the survival of the rituals of both circumcision and menstruation demonstrates their profound significance to the Jewish socio-religious and cultural system of belief and definition, and their on-going role in the business of gender and the creation of non-ambiguous male–female categories. They continue to have an impact on women's involvement in public religion and on social attitude towards "the female."

Finally, and to return to the first century ad, although Christianity inherited much from its Judaic roots, it did not embrace the need for circumcision. Formal, and informal, taboos around menstruation to some extent continued, but the ritual of male circumcision was abandoned—a fascinating development given the significance and purpose of the ritual and one that looks, at first glance, like a clean break with the past to facilitate the future and the expansion of Christianity (see, for example, Acts 10–11, 15; Romans 4; Gal. 3, 5). Whatever the pragmatics of the decision, however, a closer look at the New Testament and the justification which the early Christians chose to give for abandoning circumcision reveals much about the ritual and ironically brings us back full circle to the notion of gendered blood and the whole culture–nature: male–female scenario. For the ultimate cultic sacrifice and voluntary shedding of blood was seen to have been achieved in the figure of the male, circumcised, saviour Christ. He was the new and eternal Paschal lamb, he was the new Temple and law; through his blood the new covenant was established and by his blood sins were forgiven (see Heb. passim; 1 Cor. 5.7; Rev. 1.5, 5.6f; 14; Eph. 2; 1 John 1.7, etc.). Thinking they were breaking with the past, the early Christians re-enacted it. Depicted as a High Priest and son of the 'King of Kings . . . clad in a robe sprinkled with blood,' Christ

> . . . entered once for all into the Holy Place, taking not the blood of goats and calves but his own blood, thus securing an eternal redemption . . . He is the mediator of a new covenant . . . He has appeared once for all at the end of the age to put away sin by the sacrifice of himself . . . by the blood of the eternal covenant. (Heb. 9.12ff, 15, 26, 13.20; cf. Rev. 19.13, 16)

The old blood covenant had gone. A new one rose to replace it.

ENDNOTES

1. For a history of source criticism and other methodological approaches to the OT, in particular the Pentateuch, see Douglas A. Knight and Gene M. Tucker (eds), *The Hebrew Bible and its Modern Interpreters*, Philadelphia and Chico, Fortress, 1985, especially ch. 8; for details regarding recent debates over the dating of the Priestly literature (which vary from pre-Deuteronomic to Persian, but with the majority of scholars still looking to the exilic and post-exilic age) and discussion as to whether P is a source or redaction, see especially pp. 285–6.

2. I say "male" circumcision because this was the only form of circumcision practised among the Hebrews/Jews: the ancient geographer Strabo is certainly incorrect in his view that both male and female children were circumcised

(Geographica, XVI, 2:37, 4:9, XVII, 2:5). Even if he were correct it is clear from surveys of other cultures that female circumcision has a very different function from the male rite with which we are here concerned. On this point, see Nawal El Saadawi, The Hidden Face of Eve: Women in the Arab World, London, Zed Press, 1980.

3. Philo, De Specialibus Legibus, 1:226ff.

4. Philo, De Specialibus Legibus, 1:198ff.

5. See Sherry Ortner, "Is Female to Male as Nature is to Culture?" in Michelle Zimbalist Rosaldo and Louise Lamphere (eds), Women, Culture and Society, Stanford, University Press, CA, 1974, pp. 67–87. Opponents of her argument who are disinclined to use any universalistic model and who argue that Ortner simply swapped one set of deterministic principles (biological) for another equally inflexible set (social constructionist) include Janet Sayers, Biological Politics, London, Tavistock Publications, 1982; and Carol P. MacCormack, "Nature, Culture and Gender: A Critique" in Carol MacCormack and Marilyn Strathern (eds), Nature, Culture and Gender (Cambridge University Press, 1980), pp. 1–24. The model here presented and then applied is a modified version of Ortner's which attempts to avoid some of the obvious pitfalls of her early argument whilst at the same time acknowledging its debt to her work.

6. See Ortner, p. 71: ". . . [biological] facts and differences only take on significance of superior/inferior within the framework of culturally defined value systems"; Kirsten Hastrup, "The Semantics of Biology: Virginity," in Shirley Ardener (ed.), Defining Females, London, Croom Helm [for] the Oxford University Women's Studies Committee, 1978; p. 49: ". . . socially significant distinctions are mapped on to basic biological differences and vice versa," and MacCormack, p. 18: ". . . the link between nature and women is not a 'given.' Gender and its attributes are not pure biology. The meanings attributed to male and female are as arbitrary as are the meanings attributed to nature and culture."

7. For fuller details than is possible here of this involvement and the subsequent developments presented below, see Leonie J. Archer, "The Role of Jewish Women in the Religion, Ritual and Cult of Graeco-Roman Palestine" in Averil Cameron and Amelie Kuhrt (eds), Images of Women in Antiquity (London, Croom Helm, 1983), pp. 273–87. For women active in public capacities generally, see M.C. Astour, "Tamar the Hierodule," Journal of Biblical Literature 85 (1966), pp. 185–96; B.A. Brooks, "Fertility Cult Functionaries in the Old Testament," JBL, 60 (1941), pp. 227–53; I.J. Peritz, "Women in the Ancient Hebrew Cult," JBL 17 (1898), pp. 111–47.

8. Or at least if not the direct result they received their final and decisive impulse from the experience of the exile. Religious and social ordering had been slowly changing in the immediately preceding centuries, but the exile both accelerated and fixed these developments and marked a definite turning point. On this see further below and Leonie J. Archer, "The Virgin and the Harlot in the Writings of Formative Judaism," History Workshop Journal 24 (Autumn 1987), pp. 1–16.

9. In saying that these laws were in fact exilic, I again follow both the traditional dating within the documentary hypothesis framework and, more importantly, the internal dynamic or logic of the sociological argument here elucidated.

10. Note that only the élite of the nation had been taken into exile by Nebuchadnezzar, leaving behind "vinedressers, husbandmen, and the poorest sort of the people of the land" (2 Kings 24.14, 25.12). Of these exiles only a portion then returned to the land to start the process of purification and separation. For this see the accounts of Ezra and Nehemiah.

11. See Mary Douglas, Purity and Danger (London, Routledge, 1966), p. 124, for the way in which concern about orifices, fluids, etc., mirrors the anxieties of a "hard-pressed minority."

12. Douglas, p. 14.

13. Douglas, p. 4. Of particular importance to us here, of course, is the need to create distinct male–female categories.

14. For an analysis of the dietary laws along these lines, see Douglas, ch. 3.

15. See the constant admonitions to this effect in Ezra, Nehemiah and throughout the Priestly strands of the OT, particularly Leviticus. For the equation by the legislators of ritual cleanness with holiness, see Jacob Neusner, The Idea of Purity in Ancient Judaism, with a critique and commentary by Mary Douglas (Leiden, 1983).

16. The rules specific to men concerned excretions from the sexual organs (i.e. venereal disease) and issues of semen (Lev. 15.3–18). The first necessitated counting "seven days for his cleansing" whilst the second, obviously more common state, resulted in impurity only "until the even," i.e. the first sunset following the emission. The rules which pertained specifically to women will be treated below.

17. Douglas argues (Purity and Danger, p. 101) that women are particularly affected because their bodies serve as biological models or symbols for the purity of society—and so by implication they are the special target of such legislation. The dangers of such an argument are, however, all too obvious in that it implies an inescapable destiny for women. I prefer the focus here taken which emphasizes both the socio-economic dynamic and the cultural mapping on to the biological, in particular the patriarchal cultural mapping.

18. Here again, unlike Douglas et al., I would stress that this is just one possible interpretation of the biological facts.

19. See, for example, the analysis by Douglas of various modern societies: ". . . those holding office in the explicit part of the structure tend to be credited with consciously controlled powers, in contrast to those whose role is less explicit and who tend to be credited with unconscious powers, menacing those in better defined positions . . . [for example:] the Kachin wife. Linking two disparate power groups, her husband's and her brother's, she holds an interstructural role, and she is thought of as the unconscious, involuntary agent of witchcraft. Similarly, the father in the matrilineal Trobrianders and Ashanti, and the mother's brother in patrilineal Tikopia and Taleland, is credited with being an involuntary source of danger. These people are none of them without a proper niche in the total society. But from the perspective of one internal sub-system to which they do not belong, but in which they must operate, they are intruders . . . the kind of powers attributed to them symbolize their ambiguous, inarticulate status" (Purity and Danger, pp. 101–2).

20. For the rise of this concept/image and its use in creating distinct gender categories and social roles, see Archer, "The Virgin and the Harlot . . . ," pp. 1–16.

21. For details of this evolution, which can only be touched upon here, and the sharp impulse provided by the exile see Archer, Her Price Is Beyond Rubies: The Jewish Woman in Graeco-Roman Palestine, Sheffield (Academic Press, 1990), ch. 1 sect. d.

22. For detailed argument regarding these developments within a clear chronological framework (seventh century bc forward), together with biblical and post-biblical references too numerous to cite here, see Archer, "The Virgin and the Harlot . . . ," pp. 5–7 with notes.

23. For the way in which the law was the hallmark of Judaism—a situation very different from the earlier Hebrew religion—see Archer, "The Virgin and the Harlot . . . ," pp. 5–7, and "The Role of Jewish Women," p. 277.

24. For further details of these and the other exemptions, with full rabbinic references and secondary source citation, see Archer, "The Role of Jewish Women," pp. 277ff.

25. As much is implied by various writers of the period (see Archer, Her Price Is Beyond Rubies, ch. 1 sect. d). Note also the rabbinic view that if a woman did perform a commandment from which she was "exempt," the action was without value for she was as "one who is not commanded and fulfils" (Sot. 21a).

26. For this early history plus details of the rite's subsequent development, see Archer, Her Price Is Beyond Rubies, ch. 1 sect. b.

27. Possible alternative rituals or rites de passage suggested in my book might have included, for example, the ceremonial cutting off of the girl's first hair, given that hair in the Hebrew belief system had ritual and mystical significance (Her Price Is Beyond Rubies, ch. 1 sect. b).

28. For the significance of the operation being performed on the eighth day of the child's life rather than at any other time, see Her Price Is Beyond Rubies, ch. 1 sect. b.

29. Contrast Exod. 12.24 (5 J, early strand) with Exod. 12.44 (P). Cf. Exod. 23.17, 34.23; Deut. 16.17, all of which are pre-exilic. Note that if women did attend the Passover ceremonial in Jerusalem, they attended by virtue of some attachment to a man (husband, father, brother). See Judah Ben-Siyyon Segal, The Hebrew Passover from the Earliest Times to ad 70, London, 1963, p. 35.

30. See, for example, the later statement of Gal. 5.3. Note also the way in which God-fearers who attached themselves to the Jewish community but who were not under an obligation to fulfil the whole law were characterized by various ancient writers as "the uncircumcised" (see Emil Schurer in The History of the Jewish People in the Age of Jesus Christ, G. Vermes, F. Millar, M. Goodman (eds), Edinburgh, T. & T. Clark, III. 2, pp. 165ff).

31. It should be said that the uncircumcised Jew remained a Jew by birth (see Hull. 4b; Ab Zarah 27a, and n. 52 below), but he was denied access to the higher life, as it were, of his people (i.e. like a woman). The penalty for non-observance of the rite was karet (Gen. 17.14) which was interpreted by the rabbis to mean premature death at the hands of heaven.

32. Shabb. 135–7; Yeb. 71a; Gen Rabbah 46.12, "The sages have taught thus: in the case of an infant born without a foreskin it is necessary to cause a few drops of the blood of the covenant to flow from him on account of the covenant of Abraham." All the texts refer to "the blood of the covenant."

On this and the sacrificial character of the rite, see Geza Vermes, Scripture and Tradition in Judaism, (Leiden, 1961), pp. 190–191.

33. Exod. 4.24–6, "And it came to pass on the way at the lodging place that the Lord met him [Moses] and sought to kill him. Then Zipporah [Moses' wife] took a flint and cut off the foreskin of her son and cast it at his [Moses'/angel's?] feet, and she said "Surely a bridegroom of blood art thou to me . . . A bridegroom of blood in regard to circumcision." Later sources (Targum, Septuagint) also emphasize the all-important role which the blood of circumcision had in Moses' redemption. On the complexities of this passage and its treatment by post-biblical writers, see Vermes, Scripture and Tradition, pp. 180ff, and H. Kosmala, "The Bloody Husband," Vetus Testamentum 12 (1962).

34. Strictly speaking of course the eight-day-old child could not "voluntarily" shed his own blood, but the assumption was that if he were able to determine his own fate, he would so choose. In any case, whether it was the child's will or not, the event still marked the operation of culture over nature, albeit in this instance through the agency of others.

35. So, for example, see Mal. 2.10 ("Have we not all one father? Hath not one God created us? Why do we deal treacherously every man against his brother, profaning the covenant of our fathers?"); Amos 1.9 (the "brotherly covenant" berith achim); Ezekiel 18.4 ("Behold all souls are mine; as the soul of the father is mine, so also the soul of the son is mine").

36. Lev. Rabbah, Lev. 17.11. Note also the way in which both midrashic (rabbinic commentary) and targumic (interpretative Aramaic translation of the Bible) exegesis saw Israel as having been saved through the blood of Passover and the blood of circumcision. See Vermes, Scripture and Tradition, pp. 190–191. We might also note that in the eyes of the midrashic commentators, not only were the Hebrews in Egypt saved by the smearing of the blood of male animals on the doorposts but, in opposition, God had "punished the Egyptians with blood" because they had not allowed the daughters of Israel to ritually immerse themselves following menstruation (Ex. Rabbah 9.10).

37. So, for example, the statement of R. Akiba in Shabb. 9.1. For biblical instances of the uncleanness of the menstruant being used as a noun and metaphor for the height of defilement, see Ezek. 7.19–20; Lam. 1.17; Ezra 9.11; 2 Chron. 29.5 (note that all of these works are to be dated to the exile and beyond).

38. Lev. 15.19–32. Biblical law declared the woman unclean just for the days of bleeding, up until the close of a seven-day period (if bleeding continued thereafter she entered a different category of uncleanness); rabbinic law, however, around the turn of the eras and the first centuries of the Christian period extended the time of uncleanness to count from the day the woman expected her menses through to the close of seven clear days (i.e., days without bleeding), and totalled the whole period of impurity as a minimum of twelve days, the ruling that applies today. The emphasis of the biblical law (our concern here) was with admission to the cult, that of the rabbis with sexual activity between husband and wife, a shift that will be touched on further below. For details of the consequences of impurity, its transmission

to others, etc., see Encyclopaedia Judaica vol. 12, cols. 1141–7, vol. 13, cols. 1405–12.

39. For an analysis of the social significance of this differentiation, see Archer, Her Price Is Beyond Rubies, ch. 1 sect. b.

40. We might note that despite the wording of this particular quotation, used by the rabbis for a specific purpose, Eve is not in the main cited as the culprit for the Fall, rather the attention of the texts lies with Adam. The shift in focus to Eve only came about with Christianity and the work of the Church Fathers. On this see Archer, "The Virgin and the Harlot . . . ," p. 2 and n. 5.

41. Douglas, Purity and Danger, especially chs 7 and 9.

42. Ortner, pp. 72–3.

43. See Simone de Beauvoir, The Second Sex (London, Cape, 1968), pp. 24ff, regarding the non-function to the individual of breasts, ovarian secretions, menstrual cycle, etc., and her conclusion (p. 239) that the female ". . . is more enslaved to the species than the male, her animality is more manifest." Note the way in which I, along with Ortner (pp. 73ff), would stress that woman within this scheme of thought is seen as closer to nature and not relegated totally to that realm. As Lévi-Strauss writes, no matter how devalued woman and her designated role may be, or how denied her ability to transcend and socialize, ". . . even in a man's world she is still a person, and since insofar as she is defined as a sign she must [still] be recognized as a generator of signs" (in Elementary Structures of Kinship, Boston, Beacon Press, 1969, p. 496). The tensions inherent to this conceptual system and the woman's intermediary and interstructural role (noted already) are obvious.

44. Ortner, p. 75.

45. Note in this context de Beauvoir's comments regarding the way in which greater prestige is often accorded to the male destruction of life (e.g. warfare, hunting, etc.) than to the female creation of life (The Second Sex, pp. 58–9), and Ortner's comments thereto (p. 75). This is a particularly salient point remembering what has here been said regarding cultic sacrifice and its practitioners. In some feminist circles there have been moves towards reversing this situation by the introduction of formalized and ritualized celebrations of female creativity and the menstrual cycle. See Rosemary Radford Ruether in this volume.

46. See, for example, Josephus, Con. Ap. 2.201, "The woman, says the Law, is in all things inferior to the man"; Philo, Spec. Leg. 3:169f (quoted n. 51 below). For an argument against the spurious but oft-heard "different but equal" thesis see Leonie J. Archer, "Women in Formative Judaism" (unpublished paper, Oxford 1986).

47. See the marked frequency with which the community was reminded in the exilic and post-exilic writings of the command to "Honour thy father and thy mother," and Archer, Her Price Is Beyond Rubies, ch. 1 sect. d and ch. 2 sect. a for an analysis of both the commandment's social dynamic and the qualified nature in fact of the respect to be accorded the woman. See also n. 50 below.

48. Lévi-Strauss's labelling of the domestic unit as "biological" is of course too simplistic and indeed predisposes his own conclusion. It is also internally contradictory to his own definition which includes the domestic unit's socializing function. To follow his labelling would be to place women (and other members of the family) totally within the realm of nature. Bearing in mind these drawbacks, though, the model remains extremely useful and insightful.

49. Lévi-Strauss, p. 479, quoted in Ortner, p. 78.

50. On this see Michelle Zimbalist Rosaldo, "Woman, Culture, and Society: A Theoretical Overview," in Rosaldo and Lamphere, Women, Culture and Society, pp. 17–42; Nancy Chodorow, "Family Structure and Feminine Personality," in ibid., pp. 43–66; Ortner, "Is Female to Male . . ." The focus on women's role/status as mother also encouraged this view, for the tendency was to regard the tasks of motherhood as purely natural without recognizing that the bulk of the work involved socializing new members of the community.

51. See, for example, Spec. Leg. 3:169f, "Market places and council halls and law courts and gatherings and meetings where a large number of people are assembled, and open air life with full scope for discussion and action—all these are suitable for men both in war and peace. The women are best suited to the indoor life which never strays from the house . . . Organized communities are of two sorts, the greater which we call cities and the smaller which we call households. Both of these have their governors; the government of the greater is assigned to men under the name of statesmanship, that of the lesser, known as household management, to women . . ."

52. Regarding the question of Jewish identity, we should note that at least by Talmudic times (fifth century ad), the (ethnic) status of the child was determined by that of his or her mother and not by that of the father. So Kidd. 68b (on the basis of the second century ad mishnah), "Thy son by an Israelite woman is called thy son, thy son by a Gentile woman is not called thy son." According to Encyclopaedia Judaica vol. 10 cols. 54–5 such halachic definition of Jewish identity had been reached by Hasmonaean times (second–first centuries bc). Although more research needs to be done regarding exactly when this understanding of ethnic transmission was introduced—especially given the current debate over "Who is a Jew?"—it is certainly possible that it evolved around the time of the exile and the community's return to Palestine.

53. Although often coming from a completely different analytical perspective from the one here taken, it is interesting and revealing to note the way in which the ritual is popularly described in the secondary sources. For example, E. O. James in Myth and Ritual, S. H. Hooke, ed., London, 1933, p. 150 writes, "In most communities where the corporate attitude of mind still predominates it is necessary for the individual at some period of his [sic] life . . . to undergo a solemn initiation into the tribal society, as distinct from that of the clan or family group in which he has been born. Until this has been done the youth is excluded from the ceremonial (i.e. the social) life of the tribe. Hence the rite consists virtually in a new birth . . . as a complete and active member of society."

54. See again Lev. 12.2ff and my analysis thereof, [pp. 384–85] above. See also J.B. Segal, "Popular Religion in ancient Israel," Journal of Jewish Studies 27/1 (Autumn 1976), pp. 5–6, who descriptively rather than analytically writes: "A male infant was circumcised on the eighth day after birth because he was affected by his mother's uncleanness during the first seven days after the delivery; the eighth day was the first on which he could be approached by the male who carried out the ceremony."

55. See Gen. Rabbah 46.9 (17.8), "Only he who is himself circumcised may perform circumcision . . . An uncircumcised Israelite may not circumcise," and Song of Songs Rabbah 4.6, 1 (on Gen. 17.13), "God said, 'Shall an unclean person come and operate on the clean? Would that be right?' No; 'circumcising he shall be circumcised' . . . it befits the clean to attend the clean."

56. See the essay by Linda Sireling in this book.

57. See Encyclopaedia Judaica vol. 5 cols. 570–71 and Jewish Encyclopaedia vol. IV p. 96 for details of the proposed reform and the degree of agitation which it engendered.

58. Cf. Encyclopaedia Judaica vol. 5 col. 575, "[Circumcision] is not only a religious but also a national practice, and is observed as enthusiastically by the secularists . . . as by traditional believers. Its influence on Jewish life throughout the ages has been so strong that its observance is often the sole remaining token of affinity with Judaism, even after intermarriage, when the Jewish parent insists on the circumcision of the sons."

READING 6–4

THE SWEAT LODGE: INSIDE

William K. Powers

The sweat lodge is a characteristic religious symbol for certain native North Americans, providing the physical setting within which ritual is made to act upon the body to clear the mind and cleanse it of evil. Thus purified, the ritual participant is empowered to seek a vision in quest of self-knowledge. Emile Durkheim, in contrast to Arnold van Gennep (see Mary Douglas's article in Chapter 2), insisted on the absolute distinction between the sacred and the profane. The Oglala, however, show van Gennep to be correct. In ritual contexts, the sweat lodge is indeed considered a sacred artifact; however, when not serving its ritual function the structure is no more sacred than a children's playground, a purpose for which, Powers tells us, it is often used.

There are many kinds of dreamers among the Oglalas: some have dreamed of the eagle, bear, elk, or other animals; some have dreamed of birds. The

Source: Reprinted from Yuwipi: Vision and Experience in Oglala Religion by William K. Powers by permission of the University of Nebraska Press. Copyright © 1982 by the University of Nebraska Press.

Yuwipi man is only one kind, and he receives his first instructions about the duties of the Yuwipi man in a vision that may be incomprehensible to him and require the interpretation of another dreamer. A Yuwipi man is referred to honorifically as Tunka˘sila, just as the spirits are, or he may call himself iyeska 'interpreter' or 'medium,' because one of his functions is to interpret the meanings of visions to others, and also to relay the instructions of spirits whom only he can see, hear, and understand.

When a man receives a vision that is interpreted to mean he must become a Yuwipi man, he often serves some years as an apprentice. But the prayers, songs, and material objects he uses in his ceremonies are his personal property, because he alone has been instructed by the spirits in their specific uses. The ritual paraphernalia are sacred and are usually burned after a Yuwipi man's death or else buried with him. In some circumstances a son who has also received a vision instructing him to "walk with the pipe," as the Yuwipi man's vocation is called, may inherit his father's paraphernalia. In rare instances a Yuwipi man may bequeath his paraphernalia to an aspiring young practitioner.

Once a man has accepted the responsibility of being a Yuwipi man, he is obliged to lead a good life and to make many sacrifices. He must pray with the pipe every day and often revitalize his power by going on a vision quest. If he did not do so his power would wane, and he might even risk losing his life or that of a loved one. Although the Yuwipi man shares a close relationship with the spirits to provide long and healthy lives for all his grandchildren—that is, all his people—he is fearful of the spirits he invokes. More than the common people, he recognizes the awesome power of the spirit world, and he understands more clearly than others the spirits' absolute power. He must do nothing that offends them: he particularly must handle the pipe properly and avoid women during their menses.

Just as a Yuwipi man fears his own powers, he may be feared or mistrusted by others, because some men communicate with the spirits for evil purposes and are capable of inflicting misfortune and sickness on the people. He must learn to contend with petty jealousies, because the common people will always be watching to make sure he conducts himself properly. If he does not, they will think his power is diminishing, and his followers will leave him for a stronger Yuwipi man.

Yuwipi men cannot charge fees for their services, though they are often accused of doing so. By Oglala standards a person does not have to pay, though he will be expected to donate something to the Yuwipi man if the service enhances his life, and he must pledge to sponsor a thanksgiving ritual within a year. If such a thanksgiving is not offered the spirits will become angry, and the person the ritual benefited will be in danger.

The Yuwipi man is particularly suited and trained by the spirits to diagnose and treat "Indian sickness," illnesses that generally were common to the Indian people before the white man arrived. If a patient is afflicted with a "white man's disease" the Yuwipi man diagnoses the illness and usually recommends that the patient be treated at the public health hospital or go to a white doctor. Some Yuwipi men have been known to consult with white physicians and the Yuwipi man may conduct a ritual in the hospital. But in any case the Yuwipi man always receives credit if the sick person recovers. If the patient has a white man's disease and does not recover, the white physician is held responsible. But if he recovers from either Indian sickness or a white man's disease, the Yuwipi man receives credit for the cure because he has properly diagnosed the case.

In addition to conducting the vision quest, sweat lodge, and Yuwipi rituals, a Yuwipi man may also be asked by the tribe to supervise the sun dance or assist the sun dance director. When there are many dancers, a number of Yuwipi men may collaborate to conduct the sun dance, and each will supervise several dancers, instructing them in their duties and piercing them on the final day. Yuwipi men may be seen talking and joking together, but underlying their amiable behavior is a strong competitiveness, encouraged by their followers, who often boast of the superiority of "their" Yuwipi men.

In general appearance Yuwipi men are no different from the common people. They have no particular badge of office except a suitcase or bag in which they keep their ritual paraphernalia, which they carry only when they are about to conduct a meeting. Even during a ritual the Yuwipi man wears nothing special, and the only difference between him and the others in attendance is that he usually removes his shirt and shoes.

But though the Yuwipi man resembles the common people superficially, he is superior to them spiritually. He alone can mediate between them and the spirit world, and he alone can cure them of Indian sickness. The common people say the Yuwipi man speaks a strange language they cannot understand—a special sacred language that he uses to communicate with the spirits. He can also understand the languages of birds and animals, and it is in particular this ability to communicate with nonhumans that sets him apart from the community.

Plenty Wolf sat with his wife and son on the shady side of his log house. Though it was late in the afternoon, the sun was still hot. A light breeze played against the four-walled tent in the backyard that served as a bedroom on hot nights.

Plenty Wolf gazed straight ahead but saw very little. His eyes teared from the glaucoma that had rendered him nearly blind; it was only a matter of time before the world would be black for him. Cars sped up and down the road, but he did not hear them, for a fall from a horse when he was twenty-eight had left him almost completely deaf. This deafness was partly responsible for his seeking out a powerful Yuwipi man named Horn Chips, who put Plenty Wolf on the hill. Here the novice had a series of visions that were interpreted to mean he should walk with the pipe. He was now sixty-six years old, and for nearly forty years he had been a Yuwipi man.

His afflictions had taken their toll, and he looked much older than his age. He was small and thin, with close-cropped graying hair. His few teeth were fragile and visible only when he grinned or coughed. Plastic-rimmed glasses teetered on his bulbous nose. Time and weather had cracked his skin and wrinkled his bony hands. He wore an oversized military shirt, Levis, and black boots scraped gray at the toes. He chain-smoked, occasionally stopping to blow off the ashes, reminiscent of the days when he had smoked Bull Durham roll-your-owns, which could not be flicked like a store-bought cigarette lest they disintegrate in one's hands.

His wife, Julie, sat next to him on a metal folding chair, a remnant of a church bazaar, probably donated by some Mormon priest. The Mormons had purchased land at the junction of the Slim Buttes Road and built a church and gymnasium. They were responsible for bringing electricity to the community. The missionaries were nice young men, all blond, who wore white shirts and ties no matter how hot the weather. They chauffeured the people around the reservation, held hot dog roasts, and organized basketball and "kitten ball" games for the young people. But Julie cautioned her granddaughters and nieces, slim and beautiful teenage girls, not to "wrestle" with the Mormons. Despite their taboos against drinking, dancing, smoking, and other evils, they had a reputation for chasing young Indian girls, perhaps because of their polygynous tradition, which it was said took primacy over the other teachings of Joseph Smith.

Julie was heavyset; she wore long gingham dresses and moccasins, and usually a scarf tied gypsy style over her long silver hair. Her voice had become shrill, perhaps from shouting to make her husband understand her. As she chattered to him about the latest town gossip, it was never clear whether he even heard her. But she chirped away, her moods changing from an almost pleasant chiding of the reckless antics of the younger generation to a harangue about the neighbors' new house being too close to her yard.

Their son Basil sat on the ground Indian style, leaning against the log cabin rather like his father, gazing aimlessly into the distance, now and then combing the horizon and waiting for something, anything, to move so it could be measured and contemplated. Despite his handicaps Plenty Wolf was the first to notice the pickup coming fast toward his house, and he called his wife's attention to it by pointing with his chin. Stones flew toward both sides of the road as the truck screeched to a halt. Wayne

Runs Again climbed down and stood for a moment with his hand on the gate. Plenty Wolf could not tell who it was and quietly asked his wife. She replied that it was his nephew, Runs Again's boy, but that she couldn't recall his first name. Wayne entered the gate and walked up to Plenty Wolf. "*Hau Tunkašila,*" he said. "Hau Grandfather."

This was a sign for Julie and her son to leave, for the greeting was not the conventional *Hau kola* 'Hello friend,' or Hello uncle, which would also have been proper. The ritual greeting, the use of the honorific, signaled to everyone that there was important business to be discussed between the young man and Plenty Wolf, and this should be done in private.

Wayne came closer so he could be recognized, and the old man greeted him with "*Hau Takoja,*" Hau Grandson, the appropriate ritual response. "They said you would come," he said in Lakota, and this astonished Wayne. "The spirits," Plenty Wolf added in English, and laughed a "he-he-he" not in keeping with the dignity of his vocation. But Plenty Wolf laughed often—about gossip, about his neighbors, about his relatives, and even about the spirits. Laughing and joking with or about them did not offend the spirits because they too had a sense of humor that only he fully understood.

Wayne was flustered because the old man had expected him, and he tried to explain his reason in Lakota but faltered. "*Taku* . . ." he began, "*taku* . . . I wanna . . . *taku ociciyakin kte, Tunkašila* . . . I— uh—I wanna talk to you . . . *eyaš. . . eyaš . . . inska in* . . . my dad . . . uh . . . *lila kuja* . . . I dunno."

Plenty Wolf was patient. He said, "Smoke first. *Cannunpa.*" And he fashioned his left hand to represent the bowl of a pipe and tapped it with his right hand as if he were tamping tobacco into it. The young man understood. He took a cigarette from his shirt pocket, lit it, and handed it to Plenty Wolf. Plenty Wolf took the cigarette, puffed on it, and offered the butt end to the Four Winds, the Above, the Earth, and the Spotted Eagle, with casual flicks of his wrist toward each of the cardinal points. He returned the cigarette and told Wayne to do the same. After they had smoked Plenty Wolf asked the boy what was troubling him. Wayne began to sob profusely. When he regained his composure he talked to Plenty Wolf about the agonizing pain in his father's back that came and went. He said his father was pitiful and needed help, but that he did not know what to do. He talked about his own problems too—about the drinking and carousing, and his desire to go to college, and his problem with the girl and the baby. As he talked he stopped crying and felt relief, though Plenty Wolf remained silent during the soliloquy.

When the boy had finished, Plenty Wolf took the cigarette from him, crushed it between his fingers, and threw the ashes into the wind. He told Wayne that his father was old and understood the old ways, and that he should be prayed for. Plenty Wolf was confident that he could cure the old man and could also help the boy clear his mind of the things troubling him. But he said it would require a "sing," and that the boy would have to make some kind of sacrifice to help his father through his ordeal. Plenty Wolf told Wayne he should pledge to go on the hill—Plenty Wolf would put him there— and at the same time his father should come so the people could pray for him and ask the spirits to heal him. Wayne should kill a dog and buy cloth for offerings and some groceries; there would be a feast afterward.

But first they would have a sweat. The boy would come with him into the lodge, and Plenty Wolf would pray for him and tell the spirits his intentions. The sweat would rid his body of evil and clear his mind so he would be ready to seek a vision and gain knowledge about himself.

Architecturally, the only permanent shrine in Oglala religion is the sweat lodge. It stands, sometimes wavering in the wind, in sharp contrast to the countless Christian churches that dot the reservation—little frame boxes with identical steeples and church bells that look as if they had all been constructed by a Mission Construction Company. All are painted a sacramental white and have blue- or green-shingled roofs. It is as if they had come off an assembly line, just the way the federally funded housing projects deliver prefabricated homes intact to the owner's land.

The sweat lodge is a perfect symbol for Oglala religion; when not in use the structures look rather pitiful: a dome made of willow saplings stuck into the ground, bent over, and tied in place with cloth strips or rope. There is something exceedingly profane about them when not in use, in contrast to the white man's shrines and churches, which are perpetually sacred, set off from the rest of society in a feeble attempt to separate religion from the culture's social, political, and economic institutions. The sweat lodge reflects the Oglala principle of austerity and simplicity: the entire universe is a cathedral; everything is permanently sacred unless desecrated by human foibles that cause disharmony between humans and the rest of nature. At this time a special ritual is required to reinstate a balance among all living things, and only then are special places like the sweat lodge temporally and spatially separated from the rest of the mundane world; it is only during the ritual itself that special rules of conduct are in force and require different behavior toward nature.

When not in use, the sweat lodge becomes a playground for children, who dodge in and out of the framework, stepping into the central hole where the heated stones are placed during the ritual. It is a stopping place for multitudes of dogs, who lift their legs and declare the sacred saplings, placed there in honor of the various aspects of Wakantanka, their special territory. It is a meeting place for ants, spiders, grasshoppers, and flies seeking refuge from predatory birds who alight on the willow frame during their morning feeding. The sweat lodge is often invaded by a recalcitrant cow or a frightened horse, and it tolerates all these intrusions, along with the constant battering of the wind against its desiccated skeleton. It is partly this tolerance that makes the sweat lodge potentially sacred; like humans, it is subject to the whims of nature and must abide by its relentless impositions.

It was about four o'clock in the afternoon when Yellow Boy began throwing wood into the firepit twenty feet north of Plenty Wolf's sweat lodge. He arranged the wood in a large starlike pattern and surrounded it with the stones that had been left scattered in the ashes of a previous fire. He then piled more wood on the stones and poured on a gallon of kerosene. He lit a match, threw it on the pile, and jumped back as the flame shot up several feet before it subsided to an even-burning fire.

Wayne and his father had arrived an hour earlier, bringing the cloth they had purchased in White Clay for the tobacco offerings and flag offerings. Wayne remarked to Plenty Wolf that when he ordered the cloth at Randy's store the salesgirl said that, judging by the colors of cloth and the number of yards, it looked as if he were going to have a Yuwipi. He was a little embarrassed. Julie began the arduous task of cutting up the cloth to make the long and short strings of tobacco offerings her husband needed for the vision quest and Yuwipi.

It had taken only two days to prepare for the rituals. Wayne got credit at the local store and was able to buy meat, potatoes, bread, crackers, coffee, flour, sugar, lard, and cans of stewed tomatoes. He was instructed to obtain a pipe and, since he had no money, he went to the high school, where senior citizens had taken over a small room in the basement. A dozen of the old-timers spent their days making pipes. Large blocks of catlinite had been transported from Pipestone, Minnesota, and they used the school's power drill to make the holes in the bowls quickly. They sat around talking and smoking, filing away at the half-finished pipes. Rods of ash wood were stacked on one of the tables for the pipe stems. Business picked up in the springtime when young men would be going on vision quests or preparing for the sun dance, so they worked busily, turning out the pipes in assembly-line style. Wayne found one old man who was willing to trade a newly made pipe, a rather plain one, for a spare tire, a rim, and a jack.

As the heat of the day subtly gave way to evening, Plenty Wolf told everyone to get ready for the sweat lodge. The fire had burned down, and the stones were white-hot. Plenty Wolf led the small group of men: his son Basil, Wayne, and Plenty Wolf's son-in-law, who was a particularly good

singer and knew all Plenty Wolf's songs. Old man Runs Again was too sick, he said, to go into the sweat lodge, so Plenty Wolf told him to sit outside the lodge and lean against it so the heat from inside would help his back.

Basil, with the help of Yellow Boy, who was to serve as "janitor" for the sweat lodge, began draping blankets and tarps over the sapling framework, being careful to tuck them in neatly around the outside of the base. Once these were in place, the men began to strip off their clothing, which they piled on the ground. Naked, Plenty Wolf handed his pipe to Yellow Boy, along with tobacco and matches, and stooped to crawl through the narrow doorway left open at the east end of the lodge. Each of the naked men then crawled clockwise around the central firepit. Plenty Wolf took his place on the north side of the doorway; his son-in-law followed and sat next to him. Wayne next took his place, as he had been instructed, on the west side of the lodge, at the *catku*, or place of honor, directly opposite the doorway. Basil went in last and seated himself to the south of the doorway. All sat Indian style, legs crossed in front and heels pulled close to their bodies to keep them as far as possible from the central hole. They snuggled backward against the bare willow saplings.

Yellow Boy handed in to Plenty Wolf a galvanized bucket of water and a tin drinking cup, which Plenty Wolf placed on his right a foot from the hole. Yellow Boy stood outside the lodge leaning on a pitchfork, waiting for his next instructions. Finally Plenty Wolf spoke: "*Wana!* Now!"

Yellow Boy walked over to the firepit and picked up the first large stone, which weighed almost ten pounds. Balancing it on the pitchfork, he eased it through the doorway of the lodge, carefully dropping it to the east of the hole. While he returned for another, Plenty Wolf and Basil used wooden paddles to roll the stone into the hole, leaning it against the west side. As soon as the first stone was in place the men began to mutter in wavering voices, Hau-au-au-au, ha-ha-ha-ha, hun-un-un-un, as the heat from the first stone settled on their naked bodies. Perspiration immediately broke out, and they sniffed loudly and cleared their throats. Plenty Wolf laughed a little and called for the next stone. Again he and Basil maneuvered it into the hole, resting this one against the north side. Two more stones were handed in, and they were placed against the east and then the south side of the hole until the four stones formed a base on which the other stones would rest. The heat seemed to enliven the fresh sage on which the men sat, giving them a pleasant smothering feeling. Two more stones were handed in and placed, one on top of the other, on the four-stone base. Finally a seventh stone was rolled into the hole in a rather random way. The men sat silent, perspiring and gazing into the hole, watching each step with apparent detachment. The lodge was growing hotter and hotter; their eyes began to tear, and they cleared their wracked throats more loudly as if they were trying to spit up phlegm from their lungs.

Once the seven stones were in place, with the hole only a third of the way filled, Yellow Boy brought in smaller stones, as many as he could carry with each load. The frame of willow saplings began to feel hot and the men moved slightly forward, careful not to thrust their bare knees too close to hot stones. The stones were white and dusty, and shone red through the ash covering them. The process seemed interminable, but finally all the thirty rocks were in the hole. When a slight breeze rushed through the doorway, it was as if each man except Plenty Wolf grasped part of it and sucked it into his lungs like a drowning man's last breath before he sinks. Plenty Wolf, satisfied with the stones, called for Yellow Boy to close the doorway, and the lodge became dark except for tiny red eyes that peeped through the film of dust enveloping the stones.

Plenty Wolf began:

"Ho Tunkašila Wakantanka, in these dark days I sit with my relatives in the camp circle. Just as in former times we sit here and pray to you by name so that all our relations will be in good health, and nothing evil will happen to them."

The others replied in unison, "Hau!"

"Ho Tunkašila Wakantanka, today we offer you this pipe so that we may gain knowledge. And we ask you to help us, to help all of us because you are the strongest of all. Help us so we will be safe and well. To this end, we offer you this pipe."

Again the others replied, "Hau!"

Plenty Wolf continued to pray, and after each significant intention was offered the other men replied "Hau!" knowing precisely when to do so, as if they were following the libretto of an opera, knew when the score ended, and displayed their confidence by being the first in the audience to applaud.

Plenty Wolf continued with a lengthy prayer in which he asked Tunkašila Wakantanka to help the poor, the sick, young people who had relocated, and those who stayed on the reservation with nothing to do. He asked that the soldiers who had gone to fight across the water return safely, not only the Indian boys, but all the soldiers. He prayed that wars should end soon; that there be no more killing and no more mourning over relatives killed senselessly in fighting far away from sacred ground. He prayed for people to have food, money, and many children to help them when they became old and feeble. And he prayed that those who had to transact business with the federal bureaucrats would be spared red tape, the endless standing in lines and sitting in waiting rooms that was the bane of the people on the reservation.

Saying, "So that my relatives may walk in health, we offer you this pipe," Plenty Wolf ended his formal prayer. He took the tin cup and, joking that the handle was really hot, dipped the cup into the bucket and began to pour water on the heated stones.

Four times he threw water on the stones. Each time they hissed, with rushes of sibilant steam rolling up into the men's faces and causing them to sputter such meaningless phrases as he-he-he or hi-i-i-i and to clear their throats and nostrils and slap their bodies with their hands. As the choking steam filled the dome, Plenty Wolf's son-in-law began a song:

I send a voice above.
With the pipe, I send a voice above.
"I do this because I want to live with my relations."
Saying this over and over, I pray to Tunkašila.

The rest of the men joined in with the son-in-law, but his voice was loudest and clearest. After the first rendition he began a second, the rest again joining it. When they finished, he shouted out, "*Mitak' oyas' in!*" 'All my relations,' and each one in turn breathlessly repeated "*Ho.Mitak' oyas'in.*" Plenty Wolf quickly added the command, "Yugan yo! Open it up!" a signal to Yellow Boy to open the doorway of the lodge. Yellow boy went into action, rolling up the tarp over the doorway. Plenty Wolf added "*Tilazatanhan! Tilazatanhan!* The back too! The back too!" And Yellow Boy ran around the lodge and rolled up the tarp on the west side.

The breeze broke through the haze like a wave, lapping over the men's dripping bodies so they whimpered with delight, Ha-ha-ha-ha. They snorted and bathed in the cool air as if they could not only feel it, but taste it and smell it and hear it beating against their slippery bodies. They rapturously rubbed the wind into their arms and chests and into their scalps, and across their faces. It was briefly pleasant and cool, but the stones in the deep holes seemed to frown at such pleasure, the embers now flickering in the intruding breeze.

Plenty Wolf dipped the cup into the water bucket and passed it to Basil, who drank almost the whole cupful, then threw the remainder onto the stones, saying "*Mitak' oyas'in.*" The rest replied, "*Hau!*" They savored the water, joking about how large the stones were, and how hot. As each drank he slobbered and muttered ah! unh! in his delight. The cup, filled each time by Plenty Wolf, made the rounds of the lodge and finally was handed out to Yellow Boy, who also drank from it and said "*Mitak' oyas'in.*" The cup returned to Plenty Wolf, and the men sat savoring the coolness. Then Plenty Wolf said, "*Mitak' oyas'in. Hau. Hau. Iyohpa yo!* Close the door!" Yellow Boy closed the west side first, then rolled down the door flap.

The smell of sage once again filled the quickly heated lodge. Perspiration immediately broke out on the men, and the coolness evaporated in the darkness. Plenty Wolf took the cup and, this time more casually, sprinkled water onto the stones. The men responded to each rush of heat with ha-ha-ha-a. He began to pray:

"Ho, Grandfather. First of all, if any of us have fallen with the pipe, forgive us. Wakantanka, in these dark days one of our common boys lives upon this earth knowing that his body is one with this earth. We know that this body comes from you, Wakantanka, and the boy knows also, and he wants to take up this pipe and give thanks to you."

The rest of the men replied, "Hau!"

"And here this common boy has a father, and his father is ill. Therefore this boy wants to do some suffering for the benefit of all his relations. Therefore he has promised to take up the pipe, and live with it hereafter. Wakantanka, on this day we thank you for this opportunity, and for everything. We ask you to listen to him and give him your guidance. Tunkašila, he wants to take up this pipe so that his relations will live, and they will be free of all temptations, from distress, and from any future troubles. So tonight this boy is going to praise you with the pipe. So help him plan his future life, and do not let him be tempted by evil. We pray that he will not be discouraged in what he does, and that he will have good thoughts toward you, and patience. Make him understand what good things are yet to come in his life. And make him come back safely from where he started. Another thing, Tunkašila, a lot of men fail at this, but help this boy succeed in what he is trying to do. And if any of his relatives here have evil thoughts, please take those thoughts away. So that this boy may understand all these good things from you, and so that he may find a prosperous future, I offer you this pipe."

The rest replied, "Hau!"

"Wakantanka, this boy has stepped farther ahead than the common people, so be good to him. And give him a good plan for his future so that he may carry on. And if it is possible that you want him to serve you, so may it be. And he will thank you for helping him, and for all these things. And so, Tunkašila Wakantanka, we pray to you this way with the pipe. So let the thunders work for you, and the Four Winds, and all the animals and things that watch over the earth. So that all of this may be, I offer you this pipe."

The rest replied, "Hau!"

Plenty Wolf, now began to beat the tin cup against the bucket and led the following song:

I pray first to Wakantanka.
I pray first to Wakantanka.
I pray first to Wakantanka so that I may
live with all my relations.

Everyone joined in the second rendition, and when the song was concluded Plenty Wolf cried out "*Mitak' oyas'in,*" everybody repeated it after him, and again he called for the door flap to be opened.

The east and west flaps were opened, and the men relished the cool breeze. Plenty Wolf called out to Yellow Boy to hand in a cigarette, and the boy lit one and passed it in to Basil. Each man dragged on the smoke a few times and said "*Mitak' oyas'in*" before passing the cigarette clockwise around the circle. They did not smoke ritually, offering the butt end to each of the cardinal points. This was just casual, pleasurable smoking. The cigarette made its way around the circle, then it was offered to Yellow Boy, who smoked it down and unceremoniously threw it away.

The respite was shorter this time. Basil asked how many more times there were—that is, how many more times the lodge would be closed—as if he had lost all track of time and ritual sequence. Plenty Wolf said there would be two more times, then told Yellow Boy to close the flaps. The sweat lodge enveloped the participants in sage and steam. Plenty Wolf continued praying:

"Tunkašila Wakantanka, all these animals that watch over the earth are my friends; that is why I am walking with this pipe. And I live a life of suffering and hardship, and I recognize that this is not an easy life. And I must watch myself with every step that I take with the pipe. So I carry this pipe with me, and I sit down here and pray with you now. May all those things that this boy prays for be granted to him. Tonight he is going to stand there alone on the hill, and we pray that he will return safely when it is over. I ask you for these things."

The rest replied, "Hau!"

Now a long silence ensued. No one prayed; they just sat in the heat and darkness. Plenty Wolf occasionally muttered "Hau!" as he talked to some spirits who had arrived and were instructing him in sacred things. He finally spoke:

"In that silence the Tunkašila have said that they see us all gathering here for this occasion, and tonight, though the boy will be standing on the hill alone, he will be protected."

Turning to Wayne, he said, "The Tunkašila will be praying for you. And if you pull through successfully you should offer up a thanksgiving ceremony. Tunkašila said that is the right way to do things, the way you are doing them now. And if there is any sickness or no matter what you ask for through the pipe, they will always answer you and give you their help if you pray this way. The Tunkašila are well pleased that you are going through this. Now in the east, there are some Indians in a tipi and they are slapping their knees and saying, 'We never realized there would still be someone approaching us in this way.' It was in the midst of these men that I came to understand the ways of the pipe. No one ever came there, they said to me, but then you came to us seeking knowledge. But you did come, and you know we are good friends. Whatever you do, don't stumble and stagger with the pipe. Don't fall or turn your back on the pipe, or evil things may happen to you. No matter what bad things might happen, they told me that I must carry on the ways of this pipe faithfully, and if I do I will continue in a righteous way."

After Plenty Wolf had finished, he told Yellow Boy to open the flaps. He did so quickly, understanding that the men were exhausted.

When the flaps were open Plenty Wolf called for the pipe. Yellow Boy removed it from the sacred hill to the east of the sweat lodge, lit it, and passed it in to Basil. Each man took the pipe and smoked it, saying "*Mitak' oyas'in*" after he had finished. The pipe went out after the second man smoked it, so Plenty Wolf asked Yellow Boy to pass in the matches. It was lighted again, and the men continued to smoke.

"This is the last time," Plenty Wolf announced after Yellow Boy had smoked the pipe outside the lodge. "Close the flaps."

Again water was poured on the stones, and the men muttered, making animal sounds as the heat enveloped their bodies. Plenty Wolf's son-in-law quickly began the last song, and with it the final stage of the sweat lodge. He sang:

Someone who flies well makes a voice known.
Someone who flies well makes a voice known.
To whomever loves them and trusts in me,
I send a voice.

After two renditions of the song, Plenty Wolf called for the flaps to be opened, and the sweat lodge ended.

ASK YOURSELF

From your personal experience of your own culture think of contexts—verbal as well as physical—in which you associate right with positive qualities and left with negative qualities. Can you offer any reasons why societies should find the body to be a useful tool for representing moral qualities?

FURTHER READINGS

Willis, Roy. *Some Spirits Heal, Others only Dance: A Journey into Human Selfhood in an African Village.* New York: Berg. 1999. The author—a major authority on African ethnography—participated in the shaman-istic practices and curing rituals among the people of Central Africa. His approach to what it means to be human is original and is made all the more compelling by the empathetic insights his field research gave him.

Eilberg-Schwartz. Howard (ed.). *People of the Body: Jews and Judaism from an Embodied Perspective.* Albany: State University of New York Press, 1992. The fourteen essays in this collection examine the way Judaism con-fers meaning on the human body, especially as this understanding implicates such physical acts as sexual-ity, reproduction, menstruation, and childbirth.

Gilmore, David D. *Carnival and Culture: Sex, Symbol, and Status in Spain.* New Haven: Yale University Press, 1998. Andalusia, in the south of Spain, is the regional setting for this ethnographically precise study of con-temporary carnival in Europe. This local instance of a considerably more widespread institution provides Gilmore with a case study by which to open up avenues of interpretation for the ritual behavior and folk art of this region at the same time as contributing insights into the rituals of indulgence elsewhere in the world.

Needham, Rodney (ed.) *Right and Left.* Chicago: The University of Chicago Press, 1973. In this anthology 18 case studies from all over the world sustain Hertz' thesis

regarding the preeminence of right over left. The editor supplies a helpful introduction to dual classification in general, thereby placing the more focused concept of lateral symbolism in a wider analytical context.

Lewis, I.; Ahmed, Al-Safi; and Sayyid Hurreiz, eds. *Women's Medicine: The Zar-Bori Cult in Africa and Beyond.* Edinburgh: Edinburgh University Press, 1991. The Zar-Bori cult, which concerns itself with women's problems, is the most extensive transnational "tradi-tional" healing cult in Africa and the Middle East. This anthology depicts its various manifestations in a wide range of countries, including Tunisia, Somalia, Egypt, and Sudan.

Wilson, Elizabeth. "The Female Body as a Source of Horror and Insight in Post-Ashokan Indian Buddhism." In *Religious Reflections on the Human Body,* ed. Jane Marie Law. Bloomington: Indiana University Press, 1995, pp. 76–99. The female body in the post-Ashokan Buddhist literature of India was portrayed in horrific ways which, according to Wilson, were calculated to for-tify the celibacy of a "male counterculture." Wilson's conclusion leads her to contradict the conventional assumption that Indian Buddhism fostered gender egali-tarianism.

SUGGESTED VIDEOS

"Seven Nights and Seven Days." A ritual known as the Ndepp, performed by the Lebou people of Senegal, is the centerpiece of this documentary. It is performed in honor of ancestral spirits and to request them to permit a cure to take place. The patient in question is a young woman who, suffering from postpartum depression, refuses to take care of her child. After seven days and seven nights, and the participation of a large part of the population, the healer, Fat Seck, performs a cure. 58 minutes; $350 (sale), $75 (rental); Filmakers Library 1996, 124 East 40th Street, New York, NY 10016.

"The Dervishes of Kurdistan." In this documentary we see a remarkable expression of Muslim religious faith attested to by the manner in which devotees thrust skewers through their cheeks, plunge daggers into their sides, consume glass, and lick white-hot spoons. 52 minutes; $445 (sale), $75 (rental); Filmakers Library 1996, 124 East 40th Street, New York, NY 10016.

"Voodoo and the Church in Haiti." This documentary portrays voodoo as a complex system of beliefs integrated into the Haitian world of politics, and brings the values of West African cultures into perspective with those of the West. 40 minutes; 1989; $295 (sale), $60 (rental); Catalog #37868. "World Cultures on Film and Video," University of California Extension, Center for Media and Independent Learning, 2000 Center Street, Fourth Floor, Berkeley, CA 94704.

"Doctors of Two Worlds." Here, in this film, we have contrasted two different approaches to illness, the traditional and the modern. While an English doctor is setting up a system of modern health care in remote mountain villages in the Bolivian Highlands, local people introduce him to their traditional ways of dealing with illness, intriguing him so much that he decides to learn the methods of the local curer. Filmmaker: Natasha Solomons. 1989. £15. Length: 55 minutes. VC.RA207. Film Officer, Royal Anthropological Institute (RAI), 50 Fitzroy Street, London W1P 5HS, United Kingdom.

The belief that people can cause harm to other people or their property with an evil glance is widespread, and various symbols are used to ward off this "evil eye." In India, vehicles are protected from the evil eye with old shoes or, as in this case, pictures of shoes.

Photo courtesy of Margaret A. Gwynne

CHAPTER 7

MAGIC AND WITCHCRAFT

As we have already remarked, for Emile Durkheim the essence of magic lay in the fact that it was, in contrast to religion, an individual phenomenon. The magician–client relationship, Durkheim averred, differs fundamentally from that pertaining between a priest and a believer for whereas the former is a temporary, one-on-one, association the latter is a permanent bond between a leader who symbolizes a "moral community" and a believing member of that community. Another difference is that magic tends to be more ritualistic than ideological; it has something of the character of a pseudo-technical activity designed to achieve practical results. It was this practical feature of magic that so impressed James George Frazer, of course, when he contrasted magic with religion.

However, Frazer overstated his case when he dismissed magic as nothing more than a failed science, and it was left to the fieldworker, Bronislaw Malinowski, to put his experience among the Trobriand Islanders to good use in pointing out that magic not only had psychological functions, its rituals served as media of communication for they conveyed statements in symbolic form.

E. E. Evans-Pritchard was later to credit magic with yet another dimension, that of the moral. He observed that among the Azande magic also has a moral dimension, since rituals may be carried out to serve good ends or bad ends. Good magic works for ends society defines as good. Rituals to ensure safety at sea (as among the Trobrianders) would be an example of good magic. Bad magic, which is sometimes known as sorcery, strives to bring about ends that society defines as bad. A ritual that a sorcerer uses to cause an innocent neighbor to become ill is bad magic. Death-dealing magic in itself, however, is not necessarily bad. The Azande classify vengeance magic, which you carry out in retaliation against a witch who has slain one of your kinsfolk, as good magic even though it is lethal. This is because the execution of a "killer witch" is regarded as morally justified.

Although among the Victorian scholars Frazer is more often associated with the analysis of magic than Edward Tylor (1873:133–136), the latter also contributed to our knowledge of this field. Tylor asked himself why human beings, creatures with rational intelligences, believed in the efficacy of rituals that actually did not work. How could they maintain their faith in the face of repeated failures? To solve this problem Tylor set forth several possible answers. One was that magicians do not rely upon ritual alone to bring about the desired ends. They include those practical activities that really bring the result. For example, a magician might use magic to cure a sick person but he would also give medicine that might be empirically effective.

Belief in the existence of witches may provide some comfort in the face of misfortune, and accusing others of witchcraft empowers some people by permitting them to give voice to their frustration, malice, and feelings of victimhood. Thus, misery brought about by sickness or the death of a loved one does not have to be endured; retaliation against the perpetrators of mischief is possible. Among the Azande this was one psychological function of vengeance magic.

The social acceptability of retaliation as a sanction against a feeling of victimization is but a short remove from scapegoating. Foisting one's own faults onto another person who is then punished by the community for those flaws is a common ingredient of witchcraft accusations, especially during a period when a community is in a state of crisis. In the 15th and 16th centuries, a widespread syphilis epidemic devastated the population of Europe, and for reasons suggested in Reading 9–4 women were scapegoated as witches.

Systematically organized ideas designed to explain human experience are common features of all the world religions and many local systems of belief, but in this respect witchcraft resembles magic more than it does religion because it usually lacks religion's cosmological underpinnings. As an explanation for misfortunes witchcraft most certainly has its philosophical aspect, but witchcraft operates more as a psychologically satisfying response to the mishaps of life rather than offering a set of dogmas seeking to interpret the human experience. Ethnographers typically report that informants often seem unclear about the nature of witchcraft, even extending their ignorance to the critical notion of how precisely witches are supposed carry out their wicked activities and they note that whereas religious notions may circulate quite freely around a community witchcraft is something people rarely care to discuss in public.

But like beliefs in the sanctioning power of spirits (see Chapter 3) witchcraft also functions as force for social control. Deviance from accepted norms is held to be one mark of a witch, so that behavior considered anti-social, such as cursing another person or even a tendency to be a habitual grouse, can, when inexplicable troubles befall a community, provide fodder for accusations against the deviant.

These characteristics of witchcraft are on full display in the three selections on witchcraft in this chapter as well as in Reading 9–4. We see from them that witchcraft is widely found geographically and historically. Evans-Pritchard's Azande reside in Central Africa, where he studied their beliefs for 19 months between 1926 and 1927. Paul Boyer and Stephen Nissenbaum examine documentary materials relating to the second half of the 17th century and piece together the record of witchcraft accusation that very nearly destroyed the Massachusetts village of Salem. Jeanne Favret-Saada describes her fieldwork among French peasants from 1969 to the 1970s.

In the European tradition of witchcraft, which was exported to colonial North America in the 17th century, there was a pronounced gender bias. Women were far more likely to be accused of practicing witchcraft than were men—so much so that one can refer to "the feminization of witchcraft," a topic discussed more fully in Reading 9–4.

READING 7–1

SYMPATHETIC MAGIC

James G. Frazer

This reading presents James George Frazer's famous classification of magical thinking. Starting with the astute insight that the human mind organizes experiences by similarity and contact (a distinction that Lévi-Strauss, years later, was to reinvent as one between metaphor and metonymy), Frazer first identifies "imitative" or "homoeopathic magic" and "contagious magic," and classes both as different forms of "sympathetic magic." His distinction between imitative magic and contagious magic is illustrated by the thinking of the Azande, who prick the stalks of banana trees with the teeth of crocodiles to make the trees provide fruit as abundantly as crocodiles grow teeth (Evans-Pritchard 1937: 450). An example of contagious magic is the common practice for people to hide their hair clippings or nail parings out of concern a bad magician might use them against their former owners.

In keeping with the Victorian quest for the origins of institutions within the framework of a model of social evolution, Frazer attempted to demonstrate how magic, religion, and science were sequentially linked. In their intellectual evolution, he claimed, people first entered a stage of magic, a stage during which they sought to manipulate events independent of spirits. Hard-earned experience subsequently taught them that magic did not work, so they conceived the belief that instead of natural laws that governed the universe and which could be exploited to advantage by human human beings, there existed instead invisible agencies which controlled nature. Thus was born the age of religion. This lasted until human beings rediscovered the laws of nature, abandoned their faith in spirits, and embraced science. In Frazer's opinion, therefore, magic has a lot more in common with science than with religion. Rather than rely on the whims of spirits to grant

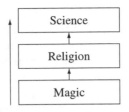

FIGURE 1   James George Frazer's Three Stages of Human Intellectual Development.

human desires the magician, like the scientist, attempts to manipulate the laws of nature to achieve his ends. From the Western point of view, he said, the difference is that the scientist bases his or her actions on empirically valid laws of nature, while the magician relies upon connections between phenomena that exist only in the imagination.

If we analyze the principles of thought on which magic is based, they will probably be found to resolve themselves into two: first, that like produces like, or that an effect resembles its cause; and, second, that things which have once been in contact with each other continue to act on each other at a distance after the physical contact has been severed. The former principle may be called the Law of Similarity, the latter the Law of Contact or Contagion. From the first of these principles, namely the Law of Similarity, the magician infers that he can produce any effect he desires merely by imitating it: from the second he infers that whatever he does to a material object will affect equally the person with whom the object was once in contact, whether it formed part of his body or not. Charms based on the Law of Similarity may be called Homoeopathic or Imitative Magic. Charms based on the Law of Contact or Contagion may be called Contagious Magic. To denote the first of these branches of magic the term Homoeopathic is perhaps preferable, for the alternative term Imitative or Mimetic suggests, if it does not imply, a conscious agent who imitates, thereby limiting the scope of magic too narrowly. For the same principles which the magician applies in the practice of his art are implicitly believed by him to regulate the operations of inanimate nature; in other words, he tacitly assumes that the Laws of Similarity and Contact are of universal application and are not limited to human actions. In short, magic is a spurious system of natural law as well as a fallacious guide of conduct; it is a false science as well as an abortive art. Regarded as a system of natural law, that is, as a statement of the rules which determine the sequence of events throughout the world, it may be called Theoretical Magic: regarded as a set of precepts which human beings observe in order to compass their ends, it may be called Practical Magic. At the same time it is to be borne in mind that the primitive magician knows magic only on its practical side; he never analyses the mental processes on which his practice is based, never reflects on the abstract principles involved in his actions. With him, as with the vast majority of men, logic is implicit, not explicit: he reasons just as he digests his food in complete ignorance of the intellectual and physiological processes which are essential to the one operation and to the other. In short, to him magic is always an art, never a science; the very idea of science is lacking in his undeveloped mind. It is for the philosophic student to trace the train of thought which underlies the magician's practice; to draw out the few simple threads of which the tangled skein is composed; to disengage the abstract principles from their concrete applications; in short, to discern the spurious science behind the bastard art.

If my analysis of the magician's logic is correct, its two great principles turn out to be merely two different misapplications of the association of ideas. Homoeopathic magic is founded on the association of ideas by similarity: contagious magic is founded on the association of ideas by contiguity. Homeopathic magic commits the mistake of assuming that things which resemble each other are the same: contagious magic commits the mistake of assuming that things which have once been in contact with each other are always in contact. But in practice the two branches are often combined; or, to be more exact, while homoeopathic or imitative magic may be practised by itself, contagious magic

will generally be found to involve an application of the homoeopathic or imitative principle. Thus generally stated the two things may be a little difficult to grasp, but they will readily become intelligible when they are illustrated by particular examples. Both trains of thought are in fact extremely simple and elementary. It could hardly be otherwise, since they are familiar in the concrete, though certainly not in the abstract, to the crude intelligence not only of the savage, but of ignorant and dull-witted people everywhere. Both branches of magic, the homoeopathic and the contagious, may conveniently be comprehended under the general name of Sympathetic Magic, since both assume that things act on each other at a distance through a secret sympathy, the impulse being transmitted from one to the other by means of what we may conceive as a kind of invisible ether, not unlike that which is postulated by modern science for a precisely similar purpose, namely, to explain how things can physically affect each other through a space which appears to be empty.

It may be convenient to tabulate as follows the branches of magic according to the laws of thought which underlie them:

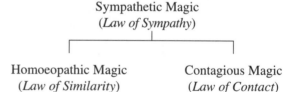

Sympathetic Magic
(*Law of Sympathy*)

Homoeopathic Magic   Contagious Magic
(*Law of Similarity*)   (*Law of Contact*)

I will now illustrate these two great branches of sympathetic magic by examples, beginning with homoeopathic magic . . .

Perhaps the most familiar application of the principle that like produces like is the attempt which has been made by many peoples in many ages to injure or destroy an enemy by injuring or destroying an image of him, in the belief that, just as the image suffers, so does the man, and that when it perishes he must die. A few instances out of many may be given to prove at once the wide diffusion of the practice over the world and its remarkable persistence through the ages. For thousands of years ago it was known to the sorcerers of ancient India, Babylon, and Egypt, as well as of Greece and Rome, and at this day it is still resorted to by cunning and malignant savages in Australia, Africa, and Scotland. Thus the North American Indians, we are told, believe that by drawing the figure of a person in sand, ashes, or clay, or by considering any object as his body, and then pricking it with a sharp stick or doing it any other injury, they inflict a corresponding injury on the person represented. For example, when an Ojebway Indian desires to work evil on any one, he makes a little wooden image of his enemy and runs a needle into its head or heart, or he shoots an arrow into it, believing that wherever the needle pierces or the arrow strikes the image, his foe will the same instant be seized with a sharp pain in the corresponding part of his body; but if he intends to kill the person outright, he burns or buries the puppet, uttering certain magic words as he does so. The Peruvian Indians moulded images of fat mixed with grain to imitate the persons whom they disliked or feared, and then burned the effigy on the road where the intended victim was to pass. This they called burning his soul . . .

Thus far we have been considering chiefly that branch of sympathetic magic which may be called homoeopathic or imitative. Its leading principle, as we have seen, is that like produces like, or, in other words, that an effect resembles its cause. The other great branch of sympathetic magic, which I have called Contagious Magic, proceeds upon the notion that things which have once been conjoined must remain ever afterwards, even when quite disserved from each other, in such a sympathetic relation that whatever is done to the one must similarly affect the other. Thus the logical basis of Contagious Magic, like that of Homoeopathic Magic, is a mistaken association of ideas; its physical basis, if we may speak of such a thing, like the physical basis of Homoeopathic Magic, is a material medium of some sort which, like the ether of modern physics, is assumed to unite distant objects and to convey impressions from one to the other. The most familiar example of Contagious Magic is the magical sympathy which is supposed to exist between a man

and any severed portion of his person, as his hair or nails; so that whoever gets possession of human hair or nails may work his will, at any distance, upon the person from whom they were cut. This superstition is world-wide . . .

READING 7–2

MEN BEWITCH OTHERS WHEN THEY HATE THEM

E. E. Evans-Pritchard

E. E. Evans-Pritchard's Witchcraft, Oracles and Magic among the Azande *is probably considered by most anthropologists to be the most influential ethnographic contribution to our understanding of witchcraft yet published. Its appearance established the benchmark for all subsequent fieldwork studies of witchcraft, especially in Africa, and his study of Zande magic ranks with Malinowski's description of magic among the Trobriand Islanders. Unlike his later book* Nuer Religion, *which is a structural-functionalist study,* Witchcraft, Oracles and Magic among the Azande, *cannot be so neatly fitted into a particular theoretical orientation for we find that witchcraft and magic are examined within several frames of reference, the most important of which are philosophical, sociological, and psychological.*

Before Evans-Pritchard Zande research, there existed reams of historical papers documenting European and New England witchcraft, and these occasionally included written accounts of how individuals reacted when accused of practicing witchcraft, but we had no notion of what suspected witches thought or felt when accused of practicing something physically impossible. Nor did we have an impartial scholar's account of what the whole business of witchcraft meant in the lives of living people. A realistic portrait of how this curious phenomenon actually worked was needed, and we got it when Evans-Pritchard book was published in 1937. In it he described

Source: E. E. Evans-Pritchard, "Men Bewitch Others When They Hate Them," in *Witchcraft, Oracles and Magic Among the Azande* (Oxford: Clarendon Press, 1968 [1937]), pp. 107–17. Reprinted by permission of Oxford University Press.

in a multitude of ethnographic detail what it meant to live in a society obsessed by witchcraft. In contrast to historical attitudes towards witchcraft by the Christian Church, which made its practice a heresy punishable by death, Zande witchcraft was a perfectly normal everyday experience in Zande life. An Azande expected to be bewitched from time to time, and his or her society provided defenses and employed counter measures to combat witches. Salem and the Azande could hardly make a stronger contrast.

Evans-Pritchard's immersion in Zande daily life enabled him to vividly describe how witchcraft beliefs control social behavior. He showed how fear of bewitchment made persons cautious about giving unnecessary offense to their neighbors—since the latter might be witches—and how fear of being accused encouraged conformity to social conventions. Readings 7–3 and 7–4 confirm this feature of witchcraft.

The sociological context and the psychological basis of witchcraft accusations are central to Evans-Pritchard's concerns in this reading. In societies where people believe in witchcraft, misfortunes are said to happen because certain ill-disposed individuals, i.e, witches cause them to occur. The Azande believe that some persons in their villages are witches and can injure others, not by performing a ritual—for there is no such thing as a ritual of witchcraft—but by psychic means. After having "uncovered" by means of a ritual of divination the identity of the witch, the victim will ask the political head of his or her community to send a deputy to confront the witch and request him or her to end the bewitchment. A witch thus accused apparently invariably complies to the request, and having been informed by the head of the community that the witch has done so the victim waits to see what happens. If health is restored, the matter ends there and then. Absolutely no reprisals can be made against the witch. Should the misfortune persist, the victim again resorts to divination, this time to determine whether the witch was lying or whether another witch has mischievously taken up where the initial witch left off. Here we should note that individuals fingered as likely culprits in the search for the witch are by no means selected at random. They are chosen from among the victim's network of social rivals, political competitors, and out-and-out-enemies. In other words, a preselected group.

Bronislaw Malinowski's influence on Evans-Pritchard, though nowhere explicitly acknowledged in this excerpt, comes across clearly enough. In its capacity as a psychological theory the former's brand of functionalism is demonstrated by the author's finding that a suf-ferer from misfortune is (a) provided with an explanation for it, and (b) given the (magical) means to counteract it. Emile Durkheim is not, however, forgotten, for in the most careful manner Evans-Pritchard pieces together all the pertinent ethnographic minutiae of Zande society and demonstrates the manner in which magic, witchcraft, and divination interconnect.

I

The notion of witchcraft is not only a function of misfortune and of personal relations but also comprises moral judgement. Indeed, Zande morality is so closely related to their notions of witchcraft that it may be said to embrace them. The Zande phrase "It is witchcraft" may often be translated simply as "It is bad." For, as we have seen, witchcraft does not act haphazardly or without intent but is a planned assault by one man on another whom he hates. A witch acts with malice aforethought. Azande say that hatred, jealousy, envy, backbiting, slander, and so forth go ahead and witchcraft follows after. A man must first hate his enemy and will then bewitch him, and unless the witch be contrite of heart when he blows out water his action will be without effect. Now since Zande interest is not in witches as such—that is to say, the static condition of being a possessor of witchcraft—but only in witch-activity, there are two consequences. Firstly, witchcraft tends to become synonymous with the sentiments which are supposed to cause it, so that Azande think of hatred and envy and greed in terms of witchcraft and likewise think of witchcraft in terms of the sentiments it discloses. Secondly, a person who has bewitched a man is not viewed by him ever afterwards as a witch but only at the time of the misfortune he has caused and in relation to these special conditions. There is no fixed attitude towards witches as there is, for instance, towards nobles. A noble is always a noble and is treated as such in every situation, but there is no like sharpness or constancy about the social personality of a witch, for he is only regarded as a witch in certain situations. Zande notions of witchcraft express a dynamic relationship of persons to other persons in inauspicious situations. Their meaning is so dependent on passing situations that a man is scarcely regarded as a witch when the situation that evoked an accusation against him has disappeared.

Azande will not allow one to say that anybody who hates another is a witch or that witchcraft and hatred are synonymous. In their representation of witchcraft hatred is one thing and witchcraft another thing. All men are liable to develop sentiments against their neighbours, but unless they are actually born with witchcraft in their bellies they cannot do their enemies an injury by merely disliking them.

It is true that an old man may say that a youth may become ill from *ima abakumba,* the consequence of an elder being angry with him, but Azande do not believe that the anger of an old man can by itself do much harm, and if an old man speaks in this vein they say that he is telling them by innuendo that he will bewitch them if they vex him. For unless an old man is a witch or sorcerer no harm can befall an unrelated person against whom he speaks in anger. His ill will might cause some slight inconvenience, as was seen to be the case with gall-bladder men, and the oracles may become confused between hatred and possession of witchcraft unless they are warned to consider only the question of actual witchcraft.

Mere feeling against a man and uttering of words against him cannot by itself seriously harm him unless there is some definite social tie between them. The curses of an unrelated man can do you no harm, but nothing is more dreadful than the curses (*motiwa*) of father and mother and uncles and aunts. Even without ritually uttering a curse a father may bring misfortune on his son simply by anger and complaint. It is also said that if a prince is continuously angered and sorrowful at the departure of a subject it will not go well with him (*motiwa gbia*). One informant told me also that if a woman goes on a journey against her husband's wishes and he sulks and pines after her it may be ill with her on her journey.

If you have any doubts whether a man who dislikes you is merely hating you or is actually bewitching you, you can ask the poison oracle, or one of the lesser oracles, to quiet them. You caution the oracle not to pay attention to spitefulness, but to concentrate upon the single issue of witchcraft. You tell it

you do not wish to know whether the man hates you, but whether he is bewitching you. For instance, you say to the rubbing-board oracle, "You observe slander and put it aside, you observe hatred and put it aside, you observe jealousy and put it aside. Real witchcraft, consider that alone. If it is going to kill me, rubbing-board oracle stick (answer 'Yes')."

Moreover, according to Zande ideas, it does not follow that a witch must injure people merely because he is a witch. As I have explained earlier, a man may be born a witch but his witchcraft-substance may remain "cool." As Azande conceive witchcraft this means that, although the man is a witch, he is a decent fellow who is not embittered against his neighbours or jealous of their happiness. Such a man is a good citizen, and to a Zande good citizenship consists in carrying out your obligations cheerfully and living all times charitably with your neighbours. A good man is good tempered and generous, a good son, husband, and father, loyal to his prince, just in his dealings with his fellow-men, true to his bargains, a law-abiding man and a peacemaker, one who abhors adultery, one who speaks well of his neighbours, and one who is generally good natured and courteous. It is not expected of him to love his enemies or to show forbearance to those who injure his family and kinsmen or commit adultery with his wives. Such a man will be thought a quiet, pleasant person but without strong character, for the Zande admires the sterner and more impulsive temperament which is roused to anger and retaliation when a man has been wronged. But if a man has suffered no wrong he ought not to show enmity to others. Similarly, jealousy is evil unless it is culturally approved as is rivalry between princes, between witch-doctors, and between singers.

II

Behaviour which conflicts with Zande ideas of what is right and proper, though not in itself witchcraft, nevertheless is the drive behind it, and persons who offend against rules of conduct are the most frequently exposed as witches. When we consider the situations that evoke notions of witchcraft and the method adopted by men to identify witches, it will at once be seen that the volitional and moral character of witchcraft is contained in them. Moral condemnation is predetermined, because when a man suffers a misfortune he meditates upon his grievance and ponders in his mind who among his neighbours has shown him unmerited hostility or who bears unjustly a grudge against him. These people have wronged him and wish him evil, and he therefore considers that they have bewitched him, for a man would not bewitch him if he did not hate him.

Now Zande moral notions are not very different from our own in their division of conduct into good and bad, but since they are not expressed in theistic terms their kinship with the codes of behaviour expounded in famous religions is not at once apparent. The ghosts of the dead cannot be appealed to as arbiters of morals and sanctions of conduct, because the ghosts are members of kinship groups and only exercise authority within these groups among the same people over whom they exercised authority when they were alive. The Supreme Being is a very vague influence and is not cited by Azande as the guardian of moral law which must be obeyed simply because he is its author. It is in the idiom of witchcraft that Azande express moral rules which mostly lie outside criminal and civil law. "Jealousy is not good because of witchcraft, a jealous man may kill some one," they say, and they speak likewise of other anti-social sentiments.

When Azande say that an action or feeling is bad they mean that it is socially deplorable and condemned by public opinion. It is bad because it may lead to witchcraft and because it brings the offending person into greater or less disrepute. This is not the place to undertake a thorough examination of Zande legal codes and moral maxims, but it may be said that the sentiments we condemn are very much the same as the sentiments they condemn; parents will inculcate in their children an opposition to them and princes will admonish their subjects to eschew them. If you hate your neighbour without due cause you show weakness of character, and people will avoid social relations with you. If you slander your neighbour you will get a bad name, and people will say that you are a liar and the prince will not believe you when you

bring a case before him. If you are greedy people will not invite you to partake of their meals, and your neighbours will often make subtle allusions to this failing in your presence and jests at your expense when you are absent, so that you will be ashamed. Similarly a man who is mean will become a target for the wit of his neighbours and will be unpopular. But the main objection to these shortcomings is that they are both the origin of witchcraft and the drive behind it, and if you ask a Zande why they are bad he will reply that they are bad because they lead to witchcraft.

III

Azande say, "Death has always a cause, and no man dies without a reason," meaning that death results always from some enmity. The strongest of men die from witchcraft due to ill will. Hence the aphorisms "They hate the elephant and it will die," and "They speak ill of the elephant and it will die." It is witchcraft which kills a man, but it is uncharitableness that drives a witch to murder.

> Azande say that witchcraft is jealousy because the heart of a man is embittered and therefore he bewitches. That man who is jealous the same is a witch. Those who know about such matters say that witchcraft always goes to injure a man because the heart of the witch is embittered against him.

Likewise greed may be the starting-point for murder, and men fear to refuse requests for gifts lest a sponger bewitches them and they say that "a man who is always asking for gifts is a witch."

Those who always speak in a roundabout manner and are not straightforward in their conversation are suspected of witchcraft. Azande are very sensitive and usually on the look-out for unpleasant allusions to themselves in apparently harmless conversation. This is a frequent occasion of quarrels, and there is no means of determining whether the speaker has meant the allusions or whether his hearer has supplied them. For example, a man sits with some of his neighbours and says, "No man remains for ever in the world." One of the old men sitting nearby gives a disapproving grunt at this remark, hearing which the speaker explains that he was talking of an old man who has just died; but others may think that he meant that he wished the death of one of those with whom he was sitting.

A man who threatens others with misfortune is certain to be suspected of witchcraft should the misfortunes befall them. A man threatens another in anger and says to him, "You will not walk this year," and then some short while afterwards the man may fall sick or have an accident and he will remember the words which were spoken to him in passion and will at once consult the oracles, placing before them the name of the speaker as the first on his list of suspects.

A spiteful disposition arouses suspicions of witchcraft. Glum and ill-tempered people, those who suffer from some physical deformity, and those who have been mutilated are suspected on account of their spitefulness. Men whose habits are dirty, such as those who defecate in the gardens of others and urinate in public, or who eat without washing their hands, and eat bad food like tortoise, toad, and house-rat, are the kind of people who might well bewitch others. The same is thought of unmannerly persons who enter into a man's hut without first asking his permission; who cannot disguise their greed in the presence of food or beer; who make offensive remarks to their wives and neighbours and fling insults and curses after them; and so on.

Not every one who displays these unpleasant traits is necessarily regarded as a witch, but it is these sentiments and modes of behaviour which make people suspicious of witchcraft, so that Azande know that those who display them have the desire to bewitch, even if they do not possess the power to do so. Since it is these traits which antagonize neighbours against those who show them it is their names which are most frequently placed before the oracles when the neighbours fall sick, and they are therefore likely to be accused frequently of witchcraft and to acquire a reputation as witches. Witches tend to be those whose behaviour is least in accordance with social demands. For though Azande do not consistently think of neighbours who have once or twice bewitched them as witches, some people are so frequently exposed by

oracles that they gain a sustained reputation for witchcraft and are regarded as witches outside specific situations of misfortune. Those whom we would call good citizens—and, of course, the richer and more powerful members of society are such—are seldom accused of witchcraft, while those who make themselves a nuisance to their neighbours and those who are weak are most likely to be accused of witchcraft.

Indeed, it is desirable to state that weakness, as well as hatred and jealousy, invites accusations of witchcraft, for there can be no doubt in the mind of any one who has lived for long among Azande that they are averse from consulting oracles about influential persons and prefer to inquire about men without influence at court and about women—that is to say, about persons who cannot easily retaliate later for the insult contained in an accusation of witchcraft. This is more evident in the oracular disclosures of witch-doctors than in the revelations of oracles. A Zande would not agree to my statement. Certainly influential men are sometimes accused of witchcraft, and often poor men are not, or very seldom, accused. I describe only a general impression of a tendency which qualifies what I have said about accusations of witchcraft being a function of equal status, for it is only a wide division of status that excludes enmities likely to lead to accusations of witchcraft.

Where Zande moral notions differ profoundly from our own is in the range of events they consider to have a moral significance. For to a Zande almost every happening which is harmful to him is due to the evil disposition of some one else. What is bad for him is morally bad, that is to say, it derives from an evil man. Any misfortune evokes the notion of injury and desire for retaliation. For all loss is deemed by Azande to be due to witches. To them death, whatever its occasion, is murder and cries out for vengeance, for the event or situation of death is to them the important thing and not the instrument by which it was occasioned, be it disease, or a wild beast, or the spear of an enemy.

In our society only certain misfortunes are believed to be due to the wickedness of other people, and it is only in these limited situations of misfortune that we can retaliate through prescribed channels upon the authors of them. Disease or failure in economic pursuits are not thought by us to be injuries inflicted on us by other people. If a man is sick or his enterprises fail he cannot retaliate upon any one, as he can if his watch has been stolen or he has been assaulted. But in Zandeland all misfortunes are due to witchcraft, and all allow the person who has suffered loss to retaliate along prescribed channels in every situation because the loss is attributed to a person. In situations such as theft or adultery or murder by violence there is already in play a person who invites retaliation. If he is known he is sued in the courts, if unknown he is pursued by punitive magic. When this person is absent notions of witchcraft provide an alternative objective. Every misfortune supposes witchcraft, and every enmity suggests its author.

IV

Looked at from this aspect it is easier to understand how Azande fail to observe and define the fact that not only may anybody be a witch, which they readily admit, but that most commoners are witches. Azande at once challenge your statement if you say that most people are witches. Notwithstanding, in my experience all except the noble class and commoners of influential position at court are at one time or another exposed by oracles as having bewitched their neighbours and therefore as witches. This must necessarily be the case, since all men suffer misfortunes and every man is some one's enemy. Every one is disliked by some one, and this somebody will some day fall sick or suffer loss and consult oracles about those who do not find favour in his eyes. But it is generally only those who make themselves disliked by many of their neighbours who are often accused of witchcraft and earn a reputation as witches.

Keeping our eyes fixed on the dynamic meaning of witchcraft, and recognizing therefore its universality, we shall better understand how it comes about that witches are not ostracized and persecuted; for what is a function of passing states and is common to most men cannot be treated with severity. The position of a witch is in no way analogous to that of a criminal in our own society, and he is certainly not an outcast living in the shadow of disgrace and shunned by his neighbours. I had certainly expected to find, not only that witchcraft was abhorrent to Azande, but that a witch, though not killed today owing to European rule, suffers social ostracism. I found that this was far from being the case. On the contrary, confirmed witches, known for miles around as such, live like ordinary citizens. Often they are respected fathers and husbands, welcome visitors to homesteads and guests at feasts, and sometimes influential members of the inner-council at a prince's court. Some of my acquaintances were notorious witches. One of those whom I knew well was my friend Tupoi of the Amozungu clan, a prominent figure at the court of Gangura. No one would suspect, from observing his social activity in the life of his district, that Tupoi is believed by every one to be a witch of long standing and of great prestige in the witch council. He is not ostracized, nor does he suffer from any disabilities. He is not even unpopular. After a while I began to hear stories about Tupoi and was surprised that such a quiet old man was believed to have committed several murders and to have brought a variety of misfortunes upon his neighbours. It was an open joke that the part of the government settlement in which he lived was unoccupied because no one wished to take the risk of living near him. It was considered wise either not to acquaint him with pending economic undertakings or, if it was impossible to prevent him from learning what was going on, to placate him and make him favourable to the undertaking. Thus a hunter would depart after game without letting Tupoi see him. When I went to shoot guinea-fowl I was generally advised to make a detour to avoid Tupoi's homestead, since my companions feared that were he to see us he would send the soul of his witchcraft to scare away the guinea-fowl. We bore Tupoi no ill will, but simply wanted to ensure that we would have something to eat. On the other hand, Tupoi was bound to know of collective expeditions, and it was usual before making them to get him, in company with other old men so as not to make it too personal, to blow water publicly to the ground in affirmation of his goodwill. People ask old men in this way to give their expeditions a blessing, but it is tacitly understood that what they request from them is that they will refrain from bewitching their hunting. One will attempt to win the favour of all old men in a neighbourhood towards large-scale hunting by distributing meat among them after a successful hunt.

Occasionally the surface of our life was broken by a violent outburst against Tupoi. Such a scene occurred a fortnight after I had arrived on my second expedition. Hearing a row going on, I came out of my hut to see what it was about, and found Zingbondo of the Avotombo clan in a towering rage and shouting out that Tupoi had killed two of his relatives that year and that he would avenge them. The quarrel was related to government road-making. Another scene was similarly derived from government labour, as are many quarrels nowadays. An old friend of mine, Badobo of the Akowe clan, remarked to his companions who were cleaning up the government road around the settlement, that he had found the stump of wood over which Tupoi had stumbled and cut himself a few days previously when he had been returning late at night from a beer feast. Badobo added to his friends that they must clear the road well, as it would never do for so important a man as Tupoi to stumble and fall if they could help it. One of Tupoi's sons heard this remark and repeated it to his father who professed to see a double meaning in it and to find a sarcastic nuance in Badobo's whole behaviour. He made a case against him before a neighbour of social standing who seems to have found Badobo's remarks innocent enough (Badobo himself assured me that they were not) and gave a decision in his favour. Whereupon Tupoi went up to Badobo and spat a huge witchcraft-spittle at his feet. There was general disgust at this act, and Badobo's friends expressed concern for him, saying, "Alas, Badobo will not recover. Tupoi has done a terrible thing to him, he has no chance of escaping death." However, Badobo did escape death, possibly because he was

a witch himself, for shortly afterwards he was observed by relatives of a dying man to spit into a gourd and to go towards the bush to hide it, evidently in order to continue his crime. Tupoi's intention was clearly to spit before Badobo in sign of goodwill, but as he had a reputation for witchcraft his action was interpreted in an unfavourable light.

Tupoi had a great failing for beer and invariably seemed to get news when I intended to give a pot or two of beer to my retainers and neighbours, and, though uninvited, he would as invariably make his appearance at the party. I found this so annoying that I strictly forbad beer to be given to him. I was not obeyed, and on inquiry I was told that no one was prepared to take the risk of passing round a gourd and leaving Tupoi out, since he was undoubtedly a witch and would harm any one who so insulted him. Yet in spite of Tupoi's reputation no one would insult him by calling him a witch, save in great anger, nor would any one mention this opinion to Tupoi's friends.

Indeed, a witch may enjoy a certain amount of prestige on account of his powers, for every one is careful not to offend him, since no one deliberately courts disaster. This was the reason for offering Tupoi beer, and this is why a householder who kills an animal sends presents of meat to the old men who occupy neighbouring homesteads. For if an old witch receives no meat he will prevent the hunter from killing any more beasts, whereas if he receives his portion he will hope that more beasts are killed and will refrain from interference. Likewise a man will be careful not to anger his wives gratuitously, for if one of them is a witch he may bring misfortune on his head by a fit of bad temper. A man distributes meat fairly among his wives lest one of them, offended at receiving a smaller portion than the others, should prevent him from killing more game.

Belief in witchcraft is a valuable corrective to uncharitable impulses, because a show of spleen or meanness or hostility may bring serious consequences in its train. Since Azande do not know who are and who are not witches, they assume that all their neighbours may be witches, and are therefore careful not to offend any of them without good cause. The notion works in two ways. A jealous man, for instance, will be suspected of witchcraft by those of whom he is jealous and will seek to avoid suspicion by curbing his jealousy. In the second place, those of whom he is jealous may be witches and may seek to injure him in return for his enmity, so that he will curb his jealousy from fear of being bewitched.

Azande say that you can never be certain that any one is free from witchcraft. Hence they say, "In consulting oracles about witchcraft no one is left out," meaning that it is best to ask the oracles about every one and to make no exceptions, and hence their aphorism "One cannot see into a man as into an open-wove basket," meaning that it is impossible to see witchcraft inside a man. It is therefore better to earn no man's enmity, since hatred is the motive in every act of witchcraft.

READING 7–3

WITCHCRAFT AND SOCIAL IDENTITY

Paul Boyer and Stephen Nissenbaum

As Western Europe witnessed the ebbing of the Great Witch Craze in the late 17th century, what Boyer and Nissenbaum call "perhaps the most exceptional event in American colonial history" exploded in violence in Salem, a tiny village in Massachusetts. Dozens of persons in 1692 were accused of practicing witchcraft and nineteen were hanged. This extraordinary episode came about when some young adolescent girls alleged that the "specters" (or phantoms) of various persons living in Salem and in outside villages periodically assaulted them by pinching and scratching parts of their bodies. No one was very clear as to what specters were exactly, but they supplied the principal evi-

Source: Reprinted by permission of the publisher from Salem Possessed by Paul Boyer and Stephen Nissenbaum, Cambridge, Mass.: Harvard University Press, Copyright © 1974 by the President and Fellows of Harvard College.

dence that convicted those accused by the girls of practicing witchcraft. Adopting a structural-functional style of analysis, reinforced by a diachronic approach, Boyer and Nissenbaum, who are historians not anthropologists, correlate the pattern of accusations made by these girls with factional alignment in the Salem community from the 1680s to 1692. Unlike the Azande, the villagers were literate and kept records of various kinds, so social and economic in the village of Salem during the time of the witchcraft accusations and trials were available for later study. Thus, while Evans-Pritchard was limited to a one dimensional—synchronic—interpretation of Zande witchcraft, historians were able to incorporate a diachronic perspective in their study, thereby giving it fuller and richer scope. The diachronic perspective enabled them to see that by the year 1692 one of the two leading families in the community, that of the Porters, had over the previous decade acquired an advantage in terms of location over their leading rivals, the Porters, who were not all pleased by their relative decline in prosperity. The Porter's land abutted the main road linking Salem to Boston, a growing commercial center, thus giving the family and its supporters greater access to this node of prosperity than the more established Putnam family whose own prosperity was waning. The synchronic approach enabled Boyer and Nissenbaum to discern that in general alleged victims and accusers tended to come from the Putnam faction, whereas the accused were related to the Porters. Their finding was that Salem witchcraft could be explained by the economic shifts that had altered the fortunes of the village's two most conspicuous families and the political antagonisms they generated.

The authors caution that the alignments were not entirely as consistent as their model suggests, but they have made a plausible case that socioeconomic success/failure in Salem and the pattern of accusations converge. Several books on Salem witchcraft had appeared prior to their own, but theirs was the first to explicitly delineate the pattern of accusations and relate it to the developing hostilities over time between the two most prominent families in the village. They also place the witchcraft prosecution within Puritan theology, since without an ideology of witchcraft to begin with the girls would have had no basis for alleging they were being assaulted by witches. Colonial New England had inherited from their forebears in England a belief in the existence of witchcraft, and in the difficult struggle to eke out a living in a harsh land the people of Salem interpreted what they believed was a massive attack by witches as rebuke by god for their own inadequacies—the negative *expression of what Max Weber characterized as Protestantism and the spirit of capitalism (Reading 11–4).*

Boyer and Nissenbaum's strategy for making sense of what occurred in Salem in 1692 is less overtly psychological than is that of Jeanne Favret-Saada in her book Deadly Words, but feelings of envy can be readily inferred from the sociological facts they present.

The inner tensions that shaped the Puritan temper were inherent in it from the very start, but rarely did they emerge with such raw force as in 1692, in little Salem Village. For here was a community in which these tensions were exacerbated by a tangle of external circumstances: a community so situated geographically that its inhabitants experienced two different economic systems, two different ways of life, at unavoidably close range; and so structured politically that it was next to impossible to locate, either within the Village or outside it, a dependable and unambiguous center of authority which might hold in check the effects of these accidents of geography.

The spark which finally set off this volatile mix came with the unlikely convergence of a set of chance factors in the early 1690's: the arrival of a new minister who brought with him a slave acquainted with West Indian voodoo lore; the heightened interest throughout New England in fortune telling and the occult, taken up in Salem Village by an intense group of adolescent girls related by blood and faction to the master of that slave; the coming-of-age of Joseph Putnam, who bore the name of one of Salem Village's two controlling families while owing his allegience to the other; the political and legal developments in Boston and London which hamstrung provincial authorities for several crucial months early in 1692.

But beyond these proximate causes lie . . . deeper and more inexorable ones . . . For in the witchcraft outburst in Salem Village, perhaps the most exceptional event in American colonial history, certainly the most bizarre, one finds laid bare the central concerns of the era. And so once again, for a final time, we must return to the Village in the sorest year of its affliction.

WITCHCRAFT AND FACTIONALISM

Predictably enough, the witchcraft accusations of 1692 moved in channels which were determined by years of factional strife in Salem Village. The charges against Daniel Andrew and Phillip English, for example, followed closely upon their election as Salem Town selectmen—in a vote which underscored the collapse of the Putnam effort to stage a comeback in Town politics. And Francis Nurse, the husband of accused witch Rebecca Nurse, was a member of the anti-Parris Village Committee which took office in October 1691 . . .

Other accusations, less openly political, suggest a tentative probing around the fringes of the anti-Parris leadership. For example, George Jacobs, Jr.—accused with several members of his family—was a brother-in-law of Daniel Andrew, whose lands he helped farm. Jacobs was close to the Porter group in other ways as well. In 1695, for example, he was on hand as the will of the dying Mary Veren Putnam was drawn up, and his name appears with Israel Porter's as a witness to that controversial document. In May 1692 Daniel Andrew and George Jacobs, Jr., were named in the same arrest warrant, and they evidently went into hiding together . . .

Another of Daniel Andrew's tenants was Peter Cloyce, whose wife, Sarah (a sister of Rebecca Nurse), was among the accused in 1692. And Michael DeRich, whose wife Mary was also charged that year, seems at one time to have been a retainer or servant in the household of the elder John Porter, and his ties to the family may well have continued into the next generation. (Mary DeRich, in turn, was a close relative—perhaps even a sister—of Elizabeth Proctor, convicted of witchcraft along with her husband John.) . . .

Indeed, as the accused are examined from the perspective of Village factionalism, they begin to arrange themselves into a series of interconnected networks. These networks were not formally organized or rigidly structured, but they were nonetheless real enough. The kinds of associations which underlay them were varied: kinship and marriage

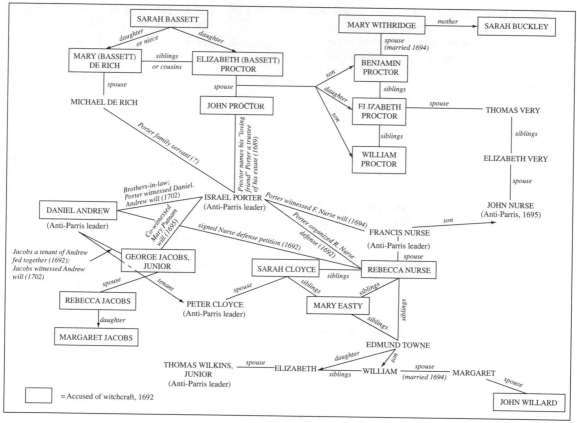

An Anti-Parris "Network."

ties were crucial, but marriage, in all likelihood, was simply the final step, the institutionalization of less tangible bonds built up gradually over a period of time. The traces of such bonds lie buried in a wide variety of sources, including real-estate transactions, court testimony, genealogies, and lists of witnesses and executors in wills and estate settlements. Ultimately, the evidence for these relationships fades off into shadowy associations which are frustratingly difficult to document with precision—although they were certainly well known at the time.

One such network, illustrated in [the accompanying chart], links Israel Porter with a startling number of "witch" families, most notably the Proctors and the Nurses . . . Other anti-Parris networks (and, for that matter, pro-Parris networks) could be reconstructed . . . Though this chart is hardly com-

plete or definitive—it could certainly be elaborated with additional research, or even extended outward to encompass additional witches—it does show the various kinds of connections which could hold such a network together. Perhaps the nature of these ties provides a key to one of the ways in which political "factions" were established, cemented, and enlarged in Salem Village (and in other communities as well) during the last part of the seventeenth century. If so, the pattern of witchcraft accusations may itself be a more revealing guide than even the maps or tax lists to the origin of political divisions in the Village.

Given all this, it is not surprising to discover a high correlation between Salem Village factionalism and the way the Village divided in 1692 over the witchcraft outbreak. There are forty-seven Villagers whose position can be determined both in 1692 (by their testimonies or other involvement in the witchcraft trials) and in 1695 (by their signatures on one or the other of the two key petitions). Of the twenty-seven of those who supported the trials by testifying against one or more of the accused witches, twenty-one later signed the pro-Parris petition, and only six the anti-Parris document. Of the twenty who registered their opposition to the trials, either by defending an accused person or by casting doubt on the testimony of the afflicted girls, only one supported Parris in 1695, while nineteen opposed him . . . In short, supporters of the trials generally belonged to the pro-Parris faction, and opponents of the trials were overwhelmingly anti-Parris.

Almost every indicator by which the two Village factions may be distinguished, in fact, also neatly separates the supporters and opponents of the witchcraft trials . . . The connection is clear: that part of Salem Village which was an anti-Parris stronghold in 1695 (the part nearest Salem Town) had also been a center of resistance to the witchcraft trials, while the more distant western part of the Village, where pro-Parris sentiment was dominant, contained an extremely high concentration of accusers in 1692.

Similarly with wealth: just as the average member of the anti-Parris faction paid about 40 percent more in Village taxes than his counterpart in the pro-Parris faction, so the average 1695–96 tax of the Villagers who publicly opposed the trials was 67 percent higher than that of those who pushed the trials forward—18.3 shillings as opposed to 11 shillings . . .

But despite all the evidence suggesting that the accusations of 1692 represented a direct and conscious continuation of factional conflict, such an explanation is ultimately insufficient. In part, this is because of the sheer mechanical difficulties in reconstructing fully those linkages that do exist. The "networks" we have postulated are difficult to pin down, for instance, because they rested on the kinds of ties and associations often reflected only in the most fragmentary way, if at all, in the written records.

Furthermore, it is simply impossible to document the position of many Salem Villagers toward the witchcraft episode. While the data available on the Village's two factions is remarkably complete, a considerably smaller proportion of the Villagers openly committed themselves one way or the other on the witchcraft issue—fewer than one hundred, on the basis of surviving testimonies . . . Of the somewhat larger number of Village men and women whose sympathies went unrecorded, some unquestionably did make their positions known at the time, since the issue was surely a matter of intense and incessant discussion in the community. But unless an individual actually committed himself on paper, by signing a complaint, a deposition, or a petition, and unless that paper was preserved in the archives, his opinions about what happened in 1692 are lost to history.

Other Villagers may have kept their silence throughout the episode and carried their opinions with them to the grave. Taking sides, after all, was a risky business. If a person seemed skeptical about the trials, he might find himself accused; if he joined in, on either side, he risked making some very powerful enemies. And nobody could be certain which side would come out on top. Samuel Parris recognized how tempting neutrality must have been for some, and he did his best to eliminate it as a viable alternative. "Here are no neuters," he insisted in September 1692; "Everyone is on one side or the other." It was a theological point Parris was making, but (as was so often the case with him) the political implications were clear. Parris was attempting to compel commitment to his own faction by posing the alternatives so starkly: Will you be God's ally, or the Devil's? An accuser, or an accused? A saint . . . or a witch? There was no middle ground, he suggested. But, for all Parris's efforts, many Villagers refused to be pressured into a possibly dangerous affirmation of their loyalties, and simply lay low.

Another kind of difficulty is posed by those Villagers who did take sides in 1692—but involuntarily: the accused witches. With very few exceptions, these people were simply not around in 1695 to sign the anti-Parris petition, either because they had been executed or because they had left the area after 1692. For this reason, it is technically impossible to associate the great majority of the accused witches with the anti-Parris faction and thus all the more difficult to establish a neat correlation between the witchcraft outbreak and the broader pattern of political conflict.

A more significant difficulty in linking Salem Village witchcraft statistically to Salem Village factionalism is the fact that—for all the probing around the fringes of the anti-Parris group—the anti-Parris leadership generally escaped prosecution in 1692. Israel Porter, Joseph Porter, Joseph Hutchinson, Joseph Putnam: none was touched by accusation in 1692—at least by any accusation permitted to reach the court. This poses a touchy problem: it is obvious that the witchcraft outbreak was intimately connected with the factional conflicts which preceded it, and yet, with only one or two exceptions, the accusations did not fall on those men who were surely the most tempting targets. Why not?

One way to answer this question is to try to identify some of the ways by which the people who were accused may be distinguished from those who were not. For example, the matter of recognized Village status: it is revealing that the three Porter brothers, none of whom was accused, were all long-time Village residents who had been born to wealth and respectability, while the one member of the family who actually was accused, their brother-in-law Daniel Andrew, was a comparative newcomer to the Village who had been born in obscurity. Or again, it is noteworthy that of the anti-Parris Village Committee elected in 1691, the three who are consistently designated "Mr." in the records (Porter, Hutchinson, Putnam) were spared, while Francis Nurse, who never advanced beyond "Goodman," saw his wife hanged a year later. (Daniel Andrew, accused but able to escape, possibly with the connivance of the authorities, was sometimes "Mr. Daniel Andrew" and sometimes not: his precise status was apparently somewhat problematical.)

Powerful men *were* accused in 1692—men addressed as "Mr.," "Captain," "Honorable," and even "Reverend," but in every instance these men were remote from the immediate Salem Village scene. (Most of them were Bostonians.) They had never been to Salem Village, and few Villagers—certainly not the afflicted girls who first named them—could have known them except by reputation. The local anti-Parris leadership may have remained immune to attack, then, precisely because it was local. It was one thing for an afflicted girl to accuse some prominent individual in Boston (or even in Salem Town) of attacking her: men like John Alden or Nathaniel Cary would have been distant and essentially symbolic figures to her. But it was something else again to lash out at members of the Salem Village gentry like Israel Porter, men whom they encountered regularly and who held a recognized position on the day-to-day scale of social status. For all the depths of factional passion, habits of deference still ran deep in Salem Village—deep enough, at any rate, to save anyone who was by blood a Porter.

This is not to suggest that the pressures to accuse such men were not intense, even unbearably so. But yet they remained "off-limits," psychologically or politically. They could not be brought down in the Village meeting or in the courts, and neither could they be brought down as witches. The catharsis which might have come through an open assault on the anti-Parris leadership was not to be achieved.

Faced with this formidable psychological barrier, the witchcraft accusations soon began to generate a powerful dynamic of their own, a dynamic which rapidly heightened the sense of general conspiracy already pervading the Village by 1692. We have earlier suggested the kinds of "networks" that linked many of the accused witches to the anti-Parris leadership. Indeed, all it takes is a slight shift in our angle of vision to perceive the victims of the witch trials in 1692 the way they must have appeared to the pro-Parris people: as the well-organized minions of those immune figures who stood poised to take over and destroy Salem Village.

The preoccupation with conspiracy was encouraged not only by Parris's sermons, but also by a cumulative body of witchcraft testimony which focused on precisely this point. One confessing witch, for example, reported that a gathering of "about six score" witches in Salem Village had decided to "pull down the Kingdom of Christ and to set up the Devil's Kingdom." (Including their non-Village sympathizers, this figure of 120 would probably be a fairly accurate estimate of the strength of the anti-Parris faction.) Deliverance Hobbs revealed that at another large assemblage of Village witches—a kind of strategy session—George Burroughs had issued instructions "to bewitch all in the Village . . . gradually, and not all at once." . . . Most alarming of all was the detailed confession of William Barker of Andover, who reported a meeting of over 300 witches in Salem Village and revealed that Satan had singled out this obscure community for assault "by reason of the people's being divided and their differing with the ministers." Evidently sensing the interest which this particular theme had aroused, Barker elaborated in a further confession from behind prison walls: "[T]he design was to destroy Salem Village, and to begin at the minister's house, and to destroy the Church of God, and to set up Satan's Kingdom, and then all will be well." . . .

Unable to attack the men they saw as responsible for this subversion, some Villagers began to see witches everywhere. But although the accusations were diverted from their most obvious targets, they were not therefore aimless or random. We have already seen that a number of the accused were linked in one way or another to the anti-Parris group, and if we could fully reconstruct all the Village "networks" many more such links would certainly emerge. For example, one destitute accused witch, Sarah Good, was denied shelter by at least one pro-Parris Salem Village family in the years before 1692. Who eventually took her and her small children in? An anti-Parris household, perhaps? We simply cannot know.

But whether or not the accused witches were openly associated with the anti-Parris group, they represented—in their careers and even, perhaps, in their manner of life—precisely what many Villagers found so disturbing about the opposition to their minister: its lack of commitment to "Salem Village," its alien and unfamiliar quality. For the people who finally accused them, at least some of these witches may well have been substitutes for other persons who were less vulnerable to attack—just as Martha Cory and Rebecca Nurse substituted, in the mind of the senior Ann Putnam, for her husband's stepmother.

READING 7–4

SYNTHETIC IMAGES

Rodney Needham

Scholars of witchcraft often view their subject as a sociological phenomenon, and like the authors of the last two readings, they are concerned to know the social dynamics linking accuser with accused. Rodney Needham, however, offers an original perspective on witchcraft, for he is interested in the mental image of the witch as it appears in indigenous collective representations around the world. He concludes that the components of that image are the spontaneous products of the brain.

Reading 7–2 shows the insights a structural-functional approach can give us, and the psychological approach Needham proposes complements it. His argument is an intriguing alternative inspired by the work of the psychiatrist Carl Jung (1875–1961). Jung, who founded the school of analytical psychology, has never received much appreciation by social anthropologists, and we should note that Needham does not advocate subscribing to the entire Jungian view. But the Jungian concept of archetype—which can be roughly defined as a genetic tendency for the brain to create certain images that are shared by all members of the species Homo sapiens and reveal themselves in dreams, myths, ritual, and art—has prompted Needham to propose a novel way of explaining an image that he characterizes as being virtually universal.

Source: Rodney Needham, "Synthetic Images," in *Primordial Characters* (Charlottesville: University Press of Virginia, 1978), pp. 23–50. Reprinted with permission of the University Press of Virginia.

From an examination of comparative ethnography Needham finds that certain attributes of thought form constant constituents of the "image" (or archetype) of the witch everywhere. He terms them "primary factors" because they would appear to be natural properties of the brain, and one might add, genetic endowments. Those primary factors that compose the image of the witch are: conceptual opposition, inversion, night, black, nocturnal familiar, flight, and aerial light.

Needham warns that his thesis is speculative and remarks that it is offered merely in an attempt to undermine the conventional approaches to witchcraft, including the structural-functional one. Perhaps one might therefore suspend the critical observation that if the Needham thesis is literally applied then ethnographic instances of societies in which where witches are not imagined to have every one of these attributes could readily be cited. The French peasants of the Bocage (Reading 7–5) are one such example.

"I have ever beleeved, and doe now know, that there are Witches." It is little more than three hundred years since a humane and learned doctor, Sir Thomas Browne, made that decided declaration. Some years later even he acted as medical witness for the prosecution in sending two old women to their deaths for the crime of witchcraft. Since his day we in the West have not been free of the obsession, for even when the last poor creature had been burnt or put to the test, the power of the collective representation survived. Historians reverted again and again to the trials and the edicts and the fulminations; folklorists traced the continued expression of ideas about witchcraft into modern society; eccentrics claimed to be, or tried to be, witches and formed themselves into covens on desolate farms and in sedate suburbs; and the anthropologists, of course, made it into one of the stock and indispensable topics of their subject.

In these regards it can be said that we are still in the power of the idea of witchcraft, just as we resort to its dramatic power in our metaphors of moral condemnation and political castigation. If it is objected that we do not actually do anything about it, this is true in the sense that we do not arrest and torture those whom we call witches, and that we do not presume to be witches those who are the victims of witch hunts. But we do not have to do and think so in order to conform to a collective representation; for neither did most people, I can conceive, in the days when such things really were done. It was the church and the state that provided the authority and the punitive means: they were the sustainers of the institution, and in this respect were parts of it. We cannot say that the authorities responded to the common conviction that there were witches, for to the common people the fearsome notion of witchcraft was not a spontaneous apprehension but had all the autonomy, generality, and coercive force of a social fact. And if we were to say that they believed in the dread powers of witchcraft, and hence collaborated in the gruesome procedures by which the authorities tried to extirpate witches, we should be on even shakier ground. In spite of the volume of contemporary reports, we do not know what the greater number of the populace believed (on the assumption that we have a clear idea of what "believe" means), but only that the collective representation was in force.

We can well conclude, moreover, that people in the past no more positively acquiesced in the execution of witches, or played any other deliberate part in the enactment of the representation, than do we today in the operation of the institutions that govern our own lives, even when the instruments of state are called representative or the corporations are called public. If we agree that people really did think there were witches, this does not justify us in imputing any particular state of mind to them. There have been crazes and scares, but these are not generically characteristic of the institution. We ourselves know, just as objectively (let us say), that hundreds of thousands of people are killed and maimed on the turnpikes; and although we regard this as deplorable, and try to make turnpikes less dangerous or to avoid the dangers if we travel on them, the knowledge and the consequent precautions do not argue for any special kind of judgment or apprehension that is distinctively associated with turnpikes. Indeed, this is much what we find when we read ethnographic accounts of societies where witches are just as real, and also just as normal an aspect of everyday life, as are turnpikes to us. There are witches, all right, and people rely on regular precautions and techniques in order to cope with them.

I have been stressing the points in these preliminary remarks in order to throw into contrast the aspect of witchcraft that I think really important and that is to be the subject of this lecture. The more normal the idea of witchcraft is taken to be, in a society where it is in force, the more striking is that aspect. The less we assume that the institution of witchcraft involves a special inner state, the more readily we shall be able to analyze the power and persistence of the complex that defines the institution. If, on the other hand, we regard the institution of witchcraft merely as a cognitive aberration, a kind of collective nightmare that can be exorcised by science, then I think we are missing some of its most interesting and instructive features. Actually, the case I intend to make first is that social anthropology, in the ways it has approached witchcraft, has tended to pass over these features and at the same time has not made a good scientific argument in any other respect.

Difficulty began with the definition of a witch, and sporadically a fair amount of literary energy went into discriminating between witch and sorcerer, the former working by some intrinsic property, the latter by recourse to material means; then in deciding whether in a certain society a mystical practitioner was the one or the other, or maybe both at the same time; and then in qualifying propositions about witchcraft according to whether a witch or a sorcerer was in question, not to mention the alternative statuses of wizard, magician, conjuror, and so on. Moreover, beyond the range of the English words there were the numerous terms in other languages that were indifferently translated as "witch" and the like, and each of these constituted a semantic problem that did not readily conduce to comparative generalizations. And against this tangled background anthropologists still found it possible to speak of "genuine" witches or of witches "proper," to differ over whether witches were essentially immoral, and, expectably enough, to become diverted by one new typological consideration after another according to the ethnographic data adduced or the cast put upon them by the anthropological commentator. At the end of the day, it remains a question if there is yet a definition of a witch that is agreeable, in the rigorous acceptation seemingly required, to anthropologists as a body. If you ask whether that really matters, the answer is that it depends on the theoretical or comparative propositions that have "witch" as their subject. We shall come to some of these in a moment. For the present occasion, I shall give the word its common, or garden, meaning of someone who causes harm to others by mystical means. If you are inclined to protest that this is altogether too rough and ready, let me invite you to wait a little until I show that this vagueness of definition has no importance for the purpose I have in view.

You may, by the way, find it interesting to keep in mind later a point about Germanic etymology. The English word *witch* comes from the Old English *wiććć,* the feminine form of *wićća,* which is rendered as a male magician, sorcerer, or wizard, and this is the end of the trail, since the source of these words is not understood. But in German the equivalent *Hexe* comes from the Middle High German *hag,* meaning a "fence," "hedge," or "enclosure"; and the Icelandic *tūnriða,* witch, means literally a female "fence-rider." There is thus a connection, which will acquire its point as we proceed, between witches and boundaries. It would be instructive to learn if this association is to be found in other linguistic traditions.

Another preliminary matter that ought to be mentioned is the almost universal premise subscribed to by anthropologists, that witches do not really exist: that is, no human beings have the secret power to inflict harm or do evil as witches are supposed to do. This is a curious presumption, though I do not maintain that it has led to any pragmatic difficulty in the study of witchcraft. It is odd because it is a flagrant instance of sheer prejudice of the kind that anthropologists are usually careful to avoid when dealing with other mystical institutions. They do not as a rule begin by declaring that God does not exist or that ancestral spirits are merely imaginary or that the benefits of blessing are illusory. They say that these notions are to be treated as social facts, and that there is simply no need to pronounce on their truth or falsity. But in the case of witchcraft there is no such compunction: witches just do not exist, and the question posed is hence why men universally but misguidedly think that they do. I must say this strikes me as pure dogma. I myself have no idea, empirically, whether any human beings possess a secret capacity to inflict harm by some immaterial and unseen means. This seems to me something of an open question. I have no evidence that there is such a power, whether generic or confined to a minority of individuals, and my inclination is to suspect that most probably there is none. But the one thing I am sure of, simply as a point of method, is that we ought not to base our investigation into witchcraft on an unsure (even unexamined) premise, let alone the premise that the essential attribute of witches—namely the malign power—does not exist.

The standard concession to reality made by anthropologists is that the idea of witchcraft must be related, as Philip Mayer has put it, to something real in human experience; but the next move is none the less to fall back on another prejudice, namely, that the reality in question consists in social and psychological strains to which the postulation of witchcraft is a social response. I am not saying that correlations of the kind cannot be made (though what they are worth is a different matter), but that the presumed locus of the reality of witchcraft corresponds in the first place to the sociological predilections of anthropologists. An extreme expression of this leaning is to be seen in an assertion, by two leading authorities, that sociological analysis "must" be employed if we wish to develop explanatory formulations which can subsume the facts from more than one society.

However that may be, the notion that witchcraft accusations point to "weak spots in the social structure" has had a considerable prevalence. Related propositions are that the accusations derive from a conflict between ideal and actual social relations; that they are a means to break relationships that have become insupportable; or that they act as a safety valve by which aggressive impulses are sublimated. The ethnographic accounts presented in these terms may be very informative, and the focus on tensions and strains can certainly contribute to a true description of social life, but the approach is nevertheless subverted by a number of considerations that cannot be countered by the improvement of fieldwork.

First, it is tautological to say that witchcraft accusations point to weak spots or to difficult relationships, for it is in part the accusations themselves that characterize the spots as weak or the relationships as uneasy. Moreover, what is needed is an independent gauge of strength and smoothness by which the ethnographer could assess these qualities in the absence of their liability to accusations; but in the nature of the case the possibility of correlating witchcraft accusations and social vulnerability, as independent variables, cannot be had. And in any case a test by concomitant variation is called for: to identify "strong" points in the social structure and to check that they are free of witchcraft accusations; and to check the "weak" points and see if they are regularly the targets of accusations. These however are tasks that in the main have not been carried out in ethnographical analyses, and lacking their results we are left without satisfactory empirical proof of the alleged connection. Finally, even if the connection could be established in particular instances, the question would remain whether the weak and difficult spots were so precisely because, for some other reason perhaps, they were conventionally regarded as the loci of witchcraft. This is a question that applies similarly to the safety valve, or sublimation, hypothesis, for we cannot know to what extent the tension or the aggression is a product of the institution itself.

As matters stand, at any rate, I think it is true to say that no sociological or psychological explanation of the differential incidence of witchcraft accusations has been borne out empirically as a general proposition that is valid for witchcraft everywhere. Witches are neighbors, or else they are distant; they are relatives, or else they cannot be relatives; they are marginal, or else they are enemies within; they are lowly misfits, or else they are secure and prosperous just because of their witchcraft; they are so categorized that not everybody can be a witch, or else they are such that anyone may be a witch. Occasionally a sociological proposition is framed in even more detailed terms: for example, that witchcraft beliefs tend to be utilized in societies in which unilineal kinship principles are employed in the formation of local residential groups larger than the domestic household. The literature of anthropology is replete with propositions like these, each perhaps persuasive in its own ethnographic setting, but none survives as a key to the institution wheresoever it may be found. No wonder that a historian such as Trevor-Roper asserts that witchcraft beliefs are inseparable from the ideology of the time. But this conclusion does not allow for, even if it does not rule out, the comparativism that is proper to social anthropology and that alone may provide a general interpretation [of] an institution that has such a global distribution. The historian's conclusion is the ethnographer's indispensable premise.

There is still one other kind of explanation, however, that seems to fare better and that is not cast in terms of jural institutions and social systems. This is the view that the idea of witchcraft provides a theory of misfortune. If that termite-riddled granary (the bane of anthropological examiners) falls on you and not on someone else, just as you happened to be sitting under it, the activity of a witch provides not only an answer to the question "Why me?" but a final and complete answer. Also it enables you to do something definite, dramatic, and perhaps personally advantageous about the source of your misfortune.

No doubt the institution of witchcraft does have these occasional uses, but they do not explain why it is that this particular institution is employed in order to explain misfortune. After all, there are many ways to do that. If misfortune strikes, you can blame an inscrutable god or capricious spirits; you can concede that it is the just retribution of your own sin, or else that it is the automatic consequence

of some unintended fault; you can put it down to bad luck (if your culture happens to have this Germanic concept), or more calculatingly you can ascribe it to chance (though this is an even more difficult notion). Theories of these kinds are legion, they are found also in societies that ascribe misfortune to witchcraft as well, and even people obsessed by witches do not blame every misfortune on their malign intervention. Why then should people hold to a theory that places responsibility for their misfortunes on other people? From a pragmatic point of view, it does not even seem a particularly desirable theory. If people think they are afflicted by an inscrutable god, they can at least band together in an attempt to placate their divine scourge by communal means that do not foster suspicion and set them one against another. But to blame individual human beings for riddled posts or failing crops or the attacks of unpredictable wild animals seems the most self-damaging theory of any.

All the same, the idea is remarkably prevalent in history and in world ethnography, and for all its apparent social disadvantages we have to accept that in fact this theory of blame is the way in which a great many peoples have chosen to think about the sources of their troubles. This fact in itself tells us something about the inclinations of human beings under stress, but I do not think the theory of misfortune hypothesis tells us anything interesting or revealing about the institution of witchcraft. In a sense, indeed, we might well not have expected it to do so, for this proposition too is tautologous by definition: ideas about witchcraft account for the blows of misfortune, after all, not for the blessings of comity.

It has taken me some little while to run through this essential introductory survey of the state of theory with regard to witchcraft, and as you see I cannot find that there is much in the way of positive results to report. This is not surprising, let alone dejecting, if only because it is a delusion to suppose that we shall do best at explaining widespread and constant social facts. We can do much better with limited and variant institutions, that is, when the weight of comparativism can least be brought to bear. If comparison is the characteristic method of social anthropology, it does not follow that we shall be very effective with it. At any rate, we have not in fact got very far in the scientific treatment of the idea of witchcraft.

It is against this background that I now want to turn to the features of witchcraft that earlier on I said struck me as interesting and as anthropologically neglected. I am not going to claim any great progress or revelation, and the matter is not one for decisive argument; but when we are so much baffled by an institution as we are in this case, an oblique attention to it, from another standpoint, may just make a difference. You will already be familiar with the features themselves, but it is perhaps when we think we are most familiar with a thing that a change of aspect can best disclose its further properties.

The aspect that I want to focus on is the image of the witch, and I shall try to make sense of its components by resort to what were introduced in the first lecture as primary factors of experience. There is, as you will see, no technique for doing this, and at points I have to rely on conjectures that are no more than plausible; but what follows is at any rate a way of thinking about witchcraft that may lead somewhere interesting.

The first reason for taking the image as the object of analysis, rather than the sociological matters that have hitherto preoccupied most anthropologists, is that amid a welter of contingent social facts (which, as we have found, have not been brought into a consistent theoretical order) this complex construction of the imagination displays a very remarkable constancy. I do not mean by this that the components of the image of the witch are always the same in number and character, from one tradition to another, but that there are characteristic features which combine polythetically (that is, by sporadic resemblances) to compose a recognizable imaginative definition of the witch.

Let us approach this representation by way of its moral component. The witch is said to do such horrible things as to eat children, practice cannibalism by secretly devouring people's organs, commit incest, and otherwise act in a vile and malevolent manner such as only the right-minded could imagine. (Eating children, incidentally, has a special vogue: Domitian charged Apollonius with it; the Romans accused the Christians; the Christians in turn the Jews.) Such particulars are infinitely elaborated on, but these are some of the major attributes. Anthropologists have frequently remarked that such conduct is grossly abnormal, or shocking, or contrary to decent norms; but I suggest that those commentators are more exact who say that morally the witch is the very opposite of the right values of society. This is not a trite point of vocabulary, but it corresponds significantly to the estimations of members of society. Typically, moral evaluations are scalar, such that actions are judged as more or less good, more or less bad. There are extreme instances at the polar ends of the scale, but at one end these are hypothetical; even societies that recognize saints concede that these exemplars have blemishes (as the saints themselves of course have to insist) and are not absolutely good. It would be both expectable and practicable, therefore, if societies were to place witches at various points toward the opprobrious end of the moral scale; certainly they would be bad, but more or less bad, and this means that they would be allowed to possess some virtues. But in fact the witch is not given the benefit of this moral nicety: the witch is absolutely and irremediably evil, a real instance of the polar type that merits utter condemnation. The witch's conduct is not merely contrasted with the ideal: there is nothing worse than the acts that the witch is imagined to perpetrate, so that the witch's conduct is strictly the opposite of the ideal. This gives us our first factor in the complex, namely, the relation of conceptual opposition.

I need not say much about this, for after Hertz a great deal has been written about polarities, complementaries, and syzygies in dual symbolic classification, especially with regard to the sets of opposed values signaled by right and left. It is important, however, not merely to isolate the relation of opposition from the moral definition of the witch, but also to stress that this relation has a fundamental character that makes it apt to the purpose of relegating the witch to the point of extreme censure. In other words, people resort to opposition as the simplest and most efficacious means of classification. They do so in innumerable institutions and contexts, including moiety systems and symmetric alliance and Manichean theologies, and witchcraft is merely one example of this proclivity.

I mentioned just now that opposite values may be signaled by the opposition of right and left. This spatial expression of nonspatial values, including moral qualities, has an analogue in a second component of the image of the witch. The behavior of the witch is commonly described as inverted, or the witch is said to embody inverted values. This is not simply a metaphor (like "opposite," for that matter), but is frequently a description of the witch's physical posture: the witch proceeds upside down, walking on his hands as the Kaguru imagine, or presents himself backwards. This imaginary inversion makes an apt picture of the perverse nature of the witch, and in itself it is both comprehensible and telling; but once again what we encounter in this component also is simply one example of the operation of a primary factor. When the Lugbara advert to the alien nature of their neighbors, members of other tribes just over the horizon, they say that the latter normally go about upside down. (It is only when you look at them that instantaneously they turn the right way up.) The Lugbara are not saying that all strange peoples are witches: they are expressing the strangeness by resorting to the image of inversion. This is in fact a very common symbolic means of marking a boundary. Similarly, many peoples imagine the world of the dead as the opposite of this, in that the spirits there speak backwards or place opposite values on things; and the Batak say also that the dead climb house-steps downwards, head first, that is, upside down. They are not saying that the spirits of the departed are witches: they are expressing the spirituality of ghosts, in opposition to terrestrial natures, by resorting to the image of inversion. The symbolic operation is the exploitation of the imaginative recourse. Inversion is an elementary mode of marking a contrast—especially at a moral or temporal boundary—and the wide extent to which it is employed, in many customs and ideologies, indicates that it is not merely a formal possibility that is available to the imagination, but that it is a positive proclivity by which men tend to be influenced in their collective representations.

Next, witches habitually go about their business at night. This looks obvious enough, for they work secretly and wish to avoid the gaze of decent people, including that of their victims. An Apache raiding party also used to travel at night, in order to gain the advantage of surprise; and burglars are supposed to operate at night in order not to be seen, either by their victims or by potential witnesses for the prosecution. But of course, there is more to the witch's association with night than a practical precaution, especially since it is doubtful that anyone does travel as a witch at night anyway. What we are dealing with is a symbolic, I dare say universal, image by which light and the absence or deprivation of light stand for opposed values and properties of innumerable kinds. The Bible is full of examples of the precellence of light and the opposite condition of darkness; mystical ideology continually resorts to the contrast; and it is a rich source of metaphor in estimating clarity of understanding and moral inclinations. As for the specific connection of witches with night, this too has analogues in other institutions. The first to come to mind is shamanism, in which it is a standard feature that the shaman holds his séance either at night or in a darkened enclosure. This is no doubt because the proceedings have to do with hidden things, with the mystical. (Recall that this word comes from the Greek *m⁻uein,* "to close the eyes.") There is no implication that a shaman is a nefarious person, acting at night in order to conceal his iniquity. Nor of course do I imply that the mystical is symbolized only by darkness, for under some aspects it is enacted in the full radiance of bright light. But the image of the witch combines both the fearsome presence of the powers of darkness and the nocturnal setting of spiritual activity.

This is sometimes symbolized by the color that is appropriate to night, namely, black. European witches used to smear themselves with soot, and witches in other cultures are on occasion distinguished by black appurtenances. In this case again, though, it is not witches alone that are symbolized by black. Our own priests wear black, so does the Mugwe of the Meru, and so also does a Gurung medium. In each instance the color, like night, stands for the mystical character of the status or the undertaking. There is no implication that all persons whose offices are symbolized by black share the horrible attributes of a witch. What particular attributes may be shared, beyond the mystical connection, is a contingent matter of local ideology. The imaginative constant is the resort to color in order to convey the significance. This general feature is nicely glossed by the example of the Kaguru witch: naturally black of skin, he is supposed to cover himself with white ashes, thus employing symbolic color in an image that is opposite to normal human appearance. So the generic factor is color, we may say, while the specific mystical significance is predominantly but not always conveyed by the color of darkness.

The association of a witch with night is reinforced by the usual character of the witch's animal familiar, or of the creature into which the witch can transform himself. Some of the species are the black cat in Europe, the polecat in North America, the fox in Japan, the maned wolf in Brazil, the owl in India, the hyena in East Africa, the bat in the Congo. The obvious and well-recognized attribute that they share is that they are all nocturnal. Some moreover are predators, others carrion-eaters, and yet others are menaces in the dark. These attributes are easy enough to grasp as being appropriate to the nocturnal operation and the dark character of the witch. But once more this is not a singular kind of symbolism that distinguishes only the witch. The individual species are indeed particularly apposite to the image of the witch, but the fact that the status is symbolized by animals is not. The classical demonstration of this fact in anthropology is totemism, in which the classification of men into social groups is symbolized by a parallel classification of animal species. In totemism, a clan may even be associated with a nocturnal species, but

there is no usual implication that the social group is composed of witches or that its members have the character of witches. What is happening in this institution is that in discriminating social statuses the members of totemic societies are resorting, by virtue of their tradition, to an extremely common method of symbolism. Ready examples are the animal supporters, such as the lion and the unicorn, in European heraldry; the animal "vehicles," such as the bull of Shiva, that help to identify Hindu deities; the animal-headed gods of Egypt; the birds and other species that represent nations or the states of the U.S.A.; the nicknames and emblems of military formations and sports teams; the terms of moral appraisal that ascribe the strengths and failings of animals to human beings. In all these cases, and in a great many other institutions and figures of speech, men are resorting to a mode of symbolism that has little to do with the particular social facts and a great deal to do with a natural imaginative impulsion. The animal familiar of the witch is merely one instance of the operation of this factor.

Another prominent component in the complex image that we are examining is that very often the witch is supposed to have the power of flight. There is one apparent reason for this, namely, that the action of the witch is usually considered to take place over some distance, either very rapidly or almost instantaneously, and in any case at such a range as could not be covered in the time by a normal human being. The attribute of flight is a simple way to imagine the witch at his swift work, and it is reinforced by those familiars, such as owls and bats, that as natural species are themselves actually capable of flying. That speed is a contributory feature is indicated by the example of the Kalapalo, who explain the rapidity with which a man travels (at night, incidentally) by stating that he came like a maned wolf, the creature that is associated with their witches.

We can conjecture also a negative basis to the employment of the image of flight. When we conceive the operation of some force at a distance, we have the scientific knowledge to enable us to think of a wavelike action, as in the form of a radio beam or a laser or a death ray. But in what terms could we represent such an action, on the part of a witch, if we had not this idiom of physics to rely on? The mystical task, let us consider, is to bring the malign power of one individual to bear, rapidly and over a distance, on another. Lacking the concept of wave-like force, we shall I think find ourselves conceiving that the witch comes directly into contact with his victim; and an immediate recourse is to imagine, with the inspiration of observing airborne species, that the witch flies. Sometimes this action is represented as a detached head (in certain cases with entrails hanging from it) flying through the air; examples come from as far afield as Borneo and Chile. But this image reminds us of Dürer's angels, who appear as cherubic heads equipped with wings, and these lead to a far more general significance in the imagined power of flight. It is a worldwide notion that persons of supernormal status are capable of flight: not only gods and angels and other spirits, but also men who are associated with them or who draw upon their powers; so that saints and shamans and yogis are all credited with mystical flight and sometimes (in Christian tradition, for instance) with physical levitation. Hocart has suggested furthermore that the common practice of carrying kings and other potentates so that they are never in contact with the earth is a ceremonial surrogate for the imagined gift of flight. Once more therefore we have to conclude that a prominent and universal component in the image of the witch has nothing exclusively to do with witches, but is merely one instance of a widely exploited recourse of the imagination in representing persons who possess abnormal powers.

Lastly, let me just mention one more component. I need only mention it, since it is too naturalistic a matter to be very interesting. This is the feature that a witch is supposed to emit a fiery trail or glow as he travels through the air. I am afraid all this means is that marsh gas and similar nocturnal illuminations are very commonly found in the world, and that peoples who imagine witches to fly at night are highly likely to associate their trajectories with the passage of these eerie lights. If the Trobrianders

hold that the glow is emitted from the witch's anus, this is just a dramatic touch added to the natural observation. Nevertheless, the component of the aerial light is a very common feature in the image of the witch, and it does reinforce the component of flight. It may not be symbolically so informative as other features, but it is still a contribution to the complex image of the witch. In some cases, moreover, it is a manifestation of fire, and we need no reminder of the fundamental importance everywhere of this lively symbol.

So much, and by necessity rather superficially, for certain factors that characteristically constitute the image: opposition, inversion, darkness, color, animals, flight, and nocturnal lights. I am not asserting that these features alone compose the image, or that all of them must be present, or that witches are necessarily represented by this image. The notion that I am putting forward is in fact doubly polythetic: first, in that disparate phenomena are grouped together under any one factor; second, that the disparate factors are variously and sporadically combined into the image of the witch.

In the first lecture I stressed that the primary factors are heterogeneous and that they are independent of the will. We now see these attributes manifested with special force in the synthetic image of the witch. The operative factors include the relational abstraction of opposition, the spatial metaphor of inversion, and a variety of observable phenomena of nature. The complex that they form has a global distribution and constancy that make it out of the question that each instance should be the result of individual or even traditional invention. As a collective representation, the complex is autonomous, and men have merely altered its particulars according to their circumstances—according to whether they themselves had white or black skins, or whether they had hyenas or the Japanese fox in their environment. It is as though the complex in itself, and not only the several factors out of which it is synthesized, were also primary.

The factors constitute a steady image of the witch, but they are also to be found in the constitution of other images and institutions. For example, the relations and phenomena that we have just sur-veyed can be combined, with different semantic values according to the appositeness of the materi-als, into the image of a saint or a shaman. If mysti-cal action at a distance is taken to be definitive, then this too is found in blessing and prayer and spiritual healing. So it is as though men have at their dis-posal, innately, a limited repertory of imaginative resources, and these, the primary factors, are differ-entially synthesized into distinct complexes repre-senting disparate social concerns. The factors accrete to the concern, and their meaning in combi-nation corresponds to the concern.

In the case of witchcraft, how are we to account for the synthesis, that is, for the fact that certain pri-mary factors characteristically combine into a rec-ognizable and comprehensible image? I am not at all sure that in principle we can hope to do so. We may in one case or another be able to see how it is that one feature or another is present or has a certain value (white ashes instead of black soot, incest instead of cannibalism), but these diacritical varia-tions are only secondary to the process of synthesis. Even where there is a naturalistic or demonstrable ground to the presence of a particular feature, still we cannot give this a causal expression, and the local explanation does not explain the synthesis. For example, if we assume that there is a patent sim-ilarity between the idea of a flying witch and the observation of a will-o'-the-wisp, the phenomenon does not explain the idea, since the idea exists where there is no marsh gas; and the adventitious occurrence of the nocturnal glow, apposite though it may be, does nothing to explain the polythetic syn-thesis with other factors.

Similar conclusions follow even when a causal connection can be shown to be possible between a feature of the image and some material agent. For example, it has been known for decades that Euro-pean witches used an ointment containing certain chemical substances, and that they rubbed this into their bodies, apparently into the vaginal membranes and the legs, through which the substances could have entered the blood stream. These substances included hemlock, henbane, belladonna, and aconite, drugs which could conduce to hallucinations, includ-

ing the sensation of flight. But this does not explain why witches are imagined to fly in societies that do not employ the drugs. Where the image is supported by drug-induced hallucinations, it does not explain the synthesis of the other factors that make up the total image. And in any case the hallucinations do not in themselves explain the factor of flight as an attribute of spirits and saints, shamans and heroes.

If we say then merely that the primary factors accrete around a social concern, what is the concern that underlies the image of the witch? It is articu-lated as a fear of other men, who can do evil by secret and invisible means. Certainly men have given one another ample occasion to fear other men, but this does not explain the complexity of the image of the witch or its characteristic components. Men everywhere are disposed to fear some other men, yet they adopt many ways apart from the insti-tution of witchcraft in expressing their apprehen-sion and in taking precautions against its object. Actually, it may not be right to say that the factors accrete around the concern, as though the concern came first and the image afterwards. All we know empirically is that the concern, in the form of a con-ventional unease about certain categories of per-sons, and the image, as a complex construction of the imagination given also in part by tradition, are found together. The true force of the metaphor of accretion is perhaps that the stated concern, namely, about malign mystical action at a distance, is the most constant definitive feature of the institution and also the theme that imparts a fit meaning to such features as trailing intestines or the invisible draining of the strength of the victims.

Moreover, to concentrate on the social concern, which people are conscious of and can express, leads to the view that witchcraft is a cognitive insti-tution. The burden of my argument however has been that witchcraft is a complex product of the imagination and that it provides evidence of certain proclivities of the imagination. Certainly the insti-tution has a cognitive aspect, for men reflect on their experience and they explain certain untoward events by witchcraft, but the form of the experience and the interpretation of the events are not the results of independent deliberation. If there is a "reality" to the idea of witchcraft, it is to be sought in the grounds and occasions of the image of the witch. Since the components of the image can be seen as products of factors that compose other complex images, the problematical focus is the process of synthesis that combines the components into the characteristic image. This process is not necessarily a response to experience, and we may not presume that it is otherwise determined by social facts. The synthesis may be, as I have suggested earlier, just as "primary" as are the factors that it integrates. In other words, the image of the witch is autonomous and can be conceived as an archetype of the unconscious imagination.

The concept of an archetype, in the sense of a primordial mental image, has suffered from obscurity and also from obscurantism, and it has fallen into discredit in the eyes of those for whom the work of Jung is not entirely creditable. In adverting to this concept, however, I am not trying to darken or diminish understanding but to advance analysis; and in formulating the results of comparative study by means of the word *archetype* I am not subscribing to Jung's psychology as a system. In undertaking the present investigation, I was not committed in advance to a Jungian view of the unconscious. My question was, How is social anthropology possible? The outcome, so far as the institution of witchcraft is concerned, is the notion of a psychic constant in the form of an autonomous image to which the human mind is naturally predisposed. *Archetype* happens to be the right word to denote this complex product of the unconscious.

There is in particular a distinction of method to be made. Typically, I take it, Jung's ideas on archetypes were derived from correspondences between images in the dreams or fantasies of patients and in alchemical manuscripts and hermeneutic sources. For the social anthropologist, on the other hand, the major sources are the reports of world ethnography, an incomparably vaster field of evidence and one that the comparativist nevertheless manages to comprehend as the widest testimony to the collective forms of human experience. As for the present investigation, moreover, there is a marked contrast between Jung's studies and the approach that I have

outlined. I think I am right in saying that Jung's analyses of what he regarded as archetypes were not only culturally limited but were also highly particularistic, and even idiosyncratic, in that each archetype was interpreted in terms of its own proper significance. My own method, though, has been to investigate the archetype of the witch by analysis into primary factors that are not exclusively associated with witchcraft. If I have on occasion referred to the products of these factors (particular colors, sides, sounds, textures) as semantic units, this was with the explicit gloss that the units could carry variable and even opposite meanings from one cultural context to another. In postulating a repertory of primary factors, I have presented a possibility that so far as I know Jung was not concerned with; and by concentrating on the principles of synthesis that constitute primary factors into archetypes and that discriminate one archetype from another, I have taken what appears to be a quite different direction of research.

Nevertheless, both of these approaches to the topic of archetypes are exercises in depth psychology. If the evidence of the social anthropologist consists in the first place of social facts and collective representations, this affords him only an advantage; for as social facts these representations have a relative autonomy, a generality, and a coercive force that objectify them for the purposes of analysis and comparison. Durkheim was quite right, I think, in propounding the notion of an entirely formal psychology that would be a sort of common ground for individual psychology and for sociology, and in suggesting that the comparative study of collective representations might seek the "laws of collective ideation" or of "social mentality" in general. This enterprise would lead, hypothetically, to the establishment of propositions that were valid equally for the individual and for the collective, with an exclusive substantive locus in neither.

The essential, if we are to say anything fundamental about human nature, is to find the common term of individual and collective. I have spoken here as though "the imagination" were in effect such a common term; and in analyzing the image of the witch I have alluded to properties that can be common both to individual consciousness and to collective representations. But these properties are such as, empirically, must inhere in some locus or entity or system of phenomena that is common to both types of manifestation of the imagination. According to received ideas, which I have no reason to question in this instance, this can reside only in the human organism; and the plainest and most economical inference is that this means the brain. The present state of knowledge concerning this organ, the most complicated natural system known, is, I gather, still relatively superficial and partial; and I am not relying on neurophysiology when I say that I interpret the primary factors and the modes of synthesis as spontaneous manifestations of properties of the brain. The strength of this accommodating hypothesis is that it accounts for the global distribution of the characteristic image of the witch, and at the same time for the constancy of the factors as apparently innate predispositions. It is on these premises that I find it convenient to regard the archetypes as vectors of consciousness. There is nothing in principle that is particularly difficult to accept in this metaphor. All it necessarily implies, in the first place, is that the brain responds to percepts differentially; for instance, that it responds especially to red rather than to other hues, or to percussion as distinct from more mellifluous sounds. There is some experimental support for this assumption, in addition to the weight of ethnographic indications. In some cases, in connection with certain primary factors or archetypes (such as percussion, the half man), it is moreover possible to suggest empirical grounds for their presence or their prominence.

Among the heterogeneous primary factors there falls a line that divides them into two types: those that are abstract (such as the relation of binary opposition) and those that are perceptual (such as color, texture). There is an inviting correspondence here with the contrasted functions of the cerebral hemispheres. It is tempting to link the respective factors causally to these functions: the abstract factors to the left hemisphere, the perceptual ones to

the right. A plausible hypothesis is that the comparatively restricted number of abstract factors has to do with the analytical function of the left hemisphere, and the more extensive range of the perceptual factors with the function of the right. A conceivable process is that these contrasted cerebral functions combine in an imaginative tropism, a synthetic response to natural foci of attraction among phenomena, whether social or physical, and that the product is the archetype.

With these considerations we are far beyond the present limits of proof, but I am not suggesting that it is essential to fall in with speculations of this kind in order to assent to the method that I have proposed. I suggest only that the dichotomy among the primary factors, and their synthesis into the archetype, are consistent with current opinion about the lateral functions of the brain; and that this ultimate locus is consistent with the unconscious generation of the archetypes and with the likelihood that these complex images are the products of genetically inherited predispositions.

What may lie at a deeper level of probing into the imaginative operations of the brain, in the form of neuroelectrical events, is a tantalizing sequel among further questions that propose themselves, if hardly one that a comparativist can have an opinion about. I mention it, however, in order to put us on our guard against inappropriate preconceptions when, as is almost inevitable, we do speculate on the cerebral grounds to collective representations. I am alluding to Wittgenstein's salutary comments:

> No supposition seems to me more natural than that there is no process in the brain correlated with associating or with thinking; so that it would be impossible to read off thought-processes from brain-processes. I mean this: if I talk or write there is, I assume, a system of impulses going out from my brain and correlated with my spoken or written thoughts. But why should the *system* continue further in the direction of the centre? . . . It is . . . perfectly possible that certain psychological phenomena cannot be investigated physiologically, because physiologically nothing corresponds to them.

For the more ascertainable present, let me conclude this lecture by resuming some of the main points. We have moved from the sociology of mystical crime, by way of induction from the global comparison of social facts, to certain apparent properties of the human brain. These properties are seen as determinants in the constitution of collective representations, not only of witchcraft but in effect universally and with regard to numerous other institutions. As such, they act as initial limits to the imagination, rather as do certain logical constraints on the forms of discursive reasoning. This conclusion runs contrary to the received idea of romantic individualism that, however constrained we may be by the dictates of society and the puny capacities of the human organism, we have an unfettered liberty in the exercise of the imagination. At the level of collective representations, our investigation of the image of the witch tends to reduce the scope and assurance of this comfortable assumption.

READING 7–5

THE WAY THINGS ARE SAID

Jeanne Favret-Saada

French ethnography is rich in published works on local folklore, and witchcraft and magic are repeatedly mentioned in the literature. Jeanne Favret-Saada, however, was the first anthropologist to carry out participant observation in a French society practicing witchcraft. Her book Deadly Words *is a pioneering landmark in the study of European witchcraft, which until its publication in France in 1977, had been understood only from historical documents. While many of these studies offered cogent explanations why witchcraft accusations could so quickly and devastatingly tear apart a community, they generally lacked an adequate discussion of the fears that apparently motivate individuals into accusing others.*

In contrast, by personally involving herself in the process of witchcraft, Favret-Saada, who herself is French, could delve into its psychology and in this way acquire insight into the mentality of believers. In the Bocage region of France witchcraft, as among the Azande, offers an intellectual explanation for unfortunate events. But not every misfortune, only those unusual in some way, as when a series of misfortunes occurs. Part of a witch's power is contained in words, and these are believed capable of causing physical injure. A villager, therefore, need do nothing more than direct "bad" words to a fellow villager to risk being suspected of witchcraft. If the "victim" subsequently suffers a series of misfortunes he or she will interpret it as witchcraft directed by the other party. As among the Azande the witch performs no ritual, and Evans-Pritchard has written that witchcraft is "a psychic act" (1937:21). Yet, although in their society, "a witch performs no rite, utters no spell, and possesses no medicines," we see that among the peasants of the Bocage, words are one of the ways in which witches can injure people. Since words are freighted with power any verbal exchange, however innocuous, can lead to accusations, and given this belief Favret-Saada's failure to convince her informants she was an uninvolved ethnographer who had merely come to live among them in the role of innocent observer of their activities is understandable. In contrast to Evans-Pritchard, whose informants did not regard him as in any significant way a part of the system of accusations, Favret-Saada discovered that the role of disinterested neutral was inconceivable in the Bocage. Accordingly, as her fieldwork progressed so she increasingly emerged as a contributor to their experiences of witchcraft. Her book therefore gives us a vivid sense of how people react to the presence of witchcraft in their lives. Her familiarity with Evans-Pritchard's pioneering work is evident, since she contrasts this aspect of their respective fieldwork experiences.

Source: from *Deadly Words: Witchcraft in the Bocage* by Jeanne Favret-Saada, Translated by Catherine Cullen. Cambridge: Cambridge University Press. Paris: Editions de la Maison des Sciences de L'Homme. 1980.

It seems that even the pure light of science requires, in order to shine, the darkness of ignorance.

KARL MARX (1856)

Take an enthnographer: she has chosen to investigate contemporary witchcraft in the Bocage* of Western France. She has already done some fieldwork; she has a basic academic training; she has published some papers on the logic of murder, violence and insurrection in an altogether different, tribal society. She is now working in France, to avoid having to learn yet another difficult language. Especially since in her view the symbolic shaping out of murder or aggression—the way things are said in the native culture—is as important as the functioning of political machinery.

I. THE MIRROR-IMAGE OF AN ACADEMIC

Getting ready to leave for the field, she looks through the scientific (and not so scientific) literature on contemporary witchcraft: the writings of folklorists and psychiatrists, of occultists and journalists. This is what she finds: that peasants, who are 'credulous', 'backward' and impervious to 'cause of effect', blame their misfortune on the jealousy of a neighbour who has cast a spell on them; they go to an unwitcher[†] (usually described as a 'charlatan', now and again as 'naïve') who protects them from their imaginary aggressor by performing 'secret' rituals which 'have no meaning', and 'come from another age'. The geographical and cultural 'isolation' of the Bocage is partly responsible for the 'survival' of these 'beliefs' in our time.

If that is all there is to be said about witchcraft (and however much you try to find out from the books of folklorists or the reports of trials in the French press over the last ten years, you will learn no more), you may wonder why it seems to be such an obsession. To judge by the public's immense curiosity, the fascination produced by the very word 'witchcraft', the guaranteed success of anything written about it, one wonders what journalistic scoop could ever find a greater public.

Take an ethnographer. She has spent more than thirty months in the Bocage in Mayenne, studying witchcraft. 'How exciting, how thrilling, how extraordinary . . .!' 'Tell us all about the witches', she is asked again and again when she gets back to the city. Just as one might say: tell us tales about ogres or wolves, about Little Red Riding Hood. Frighten

us, but make it clear that it's only a story; or that they are just peasants: credulous, backward and marginal. Or alternatively: confirm that *out there* there are some people who can bend the laws of causality and morality, who can kill by magic and not be punished; but remember to end by saying that they do not really have that power: they only believe it because they are credulous, backward peasants . . . (see above).

No wonder that country people in the West are not in any hurry to step forward and be taken for idiots in the way that public opinion would have them be—whether in the scholarly version developed by folklorists, or in the equally hard faced popular version spread by the media.

To say that one is studying beliefs about witchcraft is automatically to deny them any truth: it is just a belief, it is not true. So folklorists never ask of country people: 'what are they trying to express by means of a witchcraft crisis?', but only 'what are they hiding from us?' They are led on by the idea of some healer's 'secret', some local trick, and describing it is enough to gratify academic curiosity. So witchcraft is no more than a body of empty recipes (boil an ox heart, prick it with a thousand pins, etc.)? Grant that sort of thing supernatural power? How gullible can you be?

Similarly, when the reporter, that hero of positivist discourse, goes along on behalf of a public assumed to be incredulous, and asks country people whether they 'still believe' in spells, the case is decided in advance: yes, people do still believe in spells, especially if you go to the Lower Berry or the Normandy Bocage. How convenient that there should be a district full of idiots, where the whole realm of the imaginary can be held in. But country people are not fools: they meet these advances with obstinate silence.

But even their silence about things to do with witchcraft; and more generally about anything to do with illness and death, is said to tell us about their status: 'their language is too simple', 'they are incapable of symbolizing', you won't get anything out of them because 'they don't talk': that is what I was told by the local scholarly élite. Why not say they are wild men of the woods, since they live in a 'bocage'; animals, even? 'Medicine is a veterinary art round here' a local psychiatrist once told me.

So all that was known about witchcraft is that it was unknowable: when I left for the field, knowledge of the subject boiled down to this. The first question I asked myself when I met the peasants, who were neither credulous nor backward, was: is witchcraft unknowable, or is it just that those who say this need to block out all knowledge about it in order to maintain their own intellectual coherence? Does the 'scholar' or the 'man of our own age' need to comfort himself with the myth of a credulous and backward peasant?[1]

The social sciences aim to account for cultural differences. But can this be achieved by postulating the existence of a peasant who is denied all reality save that he is the mirror-image of an academic?

Whenever folklorists or reporters talk of witchcraft in the country, they always do so as if one were facing two incompatible physical theories: the pre-logical or medieval attitude of peasants, who wrongly attribute their misfortunes to imaginary witches; and ours, the attitude of educated people who know how to handle causal relations correctly. It is said or implied that peasants are incapable of this either because of ignorance or of backwardness. In this respect, the description given of the peasant and the '*pays*', the canton, that determines him is governed by a peculiar set of terms which necessarily imply that he is incapable of grasping causal relations. Witchcraft is put forward as a nonsense theory which peasants can afford to adopt because it is the local theory. The folklorist's job is then to underline the difference between his own theory (which also happens to be a 'true' one) and the peasant's, which is only a belief.[2]

But who can ignore the difficulties involved in postulating the co-existence of two incompatible physical theories which correspond to two ages of humankind? Do you really have to do thirty months of fieldwork to be in a position to say that country people are just as well able to cope with causal relations as anyone else, and to make the suggestion that witchcraft cannot be reduced to a physical theory, although it does indeed imply a certain kind of causality?[3]

II. WORDS SPOKEN WITH INSISTENCE

I began by studying the words used to express biological misfortunes, and used in ordinary conversation; about death, sterility, and illness in animals and humans. The first thing one notices is that they distinguish between ordinary misfortunes and their extraordinary repetition.

In the Bocage, as anywhere else in France, ordinary misfortunes are accepted as 'one-off'; so, a single illness, the loss of one animal, one bankruptcy, even one death, do not call for more than a single comment: *'the trouble with him is that he drinks too much'; 'she had cancer of the kidneys'; 'my cow was very old'.*

An onslaught by witchcraft, on the other hand, gives a pattern to misfortunes which are repeated and range over the persons and belongings of a bewitched couple: in succession, a heifer dies, the wife has a miscarriage, the child is covered in spots, the car runs into a ditch, the butter won't churn, the bread won't rise, the geese bolt, or the daughter they want to marry off goes into a decline . . . Every morning, the couple ask anxiously: *'What on earth will happen next?'* And every time some misfortune occurs: always unexpected, always inexplicable.

When misfortunes occur like this in series, the countryman approaches qualified people with a double request: on the one hand for an interpretation, and on the other for a cure.

The doctors and vets answer him by denying the existence of any series: illnesses, deaths and mechanical breakdowns do not occur for the same reasons and are not treated in the same way. These people are the curators of objective knowledge about the body, and they can claim to pick off one by one the causes of the misfortunes: go and disinfect your stables, vaccinate your cows, send your wife to the gynaecologist, give your child milk with less fat in it, drink less alcohol . . . But however effective each separate treatment may be, in the eyes of some peasants it is still incomplete, for it only affects the cause and not the origin of their troubles. The origin is always the evil nature of one or more witches who hunger after other people's misfortunes, and whose words, look and touch have supernatural power.

Faced with a bewitched, one can imagine that the priest is in a more awkward situation than the doctor, for evil, misfortune and the supernatural mean something to him. But what they mean has become singularly blurred by many centuries of theological brooding. The dividing line between the ranges of the natural and the supernatural has been fixed by Catholic orthodoxy; but the reasons given have scarcely been assimilated, especially since each late pronouncement does not categorically cancel former ones. So theological knowledge is no more unified in the mind of a country priest than it is in the body of doctrine.[4]

Hearing the various stories told in his parish, the priest can choose between three different and mutually exclusive types of interpretation:

1. He can dismiss these misfortunes as part of the natural order, and so deny them any religious significance: by doing so he sides with medical ideology, and in effect says the bewitched are raving or superstitious people.
2. He can acknowledge that these misfortunes do pertain to the supernatural order, but are an effect of divine love: so the bishop of Séez preaches 'good suffering' to a congregation of '*luckless*' peasants[5]. A universally aimed (Catholic) discourse can turn him who is '*luckless*' into the most lucky. The man whom God loves best and so chastises, is only a victim in the eyes of the world. This reversal of appearances sometimes has its effect.
3. The priest can meet the peasant on his own ground and interpret his misfortunes as the work of the devil. He is permitted to do this by at least one branch or stratum of theology. He then has two alternatives.

He may consult, as he is supposed to, the diocesan exorcist, the official expert in diabolical matters appointed by the hierarchy. But in Western France, the priest knows very well that he is not likely to

convince the expert, who has held this position for thirty years precisely because he is sceptical about the devil's interest in so-called 'simple' peasants: you have to be clever to interest the devil. So the diocesan exorcist, in the elitist style of any country priest who has risen in the Church or any peasant who has risen in society, offers the positivist interpretation. He refuses to give any religious meaning to the peasant's misfortune except by mentioning 'good suffering' or saying he will pray for him. Like the doctor, he refuses the peasant's request for a meaning by advising the man to consult a psychiatrist, to live a more balanced life, and to apply better the rules of the experimental method. The village priest knows in advance that to send a bewitched to the diocesan exorcist is to ask him to take his troubles elsewhere, and in effect to direct him to a doctor by way of the ecclesiastical hierarchy.

Alternatively, the priest comes and exorcises the farm and its inhabitants without consulting the hierarchy. As a more or less willing distributor of blessings and medals, holy water and salt, he plays the role in his parish of a small-scale unwitcher who protects people from evil spells without sending them back to the witch.

'*If it's a small spell, it works*': the series of misfortunes stops and everything returns to normal. It works, but the origin of the misfortune and its repetition are still not satisfactorily symbolized. For when the peasant talks about being bewitched to anyone who is willing to listen, what he wants acknowledged is this: *if such repetitions occur, one must assume that somewhere someone wants them to*. I shall show later that witchcraft consists in creating a misunderstanding about who it is that desires the misfortunes of the bewitched. Note here that the Church's rite merely clouds the issue by attributing the evil to some immaterial spirit included by half-hearted theology in a list of '*preternatural facts*'. For the victim, the witch is some familiar person (a neighbour, for example) whose aims he can at least hope to discover.

If '*it doesn't work*': if the priest '*isn't strong enough*' because his parishioner is '*caught tight*' in the spells, the bewitched is left with his question: why this series of events, and why in my home? What is at stake here, my sanity or my life? Am I mad, as the doctor says, or does someone have it in for me to the point of wanting me to die?

It is only at this point that the sufferer can choose to interpret his ills in the language of witchcraft. Some friend, or someone else who has noticed him moving deeper into misfortune and seen the ineffectiveness of approved learning makes the crucial diagnosis: *'Do you think there may be someone who wishes you ill?'*[6] This amounts to saying: 'you're not mad, I can see in you the signs of a similar crisis I once experienced, and which came to an end thanks to this unwitcher.'

The priest and the doctor have faded out long ago when the unwitcher is called. The unwitcher's task is first to authenticate his patient's sufferings and his feeling of being threatened in the flesh; second, it is to locate, by close examination, the patient's vulnerable spots. It is as if his own body and those of his family, his land and all his possessions make up a single surface full of holes, through which the witch's violence might break in at any moment. The unwitcher then clearly tells his client how long he still has to live if he stubbornly remains defenceless. He is a master of death; he can tell its date and how to postpone it. A professional in supernatural evil, he is prepared to return blow for blow against *'the person we suspect'*, the alleged witch, whose final identity is established only after an investigation, sometimes a long one. This is the inception of what can only be called a cure. The séances later are devoted to finding the gaps which still need sealing, as they are revealed day by day in the course of life.[7]

III. WHEN WORDS WAGE WAR

In the project for my research I wrote that I wanted to study witchcraft practices in the Bocage. For more than a century, folklorists had been gorging themselves on them, and the time had come to understand them. In the field, however, all I came across was language. For many months, the only empirical facts I was able to record were words.

Today I would say that an attack of witchcraft can be summed up as follows: a set of words spoken in a crisis situation by someone who will later be designated as a witch are afterwards interpreted as having taken effect on the body and belongings of the person spoken to, who will on that ground say he is bewitched. The unwitcher takes on himself these words originally spoken to his client, and turns them back on to their initial sender, the witch. Always the *'abnormal'* is said to have settled in after certain words have been uttered, and the situation persists without change until the unwitcher places himself like a screen between the sender and the receiver. Unwitching rituals—the actual 'practices'—are remarkably poor and contingent: this ritual or that, it makes no difference, any one will do. For if the ritual is upheld it is only through words and through the person who says them. So perhaps, I was not entirely mistaken when I said I wanted to study practices: the act, in witchcraft, is the word.

That may seem an elementary statement, but it is full of implications. The first is this: until now, the work of ethnographers has relied on a convention (one too obvious to be stated) about the use of spoken words. For ethnography to be possible, it was necessary that the investigator and the 'native' should at least agree that speech has the function of conveying information. To be an ethnographer is first to record the utterances of appropriately chosen native informants. How to establish this information-situation, the main source of the investigator's knowledge, how to choose one's informants, how to involve them in a regular working relationship . . . the handbooks always insist on this truly fundamental point in fieldwork.[8]

Now, witchcraft is spoken words; but these spoken words are power, and not knowledge or information.

To talk, in witchcraft, is never to inform. Or if information is given, it is so that the person who is to kill (the unwitcher) will know where to aim his blows. 'Informing' an ethnographer, that is, someone who claims to have no intention of using the information, but naïvely wants to know for the sake of knowing, is literally unthinkable. For a single word (and only a word) can tie or untie a fate, and whoever puts himself in a position to utter it is formidable. Knowing about spells brings money, brings more power and triggers terror: realities much more fascinating to an interlocutor than the innocent accumulation of scientific knowledge, writing a well-documented book, or getting an academic degree.

Similarly, it is unthinkable that people can talk for the sake of talking. Exchanging words just to show that one is with other people, to show one's wish to communicate, or what Malinowski called 'phatic communication' exists in the Bocage as it does anywhere else.[9] But here it implies strictly political intentions: phatic communication is the expression of zero-aggressiveness; it conveys to one's interlocutor that one might launch a magic rocket at him, but that one chooses not to do so for the time being. It is conveying to him that this is not the time for a fight, but for a cease-fire. When interlocutors for whom witchcraft is involved talk about nothing (that is about anything except what really matters) it is to emphasize the violence of what is not being talked about. More fundamentally, it is to check that the circuit is functioning, and that a state of war does indeed hold between the opponents.[10]

In short, there is no neutral position with spoken words: in witchcraft, words wage war. Anyone talking about it is a belligerent, the ethnographer like everyone else. There is no room for uninvolved observers.

When Evans-Pritchard, founder of the ethnography of witchcraft, studied the Zande, he made it his practice to interpret the events of his life by means of schemes about persecution, consulting oracles and submitting to their decisions: 'I was aided in my understanding of the feelings of the bewitched Azande', he says, 'by sharing their hopes and joys, apathy and sorrows [. . .]. In no department of their life was I more successful in "thinking black" or as it should more correctly be said "feeling black" than in the sphere of witchcraft. I, too, used to react to misfortunes in the idiom of witchcraft, and it was often an effort to check this lapse into unreason' (1937). But we learn from his book that actually the Zande had given him the position of 'Prince without portfolio', which is no slight consolation if one remembers that in Zande society, a prince can only be bewitched by another prince (a rather reassuring

thought for an ethnographer established many miles from the court) and that by not giving him of portfolio, the Zande were exempting Evans-Pritchard from having to play the role, so important for the effectiveness of the cure, of symbolic guarantee of the return to order.

In other words, the ethnographer could not himself possibly be involved in a case of witchcraft.[11] In the Bocage, the situation happens to be less comfortable: nobody ever talks about witchcraft to gain knowledge, but to gain power. The same is true about asking questions. Before the ethnographer has uttered a single word, he is involved in the same power relationship as anyone else talking about it. Let him open his mouth, and his interlocutor immediately tries to identify his strategy, estimate his force, guess if he is a friend or foe, or if he is to be bought or destroyed. As with any other interlocutor, speaking to the ethnographer one is addressing either *a subject supposed to be able* (a witch, an unwitcher) *or unable* (a victim, a bewitched person).

It follows that wanting to know could only be— for me as for anyone else— in the name of a force which I claim to have or which my interlocutor credits me with. If I were not equipped to confront it, no one would believe I could survive unharmed, or even survive it at all.

'Are you strong enough?' I was often asked when I tried to establish an information-relationship, that is to get people who had experience of witch stories to tell me about them. A mere desire for information is the sign of a naïuve or hypocritical person who must at once be frightened off. The effect that the person telling the story is trying to achieve is either to fascinate or to frighten; nobody would talk about it who did not hope to fascinate. If my interlocutor is successful, he says I have *'weak blood'* and advises me to change my course of research towards folk song or the ancient papegai festival. If he fears that he has not brought it off, he anxiously asks me how I can bear to hear such stories every day, and offers various assumptions: *'You've got strong blood',* or else *'you've got something'* (to protect yourself with). He then tries to identify my fetishes, to find out whether or not they

are *'stronger'* than his own. Otherwise, he may identify me with a certain unwitcher who has just died, a double-edged compliment which I am bound to appreciate: to say that my *'hands tremble like Madame Marie's'* means that, like her, I'm *'quite strong'*—but also that in the end she met her master in witchcraft, and he did away with her quite recently.

As you can see, this is not exactly a standard situation, in which information is exchanged and where the ethnographer may hope to have neutral knowledge about the beliefs and practices of witchcraft conveyed to him. For he who succeeds in acquiring such knowledge gains power and must accept the effects of this power; the more one knows, the more one is a threat and the more one is magically threatened. So long as I claimed the usual status of an ethnographer, saying I wanted to know for the sake of knowing, my interlocutors were less eager to communicate their own knowledge than to test mine, to try to guess the necessarily magic use I intended to put it to, and to develop their force to the detriment of my own. I had to accept the logic of this totally combative situation and admit that it was absurd to continue to posit a neutral position which was neither admissible or even credible to anyone else. When total war is being waged with words, one must make up one's mind to engage in another kind of ethnography.[12]

ENDNOTES

Bocage: countryside of Western France marked by intermingling patches of woodland and heath, small fields, tall hedgerows and orchards.

†*Unwitcher*: The Bocage natives use the word *désorcelleur* rather than the more usual *désensorcelleur* [ensorceller = to bewitch]. I have translated it by *unwitcher* rather than *unbewitcher*. Similarly, *désorceller* is translated as *to unwitch* and *désorcellage* or *d&sorcellement* as *unwitching* or *unwitchment*.

1. I have published an earlier version of the above: Jeanne Favret, 'Racontez-nous des histoires de sorciers', in *Le Monde*, 6–7 October 1974. Appendix I. (*The explorer of darkness*, cf. p. 225) reproduces a comment I wrote on a television report about witchcraft in the Berry: 'Sorciers et paysans', in *Critique*, No. 299, April 1972.

2. Arnold Van Gennep introduces the subject 'Magic and Witchcraft' in his well-known *Manuel du folklore français contemporain* (1938) as follows: 'When one looks more closely at the facts, almost the whole of French folklore could be substituted here, since the acts and concepts which are designated *popular* [i.e. the subject of folklore] contrast exactly with acts and concepts which are designated *scientific*, through a *mistaken application of the law of causality*. The importance of this *'logical error'* has varied with time . . .' I have italicized what goes without saying for Van Gennep. Appendix II, *Ignorance as a profession* (cf. p. 227) analyses the folklorists' attitude to witchcraft.

3. In theory, anthropology is a more sophisticated discipline than folklore. However, its remarkable naïveté is illustrated by the fact that it was not until 1966 that a distinguished researcher, Edmund Leach, put his own reputation at stake by criticizing the dictum (which had so far been totally accepted) according to which some primitive people ignored the causal relation between copulation and birth. Cf. Edmund Leach (1967).

4. Sometimes the dogma changes, but it is always expressed in an a-historical form and guaranteed by the infallibility of the Supreme Pontiff: 'The dogmatic truth consists in effacing its historical trace from writing', writes Pierre Legendre (1974). Anyone could lose their way in it, and the country priest must have a hard time trying to find the religious code which is appropriate to the dramatic situation presented to him by the bewitched. For although the priest is concerned with dogma, he is much more concretely involved in the a-theoretical use that the ecclesiastical hierarchy makes of an institution there, that of the diocesan exorcist) at the particular point in time when the bewitched comes to consult him.

5. To use one of their own expressions.

6. An essential character, whom I have called the *annunciator*.

7. I have published an early draft of the above, although it now seems to me confused and inadequate; cf. Jeanne Favret (1971).

8. The anthropologist's task is like learning an unknown symbolic code which must be taught him by the most competent speaker he can find. Cf. for example: Royal Anthropological Institute (1971), S. F. Nadel (1951), John Beattie (1964).

9. Under the term 'phatic communion', as part of 'ordinary conversation', Malinowski identified a particular type of discourse which is not aimed at giving information, but at a communion through words: 'inquiries about health, comment on the weather, affirmations of some supremely obvious state of things' . . . (B. Malinowski, 1923). These remarks are exchanged in order to establish and maintain communication between the speakers. On this problem, see also T. Todorov (1970), E. Benveniste (1970), R. Jakobson (1960).

10. R. Jakobson (op. cit.) remarks that the prototype of this kind of utterance is *'Hallo, can you hear me?'*

11. He only recounts one incident (p. 460) in which the Zande were able to say he was bewitched.

12. It is not surprising that Clausewitz (1968) was an important point of reference at the beginning of my work: war as a supremely serious game, trying to dictate its laws to the enemy; as an extension of a duel on a wider scale and over a longer span; as a continuation of politics through other means, and so on. It was not always easy to decide which one was speaking: the discourse of war or the discourse of witchcraft, at least until I realized that it was meaningless to think of witchcraft in terms of the categories of game theory.

RELIGION IN THE NEWS

PASTOR AND WIFE ARE ACQUITTED ON ALL CHARGES IN SEX-ABUSE CASE

By TIMOTHY EGAN

Allied with fear, unreasoning prejudice in a society, which the above readings demonstrate, motives witchcraft; but these sentiments are not restricted to witchcraft. Contemporary American society reveals these forces at work, and we obtain a useful insight into how they operate—and the devastating impact they have on peoples' lives as well as on society itself—by examining them in a non-witchcraft context. Just as men and women in Massachusetts found themselves at the mercy of unjust accusations launched at them by irresponsible girls aided and abetted by adults with a political agenda, so three hundred years later were citizens of the same state (and other American states) preyed upon by the unscrupulous. In both cases social control and the exercise of power dominated the process, the principal difference being in the nature of the alleged offence. In the one case the accusations were couched in the idiom of witchcraft, in the other in that of sexual abuse.

Sexual abuse can occur. Witchcraft, as it is described in these readings, is impossible. But although the accusations leveled at the Robersons included acts that were possible, the authorities' evidence was only marginally more convincing than the spectral evidence the judicial authorities had relied on in Salem three hundred years before. "Normal rules of procedure usually do not apply" in the case of the sexual abuse of children, one lawyer was quoted as saying, and prosecutors trusted the memories of very young children, "which can be easily influenced and [are] prone to the flights of fancy." Just as vendettas between adults encouraged the Salem girls to point their fingers at likely scapegoats, who at least at the beginning of the craze were individuals marginal to society, so, too, do we find here that the greater part of those arrested were poor and mentally retarded individuals. In yet another parallel, just as in Salem, persons who dared to speak out against the outrages were themselves accused—exactly as was Mr. Roberson after he publicly upbraided the local police officer.

SEATTLE, Dec. 11 — After less than a full day of deliberation, a jury has acquitted a lay pastor and his wife of all charges of sexual abuse of children in a trial that critics say demonstrated the worst aspects of police misconduct in such cases.

The defendants, Robert and Connie Roberson, ran a food bank and a Pentecostal church in the central Washington town of Wenatchee. They were accused of being at the center a sex ring in which children were ritualistically raped and abused by Mr. Roberson and dozens of members of his congregation.

There was no physcial evidence used to support the charges. The main witness was the 13-year-old foster daughter of a police officer, Robert Perez, who investigated the Robersons. He has been on a two-year campaign against what he said was a widespread sex ring in the small town.

Mr. Roberson was arrested and charged with 11 counts of child sex abuse shortly after he publicly criticized Mr. Perez. The preacher's 5-year-old daughter was taken from him at the time of his arrest, last spring. The authorities said Mr. Roberson, who is not ordained, had also molested the girl.

But the girl, in court testimony last week, said no such abuse ever took place. On Friday, Judge T. W. Small of Douglas County Superior Court dismissed the two charges of alleged abuse of Mr. Roberson's daughter.

Today a jury in Waterville, a small town across the Columbia River from Wenatchee, found the Robersons not guilty on the remaining 14 counts. It was a stunning rebuke of Detective Perez, who said dozens of adults in the Wenatchee area had systematically abused their own children and the children of their friends and neighbors.

"They overstepped the bounds of decency," Robert Van Siclen, the Robersons' lawyer, said after the verdict was read this afternoon in reference to the Wenatchee police. "They let objectivity get out of the way, and they let the checks and balances that ought to have at the investigative level get away from them."

RELIGION IN THE NEWS

PASTOR AND WIFE ARE ACQUITTED ON ALL CHARGES IN SEX-ABUSE CASE
continued

Mr. Perez's stepdaughter named 23 "adults who she said were involved in sexually abusing herself or other children.

During her testimony, the girl also said that shortly before she took the stand against Mr. Roberson last week, Mr. Perez twisted her arm, causing a bruise. She also said that Mr. Perez had thrown her to the floor several weeks earlier.

In his testimony, Mr. Perez denied pressuring his stepdaughter to testify against the Robersons.

As the verdict was read today, Mrs. Roberson wept. Afterward, she said she felt like a bad dream was over.

"If you ever have that dream where you're falling off a cliff, and you either hit bottom or wake up — that's exactly the way it was," she told reporters. "Falling, and falling and finally coming to an end."

In all, more than 40 adults have been arrested, and at least 20 are in prison as a result of investigations by Mr. Perez over the last two years. Most of the those arrested are poor and mentally retarded, and were living on welfare at the time they were charged. They were given long jail sentences after pleading guilty. Their lawyers said they were coerced by Mr. Perez.

Critics of the Perez investigation recalled the McMartin Preschool case of 1983, in which teachers were charged, with mass sexual abuse of children in their care in Southern California, but juries threw out all the charges.

The Justice Department may have the final say in most of the Wenatchee cases. Earlier this year Gov. Mike Lowry of Washington and the Speaker of the state House of Representatives, Clyde Ballard, asked Federal officials whether they would review some of the cases.

Attorney General Janet Reno said the Justice Department had completed its look at the Wenatchee cases, and would soon announce whether there will be a formal investigation of the cases. Federal officials were asked to examine whether the civil rights of some of those accused of sex crimes had been violated.

One Justice Department lawyer who is not involved in the review, Paul-Noel Chretien, said the Wenatchee case was reminiscent of the McMartin case. Normal rules of procedure and evidence usually do not apply, Mr. Chretien said in a recent essay in The Wall Street Journal, Instead, prosecutors rely almost entirely on the memory of a child, which can be easily influenced and is prone to flights of fancy, he said.

Wenatchee police had no comment on the verdict today. Mr. Perez was promoted to detective from patrolman in January 1994. Over the next two years at his direction, a series of sensational arrests took place, bringing much notoriety to the town.

One of the few early critics of Mr. Perez was Mr. Roberson. He said in court testimony last week that charges were brought against him because of a vendetta by Mr. Perez. After complaining about Mr. Perez's cases to a judge, Mr. Roberson said the detective told him: "We warned you, Roberson. We warned you."

Shortly after that threat, said Mr. Roberson, he was charged with raping and abusing children in the basement of this church, while other adults watched. The primary basis for the charges was Mr. Perez's stepdaughter.

The lone adult to testify against Mr. Roberson, Gary Filbeck, is a convicted child rapist whose testimony was the result of a plea bargain. Multiple counts of first-degree rape were reduced to misdemeanors in return for Mr. Filbeck's testimony that he saw Mr. Roberson abuse two girls near the church altar.

Source: Reprinted with the permission of *The New York Times*, National. December 12, 1995.

ASK YOURSELF

The "Religion in the News" reading makes no explicit reference to witchcraft. Compare the readings on Zande witchcraft and Salem witchcraft with the persecution inflicted upon the Robersons in order to detect any other parallels between the three cases. What differences seem to exist between them and what similarities? When you have made up your mind decide if you think what happened to the Robersons justifies the use of the label "witchcraft accusations."

FURTHER READINGS

Briggs, Robin. *Witches and Neighbors: The Social and Cultural Context of European Witchcraft.* London and New York: Viking, 1996. In this excellent study, Briggs brings to bear a rangeof analytical perspectives on witchcraft in the 16th and 17th centuries in Europe. Topics included are the tensions generated between the genders, spouses, kin, and neighbors in local village communities in France and Germany. Briggs's account includes psychological and sociological approaches.

Macfarlane, A.D.J. *Witchcraft in Tudor and Stuart England: A Regional and Comparative Study.* New York: Harper & Row, 1970. Adopting a structural-functional perspective, the author analyzes documentary data from the sixteen and seventeenth centuries to examine possible connections between the rise of witchcraft accusations and a set of sociological variables he isolates. In doing so he demonstrates how scapegoating and guilt are implicated in this institution.

Malinowski, Bronislaw. *Argonauts of the Western Pacific.* Prospect Heights, IL: Waveland Press, 1984 (1922). In this, one of the classic ethnographies, Malinowski gives case material for his hypothesis regarding the psychological function of magic, including the use of magic to promote safety when travelling across the sea on trading expeditions. Specifically, he discusses weather magic to still the wind and beauty magic to enhance traders' self-esteem. He also makes clear the dominant importance of spells in Trobriand magic (Reading 5–4).

Watson, C. W., and Roy Ellen, eds. *Understanding Witchcraft and Sorcery in Southeast Asia.* Honolulu: University of Hawaii Press, 1993. With 10 independent contributions from such places as Thailand, Malaya, eastern Indonesia, and Java, this volume offers abundant case material for comparison and contrast. The introduction by the editors is an excellent cross-cultural overview of witchcraft and sorcery.

SUGGESTED VIDEOS

"Magical Death." Shamans in a Yanomamo village practice harmful magic against the enemies of visitors they are receiving in order to display the goodwill they bear their guests. Shown in this documentary is the use of hallucinogenic snuff by shamans, and the interrelatedness of religion and politics. 28 minutes; 1973. Documentary Educational Resources, 5 Bridge Street, Watertown, MA 02172.

"Three Sovereigns for Sarah." Adhering closely to the explanation offered by Boyer and Nissenbaum (see Reading 7–3) for the astounding outbreak of witchcraft accusations that benighted the village of Salem in 1692, this reconstruction of events as seen through the eyes of Sarah Cloyce, one of the alleged witches, highlights the sociological nature of witchcraft, while giving full measure of appreciation to its intellectual and emotional aspects. 3 hours; 1985; Nightowl Productions.

"Witchcraft Among the Azande." Although filmed half a century after Evans-Pritchard's fieldwork, this is the visual counterpart of the anthropologist's written account of Zande beliefs. It describes what is done when an individual is bewitched and what social situations may lead to a charge of witchcraft, and it portrays the trial of an adulterous couple whose guilt is adjudicated by the poison oracle. 52 min. $445; Disappearing World Series, Filmakers Library 1996, 124 East 40th Street, New York, NY 10016

For the Tetum people of East Timor, in the western Pacific, burying the dead is an occupation that can be carried out only by relatives related by marriage to the dead person. Here one of the female relatives of a deceased person dresses another in preparation for the burial ritual.

Photo courtesy of David Hicks

CHAPTER 8

DEATH

Death is a human universal, and although we may temporarily stave off sickness, accidents, social failure, and other troubles, we know that death is inevitable. One response human beings make to this reality is to maintain that life does not end when one's last breath is taken, and for many people, belief in an immaterial self that survives the annihilation of the body is an attractive alternative to accepting the reality of final extinction.

Although for the individual death is (usually) the ultimate misfortune, Robert Hertz, in 1907, argued that death should be regarded as no less a threat to the integrity of society itself. The individual is more than just a product of nature, he pointed out, since he or she is also a product of cultural conditioning. Hertz (1960) proposed that for the sociologist, death should be regarded as a construct made by society — a collective representation, he termed — rather than simply a natural fact, because death was open to different definitions in different societies. Developing Durkheim's suggestion that society = god, Hertz argued that society-as-god construes the demise of even one of its members as an affront to what it sees as its divine-like authority to create the individual as a social personage, and that if we follow this line of reasoning it is entirely consistent that society should refuse to concede that some force outside its influence—in this case, nature—assumes the responsibility for destroying the creature that society has created as a human being. Accordingly, society's response to the death of one of its members is to reassert its dominion over the individual's destiny by, in effect, taking credit for removing its human creation from its living membership. This assertion of authority cannot, of course, be accomplished at the level of natural reality. Society cannot literally restore life to the corpse. But it can do so symbolically, that is to say, in ritual form. Hence the performance of rituals that accompany the death of a person, and hence the importance of these death rituals in the majority of societies.

Robert Hertz discovered most of the data for his famous study of death as a collective representation in the ethnography of what is known as *double burial* or *secondary burial*. In a double burial, the recently deceased's corpse is first of all provisionally disposed of, and then after a period of time has lapsed it is permanently laid to rest. In its ethnographic details, the ritual of double burial varies across cultures. The Merina of Madagascar bury their death in the ground and later dig up the remains before housing them in a sepulcher; among the people of East Timor trees traditionally served as the preliminary receptacle for the corpse. Hertz also noted that death rituals involved two social categories besides that of the corpse. These were the soul and the surviving kin; in the collective representation of death each had its part to play.

The triadic structure of this ritual — two burials separated by a period of time—found an echo one year later with the publication of Arnold van Gennep's *Rites of Passage* in 1908, and Hertz's description of the liminal stage (though Hertz did not identify the second stage by that term) might have come right out of the pages of this book. Hertz described the behavior of the soul during the transitional stage as being "betwix and between" two existences, lost to the world of the living yet not established in the world of the dead either. Which was exactly van Gennep's point.

READING 8-1

THE CONTEMPORARY AMERICAN FUNERAL RITUAL

Walter W. Whitaker III

Death rituals are devised by, and for the benefit of, the living. The dead person is the focus of community attention for a short while as the survivors perform the obsequies and impart meaning into the biological event. The

Source: Walter W. Whitaker III, "The Contemporary American Funeral Ritual," in *Rituals and Ceremonies in Popular Culture,* ed. Ray B. Browne (Bowling Green, Ohio: Bowling Green University Popular Press, 1980), pp. 316–325. Reprinted with permission by the publisher.

importance of death to the survivors comes across vividly in Whitaker's description of the death ritual as it is carried out in the United States. Whitaker depicts a standard enactment of the ritual activities, without religious overtones. Into the "generic" funeral structure, the faithful of different religious persuasions may add further meaning according to their beliefs by inserting their own distinctive symbols.

When speaking of the "Last Rite," we often compare it to the game of roulette: "round and round she goes and where she stops, nobody knows!" Death is that way, but the mores of the funeral ritual are apparent to all, even to the inane ethnic in the joke when he reads his first obituary column: "My gosh, they all died in alphabetical order!"

The organized ritual centering around death symbolically marks the end of another's time on the "living" plane, but more importantly it helps those of us who remain to organize our relationship with the deceased, to remember the deceased within a framework (both in time to come and during the bereavement period) which is representative for the time that we are aware, and also to celebrate the death with decorum. The unification of these factors within the ritual leads to a more subtle importance. Whenever a person dies, the survivors experience a vast amount of frustration, and as Freud suggests, that frustration will quite naturally lead to aggression, whether directed toward a higher godlike power which the bereaved suspects has let him or her down, or toward the people or earthly powers with which you must deal daily, or most prevalently aggression (in the form of guilt or withdrawal) directed toward oneself. Through brevity and propriety the funeral ritual becomes a basic way to channel this aggression effectively into an attitude which is both productive and supportive.

In dealing with what the funeral ritual does, it is first necessary to decide whether it is a ritual or merely an event of culmination. There is a number of criteria which a ritual must entail: it must be symbolic, repetitive, stereotypical and a complexly patterned event. Symbolically, the event celebrates the loss of an individual to his community. The funeral is repetitive in that it is nearly identical wherever you may travel in the United States. In a survey of 8,227 American funeral directors, it was found that 94% of the funerals had both the viewing of the body and a graveside service.[1] The ritual specialists (the doctor, the funeral director and the spiritual leader) enhance the ritual stereotypically. The funeral ritual is also a complexly patterned event in that it has both secular and sacred aspects. For this study I have broken the pattern down into five distinct areas: the post death activities, the viewing of the body (the wake, for some ethnic groups), the religious ceremony, the graveside disposition and the post funeral socialization. These five segments do something that no one person can achieve for the survivors: they lend dignity to the deceased and help to reorganize the survivors' existence.[2] This ultimate rite of passage for the deceased is also a rite of passage for the survivors and it culminates in a rite of unity for them.

POST DEATH ACTIVITIES

The post death activities begin with the declaration by a responsible individual (pathologist, doctor or coroner) that a person has fulfilled the legal qualifications for being pronounced dead. The qualifications may vary from state to state, but it is at this point that the ritual specialists begin their task of helping the survivors.

The ritual specialists come from many professional areas in the community. They could be the doctor who was treating the patient (because of Americans' attempts to achieve immortality, approximately 40% of them die in the hospital[3]), the nurse who helps to fill out the forms, the coroner or the policeman who was at the scene of death (the second most popular way to make the transition, with approximately 23%, is by the way of accidents[4]), and most importantly, that American small businessman, the funeral director. These people have two things in common as ritual specialists: 1) they have had some sort of professional training in dealing with the survivors and 2) they must objectify the deceased for their own mental health.

The ritual is initiated by one of the ritual specialists in locating and notifying a responsible survivor. Unless other arrangements have been made (donation of the body to a medical center or the deceased is a member of a funeral society), the responsible survivor will contact a funeral director. The funeral director is selected in a number of ways. The director could have dealt with the family on a previous occasion, could have been recommended by a friend to the responsible survivor or he may have a monopoly in the community (25% of the 8,227 funeral directors surveyed in 1971 stated that they had the only funeral home in the community[5]). Because of the psychological factor of wanting to get over this initial hurdle of the ritual as quickly as possible, the responsible survivor will select the funeral director with little shopping around. Leroy Bowman suggests that "the family doesn't hire a funeral director to weep with it; it hires and wants a normal mind to guide and advise its abnormal minds in every . . . manner that it may show proper respect to its deceased according to customs and caste."[6]

The number of things which must be done in preparation of the viewing of the body does require a normal mind. At the initial contact with the funeral director, the responsible survivor must do a number of things. The first is to give the funeral director permission to obtain the body. After this permission is granted, the director and the survivor must prepare the death notice which will appear in the obituary column of the newspaper or elsewhere. The next step is most important and probably causes the most controversy concerning the funeral director: the responsible survivor must select a casket.

In the economic aspect of the funeral, it should be pointed out that the price of pick-up, embalming, cosmetics and the rental of the home and vehicles for the funeral is included in the purchase price of the casket. The reasoning behind this package is that the buyer does not see the preparation of the body but does see something tangible in the casket.

For the buyer most of the funeral director's services are pretty intangible (maintenance of the vehicles and the funeral home, twenty-four hour availability, buying and stocking a wide economic range of caskets and, most importantly, his emotional support) and therefore the buyer does appreciate it when he or she receives something definitive, such as the casket or other tangible "extras." For instance, a funeral home in Pittsburgh supplies a briefcase which will hold the guest register, the documents which certify the individual's death and a large exterior pocket designed to hold the letters of condolence. Another relatively new practice has been initiated by one of the casket companies—they are presently offering to plant a memorial tree for anyone purchasing their casket.

After the selection of the casket, the funeral director must begin his work. He must retrieve the body and transport it to the preparation room of the funeral home. This room is reminiscent of the operating theatre in the hospital and it is here that the embalming process takes place. After washing the exterior of the body, the funeral director must "clean" the interior. The first step is Arterial Embalming. By a gentle, systematic pressure, a diluted embalming fluid and tint are forced into the veins and arteries to replace the blood. The embalming fluid partially restores a natural color to the body and will preserve the body long enough for it to be viewed. Therefore this portion of the process is primarily for cosmetic purposes. The body is not embalmed for preservation, as it was in ancient times; it is embalmed to give a representation of the person as he or she existed in life and for sanitation and disinfection. A study by Snell Laboratories concluded that microbial flora was reduced 99% within two hours of completion of the embalming process.[7] The second part of the process has an exceptionally violent nature. In cavity embalming the Trocar is "stabbed" into each of the organs and through the conjunction of a vacuum apparatus the gases and fluids trapped in the organs are reduced and/or removed. These gases and fluids contain colon bacilli which are the primary source of decomposition. The fluids and gases are replaced by vaporous formaldehyde which enhances preservation and sanitation. The violence of the process helps the funeral director emotionally create an object from the once living body. By thus creating an object out of a former living human being he can remove himself from the human involvement and be less subjective. Therefore he can go on to be professionally supportive of the survivors.

Upon completion of the embalming process, the body is once again washed, and while the funeral director is waiting for the tissues to firm (firm tissues being a sign of preservation) he will cap the eyes so that they will not accidentally open. It is also necessary to close the mouth. There are several ways this can be accomplished but the end result for the funeral director is an image of restful repose. Before dressing the body the cosmetics will be applied and the hair done as required. Quite often the funeral director will not have known the deceased and will require a photograph to make the corpse look like himself/herself while alive.

After being dressed the body is placed in the casket and taken to the funeral home's viewing area. The director must then display the appropriate religious symbols for the deceased. He is also responsible for receiving the floral displays and their arrangement. This can quite often be a problem because the director does not know the true hierarchy within the family and could unintentionally slight someone by misplacing a floral arrangement.

At this point the funeral director's handiwork is ready for display.

THE VIEWING OF THE DECEASED

The body is first seen by the responsible survivor before normal viewing hours. This ritual has a two-fold purpose. The funeral director gets a final approval in case he has made a minor error (by parting the hair on the wrong side or neglecting to put a piece of jewelry on the body). It is also to lessen the shock of death. This initial viewing is the worst for the spouse, or someone else very close, because at this point it is impossible to deny the death. One of the widows interviewed by Robert Weiss stated that this initial viewing created a realization that the "loss suddenly became almost unbearable." Weiss found that 52% of the widows he talked to felt that this viewing of the body was a negative experience.[8] There is an anomalous reaction which funeral directors dread. The spouse sometimes will attempt to crawl into the casket to be close to the loved one. The funeral director has no way to anticipate this action because it is quite common for the spouse (and other close family members) to approach the coffin and touch the deceased or even give the corpse a kiss. This touching and kissing is also a way for the bereaved to realize that the body is dead because the temperature of the corpse will be at that of the room rather than the normal 98.6 degrees. This viewing also helps the spouse, or other close persons, to prepare to deal with the visitors.

These series of shocks and realizations quite often lead to the return of that other ritual specialist, the family doctor. He is the source of medication and pertinent information. At this time the widow[9] develops an almost morbid interest in the why of her husband's death, while the widower will not ask such questions of the doctor.[10]

After the proper explanations and medications have been given, the responsible survivor is faced with the viewing hours during which the friends and family will come to the funeral home to pay their last respects. This tradition is historically based and serves a useful purpose. For example, invariably a new king could not take the throne until he had displayed the late king to the subjects. This was proof that he was actually dead and the next in line to the throne was not trying to usurp authority. Two separate studies[11] have demonstrated that the survivors generally do not approve of closed casket funerals and they are uncomfortable when the body of the deceased is not available for any of several reasons; undoubtedly this accounts for the great efforts expended in trying to recover the bodies of people in unusual accidents.

The practice is, further, an American political statement. In our striving for equality (even though individual funerals are by no means equal) and our rejection of even the faintest hint of any kind of caste system, Americans feel that every one of us, from president to pauper, has the right to a *proper* burial. This democratic urge is undoubtedly one of the reasons that the funeral ritual is relatively standard across the United States.

One of the standards of this common funeral ritual is the brief viewing hours. They are normally for a couple of hours in the afternoon and couple of hours in the evening for two days (Jewish tradition is an exception in that it has only one day for viewing the body). These short viewing times are beneficial to all the survivors.

The viewings are normally quite solemn and the visitors dress up out of respect for the deceased. They are there for three reasons. They want to share their love for the deceased with the responsible survivor. They wish to display the importance of the survivor to the community (Weiss suggests that the visitor's status reflects the status of the deceased and the more important the visitor, the better the widow will feel[12]). And most importantly, they wish to express a continuation of affection for the responsible survivor.

This continued affection is normally expressed in the action of reorganizing the memories of the deceased. This organization is probably the most important facet of this portion of the ritual. Each survivor in attendance will probably have many memories of the deceased, and there is something of a compulsion to share them with the other survivors. The survivors are justifying their presence and also channeling the aggression into a supportive and positive reaction to the death. This compulsion usually proceeds to a point where, even in their grief, the survivors will begin to tell humorous anecdotes. This is not a negative reaction but actually a comfort to the other survivors because the levity is an attempt to balance the grief.[13]

It can be seen that viewing the body accomplishes two things: it establishes the reality of death and brings the mourners together.

THE RELIGIOUS CEREMONY

The religious ceremony in the funeral ritual entails the most variety because man has attempted to make his peace with God in many various ways. It can vary in type (Catholic, Protestant, Jewish, or other), place (the funeral home, the cemetery chapel or any church) and spiritual leader (priest, clergyman, rabbi, or other religious leader, or layman). Even with all the different options there are many similarities to the ceremony itself. It would seem to follow that the decrease in religious commitment would also be reflected in a changed funeral ritual too. But in actuality fewer than 2% of the funerals conducted in the United States have neither a public nor a private religious service.[14]

The major differences lie basically in performance and organization. The Catholic Church has laid down specific rules which the priest must and will follow explicitly. The Protestant clergyman or the layman is free to follow the procedure of his or her choice (I was told by one funeral director that once you know a clergyman's routine it will not vary unless the family specifically requests it). Judaism requires that a *minyan* (ten adult Jewish males) say the *Kaddish* (the mourning prayer) during shivah (the seven days of mourning following a person's death); other religious creeds have their own particularities. The particularities do not have as much importance in the American funeral as the similarities.

The basic factors for any of the morning services is that they follow a formal and solemn format which is a relatively short time period of approximately thirty minutes. The sacredness which is involved is obvious. The meeting place is most usually somewhere reserved for reverence (even when the funeral home is used for the chapel, it has the trappings of the church, such as pulpit, font or other sacred icons) and the officiating spiritual leader has somehow gained the respect of his community in being capable of representing some higher power. The formally attired survivors are arranged backward from the closed casket which dominates the front of the meeting place. Their seating order, radiating from front to back, reflects their closeness to the deceased when he was alive.

This same order will be reflected in the funeral procession whether it leaves from the funeral home or the church. By following this procedure the survivors have done their best to insure the deceased a place with the higher power which they have agreed to revere for the time being. In ranking themselves behind the casket, they have also agreed, symbolically, that they too will follow the deceased in their good time.

THE GRAVESIDE DISPOSITION

The graveside disposition actually begins with the funeral procession beginning at the church or the funeral home. This last ride for the deceased marks the beginning of the end of the formal portion of the funeral ritual. It is the final step in which the deceased is the central figure. The ride is slow, somber and dignified as befits respect for the dead. The cars arrive at the cemetery with their little flags fluttering, marking that they are part of the procession (actually the flags are for the police escort so that no one will get lost) which honors the deceased.

Upon arrival at the gravesite, everyone gathers around in the same order that was held at the church and in the procession to witness the pall bearers bringing the casket to the gravesite. When the casket has been positioned among the flowers, if there are any, a short prayer is said by the spiritual leader and a eulogy by him or by a close friend or family member is intoned followed by the benediction by the spiritual leader.

Almost without warning the formalities are over and each survivor is thrown back into the chaos of having to live his or her life without the deceased. Grief is not complete and many survivors are not satisfied with the outcome but the formal portion of the funeral ritual is complete. It is easy to parallel the graveside brevity to the brevity of the whole process.[15] The bereaved are now on their own and are no longer attended to by any of the ritual specialists.

THE POST FUNERAL SOCIALIZATION

The formal funeral is complete but the survivors, wary of being alone with their grief, must have one last step to make the ritual complete: the post funeral socialization. This portion of the funeral ritual is for the survivors and their return to the reality of living life. It is a throwback to the days before the science of embalming restricted the care of the dead to the funeral home. The home of the deceased was the focal point of the funeral ritual. This socialization permitted then, and still permits, the survivors to restore "life" to the home of the deceased and it also was a deliberately relaxed period as distinguished [from] the formal structure of the early parts of the ritual. The activity of re-organization that was found in the earlier portion of the ritual when the body was being viewed continues here within a different sort of framework.

The ritual and its welcome disorganization begin in the cemetery when the survivors disband and go to their cars to separate and then later draw back together at the post-funeral socialization for self and community. The survivors will generally return home momentarily to change from their formal attire and to get their contribution for the communal feeding that will be served at the home of the deceased. There might be a second socialization by the peers of a young deceased. This is normally done because they are not as close to the family as they are to the deceased. Of course many people attend both socializations, therefore uniting the two groups of mourners. The necessity of the two inheres in the necessity of the socialization requiring a sense of comfort for all attendees.

Some of these implements of comfort are the relaxed attire, the freedom to go to the place of socialization at one's own choice of time, the permissiveness of eating as much as one chooses, and, most important, generally the presence of alcohol. Even in households which do not maintain a liquor cabinet or permit drinking under normal circumstances, one will find an abundance of liquor, which will be used for both its positive and negative aspects. It will be a relaxant and will symbolically celebrate life, as is found in communion. It is also used in its capacity as a depressant. Alcohol, by its very nature, can help to bring a true grief and a moribund nature to the surface. The combination of these two effects helps the survivors to release tension which has been suppressed over the events of the last few days.

This suppression is also released through humor. For some reason the release of anguish surfaces as hilarity,[16] though this hilarity is probably closer to hysteria.

Between the condiments and the place of socialization two things happen: the survivors achieve a renewed sense of community and a personal reorganization of their memories and a sense of how they can go on living without the deceased.

CONCLUSION

It is easy to see that the funeral ritual is structured for use in a number of aspects. The first and foremost is, of course, its capacity for enabling us to handle our grief. Norman Linzer breaks grief down to four major areas: need, value, structure and role.[17] The funeral ritual satisfies all these aspects. The need is in that it rechannels our psychological aggressions and frustrations. The value lies in the fact that the funeral ritual is successful in what it does. The structure is in the idea that the whole community understands and accepts the ritual. The roles are fulfilled by the ritual specialists and the mourners, each "knows the duties which they are to perform. Therefore the funeral ritual explores and satisfies our own personal fear of death."

Another aspect is that it brings us back to our popular, daily entertainments, making them very familiar and therefore comforting and satisfying. Consider the common formula that entertainment (television drama and comedy and most films) shares. The situation is set up; a conflict occurs; there is a climax and a resolution. The portions of the funeral ritual follow this "formulaic" pattern. The post-death activities set the situation; the viewing of the body is the secular conflict which

parallels the sacred conflict of the religious ceremony; the graveside disposition can be considered
the climax of the event, and the post-funeral socialization forces the individual to resolve the death for
himself or herself and the community.

If we combine the psychological aspects of grief
and the sociological familiarities it is found that the
funeral ritual serves two purposes. It provides a
comfort for the deceased (who wants to die "alone")
and it resolves a portion of the guilt of the survivors.
This resolution is for the individual and the community.

This generalization of the ritual does not deny
the individuality of any funeral, but its purpose is to
provide a systematic framework which is both recognizable and comforting as a sum total.

ENDNOTES

1. Vanderlyn Pine, *Caretaker of the Dead: The American
   Funeral Director* (New York: Irvington, Inc. 1975),
   pp. 201–03.
2. It should be noted that my concentration is on the individual
   rather than the equally important economic and theological
   aspects.
3. Herman Feifel, ed. *New Meanings of Death* (New York:
   McGraw-Hill, 1977), p. 234.
4. Ibid., p. 236.
5. Pine, p. 192.
6. Leroy Bowman, *The American Funeral: A Study in Guilt,
   Extravagance and Sublimity* (Washington: Public Affairs
   Press, 1959), p. 32.
7. Embalming: *Ancient Art/Modern Science* (U.S.A.: The
   Embalming Chemical Manufacturers Assoc. n.d.) p. 12.
8. Robert S. Weiss, Ira O. Glick and C. Murray, *The First Year
   of Bereavement* (New York: John Wiley, 1974), pp. 108–11.
9. Ibid., p. 112.
10. Ibid., pp. 204–06.
11. Richard A. Kalish and David K. Reynolds, *Death and Eth-
    nicity: A Psychocultural Study* (Los Angeles: Univ. of
    Southern Calif. Press, 1976). Paul C. Rosenblatt, R. Patricia
    Walsh and Douglas A. Jackson, *Grief and Mourning in
    Cross Cultural Perspective* (U.S.A.: H.R.A.F. Press, 1976).
12. Weiss, p. 115.
13. Elizabeth Kubler-Ross, *Questions and Answers on Death
    and Dying* (New York: MacMillan Co., 1974), pp. 154–163.
14. Pine, p. 205.
15. It may be interesting to note that weather will dictate how
    quickly the survivors disperse. In cold or wet weather they
    will be out of the cemetery within fifteen minutes. On a
    balmy summer day they will take up to forty-five minutes.
16. Bowman, p. 6.
17. Norman Linzer, ed. *Understanding Grief and Bereavement*
    (USA: Yeshiva Univ. Press, 1977), pp. 245–46.

READING 8–2

"VOODOO" DEATH

Walter B. Cannon

*Walter B. Cannon, a professor of physiology at Harvard
University from 1906 to 1942, studied the problem of
traumatic shock experienced by soldiers during the First
World War, and for much of his career continued to refine
his understanding of how emotional states exert an influence on the bodily functions of human beings. In this
reading, one that has attained classic standing in the
anthropological literature, he brings his experience of
trying to heal shell-shocked soldiers to bear on the curious phenomenon of death brought about by thought and
emotion.*

*The part played by magic or religious concepts in
bringing about the death of otherwise healthy individuals
is the theme of this reading. The power of society to control the minds of its members can be overwhelming,
Cannon contends, to the extent that once a believer is
convinced of having been bewitched that person may
actually induce his or her own death. In this article,
Cannon proposes a model demonstrating the physiological responses the body makes to such threats, and concluding that in effect the bodily processes wear down.
Finding itself in a situation of extreme danger, the body
readies itself for the most appropriate response to make,
whether "fight or flee." The sympathico-adrenal system
goes quickly into action, freeing sugar from the liver,
increasing the rate at which the heart beats, contracting
certain critical blood vessels, dilating the bronchioles,
and discharging adrenalin. But someone lacking a sufficiently strong willpower who finds that he has been
bewitched may find he cannot resist the collective
"wisdom" of his colleagues that his death is inevitable.
Stricken into immobility he is unable to fight or flee. All
the while, however, his organs, still in their fight or flee
mode, become ever-increasingly stimulated until they
reach the point at which some of the vital organs begin to
break down. The dissolution continues until his organs*

Source: Walter B. Cannon, " 'Voodoo' Death." Reproduced by
permission of the American Anthropological Association from
American Anthropologist 44:2, April–June 1942, pp. 169–81.
Not for further reproduction.

have reached a state in which they cannot stop breaking down—the point of no return — and death befalls.

This article opened a new line of research into how collective representations may cooperate with psychology to bring about death, and its intrinsic importance encouraged other researchers to reconsider the problem Canon had identified. Several alternative theories have been proposed, but all, except for one that asserts poisoning is the culprit (Clune 1973), vary from Cannon's thesis only by claiming an especially privileged influence for one or other of the factors he originally detected. According to C. P. Richter(1957) the cause of "voodoo" death is not the collapse of the body resulting from the "fight or flee" stimulation, but rather the victim's giving up his or her will to live. In David Lester's (1972) view these deaths result from the victim having an abnormally high level of susceptibility to suggestion when in a condition of extreme vulnerability, and for Barbara W. Lex (1974) the "tuning" of the nervous system is to blame.

In records of anthropologists and others who have lived with primitive people in widely scattered parts of the world is the testimony that when subjected to spells or sorcery or the use of "black magic" men may be brought to death. Among the natives of South America and Africa, Australia, New Zealand, and the islands of the Pacific, as well as among the negroes of nearby Haiti, "voodoo" death has been reported by apparently competent observers. The phenomenon is so extraordinary and so foreign to the experience of civilized people that it seems incredible; certainly if it is authentic it deserves careful consideration. I propose to recite instances of this mode of death, to inquire whether reports of the phenomenon are trustworthy, and to examine a possible explanation of it if it should prove to be real.

First, with regard to South America. Apparently Soares de Souza (1587) was first to observe instances of death among the Tupinambás Indians, death induced by fright when men were condemned and sentenced by a so-called "medicine man." Likewise Varnhagen (1875) remarks that generally among Brazilian Indian tribes, the members, lacking knowledge, accept without question whatever is told them. Thus the chief or medicine man gains the reputation of exercising supernatural power. And by intimidation or by terrifying augury or prediction he may cause death from fear.

There is like testimony from Africa. Leonard (1906) has written an account of the Lower Niger and its tribes in which he declares:

> I have seen more than one hardened old Haussa soldier dying steadily and by inches because he believed himself to be bewitched; no nourishment or medicines that were given to him had the slightest effect either to check the mischief or to improve his condition in any way, and nothing was able to divert him from a fate which he considered inevitable. In the same way, and under very similar conditions, I have seen Kru-men and others die in spite of every effort that was made to save them, simply because they had made up their minds, not (as we thought at the time) to die, but that being in the clutch of malignant demons they were bound to die.

Another instance of death wrought by superstitious fear in an African tribe is reported by Merolla in his voyage to the Congo in 1682 (cited by Pinkerton, 1814). A young negro on a journey lodged in a friend's house for the night. The friend had prepared for their breakfast a wild hen, a food strictly banned by a rule which must be inviolably observed by the immature. The young fellow demanded whether it was indeed a wild hen, and when the host answered "No," he ate of it heartily and proceeded on his way. A few years later, when the two met again, the old friend asked the younger man if he would eat a wild hen. He answered that he had been solemnly charged by a wizard not to eat that food. Thereupon the host began to laugh and asked him why he refused it now after having eaten it at his table before. On hearing this news the negro immediately began to tremble, so greatly was he possessed by fear, and in less than twenty-four hours was dead.

Also in New Zealand there are tales of death induced by ghostly power. In Brown's New Zealand and Its Aborigines (1845) there is an account of a Maori woman who, having eaten some fruit, was told that it had been taken from a tabooed place; she exclaimed that the sanctity of the chief had been profaned and that his spirit would kill her.

This incident occurred in the afternoon; the next day about 12 o'clock she was dead. According to Tregear (1890) the tapu (taboo) among the Maoris of New Zealand is an awful weapon. "I have seen a strong young man die," he declares, "the same day he was tapued; the victims die under it as though their strength ran out as water." It appears that among these aborigines superstitions associated with their sacred chiefs are a true though purely imaginary barrier; transgression of that barrier entails the death of the transgressor whenever he becomes aware of what he has done. It is a fatal power of the imagination working through unmitigated terror.

Dr. S. M. Lambert of the Western Pacific Health Service of the Rockefeller Foundation wrote to me that on several occasions he had seen evidence of death from fear. In one case there was a startling recovery. At a Mission at Mona Mona in North Queensland were many native converts, but on the outskirts of the Mission was a group of non-converts including one Nebo, a famous witch doctor. The chief helper of the missionary was Rob, a native who had been converted. When Dr. Lambert arrived at the Mission he learned that Rob was in distress and that the missionary wanted him examined. Dr. Lambert made the examination, and found no fever, no complaint of pain, no symptoms or signs of disease. He was impressed, however, by the obvious indications that Rob was seriously ill and extremely weak. From the missionary he learned that Rob had had a bone pointed at him by Nebo and was convinced that in consequence he must die. Thereupon Dr. Lambert and the missionary went for Nebo, threatened him sharply that his supply of food would be shut off if anything happened to Rob and that he and his people would be driven away from the Mission. At once Nebo agreed to go with them to see Rob. He leaned over Rob's bed and told the sick man that it was all a mistake, a mere joke—indeed, that he had not pointed a bone at him at all. The relief, Dr. Lambert testifies, was almost instaneous; that evening Rob was back at work, quite happy again, and in full possession of his physical strength.

A question which naturally arises is whether those who have testified to the reality of "voodoo" death have exercised good critical judgment. Although the sorcerer or medicine-man or chief may tacitly possess or may assume the ability to kill by bone-pointing or by another form of black magic, may he not preserve his reputation for supernatural power by the use of poison? Especially when death has been reported to have occurred after the taking of food may not the fatal result be due to action of poisonous substances not commonly known except to priests and wizards? Obviously, the possible use of poisons must be excluded before "voodoo" death can be accepted as an actual consequence of sorcery or witchcraft. Also it is essential to rule out instances of bold claims of supernatural power when in fact death resulted from natural causes; this precaution is particularly important because of the common belief among aborigines that illness is due to malevolence. I have endeavored to learn definitely whether poisoning and spurious claims can quite certainly be excluded from instances of death, attributed to magic power, by addressing enquiries to medically trained observers.

Dr. Lambert, already mentioned as a representative of the Rockefeller Foundation, wrote to me concerning the experience of Dr. P. S. Clarke with Kanakas working on the sugar plantations of North Queensland. One day a Kanaka came to his hospital and told him he would die in a few days because a spell had been put upon him and nothing could be done to counteract it. The man had been known by Dr. Clarke for some time. He was given a very thorough examination, including an examination of the stool and the urine. All was found normal, but as he lay in bed he gradually grew weaker. Dr. Clarke called upon the foreman of the Kanakas to come to the hospital to give the man assurance, but on reaching the foot of the bed, the foreman leaned over, looked at the patient, and then turned to Dr. Clarke saying, "Yes, doctor, close up him he die" (i.e., he is nearly dead). The next day, at 11 o'clock in the morning, he ceased to live. A postmortem examination revealed nothing that could in any way account for the fatal outcome.

Another observer with medical training, Dr. W. E. Roth (1897), who served for three years as government surgeon among the primitive people of north-central Queensland, has also given pertinent testimony. "So rooted sometimes is this belief on the part of the patient," Roth wrote, "that some enemy has 'pointed' the bone at him, that he will actually lie down to die, and succeed in the attempt, even at the expense of refusing food and succour within his reach: I have myself witnessed three or four such cases."

Dr. J. B. Cleland, Professor of Pathology at the University of Adelaide, has written to me that he has no doubt that from time to time the natives of the Australian bush do die as a result of a bone being pointed at them, and that such death may not be associated with any of the ordinary lethal injuries. In an article which included a section on death from malignant psychic influences, Dr. Cleland (1928) mentions a fine, robust tribesman in central Australia who was injured in the fleshy part of the thigh by a spear that had been enchanted. The man slowly pined away and died, without any surgical complication which could be detected. Dr. Cleland cites a number of physicians who have referred to the fatal effects of bone pointing and other terrifying acts. In his letter to me he wrote, "Poisoning is, I think, entirely ruled out in such cases among our Australian natives. There are very few poisonous plants available and I doubt whether it has ever entered the mind of the central Australian natives that such might be used on human beings."

Dr. Herbert Basedow (1925), in his book, *The Australian Aboriginal,* has presented a vivid picture of the first horrifying effect of bone pointing on the ignorant, superstitious and credulous natives, and the later more calm acceptance of their mortal fate:

The man who discovers that he is being boned by any enemy is, indeed, a pitiable sight. He stands aghast, with his eyes staring at the treacherous pointer, and with his hands lifted as though to ward off the lethal medium, which he imagines is pouring into his body. His cheeks blanch and his eyes become glassy and the expression of his face becomes horribly distorted. . . . He attempts to shriek but usually the sound chokes in his throat, and all that one might see is froth at his mouth. His body begins to tremble and the muscles twist involuntarily. He sways backwards and falls to the ground, and after a short time appears to be in a swoon; but soon after he writhes as if in mortal agony, and, covering his face with his hands, begins to moan. After a while he becomes very composed and crawls to his wurley. From this time onwards he sickens and frets, refusing to eat and keeping aloof from the daily affairs of the tribe. Unless help is forthcoming in the shape of a counter-charm administered by the hands of the Nangarri, or medicine-man, his death is only a matter of a comparatively short time. If the coming of the medicine-man is opportune he might be saved.

The Nangarri, when persuaded to exercise his powers, goes through an elaborate ceremony and finally steps toward the awestricken relatives, holding in his fingers a small article—a stick, a bone, a pebble, or a talon—which, he avows, he has taken from the "boned" man and which was the cause of the affliction. And now, since it is removed, the victim has nothing to fear. The effect, Dr. Basedow declares, is astounding. The victim, until that moment far on the road to death, raises his head and gazes in wonderment at the object held by the medicine-man. He even lifts himself into a sitting position and calls for water to drink. The crisis is passed, and the recovery is speedy and complete. Without the Nangarri's intervention, the boned fellow, according to Dr. Basedow, would certainly have fretted himself to death. The implicit faith which a native cherishes in the magical powers of his tribal magician is said to result in cures which exceed anything recorded by the faith-healing disciples of more cultured communities.

Perhaps the most complete account of the influence of the tribal taboo on the fate of a person subjected to its terrific potency has come from W. L. Warner, who worked among primitive aborigines in the Northern Territory of Australia. In order to provide a background for his testimony I quote from William James' *Principles of Psychology* (1905):

> A man's social me is the recognition which he gets from his mates. We are not only gregarious animals, liking to be in sight of our fellows, but we have an innate propensity to get ourselves noticed, and noticed favorably, by our kind. No more fiendish punishment could be devised, were such a thing physically possible, than that one should be turned loose in society and remain absolutely unnoticed by all the members thereof. If no one turned round when we entered, answered when we spoke, or minded what we did, but if every person we met "cut us dead," and acted as if we were non-existing things, a kind of rage and impotent despair would ere long well up in us, from which the cruellest bodily tortures would be a relief; for these would make us feel that, however bad might be our plight, we had not sunk to such a depth as to be unworthy of attention at all.

Now to return to the observations of Warner regarding the aborigines of northern Australia, creatures too ignorant, he assured me, to know about poisons. There are two definite movements of the social group, he declares, in the process by which black magic becomes effective on the victim of sorcery. In the first movement the community contracts; all people who stand in kinship relation with him withdraw their sustaining support. This means everyone he knows—all his fellows—completely change their attitudes towards him and place him in a new category. He is now viewed as one who is more nearly in the realm of the sacred and tabu than in the world of the ordinary where the community finds itself. The organization of his social life has collapsed and, no longer a member of a group, he is alone and isolated. The doomed man is in a situation from which the only escape is by death. During the death illness which ensues, the group acts with all the outreachings and complexities of its organization and with countless stimuli to suggest death positively to the victim, who is in a highly suggestible state. In addition to the social pressure upon him the victim himself, as a rule, not only makes no effort to live and to stay a part of his group but actually, through the multiple suggestions which he receives, cöperates in the withdrawal from it. He becomes what the attitude of his fellow tribesmen wills him to be. Thus he assists in committing a kind of suicide.

Before death takes place, the second movement of the community occurs, which is a return to the victim in order to subject him to the fateful ritual of mourning. The purpose of the community now, as a social unit with its ceremonial leader, who is a person of very near kin to the victim, is at last to cut him off entirely from the ordinary world and ultimately to place him in his proper position in the scared totemic world of the dead. The victim, on his part, reciprocates this feeling. The effect of the double movement in the society, first away from the victim and then back, with all the compulsive force of one of its most powerful rituals, is obviously drastic. Warner (1941) writes:

> An analogous situation in our society is hard to imagine. If all a man's near kin, his father, mother, brothers and sisters, wife, children, business associates, friends and all the other members of the society should suddenly withdraw themselves because of some dramatic circumstance, refusing to take any attitude but one of taboo and looking at the man as one already dead, and then after some little time perform over him a sacred ceremony which is believed with certainty to guide him out of the land of the living into that of the dead, the enormous suggestive power of this two-fold movement of the community, after it has had its attitudes crystallized, can be somewhat understood by ourselves.

The social environment as a support to morale is probably much more important and impressive among primitive people, because of their profound ignorance and insecurity in a haunted world, than among educated people living in civilized and well protected communities. Dr. S. D. Porteus, physician and psychologist, has studied savage life extensively in the Pacific islands and in Africa; he writes:

Music and dance are primitive man's chief defenses against loneliness. By these he reminds himself that in his wilderness there are other minds seconding his own . . . in the dance he sees himself multiplied in his fellows, his action mirrored in theirs. There are in his life very few other occasions in which he can take part in concerted action and find partners. . . . The native aboriginal is above all fear-ridden. Devils haunt to seize the unwary; their malevolent magic shadows his waking moments, he believes that medicine men know how to make themselves invisible so that they may cut out his kidney fat, then sew him up and rub his tongue with a magic stone to induce forgetfulness, and thereafter he is a living corpse, devoted to death. . . . So desperate is this fear that if a man imagines that he has been subjected to the bone pointing magic of the enemy he will straight away lie down and die.

Testimony similar to the foregoing, from Brazil, Africa, New Zealand and Australia, was found in reports from the Hawaiian Islands, British Guiana and Haiti. What attitude is justified in the presence of this accumulation of evidence? In a letter from Professor Lévi-Bruhl, the French ethnologist long interested in aboriginal tribes and their customs, he remarked that answers which he had received from inquiries could be summed up as follows. The ethnologists, basing their judgment on a large number of reports, quite independent of one another and gathered from groups in all parts of the world, admit that there are instances indicating that the belief that one has been subjected to sorcery, and in consequence is inevitably condemned to death, does actually result in death in the course of time. On the contrary, physiologists and physicians—men who have had no acquaintance with ethnological conditions—are inclined to consider the phenomenon as impossible and raise doubts regarding clear and definite testimony.

Before denying that "voodoo" death is within the realm of possibility, let us consider the general features of the specimen reports mentioned in foregoing paragraphs. First, there is the elemental fact that the phenomenon is characteristically noted among aborigines—among human beings so primitive, so superstitious, so ignorant that they are bewildered strangers in a hostile world. Instead of knowledge they have a fertile and unrestricted imagination which fills their environment with all manner of evil spirits capable of affecting their lives disastrously. As Dr. Porteus pointed out, only by engaging in communal activities are they able to develop sufficient esprit de corps to render themselves resistant to the mysterious and malicious influences which can vitiate their lives. Associated with these circumstances is the fixed assurance that because of certain conditions, such as being subject to bone pointing or other magic, or failing to observe sacred tribal regulations, death is sure to supervene. This is a belief so firmly held by all members of the tribe that the individual not only has that conviction himself but is obsessed by the knowledge that all his fellows likewise hold it. Thereby he becomes a pariah, wholly deprived of the confidence and social support of the tribe. In his isolation the malicious spirits which he believes are all about him and capable of irresistibly and calamitously maltreating him, exert supremely their evil power. Amid this mysterious murk of grim and ominous fatality what has been called "the gravest known extremity of fear," that of an immediate threat of death, fills the terrified victim with powerless misery.

In his terror he refuses both food and drink, a fact which many observers have noted and which, as we shall see later, is highly significant for a possible understanding of the slow onset of weakness. The victim "pines away"; his strength runs out like water, to paraphrase words already quoted from one graphic account; and in the course of a day or two he succumbs.

The question which now arises is whether an ominous and persistent state of fear can end the life of a man. Fear, as is well known, is one of the most deeply rooted and dominant of the emotions. Often, only with difficulty can it be eradicated. Associated with it are profound physiological disturbances, widespread throughout the organism. There is evidence that some of these disturbances, if they are lasting, can work harmfully. In order to elucidate that evidence I must first indicate that great fear and great rage have similar effects in the body. Each of these powerful emotions is associated with ingrained instincts—the instinct to attack, if rage is present, the instinct to run away or escape, if fear is present. Throughout the long history of human beings and lower animals these two emotions and their related instincts have served effectively in the struggle for existence. When they are roused they bring into action an elemental division of the nervous system, the so-called sympathetic or sympathico-adrenal division, which exercises a control over internal organs, and also over the blood vessels. As a rule the sympathetic division acts to maintain a relatively constant state in the flowing blood and lymph, i.e., the "internal environment" of our living parts. It acts thus in strenuous muscular effort; for example, liberating sugar from the liver, accelerating the heart, contracting certain blood vessels, discharging adrenaline and dilating the bronchioles. All these changes render the animal more efficient in physical struggle, for they supply essential conditions for continuous action of laboring muscles. Since they occur in association with the strong emotions, rage and fear, they can reasonably be interpreted as preparatory for the intense struggle which the instincts to attack or to escape may involve. If these powerful emotions prevail, and the bodily forces are fully mobilized for action, and if this state of extreme perturbation continues in uncontrolled possession of the organism for a considerable period, without the occurrence of action, dire results may ensue (cf. Cannon, 1929).

When, under brief ether anesthesia, the cerebral cortex of a cat is quickly destroyed so that the animal no longer has the benefit of the organs of intelligence, there is a remarkable display of the activities of lower, primary centers of behavior, those of emotional expression. This decorticate condition is similar to that produced in man when consciousness is abolished by the use of nitrous oxide; he is then decorticated by chemical means. Commonly the emotional expression of joy is released (nitrous oxide is usually known as "laughing gas"), but it may be that of sorrow (it might as well be called "weeping gas"). Similarly, ether anesthesia, if light, may release the expression of rage. In the sham rage of the decorticate cat there is a supreme exhibition of intense emotional activity. The hairs stand on end, sweat exudes from the toe pads, the heart rate may rise from about 150 beats per minute to twice that number, the blood pressure is greatly elevated, and the concentration of sugar in the blood soars to five times the normal. This excessive activity of the sympathico-adrenal system rarely lasts, however, more than three or four hours. By that time, without any loss of blood or any other event to explain the outcome, the decorticate remnant of the animal, in which this acme of emotional display has prevailed, ceases to exist.

What is the cause of the demise? It is clear that the rapidly fatal result is due to a persistent excessive activity of the sympathico-adrenal system. One of my associates, Philip Bard (1928), noted that when the signs of emotional excitement failed to appear, the decorticate preparation might continue to survive for long periods; indeed, its existence might have to be ended by the experimenter. Further evidence was obtained by another of my associates, Norman E. Freeman (1933), who produced sham rage in animals from which the sympathetic nerves had been removed. In these circumstances the behavior was similar in all respects to the behavior described above, excepting the manifestations dependent upon sympathetic innervation. The remarkable fact appeared that animals deprived of their sympathetic nerves and exhibiting sham rage, so far as was possible, continued to exist for many hours without any sign of breakdown. Here were experiments highly pertinent to the present inquiry.

What effect on the organism is produced by a lasting and intense action of the sympathico-adrenal system? In observations by Bard, he found that a prominent and significant change which became manifest in animals displaying sham rage was a gradual fall of blood pressure towards the end of the display, from the high levels of the early stages to the low level seen in fatal wound shock. In Freeman's research he produced evidence that this fall of pressure was due to a reduction of the volume of circulating blood. This is the condition which during World War I was found to be the reason for the low blood pressure observed in badly wounded men—the blood volume is reduced until it becomes insufficient for the maintenance of an adequate circulation (see Cannon, 1923). Thereupon deterioration occurs in the heart, and also in the nerve centers which hold the blood vessels in moderate contraction. A vicious circle is then established; the low blood pressure damages the very organs which are necessary for the maintenance of an adequate circulation, and as they are damaged they are less and less able to keep the blood circulating to an effective degree. In sham rage, as in wound shock, death can be explained as due to a failure of essential organs to receive a sufficient supply of blood or, specifically, a sufficient supply of oxygen, to maintain their functions.

The gradual reduction of blood volume in sham rage can be explained by the action of the sympathico-adrenal system in causing a persistent constriction of the small arterioles in certain parts of the body. If adrenaline, which constricts the blood vessels precisely as nerve impulses constrict them, is continuously injected at a rate which produces the vasoconstriction of strong emotional states, the blood volume is reduced to the degree seen in sham rage. Freeman, Freedman and Miller (1941) performed that experiment. They employed in some instances no more adrenaline than is secreted in response to reflex stimulation of the adrenal gland, and they found not only marked reduction of the blood plasma but also a concentration of blood corpuscles as shown by the percentage increase of hemoglobin. It should be remembered, however, that in addition to this circulating vasoconstrictor agent there are in the normal functioning of the sympathico-adrenal system the constrictor effects on blood vessels of nerve impulses and the coöperation of another circulating chemical substance besides adrenaline, viz., sympathin. These three agents, working together in times of great emotional stress, might well produce the results which Freeman and his collaborators observed when they

injected adrenaline alone. In the presence of the usual blood pressure, organs of primary importance, e.g., the heart and the brain are not subjected to constriction of their vessels, and therefore they are, continuously supplied with blood. But this advantage is secured at the deprivation of peripheral structures and especially the abdominal viscera. In these less essential parts, where constriction of the arterioles occurs, the capillaries are ill-supplied with oxygen. The very thin walls of capillaries are sensitive to oxygen want and when they do not receive an adequate supply they become more and more permeable to the fluid part of the blood. Thereupon the plasma escapes into the perivascular spaces. A similar condition occurs in the wound shock of human beings. The escape of the plasma from the blood vessels leaves the red corpuscles more concentrated. During World War I we found that the concentration of corpuscles in skin areas might be increased as much as fifty per cent (cf. Cannon, Fraser and Hooper, 1917).

A condition well known as likely to be harmful to the wounded was a prolonged lack of food or water. Freeman, Morison and Sawyer (1933) found that loss of fluid from the body, resulting in a state of dehydration, excited the sympathico-adrenal system; thus again a vicious circle may be started, the low blood volume of the dehydrated condition being intensified by further loss through capillaries which have been made increasingly permeable.

The foregoing paragraphs have revealed how a persistent and profound emotional state may induce a disastrous fall of blood pressure, ending in death. Lack of food and drink would collaborate with the damaging emotional effects, to induce the fatal outcome. These are the conditions which, as we have seen, are prevalent in persons who have been reported as dying as a consequence of sorcery. They go without food or water as they, in their isolation, wait in fear for their impending death. In these circumstances they might well die from a true state of shock, in the surgical sense—a shock induced by prolonged and tense emotion.

It is pertinent to mention here that Wallace, a surgeon of large experience in World War I, testified

(1919) to having seen cases of shock in which neither trauma nor any of the known accentuating factors of shock could account for the disastrous condition. Sometimes the wounds were so trivial that they could not be reasonably regarded as the cause of the shock state; sometimes the visible injuries were negligible. He cites two illustrative instances. One was a man who was buried by the explosion of a shell in a cellar; the other was blown up by a buried shell over which he had lighted a fire. In both the circumstances were favorable for terrifying experience. In both all the classic symptoms of shock were present. The condition lasted more than 48 hours, and treatment was of no avail. A postmortem examination did not reveal any gross injury. Another remarkable case which may be cited was studied by Freeman at the Massachusetts General Hospital. A woman of 43 years underwent a complete hysterectomy because of uterine bleeding. Although her emotional instability was recognized, she appeared to stand the operation well. Special precautions were taken, however, to avoid loss of blood, and in addition she was given fluid intravenously when the operation was completed. That night she was sweating, and refused to speak. The next morning her blood pressure had fallen to near the shock level, her heart rate was 150 beats per minute, her skin was cold and clammy and the measured blood flow through the vessels of her hand was very slight. There was no bleeding to account for her desperate condition, which was diagnosed as shock brought on by fear. When one understands the utter strangeness, to an inexperienced layman, of a hospital and its elaborate surgical ritual, and the distressing invasion of the body with knives and metal retractors, the wonder is that not more patients exhibit signs of deep anxiety. In this instance a calm and reassuring attitude on the part of the surgeon resulted in a change of attitude in the patient, with recovery of a normal state. That the attitude of the patient is of significant importance for a favorable outcome of an operation is firmly believed by the well-known American surgeon, Dr. J. M. T. Finney, for many years Professor of Surgery at the Johns Hopkins Medical School.

He (1934) has publicly testified, on the basis of serious experiences, that if any person came to him for a major operation, and expressed fear of the result, he invariably refused to operate. Some other surgeon must assume the risk!

Further evidence of the possibility of a fatal outcome from profound emotional strain was reported by Mira (1939) in recounting his experiences as a psychiatrist in the Spanish War of 1936–39. In patients who suffered from what he called "malignant anxiety," he observed signs of anguish and perplexity, accompanied by a permanently rapid pulse (more than 120 beats per minute), and a very rapid respiration (about three times the normal resting rate). These conditions indicated a perturbed state deeply involving the sympathico-adrenal complex. As predisposing conditions Mira mentioned "a previous lability of the sympathetic system" and "a severe mental shock experienced in conditions of physical exhaustion due to lack of food, fatigue, sleeplessness, etc." The lack of food appears to have attended lack of water, for the urine was concentrated and extremely acid. Towards the end the anguish still remained, but inactivity changed to restlessness. No focal symptoms were observed. In fatal cases death occurred in three or four days. Postmortem examination revealed brain hemorrhages in some cases, but, excepting an increased pressure, the cerebrospinal fluid showed a normal state. The combination of lack of food and water, anxiety, very rapid pulse and respiration, associated with a shocking experience having persistent effects, would fit well with fatal conditions reported from primitive tribes.

The suggestion which I offer, therefore, is that "voodoo death" may be real, and that it may be explained as due to shocking emotional stress—to obvious or repressed terror. A satisfactory hypothesis is one which allows observations to be made which may determine whether or not it is correct. Fortunately, tests of a relatively simple type can be used to learn whether the suggestion as to the nature of "voodoo death" is justifiable. The pulse towards the end would be rapid and "thready." The skin would be cool and moist. A count of the red blood corpuscles, or even simpler, a determination by means of a hematocrit of the ratio of corpuscles to plasma in a small sample of blood from skin vessels would help to tell whether shock is present; for the "red count" would be high and the hematocrit also would reveal "hemoconcentration." The blood pressure would be low. The blood sugar would be increased, but the measure of it might be too difficult in the field. If in the future, however, any observer has opportunity to see an instance of "voodoo death," it is to be hoped that he will conduct the simpler tests before the victim's last gasp.

REFERENCES

Bard, P. A diencephalic mechanism for the expression of rage with special reference to the sympathetic nervous system (*American Journal of Physiology,* 1928, 84), pp. 490–513.

Basedow, H. *The Australian Aboriginal* (Adelaide, 1925), pp. 178–179.

Brown, W. *New Zealand and Its Aborigines* (London, 1845), p. 76.

Cannon, W. B. *Traumatic Shock* (New York, 1923).

____. *Bodily Changes in Pain, Hunger, Fear and Rage* (New York, 1929).

Cannon, W. B., John Fraser, and A. N. Hooper. Report No. 2 of the Special Investigation Committee on Surgical Shock and Allied Conditions, Medical Research Committee, on Some Alterations in the Distribution and Character of the Blood in Wound Conditions (London, 1917), pp. 24–40.

Cleland, J. B. (*Journal of Tropical Medicine and Hygiene,* 1928, 31), p. 233.

Finney, J. M. T. Discussion of papers on shock. (*Annals of Surgery,* 1934, 100), p. 746.

Freeman, N. E. Decrease in blood volume after prolonged hyperactivity of the sympathetic nervous system (*American Journal of Physiology,* 1933, 103), pp. 185–202.

Freeman, N. E., H. Freedman, and C. C. Miller. The production of shock by the prolonged continuous injection of adrenalin in unanesthetized dogs (*American Journal of Physiology,* 1941, 131), pp. 545–553.

Freeman, N. E., R. S. Morison, and M. E. Mack. Sawyer. The effect of dehydration on adrenal secretion and its relation to shock (*American Journal of Physiology,* 1933, 104), pp. 628–635.

James, W. *Principles of Psychology* (New York, 1905), pp. 179–180.

Leonard, A. G. *The Lower Niger and Its Tribes* (London, 1906), p. 257 et seq.

Mira, F. Psychiatric experience in the Spanish war. (*British Medical Journal,* 1939, i), pp. 1217–1220.

Pinkerton, J. *Voyages and Travels* (1814, 16), p. 237 et seq.

Porteus, S. D. Personal communication.

Roth, W. E. *Ethnological Studies among the North-West-Central Queensland Aborigines* (Brisbane and London, 1897), p. 154.

Soares de Souza, G. *Tratado Descriptivo do Brasil in 1587* (Rio de Janeiro, 1879), pp. 292–293.

Tregear, E. *Journal of the Anthropological Institute* (1890, 19), p. 100.

Varnhagen, F. A. *Historia Geral do Brasil* (1875, 1), pp. 42–43.

Wallace, Sir Cuthbert. *Introduction to Report No. 26 to Medical Research Committee, on Traumatic Toxaemia as a Factor in Shock* (London, 1919), p. 7.

Warner, W. L. *A Black Civilization, a Social Study of an Australian Tribe* (New York and London, 1941) p. 242.

READING 8–3

SYMBOLIC ASSOCIATIONS OF DEATH

Peter Metcalf and Richard Huntington

The funeral ritual provides the topic for this comparative study of death. Peter Metcalf, a professor of anthropology at the University of Virginia, ethnographer of the Berawan of Borneo, and Richard Huntington, an applied anthropologist who has written an important study on the Bara of Madagascar, bring their ethnographic knowledge to bear on the problem of what features or traits of death rituals might be considered universal. By reassessing in light of their own ethnography the findings of Hertz, Gennep, Turner, Leach, and Needham they isolate four cultural traits that they argue recur cross-culturally: the use of certain colors, the arrangement of mourners' hair, noise (especially percussion), and symbols of rotting.

Though often intense, emotional reactions to death are too varied and shifting to provide the foundation for a theory of mortuary ritual. A recent cross-cultural study concluded that grief is shown at

Source: Peter Metcalf and Richard Huntington, "Symbolic Associations of Death," in *Celebrations of Death: The Anthropology of the Mortuary Ritual,* 2nd ed. © Cambridge University Press, 1991. Reprinted with the permission of Cambridge University Press.

funerals in most societies, but not all. Even this weak result was achieved only by defining grief so widely as to include virtually any negative emotion, namely, "sorrow, mental distress, emotional agitation, sadness, suffering, and related feelings" (Rosenblatt, Walsh, and Jackson, 1976: 2). These authors approach funeral practices assuming that they fulfill certain panhuman needs to perform "psychological work." But the need to release aggression, or break ties with the deceased, or complete any other putatively universal psychic process does not serve to explain funerals. The shoe is on the other foot. Whatever mental adjustments the individual needs to make in the face of death he or she must accomplish as best he or she can through or around such rituals as society provides. No doubt the rites frequently aid adjustment. But we have no reason to believe that they do not obstruct it with equal frequency.

Despite the perennial appeal of such theorizing, something more is needed to explain the remarkable richness and variety of funeral rituals. In succeeding chapters, we turn away from emotion in order to explore the meaning of these rites in social terms. But we are not yet ready to leave behind the nagging issue of universal, or at least general, features of behavior. Are there not regular features of funerals that crop up again and again?

Indeed there are. One obvious example is color symbolism. Although it would be an error to assume that our cultural association of black with death and mourning is universal, there is a wide distribution among the cultures of the world of the use of black to represent death. Turner (1967) suggests that there exists an almost universal color triad of red, white, and black. In many societies, white relates to such things as purity and fertility, red to both good and evil aspects of power and life, and black to decomposition and death. Turner suggests that the wide distribution of this symbolic color triad may relate to the association of these colors with bodily fluids, especially white with milk and semen, and red with blood. Black, he notes, is rarely associated with a bodily excretion, but tends to be associated with loss of conscious-

ness, such as when one faints or "blacks out" (Turner 1967: 89).

Throughout the world, black often provides the funeral hue. But there are many exceptions. White is sometimes appropriate in Christian funerals to symbolize the joy of eternal life, which the Resurrection promises to each believer. Some of the peoples of Madagascar provide another exception: Their funeral color is red. An important item in their funeral rituals is a large number of expensive, brightly colored, striped shrouds. These come in many colors, but they are always called the "red cloths." Red is used in these funerals to represent "life" and vitality in opposition to death. In both these exceptions, the funeral use of white or red is in symbolic opposition to the blackness of death. But in parts of Borneo white is the color of mourning because it is directly associated with the pallor of death and the whiteness of bones. . . .

A second example concerns the mourners' hair. As Edmund Leach (1958) notes, practices involving special cutting of the hair have a worldwide distribution, and they are particularly prominent in funeral ceremonies. Frequently survivors are enjoined to shave their heads as a sign of mourning. Elsewhere, the custom is reversed; the mourners, especially men, forgo their usual habits of shaving and trimming beards, mustaches, and hair and hence emphasize a hirsute dishevelment for the time of mourning. And it need not be one way or the other. Often in a single society, even within a family, some mourners shave entirely while others put away their razors. Hence there is a generality about the use of such practices, but not about their meaning.

In this chapter, we examine two additional symbolic items having a wide distribution and association with death rituals. The first is what we may call a purposeful noisiness, the second relates to symbols of rotting. At first sight, these two items appear dissimilar, and their selection consequently arbitrary. Whereas the former seems mysterious and unaccountable, the latter seems obvious (although we must remember that it is possible for decay to be cheated, for instance by cremation of the corpse). But however dissimilar, it is an empirical feature that din and corruption are constantly associated, as Lévi-Strauss has demonstrated in his monumental mythological studies (1973: 296–475, specifically 310, 396).

DRUMMING: SYMBOL OF DEATH, LIMINALITY, OR DIVINITY?

In many parts of the world, funerals are noisy affairs. . . . It is also very much the case among the Berawan, a small ethnic group of central northern Borneo, to whom we shall turn for case material at several places in succeeding chapters. The Berawan comprise just four communities, each of several hundred people and occupying a single massive wooden longhouse. Great tracts of dense rain forest separate the villages from one another, and in precolonial times each was a sovereign political unit. The Berawan gain their livelihood by growing hill rice in clearings made anew each year, by foraging in the jungle, and by fishing in the great rivers that also provide the only means of transportation in the interior.

During funerals, the Berawan gather great crowds of people into their longhouses. Drinking and socializing are enjoined upon the guests, and all but the close kin are encouraged to enjoy themselves as gustily as possible. The general hubbub can be heard half a mile away through the quiet forest. But not satisfied with that, the Berawan have additional ways to make noise at funerals. There is the great brass gong that is used initially to announce that a death has occurred. A special tattoo is used, and the deep reverberations can often be heard several miles away, summoning people from their farms. Then there is the large drum that can only be played during funerals. Its boom can be heard day and night, producing rhythms that are proscribed at other times. The same rhythms are played on gongs large and small, which together make up an orchestra with several players. The larger gongs are hung vertically, and struck with a padded mallet to produce a deep, resonant sound. The smaller gongs are strung horizontally in descending order of size on two strands of rattan stretched across a frame. The player holds a piece of

firewood in each hand and plays rapid tinkling figures, further augmented by the staccato clatter of children beating on bamboo slit gongs.

But even the music of the gongs and drums is lost in the din of games in which noise is supposedly only a by-product. Tops are played outside, in an arena overviewed by the veranda of the longhouse, which provides a grandstand. Men compete to see who can fling their own top in such a way as to knock a target top set spinning in the center of the arena out of the area of play. The men jostle for position to take a shot, holding their heavy hardwood tops in the upraised hands. When they throw them, a dull moaning whirr is heard. If the shot is well judged, the two tops make a loud clack on impact, and the target goes flying out of the ring. Then a great roar of approval goes up from the veranda. The men must remain alert to avoid being hit by a ricocheting top.

Meanwhile, another game played inside the house uses rice pestles. This is a game in which women excel, though men may play. The pestles are hardwood poles about five feet long and three inches wide at each end, tapering slightly to the middle. Normally they are used to pound rice free of its husk, in conjunction with a mortar that consists of a heavy slab of hardwood with a hemispherical indentation about six inches in diameter. In the game, two pestles are placed side by side across two bulks of timber such that they are about four inches above the floor. A woman sits on each side, grasping the adjacent ends of each pestle in either hand. The two women begin to beat the pestles, two strokes downward onto the bulks of timber, then two sideways, clashing the pestles one against the other. The player stands off to one side, flexing her knees and bobbing her head to get the rhythm. Then she dances nimbly across the clashing poles, trying to execute fancy steps without getting a blow on the ankle. This game is invariably played indoors on the raised plank floor of the longhouse, which provides a massive sounding board for the crashing of the pestles. This activity is in addition to the regular pounding of rice, which is a continuous chore during funerals due to the number of guests to be fed.

Finally, when the corpse is moved out of the longhouse to the barge that will carry it to the graveyard, a series of shotgun blasts punctuate the wailing of the womenfolk.

All this cacophony at Berawan funerals would come as no surprise to Rodney Needham, whose paper "Percussion and Transition" (1967) first pointed out how widespread this phenomenon is. He expands upon an idea originally stated in "The Origin of Bell and Drum" by Maria Dworakowska (1938), who argues that the use of bells and gongs at funerals derived from the use of drums, which in turn originated from "coffin-logs." Hence the association of these instruments with the dead. Needham accepts this association, shorn of its historical speculation, but criticizes it as too narrow. First, the list of instruments is too restricted: drums, gongs, bells, xylophones, metallophones, rattles, rasps, stamping tubes, sticks, resounding rocks, clashing anklets, and other objects are all used in these contexts. Berawan funerals could add a couple more items to the list, as we have seen. Needham shows that the only feature shared by these instruments, if such they may be called, is percussion. Not all of them are capable of producing a melody, or even a rhythm, so these attributes are not the relevant ones. Second, he shows that such percussive noise is not restricted to funerals. It is found at weddings and birth feasts, initiations and harvest festivals, and all manner of rites of passage.

Needham states his conclusion as follows: There is a connection between percussion and transition. As to why this connection exists, Needham is unable to offer an explanation, and he is pessimistic that anthropology is capable of finding one. So universal is the phenomenon, he believes, that its grounds must be sought in the "general psychic character of mankind" (1967: 394).

Concerning the association that Needham points out, we can make surmises similar to those concerning color and hair symbolism. A percussive noise seems to punctuate and divide time ("mark time") the way a line or a wall demarcates space. Hence it is a natural symbol for marking a temporal change in status, especially one as irreversible as death. Fur-

thermore, the drumbeat has an obvious affinity with the heartbeat and rhythm of life. Or equally, it can resound with the hollow finality of death. There is plenty of room for multiple symbolizations.

Another aspect of percussion, in addition to its rhythmic characteristics is its potential for making loud noise. Noise or silence, individually or in alternation, provide, like white and black, shaven and hairy, opportunities for symbolic representation and heightened drama. In another well known and intriguing paper, Needham (1964) traces the connections that hunting peoples of Malaya and Borneo make between "Blood, Thunder, and the Mockery of Animals." Thunder in Malaysia, he writes, is "an appalling natural phenomenon, seeming to crack and reverberate menacingly on the very surface of the forest canopy and shaking the guts of the human beings cowering underneath" (1964: 281). The great noise of thunder has, in many such places, associations with power and divinity. Noise is sometimes seen to facilitate communication between humans and the supernatural, as when the psalmist enjoins "Make a Joyful noise unto The Lord, all ye lands" (Psalm 100).

Cosmological and calendrical events such as solar eclipses and new years are characteristically greeted in many cultures with the loudest clatter the technological level permits (Lévi-Strauss 1969: 287). Over the centuries, fireworks, gunshots, horns, and sirens have been added to the initial stock of drums, bells, and gongs. In the din of the modern world, we may forget how extraordinary and rare truly loud noise was to most of the previous generations on the earth. It continues to connote power, as with electronically amplified music and roaring car engines, but it has lost its sacred character.

Our problem in dealing with the significance of noise is to cope with too many associations, not too few. Already we have three correlations of increasing generality: drums and death, percussion and transition, loud noise and supernatural power. There is little point in discussing which is the correct correlation. For instance, all are present in the Berawan events mentioned above. There is the great drum that resounds only for death. There are the gunshots that specifically punctuate the transition to the graveyard, and there is the continuous tumult of games and music associated with the presence of spirits of the dead. Many threads of significance are woven together in the Berawan use of noise. As van Gennep noted, the funeral is, of all rites of passage, the one with the greatest emphasis on liminality. It is not surprising that symbols used at the funeral are often vague and indeterminate, and yet connote mystery and power. Death and liminality must, of their very natures, retain a certain elusiveness.

RITUAL ACTIONS AND DAILY ACTIVITIES

Noise production is a cultural feature, yet its use in funerals achieves the same kind of universality as the emotion of grief. Percussive noise is frequently found in rituals of transition, and examples can be found in every region of the globe. But that does not imply that all societies use noise in this way or use it to a similar extent.

It follows that the observation of the quasi universality of grief and percussive noise at funerals does not exhaust those topics. Contrary to Needham's formulation, the variation that occurs from one society to another, and one culture area to another, is equally demanding of explanation, and implies a cultural dynamic rather than a psychic universal. As an example of this, we examine the special propensity for percussion that is found in Southeast Asia, and we draw on the work of Marie Jeanne Adams (1971, 1977).

Adams is concerned with repeated patterns of behavior occurring in ritual contexts that seem to parallel everyday work activities. The similarities are often striking, but Adams is careful to avoid the implication that either is derived from the other. On that score, we simply have no evidence. However derived, these recurring actions appear to lend a power and intensity to the rituals that is difficult for the outsider to grasp.

Adams pays particular attention to pounding: a very simple technical process to be sure, but especially pervasive in Southeast Asia. Pounding actions

figure prominently in the production and preparation of many foods. Breaking up the ground prior to planting is often accomplished with a heavy digging stick that relies more on momentum than sharpness for its effect. Alternatively, in irrigation agriculture particularly, buffalo are used to pound the topsoil in the newly flooded plots with their hooves. Even in slash-and-burn systems, where no soil preparation occurs as such, the seeds are planted in shallow conical holes made with a heavy dibble.

Many foods are inedible without preparation involving pounding. Most obvious in this connection is rice, which must have its husk removed before cooking. For those accustomed to agriculture based on wheat, grinding is the process that immediately comes to mind. But in Southeast Asia the grinding of rice is associated with the Chinese. Indigenous peoples prefer some kind of pounding technique usually involving a pestle and mortar. The rhythmic thump of the women pounding rice is often the first noise that one hears on approaching a village. In some societies employing sago, the woody part of the palm is separated from the nutritious part by beating.

But even foods that can be cooked just as they come from the ground are often preferred in some processed form involving homogenization by pounding. The favored way of eating many kinds of beans is to beat them into a paste. Corn, peanuts, and edible seeds are reduced to crushed powder. Fruit such as bananas are preserved by drying and then pounded into a thick paste. Fish are dried and then pulverized.

In trades, crafts, and all manner of technical processes, pounding constitutes an important step. In the making of rope and yarn, vegetable fibers are obtained by prolonged beating of the raw material to remove pulpy parts of the plant. We need hardly point out the importance of this technology for everything from fishing to house building. Pottery techniques in general spurn the wheel or hand molding, and instead employ the paddle-and-anvil method. Surprisingly, weaving also involves a good deal of beating. Heavy flat wooden wands are used to close up the weft and make the fabric tight and hard wearing. Sharing some of the features of weaving and fiber making is the production of bark cloth. In this process, beating is employed only to soften woody fibers, not to order them in strands.

Metalworking involves much beating. Without modern furnaces, iron cannot be brought to its melting point, and so must be worked by hammering the red-hot ingot. Iron for blades is produced by layering ingot on top of ingot and then beating them wafer thin. But even with metals that could be cast, like brass and silver, hammering methods of working are preferred. Decorative patterns are punched onto the finished product.

One final example. Anyone who has watched women washing clothes in Southeast Asia will have noticed the way that the women roll them into a ball, soak them in water, and then beat them on a stone. Alternatively, they swing the wet cloth over their heads and bring it down smartly on a washboard or a convenient rock. Seldom do they employ the rubbing actions that come most naturally to Westerners.

Pounding actions appear with equal frequency in ritual contexts in Southeast Asia. The Berawan again provide an example. At funerals, drums, gongs large and small, slit gongs, and rice pestles are all unambiguously pounded. At other festivals, such as weddings, the gongs are played (using different rhythms), but the big drum and the funeral games are prohibited. This lesser level of percussion is consonant with the relative unimportance and ritual simplicity of all life-crisis markers other than death. The only rites that compete with funerals in terms of duration and complexity are headhunting festivals, and they have their own peculiar percussive practices.

When new heads are brought into the house, the men break into a stamping dance quite unlike the graceful, light-footed warrior's dance seen on other occasions. Also the felicitous opportunity is taken to expel evil influence from the house in the following manner. A crowd of people, mostly women, line up at one end of the longhouse veranda armed with rice pestles, canoe paddles, or heavy sticks. Together they march down the veranda, pounding these implements on the floor. Three times they go up and down the house, supposedly driving bad spirits before them.

We cannot conclude that these pounding actions in ritual derive in any simple way from similar ones in everyday life. That this cannot be the entire cause for their occurrence has already been shown by Needham, for the worldwide use of percussion cannot be explained by localized technologies of food production. However, it is still possible that the special frequency and importance of pounding technologies in Southeast Asia augments a universal resort to percussion for making noise. Though drums and gongs may be very widely employed at funerals, there is a particular intensity to the crashing, clanging, booming noisiness of Berawan rites.

Moreover, there may be cultural differences of emphasis in the significance of noise. The reason that is given by Berawan for the restriction on the playing of tops to funerals is that the whirring noise that they make is like the speech of ghosts. Normally it would be dangerous to attract ghosts with such noises, but at funerals the generations of the dead are invited anyway. Percussion is associated in the same way with the presence of the ancestors. Drumming and gong playing cease at the moment when this intercourse is broken off and the souls of the living are summoned back to the longhouse away from the departing dead.

LIMINALITY AND THE CORPSE

We cannot leave this consideration of the general and the particular in funeral practices without considering the corpse. It is our thesis throughout that attention to the symbolic attributes of the dead body provides insights into a culture's understanding of the nature of death. These attributes have the same kind of quasi universality and subtle variability in connotation as do color symbolism and the use of percussive noise.

Corpse symbolism is a special case of the use of the human body as a symbol. As we have mentioned, Hertz's essay on the representation of positive and negative moral qualities through the opposition of the right and left hands is one of the classic studies in body symbolism. The mourning usages involving shaving the head or letting the beard grow touch on another aspect. Throughout history and in most cultures, the human body has been used to represent moral and social verities. In connection with circumcision and scarification at initiation, van Gennep writes that "the human body has been treated like a simple piece of wood which each has cut and trimmed to suit him" (1960: 72). If the human body in life provides such a reservoir of moral representations, this same body after death carries its own possibilities for symbolic expression. The surprising thing about corpse symbolism is how widely it is used in contexts divorced from death per se. Van Gennep saw that an immense variety of rites involve a rebirth in a new status, either for the individual or the whole society. But birth in the new condition presupposes death in the former, so that all liminal conditions involve deathly, terminal representations. Turner has paid great attention to the recurring symbols of liminality:

The symbolism attached to and surrounding the liminal persona is complex and bizarre. Much of it is modeled on human biological processes. . . . They give an outward and visible form to an inward and conceptual process. . . . The symbols . . . are drawn from the biology of death, decomposition, catabolism, and other physical processes that have a negative tinge. [Turner 1967: 98]

In Turner's view, it is the process of rotting, of dissolution of form, that provides the metaphor of a social and moral transition. Hence the prevalence of disagreeable remainders of dissolution at otherwise optimistic rites such as initiations and installations. Following Turner, one could argue that the corpse is associated with death because its decay is a metaphor of liminality. However, the direct connection between the two is so obvious as to hardly require such sophistry. Whether death or liminality is seen as primary depends upon whether one begins with funerals or other rites of passage. It is useful to explain liminality in initiation rites as deathlike, but it is tautologous in connection with funerals. However, Turner shows us a way to pursue the symbol-

ism of the corpse by focusing upon the process of dissolution. Though, like percussive sound, corruption is a nearly universal symbol, it varies greatly in its metaphorical significance.

ROTTING, FERMENTING, DYEING, AND DISTILLING

Adams (1977) shows that in Southeast Asia there are strong parallels between certain manufacturing processes and the whole format of mortuary rites. Blue-black dye is the most common color used for decorating cloth in Southeast Asia. Its preparation from indigo is widely practiced, and one of the simplest methods is that employed by the Meo of Thailand (Bühler 1972). Two pits are dug side by side, but at slightly different elevations. In the higher pit, the roots and stems of the indigo plant are soaked in water and left to rot. The liquid is then drained by a bamboo connecting pipe to the lower pit. Lime is added, and after a week or so of fermentation, a sediment forms. This is the dye, recovered by draining the pit. Elsewhere in Southeast Asia, clay pots are used to hold the liquids, but the process is the same.

In the preparation of hemp for cordage, the hemp stalks are left to rot in water for some weeks, after which the useful fibers can be separated from woody or pulpy material. Fermentation is widely employed as a means of rendering toxic food edible, or of preserving perishable foods. Fish and vegetables are stored for future consumption by means of partial anaerobic rotting in tightly sealed containers. These techniques were probably even more common 100 years ago, when rice was a less available staple and root crops made up a larger part of the diet of Southeast Asians (Pelzer 1945: 6–8). Even where not strictly necessary, fermented foods are often preferred because of their astringent flavor, such as shrimp paste and fermented tea leaves for chewing.

All these techniques involve decomposition—decomposition to produce useful things like dye and hemp or tasty things like shrimp paste and pickles. But there is a formal symmetry between these techniques and rotting in a less utilitarian context, the secondary treatment of the dead. Both involve the three stages of preparation, decomposition, and extraction.

The Berawan of Borneo do not prepare dyes and only occasionally ferment foods. The most familiar process of this kind for them is the making of rice wine, which is consumed in large quantities at social gatherings. Rice is first washed, cooked by boiling, and sprinkled with yeast. Then it is rolled into tight balls, which are stacked in large earthenware jars. The jars are sealed and left for some days, during which time a watery liquid runs off the balls of fermenting rice and collects in the bottom. When the crowd is assembled and the party about to start, the jars are opened. The remains of the rice balls are picked out and squeezed to remove the last drops of the liquor. The rice wine is now ready for consumption, after straining to remove the sediment. One characteristic Berawan method of treatment of corpses is wholly similar. After washing and dressing, the corpse is stored in a sealed jar. Decomposition proceeds similarly, except that it is the sediment that people wish to retain this time, not the liquids. The latter are drained off by means of a bamboo tube inserted in the bottom of the jar. The bones are removed from the jar finally, and placed in a smaller container for final storage. The jars used for rice wine are identical to those used for primary storage of corpses. Often several such jars are kept in the kitchen of a family apartment, and occasionally one is seen standing upside down. If one inquires why, the answer may be: Grandmother (or grandfather) has picked out this one for herself, and does not want it used for wine (Metcalf 1987).

All these processes of fermentation or rotting produce a strong smell, often a nauseating smell. Making indigo dye is infamously stinky, and many Westerners dislike the preserved foods that we mentioned because of their pungent scent. The familiarity that Southeast Asians have with such smells may indicate different attitudes to corpses. It was not our experience that the Berawan were indifferent to these smells of decomposition, but they did show fortitude in the presence of corpses. Rotting does not have the wholly negative connotations for them that

it does for us. Consequently, there may be a radically different set of attitudes to the decomposition of corpses than those found in the West.

A second feature of Southeast Asian uses of techniques of decomposition is the notion of extraction. In the making of indigo, hemp, rice wine, and so on, raw materials are refined to produce valuable finished products that are of less bulk. From something perishable, inconveniently bulky, and useless in its present form, something long lasting, compact, and useful is obtained. The bones of the deceased partake of this nature, so that it is logical to take the time to recover them and store them with the other ancestors, from where they may exercise a benign influence upon their descendants. We cannot show that secondary burial rites like those found in Borneo evolved out of techniques for processing dyes. Nevertheless, the parallels are there, and they are striking. It may be that at some subconscious level, familiarity with practical techniques of distillation and fermentation makes the practice of secondary treatment of the dead more acceptable to Southeast Asians than it is to other peoples. If at some remote period, such practices were more widely distributed in the world, it may explain their persistence in some parts of Southeast Asia. These are the strongest statements that we can make.

Finally, it is worth noticing that this analogy is not inconsistent with Hertz's analysis of secondary treatment. Hertz pointed out that in these rites the fate of the corpse provides a model for the fate of the soul. Adams would only add that both are refined: the body to ossiferous relics, the soul to perfect spirit.

THE UNIVERSAL AND THE PARTICULAR

In the first part of the book, we have rejected the possibility of a simple panhuman explanation of the forms of funeral rites. Although we may posit a general psychic unity of mankind, the identification of vague quasi universals does not preclude variation at levels lower than that of the whole species. In trying to understand why Berawan funerals are so noisy, we were led to examine the worldwide use of percussion, the special propensity for pounding in Southeast Asia, and items of belief peculiar to the Berawan. Great care is needed to sort out the nature of variation from one place to another. Hence the need for case studies. Placed in the context of a particular ideological, social, and economic system, rituals of death begin to make sense in a way that they cannot if we pursue elusive cultural universals.

Caution is doubly necessary in connection with death rites because of an odd paradox. Contrary to what one might expect, conceptions of death are not only elusive, but also highly variable. Rivers remarked many years ago:

> Death is so striking and unique an event that if one had to choose something which must have been regarded in essentially the same light by mankind at all times and in all places, I think one would be inclined to choose it in preference to any other, and yet I hope to show that the primitive conception of death . . . is different, one might say radically different, from our own. [Rivers 1926: 40]

Meanwhile, concepts of life, which seems so much more complex a notion, have a certain universal familiarity about them. Ethnographers the world over constantly report the same symbols occurring in rites designed to promote fertility and the preservation of life, and the museums are full of life-promoting charms and ritual equipment. Death is more intangible:

> . . . on the whole there does commonly seem to be a contrast between a relatively patent and apprehensible conception of life and a more obscure and perplexing conception of death. One reason for this readily suggests itself. We have our being in a life that we know; we are struck down into a death that we can only surmise. [Needham 1970: xxxv]

REFERENCES

Adams, M. J. 1971. "Work Patterns and Symbolic Structures in a Village Culture, East Sumba, Indonesia." Southeast Asia 1(4): 320–34.

____. 1977. "Style in Southeast Asian Materials Processing: Some Implications for Ritual and Art." In H. Lechtman and R. Merrill (eds.) Material Culture: Studies, Organization,

and Dynamics of Technology, pp. 21–52. St. Paul: West Publishing.

Buhler, A. 1972. "Hanfverarbeitung und Batik bei den Meau in Nord-Thailand." Ethnologische Zeitschrift 1: 61–81.

Dworakowska, M. 1938. "The Origin of Bell and Drum." Prace etnologiczne 5. Warsaw: Nakladem Towarzystwa Naukowego Waszawkiego.

Gennep, A. van 1960. The Rites of Passage. Translated by M. Vicedom and S. Kimball. Chicago: University of Chicago Press.

Leach, E. 1958. "Magical Hair." Journal of the Royal Anthropological Institute 88(2): 149–64.

Lévi-Strauss, C. 1969. The Raw and the Cooked. New York: Harper & Row.

____. 1973. From Honey to Ashes. New York: Harper & Row.

Metcalf, P. 1981. "Meaning and Materialism: The Ritual Economy of Death." Man 16:563–78.

Needham, R. 1967. "Percussion and Transition." Man N.S. 2:606–14.

____. 1970. "Editor's Introduction." In A. M. Hocart. Kings and Councillors: An Essay in the Comparative Anatomy of Human Society, pp. xii–xcix. Chicago: Chicago University Press.

Pelzer, K. J. 1945. Pioneer Settlement in the Asiatic Tropics. New York: American Geographical Society.

Rivers, W. H. R. 1926. Psychology and Ethnology. London: Kegan Paul.

Rosenblatt, P. C., R. Walsh, and A. Jackson, 1976. Grief and Mourning in Cross-Cultural Perspective. New Haven: Human Relations Area File.

Turner, V. 1967. The Forest of Symbols. Ithaca: Cornell University Press.

READING 8–4

MAKING THE KING DIVINE: A CASE STUDY IN RITUAL REGICIDE FROM TIMOR

David Hicks

Symbolic *death is the theme here. Symbolically "killing" their king is how the people of Bemalai, a community in*

Source: David Hicks, "Making the King Divine: A Case Study in Ritual Regicide from Timor," *Journal of the Royal Anthropological Institute* 2 (1996), pp. 611–24. Reprinted by permission of the Royal Anthropological Institute of Great Britain and Ireland.

East Timor, replenish their depleted reservoir of fertility and life. They do so in a ritual manner not unlike that of the Ainu (Reading 10–3). The king must die so that humanity can live. But, we learn, the king has to die so that the Bemalai divinity also can live. As among the Ainu, the relationship between humanity and its divinity is one of reciprocity, and its locus resides in the sacrifice.

The approach adopted in this study of ritual regicide combines looking for formal relations in the structural style of Claude Lévi-Strauss (see Introduction to Chapter 2) and Edmund Leach (Reading 2–2) with Emile Durkheim's theory on how rituals originated. By combining the insights of these scholars the article suggests how collective rituals may revive the notion of god in the minds of believers.

A central feature of Durkheim's thesis regarding the origin of religion was his argument that the concept of a divinity as a "category of understanding" owed its genesis to dispositions aroused by human beings coming together in ritual (1960: 420–1). Repetitions of ritual performances, he concluded, renewed these dispositions. As Bloch (1986: 7) puts it, "Durkheim sees ritual as the device by which the categories of understanding organising our perception of nature and of society are created and given their categorical, hence inevitable, and compulsive nature." Durkheim appears to have been uncertain about the process by which this might occur;[1] yet, curiously, thirteen years earlier in their work on sacrifice, his collaborators on the *Année Sociologique,* Hubert and Mauss (1898), had come close to hinting at one possibility.

Hubert and Mauss claimed to have isolated as the defining element of sacrifice the communication between the "profane" and "sacred" brought about by the consecration of a victim whom the act destroyed. They appear to have thought that the exemplary sacrifice was that of a god who, through unqualified self-abnegation, offers himself to humankind, in this way bestowing the benefit of life, or a revival of life, upon mortals. At the same time, Hubert and Mauss recognized that the gods whom human beings create also have needs ("la matière immortelle"). It is therefore all the more unexpected that in seeking to disclose what has

been referred to as the "grammar" of sacrificial rituals (Evans-Pritchard 1964: viii), they seem to have ignored the opposite, yet complementary, mode of sacrifice in which a representative of humanity offers his or her life up for the benefit of divinity. The Word might become Flesh, so to speak; but the Flesh might also become the Word.

In this article I propose one possible way in which the sacrifice of a human figure representing a deity might operate as a strategy for evoking the concept of god. To this end, I shall try to combine Durkheim's equation of god and society with certain insights derived from Hubert and Mauss.[2] The sacrificial figure I shall discuss occupies the office known in anthropology as "divine kingship."

The term "divine king" is, of course, open to various interpretations (see Feeley-Harnik 1985; Needham 1980: 66–78; Young 1966: 135–6). Some idea of the diversity of the attributes and powers of divine kings and the advantages to be gained from the use of a more generalizing term such as "sacred king" or "sacred chief," can be gauged from the collection of articles edited by de Heusch (1990b) whose own contribution (1990a) argues in favour of discarding this over-restrictive and culture-bound designation. However, the term "divine king" has become well entrenched in the anthropological literature, and I shall adhere to the convention for the purposes of this article.[3]

There are also many critiques of Durkheim's theories of the sociological nature of belief and ritual, and of Hubert and Mauss's thesis on sacrifice. Valeri (1985: 65), for example, in explicating Hawaiian kingship and sacrifice, has sought to resolve the problem of the relationship between reciprocity and inequality in the sacrificial oblation: why, as he puts it, do human beings seem to give little in exchange for much? I shall return to Valeri's position later, though by way of rehearsal I might note that my own findings tend to support his argument that sacrifice creates a bond of "mutual indebtedness" between the human and the divine (Valeri 1985: 66–7) rather than, as Durkheim, Mauss and Hubert seem to imply, a hierarchical relationship. On the contrary, I shall analyse here a ritual in which god, "society," and the scapegoat figure of the divine king become merged by the ritual performance itself into a single moral entity in which any sense of hierarchy has been effaced.[4]

I

Adjoining each other in central Timor are two ethnic groups, the Tetum and the Ema.[5] Their languages are distinct but share many lexical features and are congeners within the wider Austronesian linguistic family. However, the closest resemblances between the two peoples can be seen at the ideational and institutional levels. These resemblances include a prevailing dualistic mode of organizing important symbolic categories such as human being/spirit, masculine/feminine, dry/wet and dry season/wet season; a supreme dual godhead comprised of a father god and a mother god; a belief in a force known as lulik (sacred, forbidden, spiritual energy); a conception of human existence as cyclical; a hierarchy of ranks including chiefs of various categories; asymmetric alliance between established sets of affines; and marriages in which wife-takers give buffaloes to their wife-givers who reciprocate with pigs (Brandewie & Asten 1976; Cinatti 1965; Clamagirand 1980; Grijzen 1904; Renard-Clamagirand 1982; Vroklage 1952; Wortelboer 1952).[6]

Along the north coast of central Timor is a lagoon known as Bemalai.[7] It is approximately two kilometres long and one kilometre wide, and abounds in fish and crustaceans as well as being the haunt of crocodiles. Near it lie two villages—one Tetum-speaking and the other Ema-speaking—which share a common history and mythology telling of a bloody rivalry over the lagoon's resources. With the passage of time this violence seems to have become channelled into a co-operative, yet also competitive, calendrical ritual called the sau-biu[8] at the climax of which a surrogate of the king of one village (Balibo) is symbolically done to death and then restored to life (King 1965: 111–12). The two communities are the aforementioned Tetum village of Balibo, inhabited by comparatively recent immigrants to the region, and the Ema village of Atabae, whose people comprise the autochthonous population. The two communities become a single social entity when, every few years, their inhabitants converge on Bemalai, whose resources each village continues to claim as its own, and express their shared ideas and institutions in a performance of the sau-biu ritual.

The principal authorities on the Northern Tetum are Brandewie and Asten (1976), Grijzen (1904), Vroklage (1952) and Wortelboer (1952). Renard-Clamagirand[9] is the only authority on the Ema. Although their respective ethnographies do not specifically deal with these two villages—Renard-Clamagirand's fieldwork was carried out at Marobo, a community to the southeast of Bemalai, while the reports of the other authors refer to the Tetum region as a whole—they are nevertheless consistent with the data reported from Bemalai, such variation as may occur being in the nature of procedural mutations rather than radical differences in beliefs or institutions. Thus, whereas in one ritual carried out at Marobo the rainy season is opened by the blowing of a horn (Renard-Clamagirand 1982: 290), in the equivalent Bemalai ritual it is signalled by dancing, shouting and singing (King 1965: 115). The concept of a source from which human life originates is reified at Marobo as an altar with a bamboo arising from it (Renard-Clamagirand 1982: 270–1) and, at Bemalai, as an altar comprised of a tree trunk with a fishing net cast around it. This tree trunk represents the sacred banyan tree that stands in the centre of every ancestral village (Cinatti 1965: 40). In fundamental socio-cultural particulars, however, Marobo and Atabae are unquestionably part of the same tradition. As for Balibo, data relating to that village suggest it is an entirely typical northern Tetum village.

The published ethnography on the Bemalai ritual consists of Cinatti (1965), King (1963; 1965) and Vondra (1968). My analysis is based upon their findings, supplemented by data from Pascoal (1967) and Duarte (n.d.; pers. comm.). The latter, during research I carried out among Timorese refugees in Lisbon, kindly permitted me access to an unpublished Bemalai text which he had collected in the field.[10]

Since all these accounts describe ritual performances during the 1960s, this decade will serve as my "ethnographic present." Regrettably, the data they provide are the only extant information on this singular institution which, following upon the calamitous dissolution of traditional Timorese societies brought about by the Indonesian occupation, is almost certainly defunct.

The purposes of the ritual are, among others, to "commemorate the myth of the creation of Bemalai" (King 1965: 110), to "recreate the myth" (King 1965: 111), and to "ensure a continuation of an abundant supply of fish" (Cinatti 1965: 110).[11] The sacrifice also "lifts the prohibitions prescribed by the sacred character of the lagoon" (Cinatti 1965: 41). Shared assumptions about fecundity, gender, hierarchy, political and spiritual authority, asymmetric alliance and matters of cosmology enable the two communities to transcend their socio-cultural individualities and achieve, albeit temporarily, a common identity as a unified collectivity headed by a single ruler. These considerations find ritual expression in symbols (gestures, words and objects) employed to transform this ruler, whose local eminence merits the designation of "king," into his divine counterpart, the "lord of the water" (*we na'in*). The sacrifice of the king's blood regenerates this divinity (and the spirit world in general) thereby inducing the spirit world to reciprocate with the gift of fecundity and bringing advantages to divinity and mortals alike. It is an "operation whereby the Timorese establish a relationship with the sacred spirit . . . thus utilizing benefits which before were prohibited" (Cinatti 1965: 51).

In their interpretation of Tetum social and symbolic categories, Brandewie and Asten (1976: 19) delineate "the dualistic character of [the Tetum's] outlook" and emphasize "the implications of alliance and of dualism" in the Tetum "social world" and "symbol-world." The fact that Asten is himself a member of the Tetum ethnic group adds a special authority to their contentions, and Renard-Clamagirand (1982) is equally insistent about the pervasiveness of dualism as an organizing principle among the Ema. Inevitably, therefore, the Bemalai ritual exploits this dualistic form of classification, and in doing so elaborates the important notion that human experience can be conceived of as incorporating a cyclical movement between human and spiritual modes of existence.

Although the contrast between human being and spirit does not appear to find explicit expression in indigenous terminology, the term ema in the Tetum language is glossed by Brandewie and Asten (1976: 19) as "man" or "people," by which they evidently mean "human being." It is also the self-referencing designation used by the Ema (Clamagirand 1980: 135). However, while there is a Tetum term, *hu,* which encompasses the notions of "spirit" and "breath" (Duarte 1964: 104), neither language apparently includes a generic term for spirit beings. Nevertheless, as we shall see, the conceptual contrast between "human being" and "spirit" continually finds expression in ritual and myth among both groups (Grijzen 1904; Renard-Clamagirand 1982).

The interaction between the denizens of a visible world inhabited by human beings and those of an invisible world inhabited by spirits is critical in Tetum and Ema cosmologies (Grijzen 1904: 74–86; Renard-Clamagirand 1982). While the abode of the spirits may be variously described as underground, across the sea, in the sky, or on top of a mountain, both populations regard it as the source of life, fertility and prosperity. Ritual, such as the one at Bemalai, provides the instrument by which humans can tap this source (Grijzen 1904: 74–80; Renard-Clamagirand 1982: 291), and myth shows how this might be done. In myth, the water divinity is usually hypostatized as a crocodile or large fish ailing from some injury which is cured by a human being who enters the spiritual world, restores vigour to the divinity, and then returns to the human world. Such is the plot of two myths concerning Bemalai (see Duarte n.d.; Pascoal 1967: 132–7). The moment of transformation in both directions is typically effected by the hero closing his eyes as though dying and opening them as though revivified—precisely as does the human victim who "dies" and is "restored to life" in the ritual of regicide.

After being revitalized, the deity rewards the hero with a herd of buffaloes that miraculously keeps growing. Duarte's text stipulates that the pig and buffalo killed during the ritual of regicide be female, thereby confirming the femininity-fertility association so strongly emphasized by Renard-Clamagirand (1982: 269). As though to reinforce this connexion the myth enjoins that the buffalo be dispatched by a spear thrust through the vaginal opening.[12]

For both populations at Bemalai, images of fertility, femininity and water are combined in the institution of asymmetric alliance. This institution, like the existential cycle itself, is conceived of in terms of "an image of a flow of life which circulates by means of women" (Clamagirand 1980: 145), an Ema metaphor which Fox (1980: 12–13) renders as "the idea of a return or reunion of life," and one whose Tetum counterpart is the image of a stream of water flowing downhill or of water in a canal surrounding and linking different areas of a rice field (Brandewie & Asten 1976: 21). Just as the canal enables the water to flow, so does the affinal bond enable the life which women nurture to be transmitted from wife-givers to wife-takers (Brandewie & Asten 1976: 21; Clamagirand 1980: 145).

To perpetuate the cycle, the people of Bemalai procure the resources of life, fertility and prosperity from their god at the same time as they infuse energy into this being.[13] When human beings carry out rituals to replenish themselves and their divinity they seek life, fertility and prosperity where they also find death. As Renard-Clamagirand (1982: 293) phrases it, "The rites tend to renew the sacred time of the origins of the community so that, replenished at the source, it can perpetuate itself." The connexion between the world of the living and that of the dead is made at places which link the two worlds (Grijzen 1904: 75–8; Renard-Clamagirand 1982), principally at the altar, which is a "symbol of gushing life. . . a point of contact between the world of the dead and that of the living. . ." (Renard-Clamagirand 1982: 270–1).

II

Until the 1950s the sau-biu used to be performed every August (Duarte 1989) at the time of transition from dry season to wet season (Cinatti 1965: 32). Just as water is associated with femininity and fertility, so rain is considered "fecund and logically associated with 'Woman' who is the source of life" (Renard-Clamagirand 1982: 296). Since dryness is associated with males, the climatic transition may be interpreted as a transition from the masculine half of the year to the feminine half of the year.

Preparations for the ritual begin when villagers notice dead fish and prawns floating in the water. These are believed to indicate a "waning" of the water's lulik, which in this context refers to its vitality or spiritual energy. Since life is thought to issue from divinity, this ebbing of nature's vitality is construed as a sign that the water divinity—as in the myths—requires revitalization (King 1965: 110).

The man selected as the king's surrogate (ordinarily a member of the same descent group as the Balibo ruler) must be a healthy adult in whom the generative forces of masculinity are self-evident. The surrogate king is joined at the altar by two female animals, and the image conveyed is one of life-sustaining fertility and reproduction brought about by the union of the two genders.

A priest (corresponding to Hubert and Mauss's sacrificateur) from Balibo selects the day on which the ritual is to commence. On the final day before the ritual workers from both communities begin constructing a bridge across the lagoon to facilitate movement between the two groups. Then, as the sun begins to set, distinctions of rank and ethnicity are set aside as aristocrats and commoners of the two villages intermingle in boisterous camaraderie beside the water until dawn.

The surrogate king meanwhile retires some distance away to a hut constructed specially for this occasion. Once inside, he is no longer permitted to hold conversation with anyone, nor to eat or drink (King 1965: 113); his seclusion presumably signals a condition of liminality between the world of humans and that of spirits.

Ritual and myth at Bemalai put the contrast between silence and noise to symbolic use, and noise is a marker between temporal periods, separating the wet season from the dry season and evoking notions of the regeneration of nature (Renard-Clamagirand 1982: 233, 290). Accordingly, when on the following morning attendants escort the surrogate king to the water's edge, silence prevails. Some participants gather there while others congregate around the altar where the human victim awaits his deification. He kneels at the centre of the net, holding a wooden sceptre, while behind him the sacrificer, staff in hand, pretends to strike the surrogate king a blow on the head. As the victim slumps to the ground in simulated death, his hands are tied together, his sceptre is wrapped up in the fishing net, and cloth is bundled under his head as is done with a corpse being prepared for burial. This "burial" incorporates him into the world of the spirits, and his entry there revives the moribund water god in whose identity he is apotheosized. As god, the king is at this moment the spirit of a culture hero who figures in a myth which I shall shortly discuss (Cinatti 1965: 40).

The pig is now metonymically identified with the human sacrifice by being brought close to the dead king; and the identification metaphorically reinforced by the sacrificer plunging a knife into the creature's heart. The silence continues as the sacrificer squeezes blood from the wound into the lagoon, in an act called "giving to the [lord of the] water" (King 1965:113).

No sooner has the flow of blood ceased than ethnic and social distinctions reassert themselves with the appearance of a fleet of decorated boats. These slip out from the bank and move in a cortege across the surface of the water. Nobles from Balibo occupy the leading boat, a ceremonial craft, which is followed by a more utilitarian vessel at whose prow stands a fisherman, net in hand, ready to cast. The helmsmen guide the boats gently to ensure that the water is not disturbed unnecessarily nor the silence broken. Commoners from Balibo crowd silently into other boats. When the boat carrying the leading fisherman has lined up behind the one containing the nobles, the fisherman slings out his net.

As fishermen in the other boats follow suit, the nobles of Atabae put out in their boats and begin competing with those of Balibo to gather in fish. Commoners unable to get into the boats swarm from the banks into the shallows, dancing, shouting and singing "to stir up the mud and make the fish drunk" (King 1965: 115). This cacophony brings the period of silence to a close.

Each time he catches a fish, a fisherman exultantly cries out "bal'balum" ("my part") to the god, in this way asserting humanity's rights to the catch (the analogy between the king "caught" in the net and the fish being netted seems obvious) and with that right established, the men of Balibo and Atabae continue their rivalry over the course of the next few days in a furious spate of non-stop fishing, while their womenfolk watch from the bank.

For Ema and Tetum alike, breath can transmit life, fertility and prosperity from spirits to human beings (Clamagirand 1980: 144; Duarte 1964: 109; Renard-Clamagirand 1982: 274, 286). Accordingly, as the seasonal transition is accomplished, the sacrificer breathes an infusion of life into the mouth of the king, thereby revitalizing him and returning him to his human condition.

The second liminal period now begins. The surrogate king has been removed from the spiritual world, but has not yet been reintegrated into that of humanity. As a step towards this, the sacrificer cuts the bonds restraining the victim as soon as the first fish has been netted and, freed from his constraints, the surrogate king struggles into a squatting position. Taking pains to keep his back to the water (his domain when he was a god, but now alien territory), the surrogate king places the staff, which in the meantime has been snapped in two, under the net. With eyes downcast, he follows the sacrificer who, with arms horizontally extended, carries an unsheathed ceremonial sword on his upturned palms as he steps over to the banyan tree. Here, the third, and final, sacrifice is to be offered.

In this sacrifice, human being and beast are made symbolically equivalent, and masculinity and femininity are conjoined. As the surrogate king sits down near the beast, the sacrificer places some areca and betel on the buffalo's tongue with the tip of his sword and then offers some to the man, who stuffs it into his mouth. Offering betel and areca is a common Tetum and Ema procedure for contacting spirits (cf. Grijzen 1904: 77; Renard-Clamagirand 1982: 277). As the sacrificer backs away, the king chews for a few moments before spitting betel juice several times. He continues chewing as the priest thrusts a sword (replacing the spear of mythology) into the vaginal opening of the buffalo.

After butchering the carcass, and obedient to the protocols of status and hierarchy, the sacrificer sets aside a certain portion of the meat for himself and then allocates equal portions to the participants from Balibo (King 1965: 116). The king and his family are privileged to eat their portions first.[14] Since the king of Bemalai not only literally feeds his people by providing the buffalo but also shares a common identity with the beast,[15] this moment in the ritual seems to correspond to Feeley-Harnik's "juncture" at which "ritual and politics meet in food" (1985: 288), and recalls her argument that the Fijian stranger-king offers local residents "cooked men," that is, sacrificial victims, to consume. The surrogate king now brings the ritual to an end, and is reincorporated into the human world, by tossing the entrails of the buffalo into the water "as an offering" to nourish the water god (Vondra 1968: 47). Having done this, he can walk along the bank, mix with other human beings, and freely accept betel-chew, fish and tobacco.

Sitting with his back against the banyan (the symbolic roots of the social collectivity of Bemalai community), a story-teller known as the "lord of the word" (*lia na'in*) narrates two complementary myths that describe the origins of the lagoon, the water god and of the ritual itself (Cinatti 1965: 39–40; King 1965: 111).

Myth A

On behalf of their respective peoples two great chiefs from Atabae and Balibo attempted to negotiate a common boundary between their two groups, but failed to reach agreement and began brawling.

As they were clubbing each other with staffs, a woman came along carrying a water jar on her head. One man—or perhaps the two of them together—knocked it off [in King (1965: 111) the culprit is the Balibo man; in Vondra (1968: 46) it is the man from Atabae], breaking the container in half. The spilt water formed a lagoon, which separated the two men and formed the boundary between their two communities.

This myth accounts for the division between the people of Balibo and the people of Atabae, a disjunction analogous to the separation of the dry season from the wet season (cf. Renard-Clamagirand 1982: 296). It also highlights the discord which, by breaking the jar and spilling the water, divides the hitherto homogeneous topographic and ethnic landscape. It should also be pointed out that the myth, with its references to a "superabundance" of water, is narrated at a time of year when the rains of the—always unreliable—wet season are anxiously awaited.

The second tale accounts for the origin of divinity, which it defines in terms of the king's genealogy, and accounts also for the ritual in which people transform a king into a god.

Myth B

Four brothers founded a community. Three of them contested the ownership of a sacred water jar which their ancestors had carried from their land of origin. The jar broke and the waters that poured out swamped the entire community. Only the fourth brother, until then a marginal figure, was saved. He became the owner of the lagoon, the lord of the water, a divinized man. Through a ritual of consecration the spirit of the fourth brother would, in later generations, become reincarnated in the person of the king of Balibo. As a reminder of this episode members of each subsequent generation were to be shown a staff that rises vertically from the middle of the lagoon, and which, so informants claim, is the top of the main pillar of a sacred house which stood at the centre of the drowned community. It represents, they add, the axis of the world.

If Myth A explains the origins of the lagoon and the dual character of the social collectivity of Bemalai, Myth B focuses more upon the community's unity and introduces the origin of the notion of man-as-god.

III

The king has to die at Bemalai, I would argue, because only he represents the entire society and can therefore mediate the division between humans and spirits, and between society and nature.[16] For ordinary persons, contact with religious forces may, as Hubert and Mauss (1898: 134) claim, be dangerous; but kings are not ordinary persons—and divine ones are presumably even less so. The Tetum term for the king is *liurai*. This may be literally translated as "more than the earth," (*liu* [more than] + *rai* [earth]), a gloss that suggests a certain estranged quality in keeping with the king's divine potential. It is also in keeping with the alien origins some Timorese attribute to kings and their families (cf. Sahlins 1983). At Bemalai, only ritual makes a king divine; as Hubert and Mauss pointed out: *"la victime n'arrive pas nécessairement au sacrifice avec une nature religieuse, achevée et définie; c'est le sacrifice lui-même qui la lui confère"* (1898: 133). The Bemalai victim becomes divine by transcending metaphysical, gender ("The chiefs conjoin [the] two powers" associated with masculinity and femininity [Renard-Clamagirand 1982: 297]), and affinal distinctions,[17] as a consequence of which his death and resurrection are made to correspond to the cyclical reproduction of the society for which he stands.

As encompassing representative of an (albeit temporary) social collectivity, a representative who transcends male and female, symbolizes affinal unity, and provides the counterpart of the local god, the king transcends these contrasts. He is therefore suitably positioned to reconcile them in an act of creativity set in motion by a ritual that transforms a human being into a spirit controlling fertility and life, and then back again into a human being (Cinatti 1965: 41). By his self-sacrifice, the king is also offering up himself-as-society to the divinity who, revivified by the gift,[18] is thereby afforded the opportunity of reciprocating with the gift of life to both society and nature in what Hocart called a "communal pursuit of fertility" (1970: 217). By conjoining the spiritual and human orders, the king helps his fellow spirits and fellow-humans alike, ensuring that both receive life (Cinatti 1965: 41).[19] Furthermore, as oblation and mediator between human and spiritual and between nature and society, the king-as-divinity serves as a metaphor of the cosmos itself.[20] The ensuing regenerative interaction between spiritual and human is made possible only by the sacrifice of someone who represents the total dual community and has power over the natural resources of the lagoon. Renard-Clamagirand (Clamagirand 1980: 150) has made a special point of noting that the Ema associate the liurai with the increase of animal resources, adding that "at the collective level, rituals . . . attempt to obtain additional animals from the Liurai who has power over them and is their source." The connexion between rulers and life-sustaining largesse is reinforced by the ritual function of another category of Ema leader, the bei, who is "directly responsible for the well-being of the community and who ensures it receives the nourishment it needs" (Renard-Clamagirand 1982: 289).

That ritual serves as a device for integrating smaller units into a larger aggregation among the Ema is at no time more evident than when the rainy season commences:

It is through [the songs and dances which accompany the arrival of the rains] that the unity of the group is manifested and forged. In effect, these festivals are the occasion on which the ties that unite all the participants are tightened and, as a result, social cohesion is reaffirmed (Renard-Clamagirand 1982: 289).

IV

In calling attention to the sociological approach to divine kingship taken by scholars such as Evans-Pritchard (1948) and Seligman (1934), Vaughan suggests that [t]he concept of a divine king is the consequence of a world view which holds that the king and his kingdom are one; therefore, prosperity and failings in either must be present in both. Consequently, a king can be held responsible for all conditions in the kingdom. Should he be weak or ill, the kingdom will be in danger; or should the kingdom be in failing circumstances, there must be something wrong with the king. Finally, a change in the person of the king will change the conditions in the kingdom. (1987: 122–3)

As we have seen, while the Bemalai king does indeed symbolize his "kingdom," he is certainly no ailing symbol of the society he heads. As the dry season draws to a close, it must seem to the people living around the lagoon that it is nature and the divinity of the water that are losing vitality rather than society's most prominent member. On the contrary, the life-bestowing potency of a surrogate in all the virility of healthy manhood has to be tapped in order to revivify an ailing natural world and divinity, and replenish society with the means of reproducing itself.

In contrast to the Jukun king (Young 1966: 148) and certain other sovereigns described in the literature, whose divinity appears to have endured for their entire lifetimes, the Bemalai king's divinity is short-lived and cyclical. Reanimated in ritual, the king becomes a spirit and is then returned to mortal flesh, thereby permitting the natural world to continue its own cyclical progression into another wet season. In their distinctive way, the Timorese appear to be saying that "the Word" is altogether too remote to help them in their perennial quest for fertility and that mere flesh, even in the guise of a king, lacks sufficient inspiration to generate the resources required. Accordingly, one who is simultaneously god and king must be conjured up if their quest is to bear fruit. And since the people of Bemalai lagoon have no divine king to call upon, in a ritual performed every few years besides its waters, they must perforce make one.

In his formulation of Hawaiian kingship, Valeri (1985: 344–46) has maintained that communal rituals can be interpreted as a procedure for making

participants conscious of their society's basic concepts and principles. But rather than putting themselves in a position of merely "receiving messages," as Lévi-Strauss (1958) or Leach (1969) might have claimed, ritual allows them to act out the "only experience they can have of society manifesting itself as unity and multiplicity, that is, of the unity of the species realized as a coordinated complex of social actors" (1985: 345). Valeri (1985: 348) concludes that, in their rituals, Hawaiians introject the complex of links between their image of themselves as a society, the principles that order their society, and the acquisition of land as a source of life. If my interpretation of the sau-biu ritual is correct, then it supports Valeri's argument, for the symbols which define the ritual suggest that those who perform it are as concerned with asserting control over natural resources as the Hawaiians and are acting out the same kinds of concepts as those Valeri has identified.

It would therefore seem that by sacrificing their king the people of Bemalai not only bring land, control over fertility, life, divinity, and kingship into a synthetic unity, but make it possible for them to sacrifice themselves as a collectivity ("society") by transforming king and society into a god who, revitalized by the sacrifice, reasserts his power to restore life. In performing this, the ultimate act of self-abnegation, the collectivity impresses upon its members its power to recreate itself as a divinity and hence restore itself to life. In this sense the king is no more divine than the society he represents; but no less divine than the god he becomes.[21]

Their calendrical ritual thus allows the people who convene at the lagoon to recreate periodically their society in the image of their god. Like all divinities, their god depends upon human beings for existence, and making their king divine is their way of realizing this god-making capacity. Durkheim understood the concepts of god and society to be related metaphorically, but did not explain how their common identity might, in practice, be conserved in the imaginations of believers or generated in the first place. The ritual analysed here suggests one possible explanation. Society, in the form of a king, becomes divinized by ritual,[22] and since god, originally conceived of in myth, is recreated every time the ritual is repeated, periodically sacrificing its king is one way by which a society renews its concept of divinity and its own existence as an abstract collectivity.

ENDNOTES

I am grateful to the Wenner-Gren Foundation for Anthropological Research and the American Philosophical Society for making it possible for me to carry out research inquiries in Lisbon. My thanks also go to Simon Harrison, Declan Quigley, Gregory L. Forth, Rodney Needham, Colin Scott, W. Arens, Hushang Philsooph, Jennifer Callans, David Buchman and Darlene Malbon for helpful criticism of earlier drafts of this article. I wish also to render thanks to the late Father Jorge Barros Duarte, a generous and lamented custodian of Timorese culture, for his enthusiastic and sustained interest in my work. Preliminary versions of this article were read at the University of Mainz, the Colóquio International "Antropologia Timorense: Produções, Linguagens" in Lisbon, McGill University, and Holy Cross College, and I thank Karl-Heinz Köhl, Henri Campagnolo, Maria-Olímpia Campagnolo, Jérôme Rousseau and Susan Rodgers for inviting my contributions.

1. Evans-Pritchard (1965: 64, 68), for one, dismissed Durkheim's "cause" as nothing more than a form of "crowd psychology." "He is claiming that spirit, soul, and other religious ideas and images are projections of society, or of its segments, and originate in conditions bringing about a state of effervescence . . . fundamentally Durkheim elicits a social fact from crowd psychology" (1965: 68). For further elaboration of this approach see Lukes (1985: 462–5, 483) who has also alerted us to Durkheim's failure to appreciate the complexity of the social realities to which religious phenomena relate and his tendency to accord them a greater unitary character than they actually possess.

2. Cf. de Heusch (1985: 1–25) for an evaluative overview of Hubert and Mauss's work on sacrifice in light of African ritual, including Evans-Pritchard's (1956) classic study of Nuer sacrifice in which, he points out, the author made his thesis conform to Hubert and Mauss's schema.

3. See also Beidelman (1966), Carlson (1993), Evans-Pritchard (1948), Richards (1969), Young (1966) and Vaughan (1987). Beidelman's review of "sacrifice and sacred rule" in Africa (1987) complements that of Feeley-Harnik (1985)—as well as providing Robertson Smith with the credit often withheld from him.

4. Girard (1992) has also recently raised doubts about certain of these three scholar's assumptions, for while he considers their emphasis on the sociological function of the sacrifice to be justified, he, like Muller (1980), insists that it is a scapegoating device whose character is essentially violent. Hubert and Mauss's addiction to a diachronic style of analysis has been reassessed by de Heusch who has called into question "their ambition" to reduce all sacrifice to a rite-of-passage schema based on a vague typology contrasting pro-

fane and sacred (de Heusch 1985: 15, 213). As I try to demonstrate in this article, this schema is by no means incompatible with a sacrificial ritual, but de Heusch's objection offers a salutary caveat.

5. One of the largest ethnic groups on Timor, the Tetum, are usually classified into three branches: the northern, southern and eastern (Hicks 1984: 7). My own fieldwork was among the eastern branch, but I have not drawn on my data on this population for the present analysis.

6. All quotations from Renard-Clamagirand (1982) and Cinnati (1965) in this article are my translations.

7. Be + malai. In Tetum: *be* or *we* = "liquid," "water," "source," "point of origin." The Ema variant is *beu* (Renard-Clamagirand 1982: 230). *Malai* is a term in common use throughout eastern Timor and connotes "stranger" or "foreigner."

8. *Sau'*[n] 5 the lifting of a ritual interdiction; the meaning of biu has not been recorded. The ritual continued to be enacted until at least well into the 1960s.

9. Renard-Clamagirand and Clamagirand are the same person. Except when specifically citing works published under the name Clamagirand I refer to this author as Renard-Clamagirand.

10. The ethnographic data from Bemalai, it might be noted, lend themselves to interpretation from several alternative perspectives including the ecological and political, as well as the structural, in addition to suggesting insights into several anthropological problems such as the theoretical relationship between ritual and myth (see Hicks 1992).

11. Since I am dependent upon the reports of other authors, it might be worth remarking that in my discussions concerning Bemalai with Duarte, who was himself a Tetum-speaking Timorese and very familiar indeed with Bemalai, he ventured no misgivings of any kind about the accuracy of Cinatti's depiction of the ritual—or indeed of any of the others—and that although there are some minor differences of ethnographic detail between the five authors, there is a general, indeed quite striking, concordance on all substantial matters of fact and interpretation.

12. Precept and practice may not always coincide; and in the event it does not, and a male buffalo is sacrificed, the beast is immolated by a sword thrust in its left side, that is, its "female side," in this way maintaining the feminine connotations of the sacrifice.

13. The recent past for the Ema is associated with "the transmission of life via the vital energy released and recirculated at death while mythical time is associated with the source of vital energy which supplies 'extra' life to reactivate the life cycle" (Clamagirand 1980: 150).

14. See Sahlins's characterization of the stranger-king of Fiji as the "feeder of the people and their food . . . the sacred . . . chief [who is] domesticated ritually" by dying and being reborn (1983: 87). In this context it might be recalled that the king of Bemalai belongs to what is considered to be the immigrant population.

15. Cf. Girard: "The sacred king is also a monster. He is simultaneously god, man and savage beast" (1992: 252).

16. Since neither the Tetum nor the Ema language apparently has terms for "society" and "nature," it might be objected that a contrast between society and nature is merely an ana-

lytical contrivance; but it is clear that the ritual and its attendant beliefs implicitly entail this conceptual distinction.

17. Although Feeley-Harnik (1985: 297) has observed that "One of the most striking features of the literature on divine kingship is the absence of attention to women," we have seen that inflections of the feminine occur frequently in the ritual and accompanying myths at Bemalai. In myth, the conflict between the woman and the two men creates two separate communities, the occasion of the ritual is at the beginning of the feminine season, two female beasts are sacrificed, and the ritual is replete with implications of fertility and femininity.

18. "The sacrifice . . . restores to the spirit . . . the sacred energy enjoyed by human beings during the fishing and the commensality that derives from it" (Cinatti 1965: 41).

19. "The object of the ritual is to make the macrocosm bound in the objects of men's desires. But the spirit of the macrocosm resides in the victim, and so prosperity is to be attained by making that microcosm prosperous and bountiful" (Hocart 1970: 202).

20. Cf. Hocart (1970: 69): "Man is not a microcosm; he has to be made one in order that he may control the universe for prosperity. The ritual establishes an equivalence that was not there. If it were there already there would be no point in having a ritual; man would merely have to behave as he wished the world to behave, and there would be no need of words, of altars, and other methods of effecting the identity."

21. Cf. Galey (1990: 3): "Neither the divine nor the king are in themselves the ultimate values of society. They are merely expressions of the principles governing its identity. And as we are dealing with relations and not with substances bounded once and for all in a closed set of meaning, the principles may change and the relations be transformed. Thus, to fancy that kingship lives either below or above the limits of society is to misconceive fatally both the nature of kingship and that of society."

22. Lehmann (1993: 30) has recently reminded us that although "Durkheim is widely known for his theory that 'God' is really society . . . he believed, equally, that society is really God."

REFERENCES

Beidelman, T. O. 1966. Swazi royal ritual. *Africa* 36, 373–405.
_____. 1987. Sacrifice and sacred rule in Africa. *Am. Ethnol.* 14, 542–51.
Bloch, M. 1986. *From blessing to violence: history and ideology in the circumcision ritual of the Merina of Madagascar.* Cambridge: Univ. Press.
Brandewie, E. & S. Asten 1976. Northern Belunese (Timor) marriage and kinship: a study of symbols. *Philip. Q. Cult. Soc.* 4, 19–30.
Carlson, R. G. 1993. Hierarchy and the Haya divine kingship: a structural and symbolic reformulation of Frazer's thesis. *Am Ethnol.* 20, 312–35.
Cinatti, R. 1965. A Pescaria da Be-Malai: mito e rito. *Geographica* 1, 32–51.

Clamagirand, B. 1980. The social organization of the Ema of Timor. In *The flow of life: essays on Eastern Indonesia* (ed.) J.J. Fox. Cambridge, MA: Harvard Univ. Press.
Duarte, J. B. 1964. Barlaque. Seara 2, (N.S.) (3), 1–4.
_____. n.d. A nascente "Lulik" de "Corluli." Unpublished ms.
Durkheim, E. 1960 (1912) *Les formes élémentaires de la vie religieuse: le système totémique en Australie.* Paris: Presses Universitaires de France.
Evans-Pritchard, E. E. 1948. The divine kingship of the Shilluk of the Nilotic Sudan (Frazer Lecture 1948). Cambridge: Univ. Press. Reprinted in E.E. Evans-Pritchard *Essays in social anthropology.* London: Faber & Faber.
_____. 1956. *Nuer religion.* Oxford: Clarendon Press.
_____. 1964. Foreword. In *Sacrifice: its nature and function* [by] Henri Hubert and Marcel Mauss (trans.) W.D. Halls. Chicago: Univ. of Chicago Press.
_____. 1965. *Theories of primitive religion.* Oxford: Clarendon Press.
Feeley-Harnik, G. 1985. Issues in divine kingship. *Ann. Rev. Anthrop.* 14, 273–313.
Fox, J.J. 1980. Introduction. In *The flow of life: essays on Eastern Indonesia* (ed.) J.J. Fox. Cambridge, MA: Harvard Univ. Press.
Galey, J.-C. 1990. Introduction. In *Kingship and the kings* (ed.) J.-C. Galey. London: Harwood Academic.
Girard, R. 1992. *Violence and the sacred* (trans.) P. Gregory. Baltimore: Johns Hopkins Press.
Grijzen, H. J. 1904. Mededeelingen omtrent Beloe of Midden-Timor. In *Verhandelingen van het Bataviaasch Genootschap van Kunsten en Wetenschappen* 54. Batavia: Albrecht and Co., The Hague: Martinus Nijhoff.
Heusch, L. de. 1985. *Sacrifice in Africa: a structuralist approach* (trans.) L. O'Brien & A. Morton. Bloomington: Indiana Univ. Press.
_____. 1990a. Nkumi et Nkumu: la sacralisation du pouvoir chez les Mongo (Zaire). In L. de Heusch (ed.) 1990b.
_____. (ed.) 1990b. *Chefs et rois sacrés: systèmes de pensées en Afrique Noire.* Paris: L'Ecole Pratique des Hautes Etudes.
Hicks, D. 1984. *A maternal religion: the role of women in Tetum myth and ritual.* Dekalb: Center for Southeast Asian Studies, Northern Illinois University.
_____. 1992. Mythos und Ritual: eine Fallstudie aus Timor. In *Mythen im Kontext: ethnologische Perspektiven* (ed.) K.-H. Kohl. Frankfurt/Mainz: Qumran im Campus Verlag.
Hocart, A. M. 1954. *Social origins.* London: Watts.
_____. 1970. *Kings and councillors: a study in the comparative anatomy of human society* (ed.) R. Needham. Chicago: Univ. of Chicago Press.
Hubert, H. & M. Mauss 1898. Essai sur la nature et la fonction du sacrifice. *Année sociol.* 2, 29–138.
King, M. 1963. *Eden to paradise.* London: Hodder & Stoughton.
_____. 1965. Fishing rites at Be-Malai, Portuguese Timor. *Rec. S. Austr. Mus.* 15, 109–17.
Leach, E. 1969. *Genesis as myth and other essays.* London: Cape.

Lehmann, J. M. 1993. *Deconstructing Durkheim: a post-post-structuralist critique.* New York: Routledge.

Lévi-Strauss, C. 1958. *Anthropologie structurale.* Paris: Plon.

Lukes, S. 1985. *Emile Durkheim: his life and work; a critical and historical study.* Stanford: Univ. Press.

Muller, J.-C. 1980. *Le roi bouc émissaire: pouvoirs et rituels chez les Rukuba du Nigéria central.* Paris: L'Harmattan.

Needham, R. 1980. *Reconnaissances.* Toronto: Univ. Press.

Pascoal, E. 1967. *Alma de Timor vista na sua fantasia: lendas, fabulas e contos.* Braga: Barbosa & Xavier.

Renard-Clamagirand, B. 1982. *Marobo: une société Ema de Timor.* Paris: Centre National de la Recherche Scientifique.

Richards, A. I. 1969. Keeping the king divine. *Proc. R. anthrop. Inst.* 1968, 23–35.

Sahlins, M. 1983. Raw women, cooked men, and other "great things" of the Fiji Islands. In *The ethnography of cannibalism* (eds) P. Brown & D. Tuzin. Washington, DC: Society for Psychological Anthropology.

Seligman, C. G. 1934. *Egypt and Negro Africa.* London: G. Routledge & Sons.

Valeri, V. 1985. *Kingship and sacrifice: ritual and society in ancient Hawaii* (trans.) P. Wissing. Chicago: Univ. of Chicago Press.

Vaughan, J. H. 1987. A reconsideration of divine kingship. In *Explorations in African systems of thought* (eds) I. Karp & C.S. Bird. Bloomington: Indiana Univ. Press.

Vondra, J. G. 1968. *Timor journey.* Wellington/Auckland: A.H. & A.W. Reed.

Vroklage, B. A. C. 1952. *Ethnographie der Belu in Zentral-Timor.* Leiden: E.J. Brill.

Wortelboer, W. 1952. Monotheisme bij de Belu's op Timor? *Anthropos* 47, 290–2.

Young, M. W. 1966. The divine kingship of the Jukun: a re-evaluation of some theories. *Africa* 36, 135–53.

ASK YOURSELF

At the end of their reading, Metcalf and Huntington contrast Western attitudes regarding death with those regarding life, and they suggest that death is more "intangible" than life. What happens after death is unknowable—other than for those for whom a firm faith brings conviction—but does life have the same meaning for everyone? What are your own thoughts about life and death. Does life have a meaning? Does death have a purpose?

FURTHER READINGS

Hertz, Robert. "The Collective Representation of Death." In *Death and the Right Hand,* trans. Rodney and Claudia Needham. London: Cohen and West, 1960, pp. 27–86. Like Arnold van Gennep's book on rites of passage, this essay has served as the inspiration for innumerable studies of death in a range of societies.

Justice, Christopher. *Dying the Good Death: The Pilgrimage to Die in India's Holy City.* Albany: State University of New York Press. 1997. A study of beliefs regarding death and dying in the context of Hinduism as focused on the holy city of Benares (also known as Varanasi), which lies on the sacred river of the Ganges. Benares has some 1,500 temples, palaces, and shrines, and is a great center for pilgrimages.

Martin, Emily. "Gender and Ideological Differences in Representations of Life and Death." In *Death Ritual in Late Imperial and Modern China,* ed. James L. Watson and Evelyn D. Rawski. Berkeley: University of California Press, 1988, pp. 164–79. The argument that death in Chinese society is conceived differently according to gender is the theme of this provocative essay.

Lex, Barbara. "Voodoo Death: New Thoughts on an Old Explanation." *American Anthropologist* 76:818–823. 1974. Lex critically examines previous arguments (including that of Cannon), and offers her own explanation. She confirms Cannon's argument that suggestion is involved but contends that it is only one aspect of the complex emotional-interactional forms characteristic of human biology.

Metcalf, Peter, and Richard Huntington. *Celebrations of Death: The Anthropology of Mortuary Ritual,* 2nd ed. Cambridge: University of Cambridge Press, 1991.

This is the most useful of current cross-cultural studies of death yet published, in part because it includes especially acute insights into the work of van Gennep and Hertz.

Pearson, Mike Parker. *The Archaeology of Death and Burial.* Thrupp, Stroud, Gloucestershire, England: Sutton Publishing Limited for Texas A&M University Anthropology Series. 2000 (1999). Bringing a cultural anthropological perspective to bear upon archaeological research, the author discusses such topics as the body, status, gender, kinship, politics, and human experience within the context of death. His study offers a number of thought-provoking suggestions about how these two branches of learning can mutually engage their respective interests.

SUGGESTED VIDEOS

"Final Rest." The Beecher Funeral Home in upstate New York is the focus for this documentary, whose staff take us step by step through the process of arranging for one person's final rest. In following the decisions the deceased's survivors must make—among them the choice of casket, music, and prayer cards—this poignant video brings home the psychological and sociological reality of death, forcing viewers to contemplate their own attitudes to their own inevitable demise. 25 minutes; 1991; $295 (sale); $55 (rental); Filmakers Library, 124 East 40th Street, New York, NY 10016.

"Senhora Aparecida." In the Portuguese village of Senhora Aparecida, near Oporto, every 15th of August a procession is carried out in which penitents are carried in coffins to the local chapel. A Portuguese film crew arrives on the scene only to discover that the new, young priest who has taken over the parish has "modern" ideas about how religion should be practiced in the village. So he plans to abolish the ritual, and we see what happens! 55 minutes; 1996; $195 (sale); $50 (rental); Documentary Educational Resources, 101 Morse Street, Watertown, MA 02172.

"Good-bye Old Man." A last request of an Australian Aborigine, a member of the Tiwi tribe, was that a film be made of the bereavement ritual that would be carried out after he died. This film portrays his family's preparation of the event. Commentary by Thomas Woody Minipini, a participant. Filmmaker: David MacDougall. Color, 70 minutes, 1977. Film Officer, Royal Anthropological Institute (RAI), 50 Fitzroy Street, London W1P 5HS, United Kingdom.

The entry archway to the building where local members of the Maori population, in New Zealand, meet to discuss affairs and perform funeral services. It spotlights the belief in masculine procreative potential and the attention Maori religion gives to fertility and procreation—two universal themes in religion. Red is a Maori symbol for life. *Photo courtesy of Maxine Hicks*

CHAPTER 9

SEXUALITY AND GENDER

Sex exerts such a far-reaching influence upon human beings that the societies in which they live must find some accommodation with it. One accommodation society reaches with human sexuality is to put its own construction of gender on the biological differences between male and female, and as cultures vary, so, too, may their notions of gender. In this cultural construction of gender the biological differences between the two sexes may be fully acknowledged, and sexuality and gender converge. Or the natural differences may be minimized, in which case the cultural construction of sexuality may be pronounced. The pervasive role religion plays in society inescapably means that sexuality and gender find generous expression in ritual and belief.

Gender in religion can be expressed in straightforward fashion. A cosmos might be governed by a male deity or a female deity; or certain rituals will emphasize masculine or feminine interests. More on the complex side are metaphysical concerns involving life and death. The meaning of life may be embodied in sexual metaphor, with life said to flow from the creative union of male and female. Fertility, then, enters the equation, as noted in Chapter 8, and its counterpart, infertility, (see Chapter 9), and this binary contrast itself sets up the fundamental opposition between life and death.

In reconstituting the sexuality that nature has provided human beings, certain societies are not satisfied with two genders, and whatever the sexual attributes of individuals they permit biological females to identify themselves as culturally masculine, and biological males to identify themselves as culturally feminine. Such persons are known as *transsexuals,* and they enact social roles more usually played by the opposite sex. A transsexual may or may not be a *transvestite* (or *cross-dresser*), i.e., a person sexually stimulated by wearing clothing worn by the opposite sex, but whether this is the case or not, ritual is a common outlet for their sexual inclinations. Just as an ordinary person can become transformed into a potential shaman by experiencing a vision (Reading 5–3), so, too, among certain Native American tribes in traditional times, could a person become a *berdache*. A berdache was usually a male who had become a transvestite and transsexual, and enjoyed many of the same rights and duties as women. Berdaches were permitted to dress, style their hair, and speak like women and to cook, do needlework, and carry out other female activities. Another American tribe, the Mohave of California, traditionally allowed men to assume female gender (and vice versa) in a transformation ritual in the course of which the initiate changed names and put on fresh clothes appropriate to his new gender. So thorough was this transformation the persons involved could even marry someone of the opposite sex. Reading 9–3 furnishes us with a contemporary version of the berdache from India, male transvestites called *hijras.*

Comparative studies reveal a striking variability in the way in which religious beliefs blend with gender. Leonie J. Archer's article (Reading 6–3) has already alerted us to the ritual expression of the misogynistic trend in the Judaeo-Christian tradition, a prejudice Peggy Reeves Sanday (Reading 9–1) considers from a rather different angle. Sanday detects an obscured goddess lurking in the Judaeo-Christian tradition, under the trappings of the masculine deity, and in this she anticipates Reading 9–2, in which Eric Wolf describes the way in which the Virgin Mary has been elevated to the status of a goddess in Latin America. Femininity had a considerably less exalted status in the history of European witchcraft, however, as Stanislav Andreski (Reading 9–4) makes all too apparent. Andreski, a former professor of sociology at the University of Reading, in England, describes how sexual bias brought death to thousands of women the 15th, 16th, and 17th centuries. In Salem, for example, where the European bias against women continued in full force, of the 19 "witches" hanged, no fewer than 13 were women. Indeed, even if we move outside the European tradition we still find this prejudice. Although Zande witches are as likely to be men as women, the Nupe, Tallensi, Yoruba, Luvale, and many other African ethnic groups, routinely regard witchcraft as a feminine trait. In Southeast Asia, the Balinese have as their nightmarish symbol of evil Rangda the witch, who is an old woman.

If this association is as widespread as it might appear, why should the female sex tend to be the most vulnerable to accusations of victimizing others? Several plausible reasons have been suggested, but none entirely convincing. A structural-functional view, the most generally popular one, perhaps, is that to compensate for womens' relative lack of political influence and economic power, society implicitly foists illicit, clandestine mystical powers upon the female sex. Such power is not necessarily identified as witchcraft, but it often is. Women's inferior social status, it might be remarked, is also frequently cited as an explanation for the predominance of spirit possession among women in certain societies.

A psychological explanation for the association between witchcraft and women in New England was proposed by the historian John Putnam Demos (1983). His theory derives from Dorothy Dinnerstein's (1990) research into the origins of anti-female attitudes in Europe and North America. Dinnerstein sought the answer in child developmental psychology, and finds it in the fact that the infant's first experiences are entirely of and with its mother. Many of these experiences are positive: The mother creates the baby's sense of security and provides milk, caresses, and soothing noises. Some experiences, though, are negative: At times circumstances oblige the mother to withhold these delights and even so can never gratify her infant's every craving. Dependent on its mother for its very existence, the infant has no choice but to accede to her power, at the same time as it finds it impossible to entirely separate itself psychologically from her. Nor can the growing infant place its mother neatly into any niche in its emerging framework of human categories. So the mother is, and remains, unclassifiable. Here, though at the level of the individual, Dorothy Dinnerstein is echoing Mary Douglas's discussion of taboo and symbolic classification (Reading 2–4). As the infant develops into a child, it projects this quality of "unclassifiability" from the mother onto all women, and so by the time they have become adult, both men and women alike have come to invest the female sex with a quality that Dinnerstein calls the "magically formidable" qualities of all mothers. She identifies them as ambiguity, power, malevolence, and mysteriousness, qualities that Demos concludes were the very same ones that the New England puritans attributed to their witches.

Putnam returns to Dinnersteins' thesis to explain why New Englanders were less ready to stereotype males as witches. By the time an infant realizes the existence of what has up until then been a marginal figure, its father, it will have already passed the earlier, critical stage of developing self-awareness and will have grown completely accustomed to itself as an independent being. With its sense of individuality secured, Dinnerstein says, the infant is by now able to classify the second person in its life as an individual much like itself. Thus the figure of father is not perceived as at all ambiguous or mysterious, nor are there any unpleasant experiences to cast a shadow on him. He is no threat.

READING 9–1

EPILOGUE

Peggy Reeves Sanday

This is an inquiry into the manner in which religious ideas influence other collective representations. More precisely, it attempts to show how the privileged status of a male deity reinforces male domination in a particular tradition. That tradition is Judeo-Christianity. Peggy Reeves Sanday's thesis is that masculine dominance in Western societies is sustained by the Judaeo-Christian belief in a single male deity. Her argument is that the polytheistic beliefs of Mesopotamia privileged female divinities, but that subsequently Israel with its single masculine divinity, Yahweh, almost completely eradicated the Mesopotamian interest in goddesses. Neverthe-

Source: Peggy Reeves Sanday, "Epilogue," in *Female Power and Male Dominance: On the Origins of Sexual Inequality,* © Cambridge University Press 1981. Reprinted with the permission of Cambridge University Press.

less, she claims, a careful scrutiny of the Book of Genesis indicates that some traces of a belief in female deities persists, even though the supreme deity is masculine.

The strength of this reading lies in the scholarly care with which the author has analyzed the Scriptures and the skill with which she marshals her facts in developing her argument. In support of it she discloses the diachronic process by which the male divinity came to replace a pre-existing female divinity during biblical times and so produce the gender pattern discernible today. Sanday has undoubtedly identified a connection, but her cause-and-effect argument is open to the usual "chicken-and-egg" criticism. How do we know it was not gender bias that brought about the triumph of the male god instead of the other way around? Then again, how does her assumption that Christianity elevates a male god over a female one handle the ethnographic evidence given by such modern female goddesses in Christian "practical religion" as the Virgin of Guadalupe (see Reading 9–2)?

My goal in these last few pages is to dwell briefly on the genesis of two of the guiding symbols of Western male dominance—the patriarchal, decidedly masculine God and the sexual, inferior female who tempts the male from the path of righteousness. The story that I reconstructed includes a familiar theme: Collective sentiments centering on maleness and masculine symbols acquire coercive power by defining females as the "other" and feminine symbols as evil.

No doubt, many believe that the secularized society in which we live has liberated us from the directive power of such symbols. I disagree. Feminist theologian Carol P. Christ states the argument clearly. Symbols associated with the religious rituals of birth, marriage, and death—rituals we all attend—"cannot fail to affect the deep or unconscious structures of the mind of even a person who has rejected these symbolisms on a conscious level—especially if the person is under stress." She continues: "Religions centered on the worship of a male God create 'moods' and 'motivations' that keep women in a state of psychological dependence on men and male authority." A woman can never have her full sexual identity affirmed as being in the image and likeness of God, an experience freely available to every man and boy of her culture.[1]

We have little information on how boys and girls are affected by prevailing religious symbols. My experience in observing my son and daughter has been instructive. Upon reading the Biblical passage "So God created man in his own image, in the image of God he created him; male and female he created them" (Genesis 1:27),[2] my son exclaimed: "How could God have created a female in his own image if God was male?" His solution to this puzzle is not unlike that of the Gnostic Christians, discussed in the last section of this chapter. "Obviously, God must have been part female in order to have created male and female in his own image," my son declared. So far, my daughter has shown no interest in the question of who God is. Her personal identity is tied up with symbols of her own making: teddy bears, sunshine, and flowers. Having abandoned public symbols of femininity, she seems quite free to inform teachers who do not know better that fourth-grade girls should be treated no differently than fourth-grade boys.

To some extent all of us look to symbol systems to discover how to behave. Personal identities are inextricably linked with social form. Religious symbols and social form are part of the same underlying blueprint. Though we may reject the messages implied by the former, we cannot escape being guided by the latter.

Today, feminists seek to change the blueprint. Feminist theologians hope to change the guiding sacred symbols, other feminists work for change in the secular domain. Both seek to change the script that directs our behavior. In these last few pages, I want to look at the historic origins of the sacred part of this script. The story I have pieced together focuses on a narrow historical issue: the fate of goddess worship in Biblical popular culture and early Christianity.

THE GODDESS AND YAHWEH CULTS IN CANAAN

When the semi-nomadic Hebrew tribes entered Canaan *ca.* 1300 B.C., they brought Yahweh, origi-nally a tribal god who symbolized the collective identity of the Judeans. In Canaan, the Hebrews worshipped Yahweh as well as Canaanite gods and goddesses. The priests of the Yahweh cult argued that "awhoring after foreign gods" brought Yahweh's wrath upon the people and caused the destruction of Hebrew cities in Canaan.[3] For example, Jeremiah claimed that the "God of Israel" had said to him:

You have seen all the evil that I brought upon Jerusalem and upon all the cities of Judah. Behold, this day they are a desolation, and no one dwells in them, because of the wickedness which they committed, provoking me to anger, in that they went to burn incense and serve other gods that they knew not, neither they, nor you, nor your fathers (Jeremiah 44:1–3).

One of the "gods" worshipped by the Hebrew people was a goddess called the "Queen of Heaven." When Jeremiah brought the message of the Lord's wrath to Judean refugees in Egypt, they answered that it was the Queen of Heaven, not Yahweh, upon whom they depended for prosperity and to whom they offered worship. In response to Jeremiah's message from the Lord, they countered:

As for the word which you have spoken to us in the name of the Lord, we will not listen to you. But we will do everything that we have vowed, burn incense to the queen of heaven and pour out libations to her, as we did, both we and our fathers, our kings and our princes, in the cities of Judah and in the streets of Jerusalem; for then we had plenty of food and prospered, and saw no evil. But since we left off burning incense to the queen of heaven and pouring our libations to her, we have lacked everything and have been consumed by the sword and by famine (Jeremiah 44:16–18).

That "Queen of Heaven" was modeled after one of the most famous and powerful of the ancient Near Eastern goddesses, Inanna, the tutelary deity of a Sumerian city–state. The Sumerians flourished in southern Babylonia from the beginning of the fourth to the end of the third millenium B.C.[4] They were a migrating people who came from another land and settled on the Tigris–Euphrates plain in an area inhabited by an indigenous agricultural people and by warlike Semitic nomads who posed a constant threat to Sumerian political stability. The Tigris–Euphrates plain was a hot, arid, barren land with "the hand of God against it." The Sumerians almost literally built their civilization out of dust and clay, because there was nothing else there except the waters of the Tigris–Euphrates, which were channeled into the arid fields, turning Sumer into "a veritable Garden of Eden."[5]

Little is known about the secular power of women in Sumerian culture. In religion, however, female deities were venerated and worshipped from the beginning to the end of Sumer's existence. The Sumerian Inanna, whose exploits and deeds were recorded in many of the Sumerian epic tales and whose image is left in Sumerian art, provided the prototype for the goddess who was to play a central role in the religious ritual and popular consciousness of all ancient Near Eastern peoples.[6] She is variously described as "the queen of heaven, the goddess of light and love"; "the ambitious, aggressive, demanding goddess of love . . . and war"; and "the tutelary deity of Erech . . . a goddess who throughout Sumerian history was deemed to be the deity primarily responsible for sexual love, fertility, and procreation . . ."[7]

Progress, rivalry, and superiority are native to the philosophy and psychology of the Near East.[8] All of these attributes are reflected in Inanna's personality. In many ways she is the symbol of the Sumerian personality "writ large." The intense rivalry between the Sumerian city–states is found in the relationship between Inanna and her spouse as well as between numerous Sumerian male and female deities. In the epic tales Inanna is depicted as struggling to maintain superiority over a competitive husband or a jealous sister. The contrast between the natural aridity of the Sumerian desert and the lushness created by irrigation is repeated in the duality of Inanna's personality. She is variously represented as a union of opposites: of good and evil, of life giving and life taking, of boundless rage and all-embracing love.

Inanna did not disappear with the fall of Sumerian civilization. Though her name was changed, her character remained in the form of Ishtar of Akkad and Anath of Canaan.[9] Following their penetration of Canaan, the Hebrew tribes worshipped Anath and Asherah, believed to be Anath's mother. Asherah was the chief goddess of the Canaanite pantheon. She figured prominently as the wife of El, the chief god. Her full name was Asherah of the Sea, suggesting that her domain was the sea. Her husband's domain was heaven. She was referred to also as "Goddess" and "Progenitress of the Gods." Her children included Baal as well as Anath.[10]

Anath exhibits many features in common with Inanna. She is described as the goddess of "love and war, virginal and yet wanton, amorous and yet given to uncontrollable outbursts of rage and appalling acts of cruelty."[11] Anath is not mentioned by name in the Bible. However, the "Queen of Heaven" referred to in Jeremiah (44:15–19) is believed to be Anath. Anath may also be the same as the goddess Astarte who is mentioned by name in the Bible.[12]

Archeological evidence leaves no doubt of the importance of goddess worship among the Canaanite Hebrews. The Canaanite fertility cults attracted the infiltrating Israelite tribes for centuries. Even in Jerusalem, the center of the worship of Yahweh, a sanctuary of one of the Canaanite cults was found containing hundreds of the mother goddess figurines.[13]

The Hebrews entered into Canaan, *ca.* 1350 B.C., as animal pastoralists and changed from a life of semi-nomadism to sedentary farming. Their adoption of agriculture meant that they had to establish a relationship with the soil. They became dependent upon rainfall and on the rotation of the seasons for crops and concerned about fertility—a concern basic to the Canaanite religion of Baal and his consort Anath.

The purpose of the eroticized Canaanite religion was to preserve and enhance the fertility upon which people were dependent for their existence in the precarious environment of the Fertile Crescent. This religion catered to the human desire for security by seeking to control the gods in the interest of human well-being. As such, this religion was dia-metrically opposed to the cult of Yahweh, which the Judean tribes brought from Egypt.

The development of the Yahweh cult among the Hebrews was closely connected with the political ascendency of Moses and the migration of the Hebrews from Egypt. Before the Exodus from Egypt, Yahweh was the tribal god of the Judeans, one of the Hebrew tribes. The cult of Yahweh was extended in Egypt to include other Hebraic tribes absorbed by Judah.

One of the members of the absorbed tribes was Moses, who became an ardent protagonist of Yahweh.[14] Moses was both a religious and political leader. He revealed Yahweh to his people as a redeeming power who makes exclusive, ethical demands on man's will. At the same time, through the mechanism of the covenant, Moses united Yahweh and the Judean tribes into a single ethical community.

When the Israelites entered Canaan, only Judah, the confederacy that settled in the south, had adopted Yahweh. Judah came to dominate all the Hebrew tribes in Canaan during the time of David in response to the threat of the Philistines, who invaded Canaan after the coming of the Israelite tribes. Yahweh then became the god of all Israel. Until then the Hebraic tribes who had settled in the northern region of Canaan thought of Yahwism as a southern cult—specifically, a Judean cult—rather recently come to Israel, and intimately associated with Moses.[15]

The expansion of Yahwism did not bring about the end of goddess worship among the Hebrews. Goddesses fulfilled different needs than did Yahweh and, hence, could be strictly separated. Those who believed in the goddesses saw no incompatibility between the control exercised by the goddesses over certain areas of human life and nature and the rule Yahweh exercised over others.[16]

This is another example of an outer-oriented people embracing an inner orientation. Like the Dahomeans, the Hebrews entered a new land as an animal-oriented people and conquered a group of indigenous agriculturalists. Agriculture made the Hebrews dependent on their environment in a new

way. If, as so often is the case, women were the main cultivators, one can imagine Hebrew women being attracted to the fertility cults both because they accorded women a special place and because they guaranteed agricultural success. Like the Dahomeans, the Hebrews probably saw no reason for assimilating different cult figures.

Eventually, however, the inherent conflict between the Yahwist and the fertility cults proved too great for both to survive. The people of Israel were forced to resolve a basic question: Was the meaning of human life in Canaan to be disclosed in relation to divine powers within nature or in relation to the Lord of history?[17] This question was not resolved in practice for centuries. In theory, however, it was resolved very early by the Hebrew prophets who, like Moses, sought to form the Hebrew tribes into one social body, united by one set of laws, and led by one religious figure—the Lord God.

ADAM AND EVE: MIGRATING MEN AND FOREIGN GODDESSES

Many biblical stories repeat the theme of a vengeful, jealous god who violently punishes his people for "awhoring after foreign gods." The most widely known of the Hebrew creation stories, the story of Adam and Eve in the Garden of Eden, does not, at least on the surface, depict the wrath of God as violent. Rather, this story appears to tell of man's vulnerability and subordination to a superior being. A close reading, however, suggests that it contains themes that resolve the conflict between Yahwism and goddess worship.

The Garden of Eden story offers a prologue to what is known as the Yahwist epic, the earliest of the four major documents that make up the Pentateuch, or the "Five Books of Moses."[18] The Yahwist is the name given to a Judean prophet who lived during the reign of Solomon (ca. 961–922 B.C.).[19] This was a crucial period in Israel's history, a time when the disparate Hebrew tribes had achieved unification. Solomon, the son of David, had built a great colonial empire. He is also said to have had 700 wives and 300 concubines. He used these unions to establish close political and cultural ties with surrounding peoples. Solomon allowed his wives to practice their native religion, going so far as to build special shrines for them in Jerusalem, his capital city. Although Solomon probably regarded himself as a loyal worshipper of Yahweh, his broad-minded hospitality led him to incorporate elements of the Baalist religion in his Mosaic heritage.

The age of Solomon was simply another chapter in a long-standing conflict between Mosaic faith and surrounding religions. It was not Yahweh's intention that Israel should become a great nation in the sense of a vast colonial empire. Rather, Israel was to remain separated from other nations by the covenant calling. But it was difficult to maintain faithfulness to the Mosaic tradition when the gods of the Fertile Crescent made irresistible claims upon men's lives. Incited by expansion and success, the tendency during Solomon's reign was toward tolerance and compromise. To draw Israel back to her distinctive faith, to keep this faith from falling into oblivion among the religions of the Fertile Crescent, Yahweh's uncompromising, jealous demand for absolute allegiance was essential.[20]

In addition to the threats from without, ancient antagonisms between the northern and southern tribes threatened to weaken if not destroy the Mosaic tradition. Although united by David, the northern and southern kingdoms split apart immediately after Solomon's death in 925 B.C.[21] In this climate of great promise and great threat, the prophet who scholars call the Yahwist, or J, emerged as the champion of the Mosaic faith. The Yahwist saw his mission as one of promulgating the unity of the Hebrew people by recording their history in a manner that would give literary expression to the Mosaic tradition. As a Judean, the Yahwist must have been a loyal follower of Yahweh. His purpose "was to confess Israel's faith in Yahweh, whose saving deeds had been manifested in Israel's history."[22] The Yahwist was mainly interested in the events of the Exodus and the struggles of Israel to become a nation in Canaan.

Drawing on traditions appropriated by Israel from Canaanite cult legends, some of which are traceable to Sumerian prototypes, the Yahwist recast Canaanite traditions in Mosaic terms. Stories that were originally Canaanitish were simply made Israelitish. Religious tales originally connected with the Canaanite god Baal, the goddess Anath, or the Babylonia god Marduk and the goddess Tiamat were told of Yahweh.[23] In the Yahwist epic Yahweh appears throughout as the one great God, the Creator, the only God for Israel. He controls the forces of nature and the forces of history. He is a moral God who, in the words of one Biblical scholar, "demands righteousness, rewards faith and kindness, innocence and unselfishness, but punishes wickedness and oppression." In return for making Israel "a great and prosperous nation," Yahweh demands complete loyalty.[24]

The Garden of Eden story captures the Mosaic meaning of the Exodus from Egypt and the entrance into Canaan. Within the context of paradise, the Yahwist spells out the consequences for those who refuse to acknowledge the sovereignty of their creator and savior in their new land. The motifs of the story, though they are drawn from a wide range of ancient Near Eastern oral and literary traditions, are woven by the Yahwist so as to impress on men's minds the debt they owe to their creator.

The events of the Garden of Eden story begin in a desert environment in which there was no man to till the ground:

In the day that the Lord God made the earth and the heavens, when no plant of the field was yet in the earth and no herb of the field had yet sprung up—for the Lord God had not caused it to rain upon the earth, and there was no man to till the ground (Genesis 2:5).

This description is consonant with the Hebrew's sojourn in the Sinai desert, where water was scarce, there was no food, and existence was precarious. Because they were not agriculturalists but pastoral nomads at the time, there literally was no man to till the ground.

Next in the story there is a shift to an oasis environment, in which man is formed from the ground and becomes a living being: "But a mist went up from the earth and watered the whole face of the ground—then the Lord God formed man of dust from the ground, and breathed into his nostrils the breath of life; and man became a living being" (Genesis 2:6–7). After their sojourn in the Sinai Desert, Moses leads his people to the oasis of Sinai, which would be like a place where water would come from the ground as "a mist went up from the earth." It is at the oasis of Sinai where Moses establishes a covenant with Yahweh, thereby forming Israel as a nation. Thus, the theme of forming man from the dust can have two meanings. It may imply the formation of Israel as a nation and it may signify the new bond the Hebrews were soon to forge between man and earth as agriculturalists in Canaan.

The following is a description of the land where the Lord God puts the man he has formed:

> And the Lord God planted a garden in Eden, in the east; and there he put the man whom he had formed. And out of the ground the Lord God made to grow every tree that is pleasant to the sight and good for food, the tree of life also in the midst of the garden, and the tree of the knowledge of good and evil (Genesis 2:8–9).

The garden "in the east" is reminiscent of the "land flowing with milk and honey," which the Lord gave to his chosen people after he had delivered them from bondage and bound them to follow his laws. The "tree of the knowledge of good and evil" symbolizes the Canaanite goddess Asherah, whose places of worship were marked by trees and whose image was frequently carved from a trunklike form.[25] The union of good and evil in the goddess symbol is like the union of these qualities in the Sumerian Inanna and the Canaanite Anath.

Upon putting Adam in the Garden, the Lord God commanded him, "You may freely eat of every tree in the garden; but of the tree of knowledge of good and evil you shall not eat, for in the day that you eat of it you shall die" (Genesis 2:16–17). The Hebrew tribes were called upon to be God's servants in exchange for the land of Canaan; so when Adam is transferred to the Garden of Eden, his is called to a state of service to God. He is forbidden to partake of the goddess symbol—the tree of knowledge of

good and evil. The act of eating in this passage has been frequently equated with sexuality. In fact, ritual sex was common in sacred Canaanite shrines marked by the tree symbol of the goddess. Thus, eating of the fruit suggests engaging in sexual intercourse at a sacred shrine.

Because the man is alone in this new realm, the Lord God makes a "helper fit for him" (Genesis 2:18). She is called "Woman, because she was taken out of Man" (Genesis 2:23). Making Eve out of Adam's rib is tantamount to declaring that a proper mate is to be taken from within the man's culture. This is consonant with the Old Testament assertion that the land of Palestine was a gift to the pure-blood descendants of Israel. The people of Israel were not supposed to marry foreign women; they were to be a people of pure religion, living in isolation in their Promised Land.[26] Neither in fantasy nor in reality, however, did the Jews follow these prescriptions.

The identity of Eve presents something of an enigma. She may represent Canaanite women married to Hebrew men, who introduced their husbands to the worship of foreign gods and goddesses. Another possibility is that Hebrew women and not men were attracted to the foreign religion because women held an inferior role in the Yahweh cult.[27] Both possibilities place women in the position of enticing men away from the cult of Yahweh.

The fall from grace involves Eve and two ancient Canaanite sacred symbols, the serpent and the tree. When the serpent entices Eve to eat of the forbidden fruit, it says: "For God knows that when you eat of it your eyes will be opened, and you will be like God, knowing good and evil" (Genesis 3:5). Participation in the Canaanite religion meant being like God. Ritual sex was practiced as a form of worship. Male and female sacred prostitutes were present at the shrines and the gods were worshipped in sexual rites. Divine powers were disclosed in the mystery of fertility. The purpose of religion was to preserve and enhance the fertility upon which people depended for their existence. Sacred rites were performed to control the gods in the interest of human well-being.[28]

The tension between being "like" God and serving God is dramatically resolved in the Garden of Eden. God's anger, his jealousy, and his power are mightily expressed, first toward the serpent, then toward Eve, and finally toward Adam. The serpent is reduced to biting the dust and, curiously, God puts enmity between the serpent and Eve—between his seed and her seed (Genesis 3:15)—suggesting that the serpent also represents Canaanite men. Both Adam and Eve are made servants to the will of God. Both are forced out of the Garden (and consequently out of Canaanite sacred sanctuaries) to a life of pain, sorrow, and toil. Lest they be drawn back to their old ways, God installs at the east of the Garden of Eden "the cherubim, and a flaming sword which turned every way, to guard the way to the tree of life" (Genesis 4:24).

And so at the level of allegory and the piling up of metaphors, the competing pulls of two powerful religions, both serving the needs of the Hebrews in Canaan, are resolved. These two religions maintained a relative balance as long as the Hebrews did not face destruction from foreign oppressors. The threat from their borders reminded them that they had turned from their leader. To recoup their forces, they admitted their fall from the covenant pact and rationalized it by shifting the blame onto the practice of Canaanite fertility rites by Hebrews. To control their tendencies in non-Yahwistic directions, the Hebrew prophets attempted to submerge all reference to fertility and to other deities in the books that became their law.

IN GOD'S IMAGE

The sex-role plan codified in the Garden of Eden story is one with which we are all familiar. Less well known is the egalitarian relationship between the sexes implicit in the first chapter of Genesis. Having created all else:

Then God said, "Let us make man in our image, after our likeness; and let them have dominion over the fish of the sea, and over the birds of the air, and over the cattle, and over all the earth, and over every creeping thing that creeps upon the earth. So God created man in his own image, in the image of God he created him; male and female he created them (Genesis 1:26–7).

Chapter 1 of Genesis is attributed to the Priestly Writer (P), whose document (referred to as the Priestly Code) was written during and after the Jewish exile in Babylonia (ca. 597–538 B.C.) and adopted later in Jerusalem. The Priestly Writer, like the Yahwist, was concerned with writing a history of God's dealings with his people, beginning—as had the Yahwist—with creation. P incorporated the Yahwist epic (as well as the Epic of the Northern Kingdom attributed to E) into his comprehensive presentation, which explains why the Yahwist version of creation follows P's version.[29]

Scholars have commented on the resemblance between P's version of creation and the Babylonian creation myth. The Babylonian "Genesis" begins when nothing except the divine parents, Apsu and Tiamat, and their son Mammu existed. Apsu was the primeval sweetwater ocean, Tiamat was the saltwater ocean, and Mammu probably represented the mist rising from the two bodies of water. P's version of creation begins when "the earth was without form and void, and darkness was upon the face of the deep" (Genesis 1:2). The word for deep in the Hebrew text is *tchôm,* which scholars say is the Hebrew translation of *ti⁻amat,* which also means watery deep. The theme of "the Spirit of God . . . moving over the face of the waters" (Genesis 1:2) could refer to Apsu, who mingles his waters with those of Tiamat to beget heaven and earth in the Babylonian tale.[30] P's exclusion of the Babylonian divine figures as such from his version of creation is explained by the Hebrew emphasis on monotheism.

Whereas the Babylonian "Genesis" describes warfare and conflict between the divine parents and their offspring, a sense of peace and order prevails in the Priestly account. In Genesis, male and female are created "in our image" (suggesting divine parents) and both sexes are given dominion "over every living thing" (Genesis 1:27–8). Humans and animals alike are given only vegetable food to eat, suggesting that bloodshed and slaughter are not part of the divine plan.[31] Completing this sense of peace and order is the last verse, which ends with the formula: "And God saw everything that he had made, and behold, it was very good" (Genesis 1:31).

Life for the Judean exiles in Babylon was prosperous. Even after the Jews were able to return to Judah, many preferred to stay on in Babylonia. In Babylonia the Jews became active in agriculture as well as in a variety of lucrative trades. Since Babylonia was a much richer country than Judea, the economic position of the Babylonian Jews was considerably better than that of their Judean counterparts.[32]

Within this climate, the sense of belonging to the covenant community flourished rather than weakened. The exiles, many of whom were priests, preserved the sacred writings they had brought with them from Jerusalem. The people continued to look to the priests for exposition of Israel's faith.

The exile was a time for consolidating Israel's history. The Priestly Writer fused together old traditions, including the Yahwist epic, and added his own material. In this manner, the story of Israel was presented in full as a comprehensive unity.

THE EARLY CHRISTIANS

The early Christians recognized both the utopia described in the Priestly version of creation and the divinely ordained chain of authority described in the Yahwist version. Christians known as the "Gnostics" preferred the Priestly version; those called "orthodox" emphasized the Yahwist version.[33] Gnostic texts "abound in feminine symbolism" applied to God. This symbolism is derived from Biblical texts in some instances and is reminiscent of ancient Near Eastern goddess symbols in others. For example, several Gnostic theologians concluded from their interpretation of Genesis 1:26–7 that God is dyadic ("Let us make humanity") and that "humanity, which was formed according to the image and likeness of God (Father and Mother) was masculo-feminine."[34]

Another Gnostic text (1 of the 52 found in 1945 in the Upper Egyptian desert near the town of Nag Hammadi) is written in the words of a feminine divine whose dualistic nature recalls the Sumerian Inanna and the Canaanite Anath. She says:

> I am the first and the last. I am the honored one and the scorned one. I am the whore, and the holy one. I am the wife and the virgin. I am (the mother) and the daughter . . . I am she whose wedding is great, and I have not taken a husband . . . I am knowledge, and ignorance . . . I am shameless; I am ashamed. I am strength, and I am fear . . . I am foolish, and I am wise . . . I am godless, and I am one whose God is great (Thunder, Perfect Mind 13.16–16.25).[35]

Like Hebrew prophets, the orthodox Christians described God in monistic, masculine, and authoritarian terms. These Christians rejected Gnostic writings for their select list of 26 that comprise the New Testament collection. By the time their selection process was concluded (ca. A.D. 200), "virtually all the feminine imagery for God (along with any suggestion of an androgynous human creation) had disappeared from 'orthodox' Christian tradition."[36] Orthodox Christians looked to Genesis 2 for their endorsement of the domination of women. For example, in the pseudo-Pauline letter to Timothy, we read:

Let a woman learn in silence with full submissiveness. I do not allow any woman to teach or to exercise authority over a man; she is to remain silent, for Adam was formed first, then Eve and furthermore, Adam was not deceived, but the woman was utterly seduced and came into sin . . ." (2 Timothy 2:11–14).[37]

The orthodox version of the life of Christ also places women in a subordinate role. In sharp contrast, women play a central role in Gnostic accounts. For example, The Gospel of Philip (one of the Nag Hammadi texts) tells of the rivalry between the male disciples and Mary Magdalene because she is first among the Savior's companions. Christ, it is said:

> (loved) her more than (all) the disciples and used to kiss her (often) on her (mouth). The rest of (the disciples were offended) by it . . . They said to him, "Why do you love her more than all of us?" The Savior answered and said to them, "Why do I not love you as much as (I love) her?" (63.32–64.5).[38]

Another text, The Dialogue of the Savior, identifies Mary Magdalene as one of three disciples chosen to receive special teaching. This text singles Mary out for praise because "she spoke as a woman who knew the All" (139:12–13).[39]

Jealousy and misogyny are traits that Gnostic writers ascribe to the Jewish God and to the disciple Peter. One Gnostic author says that the masculine God of Israel is a jealous God who, after his Mother had departed, declared: "I am a jealous God, and besides me there is no one." The author of The Apocryphon of John interprets this statement to mean that there is more than one God. "For," this author explains, "if there were no other one, of whom would he be jealous" (13.8–14).[40]

The author of The Gospel of Mary alludes to Peter's jealous feelings toward Mary because of her position among the disciples. For example, in response to the disciples' eagerness to listen to what Mary could tell them about the Lord after the Crucifixion, the infuriated Peter asks: "Did he really speak privately with a woman, (and) not openly to us? Are we to turn about and all listen to her? Did he prefer her to us?" (17.18–18.15). In another text, Mary says to Jesus that she dares not speak freely because "Peter makes me hesitate; I am afraid of him, because he hates the female race" (Pistis Sophia 36.71).[41]

Many Gnostic communities were egalitarian in structure. According to Irenaeus, the Bishop of Lyon (ca. 180), who wrote polemics denouncing them as heretics, the Gnostics—male and female together—decided by lot who would take the role of priest, offer the sacrament, act as bishop, read the Scriptures for worship, and address the group as a prophet. Such practices prompted the North African theologian Tertullian (ca. 190) to say: "Those women among the heretics . . . teach, they engage in discussion; they exorcise; they cure," they may even baptize and act as bishops![42]

Orthodox Christians organized themselves into a strict order of ranks—bishops, priests, deacons, laity. The bishop acted as a "monarch," disciplinarian, and judge over the laity. This dominance—subordination relationship also extended to the rela-

tionship between the sexes. By the late second century, Elaine Pagels says, "Orthodox Christians came to accept the domination of men over women as the proper, God-given order—not only for the human race, but also for the Christian churches."[43] In his letter to the disorderly Corinthian community, the apostle Paul reminds the people of the divinely ordained chain of authority. He says: "But I want you to understand that the head of every man is Christ, the head of woman is her husband, and the head of Christ is God" (1 Corinthians 11:3).

The Gnostics criticized the authoritarian structure of the orthodox church. Thinking of themselves as "children of the Father" who joined together as equals, "enjoying mutual love, spontaneously helping one another," Gnostics referred to "ordinary Christians" as offspring of the "demiurge" who "wanted to command one another, out-rivaling one another in their empty ambition."[44] Throughout the early Christian period, orthodox Christian leaders (all of whom were male) worked to suppress Gnostic teaching. Gnostics were referred to as "agents of Satan," "heretics," "worldly," "without authority," and "without discipline."[45]

The bishops mounted a prolonged campaign against heresy. The climate of the times was one in which might determined right. By the fourth century, when Christianity became an officially approved religion, the orthodox bishops, who had previously been persecuted by the police, took command of them. They burned copies of books denounced as heretical and treated possession of such books as a criminal offense. Fortunately, someone in Upper Egypt, possibly a monk from a nearby monastery, hid the banned books to protect them from destruction. The books remained buried for some 1,600 years until discovered in 1945 by an Arab peasant.[46]

The forces that favored the ascendancy of the orthodox pattern and the suppression of the Gnostic pattern repeat a familiar theme—male dominance is endorsed in a climate of social stress and competition by populations that have adopted male religious symbolism. As the Israelites sought to preserve the integrity of their masculine God and, hence, themselves in the face of adversity in Canaan, the orthodox Christians fought to establish their church in the face of religious persecution. Stories about the martyrs were circulated widely among the orthodox communities to warn all Christians of their common danger and to strengthen the communities internally and in relation to one another.[47]

The orthodox Christian church gained strength from the death of its members. Tertullian boasted to the Roman prosecutor that "the oftener we are mown down by you, the more we grow in numbers: the blood of the Christians is seed!"[48] When Ignatius, Bishop of Antioch and a great opponent of heresy, was condemned, he embraced the death sentence with joyful exultation. He saw in it an opportunity to "imitate the passion of my God." Writing to the Christians in Rome, Ignatius said: "Allow me to be eaten by the beasts, through whom I can attain to God." Ignatius was outraged at the Gnostic belief that since Christ was a spiritual being, he only appeared to suffer and die. If Christ's "suffering was only an appearance," Ignatius said, "then why am I a prisoner, and why do I long to fight with the wild beasts? In that case, I am dying in vain."[49] Clearly, Ignatius did not die in vain. The question before us now is: Did the Gnostic Christians live in vain?

Gnostic theology and Hebrew goddess worship treat female power as part of the God-given order. The religious symbols found in these traditions create "moods" and "motivations" encouraging psychological independence and reciprocity between the sexes. These symbols have an obvious appeal for those who are unable to accept a dominance–subordination relationship between the sexes. Today, after some 2,000 years of relative obscurity, female supernatural symbols are resurfacing as women seek new guideposts. Beaten down by men, women who have had "enuf" cry out in a contemporary play, "I found God in myself and I loved her fiercely."[50] A new theology is emerging that focuses on birth, maternity, and union with nature as religious experiences. The resurrection of goddess symbols by contemporary feminists shows, once again, that people seek to align sacred and secular sex-role plans.

The seeds of sexual equality and male dominance existed from the beginning of written history in the Near East. Populations jostling each other for power strengthened domination by males and weakened sexual equality. The cultural configuration underlying male dominance provides the core values by which most of us live and think. However, the idea of sexual equality and female power was not completely obliterated from the Western consciousness. Throughout the centuries these ideas have remained, clothed in the imagery of art and literature, to remind us of other possibilities.

The inclusion of other possibilities, no matter how buried these may be, is one of the reasons that Judaism and Christianity have survived as great traditions. If a people can find alternatives within their cultural tradition enabling them to meet current exigencies, they are strengthened and so is their culture. Today's exigencies suggest that we may have taken the domination of nature too far. As a young feminist said to me, we are experiencing a backlash from nature. Pollution and the depletion of natural resources, together with the knowledge that the technology of male dominance has given us the wherewithal to destroy all life on earth, have created a different kind of stress. The ethic that sanctions control and dominion is now the problem, not the solution. Our hopes for social survival no longer rest on domination but on harmonizing competing forces.

ENDNOTES

1. See Carol P. Christ (1979:273–87).
2. All Biblical quotes are taken from *The New Oxford Annotated Bible* (1973).
3. The phrase "awhoring after foreign gods" is attributed by Patai (1967:278) to the Biblical authors.
4. Kramer (1961:vii–viii).
5. Kramer (1957:71).
6. Patai (1967:187).
7. Kramer (1961:86; 1963:153, 140).
8. Kramer (1961:74–5).
9. Patai (1967:187, 278).
10. Ibid., pp. 32–3.

11. Ibid., p. 61.
12. Ibid., pp. 54, 58.
13. Kenyon (1978:76); see also Patai (1967:60).
14. Meek (1960: 116–17).
15. Ibid., p. 117.
16. Patai (1967:271).
17. See Anderson (1975:136–64) on "The Struggle between Faith and Culture"; see Simpson (1952c:441–2).
18. See The New Oxford Annotated Bible (1973:xxvii). See also Anderson (1975:207).
19. See discussion of J1 and J2 documents in Simpson (1952c:441–8) and of JEDP documents in Simpson (1952b: 194–200).
20. Anderson (1975:194–7).
21. Kenyon (1978:67).
22. Anderson (1975:208).
23. Bewer (1933:60).
24. Ibid., p. 71.
25. Patai (1967:34–43).
26. See Leach on "The Legitimacy of Solomon" in Lane (1970: 248–92).
27. See *The New Oxford Annotated Bible* (1973:972) for a comment on the attraction of women to the worship of the "Queen of Heaven."
28. Anderson (1975:146).
29. Ibid., pp. 207, 422–36.
30. See Simpson (1952c:450) for similarities between the Babylonian creation myth and Chapter 1 of Genesis.
31. For a commentary on the meaning of peace in Chapter 1 of Genesis, see Simpson (1952a:487) and Von Rad (1961:59).
32. Patai (1971:13–14).
33. The description of competing sex-role plans among the early Christians in this section uses information presented by Elaine Pagels (1976, 1979) in her analysis of the Jewish and Christian Gnostic texts discovered in 1945 by an Arab peasant in Upper Egypt and believed to be dated the first and second centuries A.D. For the texts themselves see The Nag Hammadi Library (1977).
34. Pagels (1979:56).
35. Ibid., pp. 55–6.
36. Pagels (1976:298–9).
37. Ibid., p. 303.
38. Pagels (1979:64).
39. Ibid.
40. Ibid., p. 58.
41. Ibid., p. 65.
42. Ibid., p. 42. According to Pagels (1979:66), "gnostics were not unanimous in affirming the equality of women—nor were the orthodox unanimous in denigrating them." Clement of Alexandria (ca. 180), Pagels says, demonstrated "that even orthodox Christians could affirm the feminine in God—and the active participation of women." Most Christians, however, adopted the position of Clement's contemporary, Tertullian, who wrote: "It is not permitted for a woman to speak in the church, nor is it permitted for her to teach, nor to baptize, nor to offer (the eucharist), nor to claim for herself a share in any masculine function—least of all, in priestly office" (ibid., pp. 68–9).
43. Pagels (1976.301–2).
44. Pagels (1979:40–1).

45. Ibid., p. 42.
46. Pagels (1979:xviii–xix). See pages xiii–xvii for an account of the discovery of the texts and their eventual publication in English.
47. Ibid., pp. 98–9.
48. Ibid., p. 101.
49. Ibid., pp. 82–3.
50. From Ntosake Shange's play "For Colored Girls Who Have Considered Suicide When the Rainbow is Enuf." Original cast album, Buddah Records, 1976.

REFERENCES

Anderson, Bernhard, W. 1975. *Understanding the Old Testament.* 3rd ed. Englewood Cliff, N.J.: Prentice-Hall.

Bewer, Julius A. 1933. *The Literature of the Old Testament.* New York: Columbia University Press.

Christ, Carol. 1979. Why women need the goddess: phenomenological, psychological, and political reflections. In *Womanspirit Rising,* C.P. Christ and J. Plaskow, eds., pp. 273–87. San Francisco: Harper & Row.

Kenyon, Kathleen M. 1978. *The Bible and Recent Archaeology.* Atlanta: John Knox Press.

Kramer, Samuel N. 1957. *The Sumerians.* Scientific American (October):71–83.

____. 1961. *Sumerian Mythology.* New York: Harper & Row.

____. 1963. *The Sumerians.* Chicago: University of Chicago Press.

Lane, Michael, ed. 1970. *Introduction to Structuralism.* New York: Basic Books.

The Nag Hammadi Library. 1977. Translated by members of the Coptic Gnostic Library Project of the Institute for Antiquity and Christianity, directed by James M. Robinson. San Francisco: Harper & Row.

Meek, T. James. 1960. *Hebrew Origins.* New York: Harper & Brothers.

The New Oxford Annotated Bible. 1973. Herbert G. May and Bruce M. Metzer, eds. Rev. standard version. New York: Oxford University Press.

Pagels, Elaine H. 1976. Whatever became of God the Mother? Conflicting Images of god in early Christianity. *Signs* 2:293–303.

Patai, Raphael. 1967. *The Hebrew Goddess.* New York: KTAV.

Leach, Edmund. 1970. The Legitimacy of Solomon. In Lane, 1970: 248–92.

Simpson, Cuthbert A. 1952a. Exegesis to the Book of Genesis. In *The Interpreter's Bible,* Vol. 1, pp. 465–829. New York: Abingdon Press.

____. 1952b. The Growth of the Hexateuch. In *The Interpreter's Bible,* vol. 1, pp. 185–200. New York: Abingdon Press.

____. 1952c. Introduction to the Book of Genesis. In *The Interpreter's Bible,* vol. 1, pp. 439–57. New York: Abingdon Press.

Von Rad, Gerhard. 1961. *Genesis.* Translated by John H. Marks. Philadelphia: Westminster Press.

READING 9–2

THE VIRGIN OF GUADALUPE: A MEXICAN NATIONAL SYMBOL

Eric R. Wolf

Although not forged in any distinctive theoretical mold or conforming to any special analytical method, the significance of Eric Wolf's article transcends the ethnographic details of the region he discusses. Seven years before Victor Turner introduced his concept of a dominant *symbol, Wolf, a leading anthropological expert on peasant societies of Latin America, had examined exactly such a symbol in Mexico. This was the Virgin of Guadalupe. He characterized her as a* master *symbol, but dissects Mexico's most important religious symbol into much the same components as Turner does with the Ndembu milk tree. The tree coordinates disparate (indeed contradictory) values, channels intense emotions of fundamental concern to society, and stimulates behavior necessary for effective social life. Wolf's discussion also reflects on a matter Sanday raises in Reading 9–1, i.e., divine syncretism. The Christian peasants in the 16th century, while ostensibly worshiping Our Lady of Guadalupe, in fact, had assimilated her into their existing goddess, Tonantzin.*

Wolf's article never generated the same excitement as did Turner's study of the milk tree, possibly because he made no attempt to demonstrate its potential relevance for other religious traditions or perhaps because he did not develop his insights in subsequent theoretical papers, as did Turner. But he none the less gives us convincing explanation for why Our Lady of Guadalupe holds the place she does in Mexican religion, and offers a provocative counterpoint to Reading 9–1.

Occasionally, we encounter a symbol which seems to enshrine the major hopes and aspirations of an entire society.[1] Such a master symbol is represented

Source: Eric R. Wolf, "The Virgin of Guadalupe: A Mexican National Symbol." Reproduced by permission of the American Folklore Society from *Journal of American Folklore* 71:279, January–March 1958. Not for further reproduction.

by the Virgin of Guadalupe, Mexico's patron saint. During the Mexican War of Independence against Spain, her image preceded the insurgents into battle.[2] Emiliano Zapata and his agrarian rebels fought under her emblem in the Great Revolution of 1910.[3] Today, her image adorns house fronts and interiors, churches and home altars, bull rings and gambling dens, taxis and buses, restaurants and houses of ill repute. She is celebrated in popular song and verse. Her shrine at Tepeyac, immediately north of Mexico City, is visited each year by hundreds of thousands of pilgrims, ranging from the inhabitants of far-off Indian villages to the members of socialist trade union locals. "Nothing to be seen in Canada or Europe," says F. S. C. Northrop, "equals it in the volume or the vitality of its moving quality or in the depth of its spirit of religious devotion."[4]

In this paper, I should like to discuss this Mexican master symbol, and the ideology which surrounds it. In making use of the term "master symbol," I do not wish to imply that belief in the symbol is common to all Mexicans. We are not dealing here with an element of a putative national character, defined as a common denominator of all Mexican nationals. It is no longer legitimate to assume "that any member of the [national] group will exhibit certain regularities of behavior which are common in high degree among the other members of the society."[5] Nations, like other complex societies, must, however, "possess cultural forms or mechanisms which groups involved in the same over-all web of relationships can use in their formal and informal dealings with each other."[6] Such forms develop historically, hand in hand with other processes which lead to the formation of nations, and social groups which are caught up in these processes must become "acculturated" to their usage.[7] Only where such forms exist, can communication and coördinated behavior be established among the constituent groups of such a society. They provide the cultural idiom of behavior and ideal representations through which different groups of the same society can pursue and manipulate their different fates within a coordinated framework. This paper, then, deals with one such cultural form, operating on the symbolic level. The study of this symbol seems particularly rewarding, since it is not restricted to one set of social ties, but refers to a very wide range of social relationships.

The image of the Guadalupe and her shrine at Tepeyac are surrounded by an origin myth.[8] According to this myth, the Virgin Mary appeared to Juan Diego, a Christianized Indian of commoner status, and addressed him in Nahuatl. The encounter took place on the Hill of Tepeyac in the year 1531, ten years after the Spanish Conquest of Tenochtitlan. The Virgin commanded Juan Diego to seek out the archbishop of Mexico and to inform him of her desire to see a church built in her honor on Tepeyac Hill. After Juan Diego was twice unsuccessful in his efforts to carry out her order, the Virgin wrought a miracle. She bade Juan Diego pick roses in a sterile spot where normally only desert plants could grow, gathered the roses into the Indian's cloak, and told him to present cloak and roses to the incredulous archbishop. When Juan Diego unfolded his cloak before the bishop, the image of the Virgin was miraculously stamped upon it. The bishop acknowledged the miracle, and ordered a shrine built where Mary had appeared to her humble servant.

The shrine, rebuilt several times in centuries to follow, is today a basilica, the third highest kind of church in Western Christendom. Above the central altar hangs Juan Diego's cloak with the miraculous image. It shows a young woman without child, her head lowered demurely in her shawl. She wears an open crown and flowing gown, and stands upon a half moon symbolizing the Immaculate Conception.

The shrine of Guadalupe was, however, not the first religious structure built on Tepeyac; nor was Guadalupe the first female supernatural associated with the hill. In pre-Hispanic times, Tepeyac had housed a temple to the earth and fertility goddess Tonantzin, Our Lady Mother, who—like the Guadalupe—was associated with the moon. Temple, like basilica, was the center of large scale pilgrimages. That the veneration accorded the Guadalupe drew inspiration from the earlier worship of Tonantzin is attested by several Spanish

friars F. Bernardino de Sahagún, writing fifty years after the Conquest, says: "Now that the Church of Our Lady of Guadalupe has been built there, they call her Tonantzin too. . . . The term refers . . . to that ancient Tonantzin and this state of affairs should be remedied, because the proper name of the Mother of God is not Tonantzin, but Dios and Nantzin. It seems to be a satanic device to mask idolatry . . . and they come from far away to visit that Tonantzin, as much as before; a devotion which is also suspect because there are many churches of Our Lady everywhere and they do not go to them; and they come from faraway lands to this Tonantzin as of old."[9] F. Martín de León wrote in a similar vein: "On the hill where Our Lady of Guadalupe is they adored the idol of a goddess they called Tonantzin, which means Our Mother, and this is also the name they give Our Lady and they always say they are going to Tonantzin or they are celebrating Tonantzin and many of them understand this is the old way and not in the modern way. . . ."[10] The syncretism was still alive in the seventeenth century. F. Jacinto de la Serna, in discussing the pilgrimages to the Guadalupe at Tepeyac, noted: ". . . . it is the purpose of the wicked to [worship] the goddess and not the Most Holy Virgin, or both together."[11]

Increasingly popular during the sixteenth century, the Guadalupe cult gathered emotional impetus during the seventeenth. During this century appear the first known pictorial representations of the Guadalupe, apart from the miraculous original; the first poems are written in her honor; and the first sermons announce the transcendental implications of her supernatural appearance in Mexico and among Mexicans.[12] Historians have long tended to neglect the seventeenth century which seemed "a kind of Dark Age in Mexico." Yet "this quiet time was of the utmost importance in the development of Mexican Society."[13] During this century, the institution of the hacienda comes to dominate Mexican life.[14] During this century, also, "New Spain is ceasing to be 'new' and to be 'Spain.' "[15] These new experiences require a new cultural idiom, and in the Guadalupe cult, the component segments of

Mexican colonial society encountered cultural forms in which they could express their parallel interests and longings.

The primary purpose of this paper is not, however, to trace the history of the Guadalupe symbol. It is concerned rather with its functional aspects, its roots and reference to the major social relationships of Mexican society.

The first set of relationships which I would like to single out for consideration are the ties of kinship, and the emotions generated in the play of relationships within families. I want to suggest that some of the meanings of the Virgin symbol in general, and of the Guadalupe symbol in particular, derive from these emotions. I say "some meanings" and I use the term "derive" rather than "originate," because the form and function of the family in any given society are themselves determined by other social factors: technology, economy, residence, political power. The family is but one relay in the circuit within which symbols are generated in complex societies. Also, I used the plural "families" rather than "family," because there are demonstrably more than one kind of family in Mexico.[16] I shall simplify the available information on Mexican family life, and discuss the material in terms of two major types of families.[17] The first kind of family is congruent with the closed and static life of the Indian village. It may be called the Indian family. In this kind of family, the husband is ideally dominant, but in reality labor and authority are shared equally among both marriage partners. Exploitation of one sex by the other is atypical; sexual feats do not add to a person's status in the eyes of others. Physical punishment and authoritarian treatment of children are rare. The second kind of family is congruent with the much more open, mobile, manipulative life in communities which are actively geared to the life of the nation, a life in which power relationships between individuals and groups are of great moment. This kind of family may be called the Mexican family. Here, the father's authority is unquestioned on both the real and the ideal plane. Double sex standards prevail, and male sexuality is charged with a desire to exercise domination. Chil-

dren are ruled with a heavy hand; physical punishment is frequent.

The Indian family pattern is consistent with the behavior towards the Guadalupe noted by John Bushnell in the Matlazinca speaking community of San Juan Atzingo in the Valley of Toluca.[18] There, the image of the Virgin is addressed in passionate terms as a source of warmth and love, and the pulque or century plant beer drunk on ceremonial occasions is identified with her milk. Bushnell postulates that here the Guadalupe is identified with the mother as a source of early satisfactions, never again experienced after separation from the mother and emergence into social adulthood. As such, the Guadalupe embodies a longing to return to the pristine state in which hunger and unsatisfactory social relations are minimized. The second family pattern is also consistent with a symbolic identification of Virgin and mother, yet this time within a context of adult male dominance and sexual assertion, discharged against submissive females and children. In this second context, the Guadalupe symbol is charged with the energy of rebellion against the father. Her image is the embodiment of hope in a victorious outcome of the struggle between generations.

This struggle leads to a further extension of the symbolism. Successful rebellion against power figures is equated with the promise of life; defeat with the promise of death. As John A. Mackay has suggested, there thus takes place a further symbolic identification of the Virgin with life; of defeat and death with the crucified Christ. In Mexican artistic tradition, as in Hispanic artistic tradition in general,[19] Christ is never depicted as an adult man, but always either as a helpless child, or more often as a figure beaten, tortured, defeated and killed. In this symbolic equation we are touching upon some of the roots both of the passionate affirmation of faith in the Virgin, and of the fascination with death which characterizes Baroque Christianity in general, and Mexican Catholicism in particular. The Guadalupe stands for life, for hope, for health; Christ on the cross, for despair and for death.

Supernatural mother and natural mother are thus equated symbolically, as are earthly and other-worldly hopes and desires. These hopes center on the provision of food and emotional warmth in the first case, in the successful waging of the Oedipal struggle in the other.

Family relations are, however, only one element in the formation of the Guadalupe symbol. Their analysis does little to explain the Guadalupe as such. They merely illuminate the female and maternal attributes of the more widespread Virgin symbol. The Guadalupe is important to Mexicans not only because she is a supernatural mother, but also because she embodies their major political and religious aspirations.

To the Indian groups, the symbol is more than an embodiment of life and hope; it restores to them the hopes of salvation. We must not forget that the Spanish Conquest signified not only military defeat, but the defeat also of the old gods and the decline of the old ritual. The apparition of the Guadalupe to an Indian commoner thus represents on one level the return of Tonantzin. As Tannenbaum has well said, "The Church . . . gave the Indian an opportunity not merely to save his life, but also to save his faith in his own gods."[20] On another level, the myth of the apparition served as a symbolic testimony that the Indian, as much as the Spaniard, was capable of being saved, capable of receiving Christianity. This must be understood against the background of the bitter theological and political argument which followed the Conquest and divided churchmen, officials, and conquerors into those who held that the Indian was incapable of conversion, thus inhuman, and therefore a fit subject of political and economic exploitation; and those who held that the Indian was human, capable of conversion and that this exploitation had to be tempered by the demands of the Catholic faith and of orderly civil processes of government.[21] The myth of the Guadalupe thus validates the Indian's right to legal defense, orderly government, to citizenship; to supernatural salvation, but also to salvation from random oppression.

But if the Guadalupe guaranteed a rightful place to the Indians in the new social system of New Spain, the myth also held appeal to the large group of disinherited who arose in New Spain as illegitimate offspring of Spanish fathers and Indian mothers, or through impoverishment, acculturation or loss of status within the Indian or Spanish group.[22] For such people, there was for a long time no proper place in the social order. Their very right to exist was questioned in their inability to command the full rights of citizenship and legal protection. Where Spaniard and Indian stood squarely within the law, they inhabited the interstices and margins of constituted society. These groups acquired influence and wealth in the seventeenth and eighteenth centuries, but were yet barred from social recognition and power by the prevailing economic, social and political order.[23] To them, the Guadalupe myth came to represent not merely the guarantee of their assured place in heaven, but the guarantee of their place in society here and now. On the political plane, the wish for a return to a paradise of early satisfactions of food and warmth, a life without defeat, sickness or death, gave rise to a political wish for a Mexican paradise, in which the illegitimate sons would possess the country, and the irresponsible Spanish overlords, who never acknowledged the social responsibilities of their paternity, would be driven from the land.

In the writings of seventeenth century ecclesiastics, the Guadalupe becomes the harbinger of this new order. In the book by Miguel Sánchez, published in 1648, the Spanish Conquest of New Spain is justified solely on the grounds that it allowed the Virgin to become manifest in her chosen country, and to found in Mexico a new paradise. Just as Israel had been chosen to produce Christ, so Mexico had been chosen to produce Guadalupe. Sánchez equates her with the apocalyptic woman of the Revelation of John (12:1), "arrayed with the sun, and the moon under her feet, and upon her head a crown of twelve stars" who is to realize the prophecy of Deuteronomy 8:7–10 and lead the Mexicans into the Promised Land. Colonial Mexico thus becomes the desert of Sinai; Independent Mexico the land of milk and honey. F. Francisco de Florencia, writing in 1688, coined the slogan which made Mexico not merely another chosen nation, but the Chosen Nation: *non fecit taliter omni nationi,*[24] words which still adorn the portals of the basilica, and shine forth in electric light bulbs at night. And on the eve of Mexican independence, Servando Teresa de Mier elaborates still further the Guadalupan myth by claiming that Mexico had been converted to Christianity long before the Spanish Conquest. The apostle Saint Thomas had brought the image of Guadalupe-Tonantzin to the New World as a symbol of his mission, just as Saint James had converted Spain with the image of the Virgin of the Pillar.

The Spanish Conquest was therefore historically unnecessary, and should be erased from the annals of history.[25] In this perspective, the Mexican War of Independence marks the final realization of the apocalyptic promise. The banner of the Guadalupe leads the insurgents; and their cause is referred to as "her law."[26] In this ultimate extension of the symbol, the promise of life held out by the supernatural mother has become the promise of an independent Mexico, liberated from the irrational authority of the Spanish father-oppressors and restored to the Chosen Nation whose election had been manifest in the apparition of the Virgin on Tepeyac. The land of the supernatural mother is finally possessed by her rightful heirs. The symbolic circuit is closed. Mother; food, hope, health, life; supernatural salvation and salvation from oppression; Chosen People and national independence— all find expression in a single master symbol.

The Guadalupe symbol thus links together family, politics and religion; colonial past and independent present; Indian and Mexican. It reflects the salient social relationships of Mexican life, and embodies the emotions which they generate. It provides a cultural idiom through which the tenor and emotions of these relationships can be expressed. It is, ultimately, a way of talking about Mexico: a "collective representation" of Mexican society.

ENDNOTES

1. Parts of this paper were presented to the Symposium on Ethnic and National Ideologies, Annual Spring Meeting of the American Ethnological Society in conjunction with the Philadelphia Anthropological Society, on 12 May 1956.

2. Niceto de Zamacois, *Historia de México* (Barcelona-Mexico, 1878–82), VI, 253.

3. Antonio Pompa y Pompa, *Album del IV centenario guadalupano* (Mexico, 1938), p. 173.

4. F. S. C. Northrop, *The Meeting of East and West* (New York, 1946), p. 25.

5. David G. Mandelbaum, "On the Study of National Character," *American Anthropologist,* LV (1953), p. 185.

6. Eric R. Wolf, "Aspects of Group Relations in a Complex Society: Mexico," *American Anthropologist,* LVII (1956), 1065–1078.

7. Eric R. Wolf, "La formación de la nación," *Ciencias Sociales,* IV, 50–51.

8. Ernest Gruening, *Mexico and Its Heritage* (New York, 1928), p. 235.

9. Bernardino de Sahagún, *Historia general de las cosas de nueva españa* (Mexico, 1938), I, lib. 6.

10. Quoted in Carlos A. Echánove Trujillo, *Sociología mexicana* (Mexico, 1948), p. 105.

11. Quoted in Jesús Amaya, *La madre de Dios: genesis e historia de nuestra señora de Guadalupe* (Mexico, 1931), p. 230.

12. Francisco de la Maza, *El guadalupismo mexicano* (Mexico, 1953), pp. 12–14, 143, 30, 33, 82.

13. Lesley B. Simpson, "Mexico's Forgotten Century," *Pacific Historical Review,* XXII (1953), 115, 114.

14. François Chevalier, *La formation des grands domaines au Mexique* (Paris, 1952), p. xii.

15. de la Maza, p. 41.

16. María Elvira Bermúdez, *La vida familiar del mexicano* (Mexico, 1955), chapters 2 and 3.

17. For relevant material, see: Bermúdez; John Gillin, "Ethos and Cultural Aspects of Personality," and Robert Redfield and Sol Tax, "General Characteristics of Present-Day Mesoamerican Indian Society," in Sol Tax, ed., *Heritage of Conquest* (Glencoe, 1952), pp. 193–212, 31–39; Gordon W. Hewes, "Mexicans in Search of the Mexican'," *American Journal of Economics and Sociology,* XIII (1954), 209–223; Octavio Paz, *El laberinto de la soledad* (Mexico, 1947), pp. 71–89.

18. John Bushnell, "La Virgen de Guadalupe as Surrogate Mother in San Juan Atzingo," paper read before the 54th Annual Meeting of the American Anthropological Association, 18 November 1955.

19. John A. Mackay, *The Other Spanish Christ* (New York, 1933), pp. 110–117.

20. Frank Tannenbaum, *Peace by Revolution* (New York, 1933), p. 39.

21. Silvio Zavala, *La filosofía en la conquista de America* (Mexico, 1947).

22. Nicolas León, Las castas del México colonial o Nueva España (Mexico, 1924); C E. Marshall, "The Birth of the Mestizo in New Spain," *Hispanic American Historical Review,* XIX (1939), 161–184; Wolf, "La formación de la nación," pp. 103–106.

23. Gregorio Torres Quintero, *México hacía el fin del virreinato español* (Mexico, 1921); Eric R. Wolf, "The Mexican Bajío in the Eighteenth Century," *Middle American Research Institute Publication* XVII (1955), 180–199; Wolf, "Aspects of Group Relations in a Complex Society: Mexico."

24. de la Maza, pp. 39–40, 43–49, 64.

25. Luis Villoro, *Los grandes momentos del indigenismo en México* (Mexico, 1950), pp. 131–138.

26. Luis González y González, "El optimismo nacionalista como factor en la independencia de México," Estudios de historiografía americana (Mexico, 1948), p. 194.

READING 9-3

THE HIJRAS OF INDIA: CULTURAL AND INDIVIDUAL DIMENSIONS OF AN INSTITUTIONALIZED THIRD GENDER ROLE

Serena Nanda

The hijra are neither men nor women. Blending social attributes of both sexes, they form a third gender in some Indian societies, an ambiguous status consistent with their role as followers of the Mother Goddess, Bahuchara Mata, and with the sacred power they are considered to possess. In this reading Serena Nanda, who carried out fieldwork among the Hijras, describes the ritual significance of these ambivalent figures, and in particular brings to our attention the social tensions a third gender can engender. We find that prostitution combines with the religious role of hijras, undercutting their religious credibility and inflicting the hijras themselves with problems. Nanda's description clearly establishes the local social environment in which these figures from the third gender operate.

The hijra (eunuch/transvestite) is an institutionalized third gender role in India. Hijra are neither male nor female, but contain elements of both. As devotees of the Mother Goddess Bahuchara mata, their sacred powers are contingent upon their asexuality. In reality, however, many hijras are prostitutes. This sexual activity undermines their culturally valued sacred role. This paper discusses religious meanings of the

Source: From "The Hijaras of India" by S. Nanda in the *Journal of Homosexuality II (3/4)*, 1985, pp. 35–54. Copyright © 1986 by The Haworth Press. Reprinted by permission.

hijra role, as well as the ways in which individuals and the community deal with the conflicts engendered by their sexual activity.

The hijra, an institutionalized third gender role in India, is "neither male nor female," containing elements of both. The hijra are commonly believed by the larger society to be intersexed, impotent men, who undergo emasculation in which all or part of the genitals are removed. They adopt female dress and some other aspects of female behavior. Hijras traditionally earn their living by collecting alms and receiving payment for performances at weddings, births and festivals. The central feature of their culture is their devotion to Bahuchara Mata, one of the many Mother Goddesses worshipped all over India, for whom emasculation is carried out. This identification with the Mother Goddess is the source both of the hijras' claim for their special place in Indian society and the traditional belief in their power to curse or confer blessings on male infants.

The census of India does not enumerate hijras separately so their exact numbers are unknown. Estimates quoted in the press range from 50,000 (*India Today,* 1982) to 500,000 (*Tribune,* 1983). Hijras live predominantly in the cities of North India, where they find the greatest opportunity to perform their traditional roles, but small groups of hijras are found all over India, in the south as well as the north. Seven "houses," or subgroups, comprise the hijra community; each of these has a guru or leader, all of whom live in Bombay. The houses have equal status, but one, Laskarwallah, has the special function of mediating disputes which arise among the others. Each house has its own history, as well as rules particular to it. For example, members of a particular house are not allowed to wear certain colors. Hijra houses appear to patterned after the *gharanas* (literally, houses), or family lineages among classical musicians, each of which is identified with its own particular musical style. Though the culturally distinct features of the hijra houses have almost vanished, the structural feature remains.[1]

The most significant relationship in the hijra community is that of the *guru* (master, teacher) and *chela* (disciple). When an individual decides to (formally) join the hijra community, he is taken to Bombay to visit one of the seven major gurus, usually the guru of the person who has brought him there. At the initiation ritual, the guru gives the novice a new, female name. The novice vows to obey the guru and the rules of the community. The guru then presents the new chela with some gifts.

The chela, or more likely, someone on her behalf, pays an initiation fee and the guru writes the chela's name in her record book. This guru-chela relationship is a lifelong bond of reciprocity in which the guru is obligated to help the chela and the chela is obligated to be loyal and obedient to the guru.[2] Hijras live together in communes generally of about 5 to 15 members, and the heads of these local groups are also called guru. Hijras make no distinctions within their community based on caste origin or religion, although in some parts of India, Gujerat, for example, Muslim and Hindu hijras reportedly live apart (Salunkhe, 1976), In Bombay, Delhi, Chandigarh and Bangalore, hijras of Muslim, Christian, and Hindu origin live in the same houses.

In addition to the hierarchical guru-chela relationship, there is fictive kinship by which hijras relate to each other. Rituals exist for "taking a daughter" and the "daughters" of one "mother" consider themselves "sisters" and relate on a reciprocal, affectionate basis. Other fictive kinship relations, such as "grandmother" or "mother's sister" (aunt) are the basis of warm and reciprocal regard. Fictive kin exchange small amounts of money, clothing, jewelry and sweets to formalize their relationship. Such relationships connect hijras all over India, and there is a constant movement of individuals who visit their gurus and fictive kin in different cities. Various annual gatherings, both religious and secular, attract thousands of hijras from all over India.[3]

The extant literature on the hijras is scant, confusing, misleading, contradictory, and judgmental. With few exceptions (Salunkhe, 1976; Sinha, 1967) it lacks a basis in fieldwork or intensive interviewing. A major dispute in that literature has been whether or not the hijra role encompasses homosexuality.

In my view, the essential cultural aspect of the hijra role is its asexual nature. Yet, empirical evidence also indicates that many hijras do engage in homosexual activity. This difference between the cultural ideal and the real behavior causes a certain amount of conflict within the community. The present paper, based on a year's fieldwork among hijra communes in various parts of India, examines both the cultural ideal of asexuality and the behavioral dimension of homosexuality, and how the conflict is experienced and handled within the community.

CULTURAL DIMENSIONS OF THE HIJRA ROLE

Hijras as Neither Man nor Woman

A commonly told story among hijras, which conceptualize them as a separate, third gender, connects them to the Hindu epic, the *Ramayana:*

> In the time of the Ramayana, Ram . . . had to leave Ayodhya (his native city) and go into the forest for 14 years. As he was going, the whole city followed him because they loved him so. As Ram came to . . .the edge of the forest, he turned to the people and said, "Ladies and gents, please wipe your tears and go away." But these people who were not men and not women did not know what to do. So they stayed there because Ram did not ask the to go. They remained there 14 years and snake hills grew around them. When Ram returned from Lanka, he found many snake hills. Not knowing why they were there he removed them and found so many people with long beards and long nails, all meditating. And so they were blessed by Ram. And that is why we hijras are so respected in Ayodhya.

Individual hijras also speak of themselves as being "separate," being "neither man nor woman," being "born as men, but not men," or being "not perfect men." Hijras are most clearly "not men" in relation to their claimed inability and lack of desire to engage in the sexual act as men with women, a consequence of their claimed biological intersexuality and their subsequent castration. Thus, hijras are unable to reproduce children, especially sons, an essential element in the Hindu concept of the normal, masculine role for males.

But if hijras are "not men," neither are they women, in spite of several aspects of feminine behavior associated with the role. These behaviors include dressing as women, wearing their hair long, plucking (rather than shaving) their facial hair, adopting feminine mannerisms, taking on women's names, and using female kinship terms and a special, feminized vocabulary. Hijras also identify with a female goddess or as wives of certain male deities in ritual contexts. They claim seating reserved for "ladies only" in public conveyances. On one occasion, they demanded to be counted as women in the census.[4]

Although their role requires hijras to dress like women, few make any real attempt to imitate or to "pass" as women. Their female dress and mannerisms are exaggerated to the point of caricature, expressing sexual overtones that would be considered inappropriate for ordinary women in their roles as daughters, wives, and mothers. Hijra performances are burlesques of female behavior. Much of the comedy of their behavior derives from the incongruities between their behavior and that of traditional women. They use coarse and abusive speech and gestures in opposition to the Hindu ideal of demure and restrained femininity. Further, it is not at all uncommon to see hijras in female clothing sporting several days growth of beard, or exposing hairy, muscular arms. The ultimate section of hijras to an abusive or unresponsive public is to lift their skirts and expose the mutilated genitals. The implicit threat of this shameless, and thoroughly unfeminine, behavior is enough to make most people give them a few cents so they will go away. Most centrally, as hijras themselves acknowledge, they are not born as women, and cannot reproduce. Their impotence and barrenness, due to a deficient or absent male organ, ultimately precludes their being considered fully male; yet their lack of female reproductive organs or female sexual organs precludes their being considered fully female.

Indian belief and the hijra's own claims commonly attribute the impotence of the hijra as male to a hermaphroditic morphology and physiology.

Many informants insisted "I was born this way," implying hermaphoditism; such a condition is the standard reason given for joining the community. Only one of 30 informants, however, was probably born intersexed. Her words clearly indicate how central this status is to the hijra role, and make explicit that hijras are not males because they have no male reproductive organs:

> From my childhood I am like this. From birth my organ was very small. My mother tried taking me to doctors and all but the doctors said, "No, it won't grow, your child is not a man and not a woman, this is God's gift and all. . . From that time my mother would dress me in girl's clothes. But then she saw it was no use. So she sent me to live with the hijras. I am a real hijra, not like those others who are converts; they are men and can have children, so they have the (emasculation) operation, but I was born this way. (Field notes, 1981–2)

Hijra Impotence and Creative Asceticism

If, in Indian reality, the impotent male is considered useless as a man because he is unable to procreate, in Indian mythology, impotence can be transformed into generativity through the ideal of *tapasya,* or the practice of asceticism. *Tapas,* the power that results from ascetic practices and sexual abstinence, becomes an essential feature in the process of creation. Ascetics appear throughout Hindu mythology in procreative roles. In one version of the Hindu creation myth, siva carries out an extreme, but legitimate form of tapasya, that of self-castration. Because the act of creation he was about to undertake had already been accomplished by Brahma, Siva breaks off his linga (phallus), saying, "there is no use for this linga . . . " and throws it into the earth. His act results in the fertility cult of lingaworship, which expresses the paradoxical theme of creative asceticism (O'Flaherty, 1973). This theme provides one explanation of the positive role given the hijras in Indian society. Born intersexed and impotent, unable themselves to reproduce, hijras can, through the emasculation operation, transform their liability into a source of creative power which enables them to confer blessings of fertility on others.

The link between the Hindu theme of creative asceticism and the role and power of the hijras is explicitly articulated in the myths connecting them to their major point of religious identification—their worship of Bahuchara Mata, and her requirement that they undergo emasculation. Bahuchara was a pretty, young maiden in a party of travelers passing through the forest in Gujerat. The party was attacked by thieves, and, fearing they would outrage her modesty, Bahuchara's drew her dagger and cut off her breast, offering it to the outlaws in place of her body. This act, and her ensuing death, led to Bahuchara's deification and the practice of self-mutilation and sexual abstinence by her devotees to secure her favor.

Bahuchara has a special connection to the hijras because they are impotent men who undergo emasculation. This connection derives special significance from the story of King Baria of Gujerat. Baria was a devout follower of Bahucharaji, but was unhappy because he had no son. Through the goddess' favor a son, Jetho, was born to him. The sun, however, was impotent. The King, out of respect to the goddess, set him apart for her service. Bahuch-haraji appeared to Jetho in a dream and told him to cut off his genitalia and dress as a woman, which he did. This practice has been followed by all who join the hijra cult (Mehta, 1945-1946).

Emasculation is the *dharm* (caste duty) of the hijras, and the chief source of their uniqueness. The hijras carry it out in a ritual context, in which the client sits in front of a picture of the goddess Bahuchara and repeats her name while the operation is being performed. A person who survives the operation becomes one of Bahuchara Mata's favorites, serving as a vehicle of her power through their symbolic rebirth. While the most popular image of Bahuchara is that of the goddess riding on a cock, Shah (1961) suggests that her original form of worship was the *yantra,* a conventional symbol for the vulva. A relation between this representation of the goddess and emasculation may exist: emasculation certainly brings the hijra devotee into a closer identification with the female object of devotion.

Identification of the hijras with Bahuchara specifically and through her, with the creative powers of the Mother Goddess worshipped in many different forms in India, is clearly related to their major cultural function, that of performing at homes where a male child has been born. During these performances the hijras, using sexual innuendoes, inspect the genitals of the infant whom they hold in their arms as they dance. The hijras confer fertility, prosperity, and health on the infant and family.

At both weddings and births, hijras hold the power to bless and to curse, and families regard them ambivalently. They have both auspicious functions and inauspicious potential. In regard to the latter, charms are used during pregnancy against eunuchs, both to protect against still birth, and a transformation of the embryo from male to female. Hiltebeitel (1980) suggests that the presence of eunuchs at birth and weddings:

> marks the ambiguity of those moments when the non-differentiation of male and female is most filled with uncertainty and promise—in the mystery that surrounds the sexual identity of the still unborn child and on that (occasion) which anticipates the re-union of male and female in marital sex. (p. 168)

Thus, it is fitting that the eunuch-transvestites, themselves characterized by sexual ambiguity, have ritual functions at moments that involve sexual ambiguity.

The eunuch-transvestite role of the hijras links them not only to the Mother Goddess, but also to Siva, through their identification with Arjuna, the hero of the Mahabharata. One origin myth of the hijras is the story of Arjuna's exile. He lives incognito for one year as part of the price he must pay for losing a game of dice, and also for rejecting the advances of one of the celestial nymphs. Arjuna decide to hide himself in the guise of a eunuch-transvestite, wearing bangles made of white conch, braiding his hair like a woman, clothing himself in female attire, and serving the ladies of the King's court (Rajagopalachari, 1980). Some hijras say that whoever is born on Arjuna's day, no matter where in the world, will become a hijra. Hiltebeitel (1980) makes a persuasive case for the identification of Arjuna with Siva, especially in his singer/dancer/eunuch/transvestite role.

The theme of the eunuch state is elaborated in a number of ways in the Mahabharata, and it is Arjuna who is the theme's central character. Arjuna, in the disguise of eunuch-transvestite, participates in weddings and births, and thus provides a further legitimatization for the ritual contexts in which the hijra performs. At one point,, for example, Arjuna in this disguise helps prepare the King's daughter for her marriage and her future role as mother-to-be. In doing this, he refuses to marry the princess himself, thus renouncing not only his sovereignty, but also the issue of an heir. His feigned impotence paves the way for the birth of the princess' child, just as the presence of the impotent hijras at the home of the male child paves the way for the child's fertility and the continuation of the family line.

This evidence suggests that intersexuality, impotence, emasculation and transvestism are all variously believed to be part of the hijra role, accounting for their inability to reproduce and the lack of desire (or the renunciation of the desire) to do so. In any event, sexual abstinence, which Hindu mythology associates with the powers of the ascetic, is in fact, the very source of the hijras' powers. The hijras themselves recognize this connection: They frequently refer to themselves as *sannyasin,* the person who renounces his role in society for the life of a holy wanderer and begger. This vocation requires renunciation of material possessions, the duties of caste, the life of the householder and family man, and, most particularly, the renunciation of sexual desire (*kama*). In claiming his vocation, hijras point out how they have abandoned their families, live in material poverty, live off the charity of others, and "do not have sexual desires as other men do."

Hijras understand that their "other-worldliness" brings them respect in society, and that if they do not live up to these ideals, they will damage that

respect. But just as Hindu mythology contains many stories of ascetics who renounce desire but nevertheless are moved by desire to engage in sexual acts, so, too, the hijra community experiences the tension between their religious, ascetic ideal and the reality of the individual human's desire and sexuality.

INDIVIDUAL DIMENSIONS OF THE HIJRA ROLE

Hijras as Homosexuals

The remainder of this paper focuses on the sexual activities of hijras, and the ways in which the community experiences the conflict between the real and the ideal.

A widespread belief in India is that hijras are intersexed persons claimed or kidnapped by the hijra community as infants. No investigator has found evidence to support this belief. Given the large and complex society of India, the hijra community attacks different kinds of persons, most of whom join voluntarily as teenagers or adults. It appears to be a magnet for persons with a wide range of cross-gender characteristics arising from either a psychological or organic condition (Money & Weideking, 1980). The hijra role accommodates different personalities, sexual needs, and gender identities without completely losing its cultural meaning.

While the core of the positive meaning attached to the hijra role is linked to the negation of sexual desire, the reality is that many hijras do, in fact, engage in sexual activities. Because sexual behavior is contrary to the definition of the role such activity causes conflict for both the individuals and the community. Individual hijras deal with the conflict in different ways, while the community as a whole resorts to various mechanisms of social control.

Though it is clear from the literature that some hijras engage in homosexual activity, there has been controversy over the centrality of this activity in the institutionalization of the role in India.[5] In his psychoanalytical study of high castes in a village in

Rajasthan, Carstairs (1957) asserted that the hijra role is primarily a form of institutionalized homosexuality that developed in response to tendencies toward latent homosexuality in the Indian national character. Morris Opler (1960) contested both Carstairs' evaluation of Indian character and his assertion that hijras are primarily conceptualized as homosexuals or that they engaged in any sexual activity.

Opler argued that the cultural definition of their role in Indian society was only one of performers. Sinha (1967), who worked in Lucknow in North India, acknowledged their performing role, but treated hijras primarily as homosexuals who join the community specifically to satisfy their sexual desires. Lynton and Rajan (1974), who interviewed hijras in Hyderabad, indicate that a period of homosexual activity, involving solicitation in public, sometimes precedes a decision to join the hijras. Their informants led them to believe, however, that sexual activity is prohibited by hijra rules and that these are strictly enforced by the community elders. Freeman (1979), who did fieldwork in Orissa at the southern edge of North Indian culture, discusses hijras as transvestite prostitutes and hardly mentions their ritual roles.

My own data (Nanda, 1984), gathered through fieldwork in Bangalore and Bombay, and in several North Indian cities, confirm beyond doubt that, however deviant it may be regarded within the hijra community, hijras in contemporary India extensively engage in relations with men. This phenomenon is not entirely modern: 19th-century accounts (Bhimbhai, 1901; Fardi, 1899) claim that hijras were known to kidnap small boys for the purposes of sodomy or prostitution. Such allegations still find their way into the contemporary popular press (*India Today,* 1982).

Although hijras attribute their increased prostitution to declining opportunities to earn a living in their traditional manner, eunuch-transvestites in Hindu classical literature also had the reputation of engaging in homosexual activity. The classic Hindu manual of love, the *Kamasutra* specifically outlines sexual practices that were considered appropriate

for eunuch-transvestites to perform with male partners (Burton, 1962).[6] Classical Hinduism taught that there was a "third sex," divided into various categories, two of which were castrated men, eunuchs, and hermaphrodites, who wore false breasts, and imitated the voice, gestures, dress and temperaments of women. These types shared the major function of providing alternative techniques of sexual gratification (Bullough, 1976). In contemporary India, concepts of eunuch, transvestite and male homosexual are not distinct, and the hijras are considered all of these at once (O'Flaherty, 1980).

The term hijra, however, which is of Urdu origin and the masculine gender, has the primary meaning of hermaphrodite. It is usually translated as eunuch, never as homosexual. Even Carstairs' informants, among whom the homosexuality of the hijras was well known, defined them as either drum players at the birth of male children, or eunuchs, whose duty was to undergo castration. In parts of North India, the term for effeminate males who play the passive role in homosexual relations is *zenanas* (women); by becoming a hijra, one removes oneself from this category (see also Lynton & Rajan, 1974). Furthermore, a covert homosexual subculture exists in some of the larger cities in North India (Anderson, 1977), but persons who participate in it are not called hijras. In fact, as in the other cultures (Carstairs, 1980; Wikan, 1977) men who play the insertor role in sexual activities between men have no linguistically or sociologically distinguished role. Unlike western cultures, in India sexual object choice alone does not define gender. In some South Indian regional languages, the names by which hijras are called, such as *kojja* in Telegu (Anderson, 1977) or *potee* in Tamil, are, unlike the term *hijra,* epithets used derogatorily to mean a cowardly or feminine male or homosexual. This linguistic difference, however, is consistent with the fact that in South India the hijras do not have the cultural role which they do in North India.

According to my research, homosexual activity is widespread among hijras, and teenage homosexual activity figures significantly in the lives of many individuals who join the community. As Sinha's interviews also indicate (1967), hose hijras who engage in homosexual activity share particular life patterns before joining the community. Typically such individuals liked during childhood to dress in feminine clothes, play with girls, do traditionally female work, and avoid the company of boys in rough play. In lower class families, the boy's effeminacy is both ridiculed and encouraged by his peers, who may persuade him to play the insertee role for them, possibly with some slight monetary consideration. At this stage the boy lives with his family, though in an increasingly tense atmosphere. He thinks of himself as a male and wears male clothing, at least in public. As his interest in homosexual activity increases, and his relations with his family become more strained, he may leave home. In most cases their families make serious attempts to inhibit their feminine activity with scoldings, surveillance, restrictions, and beatings, so that the boy finally has no choice but to leave.[7]

There are two modes of sexual relations among hijras. One is casual prostitution, the exchange of sexual favors with different men for a fixed sum of money, and the other is "having a husband." Hijras do not characterize their male partners as homosexuals; they quite explicitly distinguish them as being different than homosexuals. One hijra, Shakuntala, characterizes the customers in the following way:

> these men . . . are married or unmarried, they may be the father of many children. Those who come to us, they have no desire to go to a man . . . they come to us for the sake of going to a girl. They prefer us to their wives . . . each one's tastes differ among people. . . . It is God's way; because we have to make a living, he made people like this so we can earn. (Field notes, 1981–2)

Shakuntala clearly expressed a feminine gender identity and was, in fact, the person who came closest to what would be called in the west a transsexual; that is, experiencing himself as a "female trapped in a male body." She remembered having felt that she was a female since childhood, liking to dress in female clothing, doing woman's work

inside the house and playing with girls rather than boys. She was introduced to homosexual activity in her teens, which she claims "spoiled" her for the normal, heterosexual male role. She has a very maternal, nurturing temperament, and emphasizes the maternal aspect of the guru role to her young chelas.[8] She is currently involved in a long-term, monogamous relationship with a young man who lies in her neighborhood and whom she hopes will "marry" her. She underwent the emasculation operation because she wanted "to become more beautiful, like a woman." She was the only hijra interviewed who was taking hormones "to develop a more feminine figure." She always dressed as a woman and was very convincing in a feminine role, not exhibiting the more flamboyant mannerisms and gestures of the typical hijra. Because of her strong attachment to her present boyfriend, she is sometimes criticized by her hijra friends:

> Those people, like Shakuntala, with husband fever, they are mad over their husbands, even to the point of suicide. If that fellow even talks to a[nother] girl, immediately they'll fight with him. If he is out at night, even if it is three o'clock in the morning, they'll go in search of him. They won't even sleep till he returns. (Field notes, 1981–2)

This devotion to one man is seen as typical of Shakuntala's extremely feminine identification.

Not all hijras who engage in sexual relations with other men express such complete feminine identification. One hijra, for example, explained the attraction of men to hijras on different grounds:

> See, there is a proverb, "for a normal lady [prostitute] it is four annas and for a hijra it is twelve annas." These men, they come to us to have pleasure on their own terms. They may want to kiss us or do so many things. For instance, the customer will ask us to lift the legs (from a position lying on her back) so that they can do it through the anus. We allow them to do it by the back [anal intercourse], but not very often. (Field notes, 1981–2).

This statement suggests that the attraction of the hijras is that thcy will engage in forms of sexual behavior in which Indian women will normally not engage. Several of my non-hijra male informants confirm this view.

Having a husband is the preferred alternative for those hijras who engage in sexual relations. Many of my informants have, or recently had, a relatively permanent attachment to one man whom they referred to as their husband. They maintain warm and affectionate, as well as sexually satisfying and economically reciprocal, relationships with these men, with whom they live, sometimes alone, or sometimes with several other hijras. Lalitha, a very feminine looking hijra in her middle thirties, has had the same husband for nine years. He used to come for prostitution to the hijra commune in which Lalitha lived and then they lived together in a small house until he got married. Now Lalitha has moved back with the hijras, where she cooks their meals in return for free food and lodging, but she still maintains her relationship with her "husband":

> My husband is a Christian. He works in a cigarette factory and earns 1000 rupees a month. He is married to [another] woman and has got four children. I encouraged him to get married and even his wife and children are nice to me. His children call me *chitti* [mother's sister] and even his wife's parents know about me and don't say anything. He gives me saris and flowers and whenever I ask for money he never says no. When he needs money, I would give him also. (Field notes, 1981–2).

Hijras who have husbands do not break their ties with the hijra community, although sometimes their husbands urge them to do so. Sushila, an attractive, assertive, and ambitious hijra in her early thirties has a husband who is a driver for a national corporation headquarters and earns 600 rupees a month. She continues to be very active in the local hijra community, however, and even refuses to give up practicing prostitution in spite of her husband's objections:

> My husband tells me "I earn enough money. Why do you go for prostitution?" I tell him, "you are here with me today. What surety is there you will be with me forever? I came to you from prostitution, and if you leave me I'll have to go back to it. Then all those other hijras will say, 'Oh, she lived as a wife and now look at her

fate, she has come back to prostitution.'" So I tell him, "don't put any restrictions on me; now they all think of me as someone nice, but when I go back to prostitution, they will put me to shame." If he gives me too much back talk, I give him good whacks. (Field notes, 1981–2)

Sushila is saving the money she makes from prostitution and from that her husband gives her so that she can buy a business, probably a bathhouse for working class men. In Bangalore, bathhouses are commonly run by hijras.

Although many hijras complain that it is hard for them to save money, some have a good business sense and have invested in jewelry and property so that they can be relatively independent financially in their old age. For hijras who are not particularly talented singers and dancers, or who live in cities where their ritual performances are not in demand, prostitution provides an adequate way of earning a living. It is a demanding and even occasionally dangerous profession, however, because some customers turn out to be "rowdies." Although a hijra living in a commune has to pay 50% of her fees from prostitution to her household head, few of the younger hijra prostitutes can afford their own place; and living with others provides a certain amount of protection from rough customers and the police. In spite of the resentment and constant complaints by younger hijra prostitutes that they are exploited by their elders, they are extremely reluctant to live on their own.

Hijra Sexuality as a Source of Conflict

The attraction that the hijra role holds for some individuals is the opportunity to engage in sexual relations with men, while enjoying the sociability and relative security of an organized community; these advantages are apparent in contrast to the insecurity and harassment experienced by the effeminate homosexual living on his own. But, whether with husbands or customers, sexual relations run counter to the cultural definitions of the hijra role, and are a source of conflict within the community. Hijra elders attempt to maintain control over those who would "spoil" the hijras' reputation by engaging in sexual activity.

Hijras are well aware that they have only a tenuous hold on respectability in Indian society, and that this respectability is compromised by even covertly engaging in sexual relations. Ascetics have always been regarded with skepticism and ambivalence in Indian society. While paying lip service to the ascetic, conventional Hinduism maintained a very real hostility to it. It classed the non-Vedic ascetic with the dregs of society, "such as incendiaries, poisoners, pimps, spies, adulterers, abortionists, atheists and drunkards"; these fringe members of society found their most respectable status among the Siva sects (O'Flaherty, 1973, p. 67). This ambivalence toward ascetics accurately describes the response of Indian society to the hijra as well, who are also, not coincidentally, worshippers of Siva. In addition, the notion of the false ascetic (those who pretend to be ascetics in order to satisfy their lust) abounds in Hindu mythology. This contradictory attitude, a high regard for asceticism coupled with disdain for those who practice it, characterizes contemporary as well as classical India. Even those families who allow the hijras to perform at births and weddings ridicule the notion that they have any real power.

Indian audiences express their ambivalence toward the hijras by challenging the authenticity of hijra performers. The hijras' emasculation distinguishes them from *zenanas,* or practicing effeminate homosexuals, who do not have the religious powers ascribed to the hijras, but who sometimes impersonates them in order to earn a living. Thus, hijras state that emasculation is necessary because, when they are performing or asking for alms, people may challenge them. If their genitals have not been removed, they will be reviled and driven away as impostors. Hijra elders themselves constantly deride those "men who are men and can have children" and join their community only to make a living from it, or to enjoy sexual relations with men. The parallel between such "fake" hijras and the false ascetics is clear.

Hijras consider sexual activity offensive to the hijra goddess, Bahuchara Mata. Upon initiation into the community, the novice vows to abstain from sexual relations or to marry. Hijra elders claim that all hijra houses lock their doors by nine o'clock at night, implying that no sexual activities occur there. In the cities where hijra culture is strongest, hijras who practice prostitution are not permitted to live with hijras who earn their living by traditional ritual performances. Those who live in these respectable or "family" houses are carefully watched to see that they do not have contact with men. In areas more peripheral to the core of hijra culture, including most of South India, prostitutes do live in houses with traditional hijra performers, and may, in fact, engage in such performances themselves whenever they have an opportunity to do so.

Sexually active hijras usually assert that all hijras join the community so that they can engage in sexual relations with men. As Sita, a particularly candid informant, said:

> Why else would we wear saris? Those who you see how are aged now, when they were young they were just like me. Now they say they haven't got the sexual feeling and they talk only of God and all, but I tell you, that is all nonsense. In their younger days, they also did this prostitution and it is only for the sexual feeling that we join. (Field notes, 1981-2)

The hijras who most vehemently denied having sexual relations with men were almost always over 40. It appears that as they get older, hijras give up sexual activity. Such change over the life cycle parallels that in India generally; in the Hindu cultural ideal, women whose sons are married are expected to give up sexual activity. In fact, not all women do so, but there is a social pressure to do so. People ridicule and gossip about middle aged women who act in ways that suggest active sexual interest (Vatuk, 1985). The presentation of self as a non-sexual person that occurs with age also appears among the hijras. The elderly ones may wear male clothing in public, dress more conservatively, wearing white rather than boldly colored saris, act in a less sexually suggestive manner, and take on household domestic roles that keep them indoors.

Although hijra elders are most vocal in expressing disapproval of hijras sexual relations, even younger hijras who have husbands or practice prostitution admit that such behavior runs counter to hijra norms and lowers their status in the larger society. Hijra prostitutes say that prostitution is a necessary evil for them, the only way for them to earn a living. They attribute the frequency of hijra prostitution to the declining economic status of the hijras in India since the time of Independence. At that time the rajas and nawobs in the princely states, who are important patrons of hijra ritual performances, lost their offices. Hijras also argue that in modern India, declining family size and the spread of Western values, which undermine belief in their powers, also contributes to their lowered economic position, making prostitution necessary.

INDIA AS AN ACCOMMODATING SOCIETY

India is characteristically described as a sexually tolerant society (Bullogh, 1976; Carrier 1980). Indeed, the hijra role appears to be elastic enough to accommodate a wide variety of individual temperaments, identities, behaviors, and levels of commitment, and still function in a culturally accepted manner. This elasticity derives from the genius of Hinduism: although not every hijra lives up to the role at the highest level, the role nonetheless gives religious meaning to cross-gender behavior, that is despised, punished and pushed beyond the pale of the cultural system in other societies.

Several different aspects of Hindu thought explain both the ability of Indian society to absorb an institutionalized third gender role, as well as to provide several contexts within which to handle the tension between the ideal and real aspects of the role. Indian mythology contains numerous examples of androgynes (see O'Flaherty, 1980), impersonators of the opposite sex, and among both deities and humans individuals with sex changes. Myths are an important part of popular culture. Sivabhaktis (worshipers of Siva) give hijras special respect because one of the forms of Siva is Ardhanarisvara, ("the lord who is half woman"). Hijras also associate themselves with Vishnu, who transforms himself into Mohini, the most beautiful woman in the world, in order to take back the sacred nectar from the demons who have stolen it. Further, in the worship

of Krishna, male devotees may imagine themselves to be female, and even dress in female clothing; direct identification with Krishna is forbidden, but the devoted may identify with him indirectly by identifying with Radha, that is, by taking a female form. Thousands of hijras identify themselves as Krishna's wives in a ritual performed in South India. These are only a few of the contexts within which the hijras link themselves to the Great Tradition of Hinduism and develop a positive definition for their feminine behavior.

In handling the conflict between the real and the ideal, hijras and other groups in the Indian population are confronted with the seemingly conflicting value which Hinduism places on both eroticism and procreation, on the one had, and non-attachment and asceticism, on the other. Both Hinduism and Islam are what Bullough calls "sex-positive" religions (1976). Both allow for the tolerance of a wider range of sexual expression than exists in western culture with its restrictive Judeo-Christian, religious heritage. Hinduism explicitly recognizes that humans achieve their ultimate goals—salvation, bliss knowledge and (sexual) pleasure—by following many different paths because humans differ in their special abilities and competencies. Thus, Hinduism allows a different ethic according to one's own nature and affords the individual temperament the widest latitude, from highly idealistic morality, through genial toleration, and, finally, to compulsive extremes (Lannoy, 1975).

Hindu thought attempts to reconcile the value conflict between sexuality and chastity through the concept of a life cycle with four stages. Each stage has its appropriate sexual behavior: In the first stage one should be a chaste student, in the second stage a married householder, in the third a forest dweller preparing for withdrawal from society, and in the final stage, a sannyasin, the ascetic who has renounced everything. Thus, the Hindu ideal is fully integrated life in which each aspect of human nature, including sexuality, has its time. Hijras implicitly recognize these stages in their social organization through a hierarchy in which one begins as a chela and moves into the position of guru as one gets older, taking on chelas and becoming less sexually active.

Hindu mythology also provides some contexts within which the contradictions between the ascetic idea and the sexual activity are legitimate: Siva himself is both the great erotic and the great ascetic. In myths he alternates between the two forms. In some mythic episodes Siva is unable to reconcile his two roles as ascetic and householder, and in others he is a hypocritical ascetic because of his sexual involvement with Parvati, his consort (O'Flaherty, 1973). Indian goddesses as sexual figures also exist in abundance and in some stories a god will take on a female form specifically to have sexual relations with a male deity.

Where Western culture feels uncomfortable with contradictions and makes strenuous attempts to resolve them, Hinduism allows opposites to confront each other without a resolution, "celebrating the idea that the universe is boundlessly various, and . . . that all possibilities may exist without excluding each other" (O'Flaherty, 1973, p. 318). It is this characteristically Indian ability to tolerate, and even embrace, contradictions at social, cultural and personality levels, that provides a context for hijras. Hijras express in their very bodies the confrontation of femaleness and maleness as polar opposites. In Indian society they are not only tolerated but also valued.

ENDNOTES

1. I would like to thank Veena Oldenburg for calling this to my attention. A similar pattern exists among the courtesans in North India (Oldesnburg, 1984).
2. Alan Roland (1982) has insightfully examined some of the emotional and psychological aspects of hierarchy within the Hindu joint family, and many of his conclusions could well be applied to the hijra hierarchy.
3. Some of these religious occasions are participated in by non-hijras as well, while others celebrate events specific to the hijra community, such as the anniversary of the deaths of important gurus.
4. More recently, hijras have been issued ration cards for food in New Delhi, but must apply only under the male names.
5. A more detailed description of this literature is found in Nanda (1984) and Nanda (in press).
6. "Mouth Congress" is considered the appropriate sexual activity for eunuchs disguised as women, in the Kama Sutra. An Editor's note (Burton, 1962, p. 124) suggests that this practice is no longer common in India, and is perhaps being replaced by sodomy, which has been introduced since the Muslim period.
7. Social class factors are relevant here. Boys who are born with indeterminate sex organs (I came across three such cases by hearsay) to upper middle class families would not be likely to join the hijras. In two of these cases the men in question were adults; one had been sent abroad to develop his career in science with the expectation that he would not marry, but at least would have the satisfaction of a successful and prestigious career. The other was married by his parents to a girl who, it was known, could not have children. The third is still a toddler and is being brought up as a boy. I also had the opportunity to interview a middle-aged, middle-class man who was desperately trying to find a doctor to perform the transsexual operation on him in a hospital. He chose not to join the hijras because of their "repuration" but envied them their group life and their ability to live openly as women.
8. Gurus are sometimes considered like mothers, sometimes like fathers, and sometimes like husbands. Their female aspect is related ot the nurturing and care and concern they have for their chelas; the male aspect refers more to the authority they have over their chelas and the obediece and loyalty that is due them.

REFERENCES

Anderson, C. (1977). *Gay men in India.* Unpublished manuscript, University of Wisconsin.

Bhimbhai, K. Pavayas. (1901). Gujarat population, Hindus. In J. M. Campbell (Compiler), *Gazetteer of the Bombay Presidency, 4,* part 1. Bombay: Government Central Press.

Bradford, N. J. (1983). Transgenderism and the cult of Yellamma: Heat, sex and sickness in South Indian ritual. *Journal of Anthropological Research, 39,* 307–322.

Bullough, V. L. (1976). *Sexual variance in society and history.* Chicago: University of Chicago Press.

Carrier, J. (1980). Homosexual behavior in cross cultural perspective. In J. Marmor (Ed.), *Homosexual behavior: A modern reappraisal* (pp. 100–122). New York: Basic Books.

Carstairs, G. M. (1957). *The twice born.* London: Hogarth Press.

Faridi, F. L. (1899). Hijras. In J. M. Campbell (Compiler), *Gazatteer of the Bombay Presidency, 9,* part 2. Bombay: Government Central Press.

Freeman, J. M. (1979). *Untouchable: An indian life history.* Stanford, CA: Stanford University Press.

Hiltebeitel, A. (1980). Siva, the goddess, and the disguises of the Pandavas and Draupadi. *History of religions, 20*(1/2), 147–174.

India Today. Fear is the key. (1982, September 15), pp. 84–85

The Kama Sutra of Vatsyayana. (1964). (R. F. Burton, Trans.). New York: E. P. Dutton.

Lannoy, R. (1975). *The speaking tree.* New York: Oxford University Press.

Lynton, H. S., & Rajan, M. (1974). *Days of the beloved.* Berkley: University of California Press.

Mark, M. E. (1981). *Falkland Road: Prostitutes of Bombay.* New York: Knopf.

Mehta, S. (1945–1946). Eunuchs, pavaiyas and hijras. *Gufarat ahitya Sabha.* Amdavad, Karyavahi, Part 2, Ahmedabad.

Money, J., & Wiedeking, C. (1980). *Handbook of human sexuality* (pp. 270–284). B. B. Wolman & J. Money (Eds.), Englewood Cliffs, N. J.: Prentice-Hall.

Nanda, S. (1984). The hijras of India: A preliminary report. Medicine and Law, 3, 59–75.

Nanda, S. (in press). Dancers only? In Murray (Ed.), *Cultural diversity and homosexualities.* New York: Longman.

O'Flaherty, W. (1973). *Asceticism and eroticism in the mythology of Siva.* London: Oxford University Press.

O'Flaherty, W. (1980). *Women, androgynes, and other mythical beasts.* Chicago: University of Chicago Press.

Oldenburg, V. (1984). *The making of colonial Lucknow.* Princeton, N. J.: Princeton University Press.

Opler, M. (1960). The hijras (hermaphrodites) of India and Indian national character: A rejoinder, *American Anthropologist, 62,* 505–511.

Rajagopalachary, C. (1980). Mahabharata. Bombay: Bharatiya Vidya Bhavan.

Roland, A. (1982). Toward a psychoanalytical psychology of hierarchical relationships in Hindu India. *Ethos, 10*(3), 232–253.

Salunkhe, G. (1976, August 8). The cult of the hijras. *Illustrated Weekly,* pp. 16–21.

Shah, A. M. (1961). A note on the hijras of Gujerat. *American Anthropologist, 61,* 1325–1330.

Sinha, A. P. (1967). Procreation among the eunuchs. *Eastern Anthropologist, 20,* 168–176.

The Tribune, (1983, August 26). Five eunuchs in India, Pak. P 2.

Vatuk, S. (1985). South Asian cultural conceptions of sexuality. In J. K. Brown & V. Kerns (Eds.), *In her prime: A new view of middle-aged women* (pp. 137–152).

Wikan, U. (1977). Man becomes woman: Transsexualism in Oman as a key to gender roles. *Man, 12,* 304–319.

READING 9–4

THE SYPHILITIC SHOCK

Stanislav Andreski

During the 16th and 17th centuries Europe was host to what historians would later describe as "The Great Witch Craze," an astounding epidemic of violence perpetrated against hundreds of thousands of persons of both sexes,

---

Source: 1982 (May), *Encounter* (London, England).

children as well as adults, who were presumed to be witches. Various explanations have been proposed but as the following reading shows each is open to serious objection. Stanislas Andreski puts forward a hypothesis that defies any easy labeling. It is not framed in structural-functional, cultural-material, or evolutionist terms, but combines psychology, medical knowledge, social conditions, and moral strictures as they interacted over a time-period of roughly 150 years. The terms of his thesis are two: (a) considerably more females than males were accused of being witches; and (b) the rise in accusations coincided with the introduction of syphilis from the newly discovered continent of America.

Andreski was the first scholar to notice how these two phenomena coincided in time, and the argument he puts forward is plausible. The critical eye he turns on earlier hypotheses is acute, and his criticisms of witchcraft explanations advanced by two other scholars, Keith Thomas and Alan MacFarlane, are to the point. Yet, although Andreski's thesis might be correct, and he argues his case logically and apparently with the facts on his side, one wonders why in the countless court cases and philosophical/theological discussions about witchcraft throughout that period syphilis hardly ever receives a mention. And again, while in most other respects the Salem horror was of a piece with European witchcraft, syphilis seems to have been entirely absent from the region.

The Witch Hunts of the 16th and 17th century present one of the most bizarre and gruesome spectacles to be found in the history of mankind. My interest was drawn to this extraordinary phenomenon in connection with a critique of Max Weber's concept of rationalisation which can be shown as misleading on various other grounds as well, but which the evidence of the Witch Hunts suffices to discredit. For how can we speak of the European outlook or the Western way of life becoming more "rational" or "rationalised" during the era when people were in the grip of a mania which fits better the label of irrationality than any other form of mass behaviour recorded by history?

Unless we want to make it synonymous with the lack of knowledge or with error (and therefore superfluous as a concept) we must define irrationality as an attitude to knowledge, characterised by the inclination to hold on to a belief or to persist in the choice of a means to a given end, despite the availability of the knowledge which shows it to be erroneous. With this definition, we cannot say that the Dobu islanders' beliefs about witchcraft were irrational since, given their knowledge, they had no good reasons for regarding them as false. In contrast, we can assert that the striking spread of preoccupation with witchcraft in Europe after 1500, which continued for more than a century, did constitute a growth of irrationality because it occurred despite the accumulation of knowledge. We cannot explain Isaac Newton's credulity by supposing that he did not know enough to appreciate the reasons which led Francis Bacon or Michel de Montaige to incredulity a century earlier. The eagerness to silence the critics by censorship and persecution suggests that the theoreticians of witch hunts did not feel completely secure in their beliefs. As is well known, anyone who criticised the beliefs or procedures was accused of being in league with devils and witches, and therefore a witch himself.

There are many gripping and exhaustive accounts of the facts but the explanations are few, and even the most ingenious of them seem to me inadequate—at least in the sense that although they may explain a particular feature within a given region, they fail to account for the generality of the phenomenon. However, might we not suppose that there is no need for a general explanation because the same kind of behaviour was prompted by different circumstances in each region? I don't see how one could refute conclusively such an interpretation; but it seems very improbable that a clustering of such activities could be due to sheet coincidence. However, perhaps we could be satisfied with regarding it simply as a wave of imitation, with the added (and well-founded) assumption that absurdity does not preclude imitation.

This point raises great difficulties. The propensity to imitate undoubtedly constitutes one of the most fundamental characteristics of our species, ineradicably rooted in its social nature. For any single individual, this propensity provides a sufficient explanation of why he resembles in so many

ways those among whom he lives. On the collective level, moreover, there is something which might be called the momentum of a wave of imitation. Once a pattern of behaviour has been widely imitated, it acquires a self-perpetuating force which is (at least partly) independent of the circumstances which promoted it initially. This factor must be taken into account despite our inability to assess its weight within a degree of approximation which is better than very rough. However, the propensity to imitate—which is universal and probably constant among large populations—cannot explain why in a given time and place a certain pattern is imitated rather than another. We must, therefore, search for factors which might have predisposed people to imitate what they did. Our explanation, moreover, must be in terms of phenomena of the same order of generality as the explanadum.

I wish to make clear that I am offering no explanation of why people believe in magic or in witchcraft, which is a special form of it. I merely note that in all pre-scientific cultures people think that you can harm or help other persons (on yourself, for that matter) by pronouncing certain words ("incantations") or performing certain acts ("rituals"). Many illustrious thinkers—from Herbert Spencer and Edward Tylor to Emile Durkheim and Bronislaw Malinowski—have addressed themselves to the task of explaining the universality of such beliefs, and I have nothing new to add on this question. My sole purpose here is to explain the changes which occurred in Europe during the 16th and 17th centuries.

There is a consensus among the historians that the Witch Craze was not a continuation of the tradition but something unprecedented in its intensity which was connected with a striking change in the attitude of the Church. According to Hugh Trevor-Roper:

"In the eighth century, we find St Boniface, the English apostle of Germany, declaring roundly that to believe in witches and werewolves is unchristian. In the same century Charlemagne decreed the death penalty for anyone who, in newly converted Saxony, burnt supposed witches. Such burning, he said, was 'a pagan custom.' In the next century, St. Agobard, Bishop of Lyon, repudiated the belief that witches could make bad weather and another unknown Church dignitary declared that night-flying and metamorphosis were hallucinations and that whoever believed in them 'is beyond doubt an infidel and a pagan.' This statement was accepted into the canon law and became known as the *canon Episcopi or capitulum Episcopi*. It remained the official doctrine of the Church. In the eleventh century the laws of Kin Coloman of Hungary declined to notice witches 'since they do not exist', and the twelfth-century John of Salisbury dismissed the idea of a witches' sabbat as a fabulous dream. In the succeeding centuries, when the craze was being built up, all this salutary doctrine would have to be reversed. The laws of Charlemagne and Coloman would be forgotten; to deny the reality of night-flying and metamorphosis would be officially declared heretical; the witches' sabbat would become an objective fact, disbelieved only (as a doctor of the Sorbonne would write in (1609) by those of unsound mind; and the ingenuity of churchmen and lawyers would be taxed to explain away the inconvenient text of canon law, the *canon Episcopi. . . .*"

The oldest explanation—which goes back to the wonderfully brave eye-witness critics of this practice—attributes it to ignorance and stupidity. No doubt the general ignorance of the population still uninfluenced by the discoveries of science constituted a general underlying condition: but we have no evidence that ignorance or stupidity increased in other fields of culture. So we would have a perfectly circular explanation if we took the persecution of witches as evidence of the state of mind to which this practice is attributed.

Like many people after them, the 18th-century philosophers regarded Witch Trials as a relic of the barbarian past to which the Enlightenment based on science had put an end. Their view of why these trials ceased is perfectly tenable because it is true that this occurred at the time when the discoveries of science began to influence the outlook of all educated persons. However, because historical research was only in its very beginnings, these thinkers did not know that the two centuries which preceded theirs did not represent a fair picture of the

earlier times, and that never before had the Europeans been so obsessed with this particular superstition as during the two centuries which witnessed the birth of science and revival of scholarship and philosophy. The great intensification of the persecutions at such a time demands a specific explanation which cannot be in terms of sheer inertia of tradition. On the other hand, the common acceptance of the belief in witchcraft was an underlying and pre-existing condition without which the said intensification could not have occurred, and which can be attributed to cultural inertia and some very widely spread mental tendencies. However, inertia of old beliefs may have accounted up to a point for the behavior of peasants but not for the well-documented change in the attitude of the intellectuals who abandoned the limited scepticism of their predecessors, became just as (if not more) obsessed with the fear of witches as the peasants, and played a crucial role in inciting and organising the hunts.

EXPLANATIONS

Let me begin a brief survey of the explanations of the great Witch-Hunt with the latest, which also happens to be the flimsiest.

In her book, *Die Hexen der Neuzeit*,[2] Claudia Flonegger interprets the Witch Trials as a part of the process (if not a deliberate method) of lowering women's status and bolsteting up patriarchy. Although not all historians would agree with her assessment of the trend, let us assume that she is right in what she says about the changes in "the position of women." Even if we admitted that the wave of Witch Trials did contribute to a lowering of this position, it would not follow that one would have discovered their hidden purpose. Such a conclusion would be warranted only if we had grounds for believing that Witch Trials were motivated (if not entirely, then at least to a large extent) by the desire to subjugate the female population.

The first reason for rejecting such a surmisal is that too many men and boys were burnt. It is true—and it is a fact which I shall endeavour to explain—that at the beginning of the 16th century, not only did the number of the victims drastically increase, but also the sex ratio among them changed to women's disadvantage. None the less, in absolute numbers the number of male victims also seems to have increased, and they constituted (according to the estimates summarized by Jean Delumeau[3]) about one-fourth or one-fifth of the total number. Even if it is true (as some historians maintain) that males constituted only 10% or 15% of the victims, it is scarcely conceivable that so many men would have been burnt if the aim were to frighten women into submission.

An equally strong argument against viewing witch-burning as a strategy of "sex war" is that resorting to it would be as rational as using a sledge-hammer to crack a nut: it is better to have a slave than a corpse, and there is no need for torture and burning when simple beating would be enough for the purpose. The Moslems have always maintained women in much greater subjection without a recourse to the methods of the witch hunters. In our own days, Khomeini and his faithful have been able to roll back in Iran the world-wide tide of women's emancipation and to put them back into a very inferior position with the aid of intimidation backed up by a few stonings.

More ingenious is the explanation put forth by Keith Thomas.[4] As is fashionable nowadays, Thomas turns to the economic factors but he adds an interesting application of some psychological or psychoanalytic concepts. The influence of capitalism upon rural life, according to hi thesis, led to the destruction of village solidarity and a clash between the duty to help the unfortunate neighbours and the pursuit of self-enrichment. People who were growing rich no longer complied with this duty, but the tradition was still strong enough to make them feel guilty about keeping all their wealth for themselves. Now, according to the psychoanalysts, when feelings of guilt are repressed from the consciousness, they tend to be "projected" on to those who have been wronged. The wrongdoer denies that he has wronged them, and not only imputes to the wronged hostile feelings towards him, but also convinces himself that they are actively doing or have done

something to harm him. Refusing help to poor old women would be especially likely to make the budding capitalists feel guilty, and therefore poor old women would be the most common objects of a "projection" which would then prompt suspicions and accusations. Thomas backs his thesis by an examination of the materials from the English courts, where he finds that a victim of accusation has often been previously refused aid.

Although it is quite possible that situations of this kind did on some occasions trigger off a victimisation, as a general explanation Thomas' thesis seems inadequate despite its ingenuity. Firstly, on psychological grounds. A "projection" of guilt could have prompted avoidance or further harassment of the wronged without going to such extremes. It could also have led to an espousal of a belief which justified the refusal to help and removed the feelings of guilt. Indeed, the link between John Calvin's doctrine of predestination and the development of capitalism probably rested on its appeal as a justification for leaving the poor to their fate, on the grounds that they are poor because they have been damned by God. Perhaps quite often the process of "repressing" and "projecting" such guilt feelings might have determined who was picked up for victimisation once the hunt was on; but it is difficult to imagine how it could have produced the widely shared obsessional fear which constituted the necessary background of these events.

A comparative view yields an even more decisive argument against accepting Keith Thomas' thesis as a general explanation. If the Witch Craze had been a by-product of development of Capitalism, it should have been most virulent where this development started earliest or went furhest—Italy, the Low Countries, and England—and this was not the case. Indeed, though affected, these countries suffered a good deal less than France and Germany where the village community was much less (indeed, hardly at all) disturbed by new capitalist enterprise. Furthermore, in neither of these countries had there been a clustering of the trials around the centres of capitalism—the Hanseatic cities or

Paris—while many of the bloodiest persecutions occurred in remote rural areas like the foothills of the Alps or Aquitaine. It appears from the not exactly comparable estimates made by A. Macfarlane and G.F. Black,[5] that about 20 times more witches were burnt in rustic and sparsely inhabited Scotland than in the five counties round London, the population of which was not much smaller. The craze reached Poland late and began to rage only during the 17th century when the cities were decaying and the very rudimentary capitalism was in full regression.

The final argument against Keith Thomas' thesis as a general explanation is that what he says about the social positions of the victims he has studied does not seem to apply to other samples. Soldan, Heppe and Bauer[6] give long lists of victims in various places in Germany where we find traders, artisans, squires, priests, burgomasters and even a High Court judge. Only the high nobility are absent. In her study of Luxembourg, Dupont-Bouchat[7] found mayors, magistrates, and rich merchants, while E.W. Monter[8] found wives of men of equivalent rank among the victims of the trials in the Jura.

The same argument applies with an even greater force against the view put forth by Jeanne Favret[9] that the Witch Hunts formed a part of (or were a manifestation of) "class conflict."

The persecutions, she argues, were instigated not by peasants but by the judges, whose motive was fear of the counter-culture of the weak. This last point is an unwarranted extrapolation of a notion which was perhaps not without applicability to the recent situation in France and a few other countries in 1968 when the "hippies" were throwing gauntlets to the "squares." Perhaps also the ideas and the way of life of the anarchist and communist groups, which have kept on springing up since the French Revolution, could be regarded as a "counter culture" which presented a challenge to the established culture and, therefore, inspired fear in the official circles. As far as the old Europe is concerned, there is no evidence that the folkways of peasants (let alone of the starving vagabonds) were regarded as a danger or a challenge by royalty and the nobility.

Nor could the rebellious peasants think of any innovations, and they justified their complaints by traditional references to the Bible. True, the nobility did have reasons to fear the numerical strength of the peasants; but they always took good precautions to keep them under the yoke, and did not need the pretext of witchcraft to mete out atrocious punishment. The sanguinary reprisals against peasant uprisings and banditry claimed many more victims than the Witch Trials: instead of individual burnings, entire fields were covered with impaled rebels. The Witch Hunts, moreover, would have been a very inappropriate method of nipping resistance in the bud because they were biased not against the most dangerous category—young me—but against the least dangerous—old women. True, even lonely and poor old women were evidently regarded as dangerous by powerful and rich men: but the question is *why*?

Favret is on safer ground when she claims that most of the processes were initiated by the judges or judicial officials. This is confirmed by Baschwitz and Mandrou;[10] and it is hardly surprising since they had the power. On the other hand, there are many examples of popular initiative and lynchings even when the trials were already forbidden by the princes or the parliament as was the case in Poland. The "Witch-Finder General", Matthew Hopkins, for example, started a business after the Civil War, traveling to various places in England at the request of the local population in the grip of a panic, and receiving payment from them piece-rate. The fact that most of the victims were peasants (57% on Delumeau's reckoning) proves no bias against them since everywhere they constituted at least 8/10ths (if not 9/10ths) of the population. In any case, too many victims were of respectable status to permit an interpretation of the Witch Trials as a method of keeping down the poor.

Alan Macfarlane's explanation is also economic but he combines it (in contrast with Keith Thomas) with some ideas brought from anthropology rather than psychoanalysis.[11] He also thinks that the wave of Witch Trials was caused by "the rise of capitalism" but sees the connection as the opposite of a

Class Conflict. His materials show that the accusations were usually made against neighbours or at least persons with whom the accusers had been in close contact. This means that the Witch Hunts were a grass-roots movement rather than something engineered "from above", which is the opposite of the picture given by Mandrou.[12] Personally, I doubt whether either of them is wrong about the cases which he examined; it seems to me clear that their materials simply illustrate the variations which did in fact occur.

Macfarlane takes his clue from the studies of Witchcraft in contemporary Africa where the anthropologists have noticed that (contrary to what might be expected *a priori*) townsmen, who appear to be modernised, engage in witchcraft more readily than people who have remained in tribal villages hardly touched by the science-based civilisation. This paradox was first reported by Monica Hunter-Wilson in 1935, in her book, *Reaction to Conquest.* Her explanation was that witchcraft is more tempting when additional curb are put on physical violence, while everyday conflicts become more intractable owing to the absence or irrelevance of regulation by deeply-rooted customs. Many later studies have corroborated this view. Macfarlane applies this interpretation to the England of the 17th century and maintains that the penetration or monetary economy into the villages dislocated the traditional structure, bred more frequent and intense conflicts, and thereby stimulated Witchcraft.

The first objection against Macfarlane's thesis is the same as against Keith Thomas': namely, that a comparative survey reveals little (if not an inverse) connection between the development of capitalism and the dimensions of the persecutions. The second weakness of the thesis is the assumption that an increase in the number of trial indicates more frequent recourse to witchcraft. We may believe the anthropologists who tell us that they have observed such an increase in Africa. About the 17th century we have no statements from independent observers, trained in objectivity and free to report. Confessions wrung out by torture tell us nothing except what the tormentors wanted to hear. Nor does the number of accusations prove anything about the frequency of the practice. For how can I know that someone is bewitching me in secret unless his incantations and rites do in fact produce the desired effect? On the other hand, if people are in the habit of attributing their ills to witchcraft, then any increase in misfortunes will prompt an increase in the number of accusations.

Nor can we presume that there is a close connection between intensity of conflicts and frequency of accusations, unless we have grounds for presupposing that the beliefs are unchanging. You can have plenty of conflict of the most murderous kind without any accusations of witchcraft. The intensification of the practice of witchcraft in African cities during recent decades has produced no court proceedings against witches because officials regarded it all as a superstition. So we can infer nothing about the practice from the court records. All we know is that the fear spread, and people became more eager to search for witches and to punish them.

We must bear in mind that the changes in the European societies of the 17th century were very much slower than the upheaval wrought in the lives of African tribesmen by the impact of fully fledged industrial civilisation. And for this reason they could not have brought disorientation and uprooting on the same scale. We have, therefore, no grounds for even suspecting that the same causal link was involved. Some historians' love for the word "Revolution" should not lead us to forget that economic changes in the previous centuries to which this label is often affixed (including the so called Industrial Revolution) were so slow that they escaped the notice of most people who lived through them. We must conclude, therefore, that, though interesting and ingenious, Macfarlane's thesis offers no adequate explanation.

More plausible is H. R. Trevor-Roper's view[13] linking the Witch Craze with the Wars of Religion. Whereas the changes in the economy (other than natural calamities) were almost imperceptible, wars did bring violent shocks and upheavals, and evoked waves of emotion of an altogether different dimension from what might be generated by the slow process of commercialization of personal relations and disintegration of village solidarity. One can well imagine how, faced with devastation and slaughter, gripped by fear and inclined to look for scapegoats, superstitious people would succumb to an obsession with witches. And it is true that the biggest hunts occurred in Germany, which was more devastated by the wars than any other country. On the other hand, the correspondence is only very broad—by country (in the sense of a cultural area) and epoch—and is not evident region-by-region and year-by-year, as many of the big Witch Hunts took place in regions unscourged by wars. Furthermore, we cannot explain something unprecedented by something of much more common occurrence— many wars, just as sanguinary as those of the 16th and the 17th centuries, have been waged before, and since, without provoking Witch Hunts. Another weakness of this explanation is that no one has shown what the psychological mechanism would be which would link fighting and war with an obsession with witches. The soldiers of those times were habitual looters and rapists, inclined to maltreat all defenseless people. But why should they have wanted to burn women rather than merely abuse them? Nor do we have any grounds for supposing that the civilians must have become obsessed with fear of witches because they lived in fear of the soldiers. In most wars civilians were afraid of soldiers' depredations, but even at the height of the Witch Craze there is no evidence that anyone blamed witches for causing wars or the havoc wrought by these, although they were held responsible for disease. This is perfectly understandable: people could see the soldiers killing, burning and looting— there was no mystery about it—but they knew nothing about bacteria.

Trevor-Roper's thesis could be defended by pointing out that he speaks of the War of Religion rather than wars pure and simple. But what are "wars of religion"? The explanation clearly falls short if we mean thereby wars between collectivities holding different religions, because no one claims that the wars between the Christians and the Moslems or the Catholics and the Greek-Orthodox provoked waves of witch-hunting. However, the distinguishing feature which the historians have in mind when they use the expression in question is wars accompanied by forcible conversions or by extermination of heretics. Thus restricted, the thesis becomes more defensible but remains, none the less, defective because there seems to be no covariation before the 16th century. One of the most ferocious wars of religion was the crusade against the Albigenses in the 13th century; yet there is no evidence that it was accompanied by witch hunts as distinct from the persecution of the heretics. The same can be said about the wars against the Hussites and the sanguinary suppression of the Lollards by Henry V in the 15th century. At the other end (as Kurt Baschwitz emphasizes), witch trials went on after the Peace of Westphalia.[14]

Like Stalin's chief prosecutor, Andrei Vishinsky, the Medieval and Renaissance theologians and lawyers were unsparing in heaping up reasons for a condemnation: witches were held to be guilty of heresy in the shape of the pact with Satan, while heretics were commonly accused of witchcraft and sexual vice, especially sodomy and incest, as well as of theft, robbery, arson, poisoning the wells and what-not. The practice of burning people alive was used extensively in Spain to force the conversion of Jews and Moslems before it was employed in Witch Hunts. Spain, however, never experienced the massive witch hunts of the kind that afflicted northern Europe. Consequently, despite its prominent role in many witch trials, we cannot regard the Inquisition as the sole instigator in view of the fact that it rejected this role in the country where it developed fastest and furthest. In any case, many more persons were put to death for heresy than for witchcraft. To punish someone for heresy there was no need to trump up charges on another score. Why, then, should a suppression of heresy lead to a hunt for witches?

Though indiscriminate in heaping up abuse, the persecutors discriminated between witches and heretics in penal procedure. A heretic could often save his skin by recantation and repentance (as did Galileo) whereas to a witch this escape route was normally closed. Heretics and rebels were very often burnt or impaled summarily on flimsy evidence, without waiting for their confessions. This could be done because many of them had in fact done or said what they were accused of. Extracting confessions through torture was essential if witches were to be found at all, as there could have been no proper evidence because the victims could not have done what they were accused of.

The weightiest argument against explaining witch hunts in terms of any form of "struggle for power" stems from the predominance of women among the victims and the inclusion of a good number of children, which is exactly the contrary to what happens in wars and political or religious persecutions. Usually only men are killed, while women and children are enslaved or otherwise illused. With extremely few exceptions, not only the top leaders but also all the lower-rank organizers and preachers of all religious or political movements noted in history have been men; which explains the aforementioned fact that repression has always been directed mainly at men. The Witch Hunters, in contrast, more often picked on women who, moreover, were commonly single and poor, or at least neither rich nor powerful, and therefore of all kinds of people were the least likely to represent a danger to the authorities. Soldan, Heppe and Bauer[15] give lists of victims of trials in various German cities. Among these about every fifteenth person is a child; e.g. a blind beggar girl aged 11, two brothers aged 10 and 11, a shoemaker's apprentice aged 13. On the other hand, in the same series of trials, we also find a gravedigger aged 42, a mother of three children aged 24, a single woman aged 32, a burgomaster's wife and a priest of unspecified age. The two youngest victims were aged 6 and 8. With victims of this kind, it is completely implausible to interpret the Witch Hunts as some kind of a purge or repression of enemies. (We must also bear in mind that any form of such an interpretation contradicts flatly the explanations offered by Keith Thomas and Alan Macfarlane.)

A slight variant along the lines of a political explanation is the view (the most widely held among the British historians) that the Witch Hunts were the outcome of the momentum of the machinery of repression which, once set up by the Church for purpose of hunting heretics, went on grinding lesser deviants perhaps because the inquisitors found themselves with nothing to do once heresy had been stamped out but wanted to keep themselves in business. This explanation rests upon an implicit assumption that no other potential victims were available, and this is rather far-fetched. Even if they ran out of known heretics, why couldn't the inquisitors pick on suspects, sinners, usurers, or some ethnic or occupational category? Moreover it would be easy to find victims whose possessions were a little more substantial than what most people accused of witchcraft had. Persecutions of Jews often brought substantial booty, but witch hunts were only occasionally profitable, and then mostly only to low-grade personnel like executioners to whom a few odd household goods made a difference. So an economic motive for keeping the repression going can be ruled out. On the other hand, the explanation in terms of the momentum of repression does not fit the crucial fact of the shift in the sex ratio among the victims after 1500. After that date heretics continued to be mostly women. There are many historical examples of the machinery of terror acquiring a momentum of its own and overshooting the purpose for which it was set up— they range from the carnage launched by the ancient Chinese emperor Wu to Stalin's purges and the rule of Idi Amin in Uganda. In all such cases, however, the overwhelming majority of the victims were men. The shift in the sex ratio is unique.

The Protestants' addiction to witch-hunting provides an equally decisive argument against any explanation invoking the inertia of the institutions, because the Reformation consisted above all of the destruction of the hierarchic edifice of the Church, including the Inquisition. Owing to the absence of centralised control the Witch Hunts in Protestant lands tended to be grass-roots affairs (which, incidentally, may account for the difference between the findings of Mandrou and those of Thomas and Macfarlane); but obsessive fear was just as much in evidence. Luther, Calvin and their followers discarded many of the deeply-rooted tenets of the old Church but fully upheld the notions about witches.

Why? This agreement not only could not stem from but was actually contrary to their idea of going back to the Bible (since no justification could be found there for the persecutions). The teachings of the New Testament are wholly opposed to sanguinary barbarities, and it disregards this particular superstition. True, the Old Testament mentions witches but only casually and bears no trace of an obsession with danger from them. The doctrinal justification for the persecutions was provided by the Catholic theologians whom Luther and Calvin execrated. In Scotland the bloodiest hunts were carried out by the Calvinist zealots following in the footsteps of John Knox; so that there the greatest carnage occurred after the destruction of the old machinery of repression. An explanation in terms of "momentum" can, then, be dismissed. The concordance of attitudes between embattled enemies can cease to be shrouded in mystery only if we can discover circumstances which affected them all regardless of their affiliations and their hate for one another.

In his erudite and massive Ph.D. thesis (submitted to the University of Reading under the title "The Politics of Danger"), Ronald Vanelli presents witchcraft accusations as a scapegoating mechanism which off-loads tensions generated by conflicts which threaten some people's self-image, status, and power. Although the work offers many valuable sidelights, the defect of this view is that it attempts to explain something which is far from ubiquitous by a factor which is (since in every human society there are struggles for esteem and power). Nor is there any evidence that "threats to self-image" were more common where persecutions of witches were taking place than elsewhere. The focus on dangers to esteem and self-esteem stems, I suspect, from a culturally self-centered outlook of a denizen of an affluent and well-medicated society, able to forget about the dangers which inspired the most pervasive fear in earlier times, as they still do in the less fortunate parts of the globe: famine and disease.

The word "disease" provides the clue: but, before following it, we must glance at one more interpretation. Writing before the present fad and fashion of always seeking economic or political explanation Margaret Murray [16] depicted the Witch Hunts as a repressive action of the Christian Churches against the remnants of the pre-Christian religions. Persons burnt as witches were, according to Murray, the priests and, above all, priestesses of the old religion. Their rituals were misrepresented and dubbed as witchcraft. The reunions labeled as "Witches' Sabbaths" did in fact take place, although not in the form described by the demonologists but rather as regular worship of the old pagan gods. The numerical predominance of women among the victims is explained by their greater attachment to the tradition and the central role of home worship in the pre-Christian religions which had more priestesses than priests.

However is seems highly implausible that the Church would have waited so many centuries—in the former domains of the Roman Empire more than a thousand years—before launching an attack on the pagan priesthoods. An even greater weakness stems from the assumption that there was a good deal of truth in the confessions. True, Margaret Murray and her followers rely on records from English courts where the dreadful tortures employed on the Continent were not used. Nevertheless, the accused were locked up in cold, dark and damp dungeons; they were starved, deprived of sleep and beaten. Friedrich Spee, one of the brave opponents (whose book inaugurated the waning of the hunts and who had been a confessor of the accused), wrote:

> "We would all have confessed to being witches if we had been tortured. . . ."[17]

Furthermore, many victims admitted flying on broomsticks, causing storms, and performing other impossible deeds. Why then should we assume that there must be some truth in what they said about acts which we deem possible? Under torture, many

Jews have confessed to "poisoning the wells", killing little Christian boys, and squeezing their blood into Passover bread. Following Murray's method we would have to assume that, because such deeds were physically possible, there must have been some truth in the confessions, despite the obvious untruth of the confessions about making Christ's blood flow by piercing the Eucharist with a knife or causing pestilence.

Keith Thomas, Jean Delumeau, and some other historians who have examined the same materials say that Margaret Murray and her followers make a very arbitrary selection of very late documents. As I have not studied these sources, I have no opinion on this matter; but it seems to me impossible that an organised religion could be widely practised for a thousand years without being detected and attacked by the Church until the 16th century. As a matter of fact, the pre-Christian religions were suppressed by Draconian punishments much earlier. Charlemagne slaughtered the pagan priests in Saxony. In the 11th century there was a large uprising in Poland led by pagan priests which was drowned in blood. It might have been prompted by the dreadful punishments ordered by Kin Boleslaw the Valiant (Chrobry) for non-compliance with the rules of Christianity: such as pulling out teeth for eating meat on Fridays, or cutting off the tongue for blasphemy. There are records of campaigns against pagan priests in Scandinavia; but they all took place soon after the implantation of Christianity. As there is no shred of evidence of a pagan threat to Christianity in the 16th century. Margaret Murray's thesis is untenable, particularly as the authors of demonological treatises speak of the plague of witches as something new.

In view of the fact that all the hitherto advanced explanations are either inadequate or simply false, as well as mutually contradictory, we would be faced with a complete mystery if no more plausible explanation could be devised. I contend, however, that there is an explanation which fits the data much better than any of the preceding and subsumes those of their points which retain some validity.

The Fatal Clue

The inclination to seek the causes of illness in witchcraft is by no means a peculiarity of Europeans in early modern times but an almost universal (if not absolutely universal) feature of all pre-scientific cultures, although the role of witchcraft varies greatly in details and importance. While the Pygmies of the Congo pay scant attention to witchcraft, the Azande (to take another African example) see in it the cause of all illness. The Europeans of the 16th century did not go so far as the Azande and, acquainted with the works of Hippocrates through the writings of Galen, they conceived of other causes of disease such as bad air or food. However, even the most enlightened of them (who regarded the stories of witches flying on broomsticks and feasting with Satan as fairy tales) did not deny that illness *could* be caused by witchcraft. To understand their outlook we must bear in mind that, as scientific medicine did not yet exist, there were no compelling reasons for excluding this possibility. Indeed, the practice of medicine was still thoroughly mixed up with magic. Given the state of knowledge and the nature of the beliefs, it was inevitable that any epidemic would fan the fear of witches and prompt a multiplication of suspicions, accusations and persecutions. The epidemic which coincided chronologically with the Witch Craze was that of syphilis.

Syphilis was either brought to Europe by the sailors of Columbus or underwent a mutation at the beginning of the 16th century which greatly increased its virulence.[18] Perhaps a milder strain existed in the Old World before a more powerful variant was brought from America. Be this as it may, there is no doubt that there was a terrible epidemic from the beginning of the 16th century until the second half of the 17th. Innumerable sources bear ample witness to the havoc it wrought and the dread it inspired. It was known from the beginning that it was transmitted through copulation. The following extract from an entry on The Harlot in an anonymous book called *The Profane State.*, published during the reign of Charles I, illustrates the common notions:

"She [the harlot] *dieth commonly of a lothsome disease.* I mean that disease, unknown to Antiquity, created within some hundreds of years, which took the name from Naples. When hell invented new degrees in sinnes, it was time for heaven to invent new punishments. Yet is this new disease now grown so common and ordinary, as if they meant to put divine Justice to a second task to find out a newer. And now it is high time for our Harlot, being grown lothsome to her self, to runne out of her self by repentance.

Some conceive that when King Henrie the eighth destroyed the publick Stews in the Land (which till his time stood on the banks side on Southwark next the Bear-garden, beasts and beastly women being very fit neighbours) he rather scattered than quenched the fire of lust in this kingdom, and by turning the flame out of the chimney where it had a vent, more endangered the burning of the Commonwealth. But they are deceived: for whilst the Laws of the Land tolerated open uncleannesse, God might justly have made the whole State do penance for whoredome; whereas now that sinne though committed, yet not permitted, and though (God knows) it be too general, it is still but personall."

Although it might have been counter-productive rather than helpful for avoiding contagion, and must have had deleterious effects on health in other ways, the closing of public baths is a measure of the fear of syphilis. Medieval towns had public baths where all orders of society (or almost all) were wont to go and wallow collectively, male and female naked together. These became very rare or disappeared altogether. For example, in Frankfurt, which had 40 such establishments in 1400, there were only 9 in 1530. In the same period, wooden bathtubs disappeared from inns and hotels throughout Europe. Only in Finland and in Budapest under the Ottoman rule did the public town-baths survive. The public baths which came into existence in France in the late 17th century (that is, when the epidemic of syphilis was on the wane) were public only in the sense that anyone could go in for a high fee—which meant that they were available only to the rich—but the bathing was individual.

An illness caught through sin, which was not only fatal but also repulsive, would inevitably evoke harrowing feelings of shame, guilt, and rage against the partner presumed to have transmitted the disease. The psychological mechanism of generalisation and stereotyping would tend to produce in the sufferers a hostile attitude to the other sex, which through imitation and the stimulus of generalized fear would spread among healthy individuals as well. Furthermore, according to psychoanalytic theory, the stronger the feelings of guilt, the more likely they are to be projected—that is repressed from consciousness and imputed to others. The belief in witchcraft constituted a particularly suitable vehicle for such a projection, permitting a displacement of the feelings of guilt by a grievance about being bewitched. These mechanisms would operate in women as well as men; but men ruled and therefore their inclinations determined the course of events.

Crucially important was the fact that public opinion was molded chiefly by the clergy, who were under the obligation to lead exemplary lives and in the Catholic Church to observe chastity. They therefore had reason to feel guilt and shame with special poignancy and would be particularly prone to seek scapegoats on whom these feelings could be projected, and who could be sacrificed in expiation. The strength of these feelings would fuel the psychological mechanism of generalization and stereotyping through which the hate against the partner, from whom the disease might have been contracted, would be extended to others. In principle, the process of generalisation of attitudes can operate upon any common feature. But, here, since all the resentment came from the consequences of the sexual act, the stereotype would be naturally extended to the entire opposite sex, while the most defenseless members thereof would be most likely to be picked on as scapegoats.

To repeat, there is no reason to suppose that this mechanism did not operate among women. It is very likely that the epidemic of syphilis did evoke among women a ground-swell of resentment against men, particularly perhaps against the priests and monks who abused their influences to lead them into sin. Perhaps if the women had had more power, there would have been more male victims of Witch Hunts, but since all the power lay in men's hands, only they were able to give vent to their desire to find scapegoats. It is possible, nevertheless, that some trials of men—especially of clergyment—were instigated by women. The famous affair of Loudun in France in the middle of the 17th century appears to be an example. As I said earlier, there are ample grounds for rejecting the view that Witch Trials were a consciously employed method of subjugating women. Nevertheless, the extent to which one sex can inflict sufferings on the other must reflect their relative power, even when the motives and actions are irrational and self-damaging. We might, therefore, take the sex ratio of the victims as a rough indication of the imbalance of power between the sexes. It was the sexual nature of the disease that directed the search for scapegoats against women, while during other plagues religious or ethnic minorities suffered. The outbreaks of bubonic plague were regularly followed by massacres of Jews.

The more defenseless an individual the more likely he or she is to be picked on as a scapegoat. Thus, in the partrilineal and patriarchal tribes of Africa more accusations are leveled against women than against men—which is not the case in the matrilineal tribes. This does not mean that such accusations are a deliberate method of "keeping women down", which would presuppose that the men do not truly believe in witchcraft. In many tribes in Africa and elsewhere, deliberate tricks are employed for keeping the women under control by so-called secret societies—secret not in the sense that their existence or membership is secret but only that they keep secrets. One of these is that they imitate the voice of the spirit with a device known as a bull-roarer. When this spirit wanders about the village all women and girls as well as uninitiated boys must hide, and any of them who peeps out is killed on the spot. Any initiated man who is divulged this secret to a woman or an uninitiated boy would also be killed.

The ground for attacks against women when syphilis struck was prepared by the change in atti-

tude towards them which took place during the two preceding centuries, and which Jean Delumeau calls "demonisation." Although there is no trace of it in the sayings of Jesus Christ, the idea that women are a source of evil has been present in the Christian tradition at least since St Augustine, and formed a part of the cluster of values which extolled chastity and deprecated pleasures of the flesh. This attitude, however, underwent a drastic reinforcement during the 14th and 15th centuries and reached a frenzy during the 16th. The latter change lends force to my thesis but the reinforcement during the 14th and 15th centuries calls for another explanation—which can be found if we look at the tightening up on celibacy of the clergy and the multiplication of the monastic orders which occurred during that time. The connection between the two trends is perfectly understandable in the light of psychiatry. The more stringent observance of chastity would cause the priests and monks to be more tormented by carnal desire. The aggressive impulses generated by this frustration would be directed at the objects of desire, while the repressed feelings of guilt (for indulging in sinful thoughts or acts) would (through a process of projection) lead to imputation of evil proclivities to all women, above all of wanting to tempt, tease and lead holy men to perdition.[19]

The advance of sacerdotal celibacy stretched over a thousand years: from the Synod of 384 which advised the higher ranks of the clergy to remain celibate (without, however, prescribing any punishment for non-compliance) to the Counter-Reformation when celibacy began to be enforced effectively. Important steps were taken by the Synods during the 11th and 12th centuries which prohibited the sons of priests taking over their fathers' offices, and later excluded them altogether from entering priesthood. Married priests were forbidden to celebrate mass. In 1139 the Lateran Council declared marriages of the higher clergy invalid, and penalized married priests of the lower orders by depriving them of benefices and legal immunities. [20] After the fourth Lateran Council in 1215, through the tireless vigilance of Innocent III. Open marriage of priests ceased except in outlying regions where inspection was difficult. This however, did not mean that chastity was observed. This is what the 19th-century historian Henry C. Lea says on the subject of concubinage:

"However deplorable such an alternative might be in itself, it was surely preferable to the mischief which the unquenched and ungoverned passions of a pastor might inflict upon his parish; and the instances of this were too numerous and too glaring to admit of much hesitation in electing between the two evils. Even Gerson, the leader of mystic ascetics, who recorded his unbounded admiration for the purity of celibacy in his *Dialogus Naturae et Sophiae de Castitate Clericorum,* saw and appreciated its practical evils, and had no scruple in recommending concubinage as a preventive, which, though scandalous in itself, might serve to prevent greater scandals. It therefore requires no great stretch of credulity to believe the assertion of Sleidan, that in some of the Swiss Cantons it was the custom to oblige a new pastor, on entering upon his functions, to select a concubine, as a necessary protection to the virtue of his female parishioners, and to the peace of the families entrusted to his spiritual direction. Indeed, we have already seen (p.261), on the authority of Council of Valladolid in 1322, that such a practice was not uncommon in Spain."

Lea goes on to emphasize:

"In thus reviewing the influences which a nominally celibate clergy exercised over those entrusted to their care, it is perhaps scarcely too much to conclude that they were largely responsible for the laxity of morals which is a characteristic of mediaeval society. No one who has attentively examined the records left to us of that society can call in question the extreme prevalence of the licentiousness which everywhere infected it. Christianity had arisen as the great reformer of a world utterly corrupt. How earnestly its reform was directed to correcting sexual immorality is visible in the persistence with which the Apostles condemned and forbade a sin that the Gentiles scarcely regarded as a sin. The early Church was consequently pure, and its very asceticism is a measure of the energy of its protest against the all-pervading licence which surrounded it. Its teachings, as we have seen, remained unchanged. Fornication continued to be a mortal sin, yet the period of its unquestioned domination over the conscience of Europe was the very period in which licence among the Teutonic races was most unchecked. A Church which, though founded on the Gospel, and wielding the illimitable power of the Roman hierarchy, could yet allow the feudal principle to extend to the *"jus primae noctis"* or *"droit de marquette"* and whose ministers in their character of temporal seigneurs could even occasionally claim the disgusting right themselves, was evidently exercising its influence not for good but for evil.[21]

It was not until the 16th century and, finally, at the Council of Trent (1545–1563) that the final curbs were put on concubinage; thenceforth unchastity of priests and monks had to be clandestine, and it appears to have become much rarer. It is usually said that the new strictness was a response to the Protestant challenge. This is on the whole true; but the impact of syphilis must have played an important part in this change. In my previous ENCOUNTER article, I have given reasons for linking the rise of Puritanism as well as for the introduction of a stronger dose of Puritanism, in the wider sense, into the Catholic Church, with the epidemic. Here I should like to add that it must have made the obligation of chastity much easier to enforce because sinners would be likely to be detected by the visible symptoms of the disease.

It appears, therefore, that the lay clergy began to suffer from serious sexual frustration only in the 16th century. None the less, chastity was becoming more widely practised in earlier times because the three preceding centuries saw the great multiplication of the monastic orders and the tightening up of the discipline on this score within them. Indeed, the monks were the chief helpers of the Popes in their struggle to impose celibacy on the lay clergy. And as for the "demonisation" of women, we must remember that before 1500 nearly all writers and all theologians were monks.

MONKS & CELIBACY

An objection to the foregoing argument might be raised on the ground that although their clergy were allowed to marry, the Protestants also burned witches. The thesis, however, can be saved by taking into account the following considerations.

The first is that the Catholics burned more witches than the Protestants—perhaps twice or three times as many. Secondly, the demonisation of women had gone very far by the time of the Reformation; and the Protestants inherited this tradition. Thirdly, the Protestant theologians shared with the Catholics the anti-hedonist principles. They abolished celibacy of the clergy not because they approved of indulgence in pleasures but as a way of stopping fornication. The abolition of confessions and absolutions, moreover, made it more difficult to get rid of feelings of guilt. We can plausibly surmise that this factor would tend to foster "projection" and "scapegoating", and would counteract in some measure the contrary effects of the abolition of celibacy. A much stricter enforcement of premarital chastity and marital fidelity—in combination with the puritanical refusal ever to discuss matters pertaining to sexual intercourse—would also tend to generate enough hang-ups to stimulate demonisation of women. Furthermore, the absence of a powerful hierarchy made the Protestant, clergy more vulnerable to castigation by their own flock for not living up to what they preached. Thus, any sign of having caught syphilis might bring upon a Protestant clergyman an even prompter punishment than in the case of a Catholic. None the less, although John Calvin and other Protestant theologians supported the hunts for witches, the chief theorists of the persecution were all Catholics and nearly all were monks. Monks played a crucial role in nearly all the hunts which took place in the Catholic lands, the Dominicans being particularly prominent.

The Witch Craze did not spread to the lands of the Orthodox Church: neither Russia nor the principalities of Wallachia and Moldavia were affected. The ferocious persecution of the Old Believers in Russia was accompanied by no witch hunts—which provides another argument against the view that they were a by-product of a fight against heresies. The schism between the Eastern and Western Churches occurred before the celibacy of the clergy was established: and the Orthodox priests contin-

ued to marry. As the schism occurred several centuries before the demonisation of women reached a high pitch in the West, the Eastern Church was not affected by this tradition, in contrast to the Protestant denominations. True, the Orthodox bishops were celibate, but they normally underwent voluntary castration before promotion; an entrant into the priesthood had a choice between ambition and marriage. Being castrated, the higher clergy of the Orthodox Church could not have suffered so much from frustration and guilt as did their Western equivalents. Consequently, there must have been less scope within their minds for the operations of the mechanisms of projection and scapegoating, which underlay the demonisation of women and the Witch Hunt in the West.

The same factor explains why the Witch Craze never spread to the lands of Islam, where the mullahs were hardly likely to suffer from severe sexual frustration (they usually had many wives). Furthermore, you cannot demonise women when their position is so low that they are little more than chattels. Cloistered in purdah, covered up by chadors and yashmaks from head to foot, women could hardly be seen as temptresses by polygamous Moslem theologians.

Nor did the Witch Craze infect the Jews, although they were close witnesses of these happenings. Significantly, from the viewpoint of the present thesis, rabbis are not only allowed but are obliged to marry: even a widowed rabbi will not be accepted by his community unless he remarries.

It is likely that the proportion of priests and monks who were suffering from severe sexual frustration was much greater when entry into their ranks was the only avenue to freedom from want and a respectable status for men of humble origin. Many younger sons of better-off families, were forced to take the vows against their will, and only in an ecclesiastic career could a man of intellectual disposition find an opportunity to devote himself to study. When it became possible to attain either of these goals in other walks of life, the entrants would be more self-selected in respect of their tolerance of chastity, that is, a weaker sexual appetite. Psychoanalytic theory suggests that lesser sexual frustration would diminish the inclination to demonise women. [22]

OF LUST & DISEASE

The sources bear ample witness to the preoccupation of the Witch Hunters with lust and disease. The Emperor Maximilian I, who, in 1495, declared syphilis to be God's punishment for men's sins, became very worried about depredations caused by witches. In 1508 he sought advice on this matter from Abbot Trithemius, who in that year published a book called *The Enemy of Witchcraft*. There he wrote:

> "It is a repulsive breed, that of the witches, especially the female among them, who, with the help of evil spirits or magic potions, bring to mankind endless harm. . . . Mostly they make people possessed by demons and let them be tormented by unheard-of pains. . . . Hearken, they even indulge in carnal intercourse with demons. . . . Unfortunately, the number of these witches is very great, and even in the smallest village you can find a witch. . . . People and cattle die through the wickedness of these women and nobody understands that it all comes from witches. Many people suffer most dreadful illnesses and do not know that they are bewitched."

This passage, incidentally, suggests that the theologians were even more inclined than the common folk to attribute disease to witchcraft. Writing seventy years later, Jean Bodin declares:

> . . . there are fifty women witches to one man. This happens, in my opinion, not in consequence of the weakness of this sex, because we can see untamable stubbornness in most of them. . . . It would be more correct to say that it is the force of bestial lust which pushes the women to these extremes in order to assuage her desires or to take revenge. . . .[23]

Equally eloquent in linking lust and disease with witchcraft is the most influential manual of witch hunters, *The Hammer of Witches (Malleus Maleficarum)* written by two German monks, Jacobus Sprenger and Heinrich Kramer, alias Insistoris.[24] Here are a few quotations:

> "All witchcraft comes from carnal lust, which is in women insatiable, these women satisfy their filthy lusts not only in themselves, but even in the mighty ones of the age, of whatever state and condition; causing by all sorts of witchcraft the death of their souls through the excessive infatuation of carnal love, in such a way that for no shame or persuasion can they desist from such acts."

> ". . . these wretches furthermore afflict and torment men and women, beasts of burthen, herdbeasts, as well as animals of other kinds, with terrible and piteous pains and sore diseases, both internal and external; they hinder men from performing the sexual act and women from conceiving, whence husbands cannot know their wives nor wives receive their husbands."

> ". . . when girls have been corrupted, and have been scorned by their lovers after they have immodestly copulated with them in the hope and promise of marriage with them and have found themselves disappointed in all their hopes and everywhere despised, they turn to the help and protection of devils; either for the sake of vengeance by bewitching those lovers or the wives they have married, or for the sake of giving themselves up to every sort of lechery. Alas! Experience tells us that there is no number to such girls, and consequently the witches that spring from this class are innumerable."

> "Although far more women are witches than men, as was shown in the First Part of the work, yet men are more often bewitched than women. And the reason for this lies in the fact that God allows the devil more power over the venereal act, by which the original sin is handed down, than over the other human actions."

General acceptance of the notion that men are bewitched more often than women might have been helped by the fact that men succumb to syphilitic psychoses more often than women. As might be expected, Sprenger and Kramer took a dim view of the nature of love:

> "Philocaption, or inordinate love of one person for another, can be caused in three ways. Sometimes it is due merely to lack of control over the eyes; sometimes to the temptation of devils; sometimes to the spells of necromancers and witches, with the help of devils."

Not unlike other demonologists, our authors displayed great flights of imagination on the subjects of sexual relations between witches and devils:

". . . our principal subject is the carnal act which Incubi in an assumed body perform with witches: unless perhaps anyone doubts whether modern witches practise such abominable coitus; and whether witches had their origin in this abomination."

"For it was possible for the devils to lie down themselves by the side of the sleeping husbands, during the time when a watch was being kept on the wives, just as if they were sleeping with their husbands."

". . . to return to the question whether witches had their origin in these abominations, we shall say that they originated from some pestilent mutual association with devils, as is clear from our first knowledge of them. But no one can affirm with certainty that they did not increase and multiply by means of these foul practices, although devils commit this deed for the sake not of pleasure but of corruption. And this appears to be the order of the process. A Succubus devil draws the semen from a wicked man; and if he is that man's own particular devil, and does not wish to make himself an Incubus to a witch, he passes that semen on to the devil deputed to a woman or witch; and this last, under some constellation that favours his purpose that the man or woman so born should be strong in the practice of witchcraft, becomes the Incubus to the witch."

"Husbands have actually seen Incubus devils swiving with their wives, although they have thought that they were not devils but men. And when they had taken up a weapon and tried to run them through, the devil has suddenly disappeared, making himself invisible. And then their wives have thrown their arms about them, although they have sometimes been hurt, and railed at their husbands, mocking them and asking them if they had eyes, or whether they were possessed of devils.

". . . these Incubus devils will not only infest those women who have been generated by means of such abominations, or those who have been offered to them by mid-wives, but that they try with all their might, by means of witches who are bawds or hot whores. to seduce all the devout and chaste maidens in that whole district or town."

"With the exception, therefore, of these three classes of (holy) men, no one is secure from witches.

For all others are liable to be bewitched, or to be tempted and incited by some witchery."

". . . in times long past the Incubus devils used to infest women against their wills. But the theory that modern witches are tainted with this sort of diabolic filthiness is not substantiated only in our opinion, since the expert testimony of the witches themselves, has made all these things credible; and that they do not now, as in times past, subject themselves unwillingly, but willingly embrace this most foul and miserable servitude."

The authors blame the evils of the world on women, remarking plaintively:

". . . for this age is dominated by women. . . and when the world is now full of adultery, especially among the most highly born; when all this is considered, I say, of what use is it to speak of remedies to those who desire no remedy?"

As for the following passages, they lend a particularly strong support to my thesis because all the effects of witchcraft listed by the authors fall under the headings of disturbances of the reproductive functions, other related illnesses and insanity!

". . . apart from the methods by which they injure other creatures, they have six ways of injuring humanity. And one is, to induce an evil love in a man for a woman, or in a woman for a man. The second is to plant hatred or jealousy in anyone. The third is to bewitch them so that a man cannot perform the genital act with a woman, or conversely a woman with a man, or by various means to procure an abortion, as has been said before. The fourth is to cause some disease in any of the human organs. The fifth, to take away life. The sixth, to deprive them of reason."

"How witches impede and prevent the power of procreation . . . when they directly prevent the erection of the member which is accomodated to fructification. And this need not seem impossible, when it is considered that they are able to vitiate the natural use of any member. Secondly, when they prevent the flow of the vital essences to the members in which resides the motive force, closing up the seminal ducts so that it does not reach the generative vessels, so that it cannot be ejaculated, or is fruitlessly spilled."

"How, as it were, they deprive man of his vital member. . . . A similar experience is narrated by a certain venerable Father from the Dominican House of Spires, well known in the Order for the honesty of his life and for his learning. 'One day he says, 'while I was hearing confessions a young man came to me and, in the course of the confession, woefully said that he had lost his member. Being astonished at this, and not being willing to give it easy credence, since in the opinion of the wise it is a mark of lightheartedness to believe too easily, I obtained proof of it when I saw nothing on the young man's removing his clothes and showing the place. Then, using the wisest counsel I could, I asked whether he suspected anyone of having bewitched him. And the young man said that he did suspect someone, but that she was absent, and living in Worms. Then I said: I advise you to go to her as soon as possible and try your utmost to soften her with gentle words and promises, and he did so. For he came back after a few days and thanked me, saying that he was whole and had recovered everything. And I believed his words, but again proved them by the evidence of my eyes.'"

Nor was the evidence for a misogynist persecution mania un-recorded:

". . . witches who in this way sometimes collected male organs in great numbers, as many as twenty or thirty members together, and put them in a bird's nest, or shut them up in a box, where they move themselves like living members."

"In Ratisbon, a man was being tempted by the devil in the form of a woman to copulate, and became greatly disturbed when the devil would not desist. But it came into the poor man's mind that he ought to defend himself by taking Blessed Salt, as he had heard in a sermon. So he took some Blessed Salt on entering the bath-room; and the woman looked fiercely at him and cursing whatever devil had taught him to do this, suddenly disappeared. For the devil can, with God's permission, present himself either in the form of a witch, or by possessing the body of an actual witch. . . .

". . . some are protected against all sorts of witchcrafts, so that they can be hurt in no way; and others are particularly rendered chaste by the good Angels with regard to the generative function.

"Similarly. St Gregory, in the first book of his *Dialogues,* tells of the Blessed Abbot Equitius. This man, he says, was in his youth greatly troubled by the provocation of the flesh; but the very distress of his temptation made him all the more realous in his application to prayer. And when he continuously prayed Almighty God for a remedy against this affliction, an Angel appeared to him one night and seemed to make him a eunuch, and it seemed to him in his vision that all feeling was taken away from his genital organs: and from that time he was such a stranger to temptation as if he had no sex in his body."

My final quotation reveals the authors' hankering after a release from the torments of sexual frustration through castration (as was permitted in the Eastern Church):

Again, in the *Lives of the Fathers* collected by that very holy man St Heraclides, in the book which he calls *Paradise,* he tells of a certain holy Father, a monk named Helias. This man was moved by pity to collect thirty women in a monastery, and began to rule over them. But after two years, when he was thirty years old, he fled from the temptation of the flesh into a hermitage, and gasting there for two days, prayed to God saying: 'O Lord God, either slay me, or deliver me from this temptation.' And in the evening a dream came to him, and he saw three Angels approach him; they asked him why he had fled from the Monastery of virgins. But when he did not dare to answer, for shame, the Angels said: If you are set free from temptation, will you return to your cure of those women? And he answered that he would willingly. They then exacted an oath to that effect from him, and made him a eunuch. For one seemed to hold his hands, another his feet, and the third cut out his testicles with a knife; though this was not really so, but only seemed to be. And when they asked if he felt himself remedied, he answered that he was entirely delivered. So, on the fifth day, he returned to the sorrowing women and ruled over them for the forty years that he continued to live, and never again felt a spark of that first temptation.

"No less a benefit do we read to have been conferred upon the Blessed Thomas, a Doctor of our Order, whom his brothers imprisoned for entering that Order; and, wishing to tempt him, they sent him a seductive and sumptuously adorned harlot. But when the Doctor had looked at her, he ran to the material fire, and snatching up a lighted torch, drove the engine of the fire of lust out of his prison; and, prostrating himself in a prayer for the gift of chastity, went to sleep. Two Angels then appeared to him, saying: Behold, at the bidding of God we gird you with a girdle of chastity, which cannot be loosed by any other such temptation; neither can it be acquired by the merits of human virtue, but it is given as a gift by God alone. And he felt himself girded, and was aware of the touch of the girdle, and cried out and awaked. And thereafter he felt himself endowed with so great a gift of chastity, that from that time he abhorred all the delights of the flesh, so that he could not even speak to a woman except under compulsion, but was strong in his perfect chastity."

The date of publication of *Malleus* (1486), which was several years before the panic about syphilis spread, might be seen as an argument against linking Witch Hunting with the epidemic. I do not believe that this is so. At any particular time there are a number of eccentries who attempt to propagate all kinds of out-of-the-way opinions. Although even what can be conceived by deviants is broadly limited by the culture in which they live, the narrower determination of beliefs by general circumstances occurs mainly on the level of selection through which some notions are given wide currency while others are consigned to insignificance or oblivion. The arrival of syphilis coincided with a radical change in the reception of *Malleus*. The first printing in 1486 was opposed by the clergy and was carried out with the help of a forged letter of approval. When Sprenger died in 1495 in Cologne he was buried without a mass. Krämer was expelled from more than one place by the local ecclesiastical authorities; he was suspended, and rehabilitated only in 1495 which happened to be the same year in which Emperor Maximilian bewailed the arrival of the new disease. Krämer was given a Papal commission in 1500 and died as an inquisitor in 1505. Their book was reissued 16 times in Germany, 11 times in France, and twice in Italy. It had six editions in England between 1584 and 1669.

In a book published in 1560 Pierre Boaistual [25] records this attribution of physical deformities to sexual misdemeanours:

"It is certain that most often these monstrous creatures come from God's judgment, justice, punishment and curse, which permit that fathers and mothers produce such monstrosities through their horrible sins, as they rush indiscriminately like stupid beasts wherever their lust leads them without regard to time or place or other laws ordained by nature."

In a few cases I have come across—and I am confident that many more could be found by specialists who examined the sources from this angle—the reference to venereal disease is pretty obvious. Soldan, Heppe and Bauer, for example, report a trial of a prior's housekeeper who was accused by two priests of having caused through witchcraft their "illness in the most secret parts of the body...."

It seems odd that the modern historians prate about economic and political bases when the treatises of witch-finders hardly refer to such matters but are full of pronouncements about lust, copulation, and disease. The monastic theologians displayed vivid imagination on the subject of witches and devils' sexual activities or the torments which lascivious people will suffer in hell. One of the favorite themes was how sinful women are punished on the organs used for sinning. A good deal of attention was given to the large size of the devil's penis, the swiftness with which he can alternate between intromission and cunnilinctus, or the witches' manner of kissing him on the anus.

An explanation of a pattern of behaviour may refer to circumstances unknown to the doers, but it ought at the same time to account for what they keep on saying: in this case why the writers who provided the justification of witch-hunting went on and on about sexual intercourse and disease, and why they advocated remedies involving prurient sadism. All this becomes easy to understand in the light of a psychoanalytic interpretation of the consequences of celibacy and syphilis.

Syphilis must have also stimulated witchcraft accusations in another way. It made them useful as a quite rational method of disavowing sin, and disclaiming responsibility for the visible sinful symptoms which could be attributed to being bewitched instead of having engaged in illicit copulation.

Nevertheless, the tone of the writings clearly suggests that the fear was genuine. It would be a fatuous error to imagine that witch-hunts were some kind of "psycho therapy" designed to alleviate guilt feelings. On the contrary, it is reasonable to suppose that taking part in the gruesome proceedings might have prompted additional feelings of guilt which would be repressed from consciousness, and through still more projection provide a further stimulus to ferocity.

The Witch Mania must also have been stimulated by the impact of the psychoses caused by syphilis: general paresis or *dementia paralytica,* tabes, and cerebral syphilis. Here are a few quotations from a well known modern textbook of psychiatry (1950):[26]

> "*Dementia paralytica* may be defined as an organic disease of the brain, of an inflammatory and degenerative nature, manifesting itself in progressive mental deterioration, and accompanied by certain definite physical signs. . . .
>
> The disease is world-wide, although it is less common in tropical countries. . . . *Dementia paralytica* usually manifests itself at any time from five to twenty years after infection. . . . The average rate at which the disease develops varies between 30 and 50 years, but cases below 30 and above 50 are relatively infrequent. Males are more often affected than females, in the proportion of four to one, but this variation does not occur in cases of juvenile general paralysis, where the sexes seem to be equally affected. . . . Remissions may occur at any time during the course of the disease, which may come even to an apparent standstill. . . .
>
> . . . The disease is commonly insidious in its development, and is characterised by episodes of strange behavior, not at all in harmony with the previous character of the individual. . . . All the aesthetic feelings become lost. The relatives and friends cannot understand the alteration in the patient's personality, but

feel that he is utterly different from what he formerly was. . . . During the progress of the disease the memory is progressively impaired, not only of recent events, but more remote ones. . . . There is disorientation, particularly for time. . . .

> Grandiose delusions, which are in this disease of a bizarre type, are not so common as has been generally supposed, Indeed, in some cases, instead of a feeling of well-being and euphoria, a state of intense depression is present, even amounting to stupor with mutism. The feature of the depression is the frequency with which absurd nihilistic ideas are expressed. Patients claim that they are dead, that their blood has ceased to circulate, that they have no pulse, that their bodies are utterly destroyed. The ideas of the depressive type are as fantastic and grotesque as those of the grandiose variety . . . any type of mental picture may appear—cases, for instance, in which hallucinations are prominent, cases showing alternating elation and depression and cases in whom persecutory delusions are in the forefront . . . the first evidence of a general paralytic process may be the occurrence of a convulsive seizure, but more usually these seizures occur during the course of the disease."

One can well imagine how people showing the derangements described above would be seen as "possessed", or "bewitched", or having relations with the devil, particularly as nothing was known about the causation. On the latter point, Henderson and Gillespie say:

> "During the past century this disease has been investigated from many different aspects, and its identity has been well established on clinical, pathological and serological grounds. For many years it has been recognised that many of those who ultimately suffered from this disease had at one time contracted a syphilitic infection, but there were many competent observers who stated that the condition could occur quite independently of any syphilitic infection—for instance from head injury, alcoholism of an erratic mode of life. The theory of the syphilitic causation of this disease was at first based entirely on statistics, but after Kraft-Ebing had had the temerity to inoculate general paralytics with syphilitic virus without infecting them, the conception of the syphilitic origin of the disease was greatly strengthened. This theory soon received further support from a series of researches on

the cerebro-spinal fluid, originated by Widal and Sicard, and carried on by many others until Wassermann demonstrated antibodies in the cerebro-spinal fluid and blood serum of those known to be suffering from syphilitic disease affecting the nervous system.

In 1913 Noguchi and Moore announced that in 14 out of 70 cases of general paralysis they had been able to demonstrate the *Treponema pallidum* in the brain cortex. These findings have been confirmed by many other observers. It can thus be definitively stated: 'No syphilis, no paresis.' While this is so, it does not necessarily mean that syphilis invariably leads to an affection of the nervous system; it has been estimated that approximately only 2% of syphilitics ever develop general paralysis. Why it develops in one case and not in another has been constantly discussed, but we still do not know whether it is a matter of a special strain of the organism or of a specially susceptible nervous system."

The lack of regularity in the development of the disease would facilitate attributions to occult forces. The same applies to cerebral syphilis. According to Henderson and Gillespie:

> "In the early stages of his illness the patient may complain of a certain nervous uneasiness, may feel dull, changed, mixed up in the head and complain of difficulty in thinking. The emotional condition is variable; at one time the patient is excited, irritable and resistive, while at another time he may be depressed, anxious and easily frightened. . . . The delirium which sets in is of the usual kind. It is a hallucinatory state with fear, and with great difficulty in comprehension and in attention. The patient is imperfectly oriented for time and place. . . . It is estimated that in the absence of head injury, upwards of 90% of all cases of ocular palsy in adults are caused by syphilis or by brain tumor."

Tabes was likely to prompt accusations, as can be seen from the following quotation:

> "A certain number of patients with *tabes dorsalis* develop general paralysis at a later date; but mental symptoms of other kinds may also develop in tabetics who show neither the physical nor the mental symptoms of general paralysis. The commonest non-paralytical syndromes appearing in tabetics are, according to Otto Meyer, chronic hallucinatory para-

noid states, depressive psychoses, circular psychoses, acute hallucinatory confusion, hallucinatory anxious states and various types of dementia. Kraepelin believes that there is a psychosis which is commoner than any other in tabes, and which has a course, symptomatology and outcome distinct from general paralysis. This psychosis consists in an acute hallucinatory excitement. The patient suddenly becomes fearful, agitated, hears distinct voices and is accused of numerous crimes. The onset is sudden and later in life and often at a later stage in the course of tabes than general paralysis is accustomed to appear. Memory, retention and orientation remain intact, and speech and writing do not present the specific disturbances seen in cases of general paralysis. The symptoms may subside in a few months, or remain indefinitely."

Given the ignorance of the causes, coupled with the unquestioned belief that Witchcraft can cause disease and possession, it would be strange if a spectacular eruption of the derangements described above did not foster the notion that witches were proliferating and intensifying their nefarious activities.

Moreover, these diseases multiplied the number of people whose strange behaviour aroused suspicions, as well as the number of paranoiacs eager to issue accusations. The ratio of male to female sufferers from these psychoses is 4-to-1, according to Henderson and Gillespie, which would fuel the tendency to demonise women. It may not be a coincidence that this is a rough converse of the sex ratio among the victims of the trials, as estimated by Delumeau. Persecutory hallucinations, caused by syphilitic psychoses, may have prompted much of the preaching and theorizing about Witches and Satan. (This might have been the case with Jean Bodin.)

Although neurotic difficulties connected with his celibacy might have had something to do with it, Sir Isaac Newton's acceptance of the current beliefs about witches might be explained as due to the intensity of his preoccupation with mathematical theories: this did not leave him enough mental energy for a critical examination of matters unrelated to his studies, so that his writings about witches were a kind of self-indulgence. In contrast. Jean Bodin (1530–96) was perhaps the greatest innovator in the study of society between Macchiavelli and

Montesquieu; he was not generally inclined to receive uncritically the current opinions about human behaviour, and was well acquainted with good arguments to the contrary. Indeed, one of his two works on Witchcraft was a polemic against Johannes Weyer—a brave author who criticised the current beliefs about witches on good grounds of commonsense logic. What is even more incongruous, Bodin wrote a work called *Heptaplomeres,* which he kept hidden during his life and which was only published in 1914: there he advocates the equality of religions before the law and appears to be an agnostic. Yet at the age of 48 he wrote his bloodthirsty treatise on witches; after that he wrote only a book on nature which is regarded by later commentators as showing a conspicuous decline of his mental powers.

Bodin writes about witches making men impotent. The treaties was printed two years after his marriage at 46. (Of his three children, one died early, another was mentally defective, and the third insane.) According to some of his biographers he remained a bachelor until then, including his years at the licentious French court, while others say that he was a defrocked Carmelite monk who had earlier married and divorced a woman of ill repute. In either case he had a good chance of contracting syphilis. The difference in quality between his earlier and later works indicates a deterioration of the brain which cannot be attributed to normal senility as he died at the age of 66. The man who adumbrated the quantity theory of money and who could see (contrary to the universally held belief) that gold does not constitute real wealth, would not accept the plain logic of Weyer's arguments; e.g., that if the powerful witches could manage to do all the things attributed to them, then surely they would also be able to escape from prison or avoid arrest. Bodin's fulminations also show the common feature of neurotic and psychotic obsessions: namely, the exclusion of any possibility of a refutation by the facts. He insists that evidence which in other matters would be sufficient for a verdict of "not guilty", must not be accepted in witch trials. His views on this matter were generally followed.

By taking into consideration the medical factor one can also explain why the Witch Craze affected Spain and Italy less than the countries to the north, and southern Italy less than northern. In 1917 J. Wagner-Jauregg (in Vienna) began to treat patients by infecting them with malaria, and until the discovery of penicillin this was the only effective cure for syphilis. Naturally acquired malaria has the same effect. Henderson and Gillespie report that syphilitic psychoses are rare in the tropics; nowadays malaria is rare outside tropical zones. In the earlier centuries, however, it was common in the southern parts of Europe. Consequently, the impact of syphilis could not have had there the same devastating force which it had further north. In addition to the cultural factors mentioned earlier, malaria may also have impeded the spread of the Witch Craze to the Balkans.

It remains to be added that, owing to the unfreedom of women, the ruling elites of the Islamic states should not have suffered from syphilis as much as their Christian equivalents. All important Moslem men had harems, guarded by eunuchs, containing women recruited as virgins and well-inspected beforehand. Such men had little incentive for adultery or brothel-crawling, and their wives and concubines had no opportunities for straying. Consequently, the Moslem magnates were unlikely to catch venereal disease, which was rife among the nobility and royalty of Europe, actually caused the dying out of a number of dynasties, and must have contributed to the bizarre behaviour of monarchs like Henry VIII and Ivan the Terrible.

In contrast to the historical processes invoked in other explanations, the epidemic of syphilis shows a perfect chronological correspondence with the Witch Craze. Trials, which were sporadic during the preceding centuries, multiplied enormously after 1500 and at the same time the sex ratio among the victims swung drastically against women. The epidemic of syphilis struck a few years earlier. Witch-hunting petered out gradually and at different times in various parts of Europe during the second half of the 17th century, and ceased altogether during the 18th. This was also the time when syphilis began to assume somewhat milder forms. According to W. H. McNeill's study of plagues:[27]

> "By the end of the (16th) century, syphilis began to recede. The more fulminant forms of infection were dying out, as the normal sorts of adjustment between host and parasite asserted themselves, i.e. as milder strains of the spirochete displaced those that killed off their hosts too rapidly, and as the resistance of European populations to the organism increased."

As the historian of medicine Charles Singer says, considerable progress was made around 1700 in the treatment:[28]

> "Its treatment by mercury had been practised at least as early as the fifteenth century, perhaps as an inheritance from the Arabic-speaking physicians. During the sixteenth and seventeenth centuries various other remedies were tried; much quackery arose around them. In the eighteenth century the accumulated experience of generations returned again to mercury. Satisfactory methods of administration were evolved and the treatment became standardized. It hardly changed until the twentieth century."

Development of the disease became as a rule slower, and its most vivid manifestations (like the rotting away of the flesh) came later and more rarely.

The medical interpretation accounts also for some other coincidences noted by historians, which up till now have appeared completely mysterious. In his studies of the persecutions in Germany, H. C. Erik Midelfort[29] maintains that the regions where these were the most severe were distinguished by an unusually high ratio of single women. This connection becomes explicable when we bear in mind that such a ratio would encourage fornication and, therefore, increase contagion and panic. We can also account for the numerous instances of witch hunts following in the wake of military campaigns—which led many historians as we saw earlier to follow a wrong track in the search for an explanation. The link is clear: soldiers have always been the most effective spreaders of venereal disease, particularly in the epoch when they regarded

rape as their natural right. The special victimization of midwives, noted in most histories of the persecutions, also ceases to be inexplicable: during the epidemic the number of stillbirths, infantile deaths, and children born with deformations must have increased dramatically; and midwives would be the obvious scapegoats.

It is possible that some of the witches execrated as "ugly" were syphilitic; some might have been in fact agents of contagion. Nor should we assume that all the women described as "old" must have been sexually inactive; in those days every woman over thirty would be called old. Among the tormentors' prurient sadistic enjoyments was the practice of poking the victims with their fingers all over the naked body in search of insensitive spots which were regarded as a proof of being a witch. As syphilitic do, in fact, develop insensitive spots, this practice constitutes another pointer to the connection between the persecutions and the disease.

It is also possible that some of the accused were retired prostitutes. It would, however, be a gross error to imagine that the Witch Hunts might have been some rational method of extirpating the carriers of the disease. Once the fear and hatred of women became widespread, the choice of scapegoats would become quite random or determined by circumstances which had nothing to do with the danger of contagion. After the outbreaks of bubonic plague or cholera, we know that the mobs did not pick on soldiers but on Jews, or Gypsies, or some other defenseless minority.

Apart from accounting for the already mentioned characteristics of the craze, my thesis—unlike other interpretations—also explains classless character as well as the intellectual current which accompanied the persecutions. If the craze was a mere parish-pump affair (as Thomas and Macfarlane try to tell us), why did prestigious authorities (including King James I) write books calling for general persecutions? On the other hand, if it was a clearly repressive action against the common folk organised by the ruling class (as Favret and, to some extent, Mandrou see it), then why did so many ordinary people launch the accusations, ask the authorities for help in finding witches, and even proceed to lynch the suspects? If it was a by-product of the functioning of the Church's repressive machinery, then why did so many authors write about witches? And why did their books find so many buyers, even when the authors were Catholic and the readers were Protestant? There is no way in which the demand for the English editions of the *Malleus* in the 17th century could be explained by the momentum of the Papal Inquisition. Such an explanation would not be valid even for a Catholic Land. In modern totalitarian states, writings of the rulers and their propagandists can be distributed in large numbers to bookshops and libraries although not a soul wants to buy or read them. In the 16th and the 17th century, however, printing and bookselling was a small business wholly dependent on private buyers. The literature therefore provides a reliable indication of the state of mind of the literate classes.

In my previous encounter article, I have tried to show that the impact of syphilis played a crucial role in the rise of Puritanism as well as in the "purification" of the Catholic Church. The influence on the Lutheran and the Anglican Churches must have been similar.

One could also look at puritanism as an adaptive reaction which permitted the preservation of healthy genetic lines and the growth of population despite the disease. People of stern morals, who avoided fornication and adultery and who chose as spouses persons of similar conduct, had a much better chance of a long life and of producing a large and healthy progeny, whereas libertines died young and left a few sickly descendants. Owing to the pressure of the population upon resources, and the high death rate among the physically or financially weak—aggravated below the upper classes by a vicious circle of poverty and debility—the lines contaminated by syphilis were constantly eliminated and replaced by the offspring of families with stern sexual morals. Thus, there was a biological selection for puritanism. As morals among the upper classes were laxer than among the lower, the degeneration and dying out of noble families must have

fostered an upward social mobility which facilitated Europe's cultural innovation.

My thesis, like a weather map, can account only for broad trends and conditions, and leaves out of consideration the local variations which may have been due to chance factors such as the character of individuals in crucial social or political positions. Still, detailed research into primary sources from the proffered viewpoint might also reveal closer co-variation between the epidemic and the intensity of persecutions, and thus account for local differences.

As it stands, my thesis explains the following features of the great Witch Craze which up till now have appeared as inexplicable: (*1*) its duration: (*2*) the geographical extension; (*3*) its generality and classlessness; (*4*) its bias against women; (*5*) its contrariety to the direction of the intellectual progress occurring at the time; (*6*) its bias against midwives; (*7*) its loose association with wars; (*8*) the prominent role of monks and Puritans in the hounding and the greater ferocity of the former. I hope that the foregoing comparative analysis will stimulate research into primary sources which will throw more light on the interplay of the factors surveyed here.

Let me recapitulate. The underlying permanent condition was the prevalence of the belief that Witchcraft works and can cause disease. One of the preparatory conditions was the existence of the machinery of repression forged against heretics by the Church. The second preparatory condition was the demonisation of women, which was an exacerbation of an old ingredient of the Christian tradition, and a consequence of the tightening up of celibacy. The precipitating factor was the arrival of syphilis at the beginning of the 16th century which evoked panic and a search for scapegoats, chosen with preference for the most defenseless members of the subjugated sex. A host of inexplicable psychoses and congenital malformations provided an additional stimulus for Witch Hunts. During the closing decades of the 17th century, and to an even greater extent during the early part of the 18th, there was an abatement of the severity of the disease. This, together with the growing influence of a more advanced body of scientific knowledge and the decline of the influence of celibate clergy, led to the disappearance of the mania among Europe's educated classes, which brought the trials to an historic end.

ENDNOTES

1. H. R. Trevor-Roper, *Religion, the Reformation and Social Change* (1967), pp. 92–3.
2. Claudia Honegger, *Die Hexen der Neuzeit,* (Franfurt, Suhrkamp Veriage, 1978).
3. Jean Delumeau, *La Peur en Occident* (Paris, Fayard, 1978).
4. Keith Thomas, *Religion and the Decline of Magic* (1971).
5. A survey of these and other estimates can be found in Delumeau, *La Peur en Occident,* p. 456.
6. Willhelm Gottlieb Soldan, *Geschichte der Hexenprozesse: Aus den Ouellen dargestellt* (Stuttgart, 1843: ed. Heppe, 1880; rev. ed. Bauer, Munich 1912).
7. As summarised in Delumeau, *La Peur en Occident.*
8. E. William Monter, "Witchcraft in Geneva". *Journal of Modern History,* vol. 43 (1971).
9. Jeanne Favret, "Sorciéres et Lumiéres", *Critique* Vol. 27 (1971).
10. Kurt Baschwitz, *Hexen und Hexenprozesse* (dtv, Munich): Robert Mandroud, *Magistrants et sorciers en France au XVIIe siècle: Une analyse de psychologic historique* (Paris, 1968).
11. Alan Macfarlane, *Witchcraft in Tudor and Stuart England* (1970).
12. Robert Madrou. *"Magistrats et sorciers . . .".*
13. The European Witch-craze of the Sixteenth and Seventeenth Centuries", first published in ENCOUNTER (May–June 1967) and reprinted in Trevor-Roper's *Religion, the Reformation and Social Change.*
14. Baschwitz, *Hexen und Hexenprozesse.*
15. Soldan, *Geschichte der Hexenprozesse.*
16. Margaret Murray, *The Witch-Cult in Western Europe: A Study in Anthropology* (1921).
17. Baschwitz, *Hexen und Hexenprozesse.*
18. A brief description of the effects of syphillis (with a number of quotations from contemporary sources and references) can be found in my previous article in ENCOUNTER (October 1980), pp. 76–81.
19. Although he created many of them, Freud did not use the concepts employed here to provide an explanation of the Witch Mania when he touched upon this subject. His essay offered an interpretation of a case of possession of a Bohemian gentleman in the 17th century on the basis of personal documents found by Freud's friend. Sigmund Freud, "Eine Teufelsneurose im siebzehnten Jahrundert," *Gesammelte Werken,* Vol. 13, (1950).
20. See H. E. Feine, *Kirchliche Rechtsgeschichte* (Vienna Bohlaus, 1954).
21. Henry C. Lea, *History of Sacerdotal Celibacy in the Christian Church* (1932), pp. 299–300.
22. Gregorio Maranon, *Tres estudios sobre la vida sexual* (Madrid).
23. Quotations in Baschwitz and in Delumeau; The translations are mine.
24. Jacobus Sprenger and Heinrich Kramer, *Malleus Mareficarum* (London, The Follo Society, 1968), pp. 29, 18–19, 51, 172, 176, 75, 71, 77, 80, 80–81, 45, 76, 177, 83, 87, 90–91, 93, 42, 44, 44.
25. As quoted by Delumeau, *La Peur en Occident,* p. 89: the translation is mine.
26. Henderson and R. d. Gillespie, *A Textbook of Psychiatry for Students and Practitioners* (Oxford University Press, 1950), pp. 466–9, 464–5, 493–5, 497.
27. W. H. McNeill, *Plagues and People* (1976), p. 220.
28. Charles Singer, *A Short History of Medicine* (Clarendon Press, 1928), p. 162.
29. H. C. Erik Midelfort, *Witch Hunting in Southwestern Germany,* 1562-1684 (Stanford, 1972).

ASK YOURSELF

Ascribing different social values to women and men is a typical feature of many societies. As Sanday discovered on the pages of the Bible, in Western society this difference can often be quite subtle, as feminists have also claimed. Females, they note, are frequently covertly as well as overtly assigned lower standing than males. Test this claim by thinking about ritual situations—religious as well as nonreligious—in your own community where women and girls are relegated to what one might interpret as positions of ritual inferiority to males.

FURTHER READINGS

Caldwell, Sarah. *Oh Terrifying Mother: Sexuality, Violence and Worship of the Goddess Kali.* Oxford: Oxford University Press. 1999. The author analyses a South Indian ritual in which male actors become possessed by the Hindu goddess Bhagvati.

Eliberg-Schwartz, Howard. *The Savage in Judaism: An Anthropology of Israelite Religion and Ancient Judaism.* Bloomington: Indiana Press. 1990. This is a brilliant assessment of how the approaches taken by anthropologists to the interpretation of "primitive" or "savage" religions provides important insights into that faith.

Haliczer, Stephen. *Sexuality in the Confessional: A Sacrament Profaned.* Oxford: Oxford University Press, 1996. Haliczer describes how, during and after the Counter-Reformation in the 16th century, the Catholic Church not only failed to end the practice of priests using the confessional for propositioning penitents but, through the work of the Inquisition, may have actually "eroticized" the sacrament of penance. An engrossing, fascinating read.

Herdt, Gilbert H. *Guardians of the Flutes: Idioms of Masculinity.* New York: McGraw-Hill, 1981. The rituals of the Sambia, a New Guinea population, express metaphysical beliefs about the nature of masculinity and femininity. Gender classification is exceptionally rigorous among them, with males from an early age keeping their distance from females and homosexuality being a prominent feature of Sambia ritual.

SUGGESTED VIDEOS

"Flowers for Guadalupe: The Virgin of Guadalupe in the Lives of Mexican Women." The importance of the Virgin of Guadalupe as a liberating symbol for Mexican women today provides this documentary with its theme. It follows a women's pilgrimage from Queretaro State for several arduous days over rough terrain and inclement weather to the Virgin's shrine in Mexico City. 57 minutes; $395 (sale), $75 (rental); The Filmakers Library, 124 East 40th Street, New York, NY 10016.

"Guardians of the Flutes: The Secrets of Male Initiation." As remarked above, for the Sambia, gender distinction is a fundamental fact of culture. When still very young, boys leave their mothers and move to a "boy's house" where they live until old enough to be ritually incorporated into manhood, a process that causes them to undergo agonizing initiations. The documentary shows their initiation rituals, which involve the boys being thrashed, deprived of food and sleep, and having ginger root rubbed into their wounds. 55 minutes; 1996; $395 (sale), $75 (rental); Filmakers Library, 124 East 40th Street, New York, NY 10016.

"Fatmawati's Wedding: The Wedding Of Two Sisters, The Preparations And Traditional Ceremonies." Filmmaker and anthropologist: Fiona Kerlogue. Color. 50 minutes, 1998. In portraying preparations for the wedding of two sisters in eastern Sumatra, Indonesia, in December 1996, this film demonstrates the importance of women in ritual exchanges and purification rituals. Film Officer, Royal Anthropological Institute (RAI), 50 Fitzroy Street, London W1P 5HS, United Kingdom.

On the island of Bali in Indonesia, water resources management combined with religious belief have produced this luxuriant rice crop, waiting to be dedicated to the goddess Dewi Sri before being harvested. *Photo courtesy of David Hicks*

CHAPTER 10

THE NATURAL ENVIRONMENT

In contemporary Western thought, nature and culture are typically conceived of as quite different categories. Indeed, for many distinguished writers, one famous example being Claude Lévi-Strauss, nature and culture are not only separate categories, they actually oppose each other. The first reading in this chapter informs us that the Tukano, of South America, do not make these conceptualizations. For them, they—human beings—are part of nature. This attitude is similar to what scholars of the 19th century believed was typical of nonliterate peoples, that is, that they regarded themselves as being of a piece with their natural environment. Tylor's notion of animism—for him the first religion—included the assumption that early *Homo sapiens* had invested animals and plants with souls, which meant that, for them, other living things were hardly different from human beings. For Durkheim and Freud totemism was the earliest form of religion, and totemic beliefs included the notion that human beings could be identified in some way with natural objects. Today the term *totemism* is generally used in the context of a symbolic classification in which a set of social groups corresponds to a parallel set of natural categories, such as animals or plants, with both cultural and natural sets being incorporated into local cosmological notions. Whether or not used totemically to convey distinctions between such social groups, animals and plants provide cultures with a wealth of resources for symbolism. In the Christian tradition, the lamb symbolizes (among other things) innocence, and the snake symbolizes evil. In the myths of certain South American Indians, the jaguar is the master of fire, a threat to human beings, and the anteater, his rival, is humanity's benefactor.

Religious concerns with the natural environment are not confined to symbolic classification and myth. Especially among peoples who hunt and fish, or whose demographic situation necessitates that they carefully husband their food supply and energy, ritual can play a practical role. This becomes clear in the article by Rappaport (Reading 10–2), who with some subtlety demonstrates how an ethnographic focus on material aspects of society can give us interesting insights into ritual practices. Omar Khayyam Moore (1957) had earlier suggested how ritual might be looked at from an ecological perspective when he drew attention to the divination technique of the Montagnais-Naskapi, a people living in the forests of Labrador, in Canada. Rituals of divination foretell future events or reveal occult knowledge by using an augury or spiritual agency, and the particular form used by the Montagnais-Naskapi is known as scapulimancy. Before going caribou hunting the Montagnais-Naskapi would place a shoulder blade in a fire and after withdrawing it would try and interpret the pattern of scorch marks, which they believed could provide them with clues as to the location of their prey. To the anthropologist these patterns result from chance rather than divination, of course, and Moore argues that by surrendering their knowledge of the best hunting grounds to chance when deciding where to hunt on any particular day the Montagnais-Naskapi reduced the depletion of game that overhunting in territory they knew by experience to be popular with the caribou would bring about.

Among the material concerns addressed ritually in many societies is fertility. Fertility is the means to life, and thus it is only to be anticipated that the quest for fertility should be a recurring motif in ritual. As the English anthropologist Arthur Maurice Hocart (1954, 19) put it, "[Rituals] have as their purpose to produce or increase the necessaries of life. They are acts of creation. They create more witchetty grubs, more buffaloes, more clouds, or whatever the desired objects might be. The cosmic rites create more of everything that man may need, and as the food supply depends on the proper working of the whole world, such ceremonies create the world." Control over this essential thing is typically attributed to spirits, as we see in the Ainu bear ritual discussed in Reading 10–3.

Balinese symbolic classification (Chapter 2) and spirits (Chapter 3) are cultural constructs that fit in neatly with the Balinese natural environment, and nowhere is this more evident than in their agricultural practice, so before embarking on our readings let us take a quick look at an especially instructive example of how thoroughly ritual, belief, and the natural environment can, in certain societies, blend into a coherent whole.

In Bali two crops of wet rice each year are normal. These are cultivated in irrigated fields that, because of the mountainous nature of much of central Bali, usually are terraces excavated by back-breaking labor out of steep slopes down which cascade streams whose water is channeled through canals onto the fields. Rice demands the utmost attention to its needs, be they biological, technical or—for the Balinese—ritual. To the farmer each of these needs is essential for fertility and as in coordination they must be directed towards the single goal of successfully exploiting the rice's 105-day cycle of growth and decay. To attain this goal the supply of water must be meticulously regulated. This is where the many thousands of temples found on Bali come in.

The rice cycle begins when farmers plow into the dry soil of their fields the weeds that have accumulated since the previous crop was harvested. The fields are then flooded, and although the land remains under water for most of the growing period, the farmers gradually decrease the height of the water until by harvest time their fields have become quite dry. Following harvesting, the fields are allowed to remain in this condition and wild grasses spring rapidly up until several weeks later the farmers churn them into the soil, in this way replenishing it with their nutrients. The cycle has begun again.

Bali's climate permits farmers to plant in virtually any month they choose, and nature provides adequate water. Experience, however, has taught farmers that for maximum productivity the amount of water allowed to flood a field should be kept reasonably constant and assured throughout the year. These stipulations create a major predicament. If left to their own devices, farmers would tap their local source of water whenever they wished. Those living higher up a valley would be the first to exploit all the water resources, and farmers lower down would lack for water. So, over the centuries the Balinese have worked out a system that not only prevents self-destructive greed and waste but enables the best use to be made of this treasured resource so that everyone in a neighborhood benefits and no water is squandered. The system mandates staggering the supply of water received by neighboring farmers who rely upon the same source of water. At any given moment some fields will be dry while others will be inundated, which means there is a sufficient and constant supply of water available for all, whether the farmers are high up a valley or on the plains of the coast. But because streams interconnect with each other and run down valleys for many miles the water they contain has to be allocated over hundreds of square miles. To ensure cooperation across what in practice is almost the entire arable surface of Bali, farmers take advantage of their network of temples. From the smallest neighborhood (where fields stand adjacent) to districts (composed of several neighborhoods) to extensive regions (composed of districts) farmers are brought into one huge pan-Balinese system of water management.

How do temples perform this feat? We shall start at the neighborhood, where several farmers share a canal in common. The rice-cultivating group they comprise is known as the *tempek,* under the supervision of whose head its members sacrifice offerings to the rice goddess, Dewi Sri, at tiny shrines in their fields, and plant and harvest as a group. This *tempek* links up with neighboring *tempek* to form a larger unit known as the *subak.* A *subak* owns two kinds of temple. One is located near the dam that controls the water supply of the *subak.* The other is located in the rice fields. At set times during the rice cycle the several *tempek* within each *subak* offer sacrifices to Dewi Sri at the temples, each *tempek* following a different ritual schedule. This is determined by the leader of the *subak,* and it also regulates the schedule of agricultural activities. The flooding and draining of the fields is thus staggered among the *tempek* components of the *subak* so that the supply of water is never exhausted by any one *tempek,* but each gets its fair share.

At a higher level of cooperation, groups of *subak* that rely on the same source of water—a stream or river—and worship at the same temple also stagger rituals at different times, and regulate their schedule of water in tandem. Such groups of *subak* tend to occupy the same valley, and coordination is brought about by the leaders of the different *subak* travelling

to "mountain temples," which are temples situated near the top of the valley. They visit them when the social groups that own the temples are commemorating their foundation in an annual ritual anniversary. During this assembly the heads of the mountain temples decide the schedule for staggering the temple rituals of each *subak* in the valley. These, of course, also determine the schedule of rice cultivation and water allocation for each *subak,* thus ensuring no *subak* wastes water and no *subak* lacks any at the proper time.

A Balinese year lasts 210 days, and once a year the heads of the mountain temples themselves travel. They go high into the mountains to visit a pair of "water temples" located near sacred lakes at the top of Bali. It is these water temples that ultimately coordinate the rice-growing and water-management schedules for the entire island. Pura Batu Kau is the master temple for the lesser temples in western Bali, while Ulun Danau fulfills the same function for eastern Bali. Their respective heads and visitors have the authority to decide how to stagger the ritual schedules for all Bali's mountain temples, a decision that, in effect, determines the rice and water cycles for the entire island.

At the same time as they plant rice seeds in the "womb" of the soil, farmers offer Dewi Sri meat, drink, and flower petals as a way of encouraging her to make the crop fertile. Later "when the rice is pregnant" they sacrifice additional offerings to encourage her to make the rice seeds grow healthily in the earthy "womb." Then comes the "birth ritual" when the rice first appears on the stalks and the celebrants sing songs to charm the "baby" rice. An essential component of these rituals consists of an aspersion with holy water, for the Hindu notion of purity has penetrated the Balinese ecology of rice cultivation, and it is believed that dire consequence will befall if the rice is not pure. The water used in this purification is sanctified in the system of temple networks and symbolizes the connections between them. It also originates in it, for Brahman priests from the two water temples bless the water that they draw from the sacred lakes and convey it down to the mountain temple priests. In their turn, they use it to make the water in their own localities holy before sending it down the valley to the temples of the various *subak* where every month the holy water is aspersed onto the rice fields within every *subak*. Creating holy water is a ritual act in which all who participate are made aware that they as individuals, their fields, and their temples are contributing to an indivisible whole that embraces all Bali.

This network of relationships is supported by other religious institutions. One of the most important is the great council temple, which administers a hamlet, but also plays its part in fostering communal prosperity by carrying out its own distinctive rice ritual. To focus the entire spiritual force of its temple on the growth of the rice, 25 days before the farmers plan to harvest, its leader invites Dewi Sri and her fellow deities to take up temporary residence in their council temple shrine. Over 3 days they regale their spiritual guests with huge quantities of food and drink hoping thereby to persuade the gods to bring succulence and strength-giving vitality to the baby rice as it grows in the womb of the earth that they—the farmers—have kept constantly moist with water. By doing so the Balinese keep their path open to fertility and life.

READING 10–1

COSMOLOGY AS ECOLOGICAL ANALYSIS: A VIEW FROM THE RAIN FOREST

G. Reichel-Dolmatoff

Few societies reveal a more harmonious blend of cosmological notions, myth, ritual, shamanism, and ecology than the Tukano of the northwest Amazon. In this reading, G. Reichel-Dolmatoff, an author of several classic studies of these people's way of life, describes how the Tukano

Source: G. Reichel-Dolmatoff, "Cosmology as Ecological Analysis: A View from the Rain Forest," *Man* 11 (1976), pp. 307–18. Reprinted by permission of the Royal Anthropological Institute of Great Britain and Ireland.

efficiently exploit the limited resources of their natural environment by making their cosmological beliefs function as an indigenous version of modern systems analysis. He emphasizes just how limited are local natural resources, and notes that the Tukano are prevented from expanding their territory by the presence of other ethnic groups. The amount of exploitable land available cannot, therefore, be increased, and so they have had to adjust their mental attitudes to cope with this restriction, and evolve a society that, if it is to survive, has to adapt to it. This article suggests that the Tukano make strenuous efforts to match their expectations to the limitations imposed by the natural environment, and their society has developed a formidable number of taboos to prevent their natural resources from being depleted. These taboos include prohibitions found in other societies, for example, physical violence between people, but the Tukano have incorporated these rules, which for Westerners would be classed as part of the legal system, into their religion, and instead of policemen to keep order, they have shamans. The exchange of women between groups of men in the Tukano marriage system is as much as part of their system of belief and ritual as it is a feature of the kinship system, and acts of cooperation between individuals are regarded as essential to the conservation of ecological balance.

Ecological balance is intrinsic to the Tukano's all-embracing concept of the cosmos, as is their belief in the finiteness of the energy that flows through the cosmos. Unlike the Western idea of an expanding universe, the Tukana cosmos is finite. Thus when hunters kill game, the energy expended by the death must be returned to nature so that life and death may remain balanced. Finiteness and balance are sustained by these taboos, and the result of this logic, Reichel-Dolmatoff points out, is that Tukano cosmology bears a remarkable resemblance to modern systems analysis in that the Tukano have constructed their cosmos in the form of a system in which the amount of energy expended is directly related to the amount of energy input the cosmic system receives. Fertility, necessary for life, and sex, through which fertility comes about, are necessary components of this system, and the interaction between males and females acts as a metaphor for the union of opposites that helps energy to flow through the system.

I

Until relatively recent times the cultural image of the Indian tribes of tropical America has been that of a group of rather primitive and hostile peoples whose contribution to human thought had been negligible and whose level of social complexity had remained far below that of most aboriginal societies of the Old World. In fact, only the higher civilisations of America—the ancient Mexicans, Mayas and Peruvians—were occasionally credited with having created fairly elaborate social, political and religious institutions, but even in their case seldom has there been explicit discussion of native philosophical systems, or something approaching an integrated world-view. Sometimes one was almost led to believe that the tropical forest Indians were fossil societies; societies which, in a sense, were incomplete; which had not evolved and had nothing to teach us. They were "out of the mainstream" some people said, and those of us who made these societies the subject of their studies struggled against the stigma of working somewhat "out of the mainstream."

In the more recent past, however, this image has undergone a notable change. Ethnological research among the surviving tribes of the tropical rain forest has begun to reach a depth and breadth of inquiry that were formerly unthought of, and these newly gained insights are beginning to shed an entirely new light upon the intellectual achievements of the aboriginal peoples of the Amazon Basin, the Orinoco Plains and many other regions of the American Tropics, a vast area covering more than six million square kilometers. It seems that the old stereotypes are disappearing at last; and instead we are presented with a new image: the Indian, not only as a highly pragmatic thinker and an individual with a sound sense of reality, but also, the Indian as an abstract philosopher, a builder of intricate cosmic models, and a planner of sweeping moral designs. Also at the same period, in view of current interest in natural resources, many scientists and technologists who have turned their attention to the tropical rain forest areas of the world, have become concerned with the many problems of ecological adaptation which traditional societies have had to solve in these environments. In the case of the Amazon Basin it takes a healthy and energetic society to cope with the rigorous climatic conditions and with the management of easily depleted natural resources, a society that would develop not only a set of highly

adaptive behavioural rules for survival—framed within effective institutional bodies—but, more important still, a society with a coherent belief system, with a foundation of strongly motivating values which would make endurable the problems of man's existence in an unpredictable world.

In this lecture it is my purpose to describe and examine some aspects cf adaptive behaviour as I have been able to observe it n the course of my contacts with several Indian g oups in the Colombian lowlands. I should add he e that by "adaptive" I mean anything that increas es the probability of survival of the individual or the group. In the following I shall mainly refer to the Tukano Indians of the Northwest Amazon, especially the Desana (Eastern Tukano), and my chief concern will be to trace some connexions that exist between the cosmological concepts of these Indians, and the realities of adaptation to a given physical environment. In doing so I shall try to demonstrate that aboriginal cosmologies and myth structures, together with the ritual behaviour derived from them, represent in all respects a set of ecological principles and that these formulate a system of social and economic rules that have a highly adaptive value in the continuous endeavour to maintain a viable equilibrium between the resources of the environment and the demands of society.

II

The Tukano Indians occupy a large area in the central portion of the northwest Amazon, mainly on the Vaupés River, a major affluent of the Rio Negro. Although most of the country is flat and densely forested, a transitional terrain of hilly uplands lies on the western fringe, while towards the north the forest is sometimes broken by stretches of grassy, tree-strewn savanna country. Although this rain forest area has often been described as a rather homogeneous region, many environmental differences exist which have considerable bearing upon the range and success of human adaptive responses. Game animals, amphibians and reptiles, edible fruits, nuts and insects, and suitable horticultural lands are not evenly distributed and considerable resource fluctuation can be said to exist within and among subregions.

The Tukano are bound to their rain forest habitat by a number of circumstances. In the first place, according to myth and tradition, the land inhabited by them at present was originally peopled by their forefathers in ancient, heroic times, and was handed on to their descendants as a solemn investiture in a perpetual trust. These tribal ancestors whose names and deeds are remembered in myths and genealogical recitals had given proper designations to the rivers and the hills, the rocks and the rapids and to all other notable natural features. This, then, continues to be their country, the homeland of the ancients. It is of interest to observe here that, although the Tukano habitat can, to a large degree, be described as a truly "natural environment," they themselves perceive it as a man-made environment, transformed and structured in the past not so much by any exploitative activities of their ancestors, but by having been imbued by them with symbolic meaning. There is, then, a time-perspective to their understanding of the environment.

In the second place, Tukano territory is surrounded by lands occupied by other people, be they tribal Indians or be they Colombian or Brazilian settlers, and both these neighbouring groups are quite unwilling to accept immigrants, much less invaders. The Tukano, then, must of necessity exist within the limitations of their given environment and must make the best of it. They have to rely utterly upon their local resources and upon their own traditional skills for exploiting them.

The traditional settlement pattern consists of widely scattered large and well-built communal houses, occupied by extended families whose members derive much of their basic food supply from cultivating manioc gardens. However, seasonal hunting, fishing and gathering play an important part in their economic and social life. Tukano society is divided into more than twenty named exogamic groups; descent is patrilineal and residence is patrilocal, with cross-cousin marriage said to be preferred. Marriage between these different units implies a rigidly structured relationship which

is expressed in many forms of reciprocity and exchange. Most of these activities, both social and economic, are closely connected with ceremonies directed by the shaman who also officiates at the rituals of the life cycle and is active as a healer of illness. Warfare is not institutionalised.

Here is a brief summary of how the Tukano imagine the origin and structure of the universe and the elementary forces that animate it. The creator was the Sun-Father, an anthropomorphic god who designed a three-layered cosmos consisting of a flat earth, a celestial vault, and a place of bliss situated under the earth. He then peopled the land and created animals and plants, giving to each species a set of rules according to which they were to live and multiply. However, the Sun-Father created only a limited number of animals and plants, placing both categories under the constant care of specific spirit-beings who were to guard and protect them against eventual abuses. What is more, he assigned to his creation only a restricted, roughly circular, stretch of land, limited on all sides by permanent landmarks. In other words, the creation of the Tukano universe was not conceived as an all-embracing or expanding system, but was a limited, well-defined proposition with finite and restricted resources. Nor was it accomplished as a single act limited in time: it still continues uninterruptedly because, ever since its initiation, the Sun-Father exercises a fertilising action upon it. It is the energy of the sun, imagined by the Tukano in terms of seminal light and heat, that causes plants to grow and fruit to ripen, that makes mankind and animals reproduce, and that is thought to be creative not only in a germinal, biological sense, but also in the sense of spiritual illumination and the attainment of esoteric wisdom. The essence of this force is imagined as a masculine power that fertilizes a feminine element that is this world. In Tukano thought, the biosphere has both male and female aspects, but seen in its totality, it has primarily a feminine character over which the sun exercises his power.

The seminal energy of the sun is thought to constitute a huge circuit in which the entire cosmos participates. This circuit is imagined as having a limited quantity of procreative energy that flows continuously between man and animal, between society and nature. Since the quantity of energy is restricted, man may remove what he needs only under certain conditions and must convert his quantum of "borrowed" energy into an essence than can be reincorporated into the circuit. For example, when an animal is killed or when a crop is harvested the energy of the local fauna and flora are thought to be diminished; however, as soon as the game or fruit are converted into nourishment, the energy is conserved, now on the level of society, because the consumers of the food have now acquired a reproductive life force that previously belonged to an animal or plant.

III

The striking point about these ideas is that this bears a remarkable resemblance to modern systems analysis. In terms of ecological theory, the Tukano thus conceive the world as a system in which the amount of energy output is directly related to the amount of input the system receives. According to the Tukano, the system handles these inputs in two ways: sexual energy which has been repressed in the individual, returns directly to the capital of total energy in which the biotic components of the system participates; mere health and well-being, resulting from controlled food consumption, represent an input which energises also the abiotic components of the system, for example, the movements of the stars or meteorological phenomena. The individual should never cause a disturbance in this general equilibrium, that is, he should never use energy without restoring it as soon as possible. The entire system is largely derived from the model of sexual physiology. The Tukano concept of solar energy includes a large number of things to which a seminal symbolism is attributed because of their colour, shape, texture or other characteristics; while a number of other things are associated with a female concept of fecundity and gestation. The associations of images and symbols are interpreted by the Tukano on various levels of abstraction and eventu-

ally dissociate themselves farther and farther from natural and physiological facts until, at a higher cognitive level, they come to constitute a systems theory of balanced, finite energy flow.

This cosmological model of a system which constantly requires rebalancing in the form of inputs of energy retrieved by individual effort, constitutes a religious proposition which is intimately connected with the social and economic organisation of the group. In this way, the general balance of energy flow becomes a religious objective in which native ecological concepts play a dominant organisational role. To understand the structure and functioning of the ecosystem becomes therefore a vital task to the Tukano. It follows that the Indian's ethnobiological knowledge of the natural environment is not casual and is not something he assimilates through gradually increasing familiarity and repeated sense experience; it is a structured, disciplined knowledge which is based upon a long tradition of enquiry and which is acquired of necessity as part of his intellectual equipment for biological and cultural survival.

Among the Indians there is usually little interest in new knowledge that might be used for exploiting the environment more effectively and there is little concern for maximising short-term gains or for obtaining more food or raw-materials than are actually needed. But there is always a great deal of interest in accumulating more factual knowledge about biological reality and, above all, about what the physical world requires from man. This knowledge, the Indians believe, is essential for survival because man must bring himself into conformity with nature if he wants to exist as part of nature's unity, and must fit his demands to nature's availabilities.

Animal behaviour is of greatest interest to the Indians because it often constitutes a model for what is *possible* in terms of successful adaptation. On the one hand, the Indians have a detailed knowledge of such aspects as seasonal variation and microdistributions of the animal and plant species of their habitat. They have a good understanding of ecological communities, of the behaviour of social insects, of bird flocks, the organisation of fish schools, the patterns of fish runs, and other forms of collective behaviour. Such phenomena as parasitism, symbiosis, commensalism and other relationships between co-occurring species have been well observed by them and are pointed out as possible models of adaptation. On the other hand, myths and tales abound with accounts of visits to the animal world, of people turning into animals in order to learn more about their habits, or of animals teaching men how to make use of certain resources. Shamanistic wisdom often contains detailed descriptions of such contacts and exchanges, and many shamans claim to have acquired part of their specific knowledge from animals which revealed to them some unexpected food resource, a cure for an illness, or a practical procedure in solving some everyday problem. Some of this wisdom may then be considered esoteric and secret, remaining the private property of a shaman, but often enough this specialised knowledge of animal behaviour becomes part of prescribed patterns of human action and interaction because of its obvious adaptive value. Moreover, mythology emphatically tells of animal species which have become extinct or which were punished or degraded for *not* obeying certain prescribed rules of adaptive significance. Thus, gluttony, improvidence, aggressiveness and all forms of overindulgence are punished by the superior forces, to serve as examples not only to the animal community, but also to human society. Animals, then, are metaphors for survival. By analysing animal behaviour the Indians try to discover an order in the physical world, a world-order to which *human* activities can then be adjusted.

In Tukano culture, the individual person is conscious that he forms part of a complex network of interactions which include not only society but the entire universe. Within this context of an essential interrelatedness of all things, a person has to fulfil many functions that go far beyond his or her social roles and that are extrasocietal extensions of a set of adaptive norms. These rules or norms, then, guide a person's relationships not only with other people—past or present, kin or ally—but also with animals, plants, as a matter of fact with all biotic and non-biotic components of the environment.

The rules the individual has to follow refer, above all, to cooperative behaviour aimed at the conservation of ecological balance as the ultimately desirable quality. Thus the relationship between man and his environment is being formulated not only on a cognitive level, but clearly it also constitutes an affective personal relationship in which individual animals and plants are treated with respect and caution.

The Tukano are quite aware of the fact that, in order to maintain a stable balance of input and output, a number of regulatory mechanisms have to be instituted and, what is more, have to be fully respected by all members of the society. These social controls of necessity possess marked adaptive implications and must be enforced primarily in those aspects of existence which, to a large degree, determine survival. I shall mention here: population growth, the exploitation of the physical environment, and aggression in interpersonal relations. It is quite clear to the Tukano that, in order to ensure individual and collective survival and well-being, adaptive rules have to be established to adjust the birth-rate, the harvest-rate, and to counterbalance all socially disruptive behaviour.

IV

I shall first turn to the problem of population growth and regulations. Two mechanisms are used by the Indians to control the birth-rate: oral contraceptives and sexual continence. Tukano women use herbal concoctions which, in varying concentrations, cause temporary sterility, and by this means they manage to space their offspring over several years in such a way that when a woman has her second child the first is already sufficiently independent not to be a bother. The number of children is kept low and couples with many children are criticised quite openly as socially irresponsible. It may be added here that the old and infirm, as soon as they cease to collaborate in the food quest of their household group, are eliminated by being abandoned in the forest or on an island in the river.

The second mechanism is abstention. Sexual abstinence and sexual repression are practised on many occasions and are among the most important prerequisites to many ritual activities. It is important to point out here that, in Tukano thought, food and sex are closely related and are symbolically equivalent. This idea of relationship between caloric and sexual appetite is expressed in many ways; on a metaphorical level sexual intercourse and eating are equated, and in ritual exchange certain foodstuffs come to represent the exchange of women. Since strict exogamic rules constitute the main organising principle in Tukano society, the consumption or avoidance of certain foods are geared to the concept of exogamy in such a way that dietary restrictions come to stand for sexual restrictions. The selective use of certain foods may thus be said to be subject to the laws of *exophagy,* which determine the permissibility of certain foods under diverse circumstances. There are "male" and "female" foods and food preparations, and these rules refer not only to animal-derived foods, but also to vegetable foods.

These aspects are best illustrated by the ideas that guide the activities of the hunter. All game animals are subject to the Master of Animals, a dwarf-like spirit-being with marked phallic attributes. This supernatural gamekeeper jealously guards his flock consisting of deer, tapir, peccary, agouti, paca, monkeys and all other animal species that are a common food resource of the Indians. The Master of Animals is directly their protector and procreator and they all live inside steep rocky hills or in deep pools in the river, both dwelling-places being imagined as large store-houses teeming with game and fish. In order to obtain the supernatural Master's permission to kill a game animal, the prospective hunter must undergo a rigorous preparation which consists of sexual continence, food restrictions, and purification rites ensuring cleansing the body by bathing and emetics. For some days before going on a hunting excursion, the man should refrain from all sexual relations and, what is more, he should not have had any dreams with an erotic content. Moreover, it is necessary that none of the women who

live in his household is menstruating. Another mechanism that restricts overhunting is this: According to cosmological myths all game animals are associated with certain constellations, as defined by the Tukano. However, a species can only be hunted *after* its constellation has risen over the horizon, and it is said that the animals cry and weep with fear when they realise that their time is approaching. It may be mentioned here also that the hunt itself is more than a mere food quest in that it is imagined as a courtship in which the prey has to be seduced to submit to the hunter.

Whenever game is scarce, the shaman must visit the Master of Animals in a narcotic trance and try to obtain from him the release of some of his charges. He will not ask for individual animals but rather for herds or for a good hunting season and in return he promises to send to the Master's abode the souls of persons who, at their death, must return to this great store-house to replenish the energy of those animals the supernatural gamekeeper gives to the hunters. The Master of Animals and his numerous personifications are thus conceived as administrators of usufruct rights; since game resources are limited, restrictive rights to their use are instituted by these spirit-beings, and it falls to the shaman to become the mediator.

From the examples I have mentioned it is obvious that the combination of all these prerequisites represents in itself a body of highly adaptive rules which notably restrict the activities of any hunter or fisherman. A person cannot go hunting or fishing simply any time he needs food, but only after having undergone a more or less anxiety-charged period of preparation, the purpose of which is to avoid overhunting. Illness or misfortune in hunting are almost always attributed to neglect of any of the numerous rules a hunter has to observe.

Food restrictions are not only observed in connexion with economic activities, but are a standard practice on most ritual occasions and in many other everyday circumstances. For example, a man whose wife is expecting a child should eat neither tapir, peccary nor monkey meat because this might affect the good health of his yet unborn offspring. A man whose hunting or fishing gear has become polluted from being casually touched by a woman, must observe a liquid diet for several days. When fish run to spawn, those present in one's stretch of the river should not be eaten, nor are birds' eggs ever collected for food, and the flesh of some reptiles is avoided during their breeding season. All these interdictions are verbalised by the Indians in terms of dangers to the consumer's health. Especially strict prohibitions keep people from eating normally while engaged in the acquisition of esoteric knowledge and, similarly, all rituals of the individual life cycle involve temporary dietary restrictions. In summary, during pregnancy, childbirth and menstruation; during mourning periods, or while gathering medicinal herbs; during the couvade or while engaged upon the preparation of poisons, narcotics or love potions, people carefully control their food intake and, as a general rule, refrain from eating the meat of game animals.

Similar prohibitions restrict the gathering of wild fruits and nuts, of honey and of edible insects. Even the extraction of raw-materials used in technological manufactures is controlled by ritual restrictions. The gathering of thatch for a roof, of clay for pottery making, or of scarce woods or fibres for a number of specific end products, are subject to permits which have to be obtained from the spirit-owners of the respective resources.

This complex of dietary and sexual restrictions is closely related to the control of aggressive attitudes. The principal mechanism which checks socially disruptive behaviour is the organisation into exogamic groups which are linked by alliances and stand in a relationship of reciprocal exchange. Besides exchanging women, these complementary units will give and receive foods, raw-materials or manufactured goods, and on these periodic occasions which constitute highly formalised rituals, the dances, songs and ceremonial dialogues emphasise over and over again the paired linkages that unite Tukano society.

It appears from the foregoing that the Tukano definition of what constitutes carrying capacity, refers mainly to a certain balance of protein-rich food resources such as game, fish and wild fruits. Environmental degradation is interpreted *not* in terms of soil exhaustion, but in terms of the eventual depletion of game and of increased walking time. Because of the relative scarcity of protein resources restrictive rights to their use have to be established in order to avoid frequent relocation of settlements. Propitious conditions for horticultural activities are perhaps not plentiful, but land for productive garden plots *is* available. However, the nutrient content of practically all vegetable foods of the rain forest is very low and carrying capacity is therefore determined by the existence of protein resources, and population size and density are functions thereof.

The three aspects I have mentioned—population growth, the exploitation of the physical environment and the control of aggression—can be reduced to one single problem, that is, the maintenance of a balanced ecosystem. The Indians know that their daily existence depends upon the proper functioning of these adaptive interactions. The question arises, how can a people be made to follow these prescriptions and regulations which impose such severe restrictions upon their social behaviour and their biological needs?

V

The mechanisms which, in the native groups I am concerned with here, enforce the rules are closely related to the aboriginal theory of disease. To begin with, the specific bodily or mental conditions which, according to the Tukano, constitute illness and which manifest themselves through a large number of signs and symptoms, are always thought to be caused by an agent external to the body. The possible pathogenic agencies fall into three categories (1) the revenge of game animals; (2) the illwill of other people; and (3) the malevolence of supernatural beings such as the Master of Animals or other spirit-beings.

This malevolence of people and animals is not an arbitrary force that blindly strikes its unsuspecting victim. On the contrary, illness is always interpreted as a quite natural consequence of a person's breach or neglect of cultural norms. Apart from its being socially and emotionally disturbing, illness is, in the Tukano view, nothing but a reaction to the ecologically inadequate behaviour of the patient, to his maladaptive performance. It is the patient who causes the disease, by making himself vulnerable to it. The diagnosis the shaman establishes has, therefore, two different aspects: One refers to the patient's complaints, to the symptoms he has developed; the other aspect refers to the question *why* the person became a victim of the disease. And here we can recognise another important aspect of the shaman's function, an aspect that is closely related to the problem of ecological adaptation.

In shamanistic practice illness is taken to be the consequence of a person's upsetting a certain aspect of the ecological balance. Overhunting is a common cause and so are harvesting activities in which some relatively scarce natural resource has been wasted. The delicate balance existing within the natural environment, between nature and society, and within society itself, constitutes a series of systems in which any disturbance, however slight, is bound to affect the whole. For example, meddling with certain women who should be avoided is the same kind of affront as eating certain fish that should not be eaten; while killing too many animals of a certain species must always be avoided. These are offences the consequence of which is likely to be an illness. In the diagnostic process, which is often accompanied by divinatory practices, the shaman is interested in the patient's illness not so much as a function of biology, but rather as a symptom of a disorder in the energy flow. His main concern is about the relationship between society and the supernatural Masters of game, fish and wild fruits, on whom depend success in harvesting and who command many pathogenic agents. To the shaman it is therefore of the essence to diagnose correctly the causes of the illness, to identify the exact quality of the inadequate relationship (be it adultery, overhunting, or any other overindulgence or waste), and then to redress the balance by communicating with the spirits and by establishing reconciliatory contacts with the game animals. To mention just one example of how a diagnosis is

established: A man who has killed too many animals of a certain species, will appear in the shaman's dream or trance states in the shape of that animal and the image will be accompanied by a certain luminosity, a certain degree of light. It is quite remarkable that differences in high or low light intensity are recognised to be very important in the flow of solar energy, as understood by the Tukano, and that shamans will mention in their spells and incantations up to seven shades of "yellow light" that energise the biosphere.

In summarising this aspect I want to emphasise that the shaman as a healer of illness does not so much interfere on the individual level, but operates on the level of those supra-individual structures that have been disturbed by the person. To be effective, he has to apply his treatment to the disturbed part of the ecosystem. It might be said then that a Tukano shaman does not have individual patients; his task is to cure a social malfunctioning. The diseased organism of the patient is secondary in importance and will be treated eventually, both empirically and ritually, but what really counts is the re-establishment of the rules that will avoid overhunting, the depletion of certain plant resources, and unchecked population increase. The shaman becomes thus a truly powerful force in the control and management of resources.

The shaman then interferes quite directly with hunting, fishing, gathering and most other harvesting activities. For example, a shaman will personally control the quantity and concentration of fishpoison to be used on a certain stretch of river; he will determine the number of animals to be killed when a herd of peccary is reported, and he will decide on a suitable harvesting strategy for the gathering of wild fruits. He will determine *which* fish have to be thrown back into the water after a haul has been made, and occasionally he even might completely prohibit the killing of certain animals in a restricted area of the forest. He will also control such technological activities as the construction of a communal house, the manufacture of a canoe, or the opening of a trail. All these activities obviously affect the natural environment since trees have to be felled and many plants have to be destroyed or used in the process, and the shaman's role as a protector of game and plant-life explains why animals and plants figure so prominently as his spirit-helpers. All this, I should like to point out here, is not speculation; the Indians are quite explicit in these matters and explain that the spirit-owners of nature must not be angered and that it is the shaman's task to reconcile them.

The very large denotative vocabulary of a shaman expresses his great concern with establishing the complete inventory of the ecosystem. In order to be able to administer this great store-house, he has to know, name and categorise all its contents. This knowledge eventually provides him with the criteria for ecological planning and this, of course, is problem-solving by anticipation.

The fact that many daily activities such as hunting, fishing, gathering, the clearing of a new field or the curing of a disease are subject to divinatory practices in order to locate the most propitious spot or time, or to find the most effective procedure in coping with this or that predicament, gives the shaman ample opportunity to protect wild-life by random scheduling of hunting excursions whenever he thinks that a certain species is endangered, or to channel any other exploitative activity in directions he believes to be best. I know of several cases where shamans initiated limited migratory movements by asking people to abandon their homes in order to avoid an approaching epidemic or the presence of evil spirits, both calamities being revealed in divinatory trance. The true reason, however, seems to have been the advanced depletion of protein resources. In view of the observation of a number of related cases, it seems not unlikely that shamanistic divinatory practices operate with models and that, in this manner, many adaptive changes are being introduced by shamans.

One might ask here: how far is a shaman actually conscious of his role as an ecological broker? Does he always act quite rationally and with an adequate understanding of ecological principles? There exist, of course, differences. Some shamans, notably the younger and less experienced ones, tend to verbalise their conceptions in quite simplistic terms by saying that overhunting and overharvesting are

bound to annoy both the spirits and the game animals, and that illness will be the punishment. They will readily point out changes in prey abundance and will attribute the biotic impoverishment of certain restricted areas to the action of vengeful spirits. Others however will not make use of these mystical interpretations but will blame greed and ignorance for the depletion of protein resources. They will attribute some (if not all) diseases to nutritional deficiencies and will state quite plainly that protein resources are scarce and have to be protected. To be sure, the fact that most economic activities are accompanied by rituals does not mean that the shaman simply asks the supernatural forces for abundance, for plenty, for a maximum amount of what the environment can produce, but rather that occasions are being provided for stock-taking, for weighing costs and benefits, and for the eventual redistribution of resources. At these moments the shaman's book-keeping shows the general system inputs and outputs. In point of fact, most shamanistic activities such as curing rituals, rain-making, the periodic reaffirmation of alliances or food exchange between exogamic groups might be viewed as rituals concerned with resource management and ecological balance. This fact has sometimes been obscured by a tendency to describe native shamans in terms of mere witchdoctors or religious fanatics.

VI

The Tukano and many other Colombian tribes believe that the entire universe is steadily deteriorating. Thus it is thought that formerly people were healthier, stronger and more intelligent than they are at present; that animals and fruits were larger and that they were more abundant than now. The Indians will point out stretches of forest, rivers or lagoons saying that in former times animal life was plentiful there. It is true that, at present, this feeling of impending doom is partly justified; in many parts the world of the rain forest Indians *is* on the wane. But the Indian's sense of entropy, of the tendency toward disorder and chaos, does not seem to be a consequence of his present plight, but rather represents an existential anxiety that forms part of native cosmology and philosophy, and that is based upon the close and daily observation of the biological cycles of growth and decline. The important point is that this idea of increasing disorder is always followed by the institutionalised resolution to *recreate* the world and to re-establish its order and purpose as stated in cosmological tradition. This continuous cycle of ritual creation, destruction and re-creation can be found in many tropical forest societies and is indeed an important mechanism of cultural and biological survival.

In the course of these ceremonial occasions, when the universe and all its components are being renewed, one goal becomes of central importance: the reaffirmation of links with past and future generations, together with the expression of concern about the future well-being of society. The emphasis of the ritual is upon unifying the social group, upon continuity, upon the close bonds of identity that unite society with the past and make it the foundation of the future. It seems that this sense of union provides deeply motivating values and strong incentives for ecological responsibility. The lengthy genealogical recitals and the ritual dialogues have a powerful cohesive function, and in many of these rituals animal and plant-spirits are thought to participate, expressing by their presence their interrelatedness and interdependency. It must be pointed out here that the ritual re-creation of the universe is generally accompanied by the collective use of narcotics of plant origin. During these drug-induced trance states, or other forms of dissociate phenomena, the participants establish contact with the mythical past, in fact, they see themselves return to the time of divine Creation and thus take part in it. It is clear that, here again, the officiating shaman can adaptively orient the interpretations of the visions people project upon the vivid background of their hallucinations.

During most or all of these rituals which can be said to be essentially concerned with ecological balance, the recital of myths and genealogies is of great importance. These myths explain man's nature and trace man's destiny from birth and infancy through maturity to decline and death; from the sin of incest to chaos and near-destruction, and hence to a new order and the establishment of law. These myths and tales, I should like to emphasise here, are not mere "literature"; they represent a truly remarkable effort at intellectual interpretation, at providing a cognitive matrix for life. They are a guide for survival because they establish rules of conduct, not only for ritual occasions but for everyday life; a fact which sometimes goes unnoticed as long as one has not discovered the metaphorical code in which the myths are transmitted.

The cosmological myths which express the Tukano world-view do not describe Man's Place in Nature in terms of dominion, of mastery over a subordinate environment, nor do they in any way express the notion of what some of us might call a sense of "harmony with nature." Nature, in their view, is not a physical entity apart from man and, therefore, he cannot confront it or oppose it or harmonise with it as a separate entity. Occasionally man can unbalance it by his personal malfunctioning as a component, but he never stands apart from it. Man is taken to be a part of a set of supra-individual systems which—be they biological or cultural—transcend our individual lives and within which survival and the maintenance of a certain quality of life are possible only if all other life forms too are allowed to evolve according to their specific needs, as stated in cosmological myths and traditions.

In closing, I should like to note the following. Until quite recently ethnologists and archaeologists have attempted to explain cultural evolution and change in terms of linear cause-and-effect models and this approach is still used by most specialists in these fields. Gregory Bateson was the first ethnographer to sense the need for a systems theory model to account for his ethnographical data, although his now classic monograph on New Guinea was written long before the formal aspects of systems theory had been developed.

Archaeologists have been particularly prone to dependence on cause-and-effect explanations and models constructed on the principles of linear causality, and these trends have been emphasised in the intellectual movement called "New Archaeology." It is only recently that Flannery has noted that two very different kinds of explanatory models are used by the "New Archaeology." One of these schools is explicit in its adherence to linear causality. Flannery has applied the term "law-and-order" archaeology to this school. The other less popular trend has been an application of systems theory to account for cultural change, attributing its dynamics to very slow deviations which originate in a part of the system and then develop into major modifications. It seems that this approach is far more likely to produce significant models than is "law-and-order" archaeology.

It is striking then that in the last decade ethnographers and archaeologists are coming to accept as the only kind of explanatory model which can be used to handle ecological relationships the kind of overall systems model which was adopted by "primitive" Indians a very long time ago.

READING 10–2

RITUAL REGULATION OF ENVIRONMENTAL RELATIONS AMONG A NEW GUINEA PEOPLE[1]

Roy A. Rappaport

The cultural-materialist perspective from which Roy Rappaport interprets Tsembaga ritual complements that of Reichel-Dolmatoff's in certain respects. Although lacking the cosmological underpinnings and intrusive weight of ancestral sanctions, the Tsembaga have managed to create a system by which ritual conserves natural resources, reduces warfare between local groups to levels

Source: Roy A. Rappaport, "Ritual Regulation of Environmental Relations among a New Guinea People," *Ethnology* Vol. 6, no. 1 Jan. 1967, pp. 17–30. Reprinted with permission.

that do not threaten to jeopardize them, adjusts the ratio between the land and its human occupants, and guarantees that individuals can have high-quality protein when they most require it.

As a respected contribution to materialist interpretations of social phenomena, Rappaport's article provides a salutary approach to that offered by structural-functionalists, Malinowskian functionalism, and structuralists who all too frequently write as though rituals and beliefs form a closed circuit quite unaffected by, or without a bearing on, material factors. This study therefore is especially useful in showing that rituals may serve other purposes than those proposed by scholars of the above approaches. One caveat needs to be registered, however. The merits of Rappaport's demonstration rely very much upon the quality of his ethnography, which as we see is impressive. Other exponents of this approach have laid claims for its validity on the basis of ethnographic data of less reliability than those we are presented with here.

Most functional studies of religious behavior in anthropology have as an analytic goal the elucidation of events, processes, or relationships occurring within a social unit of some sort. The social unit is not always well defined, but in some cases it appears to be a church, that is, a group of people who entertain similar beliefs about the universe, or a congregation, a group of people who participate together in the performance of religious rituals. There have been exceptions. Thus Vayda, Leeds, and Smith (1961) and Vogt (1952) have clearly perceived that the functions of religious ritual are not necessarily confined within the boundaries of a congregation or even a church. By and large, however, I believe that the following statement by Homans (1941: 172) represents fairly the dominant line of anthropological thought concerning the functions of religious ritual:

> Ritual actions do not produce a practical result on the external world—that is one of the reasons why we call them ritual. But to make this statement is not to say that ritual has no function. Its function is not related to the world external to the society but to the internal constitution of the society. It gives the members of the society confidence, it dispels their anxieties, it disciplines their social organization.

No argument will be raised here against the sociological and psychological functions imputed by Homans, and many others before him, to ritual. They seem to me to be plausible. Nevertheless, in some cases at least, ritual does produce, in Homans' terms, "a practical result on the world" external not only to the social unit composed of those who participate together in ritual performances but also to the larger unit composed of those who entertain similar beliefs concerning the universe. The material presented here will show that the ritual cycles of the Tsembaga, and of other local territorial groups of Maring speakers living in the New Guinea interior, play an important part in regulating the relationships of these groups with both the nonhuman components of their immediate environments and the human components of their less immediate environments, that is, with other similar territorial groups. To be more specific, this regulation helps to maintain the biotic communities existing within their territories, redistributes land among people and people over land, and limits the frequency of fighting. In the absence of authoritative political statuses or offices, the ritual cycle likewise provides a means for mobilizing allies when warfare may be undertaken. It also provides a mechanism for redistributing local pig surpluses in the form of pork throughout a large regional population while helping to assure the local population of a supply of pork when its members are most in need of high quality protein.

Religious ritual may be defined, for the purposes of this paper, as the prescribed performance of conventionalized acts manifestly directed toward the involvement of nonempirical or supernatural agencies in the affairs of the actors. While this definition relies upon the formal characteristics of the performances and upon the motives for undertaking them, attention will be focused upon the empirical effects of ritual performances and sequences of ritual performances. The religious rituals to be discussed are regarded as neither more nor less than part of the behavioral repertoire employed by an aggregate of organisms in adjusting to its environment.

The data upon which this paper is based were collected during fourteen months of field work among the Tsembaga, one of about twenty local groups of Maring speakers living in the Simbai and Jimi Valleys of the Bismarck Range in the Territory of New Guinea. The size of Maring local groups varies from a little over 100 to 900. The Tsembaga, who in 1963 numbered 204 persons, are located on the south wall of the Simbai Valley. The country in which they live differs from the true highlands in being lower, generally more rugged, and more heavily forested. Tsembaga territory rises, within a total surface area of 3.2 square miles, from an elevation of 2,200 feet at the Simbai river to 7,200 feet at the ridge crest. Gardens are cut in the secondary forests up to between 5,000 and 5,400 feet, above which the area remains in primary forest. Rainfall reaches 150 inches per year.

The Tsembaga have come into contact with the outside world only recently; the first government patrol to penetrate their territory arrived in 1954. They were considered uncontrolled by the Australian government until 1962, and they remain unmissionized to this day.

The 204 Tsembaga are distributed among five putatively patrilineal clans, which are, in turn, organized into more inclusive groupings on two hierarchical levels below that of the total local group.[2] Internal political structure is highly egalitarian. There are no hereditary or elected chiefs, nor are there even "big men" who can regularly coerce or command the support of their clansmen or co-residents in economic or forceful enterprises.

It is convenient to regard the Tsembaga as a population in the ecological sense, that is, as one of the components of a system of trophic exchanges taking place within a bounded area. Tsembaga territory and the biotic community existing upon it may be conveniently viewed as an ecosystem. While it would be permissible arbitrarily to designate the Tsembaga as a population and their territory with its biota as an ecosystem, there are also nonarbitrary reasons for doing so. An ecosystem is a system of material exchanges, and the Tsembaga maintain against other human groups exclusive access to the resources within their territorial borders. Conversely, it is from this territory alone that the Tsembaga ordinarily derive all of their foodstuffs and most of the other materials they require for survival. Less anthropocentrically, it may be justified to regard Tsembaga territory with its biota as an ecosystem in view of the rather localized nature of cyclical material exchanges in tropical rainforests.

As they are involved with the nonhuman biotic community within their territory in a set of trophic exchanges, so do they participate in other material relationships with other human groups external to their territory. Genetic materials are exchanged with other groups, and certain crucial items, such as stone axes, were in [the] past obtained from the outside. Furthermore, in the area occupied by the Maring speakers, more than one local group is usually involved in any process, either peaceful or warlike, through which people are redistributed over land and land redistributed among people.

The concept of the ecosystem, though it provides a convenient frame for the analysis of interspecific trophic exchanges taking place within limited geographical areas, does not comfortably accommodate intraspecific exchanges taking place over wider geographic areas. Some sort of geographic population model would be more useful for the analysis of the relationship of the local ecological population to the larger regional population of which it is a part, but we lack even a set of appropriate terms for such a model. Suffice it here to note that the relations of the Tsembaga to the total of other local human populations in their vicinity are similar to the relations of local aggregates of other animals to the totality of their species occupying broader and more or less continuous regions. This larger, more inclusive aggregate may resemble what geneticists mean by the term population, that is, an aggregate of interbreeding organisms persisting through an indefinite number of generations and either living or capable of living in isolation from similar aggregates of the same species. This is the unit which survives through long periods of time while its local ecological (*sensu stricto*) subunits, the units more or less independently involved in

interspecific trophic exchanges such as the Tsembaga, are ephemeral.

Since it has been asserted that the ritual cycles of the Tsembaga regulate relationships within what may be regarded as a complex system, it is necessary, before proceeding to the ritual cycle itself, to describe briefly, and where possible in quantitative terms, some aspects of the place of the Tsembaga in this system.

The Tsembaga are bush-fallowing horticulturalists. Staples include a range of root crops, taro (*Colocasia*) and sweet potatoes being most important, yams and manioc less so. In addition, a great variety of greens are raised, some of which are rich in protein. Sugar cane and some tree crops, particularly *Pandanus conoideus,* are also important.

All gardens are mixed, many of them containing all of the major root crops and many greens. Two named garden types are, however, distinguished by the crops which predominate in them. "Taro-yam gardens" were found to produce, on the basis of daily harvest records kept on entire gardens for close to one year, about 5,300,000 calories[3] per acre during their harvesting lives of 18 to 24 months; 85 per cent of their yield is harvested between 24 and 76 weeks after planting. "Sugar-sweet potato gardens" produce about 4,600,000 calories per acre during their harvesting lives, 91 per cent being taken between 24 and 76 weeks after planting. I estimated that approximately 310,000 calories per acre is expended on cutting, fencing, planting, maintaining, harvesting, and walking to and from taro-yam gardens. Sugar-sweet potato gardens required an expenditure of approximately 290,000 calories per acre.[4] These energy ratios, approximately 17:1 on taro-yam gardens and 16:1 on sugar-sweet potato gardens, compare favorably with figures reported for swidden cultivation in other regions.[5]

Intake is high in comparison with the reported dietaries of other New Guinea populations. On the basis of daily consumption records kept for ten months on four households numbering in total sixteen persons, I estimated the average daily intake of adult males to be approximately 2,600 calories, and that of adult females to be around 2,200 calories. It may be mentioned here that the Tsembaga are small and short statured. Adult males average 101 pounds in weight and approximately 58.5 inches in height; the corresponding averages for adult females are 85 pounds and 54.5 inches.[6]

Although 99 per cent by weight of the food consumed is vegetable, the protein intake is high by New Guinea standards. The daily protein consumption of adult males from vegetable sources was estimated to be between 43 and 55 grams, of adult females 36 to 48 grams. Even with an adjustment for vegetable sources, these values are slightly in excess of the recently published WHO/FAO daily requirements (Food and Agriculture Organization of the United Nations 1964). The same is true of the younger age categories, although soft and discolored hair, a symptom of protein deficiency, was noted in a few children. The WHO/FAO protein requirements do not include a large "margin for safety" or allowance for stress; and, although no clinical assessments were undertaken, it may be suggested that the Tsembaga achieve nitrogen balance at a low level. In other words, their protein intake is probably marginal.

Measurements of all gardens made during 1962 and of some gardens made during 1963 indicate that, to support the human population, between .15 and .19 acres are put into cultivation per capita per year. Fallows range from 8 to 45 years. The area in secondary forest comprises approximately 1,000 acres, only 30 to 50 of which are in cultivation at any time. Assuming calories to be the limiting factor, and assuming an unchanging population structure, the territory could support—with no reduction in lengths of fallow and without cutting into the virgin forest from which the Tsembaga extract many important items—between 290 and 397 people if the pig population remained minimal. The size of the pig herd, however, fluctuates widely. Taking Maring pig husbandry procedures into consideration, I have estimated the human carrying capacity of the Tsembaga territory at between 270 and 320 people. Because the timing of the ritual cycle is bound up with the demography of the pig herd, the place of the pig in Tsembaga adaptation must be examined.

First, being omnivorous, pigs keep residential areas free of garbage and human feces. Second, limited numbers of pigs rooting in secondary growth may help to hasten the development of that growth. The Tsembaga usually permit pigs to enter their gardens one and a half to two years after planting, by which time second-growth trees are well established there. The Tsembaga practice selective weeding; from the time the garden is planted, herbaceous species are removed, but tree species are allowed to remain. By the time cropping is discontinued and the pigs are let in, some of the trees in the garden are already ten to fifteen feet tall. These well-established trees are relatively impervious to damage by the pigs, which, in rooting for seeds and remaining tubers, eliminate many seeds and seedlings that, if allowed to develop, would provide some competition for the established trees. Moreover, in some Maring-speaking areas swiddens are planted twice, although this is not the case with the Tsembaga. After the first crop is almost exhausted, pigs are penned in the garden, where their rooting eliminates weeds and softens the ground, making the task of planting for a second time easier. The pigs, in other words, are used as cultivating machines.

Small numbers of pigs are easy to keep. They run free during the day and return home at night to receive their ration of garbage and substandard tubers, particularly sweet potatoes. Supplying the latter requires little extra work, for the substandard tubers are taken from the ground in the course of harvesting the daily ration for humans. Daily consumption records kept over a period of some months show that the ration of tubers received by the pigs approximates in weight that consumed by adult humans, i.e., a little less than three pounds per day per pig. If the pig herd grows large, however, the substandard tubers incidentally obtained in the course of harvesting for human needs become insufficient, and it becomes necessary to harvest especially for pigs. In other words, people must work for the pigs and perhaps even supply them with food fit for human consumption. Thus, as Vayda, Leeds, and Smith (1961: 71) have pointed out, there can be too many pigs for a given community.

This also holds true of the sanitary and cultivating services rendered by pigs. A small number of pigs is sufficient to keep residential areas clean, to suppress superfluous seedlings in abandoned gardens, and to soften the soil in gardens scheduled for second plantings. A larger herd, on the other hand, may be troublesome; the larger the number of pigs, the greater the possibility of their invasion of producing gardens, with concomitant damage not only to crops and young secondary growth but also to the relations between the pig owners and garden owners.

All male pigs are castrated at approximately three months of age, for boars, people say, are dangerous and do not grow as large as barrows. Pregnancies, therefore, are always the result of unions of domestic sows with feral males. Fecundity is thus only a fraction of its potential. During one twelve-month period only fourteen litters resulted out of a potential 99 or more pregnancies. Farrowing generally takes place in the forest, and mortality of the young is high. Only 32 of the offspring of the above-mentioned fourteen pregnancies were alive six months after birth. This number is barely sufficient to replace the number of adult animals which would have died or been killed during most years without pig festivals. The Tsembaga almost never kill domestic pigs outside of ritual contexts. In ordinary times, when there is no pig festival in progress, these rituals are almost always associated with misfortunes or emergencies, notably warfare, illness, injury, or death. Rules state not only the contexts in which pigs are to be ritually slaughtered, but also who may partake of the flesh of the sacrificial animals. During warfare it is only the men participating in the fighting who eat the pork. In cases of illness or injury, it is only the victim and certain near relatives, particularly his co-resident agnates and spouses, who do so.

It is reasonable to assume that misfortune and emergency are likely to induce in the organisms experiencing them a complex of physiological changes known collectively as "stress." Physiological stress reactions occur not only in organisms which are infected with disease or traumatized, but also in those experiencing rage or fear (Houssay *et al.* 1955: 1096), or even prolonged anxiety (National Research Council 1963: 53). One important aspect of stress is the increased catabolization of protein (Houssay *et al.* 1955: 451; National Research Council 1963: 49), with a net loss of nitrogen from the tissues (Houssay *et al.* 1955: 450). This is a serious matter for organisms with a marginal protein intake. Antibody production is low (Berg 1948: 311), healing is slow (Large and Johnson 1948: 352), and a variety of symptoms of a serious nature are likely to develop (Lund and Levenson 1948: 349; Zintel 1964: 1043). The status of a protein-depleted animal, however, may be significantly improved in a relatively short period of time by the intake of high quality protein, and high protein diets are therefore routinely prescribed for surgical patients and those suffering from infectious diseases (Burton 1959: 231; Lund and Levenson 1948: 350; Elman 1951: 85ff; Zintel 1964: 1943ff).

It is precisely when they are undergoing physiological stress that the Tsembaga kill and consume their pigs, and it should be noted that they limit the consumption to those likely to be experiencing stress most profoundly. The Tsembaga, of course, know nothing of physiological stress. Native theories of the etiology and treatment of disease and injury implicate various categories of spirits to whom sacrifices must be made. Nevertheless, the behavior which is appropriate in terms of native understandings is also appropriate to the actual situation confronting the actors.

We may now outline in the barest of terms the Tsembaga ritual cycle. Space does not permit a description of its ideological correlates. It must suffice to note that Tsembaga do not necessarily perceive all of the empirical effects which the anthropologist sees to flow from their ritual behavior. Such empirical consequences as they may perceive, moreover, are not central to their rationalizations of the performances. The Tsembaga say that they perform the rituals in order to rearrange their relationships with the supernatural world. We may only reiterate here that behavior undertaken in reference to their "cognized environment"—an environment which includes as very important elements the spirits of ancestors—seems appropriate in their "operational environment," the material environment specified by the anthropologist through operations of observation, including measurement.

Since the rituals are arranged in a cycle, description may commence at any point. The operation of the cycle becomes clearest if we begin with the rituals performed during warfare. Opponents in all cases occupy adjacent territories, in almost all cases on the same valley wall. After hostilities have broken out, each side performs certain rituals which place the opposing side in the formal category of "enemy." A number of taboos prevail while hostilities continue. These include prohibitions on sexual intercourse and on the ingestion of certain things—food prepared by women, food grown on the lower portion of the territory, marsupials, eels, and, while actually on the fighting ground, any liquid whatsoever.

One ritual practice associated with fighting which may have some physiological consequences deserves mention. Immediately before proceeding to the fighting ground, the warriors eat heavily salted pig fat. The ingestion of salt, coupled with the taboo on drinking, has the effect of shortening the fighting day, particularly since the Maring prefer to fight only on bright sunny days. When everyone gets unbearably thirsty, according to informants, fighting is broken off.

There may formerly have been other effects if the native salt contained sodium (the production of salt was discontinued some years previous to the field work, and no samples were obtained). The Maring diet seems to be deficient in sodium. The ingestion of large amounts of sodium just prior to fighting would have permitted the warriors to sweat normally without a lowering of blood volume and consequent weakness during the course of the fighting. The pork belly ingested with the salt would have provided them with a new burst of energy two hours or so after the commencement of the engagement. After fighting was finished for the day, lean

pork was consumed, offsetting, at least to some extent, the nitrogen loss associated with the stressful fighting (personal communications from F. Dunn, W. MacFarlane, and J. Sabine, 1965).

Fighting could continue sporadically for weeks. Occasionally it terminated in the rout of one of the antagonistic groups, whose survivors would take refuge with kinsmen elsewhere. In such instances, the victors would lay waste their opponents' groves and gardens, slaughter their pigs, and burn their houses. They would not, however, immediately annex the territory of the vanquished. The Maring say that they never take over the territory of an enemy for, even if it has been abandoned, the spirits of their ancestors remain to guard it against interlopers. Most fights, however, terminated in truces between the antagonists.

With the termination of hostilities a group which has not been driven off its territory performs a ritual called "planting the *rumbim*." Every man puts his hand on the ritual plant, *rumbim* (*Cordyline fruticosa* (L.), A. Chev; *C. terminalis,* Kunth), as it is planted in the ground. The ancestors are addressed, in effect, as follows:

> We thank you for helping us in the fight and permitting us to remain on our territory. We place our souls in this *rumbim* as we plant it on our ground. We ask you to care for this *rumbim*. We will kill pigs for you now, but they are few. In the future, when we have many pigs, we shall again give you pork and uproot the *rumbim* and stage a *kaiko* (pig festival). But until there are sufficient pigs to repay you the *rumbim* will remain in the ground.

This ritual is accompanied by the wholesale slaughter of pigs. Only juveniles remain alive. All adult and adolescent animals are killed, cooked, and dedicated to the ancestors. Some are consumed by the local group, but most are distributed to allies who assisted in the fight.

Some of the taboos which the group suffered during the time of fighting are abrogated by this ritual. Sexual intercourse is now permitted, liquids may be taken at any time, and food from any part of the territory may be eaten. But the group is still in debt to its allies and ancestors. People say it is still the time of the *bamp ku,* or "fighting stones," which are actual objects used in the rituals associated with warfare. Although the fighting ceases when *rumbim* is planted, the concomitant obligations, debts to allies and ancestors, remain outstanding; and the fighting stones may not be put away until these obligations are fulfilled. The time of the fighting stones is a time of debt and danger which lasts until the *rumbim* is uprooted and a pig festival (*kaiko*) is staged.

Certain taboos persist during the time of the fighting stones. Marsupials, regarded as the pigs of the ancestors of the high ground, may not be trapped until the debt to their masters has been repaid. Eels, the "pigs of the ancestors of the low ground," may neither be caught nor consumed. Prohibitions on all intercourse with the enemy come into force. One may not touch, talk to, or even look at a member of the enemy group, nor set foot on enemy ground. Even more important, a group may not attack another group while its ritual plant remains in the ground, for it has not yet fully rewarded its ancestors and allies for their assistance in the last fight. Until the debts to them have been paid, further assistance from them will not be forthcoming. A kind of "truce of god" thus prevails until the *rumbim* is uprooted and a *kaiko* completed.

To uproot the *rumbim* requires sufficient pigs. How many pigs are sufficient, and how long does it take to acquire them? The Tsembaga say that, if a place is "good," this can take as little as five years; but if a place is "bad," it may require ten years or longer. A bad place is one in which misfortunes are frequent and where, therefore, ritual demands for the killing of pigs arise frequently. A good place is one where such demands are infrequent. In a good place, the increase of the pig herd exceeds the ongoing ritual demands, and the herd grows rapidly. Sooner or later the substandard tubers incidentally obtained while harvesting become insufficient to feed the herd, and additional acreage must be put into production specifically for the pigs.

The work involved in caring for a large pig herd can be extremely burdensome. The Tsembaga herd just prior to the pig festival of 1962–63, when it numbered 169 animals, was receiving 54 per cent of all of the sweet potatoes and 82 per cent of all of the manioc harvested. These comprised 35.9 per cent by weight of all root crops harvested. This figure is consistent with the difference between the amount of land under cultivation just previous to the pig festival, when the herd was at maximum size, and that immediately afterwards, when the pig herd was at minimum size. The former was 36.1 per cent in excess of the latter.

I have estimated, on the basis of acreage yield and energy expenditure figures, that about 45,000 calories per year are expended in caring for one pig 120–150 pounds in size. It is upon women that most of the burden of pig keeping falls. If, from a woman's daily intake of about 2,200 calories, 950 calories are allowed for basal metabolism, a woman has only 1,250 calories a day available for all her activities, which include gardening for her family, child care, and cooking, as well as tending pigs. It is clear that no woman can feed many pigs; only a few had as many as four in their care at the commencement of the festival; and it is not surprising that agitation to uproot the *rumbim* and stage the *kaiko* starts with the wives of the owners of large numbers of pigs.

A large herd is not only burdensome as far as energy expenditure is concerned; it becomes increasingly a nuisance as it expands. The more numerous pigs become, the more frequently are gardens invaded by them. Such events result in serious disturbances of local tranquillity. The garden owner often shoots, or attempts to shoot, the offending pig; and the pig owner commonly retorts by shooting, or attempting to shoot, either the garden owner, his wife, or one of his pigs. As more and more such events occur, the settlement, nucleated when the herd was small, disperses as people try to put as much distance as possible between their pigs and other people's gardens and between their gardens and other people's pigs. Occasionally this reaches its logical conclusion, and people begin to leave the territory, taking up residence with kinsmen in other local populations.

The number of pigs sufficient to become intolerable to the Tsembaga was below the capacity of the territory to carry pigs. I have estimated that, if the size and structure of the human population remained constant at the 1962–1963 level, a pig population of 140 to 240 animals averaging 100 to 150 pounds in size could be maintained perpetually by the Tsembaga without necessarily inducing environmental degradation. Since the size of the herd fluctuates, even higher cyclical maxima could be achieved. The level of toleration, however, is likely always to be below the carrying capacity, since the destructive capacity of the pigs is dependent upon the population density of both people and pigs, rather than upon population size. The denser the human population, the fewer pigs will be required to disrupt social life. If the carrying capacity is exceeded, it is likely to be exceeded by people and not by pigs.

The *kaiko* or pig festival, which commences with the planting of stakes at the boundary and the uprooting of the *rumbim,* is thus triggered by either the additional work attendant upon feeding pigs or the destructive capacity of the pigs themselves. It may be said, then, that there are sufficient pigs to stage the *kaiko* when the relationship of pigs to people changes from one of mutualism to one of parasitism or competition. A short time prior to the uprooting of the *rumbim,* stakes are planted at the boundary. If the enemy has continued to occupy its territory, the stakes are planted at the boundary which existed before the fight. If, on the other hand, the enemy has abandoned its territory, the victors may plant their stakes at a new boundary which encompasses areas previously occupied by the enemy. The Maring say, to be sure, that they never take land belonging to an enemy, but this land is regarded as vacant, since no *rumbim* was planted on it after the last fight. We may state here a rule of land redistribution in terms of the ritual cycle: *If one of a pair of antagonistic groups is able to uproot its* rumbim *before its opponents can plant their* rumbim*, it may occupy the latter's territory.*

Not only have the vanquished abandoned their territory; it is assumed that it has also been abandoned by their ancestors as well. The surviving members of the erstwhile enemy group have by this time resided with other groups for a number of years, and most if not all of them have already had occasion to sacrifice pigs to their ancestors at their new residences. In so doing they have invited these spirits to settle at the new locations of the living, where they will in the future receive sacrifices. Ancestors of vanquished groups thus relinquish their guardianship over the territory, making it available to victorious groups. Meanwhile, the *de facto* membership of the living in the groups with which they have taken refuge is converted eventually into *de jure* membership. Sooner or later the groups with which they have taken up residence will have occasion to plant *rumbim,* and the refugees, as co-residents, will participate, thus ritually validating their connection to the new territory and the new group. A rule of population redistribution may thus be stated in terms of ritual cycles: *A man becomes a member of a territorial group by participating with it in the planting of* rumbim.

The uprooting of the *rumbim* follows shortly after the planting of stakes at the boundary. On this particular occasion the Tsembaga killed 32 pigs out of their herd of 169. Much of the pork was distributed to allies and affines outside of the local group.

The taboo on trapping marsupials was also terminated at this time. Information is lacking concerning the population dynamics of the local marsupials, but it may well be that the taboo which had prevailed since the last fight—that against taking them in traps—had conserved a fauna which might otherwise have become extinct.

The *kaiko* continues for about a year, during which period friendly groups are entertained from time to time. The guests receive presents of vegetable foods, and the hosts and male guests dance together throughout the night.

These events may be regarded as analogous to aspects of the social behavior of many nonhuman animals. First of all, they include massed epigamic, or courtship, displays (Wynne-Edwards 1962: 17). Young women are presented with samples of the eligible males of local groups with which they may not otherwise have had the opportunity to become familiar. The context, moreover, permits the young women to discriminate amongst this sample in terms of both endurance (signaled by how vigorously and how long a man dances) and wealth (signaled by the richness of a man's shell and feather finery).

More importantly, the massed dancing at these events may be regarded as epideictic display, communicating to the participants information concerning the size or density of the group (Wynne-Edwards 1962: 16). In many species such displays take place as a prelude to actions which adjust group size or density, and such is the case among the Maring. The massed dancing of the visitors at a *kaiko* entertainment communicates to the hosts, while the *rumbim* truce is still in force, information concerning the amount of support they may expect from the visitors in the bellicose enterprises that they are likely to embark upon soon after the termination of the pig festival.

Among the Maring there are no chiefs or other political authorities capable of commanding the support of a body of followers, and the decision to assist another group in warfare rests with each individual male. Allies are not recruited by appealing for help to other local groups as such. Rather, each member of the groups primarily involved in the hostilities appeals to his cognatic and affinal kinsmen in other local groups. These men, in turn, urge other of their co-residents and kinsmen to "help them fight." The channels through which invitations to dance are extended are precisely those through which appeals for military support are issued. The invitations go not from group to group, but from kinsman to kinsman, the recipients of invitations urging their co-residents to "help them dance."

Invitations to dance do more than exercise the channels through which allies are recruited; they provide a means for judging their effectiveness. Dancing and fighting are regarded as in some sense equivalent. This equivalence is expressed in the similarity of some pre-fight and pre-dance rituals, and the Maring say that those who come to dance come to fight. The size of a visiting dancing contingent is consequently taken as a measure of the size of the contingent of warriors whose assistance may be expected in the next round of warfare.

In the morning the dancing ground turns into a trading ground. The items most frequently exchanged include axes, bird plumes, shell ornaments, an occasional baby pig, and, in former times, native salt. The *kaiko* thus facilitates trade by providing a market-like setting in which large numbers of traders can assemble. It likewise facilitates the movement of two critical items, salt and axes, by creating a demand for the bird plumes which may be exchanged for them.

The *kaiko* concludes with major pig sacrifices. On this particular occasion the Tsembaga butchered 105 adult and adolescent pigs, leaving only 60 juveniles and neonates alive. The survival of an additional fifteen adolescents and adults was only temporary, for they were scheduled as imminent victims. The pork yielded by the Tsembaga slaughter was estimated to weigh between 7,000 and 8,500 pounds, of which between 4,500 and 6,000 pounds were distributed to members of other local groups in 163 separate presentations. An estimated 2,000 to 3,000 people in seventeen local groups were the beneficiaries of the redistribution. The presentations, it should be mentioned, were not confined to pork. Sixteen Tsembaga men presented bridewealth or child-wealth, consisting largely of axes and shells, to their affines at this time.

The *kaiko* terminates on the day of the pig slaughter with the public presentation of salted pig belly to allies of the last fight. Presentations are made through the window in a high ceremonial fence built specially for the occasion at one end of the dance ground. The name of each honored man is announced to the assembled multitude as he charges to the window to receive his hero's portion. The fence is then ritually torn down, and the fighting stones are put away. The pig festival and the ritual cycle have been completed, demonstrating, it may be suggested, the ecological and economic competence of the local population. The local population would now be free, if it were not for the presence of the government, to attack its enemy again, secure in the knowledge that the assistance of allies and ancestors would be forthcoming because they have received pork and the obligations to them have been fulfilled.

Usually fighting did break out again very soon after the completion of the ritual cycle. If peace still prevailed when the ceremonial fence had rotted completely—a process said to take about three years, a little longer than the length of time required to raise a pig to maximum size—*rumbim* was planted as if there had been a fight, and all adult and adolescent pigs were killed. When the pig herd was large enough so that the *rumbim* could be uprooted, peace could be made with former enemies if they were also able to dig out their *rumbim*. To put this in formal terms: *If a pair of antagonistic groups proceeds through two ritual cycles without resumption of hostilities their enmity may be terminated.*

The relations of the Tsembaga with their environment have been analyzed as a complex system composed of two subsystems. What may be called the "local subsystem" has been derived from the relations of the Tsembaga with the nonhuman components of their immediate or territorial environment. It corresponds to the ecosystem in which the Tsembaga participate. A second subsystem, one which corresponds to the larger regional population of which the Tsembaga are one of the constituent units and which may be designated as the "regional subsystem," has been derived from the relations of the Tsembaga with neighboring local populations similar to themselves.

It has been argued that rituals, arranged in repetitive sequences, regulate relations both within each of the subsystems and within the larger complex system as a whole. The timing of the ritual cycle is largely dependent upon changes in the states of the components of the local subsystem. But the *kaiko,* which is the culmination of the ritual cycle, does more than reverse changes which have taken place within the local subsystem. Its occurrence also affects relations among the components of the regional subsystem. During its performance, obligations to other local populations are fulfilled, support for future military enterprises is rallied, and land from which enemies have earlier been driven

is occupied. Its completion, furthermore, permits the local population to initiate warfare again. Conversely, warfare is terminated by rituals which preclude the reinitiation of warfare until the state of the local subsystem is again such that a *kaiko* may be staged and completed. Ritual among the Tsembaga and other Maring, in short, operates as both transducer, "translating" changes in the state of one subsystem into information which can effect changes in a second subsystem, and homeostat, maintaining a number of variables which in sum comprise the total system within ranges of viability. To repeat an earlier assertion, the operation of ritual among the Isembaga and other Maring helps to maintain an undegraded environment, limits fighting to frequencies which do not endanger the existence of the regional population, adjusts man-land ratios, facilitates trade, distributes local surpluses of pig throughout the regional population in the form of pork, and assures people of high quality protein when they are most in need of it.

Religious rituals and the supernatural orders toward which they are directed cannot be assumed *a priori* to be mere epiphenomena. Ritual may, and doubtless frequently does, do nothing more than validate and intensify the relationships which integrate the social unit, or symbolize the relationships which bind the social unit to its environment. But the interpretation of such presumably *sapiens*-specific phenomena as religious ritual within a framework which will also accommodate the behavior of other species shows, I think, that religious ritual may do much more than symbolize, validate, and intensify relationships. Indeed, it would not be improper to refer to the Tsembaga and the other entities with which they share their territory as a "ritually regulated ecosystem," and to the Tsembaga and their human neighbors as a "ritually regulated population."

ENDNOTES

1. The field work upon which this paper is based was supported by a grant from the National Science Foundation, under which Professor A. P. Vayda was principal investigator. Personal support was received by the author from the

National Institutes of Health. Earlier versions of this paper were presented at the 1964 annual meeting of the American Anthropological Association in Detroit, and before a Columbia University seminar on Ecological Systems and Cultural Evolution. I have received valuable suggestions from Alexander Alland, Jacques Barrau, William Clarke, Paul Collins, C. Glen King, Marvin Harris, Margaret Mead, M. J. Mcggitt, Ann Rappaport, John Street, Marjorie Whiting, Cherry Vayda, A. P. Vayda and many others, but I take full responsibility for the analysis presented herewith.

2. The social organization of the Tsembaga will be described in detail elsewhere.

3. Because the length of time in the field precluded the possibility of maintaining harvest records on single gardens from planting through abandonment, figures were based, in the case of both "taro-yam" and "sugar-sweet potato" gardens, on three separate gardens planted in successive years. Conversions from the gross weight to the caloric value of yields were made by reference to the literature. The sources used are listed in Rappaport (1966: Appendix VIII).

4. Rough time and motion studies of each of the tasks involved in making, maintaining, harvesting, and walking to and from gardens were undertaken. Conversion to energy expenditure values was accomplished by reference to energy expenditure tables prepared by Hipsley and Kirk (1965: 43) on the basis of gas exchange measurements made during the performance of garden tasks by the Chimbu people of the New Guinea highlands.

5. Marvin Harris, in an unpublished paper, estimates the ratio of energy return to energy input ratio on Dyak (Borneo) rice swiddens at 10:1. His estimates of energy ratios on Tepotzlan (Meso-America) swiddens range from 13:1 on poor land to 29:1 on the best land.

6. Heights may be inaccurate. Many men wear their hair in large coiffures hardened with pandanus grease, and it was necessary in some instances to estimate the location of the top of the skull.

BIBLIOGRAPHY

Berg, C. 1948. Protein Deficiency and Its Relation to Nutritional Anemia, Hypoproteinemia, Nutritional Edema, and Resistance to Infection. Protein and Amino Acids in Nutrition, ed. M. Sahyun, pp. 290–317. New York.

Burton, B. T., ed. 1959. The Heinz Handbook of Nutrition. New York.

Elman, R. 1951. Surgical Care. New York.

Food and Agriculture Organization of the United Nations. 1964. Protein: At the Heart of the World Food Problem. World Food Problems 5. Rome.

Hipsley, E., and N. Kirk. 1965. Studies of the Dietary Intake and Energy Expenditure of New Guineans. South Pacific Commission, Technical Paper 147. Noumea.

Homans, G. C. 1941. Anxiety and Ritual: The Theories of Malinowski and Radcliffe-Brown. American Anthropologist 43: 164–172.

Houssay, B. A., et al. 1955. Human Physiology. 2nd ed. New York.

Large, A., and C. G. Johnston. 1948. Proteins as Related to Burns. Proteins and Amino Acids in Nutrition, ed. M. Sahyun, pp. 386–396. New York.

Lund, C. G., and S. M. Levenson. 1948. Protein Nutrition in Surgical Patients. Proteins and Amino Acids in Nutrition, ed. M. Sahyun, pp. 349–363. New York

Moore, O. K. 1957 Divination—a New Perspective. American Anthropologist 59: 69–74.

National Research Council. 1963. Evaluation of Protein Quality. National Academy of Sciences—National Research Council Publication 1100. Washington.

Rappaport, R. A. 1966. Ritual in the Ecology of a New Guinea People. Unpublished doctoral dissertation, Columbia University.

Vayda, A. P., A. Leeds, and D. B. Smith. 1961. The Place of Pigs in Melanesian Subsistence. Proceedings of the 1961 Annual Spring Meeting of the American Ethnological Society, ed. V. E. Garfield, pp. 69–77. Seattle.

Wayne-Edwards, V. C. 1962. Animal Dispersion in Relation to Social Behaviour. Edinburgh and London.

Zintel, Harold A. 1964. Nutrition in the Care of the Surgical Patient. Modern Nutrition in Health and Disease, ed. M. G. Wohl and R. S. Goodhart, pp. 1043–1064. Third ed. Philadelphia.

READING 10–3

AINU WORLDVIEW AND BEAR HUNTING STRATEGIES

Takashi Irimoto

Unlike the Tukano, the Ainu, who reside on the island of Hokkaido, in Japan, do *regard nature and culture as separate categories yet they, too, place great emphasis on fertility, and employ ritual to achieve it. Fertility is obtained through reciprocity between human beings and nature, represented by the bear, and Tahaski Irimoto, in this reading, explains how the bear cult and the sacrifice of a member of this species provides the Ainu with the means of satisfying both human need and the need of the*

Source: Takashi Irimoto, "Ainu Worldview and Bear Hunting Strategies," in *Shamanism and Northern Ecology* (Religion and Society 36), ed. Juha Pentikäinen (Berlin: Mouton de Gruyter, 1996), pp. 293–303. Reprinted with permission by Mouton de Gruyter, A Division of Walter de Gruyter & Co. Publishers.

spirits who are the forces behind the natural world. A spirit, incarnated materially as a bear, sacrifices itself to humanity in two situations. One is during hunting, when the bear spirit is brought into the human world. The other is when a baby bear, raised by the community, is ritually slain and its spirit dispatched to the other world as an offering. In this reciprocity between the two worlds, the needs of the spirits, which are conceived to be as urgent as those of human beings, are also met, and a relationship of balance—though of a different sort to that described for the Tukano—is maintained.

1.1. INTRODUCTION

The Ainu worldview will be analyzed in this paper in relation to the symbolism of hunting and Ainu behavioral strategies in hunting. The behavioral strategy is defined here as a strategy to adjust the man-nature relationships through behavioral operation. The hunting behavior is based on the reality of nature as well as the symbolised nature in human cognition. Thus, behavioral strategies in hunting can be understood as dynamic processes of interaction between human thought and behavior.

There has been various information regarding Ainu hunting in different fields of study, such as technology, ecology, religion, ritual, language, and myth (Irimoto 1987: 1–218; 1988a: 1–96). However, in this paper, primarily based on information from the Ainu of the Saru River region, in Hokkaido, Japan, I examined the data thoroughly with special reference to hunting behavior, from ecological and ethno-ecological viewpoints, to discover Ainu behavioral strategy in bear hunting.

1.2. THE SYMBOLISM OF HUNTING STRATEGIES

The Ainu imagined hunting to be a visit of the spirit (*kamui*) of the game animal, from the world of kamui (*Kamui moshir*) to the world of man (*Ainu moshir*). Thus, bear hunting is a human behavioral operation through which the bear spirit is enabled to visit the world of man.

Ainu hunting technology was characterized by the use of arrow poisons (aconite-based), automatic devices (spring-bows), hand bows and hunting dogs. The arrow poisons and dogs were considered *Surku Kamui* (Kamui of Aconite) and *Mintar-uskur* (Kamui of Yard), respectively, and they served as messengers used by *Ape huchi* (Old Woman of fire; i.e. *Kamui huchi,* Kamui of Old Woman) to contact *Kimun kamui* (Kamui of Mountains; i.e. good bear).

1.2.1. The Symbolism of Aconite

The procedures for obtaining aconite plants were as follows (Watanabe 1952/53: 262): the hunter, after obtaining permission to collect plants from the village chief (*kotan-kor-kur*) who controlled the gathering area, prayed to the Kamui of Fire (*Ape huchi*) and the Kamui of Water (*Wakka-ush-kamui*). Then, on the gathering ground, the Ainu offered home-brewed beer and *inau* (offering sticks with wooden shavings attached) to *Monorush kamui* and the Kamui of Fox (*Chironnup kamui*) and asked these to be granted the spirit of the Kamui of Aconite (*Surku Kamui*). Here, the *Monorush kamui* was the spirit that controlled the Kamui of Aconite. Munro (Munro: F10, N1:13) noted the Kamui of Fire (*Kamui huchi*) as the object of prayer at the village chief's house, and the Kamui of Forest (*Shiramba kamui*) and the Kamui of Hunting (*Hash-inau-uk kamui*) as the objects of prayer on the gathering ground.

The Kamui of Fire (*Ape huchi; Kamui huchi*) was the deity who first descended from the world of kamui (*Kanto; Kamui moshir*) to the world of man (*Ainu moshir*), as the guardian of this world, when the world of man was created. She was the deity and the mediator who transmitted the imperfect words of man to the other kamuis (Kubodera 1977: 42). Thus, it is revealed here that the prayer for the Kamui of Fire, before collecting aconite, was the transmission of the words of man to the *Monorush kamui*. The role of the Kamui of Fire as a mediator can also be found in the prayer for the Kamui of Hunting, the Kamui of Forest, and the Kamui of Altar, before departing for hunting trips.

In the Ainu hunting tradition, the role of the Kamui of Aconite, as an arrow poison, was the messenger from the Kamui of Fire to the Kamui of Mountains (*Kimun kamui;* i.e. the good bear) for invitation. Thus, the Kamui of Mountains, after being shot by the poisoned arrow, described himself in the myth as follows: "Then / the Kamui of Aconite / appeared in front of me. / As the Kamui of Fire's / messenger, (her) words were / as follows: / 'Oh, the important great God! / peacefully / come to be enjoyed in my place, / and so / comfortably enjoying yourself by hearing stories / when we see together / (it) should be. / The Kamui of fire / sent me / I came / so' " (*Kamui-yukar* 6, Kubodera 1977: 67).

The Kamui of Mountains (i.e. Bear) initially rejected this invitation, but the Kamui of Pine Resin (*Unkotuk kamui*) appeared to take away his freedom as described below. That is, "The Kamui of Pine Resin / appeared, / (with) the Kamui of Aconite / together / on my legs / on my hands / clung to my feet / took away my freedom by catching in my hands" (*Kamui-yukar* 6, Kubodera 1977: 67). Then, the Kamui of Mountains fell down to find himself on the branch of the tree, with his hands and legs hanging down, seeing an old bear lying on the ground below. The Kamui of Pine Resin appearing here was the resin of the pine tree which had been used to fix the aconite poison on the bamboo arrow head, either by being mixed with the aconite, or by being applied.

In the other myth (Kayano 1977: 150–151; 1978: 156), the Kamui of Pine Resin and the Kamui of Aconite appeared as so beautiful a Woman of Pine Resin (*Unkotuk katkemat*) as was never seen in the world of kamui, and as so good-looking Woman of Aconite (*Surku katkemat*) as was never found in the world of man. And they caught in hands and clung to legs, and tempted the Kamui of Mountains with their good fragrance. Although they were well spoken and gently-behaved, this active role of the Kamui of Aconite and the Kamui of Pine Resin in taking away the freedom of the bear was significant and corresponded to the real effect of aconite on the bear, i.e. walking unsteadily on its feet after being shot by a poisoned arrow (Irimoto 1988; field data KK 1914m Biratori).

1.2.2.   The Symbolism of the Dog

The symbolic role of the hunting dog in the Ainu view was as the messenger of the Kamui of Fire (*Ape huchi*) to the Kamui of Mountains (*Kimun kamui,* or the good bear), bringing words of invitation. In the myth (*Kamui-yukar* 16; *Pon moyak isoitak; Kamui-yukar* 17; *Apa-samun kamui isoitak,* Kubodera 1977), a raccoon dog, who was believed to be a servant of the bear, told about hunting dogs attacking the bear's den, or the dwelling of the raccoon dog and his uncle bear: "Dogs / at the / door of (our) house / lining up their heads, hastly, each by each / 'the Kamui of Fire / sent me / (so, I) came here' / saying so / (, and then) wanting to give the message / just like fighting together / (dogs) gave the message."

Besides the term of *seta* for the dog, it was called *mintar-us-kur,* or the Kamui (spirit) residing in the yard (Chiri 1962: 140) in the Bihoro region, *Ape-huchi mintar-us-kur,* or the Kamui (spirit) residing in the yard of the Kamui of Fire (Sarashina 1976: 334) in the regions of Tokachi, Kushiro, and Kitami, and *Apa-cha-punki,* or the guard at the door (Chiri 1962: 137) in the Bihoro region. In the Saru River region a dog killed in hunting was given a special funeral with two *chehorokakep,* or the backward shaven *inau,* to be sent by the words: "Since you were the person descended from the most important ancestral God, you would go to the world of the ancestral God of the wolf" (Sarashina 1976: 335). Also, in the Abashiri region, the skull of the dog was preserved with *inau-kike,* wood shavings, to pray as *Mintara-kor-kamui,* or the Kamui of Yard. Therefore, it is revealed here that the dog resided at a place near the Kamui of Fire and that it was interpreted as the kamui guarding the site.

The dog was also believed to have the ability to work in two worlds: that of the dead and the living. That is, the dead people's souls, or the ghosts which came from the underworld to the upper world (*Kanna-moshir:* upper world seen from the underworld; i.e. this living world) could not be seen by the living people; only the dog was able to detect them and therefore barked. On the contrary, when living people happened to visit the underworld, they could not be seen by the dead people and were treated as a ghost. In this case also, only the dog could detect them and it barked (Batchelor 1901: 570–571).

The role of the dog as a messenger between the world of kamui and the world of man can also be noted in the metaphorical expressions used in Ainu plant nomenclature (Yamada 1986: 160–161). Then, the role of the dog in bear hunting, as a messenger of the Kamui of Fire to the Kamui of Mountains, is the application of this general symbolic role of the dog in Ainu thought.

1.2.3. The Symbolism of the Bear and the Reciprocity between the Ainu and the Kamui

Before starting on a hunting trip, the Ainu prayed to the important kamuis for a successful hunt, including the Mountain owning Kamui (*Nupri-kor kamui*), the Kamui of Hunting (*Hashinau-uk-kamui*), the Kamui of Forest (*Shiramba kamui*), and the Kamui of Altar (*Nusa-kor kamui*). In the Saru River region, the Mountain owning Kamui (*Nupri-kor kamui*) was considered to be the chief deity of the Kimun kamui, the Kamui of Mountains, or the bear.

In the course of hunting, various taboos were observed not only by the hunters, but by their wives in the village (Irimoto 1988b: 136). Then, after the killing of the bear, the welcome reception and the sending-off ritual for the bear's spirit (*Kamui-hop-unire; iomante*) was carried out.

In Ainu thought, the *Kimun kamui* visiting the world of man, presented his meat, hide, and gall to the Ainu as gifts, and received a feast and prayers from the Ainu as return gifts. After returning to the world of kamui, the *Kimun kamui* was believed to invite other kamuis to make feasts in the world of kamui. Here, the *inau* (offering sticks with wooden shavings attached), cakes, and home-brewed beer which were presented to him from the world of man, were used in his feast. As such, the Kamui of Mountains had a much higher status, according to the myth (*Kamui-yukar 6 Nupuri-kor kamui isoitak*; *Kamui-yukar 7:8:9 Peurep-kamui isoitak,*

Kubodera 1977: 71–72, 82, 85, 93). Also, the myth (*Kamui-yukar 10 Nupuri-kor kamui kor matnepo yaieyukar,* Kubodera 1977: 94–95) related that the Kamui of Mountains would habitually come to the world of man as a guest and then return to the world of kamui to make a big feast. Thus, in reality, the hunting is the killing of an animal and the taking of its products; the Ainu justified this act by the logic of reciprocity between man and the kamui.

However, it was said that the Kamui of Mountains who visited the world of man in the next turn was not the same bear being sent off, but one of his relatives (Irimoto, field data KK 1914m Biratori). Consequently, in the farewell prayer during the sending-off ritual of the bear spirit, the Kamui of Mountains (bear spirit) was asked to speak to the ancestor of the bear, to say that his fellow should go to that *kotan* (settlement) in case he visited the world of man to again bring many gifts back to the ancestor of the bear in the world of kamui (Irimoto, field data XM 1908m; TS 1922m Niikap).

In fact, the above description is part of a positive strategy to establish a reciprocal relationship between the Ainu and the *Kimun kamui*. Here, the *Kimun kamui* is the Kamui of Mountains, or the good bear which is synonymously referred to as *no-yuk;* i.e. good-game. In contrast, the Ainu assumed the negative strategy of defending themselves against the *Wen kamui (bad kamui)* in hunting. The Bad kamui (*Wen kamui*) meant the rough bear and the man-eater, also termed *wey-yuk* (bad-game) (Chiri 1962: 152). These harmful bears were also called by special names in accordance with distinguishing features on their hide and body, such as *ikon-noka* (sword-marks; i.e. bear with sword-like marks on its hide) and *epen-kuwaus (-kamuy)* (front-putting cane-bear; i.e. bear with long front legs) (Kubodera 1977: 105; Chiri 1962: 155–156; Sarashina 1976: 357–358). Classification of the bear is based on definition of anomalies in the colour of its hide and somatological characteristics; *wey-yuk* is defined by the anomalies and thus *no-yuk* is actualized as a residual category of *wey-yuk,* (Yamada 1987: 234–235). In reality, the Ainu category of the *Kimun kamui (-no-yuk)* and then *Wen*

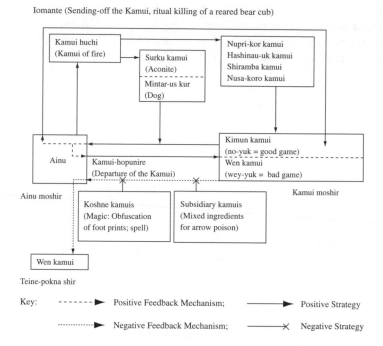

Iomante (Sending-off the Kamui, ritual killing of a reared bear cub)

FIGURE 1 **A Schematic Diagram of the Reciprocity between the Ainu and the Kamui in Relation to the Ainu Bear Hunting Strategies.**

kamui (-wey-yuk) would be a plea based on the outcome of the hunt. Thus, it is interpreted here that *Wen Kamui* was a symbol of danger and uncertainty which might cause accidents and failure in hunting.

Therefore, the Ainu operated the defensive strategy against the Bad Kamui (*Wen kamui*) in hunting by means of exorcised power of the Kamui of the Skull of the Good Fox (*Shiratki kamui*) and another subsidiary kamuis. The latter were the kamuis of the various plants being used with aconite as ingredients for arrow poison (Irimoto 1988b: 128–131). In the emergent circumstances in hunting, the hunter took magical counter-attack against the Bad Kamui, or the bad-game, with the help of *Koshne kamui*, which were even believed to be wicked spirits. Then, lastly, in the case of a hunting death caused by a bear, the *Wen kamui*, the bad bear's spirit, was banished to the *Teine-pokna shir* (the wet and underworld), or the world of eternal death, to be

prevented from going back to the world of Kamui, after it was killed in revenge. In fact, the *Teine-pokna shir,* which was generally termed as *Pokna moshir* in the underworld, was the place to which the various evil kamuis had to be expelled from the worlds of man and kamui in Ainu mythology (Yamada 1991). Therefore, this meant exclusion of the evil bear's spirit from the reciprocity between the world of Kamui (*Kamui moshir*) and the world of man (*Ainu moshir*). Generally speaking, reciprocity between the Kamui of Mountains (*Kimun kamui*; i.e. good-game) and Man (the Ainu) is established by an invitation and sending-off ritual for the bear spirit as a positive-feedback mechanism, while the Ainu denied this reciprocal relationship to the Bad Kamui (*Wen kamui*; i.e. bad-game) by defence and banishment for the evil bear's spirit as the negative-feedback mechanism in the hunting strategy.

1.3. HE BEAR FESTIVAL AS A POSITIVE FEEDBACK MECHANISM OF THE AINU HUNTING STRATEGIES

The integrated bear cult, which included capturing the bear cub, after killing the mother bear at the bear den, rearing the cub in the village, and the ritual killing of the cub (bear festival), are carried over from Ainu bear hunting activity. Although these processes are not hunting itself, they are closely connected with the Ainu view of the bear and the behavioral strategy for hunting.

The bear festival, or the sending-off ritual for the spirit of the reared bear cub (*iomante*), a term which may be distinguished from the word used for the sending-off ritual for the spirit of the hunted wild bear (*Kamui-hopunire*) (Kubodera 1977: 61; Sarashina 1976: 362), can be seen as a part of the Ainu behavioral strategy for repetition of the reciprocal relationship between man and the Kamui of Mountains (Bear). The significance of the *iomante* is that the bear cub was reared in the village for a long time. In Ainu thought, this is the prolonged stay of the Kamui of Mountains in the world of man; i.e. the continuation of the reciprocal relationship between the Ainu and the Kamui of Mountains by keeping the bear cub in the world of man.

After the killing of the bear cub, the spirit of the bear cub was believed to go back to the place of its parents (father bear and mother bear) as well as to the place of the chief of the bears (Natori 1941: 103). Thus, the bear cub can be seen as a messenger from the world of man to the world of kamui. The logic was similar in the case of a reared bird, such as the eagle owl which was ritually killed, thus assuming the role of messenger to his parents to relieve man of the difficulties that the bird had seen in the world of man.

The significant role of the young game animal in establishment of reciprocity between the worlds of man and animal has been pointed out among the Chipewyan of northern North America (Irimoto 1981: 94–99; 1983: 152–155). Here, in the case of the Chipewyan, the establishment of reciprocity was justified in the myth, and it was maintained by min-

imal usage of rituals and taboos in the real situation of hunting (Irimoto 1988c). However, in the case of the Ainu, it is revealed that the human concept of reciprocity was actualized by rearing the bear cub in the real world and by assigning him the function of special messenger between the world of man and the world of kamui.

It is true that the integrated bear cult, including the *iomante*, or the bear festival, was conditioned by the sedentism of the Ainu and the surplus of food which made the keeping of the bear cub possible (Watanabe 1964: 213; Obayashi 1964: 233). In addition to ecological conditions, the development of the bear cult had been related to social aspects among the Ainu (Watanabe 1964: 212), and possibly to cultural contact with the agriculturalists in the Amur River region who had carried out the animal breedings (Obayashi 1973: 77). Yet, the origin and the continuation of the integrated bear cult had been based on the human motivation for the repetition of reciprocity between man and the kamui. Thus, the Ainu bear festival can be understood as a part of the positive-feedback mechanisms in the behavioral strategy for hunting.

1.4. SUMMARY AND CONCLUSION

The Ainu worldview is examined with reference to the bear hunting strategies of the Ainu. Behavioral strategies for hunting include positive and negative mechanisms. The positive mechanism is to invite *Kimun kamui* (Kamui of Mountains; i.e. good game) to the world of man and to send the spirit of the slain bear to the world of kamui. The bear's gall, meat, and hide were considered gifts to the Ainu from the bear spirit, and the *inau* (offering sticks with wooden shavings attached), cakes, and home-brewed beer were considered reciprocal presents to the bear spirit. The Ainu bear festival, which involved the ritual killing of a raised bear cub, can also be understood as a positive mechanism in the Ainu hunting strategies. In this case, the Ainu used the bear cub as a special messenger to their ancestors in the world of kamui, requesting them to send another bear to the Ainu world. A negative mechanism functioned to defend the Ainu against the *Wen kamui* (evil spirit; i.e. bad game, also a symbol of danger and uncertainty in hunting). Here various plants were mixed with aconite to make an arrow poison. The spirit of these plants was believed to be capable of checking the advance of *Wen kamui*. In cases of a hunting death caused by a bear, the bad bear's spirit had to be banished to the world of eternal death after it was killed in revenge. This act can be interpreted as a denial of reciprocity between *Ainu* and *Wen kamui*. In conclusion, the Ainu operated man-nature relationships through behavioral strategies which were based on the dual symbolism of nature, and the concept of reciprocity between the two worlds.

REFERENCES

Batchelor, John
1901   *The Ainu and their folk-lore.* London: The Religious Tract Society.

Chiri, Mashiho
1962   *Bunrui Ainugo Jiten, II, Dobutsu Hen* [A Classificatory Ainu dictionary, Vol. II, Animals]. Tokyo: Nihon Jomim Bunka Kenkyujo.

Irimoto, Takashi
1981   "Chipewyan ecology," *Senri Ethnological Studies,* 8, National Museum of Ethnology.
1983   *Canada Indian no, Sekai kara* [From the world of Canadian Indians]. Tokyo: Fukuinkan Shoten.
1987   "Saru-gawa Ryuiki Ainu ni kansuru Rekishi teki Shiryo no Bunka-jinruigaku teki Bunseki: C. 1300–1867 Nen" [A cultural anthropological analysis of historical data on the Ainu of the Saru River region: C. 1300–1867 A.D.], *Bulletin of the Institute for the Study of North Eurasian Cultures, Hokkaido University,* 18.
1988a   "Saru-gawa Ryuiki Ainu no Bunka-jinruigaku teki joho ni kansuru Database" [A cultural anthropological database on the Ainu of the Saru River region], *Bulletin of the Institute for the Study of North Eurasian Cultures, Hokkaido University,* 19.
1988b   "Ainu wa ikani shite Kuma o Shuryo shitaka: Shuryo no Shocho teki imi to Kodo Senryaku [How the Ainu hunted bears: symbolism of Hunting and Behavioral Strategies], *The Japanese Journal of Ethnology,* 53(2).
1988c   "Chipewyan Ecology and Mythology with Reference to Caribou Hunting Strategies." Paper presented at the 87th Annual Meeting of the American Anthropological Association, Phoenix, Arizona, November 16-20, 1988.

Kayano, Shigeru
1977   *Hono no Uma* [Horse of flame:. Tokyo] Suzusawa shoten.
1978   *Ainu no Mingu* [Artefacts of the Ainu]. Tokyo: Ainu no Mingu Kanko Undokai.

Kubodera, Itsuhiko
1977   *Ainu Jojishi: Shinyo, Seiden no Kenkyu* [The Ainu Epics: A Study of Kamui Yukar and Oina]. Tokyo: Iwanami Shoten.

Munro, Neil
1963   Munro's Ainu Material (MSS) of the Royal Anthropological Institute of Great Britain and Ireland.

Natori, Takemitsu
1941   "Saru Ainu no Kumaokuri ni okeru Kamigami no Yurai to Nusa" [The origin of gods and the Nusa [cluster of Inau] in the Bear Festival of Saru Ainu]. *Studies from the Research Institute for Northern Culture, Hokkaido Imperial University,* 4.

Obayashi, Taryo
1973   "*Kotan* no Seikatsu to Kuma-matsuri" [Life of *Kotan,* settlement, and Bear Festival], Taiyo, 118.

Obayashi, Taryo, and Paproth, Hans-Joachim
1964   "Karafuto Orok no Kuma-matsuri" [The Orok Bear Festival on Saghalien], *The Japanese Journal of Ethnology,* 29(3).

Sarashina, Genzo, and Sarashina, Ko
1976   *Kotan Seibutsu-ki, II, Yaju, Kaiju, Gyozoku Hen* [Natural History of Kotan, Vol. II, Wild Animals, Sea Mammals, and Fishes]. Tokyo: Hosei Daigaku Shuppan-kyoku.

Watanabe, Hitoshi
1952/53 "Saru Ainu ni okeru Tennen Shigen no Riyo" [Utilization of natural resources by the Saru Ainu], *The Japanese Journal of Ethnology,* 16(3/4).
1964   "Ainu no Kuma-matsuri no Shakai teki Kino narabini sono Hatten ni kansuru Seitai teki Yoin" [Social function of the Ainu Bear Ceremony and ecological factors relevant to its development], *The Japanese Journal of Ethnology,* 29(3).
1972   *The Ainu Ecosystem.* The American Ethnological Society, Monograph 54.

Yamada, Takako
1986   "Ainu no Shokobutsu Bunrui Taikei" [Ainu classification of plants], *The Japanese Journal of Ethnology,* 51(2).
1987   "Ainu no Dobutsu Bunrui to Sekaikan" [Ainu classification of animals and cosmology], *Bulletin of the Institute for the Study of North Eurasian Cultures,* Hokkaido University, 18.
1991   "Ainu no Uchukan Saiko" [Reconsideration of Ainu cosmology], in: Tanaka, Jiro and Malcoto Kakeya (eds.) *Itani Junichiro Sensei Taikan Kinen Ronbunshu* [Papers in celebration of the retirement of Professor Itani Junichiro]. Tokyo: Heibonsha.

READING 10–4

WATER WITCHING: AN INTERPRETATION OF A RITUAL PATTERN IN A RURAL AMERICAN COMMUNITY

Evon Z. Vogt

Evon Z. Vogt was a professor at Harvard, and carried out extensive field research among the Navaho and Zuni Indians in the United States, and among peasant communities in Mexico. In this reading, which many anthropologists look upon as a classic, Vogt takes up Malinowski's claim that even though empirically ineffective magic does have an empirical function by, for example, instilling confidence in persons who believe in it. Malinowski argued on the basis of his Trobriand ethnography that ritual fills the gap in causality between empirical activity and wishes that cannot be fulfilled by it. The ritual here is water witching, which like scapulimancy is a form of divination. The author's findings confirm Malinowski's hypothesis. Despite its empirical invalidity water witching does fill the aforementioned gap and instills reassurance in otherwise uncertain situations. Vogt concludes by comparing this instance of "folk science" or "pseudoscience" to placebos employed in modern medicine.

This paper will attempt an interpretation of the phenomenon of water witching as a folk-ritual pattern which has been extraordinarily persistent in rural American culture and which has not been replaced by the services of competent ground water geologists in locating family-size wells in countless rural American communities. There is a vast literature on this waterdivining pattern,[†] but by and large the writings have centered on the problem of whether dowsing does or does not work as an empirical technique for locating underground supplies of water. The latest publication of note in this vein is the best thriller by Kenneth Roberts, *Henry Gross and his Dowsing Rod,* which, as a spirited defense

Source: The Scientific Monthly 75, September 1952, pp. 175–186.

of the empirical validity of the dowsing technique, has renewed and publicized the age-old controversy. But, so far as this writer has been able to determine, there has been no systematic attempt to analyze the phenomenon as a folk-ritual pattern functionally equivalent to the magical practices found in the nonliterate cultures of the world.

Emanating from the writings of Pareto, Malinowski, and Weber, and continuing in the present generation of theorists—notably Parsons, Kluckhohn, and Homans—a general body of theory concerning the function of ritual in the situation of human action has emerged. Briefly stated, the essence of this theory is that when human beings are confronted with situations that are beyond empirical control and that are, therefore, anxiety-producing both in terms of emotional involvement and of a sense of cognitive frustration, they respond by developing and elaborating nonempirical ritual that has the function of relieving emotional anxiety and of making some sense of the situation on a cognitive level.[2] Kroeber has recently questioned the university of this relationship by pointing out that the Eskimos, who live in a far more uncertain and anxiety-producing environment than do Malinowski's Trobriand Islanders, have little ritual as compared to the Trobrianders, whereas given Malinowski's formulation one would expect more Eskimo ritual.[3] Kroeber goes on to indicate that the arctic environment is so severe that had the Eskimos devoted much energy to the development of ritual patterns, they would long since have perished. This latter point is sound, but further analysis of Eskimo culture may reveal that, although there is little elaboration of ritual, the ritual patterns that do exist are still clustered around the greatest uncertainties of Eskimo life.

Others, notably Radcliffe-Brown,[4] have raised the issue as to whether rituals do not create anxiety (when they are not performed or are not performed properly) rather than alleviate it. Homans has treated this problem in terms of "primary" and "secondary" rituals focused around "primary" and "secondary" types of anxiety. Primary anxiety describes the sentiment men feel when they desire the accomplishment of certain results and do not possess the techniques that make these results certain; secondary anxiety describes the sentiment resulting when the traditional rites are not performed or are performed improperly.[5] Kluckhohn has carried the analysis further by demonstrating that ritual patterns have both a "gain" and a "cost" from the point of view of the continued functioning of a society, and that problems are created as well as solved by the presence of ritual patterns in a given culture.[6]

Finally, I should like to advance the theory that ritual patterns which initially emerge as responses to critical areas of uncertainty in the situation of action are elaborated and reinterpreted in terms of certain selective value-orientations in a given culture.[‡]

We are brought, then, to a dynamic conception of ritual which includes the following considerations: Ritual patterns develop as a response to emotional anxiety and cognitive frustration in a situation of uncertainty; but ritual patterns come to have both "functional" and "dysfunctional" aspects (both a "gain" and a "cost") for the continuing existence of a society as the patterns are elaborated and developed in terms of the selective value-orientations of a given culture.

In this paper I shall analyze the relationship of the water-witching pattern to the critical area of uncertainty in the location of underground water supplies, explore the functional and dysfunctional aspects of this pattern for the continuing survival of the community, and try to show how the pattern has become an expression of the value stress on "rational" environmental control in a rural American community.

FOLK RITUAL IN RURAL AMERICA

The continuing existence of a large body of folk ritual in rural American culture is a fact of common observation by anyone who has lived in such communities and by those who have done systematic research in rural areas. For example, in *Plainville, USA,* James West wrote that "many magical practices still exist for planting crops, castrating livestock, weaning, gardening, girdling trees."[7] Taylor reported that he had gathered 467 different signs and superstitions that are known and to some extent believed in rural communities.[8]

Although these magical practices are found in connection with many aspects of rural culture, including the preparation of food, the curing of illness, and the weaning of babies, they are apparently concentrated in the area of farming technology and have to do mainly with weather, crops, the care of animals, and the locating of water wells. Taylor asserted that over one fourth of his 467 signs and superstitions refer to climate and weather and that the majority refer to plants and animals in addition to weather and climate.[9]

THE WATER-WITCHING PATTERN

The phenomenon by means of which one is supposed to find underground supplies of water by the use of a divining rod is variously known as dowsing, divining, witching, and rhabdomancy. The indicator employed in water divining is called a divining rod, witching stick, dowsing rod, dipping rod, striking stick, or wand; and the practitioner may be called a diviner, dowser, witch, or finder. In current usage the word "dowsing" is more common in their literature and is used by rural people along the Eastern seaboard; "water witching" is the more common term used by rural folk who utilize the technique in the South, Middle West, and Far West.[§]

It is certain that the water-witching pattern has a respectable antiquity in Western culture and it is highly probable that the basic ideas of the technique derive ultimately from ancient divining practices that are widespread among the nonliterate cultures of the world. The "rod" is mentioned many times in the Bible in connection with miraculous performances, especially in the books of Moses. The much-quoted references to Moses' striking the rock with his rod, thus producing water for his followers in the wilderness (Numb. XX: 9-11), has been regarded by enthusiasts of water witching as a significant reference to the divining rod.[10] Herodotus mentions the use of the divining rod by the Persians, Scythians, and Medes; and Marco Polo reports it use throughout the Orient.[11]

But whatever significance one may attach to such references, authorities agree that the divining rod in its present form was in use in Germany by the first half of the sixteenth century.[12] The first complete published description is contained in Agricola's *De re metallica,* published in 1556.[13] Barrett considers that the birthplace of the modern divining rod was in the mining districts of Germany, probably in the Harz Mountains, where it was used to prospect for ore. During the reign of Queen Elizabeth (1558–1603), when German miners were imported to England to lend an impetus to the mining industry in Cornwall, they brought the *schlagruthe* ("striking rod") with them. As mining declined in Cornwall, the use of the rod was transferred to water finding.[14] At about the same time there is mention of the use of the rod for locating water supplies in France.[15]

Before the end of the seventeenth century the use of the divining rod had spread through Europe, everywhere arousing controversy. Its champions, among whom were some of the most learned men of the time, explained its operation on the principle of "sympathy" or "attraction and repulsion". Its adversaries, like Agricola, condemned its use as a superstitious and vain practice.[18] Indeed, the practice became a subject of ecclesiastical controversy when Martin Luther proclaimed in 1518 that the use of the rod violated the First Commandment,[16] and the Jesuit Father Gaspard Schott later denounced it as an instrument controlled by the devil.[17] From Europe the water-witching pattern spread to New Zealand,[18] and it is reported that as late as 1931 the government of British Columbia hired an "official" water-diviner to locate wells.°

Over the past four centuries the phenomenon has also been the subject of innumerable scientific (or allegedly scientific) investigations and controversies, beginning with Pierre Lebrum in 1692[12] and continuing off and on to the present controversy stimulated by Roberts' best-selling book.[9] The key figures in these investigations and controversies have been such men as Sir William Barrett (professor of physics in the Royal College of Science for Ireland), Henri Mager (in France), J. W. Gregory (Glasgow University),O.E. Meinzer (U.S. Geological Survey), and more recently Solco W. Tromp (professor of geology at Fouad I University, Cairo).

The core of the water-witching pattern as it is now found in rural American culture may be characterized as follows:

Equipment The most common item of equipment utilized is the witching stick, typically a Y-shaped green twig cut from a hazel, willow, or peach tree. The two forks vary from 14 to 18 inches in length, and the neck from 4 to 11 inches. The diameter of the stick may vary from one-eighth inch to almost an inch. Alternative types of wood used include maple, apple, dogwood, and beech twigs and, in the southwestern United States, twigs cut from piñon and juniper trees. There is even one case on record of a diviner who uses a leaf form the broad-leafed yucca plant.[19] Less common, but widespread, are various metallic materials used for witching, including barbed wire from the nearest fence, a clock or watch spring, and especially constructed aluminum rods. Finally, some water witches use various kinds of pendulums such as small bottles of "chemicals" suspended on a string, or a key suspended by a string from either a Bible or an arithmetic book.

Technique The most common technique is to grasp the two branches of the forked twig, one in each hand, with the neck (or bottom of the Y) pointing skyward. Usually the twig is grasped with the palms of the hands up, but an alternative method is to hold the stick with the palms down.[20] In either case, the forked twig is placed under tension in such a way that the slightest contraction of the muscles in the forearm or a slight twist of the wrists is sufficient to cause the twig to rotate toward the ground. The water witch walked over the ground in the area where a water supply is desired. When he walks over an underground supply of water, the witching stick is supposed to dip down, and a stake is then driven into the ground to mark the spot. Although most dowsers function only to locate a suitable spot to drill for a well or to dig for a spring, some also have techniques for determining the depth of the water supply. Perhaps the most common of these is to measure the distance for the place where the stick starts to dip to where it dips straight down over the water supply. Few, if any, other practitioners profess to have the sophisticated "powers" of Henry Gross that would enable them to ask questions and receive answers (by the way the rod nods) as to the quality and amount of the underground water, or to locate a water supply by "long-distance" dowsing, as Henry Gross did when he dowsed over a map of Bermuda while in New England and located water there.[9]

Ideology   Like most ritual patterns, water witching carries with it an elaborate mythology, the core of which involves two aspects: the dowser's definition of the geological situation, summarized by the belief held by dowsers that underground water occurs in two forms: *sheet water,* which underlies a total area, and *water veins,* which may vary in magnitude from "the size of a pencil" to "underground rivers" and which run through the earth like the veins in the human body. The important thing is to locate and trace these veins, because either there may be no sheet water in a given area or it may be located at so deep a level that the only way to find suitable shallow water is to "hit a vein." The most elementary knowledge of ground water geology is sufficient to prove that this dowsing concept bears little relations to known facts. The second aspect concerns the many and varied "explanations" and justifications advanced by dowsers for the efficacy of dowsing and the rationalization provided to account for failures. The "explanations" on record range from supernaturalistic interpretations (such as the notion that dowsers derive their mysterious power from Moses, "who was the first water witch") to supposedly scientific interpretations (such as the notion that the muscles of the water witch are affected by electromagnetic disturbances emanating from underground water supplies). Most of the ordinary and less articulate water witches in rural America provide explanations in terms of (1) a kind of magical principle by which the water in the green twig is attracted by the water in the ground, or (2) a theory—which they regard as "scientific"—that the dipping of the stick has something to do with "electricity" or "electrical currents" which run from the water through their bodies and into the stick causing it to dip. Equally important are the rationalizations

advanced to account for failures. These typically take the form of attributing the failure either to faulty equipment (e.g., "I couldn't find a straight stick that day") or to some aspect of the situation that negates the findings of the dowser (e.g., "I found I had a knife in my pocket which short-circuited the electric current," or"The vein dried up before they got around to drilling the well").

Institutionalization of Role   There is considerable variation in the prestige the dowser has in a rural community, depending upon various factors. But it is clear that he occupies a special role. In the first place, the basic ability to do witching is usually believed to be a skill with which one is born and which he later discovers; it cannot be acquired by training or experience. In this respect it comprises a skill which is acquired by "divine stroke," as in the "shamanistic" tradition, rather than a body of knowledge transmitted by training in a "priestly" tradition. To be sure, it is necessary for a person to have observed (or to have heard about) the basic techniques, but it is impossible for one water witch to impart the skill to another. One is either born with it or one is not.[‖] By virtue of this inborn ability, the dowser assumes a specialized role that is recognized by the total community—both by the proponents and by the adversaries of dowsing.

In the second place, the water witch is almost always paid for his service, in amounts ranging from $5 to $25 (in the Southwest) for locating each well site. In this respect, his position becomes a part-time occupation, and some dowsers derive a substantial income from their activities. It should be pointed out that some dowsers charge a set price and collect the money in businesslike fashion; others volunteer their services and take whatever contributions are offered them. But I have not yet known a water witch who was a charlatan or who performed the operation purely for the monetary gain involved. Usually they are sincere individuals who believe thoroughly in their ability to find water. Finally, it should be noted that dowsers are usually men, although women sometimes have the witching skill. Indeed, the water-diviner reported to have been employed by the government of British Columbia in 1931 was a woman.

Having described the history and general pattern of dowsing, let us turn to a more intensive treatment of water witching in terms of the concrete data from a single community—Homestead, New Mexico[¶]—where the relevant historical, geological, and social facts are well known.

WATER-WITCHING IN HOMESTEAD**

The community of Homestead was established by families from the South Plains area of western Texas and Oklahoma who settled on homesteads in the semiarid area of western New Mexico in the early 1930s. The economy focuses around the production of pinto beans on dry-land farms, supplemented by crops of corn, winter wheat, and beef cattle. Farms now average two sections in size and are scattered as far as twenty miles from the crossroads center of the community which contains the stores, school, post office, repair shops, and other service institutions. Farming technology has shifted through the years from horse-drawn implements to mechanized equipment.

The natural environment provides an unusually hazardous setting for dry-land farming. Until the homesteaders arrived, the land had been used only for grazing purposes, and the area is still regarded as submarginal farming land by authorities in the U.S. Department of Agriculture. The soil is excellent for beans, but the necessary 90-day growing season is often cut short by late spring frosts or early fall frosts at this elevation (7000 feet). Heavy windstorms in the spring add the hazard of serious wind erosion. But the basic environmental problems are those of inadequate and fluctuating rainfall and the development of water resources for livestock and household use. Annual precipitation averages 12.5–15 inches, depending upon locality and elevation, but has varied over the past two decades from 6 to 19 inches.

The people who established this community defined themselves as pioneers, leaving the "civilized" centers of Texas and Oklahoma to seek new homes on the "frontier" west of the Continental Divide. As pioneers, they emphasize many of the values characteristic of newly settled American farming communities: a stress on self-reliance and independence of the individual, a drive to subdue and control the natural environment, an abiding faith in the progressive development of their community, and a perennial optimism about the future. With these values they confronted the semiarid environment of western New Mexico and set about the business of developing dry-land farms.

One of the first critical problems the homesteaders faced was the development of adequate water supplies. When they first arrived in 1930–31, they found it necessary to haul water in barrels by team and wagon from a lake three miles from the center of the community. When the lake went dry, they hauled water from a spring seven miles distant. If a farmer had livestock, it meant that he had to haul water at least every other day. A few tried drilling wells in the early years, but it was soon discovered that, although in some places water was struck at shallow depths (80–100 feet), in others dry holes were the only result after drilling over 500 feet. At a cost of $1–$3 a foot for drilling a well, few homesteaders were willing or able to take the risk.

It was in this situation that one farmer suddenly "discovered" in 1933 that he had the "power" to witch for water. As a young boy in Texas he had observed witching. One day he simply cut a forked stick from his wife's peach tree, tried out the technique as he remembered it, and it worked. He found two water veins on his farm, traced them to a point where they crossed each other, and had a successful well drilled at this spot at a depth of 230 feet. He rapidly achieved community-wide reputation as a water witch and successfully witched 18 wells in the next few years. Six wells were dowsed by a second water witch who lived in the community for a few years, making a total of 24 wells that were located in this manner. During the same period, however, the original water witch dowsed five locations where dry holes resulted after drilling; and he often missed calculating the depth by as much as 200–400 feet. For, in addition to using the common technique for locating the water vein by walking over the ground with a forked twig and putting a stake in the ground where the rod dipped, he developed a special technique for determining the depth. He would hold a thin, straight stick (5 feet in length) over the water vein, and it would "involuntarily" nod up and down. The number of nods indicated the depth in feet to the water. During the same period 25 wells were successfully drilled without benefit of dowsing, and seven dry holes were drilled in locations that were not dowsed. (Table 1)

Table 1

	Wells Divined	Wells Not Divined
Successful wells	24	25
Dry holes	5	7

As time went on, the water witch killed his wife's lone peach tree by cutting witching sticks from it. He then made an adjustment to the New Mexican environment by shifting to the use of forked twigs from piñon trees. He explains his dowsing in terms of "electricity" and usually attributes errors to the presence of iron (like a knife in his pocket, or an old piece of farm machinery in the vicinity) or to the fact that he could not find a straight stick.

There is, of course, more than a casual relation between the early water supply problems of homesteaders and the geology of the Homestead area.[††] The community is bordered on the south by a high escarpment that exposes the upper formations underlying the area. These consist of Quaternary basalt flows which are exposed in portions of the eastern and northern parts, Tertiary sands and conglomerates which underlie the western part, and the Mesa Verde formation of Upper Cretaceous age which underlies the above formations at variable lengths. The Mesa Verde formation is about 1800 feet thick and consists of alternating gray to buff sandstones, gray clay shales, and coal.

During Tertiary time the shales and sandstones of the upper Mesa Verde formation were eroded, and subsequent deposition of the Tertiary sands and conglomerates filled the old channels. The existence of these buried channels and ridges, and recent erosion of the Tertiary formation, resulted in variations in the thickness of the Tertiary formation and the upper member of the Mesa Verde formation.

Ground water occurs in the Mesa Verde formation, which is the main aquifer, and in the Tertiary formation; small quantities may also be available in the recent alluvium in the valleys, especially in the north and northeast. Structural conditions are not well known, but there are indications of a number of faults and of one syncline, which also affect ground water supplies.

Several shallow wells near the center of the community and a few wells to the west obtain water from the Tertiary formation. These walls range in depth from 225 to 260 feet, and the yield is usually small. The erosion of the Mesa Verde formation, and subsequent deposition of the Tertiary formation, have caused the base of the Tertiary sands to be an irregular surface. This accounts for the variable depths of wells and the variation in yields. Wells drilled into the old channels are likely to yield more water than others drilled on the buried ridges of the underlying Mesa Verde formation.

The majority of wells in the Homestead area, and all the wells a mile or more east of the center of the community, obtain water from the Mesa Verde formation. The yield of these wells is generally greater than those obtaining water from the Tertiary sands, but it is necessary to drill deeper. The depth varies from about 80 feet in the Tertiary sands in the western part of the area to 800 feet in the Mesa Verde formation in the eastern portion.

Thus it is readily seen that geological conditions have resulted in substantial variations in ground water resources in different parts of the area. In some localities water is found in the Tertiary sands, usually at relatively shallow depths, but with variations running from 88 to over 300 feet. In other localities it is necessary to drill to a greater depth in to the Mesa Verde formation. And the situation is further complicated by structural conditions that are not yet well known by geologists.

In the dowsing of his own well the local water witch was over the Tertiary formation, and water in small quantities was located at 230 feet. The wells which the dowser "successfully" located were either drilled into the Tertiary formation or the farmers were willing to drill to greater depths and thus reach the Mesa Verde formation. The dry holes were cases in which the wells were either *(a)* located where the Tertiary sands did not exist and the farmer was unwilling to go deep enough to strike the Mesa Verde formation (two cases), or *(b)* located over the Tertiary formation but in places where buried channels or the presence of the syncline in the underlying Mesa Verde formation made the depth to water greater than the wells were drilled (three cases). The same geological facts account for the dry holes that resulted from drilling in locations that were not dowsed. The frequent errors in estimating depth were undoubtedly due to these same geological conditions, especially since the dowser usually named a depth that approximated, or was less than, the depth of his own well.

In addition to the water-witching pattern there are two other types of institutionalized folk ritual in Homestead: (1) the use of natural phenomena, such as the winds, clouds, or moon to predict the weather (especially the occurrence of frost) and to judge the proper time for planting crops; and (2) the use of the signs of the zodiac to know when to perform certain farming or livestock operations,‡‡ such as when to castrate calves "so they won't bleed to death," when to wean calves "so they won't bawl around for several days," §§ or when to hoe weeds "so they won't come up again." Farmers who believe in and practice these three types of folk ritual are known, respectively, as "witch men," and "sign men."

Not all the homesteaders believe in and practice these rituals. Our data indicate that opinion range from those of farmers who are wholly oriented in terms of the rational-technological methods of modern agricultural science and scoff at "those silly superstitions," to those who believe firmly in and practice all three types of ritual—e.g., the water witch who is also full of knowledge about and belief in "signs," "planting by the moon," etc. The data further indicate that, of the three areas of ritual, the water-witching pattern is the most widespread and the most persistent in the face of formal education in the theories and methods of modern science. When the recorded instances of the practice of these rituals from our running field notes for the year's period were classified, it was found that 57 per cent of the instances were in the area of water witching, 29 per cent were in the area of the use of the almanac and the signs of the zodiac, and 14 per cent referred to the use of natural phenomena to predict and control events.[21] It was further discovered that some of the most highly educated individuals in the community were having wells dowsed (for example, the principal of the school, who possesses an M.A. degree). Again, research revealed that opinion varied from utter skepticism on the part of some farmers who said that "the best witching stick is the end of a driller's bit" to complete faith in the ability of the dowser to locate water. The most frequent response was an attitude expressed by such statements as, "Well, I'm not sure I believe in it, but it don't cost any more," or "I'll always give it the benefit of the doubt." Comparative data from a recent study in the Texas Panhandle, which was initiated to provide controls over certain variables in the Homestead study, are illuminating for the analysis of water witching.[22] The Panhandle study was focused on the small community of Cotton Center (pop. 100), near the geographical center of the area that provided the families for the present population of Homestead. The kinship and intervisiting ties between the two communities are unusually close, despite the distances involved, and there is ample evidence that the cultures of the two communities are still quite similar.

Specific inquiries as to water witching and the geology and ground water resources were made in Cotton Center. The community is located in Hale County, which is extremely flat, consisting of slightly undulating hills interspersed with many poorly drained depressions that fill with water during the rainy season. Annual rainfall averages 22 inches, or almost twice the precipitation found in

Homestead. Most of the usable ground water is found in the Ogallala formation, a sandy deposit lying at or near the surface throughout the region.[23] The ground water table stands at a depth of about 125 feet below the surface, and good wells can be obtained at almost any point. Wells are located where water can be used to best agricultural advantage on the farms. Water witching is widely known, but it is almost never practiced. It can be classified as an unused skill in Cotton Center.

There is also evidence from this area of the Panhandle to indicate that the practice of water witching in Homestead is not due to selective migration—with the "superstitious people" moving west to New Mexico and leaving the families with a more rational-technological orientation behind. For, less than 25 miles to the southeast of Cotton Center in Floyd and Crosby counties, the ground water situation is more variable, there is more difficulty locating wells, and water witching is currently practiced. Indeed, there are men from Cotton Center who assist their relatives in dowsing for water in these other counties.

ALTERNATIVE THEORIES OF WATER WITCHING

There are three theories to account for the persistence of water witching in rural American culture. The first may be designated as the "technological theory," which accounts for the continuing practice of water witching on the basis of the empirical validity of the technique as a reliable method for locating wells. The second theory may be designated as the "survival theory," which assumes that water witching is a folk-ritual pattern but accounts for its continued practice by defining the pattern as a "survival" from a previous, less technically oriented phase of our cultural development. The third theory may be designated as the "functional theory," which also defines water witching as a ritual pattern but emphasizes the relationship between situations of technological uncertainty in the present scene and the pattern of water witching as ritual means of coping with situations that are beyond empirical control.

THE TECHNOLOGICAL THEORY

As indicated earlier, the controversy about water witching has centered around the problem of whether is does or does not work as a reliable empirical method for locating underground supplies of water. This theory must be examined first, because if water witching is an empirically reliable technique, it can then be regarded as part of the rational farming technology in rural American culture, and no further explanation of its continuing use is necessary.

It would be patently impossible to summarize here all the arguments pro and con on the empirical validity of water witching; our task is merely to examine the most relevant evidence. At the outset we may rule out the various "supernaturalistic" claim—as, for example, the claim that dowsers have some kind of mysterious power transmitted through the generations from Moses which enables them to find water. We may also eliminate the simple explanation of many dowsers to the effect that the water in the ground attracts and pulls the water in the freshly cut witching stick. There would appear to be no naturalistic basis for believing that water located (in some cases) as much as several hundred feet under the surface could directly affect the water in a freshly cut stick. Furthermore, as Finklestein points out, the claims of the dowsers lead one to the inevitable conclusion that if there is an empirical basis for the technique, it must be independent of the type of witching device utilized; because the same claims are made for the effectiveness of all devices.[21]

Although we may eliminate the possibility that some kind of external physical force acts directly upon the dowsing rod, there remains the possibility that some kind of external physical force is stimulating the dowser's muscles, which then contract and cause the rod to dip. In this case the rod is merely an indicator of muscular contractions and the type of witching rod used would make no difference.

This approach to the problem has recently been explored by Tromp, who presents experimental evidence indicating that some individuals are more sensitive than others to changes in the strength and polarity of electrical fields associated with both natural and artificial objects.[1] And the problem then becomes one of assessing the possibility that underground supplies of water may affect variations in electromagnetic fields to the extent that these changes in electrical field strength are registered in the dowser's muscles, stimulating them to contract, and thereby indicating the presence of underground water. As matters now stand, even Tromp does not appear to claim that dowsers can identify the cause of a particular change in electrical field strength (such as might result from the presence of underground water), but only that it exists.[24] And the judgment of competent geologists is that it is impossible that changes in electromagnetic fields caused by the *specific* presence of underground water can be registered in *specific* ways in the muscular contractions of dowsers.[¶]

The question may also be raised as to whether the dowser is not merely a sound practical geologist who knows the ground water situation from experience in a given area, and that he is responding to certain surface outcroppings or other indications of underground water when his witching stick dips. In other words, perhaps the witching stick is merely an indirect way of communicating sound geological knowledge.

It is true that many dowsers respond to certain cues in the environment while they are going through the dowsing process. For example, the dowser in Homestead utilizes anthills, and piñon trees with branches that hang down unusually far, as general guides to underground water. But our evidence indicates that these are merely cues for the dowser and have no specific connection with shallow underground water. Furthermore, the dowser makes no attempt to collect information about the location and depth of other wells in the vicinity or to utilize other types of empirical data in the location of new wells.

In other areas of the world, however, there is suggestive evidence that the dowsers occasionally do possess some sound geological knowledge and that their "successes" are due to these empirical observations that are then recorded by the witching stick.[25] But in this case it is obviously the geological observations made by the dowser (and neither the attraction of the rod by underground water nor the stimulation of the muscles of the dowser by variations in electrical fields caused by the presence of underground water) which give the technique an empirical basis.

A second approach to the problem of the empirical validity of water witching is to examine the best evidence available as to the reliability of the dowsing technique. There have been two recent relevant systematic studies. In 1939 the New South Wales Water Conservation and Irrigations Commission issued a report containing full data on wells drilled in New South Wales from 1918 to 1939. The commission drills wells and issues licenses for wells drilled by private companies, so that full statistical data are available. Table 2 gives the totals from 1918 to 1939.[26]

Table 2

	Wells Divined		Wells Not Divined	
	No. of Wells	Percentage	No. of Wells	Percentage
Bores in which supplies of serviceable water estimated at 100 gal./ hr. or over were obtained	1234	70.4	1406	83.9
Bores in which supplies of serviceable water estimated at less than 100 gal./hr. were obtained	180	10.2	88	5.3
Bores in which supplies of unserviceable water were obtained	82	4.7	55	3.3
Bores—absolute failures, no water of any kind obtained	257	14.7	126	7.5
Total	1753	100.0	1675	100.0

In 1948 P. A. Ongley, of the Medical School at the University of Otago, published the results of controlled experiments performed on 58 different New Zealand water dowsers. Not a single dowser showed any reliability in any of the experiments, which consisted of the following:

1. Asking the dowser to locate an underground stream and then return to it with his eyes closed.
2. Having the dowser locate an underground stream and then later identify which pegs were on the stream and which were not—the experiment having placed one half of a number of pegs over the underground stream designated by the dowser and the other half of the pegs off the stream.
3. Asking two or more dowsers to check one another on the location of underground water.
4. Asking the dowser to say whether a hidden bottle was full of water or empty.
5. Asking two or more dowsers to determine the depth of the water below the surface of the ground.[25]

To these observed facts, we may add the data on dowsing from Homestead which are reported in Table 1. Although the number of wells involved is small as compared to the series from New South Wales, it is plain that the same negative results are indicated. In both instances, it does not appear to make much difference whether a well is dowsed or not; if anything, there would appear to be fewer complete failures when wells are located by methods other than dowsing, indicating that chance or common sense is a little more reliable.

Finally, I have observed two cases in Homestead in which the well driller was already drilling in a water-bearing formation when the water witch appeared with his forked twig and announced (after dowsing around the immediate area of the well rig) that the driller had best move his drill since he would never hit water in the hole he was then drilling!

It is difficult to avoid the conclusion that water witching is not an empirically reliable method for locating underground supplies of water.[26] It is plain that the witching stick dips in response to muscular contractions of the dowser that are due to some type of unconscious mental or psychic processes and *not* in response to the physical presence of underground water supplies. But the question remains as to why water witching continues to be practiced if it is not an empirical method for locating water. To answer this question we must turn to the other two theories.

THE SURVIVAL THEORY

A second theory that is held implicitly, and sometimes stated explicitly, by many rural sociologists, government agricultural experts, and other observers of the rural scene is the view that water witching is one of many "superstitions" that survive among the unenlightened farmers who learned them from their fathers and grandfathers. It is firmly believed by these observers that the "superstitions" will be replaced by rational-technological methods for coping with the environment as soon as there is sufficient education in the methods of modern agricultural science. Indeed, the disposition of many of these writers is to behave as if the superstitions had already been replaced by scientific methods; and despite their prevalence in rural American culture, it is rare to find an explicit treatment of the problem in rural sociology textbooks. An exception is Sims, who writes that:

> The magical mind, rather than the scientific attitude, tends to prevail (in rural America). . . . This is an emotional and unreflective attitude which does not clearly perceive the steps between thoughts and actions. . . . Expressions of magical mindedness are seen in numerous superstitious beliefs and practices in regard to harvesting and planting.[27]

Sims goes on to argue that science will eventually cause the disappearance of ritual from the rural scene, as he writes:

> The impress of science is already marked and the agencies carrying it to the farmers persistent. . . . With much prestige already established for this method, there is every reason to think that fairly rapid headway

will be made in the immediate future. To the degree such progress is made, the magical mindedness will disappear.[27]

There is certainly a grain of truth in this explanation of water witching. It *is* a "superstitious" practice from the point of view of the educated observer, and the pattern has obviously been transmitted to the current generation of farmers from earlier generations. But does it persist *merely* because farmers are lacking in education and are "magical minded"? Two observations on the basis of Homestead data may be made here. The first is that many of the most highly educated individuals in Homestead still resort to the practice when they have a well drilled. The second is the fact that although the educational level is approximately the same in the present population of Homestead as in the population of Cotton Center in the Texas Panhandle, water witching is not utilized to locate wells in Cotton Center (where the water table stands at a uniform depth), whereas the practice flourishes in Homestead (where the underground water supply is highly variable in depth). These facts strongly suggest that there is more to the phenomenon of dowsing than that it is a "superstitious survival" from an earlier phase of cultural development.

THE FUNCTIONAL THEORY

A few rural sociological writers have given some attention to this third theory in which such practices as water witching are viewed not merely as "superstitious survivals" but as ritual responses to situations of technological uncertainty in the contemporary scene. Carl Taylor, in his *Rural Sociology,* has made the following statement:

> The reliance of the old time farmer upon the almanac was proverbial, and his belief in signs, although sometimes exaggerated, is by no means extinct.. . . The point we wish to make here is not that superstitions, signs, and charms have greater influence among rural than urban people (although this is probably the case), but that farming as an enterprise is influenced by the uncertainty of weather and seasons to such an extent that specious explanations of the causes and effects of

this uncertainty have become widespread among rural people.[8]

In the elaboration and application of this functional theory to the phenomenon of water witching, we must first specify the aspects of the Homestead situation that are technologically uncertain (and hence productive of emotional and cognitive frustration) from the point of view of modern science. It is clear that a competent ground water geologist can provide a sound general description of the geology and the water resources of the region, and that this geological knowledge indicates that ground water is available in two of the formations that underlie all or part of the region. One or the other of these aquifers can always be reached if wells are drilled deep enough. But it is equally clear that even with the most careful geological mapping, there exists a high degree of uncertainty as to the depth and amount of ground water available in any *particular* location where one may choose to drill. This factor of indeterminacy arises from the fact that surface outcroppings do not provide complete knowledge of the buried channels and ridges that resulted from erosion of the Mesa Verde formation in Tertiary times, or of the structural conditions resulting from faults. Both these geological facts result in substantial variations in the depth and quantity of ground water.

We have, then, a situation in which family-size wells on the scattered farmsteads were needed to relieve farmers of the expensive and time-consuming task of hauling water from some distance, and a situation in which there existed a zone of indeterminacy in the exact location of adequate ground water resources. The stage was set, so to speak, for the development of a method to cope with the situation. Two things happened. On the one hand, a local farmer "discovered" that he had the power to dowse wells and began to do so throughout the community; on the other, geologists from the Soil Conservation Service began to visit the community and make certain recommendations on the location of wells. The two alternative methods were in competition. But the geologists came to the community infrequently[***] and could only provide answers to the question of location and the depth to water in a given well in *general* terms, whereas the water witch was always available and could specify an *exact* location and an *exact* number of feet to water. These reassuring answers encouraged many homesteaders to drill wells. When good wells were obtained at near the depth named by the water witch, his praises were sung throughout the community. When a dowsed well was a failure (because it was not deep enough), there were readymade rationalizations to account for the failure. And the most frequent stories told about dowsing involve the cases in which a farmer tried drilling without dowsing and obtained a dry hole; then he hired the water witch to locate a well on his farm and obtained good water.

In brief, there would appear to be a functional connection between technological uncertainty in locating wells in this arid environment with a complicated geological structure and the flourishing of the water-witching pattern. This conclusion is fortified by the observed fact that the area of highest anxiety in the community—the location and development of adequate water resources—is also the area of the most persistent and most utilized ritual pattern—the water-witching technique (57 per cent of the observed instances of ritual practice)—and by the fact that water witching, which is an unused skill in the ancestral region of the Texas Panhandle, was activated and has flourishes in Homestead.

Thus, although a relationship can be demonstrated between technological uncertainty and ritual in the case of water witching, the pattern has been elaborated and rationalized in terms of one of the central value-orientations of Homestead. For in their relationships with the natural environment the homesteaders strongly emphasize an orientation which may be described as "rational mastery over nature;"[28] the environment is viewed as something to be controlled and exploited for man's material comfort. And for the adherents of water witching in the community, the pattern becomes an important expression of this value stress upon "rational" environmental control. It is part of the farming process—along with clearing the land with bulldozers, plowing, planting, and cultivating the fields with power machinery—to locate a well by witch-

ing before one employs a driller. Explanations of how dowsing works are predominantly sought in terms of the presence of metal objects which "short-circuit" the process, or in terms of technologically faulty equipment.

There are clearly certain functional "gains" in the practice of water witching for the development and continuing survival of a community like Homestead. The *certain* answers provided by the dowser relieve the farmers' anxiety about ground water resources and inspire confidence to go ahead with the hard work of developing farms. The pattern also provides a cognitive orientation to the problem of why water is found (at a certain depth) on one farm and not on another—in terms of the ideas about water veins that run irregularly under the ground.

But it is equally clear that the practice of dowsing involves certain functional "costs" in this situation. Energy and resources are invested in a technique which does not provide any better information as to the location of shallow underground water supplies than does the good judgment of individual farmers. It is also often the case that dowsed well will be located at spots that are highly inconvenient and inefficient for the most economical operation of the farm. Some farmhouses in the community have been built in inaccessible places on the sides of hills "because that is where the water witch found the water." But the homesteaders who are adherents of dowsing believe that they are being "scientific" about locating underground water. These attitudes detract from the effort of obtaining more precise geological information which, even if it does not tell the farmer in terms of so many feet how far it is to water at a given location, is at least a more promising long-range approach to the development of water resources for the community.

SOME COMPARATIVE DATA

Homestead is located in a region inhabited by four other cultural groups: Mormon, Spanish-American, Zuni, and Navaho. The water-witching pattern is part of the cultural equipment of the Mormons and the Spanish-Americans, but it is generally absent among the Navahos and Zunis. The Mormon experience with water dowsing parallels that of Homestead. The Mormon community is located in a well-watered valley at the base of a mountain range. In this valley wells can be drilled at almost any location, and ample ground water obtained at 30–40 feet. Some of the Mormon settlers have dry-land farms and ranches in the area to the south and east in which the ground water situation, with a high degree of variability in amount and depth, is comparable to that of Homestead. Although the Mormon community has a water witch, he has dowsed only five wells in the irrigated value during the past forty years. On the other hand, he has been employed to witch more than fifty wells in the dry-land farming and ranching region where the ground water situation is highly uncertain. Occasionally, the Mormon water witch is employed to dowse for the homcsteaders, and the water witch from Homestead has been employed on at least three occasions to dowse for the Mormons.

Water witching is also used by the Spanish-Americans in the area. About fifty years ago there was a practicing Spanish-American dowser, but at present the Spanish-American population does not have its own dowser. Instead, water witches from Homestead or the Mormon community dowse wells.

So far as we can determine, the water-witching pattern is unknown to the Zunis and to most Navahos, and there is no evidence that aboriginal divining techniques—such as Navaho hand-trembling—have ever been used to locate springs or wells. The only exception in the Navaho community is found in the case of three older Navahos who in the 1930s observed the techniques of the Mormon water witch. When the Navahos tried the technique themselves, the witching stick "worked" for only one of the three. This Navaho still claims to be a water witch and reports that he has (on his own initiative) dowsed three wells, two of which produced water, and one of which was a dry hole. The powers of this one Navaho water witch are not generally recognized by others in the Navaho community, and, indeed, he is usually ridiculed when he talks about dowsing. It should be noted that this dowser is the

only one of the local Navahos who has become an earnest convert to Mormonism; he is now an elder in the Mormon church.

The general absence of the pattern among the Zunis and Navahos is partly a matter of history, in that it was not a part of the cultural tradition of these groups as it was in the case of the homesteaders, Mormons, and Spanish-Americans. But it is also partly a matter of geographical situation and the use made of water resources by the Indians. Before the Indian Service began to drill wells for these two tribes, the Navahos depended upon springs, natural water holes, and lakes for water; the Zunis depended upon springs, natural lakes, and the Zuni River. Although both tribes now have wells on their reservations, the problem of locating and drilling the wells is completely in the hands of Indian Service technicians.

There is one interesting case of a highly acculturated Navaho who decided to have his own well drilled. At the suggestion of the Mormon trader, he employed the Mormon water witch and paid him $25 to locate a well. The dowser designated a location with his witching stick and told the Navaho that it would be 12 feet to water. A well driller was then employed, but the only result was a dry hole 400 feet deep which cost the Navaho $1200. The Mormon trader commented, "First time I've seen the water witch miss;" the water witch explained the situation by asserting that "the vein must have dried up," since it was several months after the dowsing took place that the well was drilled. The Navaho is thoroughly disillusioned about the powers of water-diviners.

Our conclusion is that water witching is a ritual pattern which fills the gap between sound rational-technological techniques for coping with the ground water problems and the type of control which rural American farmers feel the need to achieve. The best geological knowledge of ground water resources that is currently available still leaves an area of uncertainty in the task of predicting the exact depth to water at a *given* location in a region with a variable ground water table. The water-witching pattern provides a reassuring mode of response in this uncertain situation.

Thus, although water witching is to be regarded by the scientific observer as a nonempirical means for achieving empirical ends—and is functionally equivalent to the magical practices of nonliterate societies—it is generally viewed as a rational technological procedure by its adherents in rural communities. The technique can, therefore, best be described as a type of "folk science" or "pseudo science" in the rural American cultural tradition. As a body of pseudo-scientific knowledge, the water-witching pattern in our rural farming culture is the same order of phenomena as the pseudo-scientific practices that cluster around situations of uncertainty in other areas of our culture, as, for example, in modern medical practice where there appears to be a pattern of "fashion change" in the use of certain drugs, an irrational "bias" in favor of active surgical intervention in doubtful cases, and a general "optimistic bias" in favor of the soundness of ideas and efficacy of procedures which bolsters self-confidence in uncertain situations.[29]

ENDNOTES

Author's original footnoting has been retained.

[†]Tromp has compiled a bibliography of approximately 700 items on the subject of water divining.[1]

[‡]This theoretical point will be developed in the writer's forthcoming publication on *The Homesteaders: A Study of Value in a Frontier Community.*

[§] Roberts objects to the use of the term "water witch" on the ground that it perpetuates the idea of its association with witchcraft and prefers the term "dowsing." "Dowsing" come from the Cornish word *dowse* and the Middle English word *duschen*, both meaning to strike or to fall. "Rhabdomancy" comes from two Greek words, *Rhabdos* ("rod") and *manteia* ("divination").

[‖]However, there are reputedly differences among dowsers as to the amount of skill they possess. Thus Roberts describes Henry Gross as being a highly skilled dowser.[9] And once a dowser finds that he has the basic ability, it is possible for him to become more skilled with experience. It would be interesting to know the incidence of dowsing skill in the rural population, but no data are yet available. It is worth noting that in the community of Homestead (pop. 250) there is one dowser; and in the nearby Mormon community of Rimrock (pop. 300) there is only one. Neither community has ever been without at least one dowser. For short periods of time there have been tow in each community, but never more than two at any given time.

[¶]Homestead is a fictitious name, used to protect the anonymity of my informants.

[**] The data from Homestead are based upon a year's field experience in the community during 1949–50. Additional data on this community will be provided in the writer's forthcoming monograph on *The Homesteaders.*

[††]I am indebted to Tom O. Meeks for the geological data.

[‡‡]For the signs the homesteaders depend mainly upon *Dr. J. H. McLean's Almanac* (now in its 98th year of publication), which is distributed free through the local stores by the Dr. J. H. McLean Medicine Company, of St. Louis.

[§§]The same sign is used to judge the proper times to wean infants. Other researchers interested in the socialization process in Homestead were startled when the response to their question "When do you wean your babies?" was "I wean them when the sign is right." This would appear to be an aspect of the socialization process in rural America that has not yet been explored.

[¶¶]Personal communication from Kirtley F. Mather, April 10, 1952, as follows: "Although he Tromp claims that the results of his own experiments and those of other qualified scientists indicate 'that divining phenomena are not due to charlatanry and suggestion but really exist,' he also states that 'many diviners make the mistake of claiming that they are able to indicate certain hidden objects, underground ore deposits, water, etc. They fail to realize that many external influences can create the same physiological reaction, similar to readings with modern geophysical instruments, which could be the same under different external conditions.' My conclusion is that Tromp presents no valid evidence that there is any scientific basis other than psychological, for the procedures followed by dowsers in their efforts to locate underground water supplies."

[¶¶]For an answer to the problem of how Henry Gross was able to locate wells in Bermuda by merely dowsing over a map, the reader is referred to Nichol's review of Kenneth Roberts' book on *Henry Gross and his Dowsing Rod.* Briefly, Nichols points out that limestone islands of the Bermuda type have little fresh water, because the limestone is so permeable that the rain water runs through it rapidly and mixes with the salt water. Most of these islands have a thin lens of fresh water floating on salt water, its thickness depending on the size of the island, the permeability of the rock, and the rainfall. The problem is not that there is no fresh water in Bermuda, but that there is not very much. What there is must be developed by a "skimming" process in which wells are dug to or just below sea level and the water is pumped at a rate that will keep its level just above that of the sea, thus preventing salt water from rising into the well. So Henry Gross did not locate "domes" of fresh water in Bermuda (where there was previously nothing but rain water trapped from the runoff of roofs); he merely located wells which reached to lenses of fresh water floating on the salt water.[24]

[***] Mr. Meeks has called my attention to the fact that the Soil Conservation Service maintain only two geologists in the Southwest who give advice on locating wells; hence their visits to any given community are necessarily infrequent.

[*]REFERENCES

1. Tromp, S. W. *Psychical Physics, A Scientific Analysis of Dowsing, Radiesthesia and Kindred Divining Phenomena.* New York: Elsevier (1949).

2. Parsons, T. J. *History of Ideas,* 4, (2), 176 (1944).

3. Kroeber, A. L. *Anthropology.* New York: Harcourt, Brace (1948).

4. Radcliffe-Brown, A. R. *Taboo.* Cambridge: Cambridge Univ. Press (1939).

5. Homans, G. C. *Am. Anthrop.,* 43, (2), 164 (1941).

6. Kluckhohn, C. *Peabody Museum of Harvard University Papers,* 22, (2), (1944).

7. West, J. *Plainville, USA.* New York: Columbia Univ. Press (1945).

8. Taylor, C. C. *Rural Sociology.* New York: Harper (1933).

9. Roberts, K. *Henry Gross and his Dowsing Rod.* Garden City, N.Y.: Doubleday (1951).

10. Latimer, C. *The Divining Rod.* Cleveland: Fairbanks, Benedict (1876).

11. Raymond, R. W. *Am. Inst. Mining Engrs., Trans.,* 11, 415 (1883).

12. Ellis, A. J. *U.S. Geol. Survey Water Supply Paper 416,* Washington, D.C.: GPO (1938).

13. Agricola, Georgius. *De re metallica.* Trans. By H. C. Hoover and L. H. Hoover. London: *Mining Mag.* (1912).

14. Bartlett, W. F. *Prof. Soc. Psychical Research,* 13, 13 (1897).

15. Galien, C. *La découverte des eaux minérales de Chateau-Thierry et de leurs propriétés.* Paris: (1630).

16. Barrett, W. F., and Besterman, T. *The Divining Rod.* London: Methuen (1926).

17. Schott, G. *Magiae universalis naturae et artis, sive recondite naturalium et artificialium rerum scientia,* 4 vols. Herbipoli: 1657–59.

18. Gregory, J. W. *Smithsonian Inst. Annual Rept.* Washington, GD.C.: GPO, 325 (1928).

19. Meeks, T. O. Personal Communication. (Oct. 25, 1952).

20. Richmond, D. M. H. Water Dowsing. Unpub. ms., Dept. Sociol. and Anthrop., Washington Univ. (1951).

21. Finklestein, J. A. Functional Analysis of the Folk-Ritual System in a Small Agricultural Community. Unpub. Honor's thesis, Dept. Social Relations, Harvard Col. (1951).

22. Bailey, W. C. A Study of a Texas Panhandle Community; A Preliminary Report on Cotton Center, Texas. Unpub. ms., Values Study File, Peabody Museum, Harvard Univ. (1951).

23. White, W. N., Broadhurst, W. L., and Lang, J. W. *Ground Water in the High Plains in Texas.* Texas State Board of Water Engrs., prepared in cooperation with U.S. Geol. Survey. Austin (1940).

24. Nichols, H. B. *Sci. Monthly,* 72, 340 (1951).

25. Ongley, P. A. *New Zealand J. Sci. Technol.,* 30, (1), 38 (1948).

26. Meinzer, O. E. *Water Works Eng.,* 97, (11), 571 (1944).

27. Sims, N. LeR. *Elements of Rural Sociology.* New York: Crowell (1929).

28. Kluckhohn, F. *Social Forces,* 28, 376 (1950).

29. Parsons, T. *The Social System.* Glencoe, Ill.: Free Press (1951).

This paper is an indirect outcome of a program of laboratory research on problem solving and social interaction, sponsored by the Office of Naval Research, Group Psychology Branch.

Thanks are due to Alan R. Anderson, Maurice R. Davie, and George P. Murdock, who read preliminary drafts of this paper and made helpful suggestions which were incorporated into the final manuscript.

ASK YOURSELF

Edward Tylor thought that many nonliterate people believed animals, plants, and stones had souls, and he applied the term "animism" to these beliefs, which he considered constituted the earliest religion. Another 19th-century anthropologist, James George Frazer, discussed at length what he called "the worship of nature."

To what extent, in your opinion, are such beliefs different from the beliefs of pro-environmental advocates, like the "tree-huggers" and the Greens? And what would such advocates need to do to convert their beliefs into a religion?

FURTHER READINGS

Geertz, Clifford. "Deep Play: Notes on the Balinese Cockfight." In *The Interpretation of Cultures: Selected Essays.* New York: Basic Books, 1973, pp. 413–53. The cockerel is a prime symbol of masculine values on Bali, and Geertz interprets the most popular Balinese sport—cockfighting—as an expression of the islanders' ethos.

Harris, Marvin. *Cows, Wars, Pigs, and Witches: The Riddles of Culture.* New York: Random House, 1974. The application of the cultural-materialist perspective to ritual and belief is clearly demonstrated in the case studies in this collection. They include discussions on the sacred cow of Hinduism, the great witch craze that afflicted Europe in the 15th, 16th, and 17th centuries, and revitalization movements and their leaders (see Chapter 11). Harris's explanation of the sacred cow ("Mother Cow") is especially worth reading—if only to stir up debate! He argues that an apparently irrational obsession with what, in the Indian context, might seem to be a useless creature is a means whereby believers obtain material benefits essential to their lives.

Lansing, Stephen J. *Priests and Programmers: Technologies of Power in the Engineered Landscape of Bali.* Princeton, N.J.: Princeton University Press, 1991. Expanding on themes graphically portrayed in the video "The Three Worlds of Bali" (see below), Lansing examines the intricate ties that bind water temples, rituals, art, social relationships, and the technical aspects of intensive rice cultivation into one integrated conceptual and practical system.

SUGGESTED VIDEOS

"Dineh Nation: the Navajo Story." For the Navajo of the Sovereign Dineh Indian Reservation (in Arizona, New Mexico, and Utah) the earth ("Mother Earth") is sacred. Religious ideas forbid the Navajo from exploiting Mother Earth's natural resources, but outside agencies are carrying out strip mining and polluting the water. Navajo water wells are drying up, and the land has suffered a uranium spill larger than the Three Mile Island disaster. Thousands of Navajo have been relocated and others fenced off from their sacred land. 26 minutes, $195; Filmakers Library 1996, 124 East 40th Street, New York, NY 10016.

"The Ainu Bear Ceremony." In this ritual a bear nurtured and raised by the Ainu is ceremonially slain, and its flesh and blood are consumed by the participants. This video depicts a series of ritual activities, with commentaries on their meaning. 27 minutes, $119; Film Officer, Royal Anthropological Institute, 50 Fitzroy Street, London W1P 5HS, United Kingdom.

"The People, the Plants, and the Rules." This documentary shows the close relationship between the Pomo, a population living in northern California, and their natural environment, by focusing on the rules and responsibilities by which the Pomo orientate themselves to nature. The central figure is a famous dream weaver and doctor, Mabel McKay. 29 minutes; 1994; $175 (sale), $50 (rental); Catalog #38280. "World Cultures on Film and Video," University of California Extension, Center for Media and Independent Learning, 2000 Center Street, Fourth Floor, Berkeley, CA 94704.

"The Three Worlds of Bali." The total assimilation of Balinese rituals and beliefs into the dynamic fabric of this island society is strikingly apparent in this spectacular portrayal of the temple system, art, and the great ritual of Eka Dasa Rudra, which is performed once every Balinese century to restore the balance between good and evil. 50 minutes (approx.); Odyssey series. The Center for Visual Anthropology, Department of Anthropology, University of Southern California, Los Angeles, CA 90024.

"The Condor And The Bull." Villagers from remote hamlets high in the Andes join people from a roadside village to celebrate Peruvian Independence Day. The ritual requires that a wild condor be captured and pitted against a bull during a bullfight in the town plaza. The film depicts the ritual working out of power relations between villagers and highlanders, and shows the relationship of both to the Peruvian state. Filmmakers: Peter Getzels & Harriet Gordon. Anthropologists: Penny Harvey & Peter Getzels. Color, 56 minutes, 1990. Film Officer, Royal Anthropological Institute (RAI), 50 Fitzroy Street, London W1P 5HS, United Kingdom.

The blending of elements from two or more cultural traditions into a single new one is called *syncretism*. In Zimbabwe, southern Africa, followers of a syneretic religion combining Christianity with traditional animistic beliefs pray together in the rocky, uninhabited terrain outside the capital, Harare.

Photo courtesy of Margaret A. Gwynne

CHAPTER 11

AGENTS OF CHANGE

As I remarked in the Introduction, Max Weber is one of the two great figures in sociology, and in this chapter each reading can be studied to better effect if we have some idea of what Weber was trying to do. Recall that whereas Emile Durkheim favored a static approach to the study of society, Max Weber was willing to give social change its due weight. Further, although both great sociologists were interested in the interaction of ideas and social institutions, Durkheim's concept of "collective representations" was elaborated within the context of stable societies. Weber did not chose to ignore the fact that collective ideas and institutions could, and did, change in the course of time. This chapter deals with the part religious ideas play in social change, with each of the readings encouraging discussion of this association.

Max Weber's own reading (11–1) underscores the connection between religious ideas and social change, and it provides us with a direct avenue to the ideas contained in one of the most discussed books in sociology, his *The Protestant Ethic and the Spirit of Capitalism.* In it he argues that the rise of capitalism was stimulated by a two ideas—formalized as doctrines fundamental to Calvinism, one of the earliest branches of Christianity that emerged from the Reformation in sixteenth century Europe. These were the "calling" (or "vocation") and "predestination," and both were adopted by Protestant sects influenced by Calvinism. The most notable among these were the Puritans. Now, the traditional view held by the Catholic Church had been that the primary route to condition of holiness was through removing oneself from the world and becoming a religious recluse, like a monk. But Calvinism contended that attaining holiness came through remaining in the world and dedicating one's daily labors to god's service. While advancing himself materially the individual was working to bring about god's kingdom on earth (Anker 1999:46).

Predestination was the belief that before he ever created humanity God had already chosen those who would be saved. These were his "elect." God had not, however, announced who its members were, and in Weber's view, the Puritans felt they needed to know. So "Puritans supposedly searched for some outward empirical sign, a tangible proof, of divine hope and favor that would confirm their hope of salvation" (Anker 1999:47). That objective proof, Weber claimed, was wealth. Wealth was proof of divine favor. With this conviction enshrined as a dogma Puritans had the incentive to work hard (the famous Protestant "work ethic") and with innovative flair to acquire both wealth and the holiness it indicated. In this way a pair of religious ideas ("calling" and "predestination") had encouraged a great socioeconomic innovation called "capitalism."

Weber's thesis is among the most contested in the sociology of religion. Advocates assert Weber succeeded in identifying a convincing link between concepts; skeptics argue that capitalism and Puritanism have no necessary connection. Irrespective of its validity, however, this insight offers a healthy diachronic antidote to the Durkheimian insistence on the synchronic approach, and Weber demonstrated that scholars could say interesting things about religion as a dynamic force in a changing society.

The other three readings reveal the dynamics of such changes in operation in the form of revitalization movements, which are popular movements for radical change, often spearheaded by the charismatic figure of the prophet (see Chapter 5), and provoked by social, economic, and political upheavals. In periods of traumatic deprivation, a population may sometimes find solace in the notion that the time is approaching when their most earnestly wished-for desires will be satisfied, and revitalization may take the form of a *millenarian movement*. Such movements have often emerged in Melanesia, where they are known locally as *cargo cults*. Revitalization movements frequently fail, and this is largely because they are so often based on unrealistic expectations, so that with the intrusion of reality its adherents come to realize what they have anticipated is never going to happen, and the movement collapses. So, too, of course, does its prophet's influence. Nevertheless, some revitalization movements, such as the Church of Jesus Christ of the Latter-day Saints, do succeed, and find a resurgence of commitment and continuity of purpose.

Even in less turbulent times that affect much of society, disaffection with the status quo may emerge and galvanize individuals and groups into challenging the prevailing ritual orthodoxy. In North America and Europe such movements are commonly known as sects, new religious movements, or cults. These constitute the topic of the following chapter.

READING 11–1

JUDAISM, CHRISTIANITY, AND THE SOCIO-ECONOMIC ORDER

Max Weber

Max Weber's interest in the dynamic interplay of ideas and socioeconomic change comes across clearly in the contrast he makes between Judaism and Christianity, particularly Puritanism and Catholicism, in this reading. Weber argues that the "pariah" status of orthodox Judaism inhibited Jews from playing the sort of role Puritans did in the Industrial Revolution in 18th - century Europe. The religious ideals of the Puritan businessman could be adequately attained in his daily commercial enterprises, and his successes were a sign that God appreciated his merits. In contrast, the orthodox Jew's scrupulous adherence to the Law was his primary pursuit, while commercial success was little more than a sign God was not displeased with his activities. The revolution effected by Paul, Jesus' successor, was to break the hold the Law exercised over orthodox Judaism and make it possible for Jews, by converting to Christianity, to escape their pariah condition.

Judaism, in its postexilic and particularly its Talmudic form, belongs among those religions that are in some sense accommodated to the world. Judaism

Source: "Judaism, Christianity, and the Socio-Economic Order" from *The Sociology of Religion* by Max Weber © 1956 by J. C. B. Mohr (Paul Siebeck). English translation by Ephraim Fischoff © 1963, 1991 by Beacon Press. Reprinted by permission of Beacon Press, Boston.

is at least oriented to the world in the sense that it does not reject the world as such but only rejects the prevailing system of social classes in the world.

We have already made some observations concerning the total sociological structure and attitude of Judaism. Its religious promises, in the customary meaning of the word, apply to this world, and any notions of contemplative or ascetic world-flight are as rare in Judaism as in Chinese religion and in Protestantism. Judaism differs from Puritanism only in the relative (as always) absence of systematic asceticism. The ascetic elements of the early Christian religion did not derive from Judaism, but emerged primarily in the heathen Christian communities of the Pauline mission. There is as little justification for equating the observance of the Jewish law with asceticism as for equating it with the fulfillment of any ritual or tabooistic norms.

Moreover, the relationship of the Jewish religion to both wealth and sexual indulgence is not in the least ascetic, but rather highly naturalistic. For wealth was regarded as a gift of God, and the satisfaction of the sexual impulse—naturally in the prescribed legal form—was thought to be so imperative that the Talmud actually regarded a person who had remained unmarried after a certain age as morally suspect. The interpretation of marriage as an economic institution for the production and rearing of children is universal and has nothing specifically Jewish about it. Judaism's strict prohibition of illegitimate sexual intercourse, a prohibition that was highly effective among the pious, was also found in Islam and all other prophetic religions, as well as in Hinduism. Moreover, the majority of ritualistic religions shared with Judaism the institution of periods of abstention from sexual relations for purposes of purification. For these reasons, it is not possible to speak of an idiosyncratic emphasis upon sexual asceticism in Judaism. The sexual regulations cited by Sombart do not go as far as the Catholic casuistry of the seventeenth century and in any case have analogies in many other casuistical systems of taboo.

Nor did Judaism forbid the uninhibited enjoyment of life or even of luxury as such, provided that the positive prohibitions and taboos of the law were observed. The denunciation of wealth in the prophetic books, the Psalms, the Wisdom Literature, and subsequent writings was evoked by the social injustices which were so frequently perpetrated against fellow Jews in connection with the acquisition of wealth and in violation of the spirit of the Mosaic law. Wealth was also condemned in response to arrogant disregard of the commandments and promises of God and in response to the rise of temptations to laxity in religious observance. To escape the temptations of wealth is not easy, but is for this reason all the more meritorious. "Hail to the man of wealth who has been found to be blameless." Moreover, since Judaism possessed no doctrine of predestination and no comparable idea producing the same ethical effects, incessant labor and success in business life could not be regarded or interpreted in the sense of certification, which appears most strongly among the Calvinist Puritans and which is found to some extent in all ascetic Protestant religions, as shown in John Wesley's remark on this point. Of course a certain tendency to regard success in one's economic activity as a sign of God's gracious direction existed in the religion of the Jews, as in the religions of the Chinese and the lay Buddhists and generally in every religion that has not turned its back upon the world. This view was especially likely to be manifested by a religion like Judaism, which had before it very specific promises of a transcendental God together with very visible signs of this God's indignation against the people he had chosen. It is clear that any success achieved in one's economic activities while keeping the commandments of God could be, and indeed had to be, interpreted as a sign that one was personally acceptable to God. This actually occurred again and again.

But the situation of the pious Jew engaged in business was altogether different from that of the Puritan, and this difference remained of practical significance for the role of Judaism in the history of economics. Let us now consider what this role has been. In the polemic against Sombart's book, one fact could not be seriously questioned, namely that

Judaism played a conspicuous role in the evolution of the modern capitalistic system. However, this thesis of Sombart's book needs to be made more precise. What were the *distinctive* economic achievements of Judaism in the Middle Ages and in modern times? We can easily list: moneylending, from pawnbroking to the financing of great states; certain types of commodity business, particularly retailing, peddling, and produce trade of a distinctively rural type; certain branches of wholesale business; and brokerage, above all the brokerage of stocks. To this list of Jewish economic achievements should be added: money-changing; money-forwarding or check-cashing, which normally accompanies money-changing; the financing of state agencies, wars, and the establishment of colonial enterprises; tax-farming, naturally excluding the collection of prohibited taxes such as those directed to the Romans; banking; credit; and the floating of bond issues. But of all these businesses only a few, though very important ones, display the legal and economic forms characteristic of modern occidental capitalism in contrast to the forms characteristic of commerce in ancient times, the Middle Ages, and the earlier period in Eastern Asia. The distinctively modern legal forms include stock corporations and business organizations, but these are not of specifically Jewish provenience. The Jews may have introduced these forms into the Occident, but the forms themselves have a common oriental (probably Babylonian) origin, and their influence on the Occident was mediated through Hellenistic and Byzantine sources. In any event they were common to both the Jews and the Arabs. It is even true that the specifically modern forms of these institutions were in part occidental and medieval creations, with some specifically German infusions of influence. To adduce detailed proof of this here would take us too far afield. However, it can be said by way of example that the exchange, as a "market of tradesmen," was created not by Jews but by Christian merchants. Again, the particular manner in which medieval legal regulations were adapted to make possible rationalized economic enterprises (e.g., limited liability companies; privileged companies of all types—*Kommanditen, Maonen, privilegierte Kompagnien aller Art;* and stock companies) was not at all dependent on specifically Jewish influences, no matter how large a part Jews played in the formation of such rationalized economic enterprises. Finally, it must be noted that the characteristically modern principles of public and private financing first arose in nuce on the soil of the medieval city. Only later were the medieval legal forms of finance, which were quite un-Jewish in certain respects, adapted to the economic needs of modern states and other modern recipients of credit.

Above all, one element particularly characteristic of modern capitalism was strikingly—and perhaps completely—missing from the extensive list of Jewish economic activities. This was the organization of industrial production (*gewerbliche Arbeit*) or manufacturing in domestic industry and in the factory system. How does one explain the fact that no pious Jew succeeded in establishing an industry employing pious Jewish workers of the ghetto (as so many pious Puritan entrepreneurs had done with devout Christian workers and artisans) at times when numerous proletarians were present in the ghettos, princely patents and privileges for the establishment of any sort of industry were available for a financial remuneration, and areas of industrial activity uncontrolled by guild monopoly were open? Again, how does one explain the fact that no modern and distinctively industrial bourgeoisie of any significance emerged among the Jews to employ the Jewish workers available for home industry, despite the presence of numerous impecunious artisan groups at almost the threshold of the modern period?

All over the world, for several millennia, the characteristic forms of the capitalist employment of wealth have been state-provisioning, the financing of states, tax-farming, the financing of military colonies, the establishment of great plantations, trade, and moneylending. One finds these again and again. One finds Jews involved in just these activities, found at all times and places but especially characteristic of antiquity, as well as involved in those specifically modern legal and organizational forms of economic activity which were evolved by the Middle Ages and not by the Jews. On the other hand, the Jews were relatively or altogether absent from the new and distinctive forms of modern capitalism, the rational organization of labor, especially production in an industrial enterprise of the factory type. The Jews evinced the ancient and medieval business temper which had been and remained typical of all primitive traders, whether small businessmen or large-scale moneylenders, in antiquity, the Far East, India, the Mediterranean littoral area, and the Occident of the Middle Ages: the will and the wit to employ mercilessly every chance of profit, "for the sake of profit to ride through Hell even if it singes the sails." But this temper is far from distinctive of modern capitalism, as distinguished from the capitalism of other eras. Precisely the reverse is true. Hence, neither that which is new in the modern economic *system* nor that which is distinctive of the modern economic *temper* is specifically Jewish in origin.

The ultimate theoretical reasons for this fact, that the distinctive elements of modern capitalism originated and developed quite apart from the Jews, are to be found in the peculiar character of the Jews as a pariah people and in the idiosyncracy of their religion. Their pariah status presented purely external difficulties impeding their participation in the organization of industrial labor. The legally and factually precarious position of the Jews hardly permitted continuous, systematic, and rationalized industrial enterprise with fixed capital, but only trade and above all dealing in money. Also of fundamental importance was the subjective ethical situation of the Jews. As a pariah people, they retained the double standard of morals which is characteristic of primordial economic practice in all communities: what is prohibited in relation to one's brothers is permitted in relation to strangers. It is unquestionable that the Jewish ethic was thoroughly traditionalistic in demanding of Jews an attitude of sustenance toward fellow Jews. As Sombart correctly notes, the rabbis made concessions in these matters, even in regard to business associations with fellow Jews, but these remained nothing

more than concessions to laxity, with those who resorted to the employment of these concessions remaining far behind the highest requirements of Jewish business ethics. In any case, it is certain that economic behavior was not the realm in which a Jew could demonstrate his religious merit.

However, for the Jews the realm of economic relations with strangers, particularly economic relations prohibited in regard to fellow Jews, was an area of ethical indifference. This is of course the primordial economic ethics of all peoples everywhere. That this should have remained the Jewish economic ethic was a foregone conclusion, for even in antiquity the Jews almost always regarded strangers as enemies. All the well-known admonitions of the rabbis enjoining honor and faithfulness toward Gentiles could not change the impression that the religious law prohibited taking usury from fellow Jews but permitted it in transactions with non-Jews. Nor could the rabbinical counsels enjoining honesty and reliability in dealing with Gentiles alter the fact, which again Sombart has rightly stressed, that a lesser degree of legality was required by the law in dealing with a stranger, i.e., an enemy, than in dealing with another Jew, in such a matter as taking advantage of an error made by the other party. In fine, no proof is required to establish that the pariah condition of the Jews, which we have seen resulted from the promises of Yahweh, and the resulting incessant humiliation of the Jews by Gentiles necessarily led to the Jewish people's retaining different economic moralities for its relations with strangers and with fellow Jews.

Let us summarize the respective situations in which Catholics, Jews, and Protestants found themselves in regard to economic enterprises. The devout Catholic, as he went about his economic affairs, found himself continually behaving—or on the verge of behaving—in a manner that transgressed papal injunctions. His economic behavior could be ignored in the confessional only on the principle of *rebus sic stantibus,* and it could be permissible only on the basis of a lax, probabilistic morality. To a certain extent, therefore, the life of business itself had to be regarded as reprehensible or, at best, as not positively favorable to God. The inevitable result of this Catholic situation was that pious Jews were encouraged to perform economic activities among Christians which if performed among Jews would have been regarded by the Jewish community as unequivocally contrary to the law or at least as suspect from the point of view of Jewish tradition. At best these transactions were permissible on the basis of a lax interpretation of the Judaic religious code, and then only in economic relations with strangers. Never were they infused with positive ethical value. Thus, the Jew's economic conduct appeared to be permitted by God, in the absence of any formal contradiction with the religious law of the Jews, but ethically indifferent, in view of such conduct's correspondence with the average evils in the society's economy. This is the basis of whatever factual truth there was in the observations concerning the inferior standard of economic legality among Jews. That God crowned such economic activity with success could be a sign to the Jewish businessman that he had done nothing clearly objectionable or prohibited in this area and that indeed he had held fast to God's commandments in other areas. But it would still have been difficult for the Jew to demonstrate his ethical merit by means of characteristically modern business behavior.

But this was precisely the case with the pious Puritan. He could demonstrate his religious merit through his economic activity because he did nothing ethically reprehensible, he did not resort to any lax interpretations of religious codes or to systems of double moralities, and he did not act in a manner that could be indifferent or even reprehensible in the general realm of ethical validity. On the contrary, the Puritan could demonstrate his religious merit precisely in his economic activity. He acted in business with the best possible conscience, since through his rationalistic and legal behavior in his business activity he was factually objectifying the rational methodology of his total life pattern. He legitimated his ethical pattern in his own eyes, and indeed within the circle of his community, by the extent to which the absolute—not relativized—

unassailability of his economic conduct remained beyond question. No really pious Puritan—and this is the crucial point—could have regarded as pleasing to God any profit derived from usury, exploitation of another's mistake (which was permissible to the Jew), haggling and sharp dealing, or participation in political or colonial exploitation. Quakers and Baptists believed their religious merit to be certified before all mankind by such practices as their fixed prices and their absolutely reliable business relationships with everyone, unconditionally legal and devoid of cupidity. Precisely such practices promoted the irreligious to trade with them rather than with their own kind, and to entrust their money to the trust companies or limited liability enterprises of the religious sectarians rather than those of their own people—all of which made the religious sectarians wealthy, even as their business practices certified them before their God.

By contrast, the Jewish law applying to strangers, which in practice was the pariah law of the Jews, enabled them, notwithstanding innumerable reservations, to engage in dealings with non-Jews which the Puritans rejected violently as showing the cupidity of the trader. Yet the pious Jew could combine such an attitude with strict legality, with complete fulfillment of the law, with all the inwardness of his religion, with the most sacrificial love for his family and community, and indeed with pity and mercy toward all God's creatures. For in view of the operation of the laws regarding strangers, Jewish piety never in actual practice regarded the realm of permitted economic behavior as one in which the genuineness of a person's obedience to God's commandments could be demonstrated. The pious Jew never gauged his inner ethical standards by what he regarded as permissible in the economic context. Just as the Confucian's authentic ideal of life was the gentleman who had undergone a comprehensive education in ceremonial esthetics and literature and who devoted lifelong study to the classics, so the Jew set up as his ethical ideal the scholar learned in law and casuistry, the intellectual who continuously immersed himself in the sacred writings and commentaries at the expense of his business, which he very frequently left to the management of his wife.

It was this intellectualist trait of authentic late Judaism, with its preoccupation with literary scholarship, that Jesus criticized. His criticism was not motivated by the proletarian instincts which some have attributed to him, but rather by his type of piety and his type of obedience to the law, both of which were appropriate to the rural artisan or the inhabitant of a small town, and constituted his basic opposition to the virtuosi of legalistic lore who had grown up on the soil of the *polis* of Jerusalem. Members of such urban legalistic circles asked "What good can come out of Nazareth?"—the kind of question that might have been posed by any dweller of a metropolis in the classical world. Jesus' knowledge of the law and his observance of it was representative of that average lawfulness which was actually demonstrated by men engaged in practical work, who could not afford to let their sheep lie in wells, even on the Sabbath. On the other hand, the knowledge of the law obligatory for the really pious Jews, as well as their legalistic education of the young, surpassed both quantitatively and qualitatively the preoccupation with the Bible characteristic of the Puritans. The scope of religious law of which knowledge was obligatory for the pious Jew may be compared only with the scope of ritual laws among the Hindus and Persians, but the Jewish law far exceeded these in its inclusion of ethical prescriptions as well as merely ritual and tabooistic norms.

The economic behavior of the Jews simply moved in the direction of least resistance which was permitted them by these legalistic ethical norms. This meant in practice that the acquisitive drive, which is found in varying degrees in all groups and nations, was here directed primarily to trade with strangers, who were usually regarded as enemies. Even at the time of Josiah and certainly in the exilic period, the pious Jew was an urban dweller, and the entire Jewish law was oriented to this urban status. Since the orthodox Jew required the services of a ritual slaughterer, he had necessarily to live in a community rather than in isolation. Even today, urban residence is characteristic of orthodox Jews

when they are contrasted with Jews of the Reform group, as for example in the United States. Similarly, the Sabbatical year, which in its present form is certainly a product of postexilic urban scholars learned in the law, made it impossible for Jews to carry on systematic intensive cultivation of the land. Even at the present time,[*] German rabbis endeavor to apply the prescription of the Sabbatical year to Zionist colonization in Palestine, which would be ruined thereby. In the age of the Pharisees a rustic Jew was of second rank, since he did not and could not observe the law strictly. Jewish law also prohibited the participation of Jews in the procedures of the guilds, particularly participation in commensality with non-Jews, although in antiquity as well as in the Middle Ages commensality was the indispensable foundation for any kind of integration or naturalization (*Einbürgerung*) in the surrounding world. But the Jewish institution of the dowry, common to the Orient and based originally on the exclusion of daughters from inheritance, favored the establishing of the Jewish groom at marriage as a small merchant; and indeed, the custom still tends toward this result. Traces of this phenomenon are still apparent in the relatively undeveloped class consciousness of Jewish apprentices.

In all his other dealings, as well as those we have just discussed, the Jew—like the pious Hindu—was controlled by scruples concerning his law. As Guttmann has correctly emphasized, genuine study of the law could be combined most easily with the occupation of moneylending, which requires relatively little continuous labor. The outcome of Jewish legalism and intellectualist education was the Jew's methodical patterning of life and his rationalism. It is a prescription of the Talmud that "A man must never change a practice." Only in the realm of economic relationships with strangers, and in no other area of life, did tradition leave a sphere of behavior that was relatively indifferent ethically. Indeed, the entire domain of things relevant before God was determined by tradition and the systematic

---

[*][Before World War I. Translator's note.]

casuistry concerned with its interpretation, rather than determined by rational purposes derived from laws of nature and oriented without further presupposition to methodical plans of individual action (*nicht ein rational voraussetsungslos, aus einem "Naturrecht" heraus, selbstorientiertes methodisches Zweckhandeln*). The tendency of scrupulosity before the law to develop rationalization is thoroughly pervasive but entirely indirect.

Self-control—usually accompanied by alertness, equableness, and serenity—was found among Confucians, Puritans, Buddhists and other types of monks, Arab sheiks, and Roman senators, as well as among Jews. But the basis and significance of self-control were different in each case. The alert self-control of the Puritan flowed from the necessity of his subjugating all creaturely impulses to a rational and methodical plan of conduct, so that he might secure his certainty of his own salvation. Self-control appeared to the Confucian as a personal necessity which followed from his disesteem for plebeian irrationality, the disesteem of an educated gentleman who had received classical training and had been bred along lines of honor and dignity. On the other hand, the self-control of the devout Jew of ancient times was a consequence of the preoccupation with the law in which his mind had been trained, and of the necessity of his continuous concern with the law's precise fulfillment. The pious Jew's self-control received a characteristic coloring and effect from the situation of being piously engaged in fulfilling the law. The Jew felt that only he and his people possessed this law, for which reason the world persecuted them and imposed degradation upon them. Yet this law was binding; and one day, by an act that might come suddenly at any time but that no one could accelerate, God would transform the social structure of the world, creating a messianic realm for those who had remained faithful to his law. The pious Jew knew that innumerable generations had awaited this messianic event, despite all mockery, and were continuing to await it. This produced in the pious Jew an excessive feeling of alertness. But since it remained necessary for him

to continue waiting in vain, he nurtured his feelings of self-esteem by a meticulous observance of the law for its own sake. Last but not least, the pious Jew had always to stay on guard, never permitting himself the free expression of his passions against powerful and merciless enemies. This repression was inevitably combined with the aforementioned feeling of *ressentiment* which resulted from Yahweh's promises and the unparalleled history of his people who had sinned against him.

These circumstances basically determined the rationalism of Judaism, but this is not "asceticism" in our sense. To be sure, there are ascetic traits in Judaism, but they are not central. Rather, they are by-products of the law, which have arisen in part from the peculiar problem-complex of Jewish piety. In any case, ascetic traits are of secondary importance in Judaism, as are any mystical traits developed within this religion. We need say nothing more here about Jewish mysticism, since neither cabalism, Chassidism nor any of its other forms—whatever symtomatic importance they held for Jews—produced any significant motivations toward practical behavior in the economic sphere.

The ascetic aversion of pious Jews toward everything esthetic was originally based on the second commandment of the Decalogue, which actually prevented the once well-developed angelology of the Jews from assuming artistic form. But another important cause of aversion to things esthetic is the purely pedagogic and jussive character of the divine service in the synagogue, even as it was practiced in the Diaspora, long before the disruption of the Temple cult. Even at that time, Hebrew prophecy had virtually removed plastic elements from the cult, effectively extirpating orgiastic, orchestral, and terpsichorean activities. It is of interest that Roman religion and Puritanism pursued similar paths in regard to esthetic elements, though for reasons quite different from the Jewish reasons. Thus, among the Jews the plastic arts, painting, and drama lacked those points of contact with religion which were elsewhere quite normal. This is the reason for the marked diminution of secular lyricism and especially of the erotic sublimation of sexuality, when contrasted with the marked sensuality of the earlier Song of Solomon. The basis of all this is to be found in the naturalism of the Jewish ethical treatment of sexuality.

All these traits of Judaism are characterized by one overall theme: that the mute, faithful, and questioning expectation of a redemption from the hellish character of the life enforced upon the people who had been chosen by God (and definitely chosen, despite their present status) was ultimately refocused upon the ancient promises and laws of the religion. Conversely, it was held—although there are no corresponding utterances of the rabbis on this point—that any uninhibited surrender to the artistic or poetic glorification of this world is completely vain and apt to divert the Jews from the ways and purposes of God. Even the purpose of the creation of this world had already on occasion been problematic to the Jews of the later Maccabean period.

Above all, what was lacking in Judaism was the decisive hallmark of that inner-worldly type of asceticism which is directed toward the control of this world: an integrated relationship to the world from the point of view of the individual's proof of salvation (*certitudo salutis*), which proof in conduct nurtures all else. Again in this important matter, what was ultimately decisive for Judaism was the pariah character of the religion and the promises of Yahweh. An ascetic management of this world, such as that characteristic of Calvinism, was the very last thing of which a traditionally pious Jew would have thought. He could not think of methodically controlling the present world, which was so topsy-turvy because of Israel's sins, and which could not be set right by any human action but only by some free miracle of God that could not be hastened. He could not take as his "mission," as the sphere of his religious "vocation," the bringing of this world and its very sins under the rational norms of the revealed divine will, for the glory of God and as an identifying mark of his own salvation. The pious Jew had a far more difficult inner destiny to overcome than did the Puritan, who could be certain of his election to the world beyond. It was incumbent upon the individual Jew to make peace with

the fact that the world would remain recalcitrant to the promises of God as long as God permitted the world to stand as it is. The Jew's responsibility was to make peace with this recalcitrancy of the world, while finding contentment if God sent him grace and success in his dealings with the enemies of his people, toward whom he must act soberly and legalistically, in fulfillment of the injunctions of the rabbis. This meant acting toward non-Jews in an objective or impersonal manner, without love and without hate, solely in accordance with what was permissible.

The frequent assertion that Judaism required only an external observance of the law is incorrect. Naturally, this is the average tendency; but the requirements for real religious piety stood on a much higher plane. In any case, Judaic law fostered in its adherents a tendency to compare individual actions with each other and to compute the net result of them all. This conception of man's relationship to God as a bookkeeping operation of single good and evil acts with an uncertain total (a conception which may occasionally be found among the Puritans as well) may not have been the dominant official view of Judaism. Yet it was sufficient, together with the double-standard morality of Judaism, to prevent the development within Judaism of a methodical and ascetic orientation to the conduct of life on the scale that such an orientation developed in Puritanism. It is also important that in Judaism, as in Catholicism, the individual's activities in fulfilling particular religious injunctions were tantamount to his assuring his own chances of salvation. However, in both Judaism and Catholicism, God's grace was needed to supplement human inadequacy, although this dependence upon God's grace was not as universally recognized in Judaism as in Catholicism.

The ecclesiastical provision of grace was much less developed in Judaism, after the decline of the older Palestinian confessional, than in Catholicism. In practice, this resulted in the Jew's having a greater religious responsibility for himself. This responsibility for oneself and the absence of any mediating religious personality necessarily made the Jewish pattern of life more systematic and personally responsible than the corresponding Catholic pattern of life. Still, the methodical control of life was limited in Judaism by the absence of the distinctively ascetic motivation characteristic of Puritans and by the continued presence of Jewish internal morality's traditionalism, which in principle remained unbroken. To be sure, there were present in Judaism numerous single stimuli toward practices that might be called ascetic, but the unifying force of a basically ascetic religious motivation was lacking. The highest form of Jewish piety is found in the religious mood (*Stimmung*) and not in active behavior. How could it be possible for the Jew to feel that by imposing a new rational order upon the world he would become the human executor of God's will, when for the Jew this world was thoroughly contradictory, hostile, and—as he had known since the time of Hadrian—impossible to change by human action? This might have been possible for the Jewish freethinker, but not for the pious Jew.

Puritanism always felt its inner similarity to Judaism, but also felt the limits of this similarity. The similarity in principle between Christianity and Judaism, despite all their differences, remained the same for the Puritans as it had been for the Christian followers of Paul. Both the Puritans and the pristine Christians saw the Jews as the people who had once and for all been chosen by God. But the unexampled activities of Paul had the following significant effects for early Christianity. On the one hand, Paul made the sacred book of the Jews into one of the sacred books of the Christians, and at the beginning the only one. He thereby erected a stout fence against all intrusions of Greek, especially Gnostic, intellectualism, as Wernle in particular has pointed out. But on the other hand, by the aid of a dialectic that only a rabbi could possess, Paul here and there broke through what was most distinctive and effective in the Jewish law, namely the tabooistic norms and the unique messianic promises. Since these taboos and promises linked the whole religious worth of the Jews to their pariah position, Paul's breakthrough was fateful in its effect. Paul

accomplished this breakthrough by interpreting these promises as having been partly fulfilled and partly abrogated by the birth of Christ. He triumphantly employed the highly impressive proof that the patriarchs of Israel had lived in accordance with God's will long before the issuance of the Jewish taboos and messianic promises, showing that they found blessedness through faith, which was the surety of God's election.

The dynamic power behind the incomparable missionary labors of Paul was his offer to the Jews of a tremendous release, the release provided by the consciousness of having escaped the fate of pariah status. A Jew could henceforth be a Greek among Greeks as well as a Jew among Jews, and could achieve this within the paradox of faith rather than through an enlightened hostility to religion. This was the passionate feeling of liberation brought by Paul. The Jew could actually free himself from the ancient promises of his God, by placing his faith in the new savior who had believed himself abandoned upon the cross by that very God.

Various consequences flowed from this rending of the sturdy chains that had bound the Jews firmly to their pariah position. One was the intense hatred of this one man Paul by the Jews of the Diaspora, sufficiently authenticated as fact. Among the other consequences may be mentioned the oscillations and utter uncertainty of the pristine Christian community; the attempt of James and the "pillar apostles" to establish an ethical minimum of law which would be valid and binding for all, in harmony with Jesus' own layman's understanding of the law; and finally, the open hostility of the Jewish Christians toward Judaism. In every line that Paul wrote we can feel his overpowering joy at having emerged from the hopeless "slave law" into freedom, through the blood of the Messiah. The overall consequence was the possibility of a Christian world mission.

The Puritans, like Paul, rejected the Talmudic law and even the characteristic ritual laws of the Old Testament, while taking over and considering as binding—for all their elasticity—various other expressions of God's will witnessed in the Old Testament. As the Puritans took these over, they always conjoined norms derived from the New Testament, even in matters of detail. The Jews who were actually welcomed by Puritan nations, especially the Americans, were not pious orthodox Jews but rather Reformed Jews who had abandoned orthodoxy, Jews such as those of the present time who have been trained in the Educational Alliance, and finally baptized Jews. These groups of Jews were at first welcomed without any ado whatsoever and are even now welcomed fairly readily, so that they have been absorbed to the point of the absolute loss of any trace of difference. This situation in Puritan countries contrasts with the situation in Germany, where the Jews remain—even after long generations—"assimilated Jews." These phenomena clearly manifest the actual kinship of Puritanism to Judaism. Yet precisely the non-Jewish element in Puritanism enabled Puritanism to play its special role in the creation of the modern economic temper, and also to carry through the aforementioned absorption of Jewish proselytes, which was not accomplished by nations with other than Puritan orientations.

READING 11–2

REVITALIZATION MOVEMENTS

Anthony F. C. Wallace

In this reading—another article that has achieved the status of a classic in the anthropological literature—Anthony F. C. Wallace follows the lead of Max Weber rather than Emile Durkheim. Here we see Wallace examining the dynamic force contained within rituals and beliefs, and at the same time, taking seriously the role of the individual in bringing about religious changes. This

Source: Anthony F. C. Wallace, "Revitalization Movements." Reproduced by permission of the American Anthropological Association from *American Anthropologist* 58:2, 1956. Not for further reproduction.

he does through his study of charismatic figures. Wallace's main intention is to identity important attributes of revitalization movements and classify them into six basic categories: nativistic, revivalistic, cargo cults, vitalistic, millenarian, and messianic. These six categories are formulated within a framework he calls "the processual structure," and as a set they offer an enlightening model for understanding how religious movements arise, take hold, and decline. Social reality, however, is too messy to fit tidily into neat categories and as Wallace himself recognizes, these categories are not exclusive. As with the classification of religious practitioners (see Chapter 5) an attribute that helps define one category may also contribute to the definition of another, so though convenient as a provisional overview of these movements, Wallace's classification has to be used with care.

INTRODUCTION

Behavioral scientists have described many instances of attempted and sometimes successful innovation of whole cultural systems, or at least substantial portions of such systems. Various rubrics are employed, the rubric depending on the discipline and the theoretical orientation of the researcher, and on salient local characteristics of the cases he has chosen for study. "Nativistic movement," "reform movement," "cargo cult," "religious revival," "messianic movement," "utopian community," "sect formation," "mass movement," "social movement," "revolution," "charismatic movement," are some of the commonly used labels. This paper suggests that all these phenomena of major cultural-system innovation are characterized by a uniform process, for which I propose the term "revitalization." The body of the paper is devoted to two ends: (1) an introductory statement of the concept of revitalization, and (2) an outline of certain uniformly-found processual dimensions of revitalization movements.

The formulations are based in major part on documentary data, mostly published. Library research on the project began in 1951 with a study of the new religion initiated by Handsome Lake, the Seneca prophet, among the nineteenth century reservation

Iroquois. The Handsome Lake materials being unusually ample (a number of manuscript journals and diaries were found) provided a useful standard with which to compare the various other movements which have since been investigated. Our files now contain references to several hundred religious revitalization movements, among both western and non-western peoples, on five continents. These represent only a small portion, gathered in a quick preliminary survey of anthropological literature. An earnest attempt to collect all revitalization movements described in historical, anthropological, and other sorts of documents, would without question gather in thousands. Movements on which we have substantial data include: in North America, the Handsome Lake case (Seneca, 1799–1815), the Delaware Prophet (associated with Pontiac, 1762–1765), the Shawnee Prophet (associated with Tecumseh, 1805–1814), the Ghost Dance (1888–1896), and Peyote; in Europe, John Wesley and early Methodism (1738–1800); in Africa, Ikhnaton's new religion (ancient Egypt), the Sudanese Mahdi (the Sudan, 1880–1898), and the Xosa Revival (South Africa, 1856–1857); in Asia, the origin of Christianity, the origin of Mohammedanism (c610–650), the early development of Sikhism (India, c1500–c1700), and the Taiping Rebellion (China, 1843–1864); in Melanesia, the Vailala Madness (New Guinea, c1919–c1930); in South America, a series of terre sans mal movements among the forest tribes, from early contact to recent times.[1]

Accordingly, the formulations presented here are in an intermediate stage: a species has been recognized and certain characteristics (selected, of course, in the light of the author's theoretical interests) described, after the fashion of natural history. More abstract descriptions, in terms of the interaction of analytic variables, can only be suggested here, and other papers will present details of the dynamics of the revitalization process.

THE CONCEPT OF REVITALIZATION

A revitalization movement is defined as a deliberate, organized, conscious effort by members of a society to construct a more satisfying culture. Revitalization is thus, from a cultural standpoint, a special kind of culture change phenomenon: the persons involved in the process of revitalization must perceive their culture, or some major areas of it, as a system (whether accurately or not); they must feel that this cultural system is unsatisfactory; and they must innovate not merely discrete items, but a new cultural system, specifying new relationships as well as, in some cases, new traits. The classic processes of culture change (evolution, drift, diffusion, historical change, acculturation) all produce changes in cultures as systems; however, they do not depend on deliberate intent by members of a society, but rather on a gradual chain-reaction effect: introducing A induces change in B; changing B affects C; when C shifts, A is modified; this involves D . . . and so on *ad infinitum.* This process continues for years, generations, centuries, millennia, and its pervasiveness has led many cultural theorists to regard culture change as essentially a slow, chain-like, self-contained procession of superorganic inevitabilities. In revitalization movements, however, A, B, C, D, E . . . N are shifted into a new *Gestalt* abruptly and simultaneously in intent; and frequently within a few years the new plan is put into effect by the participants in the movement. We may note in passing that Keesing's assessment of the literature on culture change (1953), while it does not deal explicitly with the theoretical issue of chain-effects versus revitalization, discusses both types. Barnett (1953) frankly confines his discussion to innovations of limited scope in the context of chains of events in acceptance and rejection. As Mead has suggested, cultures *can* change within one generation (Mead 1955); and the process by which such transformations occur is the revitalization process.

The term "revitalization" implies an organismic analogy.[2] This analogy is, in fact, an integral part of the concept of revitalization. A human society is here regarded as a definite kind of organism, and its culture is conceived as those patterns of learned behavior which certain "parts" of the social organism or system (individual persons and groups of persons) characteristically display. A corollary of the organismic analogy is the principle of homeostasis: that a society will work, by means of coordinated actions (including "cultural" actions) by all or some of its parts, to preserve its own integrity by maintaining a minimally fluctuating, life-supporting matrix for its individual members, and will, under stress, take emergency measures to preserve the constancy of this matrix. Stress is defined as a condition in which some part, or the whole, of the social organism is threatened with more or less serious damage. The perception of stress, particularly of increasing stress, can be viewed as the common denominator of the panel of "drives" or "instincts" in every psychological theory.

As I am using the organismic analogy, the total system which constitutes a society includes as significant parts not only persons and groups with their respective patterns of behavior, but also literally the cells and organs of which the persons are composed. Indeed, one can argue that the system includes nonhuman as well as human subsystems. Stress on one level is stress on all levels. For example, lowering of sugar level (hunger) in the fluid matrix of the body cells of one group of persons in a society is a stress in the society as a whole. This holistic view of society as organism integrated from cell to nation depends on the assumption that society, as an organization of living matter, is definable as a network of intercommunication. Events on one subsystem level must affect other subsystems (cellular vis-à-vis institutional, personal vis-à-vis societal) at least as information; in this view, social organization exists to the degree that events in one subsystem are information to other subsystems.

There is one crucial difference between the principles of social organization and that of the individual person: a society's parts are very widely interchangeable, a person's only slightly so. The central nervous system cells, for example, perform many functions of coordinating information and executing adaptive action which other cells cannot do. A society, on the other hand, has a multiple-replacement capacity, such that many persons can perform the analogous information-coordination and execu-

tive functions on behalf of society-as-organism. Furthermore, that regularity of patterned behavior which we call culture depends relatively more on the ability of constituent units autonomously to perceive the system of which they are a part, to receive and transmit information, and to act in accordance with the necessities of the system, than on any all-embracing central administration which stimulates specialized parts to perform their function.

It is therefore functionally necessary for every person in society to maintain a mental image of the society and its culture, as well as of his own body and its behavioral regularities, in order to act in ways which reduce stress at all levels of the system. The person does, in fact, maintain such an image. This mental image I have called "the mazeway," since as a model of the cell-body-personality-nature-culture-society system or field, organized by the individual's own experience, it includes perceptions of both the maze of physical objects of the environment (internal and external, human and nonhuman) and also of the ways in which this maze can be manipulated by the self and others in order to minimize stress. The mazeway is nature, society, culture, personality, and body image, as seen by one person. Hallowell (1955) and Wallace (1955 and 1956) offer extended discussions of the mazeway and the related concepts of self, world view, and behavioral environment.

We may now see more clearly what "revitalization movements" revitalize. Whenever an individual who is under chronic, physiologically measurable stress, receives repeated information which indicates that his mazeway does not lead to action which reduces the level of stress, he must choose between maintaining his present mazeway and tolerating the stress, or changing the mazeway in an attempt to reduce the stress. Changing the mazeway involves changing the total *Gestalt* of his image of self, society, and culture, of nature and body, and of ways of action. It may also be necessary to make changes in the "real" system in order to bring mazeway and "reality" into congruence. The effort to work a change in mazeway and "real" system together so as to permit more effective stress reduction is the effort at revitalization; and the collaboration of a number of persons in such an effort is called a revitalization movement.

The term revitalization movement thus denotes a very large class of phenomena. Other terms are employed in the existing literature to denote what I would call subclasses, distinguished by a miscellany of criteria. "Nativistic movements," for example, are revitalization movements characterized by strong emphasis on the elimination of alien persons, customs, values, and/or material from the mazeway (Linton 1943). "Revivalistic" movements emphasize the institution of customs, values, and/or material from the mazeway (Linton 1943). "Revivalistic" movements emphasize the institution of customs, values, and even aspects of nature which are thought to have been in the mazeway of previous generations but are not now present (Mooney 1892–93). "Cargo cults" emphasize the importation of alien values, customs, and materiel into the mazeway, these things being expected to arrive as a ship's cargo as for example in the Vailala Madness (Williams 1923, 1934). "Vitalistic movements" emphasize the importation of alien elements into the mazeway but do not necessarily invoke ship and cargo as the mechanism.[3] "Millenarian movements" emphasize mazeway transformation in an apocalyptic world transformation engineered by the supernatural. "Messianic movements" emphasize the participation of a divine savior in human flesh in the mazeway transformation (Wallis 1918, 1943). These and parallel terms do not denote mutually exclusive categories, for a given revitalization movement may be nativistic, millenarian, messianic, and revivalistic all at once; and it may (in fact, usually does) display ambivalence with respect to nativistic, revivalistic, and importation themes.

Revitalization movements are evidently not unusual phenomena, but are recurrent features in human history. Probably few men have lived who have not been involved in an instance of the revitalization process. They are, furthermore, of profound historical importance. Both Christianity and Mohammedanism, and possibly Buddhism as well,

originated in revitalization movements. Most denominational and sectarian groups and orders budded or split off after failure to revitalize a traditional institution. One can ask whether a large proportion of religious phenomena have not originated in personality transformation dreams or visions characteristic of the revitalization process. Myths, legends, and rituals may be relics, either of the manifest content of vision-dreams or of the doctrines and history of revival and import cults, the circumstances of whose origin have been distorted and forgotten, and whose connection with dream states is now ignored. Myths in particular have long been noted to possess a dream-like quality, and have been more or less speculatively interpreted according to the principles of symptomatic dream interpretation. It is tempting to suggest that myths and, often, even legends, read like dreams because they *were* dreams when they were first told. It is tempting to argue further that culture heroes represent a condensation of the figures of the prophet and of the supernatural being of whom he dreamed.

In fact, it can be argued that all organized religions are relics of old revitalization movements, surviving in routinized form in stabilized cultures, and that religious phenomena per se originated (if it is permissible still in this day and age to talk about the "origins" of major elements of culture) in the revitalization process—i.e., in visions of a new way of life by individuals under extreme stress.

THE PROCESSUAL STRUCTURE

A basic methodological principle employed in this study is that of event-analysis (Wallace 1953). This approach employs a method of controlled comparison for the study of processes involving longer or shorter diachronic sequences (vide Eggan 1954 and Steward 1953). It is postulated that events or happenings of various types have genotypical structures independent of local cultural differences; for example, that the sequence of happenings following a severe physical disaster in cities in Japan, the United States, and Germany, will display a uniform pattern, colored but not obscured by local differences in culture. These types of events may be called behavioral units. Their uniformity is based on generic human attributes, both physical and psychological, but it requires extensive analytical and comparative study to elucidate the structure of any one. Revitalization movements constitute such a behavioral unit, and so also, on a lower level of abstraction, do various subtypes within the larger class, such as cargo and revival cults. We are therefore concerned with describing the generic structure of revitalization movements considered as a behavioral unit, and also of variation along the dimensions characteristic of the type.

The structure of the revitalization process, in cases where the full course is run, consists of five somewhat overlapping stages: 1. Steady State; 2. Period of Individual Stress; 3. Period of Cultural Distortion; 4. Period of Revitalization (in which occur the functions of mazeway reformulation, communication, organization, adaptation, cultural transformation, and routinization), and finally, 5. New Steady State. These stages are described briefly in the following sections.

I. *Steady State.* For the vast majority of the population, culturally recognized techniques for satisfying needs operate with such efficiency that chronic stress within the system varies within tolerable limits. Some severe but still tolerable stress may remain general in the population, and a fairly constant incidence of persons under, for them, intolerable stress may employ "deviant" techniques (e.g., psychotics). Gradual modification or even rapid substitution of techniques for satisfying some needs may occur without disturbing the steady state, as long as (1) the techniques for satisfying other needs are not seriously interfered with, and (2) abandonment of a given technique for reducing one need in favor of a more efficient technique does not leave other needs, which the first technique was also instrumental in satisfying, without any prospect of satisfaction.

II. *The Period of Increased Individual Stress.* Over a number of years, individual members of a population (which may be "primitive" or "civilized," either a whole society or a class, caste, reli-gious, occupational, acculturational, or other definable social group) experience increasingly severe stress as a result of the decreasing efficiency of certain stress-reduction techniques. The culture may remain essentially unchanged or it may undergo considerable changes, but in either case there is continuous diminution in its efficiency in satisfying needs. The agencies responsible for interference with the efficiency of a cultural system are various: climatic, floral and faunal change; military defeat; political subordination; extreme pressure toward acculturation resulting in internal cultural conflict; economic distress; epidemics; and so on. The situation is often, but not necessarily, one of acculturation, and the acculturating agents may or may not be representatives of Western European cultures. While the individual can tolerate a moderate degree of increased stress and still maintain the habitual way of behavior, a point is reached at which some alternative way must be considered. Initial consideration of a substitute way is likely, however, to increase stress because it arouses anxiety over the possibility that the substitute way will be even less effective than the original, and that it may also actively interfere with the execution of other ways. In other words, it poses the threat of mazeway disintegration. Furthermore, admission that a major technique is worthless is extremely threatening because it implies that the whole mazeway system may be inadequate.

III. *The Period of Cultural Distortion.* The prolonged experience of stress, produced by failure of need satisfaction techniques and by anxiety over the prospect of changing behavior patterns, is responded to differently by different people. Rigid persons apparently prefer to tolerate high levels of chronic stress rather than make systematic adaptive changes in the mazeway. More flexible persons try out various limited mazeway changes in their personal lives, attempting to reduce stress by addition or substitution of mazeway elements with more or less concern for the *Gestalt* of the system. Some persons turn to psychodynamically regressive innovations; the regressive response empirically exhibits itself in increasing incidences of such things as alcoholism, extreme passivity and indo-lence, the development of highly ambivalent dependency relationships, intragroup violence, disregard of kinship and sexual mores, irresponsibility in public officials, states of depression and self-reproach, and probably a variety of psychosomatic and neurotic disorders. Some of these regressive action systems become, in effect, new cultural patterns.

In this phase, the culture is internally distorted; the elements are not harmoniously related but are mutually inconsistent and interfering. For this reason alone, stress continues to rise. "Regressive" behavior, as defined by the society, will arouse considerable guilt and hence increase stress level or at least maintain it at a high point; and the general process of piecemeal cultural substitution will multiply situations of mutual conflict and misunderstanding, which in turn increase stress-level again.

Finally, as the inadequacy of existing ways of acting to reduce stress becomes more and more evident, and as the internal incongruities of the mazeway are perceived, symptoms of anxiety over the loss of a meaningful way of life also become evident: disillusionment with the mazeway, and apathy toward problems of adaptation, set in.

IV. *The Period of Revitalization.* This process of deterioration can, if not checked, lead to the death of the society. Population may fall even to the point of extinction as a result of increasing death rates and decreasing birth rates; the society may be defeated in war, invaded, its population dispersed and its customs suppressed; factional disputes may nibble away areas and segments of the population. But these dire events are not infrequently forestalled, or at least postponed, by a revitalization movement. Many such movements are religious in character, and such religious revitalization movements must perform at least six major tasks:

1. *Mazeway reformulation.* Whether the movement is religious or secular, the reformulation of the mazeway generally seems to depend on a restructuring of elements and subsystems which have already attained currency in the society and may even be in use, and which are known to the person

who is to become the prophet or leader. The occasion of their combination in a form which constitutes an internally consistent structure, and of their acceptance by the prophet as a guide to action, is abrupt and dramatic, usually occurring as a moment of insight, a brief period of realization of relationships and opportunities. These moments are often called inspiration or revelation. The reformulation also seems normally to occur in its initial form in the mind of a single person rather than to grow directly out of group deliberations.

With a few exceptions, every religious revitalization movement with which I am acquainted has been originally conceived in one or several hallucinatory visions by a single individual. A supernatural being appears to the prophet-to-be, explains his own and his society's troubles as being entirely or partly a result of the violation of certain rules, and promises individual and social revitalization if the injunctions are followed and the rituals practiced, but personal and social catastrophe if they are not. These dreams express: 1. the dreamer's wish for a satisfying parental figure (the supernatural, guardian-spirit content), 2. world-destruction fantasies (the apocalyptic, millennial content), 3. feelings of guilt and anxiety (the moral content), and 4. longings for the establishment of an ideal state of stable and satisfying human and supernatural relations (the restitution fantasy or Utopian content). In a sense, such a dream also functions almost as a funeral ritual: the "dead" way of life is recognized as dead; interest shifts to a god, the community, and a new way. A new mazeway *Gestalt* is presented, with more or less innovation in details of content. The prophet feels a need to tell others of his experience, and may have definite feelings of missionary or messianic obligation. Generally he shows evidence of a radical inner change in personality soon after the vision experience: a remission of old and chronic physical complaints, a more active and purposeful way of life, greater confidence in interpersonal relations, the dropping of deep-seated habits like alcoholism. Hence we may call these visions "personality transformation dreams." Where there is no vision (as with John Wesley), there occurs a similarly brief and dramatic moment of insight, revelation, or inspiration, which functions in most respects like the vision in being the occasion of a new synthesis of values and meanings.

My initial approach to the understanding of these visions was by way of psychoanalytic dream theory. This proved to be of some use in elucidating the meaning of the vision. From an analysis of its manifest content and from the circumstances of the dreamer's history and life situation, it is possible to make more or less plausible interpretations of the nature of the prophet's personal preoccupations and conflicts. But conventional dream theory was designed to explain the conflicts represented in ordinary night dreams. Prophetic visions, while essentially dream formations, differ in several respects from ordinary symptomatic dreams: they often occur during a waking state as hallucinatory experiences, or in an ecstatic trance rather than in normal sleep; they impress the dreamer immediately as being meaningful and important; the manifest content is often in large part rational and well considered intellectual argument and cogent moral exhortation; and recollection of them is in unusually rich detail. This brings to mind Fromm's position (1951), that many dreams are not so much symptomatic of unconscious neurotic conflict as insightful in a positive and creative sense. But this additional consideration did not seem adequately to account for the most remarkable feature of all: the transformation of personality, often in a positive therapeutic sense, which these dreams produced. Prophetic and ecstatic visions do express unconscious conflict; they sometimes reveal considerable insight, but they also work startling cures.

We therefore became interested in pursuing the dynamics of personality transformation dreams. As a type of event, they would seem to belong to a general clinical category of sudden and radical changes in personality, along with transformations occurring in psychotic breaks, spontaneous remissions, narcosynthesis, some occasions in psychotherapy, "brainwashing," and shock treatments. There are, incidentally, some interesting similarities between the physical state of prophets and converts in the vision-trance, and patients undergoing shock (Sargant 1949, 1951). Physical stress and exhaustion often seem to precede the vision-trance type of transformation, and it seems probable that chemical substances produced in the body under stress may be important in rendering a person capable of this type of experience (Hoffer, Osmond, and Smythies, 1954). The relationship of this sort of sudden personality change to slower maturational processes, on the one hand, and to what happens in rites of passage, on the other, should be points of interest to social scientists generally.

Nonclinical analogues of the prophet's personality transformation vision appear in several contexts: in accounts of individual ecstatic conversions and experiences of religious enthusiasm; in the guardian spirit quest among American Indians and elsewhere; and in the process of becoming a shaman, which is similar in many cultures all over the world. Conversion, shamanism, and the guardian-spirit vision seem to be phenomena very similar in pattern. All three of these processes are distributed globally; in many cultures all three are normal phenomena; all involve persons who are faced with the opportunity (if not necessity) of assuming a new cultural role and of abandoning an earlier role in order to reduce stress which they will not be able to resolve if they stand pat. A precipitating factor in many cases is some sort of severe physical stress, such as illness, starvation, sleeplessness, or fatigue. After the vision experience, the individual is often able to assume a new role requiring increased or differently phrased emotional independence. In the vision experience, he has invented a fictitious, nurturing, parent-like supernatural figure who satisfies much of his need for authority and protection; thus he is presumably able to loosen emotional ties to certain cultural objects, roles, and persons, and to act without undue inhibition and anxiety. Inconvenient wishes are displaced onto a fictitious but culturally sanctioned supernatural pseudo-community, leaving the personality free for relatively healthy relationships to the real world. An essential function of the vision is that the demands for energy made by transference wishes are minimized by displacement onto supernatural objects which can in fantasy be perceived as uniformly supporting and protective.

Inasmuch as many prophets were suffering from recognizable and admitted mental disorders before their transformation, which they achieved by means of a type of experience (hallucination) that our culture generally regards as pathological, the relevance of psychopathology to the vision experience needs to be explored. We have under way some observations on the case histories of a series of persons in a state mental institution who have been known to attendants for their excessive religiosity.[4] This survey, which we hope to extend to include interview materials, is not complete, but I can summarize our initial impressions. Chronic schizophrenics with religious paranoia tend to believe that they are God, Jesus, the Virgin Mary, the Great Earth Mother, or some other supernatural being. Successful prophets, on the other hand, usually do not believe that they are the supernatural, only that they have communicated with him (although their followers may freely deify them). Prophets do not lose their sense of personal identity but psychotics tend to become the object of their spiritual longing.

There are in this institution several persons who were hospitalized during the course of an experience which resembles in many respects the process of becoming a prophet. A man, burdened with a sense of guilt and inadequacy, and sensible of the need to reform his life, has a religious conversion in which he sees God or hears his voice; thereafter he displays a changed and in some ways healthier (or at least less rapidly deteriorating) personality; he undertakes an evangelistic or prophetic enterprise which is socially inconvenient to spouse, relatives, employer, warden, or other closely associated persons; he is thereupon certified as insane and hospitalized. Such frustrated prophets, being unable any longer to satisfy important human needs and suffering the obvious disapproval of the community, may also lose confidence in their relationship to the supernatural pseudo-community. They cannot return to their preconversion state because the hospital situation makes anything remotely approaching normal cultural and social participation impossible. Many therefore take the emotionally logical but unfortunate next step, and become the guardian spirit.

At this time, then, we would tentatively conclude that the religious vision experience per se is not psychopathological but rather the reverse, being a synthesizing and often therapeutic process performed under extreme stress by individuals already sick.

2. *Communication.* The dreamer undertakes to preach his revelations to people, in an evangelistic or messianic spirit; he becomes a prophet. The doctrinal and behavioral injunctions which he preaches carry two fundamental motifs: that the convert will come under the care and protection of certain supernatural beings; and that both he and his society will benefit materially from an identification with some definable new cultural system (whether a revived culture or a cargo culture, or a syncretism of both, as is usually the case). The preaching may take many forms (e.g., mass exhortation vs. quiet individual persuasion) and may be directed at various sorts of audiences (e.g., the elite vs. the down-trodden). As he gathers disciples, these assume much of the responsibility for communicating the "good word," and communication remains one of the primary activities of the movement during later phases of organization.

3. *Organization.* Converts are made by the prophet. Some undergo hysterical seizures induced by suggestion in a crowd situation; some experience an ecstatic vision in private circumstances; some are convinced by more or less rational arguments, some by considerations of expediency and opportunity. A small clique of special disciples (often including a few already influential men) clusters about the prophet and an embryonic campaign organization develops with three orders of personnel: the prophet; the disciples; and the followers. Frequently the action program from here on is effectively administered in large part by a political rather than a religious leadership. Like the prophet, many of the converts undergo a revitalizing personality transformation.

Max Weber's concept of "charismatic leadership" well describes the type of leader-follower relationship characteristic of revitalization movement organizations (1947). The fundamental element of the vision, as I have indicated above, is the entrance of the visionary into an intense relationship with a supernatural being. This relationship, furthermore, is one in which the prophet accepts the leadership, succor, and dominance of the supernatural. Many followers of a prophet, especially the disciples, also have ecstatic revelatory experiences; but they and all sincere followers who have not had a personal revelation also enter into a parallel relationship to the prophet: as God is to the prophet, so (almost) is the prophet to his followers. The relationship of the follower to the prophet is in all probability determined by the displacement of transference dependency wishes onto his image; he is regarded as an uncanny person, of unquestionable authority in one or more spheres of leadership, sanctioned by the supernatural. Max Weber denotes this quality of uncanny authority and moral ascendency in a leader as charisma. Followers defer to the charismatic leader not because of his status in an existing authority structure but because of a fascinating personal "power," often ascribed to supernatural sources and validated in successful performance, akin to the "mana" or "orenda" of ethnological literature. The charismatic leader thus is not merely permitted but expected to phrase his call for adherents as a demand to perform a duty to a power higher than human. Weber correctly points out that the "routinization" of charisma is a critical issue in movement organization, since unless this "power" is distributed to other personnel in a stable institutional structure, the movement itself is liable to die with the death or failure of individual prophet, king, or war lord.

Weber, however, is essentially discussing a quality of leadership, and one which is found in contexts other than that of revitalization movements. In consequence, his generalizations do not deal with the revitalization formula itself, but rather with the nature of the relationship of the early adherents to their prophet. Furthermore, there is a serious ambiguity in Weber's use of the charisma concept. Weber seems to have been uncertain whether to regard it as an unusual quality in the leader which is recognized and rationalized by his adherents, or whether to regard it as a quality ascribed to the leader by followers and hence as being a quality of their relationship to him, determined both by the observed and the observer in the perceptual transaction. We have used it to denote the libidinal relationship which Freud described in *Group Psychology and the Analysis of the Ego* (1922).

It would appear that the emotional appeal of the new doctrine to both the prophet and his followers is in considerable part based on its immediate satisfaction of a need to find a supremely powerful and potentially benevolent leader. For both the prophet and his followers, this wish is gratified in fantasy (subjectively real, of course); but the follower's fantasy is directed toward the person of the prophet, to whom are attributed charismatic properties of leadership (Weber 1946, 1947).

4. *Adaptation.* The movement is a revolutionary organization and almost inevitably will encounter some resistance. Resistance may in some cases be slight and fleeting but more commonly is determined and resourceful, and is held either by a powerful faction within the society or by agents of a dominant foreign society. The movement may therefore have to use various strategies of adaptation: doctrinal modification; political and diplomatic maneuver; and force. These strategies are not mutually exclusive nor, once chosen, are they necessarily maintained through the life of the movement. In most instances the original doctrine is continuously modified by the prophet, who responds to various criticisms and affirmations by adding to, emphasizing, playing down, and eliminating selected elements of the original visions. This reworking makes the new doctrine more acceptable to special interest groups, may give it a better "fit" to the population's cultural and personality patterns, and may take account of the changes occurring in the general milieu. In instances where organized hostility to the movement develops, a crystallization of counter-hostility against unbelievers frequently occurs, and emphasis shifts from cultivation of the ideal to combat against the unbeliever.

5. *Cultural Transformation.* As the whole or a controlling portion of the population comes to accept the new religion with its various injunctions, a noticeable social revitalization occurs, signalized by the reduction of the personal deterioration symptoms of individuals, by extensive cultural changes, and by an enthusiastic embarkation on some organized program of group action. This group program may, however, be more or less realistic and more or less adaptive: some programs are literally suicidal; others represent well conceived and successful projects of further social, political, or economic reform; some fail, not through any deficiency in conception and execution, but because circumstances made defeat inevitable.

6. *Routinization.* If the group action program in nonritual spheres is effective in reducing stress-generating situations, it becomes established as normal in various economic, social, and political institutions and customs. Rarely does the movement organization assert or maintain a totalitarian control over all aspects of the transformed culture; more usually, once the desired transformation has occurred, the organization contracts and maintains responsibility only for the preservation of doctrine and the performance of ritual (i.e., it becomes a church). With the mere passage of time, this poses the problems of "routinization" which Max Weber discusses at length (Weber 1946, 1947).

V. *The New Steady State.* Once cultural transformation has been accomplished and the new cultural system has proved itself viable, and once the movement organization has solved its problems of routinization, a new steady state may be said to exist. The culture of this state will probably be different in pattern, organization or *Gestalt,* as well as in traits, from the earlier steady state; it will be different from that of the period of cultural distortion.

VARIETIES AND DIMENSIONS OF VARIATION

I will discuss four of the many possible variations: the choice of identification; the choice of secular

and religious means; nativism; and the success-failure continuum.

1. *Choice of Identification.* Three varieties have been distinguished already on the basis of differences in choice of identification: movements which profess to revive a traditional culture now fallen into desuetude; movements which profess to import a foreign cultural system; and movements which profess neither revival nor importation, but conceive that the desired cultural endstate, which has never been enjoyed by ancestors or foreigners, will be realized for the first time in a future Utopia. The Ghost Dance, the Xosa Revival, and the Boxer Rebellion are examples of professedly revivalistic movements; the Vailala Madness (and other cargo cults) and the Taiping Rebellion are examples of professedly importation movements. Some formulations like Ikhnaton's monotheistic cult in old Egypt and many Utopian programs, deny any substantial debt to the past or to the foreigner, but conceive their ideology to be something new under the sun, and its culture to belong to the future.

These varieties, however, are ideal types. A few movements do correspond rather closely to one type or another but many are obvious mixtures. Handsome Lake, for instance, consciously recognized both revival and importation themes in his doctrine. It is easy to demonstrate that avowedly revival movements are never entirely what they claim to be, for the image of the ancient culture to be revived is distorted by historical ignorance and by the presence of imported and innovative elements. Importation movements, with professed intentions to abandon the ancestral ways, manage to leave elements of the ancestral culture intact, if unrecognized, in large areas of experience. And movements which claim to present an absolutely new conception of culture are obviously blinding themselves to the fact that almost everything in the new system has been modeled after traditional or imported elements or both. Although almost every revitalization movement embodies in its proposed new cultural system large quantities of both traditional and imported cultural material, for some reason each movement tends to profess either no identification at all, a traditional orientation, or foreign orientation. This suggests that the choice of identification is the solution of a problem of double ambivalence: both the traditional and the foreign model are regarded both positively and negatively.

Culture areas seem to have characteristic ways of handling the identification problem. The cargo fantasy, although it can be found outside the Melanesian area, seems to be particularly at home there; South American Indian prophets frequently preached of a migration to a heaven-on-earth free of Spaniards and other evils, but the promised-land fantasy is known elsewhere; North American Indian prophets most commonly emphasized the revival of the old culture by ritual and moral purification, but pure revival ideas exist in other regions too. Structural "necessity" or situational factors associated with culture area may be responsible. The contrast between native–white relationships in North America (a "revival" area) and Melanesia (an "importation" area) may be associated with the fact that American Indians north of Mexico were never enslaved on a large scale, forced to work on plantations, or levied for labor in lieu of taxes, whereas Melanesians were often subjected to more direct coercion by foreign police power. The Melanesian response has been an identification with the aggressor (vide Bettelheim 1947). On the other hand, the American Indians have been less dominated as individuals by whites, even under defeat and injustice. Their response to this different situation has by and large been an identification with a happier past. This would suggest that an important variable in choice of identification is the degree of domination exerted by a foreign society, and that import-oriented revitalization movements will not develop until an extremely high degree of domination is reached.

2. *The Choice of Secular and Religious Means.* There are two variables involved here: the amount of secular action which takes place in a movement, and the amount of religious action. Secular action is here defined as the manipulation of human relationships; religious action as the manipulation of relationships between human and supernatural

beings. No revitalization movement can, by definition, be truly nonsecular, but some can be relatively less religious than others, and movements can change in emphasis depending on changing circumstances. There is a tendency, which is implicit in the earlier discussion of stages, for movements to become more political in emphasis, and to act through secular rather than religious institutions, as problems of organization, adaptation, and routinization become more pressing. The Taiping Rebellion, for instance, began as religiously-preoccupied movements; opposition by the Manchu dynasty and by foreign powers forced it to become more and more political and military in orientation.

A few "purely" political movements like the Hebertist faction during the French Revolution, and the Russian communist movement and its derivatives, have been officially atheistic, but the quality of doctrine and of leader-follower relationships is so similar, at least on superficial inspection, to religious doctrine and human-supernatural relations, that one wonders whether it is not a distinction without a difference. Communist movements are commonly asserted to have the quality of religious movements, despite their failure to appeal to a supernatural community, and such things as the development of a Marxist gospel with elaborate exegesis, the embalming of Lenin, and the concern with conversion, confession, and moral purity (as defined by the movement) have the earmarks of religion. The Communist Revolution of 1917 in Russia was almost typical in structure of religious revitalization movements: there was a very sick society, prophets appealed to a revered authority (Marx), apocalyptic and Utopian fantasies were preached, and missionary fervor animated the leaders. Furthermore, many social and political reform movements, while not atheistic, act through secular rather than religious media and invoke religious sanction only in a perfunctory way. I do not wish to elaborate the discussion at this time, however, beyond the point of suggesting again that the obvious distinctions between religious and secular movements may conceal fundamental similarities of socio-cultural process and of psychodynamics, and that while all secular prophets have not had personality transformation visions, some probably have, and others have had a similar experience in ideological conversion.

Human affairs around the world seem more and more commonly to be decided without reference to supernatural powers. It is an interesting question whether mankind can profitably dispense with the essential element of the religious revitalization process before reaching a Utopia without stress or strain. While religious movements may involve crude and powerful emotions and irrational fantasies of interaction with nonexistent beings, and can occasionally lead to unfortunate practical consequences in human relations, the same fantasies and emotions could lead to even more unfortunate practical consequences for world peace and human welfare when directed toward people improperly perceived and toward organs of political action and cultural ideologies. The answer would seem to be that as fewer and fewer men make use of the religious displacement process, there will have to be a corresponding reduction of the incidence and severity of transference neuroses, or human relationships will be increasingly contaminated by character disorders, neurotic acting out, and paranoid deification of political leaders and ideologies.

3. *Nativism.* Because a major part of the program of many revitalization movements has been to expel the persons or customs of foreign invaders or overlords, they have been widely called "nativistic movements." However, the amount of nativistic activity in movements is variable. Some movements—the cargo cults, for instance—are antinativistic from a cultural standpoint but nativistic from a personnel standpoint. Handsome Lake was only mildly nativistic; he sought for an accommodation of cultures and personalities rather than expulsion, and favored entry of certain types of white persons and culture-content. Still, many of the classic revivalistic movements have been vigorously nativistic, in the ambivalent way discussed earlier. Thus nativism is a dimension of variation rather than an elemental property of revitalization movements.

A further complication is introduced by the fact that the nativistic component of a revitalization movement not uncommonly is very low at the time of conception, but increases sharply after the movement enters the adaptation stage. Initial doctrinal formulations emphasize love, co-operation, understanding, and the prophet and his disciples expect the powers-that-be to be reasonable and accepting. When these powers interfere with the movement, the response is apt to take the form of an increased nativistic component in the doctrine. Here again, situational factors are important for an understanding of the course and character of the movement.

4. *Success and Failure.* The outline of stages as given earlier is properly applicable to a revitalization movement which is completely successful. Many movements are abortive; their progress is arrested at some intermediate point. This raises a taxonomic question: how many stages should the movement achieve in order to qualify for inclusion in the category? Logically, as long as the original conception is a doctrine of revitalization by culture change, there should be no requisite number of stages. Practically, we have selected only movements which passed the first three stages (conception, communication, and organization) and entered the fourth (adaptation). This means that the bulk of our information on success and failure will deal with circumstances of relatively late adaptation, rather than with such matters as initial blockage of communication and interference with organization.

Two major but not unrelated variables seem to be very important in determining the fate of any given movement: the relative "realism" of the doctrine; and the amount of force exerted against the organization by its opponents. "Realism" is a difficult concept to define without invoking the concept of success or failure, and unless it can be so defined, is of no use as a variable explanatory of success or failure. Nor can one use the criterion of conventionality of perception, since revitalization movements are by definition unconventional. While a great deal of doctrine in every movement (and, indeed, in every person's mazeway) is extremely unrealistic in that predictions of events made on the basis of its assumptions will prove to be more or less in error, there is only one sphere of behavior in which such error is fatal to the success of a revitalization movement: prediction of the outcome of conflict situations. If the organization cannot predict successfully the consequences of its own moves and of its opponents' moves in a power struggle, its demise is very likely. If, on the other hand, it is canny about conflict, or if the amount of resistance is low, it can be extremely "unrealistic" and extremely unconventional in other matters without running much risk of early collapse. In other words, probability of failure would seem to be negatively correlated with degree of realism in conflict situations, and directly correlated with amount of resistance. Where conflict-realism is high and resistance is low, the movement is bound to achieve the phase of routinization. Whether its culture will be viable for long beyond this point, however, will depend on whether its mazeway formulations lead to actions which maintain a low level of stress.

SUMMARY

This programmatic paper outlines the concepts, assumptions, and initial findings of a comparative study of religious revitalization movements. Revitalization movements are defined as deliberate, conscious, organized efforts by members of a society to create a more satisfying culture. The revitalization movement as a general type of event occurs under two conditions: high stress for individual members of the society, and disillusionment with a distorted cultural *Gestalt*. The movement follows a series of functional stages: mazeway reformulation, communication, organization, adaptation, cultural transformation, and routinization. Movements vary along several dimensions, of which choice of identification, relative degree of religious and secular emphasis, nativism, and success or failure are discussed here. The movement is usually conceived in a prophet's revelatory visions, which provide for him a satisfying relationship to the supernatural and outline a new way of life under divine sanction. Followers achieve similar satisfaction of dependency needs in the charismatic relationship. It is suggested

that the historical origin of a great proportion of religious phenomena has been in revitalization movements.

ENDNOTES

1. The Handsome Lake project, supported largely by a Faculty Research Fellowship of the Social Science Research Council, with supplemental funds from the Behavioral Research Council and Committee for the Advancement of Research of the University of Pennsylvania, has served as a pilot study, and the larger investigation is now largely financed by the National Institute of Mental Health (U.S. Public Health Service), Grant M-883, with supplemental funds from the American Philosophical Society and the Eastern Pennsylvania Psychiatric Institute. I should like to express my appreciation to Sheila C. Steen (who has been the "field director" of the project, responsible for much of the empirical research and participant in conceptual formulation), and to research and clerical assistants Josephine H. Dixon, Herbert S. Williams, and Ruth Goodenough. Persons whose comments and suggestions on the first draft of this paper have been of value in its revision include Margaret Mead, Theodore Schwartz, Walter Goldschmidt, A. I. Hallowell, David F. Aberle, Betty S. Wallace and Ward Goodenough. The Handsome Lake movement will be described in detail in a book the writer is now preparing. For other treatments now in print, see Parker, 1913; Deardorff, 1951; Voget, 1954; and Wallace, 1952a and 1952b.

2. This article is not the place to present a general discussion of the notions of order and field, function and equilibrium, the organismic analogy, the concept of homeostasis, and certain ideas from cybernetics, learning and perception, and the physiology of stress, which would be necessary to justify and fully elucidate the assumptions on which the revitalization hypothesis is based. See however, Wallace 1953, 1955, and 1956 for further development of the holistic view and more extended discussions of the mazeway concept.

3. After we had coined the term "revitalization movement," we discovered that Marian Smith in an article on the Indian Shakers (Smith 1954) uses the closely related term "vitalistic movements" ("a vitalistic movement may be defined as 'any conscious, organized attempt on the part of a society's members to incorporate in its culture selected aspects of another culture in contact with it' "). However, she uses this term for what I would call nonnativistic revitalization movements with importation (rather than revivalistic) emphasis.

4. I should like to express my appreciation to Dr. Arthur P. Noyes, Superintendent, and Drs. Warren Hampe and Kenneth Kool of the staff of Norristown (Pa.) State Hospital, for their assistance in making this survey possible.

BIBLIOGRAPHY

Barnett, H. G.
1953   Innovation: The Basis of Culture Change. New York.

Bettelheim, B.
   1947   Individual and Mass Behavior in Extreme Situations. In Newcomb, Hartley, et al., eds., Readings in Social Psychology. New York.
Cantril, Hadley
   1941   The Psychology of Social Movements. New York.
Deardorff, M. H.
   1951   The Religion of Handsome Lake: Its Origin and Development. In Symposium on Local Diversity in Iroquois Culture, edited by W. N. Fenton, Bureau of American Ethnology Bulletin 149:79–107. Washington.
Eggan, Fred
   1954   Social Anthropology and the Method of Controlled Comparison. American Anthropologist 56:743–63.
Freud, Sigmund
   1922   Group Psychology and the Analysis of the Ego. London.
Fromm, Erich
   1951   The Forgotten Language. New York.
Hallowell, A. I.
   1955   The Self and Its Behavioral Environment. In A. I. Hallowell, Culture and Experience. Philadelphia.
Hoffer, A., H. Osmond, and J. Smythies
   1954   Schizophrenia: A New Approach. II. Result of a Year's Research. Journal of Mental Science, 100:29–45.
James, William
   1902   Varieties of Religious Experience. New York.
Keesing, Felix M.
   1953   Culture Change: An Analysis and Bibliography of Anthropological Sources to 1952. Stanford.
Knox, R. A.
   1950   Enthusiasm: A Chapter in the History of Religion, with Special Reference to the XVII and XVIII Centuries. Oxford.
Linton, Ralph
   1943   Nativistic Movements. American Anthropologist 45:230–40.
Lowe, Warner L.
   1953   Psychodynamics in Religious Delusions and Hallucinations. American Journal of Psychotherapy 7:454–62.
Mead, Margaret
   1954   Nativistic Cults as Laboratories for Studying Closed and Open Systems. Paper read at annual meeting of the American Anthropological Association.
   1955   How Fast Can Man Change? Address presented to Frankford Friends Forum, Philadelphia, 4 Dec. 1955.
Mooney, James
   1892–93 The Ghost Dance Religion. Bureau of American Ethnology Annual Report. Washington.

Parker, Arthur
   1913   The Code of Handsome Lake, the Seneca Prophet. New York State Museum Bulletin 163. Albany.
Sargant, William
   1949   Some Cultural Group Abreactive Techniques and Their Relation to Modern Treatments. Proceedings of the Royal Society of Medicine 42:367–74.
   1951   The Mechanism of Conversion. British Medical Journal 2:311 et seq.
Schwartz, Theodore
   1954   The Changing Structure of the Manus Nativistic Movement. Paper read at annual meeting of the American Anthropological Association.
Smith, Marian
   1954   Shamanism in the Shaker Religion of Northwest America. Man, August 1954, #181.
Steward, Julian N.
   1953   Evolution and Process. In A. L. Kroeber, ed., Anthropology Today. Chicago.
Voget, Fred W.
   1954   Reformative Tendencies in American Indian Nativistic Cults. Paper read at annual meeting of the American Anthropological Association.
Wallace, Anthony F. C.
   1952a   Handsome Lake and the Great Revival in the West. American Quarterly, Summer: 149–65.
   1952b   Halliday Jackson's Journal to the Seneca Indians, 1798–1800. Pennsylvania History 19: Nos. 2 and 3.
   1953   A Science of Human Behavior. Explorations No. 3.
   1955   The Disruption of the Individual's Identification with His Culture in Disasters and Other Extreme Situations. Paper read at National Research Council, Committee on Disaster Studies, Conference on Theories of Human Behavior in Extreme Situations, Vassar College.
   1956   The Mazeway. Explorations No. 6. In press.
Wallis, Wilson D.
   1918   Messiahs—Christian and Pagan. Boston.
   1943   Messiahs—Their Role in Civilization. Washington.
Weber, Max
   1930   The Protestant Ethic and the Spirit of Capitalism. Translated by Talcott Parsons. New York.
   1946   From Max Weber: Essays in Sociology. Translated and edited by H. Gerth and C. W. Mills. New York.
   1947   The Theory of Social and Economic Organization. Translated and edited by A. M. Henderson and Talcott Parsons. New York.
Williams, F. E.
   1923   The Vailala Madness and the Destruction of Native Ceremonies in the Gulf Division. Port Moresby: Territory of Papua, Anthropology Report No. 4.
   1934   The Vailala Madness in Retrospect. In Essays Presented to C. G. Seligman. London.

READING 11-3

CARGO CULTS

Peter M. Worsley

Like Anthony Wallace (Reading 11–2), Peter Worsley gives the dynamics of belief full rein in this article, and Weber's diachronic approach to religion is again vividly illustrated. Prophets are prominent features here, and Worsley examines their role in Melanesian cargo cults, and makes clear the nature of the social changes that inspire their calling. The author summarizes the main features of this form of revitalization movement, and gives us a clear picture of its genesis in the interface between indigenous and Western cultures. He draws a picture of indigenous cultures lacking the kind of material wealth possessed by the exotic, alien, Western culture, whose members seem hardly to work at all, and exhorted by charismatic religious figures to gain parity by abandoning the values and institutions that gave meaning to the lives of their members. The strategies of renewal that are the response to a people's socioeconomic crises often fail because they have misconstrued how Western societies work.

Patrols of the Australian Government venturing into the "uncontrolled" central highlands of New Guinea in 1946 found the primitive people there swept up in a wave of religious excitement. Prophecy was being fulfilled: The arrival of the Whites was the sign that the end of the world was at hand. The natives proceeded to butcher all of their pigs—animals that were not only a principal source of subsistence but also symbols of social status and ritual preeminence in their culture. They killed these valued animals in expression of the belief that after three days of darkness "Great Pigs" would appear from the sky. Food, firewood and other necessities had to be stock-piled to see the people through to the arrival of the Great Pigs. Mock wireless antennae of bamboo and rope had been erected to receive in advance the news of the millennium.

Many believed that with the great event they would exchange their black skins for white ones.

This bizarre episode is by no means the single event of its kind in the murky history of the collision of European civilization with the indigenous cultures of the southwest Pacific. For more than 100 years traders and missionaries have been reporting similar disturbances among the peoples of Melanesia, the group of Negro-inhabited islands (including New Guinea, Fiji, the Solomons and the New Hebrides) lying between Australia and the open Pacific Ocean. Though their technologies were based largely upon stone and wood, these peoples had highly developed cultures, as measured by the standards of maritime and agricultural ingenuity, the complexity of their varied social organizations and the elaboration of religious belief and ritual. They were nonetheless ill prepared for the shock of the encounter with the Whites, a people so radically different from themselves and so infinitely more powerful. The sudden transition from the society of the ceremonial stone ax to the society of sailing ships and now of airplanes has not been easy to make.

After four centuries of Western expansion, the densely populated central highlands of New Guinea remain one of the few regions where the people still carry on their primitive existence in complete independence of the world outside. Yet as the agents of the Australian Government penetrate into ever more remote mountain valleys, they find these backwaters of antiquity already deeply disturbed by contact with the ideas and artifacts of European civilization. For "cargo"—Pidgin English for trade goods—has long flowed along the indigenous channels of communication from the seacoast into the wilderness. With it has traveled the frightening knowledge of the white man's magical power. No small element in the white man's magic is the hopeful message sent abroad by his missionaries: the news that a Messiah will come and that the present order of Creation will end.

The people of the central highlands of New Guinea are only the latest to be gripped in the recurrent religious frenzy of the "cargo cults." However variously embellished with details from native myth and Christian belief, these cults all advance the same central theme: the world is about to end in a terrible cataclysm. Thereafter God, the ancestors or some local culture hero will appear and inaugurate a blissful paradise on earth. Death, old age, illness and evil will be unknown. The riches of the white man will accrue to the Melanesians.

Although the news of such a movement in one area has doubtless often inspired similar movements in other areas, the evidence indicates that these cults have arisen independently in many places as parallel responses to the same enormous social stress and strain. Among the movements best known to students of Melanesia are the "Taro Cult" of New Guinea, the "Vailala Madness" of Papua, the "Naked Cult" of Espiritu Santo, the "John Frum Movement" of the New Hebrides and the "Tuka Cult" of the Fiji Islands.

At times the cults have been so well organized and fanatically persistent that they have brought the work of government to a standstill. The outbreaks have often taken the authorities completely by surprise and have confronted them with mass opposition of an alarming kind. In the 1930s, for example, villagers in the vicinity of Wewak, New Guinea, were stirred by a succession of "Black King" movements. The prophets announced that the Europeans would soon leave the island, abandoning their property to the natives, and urged their followers to cease paying taxes, since the government station was about to disappear into the sea in a great earthquake. To the tiny community of Whites in charge of the region, such talk was dangerous. The authorities jailed four of the prophets and exiled three others. In yet another movement, that sprang up in declared opposition to the local Christian mission, the cult leader took Satan as his god.

Troops on both sides in World War II found their arrival in Melanesia heralded as a sign of the Apocalypse. The G.I.'s who landed in the New Hebrides, moving up for the bloody fighting on Guadalcanal, found the natives furiously at work preparing airfields, roads and docks for the magic ships and planes that they believed were coming from "Rusefel" (Roosevelt), the friendly king of America.

The Japanese also encountered millenarian visionaries during their southward march to Guadalcanal. Indeed, one of the strangest minor military actions of World War II occurred in Dutch New Guinea, when Japanese forces had to be turned against the local Papuan inhabitants of the Geelvink Bay region. The Japanese had at first been received with great joy, not because their "Greater East Asia Co-Prosperity Sphere" propaganda had made any great impact upon the Papuans, but because the natives regarded them as harbingers of the new world that was dawning, the flight of the Dutch having already given the first sign. Mansren, creator of the islands and their peoples, would now return, bringing with him the ancestral dead. All this had been known, the cult leaders declared, to the crafty Dutch, who had torn out the first page of the Bible where these truths were inscribed. When Mansren returned, the existing world order would be entirely overturned. White men would turn black like Papuans, Papuans would become Whites; root crops would grow in trees, and coconuts and fruits would grow like tubers. Some of the islanders now began to draw together into large "towns"; others took Biblical names such as "Jericho" and "Galilee" for their villages. Soon they adopted military uniforms and began drilling. The Japanese, by now highly unpopular, tried to disarm and disperse the Papuans; resistance inevitably developed. The climax of this tragedy came when several canoeloads of fanatics sailed out to attack Japanese warships, believing themselves to be invulnerable by virtue of the holy water with which they had sprinkled themselves. But the bullets of the Japanese did not turn to water, and the attackers were mowed down by machine-gun fire.

Behind this incident lay a long history. As long ago as 1857 missionaries in the Geelvink Bay region had made note of the story of Mansren. It is typical of many Melanesian myths that became confounded with Christian doctrine to form the ideological basis of the movements. The legend tells how long ago there lived an old man named Manamakeri ("he who itches"), whose body was covered with sores. Manamakeri was extremely fond of palm wine, and used to climb a huge tree every day to tap the liquid from the flowers. He soon found that someone was getting there before him and removing the liquid. Eventually he trapped the thief, who turned out to be none other than the Morning Star. In return for his freedom, the Star gave the old man a wand that would produce as much fish as he liked, a magic tree and a magic staff. If he drew in the sand and stamped his foot, the drawing would become real. Manamakeri, aged as he was, now magically impregnated a young maiden; the child of this union was a miracle-child who spoke as soon as he was born. But the maiden's parents were horrified, and banished her, the child and the old man. The trio sailed off in a canoe created by Mansren ("The Lord"), as the old man now became known. On this journey Mansren rejuvenated himself by stepping into a fire and flaking off his scaly skin, which changed into valuables. He then sailed around Geelvink Bay, creating islands where he stopped, and peopling them with the ancestors of the present-day Papuans.

The Mansren myth is plainly a creation myth full of symbolic ideas relating to fertility and rebirth. Comparative evidence—especially the shedding of his scaly skin—confirms the suspicion that the old man is, in fact, the Snake in another guise. Psychoanalytic writers argue that the snake occupies such a prominent part in mythology the world over because it stands for the penis, another fertility symbol. This may be so, but its symbolic significance is surely more complex than this. It is the "rebirth" of the hero, whether Mansren or the Snake, that exercises such universal fascination over men's minds.

The 19th-century missionaries thought that the Mansren story would make the introduction of Christianity easier, since the concept of "resurrection," not to mention that of the "virgin birth" and the "second coming," was already there. By 1867, however, the first cult organized around the Mansren legend was reported.

Though such myths were widespread in Melanesia, and may have sparked occasional movements even in the pre-White era, they took on a new significance in the late 19th century, once the European powers had finished parceling out the Melanesian region among themselves. In many coastal areas the long history of "blackbirding"—the seizure of islanders for work on the plantations of Australia and Fiji—had built up a reservoir of hostility to Europeans. In other areas, however, the arrival of the Whites was accepted, even welcomed, for it meant access to bully beef and cigarettes, shirts and paraffin lamps, whisky and bicycles. It also meant access to the knowledge behind these material goods, for the Europeans brought missions and schools as well as cargo.

Practically the only teaching the natives received about European life came from the missions, which emphasized the central significance of religion in European society. The Melanesians already believed that man's activities—whether gardening, sailing canoes or bearing children—needed magical assistance. Ritual without human effort was not enough. But neither was human effort on its own. This outlook was reinforced by mission teaching.

The initial enthusiasm for European rule, however, was speedily dispelled. The rapid growth of the plantation economy removed the bulk of the able-bodied men from the villages, leaving women, children and old men to carry on as best they could. The splendid vision of the equality of all Christians began to seem a pious deception in face of the realities of the color bar, the multiplicity of rival Christian missions and the open irreligion of many Whites.

For a long time the natives accepted the European mission as the means by which the "cargo" would eventually be made available to them. But they found that acceptance of Christianity did not bring the cargo any nearer. They grew disillusioned. The story now began to be put about that it was not the Whites who made the cargo, but the dead ancestors. To people completely ignorant of factory production, this made good sense. White men did not work; they merely wrote secret signs on scraps of paper, for which they were given shiploads of goods. On the other hand, the Melanesians labored week after week for pitiful wages. Plainly the goods must be made for Melanesians somewhere, perhaps in the Land of the Dead. The Whites, who possessed the secret of the cargo, were intercepting it and keeping it from the hands of the islanders, to whom it was really consigned. In the Madang district of New Guinea, after some 40 years' experience of the missions, the natives went in a body one day with a petition demanding that the cargo secret should now be revealed to them, for they had been very patient.

So strong is this belief in the existence of a "secret" that the cargo cults generally contain some ritual in imitation of the mysterious European customs which are held to be the clue to the white man's extraordinary power over goods and men. The believers sit around tables with bottles of flowers in front of them, dressed in European clothes, waiting for the cargo ship or airplane to materialize; other cultists feature magic pieces of paper and cabalistic writing. Many of them deliberately turn their backs on the past by destroying secret ritual objects, or exposing them to the gaze of uninitiated youths and women, for whom formerly even a glimpse of the sacred objects would have meant the severest penalties, even death. The belief that they were the chosen people is further reinforced by their reading of the Bible, for the lives and customs of the people in the Old Testament resemble their own lives rather than those of the Europeans. In the New Testament they find the Apocalypse, with its prophecies of destruction and resurrection, particularly attractive.

Missions that stress the imminence of the Second Coming, like those of the Seventh Day Adventists, are often accused of stimulating millenarian cults among the islanders. In reality, however, the Melanesians themselves rework the doctrines the missionaries teach them, selecting from the Bible what they themselves find particularly congenial in it. Such movements have occurred in areas where missions of quite different types have been dominant, from Roman Catholic to Seventh Day Adventist. The reasons for the emergence of these cults, of course, lie far deeper in the life-experience of the people.

The economy of most of the islands is very backward. Native agriculture produces little for the world market, and even the European plantations and mines export only a few primary products and raw materials: copra, rubber, gold. Melanesians are quite unable to understand why copra, for example, fetches 30 pounds sterling per ton one month and but 5 pounds a few months later. With no notion of the workings of world-commodity markets, the natives see only the sudden closing of plantations, reduced wages and unemployment, and are inclined to attribute their insecurity to the whim or evil in the nature of individual planters.

Such shocks have not been confined to the economic order. Governments, too, have come and gone, especially during the two world wars: German, Dutch, British and French administrations melted overnight. Then came the Japanese, only to be ousted in turn largely by the previously unknown Americans. And among these Americans the Melanesians saw Negroes like themselves, living lives of luxury on equal terms with white G.I.'s. The sight of these Negroes seemed like a fulfillment of the old prophecies to many cargo cult leaders. Nor must we forget the sheer scale of this invasion. Around a million U.S. troops passed through the Admiralty Islands, completely swamping the inhabitants. It was a world of meaningless and chaotic changes, in which anything was possible. New ideas were imported and given local twists. Thus in the Loyalty Islands people expected the French Communist Party to bring the millennium. There is no real evidence, however, of any Communist influence in these movements, despite the rather hysterical belief among Solomon Island planters that the name of the local "Masinga Rule" movement was derived from the word "Marxian"! In reality the name comes from a Solomon Island tongue, and means "brotherhood."

Europeans who have witnessed outbreaks inspired by the cargo cults are usually at a loss to understand what they behold. The islanders throw away their money, break their most sacred taboos, abandon their gardens and destroy their precious livestock; they indulge in sexual license or, alternatively, rigidly separate men from women in huge communal establishments. Sometimes they spend days sitting gazing at the horizon for a glimpse of the long-awaited ship or airplane; sometimes they dance, pray and sing in mass congregations, becoming possessed and "speaking with tongues."

Observers have not hesitated to use such words as "madness," "mania," and "irrationality" to characterize the cults. But the cults reflect quite logical and rational attempts to make sense out of a social order that appears senseless and chaotic. Given the ignorance of the Melanesians about the wider European society, its economic organization and its highly developed technology, their reactions form a consistent and understandable pattern. They wrap up all their yearning and hope in an amalgam that combines the best counsel they can find in Christianity and their native belief. If the world is soon to end, gardening or fishing is unnecessary; everything will be provided. If the Melanesians are to be part of a much wider order, the taboos that prescribe their social conduct must now be lifted or broken in a newly prescribed way.

Of course the cargo never comes. The cults nonetheless live on. If the millennium does not arrive on schedule, then perhaps there is some failure in the magic, some error in the ritual. New breakaway groups organize around "purer" faith and ritual. The cult rarely disappears, so long as the social situation which brings it into being persists.

At this point it should be observed that cults of this general kind are not peculiar to Melanesia. Men who feel themselves oppressed and deceived have always been ready to pour their hopes and fears, their aspirations and frustrations, into dreams of a millennium to come or of a golden age to return. All parts of the world have had their counterparts of the cargo cults, from the American Indian ghost dance to the communist-millenarist "reign of the saints" in Münster during the Reformation, from medieval European apocalyptic cults to African "witch-finding" movements and Chinese Buddhist heresies. In some situations men have been content to wait and pray; in others they have sought to hasten the day by

using their strong right arms to do the Lord's work. And always the cults serve to bring together scattered groups, notably the peasants and urban plebeians of agrarian societies and the peoples of "stateless" societies where the cult unites separate (and often hostile) villages, clans and tribes into a wider religio-political unity.

Once the people begin to develop secular political organizations, however, the sects tend to lose their importance as vehicles of protest. They begin to relegate the Second Coming to the distant future or to the next world. In Melanesia ordinary political bodies, trade unions and native councils are becoming the normal media through which the islanders express their aspirations. In recent years continued economic prosperity and political stability have taken some of the edge off their despair. It now seems unlikely that any major movement along cargo-cult lines will recur in areas where the transition to secular politics has been made, even if the insecurity of prewar times returned. I would predict that the embryonic nationalism represented by cargo cults is likely in future to take forms familiar in the history of other countries that have moved from subsistence agriculture to participation in the world economy.

READING 11–4

THE GHOST DANCE RELIGION

Alice Beck Kehoe

This extract from her book The Ghost Dance *by Alice Beck Kehoe gives ethnographic substance to Wallace's general discussion of that form of revitalization movement known as the revivalistic (Reading 11–2) and establishes a comparison with Worsley's analysis of cargo*

Source: "The Ghost Dance Religion," from *The Ghost Dance: Ethnohistory and Revitalization* (Fort Worth: Holt, Rinehart, and Winston, 1989), pp. 3–9, copyright © 1989 by Alice Beck Kehoe, reprinted by Permission of Holt, Rinehart and Winston, Inc.

cults. (Reading 11–3). Its substance is biographical, for it deals with a single personality called Jack Wilson, whose personal attributes and impact on his society's religious beliefs give us a compelling illustration of Max Weber's charismatic leader. We see in Kehoe's portray of this unusual man the genesis of a prophet created in part by the squalid socio economic circumstances into which his people had fallen. During a solar eclipse on January 1, 1889 Jack Wilson, a member of the Paiute tribe, suffered from a serious fever and fell unconscious. He later reported that he felt taken up to heaven and brought before God, who commissioned him to deliver a message to his fellow human. The invalid saw it was one of peace and right living, and strengthened with this gospel he regained consciousness. By dawn the next day, Jack Wilson was a man with a mission. He had become a prophet.

New Year's Day, 1892. Nevada.

A wagon jounces over a maze of cattle trails crisscrossing a snowy valley floor. In the wagon, James Mooney, from the Smithsonian Institution in faraway Washington, D.C., is looking for the Indian messiah, Wovoka, blamed for riling up the Sioux, nearly three hundred of whom now lie buried by Wounded Knee Creek in South Dakota. The men in the wagon see a man with a gun over his shoulder walking in the distance.

"I believe that's Jack now!" exclaims one of Mooney's guides. "Jack Wilson," he calls to the messiah, whose Paiute name is Wovoka. Mooney's other guide, Charley Sheep, Wovoka's uncle, shouts to his nephew in the Paiute language. The hunter comes over to the wagon.

"I saw that he was a young man," Mooney recorded, "a dark full-blood, compactly built, and taller than the Paiute generally, being nearly 6 feet in height. He was well dressed in white man's clothes, with the broad-brimmed white felt hat common in the west, secured on his head by means of a beaded ribbon under the chin. . . . He wore a good pair of boots. His hair was cut off square on a line below the base of the ears, after the manner of his tribe. His countenance was open and expressive of firmness and decision" (Mooney [1896] 1973:768–769).

That evening, James Mooney formally interviewed Jack Wilson in his home, a circular lodge ten feet in diameter, built of bundles of tule reeds tied to a pole frame. In the middle of the lodge, a bright fire of sagebrush stalks sent sparks flying out of the wide smoke hole. Several other Paiutes were with Jack, his wife, baby, and little son when Mooney arrived with a guide and an interpreter. Mooney noticed that although all the Paiutes dressed in "white man's" clothes, they preferred to live in traditional wickiups. Only Paiute baskets furnished Jack Wilson's home; no beds, no storage trunks, no pots or pans, nothing of alien manufacture except the hunting gun and knife lay in the wickiup, though the family could have bought the invaders' goods. Jack had steady employment as a ranch laborer, and from his wages he could have constructed a cabin and lived in it, sitting on chairs and eating bread and beef from metal utensils. Instead, Jack and Mary, his wife, wanted to follow the ways of their people as well as they could in a valley overrun with Euro-American settlement. The couple hunted, fished, and gathered pine nuts and other seeds and wild plants. They practiced their Paiute religion rather than the Presbyterian Christianity Jack's employer insisted on teaching them. Mooney was forced to bring a Euro-American settler, Edward Dyer, to interpret for him because Jack would speak only his native Paiute, though he had some familiarity with English. This was Mason Valley, in the heart of Paiute territory, and for Jack and Mary it was still Paiute.

Jack Wilson told Mooney that he had been born four years before the well-remembered battle between Paiutes and American invaders at Pyramid Lake. The battle had been touched off by miners seizing two Paiute women. The men of the Paiute community managed to rescue the two women. No harm was done to the miners, but they claimed they were victims of an "Indian outrage," raised a large party of their fellows, and set off to massacre the Paiutes. Expecting trouble, the Paiute men ambushed the mob of miners at a narrow pass, and although armed mostly with only bows and arrows, killed nearly fifty of the mob, routing the rest and saving the families in the Indian camp. Jack Wilson's father, Tavibo, was a leader of the Paiute community at that time. He was recognized as spiritually blessed—gifted and trained to communicate with invisible powers. By means of this gift, carefully cultivated, Tavibo was said to be able to control the weather.

Tavibo left the community when his son Wovoka was in his early teens, and the boy was taken on by David Wilson, a Euro-American rancher with sons of his own close in age to the Paiute youth. Though employed as a ranch hand, Wovoka was strongly encouraged to join the Wilson family in daily prayers and Bible reading, and Jack, as he came to be called, became good friends with the Wilson boys. Through these years with the Wilsons, Jack's loyalty to, and pride in, his own Paiute people never wavered. When he was about twenty, he married a Paiute woman who shared his commitment to the Paiute way of life. With his wages from the ranch, Jack and Mary bought the hunting gun and ammunition, good-quality "white man's" clothes, and ornaments suited to their dignity as a respected younger couple in the Mason Valley community.

As a young adult, Jack Wilson began to develop a reputation as a weather doctor like his father. Paiute believe that a young person lacks the maturity and inner strength to function as a spiritual agent, but Jack was showing the self-discipline, sound judgment, and concern for others that marked Indians gifted as doctors in the native tradition. Jack led the circle dances through which Paiute opened themselves to spiritual influence. Moving always along the path of the sun—clockwise to the left—men, women, and children joined hands in a symbol of the community's living through the circle of the days. As they danced they listened to Jack Wilson's songs celebrating the Almighty and Its wondrous manifestations: the mountains, the clouds, snow, stars, trees, antelope. Between dances, the people sat at Jack's feet, listening to him preach faith in universal love.

The climax of Jack's personal growth came during a dramatic total eclipse of the sun on January 1, 1889. He was lying in his wickiup very ill with a fever. Paiute around him saw the sky darkening although it was midday. Some monstrous force was overcoming the sun! People shot off guns at the apparition, they yelled, some wailed as at a death. Jack Wilson felt himself losing consciousness. It seemed to him he was taken up to heaven and brought before God. God gave him a message to the people of earth, a gospel of peace and right living. Then he and the sun regained their normal life.

Jack Wilson was now a prophet. Tall, handsome, with a commanding presence, Jack already was respected for his weather control power. (The unusual snow blanketing Mason Valley when James Mooney visited was said to be Jack's doing.) Confidence in his God-given mission further enhanced Jack Wilson's reputation. Indians came from other districts to hear him, and even Mormon settlers in Nevada joined his audiences. To carry out his mission, Jack Wilson went to the regional Indian agency at Pyramid Lake and asked one of the employees to prepare and mail a letter to the President of the United States, explaining the Paiute doctor's holy mission and suggesting that if the United States government would send him a small regular salary, he would convey God's message to all the people of Nevada and, into the bargain, make it rain whenever they wished. The agency employee never sent the letter. It was agency policy to "silently ignore" Indians' efforts toward "notoriety." The agent would not even deign to meet the prophet.

Jack Wilson did not need the support of officials. His deep sincerity and utter conviction of his mission quickly persuaded every open-minded hearer of its importance. Indians came on pilgrimages to Mason Valley, some out of curiosity, others seeking guidance and healing in that time of afflictions besetting their peoples. Mormons came too, debating whether Jack Wilson was the fulfillment of a prophecy of their founder, Joseph Smith, Jr., that the Messiah would appear in human form in 1890. Jack Wilson himself consistently explained that he was a messiah like Jesus but not the Christ of the Christians. Both Indians and Euro-Americans tended to ignore Jack's protestations and to identify him as "the Christ." Word spread that the Son of God was preaching in western Nevada.

Throughout 1889 and 1890, railroads carried delegates from a number of Indian nations east of the Rockies to investigate the messiah in Mason Valley. Visitors found ceremonial grounds maintained beside the Paiute settlements, flat cleared areas with low willow-frame shelters around the open dancing space. Paiutes gathered periodically to dance and pray for four days and nights, ending on the fifth morning shaking their blankets and shawls to symbolize driving out evil. In Mason Valley itself, Jack Wilson would attend the dances, repeating his holy message and, from time to time, trembling and passing into a trance to confirm the revelations. Delegates from other reservations were sent back home with tokens of Jack Wilson's holy power: bricks of ground red ocher dug from Mount Grant south of Mason Valley, the Mount Sinai of Northern Paiute religion; the strikingly marked feathers of the magpie; pine nuts, the "daily bread" of the Paiutes; and robes of woven strips of rabbit fur, the Paiutes' traditional covering. James Mooney's respectful interest in the prophet's teachings earned him the privilege of carrying such tokens to his friends on the Cheyenne and Arapaho reservations east of the mountains.

Jack Wilson told Mooney that when "the sun died" that winter day in 1889 and, dying with it, he was taken up to heaven,

> he saw God, with all the people who had died long ago engaged in their oldtime sports and occupations, all happy and forever young. It was a pleasant land and full of game. After showing him all, God told him he must go back and tell his people they must be good and love one another, have no quarreling, and live in peace with the whites; that they must work, and not lie or steal; that they must put away all the old practices that savored of war; that if they faithfully obeyed his instructions they would at last be reunited with their friends in this other world, where there would be no more death or sickness or old age. He was then given the dance which he was commanded to bring back to his people. By performing this dance at intervals, for five consecutive days each time, they would secure

this happiness to themselves and hasten the event. Finally God gave him control over the elements so that he could make it rain or snow or be dry at will, and appointed him his deputy to take charge of affairs in the west, while "Governor Harrison" [President of the United States at the time] would attend to matters in the east, and he, God, would look after the world above. He then returned to earth and began to preach as he was directed, convincing the people by exercising the wonderful powers that had been given him. (Mooney [1896] 1973:771–772)

Before Mooney's visit, Jack Wilson had repeated his gospel, in August 1891, to a literate young Arapaho man who had journeyed with other Arapaho and Cheyenne to discover the truth about this fabled messiah. Jack instructed his visitors, according to the Arapaho's notes:

> When you get home you make dance, and will give you the same.. . . . He likes you folk, you give him good, many things, he heart been sitting feel good. After you get home, will give good cloud, and give you chance to make you feel good. and he give you good spirit. and he give you all a good paint.. . .
>
> Grandfather said when he die never no cry. no hurt anybody. no fight, good behave always, it will give you satisfaction, this young man, he is a good Father and mother, dont tell no white man. Jueses [Jesus?] was on ground, he just like cloud. Everybody is alive agin, I dont know when they will [be] here, may be this fall or in spring.
>
> Everybody never get sick, be young again,—(if young fellow no sick any more,) work for white men never trouble with him until you leave, when it shake the earth dont be afraid no harm any body.
>
> You make dance for six weeks night, and put you foot [food?] in dance to eat for every body and wash in the water. that is all to tell, I am in to you. and you will received a good words from him some time, Dont tell lie. (Mooney [1896] 1973:780–781)

Seeing the red ocher paint, the magpie feathers, the pine nuts, and the rabbit skin robes from the messiah, his Arapaho friends shared this message with James Mooney. Jack Wilson himself had trusted this white man. Thanks to this Arapaho document, we know that Jack Wilson himself obeyed his injunction, "Dont tell lie": he had confided to the

Smithsonian anthropologist the same gospel he brought to his Indian disciples.

"A clean, honest life" is the core of Jack Wilson's guidance, summed up seventy years later by a Dakota Sioux who had grown up in the Ghost Dance religion. The circling dance of the congregations following Jack Wilson's gospel symbolized the ingathering of all people in the embrace of Our Father, God, and in his earthly deputy Jack Wilson. As the people move in harmony in the dance around the path of the sun, leftward, so they must live and work in harmony. Jack Wilson was convinced that if every Indian would dance this belief, the great expression of faith and love would sweep evil from the earth, renewing its goodness in every form, from youth and health to abundant food.

This was a complete religion. It had a transcendental origin in the prophet's visit to God, and a continuing power rooted in the eternal Father. Its message of earthly renewal was universalistic, although Jack Wilson felt it was useless to preach it to those Euro-Americans who were heedlessly persecuting the Indian peoples. That Jack shared his gospel with those non-Indians who came to him as pilgrims demonstrates that it was basically applicable to all people of goodwill. The gospel outlined personal behavior and provided the means to unite individuals into congregations to help one another. Its principal ceremony, the circling dance, pleased and satisfied the senses of the participants, and through the trances easily induced during the long ritual, it offered opportunities to experience profound emotional catharsis. Men and women, persons of all ages and capabilities, were welcomed into a faith of hope for the future, consolation and assistance in the present, and honor to the Indians who had passed into the afterlife. It was a marvelous message for people suffering, as the Indians of the West were in 1889, terrible epidemics; loss of their lands, their economic resources, and their political autonomy; malnourishment and wretched housing; and a campaign of cultural genocide aimed at eradicating their languages, their customs, and their beliefs.

Jack Wilson's religion was immediately taken up by his own people, the Northern Paiute, by other Paiute groups, by the Utes, the Shoshoni, and the Washo in western Nevada. It was carried westward across the Sierra Nevada and espoused by many of the Indians of California. To the south, the religion was accepted by the western Arizona Mohave, Cohonino, and Pai, but not by most other peoples of the American Southwest. East of the Rockies, the religion spread through the Shoshoni and Arapaho in Wyoming to other Arapaho, Cheyenne, Assiniboin, Gros Ventre (Atsina), Mandan, Arikara, Pawnee, Caddo, Kichai, Wichita, Kiowa, Kiowa-Apache, Comanche, Delaware (living by this time in Oklahoma), Oto, and the western Sioux, especially the Teton bands. The mechanism by which this religion spread was usually a person visiting another tribe, observing the new ceremonial dance and becoming inspired by its gospel, and returning home to urge relatives and friends to try the new faith. Leaders of these evangelists' communities would often appoint respected persons to travel to Nevada to investigate this claim of a new messiah. The delegates frequently returned as converts, testifying to the truth of the faith and firing the enthusiasm of their communities. Those who remained skeptics did not always succeed in defusing the flame of faith in others.

Never an organized church, Jack Wilson's religion thus spread by independent converts from California through Oklahoma. Not all the communities who took it up continued to practice it, when months or years passed without the hoped-for earth renewal. Much of Jack Wilson's religion has persisted, however, and has been incorporated into the regular religious life of Indian groups, especially on Oklahoma reservations. To merge into a complex of beliefs and rituals rather than be an exclusive religion was entirely in accordance with Jack Wilson's respect for traditional Indian religions, which he saw reinforced, not supplanted, by his revelations. Though the Sioux generally dropped the Ghost Dance religion after their military defeats following their initial acceptance of the ritual, older people among the Sioux could be heard occasionally singing Ghost Dance songs in the 1930s. The last real congregation of adherents to Jack Wilson's gospel continued to worship together into the 1960s, and at least one who survived into the 1980s never abandoned the faith. There were sporadic attempts to revive the Ghost Dance religion in the 1970s, though these failed to kindle the enthusiasm met by the original proselytizers.

"Ghost Dance" is the name usually applied to Jack Wilson's religion, because the prophet foresaw the resurrection of the recently dead with the hoped-for renewal of the earth. Paiute themselves simply called their practice of the faith "dance in a circle," Shoshoni called it "everybody dragging" (speaking of people pulling others along as they circled), Comanche called it "the Father's Dance," Kiowa, "dance with clasped hands," and Caddo, "prayer of all to the Father" or "my [Father's] children's dance." The Sioux and Arapaho did use the term "spirit [ghost] dance," and the English name seems to have come from translation of the Sioux. The last active congregation, however, referred to their reli-gion as the New Tidings, stressing its parallel to Jesus' gospel.

To his last days in 1932, Jack Wilson served as Father to believers. He counseled them, in person and by letters, and he gave them holy red ocher paint, symbolizing life, packed into rinsed-out tomato cans (the red labels indicated the contents). With his followers, he was saddened that not enough Indians danced the new faith to create the surge of spiritual power that could have renewed the earth, but resurrection was only a hope. The heart of his religion was his creed, the knowledge that a "clean, honest life" is the only good life.

REFERENCES

Mooney, James. *The Ghost-Dance Religion and Wounded Knee.* New York: Dover Publications, Inc., 1973. (Originally pub-lished as Part 2, Fourteenth Annual Report 1892–93, Bureau of Ethnology. Washington: Government Printing Office.) [1896]

ASK YOURSELF

The readings in this chapter illustrate religion as a force for change. They also furnish examples of religions in the process of changing. Religion can also be a conser-vative force, however, so think of current examples of beliefs and rituals being forces for the conservation of institutions and collective representation. Example: the Catholic Church's attitude to abortion. Consider, too, the social implications of religion as a source of institu-tional and ideological stability. Whether you are reli-gious or not, what are some of the ethical questions Western societies face and how do you see religious beliefs and institutions playing a role in these decisions?

FURTHER READINGS

Bax, Mart. "Marian Apparitions in Medjugorge: Rivalling Reli-gious Regimes and State-Formation in Yugoslavia." In *Reli-gious Regimes and State-Formation: Perspectives from Euro-pean Ethnology,* ed. Eric R. Wolf. Albany: State University of New York Press, 1991, pp. 29–53. A riveting account of the politics of religious devotion in Yugoslavia before the nation disintegrated.

Lewis, I. M. *Ecstatic Religion,* 2nd ed. London: Routledge, 1989. Among the author's concerns here is to account for the rise of possession cults and other manifestions of religious conviction in terms of the social circumstances that generate them.

Mooney, James. *The Ghost-Dance Religion and the Sioux Out-break of 1890,* abridged ed. Chicago: University of Chicago Press, 1965. This is the original account of one of the most interesting episodes in the tragic history of European-Indian relations in North America.

Whitehouse, Harvey. "From Mission to Movement: The Impact of Christianity on Patterns of Political Association in Papua New Guinea." *Journal of the Royal Anthropological Institute* (N.S.) 4:43–63. The author describes how missionaries, by encouraging the indigenous peoples of this Melanesian island to participate in routinized religious worship, helped trans-form tribal fragmentation into micro-nationalist movements under indigenous leadership.

SUGGESTED VIDEOS

"The Amish: Not to Be Modern." The Amish are of special interest in the context of change because of their determination not to adjust their customary ways to satisfy external pressures from the modern world. This documentary portrays life in an Amish religious community as its members engage in their daily activities over four seasons. Commentaries are provided by the Amish themselves. 57 minutes; 1985; $374 (sale), $85 (rental). Filmakers Library 1996, 124 East 40th Street, New York, NY 10016.

"Women Serving Religion." Women have traditionally played lesser roles than men in Judaism, Christianity, and Islam. Social forces, however, are rapidly altering the status quo. This documentary brings the contemporary dynamics of gender into the context of traditional religious thought and examines the influences exerted by feminism, especially in regard to the ordination of women. 29 minutes; 1996; $89.95 (sale); Catalog #KB5741; Films for the Humanities and Sciences, Video Programs, 1996 (Religion), P.O. Box 2053, Princeton, NJ 08543-2053.

"The House-Opening." After Geraldine Kawanka's husband died, she and her children left their house on Cape York Peninsula, Australia. Although traditionally a bark house would have been burnt to help the surviving kin adjust to the change in their circumstances, today a "house-opening" ceremony—imaginatively combining Aboriginal and European elements—is given. This film records the opening of the house and Geraldine's feelings. Filmmaker: Judith MacDougall. 45 minutes, 1980 Film Officer, Royal Anthropological Institute (RAI), 50 Fitzroy Street, London W1P 5HS, United Kingdom.

Followers of wiccan claim to be the descendants of witches who carried out rituals in the centuries before Christianity claimed the Western world. Here we see a modern-day witch carrying out a wiccan ritual at a fire at a gathering near Atlanta, Georgia, in 1996. The witch, Ceil Thomas, was "feeding" the fire in a gesture of union between the 20 or so participant witches and this "living" element, which is considered the source of the universe and the animating force or "spirit" in all things.

Photo courtesy of Loretta Orion

CHAPTER 12

NEW RELIGIOUS MOVEMENTS

The readings in this chapter involve modern religious movements known variously as *sects, new religious movements, alternative religions,* or *cults.* Alternative religions in the United States number several hundred, or even several thousands, depending upon the criteria for definition (Miller 1995: 5), and among those that have pushed themselves to the forefront of our awareness are the Seventh Day Adventists, Jehovah's Witnesses, the Quakers, the Church of Jesus Christ of Latterday Saints or Mormons, Shakers, Hutterites, Branch Davidians, Hare Krishna, Santerí, Voudoo, various New Age movements, the Church of Scientology, and the Satanic Churches.

In current popular usage, the terms "sect" and "cult" have acquired pejorative connotations (especially, perhaps, "cult"), largely because members of the mainstream religions see them as rival groups, and also because of the fears aroused in the minds of relatives of individuals—usually young persons—who might appear to have been brainwashed by some groups into becoming members. In some cases these fears are justified, but many allegations of mind control are, according to Miller (1995:6–7), distortions of the truth. However that may be, the terms "sect" and "cult" are also perfectly neutral scholarly words, and as such, of course, are used in this volume. A useful definition of a sect is a religious grouping set apart from the dominant religion or religions in its society by its divergence in doctrine, ritual, and social character. Members of a sect constitute a minority and are most often regarded by members who remain loyal to the parent group as being a deviant offshoot. "It is divergence and intensity of commitment . . . which serve as the indicators of sectarianism" (Wilson 1990:1). Most sects constitute a protest against the religious orthodoxy or the social establishment, and they see themselves as having rejected the conventional beliefs and behavior of the parent group. Bryan Wilson (1990:1–2), who is a British sociologist regarded as a leading authority in the field of "non-mainstream religions" (Miller 1995: 1–2) notes that a sect "maintains a degree of tension with the world which is at least an expression of indifference to it, if not of hostility towards it." A sect is also a voluntary association. Individuals make a decision to join it, they are not members from birth, unlike the practice in mainstream religions. Having elected to join, however, membership in the sect becomes the adherent's primary source of social identity. "The ideal of total allegiance is far more strongly presupposed than is the case with so-called 'mainline' religious bodies" (Wilson 1990:2).

The meaning of the term "cult" overlaps with that of "sect," but usually refers to a small, intense religious group whose ties to a conventional religion are rather more tenuous. The term is also more commonly applied to a religion that has not broken away from Christianity or Judaism, and is frequently led by a prophet or prophet-like figure (Miller 1995:1).

Why do persons decide to join sects or cults? A variety of factors could be cited. Some individuals choose to join because the beliefs of the group find resonance with their own personal views of life. Or, idealists might join thinking that as a member of the group they would stand a better chance of shaping society in ways they deem better. Others find a security in the movement that they lack in their lives. Another reason is curiosity. A new style of living offers prospects of novelty that some individuals find hard to resist. So they experiment with it, a reason, Miller (1995, 6) points out, that helps explain why the attrition rates of non-mainstream religious is high. The majority of persons in contemporary American society, however, are not prepared to invest their lives in the kind of experiment these religions offer. Life, for them, is sufficiently challenging, with its need for the individual to work and perhaps raise a family, so most people tend to be conservative. Even so, though, the attraction of alternative religions can be very compelling. Thus whereas most Christian religions are either static in membership or gradually reducing in numbers, since about 1960 significant religious decentralization has been taking place, to the numerical benefit of less conventional religions (Miller 1995, 8). Nor is there reason for thinking this trend will change any time in the near future.

Four alternative religious movements that attained celebrity in the late 20th century in the United States were the Peoples Temple, the Unification Church, the Rastafari or Rasta, and wicca. The Unification Church and the Rastafari are international in their reach, and wicca has taken hold in England as well and in the United States. Despite certain common properties, such as the degree to which they vary in the intensity with which they react to traditional religion, each new religion has its distinctive set of beliefs and rituals, and has made an impact on American culture—as we shall see in the readings that follow.

READING 12–1

APOCALYPSE AT JONESTOWN

John R. Hall

The Reverend Jim Jones' Peoples Temple is an example of a form of sect known as "apocalyptic." The term "apocalyptic" derives from "apocalypse," which denotes "revelation" or "disclosure," a meaning that derives from its use in the New Testament *where the "revelation" or the "apocalypse" of the future is revealed to St. John. In the context of a sect the term "apocalyptic" refers to a sect whose members focus with unusually intense profundity on the fact that one day the world will come to an end. Apocalyptic sects vary in the degree to which they put this belief into action, but for the Peoples Temple this belief was a controlling concept, and its destruction resulted from a religious conflict that came about between a sect willing to defend its doctrines literally to the death and representatives of the outside world who helped fulfill the sect's "emergent apocalyptic vision" (Hall 1995:205).*

Apart from the sensational manner in which the movement closed down its existence, the Peoples Temple was unique among sects in that Jim Jones combined Pentecostal Christianity with a leaning towards the Communist

Movement. "He consolidated a politically engaged movement built on the apocalyptic premise that Peoples Temple would offer an ark of refuge in the face of a prophesied U.S. drift toward race and class warfare" (Hall 1995:207). Jones created his own apocalyptic vision and that vision addressed contemporary social issues.

According to the author of this reading, a professor of sociology at the University of California, Davis, Jim Jones's Peoples Temple was an "other-worldly" sect, but one with special characteristics that led to the suicide of 900 of its followers in October 1978. Like members of most other-worldly American sects, many members of the Peoples Temple felt they were under siege from the decadent world outside; but in contrast to most, they continued to feel part of the world they were trying to escape. The resulting sense of ambivalence, John R. Hall suggests, partly explains the paranoia that increasingly infected the community over the course of its last year, and which by October had put the leadership of prophet Jim Jones under threat. It appears the "mass murder/suicide" resulted when Jones became aware of the untenability of his leadership and the congregation realized that survival on the terms they required was not possible.

The events of November 1978 at Jonestown, Guyana, have been well documented. Beyond the wealth of "facts" which have been drawn from interviews with survivors of all stripes, there remain piles of as yet unsifted documents and tapes. If they can ever be examined, these might add something further to the record, but it is unlikely they will change very much the broad lines of our understanding of Jonestown. The major dimensions of the events and the outlines of various intrigues are already clear enough. But so far we have been caught in a flood of instant analysis; some of this has been insightful, but much of the accompanying moral outrage has clouded our ability to comprehend the events themselves. We need a more considered look at what sort of social phenomenon Jonestown was, and why (and how) Reverend Jim Jones and his staff led the 900 people of Jonestown to die in mass murder and suicide. This article suggests a very plausible explanation.

"CRAZY LIKE A FOX"

The news media have sought to account for Jonestown largely by looking for parallels "in history"; yet we have not been terribly enlightened by the ones they have found, usually because they have searched for cases which bear the outer trappings of the event, but which have fundamentally different causes. Thus, at Masada, in 73 A.D., the Jews who committed suicide under siege by Roman soldiers knew their fate was death, and chose to die by their own hands rather than at those of the Romans. In World War II, Japanese kamikaze pilots acted with the knowledge that direct, tangible, strategic results would stem from their altruistic suicides, if they were properly executed. And in Hitler's concentration camps, though there was occasional cooperation by Jews in their own executions, the Nazi executioners had no intentions of dying themselves.

Besides pointing to parallels which don't quite fit, the news media have targeted Jim Jones as irrational, a madman who had perverse tendencies from early in his youth. They have labeled the Peoples Temple as a "cult," perhaps in the hope that a label will suffice when an explanation is unavailable. And they have quite correctly plumbed the key issue of how Jones and his staff were able to bring the mass murder/suicide to completion, drawing largely on the explanations of psychiatrists who have prompted the concept of "brainwashing" as the answer.

But Jones was crazy like a fox. Though he may have been "possessed" or "crazed," both the organizational effectiveness of the Peoples Temple for more than 15 years, and the actual carrying out of the mass murder/suicide show that Jones and his immediate staff knew what they were doing.

Moreover, the Peoples Temple only became a "cult" when the media discovered the mass/suicide. As an Indiana woman whose teenager died at Jonestown commented, "I can't understand why they call the Peoples Temple a cult. To the people, it was their church. . . ." It is questionable whether the term "cult" has any sociological utility. As Harold Fallding has observed, it is a value-laden term most often used by members of one religion to describe a heretical or competing religion, of which they disapprove. Of course, even if the use of the term "cult" in the press has been sloppy and inappropriate, some comparisons, for example to the Unification Church, the Krishna Society, and the Children of God, have been quite apt. But these comparisons have triggered a sort of guilt by association: in this view, Jonestown is a not so aberrant case among numerous exotic and weird religious "cults." The only thing stopping some people from "cleaning up" the "cult" situation is the constitutional guarantee of freedom of religion.

Finally, "brainwashing" is an important but incomplete basis for understanding the mass murder/suicide. There can be no way to determine how many people at Jonestown freely chose to drink the cyanide-laced Flav-r-ade distributed after Jonestown received word of the murders of U.S. Congressman Leo Ryan and four other visitors at the airstrip. Clearly over 200 children and an undetermined number of adults were murdered. Thought control and blind obedience to authority ("brainwashing") surely account for some additional number of suicides. But the obvious cannot be ignored: a substantial number of people—"brainwashed" or not—committed suicide. Insofar as "brainwashing" occurs in other social organizations besides the Peoples Temple, it can only be a necessary and not a sufficient cause of the mass murder/suicide. The coercive persuasion involved in a totalistic construction of reality may explain in part how large numbers of people came to accept the course proposed by their leader, but it leaves unanswered the question of why the true believers among the inhabitants of Jonestown came to consider "revolutionary suicide" a plausible course of action.

In all the instant analysis of Jones' perversity, the threats posed by "cults" and the victimization of people by "brainwashing," there has been little attempt to account for Jonestown sociologically, and as a religious phenomenon. The various facets of Jonestown remain as incongruous pieces of seemingly separate puzzles; we need a close examination of the case itself to try to comprehend it. In the following discussion based on ideal type analysis and *verstehende* sociology, I will suggest that the Peoples Temple Agricultural Project at Jonestown was an apocalyptic sect. Most apocalyptic sects gravitate toward one of three ideal typical possibilities: (1) preapocalyptic Adventism, (2) preapocalyptic war, or (3) postapocalyptic other-worldly grace.

Insofar as the Adventist group takes on a communal form, it comes to approximate the postapocalyptic tableau of other-worldly grace. Jonestown was caught on the saddle of the apocalypse: it had its origins in the vaguely apocalyptic revivalist evangelism of the Peoples Temple in the United States, but the Guyanese communal settlement itself was an attempt to transcend the apocalypse by establishing a "heaven-on-earth." For various reasons, this attempt was frustrated. The Peoples Temple at Jonestown was drawn back into a preapocalyptic war with the forces of the established order. "Revolutionary suicide" then came to be seen as a way of surmounting the frustration, of moving beyond the apocalypse, to "heaven," albeit not "on earth."

In order to explore this account, let us first consider the origins of Jonestown and the ways in which it subsequently came to approximate the ideal typical other-worldly sect. Then we can consider certain tensions of the Jonestown group with respect to its other-worldly existence, so as to understand why similar groups did not (and are not likely to) encounter the same fate as Jonestown.

"A PROPHET CALLS THE SHOTS"

An other-worldly sect, as I have described it in *The Ways Out,* is a utopian communal group which subscribes to a set of beliefs based on an apocalyptic interpretation of current history. The world of society-at-large is seen as totally evil, and in its last days; at the end of history as we know it, it is to be replaced by a community of the elect—those who live according to the revelation of God's will. The convert who embraces such a sect must, perforce, abandon any previous understanding of life's meaning, and embrace the new worldview, which itself is capable of subsuming and explaining the individual's previous life, the actions of opponents to the sect, and the demands which are placed on the convert by the leadership of the sect. The other-worldly sect typically establishes its existence on the "other" side of the apocalypse by withdrawing from "this" world into a timeless heaven-on-earth. In this millennial kingdom, those closest to God come to rule. Though democratic consensuality or the collegiality of elders may come into play, more typically, a preeminent prophet or messiah, legitimated by charisma or tradition, calls the shots in a theocratic organization of God's chosen people.

The Peoples Temple had its roots in amorphous revivalistic evangelical religion, but in the transition to the Jonestown Agricultural Mission, it came to resemble an other-worldly sect. The Temple grew out of the interracial congregation Jim Jones had founded in Indiana in 1953. By 1964, the Peoples Temple Full Gospel Church was federated with the Disciples of Christ. Later, in 1966, Jones moved with 100 of his most devout followers to Redwood Valley, California. From there they expanded in the 1970s to San Francisco and Los Angeles—more promising places for liberal, interracial evangelism than rural Redwood Valley. In these years before the move to Guyana, Jones engaged himself largely in the manifold craft of revivalism. Jones learned from others he observed—Father Divine in Philadelphia and David Martinus de Miranda in Brazil, and Jones himself became a purveyor of faked miracles and faith healings. By the California years, the Peoples Temple was prospering financially from its somewhat shady "tent meeting" style activities, and from a variety of other petty and grand money-making schemes; it was also gaining political clout through the deployment of its members for the benefit of various politicians and causes.

These early developments give cause to wonder why Jones did not establish a successful but relatively benign sect like Jehovah's Witnesses, or, alternatively, why he did not move from a religious base directly into the realm of politics, as did the Reverend Adam Clayton Powell, from his Harlem congregation to the U.S. House of Representatives. The answer seems twofold. In the first place, Jim Jones seems to have had limitations both as an evangelist and as a politician. He simply did not succeed in fooling key California observers with his faked miracles. And for all the political support he peddled in California politics, Jones was not always able to draw on his good political "credit" when he needed it. A certain mark of political effectiveness concerns the ability to sustain power in the face of scandal. By this standard, Jones was not totally successful in either Indiana or California: there always seemed to be investigators and reporters on the trails of various questionable financial and evangelical dealings.

Quite aside from the limits of Jones' effectiveness, the very nature of his prophecy directed his religious movement along a different path from either "worldly" politics or sectarian Adventism. Keyed to the New Testament Book of Revelations, Adventist groups receive prophecy about the apocalyptic downfall of the present evil order of the world and the second coming of Christ to preside over a millennial period of divine grace on earth. For all such groups, the Advent itself makes social action to reform "this" world's institutions irrelevant. Adventist groups differ from one another in their exact eschatology of the last days, but the groups that have survived, like the Seventh Day Adventists and Jehovah's Witnesses, have juggled their doctrines which fix an exact date for Christ's appearance. Thus they have moved away from any intense chiliastic expectation of an imminent appearance, to engage in more mundane conversionist activities which are intended to pave the way for the Millennium.

"APOCALYPSE NOW"

Reverend Jones himself seems to have shared the pessimism of the Adventist sects about reforming social institutions in this world (for him, the capitalist world of the United States). True, he supported various progressive causes, but he did not put much stake in their success. Jones' prophecy was far more radical than those of contemporary Adventist groups: he focused on imminent apocalyptic disaster rather than on Christ's millennial salvation, and his eschatology therefore had to resolve a choice between preapocalyptic struggle with "the beast" or collective flight to establish a postapocalyptic kingdom of the elect. Up until the end, the Peoples Temple was directed toward the latter possibility. Even in the Indiana years, Jones had embraced an apocalyptic view. The move from Indiana to California was in part justified by Jones' claim that Redwood Valley would survive nuclear holocaust. In the California years, the apocalyptic vision shifted to Central Intelligence Agency persecution and Nazi-like extermination of blacks. In California too, the Peoples Temple gradually became communalistic in certain respects; it established a community of goods, pooled resources of elderly followers to provide communal housing for them, and drew on state funds to act as foster parents by establishing group homes for displaced youth. In its apocalyptic and communal aspects, the Peoples Temple more and more came to exist as an ark of survival. Jonestown, the Agricultural Project in Guyana, was built beginning in 1974 by an advance crew that by early 1977 still amounted to less than 60 people, most of them under 30 years old. The mass exodus of the Peoples Temple to Jonestown really began in 1977, when the Peoples Temple was coming under increasing scrutiny in California.

In the move to Guyana, the Peoples Temple began to concertedly exhibit many dynamics of other-worldly sects, though it differed in ways which were central to its fate. Until the end, Jonestown was similar in striking ways to contemporary sects like the Children of God and the Krishna Society (ISKCON, Inc.). Indeed, the Temple bears a more than casual (and somewhat uncomfortable) resemblance to the various Protestant sects which emigrated to the wilderness of North America beginning in the seventeenth century. The Puritans, Moravians, Rappites, Shakers, Lutherans, and many others like them sought to escape religious persecution in Europe in order to set up theocracies where they could live out their own visions of the earthly millennial community. So it was with Jonestown. In this light, neither disciplinary practices, the daily round of life, nor the community of goods at Jonestown seem so unusual.

"THE JUNGLE IS ONLY A FEW YARDS AWAY"

The disciplinary practices of the Peoples Temple—as bizarre and grotesque as they may sound, are not uncommon aspects of other-worldly sects: these practices have been played up in the press in an attempt to demonstrate the perverse nature of the group, so as to "explain" the terrible climax to their life. But as Erving Goffman has shown in *Asylums,* sexual intimidation and general psychological terror occur in all kinds of total institutions, including mental hospitals, prisons, armies, and even nunneries. Indeed, Congressman Leo Ryan, just prior to his fateful visit to Jonestown, accepted the need for social control: " . . . you can't put 1,200 people in the middle of a jungle without some damn tight discipline." Practices at Jonestown may well seem restrained in comparison to practices of, say, seventeenth-century American Puritans who, among other things, were willing to execute "witches" on the testimony of respected churchgoers or even children. Meg Greenfield observed in *Newsweek* in reflecting on Jonestown, "the jungle is only a few yards away." It seems important to recall that some revered origins of the United States lie in a remarkably similar "jungle."

Communal groups of all types, not just other-worldly sects, face problems of social control and commitment. Rosabeth Kanter has convincingly shown that successful communal groups in the nineteenth-century U.S. often drew on mechanisms of mutual criticism, mortification, modification of conventional dyadic sexual mores, and other devices in order to decrease the individual's ties to the outside or personal relationships within the group, and increase the individual's commitment to the collectivity as a whole.

Such commitment mechanisms are employed most often in religious communal groups, especially those with charismatic leaders. Other-worldly communal groups, where a special attempt is being made to forge a wholly new interpretation of reality, where the demand for commitment is especially pronounced (in a word, where it is sectarian)—these groups have tremendously high stakes in maintaining commitment. These groups are likely to seek out the procedures most effective at guaranteeing commitment. After all, defection from "the way" inevitably casts doubt on the sanctity of the way, no matter how it is rationalized among the faithful. Thus, it is against such groups that the charges of "brainwashing," chicanery, and mistreatment of members are most often leveled. Whatever their basis in fact, these are the likely charges of families and friends who see their loved ones abandon them in favor of committing material resources and persona to the religious hope of a new life. Much like other-worldly sects, families suffer a loss of legitimacy in the "defection" of one of their own.

The abyss that comes to exist between other-worldly sects and the world of society-at-large left behind simply cannot be bridged. There is no encompassing rational connection between the two realities, and, therefore, the interchange between the other-worldly sect and people beyond its boundaries becomes a struggle either between "infidels" and the "faithful" from the point of view of the sect, or between rationality and fanaticism from the point of view of outsiders. Every sectarian action has its benevolent interpretation and legitimation within the sect and a converse interpretation from the outside. Thus, from inside the sect, various practices of "confession," "mutual criticism," or "catharsis" sessions seem necessary to prevent deviant worldviews from taking hold within the group. In the Peoples Temple, such practices included occasional enforced isolation and drug regimens for "rehabilitation" akin to contemporary psychiatric treatment. From the outside, all this tends to be regarded as "brainwashing," but insiders will turn the accusation outward, claiming that it is those in the society-at-large who are "brainwashed." Though there can really be no resolution to this conflict of interpretations, the widespread incidence of similar "coercive persuasion" outside Jonestown suggests that the fact it was practiced at Jonestown is not so unusual, at least within the context of other-worldly sects, or total institutions in general, for that matter.

What is unusual is the direction which coercive persuasion or "brainwashing" took. Jones worked to instill devotion in unusual ways—ways which fostered the acceptability of "revolutionary suicide" among his followers. During "white nights" of emergency mobilization, he conducted rituals of proclaimed mass suicide, giving "poison" to all members, saying they would die within the hours. According to one defector, Deborah Blakey, Jones "explained that the poison was not real and we had just been through a loyalty test. He warned us that the time was not far off when it would be necessary for us to die by our own hands." This event initially left Blakey "indifferent" to whether she "lived or died." A true believer in the Peoples Temple was more emphatic: disappointed by the string of false collective suicides, in a note to Jones he hoped for "the real thing" so that they could all pass beyond the suffering of this world. Some people yielded to Jim Jones only because their will to resist was beaten down; others, including many "seniors"— the elderly members of the Peoples Temple—felt they owed everything to Jim Jones, and provided him with a strong core of unequivocal support. Jones allowed open dissension at "town meetings" apparently because, with the support of the "seniors," he knew he could prevail. Thus, no matter what they wanted personally, people learned to leave their fates in the hands of Jim Jones, and accept what he demanded. The specific uses of coercive persuasion at Jonestown help explain how (but not why) the mass murder/suicide was implemented. But it is the special use, not the general nature of "brainwashing" which distinguishes Jonestown from most other-worldly sects.

MEAT EATERS AND BEAN EATERS

Aside from "brainwashing," a second major kind of accusation about Jonestown, put forward most forcefully by Deborah Blakey, concerns the work discipline and diet there. Blakey swore in an affidavit that the work load was excessive and the food served to the average residents of Jonestown, inadequate. She abhorred the contradiction between the conditions she reported and the privileged diet of Reverend Jones and his inner circle. Moreover, because she had dealt with the group's finances, she knew that money could have been directed to providing a more adequate diet.

Blakey's moral sensibilities notwithstanding, the disparity between the diet of the elite and of the average Jonestowner should come as no surprise: it parallels Erving Goffman's description of widespread hierarchies of privilege in total institutions. Her concern about the average diet is more the point. But here, other accounts differ from Blakey's report. Maria Katsaris, a consort of Reverend Jones, wrote her father a letter extolling the virtues of the Agricultural Project's "cutlass" beans used as a meat substitute. And Paula Adams, who survived the Jonestown holocaust because she resided at the Peoples Temple house in Georgetown, expressed ambivalence about the Jonestown community in an interview after the mass murder/suicide. But she also remarked, "My daughter ate very well. She got eggs and milk every day. How many black children in the ghetto eat that well?" The accounts of surviving members of Reverend Jones' personal staff and inner circle, like Katsaris and Adams, are suspect, of course, in exactly the opposite way as those of people like the "Concerned Relatives." But the inside accounts are corroborated by at least one outsider, *Washington Post* reporter Charles Krause. On his arrival at Jonestown in the company of U.S. Congressman Leo Ryan, Krause noted, "contrary to what the Concerned Relatives had told us, nobody seemed to be starving. Indeed, everyone seemed quite healthy." It is difficult to assess these conflicting views. Beginning early in the summer of 1977, Jones set in motion the mass exodus of some 800 Peoples Temple members from California to Jonestown. Though Jonestown could adequately house only about 500 people by then, the population quickly climbed well beyond that mark, at the same time ballooning way past the agricultural base of the settlement. The exodus also caused Jonestown to become "top heavy" with less-productive seniors and children. Anything close to agricultural self-sufficiency then became a more elusive and long-range goal. As time wore on during the group's last year of existence, Jones himself became ever more fixated on the prospect of a mass emigration from Guyana, and in this light, any sort of long-range agricultural development strategy seemed increas-

ingly irrational. According to The New York Times, the former Jonestown farm manager, Jim Bogue, suggested that the agricultural program at Jonestown would have succeeded in the long run, if it had been adhered to. But with the emerging plans for emigration, it was not followed, and thus became merely a charade for the benefit of the Guyanese government. This analysis would seem to have implications for internal conflicts about goals within Jonestown: for example, Jim Jones' only natural son, Stephan Jones, as well as several other young men in the Peoples Temple, came to believe in Jonestown as a socialist agrarian community, not as an other-worldly sect headed up by Jim Jones. Reflecting about his father after the mass murder/suicide, Stephan Jones commented, "I don't mind discrediting him, but I'm still a socialist, and Jim Jones will be used to discredit socialism. People will use him to discredit what we built. Jonestown was not Jim Jones, although he believed it was."

The "seniors" who provided social security checks, gardened, and produced handicraft articles for sale in Georgetown in lieu of heavy physical labor, as well as the fate of agricultural productivity—these both reinforce the assessment that Jim Jones' vision of the Peoples Temple approximates the "other-worldly sect" as an ideal type. In such sects, as a rule, proponents seek to survive not on the basis of productive labor (as in more "worldy utopian" communal groups), but on the basis of patronage, petty financial schemes, and the building of a "community of goods" through proselytism. This was just the case with Jonestown: the community of goods which Jones built up is valued at more than $12 million. As a basis for satisfying collective wants, any agricultural production at Jonestown would have paled in comparison to this amassed wealth.

But even if the agricultural project itself became a charade, it is no easy task to create a plausible charade in the midst of relatively infertile soil reclaimed from dense jungle; this would have required the long hours of work which Peoples Temple defectors described. Such a charade could serve as yet another effective means of social control. In the first place, it gave a purposeful role to those who envisioned Jonestown as an experimental socialist agrarian community. Beyond this, it monopolized the waking hours of most of the populace in exhausting work, and gave them only a minimal (though probably adequate) diet on which to do it. It is easy to imagine that many city people, or those with bourgeois sensibilities in general, would not find this their cup of tea in any case. But the demanding daily regimen, however abhorrent to the uninitiated, is widespread in other-worldly sects. Various programs of fasting and work asceticism have long been regarded as signs of piety and routes to religious enlightenment or ecstasy. In the contemporary American Krishna groups, an alternation of nonsugar and high-sugar phases of the diet seems to create an almost addictive attachment to the food which is communally dispersed. And we need look no later in history than to Saint Benedict's order to find a situation in which the personal time of participants is eliminated for all practical purposes, with procedures of mortification for offenders laid out by Saint Benedict in his *Rule.* The concerns of Blakey and others about diet, work, and discipline may have some basis, but they have probably been exaggerated, and in any case, they do not distinguish Jonestown from other-worldly sects in general.

COMMUNITY OF GOODS

One final public concern with the Peoples Temple deserves mention because it so closely parallels previous sectarian practice: the Reverend Jim Jones is accused of swindling people out of their livelihoods and life circumstances by tricking them into signing over their money and possessions to the Peoples Temple or its inner circle of members. Of course, Jones considered this a "community of goods" and correctly pointed to a long tradition of such want satisfaction among other-worldly sects; in an interview just prior to the mass murder/suicide, Jones cited Jesus' call to hold all things in common. There are good grounds to think that Reverend Jones carried this philosophy into the realm

of a con game. Still, it should be noted that in the suicidal end, Jones did not benefit from all the wealth the way a good number of other self-declared prophets and messiahs have done.

As with its disciplinary practices and its round of daily life, the community of goods in the Peoples Temple at Jonestown emphasizes its similarities to other-worldly sects—both the contemporary ones labeled "cults" by their detractors, and historical examples which are often revered in retrospect by contemporary religious culture. The elaboration of these affinities is in no way intended to suggest that we can or should vindicate the duplicity, the bizarre sexual and psychological intimidation, and the hardships of daily life at Jonestown. But it must be recognized that the Jonestown settlement was a good deal less unusual than some of us might like to think: the things which detractors find abhorrent in the life of the Peoples Temple at Jonestown prior to the final "white night" of murder and suicide are the core nature of other-worldly sects; it should come as no surprise that practices like those in Jonestown are widespread, both in historical and contemporary other-worldly sects. Granted that the character of such sects—the theocratic basis of authority, the devices of mortification and social control, and the demanding regimen of everyday life—predispose people in such groups to respond to the whims of their leaders, whatever fanatic and zealous directions they may take. But given the widespread occurrence of other-worldly sects, the other-worldly features of Jonestown are in themselves insufficient to explain the bizarre fate of its participants. If we are to understand the unique turn of events at Jonestown, we must look to certain distinctive features of the Peoples Temple—things which make it unusual among other-worldly sects, and we must try to comprehend the subjective meanings of these features for various of Jonestown's participants.

RACE AND IDEOLOGY

If the Peoples Temple was distinctive among other-worldly sects, it is for two reasons: first, the group was far and away more thoroughly racially integrated than any other such group today. Second, the Peoples Temple was distinctively proto-communist in ideology. Both of these conditions, together with certain personal fear of Jim Jones (mixed perhaps with organic disorders and assorted drugs), converged in the active mind of the reverend to give a special twist to the apocalyptic quest of his flock. Let us consider these matters in turn.

In the Peoples Temple, Jim Jones had consistently sought to transcend racism in peace rather than in struggle. The origins of this approach, like most of Jones' early life, are by now shrouded in myth. But it is clear that Jones was committed to racial harmony in his Indiana ministry. In the 1950s, his formation of an interracial congregation met with much resistance in Indianapolis, and this persecution was one impetus for the exodus to California. There is room for debate on how far Jones' operation actually went toward racial equality, or to what degree it simply perpetuated racism, albeit in a racially harmonious microcosm. But the Peoples Temple fostered greater racial equality and harmony than that of the society-at-large, and in this respect, it has few parallels in present-day communal groups, much less mainstream religious congregations. The significance of this cannot easily be assayed, but one view of it is captured in a letter from a 20-year-old Jonestown girl: she wrote to her mother in Evansville, Indiana, that she could "walk down the street now without the fear of having little old white ladies call me nigger."

Coupled with the commitment to racial integration, and again in contrast with most other-worldly sects, the Peoples Temple moved strongly toward ideological communism. Most other-worldly sects practice religiously inspired communism—the "clerical" or "Christian" socialism which Marx and Engels railed against. But few, if any, to date have flirted with the likes of Marx, Lenin, and Stalin. By contrast, it has become clear that, whatever the contradictions other socialists point to between Jones' messianism and socialism, the Reverend Jim Jones and his staff considered themselves socialists. In his column "Perspectives from Guyana," Jim Jones

maintained, "neither my colleagues nor I are any longer caught up in the opiate of religion. . . ." Though the practice of the group prior to the mass murder/suicide was not based on any doctrinaire Marxism, at least some of the recruits to the group were young radical intellectuals, and one of the group's members, Richard Tropp, gave evening classes on radical political theory. In short, radical socialist currents were unmistakably present in the group.

PREACHING ATHEISM

It is perhaps more questionable whether the Peoples Temple was religious in any conventional sense of the term. Of course, all utopian communal groups are religious in that they draw together true believers who seek to live out a heretical or heterodox interpretation of the meaningfulness of social existence. In this sense, the Peoples Temple was a religious group, just as Frederick Engels once observed that socialist sects of the nineteenth century paralleled the character of primitive Christian and Reformation sects. Clearly, Jim Jones was more self-consciously religious than the socialist sects were. Though he "preached atheism," and did not believe in a God that answers prayer, he did embrace reincarnation, and a surviving resident of Jonestown remembers him saying, "Our religion is this: your highest service to God is service to your fellow man." On the other hand, it seems that the outward manifestations of conventional religious activity—revivals, sermons, faith healings—were, at least in Jim Jones' view, calculated devices to draw people into an organization which was something quite different. It is a telling point in this regard that Jones ceased the practice of faith healings and cut off other religious activities once he moved to Jonestown. Jones' wife Marceline once noted that Jim Jones considered himself a Marxist who "used religion to try to get some people out of the opiate of religion." In a remarkable off-the-cuff interview with Richard and Harriet Tropp—the two Jonestown residents who were writing a book about the Peoples Temple—Jones reflected on the early years of his ministry, claiming, "what a hell of a battle that (integration) was—I thought 'I'll never make a revolution, I can't even get those fuckers to integrate, much less get them to any communist philosophy.' " In the same interview, Jones intimated that he had been a member of the U.S. Communist party in the early 1950s. Of course, with Jones' Nixonesque concern for his place in history, it is possible that his hindsight, even in talking with sympathetic biographers, was not the same as his original motives. In the interview with the Tropps, Jones hinted that the entire development of the Peoples Temple down to the Jonestown Agricultural Project derived from his communist beliefs. This interview and Marceline Jones' comment give strong evidence of an early communist orientation in Jones. Whenever this orientation originated, the move to Jonestown was in part predicated on it. The socialist government of Guyana was generally committed to supporting socialists seeking refuge from capitalist societies, and they apparently thought Jones' flexible brand of Marxism fit well within the country's political matrix. By 1973, when negotiations with Guyana about an agricultural project were initiated, Jones and his aides were professing identification with the world-historical communist movement.

THE PERSECUTION COMPLEX

The convergence of racial integration and crude communism gave a distinctly political character to what in many other respects was an other-worldly religious sect. The injection of radical politics gave a heightened sense of persecution to the Jonestown Agricultural Project. Jim Jones seems to have both fed this heightened sense of persecution to his followers, and to have been devoured by it himself. Jones manipulated fears among his followers by controlling information and spreading false rumors about news events in the United States. With actual knowledge of certain adversaries, and fed by his own premonitions, Jones spread premonitions among his followers, thereby heightening their dedication. In the process, Jones disenchanted a few,

who became Judas Iscariots, in time bringing the forces of legitimated external authority to "persecute" Jones and his true believers in their jungle theocracy.

The persecution complex is a stock-in-trade of other-worldly sects. It is naturally engendered by a radical separation from the world of society-at-large. An apocalyptic mission develops in such a way that "persecution" from the world left behind is taken as a sign of the sanctity of the group's chosen path of salvation. Though racial and political persecution are not usually among the themes of other-worldly persecution, they do not totally break the other-worldly way of interpreting experience. But the heightened sense of persecution at Jonestown did reduce the disconnection from society-at-large which is the signature of other-worldly sects.

Most blacks in the U.S. have already experienced "persecution"; if Jim Jones gave his black followers some relief from a ghetto existence (which many seem to have felt he did), he also made a point of reminding the blacks in his group that persecution still awaited them back in the ghettos and rural areas of the United States. In the California years, for example, the Peoples Temple would stage mock lynchings of blacks by the Ku Klux Klan, as a form of political theater. And according to Deborah Blakey, Jones "convinced black Temple members that if they did not follow him to Guyana, they would be put into concentration camps and killed."

Similarly, white socialist intellectuals could easily develop paranoia about their activities; as any participant in the New Left movement of the 1960s and early 1970s knows, paranoia was a sort of badge of honor to some people. Jones fed this sort of paranoia by telling whites that the CIA listed them as enemies of the state.

Jones probably impressed persecution upon his followers to increase their allegiance to him. But Jones himself was caught up in a web of persecution and betrayal. The falling out between Jones and Grace and Tim Stoen seems central here. In conjunction with the imminent appearance of negative news articles, the fight over custody of John Victor

Stoen—Grace's son whom both Jones and Tim Stoen claimed to have fathered—triggered Jones' 1977 decision to remove himself from the San Francisco Temple to Guyana.

We may never know what happened between the Stoens and Jones. According to Terri Buford, a former Jonestown insider, Tim Stoen left the Peoples Temple shortly after it became known that in the 1960s he had gone on a Rotary-sponsored speaking tour denouncing communism. Both sides have accused the other of being the progenitors of violence in the Peoples Temple. To reporters who accompanied Congressman Ryan, Jones charged that the Stoen couple had been government agents and provocateurs who had advocated bombing, burning, and terrorism. This possibility could have been regarded as quite plausible by Jones and his staff, for they possessed documents about alleged similar Federal Bureau of Investigation moves against the Weather Underground and the Church of Scientology. The struggle between Jones and the Stoens thus could easily have personified to Jones the quintessence of a conspiracy against him and his work. It certainly intensified negative media attention on the Temple.

For all his attempts to garner favor from the press, Jones failed in the crucial instance: the San Francisco investigative reporters gave horror stories about the Peoples Temple and Jones' custody battle a good deal of play. Jones may well have been correct in his suspicion that he was not being treated fairly in the press. After the mass murder/suicide, the managing editor of the *San Francisco Examiner* proudly asserted in a January 15, 1979, letter to the *Wall Street Journal* that his paper had not been "morally neutral" in its coverage of the Peoples Temple.

The published horror stories were based on the allegations by defectors, the Stoens and Deborah Blakey foremost among them. How true, widespread, exaggerated, or isolated the incidents reported were, we do not know. Certainly they were generalized in the press to the point of creating an image of Jones as a total ogre. The defectors also initiated legal proceedings against the Temple. And

the news articles began to stir the interest of government authorities in the operation. These developments were not lost on Jim Jones. The custody battle with the Stoens seems to have precipitated Jones' mass suicide threat to the Guyanese government. Not coincidentally, according to Jim Jones' only natural son, Stephan Jones, at this point the first "white night" drills for mass suicide were held (Stephan Jones connects these events with the appearance of several negative news articles).

With these sorts of events in mind, it is not hard to see how it came to be that Jim Jones felt betrayed by the Stoens and the other defectors, and persecuted by those who appeared to side with the defectors—the press and the government foremost among them. In September 1978, Jones went so far as to retain well-known conspiracy theorist and lawyer Mark Lane to investigate the possibility of a plot against the Peoples Temple. In the days immediately after he was retained by Jones, Mark Lane (perhaps self-servingly) reported in a memorandum to Jones that "even a cursory examination" of the available evidence "reveals that there has been a coordinated campaign to destroy the Peoples Temple and to impugn the reputation of its leader." Those involved were said to include the U.S. Customs Bureau, the Federal Communications Commission, the Central Intelligence Agency, the Federal Bureau of Investigation, and the Internal Revenue Service. Lane's assertions probably had little basis in fact: though several of the named agencies independently had looked into certain Temple activities, none of them had taken any direct action against the Temple, even though they may have had some cause for doing so. The actual state of affairs notwithstanding, with Lane's assertions, Jones had substantiation of his sense of persecution from a widely touted theorist of conspiracies.

The sense of persecution which gradually developed in the Peoples Temple from its beginning and increased markedly at Jonestown must have come to a head with the visit there of U.S. Congressman Leo Ryan. The U.S. State Department has revealed that Jones had agreed to a visit by Ryan, but withdrew permission when it became known that a contingent of "Concerned Relatives" as well as certain members of the press would accompany Ryan to Guyana. Among the Concerned Relatives who came with Ryan was the Stoen couple; in fact, Tim Stoen was known as a "leader" of the Concerned Relatives. Reporters with Ryan included two from the *San Francisco Chronicle,* a paper which had already pursued investigative reporting on the Peoples Temple, as well as Gordon Lindsay, an independent newsman who had written a negative story on the Peoples Temple intended to be (but never actually) published in the *National Enquirer.* This entourage could hardly have been regarded as objective or unbiased by Jim Jones and his closer supporters. Instead, it identified Ryan with the forces of persecution, personified by the Stoens and the investigative press, and it set the stage for the mass murder/suicide which had already been threatened in conjunction with the custody fight.

The ways in which the Peoples Temple came to differ from more typical other-worldly sects are more a matter of degree than of kind, but the differences together profoundly altered the character of the scene of Jonestown. Though the avowed radicalism, the interracial living, and the defector-media-government "conspiracy" are structurally distinct from one another, Jim Jones drew them together into a tableau of conspiracy which was intended to increase his followers' attachment to him, but ironically brought his legitimacy as a messiah into question, undermined the other-worldly possibilities of the Peoples Temple Agricultural Project, and placed the group on the stage of history in a distinctive relationship to the apocalypse.

VIRTUOSI OF THE COLLECTIVE LIFE

Other-worldly sects by their very nature are permeated with apocalyptic ideas. The sense of a decaying social order is personally experienced by the religious seeker in a life held to be untenable, meaningless, or both. This interpretation of life is collectively affirmed and transcended in other-worldly sects, which purport to offer "heaven-on-earth," beyond the effects of the apocalypse. Such sects

promise the grace of a theocracy in which followers can sometimes really escape the "living hell" of society-at-large. Many of Reverend Jones' followers seem to have joined the Peoples Temple with this in mind. But the predominance of blacks and the radical ideology of the Temple, together with the persistent struggle against the defectors and the "conspiracy" which formed around them in the minds of the faithful each gave the true believers' sense of persecution a more immediate and pressing, rather than "other-worldly" cast. Jones used these elements to heighten his followers' sense of persecution from the outside, but this device itself may have drawn into question the ability of the supposed charismatic leader to provide an other-worldly sanctuary. By the middle of October, a month before Congressman Ryan's trip in November 1978, Jones' position of preeminent leadership was beginning to be questioned not only by disappointed religious followers, but also by previously devoted "seniors" who were growing tired of the ceaseless meetings and the increasingly untenable character of everyday life, and by key virtuosi of collective life who felt Jones was responsible for their growing inability to deal successfully with Jonestown's material operations. Once those who were dissatisfied circumvented Jones' intelligence network of informers and began to establish solidarity with one another, the "conspiracy" can truly be said to have taken hold within Jonestown itself. If the times were apocalyptic, Reverend Jones was like the revolutionary millenarians described by Norman Cohn and Gunther Lewy. Rather than successfully proclaiming the postapocalyptic sanctuary, Jones was reduced to declaiming the web of "evil" powers in which he was ensnared, and searching with chiliastic expectation for the imminent cataclysm which would announce the beginning of the kingdom of righteousness.

Usually, other-worldly sects have a sense of the eternal about them: having escaped "this" world, they adopt the temporal trappings of "heaven," which amounts to a timeless bliss of immortality. But Jim Jones had not really established a postapocalyptic heavenly plateau. Even if he had promised this to his followers, it was only just being built in the form of the Agricultural Project. And it was not even clear that Jonestown itself was the promised land: Jones did not entirely trust the Guyanese government, and he was considering seeking final asylum in Cuba or the Soviet Union. Whereas other-worldly sects typically assert that heaven is at hand, Jones could only hold it out as a future goal, and one which became more and more elusive as the forces of "persecution" tracked him to Guyana. Thus, Jones and his followers were still within the throes of the apocalypse, still, as they conceived it, the forces of good battling against the evil and conspiratorial world which could not tolerate a living example of a racially integrated American socialist utopia.

In the struggle against evil, Jones and his true believers took on the character of what I have termed a "warring sect"—fighting a decisive Manichean struggle with the forces of evil. Such a struggle seems almost inevitable when political rather than religious themes of apocalypse are stressed, and it is clear that Jones and his staff at times acted within this militant frame of reference. For example, they maintained armed guards around the settlement, held "white night" emergency drills, and even staged mock CIA attacks on Jonestown. By doing so, they undermined the plausibility of an other-worldly existence. The struggle of a warring sect takes place in historical time, where one action builds on another, where decisive outcomes of previous events shape future possibilities. The contradiction between this earthly struggle and the heaven-on-earth Jones would have liked to proclaim (for example, in "Perspectives from Guyana") gave Jonestown many of its strange juxtapositions—of heaven and hell, of suffering and bliss, of love and coercion. Perhaps even Jones himself, for all his megalomaniacal ability to transcend the contradictions which others saw in him (and labeled him an "opportunist" for), could not endure the struggle for his own immortality. If he were indeed a messianic incarnation of God, as he sometimes claimed, presumably Jones could have either won the struggle of the warring sect against

its evil persecutors or delivered his people to the bliss of another world.

In effect, Jones had brought his flock to the point of straddling the two sides of the apocalypse. Had he established his colony beyond the unsympathetic preview of defectors, Concerned Relatives, investigative reporters, and governmental agencies, the other-worldly tableau perhaps could have been sustained with less-repressive methods of social control. As it was, Jones and the colony experienced the three interconnected limitations of group totalism which Robert Jay Lifton described with respect to the Chinese Communist revolution: (1) diminishing conversions, (2) inner antagonism (that is, of disillusioned participants) to the suffocation of individuality, and (3) increasing penetration of the "idea-tight milieu control" by outside forces. As Lifton noted, revolutionaries are engaged in a quest for immortality. Other-worldly sectarians in a way short-circuit this quest by the fiat of *asserting* their immortality—positing the timeless heavenly plateau which exists *beyond* history as the basis of their everyday life. But under the persistent eyes of external critics, and because Jones himself exploited such "persecution" to increase his social control, he could not sustain the illusion of other-worldly immortality.

On the other hand, the Peoples Temple could not achieve the sort of political victory which would have been the goal of a warring sect. Since revolutionary war involves a struggle with an established political order in unfolding historical time, revolutionaries can only attain immortality in the wide-scale victory of the revolution over the "forces of reaction." Ironically, as Lifton pointed out, even the initial political and military victory of the revolutionary forces does not end the search for immortality: even in victory, revolution can only be sustained through diffusion of its principles and goals. But as Max Weber observed, in the long run, it seems impossible to maintain the charismatic enthusiasm of revolution; more pragmatic concerns come to the fore, and as the ultimate ends of revolution are faced off against everyday life and its demands, the quest for immortality fades, and the immortality of the revolutionary moment is replaced by the myth of a grand revolutionary past.

The Peoples Temple could not begin to achieve revolutionary immortality in historical time, for it could not even pretend to achieve any victory against its enemies. If it had come to a pitched battle, the Jonestown defenders—like the Symbionese Liberation Army against the Los Angeles Police Department S.W.A.T. (strategic weapons and tactics) Team—would have been wiped out.

But the Peoples Temple could create a kind of "immortality" which is really not a possibility for political revolutionaries. They could abandon apocalyptic hell by the act of mass suicide. This would shut out the opponents of the Temple: they could not be the undoing of what was already undone, and there could be no recriminations against the dead. It could also achieve the other-worldly salvation Jones had promised his more religious followers. Mass suicide united the divergent public threads of meaningful existence at Jonestown—those of political revolution and religious salvation. It was an awesome vehicle for a powerful statement of collective solidarity by the true believers among the people of Jonestown—that they would rather die together than have the life that was created together subjected to gradual decimation and dishonor at the hands of authorities regarded as illegitimate.

Most warring sects reach a grisly end: occasionally, they achieve martyrdom, but if they lack a constituency, their extermination is used by the state as proof of its monopoly on the legitimate use of force. "Revolutionary" suicide is a victory by comparison. The event can be drawn upon for moral didactics, but this cannot erase the stigma that Jonestown implicitly places on the world that its members left behind. Nor can the state punish the dead who are guilty, among other things, of murdering a U.S. congressman, three newsmen, a Concerned Relative, and how ever many Jonestown residents did not willingly commit suicide. Though they paid the total price of death for their ultimate commitment, and though they achieved

little except perhaps sustenance of their own collective sense of honor, still those who won this hollow victory cannot have it taken away from them. In the absence of retribution, the state search for living guilty, as well as the widespread outcry against "cults," take on the character of scapegoating. Those most responsible are beyond the reach of the law: unable to escape the hell of their own lives by creating an other-worldly existence on earth, they instead sought their "immortality" in death, and left it to others to ponder the apocalypse which they have unveiled.

READING 12–2

THE UNIFICATION CHURCH

Eileen Barker

The full title of the Unification Church is the Holy Spirit Association for the Unification of World Christianity. It was founded in 1954 and although its members prefer to being known as Unificationists, Americans generally refer to them as "Moonies" because the movement's founder was called Sun Myung Moon (Barker 1995, 223).

Comparing this account of the Unification Church by Eileen Barker, a professor of sociology at the University of London, with the Peoples Temple immediately underscores the point that contemporary alternative religions can differ markedly. The Peoples Temple destroyed itself by its determination to cut itself off from the rest of society, its founder became a prophet for a relatively small cohort of followers; and although their existence ended in a foreign country, his movement could lay no claims to being an international phenomenon. In contrast, the Unification Church thoroughly integrated itself into Western capitalistic society and has made itself a political force to be reckoned with. The Unification Church's wealth is invested in multimillion-dollar corporations and through its publishing empire it offers an outlet—regardless of the

Source: University of New York Press, pages 223–229. Reprinted from *America's Alternative Religions* by Timothy Miller (Ed.), by permission of the State University of New York Press, pages 223–229, © 1995, State University of New York. All rights reserved.

fact that it is a nonestablishment religion—for conservative political views. While the core membership of the movement, Barker surmises, is unlikely to have been more than about 10,000 in the West, its impact on society has proved to be far greater than most cults, and its reach extends far outside the Western hemisphere. After all, it was founded in Korea, in 1954, by a Korean, and only reached the West in the late 1950s.

Of special interest in this account are the author's views regarding the brainwashing the Unification Church has from time to time been accused of perpetrating on its adherents. The same charge has been leveled at other cults, as I noted in the Introduction, but the Moonies have been subjected to criticism more than most. Barker is of the opinion that these accusations are mostly distortions and implies that conventional religion is also open to such a charge.

She is cautious about predicting what future awaits the Unification Church, but, unlike the followers of James Jones, it most decidedly does have a future—as do the wiccans and the Rastafari.

The Unification Church or, to give it its full title, the Holy Spirit Association for the Unification of World Christianity, was founded in Korea in 1954. Although the members prefer to be called Unificationists, they are referred to in the media and popularly known as "Moonies"—a label derived from the name of the movement's founder, Sun Myung Moon.

Moon was born in what is now North Korea in 1920 to a family which converted to Christianity when he was ten years old. It is claimed that on Easter Sunday, 1936, Jesus appeared to Moon and told him that God had chosen him for the special mission of restoring His Kingdom of Heaven on earth. For the next nine years, through prayer and spiritual communications with other religious leaders (such as Jesus, Moses, and Buddha), Moon sought to solve the fundamental questions of life and the universe, and, through spiritual communication with God Himself, he received the revelations that were later to form the basis of Unification theology.[1] Having studied electrical engineering in Japan, and then worked as an electrician in Korea, Moon started his own church after the end of World War II; but, always a controversial figure, he found himself arrested on several occasions, and spent over two and a half years in a communist labour camp, from which he was liberated by the Allies at the end of the Korean War.

Missionaries were sent by Moon to the West in the late 1950s. They met with limited success at first,[2] but, from the early 1970s, when Moon and his family came to live in the United States, the Unification Church became one of the new religions with the highest profile throughout the West. "Moonies" became familiar figures, selling literature, flowers, candy and other goods in the streets, shopping malls and airports, and "witnessing" on campuses to potential converts, inviting them to visit a local centre to learn more about the movement. Moon himself became a household name, largely as a result of his speaking at a number of rallies, his supporting Nixon's continuing presidency at the time of Watergate, and the movement's being the subject of an investigation by a congressional committee in the late 1970s.

The Unification movement has given rise to innumerable organizations and projects, among which one might, almost at random, name the Korean Folk Ballet, the Unification Theological Seminary, the Washington Institute, the *Washington Times,* the International Religious Foundation, the Collegiate Association for the Research of Principles (CARP), CAUSA, and a projected international highway that includes a tunnel between Japan and Korea. It has also acquired a number of valuable properties, including the New Yorker hotel and the old Tiffany building in Manhattan.

One of the features of the movement has always been its internationalism. Couples from different cultures, sometimes unable to speak in a common language and with little in common apart from their membership of the movement, have been married to each other; young converts have not infrequently been expected to travel to another country at a moment's notice. Unificationists are now to be found in over 150 countries throughout the world, although sometimes there may be no more than a small handful of members, occasionally living "underground" if, as in some Muslim societies, active proselytizing is illegal. Since 1989, members of the Unification Church, like members of many other new religious movements (and, indeed, mainstream American Evangelicals), have been active in eastern Europe and some of the erstwhile Republics of the Soviet Union—particularly in Russia.

Since the early 1970s, but more vociferously following the Jonestown tragedy in 1978, the media and the anticult movement have publicised a number of accusations about the church—that it was amassing large fortunes for its leaders, that it was engaged in nefarious political activities, that it brainwashed and exploited its members, that it was breaking up families and carrying out all manner of other deceptive and sinister practices. In some circles, such accusations have been taken as a justification for the expensive and illegal practice of "deprogramming" to which a considerable number of Unificationists have been, and continue to be, subjected.

Moon himself has been the object of more suspicion and enmity than almost any other contemporary religious leader. He has been attacked for his theology, which has been described as bizarre, heretical and/or blasphemous, for his political beliefs, which are strongly anti-communist, and for his accumulation of real estate and vast business empires which include the manufacture of parts for armaments in Korea. Despite a number of *amicus curiae* briefs submitted in his defence by the mainstream churches, Moon was convicted of conspiracy to evade taxes in 1982, and was sentenced to prison for eighteen months. Since his release, he has spent most of his time in the East, although he still visits the United States and has made a number of appearances both on semi-public occasions, such as at conferences that the movement has organised, and, more privately, when addressing his American followers.

Unlike many new religious movements, the Unification Church has an elaborate and comprehensive theology, based on Moon's particular interpretation of the Old and New Testaments. The more publicly accessible part of the belief system is to be found in the *Divine Principle,* a book in which his followers wrote down his teachings. This reveals that God created Adam and Eve in the hope that they could establish a God-centred family. However, before they were sufficiently mature to be married, the Archangel Lucifer, who was jealous of God's love for Adam, seduced Eve into having a spiritual sexual relationship with him. Eve then had an illicit physical relationship with Adam. The Fall was, thus, the result of the misuse of the most powerful of all forces: love; and the children born of this Lucifer-centred union have been contaminated by Fallen Nature—which is, roughly, the Unificationist equivalent of original sin.

The *Divine Principle* interprets history as a series of attempts by key figures to restore the world according to God's original plan. Jesus was meant to perform this mission, but he was murdered before he was able to marry and set the foundation for the ideal God-centred family; he was, as a consequence, able to offer only spiritual salvation to the world. According to Unification theology, a careful reading of history since the time of Jesus demonstrates that the Lord of the Second Advent was born in Korea between 1917 and 1930. Unificationists believe that Moon is this Messiah and that, through his marriage to his present wife in 1960, he has laid the foundation for establishing the Kingdom of Heaven on earth. The final battle between God and Satan has been revealed to be that taking place between "godism," as exemplified by the Unification Church, and atheistic communism. A further elaboration of the theology, centring mainly on Moon and his family, and making abundant use of significant numbers and dates, is disseminated to the members in the form of transcripts of Moon's speeches. It has frequently been stated that Moon has received many more revelations that have yet to be released.[3]

The most important Unification rite is the mass wedding ceremony, or "Blessing," during which several thousands of couples whom Moon has "matched" are married. Shortly preceding the wedding ceremony, there is the Holy Wine Ceremony, during which, it is believed, the matched couples' blood lineage is purified, enabling them to bear children untainted by Fallen Nature. The marriages are not consummated for some time (ranging from a few days to several years) after the Blessing, but when they are, there is a special "three-day ceremony" performed by each couple. Further ceremonies, equivalent in some ways to infant baptism, are performed after the birth of "blessed" children.

Members observe a Pledge service at 5 A.M. on the first day of each week, month, and year. Also on Sundays, there is a mid-morning and/or evening service which non-members might attend at some of the larger centres. Five major Holy Days (God's Day, Parents' Day, Children's Day, the Day of All Things, and True Parents' [Reverend and Mrs. Moon's] Birthday) are celebrated each year. A number of other rituals, many of them commemorating happenings and accomplishments of theological significance, have emerged during the years and become part of what is known as the Unification Tradition.[4]

While the basic tenets of Unification theology have not changed significantly since they were first taught in America in the 1960s, there have been several elaborations and a number of significant additions. It could be argued that there have been modifications in the movement's eschatology—for example, many of the early members in America were expecting an apocalyptic event in 1967. When nothing much seemed to have happened, several members left the movement, but to those who remained it was explained that it had been a misguided understanding on the part of some of the leaders that had led to an expectation of a visible change—rather than the significant spiritual change that had, it was claimed, been accomplished. With the passage of time, imminent dates of great import have continued to hold out promises (on February 23rd, 1977, Moon declared the beginning of the new age),[5] but the members' understanding of the changes anticipated for such successive date seems, at least to an outsider, to have become progressively less apocalyptic. Very generally speaking, it has been possible to observe a shift from a movement

with millennial expectations that God was going to bring about a miraculous change, to one in which a utopian ideal might be established by following the leadership of the Messiah, to a movement whose members are more reformist in their visions of the future, accepting that if changes are to take place, then they themselves are responsible for bringing these about. Moon's claims of important victories being actually accomplished continue, however. One comparatively recent such declaration was made following Moon's meeting in December 1991 with the late Kim Il Sung, the president of North Korea, who had allegedly tried to kill Moon at least three times:

> The natural subjugation of Kim Il Sung, who symbolizes all the evil, satanic qualities, including false parenthood, means false parents have finally surrendered in front of the True Parents. Father [Moon] has completely fulfilled God's dispensational history.[6]

One of the more significant additions to the theology, which was to lead to what might be termed a revivalist movement within the church, was revealed after the Reverend and Mrs. Moon's seventeen-year-old son, Heung Jin Nim, was involved in what proved to be a fatal car accident in America. Moon has told his followers that he had the power to save his son, but that he had let him die: Heung Jin Nim's death was the culmination of a final showdown between Moon and Satan, who, having been unable to "invade" Moon himself, had turned to Moon's family. Through this sacrifice, Heung Jin Nim had become the bridge between the spirit world and the physical world, and within the spirit world, we are told, "Jesus is now known as the old Christ and Heung Jin is the young Christ."[7]

Shortly after Heung Jin's death on January 2nd, 1984, a number of members began to receive messages from him from the spirit world. One of the most well known of these spiritual mediums is a British woman, Faith Jones, who reports that soon after his death, Heung Jin Nim told her, "You must become my body, Faith, I need your body to walk, talk and speak, your body must become my body."[8] Another "channel" was an American man through whom Heung Jin Nim gave a series of well-attended lectures in New York towards the end of 1987. Some of the other members were less successful—a small group in Germany left the movement after it was decided that the messages coming through from Heung Jin Nim did not match the statements made by the local leader.

Later, Heung Jin Nim took over the body of a young Unificationist from Zimbabwe who had been practically unknown to anyone outside Africa at the time. Soon, however, the news had spread that Moon and his family fully accepted that this was indeed Heung Jin Nim, and the movement took on a revivalist character as "Second Self Heung Jin Nim" spoke at meetings to the membership, making a tremendous impression on nearly all those who saw him in action. He told the Bible stories from a new, robust perspective which included some interesting African embellishments. Special meetings were convened at which particular categories of members, such as the "blessed couples," were expected to confess to their sins and were given "conditions," such as fasting or abstention from sex for varying periods of time, according to the severity of the sins. Even the most senior members of the movement did not escape his wrath at their misdemeanours, and at one time physical punishment was meted out to miscreants: Col. Pak, Moon's chief interpreter and one of his top aides, was, it is said, hit so severely that he was in hospital for several days. Second Self Heung Jin Nim also arranged for couples to conceive and bear children for other Unification couples who had found themselves unable to have children.[9]

But as time passed, Second Self Heung Jin Nim began to have revelations that differed, not just in interesting embellishments but in more fundamental ways, from Moon's revelations. Claims were made about the circumstances of the Fall, for example, that had serious implications for the movement's theodicy. About this time, Second Self Heung Jin Nim left the United States and went on a world tour of Europe and the East. His speeches were no longer distributed (as "Second Self Heung Jin Nim"). Soon after, it appears, Heung Jin Nim

left the Zimbabwe brother's body, the Zimbabwe brother returned to Zimbabwe, and the excitement of the revival died down.

An early observer of the Unification Church, John Lofland, noted that those who joined the movement on the West Coast of America in the early 1960s were "primarily white, Protestant, young (typically below age thirty-five), some had college training, most were Americans from lower-middle-class and small town backgrounds, and the rest were immigrants."[10] With the advent of the 1970s, and as the movement increasingly concentrated on converting college students, the social class and educational attainments of the membership rose. By the time of my own study in the mid-to late-1970s, those joining the movement were disproportionately male (2:1) and disproportionately from the upper-middle and middle-middle classes, and the average age of joining was 23.[11] Although the average age of membership does not increase by one year every twelve-month (due to the high turnover and the fact that new converts tend to be young), the average age of those who converted to the movement is now around the late-thirties—but the average age of all those in the movement has become much younger with the advent of a second generation. A few of the older "blessed" children are now young men and women, a handful of whom have themselves been blessed in marriage by Moon, but the majority of those born to Americans will not have reached their teens by the mid-1990s.

It has never been easy to assess the number of Unificationists at any one time. This is partly because, for different reasons, both the movement and its opponents have tended to exaggerate the figures and to discount the large turnover rate—the members because they wanted to seem more successful than they are, and the anticultists because they wanted to stress the threat of the movement and to deny the possibility that the "brainwashed" members are able to leave of their own free will. In fact, it is unlikely that there have ever been ten thousand core members at any one time in the West. Although many more may have flirted with

Unificationism for a short time, the majority of those who have joined have left within a comparatively short time. A few of those who leave do so because they have been expelled or forcibly "deprogrammed," but the vast majority leave because they themselves no longer wanted to stay—sometimes because they had become disillusioned with the leadership or because they no longer believed that what they were doing was actually going to produce the promised results. Some, still believing, have found the life too hard, or have wanted to escape from a particular situation or group of people—or, perhaps, from the partner chosen for them by Moon.[12] Yet others have just wanted to move on—to return to college, perhaps, or to enjoy more control over their own lives.[13]

The high drop-out rate among the membership, and the fact that around 90 percent of those who have been interested enough in the Unification Church to attend one of its residential seminars were perfectly capable of saying that they did not want to join the movement,[14] does, of course, seriously challenge the popular hypothesis that the Unification Church uses irresistible and irreversible techniques of brainwashing or mind control to obtain and keep its members. It would, on the contrary, seem that if sinister techniques are being used (and there is no evidence that any of the processes involved in proselytizing differ qualitatively from processes that are to be found in "outside" society), they are pretty ineffective.[15] Furthermore, comparative analysis has indicated that those who (according to a number of criteria independent of the fact that they had expressed an interest in the movement) might be considered particularly inadequate or suggestible were in fact unlikely to join, or they would join for a short period—of a week or so—and then leave.[16]

During the 1970s, it was easy to know who was and who was not a "real Unificationist," and anyone who left the movement was likely to be shunned by the remaining members. With the passage of time, however, unambiguous labels have become more difficult to apply to a number of individuals on the periphery of the movement, some of whom are not

themselves very sure whether or not they still accept enough of the movement's beliefs to continue to call themselves Unificationists, but who, nonetheless, keep in touch with the more committed membership and may attend the occasional Unificationist function. This blurring of the boundaries between "them" and "us" is in part a reflection of changes that have taken place both within the movement and in its relationship with the rest of American society.

Various levels of Unification membership have, however, existed for some time, the "core" members being those who have attracted the most attention and whose parents have been most anxious about their intensity of commitment. In America, where it has been predominantly single people rather than families who have joined the movement, the members tended to live together in communities, which have ranged in size from small apartments to the vast New Yorker hotel. Given the movement's theological position, it is not surprising that there are strict rules about the relationship between the sexes, with members segregated in dormitories and expected to regard each other as brothers and sisters whose marriage partners are chosen for them by Moon.

Around 1972 the majority of members in the West started to work full-time for the movement (sometimes for up to eighteen hours a day), often travelling in Mobile Fund-raising Teams (MFTs). Unificationists are also expected to try to bring "spiritual children" into the movement by "witnessing" to potential converts, but there are various other activities in which members may be involved, including such "missions" as public relations, working for one of the movement's publications or one of its businesses (such as the fishing industry or selling ginseng products), or organising the large number of conferences that have been arranged for theologians, clergy, academics, politicians, army personnel, and journalists. While many stories in the media have been gross distortions of the truth, there can be little doubt that life in the Unification Church has been, and continues to be, one in which the rank-and-file members have enjoyed far fewer of the material comforts of this world than they would have been likely to have done were they not members.

Towards the end of the 1970s, the category of "House Church" member was introduced to accommodate those (often older Unificationists with young families) who preferred to live in their own homes and to continue to work outside the movement. At a much less committed level are people who may be referred to as "Associates," some of whom may attend occasional services or keep spasmodically in touch with some members, but many of whom have done little more than sign a piece of paper at some time stating that they were in sympathy with one or other of the movement's tenets. More recently, "core members" have been living with their young children as self-contained units, or in semi-self-contained apartments in a centre with other Unificationists—or, in some instances, with or close by their non-Unificationist parents, having been encouraged to move to their home towns and to find outside work or to set up small businesses with other members, tithing a percentage of their income to the movement.

It would be foolhardy to anticipate what the future holds for the Unification Church, but the demographic factors of a membership which has shifted from one of young, idealistic persons, eager to sacrifice themselves for the cause of restoring the Kingdom of Heaven on earth, to a middle-aged membership with more immediate responsibilities towards their young families has meant that many changes have already occurred, only the more obvious of which have been mentioned in this short chapter. Although Moon seems to be in excellent health, he himself is aware that he cannot live forever, and he has started to make plans for a future without his presence in the physical world. His wife, twenty years his junior, has recently started to play a far more significant role in the movement. Exactly what will happen when Moon dies does, of course, remain to be seen; there are a number of possible scenarios, including the probability that there will be some schisms. But it is unlikely that the Unification Church will disappear completely from the American scene, at least within the foreseeable future.

NOTES

1. Chung Hwan Kwak, *Outline of the Principle: Level 4* (New York: HSA-UWC, 1980), 1–2.
2. J. Lofland, *Doomsday Cult: A Study of Conversion, Proselytization, and Maintenance of Faith* (New York 1966; London: Irvington, 1977) and Michael Mickler, "A History of the Unification Church in the Bay Area: 1960–74," MA thesis, Graduate Theological Union, Berkeley, California.
3. See, for example, Kwak, *Outline of the Principle*, 2.
4. Chung Hwan, *The Tradition* (New York: HSA-UWC, 1985).
5. *Reverend Sun Myung Moon Speaks on The Age of New Dispensation* 14 (May 1978): 17.
6. *Today's World* (February 1992): 36.
7. "Day of Victory of Love," talk by Sun Myung Moon on 2 January 1987, *Today's World* (March 1987): 14. See also page 8 of the original transcript of the talk and Young Whi Kim *Guidance for Heavenly Tradition*, vol. 2 (Morfelden-Walldorf: Kando, 1985), ch. 22.
8. "Faith Jones—Experiences with Heung Jin Nim," Friday, 24 February 1984. Duplicated typescript, p. 1.
9. *The Home Front: Newsletter of the 8000 Couples Blessed Family Association* (Spring 1988): 4.
10. Lofland, *Doomsday Cult*, 32.
11. E. Barker, *The Making of a Moonie: Brainwashing or Choice?* (Oxford: Basil Blackwell, 1984; reprint, Aldershot: Gregg Revivals, 1993).
12. It is perfectly possible for members to reject the partner chosen for them and to stay in the movement.
13. David G. Bromley, ed., *Falling from the Faith: Causes and Consequences of Religious Apostasy* (Beverly Hills: Sage, 1988), chs. 9 and 10.
14. Barker, *Making of a Moonie*, 146; M. Galanter, "Psychological Induction into the Large Group: Findings from a Modern Religious Sect," *American Journal of Psychiatry* 137, no. 12 (1980): 1575.
15. Barker, *Making of a Moonie*; Lofland *Doomsday Cult*; and D. Bromley and A. Shupe, *"Moonies" in America: Cult, Church and Crusade* (Beverly Hills: Sage, 1979).
16. Barker, *Making of a Moonie*, ch. 8.

SUGGESTIONS FOR FURTHER READING

Barker, Eileen. *The Making of a Moonie: Brainwashing or Choice?* Oxford: Basil Blackwell, 1984; reprint, Aldershot: Gregg Revivals, 1993.

Bromley, David, and Anson Shupe. *"Moonies" in America: Cult, Church and Crusade* Beverly Hills: Sage, 1979.

Lofland, John. *Doomsday Cult: A Study of Conversion, Proselytization, and Maintenance of Faith.* 1966. Reprint. New York and London: Irvington.

Mickler, Michael. *The Unification Church in America: A Bibliography and Research Guide.* New York: Garland, 1987.

THE TRANSFORMING INFLUENCE OF AMERICAN GATHERINGS

Loretta Orion

Since the 1960s, North America and England have witnessed the emergence of a movement whose followers refer to themselves as neopagans or witches. Neopagans perform rituals that they claim were practiced as part of a pre-Christian religion they call Wicca, *a derivative of "wiccan," which itself derives from the Old English (or Anglo-Saxon) term for female witch,* wicca, *of which the male equivalent is* wicce. *Both words, according to the* Oxford English Dictionary, *apparently derive from* wiccian, *"witch." Those who practice wiccan today claim that in pre-Christian times populations living in Europe practiced a religion called "wiccan" and that they have revived it. They believe that the "the world is alive, interconnected, and responsive to attempts to manipulate invisible (occult) forces" (Orion 1995:1), which they seek to do by an array of magical devices that they refer to as "the craft." In the United States, wicca has become the core of a host of cognate non-Christian religious and magical practices that together are known as "neopaganism." Witches consider themselves healers and practice their craft for beneficent reasons not for malevolent ones. In this respect, at least, they differ strikingly from the classical image of 16th- and 17th-century witch.*

In this, the most penetrating and detailed study of contemporary wicca beliefs and practices in the United States that has yet been made, Loretta Orion, an anthropologist who underwent initiation into a wicca group in order to carry out fieldwork, discusses neopaganism from the perspective of self-identified witches, history, and demographic characteristics. The roots of the neopagan movement in the United States can be traced to England, where during the 1930s Gerald Gardner was initiated

Source: Reprinted by permission of Waveland Press, Inc. from Loretta Orion, *Never Again the Burning Times*, pages 127-140. (Prospect Heights, IL: Waveland Press, Inc., 1995). All rights reserved.

into a coven of witches, one of nine offshoots of one founded by George Pickingill (1816–1909), a witch who claimed descent from an alleged witch called Julia Brandon, who died in 1071. Whether this tradition is true or false, Gardner created a popular movement which spread across the Atlantic. As Loretta Orion remarks, the tradition Gardner claimed to have restored was challenged after its arrival in the United States, and rival schools of witchcraft emerged. In this extract from her book, she describes her participant observation in a "Spiral Gathering" performed by one of these schools. The importance of women, (among the most celebrated witches are Margot Adler, Starhawk, and Selena Fox), the fertile interaction of both sexes, and the sense of creativity pervading the event are typical motifs of witchcraft today.

By devising large outdoor gatherings, American witches created a loosely knit national community with a shared set of beliefs and both oral and written traditions. Largely as a result of the ritual dramas that evolved at these gatherings, Americans converted Gardner's more rigid ceremonies into inventive rituals, so that the religion of witchcraft broadens into a more general Neopaganism that serves strikingly different purposes. Rather than performing established religious ceremonies, American witches employ techniques that liberate the imagination and spur improvisation and invention.[1]

In the 1970s, meetings that resembled seminars or conventions were organized in hotels for individuals who were interested in various aspects of the occult. By the mid-1970s these events had evolved into the outdoor camping festivals that I attended. The first flurry of this kind of gathering was in California in the mid-1970s. By 1985, Adler wrote, there were at least fifty annual regional or national gatherings with a pagan or Wiccan focus (1986).

The impetus for one gathering in the midwest was the tensions that were building between local groups in the Chicago area. Most of the groups were of the English-based Wiccan tradition. However, friction developed between conservative Gardnerian groups and those that had begun to modify his version of the Wiccan tradition. Eventually the Gardnerians and the innovators made their peace, and now witches of both persuasions enjoy gatherings together. They make good-hearted fun of one another's style, but I have seen no evidence of conflict.

In fact, a great deal of cross-fertilization has been the result. The stronger influence today is in the direction of softening the rigid structure of English Wicca with the spontaneity, inventiveness, playfulness, and greater political focus that distinguish the American Neopagan festival style of religious celebration. There now exists a national Neopagan community with a shared body of chants, dances, and ritual techniques (Adler 1986). Formal hierarchical English Wicca persists but, largely as a result of the gatherings, a more pervasive, distinctly American Neopaganism has emerged.

While covens consist ideally of a fairly stable membership of no more than thirteen members, the gatherings—which are more like religious retreats or conventions than intimate meetings—are attended by hundreds of individuals. Over the years Spiral Gathering in the state of Georgia once accommodated 120 guests; presently about 75 people attend. The largest gatherings—Pagan Spirit Gathering and Rites of Spring—drew from 300 to 500 participants. In the last few years 600 to 700 individuals have attended Rites of Spring. Although the faces change at gatherings, there is a core group that constitutes about half of the attendees at most gatherings.

Because the gatherings occur only once a year, and there is as much socializing as worship or magic, they resemble family reunions. Bonds are established among individuals living long distances from one another, and these are sustained through computer networks and by correspondences of several years' duration—letters and greeting cards on the sabbaths, and occasional telephone calls. I first met the Neopagans, with whom I maintain contact in these ways, at Pagan Spirit Gathering in 1983.

PAGAN SPIRIT GATHERING, 1983

My first experience at Pagan Spirit Gathering (PSG) was one of immersion in a new and strange experience. I didn't study it; instead, I allowed myself to respond to the drama and playfulness of

it. The following description is impressionistic. Although most of my comments have been formulated in retrospect, it nonetheless serves my purpose of illustrating the dramatic effects of American culture on British witchcraft.

PSG, which takes place in Wisconsin on the summer solstice in June, is organized by Selena Fox of Circle Farm in Wisconsin. For several years it had been the largest of the American gatherings, attracting 400 to 500 Neopagans from all over the country, Canada, and Europe. While other gatherings have surpassed it in size, PSG remains the most eclectic and its popularity continues to grow.[2] PSG is presently organized and run by Selena, her husband, Dennis, and a handful of volunteers, some of whom live and work at Circle.

The 1983 PSG took place in a newly mown field of straw situated on a lake near Madison, Wisconsin. The land was made available by its owner, an anonymous Neopagan. I enjoyed the comforts of my friend Deborah's recreational vehicle, while most of the attendees, over 400 of them, sheltered in tents.

Open House at Circle Farm

More than 100 of us arrived the day before the official start of the gathering to attend an open house at Circle Farm. The field surrounding the old farmhouse was dotted with tents and 20 to 30 guests who looked like hippies ranging in ages from about 20 to 70 years old.

During the afternoon Selena led a tour of her herb garden. Jim Allen, who was then Selena's partner, made Kirlian[3] photographs of our hands. We met 30 or 40 Neopagans from all over the United States, including Crystal, a flashy ceremonial magician who drew me aside to demonstrate his magical prowess.

He showed me how to dowse energy fields with bent coat hangers. Dowsing is a technique that had been used to find underground water or minerals with the use of a divining rod. Holding an L-shaped wire in each hand, Crystal approached trees, plants, Selena's dog, and people to show me how the wires would swing away as he approached the vicinity of their energy fields. It worked for me, too (perhaps by hypnotic suggestion).

Crystal pulled scarves out of nowhere and coins from behind my ears, and displayed the artifacts of his more serious magic: his ritual tools and ceremonial robe, all of which his magical order required that he create. I was also treated to a reading from his secret Book of Shadows.

That afternoon's events served as an introduction to the Neopagan concepts of immanence of divinity and energy. When Selena "introduced" her herbs to us on the tour of her garden, it was clear that in her estimation each possessed an inherent divine life force and specific affinities (sympathies) with other parts of the natural world including planets, seasons, and human organ systems.

The herb garden completely surrounded the old farm house, "protecting it with the serene and powerful energies of the plants," Selena said. "A plant should never be harvested without first gaining its permission," Selena explained, as she gently broke off a few leaves for us to taste, smell, and feel. (She had prepared the garden for the tour before we arrived.) Several of us wondered how a plant might indicate its permission to be harvested. "Oh, you can feel it," she replied. "It will either feel right or wrong to do it." Offerings of tobacco are generally appreciated by the plant spirits, she continued, and, of course, plants respond to human love and attention, as do all living things, by flourishing.

I learned that day that Neopagans include minerals and gems among the living, after watching stones and talismans reveal blue-white halos in the Kirlian photographs made of them with primitive equipment in the barn. Within a few hours of my arrival at Circle Farm, belief in Starhawk's poetic words about the consciousness of immanence had been vividly demonstrated for me: "The world and everything in it is alive, dynamic, interdependent, interacting, and infused with moving energies; a living being, a weaving dance" (Starhawk 1979).

By the time we organized a potluck supper, some "Big Name Pagans" (BNPs) arrived. Although Neopagans despise the very idea of leaders and followers, they do recognize celebrities. BNP is a tongue-

in-cheek term which refers to individuals who are recognized for their talents or services to the community. As a result of the festivals, many local musicians and organizers of large group rituals and gatherings have acquired a national reputation as BNPs. Starhawk and Margot Adler are recognized for their authorship of widely read books. Adler reported that by the end of 1985, Starhawk's first two books had sold a combined total of about eighty-thousand copies;[4] the first edition of Adler's *Drawing Down the Moon* sold thirty thousand copies.

Selena Fox is on a par with these authors because of her Circle networking service, the PSG gathering, her skills as a healer, and her talent as a performer of Neopagan music. For several years, since public interest began to gather around the emerging cult of witchcraft, Selena has been visible in the media. More recently, she has appeared on television talk shows and in courts of law as a spokesperson for the movement and protector of the religious freedoms of Neopagans, including her own right to operate a Neopagan church on Circle Farm.

The category of BNP merges into one that the Neopagans have not yet named, but I think it would be the present-day equivalent of "tribal elder." Surprisingly few of these are high priestesses or priests of the English traditional covens. An exception is Haragano, of Seattle, Washington, a wise, competent, and humorous "matriarch," whose famous psychic skills will be mentioned later. Haragano's husband, Tiller, who is a charming musician, comedian, organizer, and community peacemaker, is another example. Oz of Albuquerque is honored as an expert dancer and authoritative priestess. She creates elaborate rituals from inspirations received in trance states from the deities she serves. Amber K, a healer and organizer of the first Wiccan seminary, is another example of the Neopagan equivalent of tribal elder.

After the evening's potluck supper, more than a hundred of us gathered in the meadow where Selena led a simple but very impressive ritual. As we turned to face each direction, she invited everyone to salute the guardians of the watchtowers of the cardinal directions by singing three times, "Spirits of the north [or east, south, or west], come." When, by this simple collaboration, the circle between the worlds was established, the group sang a chant to raise energy to fill the circle. Selena invited everyone to invoke (or draw down) whatever deities were important to them by calling out their names.

When silence gradually returned, twenty or more deities had been invoked—deities of Greco-Roman, Norse, Celtic, and African derivation, as well as others I did not recognize. Selena asked the multitudes of deities to bless the gathering and those who were journeying to it.

Then Selena asked for the names of people or places the participants wished to empower with the raising of a cone of power that she was preparing to orchestrate. Theoretically, some of the energy would be directed to the desired destination by individual thoughts at the moment of their release.

Several people mentioned a baby whose kidnapping was then in the news. Another person mentioned a mock witchburning that a fundamentalist Christian group was planning to perform that weekend. Groans and sighs signaled that the group's energy (and emotional excitement) was already beginning to rise.

Selena reminded the group that while the gathering was in progress Starhawk was leading a demonstration to stop the opening of the aforementioned Livermoor nuclear power plant near the San Diablo fault line in California. I discovered later that Starhawk conducted witchcraft rituals as part of her political demonstrations and that when she and other demonstrating witches got arrested, they taught the prison inmates how to conduct rituals to raise and release energy. Blessings and protection were to be sent to the demonstrators that evening and at all the rituals throughout the gathering.

Selena then started a chant naming several goddesses: "Isis, Astarte, Diana, Hecate, Demeter, Kali, Inanna." The group moved faster and faster in a clockwise direction, or deosil (meaning following the natural rotation of the earth), while drums, tambourines, and various other percussion and wind instruments set the gradually quickening pace of singing and dancing around the circle.

At the moment when the group's energy was elevated to its peak, the chanting erupted into cheers, howls, screams, and animal calls, followed by ripples of contented laughter and sighs of exhaustion. The celebrants were content that a powerful cone of power had been created and released.

That evening was the first time I had experienced the raising and releasing of the cone of power. The orchestration of the rise to crescendo and the release of the energies of over a hundred people are impressive. Later, a high priestess described it this way: "A high priestess is a psychic cheerleader; she guides and paces the rising of the group's energy, and she must be able to feel the moment when the peak of excitement is reached and signal its release. A second in either direction can spoil the cone of power."[5]

Drummers orchestrate the rise and release of the energy for large rituals; occasionally the presiding priestess or priest leads the drumming. At some rituals I have witnessed the virtuosity of well-rehearsed groups of twenty to thirty drummers playing together. The prominence of percussion in orchestrating group energy in Wiccan rituals is uniquely American and, I would surmise, a result of the large gatherings that have developed here.

After the release of the cone of power, the group settled into silence for a few minutes before Selena asked if anyone wished to tell about any visions they had experienced during the raising and releasing of the cone of power.

I was most impressed by what Haragano reported. She "saw" three women traveling to the gathering in a red Ford Falcon. She felt that they were having problems and saw them drinking coffee in a diner while puzzling over whatever was holding them up. She said she thought she knew their names. Selena led the group in chanting the three names that Haragano provided and suggested that everyone visualize protective white light around the three women.

Two days later three women arrived at the gathering in a car they rented after leaving the red Falcon to be repaired. The names of two of the women were those that Haragano mentioned. I have been impressed several times since by Haragano's predictions and insights. "Been doing it all my life," she says; her point of view is that anyone can develop the skill. If people trust their intuition and use it a lot, it improves, as any human faculty would. Nonetheless, I found her own skill to be extraordinary.

At the gatherings I have most often seen divinatory talent put to use in Tarot readings or palm readings, but a few individuals have told me that they have been consulted to locate lost people and things by members of their local communities, generally by police departments.

When Selena directed the group to face each of the cardinal directions and bid the spirits of each direction farewell, the ritual was concluded. We dispersed into tents and campers, and the next day we packed up and moved to the festival site.

The Gathering

At the head of a tiny path, inconspicuously marked by a cloth with a barely perceptible star painted on it, a small group with a walkie-talkie greeted us. They inspected our admission pass before they directed us down the path into the site.

Gatherings are generally publicized only in Neopagan newsletters. My friend Deborah learned about PSG by reading the announcement in *Circle Network News,* published by Selena at Circle Farm. Each participant must sign a waiver in which he or she agrees not to inform the media about the event. Secrecy and security are maintained to protect participants from the intrusion of the uninitiated and unsympathetic.

We found the site and checked in, much as one would at any retreat, and then explored the grounds. It was somewhat disconcerting to see so many naked people. Fieldwork is a double-edged process, particularly when examining one's own culture. The familiar goes unnoticed, requiring no exploration or explanation. When the unfamiliar inspires the researcher to undertake a clarification, one of the first steps is to explore one's own sense of the familiar and the exotic. "Why does it seem

strange?" is the flip side of "Why do they do this?" or "What does it mean?"

Being uninitiated, though sympathetic, I found myself experiencing shock on many occasions. The sight of people in varying degrees of nudity dancing around a bonfire in the black of night in a remote field can activate fear responses in the Western mind influenced by a culture that for several hundred years has surrounded such images with the most sinister of associations. The exuberance and playfulness of the actual event contrasted so completely with these automatic responses that I experienced cognitive disorientation. Had I succumbed to depravities or was the leaping over fires and the rise and fall of ecstatic dancing and chanting as harmlessly invigorating as it seemed?

Nudity, among other things, represents freedom from cultural conventions. Neopagan gatherings, like other pilgrimages, are retreats from the constraints of quotidian existence. In sacred space (removed from the constraints of mundane existence) it is safe to shed clothing and other conventions linked with the secular world, as it is safe and efficacious to assume a different appearance by wearing masks or costumes.[6] It was not long before the costumes—ritual jewelry, robes, horned furry headdresses (to emulate the horned god), and masks—demanded more of my attention and wonder than the nudity.

In sacred space, where adornment is potent with significance, the costumes spoke clearly. Many Neopagans reveal a nostalgia for feudal grandeur in their laced bodices and flowing skirts, shirts with full sleeves, and tunics over tights. Others dress like gypsies or Native Americans. The majority, however, cannot be classified. Many people wear only an athame in a belt and sheath, a scarf, or jewelry. Those who wear shorts and tee-shirts (somewhat less than half the group) begin to look out of place, reminders of the world left behind.

Nudity at gatherings is fundamentally a symbolic statement of forsaking ordinary culture for an immersion in nature, much as it would be at a nudist beach. Although many Neopagans welcome sexual liaisons at gatherings—generally considered a deeply significant religious sacrament—nudity is not necessarily an invitation to have sex.

Because of the large number of newcomers who might not understand the sexual mores, and to protect participants from the spread of AIDS, the EarthSpirit Community was moved to issue a guide to appropriate behavior for pagan gatherings at the 1988 Rites of Spring.[7]

In the last two years, concern about AIDS has caused conflict regarding the concept of sex as sacrament. In many cases even the practice of sharing wine from a common chalice has been abandoned in favor of the use of paper cups or dispensed with entirely as too dangerous a ritual practice in large groups.

From this digression into the subject of nudity and sex, let us return now to the layout of the gathering. Covens or groups that journeyed there together set up camps around a common fire pit. Many displayed banners with the name and symbols of their group: Athanor of Boston, Silver Web of Maryland, Tribe of the Phoenix of Georgia, Circle Jerk Camp, for example. The banner belonging to the gay men's camp featured Bugs Bunny.

There were two magnificent teepees, each about twenty feet high. One had a ring of rainbows painted around the outside. We were invited to see that the inside was lined with images of various goddesses, expertly crafted in soft fabric sculpture.

A strong sense of playfulness mixed with competent creativity was becoming apparent as Deborah and I toured the camp and saw the altars people had created at their campsites, the clothing and jewelry with which they adorned themselves, and the beautiful handcrafted wares that were displayed for sale under a huge army tent labeled "Tenthenge." Overall, the camp had the appearance of a gathering of tribes of gypsies.

On the first evening of the official festival, or gathering, the fire that was to serve as the symbolic center of the ritual circle (within the larger sacred space of the entire campsite) was lit in a ceremony in which Randy, the "Fireman," was the main actor. The fire was kept burning until Randy extinguished it at the concluding ceremony on the last day of the festival.

Many people stayed to talk, drum, sing, and dance around the fire each evening. The fire served as a symbol of the group's collective spirit. The ritual circle was the focal point of the campground; the fire represented its core. Each evening another spectacular ritual drama was presented there, and all day long people brought wood to the fire.

On another evening, the EarthSpirit Community staged a purification ritual in which a larger than life "Wicker Man," an effigy of straw, was set ablaze. Participants had been invited to bring debris from their homes as a symbol of what they wished to destroy or relinquish. The trash was woven into the effigy and burned with the usual ecstatic singing and dancing.

One evening the men and women celebrated separate rituals: men's and women's mysteries. While the women splashed and sang their way through their mysteries (performed in the lake), they laughed at the sounds of the shouting, stomping men "relieving their endless aggressions."

Although all rituals are intended to effect some "healing," by which the Neopagans mean any beneficial magic, two rituals were specifically referred to in that way: the web-building ritual, described earlier, for healing the earth and a more overtly healing ritual—in terms of transforming pathological physical states—which was facilitated by Selena one evening.

To heal the physical ailments of individuals who were present, Selena instructed the group in a technique resembling therapeutic touch. Every person present was considered capable of drawing energy up from the earth down from the stars, and through their bodies to effect a healing in others present.

To heal those not present, energy was sent by releasing a cone of power, and it was conveyed by contagious magic through photographs or small belongings or symbols of the person that were brought to the ritual.

Finally, energy was released into the Earth when everyone lay down on the ground and visualized the residual energy draining out of their bodies into the "body" of the Earth. The energy source for this ritual was external to the participants; energy from the Earth or sky was "tapped," so that the participants would not be personally depleted.

One evening a talent show was staged. There are many competent musicians, bards, poets, and comedians in the Neopagan movement, and there is also a distinct style of Neopagan music—a cross between Celtic bardic songs and the folk music that was popular in the 1960s. Neopagans have a charming sense of humor about their beliefs and practices that enlivens their performances. Numerous other rituals, including two "handfasting" (marriage) ceremonies took place. On the morning of the solstice a tiny band of early risers chanted and danced while the sun rose.

Peter the Big Blue Fairy's Full Moon Ritual[8]

The most elaborate was the full moon ritual. It involved about twenty dancers, as many musicians and singers, and elaborate props. Everyone sang original chants that the entire group had learned and rehearsed each morning at the "village meeting." The ritual was designed by Peter Sonderberg who calls himself "Peter the Big Blue Fairy." Peter, who thinks of ritual as a form of theater, brought his considerable dramatic gifts and experience into the creation of this culminating ritual drama.

This ritual event is an example of the transforming influence of American culture on British Wicca. Gardner's rituals are formulae that must be performed in rigorous accord with the "ancient" traditions; otherwise, the theory goes, the gods will not be pleased or they will not come and/or the magic will not work. On the other hand, the more innovative rituals generally presented at gatherings are devised to evoke powerful responses in the participants, in whom divinity is assumed to be immanent.

The episodes of Gardner's basic ritual provided the structure for this very different one. The circle between the worlds was marked, not by one candle at each cardinal direction, but with a ring of flaming candles that the hundreds of participants were instructed to carry as they took their places in an enormous ring.

Celebrants entered through a human gate: a pregnant woman suspended on a litter between one

black man and one white man, who served as the two supports of the lintel. The celebrants entered through the elegantly portrayed opposites that are recognized in Wiccan rituals and ultimately united in the great rite or ceremony of cakes and wine: black and white; woman and man; moon and sun; the pregnant fecundity of the woman and the virility of the men.

The black and white pillars have deep roots in the Western spiritual tradition. They derive ultimately from the twin pillars constructed in the temple of Solomon. The black and white pillars can be seen in the temples of the Masonic order and other secret societies. In the Hebrew Cabala, with which many Neopagans are acquainted firsthand, and even more through its incorporation into Gardner's Wicca, the black pillar represents severity, the white, mercy; and the "Middle Pillar of Mildness," or "Middle Way," is the spiritual path between the two extremes that represent other countless complementary oppositions (Gray 1984).

When everyone had entered the circle by passing through the "doorway" framed by the black and white human pillars, the pregnant woman was lowered into a chair beside the fire. The red spirals painted on her naked breasts and pregnant belly gave her the appearance of a life-sized fertility fetish. She represented the great mother goddess.

The guardians of the watchtowers were wordlessly invoked by four dancers wearing costumes of colors evocative of the elements: air, fire, water, and earth. Each danced to the accompaniment of a small orchestra of percussion and wind instruments.

The celebrants raised energy to fill the circle by singing Peter's original chant.

And the full moon
Is her vagina spread wide.
And the full moon
Is her vagina spread wide.
And the wild realm of all possibilities,
every possibility,
Is pouring out.

The goddess was drawn down (invoked or evoked from within) by a parade of twelve women; each one embodied one aspect of the triple goddess who represents the three phases of the moon. As each one entered, she bowed before the enthroned pregnant high priestess, revealing with her dance, costume, gestures, or a short expression (such as "I am the giver of milk, she who comforts children in the dark of the night") that she represented either the new moon (maiden goddess), the full moon (matron), or the waning moon (crone). The "goddesses" then danced together: among them were "Hecate" in black-hooded cape; "Kali" with a gleaming scimitar balanced on her head; one portrayed the "Amazon" in leopard skin loin cloth, another, a businesswoman in a suit; another had flowers painted on her body; Haragano's skin was stained to look like the Venus of Willendorf. The "goddess" who entered last, a young homosexual man wearing rabbit ears and pink harem pants, represented Discordia, the goddess of chaos.

When this homage to the great mother goddess was finished, the queen of witches and goddess of the moon made her appearance. Wearing the traditional silver crown of a high priestess (with upturned crescent moon), "Diana" entered through the gate of oak branches where the human portal had been, accompanied by two men in long robes and a chorus of twelve others, all singing a song made popular by another Diana. Through the "ooo-ooo-ooo-ooo, aah-aah-aah-aah" that introduced the song, the crowd laughed softly at the spectacle of this emulation of Diana Ross and the Supremes. Because Peter the Big Blue Fairy (now one of the three Supremes singing beside Diana) was a notorious practitioner of an innovative Wiccan tradition devoted to Discordia, he was expected to be unconventional, bordering on sacrilegious.

When the priestess sang the lyrics of the love song promising that no wind or rain or any other thing could prevent her from coming to the beloved whenever she was needed, the laughter stopped. With the lyrics of the song "Ain't No Mountain High Enough," the priestess was delivering the charge of the goddess.

If you need me; call me.

No matter where you are,

No matter how far,

Just call my name.

I'll be there in a hurry.

On that you can depend and never worry.[9]

The full moon goddess was drawn down to speak with the lips of the singing priestess her covenant with the witches.[10] In the traditional charge, Aradia, avatar of the goddess, reminds the witches:

Whenever ye have need of anything,

Once in the month, and when the moon is full,

Ye shall assemble in some desert[ed] place,

Or in a forest all together join

To adore the potent spirit of your queen,

My mother, great Diana. (Leland 1899, 7)

Of course no mountain could be high enough to keep her away; the goddess *is* the mountains, the wind, rain, and all things in the universe. The invocation to draw her down reads:

Hear ye the words of the star goddess,

The dust of whose feet are the hosts of heaven

Whose body encircles the universe:

Once drawn down, Diana speaks through the lips of the priestess:

I am the beauty of the green earth,

And the white moon among the stars,

The mystery of the waters,

And the passion of human hearts.

Call unto your soul,

Arise and come unto me

For I am the soul of nature.

From me all things proceed

And unto me all things must return.

Diana sang that she realized that the beloved must follow the sun, wherever it leads. However, if one should fall short, life holds one guarantee: she will always be there.

I know you must follow the sun,

wherever it leads.

But remember,

If you should fall short of your desires,

. . . life holds for you one guarantee;

You'll always have me . . .[11]

In a similar fashion the familiar charge advises: "Keep pure your highest ideals; strive ever toward it, let naught stop you or turn you aside. . . . For mine is the secret door . . . the cup of wine of life . . . which is the Holy Grail of Immortality" (Farrar 1983, 172).

"Diana and the Supremes" sang the assurance that her love is constant.

You see my love is alive,

It's like a seed that only needs the

thought of you to grow.[12]

In the traditional ceremony the priest draws down the moon with similar references to plants:

I invoke Thee and call upon Thee

O Mighty Mother of us all,

Bringer of all Fruitfulness, by seed

and by root.

I invoke thee, by stem and by bud.

I invoke Thee by life and by love

and call upon Thee to descend into this,

Thy Priestess and Servant.

Hear with her ears, speak with her

tongue . . ." (Bell 1974, 157)

The idea that humans are linked to the divine universe through the mind is recognizable in these lyrics as well. When the moon is drawn down, human and divine are made one.

At the completion of the song/charge of the goddess, Diana took her place at the opposite side of the fire from the pregnant priestess, and the goddess was considered amply drawn down in all her aspects.

The god or sun was then drawn down as several young men danced through the gate and around the circle, wearing horned headdresses to emulate the horned god as animal, Cernunos, Dionysus, and other of his forms.[13] They cavorted like a herd of frisky ungulates. Finally they collapsed in exhaustion at the feet of the many representatives of the goddesses who were assembled in a ring around the central fire.

Then the great rite was performed. The "blessedness" that results from the conjoining of opposites was, in this case, the planting of seeds in the Earth. The goddess' representatives—except for the pregnant moon goddess and Diana, who both remained enthroned at opposite sides of the fire—gathered into large bowls the seeds that each person had been given as he or she entered the gate. Each dropped their seeds into the bowls, serving as a cauldron or chalice, and said what they wished to "plant" for the future (peace, companionship, and other boons). The many goddesses emptied the contents of the bowls as a libation onto the Earth in front of the pregnant full moon goddess around whom the "gods" crouched on the ground. The god figures quickly descended upon the seeds, planting them into the soil with a swimming, squirming, sperm-like dance. The opposites were blended: the male (seeds) penetrated the female (Earth) to initiate a transformation (new crop).

The ritual ended with the raising and releasing of a cone of power in a spiral dance. The circle of participants were led into the center to dance around the fire and spiralled back out again while singing to the beat of the drummers. With howls and cries the cone of power was released, representing, not only the energy raising of the is ritual, but the culmination of the five-day-long gathering. Excess energy was grounded—allowed to flow from the energized and exhausted bodies into the Earth—as the celebrants lay panting on the ground. Gradually drumming and chanting started up around the fire and most of the celebrants returned to their camps to feast.

On the following day Randy, the Fireman, extinguished the ritual fire as ceremoniously as he had lit it. The pagans broke down the camp and said their emotional farewells. Then these pilgrims returned home from a pilgrimage site that existed only in their memories, leaving their seeds to sprout in the deserted straw field.

ENDNOTES

1. In her revised edition of *Drawing Down the Moon* (1986), Margot Adler wrote that in the seven years since the original publication of her book festivals have completely changed the face of the Neopagan movement.
2. Often the size of a gathering is limited more by the size of available camping accommodations than popularity.
3. Kirlian photography captures the energy fields surrounding plants and animals.
4. Both of Starhawk's first books are in their second edition and have been translated into German.
5. Personal communication, Sally Cook, 1985.
6. The social dynamics operative in sacred space (liminality) will be discussed in the following chapter.
7. "Ms. Manners' Official Guide to Etiquette and All-Around Appropriate Behavior at Pagan Gatherings," was distributed at the registration desk. It included advice for appropriate behavior at rituals ("Don't touch other peoples' ritual tools"; "Don't throw cigarette butts in the ritual fire"; and such things). Advice about sex included the following: "Among Pagans, nudity is not an invitation to have sex"; "If you have a sexually transmitted disease, please be responsible and discuss this with your partner" (free condoms were provided).
8. This ritual is described elsewhere by Neopagan priestess, Oz, in "An Insider's Look at Pagan Festivals" in *Witchcraft Today: The Modern Craft Movement,* Charles S. Clifton (ed.), (St. Paul: Llewellyn Publications, 1992).
9. Lyrics of "Ain't No Mountain High Enough" by Nicholas Ashford and Valarie Simpson, © 1967, reprinted by permission of Jobete Music Company, Inc.
10. See chapter 5 for a discussion of the ritual of drawing down the moon.
11. Lyrics of "Ain't No Mountain High Enough" by Nicholas Ashford and Valarie Simpson, © 1967, reprinted by permission of Jobete Music Company, Inc.
12. Ibid.
13. Oz, whom I numbered among the BNPs above, told me that she danced with the men to embody the god (personal communication, 1994).

READING 12–4

THE RASTAFARI ABROAD

Barry Chevannes

In contrast to the Unification Church, the Rastafari came into existence as several separate cults and without the founding intervention of a prophet. However, the coronation of Haile Selassie as emperor of Ethiopia in 1930 served as the impetus for the movement's creation, and he remains a central figure in the movement, which holds as a key belief the coming repatriation of blacks in the Americas to Africa. In the United States, they are especially well-known, perhaps, for sporting long, matted hair, called "dreadlocks," and for having as a sacrament the smoking of marijuana.

A lecturer at the University of the West Indies, Barry Chavannes is an ethnographer of the Rastafari, and the description he gives of their movement depicts another type of alternative religion to that depicted in the three previous readings. The Rastafari have not embedded their beliefs in the economic mainstream of American society, like the Unification Church. Nor did they self-destruct like the Peoples Temple or make the rejection of Christianity a conspicuous feature of their religion, like the wiccans. To a far greater extent than any of these other religions the Rastafari religion originated in social conditions of deprivation. This deprivation, combined with low social status related to race, encouraged its emergence. Deriving much of its message from the history of slavery, with the transportation of black Africans from their continent of origin to the New World as its major theme, members of the underclass in western Jamaica have sought to improve their economic lives by adopting new religious beliefs.

In 1953 Rastafari was a small sect almost entirely confined to the west end of Kingston, the capital of Jamaica. Forty years later, in 1993, there were people

---

Source: Reprinted from *America's Alternative Religions,* by Timothy Miller (Ed.), by permission of the State University of New York Press, pages 297-302, © 1995, State University of New York. All rights reserved.

in many parts of the world identifying themselves as Rasta. Following a brief introduction, this chapter presents a survey of the Rastafari outside of Jamaica, including the United States, and explains the factors accounting for this internationalization.

On the coronation in 1930 of Ras Tafari Makonnen as the Emperor of Ethiopia, Haile Selassie I, certain Jamaicans influenced by the popular teachings of Marcus Garvey, but equally also influenced by traditional African-Jamaican beliefs, concluded that Tafari was none other than the Returned Messiah. They based their arguments primarily on an alleged prophecy of Garvey that black people were to look to Africa for the crowning of a king as the sign that their redemption was at hand; but they were also moved by the biblical roots of the new emperor's titles and claims: King of Kings, Lord of Lords, Elect of God, Light of the World, Conquering Lion of the Tribe of Judah—biblical titles referring to the Messiah. The Ethiopian royal family in actual fact claimed descent from the Jewish King Solomon and the Kushite Queen Sheba.

From this simple origin, the Rastafarians[1] as they eventually became known, grew into an important social and religious movement among rural migrants in the city of Kingston. The conviction that the black man, Selassie, was God was the main cornerstone on which they erected a new consciousness, for it empowered them to reject the popular conception of God as white, and of black skin color as a debility. Along with this belief came their well-known agitation for repatriation, that is the return to Africa, from where blacks were unlawfully and involuntarily forced into slavery by the Europeans. It is with this latter tenet in mind that most scholars have described the movement as millenarian, overlooking its profound impact as a cultural force in Jamaica and the African world generally. By the 1960s Rastafari became the most important social force among the urban youth and retained this position throughout the 1970s.[2]

Beginning late in the 1940s, a group of young militants, impatient with their elders, started a new trend that earned the designation "Dreadlocks," since their most distinguishing mark was their long matted hair, a symbol of their alienation from and aggressive attitude toward the society which they designated "Babylon," in reference to the biblical kingdom that had enslaved the nation of Israel.[3] By the 1970s Dreadlocks became synonymous with Rastafari.[4]

The aggressive attitude towards Jamaican society found expression in three attempts late in the 1950s to force repatriation to Africa. The last, the Claudius Henry affair,[5] was blown up into a national crisis, the aftermath of which was to have a profound impact on the cultural development of the country. Rex Nettleford made himself available both as one of the three scholars to study the Rastafari in Kingston[6] and as one of the emissaries on a technical mission to Africa to conclude arrangements for the emigration of Jamaicans there. Nettleford followed closely the developments through the 1960s and argues that Rastafari agitation was in reality a dialogue with the society over the question of the cultural identity of Jamaica.[7] Given the Eurocentric biases and orientation of the upper and middle classes, Rastafari builds on and extends the Afrocentrism of the lower-class African majority in a struggle for supremacy. As such the African majority is up against the continuing racism that values everything white and devalues everything black. Or, as he put it, Jamaican culture is the "melody of Europe and the rhythm of Africa, or 'every john crow t'ink him pickney white,' " in reference to a Jamaican proverb which alludes disapprovingly to the tendency among some blacks to think that they are white (the "john crow" being a buzzard).

The results of this struggle are still unfolding, but progress has been recorded in getting Jamaicans to shed much, though by no means all, of their colonial legacy of mental enslavement and to identify positively with being black and a part of the African diaspora.[8] Now Rastafari has become an upwardly mobile movement that has attracted members of the middle classes,[9] not only because of its struggle on the question of racial identity, but also because of its philosophy of "ital livity." "Ital livity" rejects the artificiality of modern Western consumerism and opts for relationships and activities that harmonize more closely with nature: food grown without chemical fertilizers and cooked without salt, herbal remedies instead of manufactured pills and medicines, sexual intercourse without prophylactics, and so on; and on the moral level, a life guided by principles of integrity and straightforwardness. Indeed, these are some of the achievements of the Rastafari that make the group appealing on the international level.

INTERNATIONALIZATION

As Ken Bilby has already observed, the spread of Rastafari outside of Jamaica has been due to the external migration of Jamaicans and to the internationalization of reggae music.[10] Bilby is correct of course, but to these must be added the role of the Caribbean integration movement, since Caribbeans were the first non-Jamaicans to adopt Rastafari. The circumstances facilitating this were twofold. First, there was the University of the West Indies, whose main campus located in Jamaica hosted hundreds of students from other islands. With Rastafari ideas becoming more and more commonplace in Jamaican cultural and political life throughout the 1960s and 1970s, inevitably many students were influenced and returned home the bearers of a new light. Second, there was the fleet of federal boats that used to ply the Caribbean, facilitating inter-island contact. Rastafari ideas were first taken back to St. Kitts in this way. By the time the reggae artistes were staging shows in the islands, the way had already been prepared. Dominica and Grenada were two islands in which Rastafari were making— some would say a negative—political impact by the end of the 1970s.[11]

But the first part of the world outside of the Caribbean where the Rastafari drew the attention of the establishment was Great Britain. There the children of Caribbean immigrants, confronted with racism and ethnocentricity, found in Rastafari an ideal source of cultural pride and identity, and a weapon with which to fight back. British society, unable to withstand the aggressive critique of a morally powerful social movement, at first retaliated by trying to criminalize it.[12] Both have since found common ground, and the Rastafari have been declared an ethnic group, with the right to wear their dreadlocks without fear of discrimination.[13]

Another European country to receive Caribbean migrants was the Netherlands. A few of the Surinamese who have settled in Amsterdam, Rotterdam, Utrecht, and other cities were Rastafari prior to leaving Suriname. Similarly, it is believed that many of the Rastafari in Paris were already Dreadlocks before leaving Martinique or Guadeloupe.

While migration may account for some Rastafari in the metropolitan countries, without doubt the main factor responsible for the growth of the movement there was the internationalization of reggae from a national music that evolved in Jamaica during the 1960s. During that evolution reggae became an ideal vehicle for the expression of Rastafari alienation from Jamaican society, what with the music's inherited tradition for social commentary. With Kingston already overcrowded by rural immigrants, unemployment doubling during the decade, and health, sanitation and other social conditions in the ghettoes at subhuman levels, the youth turned to the Rastafari, bringing into the movement the newly emerging music but taking from it the trenchant critique of the society. By the start of the 1970s, very few nationally recognized artists were not also Dreadlocks. Among them was Bob Marley, the charismatic genius whose exposition of reggae was to become to many a listener the sacred presentation of all that mattered about life. To them Marley's music was not about Marley, but about Jah, about Rastafari, about truth, about justice.

Reggae music first made its international debut in England among the Caribbean immigrants, and from there it developed a following in Europe, where groups such as Boney M became exponents of reggae. In between local groups and touring bands and artistes from Jamaica, reggae aficionados could satisfy their tastes with the hundreds of recordings produced by an industry whose center gradually shifted from Jamaica to Britain by the 1980s. Reggae music is no longer exclusively Jamaican, though its leading artistes and composers are, and the association with Jamaica remains.

As a result of the internationalization of reggae, Rastafari has spread as far east as Japan and Australasia. Its presence in Africa is due primarily to the "reggae ambassadors,"[14] the Rastafari artistes, whose strong sense of identity with Africa resonates through the music. Zimbabweans had camped outside the stadium in Harare days before Bob Marley's concert there. And when Nelson and Winnie Mandela visited Jamaica in 1991 they paid tribute to the many Jamaican singers and composers whose songs they said gave succor to their struggle against apartheid. If Rastafari, many of them white, may be found outside Durban,[15] chances are that others may be found in the black townships of South Africa. In Zambia, at a park outside Lusaka, every September Zambian Rastafari stage their own version of the Jamaican summer festival called "Reggae Sunsplash." And in West Africa there are Rastafari in most countries of the region, including even some that are also Islamic.[16]

Although they are by no means a major factor, mention should be made of the presence of "missionary" groups of Jamaican Rastafari on the continent. The settlement at Shehamane in Ethiopia has been well known. In gratitude to the African diaspora for their support during the Italian invasion of Ethiopia, Emperor Haile Selassie made a grant of several hundred acres of land available to all those who wished to settle there. Rastafari from Jamaica have been there since the 1950s. In Ghana, the group of Rastafari known in Jamaica as the Bobo has established a presence.[17] It is not known what success they may be having in winning over Ghanaians and other Africans.

The growth of the Rastafari in the United States, like its growth elsewhere, is due to the factors cited above. However, owing to the fact that a larger number of Americans are themselves of African origin, its rootedness promises to be far deeper in the United States than in any other industrialized country. It also is more recent. None of the publications on new religious movements in the United States in the 1980s, by Petersen, Choquette, Melton, or Ellwood, make any mention of Rastafari.[18]

Although reggae artistes from Jamaica were already touring the United States from the early 1970s, it was through an alleged criminal link that the American establishment began taking public notice of the Rastafari.[19] It began in 1979 with national exposure of a Miami-based group known as the Coptics, suspected as much for their prolific use of marihuana as for their trafficking in it. This was followed quickly by the leaking to the press of a "secret report" on the Rastas prepared as early as 1977 by the New York Police, and attributing to them the criminal violence of the Jamaican posses. What the author of the report if not the American press should have understood was that in Jamaica no one made the mistake of confusing the Rastafari and the urban youth, even though the street language and dreadlocks hair styles of the latter made them appear the same as the former. Thus, notwithstanding the rise of violent crimes in Jamaica, Rastafari has remained completely untarnished, thanks to the quiet and resourceful affirmation of "ital livity," which has become the badge of identification distinguishing "Rasta" from "Rascal," as the people themselves put it. In the United States, however, for most of the 1980s the American establishment, including the media to a large extent, tried to link the violence of the Jamaican posses to the Rastafari. Rastafari use of marihuana as a sacrament, likened to the communion wine of the Christian churches,[20] made it easier to do so.

Although much damage was done as a result of adverse publicity, Rastafari is set to win out in the end, as Americans come to understand the various aspects of the concept of livity. For this Rastafari owe much to the reggae ambassadors, in particular Bob Marley. As a new and attractive sound, reggae developed its own American following and soon many Americans were making the connection that others had been making in other parts of the world between reggae and Rasta.

Especially significant, particularly for African Americans, have been the dreadlocks. This public statement with one's hair could not be made without one's having first made an internal decision about one's identity, since dreadlocks take some time to grow.[21] Some members of the African-American intelligentsia and artistic community have taken this step, aided by increasing contact with migrant Rastafari leaders from Jamaica, or with Jamaica itself, through which the deeper dimensions of the Rasta lifestyle and position are realized.

Nevertheless, Rastafari at the international level is not the same as Rastafari in Jamaica. The most profound difference lies in the position of Haile Selassie. In Jamaica, belief in the divinity of the emperor has remained the most central aspect of Rastafari beliefs, even after his death. It could be argued that such profound impact as the Rasta movement has had in Jamaica could not have been possible without so fundamental a change in one's conception of God, that this is the origin and font of one's "emancipation from mental slavery." Outside Jamaica, on the other hand, very few hold to this belief in Haile Selassie, among them some Ethiopian Rastafari. Indeed, few non-Jamaican Rastafari would maintain the belief that he has not died. At best, most seem to think him a ruler who did much for Africa and for world peace.

Although research on the Rastafari diaspora has only just begun, it would seem that a second difference lies in the ritual process. In Jamaica, the Rastafari constitute a loose community of believers who are nurtured by a network of association formalized around a *nyabinghi,* or *binghi.* This is a ritual which brings together Dreadlocks several times a year on events in the Rastafari liturgical calendar, such as the anniversary of Haile Selassie's coronation or of his visit to Jamaica, for celebrations lasting at least three days. Ritual reasoning throughout the day and chanting to the beat of the drums at night are its main hallmarks. There is no evidence yet of formal religious worship among Rastafari outside of Jamaica, except in cities such as London and Atlanta where Jamaican Rastas have established themselves.

A third difference lies in the place of marihuana. Rastafari sacralization of this substance was culturally rooted in Jamaica. Brought to the country by Indian indentured laborers in the nineteenth cen-

tury, marihuana, or *ganja,* the Indian name it goes by in Jamaica, was incorporated into the folk pharmacopoeia as a panacea. The Rastafari modified the Indian way of smoking it, turning it into an entirely different ritual.[22] Although the complete suppression of *ganja* is impossible because of its rootedness in folk practices and beliefs, official recognition of the Rastafari has been blocked because of their use of this illegal substance. In the United States, however, not much emphasis is given to the sacramental character of *ganja,* especially not when it is assumed that its users are also quite likely addicted to dangerous substances like cocaine, crack, and heroin.

CONCLUSION

Rastafari is a Third World religion that has won adherents in other parts of the world, especially the industrialized countries. Other Third World religions making similar headway are those from India and the Middle East, the various forms and offshoots of Hinduism and Islam. Rastafari represents a first for black Africa.

As the movement spreads outside Jamaica, it will undergo change. Already certain beliefs are being modified, for example those concerning Haile Selassie's divinity and immortality. These developments will have an impact on the movement even in Jamaica itself, as efforts will be made to establish networks and linkages between all its various manifestations.

NOTES

1. They at first called themselves the "King of Kings" people. Today they prefer the designation "Rastafari" or "Rastas."
2. See Barry Chevannes, "The Rastafari and the Urban Youth," in *Perspectives on Jamaica in the Seventies,* ed. Carl Stone and Aggrey Brown (Kingston: Jamaica Publishing House, 1982).
3. See Barry Chevannes, *Rastafari: Roots and Ideology* (Syracuse: Syracuse University Press, 1994). Prior to this period most Rastafari, identifying black people as the biblical children of God, the Israelites, adopted the Nazarite vow—they combed but did not cut their hair.

4. On the significance of the hair, see "The Phallus and the Outcast," in *Rastafari and Other African-Caribbean World Views,* ed. Barry Chevannes (London: Macmillan, 1995).

5. See my "Repairer of the Breach: Reverend Claudius Henry and Jamaican society," in *Ethnicity in the Americas,* ed. Frances Henry (The Hague: Mouton, 1976).

6. See M. G. Smith, Roy Augier, and Rex Nettleford, *Report on the Rastafari Movement in Kingston, Jamaica* (Kingston: Extra-Mural Department, University of the West Indies, 1960).

7. Rex Nettleford, *Mirror, Mirror: Identity, Race and Protest* (Glasgow: Collins-Sangsters, 1970).

8. See Barry Chevannes, "The Case of Jah versus Jamaican Middle-Class Society," Institute of Social Studies Working Paper Series, no. 68 (The Hague, 1990).

9. See Frank Jan van Dijk; "The Twelve Tribes of Israel: Rasta and the Middle Class." *New West Indian Guide* 62, nos. 1 and 2 (1988).

10. Kenneth M. Bilby, "Black Thoughts from the Caribbean," *New West Indian Guide* 57, nos. 3 and 4 (1983).

11. For a survey of Rastafari in the Caribbean, see Horace Campbell, *Rastafari and Resistance: From Marcus Garvey to Walter Rodney* (London: Honsib Publishing Ltd.).

12. See E. E. Cashmore, *Rastaman* (London: George Allen and Unwin. 1979), and his "The De-Labelling Process: From 'Lost Tribe' to 'Ethnic Group,' in *Rastafari and other African-Caribbean World Views,* ed. Barry Chevannes. Cashmore argues that Rastafari and British police (society) have both undergone internal and externally propelled changes that make them now able to live together.

13. Cashmore, "The De-Labelling Process."

14. The title of a song by Third World.

15. Personal communication from a South African student at the Institute of Social Studies in The Hague, July 1989.

16. Personal communication from Neil Savishinsky.

17. The Bobo are the only Rastafari to live a communal life. They distinguish themselves from mainstream Dreadlocks principally by wearing a turban at all times and a flowing robe sometimes, and by peddling brooms made of straw.

18. William J. Petersen, *Those Curious New Cults in the 80s* (New Canaan, Conn.: Keats, 1982); Diane Choquette, *New Religious Movements in the U.S. and Canada* (Westport, Conn.: Greenwood, 1985); J. Gordon Melton, *The Encyclopedic Handbook of Cults in America* (New York: Garland, 1986); Robert S. Ellwood and Harry B. Partin, *Religious and Spiritual Groups in Modern America,* 2d ed. (Englewood Cliffs, N.J.: Prentice-Hall, 1988).

19. See Chevannes, *Rastafari Origins,* for a more detailed survey of the Rastafari in the United States.

20. The *chillum* pipe is called a "chalice." To "lick a chalice" is to partake in a communal sharing of ideas, as the chalice passes from hand to hand. This sacred ritual is called a "reasoning."

21. Even the instant dreadlocks that may now be woven by hair stylists are not without their own statement. If nothing else, blacks, as never before, are finding pleasure in their own hair.

22. Indian men smoked *ganja* using the *chillum* only; Indian women smoked tobacco using the *huka* or water pipe. The Rastafari merged the two.

SUGGESTIONS FOR FURTHER READING

Barrett, Leonard E., Sr. *The Rastafarians.* Boston: Beacon Press, 1988.

Caribbean Quarterly Monograph: Rastafari. Kingston: University of the West Indies, 1985.

Chevannes, Barry. *Rastafari: Roots and Ideology,* Syracuse: Syracuse University Press, 1994.

———, ed. *Rastafari and Other African-Caribbean World Views.* London: Macmillan, 1993.

RELIGION IN THE NEWS

AN APOCALYPTIC MYSTERY

Contemporary apocalyptic sects also occur outside the West, as this grisly example from Uganda shows. During the period of March–April, newspapers seemed to compete with one another to see which could fascinate their readers with the most explicit account of the deaths attributed to Joseph Kibwetere, a former Catholic schoolteacher-turned-cult leader. Some reports denied the massacre were sect-related; most, however, converged with this reading, which places the Movement for the Restoration of the Ten Commandments in the same category as Peoples Temple and the Branch Davidian.

THE SECT MEMBERS GAVE NO warning. In a field a few yards away from their compound, Pius Kabeireho laid bricks in the mounting heat and listened to the joyful hallelujahs wafting from the simple corrugated-iron-roofed church where the worshipers went

RELIGION IN THE NEWS

AN APOCALYPTIC MYSTERY
continued

for their morning prayers. Suddenly, just past 10 a.m. on Friday, March 17, Kabeireho heard a loud explosion, followed by the screams of children. "Mother, save me!" he says they cried. Seized by panic, he ran to the nearby police station for help. When he returned, the church was aflame, and Kabeireho gazed on the scene with terror. "I saw hundreds of charred skeletons pressed together, kneeling, with their hands clasped in prayer," he says. Amid the acrid smell of charcoal and burned flesh, Kabeireho also detected the unmistakable odor of an insecticide sold in local shops. It had been sprayed, apparently, to intensify the flames. The product's name: Doom.

The fire in Kanungu, deep in the impoverished rural highlands of southwest Uganda, was the latest horror to blight a region that has seen countless tragedies in recent years. At last count, 530 members of the Movement for the Restoration of the Ten Commandments of God died in the fire, which at first glance appeared to have been set by members of the apocalyptic cult in an act of mass suicide. In Uganda, where the legacy of a long civil war and the rampant spread of AIDS have driven thousands to seek refuge in breakaway religious movements, news of the apparent suicides provoked widespread grief. But as more information emerged last week, there were growing doubts that the sect members had willingly set themselves ablaze. Investigators are probing whether the group's leader, a messianic former Roman Catholic schoolteacher named Joseph Kibwetere, 68, had lured his unwitting flock to their deaths—then fled with associates. The prophet may have decided to eliminate his followers after the end of the world he had long predicted failed to materialize. Last Friday, police discovered the bodies of 153 more people—some strangled, other stabbed—in a mass grave beneath a cult-owned house 35 miles from Kanungu. They had been murdered two weeks earlier. "If it is true that [the Kanungu victims] were killed and the leaders are alive, I may have to go there and join in the hunt," Uganda's President Yoweri Museveni told his countrymen.

There were few clues to be found at the site of the inferno. Five days after the fire, villagers wandered, stunned, through the sect's one-story dormitories that stood alongside the burned-out church, gawking at the inner sanctum of the strangers who had lived beside them for a decade. Grass mats, robes, school report cards and notebooks containing the scribbled messages of sect members—all sworn to a code of silence—littered the ground. A heap of red earth marked the mass grave where the victims had been dumped without ceremony. The church where they died was a pile of scorched rubble and iron roofing. Just up the hill, the stench of decomposed bodies rose from a pit beneath the leaders' house. Policemen held handkerchiefs to their faces as they removed the bodies of eight men—apparently they had defied Kibwetere—who had been bludgeoned and poisoned days before the fire. "[The cult members] were all simple people looking for a better life," said a local schoolteacher who has known Kibwetere for decades, "but this man sold them lies."

He was a charismatic deceiver. Born in southwest Uganda in 1932, Kibwetere was raised as a Roman Catholic, and taught and served as an administrator in Uganda's Catholic school system. But he broke from the church in the early 1980s after claiming that he could communicate directly with God. In 1984 Kibwetere announced that Jesus and Mary had visited him and commanded him to spread the word that the Apocalypse was coming. In the year 2000 epidemics and whirlwinds would blight the earth, he wrote in the movement's book of prophecy. The calamities would be followed by three days of darkness, during which three quarters of the world's population would die. Only those who followed Kibwetere and took refuge with him inside a church that he would build—he called it the "ark"—would be assured of survival.

The preacher set up camp in Kanungu in the early 1990s, merging his sect with that of a local prophetess and former prostitute named Keledonia Mwerinde. Their followers prayed and toiled 12 hours a day in the

RELIGION IN THE NEWS

AN APOCALYPTIC MYSTERY
continued

surrounding sugar-cane and banana fields. Members handed over their property to the church and exchanged their clothes for green uniforms and white caps. Men and women were segregated, sex was forbidden and fasting two days a week was mandatory. The cultists spoke to one another only in sign language. "They explained that if someone is talking at the end of the world, he won't hear the bell summoning him to heaven," says Kabeireho, who rejected many offers to join the group. Despite the harsh conditions, and repeated allegations of cruelty to children, the sect flourished. On a 1997 government registration form, Kibwetere claimed 4,500 followers.

The approach of the millennium marked the true test of the prophet's credibility. In a notebook recovered by NEWSWEEK in the abandoned dining hall, Kibwetere excitedly announced that the dawn of "the year one" was near. "We are all waiting until December 31st," he wrote on Christmas morning. On New Year's Eve, he readied his flock for the end of the world." "We have to fill all the jerry cans with water," he wrote. "We have to be clean so that we can prepare ourselves for heaven." New Year's came and went. By mid-February, Kibwetere was again prophesying doomsday. "Buy flowers," he advised, "clean the church, and recruit other members for the special occasion." Two weeks before the inferno Kibwetere apparently had decided to take matters into his own hands. After a sect member complained that "the jerry cans are all leaking," Kibwetere responded ominously: "Don't bother with them. Soon everything will be over. We're going to make a big fire and the jerry cans will stop leaking."

Some investigators theorized that Kibwetere, depressed by the loss of his credibility, panicked. According to them, a handful of skeptical sect members apparently demanded that the leader return their property; they were murdered and tossed into the hidden pit. The killings seem to have lent new urgency to the leader's plans. Sect members sold their cattle, sugar and flour to villagers at half price. To deceive locals into believing that nothing was amiss, the sect sent out invitations to a party at the compound to be held Saturday. March 18—one day after the fire. On Thursday evening they gathered in the dining hall for a feast. The next morning they entered the church. The doors and windows were nailed shut. Then a match was struck, igniting a mixture of gasoline, sulfuric acid and insecticide. It is still unclear whether the victims knew they were about to die—or whether they believed that the "ark" would be a refuge from the imminent apocalypse. Learning the truth will be difficult, says detective Solomon Kyanmanywa, since "there were no survivors."

None except, perhaps, Kibwetere and his associates. Some believe his charred body lies among those of his followers. But a 17-year-old eyewitness has told investigators that he saw both Kibwetere and his partner Mwerinde sneaking out of the compound late Thursday night carrying small suitcases. The leaders' apparent escape has only deepened the grief of people such as Joseph Mpanimanya, 27, a taxi driver from north Uganda whose mother, father, wife and two small daughters joined the Ten Commandments of God movement last October. All perished. "I begged them not to go. I said the end of the world wasn't coming," he says, standing beside the mass grave where they lie buried. "They called me 'Satan' and said I didn't know what I was talking about." Police are now searching for more victims on the cult's properties scattered across Uganda. Until they finish their grim task, it will be impossible to gauge the full consequences of a madman's fatal delusions.

ASK YOURSELF

Several reasons were suggested in this chapter for the recruitment success of alternative religions in the United States. How many other reasons can you suggest why young people and the not-so-young would wish to abandon their settled life in mainstream society or within the embrace of established religion for life in a community on the fringes of society?

FURTHER READINGS

Luhrmann, T. M. *Persuasions of the Witch's Craft: Ritual Magic in Contemporary England.* Cambridge, Mass.: Harvard University Press, 1989. Luhrmann's penetrating analysis of covens and magical groups in the London region seeks to explain why educated persons of the middle class have become intensely involved with witchcraft and magic.

Miller, Timothy. *America's Alternative Religions,* edited by Timothy Miller. Albany: State University of New York Press. 1995. This is a scholarly collection of studies of dozens of the more prominent sects in contemporary American society. Very useful as a reference, and a mine of informative for comparative studies.

Wilson, Bryan R. *The Social Dimensions of Sectarianism: Sects and New Religious Movements in Contemporary Society.* Oxford: Clarendon Press. 1990. This scholarly collection of papers previously published by the author gives a thoughtful introduction and overview of a phenomenon that is of increasing importance in Western societies. Its regional provenance is Europe, but many of its insights have relevance to the new religious movements in the United States.

SUGGESTED VIDEOS

"Cults: Saying No under Pressure." This documentary explores various categories of cults. It examines their recruitment tactics, includes interviews with ex-cult members, and presents a recruitment vignette illustrating how cults work and how people can resist the pressure to join. The documentary also deals with satanic rituals and the similarities between these and the rituals of cults. 29 minutes; 1991; $139 (sale); Catalog #SJ229. "World Cultures on Film and Video," University of California Extension, Center for Media and Independent Learning, 2000 Center Street, Fourth Floor, Berkeley, CA 94704.

"The Heaven's Gate Cult: The Thin Line Between Faith and Reason." This ABC News *Nightline* uses the 1997 mass suicide of the Heaven's Gate cult as a starting point for a discussion among prominent cult scholars about the differences between contemporary cults and those from which the world religions developed. 20 minutes. #BRF7610. $89.95 (sale). Religion Catalogue. Films for the Humanities & Sciences, PO Box 2053, Princeton, NJ 08543-2053.

"Children of Jehovah." The Jehovah's Witnesses is a quickly growing sect in the United States. One of its key beliefs is that the end of the world is rapidly approaching when the forces of good and the forces of evil will fight for the final time. The video shows how individuals deal with the intense pressure to conform to its doctrines. Nonconformists must leave the community, and its members (including the nonconformist's own family) henceforth cuts off all communication with them. 46 minutes. #BRF6202. #129 (sale); $75 (rental). Religion Catalogue. Films for the Humanities & Sciences, PO Box 2053, Princeton, NJ 08543-2053.

"The Shakers: I Don't Want to be Remembered as a Chair." The last remaining compound of the Shakers has been reduced to nine members, who lead lives of equality, fraternity, and simplicity. The simplicity of the Shakers is shown in their furniture and basketry, which now sell for thousands of dollars. In this video the Shakers reflect upon their legacy. Will they be remembered for their furniture or for their faith? A BBC Production. 49 minutes. #BRF77443. $129 (sale); $75 (rental). Religion Catalogue. Films for the Humanities & Sciences, PO Box 2053, Princeton, NJ 08543-2053.

GLOSSARY

alternative religion   See "sect" or "cult."

animism   The idea that souls or spirits inhabit animals, plants, or inanimate objects. The term was originally coined by Edward Tylor.

archtype   The genetic tendency for the human brain to create certain images that are shared by all *Homo sapiens* and reveal themselves in dreams, myths, ritual, and art. Originally propounded by Carl Jung.

cargo cult   A popular movement for social change in New Guinea, whose followers believe that certain rituals will result in the coming of ships loaded with valuable cargo.

carnival   A period of festivity celebrated in Europe which lasted from a day to several weeks immediately before Lent (the 40-day period from Ash Wednesday to Easter Eve) characterized by license typically involving sexual indulgence, gluttony, and drunkenness.

carnavalesque   Carnival-like festivities in Europe that usually took place in May and June, or after the autumn harvest.

charisma   Personal magnetism capable of inspiring agreement, loyalty, and enthusiasm. The term is associated with Max Weber.

clan   A group based on descent from the father or the mother. In the former case the group is known as a patriclan or patrilineal clan; in the latter case the group is known as a matriclan or matrilineal clan. Clans are often said to trace their origins to a mythological being—cultural hero or totem—and they distinguish themselves from other clans in their society by observing distinctive taboos. In some societies a clan may be divided into two or more lineages.

communitas   A ritual condition in which a group of individuals interact in disregard of ordinary constraints of social structure and feel liberated from conformity to general social norms. This concept was invented by Victor Turner, who often used it in conjunction with the notion of liminality.

contagious magic   Magic based on the idea that things once in contact can influence each other even after they have been separated.

cosmos   The conception members of a society have of the entire world of nature and spirit, and humanity's place in it. Also known as cosmology.

cult   a small, intense religious group whose ties to a conventional religion are more tenuous than in the case of sects. The term is also more commonly applied to a religion that has not broken away from Christianity or Judaism, and is frequently led by a prophet or prophet-like figure.

culture Everything that people collectively do, think, make, and say.

cultural-materialism an anthropological approach emphasizing the empirical factors, such as the natural environment or technology, as the controlling determinants shaping institutions and collective representations.

culture hero A spirit, animal, quasi-human being, or inanimate object that plays an important role in shaping the human world.

descent A relationship defined by a connection to an ancestor through a series of parent–child links.

diachronic approach A perspective that considers society as it changes through time in contrast to a synchronic approach that considers society at a particular moment or period in time.

divination A ritual designed to foretell the future or interpret the past with the help of supernatural agents.

divine king A very broad term for any leader of a community who is regarded by his followers as representing in his own person the spiritual world.

dominant symbol A symbol that is regarded by its users not merely as the means to the fulfillment of the purposes of the ritual they are performing but as also representing values they regard as axiomatic. The term was coined by Victor Turner. The Ndembu milk tree and Miss America are examples.

double burial A mortuary ritual in which the corpse is provisionally laid aside and then after a period of time is permanently disposed of. Also known as *secondary burial*. The Merina of Madagascar are an example of a people performing this ritual.

ethnographer A cultural anthropologist actually in the process of collecting data in the field.

ethnography The collection of data in the field; also, a written work about a particular society.

folktale A fictional story about the adventures of animals or of animals and human beings.

functionalism Malinowski's thesis that aspects of culture function to fulfill the biological, psychological, or other needs of individuals.

imitative magic A ritual that mimics the results desired.

incorporation The final stage of a rite of passage, in which an individual is integrated into a new status in society.

informant An individual who provides an ethnographer with information.

legend A story that describes events set in a specific place in the real world, at a time less remote than the mythological past.

liminality The second stage of a rite of passage, in which an individual has no established status.

lineage A group based on descent from the father or the mother. In the former case the group is known as a patrilineage; in the latter case the group is known as a matrilineage. Lineages differ from clans in that clans typically trace their origins to a mythological being whereas lineages trace their origins to a real person who founds the lineage. This is a man in a patrilineage and a woman in a matrilineage. A number of lineages may group themselves together into a clan and therefore share the same origin myth, totem, and taboo.

magic A ritual or set of rituals intended to bring about some relatively immediate practical benefit, usually without the intervention of spirits.

messianic movement A revitalization movement characterized by an emphasis on the participation of a divine savior in human flesh.

millenarian movement A response made by a community suffering extreme socioeconomic deprivation and characterized by anticipations that the performance of new or rediscovered attitudes to life will bring about a radical improvement in living conditions.

monotheism The belief that there is only one god.

multivocal symbol A symbol which has more than one referent. The Ndembu milk tree is an example.

myth A story that describes the origins of the world, some natural phenomenon, or some aspect of culture and that contains at least one physically or humanly impossible event or situation.

neopaganism (Wicca) A modern revival of a supposedly pre-Christian religion.

New Age Movement A complex of spiritual and consciousness-raising movements dating from the 1980s and embracing a diverse range of themes, including holistic approaches to health and ecology.

new religious movement See "cult" or "sect."

nonliterate Lacking a tradition of reading and writing.

non-mainstream religion See "cult" or "sect."

origin myth A story describing the origins of some feature of the physical environment, of a society, or of a culture; often describes the appearance of a clan's culture hero and how the clan was founded.

pagan A person who is not a Christian, Muslim, or Jew.

participant observation Social anthropology's major

research tool, involving the ethnographer participating in his informants' lives as well as observing what they do and noting what they say.

pollution In its contemporary anthropological sense, defilement resulting from contact between things that should be kept apart.

polytheism The belief in the existence of many gods.

practical religion Rituals and beliefs as ordinary people put them into practice, as distinct from the theology formulated by specialists.

priest A religious specialist whose authority comes from the office he or she occupies rather than some personal endowment.

primary factors of experience A term coined by Rodney Needham to denote the capacities, proclivities, and constraints that universally make up human nature.

prophet A charismatic leader who emerges after an intense spiritual experience.

revitalization movement A popular movement for radical change, led by a charismatic figure and usually brought about by one or more social, economic, or political upheavals.

rite of passage A ritual performed at a period of transition in the life cycle of an individual or group.

ritual A stereotyped, repetitive behavior or set of behaviors, either religious or nonreligious, that uses symbols to communicate meaning.

ritual of propitiation A ritual intended to appease a spirit.

sacrifice An offering made to a spirit. Also, the ritual itself.

scapulimancy Divination using the cracks burnt into a shoulder-blade when it is put into fire.

secondary burial See *double burial.*

sect a religious grouping set apart from the dominant religion or religions in its society by its divergence in doctrine, ritual, and social character. Members of a sect constitute a minority and are most often regarded by members who remain loyal to the parent group as being a deviant offshoot.

separation The first stage of a rite of passage, in which an individual is separated from an established status.

shaman An "inspired priest," that is, a religious functionary believed to be chosen by spirits, who functions as an intermediary between the world of spirits and human beings, and performs healing rituals.

social structure The web of relationships binding members of a society.

society A group of people whose members live in the same place and whose lives and livelihoods are interdependent.

sorcery Bad magic, performed to achieve ends that society regards as bad or evil.

symbol In its simplest definition, "something that stands for something else."

synchronic approach A perspective that considers society at a particular moment or period in time in contrast with the diachronic approach that considers society as it changes through time. Favored by structural-functionalists.

structural analysis An anthropological approach, associated with Lévi-Strauss, which examines the manner in which categories of thought are ordered in a society. The approach emphasizes the operation of certain properties of classificatory thought common to all people.

structural-functionalism A perspective, associated with Emile Durkheim, A. R. Radcliffe-Brown, and E. E. Evans-Pritchard, which studies institutions and collective representations as though they constituted a coherent and stable structure.

taboo A prohibition resulting from social custom or psychological inhibition. The term comes from Polynesia and has the sense of giving a sacred or privileged quality to a person or thing, which removes it from ordinary use. Also known as *tabu.*

theology (a) The study of the nature of religious truth by rational inquiry; (b) a system or school of opinions concerning religious questions.

totem A plant, animal, or object from which members of a social group are believed to have descended, or which plays some central role in its history.

voodoo A syncretic religion practiced mainly among peoples residing in the Caribbean region, especially Haiti, and composed of Catholic ritual features and the animism and magic of slaves from Benin, West Africa. The religion involves a belief in a god who rules a large pantheon of guardian spirits, local elementals, deified ancestors, and saints. Also known as *vodoun* or *vodun.*

water witching A divinatory ritual carried out in rural America and in certain other parts of the world by means of which the practitioner is supposed to find underground supplies of water by using a divining rod. Also known as dowsing or witching.

witchcraft The belief that certain individuals, called witches, can injure others by psychic means or by the use of certain words.

GENERAL REFERENCES

Anker, Roy M. *Self-Help and Popular Religion in Early American Culture: An Interpretive Guide.* Westport, Connecticut: Greenwood Press. 1999.

Baal, J. van. Review of *Le symbolism en general* by Dan Sperber. *Bijdragen tot de Taal-en Volkenkunde* 133:163–165.

Brunner, Borgna, ed. *1998 Information Please Almanac.* Boston: Information Please LLC, 1998.

Bogoras, Waldemar, 1904–1905. *The Chukchee,* Vol. 7 of Franz Boas (ed.), *The Jesup North Pacific Expedition ("Memoirs of the American Museum of Natural History,")* Vol. 11, Parts 2 and 3. Leiden: E. J. Brill.

Clune, Francis J. "A Comment on Voodoo Deaths." *American Anthropologist* 75:312.

Cushing, Frank Hamilton. "Outlines of Zuni Creation Myths." In *Annual Report of the Bureau of Ethnology* (12), pp. 9–45.

Demos, John Putnam. *Entertaining Satan: Witchcraft and the Culture of Early New York.* New York: Oxford University Press, 1983.

Dinnerstein, Dorothy. *The Mermaid and the Minotaur: Sexual Arrangements and Human Malaise.* New York: Harper, 1990 (1976).

Durkheim, Emile. *The Elementary Forms of the Religious Life,* trans. Joseph Ward Swain. New York: The Free Press, 1965 (1915).

Eliade, Mircea. *The Myth of the Eternal Return.* New York. English translation, 1954.

Evans-Pritchard, E. E. *Witchcraft, Oracles and Magic among the Azande.* Oxford: Clarendon Press, 1937.

———. *Theories of Primitive Religion.* Oxford: Clarendon Press, 1965.

Evans-Pritchard, E. E. *The Divine Kingship of the Shilluk of the Nilotic Sudan (Frazer Lecture 1948).* Cambridge: Cambridge University Press. Reprinted in E.E. Evans-Pritchard. *Essays in Social Anthropology.* London: Faber & Faber.

Forth, Gregory. "The Pigeon and the Friarbird: The Mythical Origin of Death and Daylight in East Indonesia." *Anthropos* 87:432–441.

Geertz, Clifford. "Religion as a Cultural System." In *Anthropological Approaches to the Study of Religion,* ed. Michael Banton. Association of Social Anthropologists Monographs, no. 3. London: Tavistock Publications, 1965, pp. 1–46.

Gennep, Arnold van. *The Rites of Passage,* trans. Monika B. Vizedom and Gabrielle L. Caffee. Chicago: University of Chicago Press, 1960 (1908).

Hall, John R. "Public Narratives and the Apocalyptic Sect: From Jonestown to Mt. Carmel." In *Armageddon in Waco: Critical Perspectives on the Branch Davidian Conflict* (ed. Stuart A. Wright). Chicago: University of Chicago Press. 1995, pp. 205–235.

Hertz, Robert. "The Collective Representation of Death." In *Death and the Right Hand,* trans. Rodney and Claudia Needham. London: Cohen and West, 1960 (1907), pp. 27–86.

Hertz, Robert. "The Pre-Eminence of the Right Hand: A Study in Religious Polarity." In *Death and the Right Hand,* trans. Rodney and Claudia Needham. London: Cohen and West, 1960 (1907), pp. 89–113.

Hocart, Arthur Maurice. *Social Origins.* London: Watts & Company, 1954.

Hubert, Henri, and Mauss, Marcel. *Sacrifice: Its Nature and Function,* trans. W. D. Halls. Chicago: University of Chicago Press, 1964 (1899).

Kehoe, Alice Beck. *The Ghost Dance: Ethnohistory and Revitalization.* Fort Worth: Holt, Rinehart and Winston, 1989.

Leach, E. R. *Political Systems of Highland Burma: A Study of Kachin Social Structure.* London: The London School of Economics and Political Science, 1954.

Leach, E. R. (ed.). *Dialectic in Practical Religion.* Cambridge Papers in Social Anthropology Cambridge: Cambridge University Press. 1968.

Leach, Edmund. 1970. "The Legitimacy of Solomon." In *Introduction to Structuralism.* Michael Lane (ed.). New York: Basic Books.

Lester, David. 1972. "Voodoo Death: Some New Thoughts on an Old Phenomenon." *American Anthropologist* 74:386–390.

Lévi-Strauss, Claude. *The Raw And The Cooked: Introduction To A Science of Mythology, I* Translated from the French by John and Doreen Weightman. New York: Harper & Row, 1969.

Lex, Barbara. "Voodoo Death: New Thoughts on an Old Explanation." *American Anthropologist* 76:818–823.

Littleton, C. Scott. *The New Comparative Mythology: An Anthropological Assessment of the Theories of George Dumézil.* Third edition. Berkeley: University of California Press. 1982 (1966).

Lowie, Robert H. *Primitive Religion.* New York: Liveright, 1970 (1925).

Morphy, Howard. *Aboriginal Art.* London: Phaidon Press Ltd. 1998.

Malinowski, Bronislaw. *Magic, Science and Religion, and Other Essays.* Garden City, N.Y.: Doubleday, 1954 [1948].

Moore, O. K. 1957. "Divination—a New Perspective." *American Anthropologist* 59: 69–74.

Needham, Rodney. *Belief, Language, and Experience.* Oxford: Basil Blackwell, 1972.

———. *Circumstantial Deliveries.* Berkeley and Los Angeles: University of California Press, 1981.

———. *Exemplars.* Berkeley: University of California Press, 1985.

———. *Primordial Characters.* Charlottesville: University Press of Virginia, 1978.

———. *Symbolic Classification.* Santa Monica, California: Goodyear, 1979.

Oxford English Dictionary [*O.E.D.*] Prepared by J. A. Simpson and E. S. C. Weiner Second Edition. Oxford: Clarendon Press, 2000 (1989).

Radin, Paul. *Monotheism among Primitive Peoples.* Basel, Switzerland: Ethnographic Museum, 1954.

Richter, C. P. "On the Phenomenon of Sudden Death in Animals and Man." *Pschosomatic Medicine* 19:191–198.

Smith, Wilfred Cantwell. *The Meaning and End of Religion.* Minneapolis: Fortress Press, 1991 (1962).

Turner, Victor. *The Forest of Symbols.* Ithaca: Cornell University Press, 1967.

Turner, Victor. *Dramas, Fields, and Metaphors: Symbolic Action in Human Society.* Ithaca: Cornell University Press. 1974.

Tylor, Edward. *Primitive Culture:* Researches into the Development of Mythology, Philosophy, Religion, Language Arts, and Custom. 2d ed. Vol. 1. London: John Murray, 1873.

Weber, Max. *The Theory of Social and Economic Organization.* New York: Free Press, 1947.

Weber, Max. *The Protestant Ethic and the Spirit of Capitalism.* Trans. by Talcott Parsons New York: Scribners. 1958.

Wilson, Bryan R. *The Social Dimensions of Sectarianism: Sects and New Religious Movements in Contemporary Society.* Oxford: Clarendon Press. 1990.

INDEX